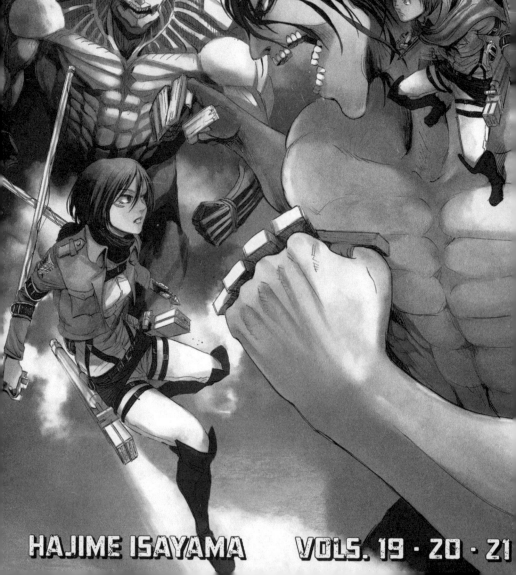

ATTACK on TITAN
OMNIBUS

HAJIME ISAYAMA   **VOLS. 19 · 20 · 21**

ATTACK on TITAN

OMNIBUS 7 (VOL. 19-21)

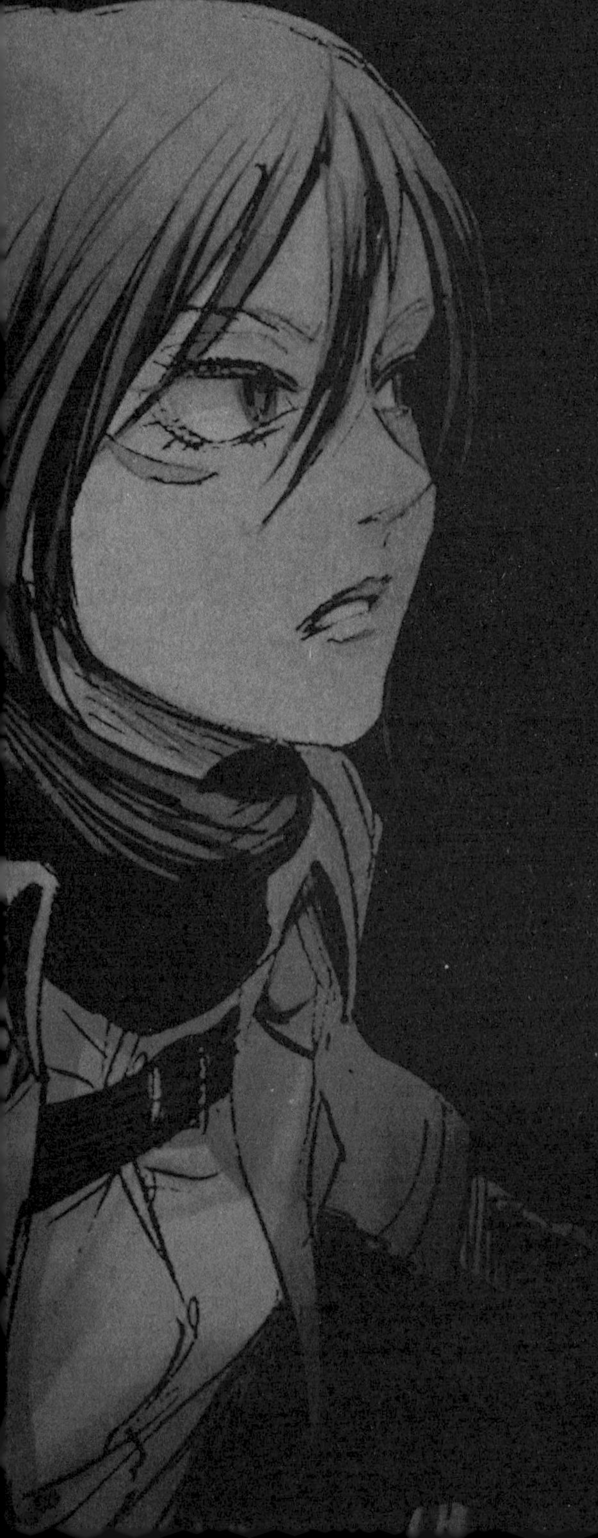

ATTACK ON TITAN 19

HAJIME ISAYAMA

"Attack on Titan" Character Introductions

104th Corps

Graduated at the top of her training corps, Mikasa is a highly talented soldier. Her parents were murdered before her eyes when she was a child, but Eren saved her life. Since then, she has made it her mission to protect him.

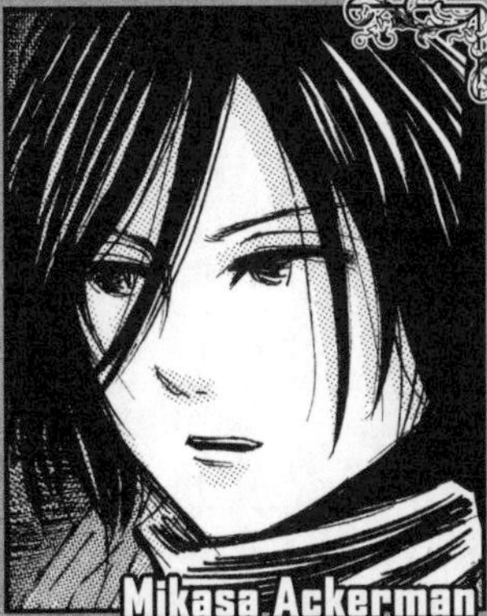

Mikasa Ackerman

Eren joined the Survey Corps out of his longing for the outside world and his hatred of the Titans. He has the power to turn himself into a Titan, but its origins are unknown.

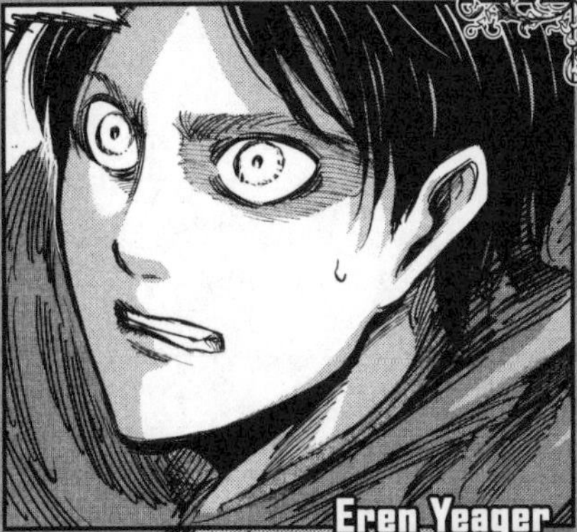

Eren Yeager

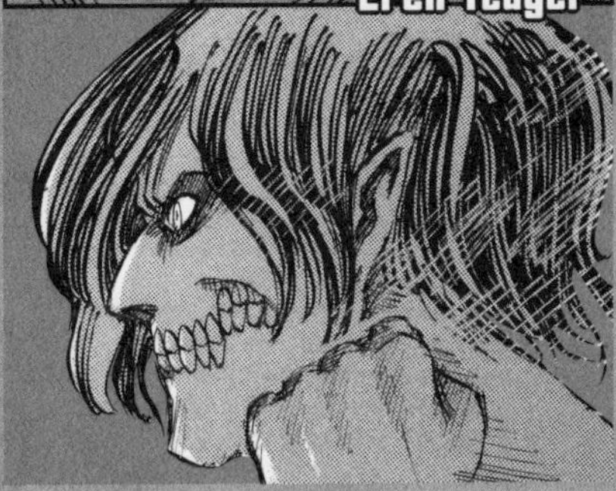

Eren and Mikasa's childhood friend. Though Armin isn't athletic in the least, he possesses both sharp observational powers and keen insight, and he exhibits an extra-ordinary ability to develop strategies.

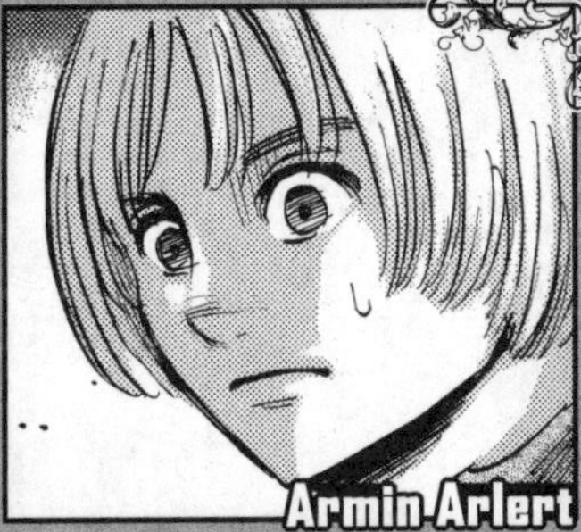

Armin Arlert

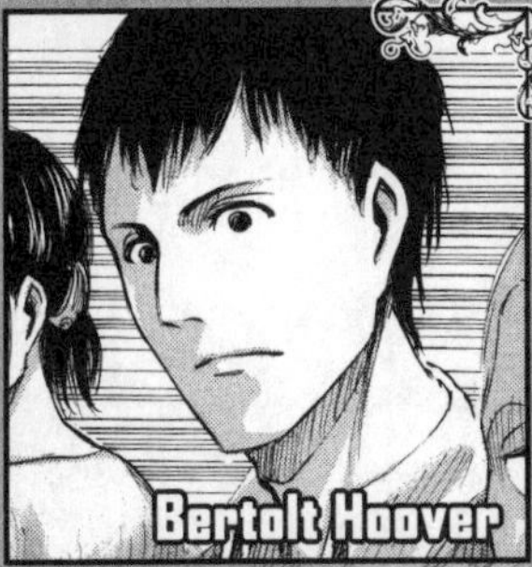

Bertolt Hoover

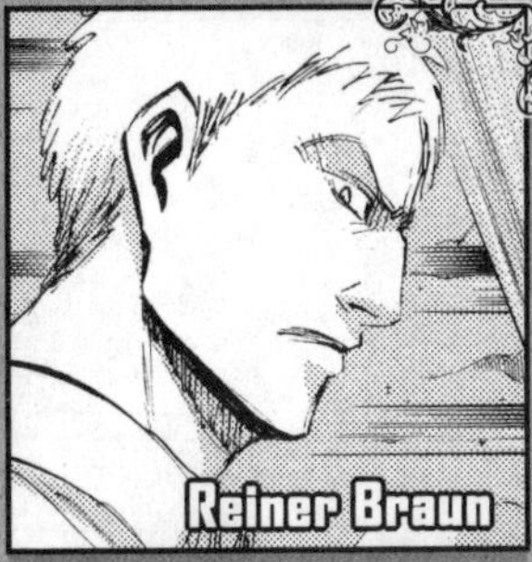

Reiner Braun

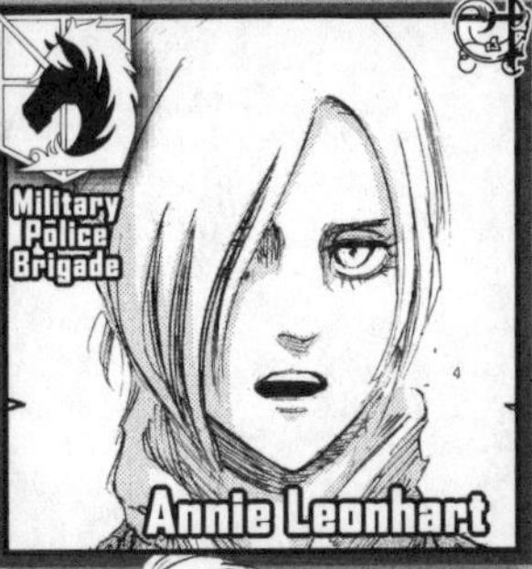
Military Police Brigade

Annie Leonhart

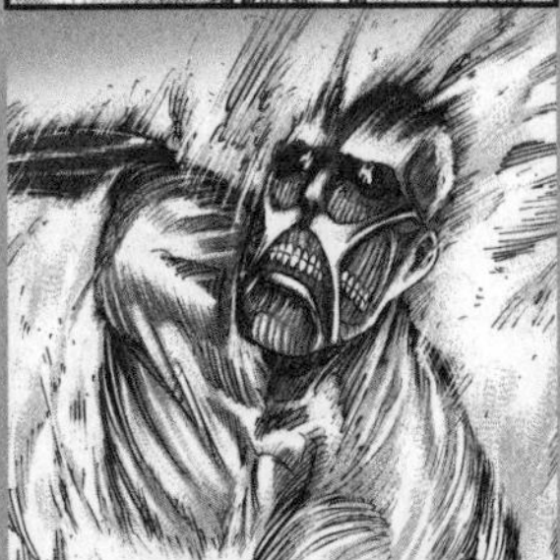

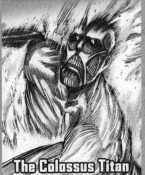

The Colossus Titan

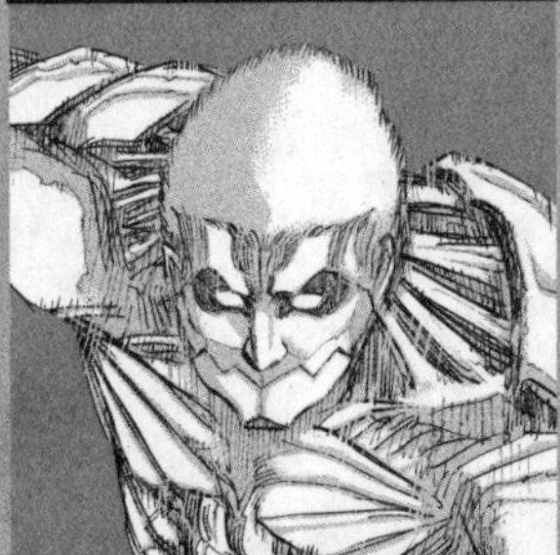

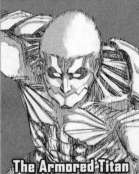

The Armored Titan

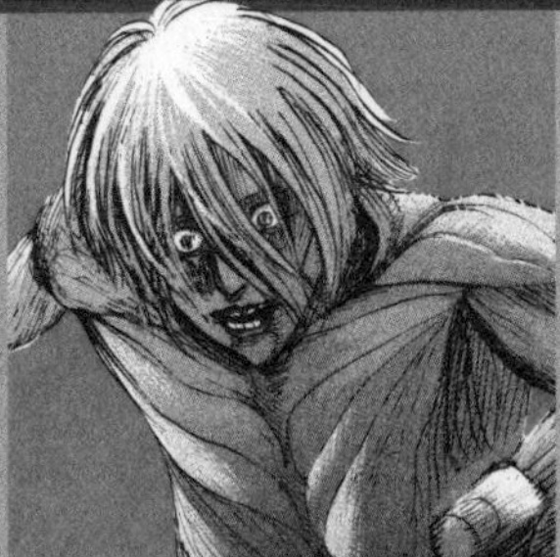

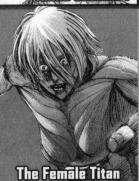

The Female Titan

Survey Corps

Soldiers who are prepared to sacrifice themselve
as they brave the Titan territory outside the wall

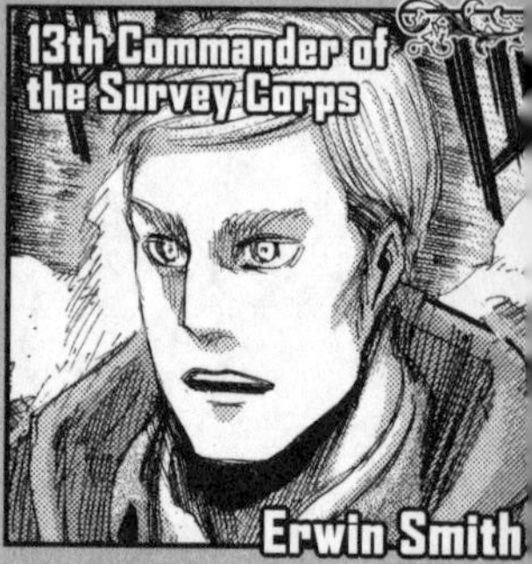

13th Commander of the Survey Corps

Erwin Smith

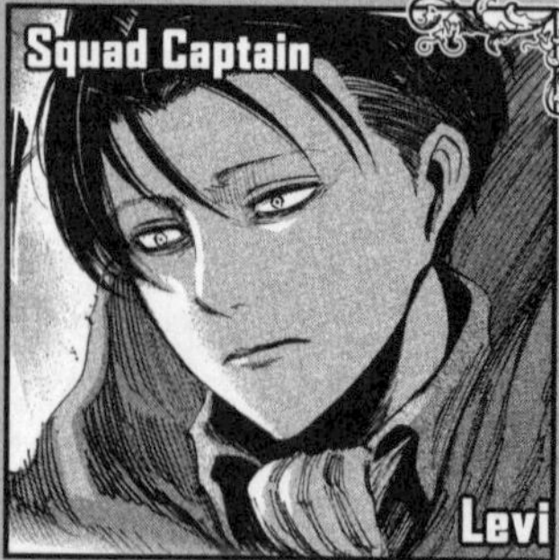

Squad Captain

Levi

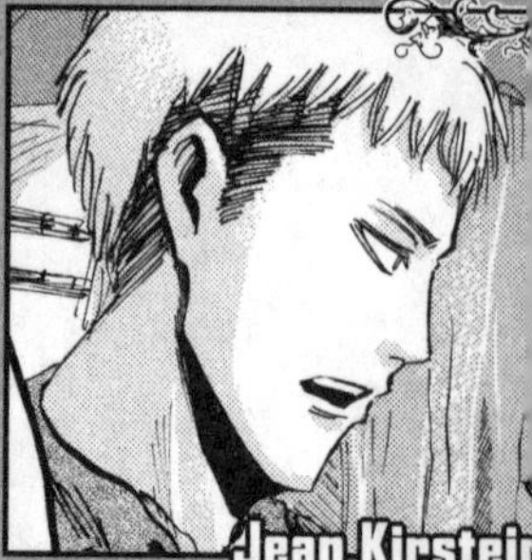

Jean Kirstein

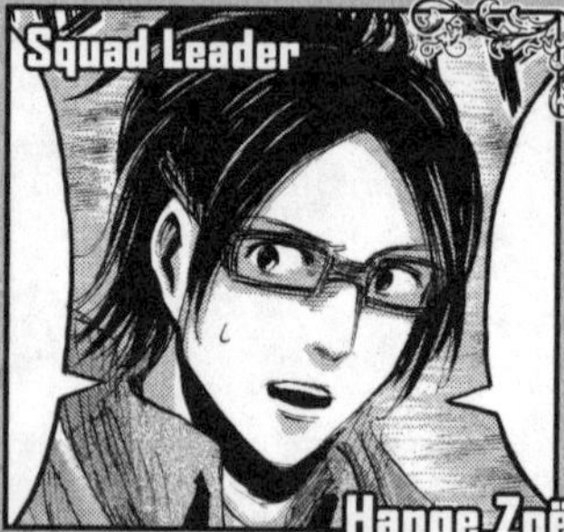

Squad Leader

Hange Zoë

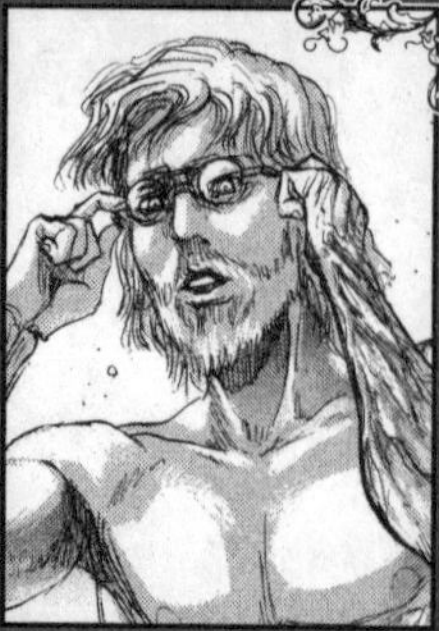

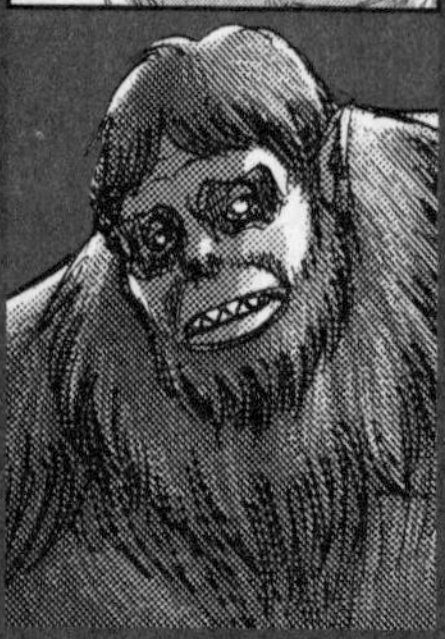

The Beast Titan

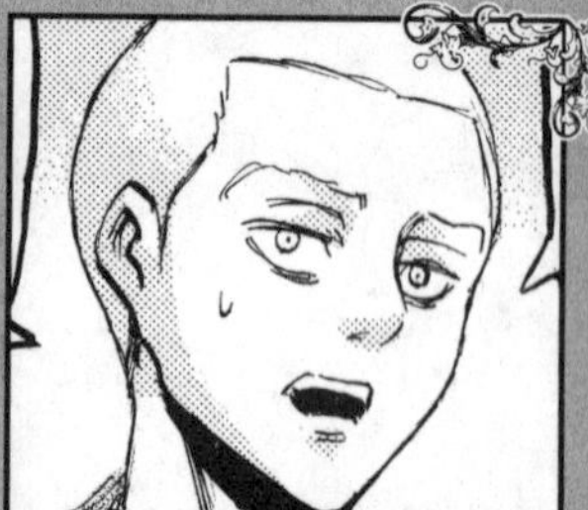

Connie Springer

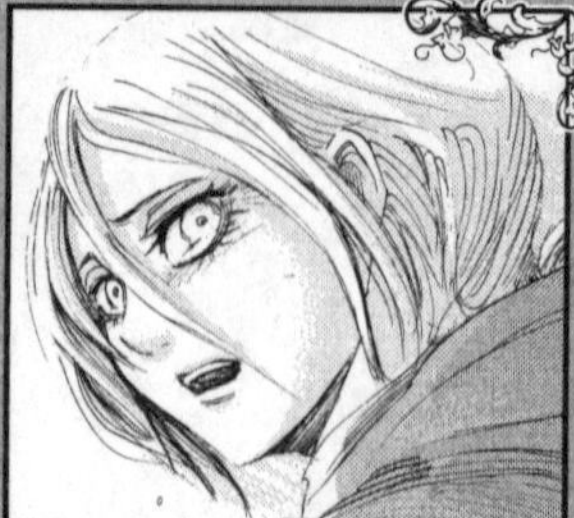

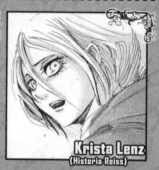

Krista Lenz

(Historia Reiss)

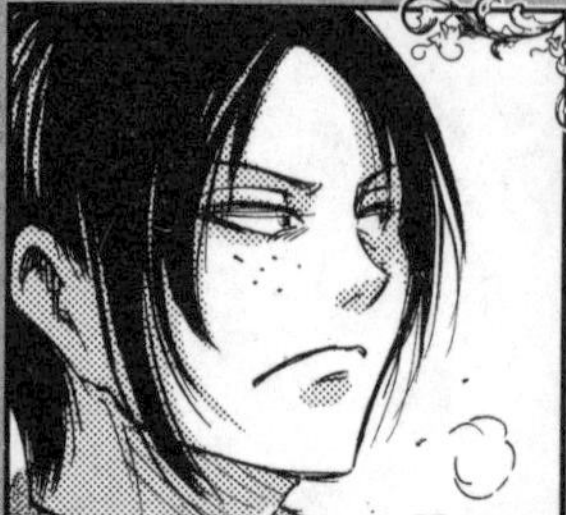

Ymir

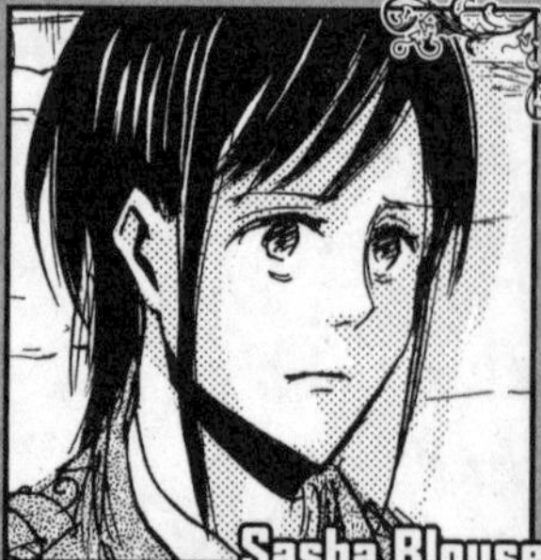

Sasha Blouse

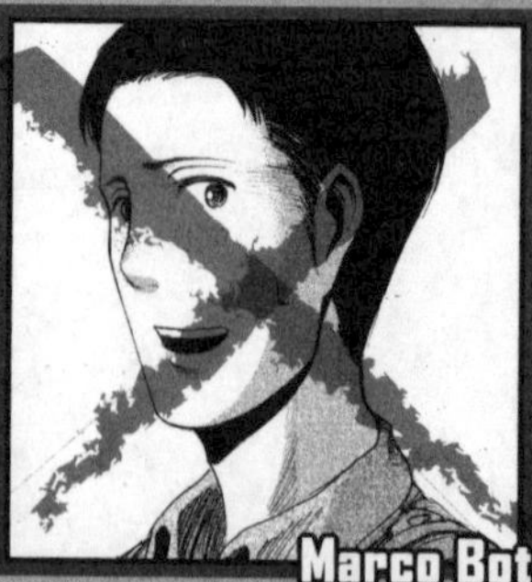

Marco Bott

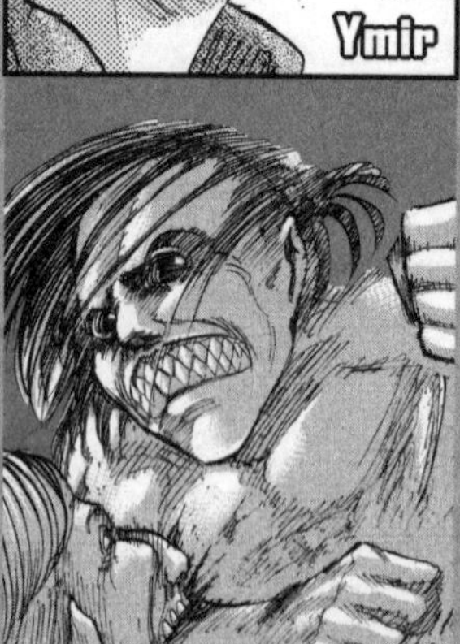

ATTACK on TITAN

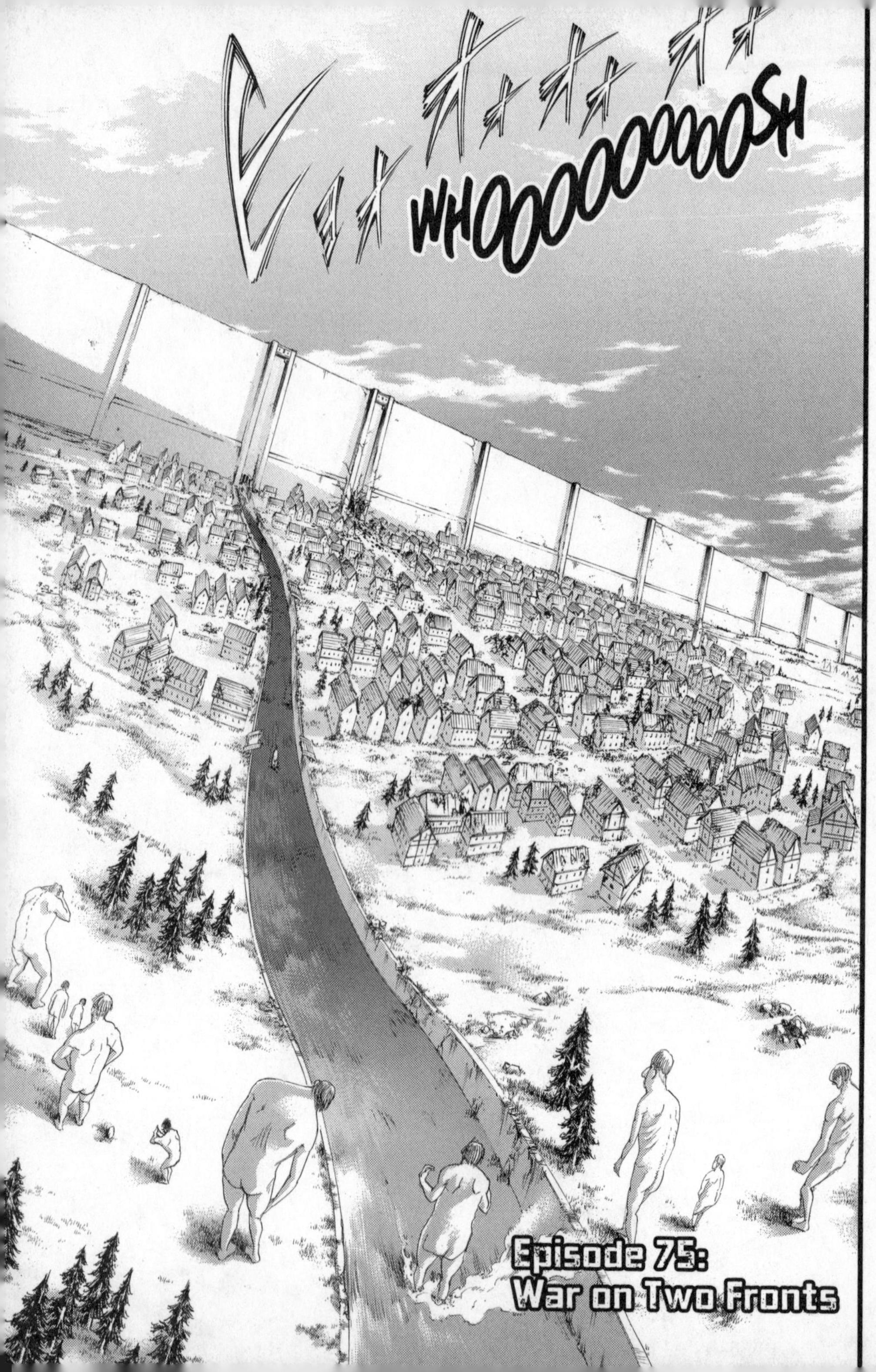
ヒュオオオオオオオオ
WHOOOOOOOOOSH
Episode 75:
War on Two Fronts

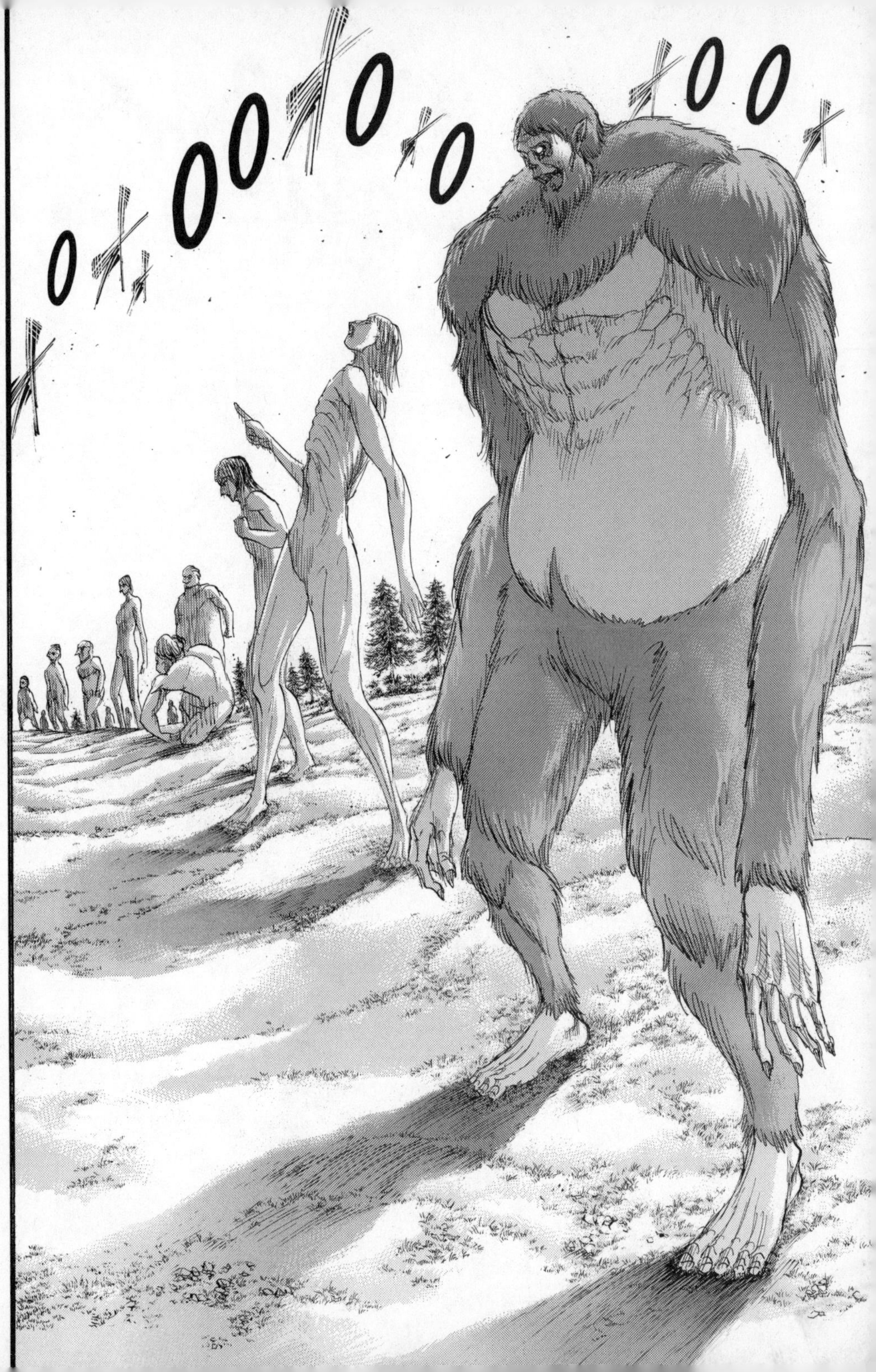

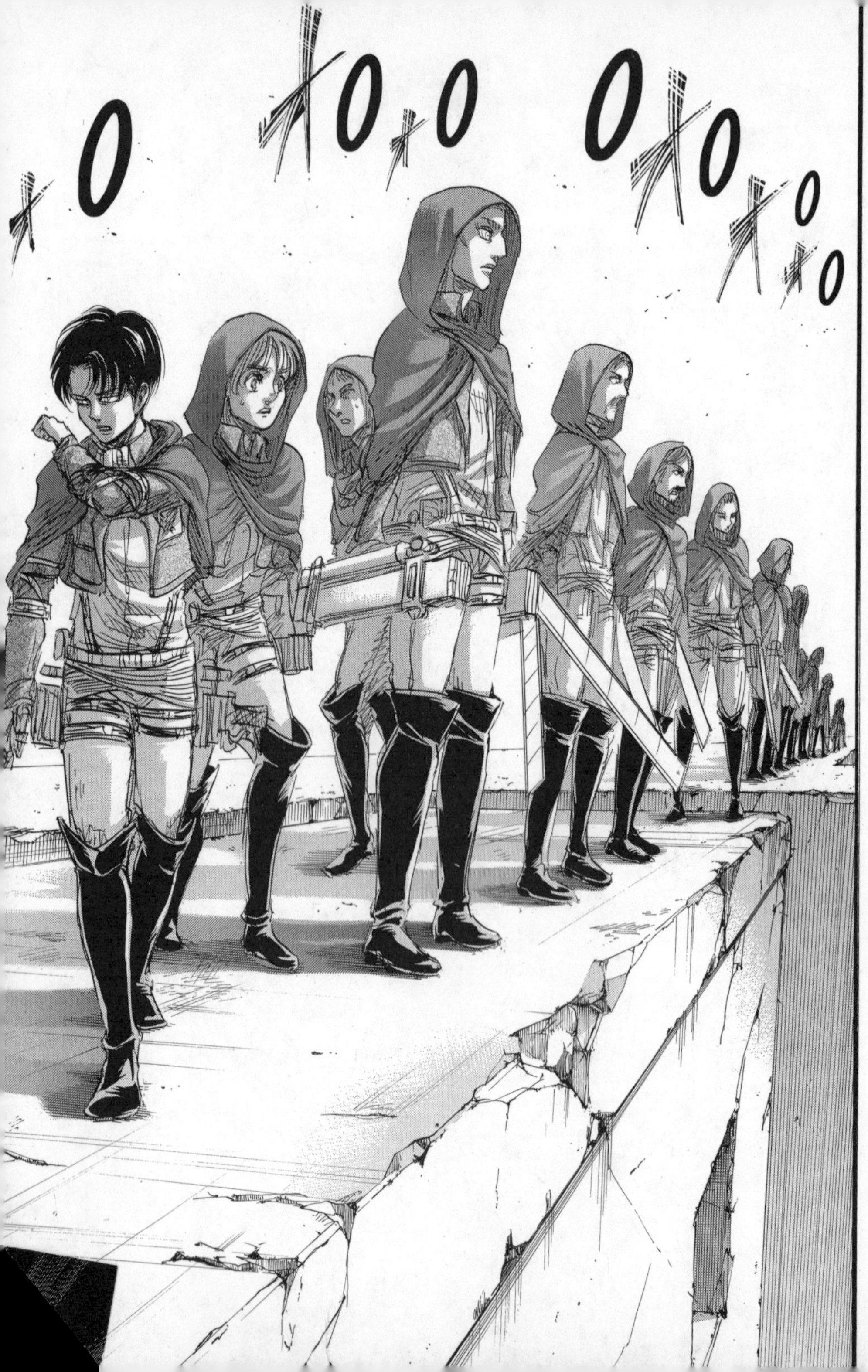
オO オOオO OオOオOオO

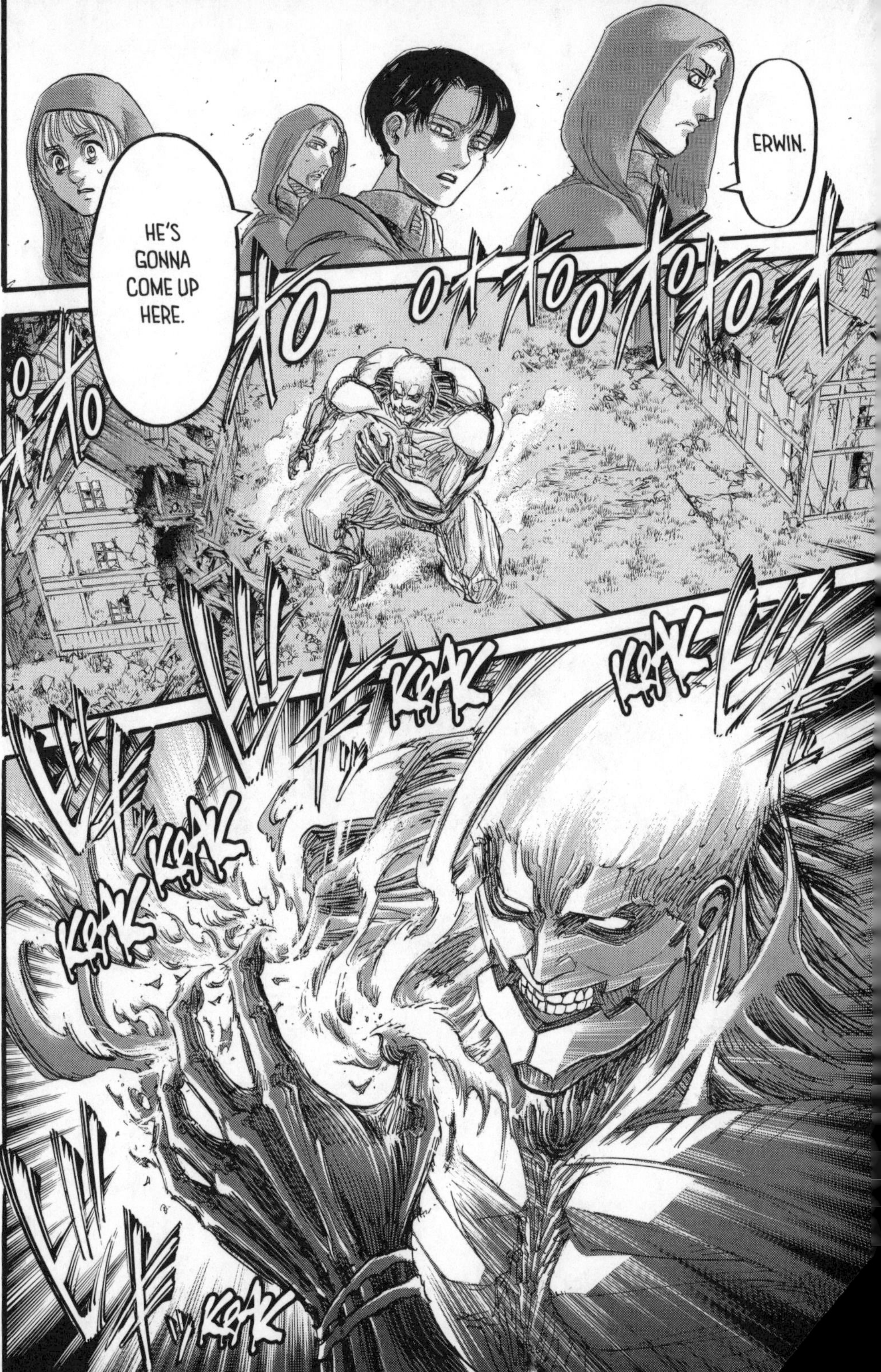
ERWIN.
HE'S GONNA COME UP HERE.
KRAK
KRAK
KRAK
KRAK
KRAK
KRAK

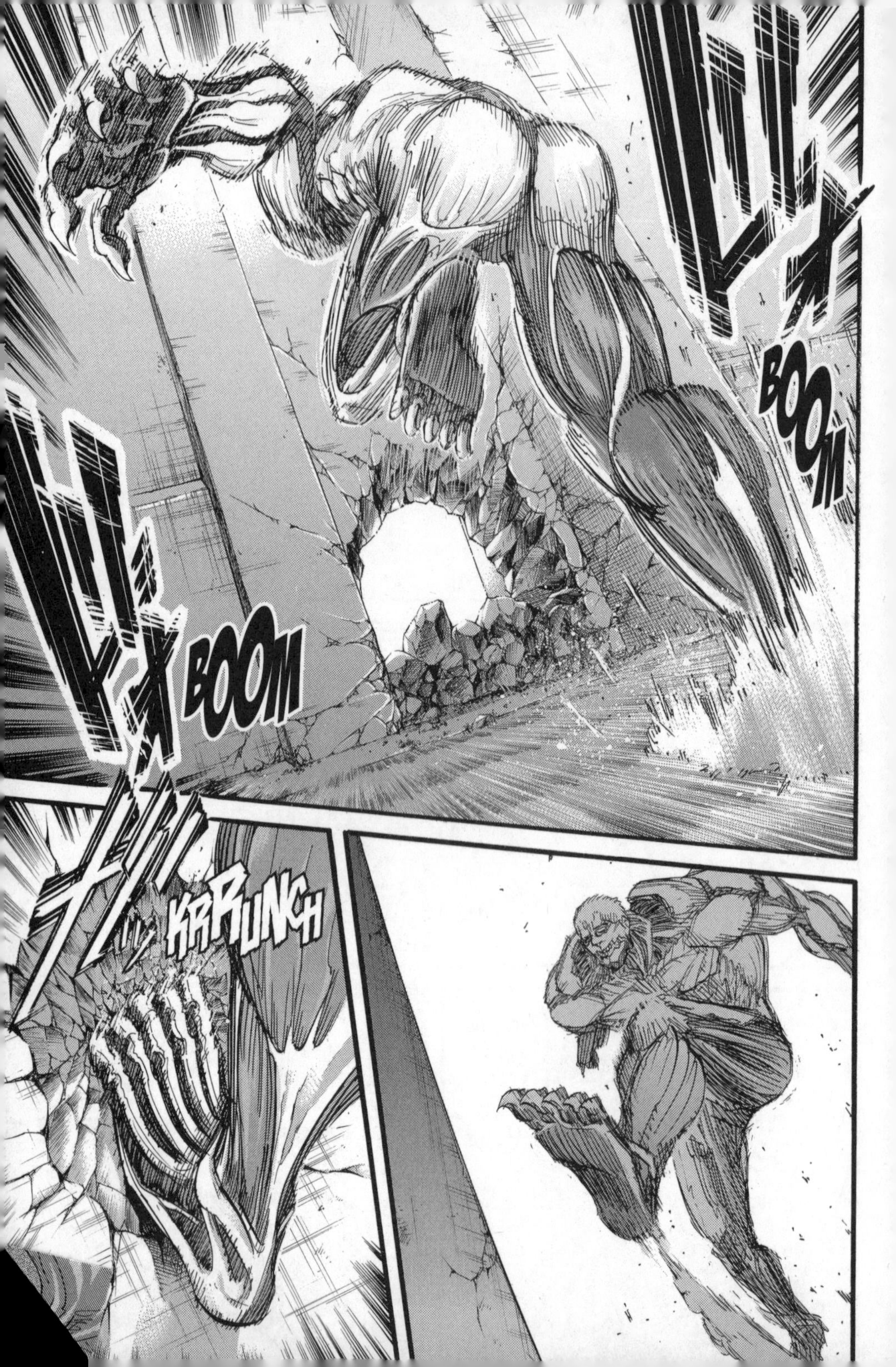
BOOM
BOOM
KRRUNCH

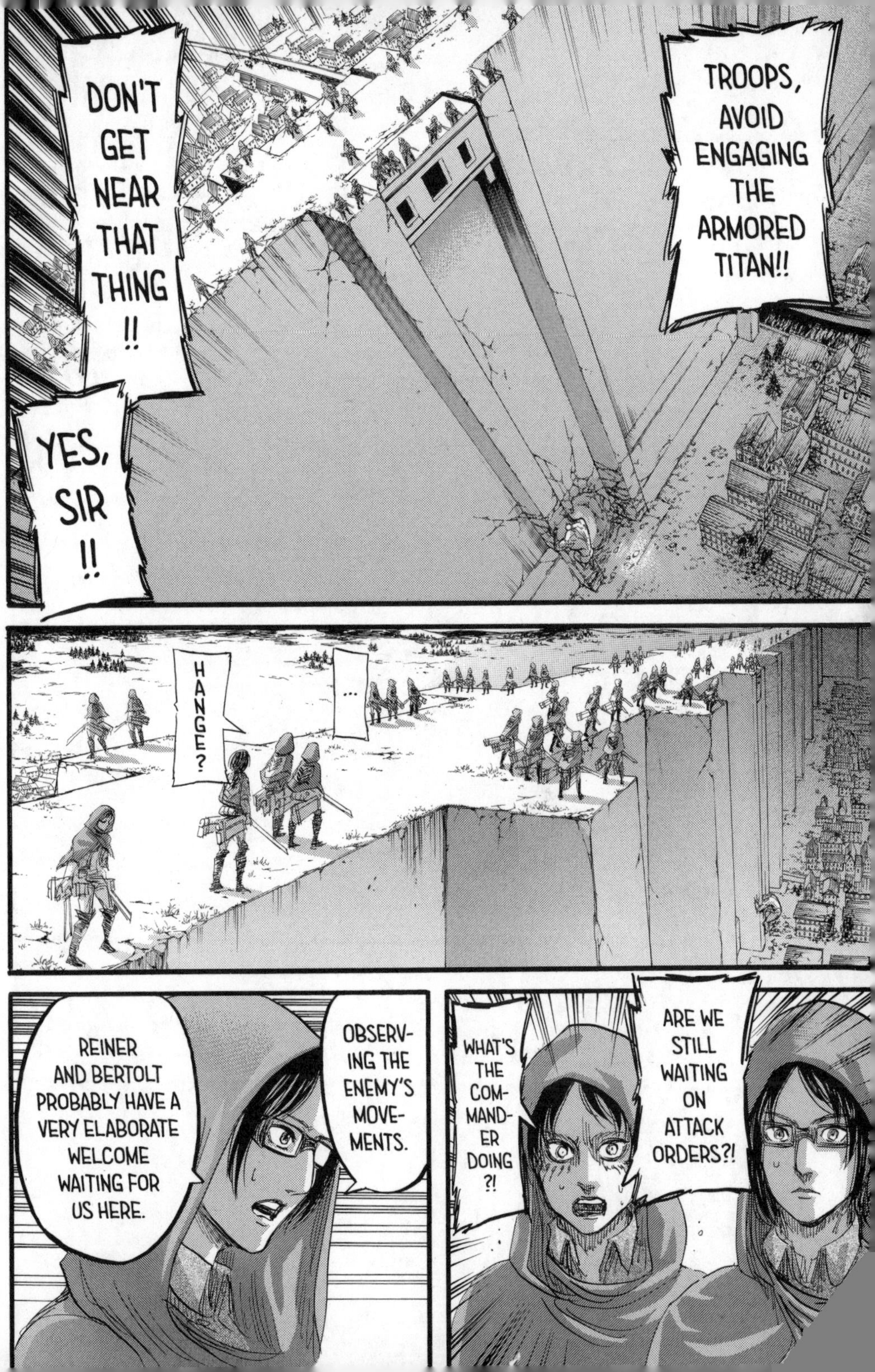
TROOPS, AVOID ENGAGING THE ARMORED TITAN!!
DON'T GET NEAR THAT THING!!
YES, SIR!!
...
HANGE?
ARE WE STILL WAITING ON ATTACK ORDERS?!
WHAT'S THE COM-MAND-ER DOING?!
OBSERV-ING THE ENEMY'S MOVE-MENTS.
REINER AND BERTOLT PROBABLY HAVE A VERY ELABORATE WELCOME WAITING FOR US HERE.

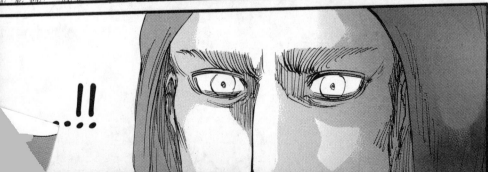

...!!

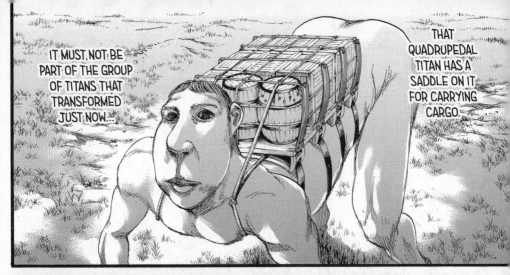

THAT QUADRUPEDAL TITAN HAS A SADDLE ON IT FOR CARRYING CARGO.

IT MUST NOT BE PART OF THE GROUP OF TITANS THAT TRANSFORMED JUST NOW...

COULD THAT MEAN IT'S AN ENEMY SCOUT?

IT COULD HAVE BEEN THE ONE THAT SPOTTED US APPROACHING AND WARNED REINER. IN THAT CASE...

CARGO?!

NO... THERE MUST BE EVEN MORE OF THEM OUT THERE.

WHAT COULD IT...

!

THAT QUADRUPEDAL TITAN IS INTELLIGENT, TOO.

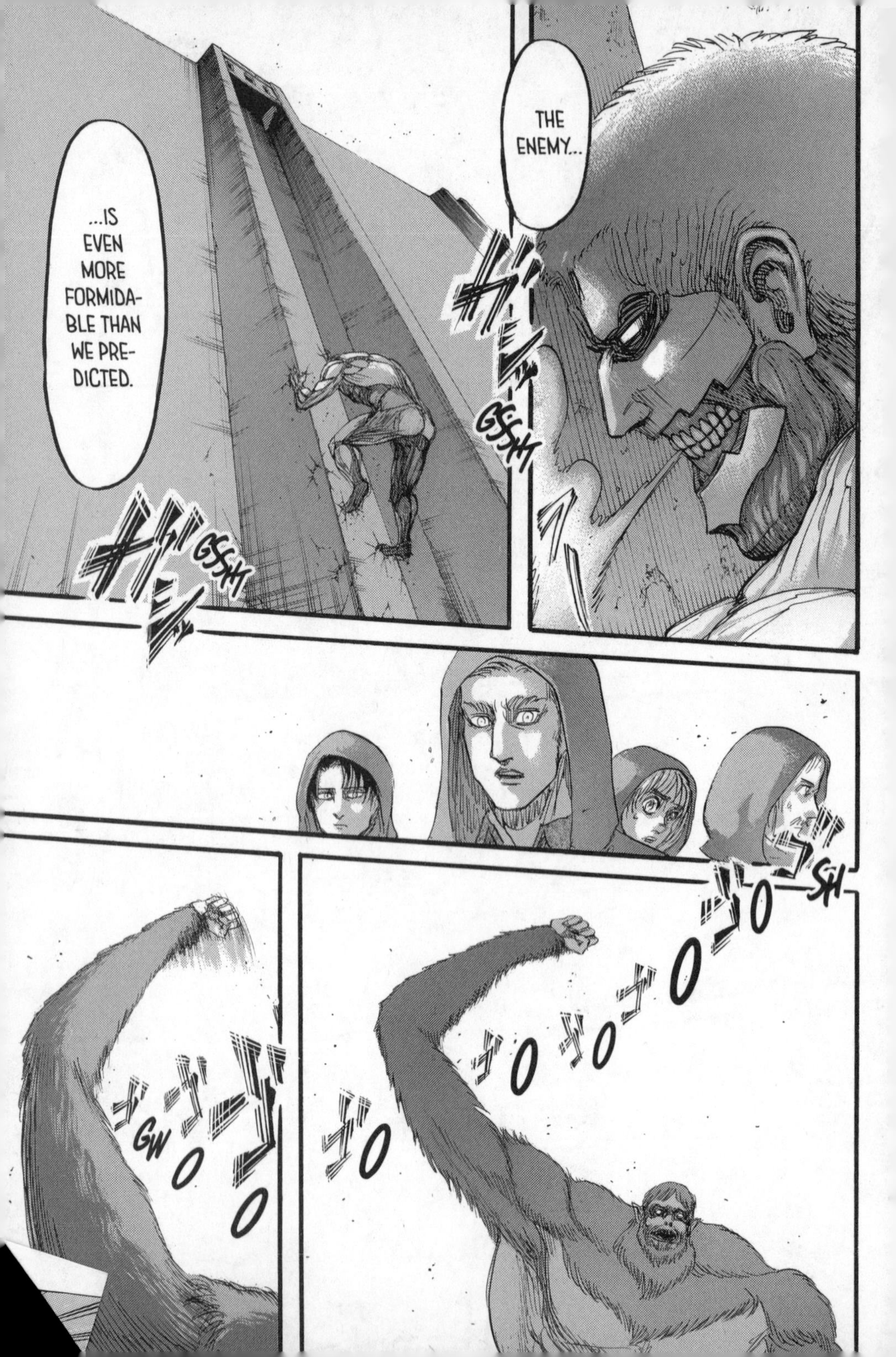
THE ENEMY...
GSSH
...IS EVEN MORE FORMIDABLE THAN WE PREDICTED.
GSSH
SH
GWOO

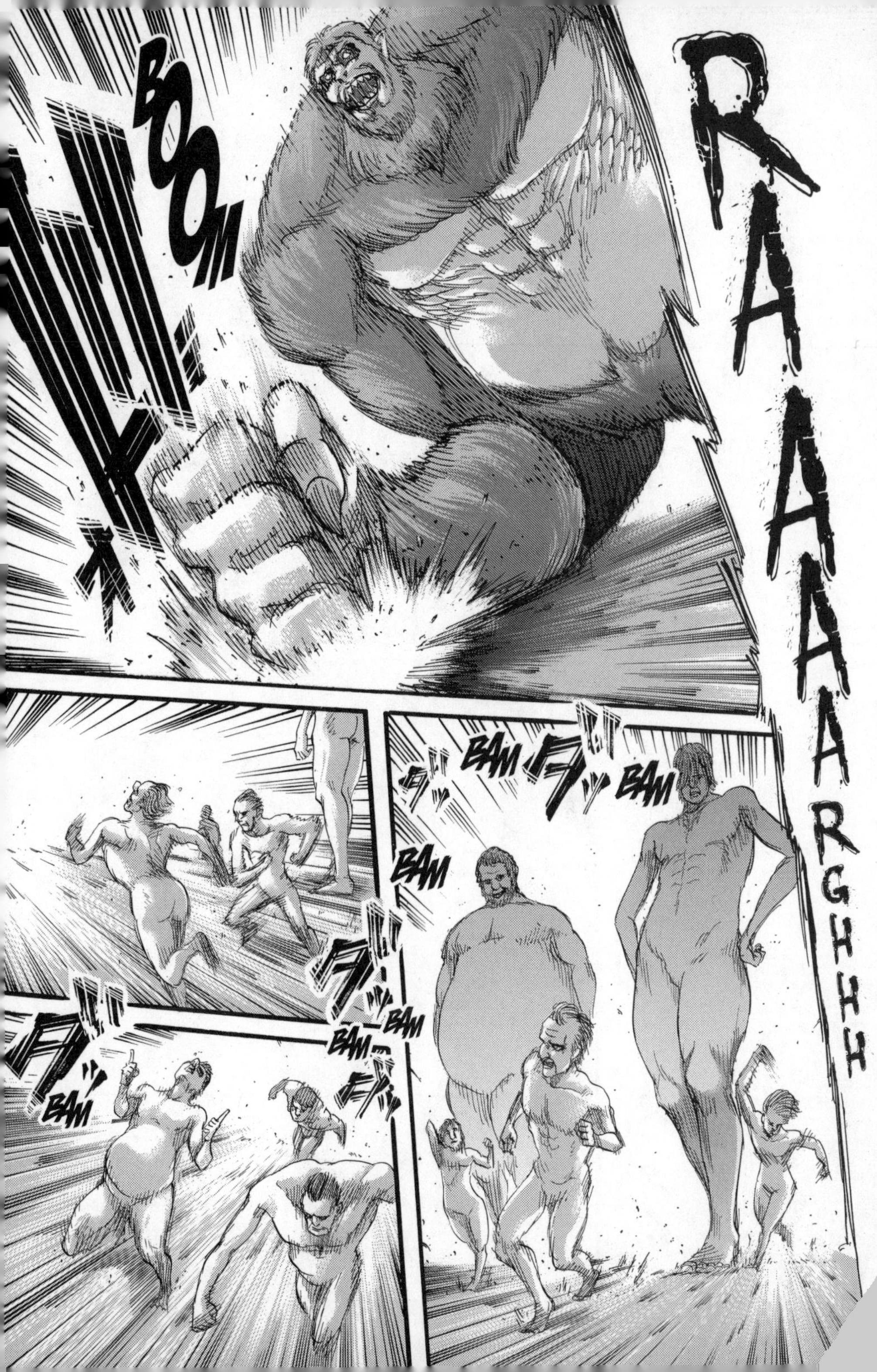
RAAAAARGHHH
BOOM
BAM
BAM
BAM
BAM
BAM
BAM

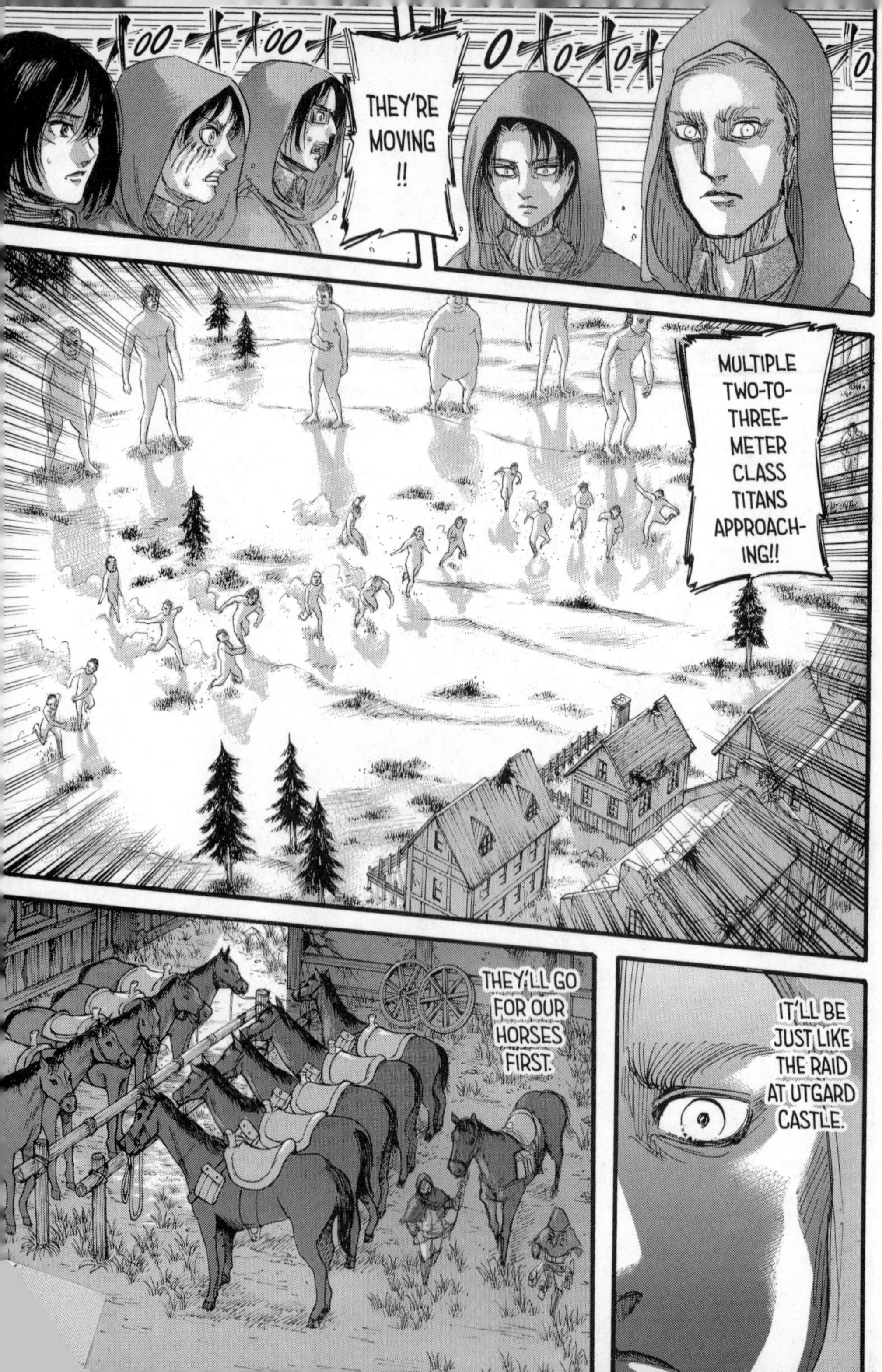
THEY'RE MOVING !!
MULTIPLE TWO-TO-THREE-METER CLASS TITANS APPROACHING!!
IT'LL BE JUST LIKE THE RAID AT UTGARD CASTLE.
THEY'LL GO FOR OUR HORSES FIRST.

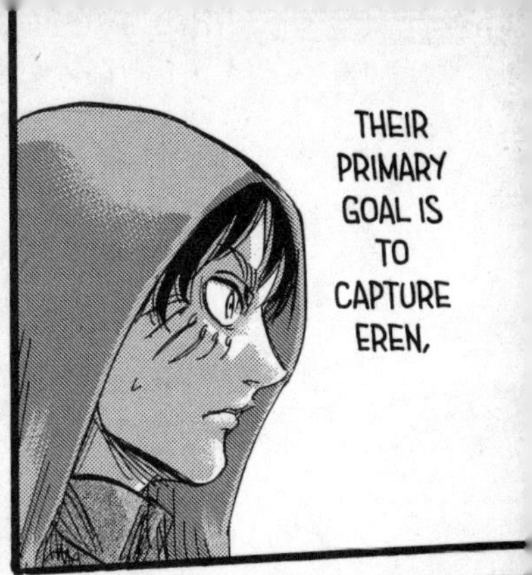
THEIR PRIMARY GOAL IS TO CAPTURE EREN,

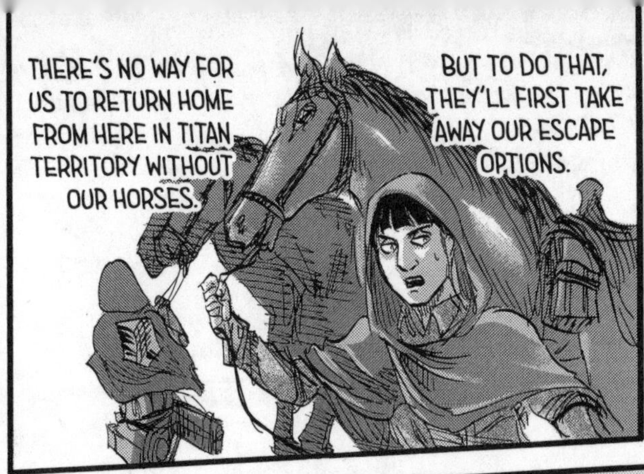
BUT TO DO THAT, THEY'LL FIRST TAKE AWAY OUR ESCAPE OPTIONS.
THERE'S NO WAY FOR US TO RETURN HOME FROM HERE IN TITAN TERRITORY WITHOUT OUR HORSES.

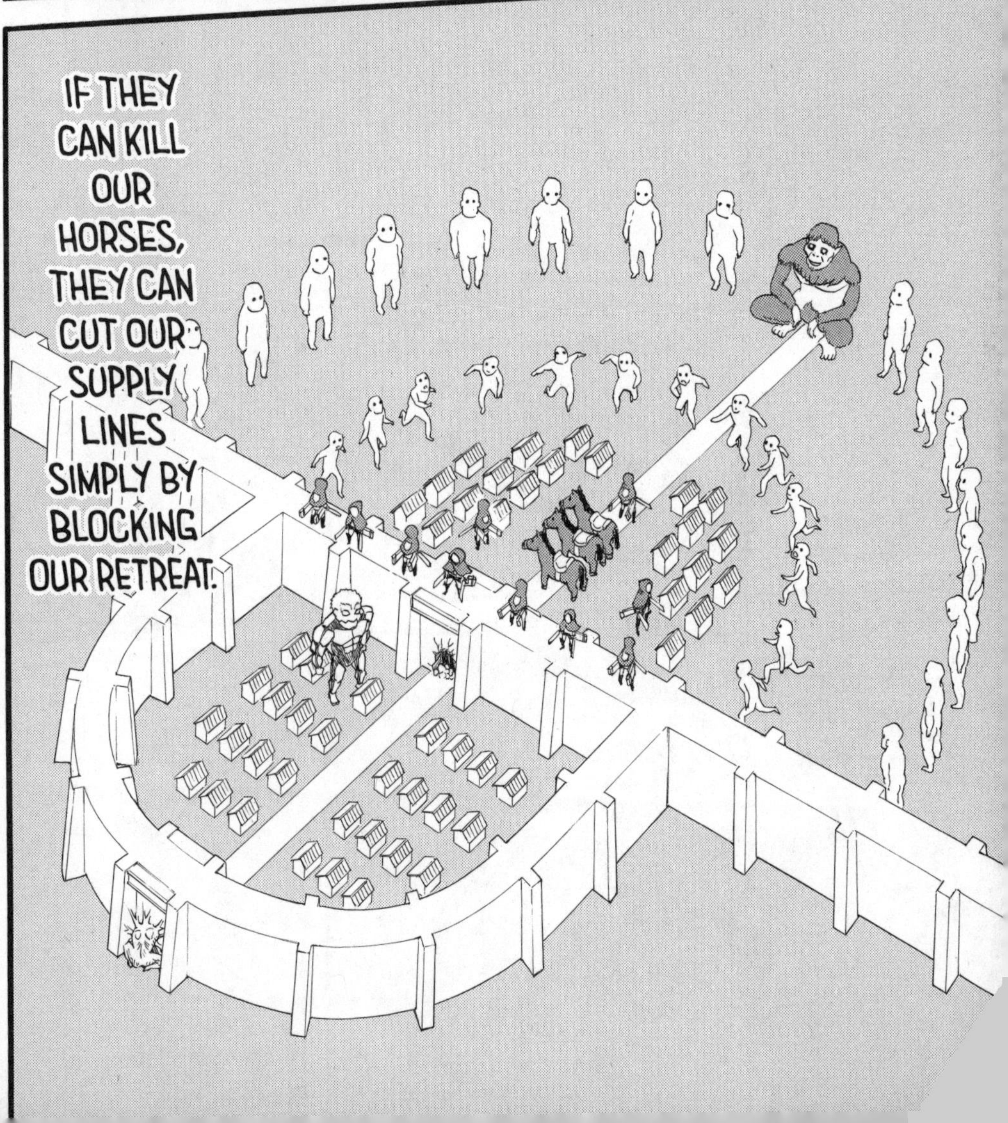
IF THEY CAN KILL OUR HORSES, THEY CAN CUT OUR SUPPLY LINES SIMPLY BY BLOCKING OUR RETREAT.

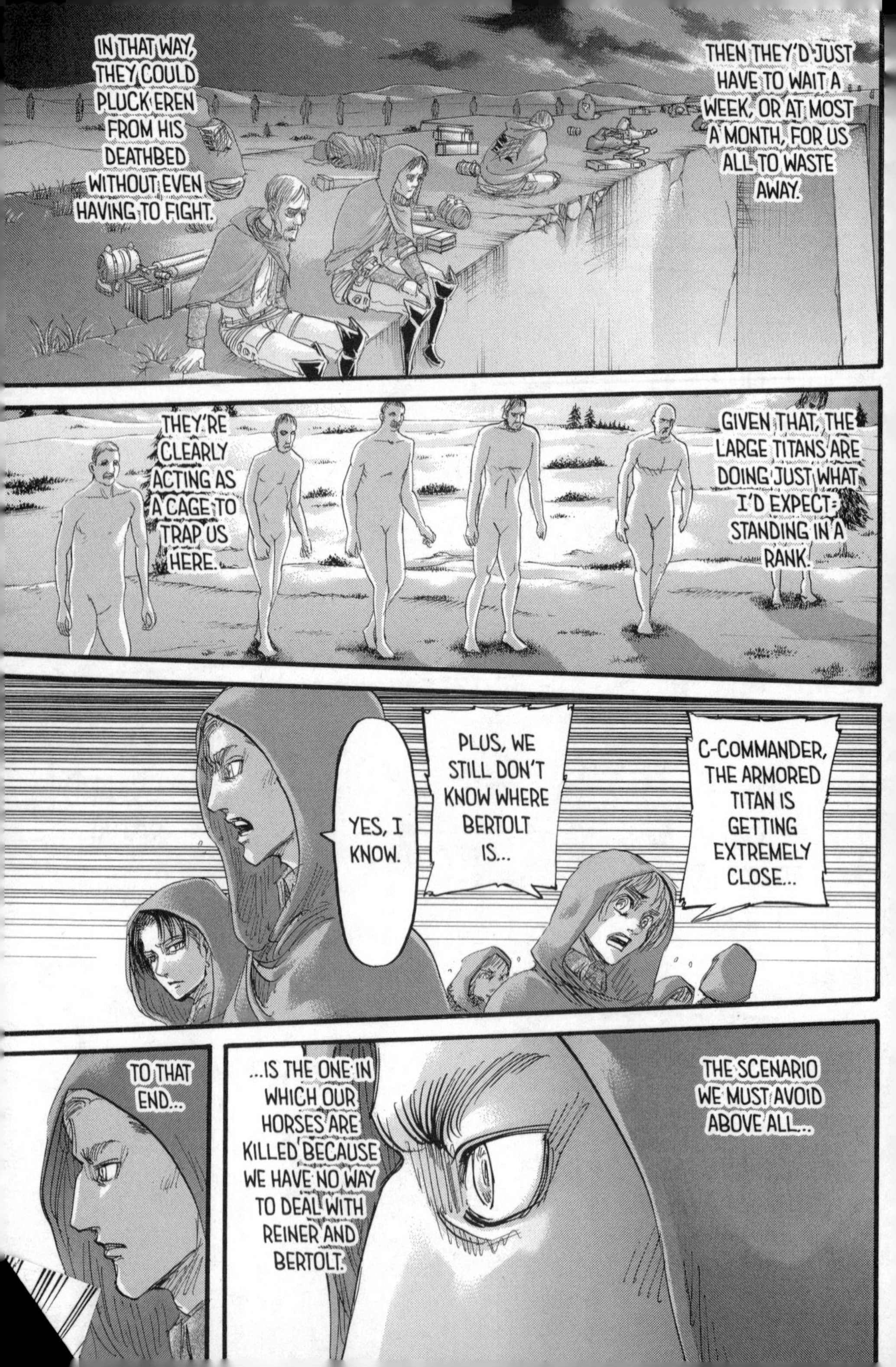
THEN THEY'D JUST HAVE TO WAIT A WEEK, OR AT MOST A MONTH, FOR US ALL TO WASTE AWAY.
IN THAT WAY, THEY COULD PLUCK EREN FROM HIS DEATHBED WITHOUT EVEN HAVING TO FIGHT.
GIVEN THAT, THE LARGE TITANS ARE DOING JUST WHAT I'D EXPECT: STANDING IN A RANK.
THEY'RE CLEARLY ACTING AS A CAGE TO TRAP US HERE.
C-COMMANDER, THE ARMORED TITAN IS GETTING EXTREMELY CLOSE...
PLUS, WE STILL DON'T KNOW WHERE BERTOLT IS...
YES, I KNOW.
THE SCENARIO WE MUST AVOID ABOVE ALL...
...IS THE ONE IN WHICH OUR HORSES ARE KILLED BECAUSE WE HAVE NO WAY TO DEAL WITH REINER AND BERTOLT.
TO THAT END...

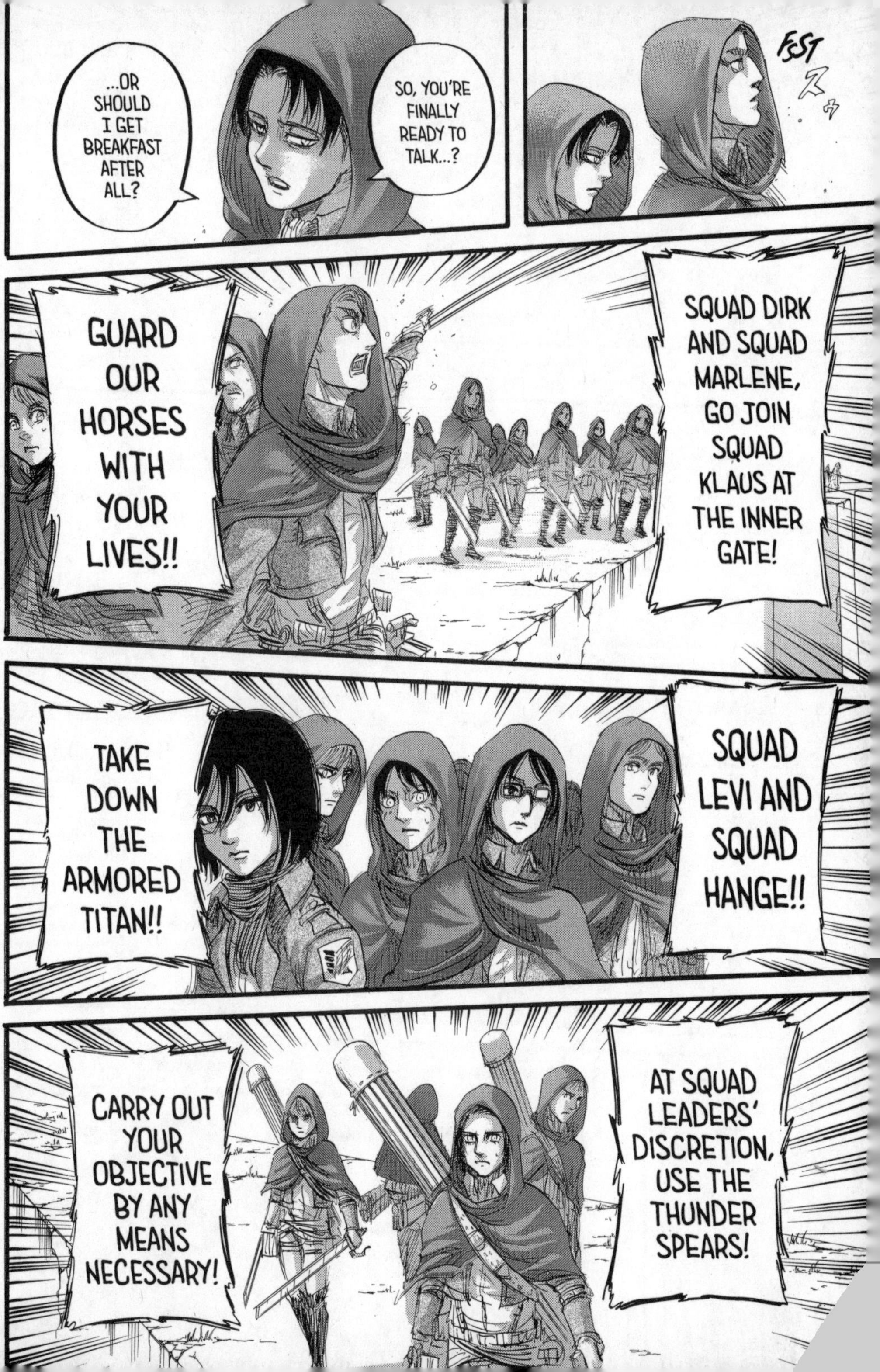
FSST
スッ
SO, YOU'RE FINALLY READY TO TALK...?
...OR SHOULD I GET BREAKFAST AFTER ALL?
SQUAD DIRK AND SQUAD MARLENE, GO JOIN SQUAD KLAUS AT THE INNER GATE!
GUARD OUR HORSES WITH YOUR LIVES!!
SQUAD LEVI AND SQUAD HANGE!!
TAKE DOWN THE ARMORED TITAN!!
AT SQUAD LEADERS' DISCRETION, USE THE THUNDER SPEARS!
CARRY OUT YOUR OBJECTIVE BY ANY MEANS NECESSARY!

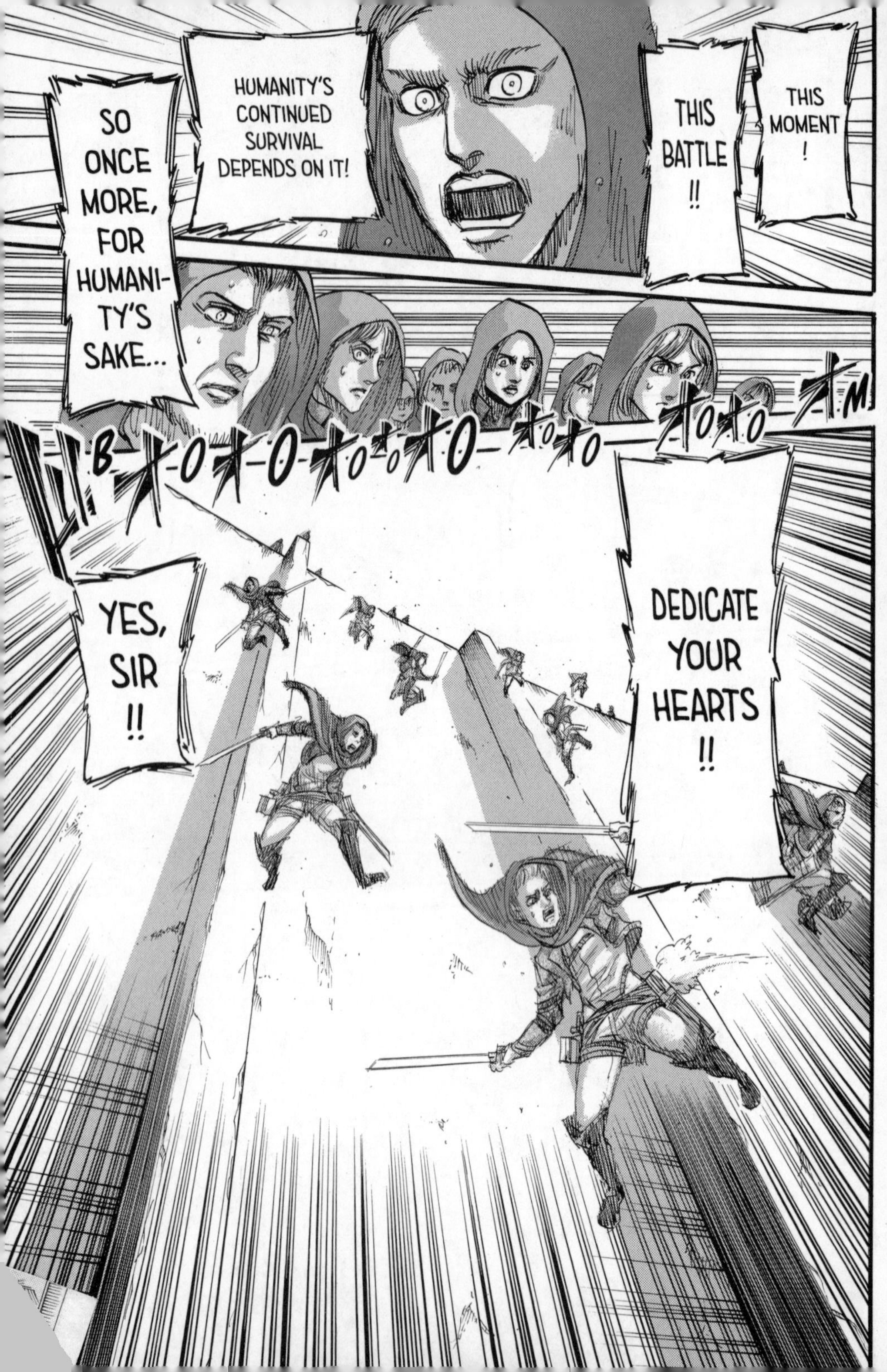

THIS MOMENT!
THIS BATTLE!!
HUMANITY'S CONTINUED SURVIVAL DEPENDS ON IT!
SO ONCE MORE, FOR HUMANI-TY'S SAKE...
BOOOOOOOOOOOOM
DEDICATE YOUR HEARTS!!
YES, SIR!!

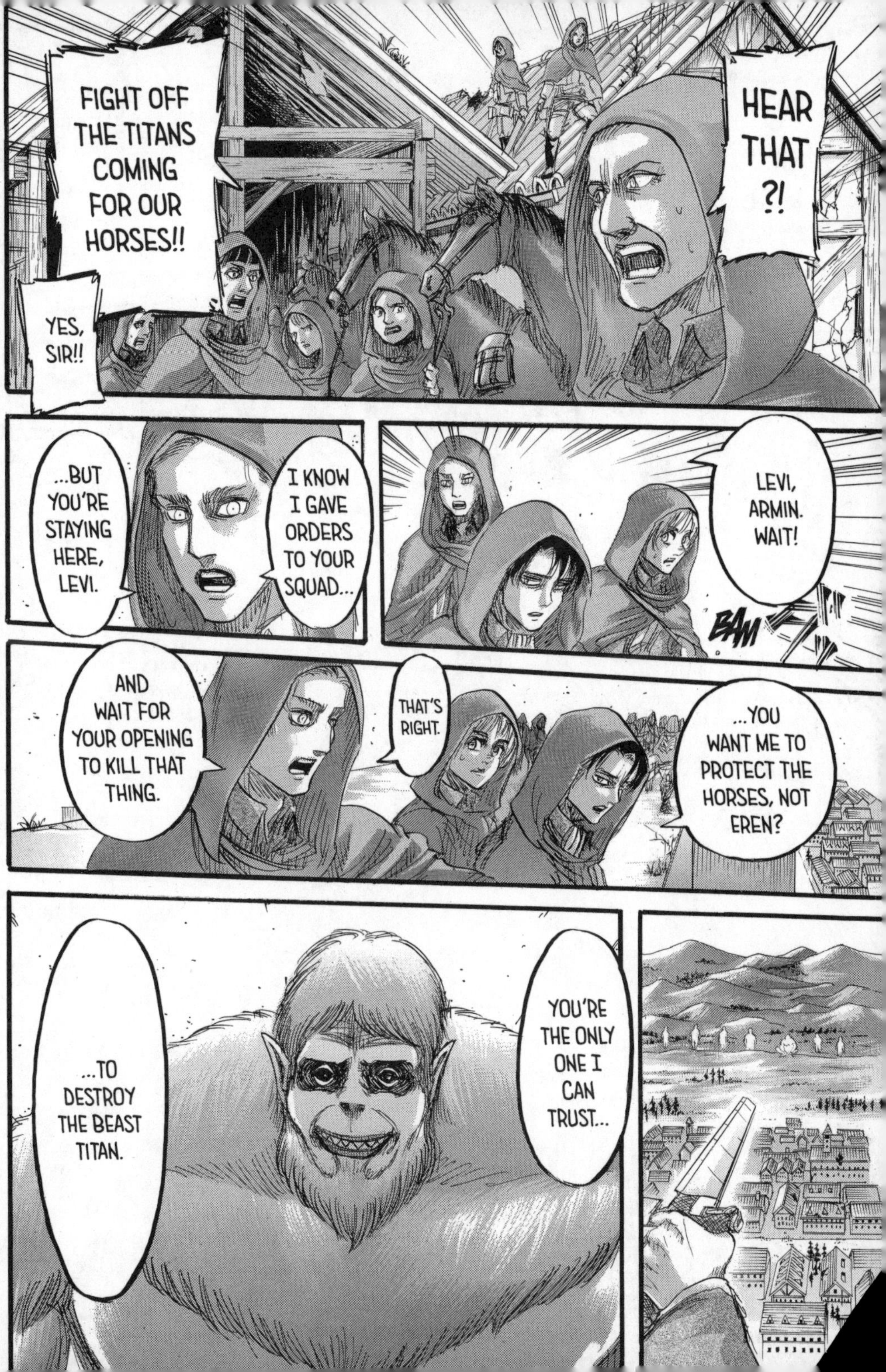
HEAR THAT?!
FIGHT OFF THE TITANS COMING FOR OUR HORSES!!
YES, SIR!!
LEVI, ARMIN. WAIT!
BAM
I KNOW I GAVE ORDERS TO YOUR SQUAD...
...BUT YOU'RE STAYING HERE, LEVI.
...YOU WANT ME TO PROTECT THE HORSES, NOT EREN?
THAT'S RIGHT.
AND WAIT FOR YOUR OPENING TO KILL THAT THING.
YOU'RE THE ONLY ONE I CAN TRUST...
...TO DESTROY THE BEAST TITAN.

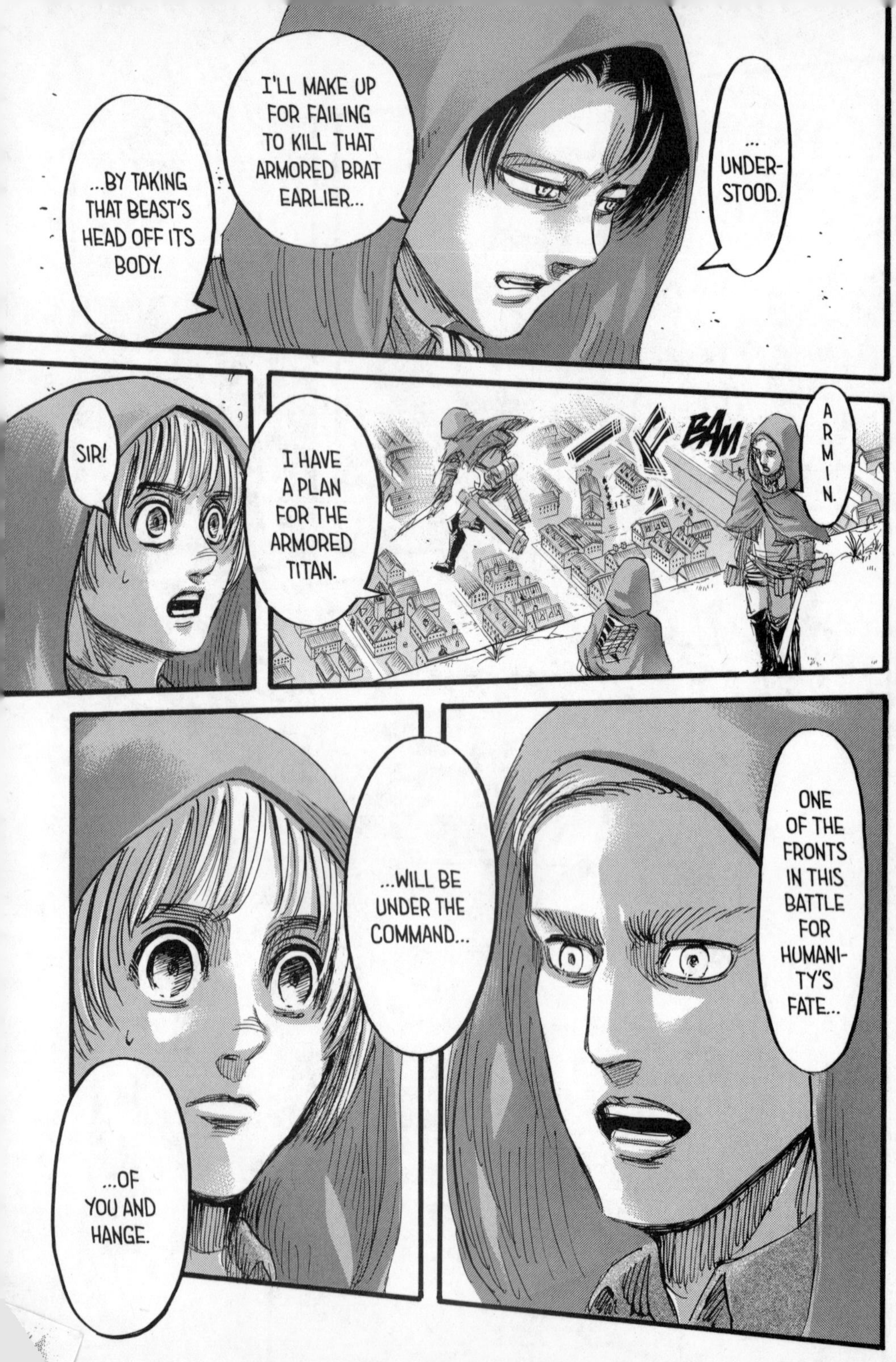
...UNDERSTOOD.
I'LL MAKE UP FOR FAILING TO KILL THAT ARMORED BRAT EARLIER...
...BY TAKING THAT BEAST'S HEAD OFF ITS BODY.
ARMIN.
BAM
I HAVE A PLAN FOR THE ARMORED TITAN.
SIR!
ONE OF THE FRONTS IN THIS BATTLE FOR HUMANITY'S FATE...
...WILL BE UNDER THE COMMAND...
...OF YOU AND HANGE.

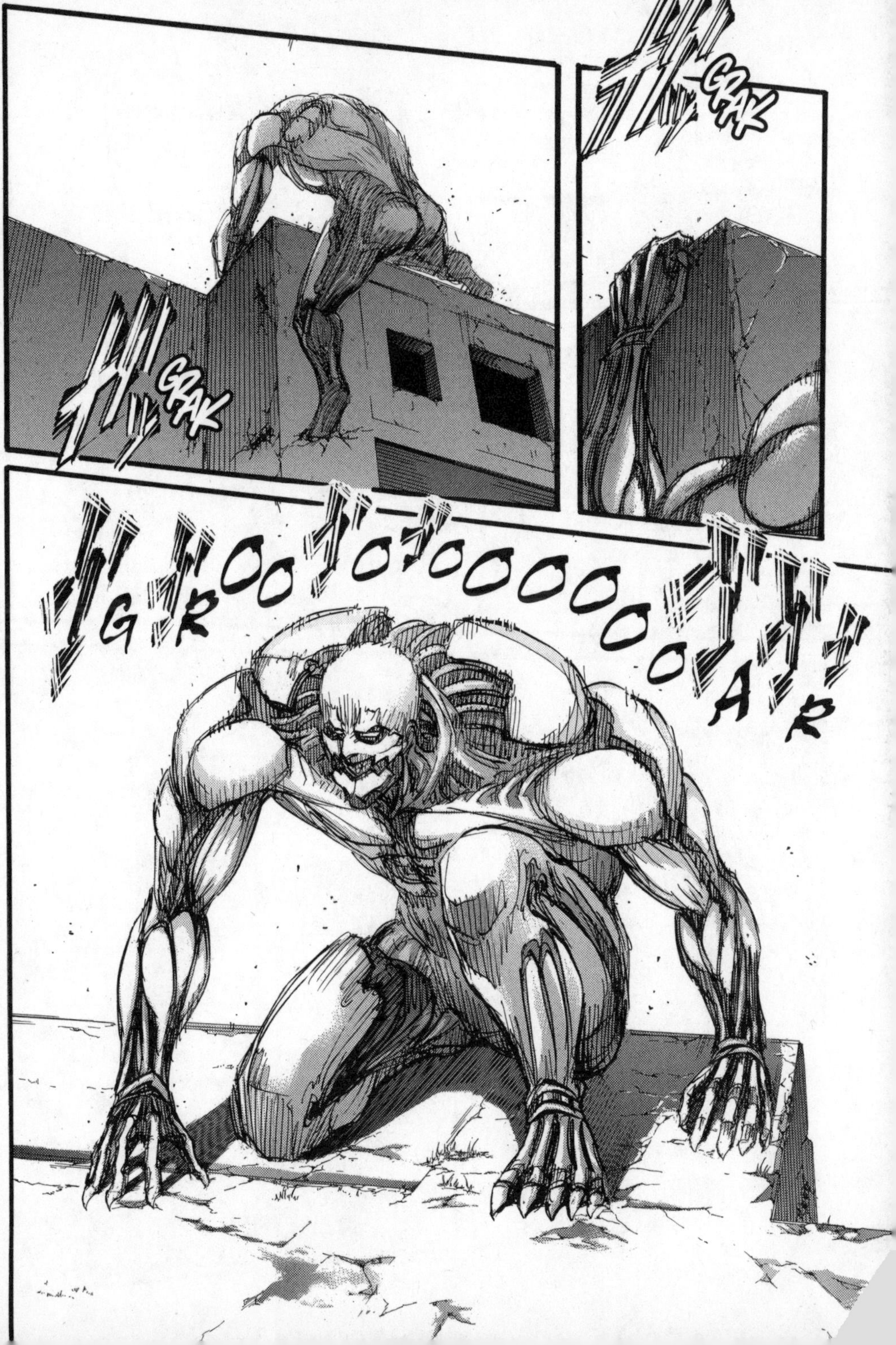
GRAK
GRAK
GROOOOOOOOOOOAR

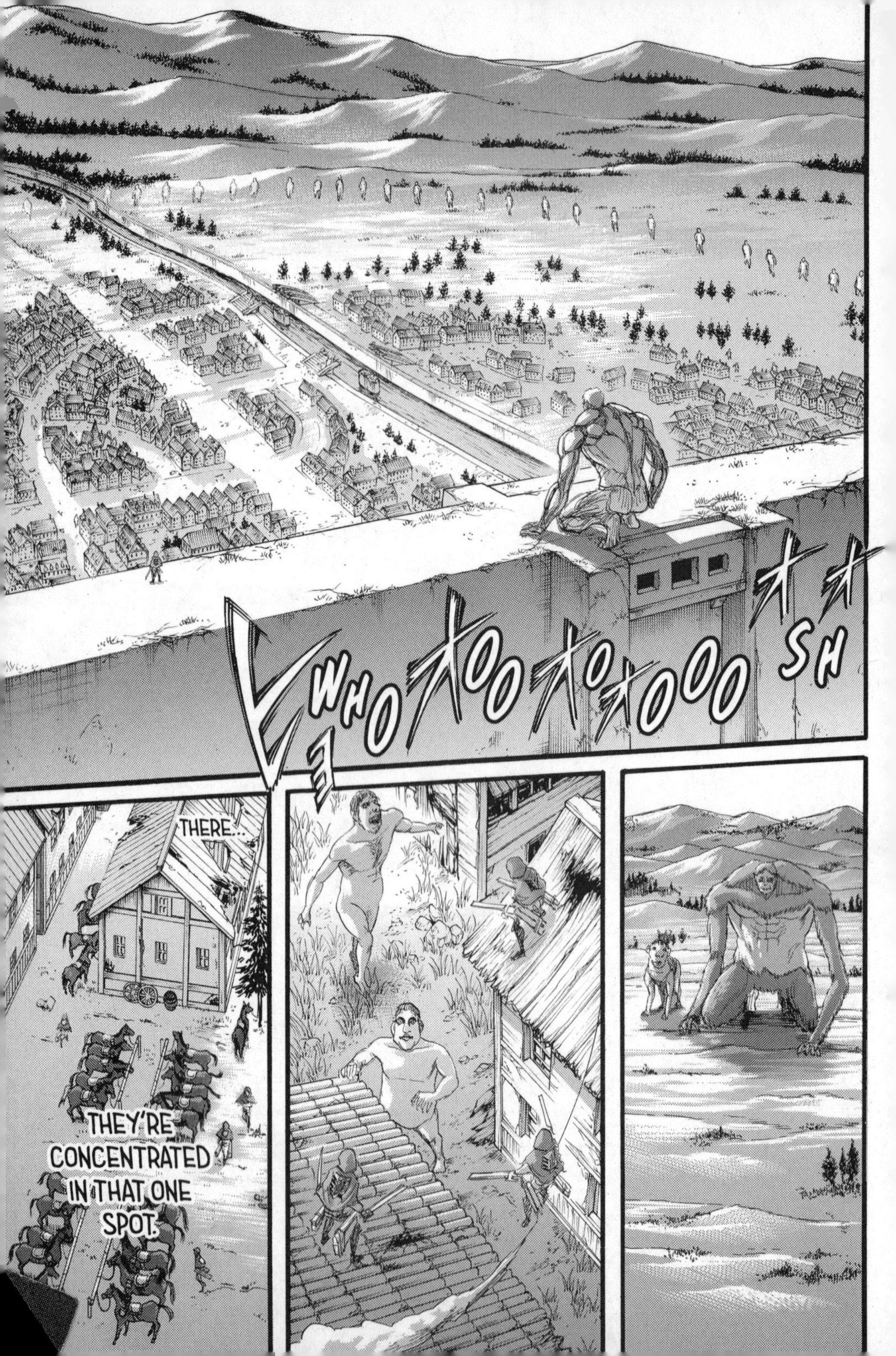
WHOOOOOOOSH
THERE...
THEY'RE CONCENTRATED IN THAT ONE SPOT.

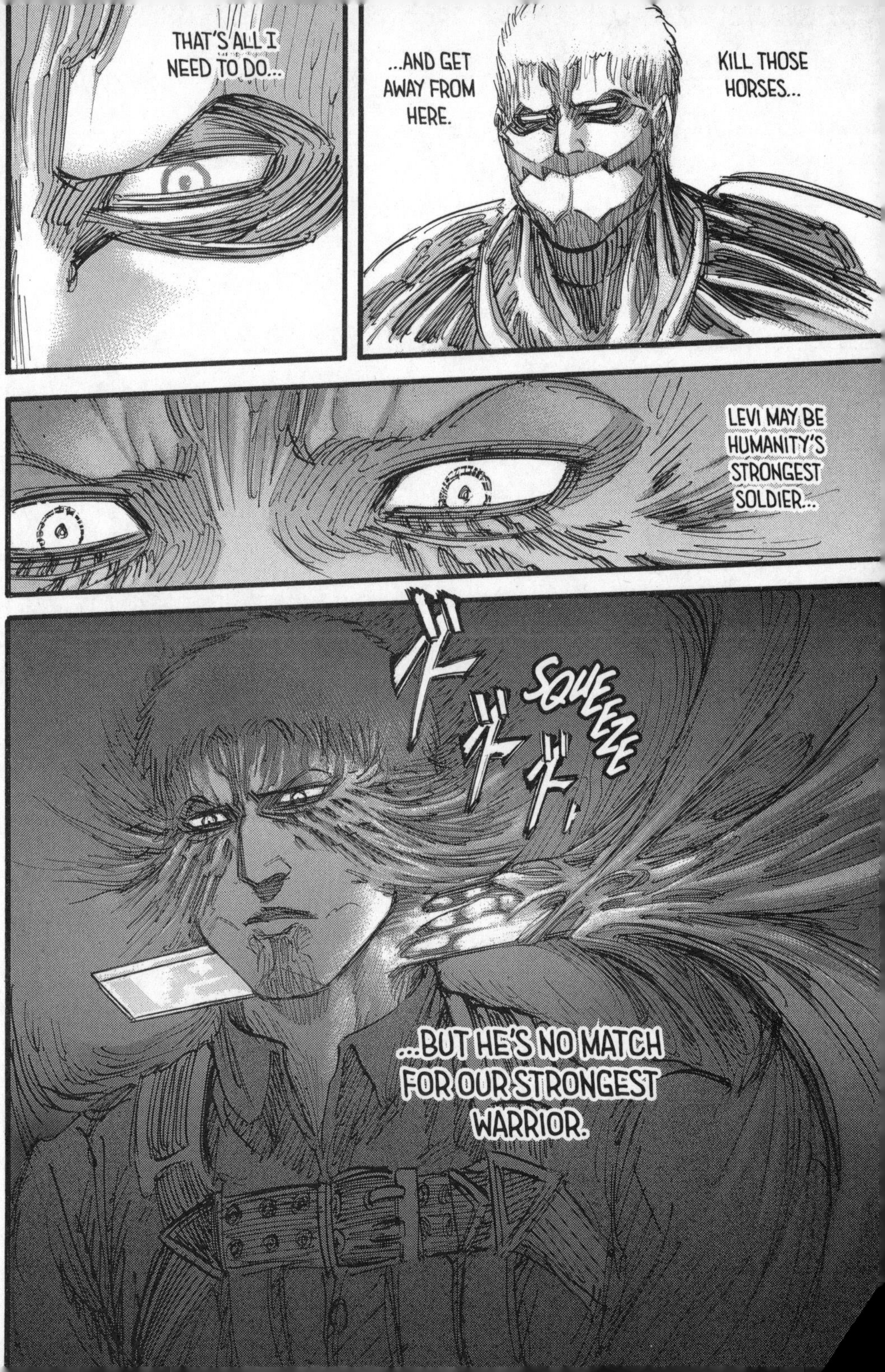
KILL THOSE HORSES...
...AND GET AWAY FROM HERE.
THAT'S ALL I NEED TO DO...
LEVI MAY BE HUMANITY'S STRONGEST SOLDIER...
SQUEEZE
...BUT HE'S NO MATCH FOR OUR STRONGEST WARRIOR.

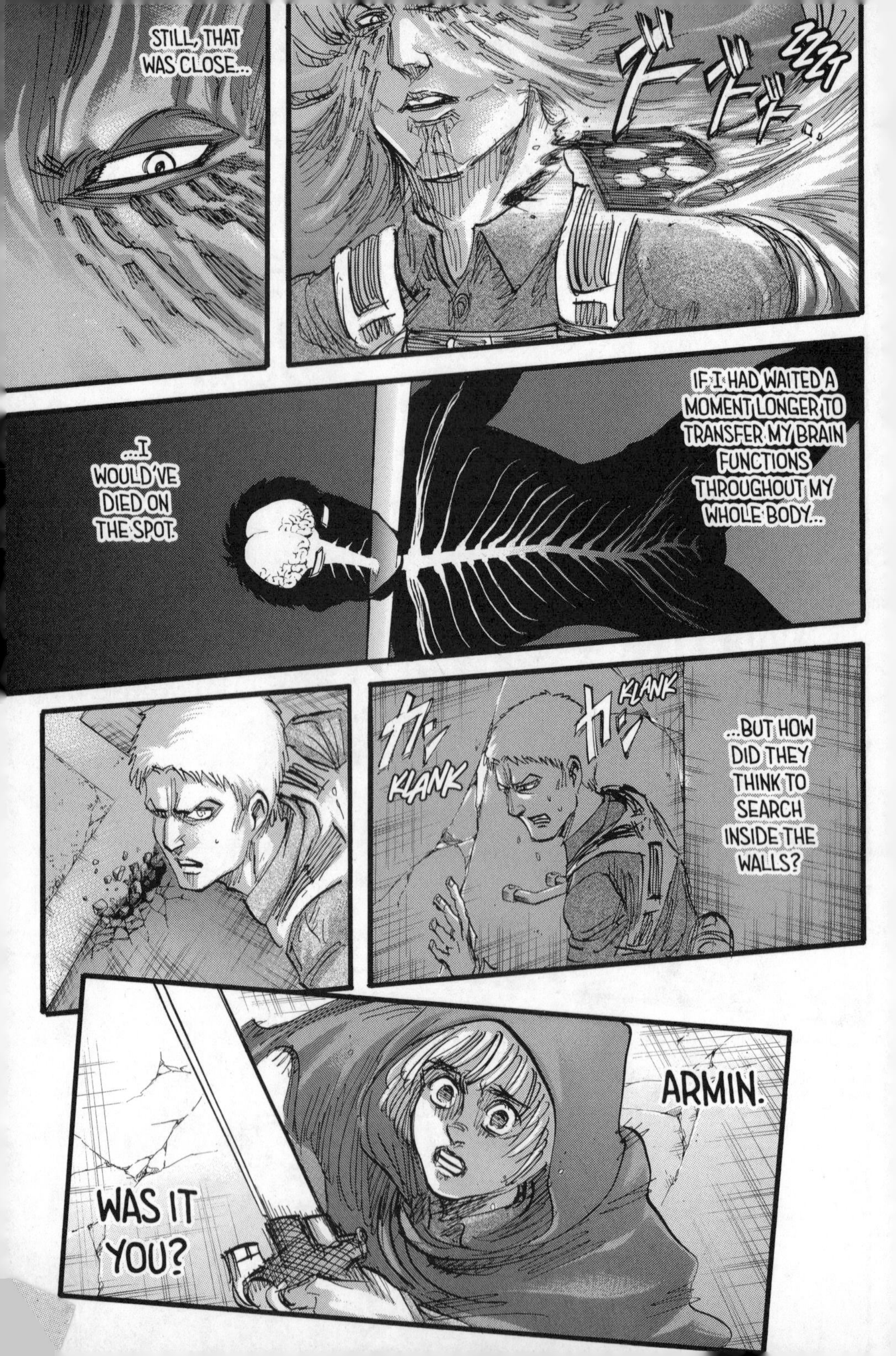
ZZZT
STILL, THAT WAS CLOSE...
IF I HAD WAITED A MOMENT LONGER TO TRANSFER MY BRAIN FUNCTIONS THROUGHOUT MY WHOLE BODY...
...I WOULD'VE DIED ON THE SPOT.
KLANK
KLANK
...BUT HOW DID THEY THINK TO SEARCH INSIDE THE WALLS?
ARMIN.
WAS IT YOU?

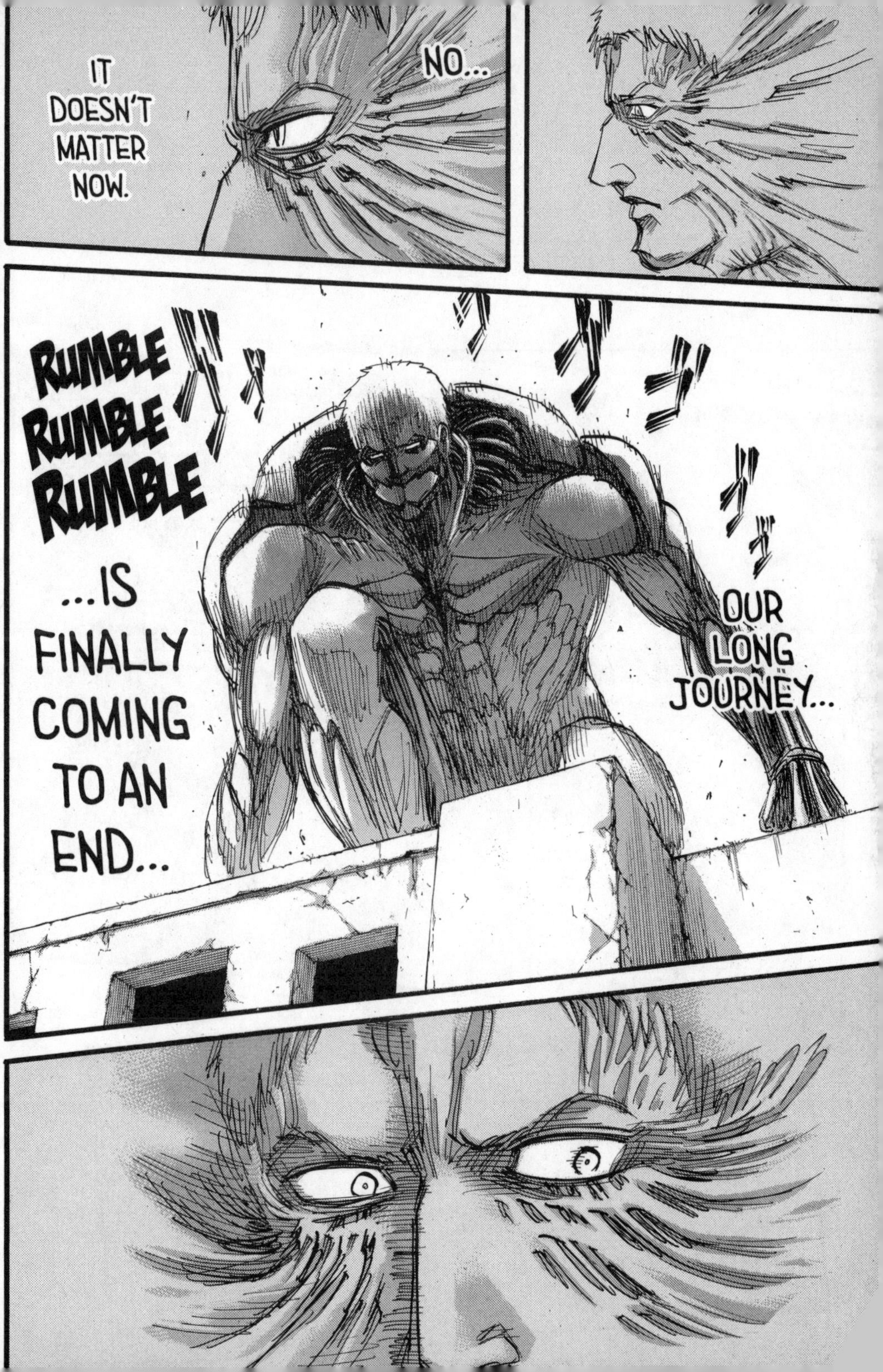
NO...
IT DOESN'T MATTER NOW.
OUR LONG JOURNEY...
RUMBLE RUMBLE RUMBLE
...IS FINALLY COMING TO AN END...

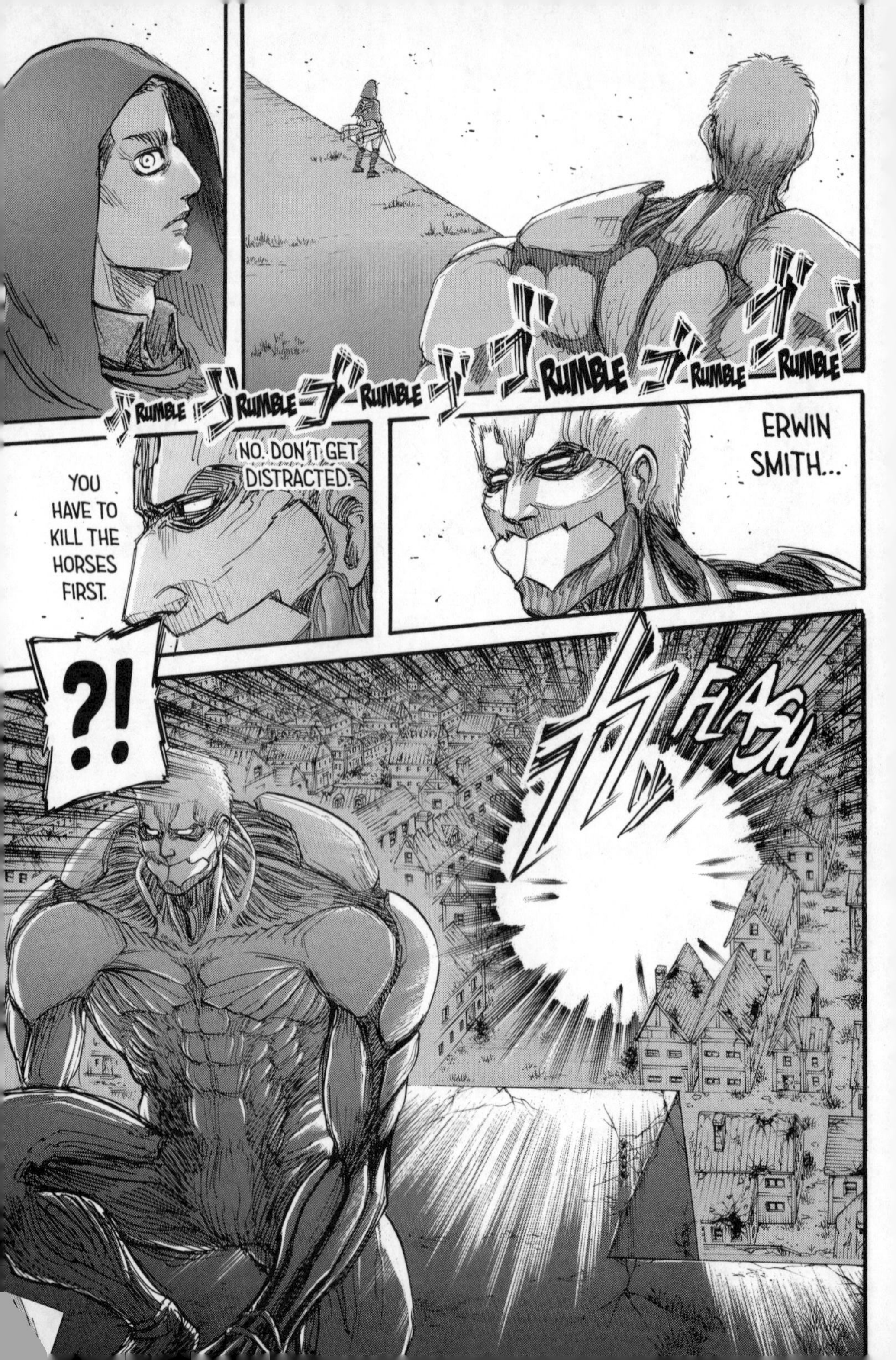
RUMBLE
RUMBLE
RUMBLE
RUMBLE
RUMBLE
RUMBLE
RUMBLE
ERWIN SMITH...
NO. DON'T GET DISTRACTED.
YOU HAVE TO KILL THE HORSES FIRST.
?!
FLASH

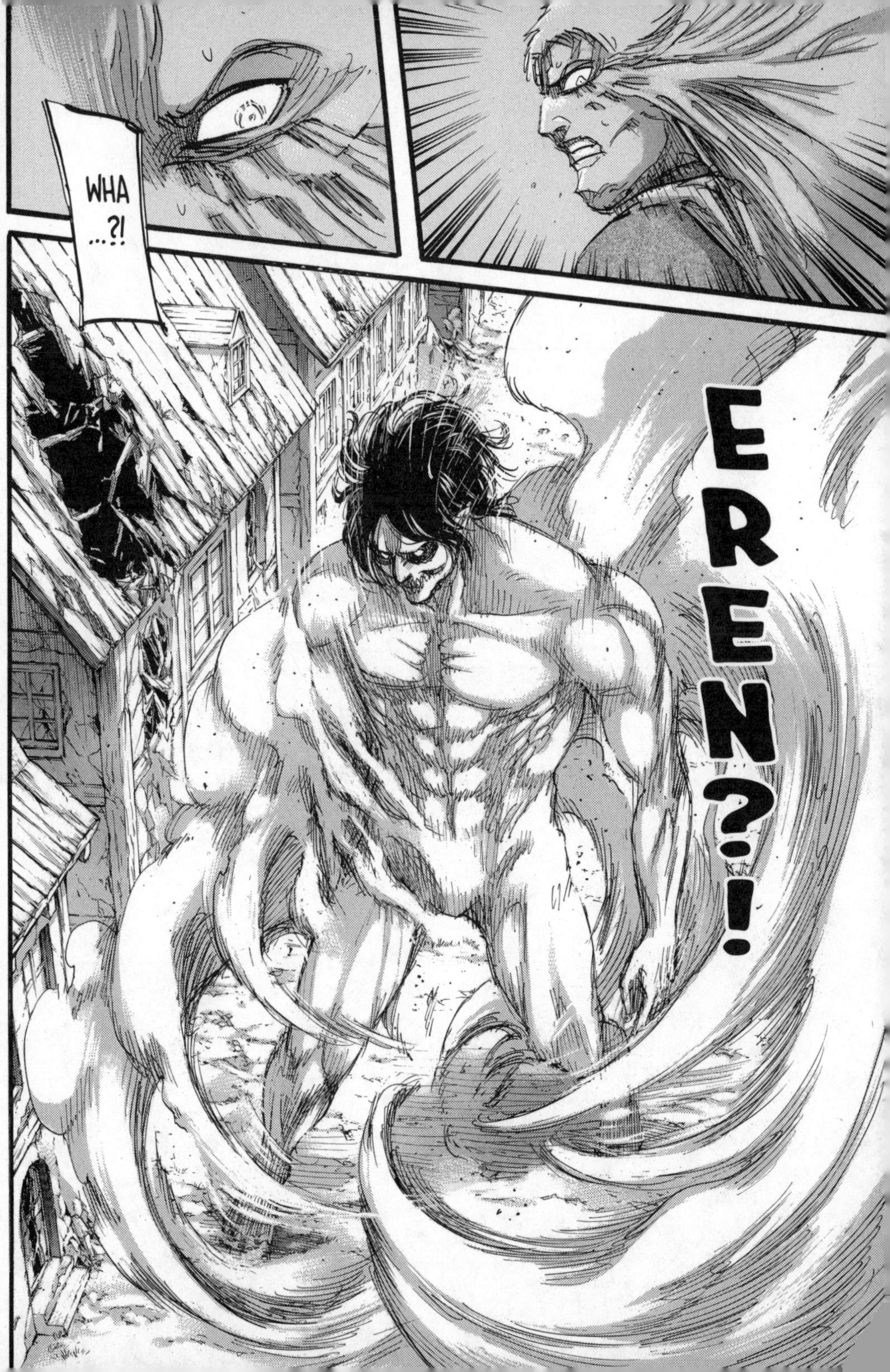
WHA ...?!
EREN?!

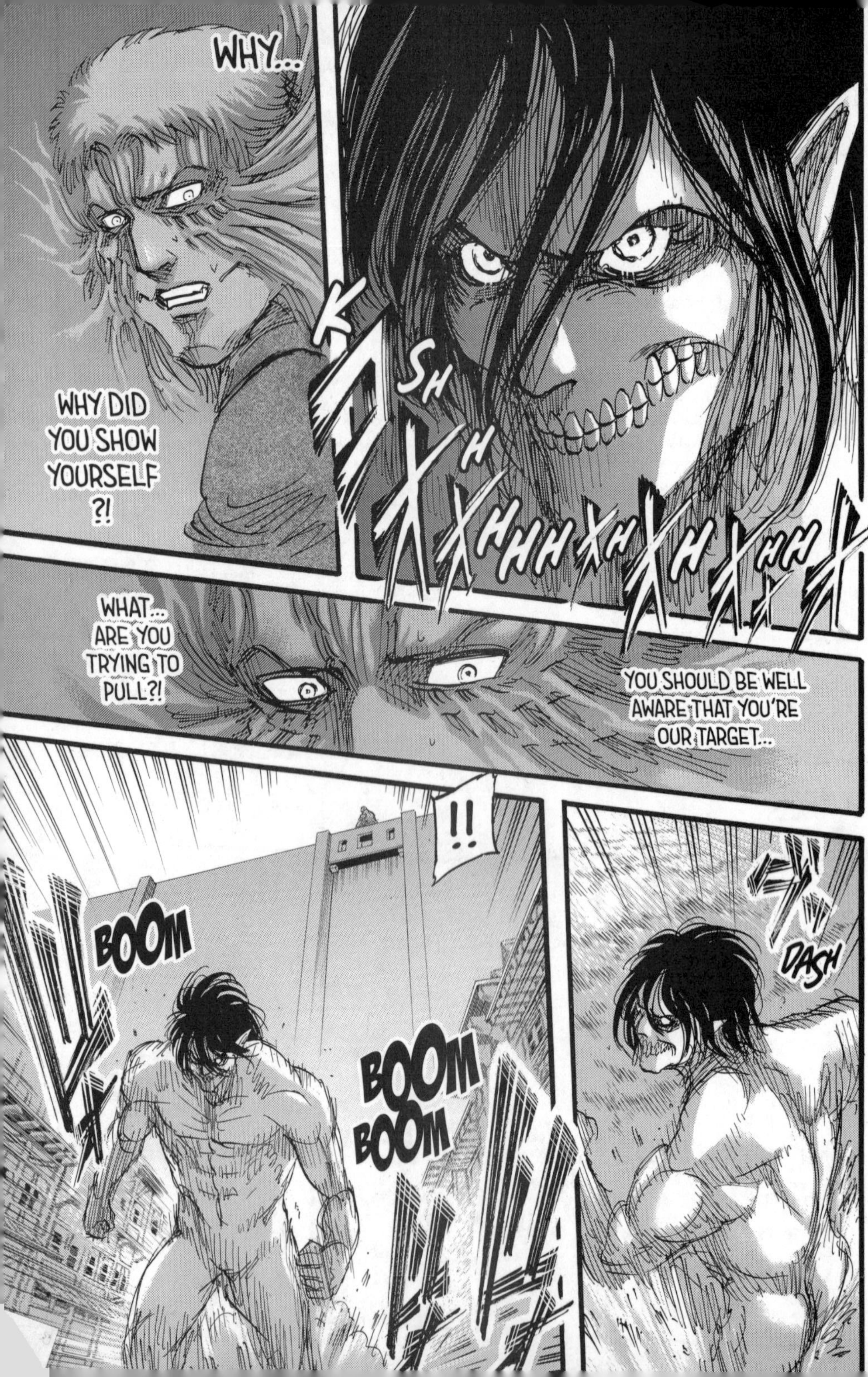
KSHH
WHY...
WHY DID YOU SHOW YOURSELF ?!
WHAT... ARE YOU TRYING TO PULL?!
YOU SHOULD BE WELL AWARE THAT YOU'RE OUR TARGET...
DASH
!!
BOOM
BOOM
BOOM
BOOM

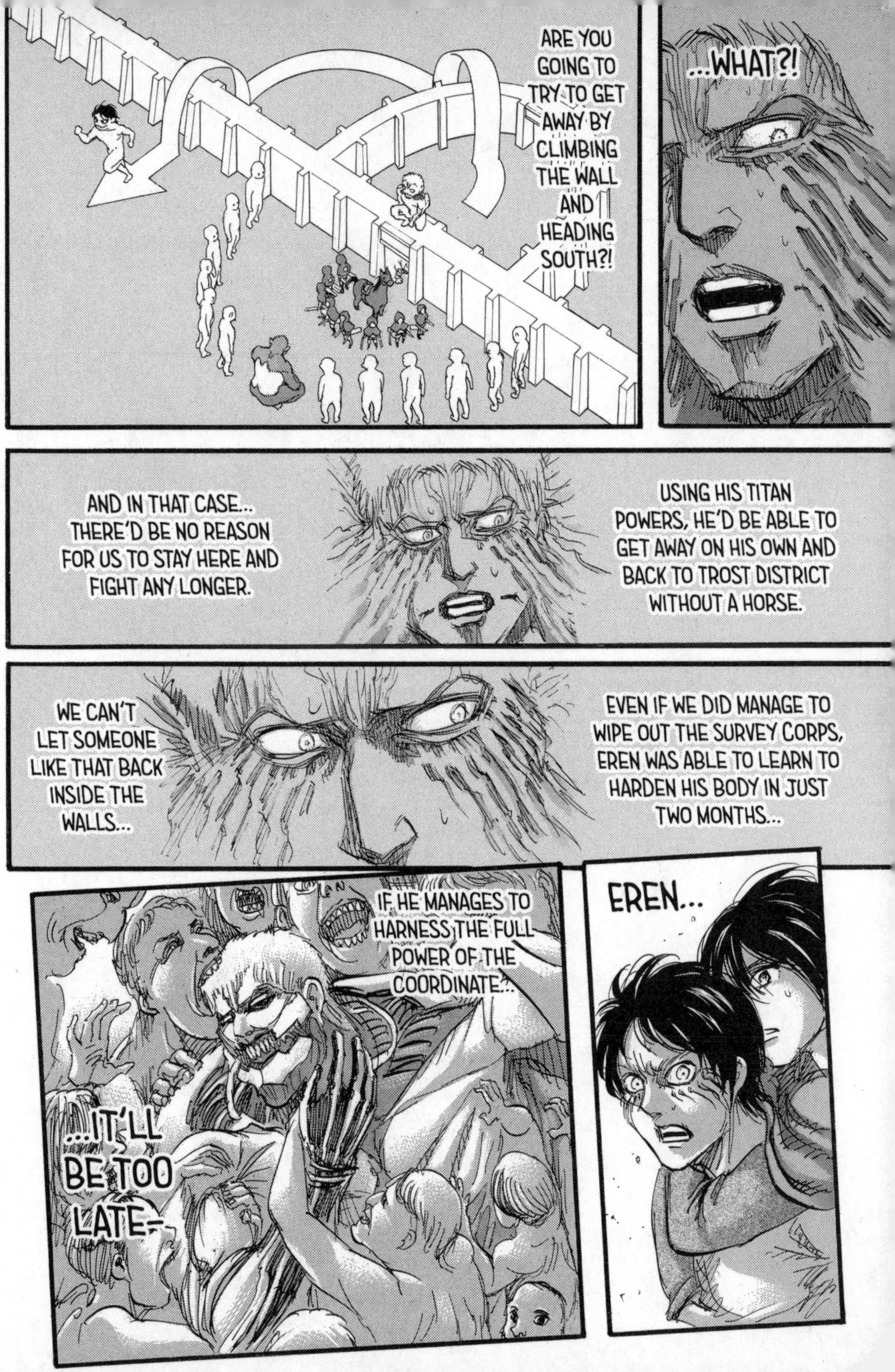
...WHAT?!
ARE YOU GOING TO TRY TO GET AWAY BY CLIMBING THE WALL AND HEADING SOUTH?!
USING HIS TITAN POWERS, HE'D BE ABLE TO GET AWAY ON HIS OWN AND BACK TO TROST DISTRICT WITHOUT A HORSE.
AND IN THAT CASE... THERE'D BE NO REASON FOR US TO STAY HERE AND FIGHT ANY LONGER.
EVEN IF WE DID MANAGE TO WIPE OUT THE SURVEY CORPS, EREN WAS ABLE TO LEARN TO HARDEN HIS BODY IN JUST TWO MONTHS...
WE CAN'T LET SOMEONE LIKE THAT BACK INSIDE THE WALLS...
EREN...
IF HE MANAGES TO HARNESS THE FULL POWER OF THE COORDINATE...
...IT'LL BE TOO LATE-

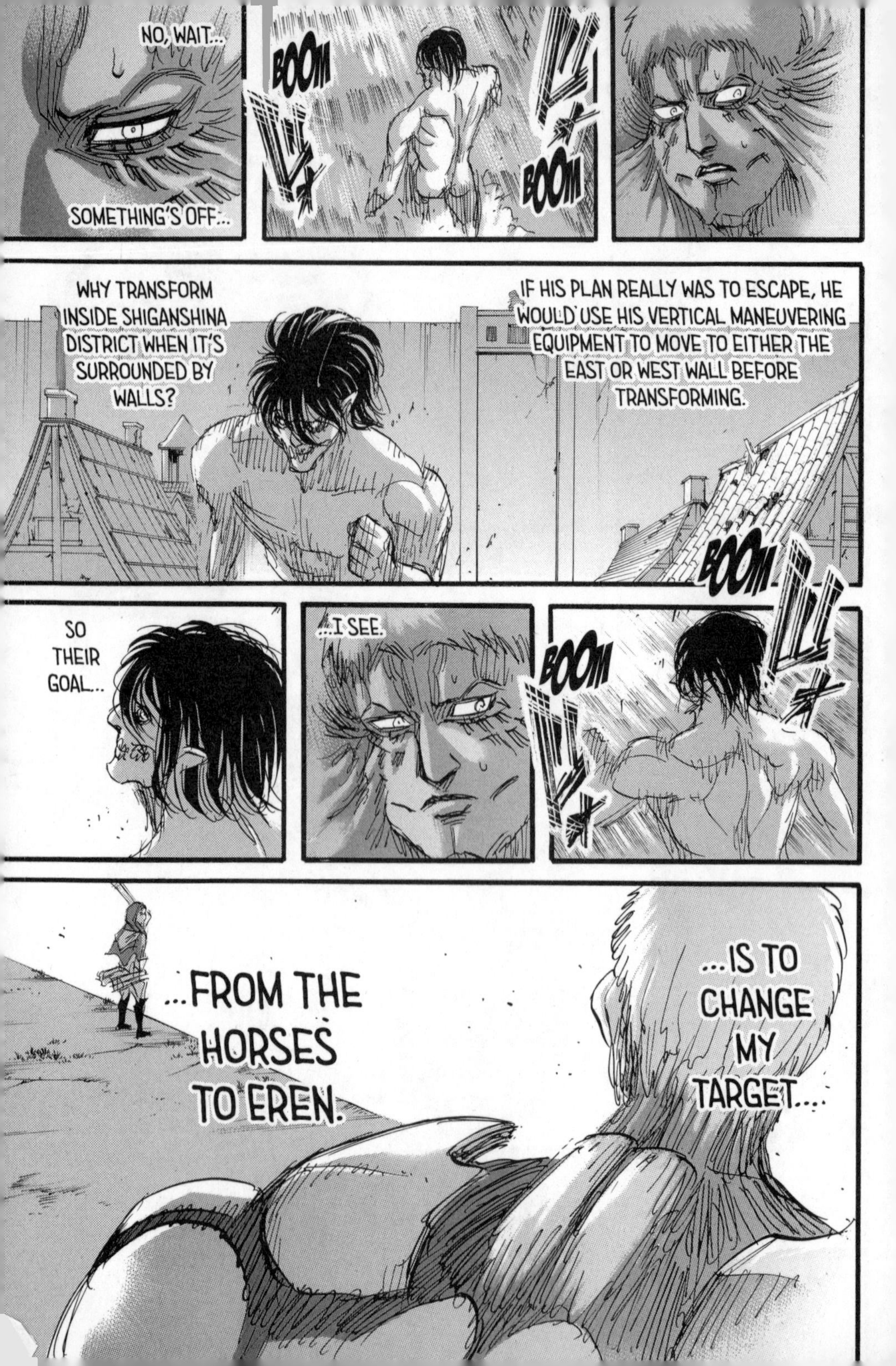
BOOM
BOOM
NO, WAIT...
SOMETHING'S OFF...
IF HIS PLAN REALLY WAS TO ESCAPE, HE WOULD USE HIS VERTICAL MANEUVERING EQUIPMENT TO MOVE TO EITHER THE EAST OR WEST WALL BEFORE TRANSFORMING.
WHY TRANSFORM INSIDE SHIGANSHINA DISTRICT WHEN IT'S SURROUNDED BY WALLS?
BOOM
BOOM
...I SEE.
SO THEIR GOAL...
...IS TO CHANGE MY TARGET...
...FROM THE HORSES TO EREN.

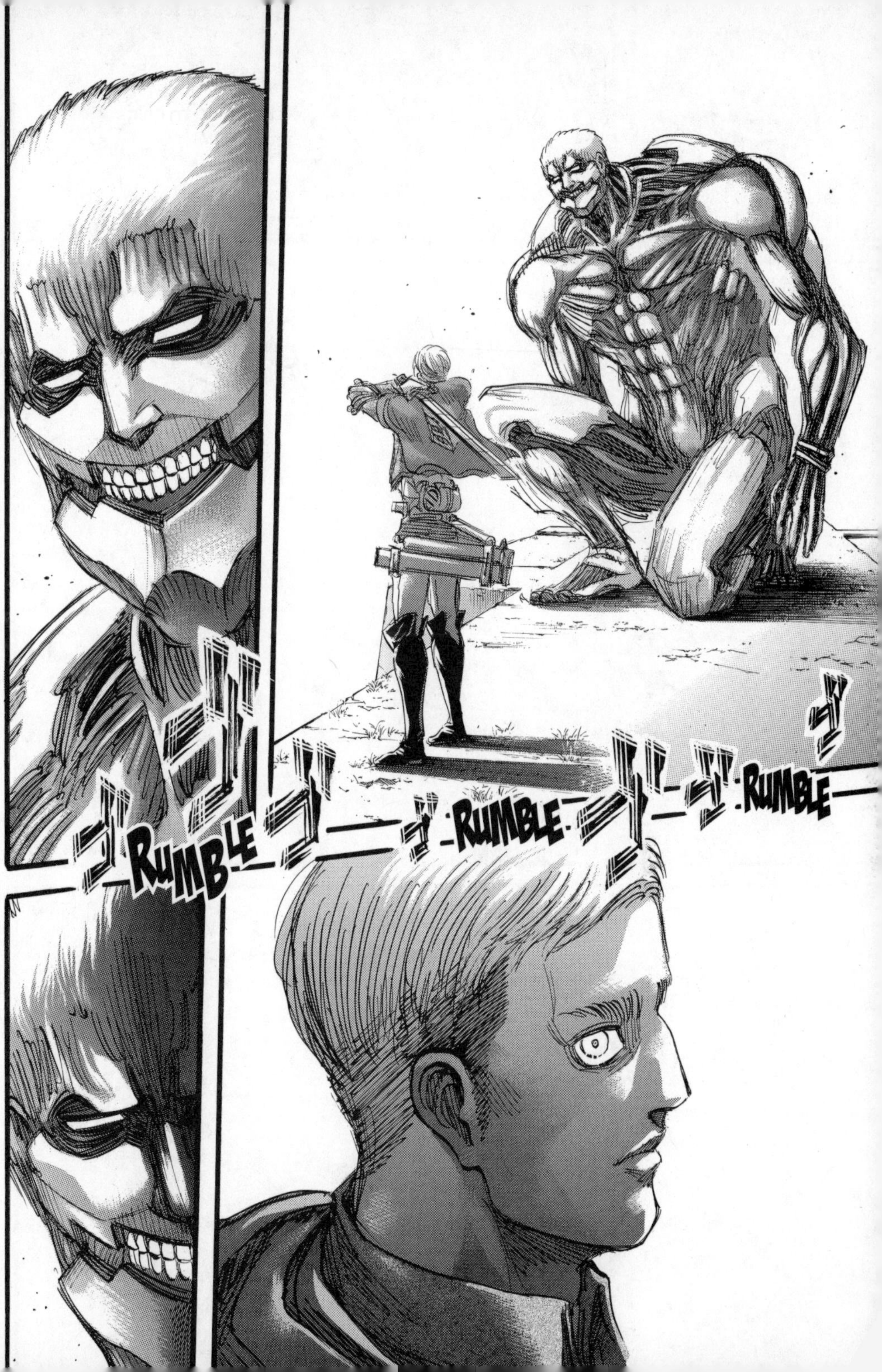
RUMBLE
RUMBLE
RUMBLE

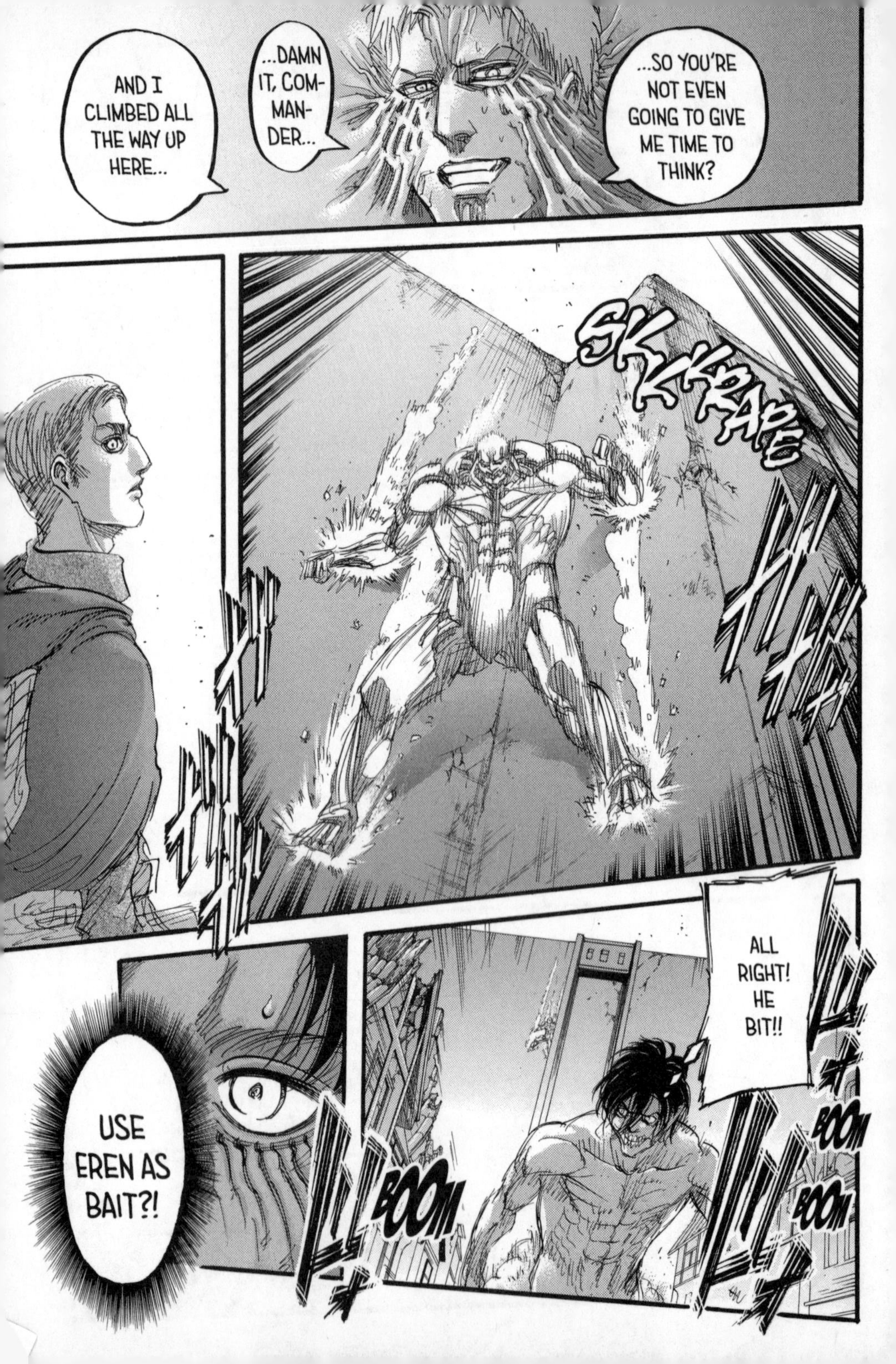

...SO YOU'RE NOT EVEN GOING TO GIVE ME TIME TO THINK?
...DAMN IT, COM-MANDER...
AND I CLIMBED ALL THE WAY UP HERE...
SKKRAPE
ALL RIGHT! HE BIT!!
BOOM
BOOM
USE EREN AS BAIT?!
BOOM

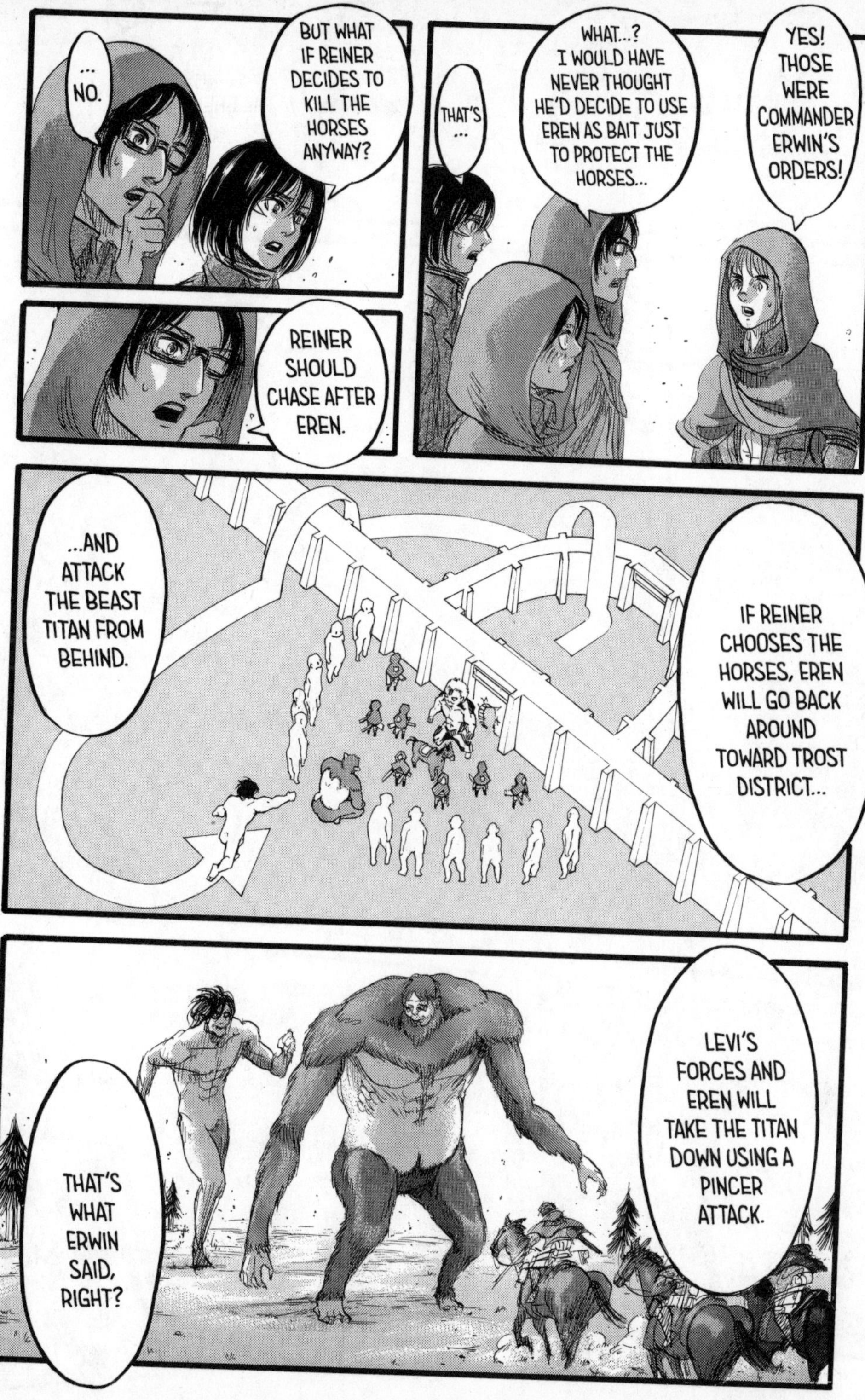
YES! THOSE WERE COMMANDER ERWIN'S ORDERS!
WHAT...? I WOULD HAVE NEVER THOUGHT HE'D DECIDE TO USE EREN AS BAIT JUST TO PROTECT THE HORSES...
THAT'S ...
BUT WHAT IF REINER DECIDES TO KILL THE HORSES ANYWAY?
... NO.
REINER SHOULD CHASE AFTER EREN.
IF REINER CHOOSES THE HORSES, EREN WILL GO BACK AROUND TOWARD TROST DISTRICT...
...AND ATTACK THE BEAST TITAN FROM BEHIND.
LEVI'S FORCES AND EREN WILL TAKE THE TITAN DOWN USING A PINCER ATTACK.
THAT'S WHAT ERWIN SAID, RIGHT?

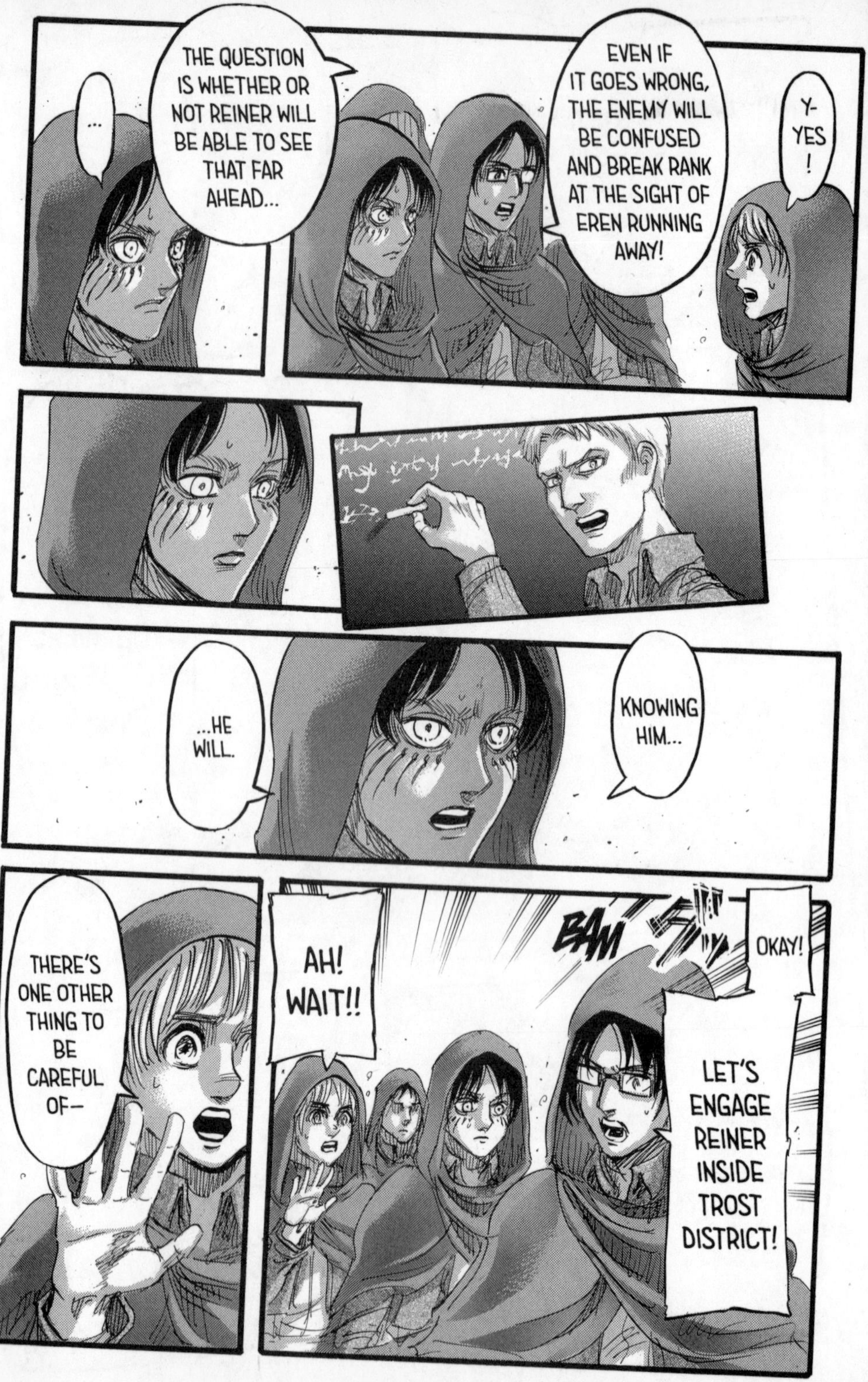

EVEN IF IT GOES WRONG, THE ENEMY WILL BE CONFUSED AND BREAK RANK AT THE SIGHT OF EREN RUNNING AWAY!
Y-YES!
THE QUESTION IS WHETHER OR NOT REINER WILL BE ABLE TO SEE THAT FAR AHEAD...
...
KNOWING HIM...
...HE WILL.
OKAY!
BAM
LET'S ENGAGE REINER INSIDE TROST DISTRICT!
AH! WAIT!!
THERE'S ONE OTHER THING TO BE CAREFUL OF—

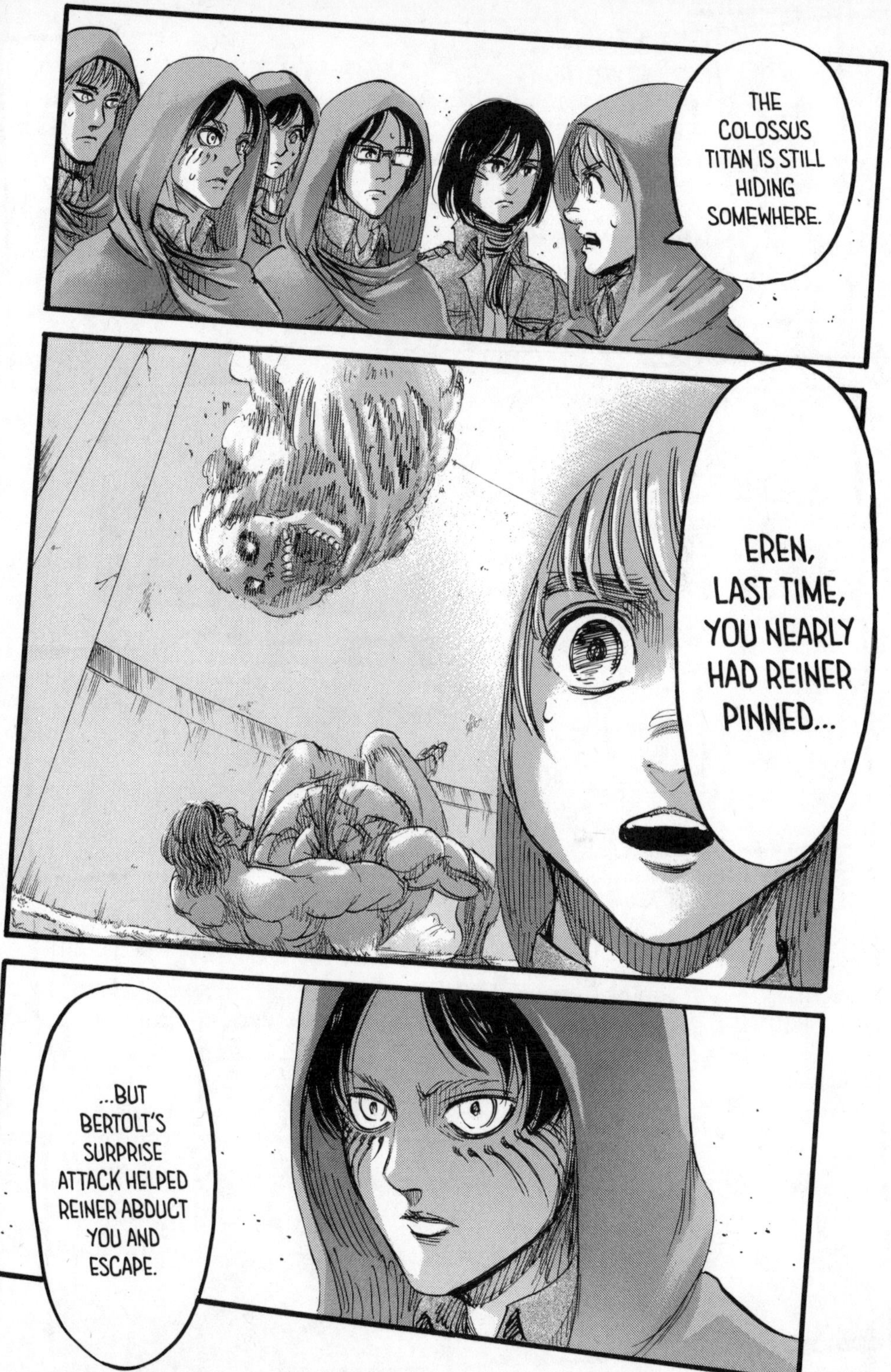
THE COLOSSUS TITAN IS STILL HIDING SOMEWHERE.
EREN, LAST TIME, YOU NEARLY HAD REINER PINNED...
...BUT BERTOLT'S SURPRISE ATTACK HELPED REINER ABDUCT YOU AND ESCAPE.

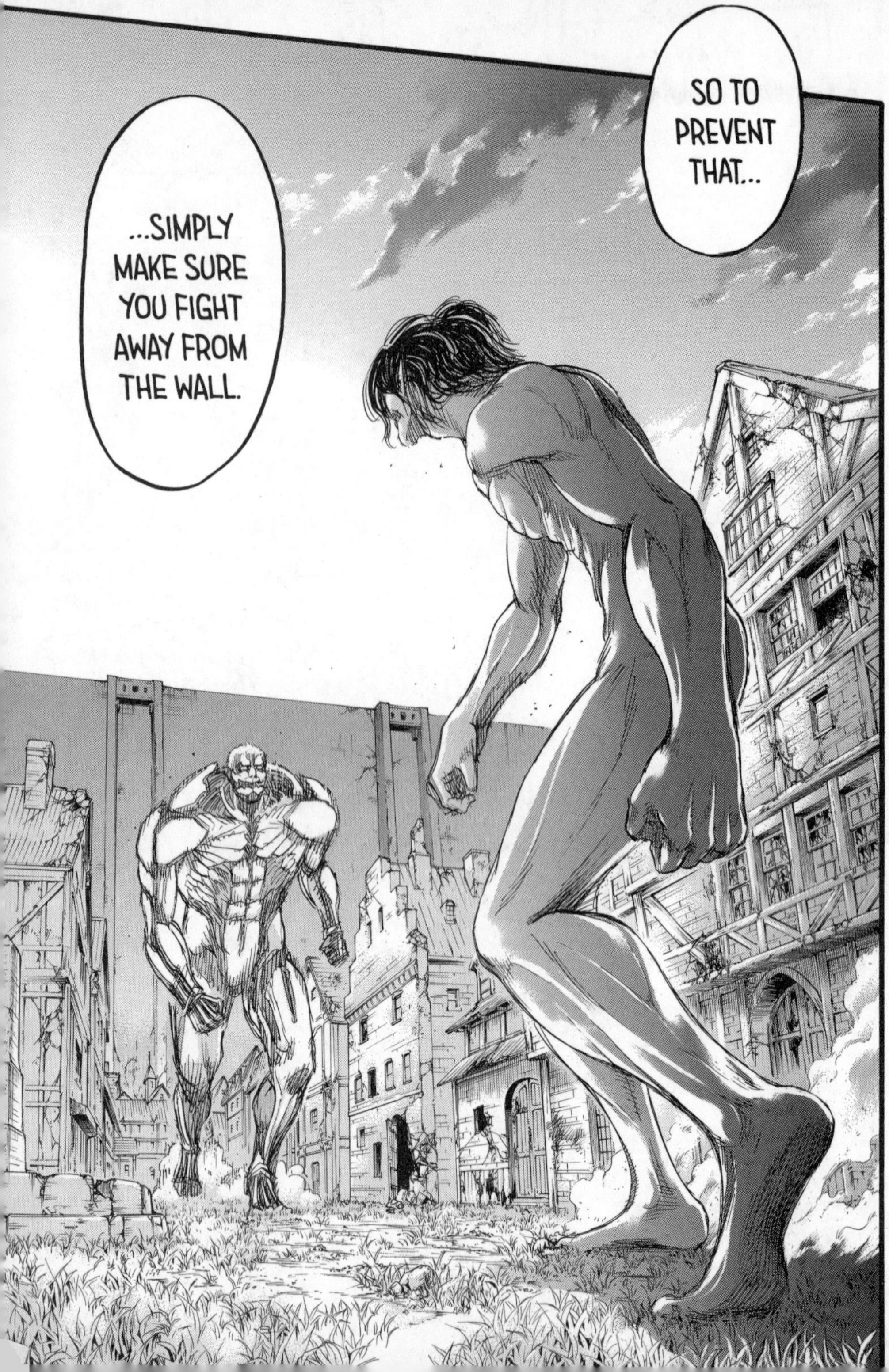
SO TO PREVENT THAT...
...SIMPLY MAKE SURE YOU FIGHT AWAY FROM THE WALL.

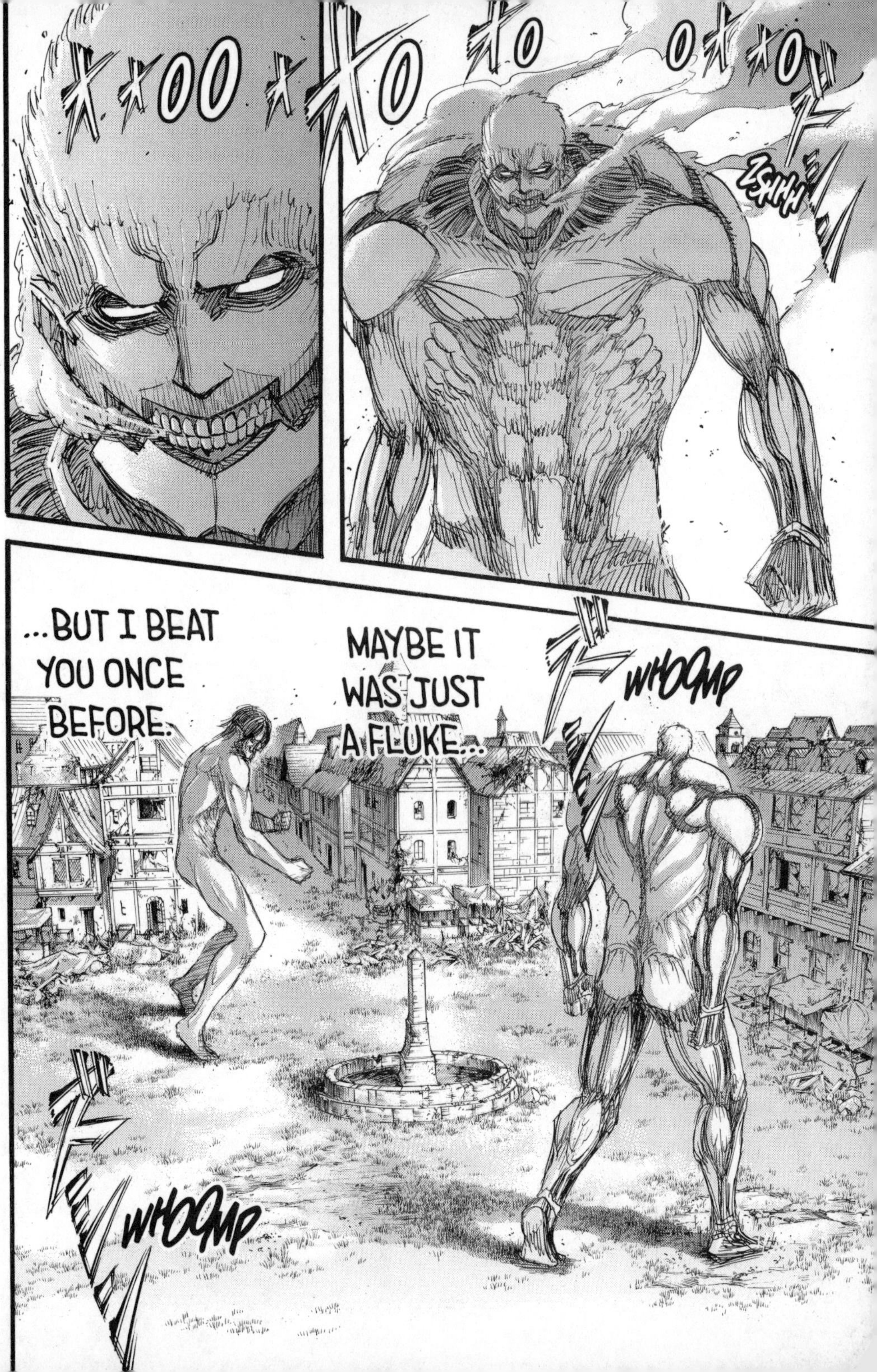
ZSHHH
MAYBE IT WAS JUST A FLUKE...
...BUT I BEAT YOU ONCE BEFORE.
WHOOMP
WHOOMP

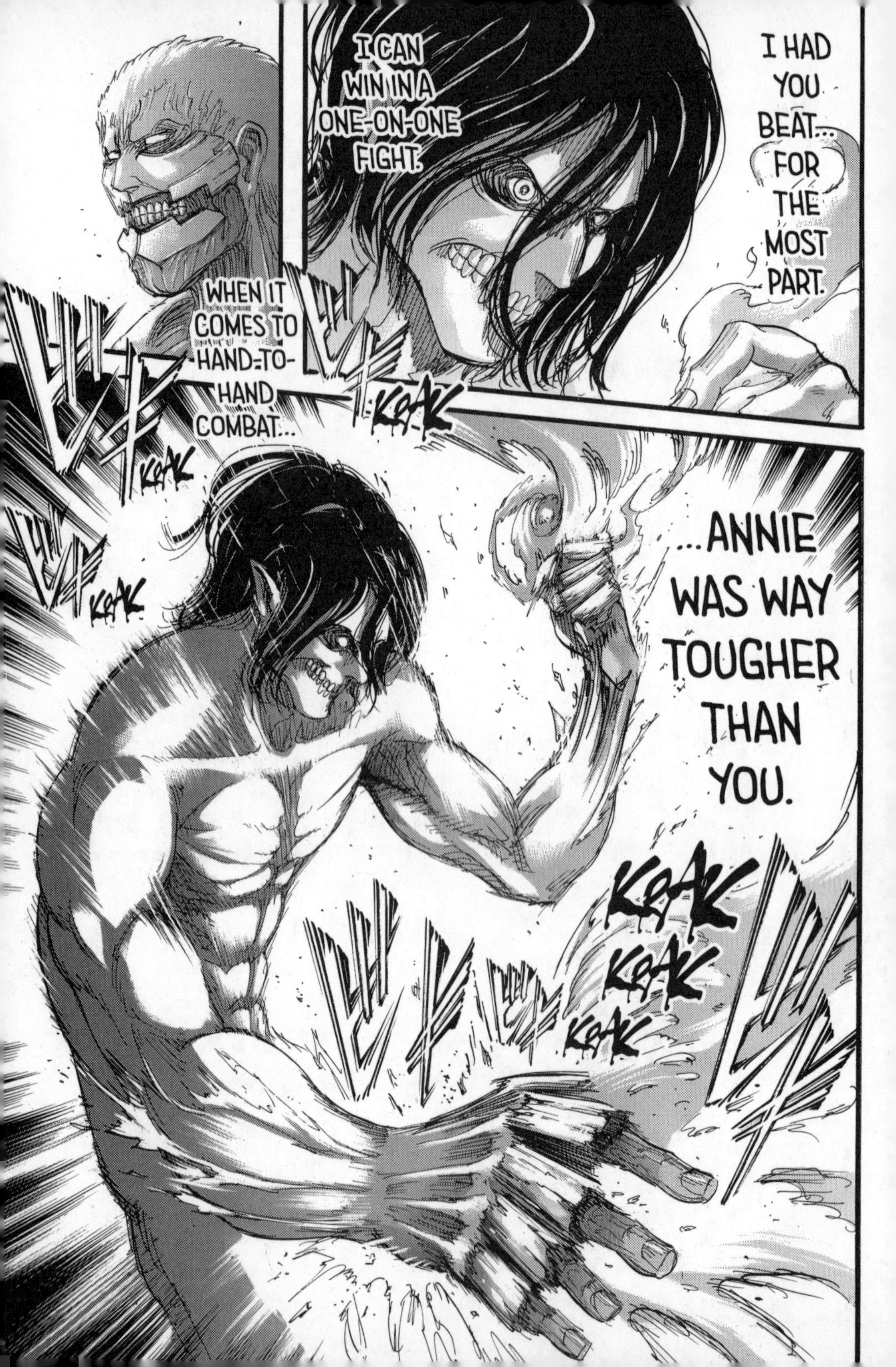
I HAD YOU BEAT... FOR THE MOST PART.
I CAN WIN IN A ONE-ON-ONE FIGHT.
KRAK
WHEN IT COMES TO HAND-TO-HAND COMBAT...
KRAK
KRAK
...ANNIE WAS WAY TOUGHER THAN YOU.
KRAK
KRAK
KRAK

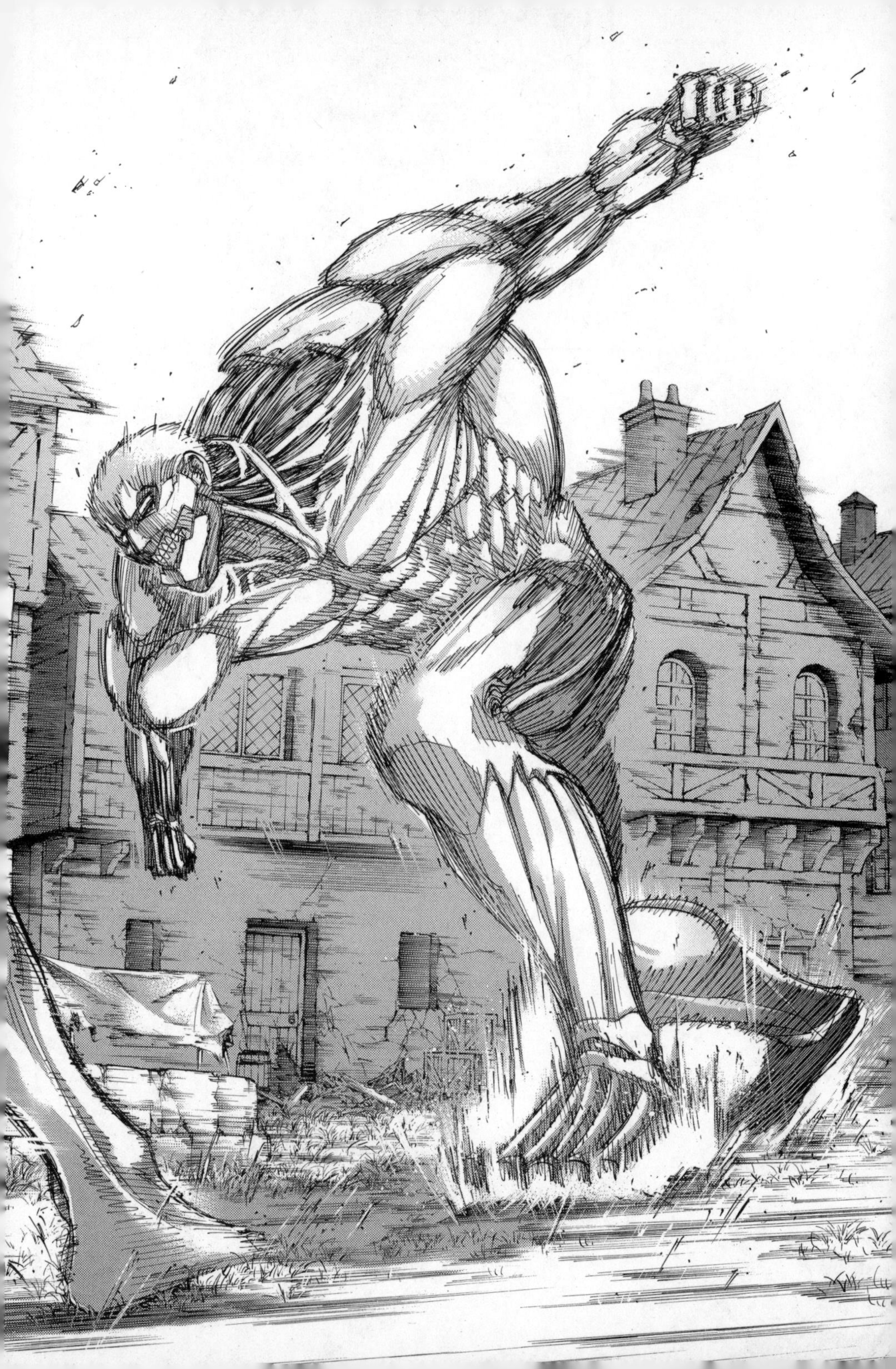

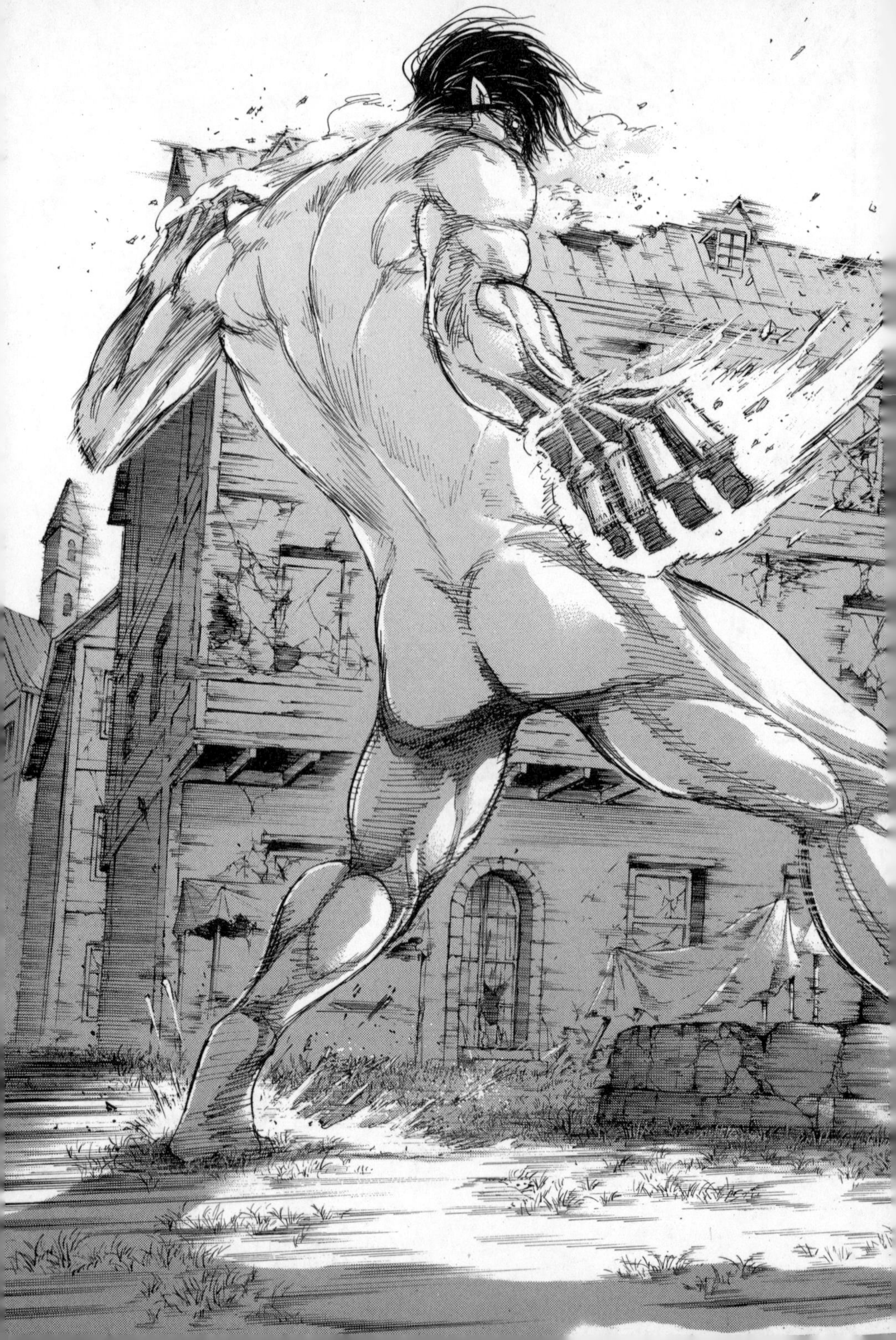

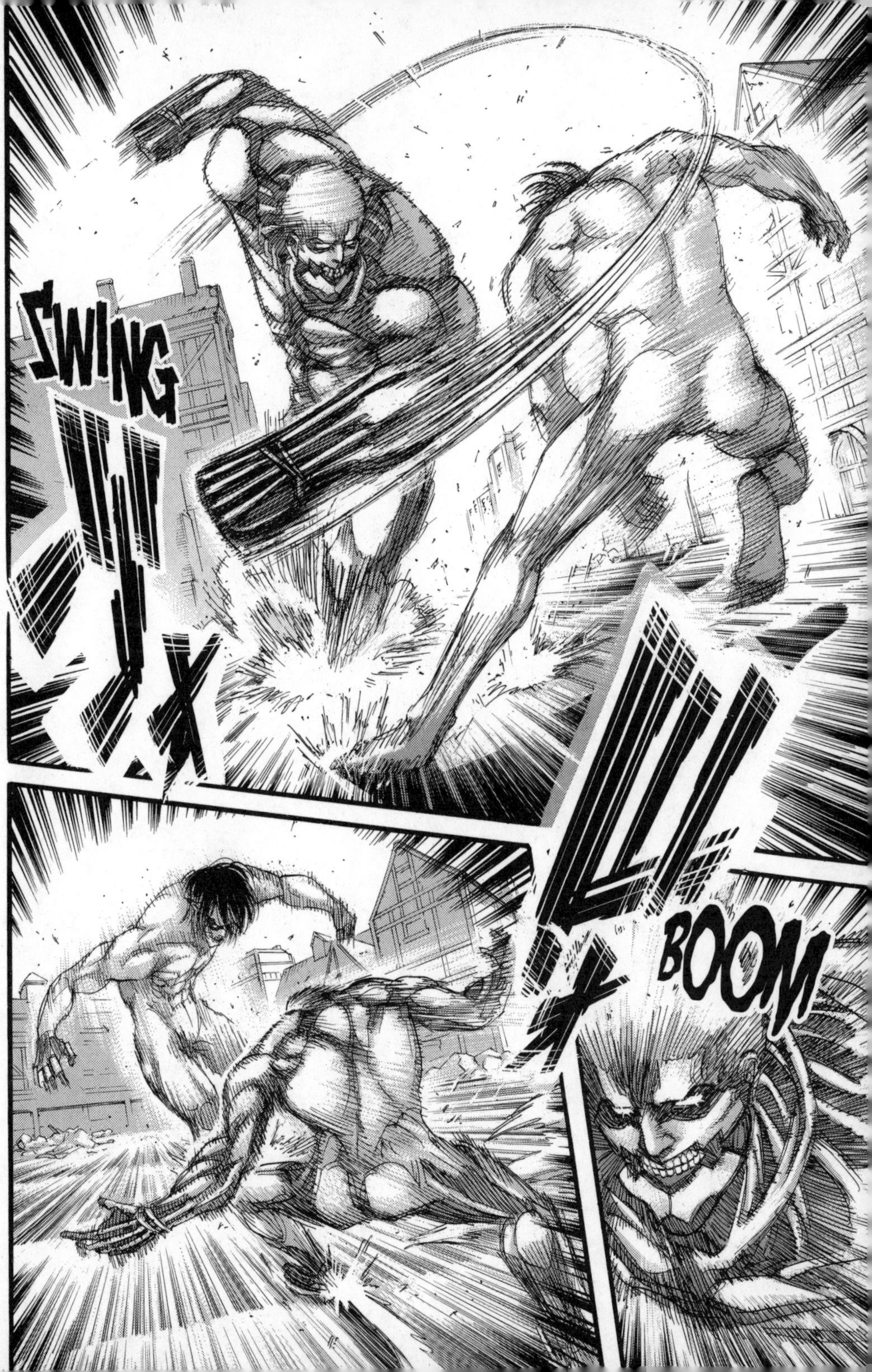
SWING
BOOM

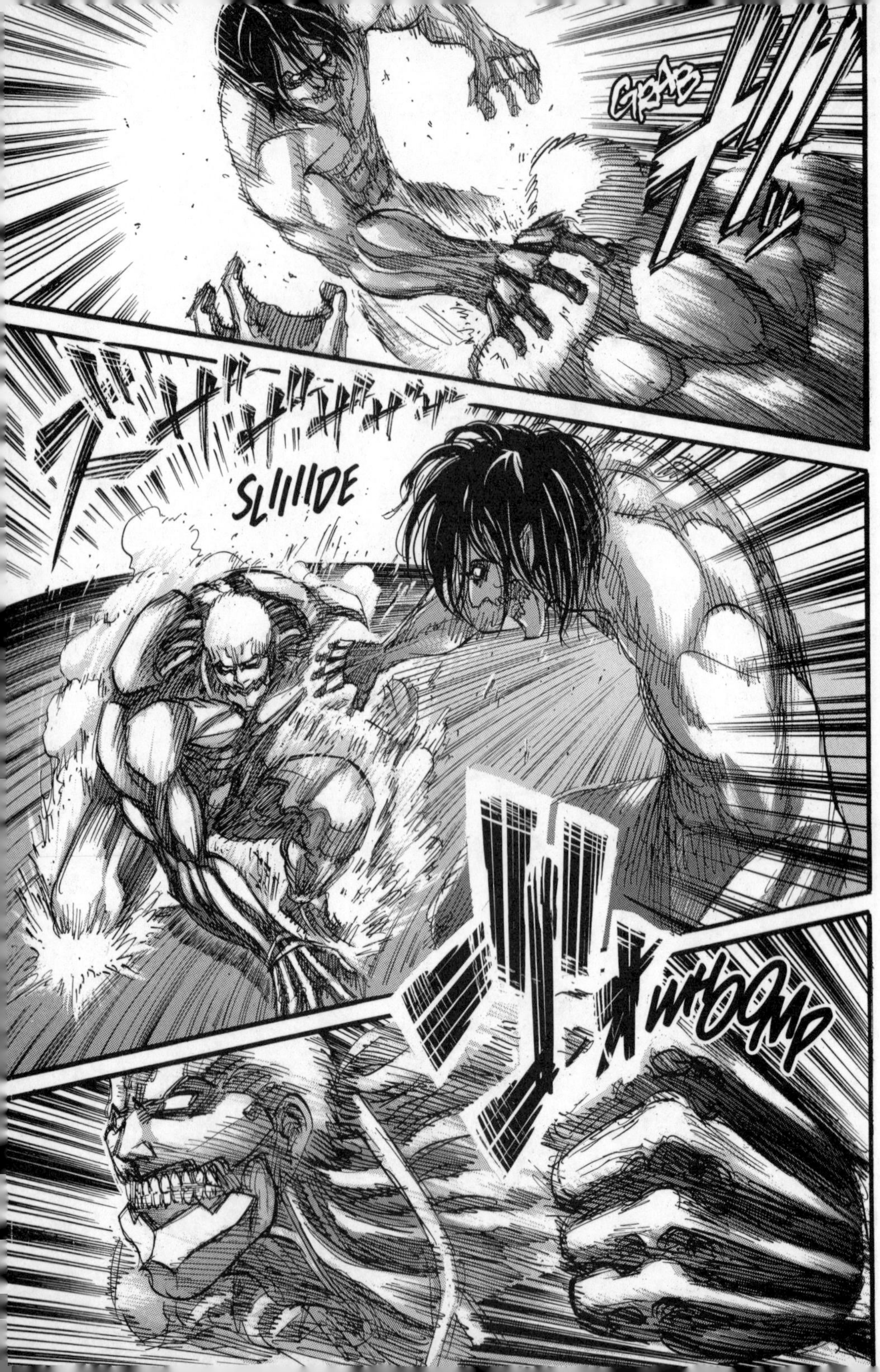
GRAB
SLIIIIDE
WHOMP

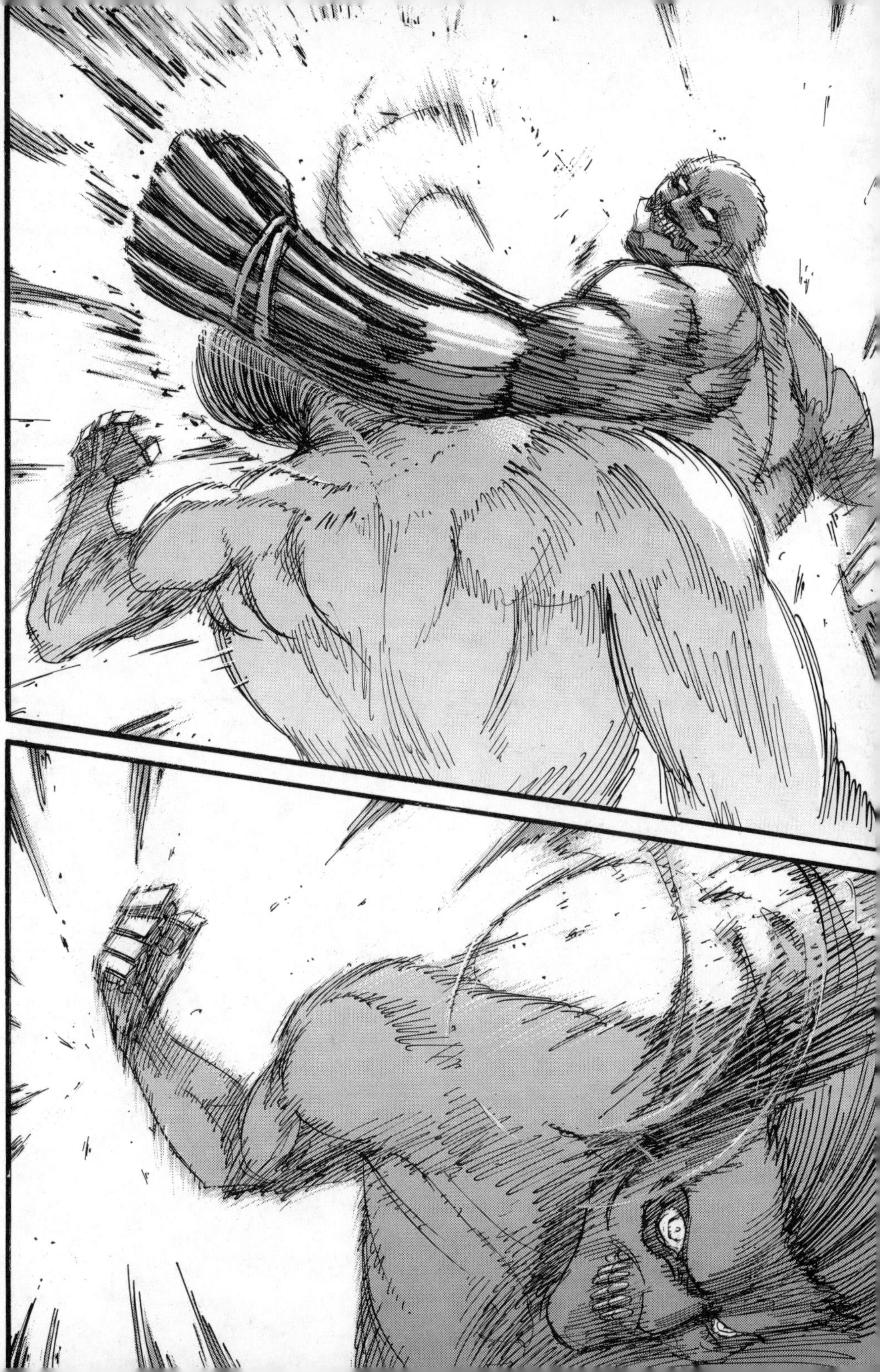

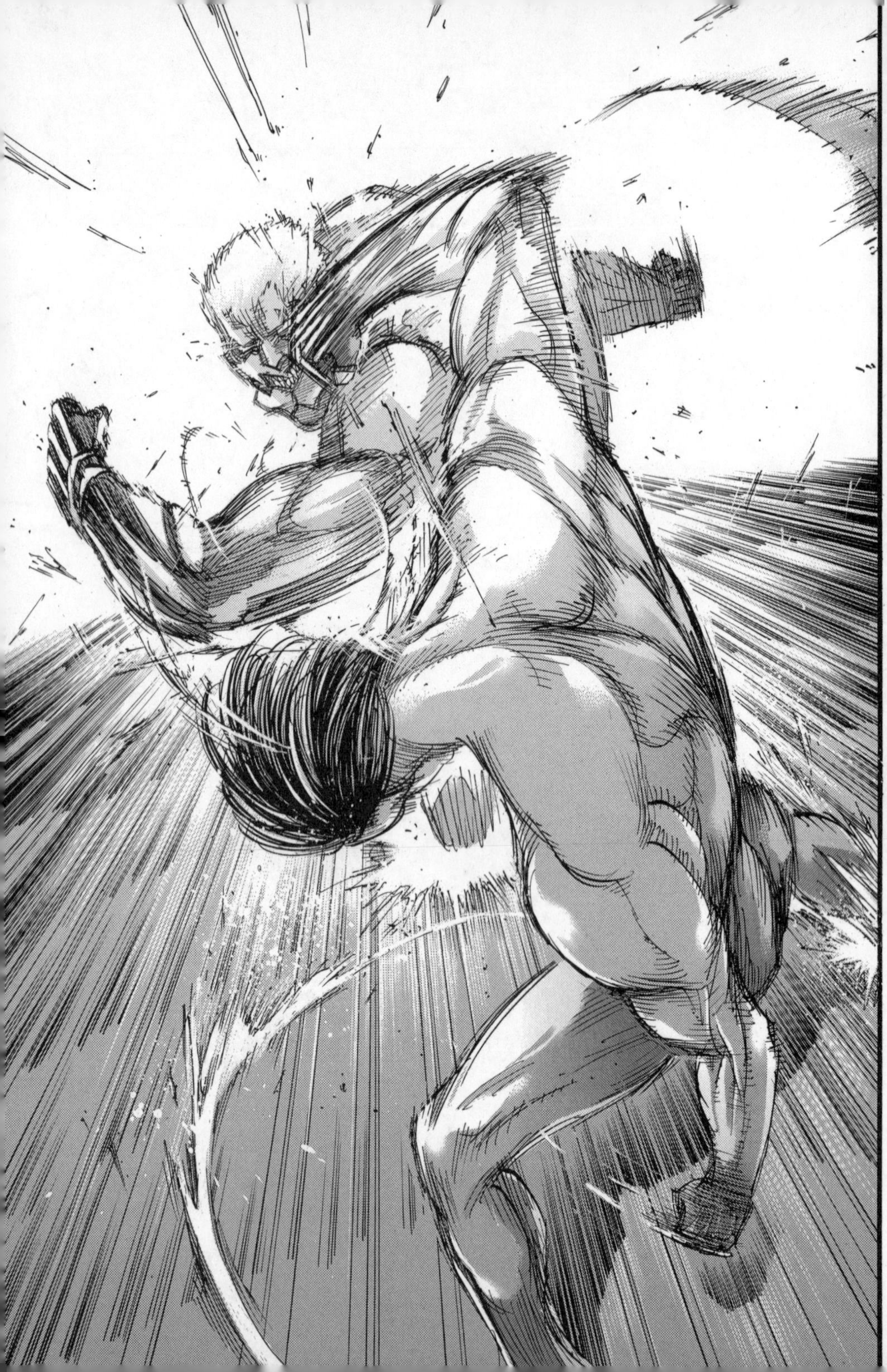

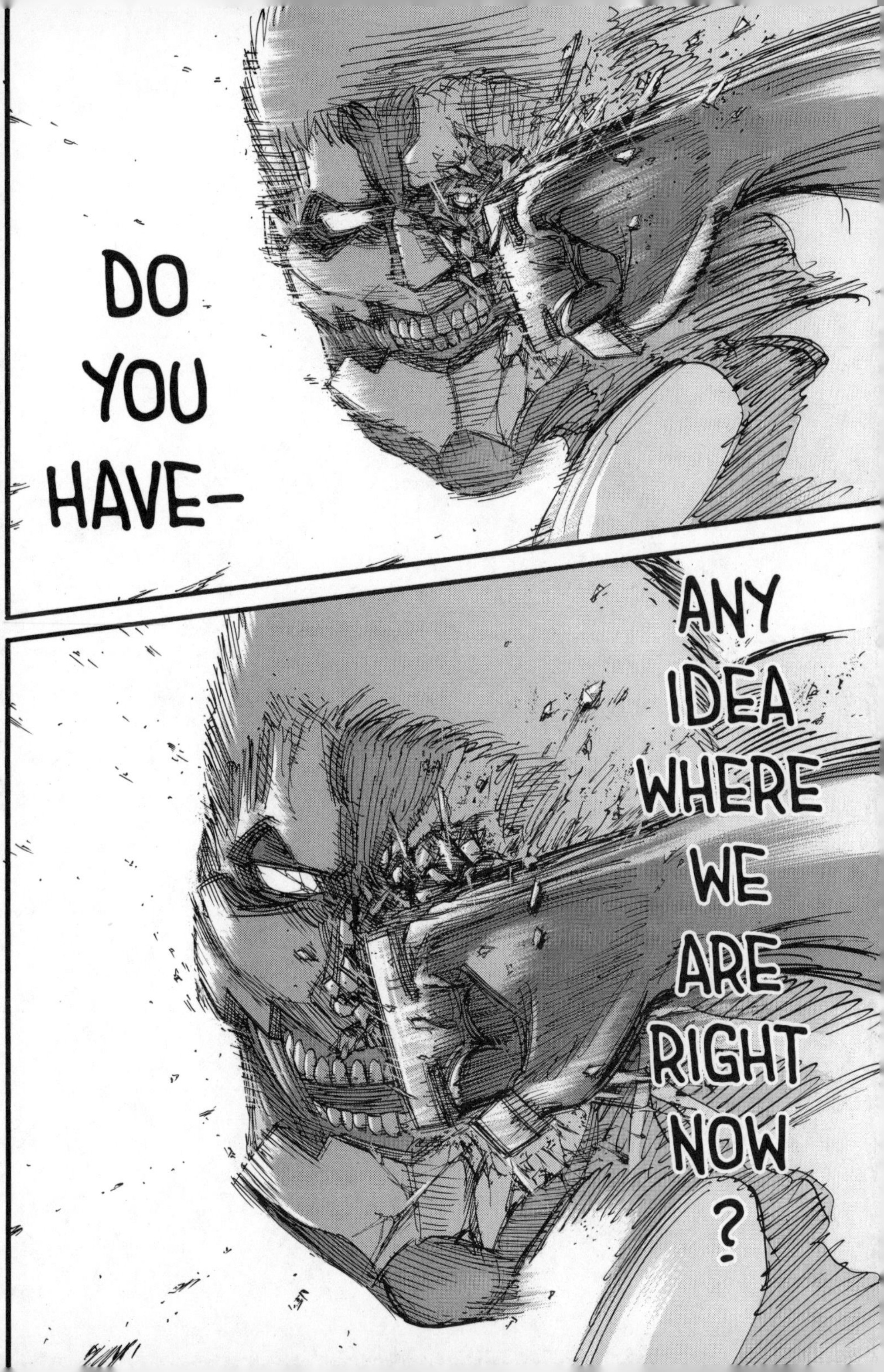
DO YOU HAVE-
ANY IDEA WHERE WE ARE RIGHT NOW ?

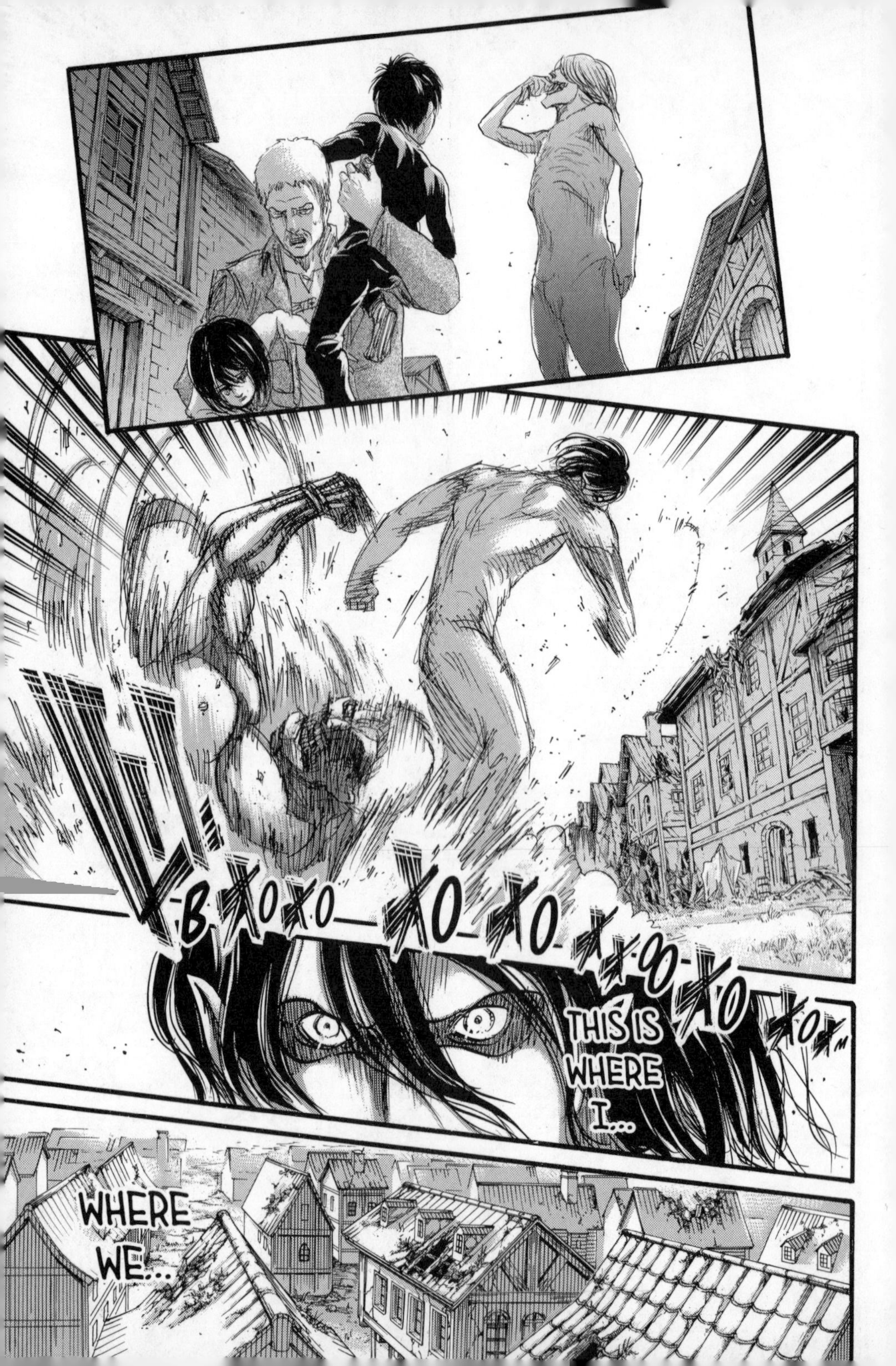
BOOOOOOOOOO
THIS IS WHERE I...
WHERE WE...

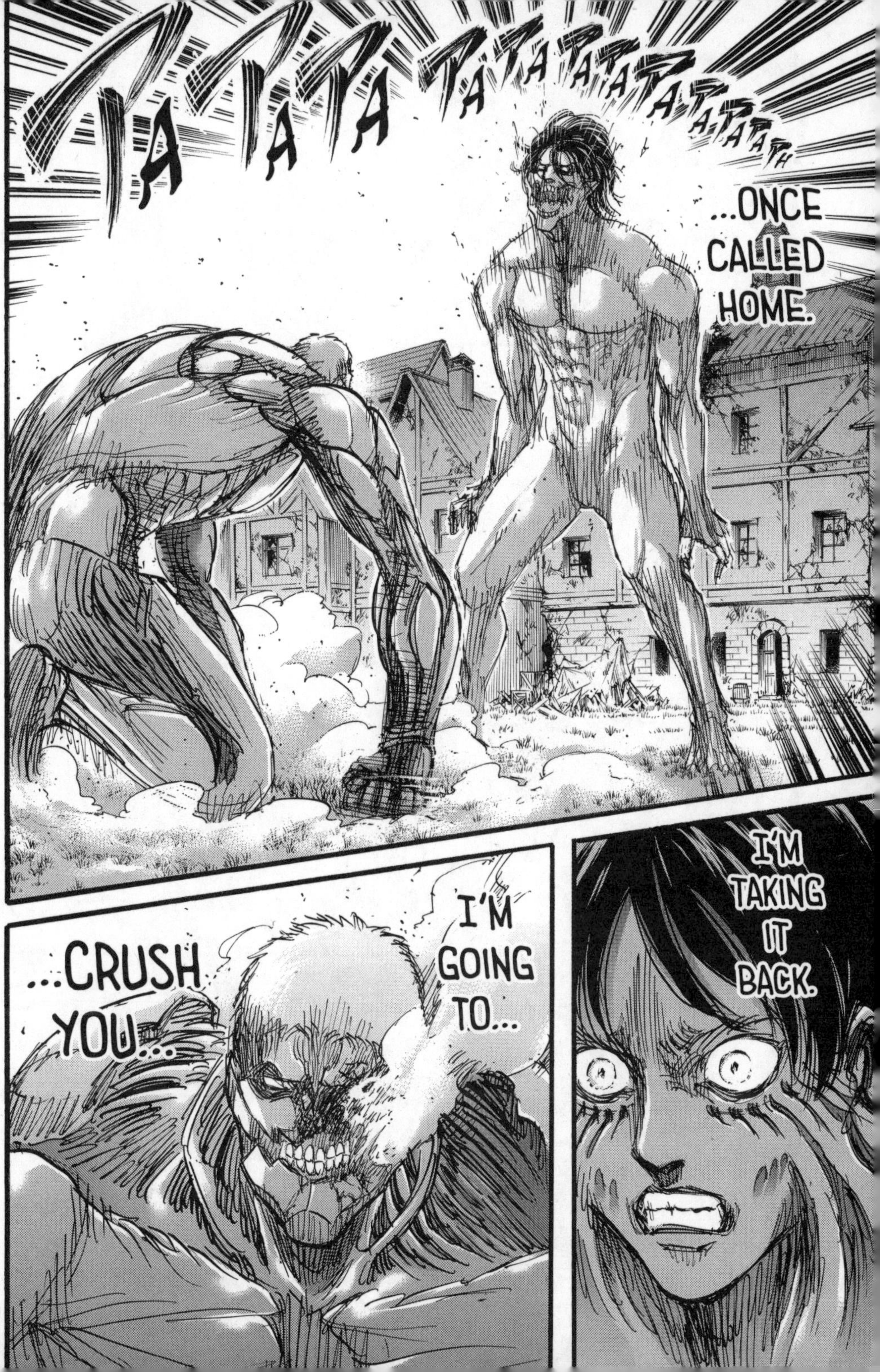
AAAAAAAAAAAAAAH
...ONCE CALLED HOME.
I'M TAKING IT BACK.
I'M GOING TO...
...CRUSH YOU...

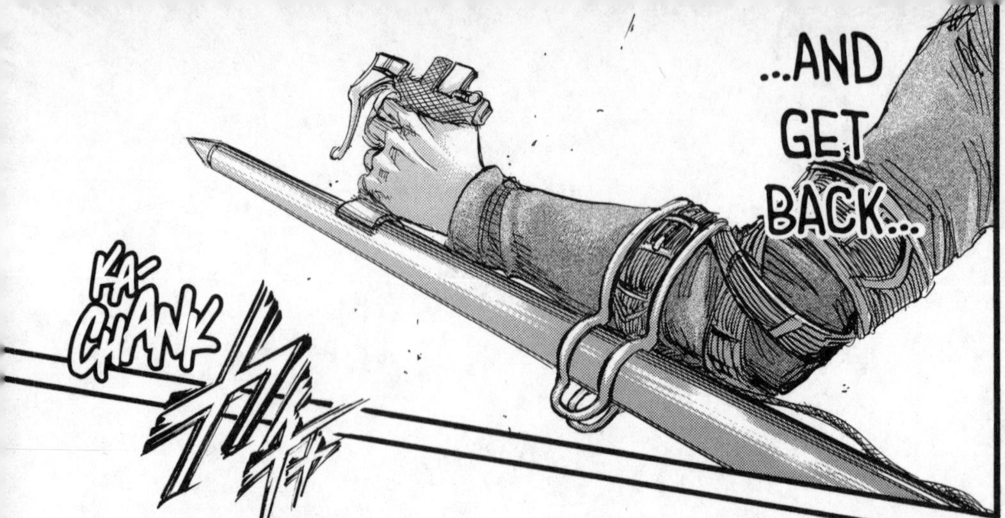
...AND GET BACK...
KA-CHANK
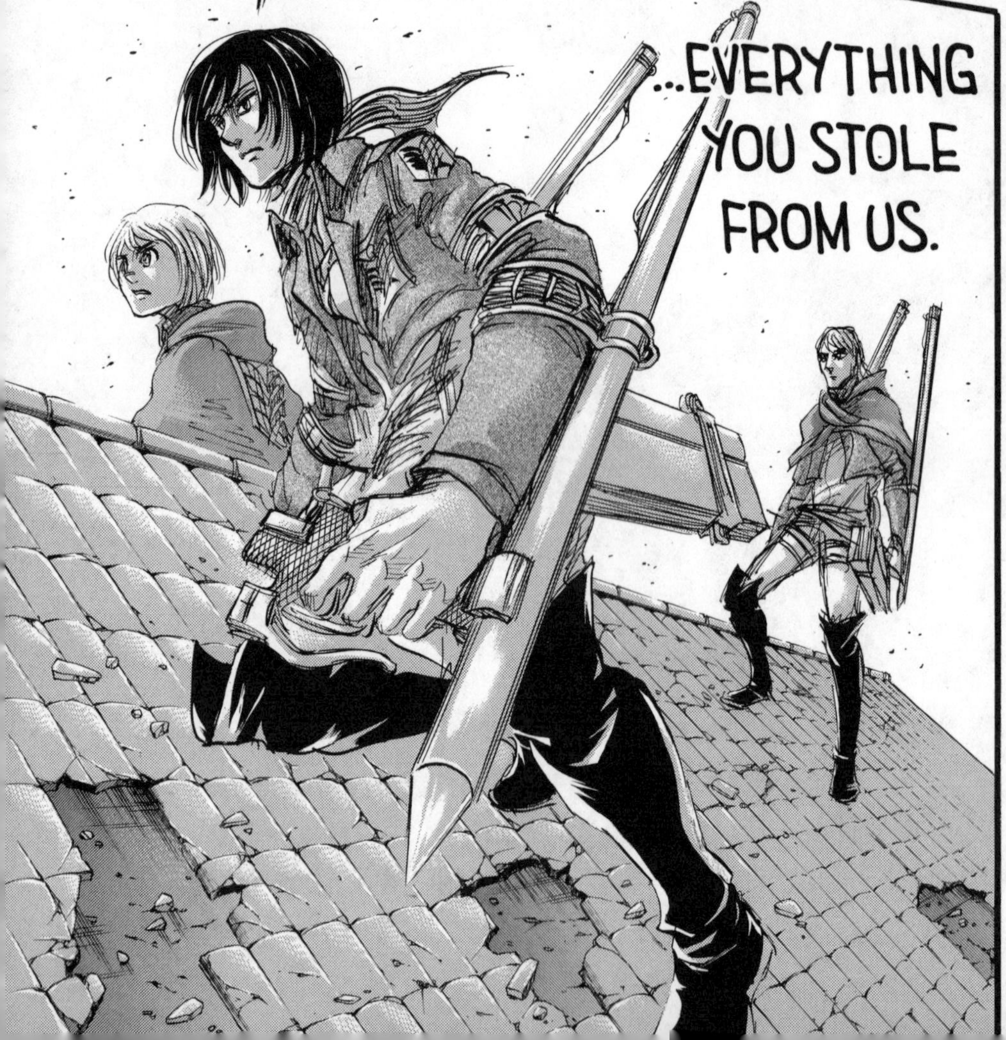
...EVERYTHING YOU STOLE FROM US.

ATTACK on TITAN

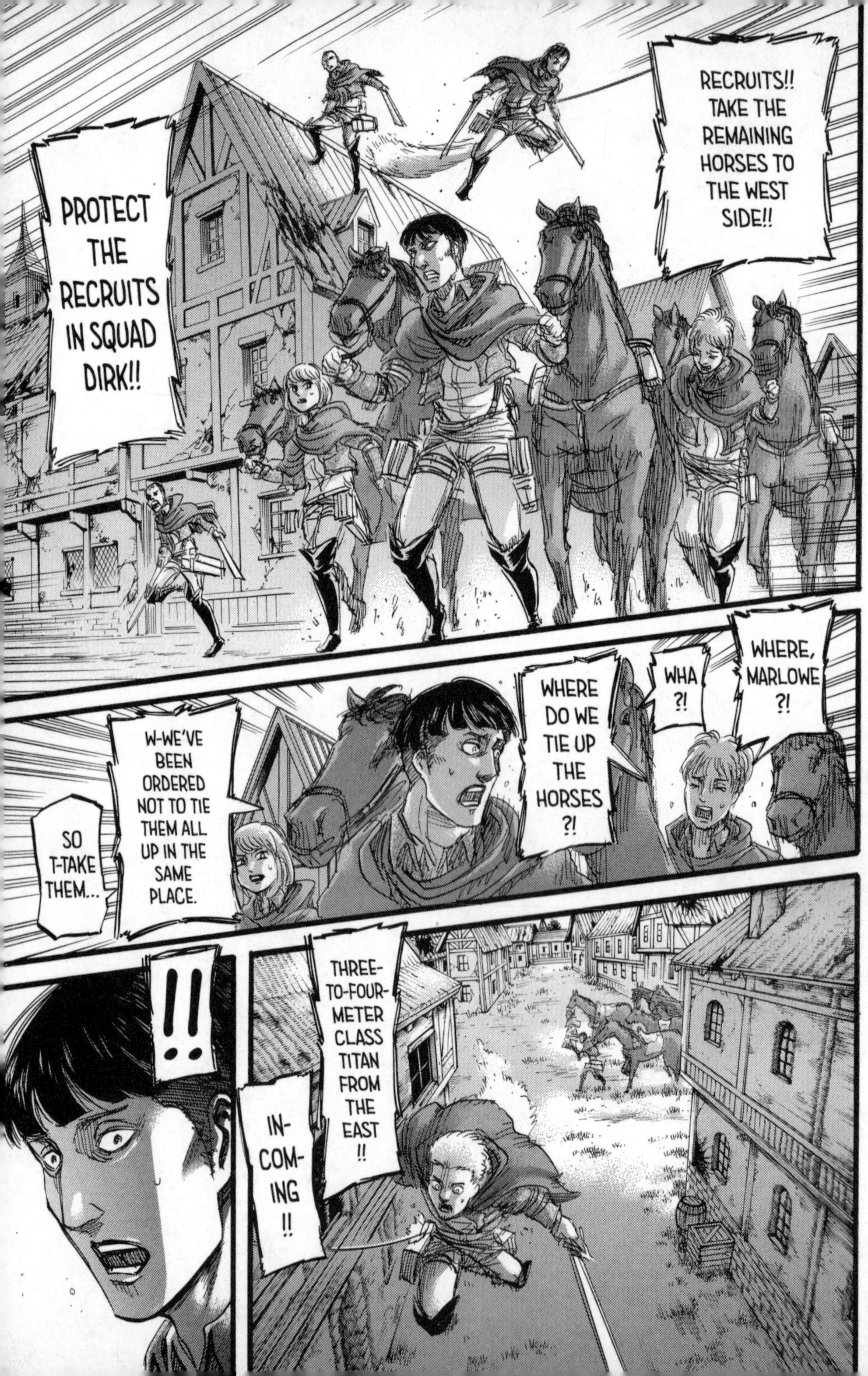
RECRUITS!! TAKE THE REMAINING HORSES TO THE WEST SIDE!!
PROTECT THE RECRUITS IN SQUAD DIRK!!
WHERE, MARLOWE?!
WHA?!
WHERE DO WE TIE UP THE HORSES?!
W-WE'VE BEEN ORDERED NOT TO TIE THEM ALL UP IN THE SAME PLACE.
SO T-TAKE THEM...
THREE-TO-FOUR-METER CLASS TITAN FROM THE EAST!!
IN-COM-ING!!
!!

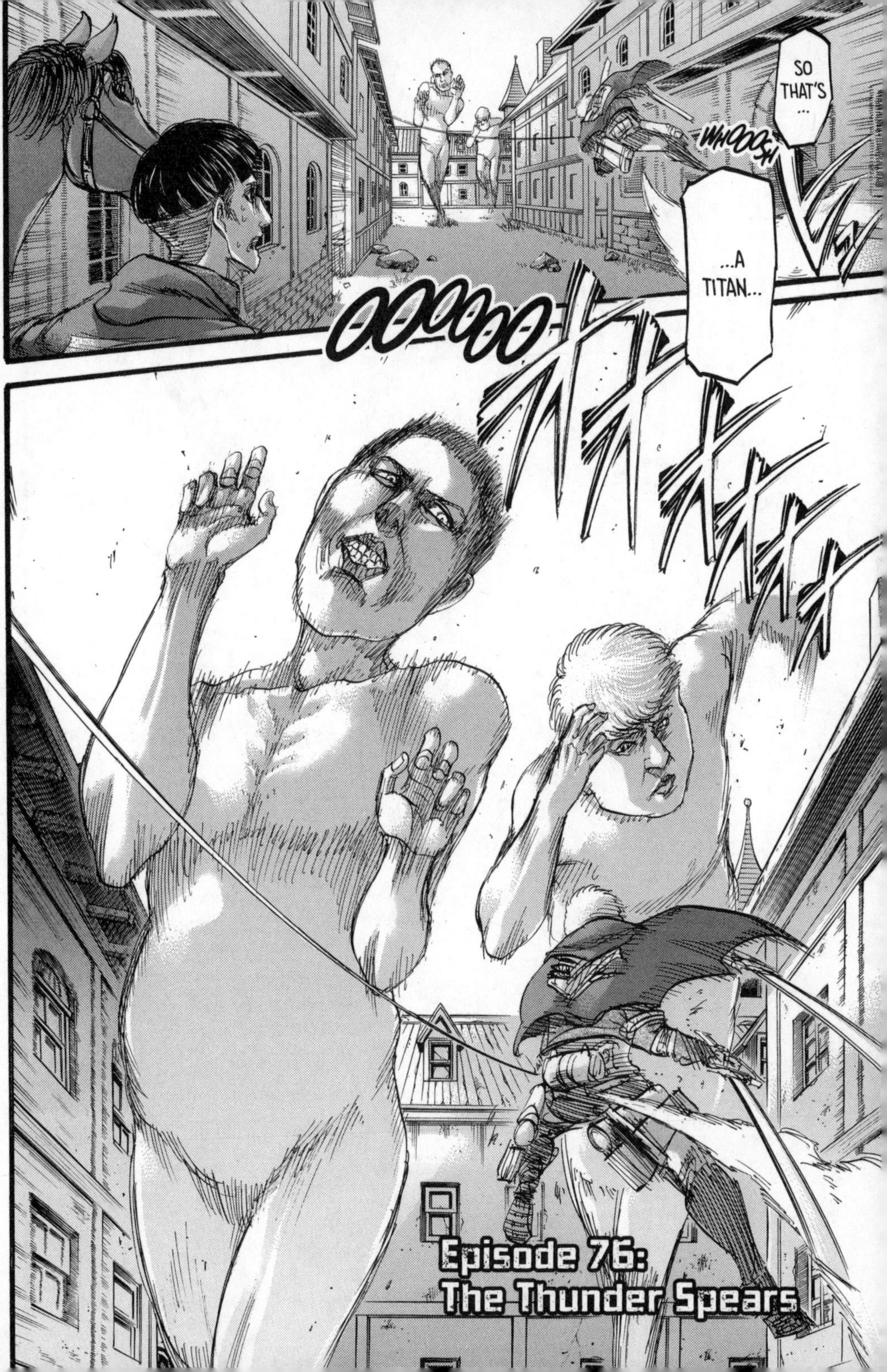
SO THAT'S ...
WHOOOSH
...A TITAN...
OOOOOO
Episode 76:
The Thunder Spears

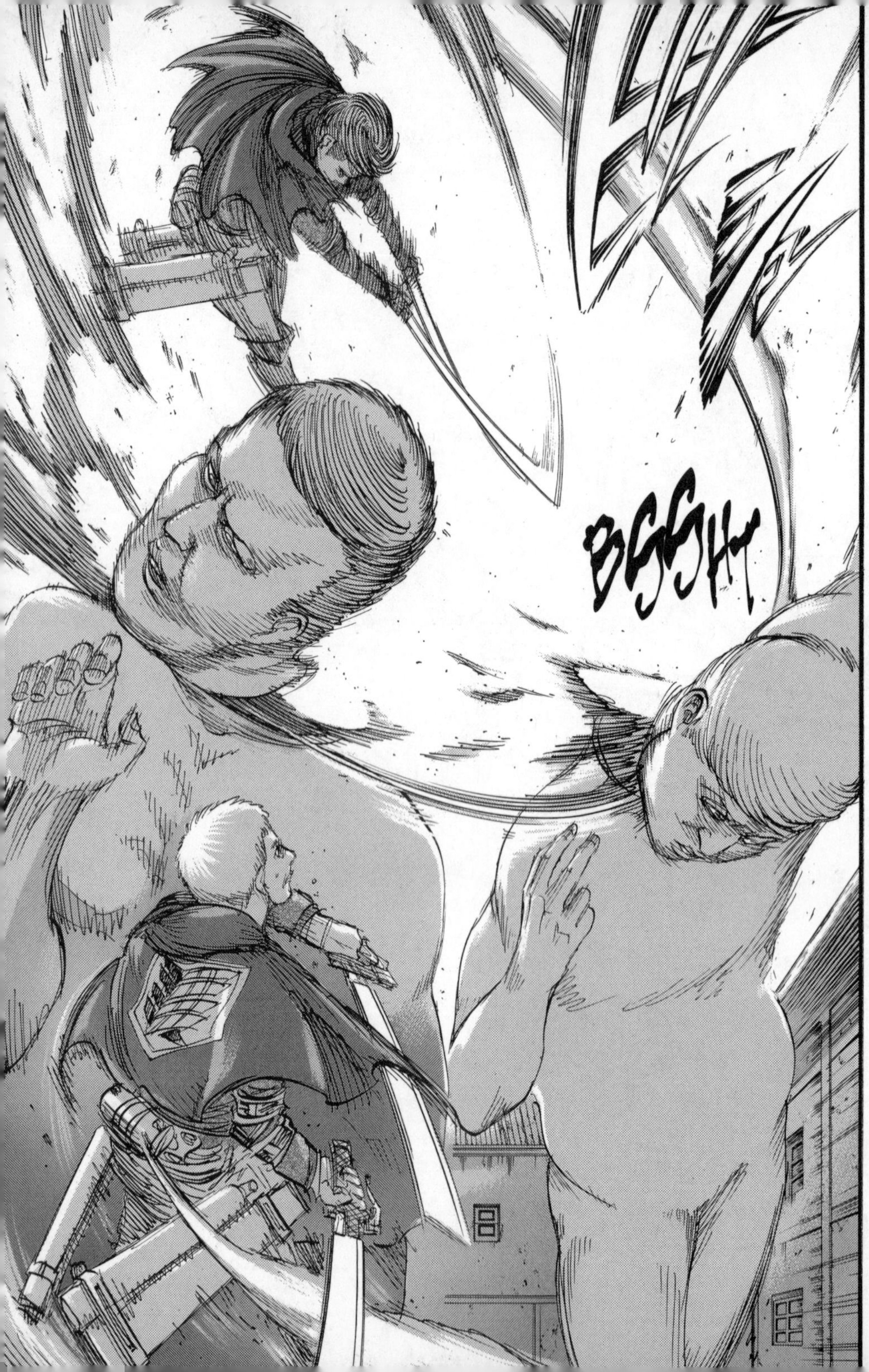
BGGHT

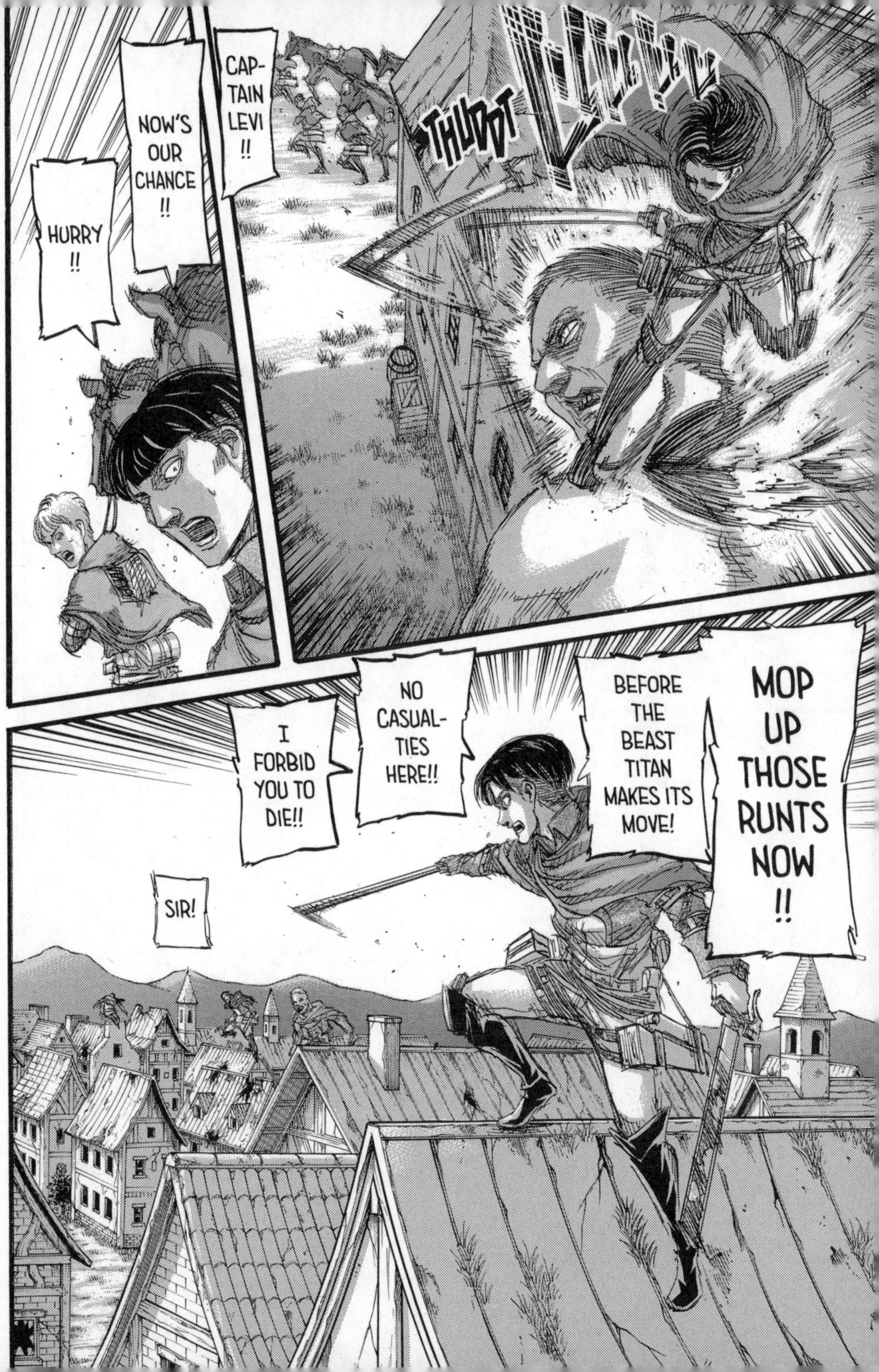
THUDDT
CAPTAIN LEVI!!
NOW'S OUR CHANCE!!
HURRY!!
MOP UP THOSE RUNTS NOW!!
BEFORE THE BEAST TITAN MAKES ITS MOVE!
NO CASUALTIES HERE!!
I FORBID YOU TO DIE!!
SIR!

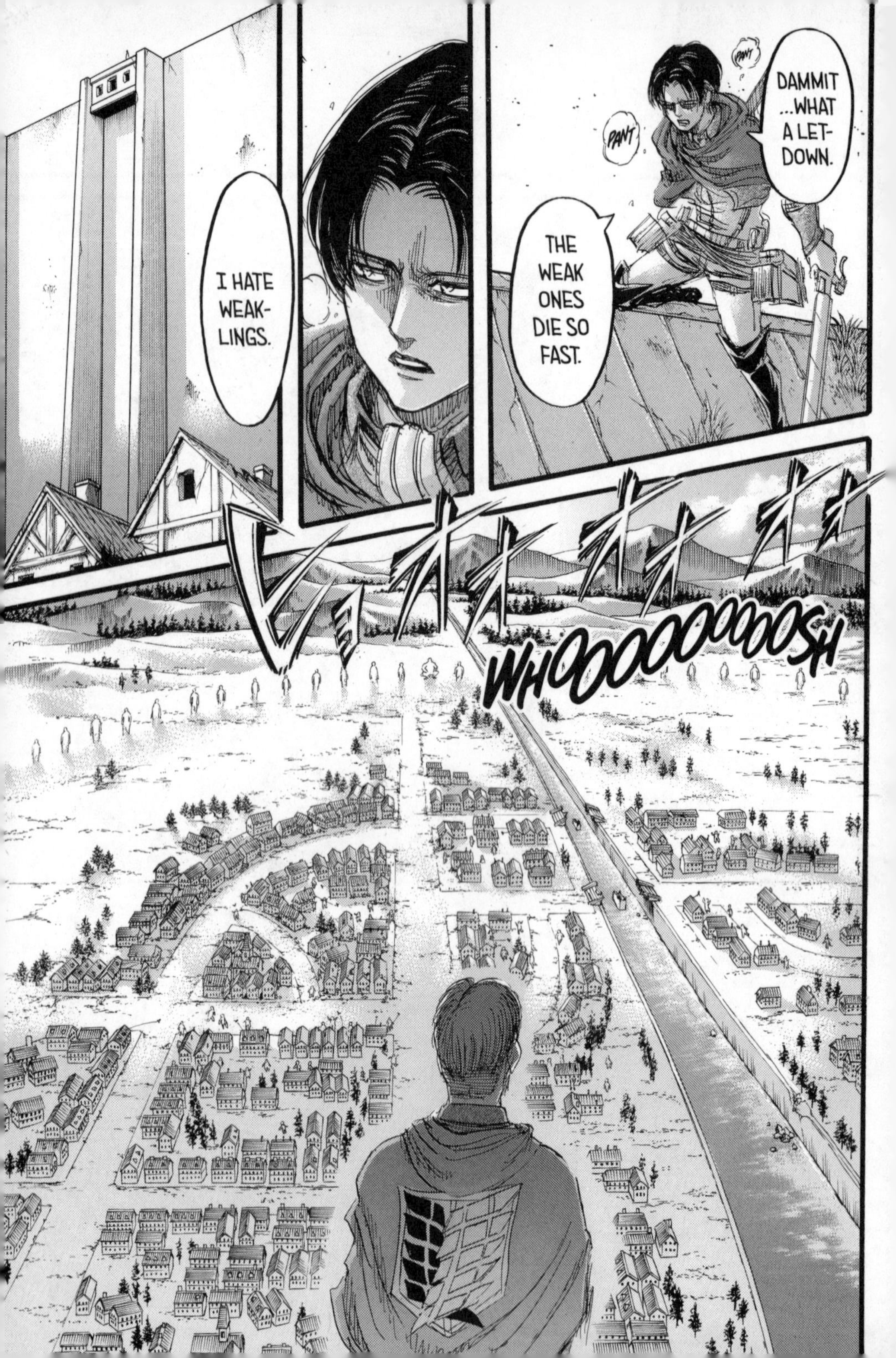
PANT
DAMMIT ...WHAT A LET-DOWN.
PANT
THE WEAK ONES DIE SO FAST.
I HATE WEAK-LINGS.
ビョオオオオオォ
WHOOOOOOOOOSH

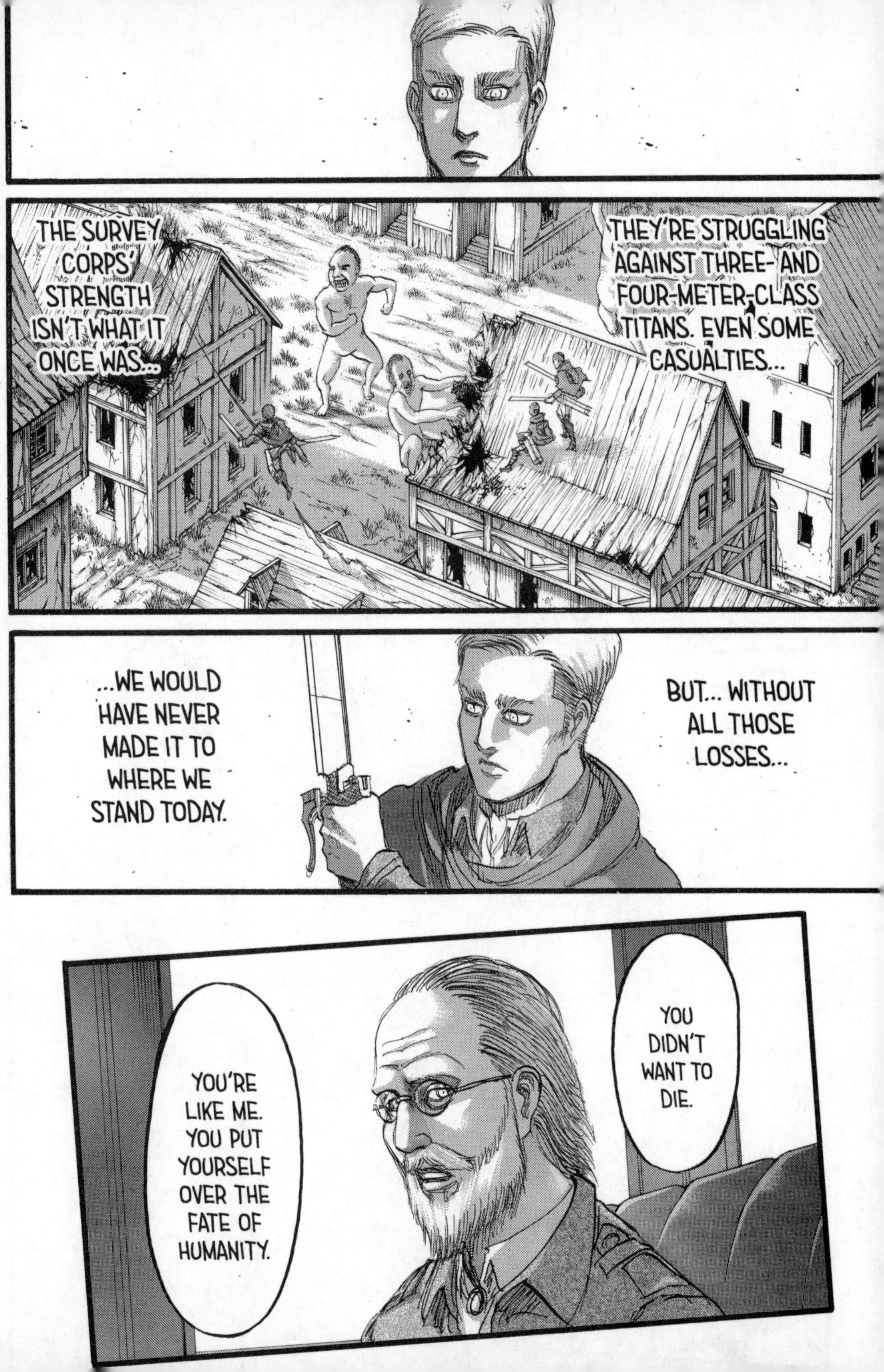
THEY'RE STRUGGLING AGAINST THREE- AND FOUR-METER-CLASS TITANS. EVEN SOME CASUALTIES...
THE SURVEY CORPS' STRENGTH ISN'T WHAT IT ONCE WAS...
BUT... WITHOUT ALL THOSE LOSSES...
...WE WOULD HAVE NEVER MADE IT TO WHERE WE STAND TODAY.
YOU DIDN'T WANT TO DIE.
YOU'RE LIKE ME. YOU PUT YOURSELF OVER THE FATE OF HUMANITY.

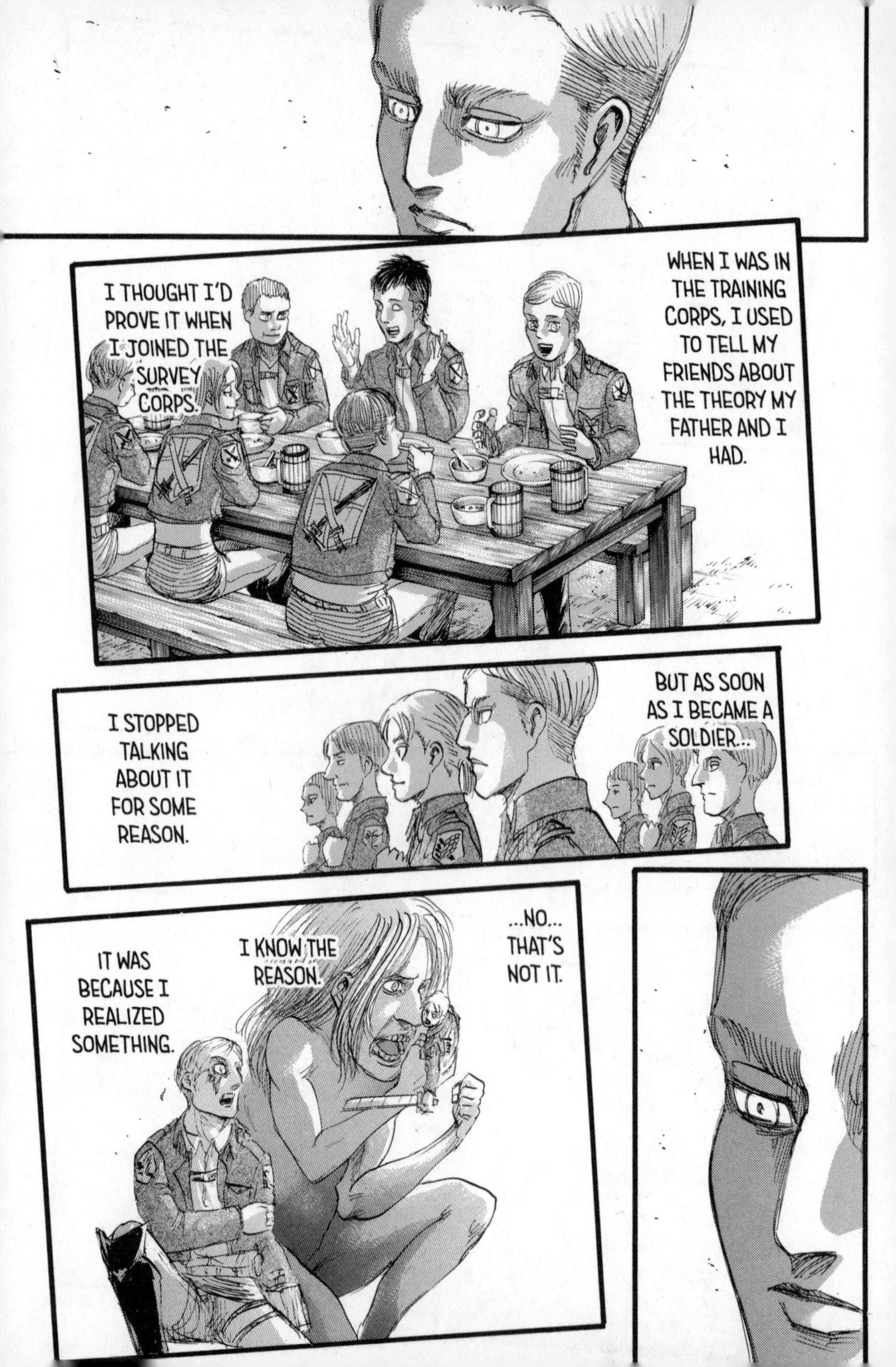
WHEN I WAS IN THE TRAINING CORPS, I USED TO TELL MY FRIENDS ABOUT THE THEORY MY FATHER AND I HAD.
I THOUGHT I'D PROVE IT WHEN I JOINED THE SURVEY CORPS.
BUT AS SOON AS I BECAME A SOLDIER...
I STOPPED TALKING ABOUT IT FOR SOME REASON.
...NO... THAT'S NOT IT.
I KNOW THE REASON.
IT WAS BECAUSE I REALIZED SOMETHING.

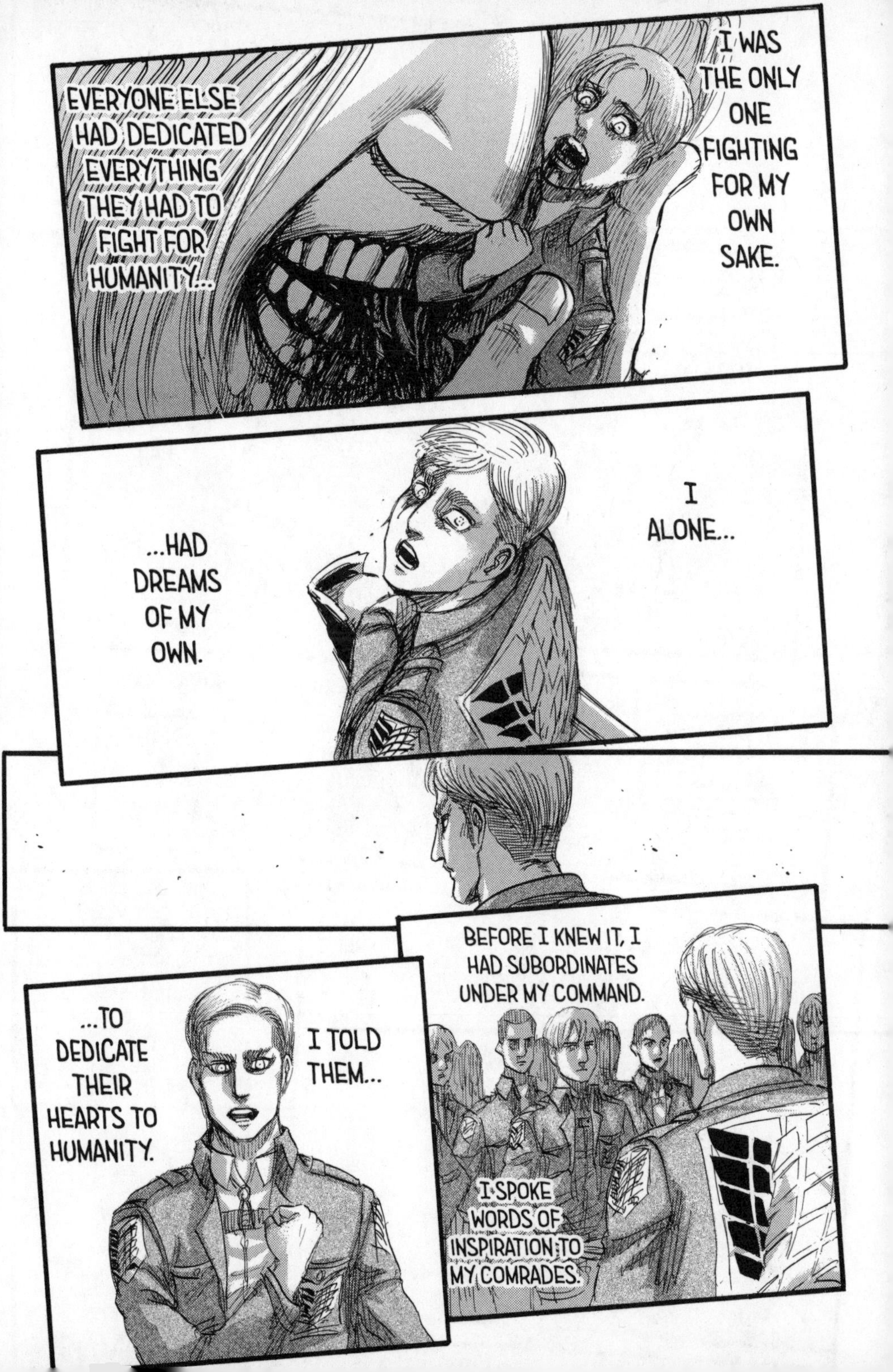

I WAS THE ONLY ONE FIGHTING FOR MY OWN SAKE.
EVERYONE ELSE HAD DEDICATED EVERYTHING THEY HAD TO FIGHT FOR HUMANITY...
I ALONE...
...HAD DREAMS OF MY OWN.
BEFORE I KNEW IT, I HAD SUBORDINATES UNDER MY COMMAND.
I SPOKE WORDS OF INSPIRATION TO MY COMRADES.
I TOLD THEM...
...TO DEDICATE THEIR HEARTS TO HUMANITY.

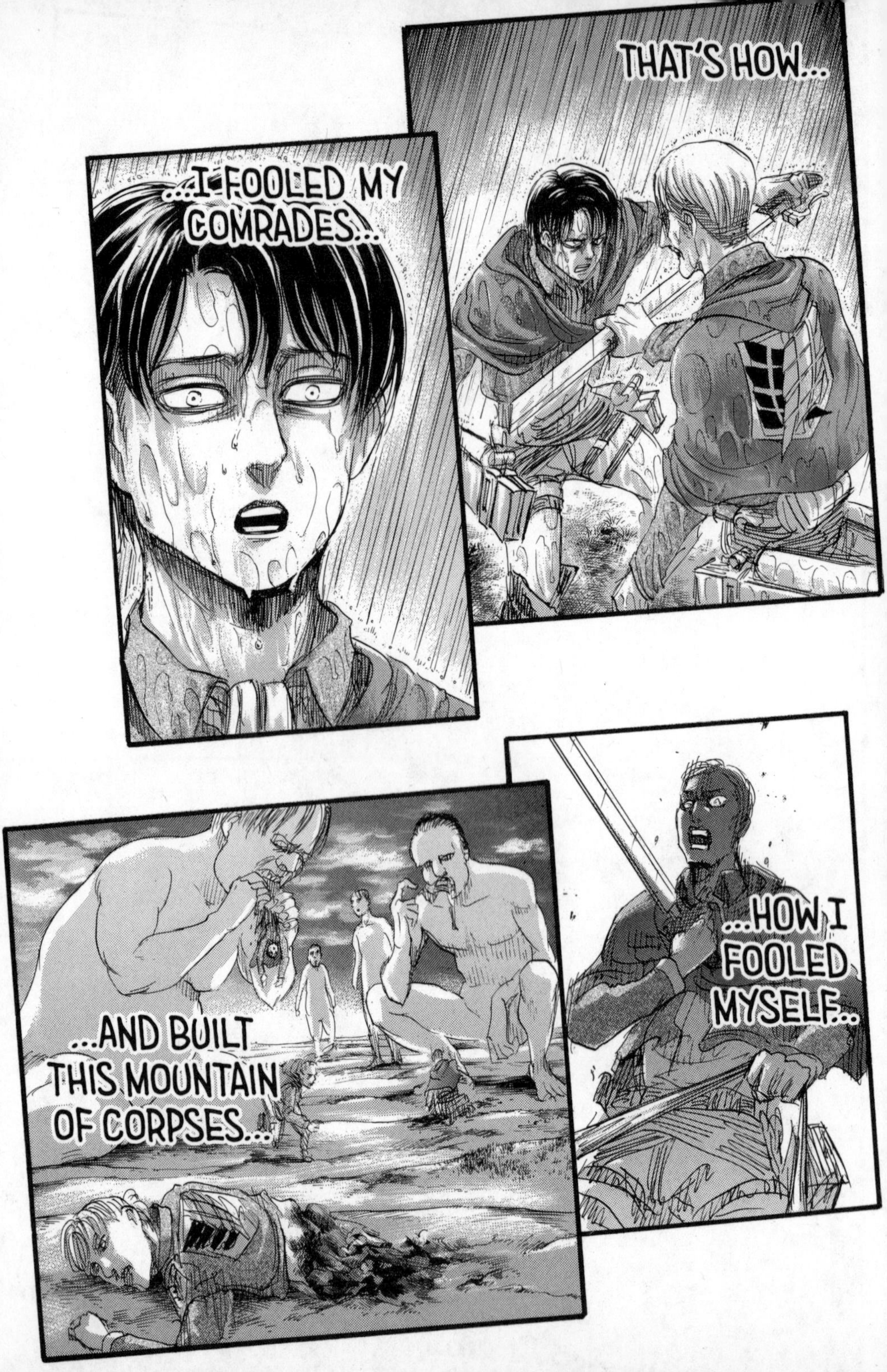
THAT'S HOW...
...I FOOLED MY COMRADES...
...HOW I FOOLED MYSELF...
...AND BUILT THIS MOUNTAIN OF CORPSES...

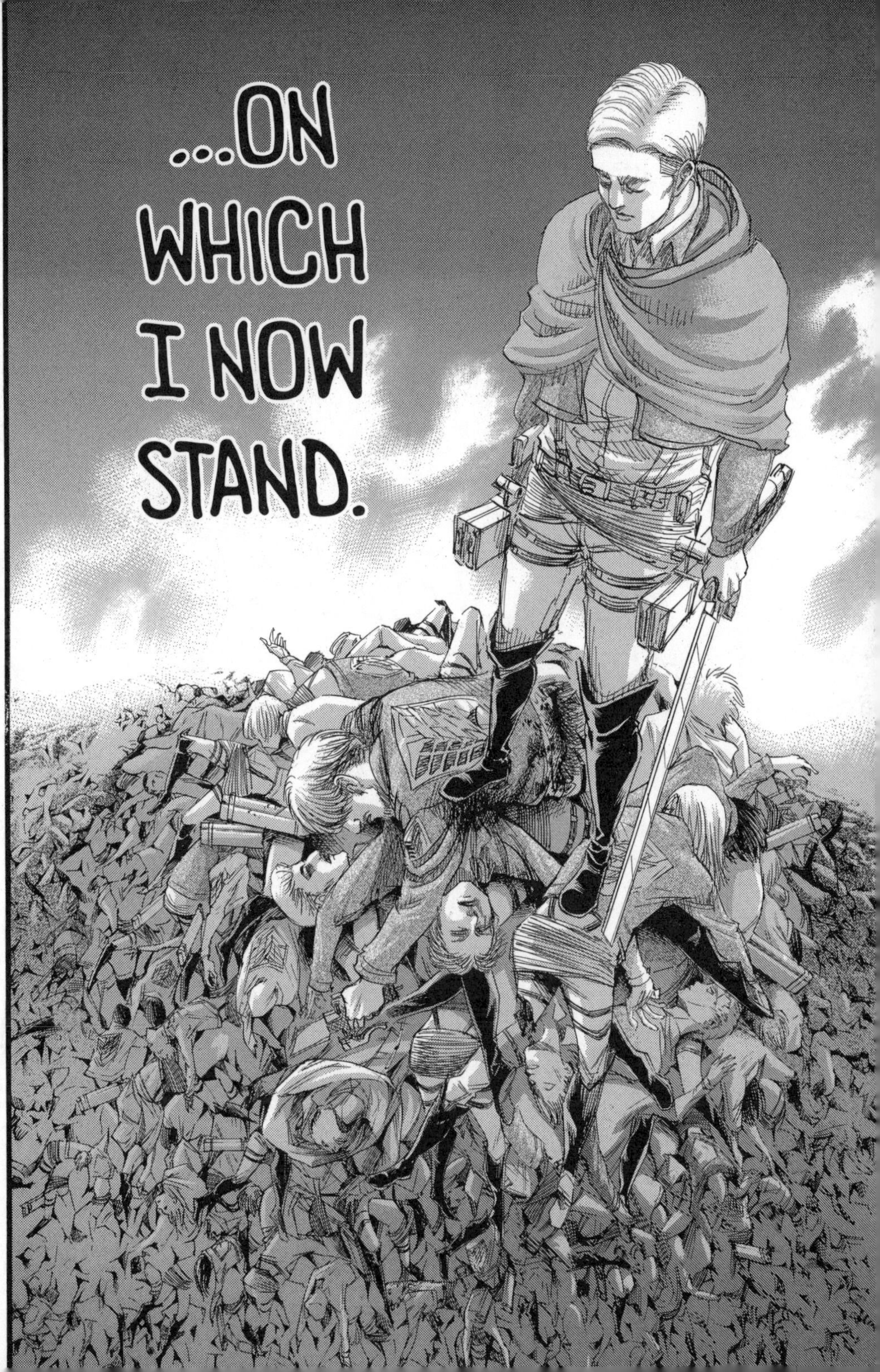
...ON WHICH I NOW STAND.

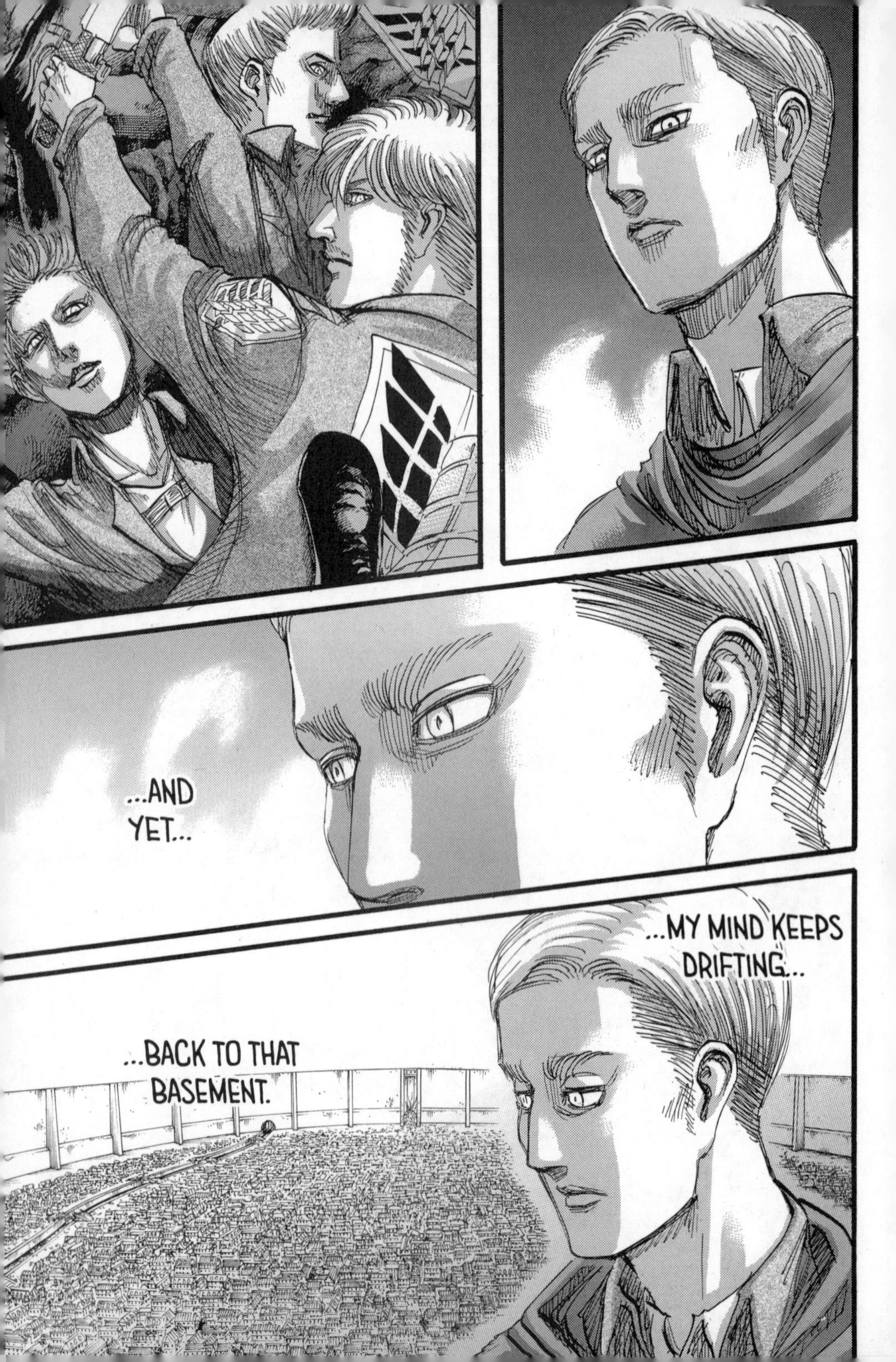
...AND YET...
...MY MIND KEEPS DRIFTING...
...BACK TO THAT BASEMENT.

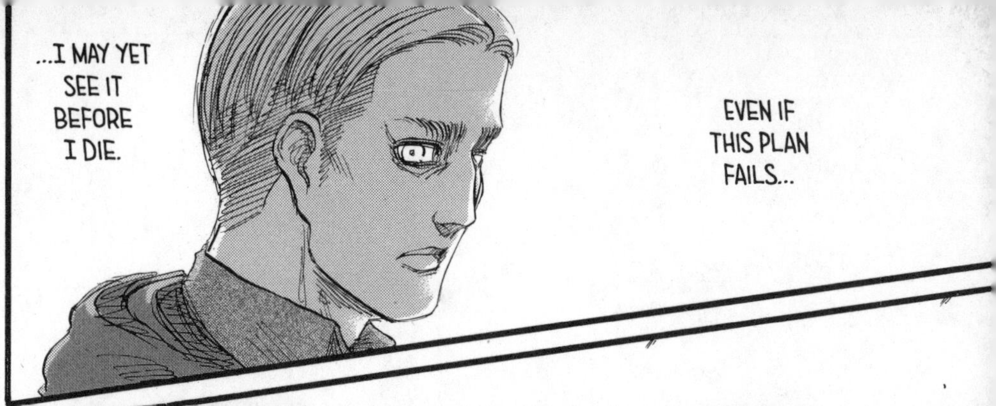
EVEN IF THIS PLAN FAILS...
...I MAY YET SEE IT BEFORE I DIE.

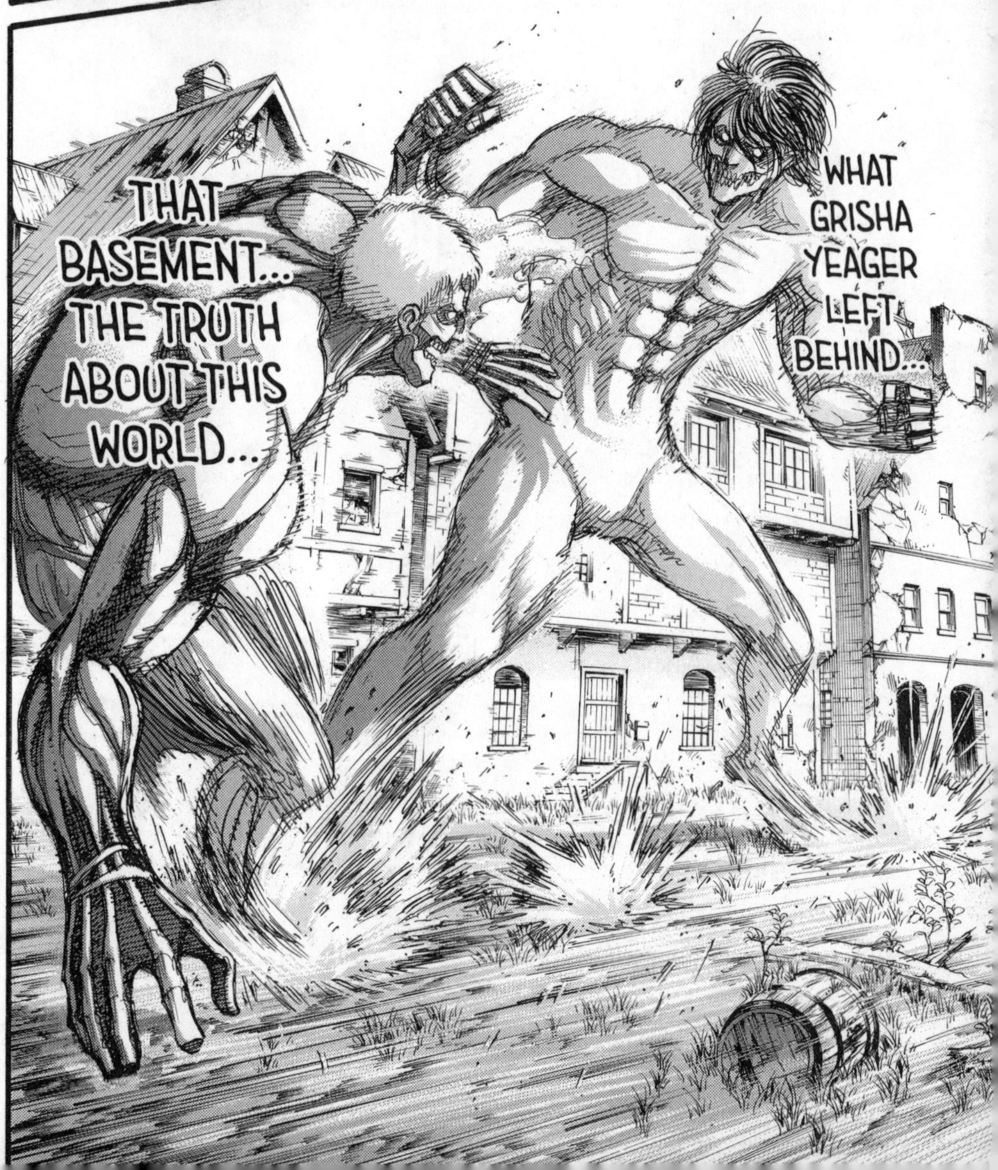
WHAT GRISHA YEAGER LEFT BEHIND...
THAT BASEMENT... THE TRUTH ABOUT THIS WORLD...

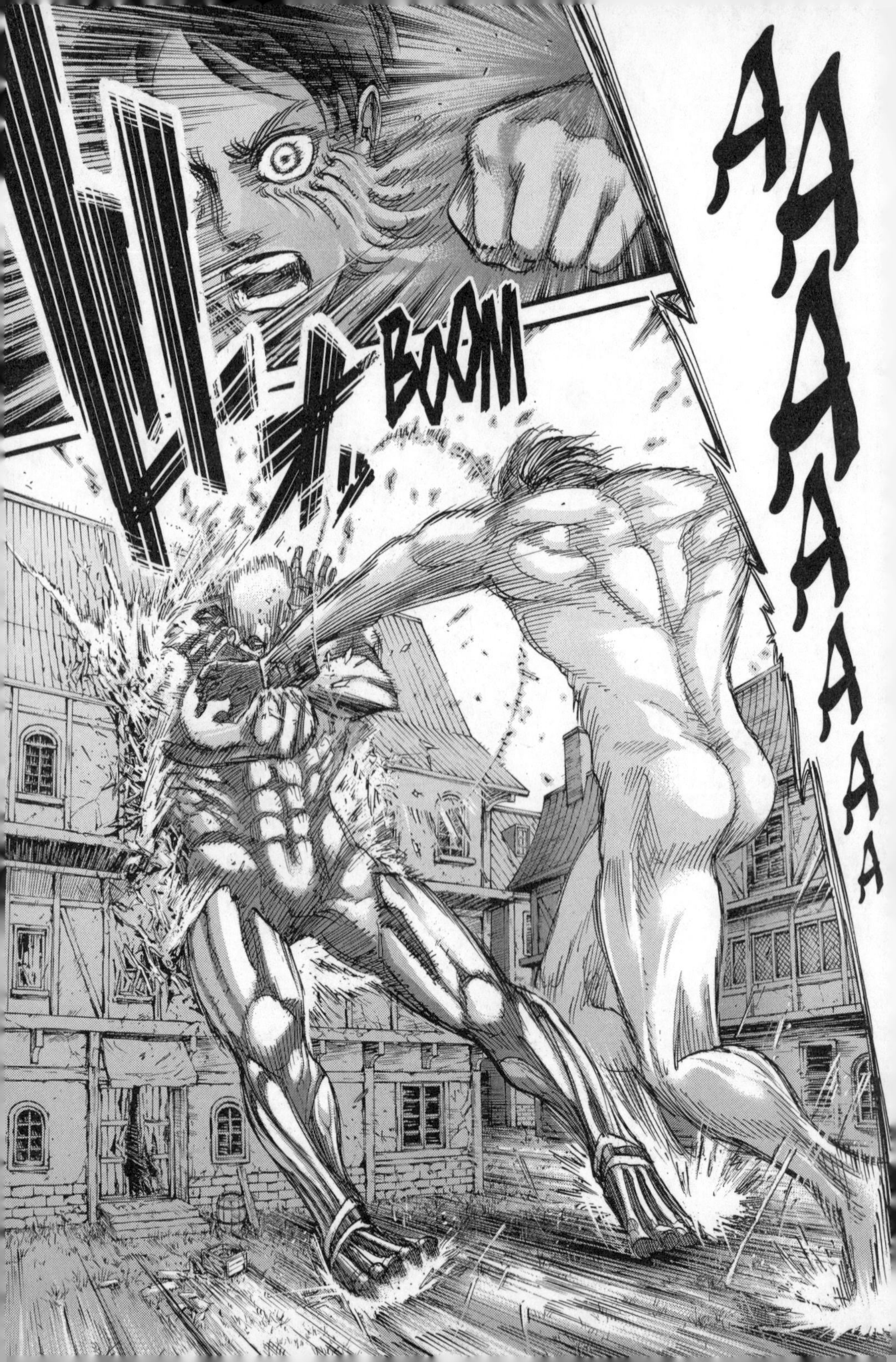
AAAAAAAAAAAAA
BOOM

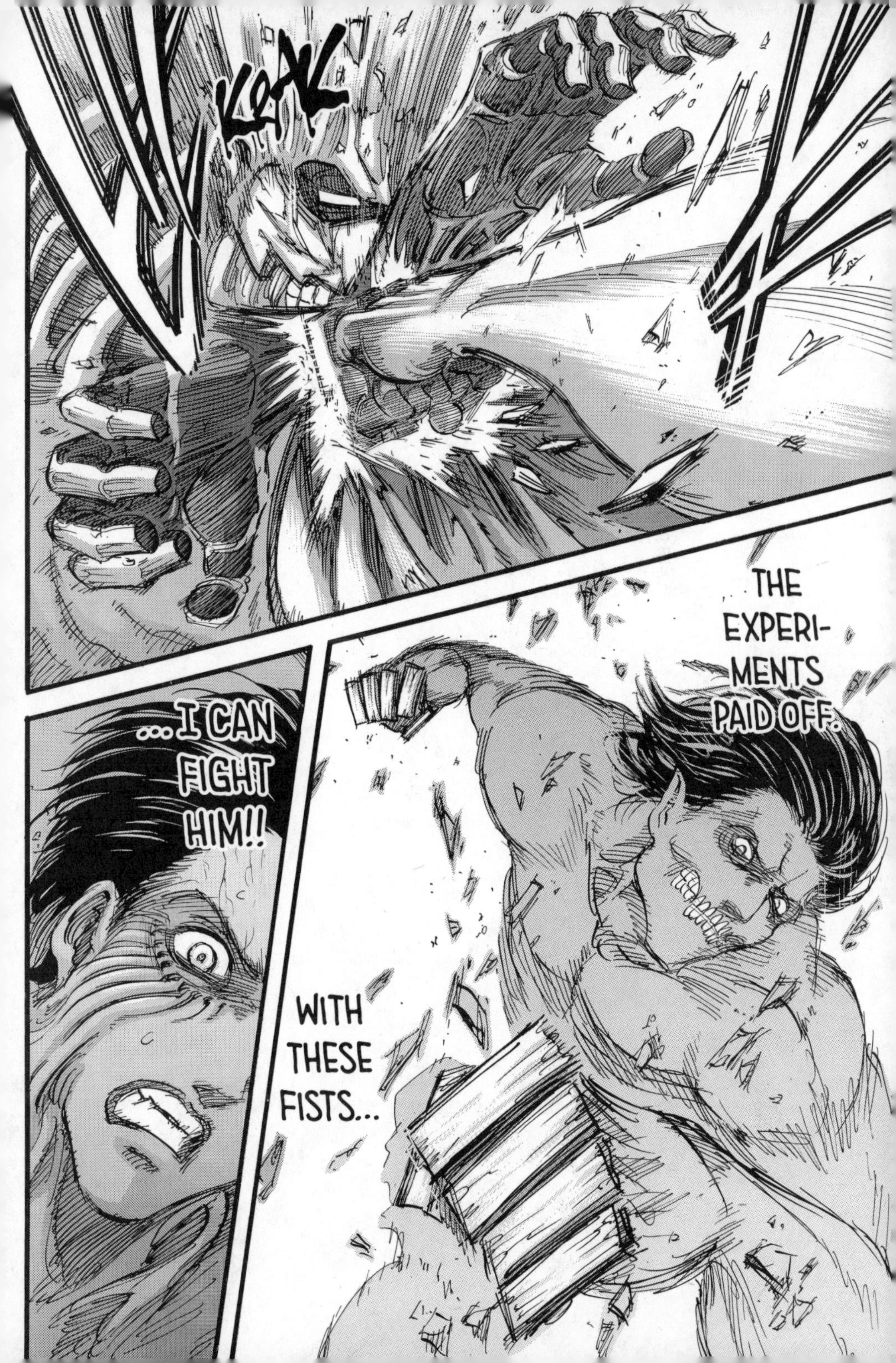
KRAK
THE EXPERI-
MENTS
PAID OFF.
WITH
THESE
FISTS...
...I CAN
FIGHT
HIM!!

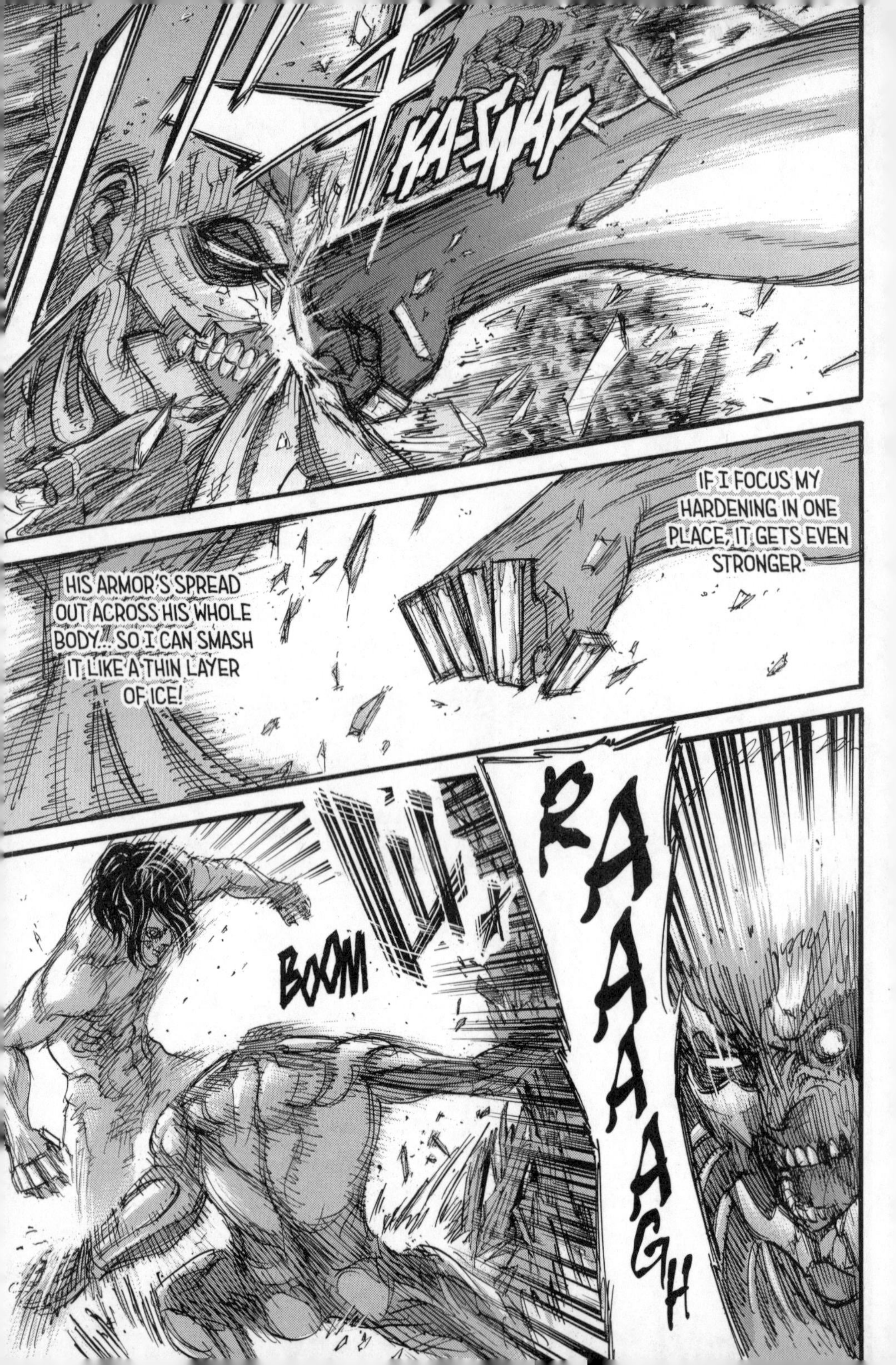
KA-SNAP
IF I FOCUS MY HARDENING IN ONE PLACE, IT GETS EVEN STRONGER.
HIS ARMOR'S SPREAD OUT ACROSS HIS WHOLE BODY... SO I CAN SMASH IT LIKE A THIN LAYER OF ICE!
RAAAAAGH
BOOM

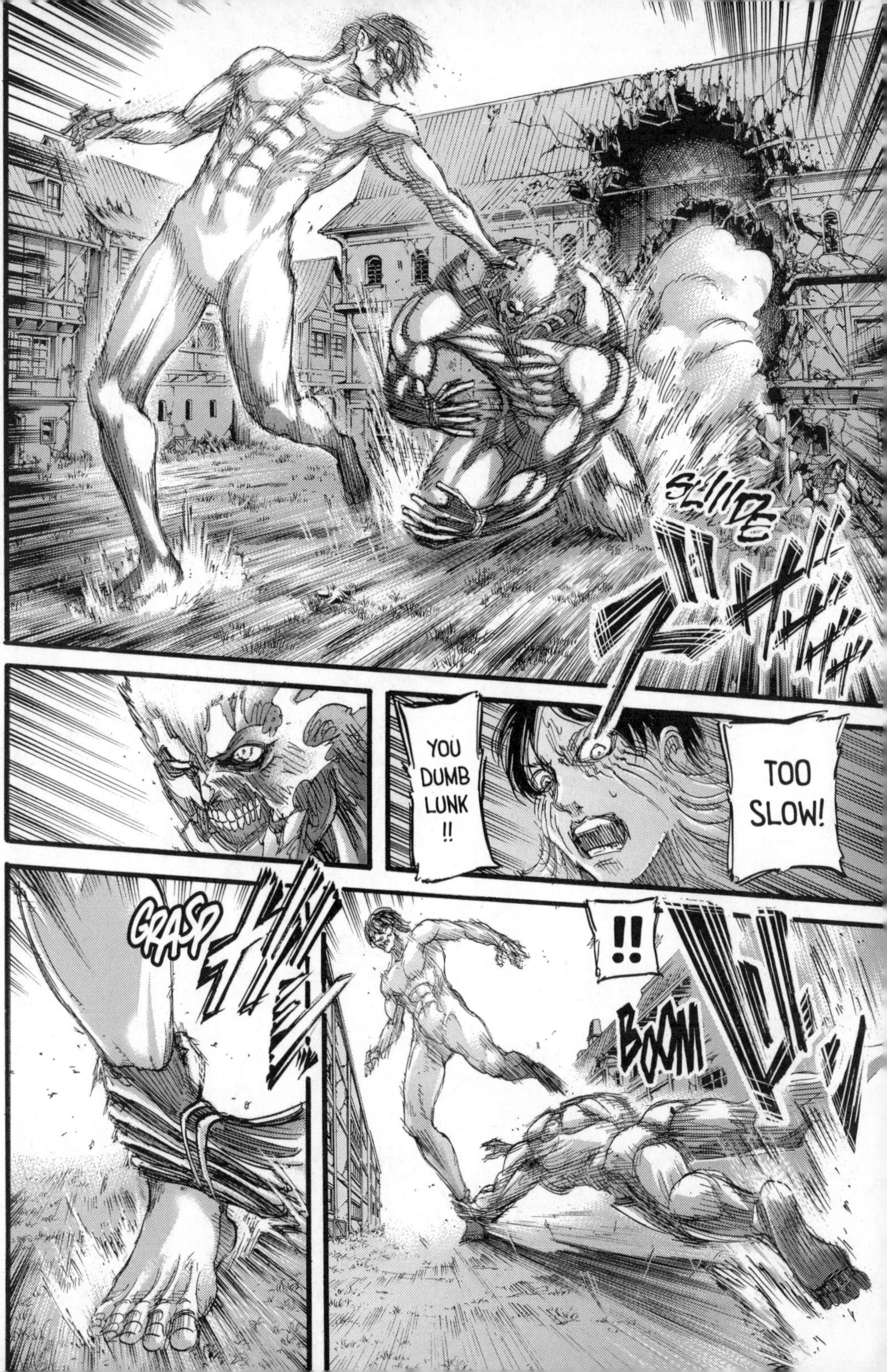
SLIIIDE
TOO SLOW!
YOU DUMB LUNK !!
!!
BOOM
GRASP

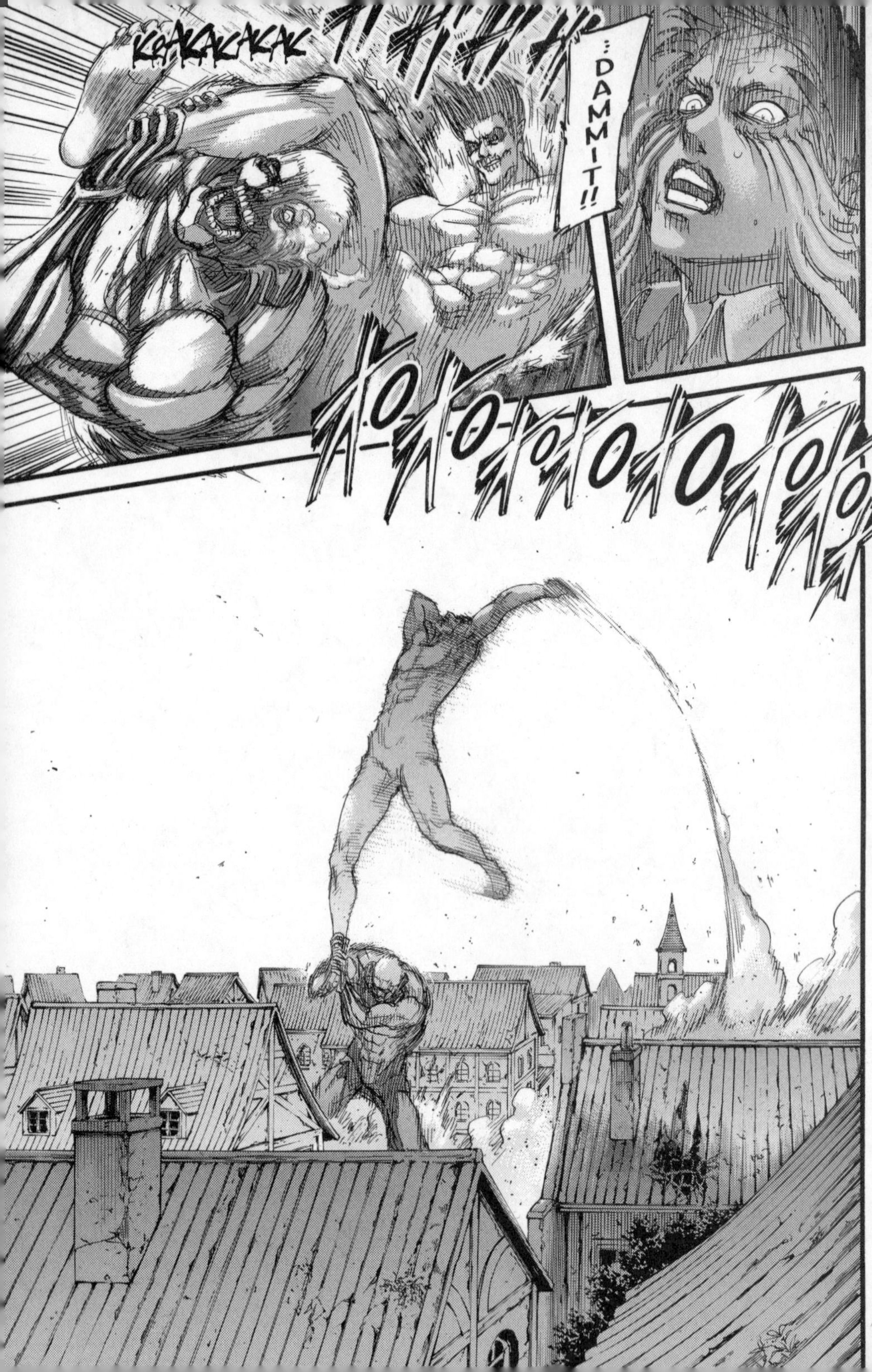

...DAMMIT!!
KRAKAKAKAK

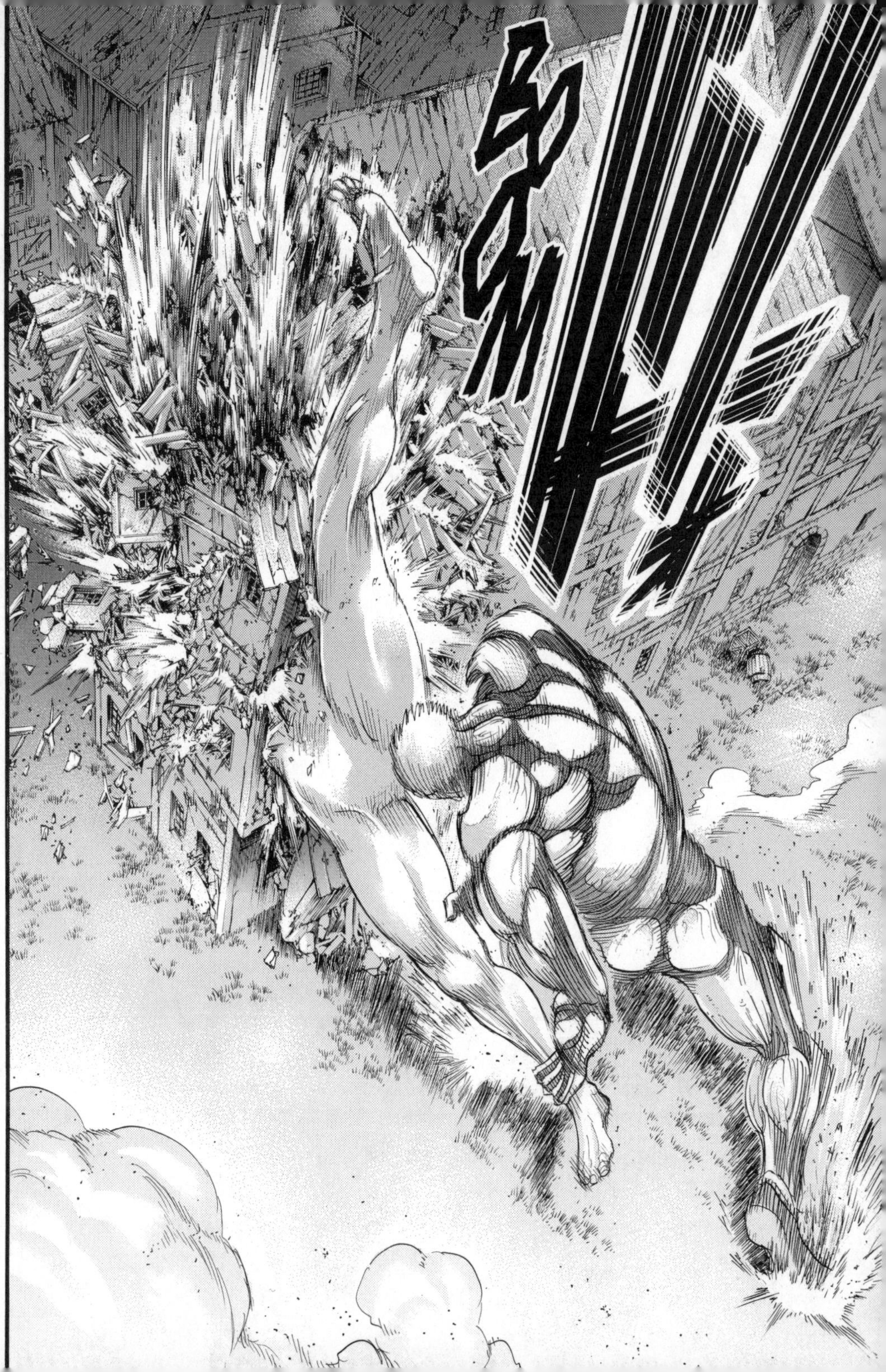
BOOM

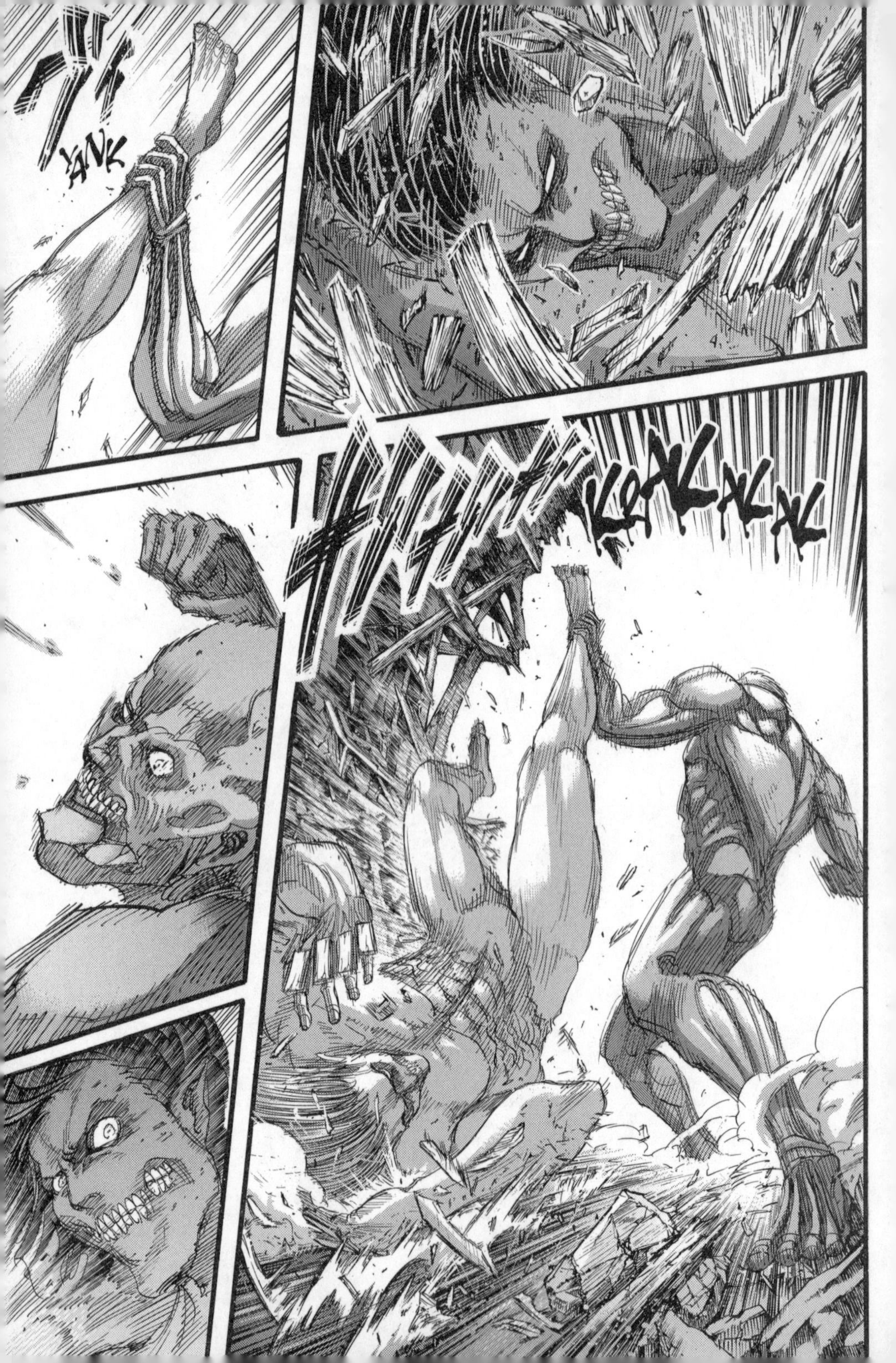
KRAKAKAKAK
YANK

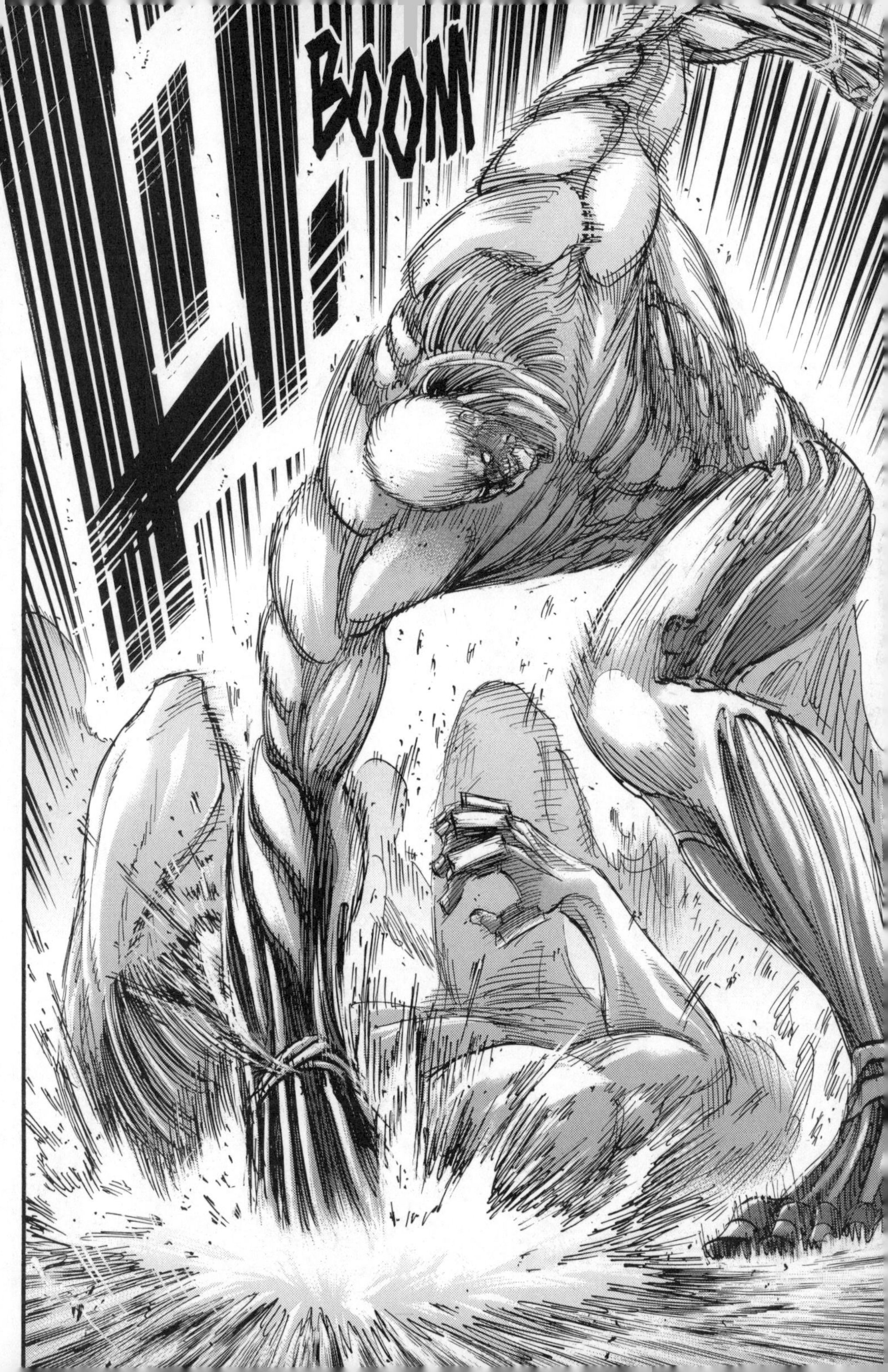
BOOM

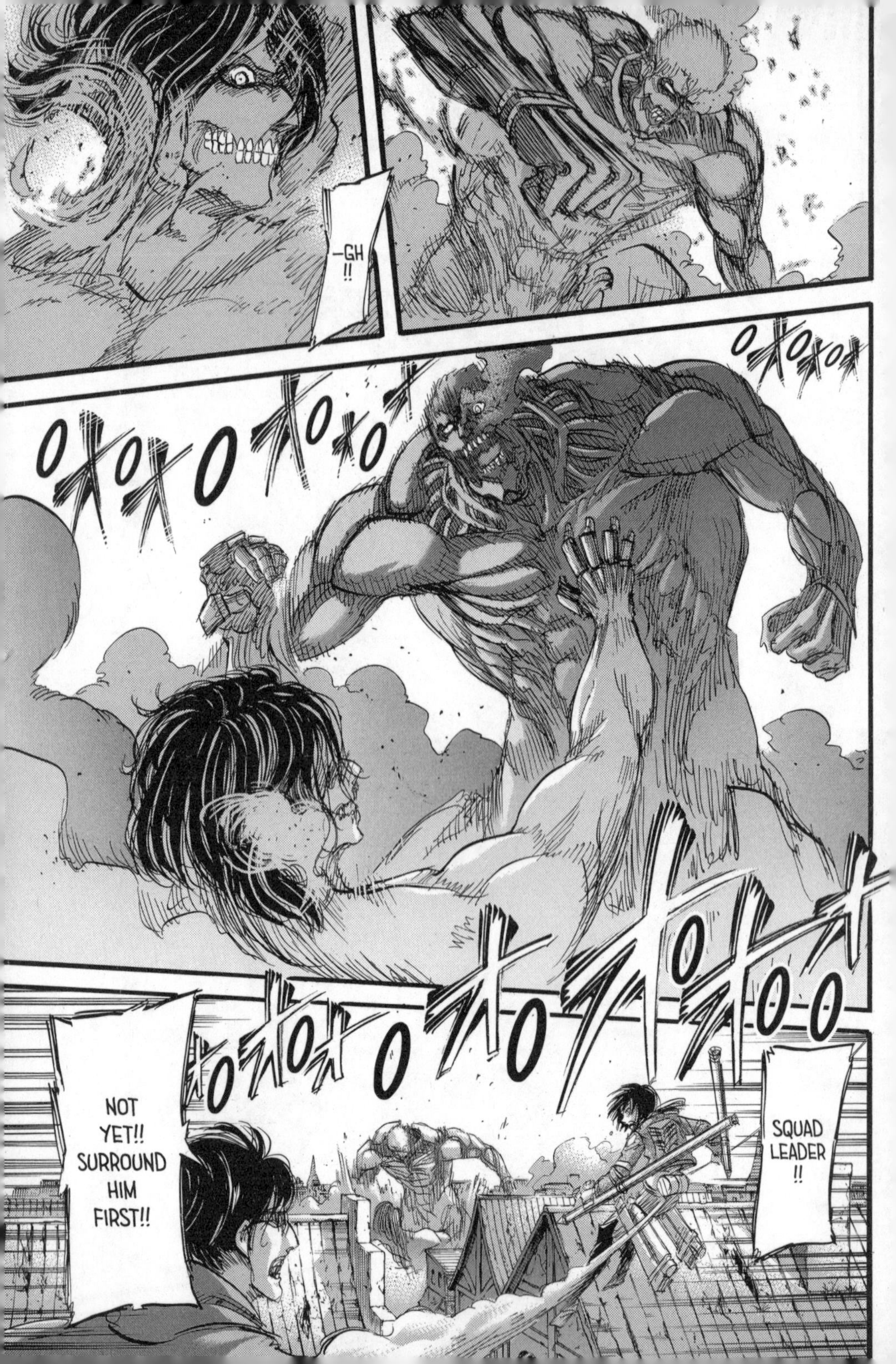
—GH!!
SQUAD LEADER!!
NOT YET!! SURROUND HIM FIRST!!

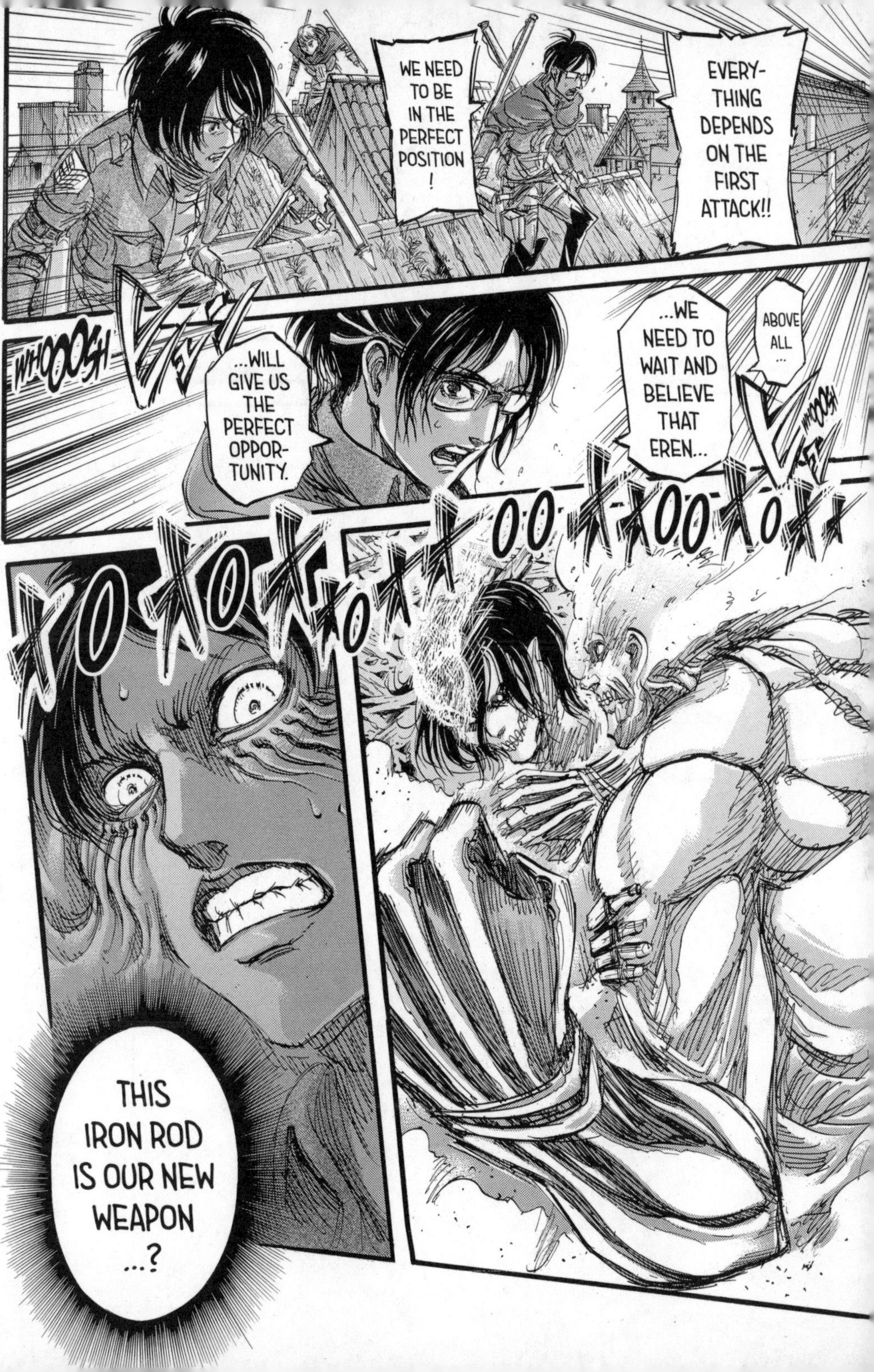
EVERY-THING DEPENDS ON THE FIRST ATTACK!!
WE NEED TO BE IN THE PERFECT POSITION!
WHOOOSH
ABOVE ALL...
...WE NEED TO WAIT AND BELIEVE THAT EREN...
...WILL GIVE US THE PERFECT OPPORTUNITY.
WHOOOSH
THIS IRON ROD IS OUR NEW WEAPON...?

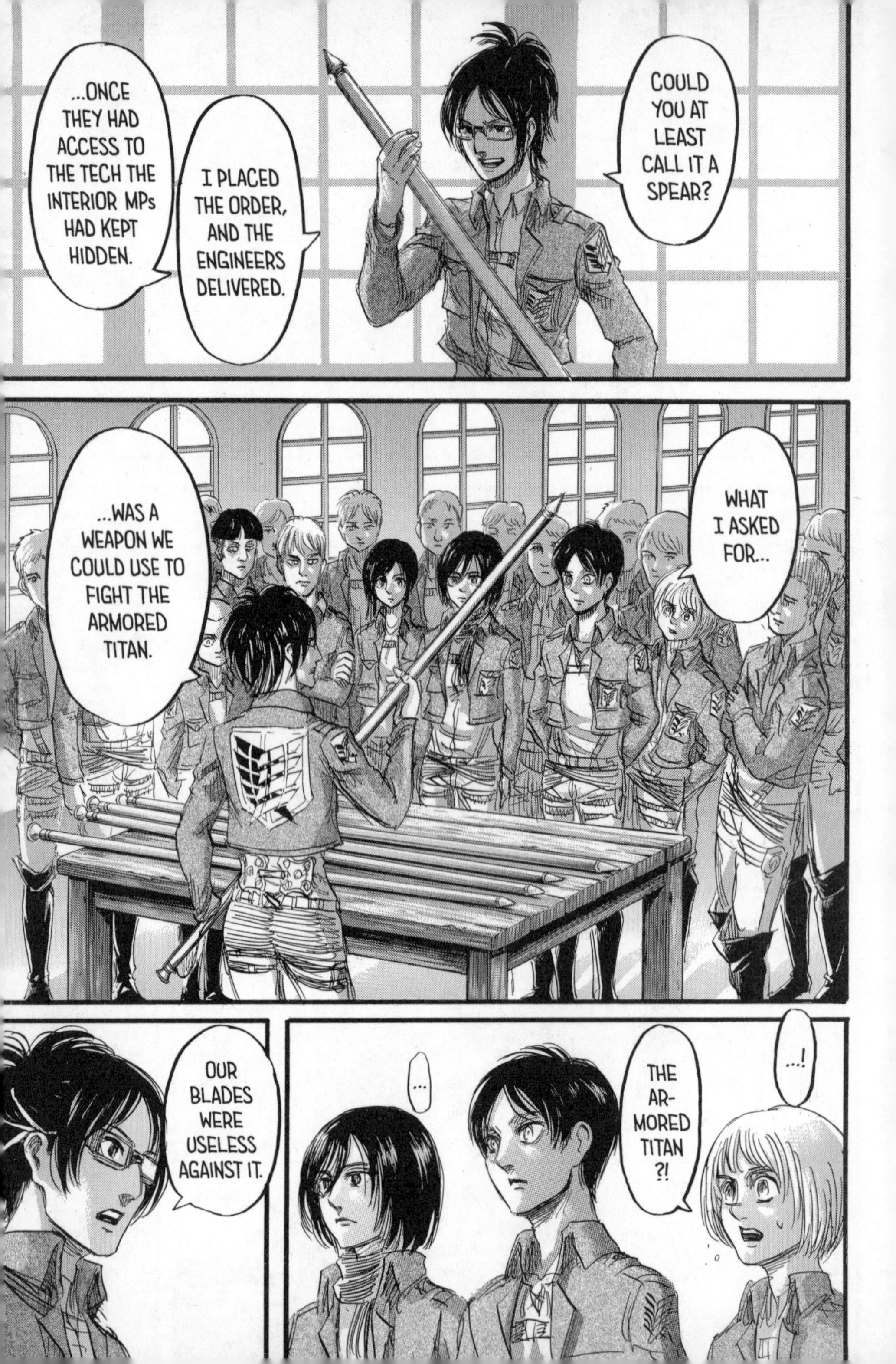
COULD YOU AT LEAST CALL IT A SPEAR?
I PLACED THE ORDER, AND THE ENGINEERS DELIVERED.
...ONCE THEY HAD ACCESS TO THE TECH THE INTERIOR MPs HAD KEPT HIDDEN.
WHAT I ASKED FOR...
...WAS A WEAPON WE COULD USE TO FIGHT THE ARMORED TITAN.
...!
THE AR-MORED TITAN?!
...
OUR BLADES WERE USELESS AGAINST IT.

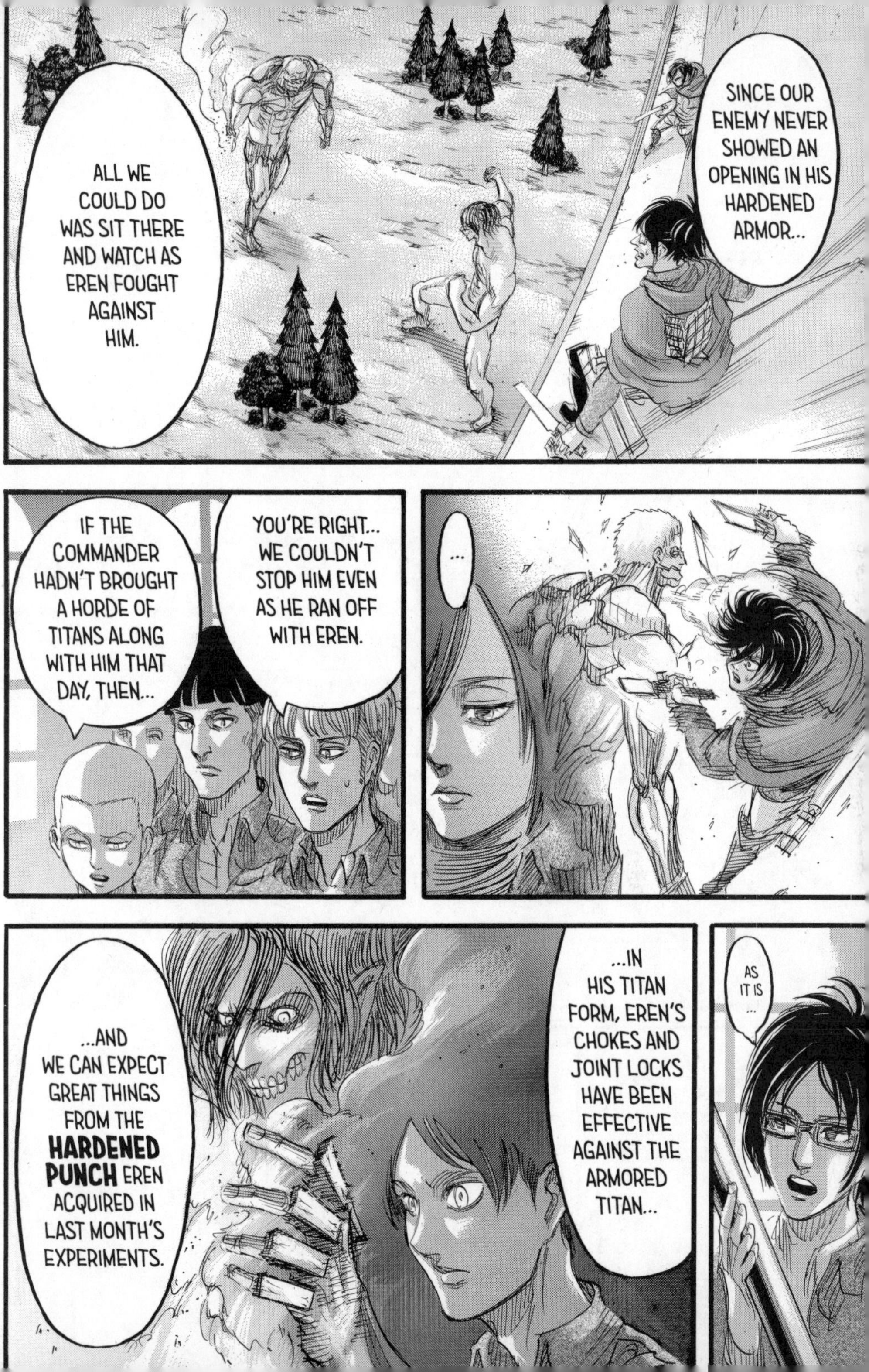
SINCE OUR ENEMY NEVER SHOWED AN OPENING IN HIS HARDENED ARMOR...
ALL WE COULD DO WAS SIT THERE AND WATCH AS EREN FOUGHT AGAINST HIM.
...
YOU'RE RIGHT... WE COULDN'T STOP HIM EVEN AS HE RAN OFF WITH EREN.
IF THE COMMANDER HADN'T BROUGHT A HORDE OF TITANS ALONG WITH HIM THAT DAY, THEN...
AS IT IS...
...IN HIS TITAN FORM, EREN'S CHOKES AND JOINT LOCKS HAVE BEEN EFFECTIVE AGAINST THE ARMORED TITAN...
...AND WE CAN EXPECT GREAT THINGS FROM THE **HARDENED PUNCH** EREN ACQUIRED IN LAST MONTH'S EXPERIMENTS.

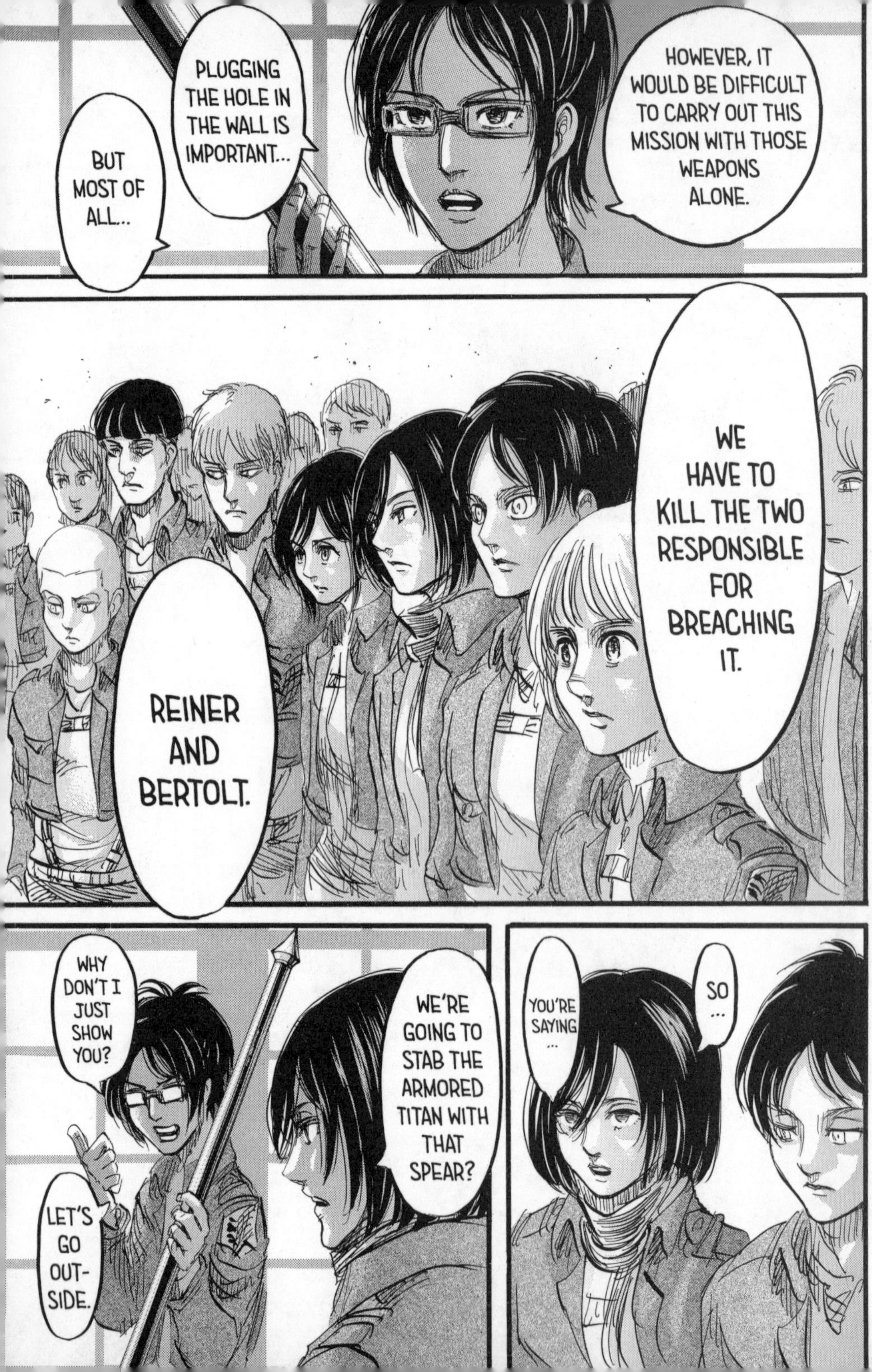
HOWEVER, IT WOULD BE DIFFICULT TO CARRY OUT THIS MISSION WITH THOSE WEAPONS ALONE.
PLUGGING THE HOLE IN THE WALL IS IMPORTANT...
BUT MOST OF ALL...
WE HAVE TO KILL THE TWO RESPONSIBLE FOR BREACHING IT.
REINER AND BERTOLT.
SO ...
YOU'RE SAYING ...
WE'RE GOING TO STAB THE ARMORED TITAN WITH THAT SPEAR?
WHY DON'T I JUST SHOW YOU?
LET'S GO OUT-SIDE.

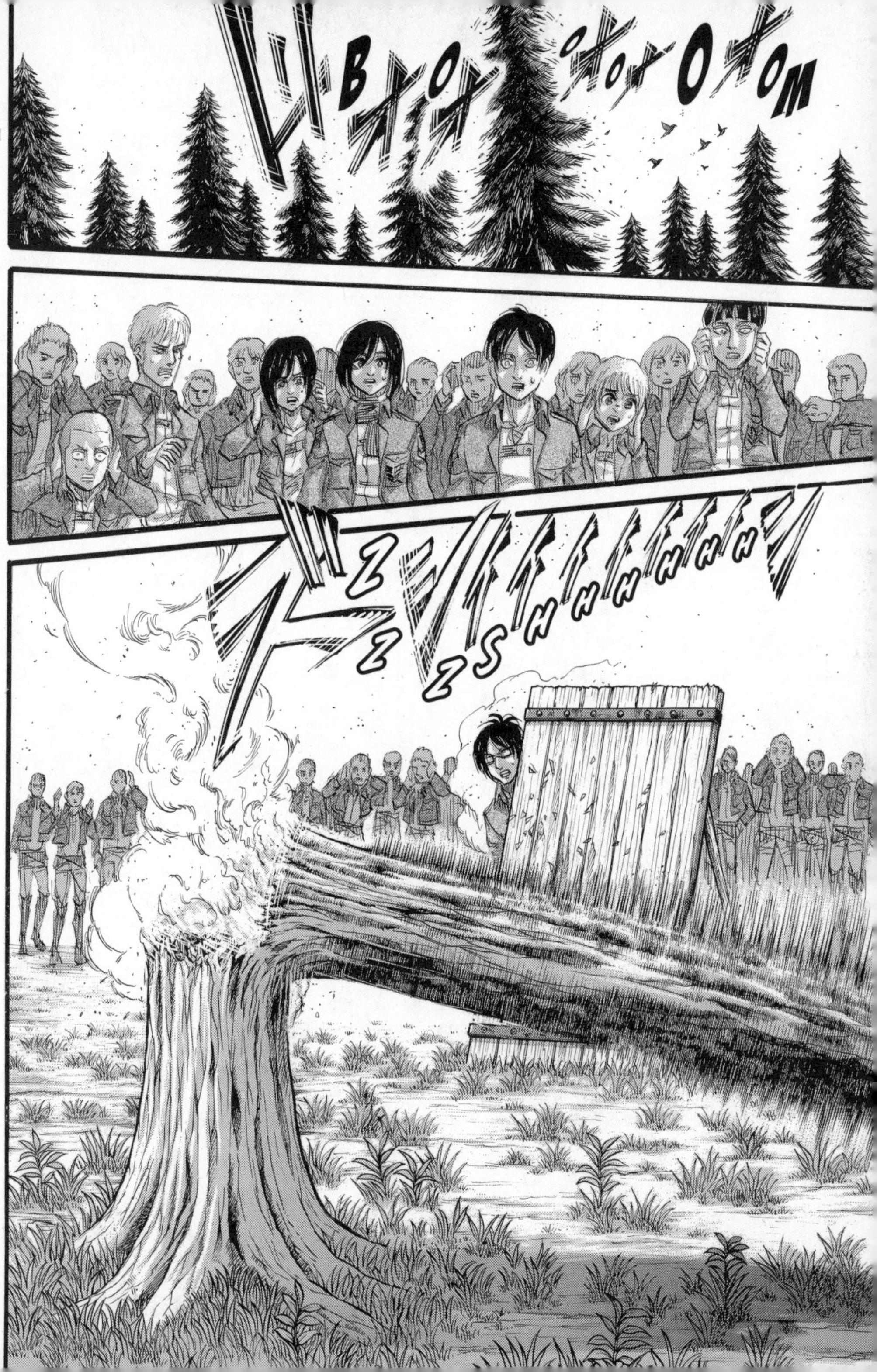
BOOM
ZZZSHHHHHHHH

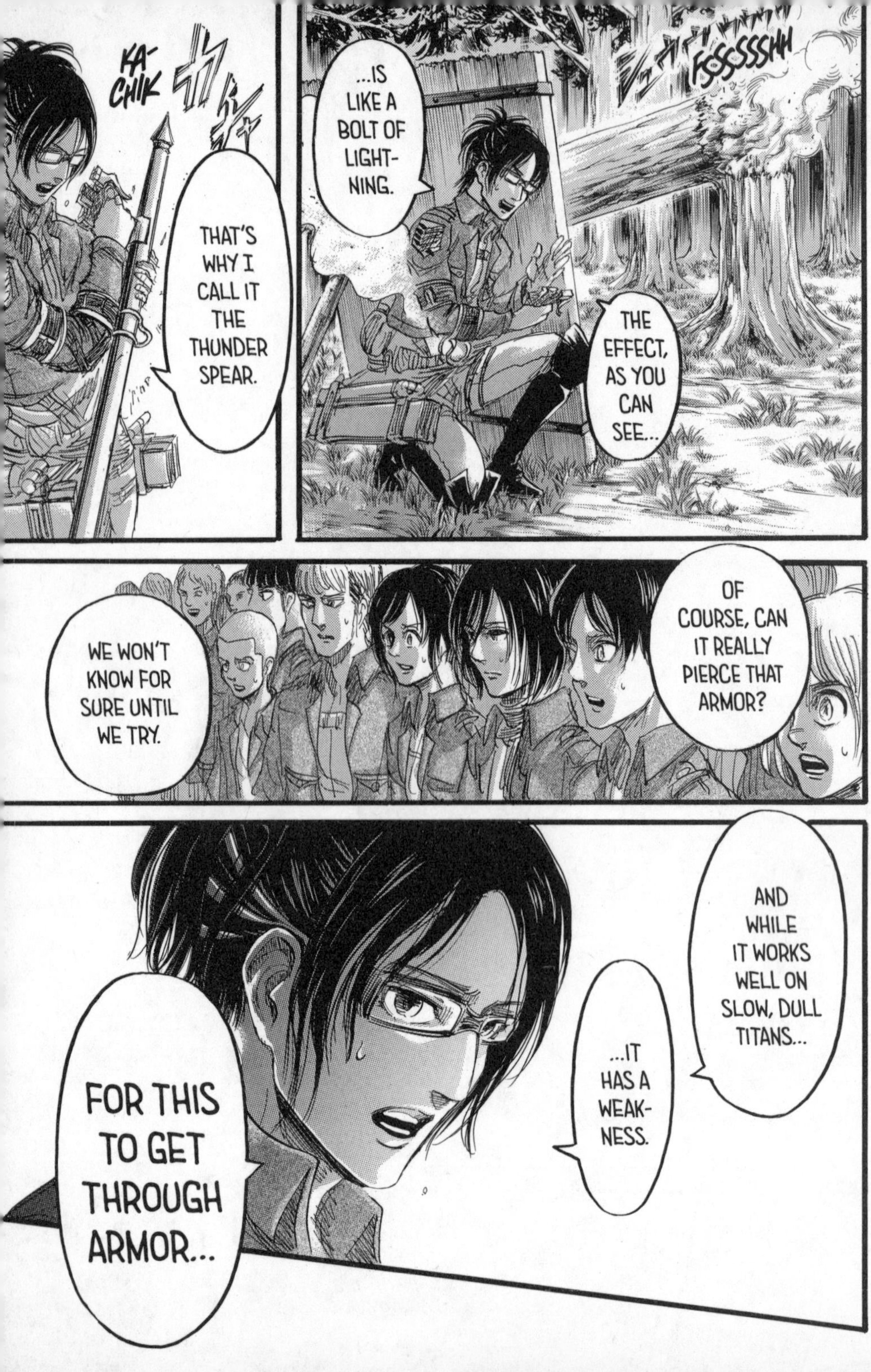
FSSSSSHH
THE EFFECT, AS YOU CAN SEE...
...IS LIKE A BOLT OF LIGHT-NING.
KA-CHIK
THAT'S WHY I CALL IT THE THUNDER SPEAR.
OF COURSE, CAN IT REALLY PIERCE THAT ARMOR?
WE WON'T KNOW FOR SURE UNTIL WE TRY.
AND WHILE IT WORKS WELL ON SLOW, DULL TITANS...
...IT HAS A WEAK-NESS.
FOR THIS TO GET THROUGH ARMOR...

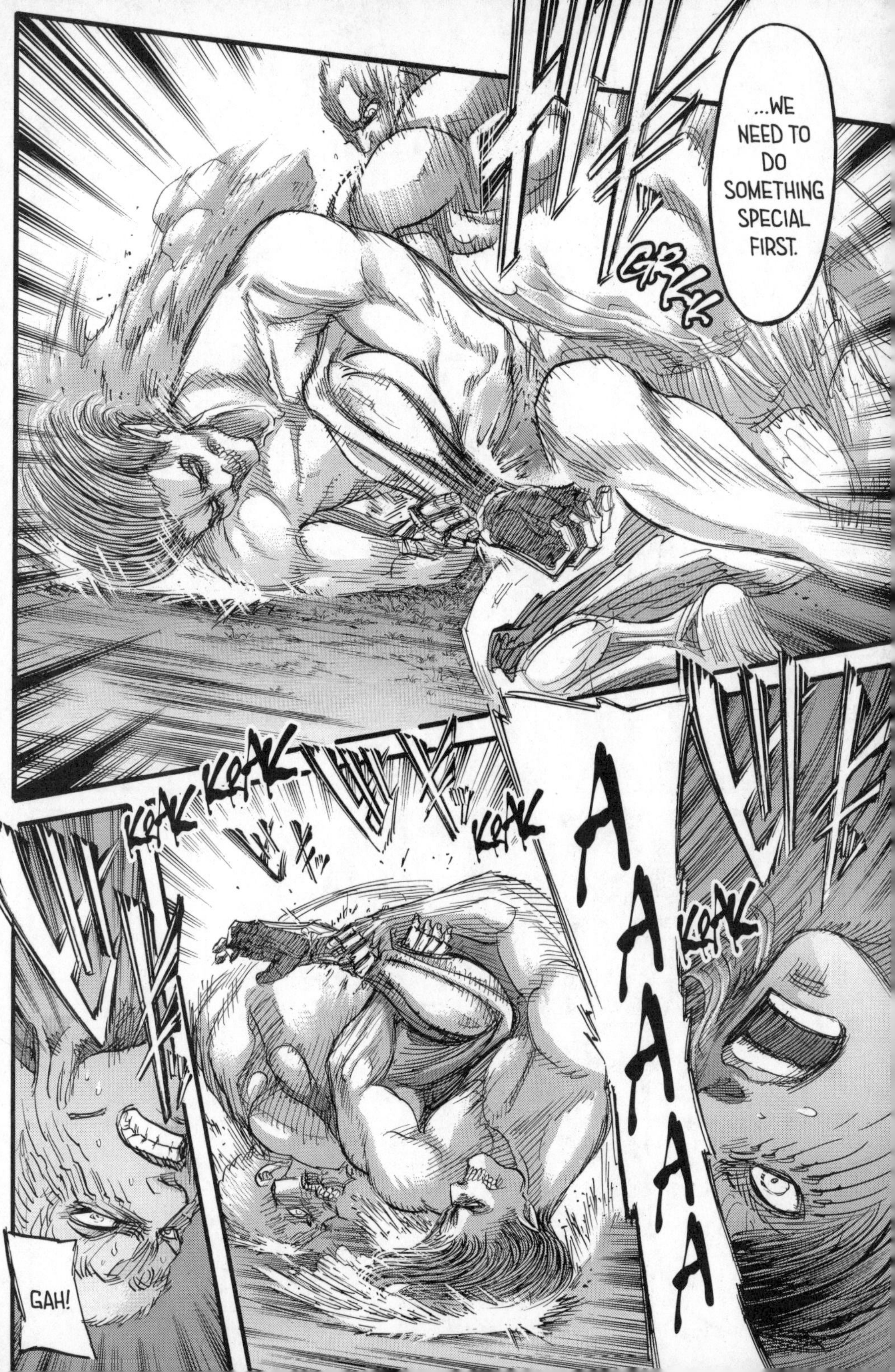
...WE NEED TO DO SOMETHING SPECIAL FIRST.
GRLK
KRAK
AAAAAAA
KRAK
KRAK KRAK
GAH!

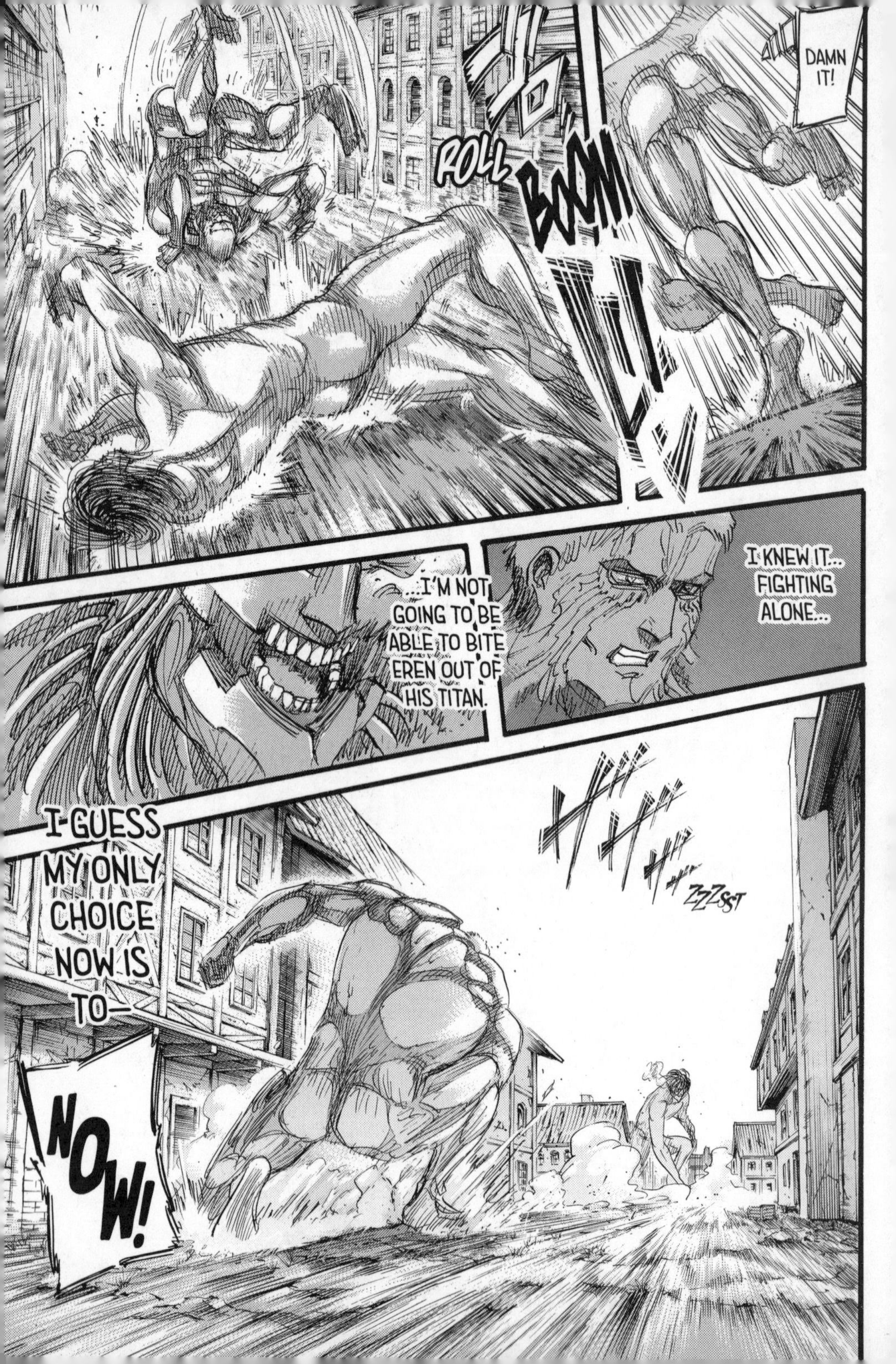
DAMN IT!
BOOM
ROLL
I KNEW IT... FIGHTING ALONE...
...I'M NOT GOING TO BE ABLE TO BITE EREN OUT OF HIS TITAN.
ZZZSST
I GUESS MY ONLY CHOICE NOW IS TO—
NOW!

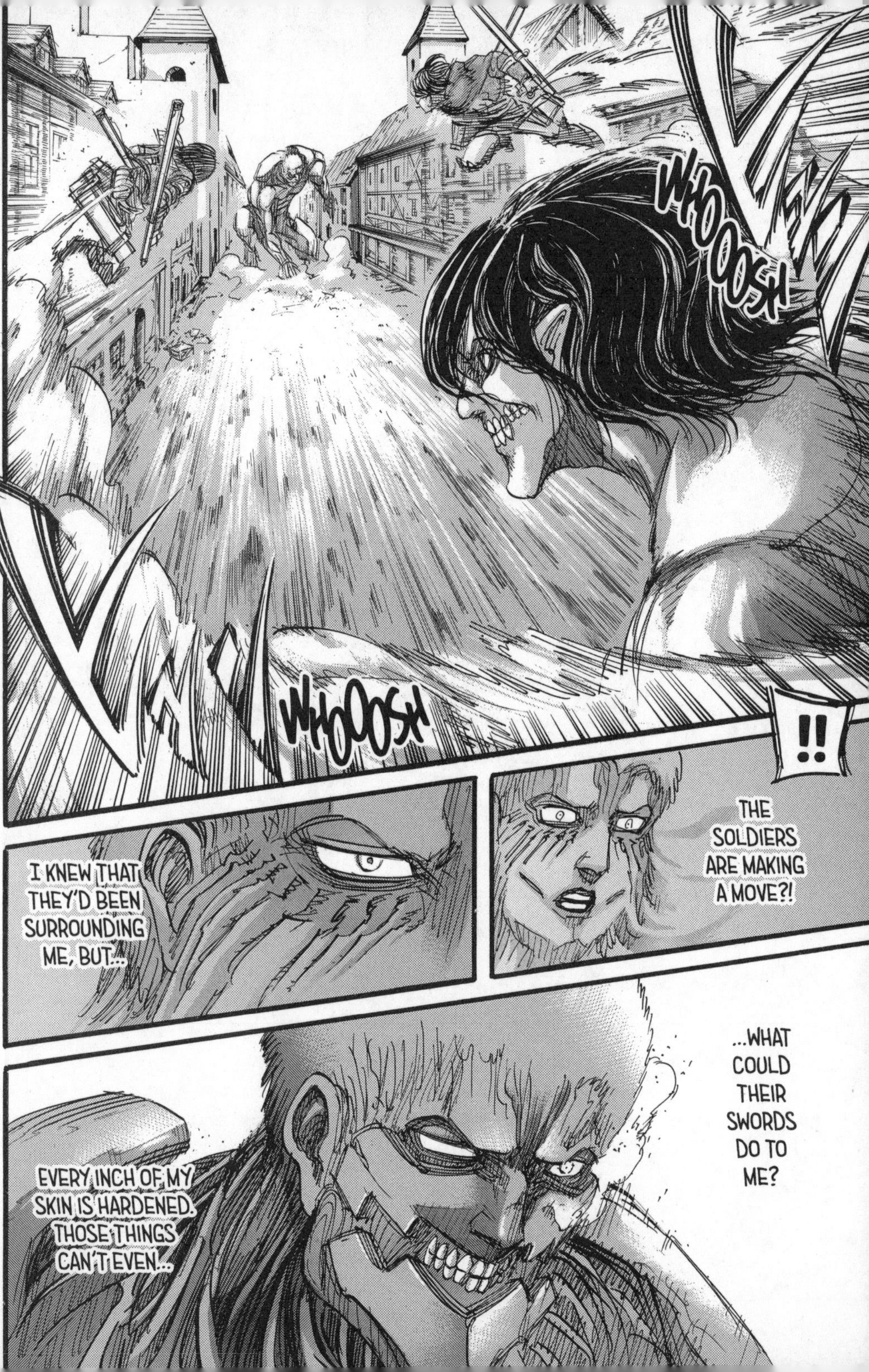
WHOOOSH
WHOOOSH
!!
THE SOLDIERS ARE MAKING A MOVE?!
I KNEW THAT THEY'D BEEN SURROUNDING ME, BUT...
...WHAT COULD THEIR SWORDS DO TO ME?
EVERY INCH OF MY SKIN IS HARDENED. THOSE THINGS CAN'T EVEN...

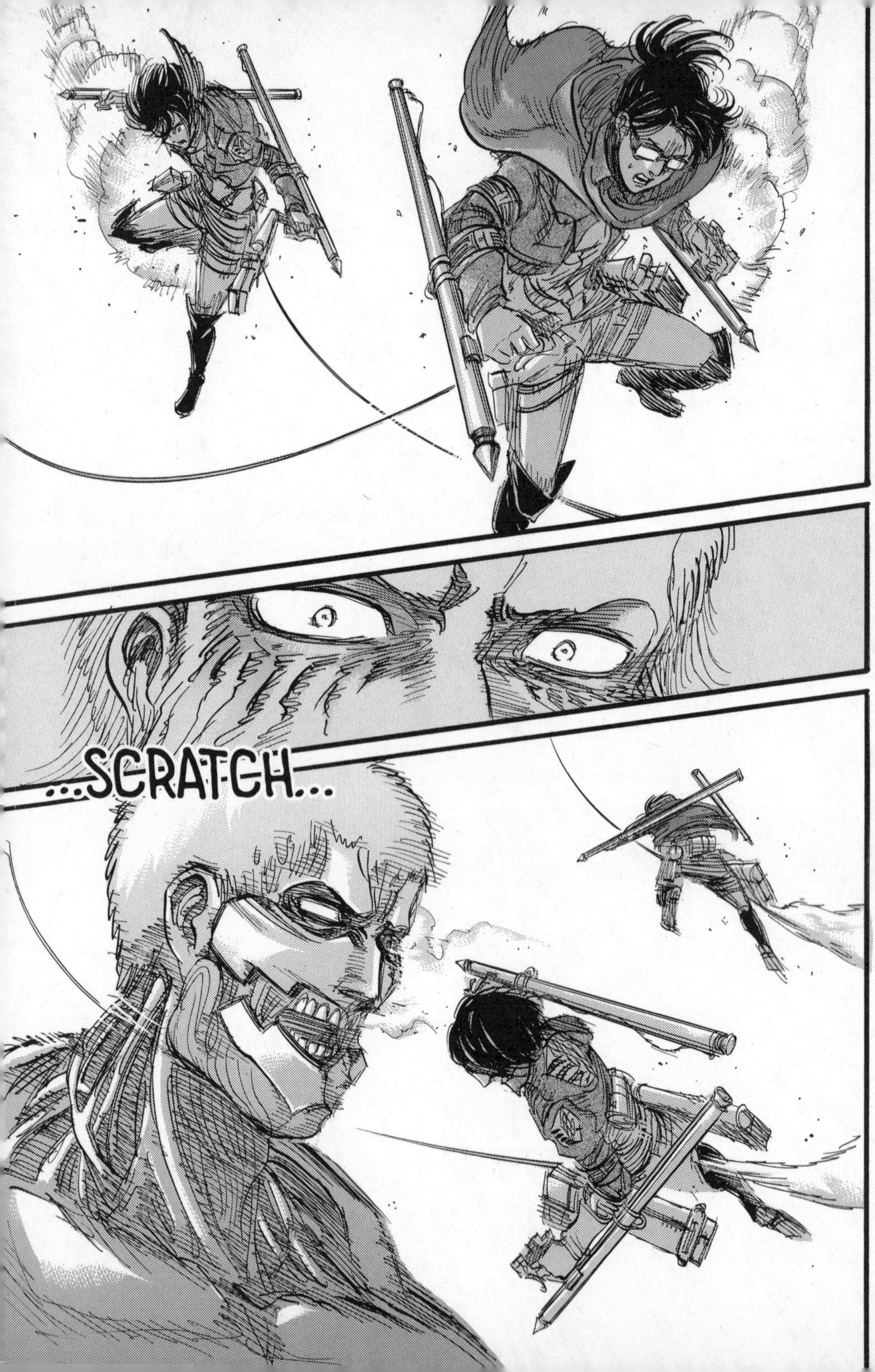
...SCRATCH...

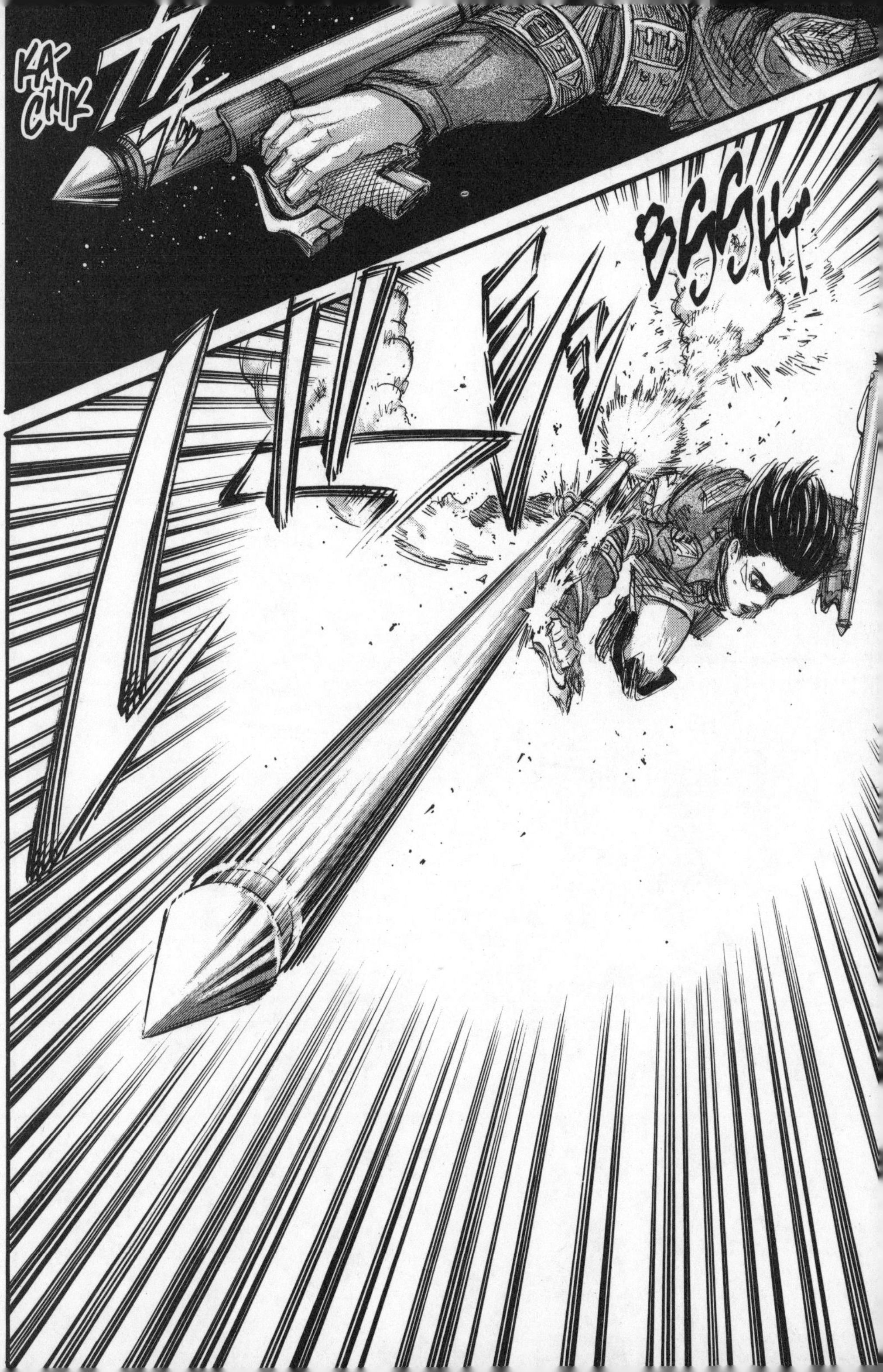
KA-CHIK
BGSSH

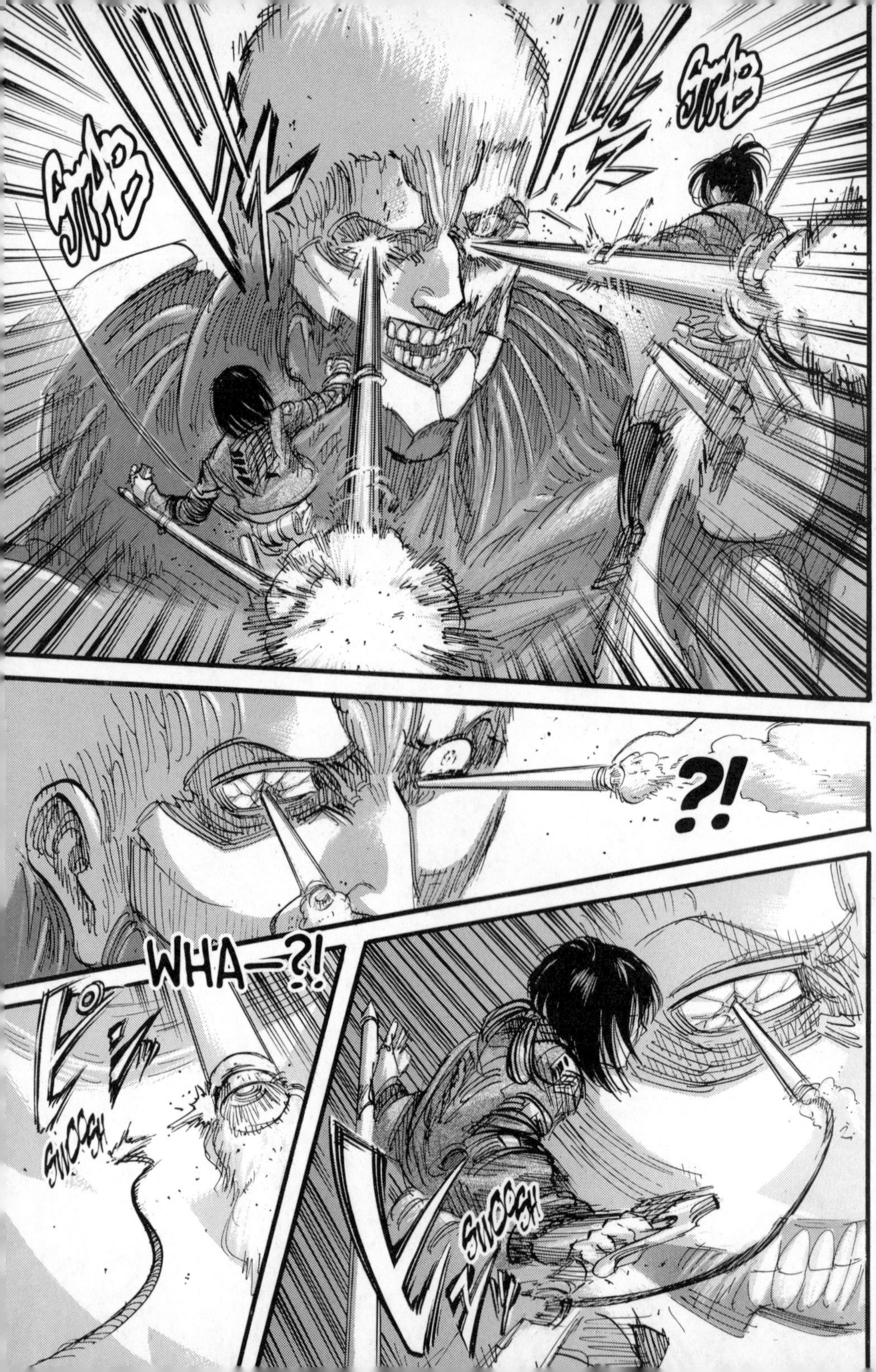

STAB
STAB
?!
SHOOSH
WHA—?!
SHOOSH

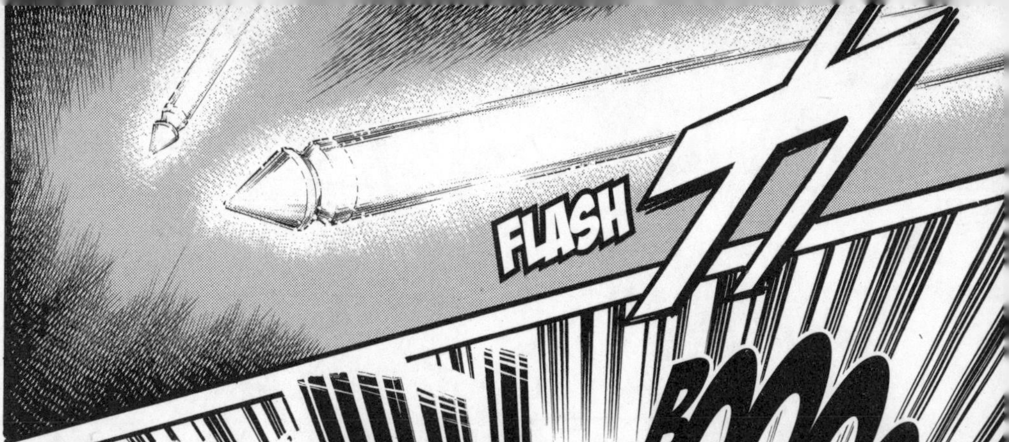
FLASH
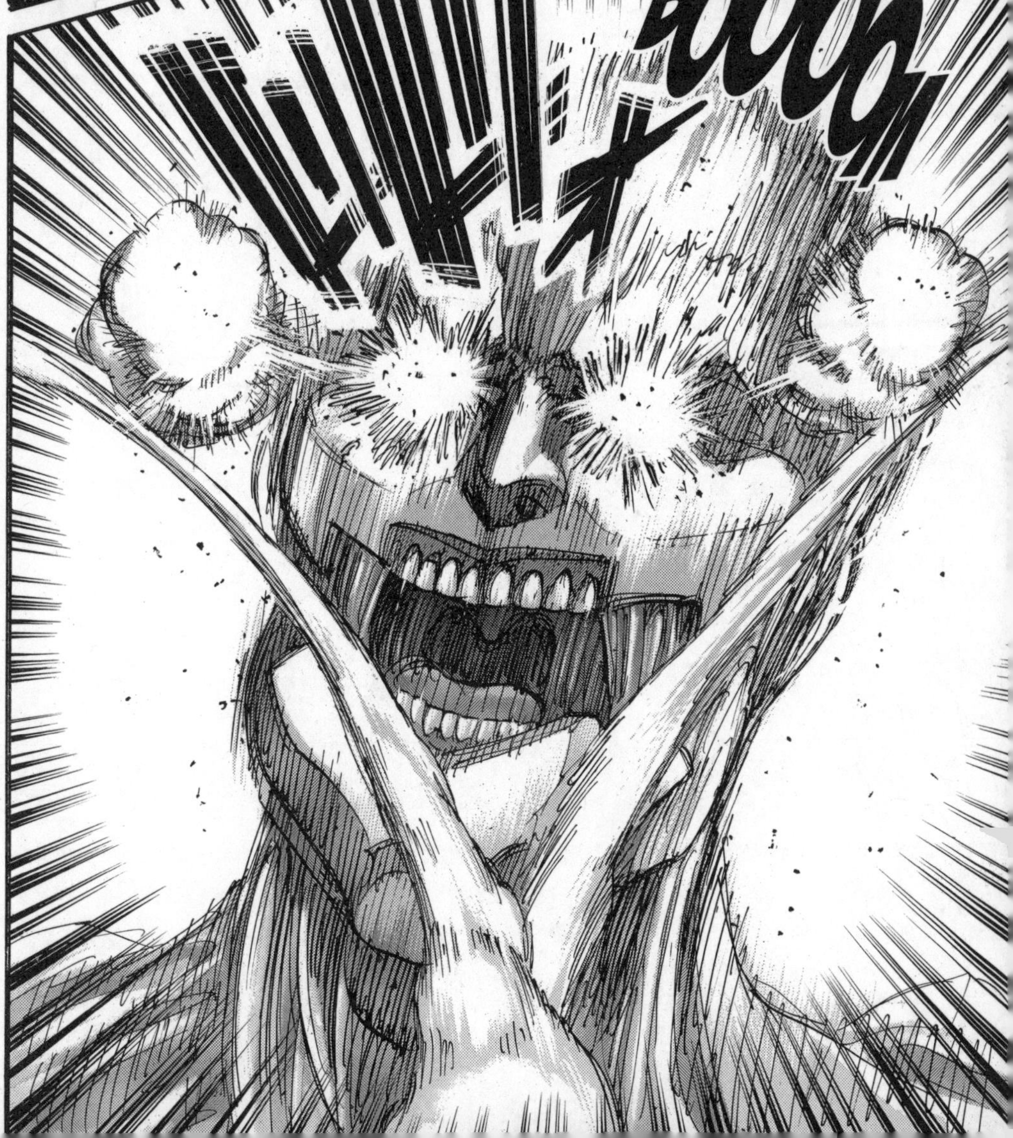
BOOOOM

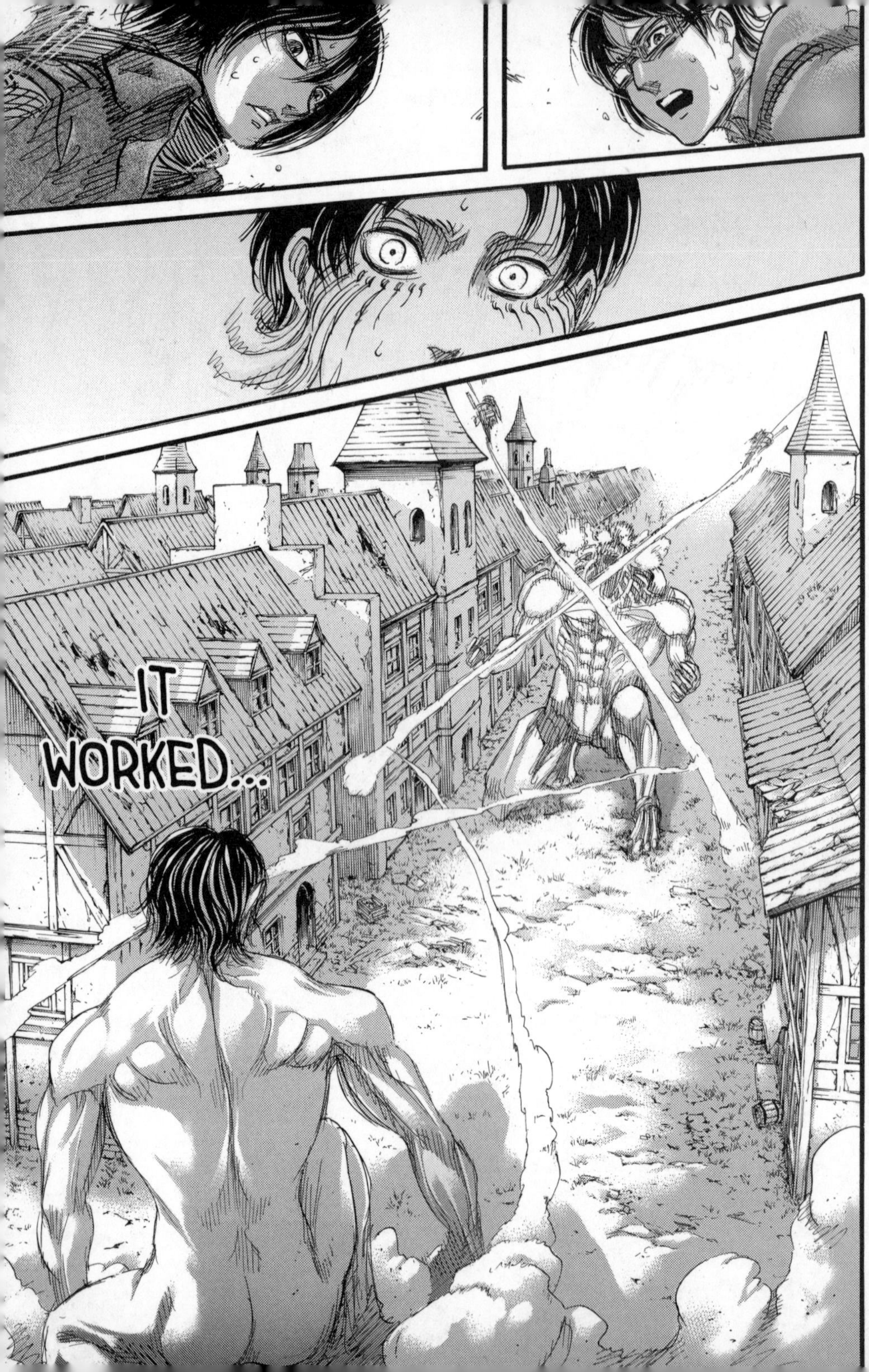
IT WORKED...

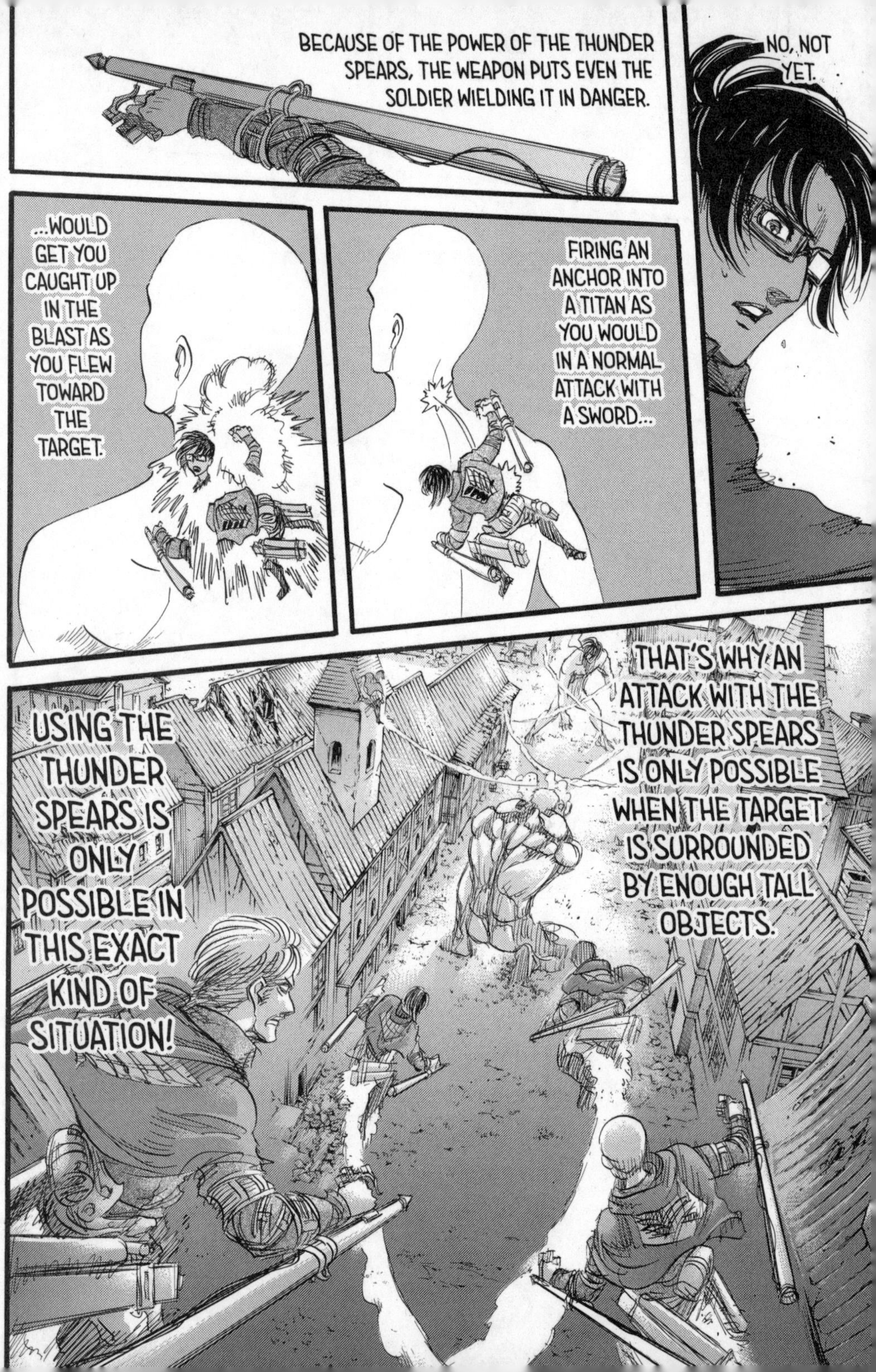
NO, NOT YET.
BECAUSE OF THE POWER OF THE THUNDER SPEARS, THE WEAPON PUTS EVEN THE SOLDIER WIELDING IT IN DANGER.
FIRING AN ANCHOR INTO A TITAN AS YOU WOULD IN A NORMAL ATTACK WITH A SWORD...
...WOULD GET YOU CAUGHT UP IN THE BLAST AS YOU FLEW TOWARD THE TARGET.
THAT'S WHY AN ATTACK WITH THE THUNDER SPEARS IS ONLY POSSIBLE WHEN THE TARGET IS SURROUNDED BY ENOUGH TALL OBJECTS.
USING THE THUNDER SPEARS IS ONLY POSSIBLE IN THIS EXACT KIND OF SITUATION!

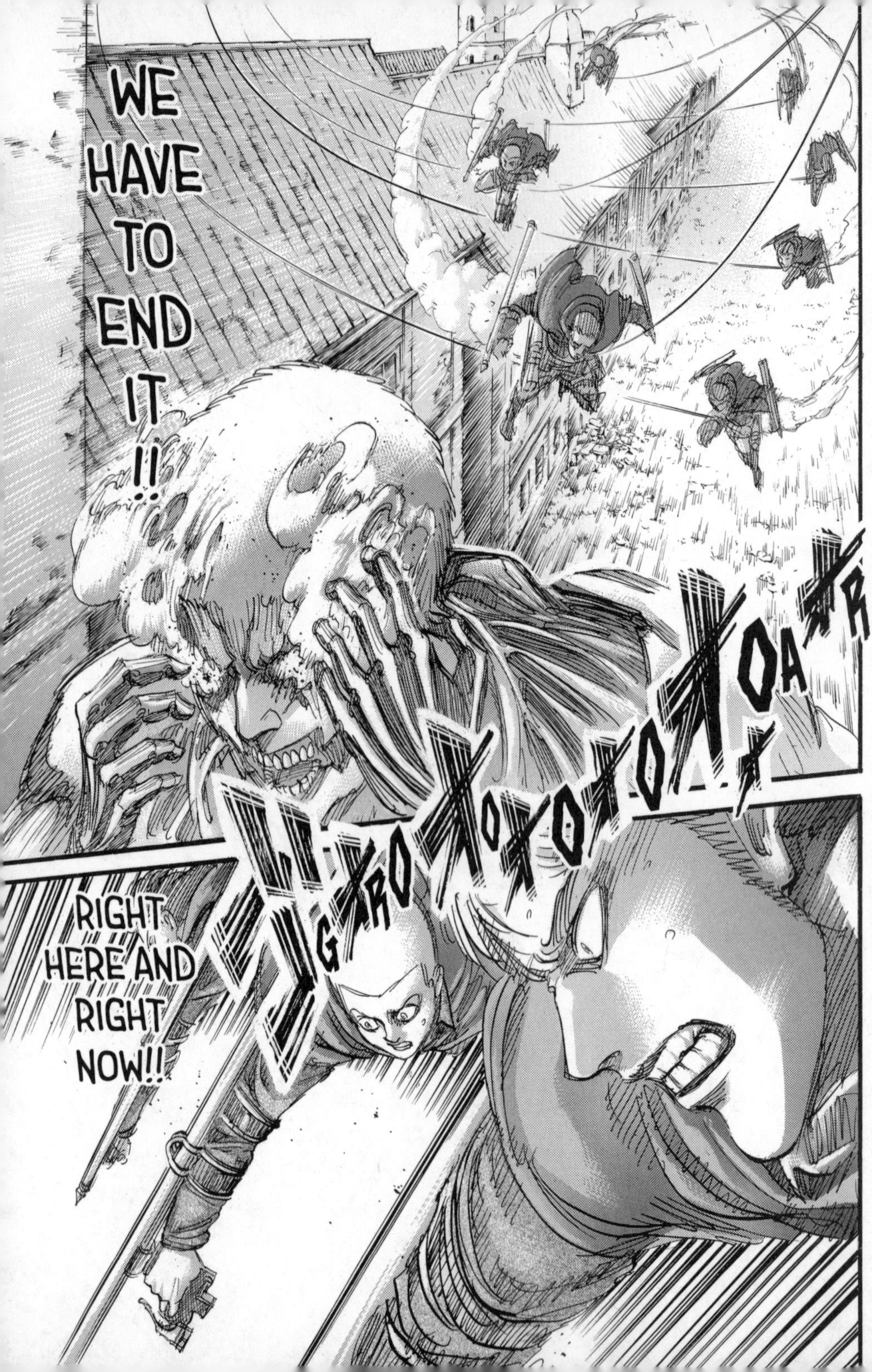
WE HAVE TO END IT!!
GROOOOOOAR
RIGHT HERE AND RIGHT NOW!!

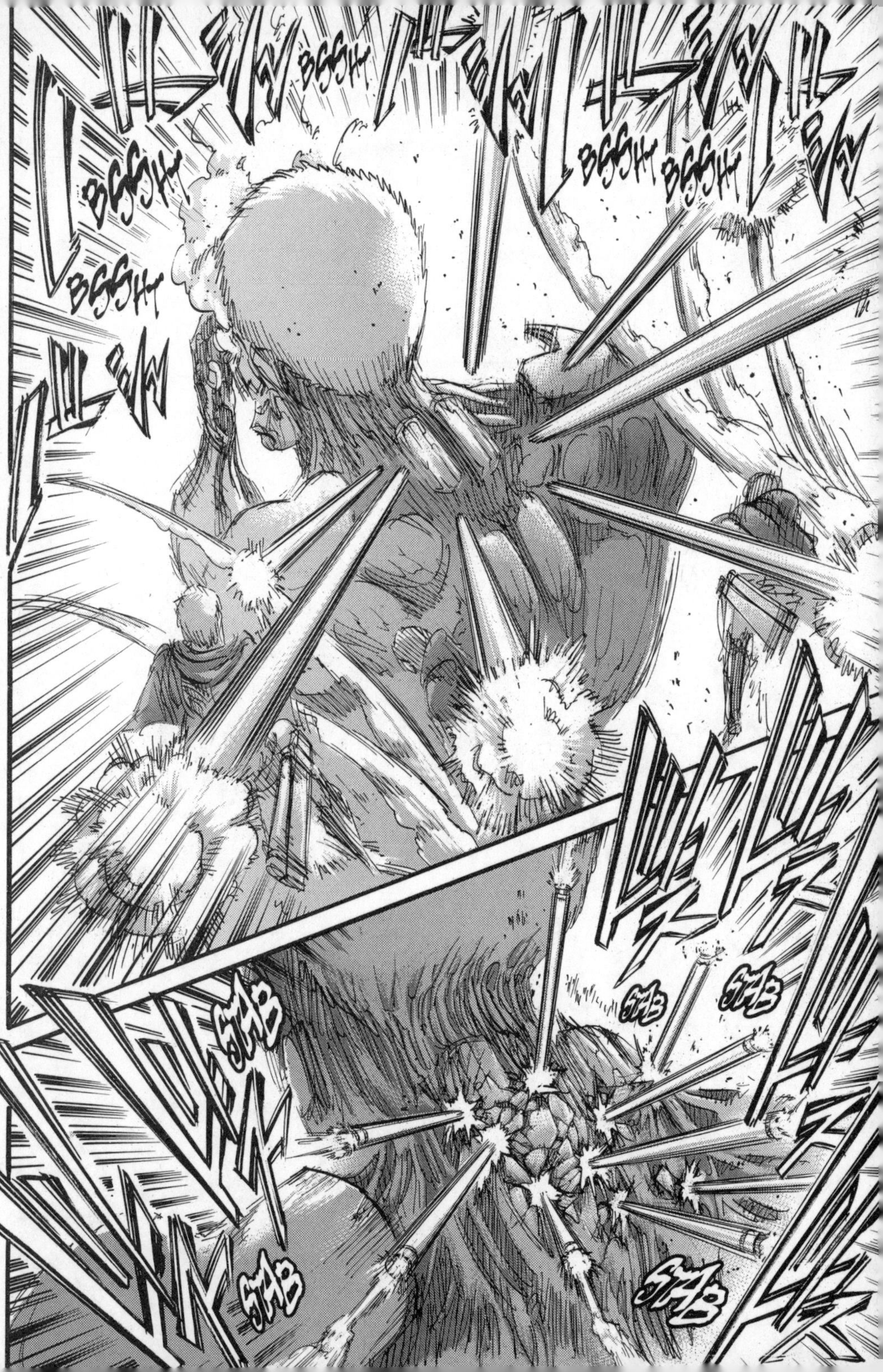
BSSH
BSSH
BSSH
BSSH
BSSH
STAB
STAB
STAB
STAB
STAB

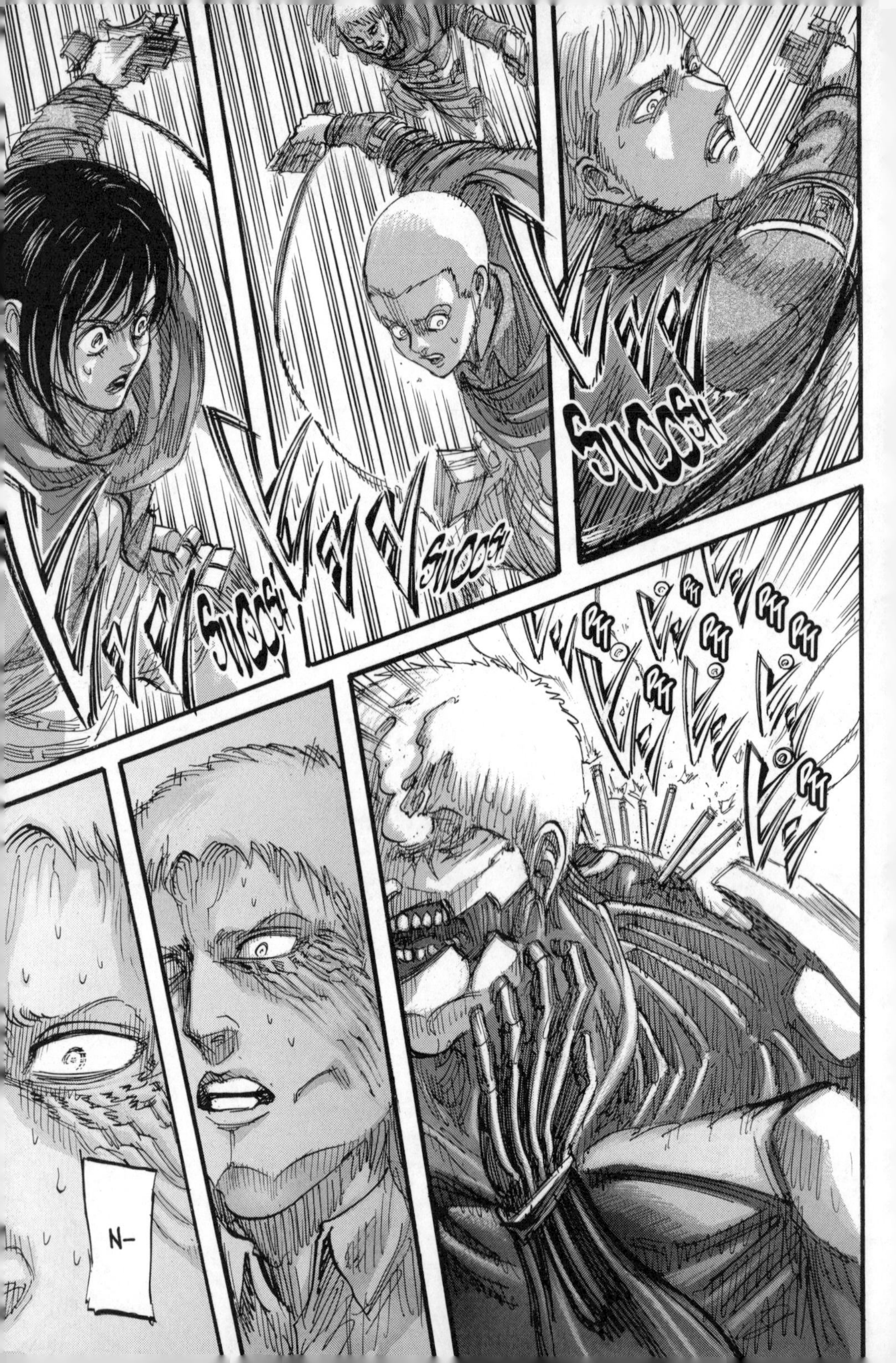
SHOOSH
SHOOSH
SHOOSH
PK PK PK PK PK PK PK PK PK PK PK
N–

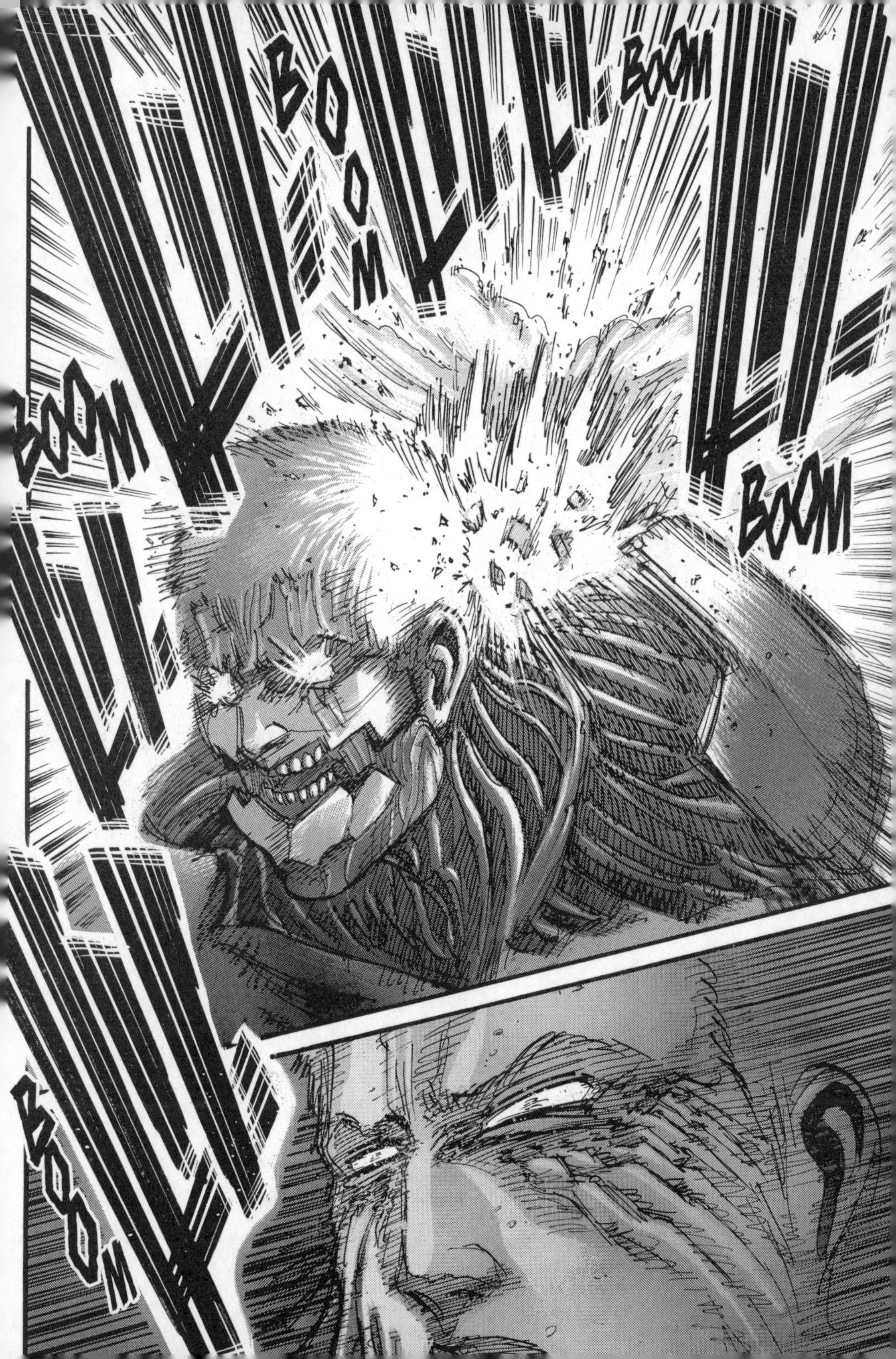
BOOM
BOOM
BOOM
BOOM
BOOOM

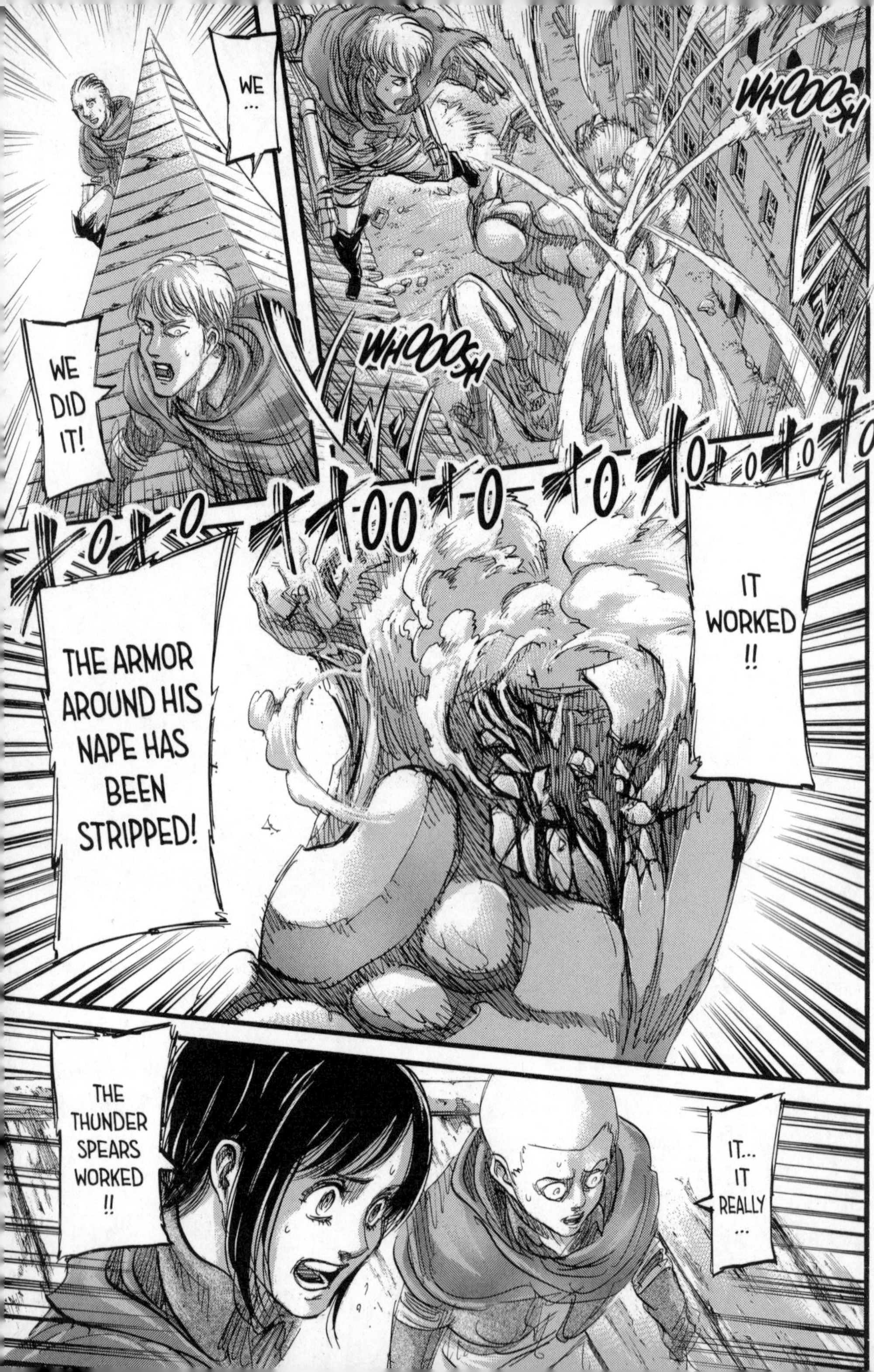
WHOOOSH
WE ...
WHOOOSH
WE DID IT!
IT WORKED !!
THE ARMOR AROUND HIS NAPE HAS BEEN STRIPPED!
IT... IT REALLY ...
THE THUNDER SPEARS WORKED !!

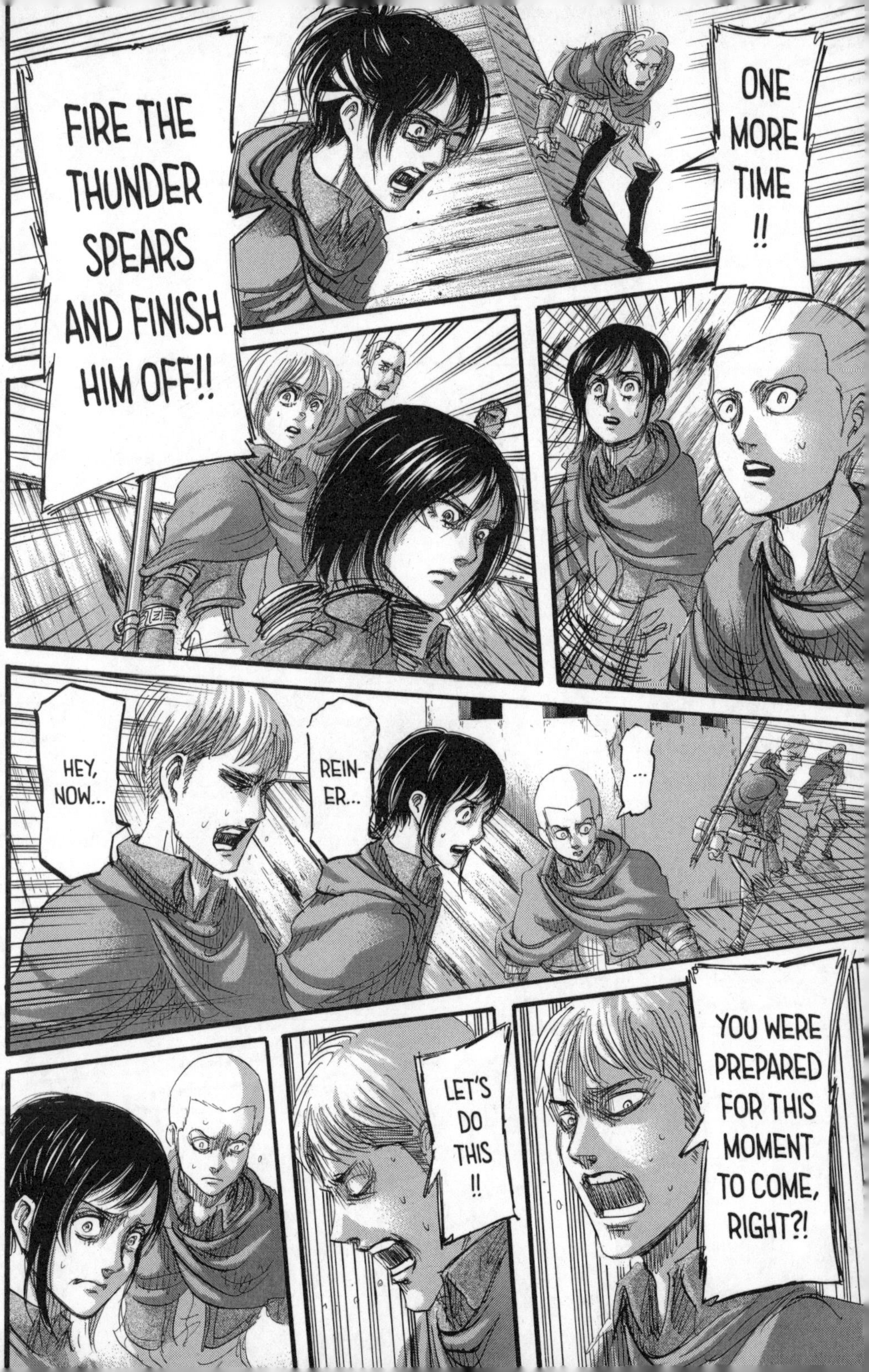
ONE MORE TIME !!
FIRE THE THUNDER SPEARS AND FINISH HIM OFF!!
...
REIN-ER...
HEY, NOW...
YOU WERE PREPARED FOR THIS MOMENT TO COME, RIGHT?!
LET'S DO THIS !!

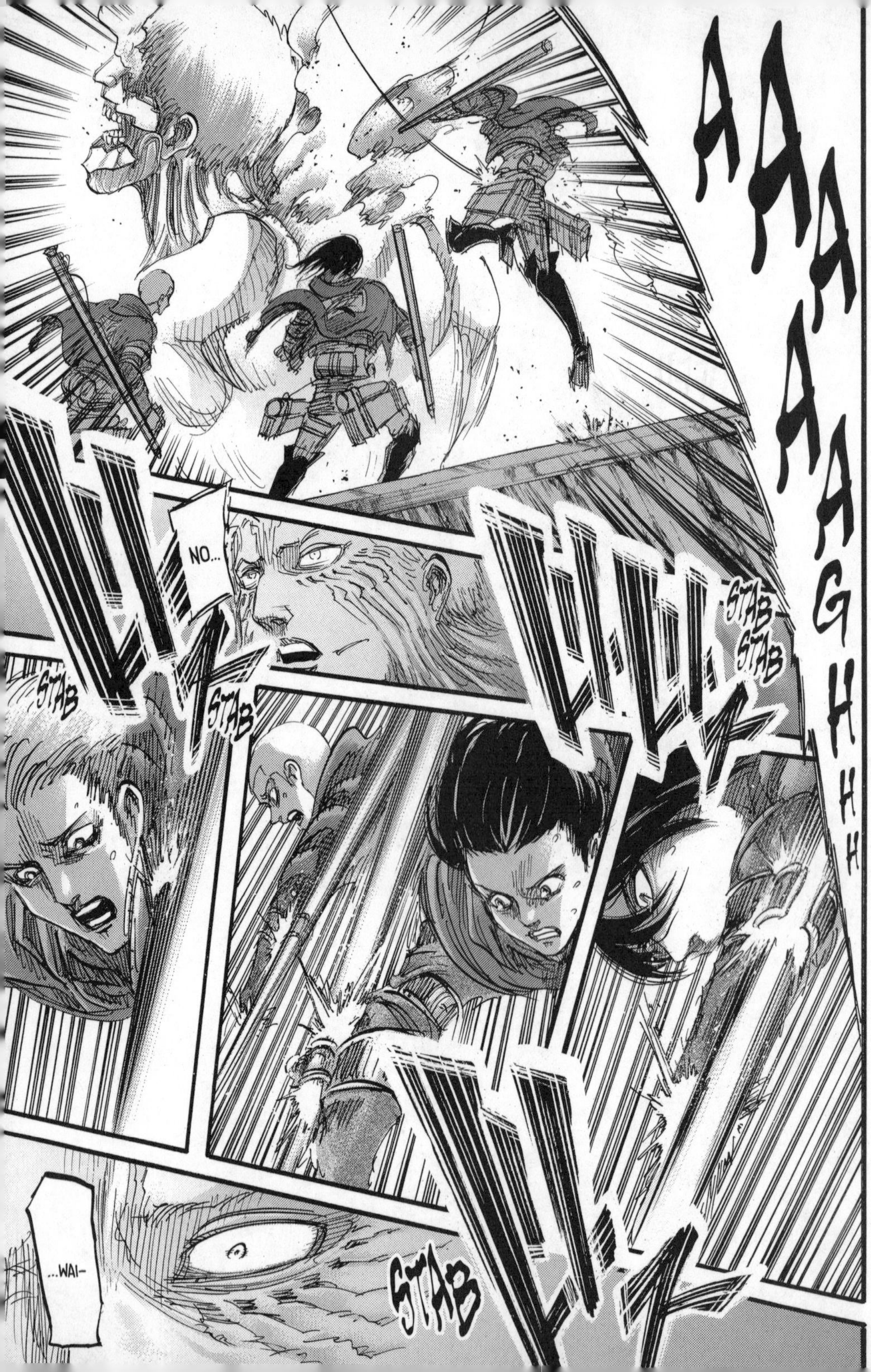

AAAAAAAGHHHH
NO...
STAB STAB
STAB
STAB
STAB
...WAI-

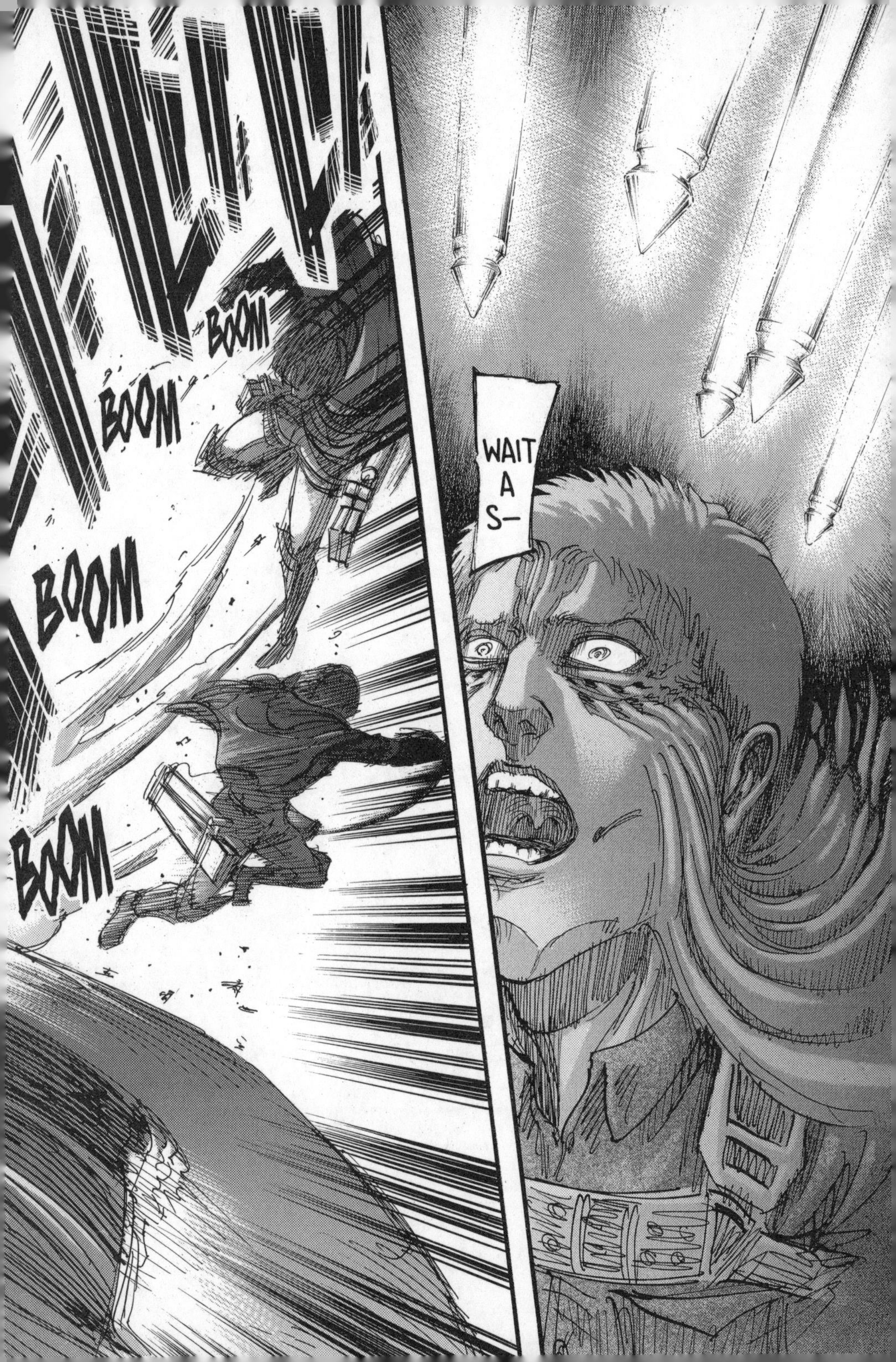
WAIT A S—
BOOM
BOOM
BOOM
BOOM

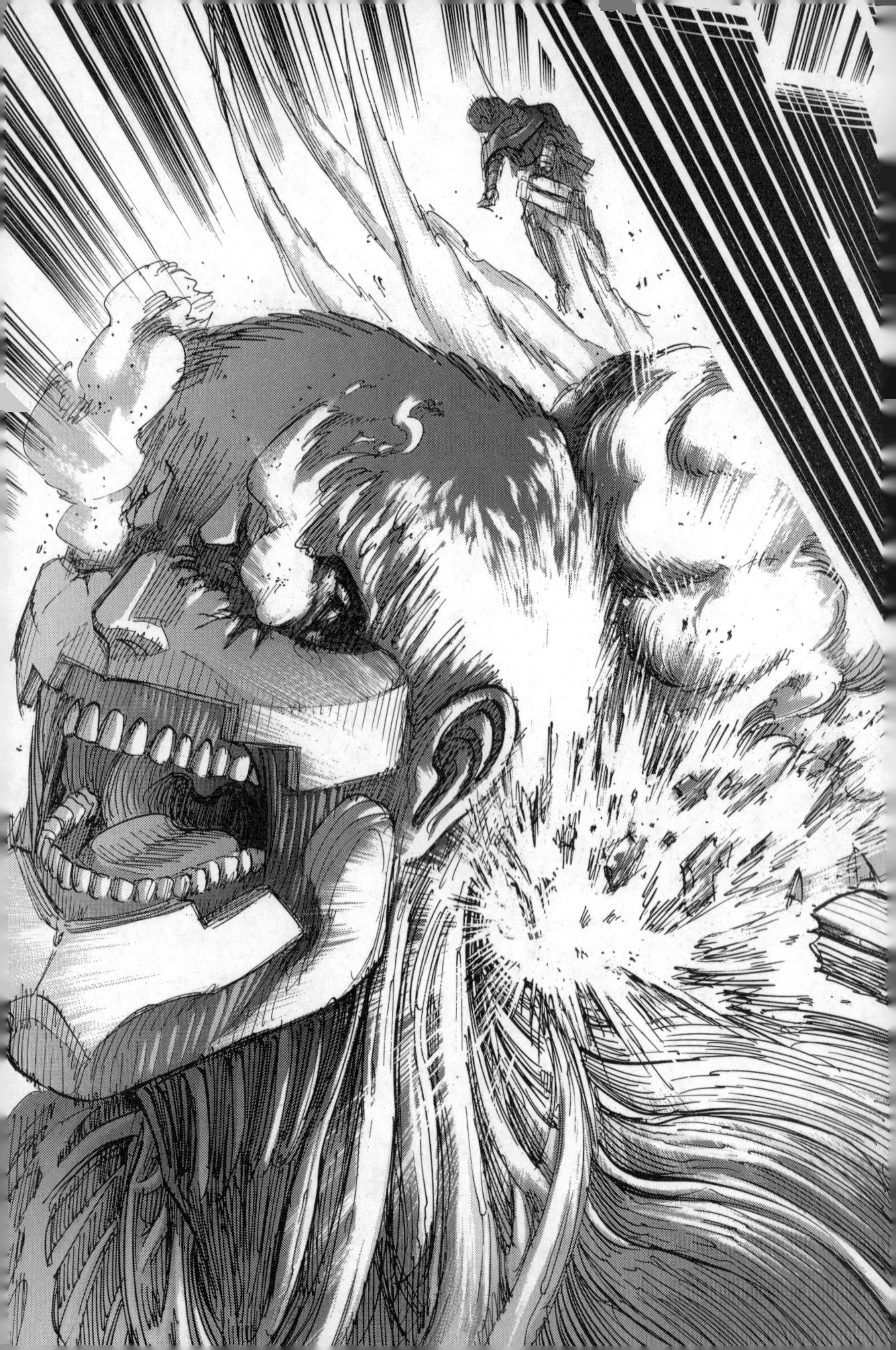

ATTACK on TITAN

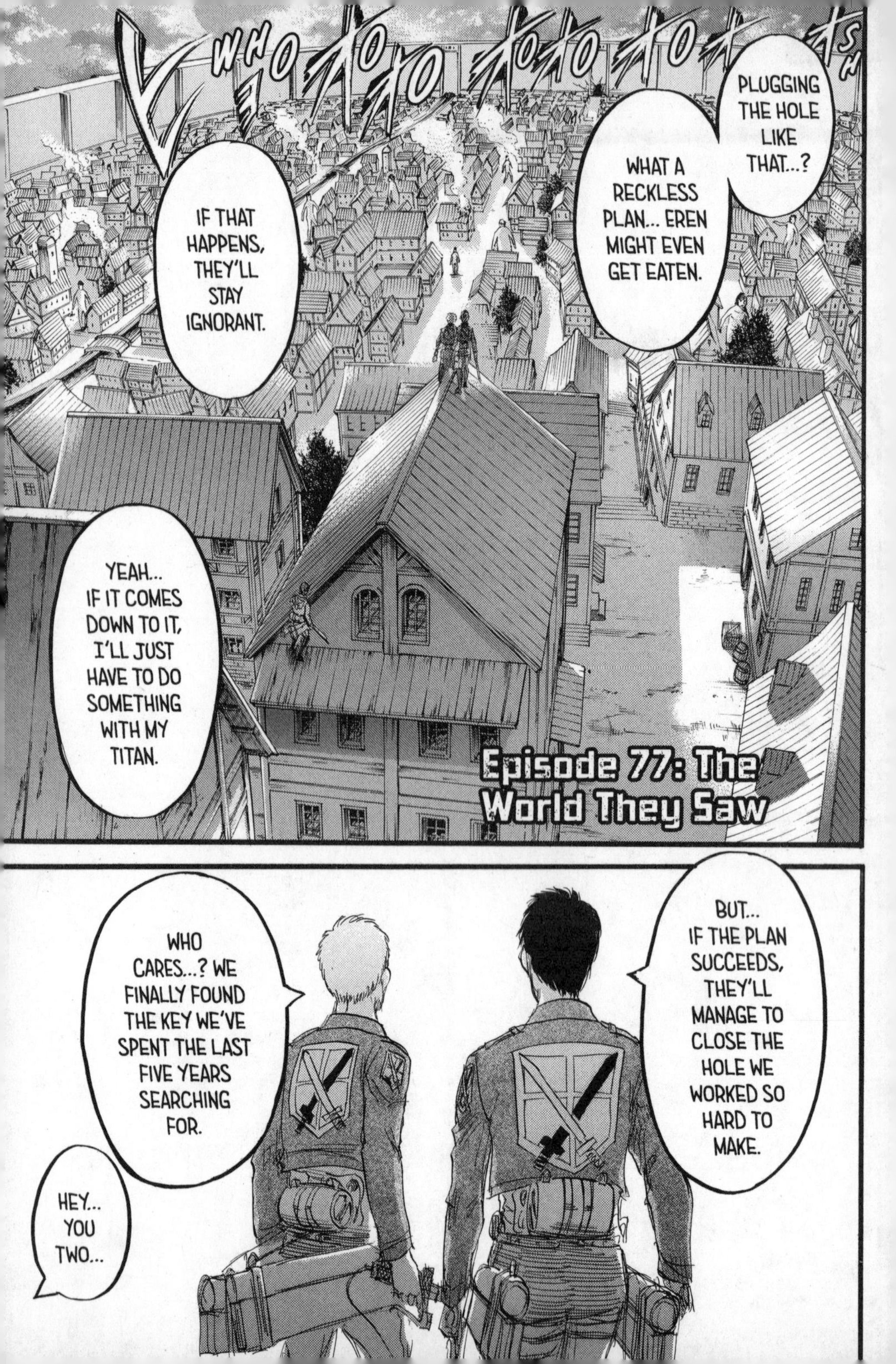

PLUGGING THE HOLE LIKE THAT...?
WHAT A RECKLESS PLAN... EREN MIGHT EVEN GET EATEN.
IF THAT HAPPENS, THEY'LL STAY IGNORANT.
YEAH... IF IT COMES DOWN TO IT, I'LL JUST HAVE TO DO SOMETHING WITH MY TITAN.
Episode 77: The World They Saw
BUT... IF THE PLAN SUCCEEDS, THEY'LL MANAGE TO CLOSE THE HOLE WE WORKED SO HARD TO MAKE.
WHO CARES...? WE FINALLY FOUND THE KEY WE'VE SPENT THE LAST FIVE YEARS SEARCHING FOR.
HEY... YOU TWO...

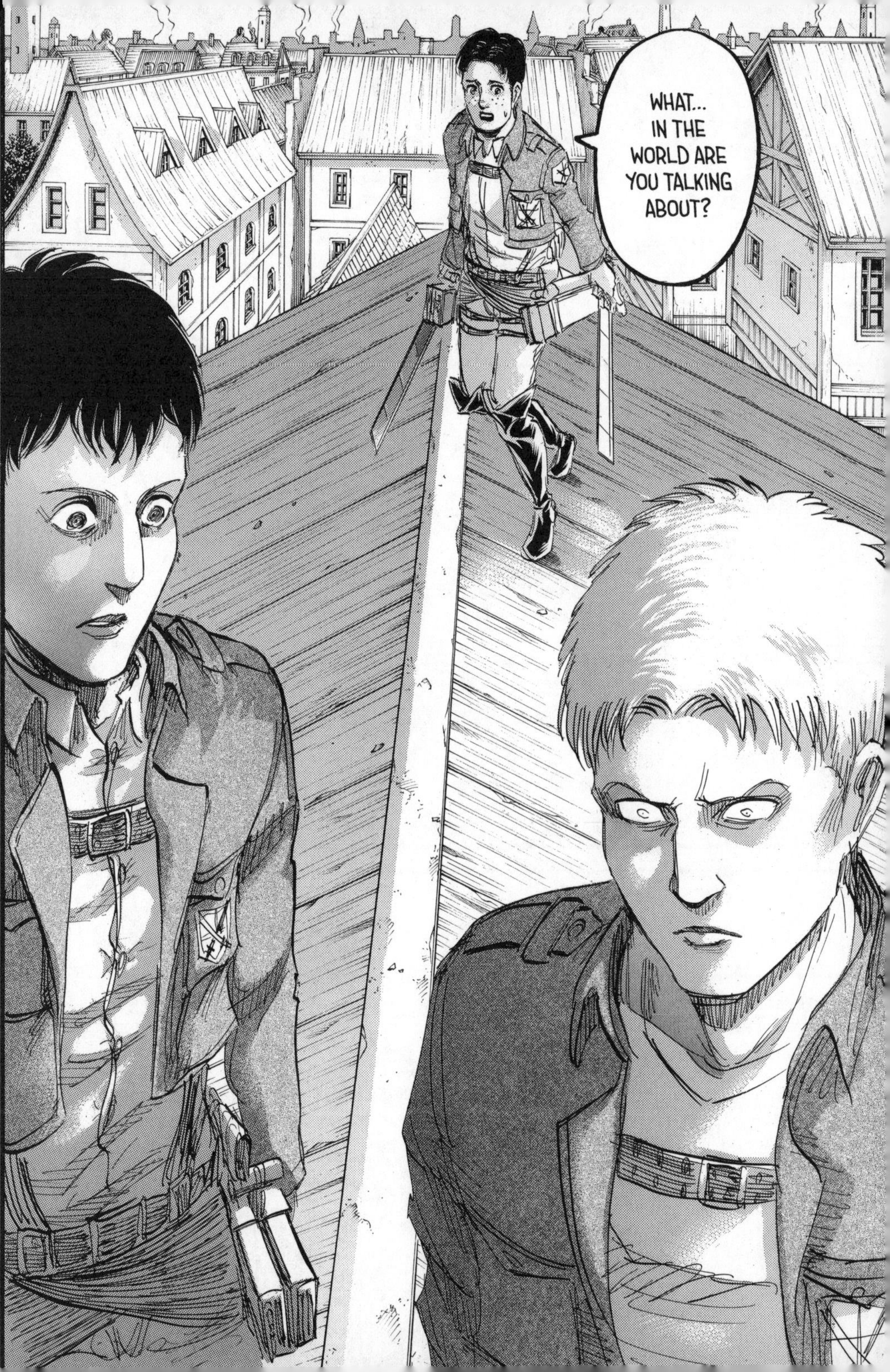
WHAT... IN THE WORLD ARE YOU TALKING ABOUT?

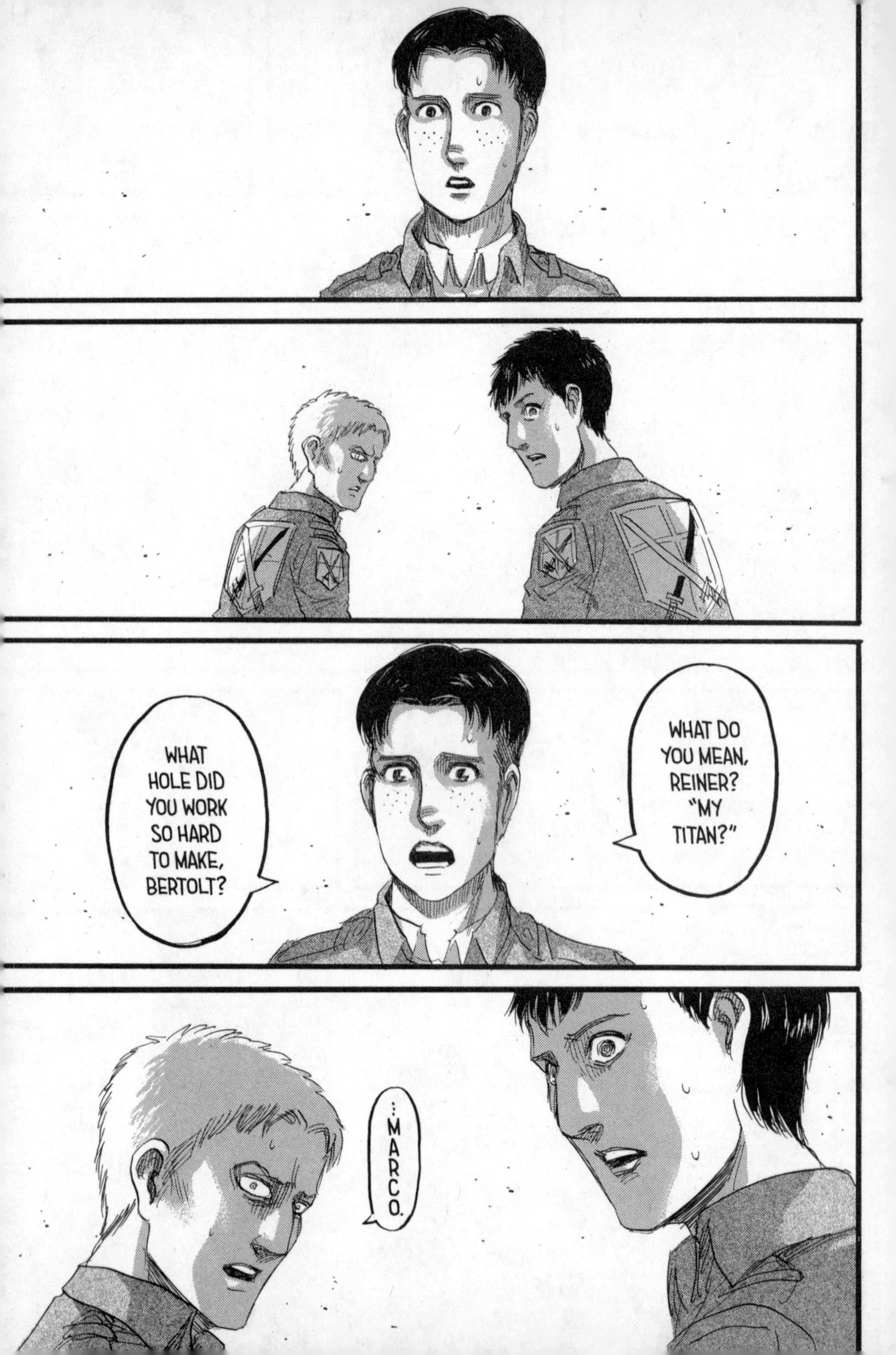
WHAT DO YOU MEAN, REINER? "MY TITAN?"
WHAT HOLE DID YOU WORK SO HARD TO MAKE, BERTOLT?
...MARCO.

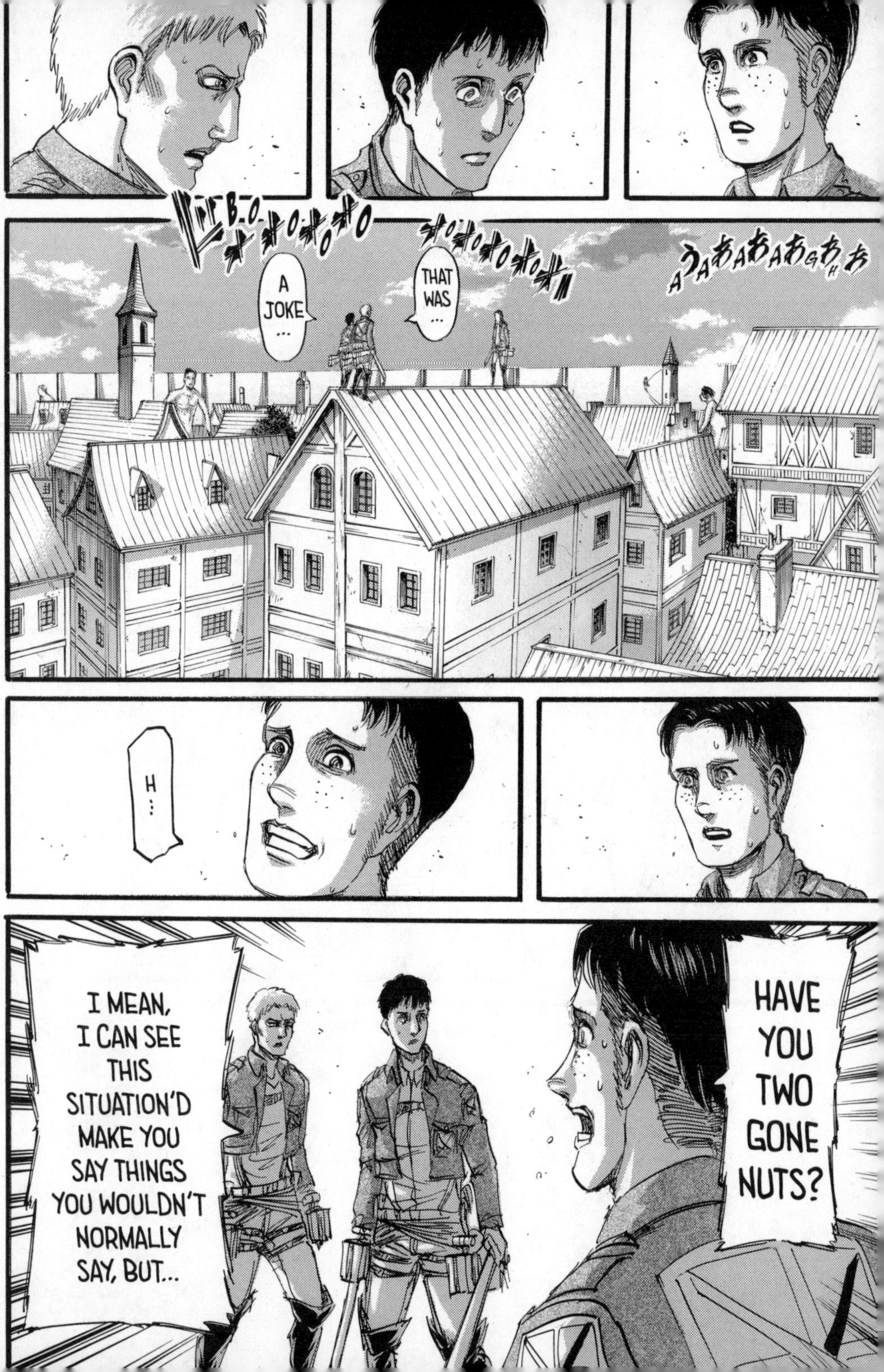
THAT WAS ...
A JOKE ...
H ...
HAVE YOU TWO GONE NUTS?
I MEAN, I CAN SEE THIS SITUATION'D MAKE YOU SAY THINGS YOU WOULDN'T NORMALLY SAY, BUT...

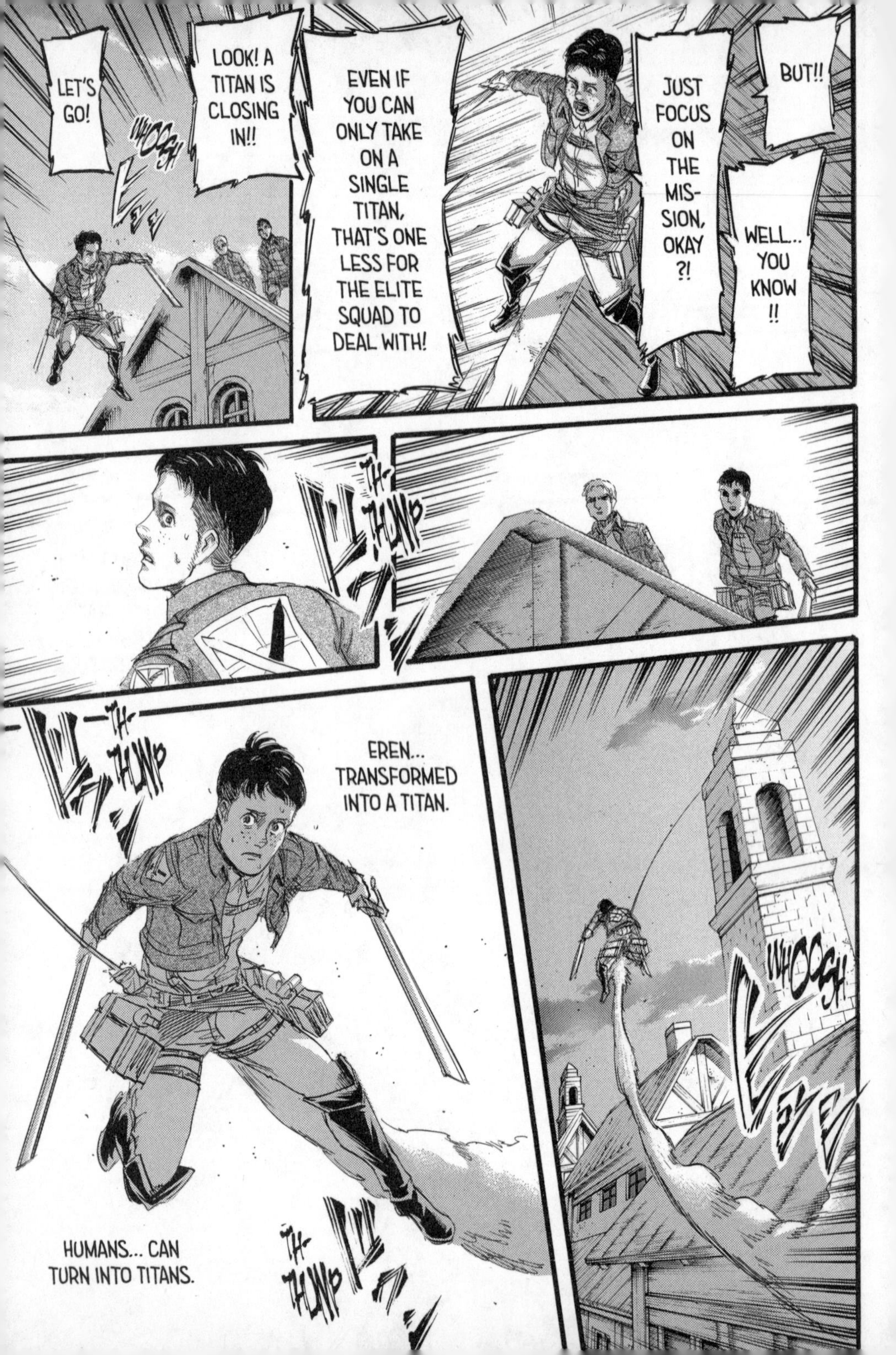
BUT!!
WELL... YOU KNOW!!
JUST FOCUS ON THE MIS-SION, OKAY?!
EVEN IF YOU CAN ONLY TAKE ON A SINGLE TITAN, THAT'S ONE LESS FOR THE ELITE SQUAD TO DEAL WITH!
LOOK! A TITAN IS CLOSING IN!!
LET'S GO!
WHOOSH
TH-THUMP
WHOOSH
TH-THUMP
EREN... TRANSFORMED INTO A TITAN.
HUMANS... CAN TURN INTO TITANS.
TH-THUMP

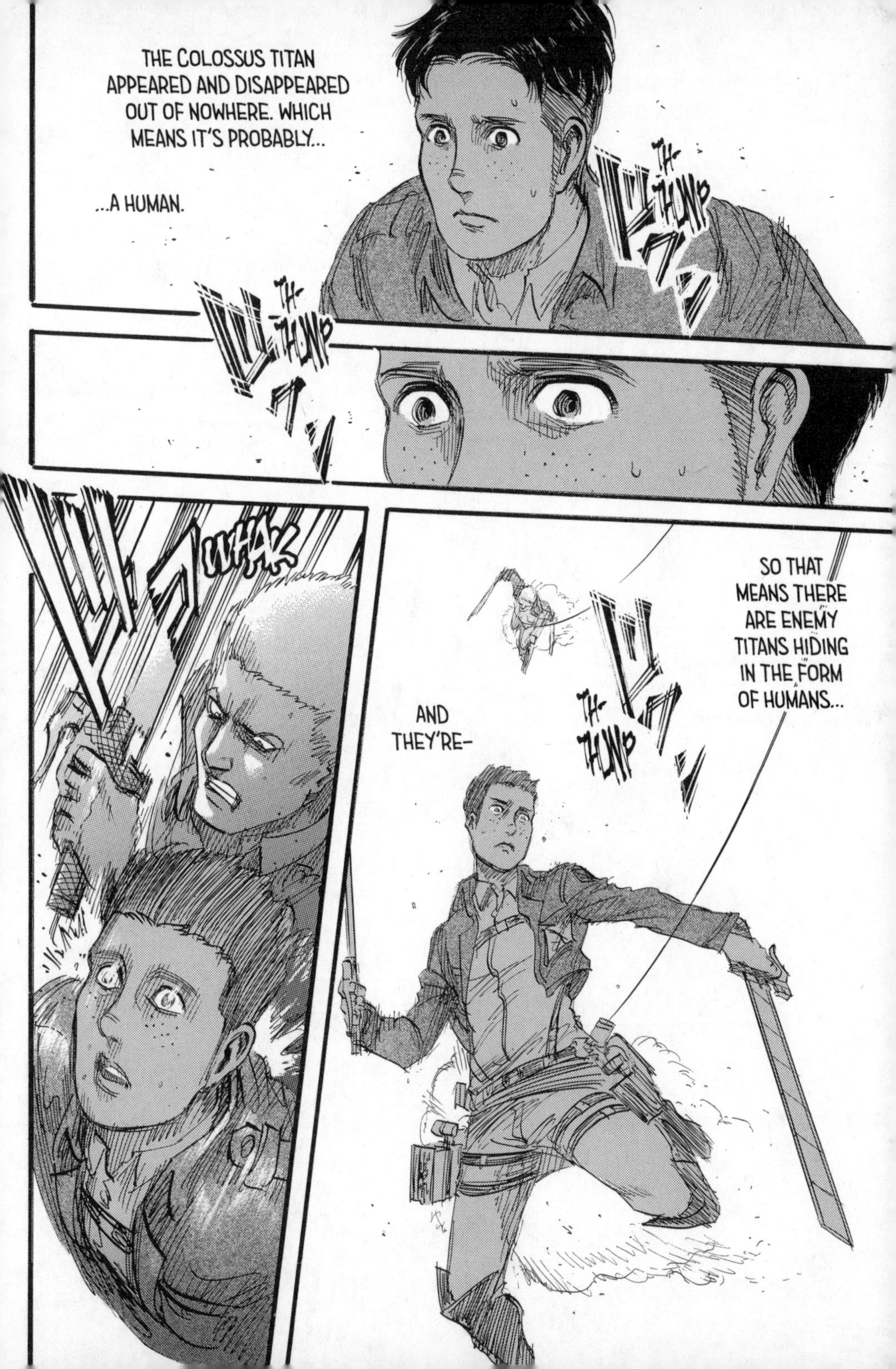

THE COLOSSUS TITAN APPEARED AND DISAPPEARED OUT OF NOWHERE. WHICH MEANS IT'S PROBABLY...
...A HUMAN.
TH-THUMP
TH-THUMP
SO THAT MEANS THERE ARE ENEMY TITANS HIDING IN THE FORM OF HUMANS...
TH-THUMP
AND THEY'RE-
WHAK

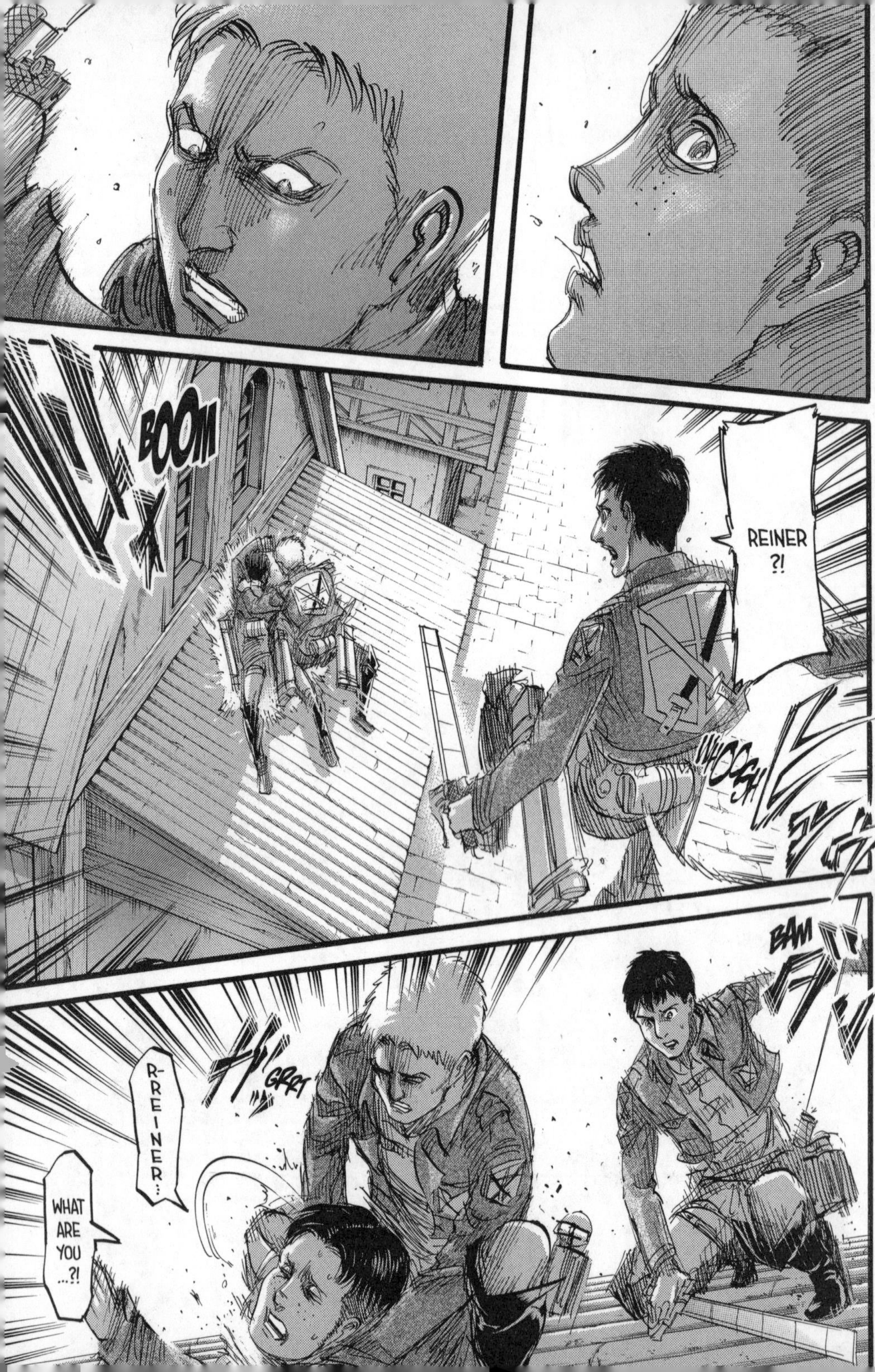
BOOM
REINER ?!
WHOOSH
BAM
GRRRT
R-REINER...
WHAT ARE YOU ...?!

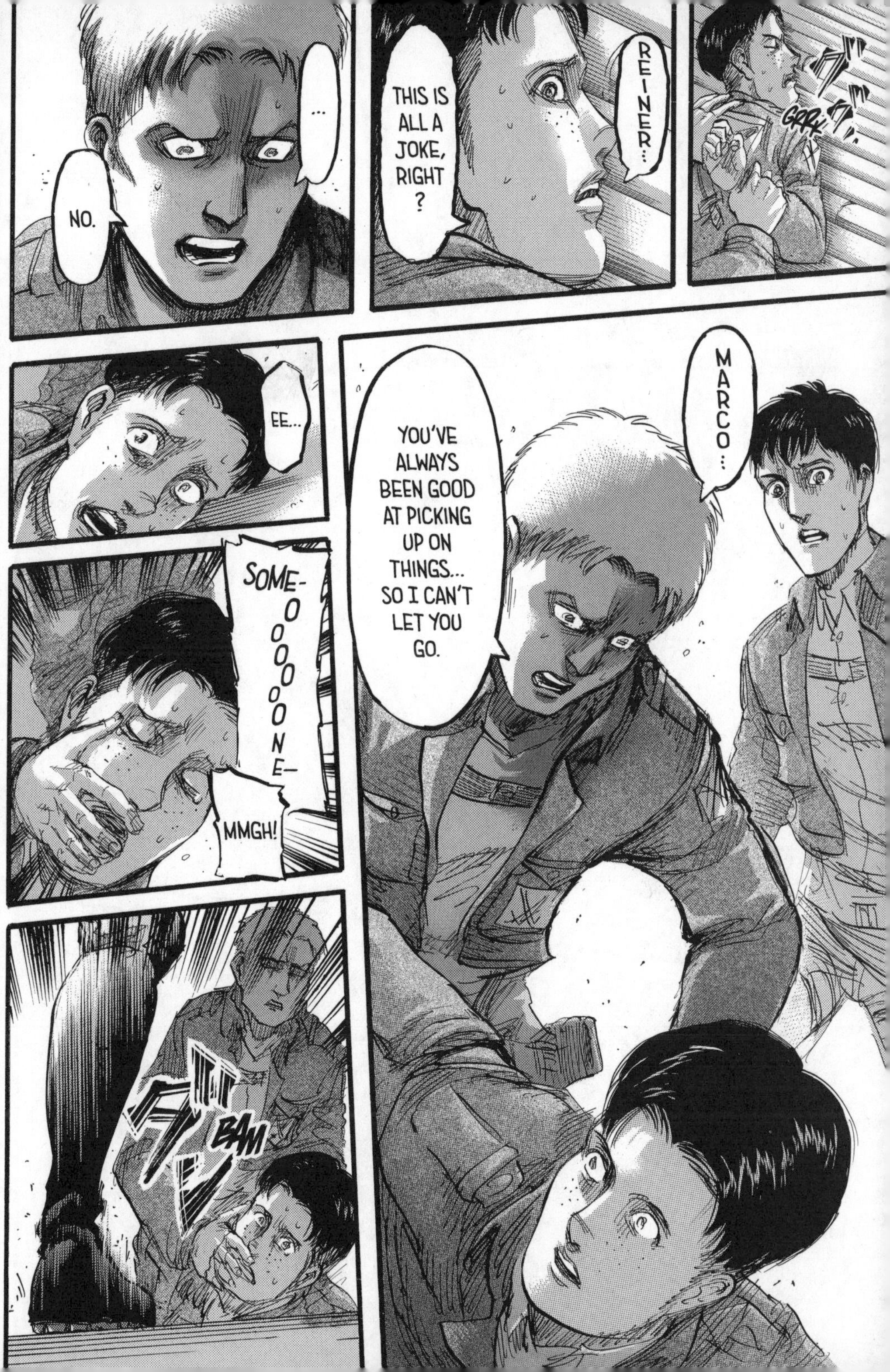
GRR
REINER...
THIS IS ALL A JOKE, RIGHT?
...
NO.
MARCO...
YOU'VE ALWAYS BEEN GOOD AT PICKING UP ON THINGS... SO I CAN'T LET YOU GO.
EE...
SOME-OOOOOOOONE—
MMGH!
BAM

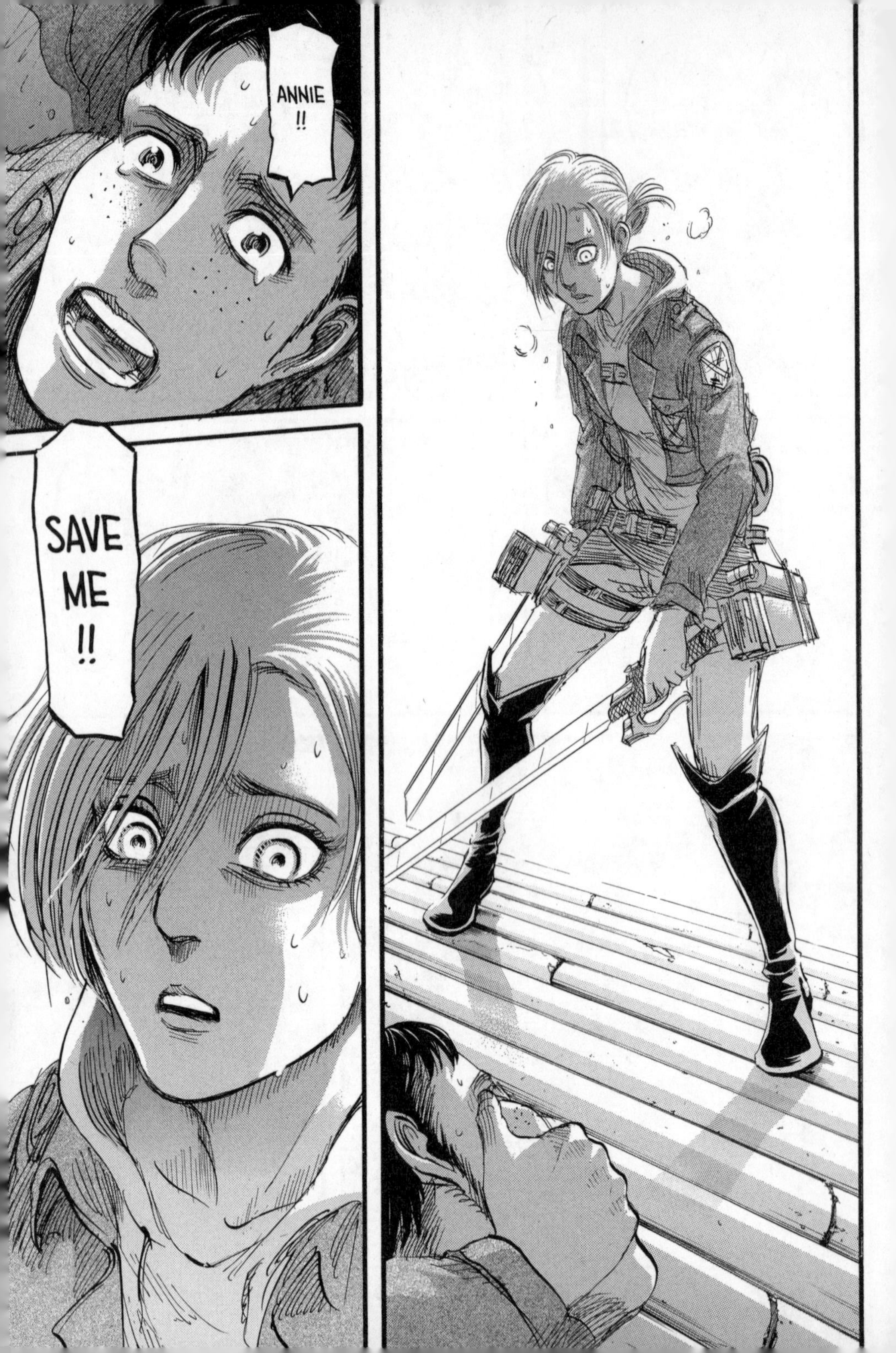
ANNIE !!
SAVE ME !!

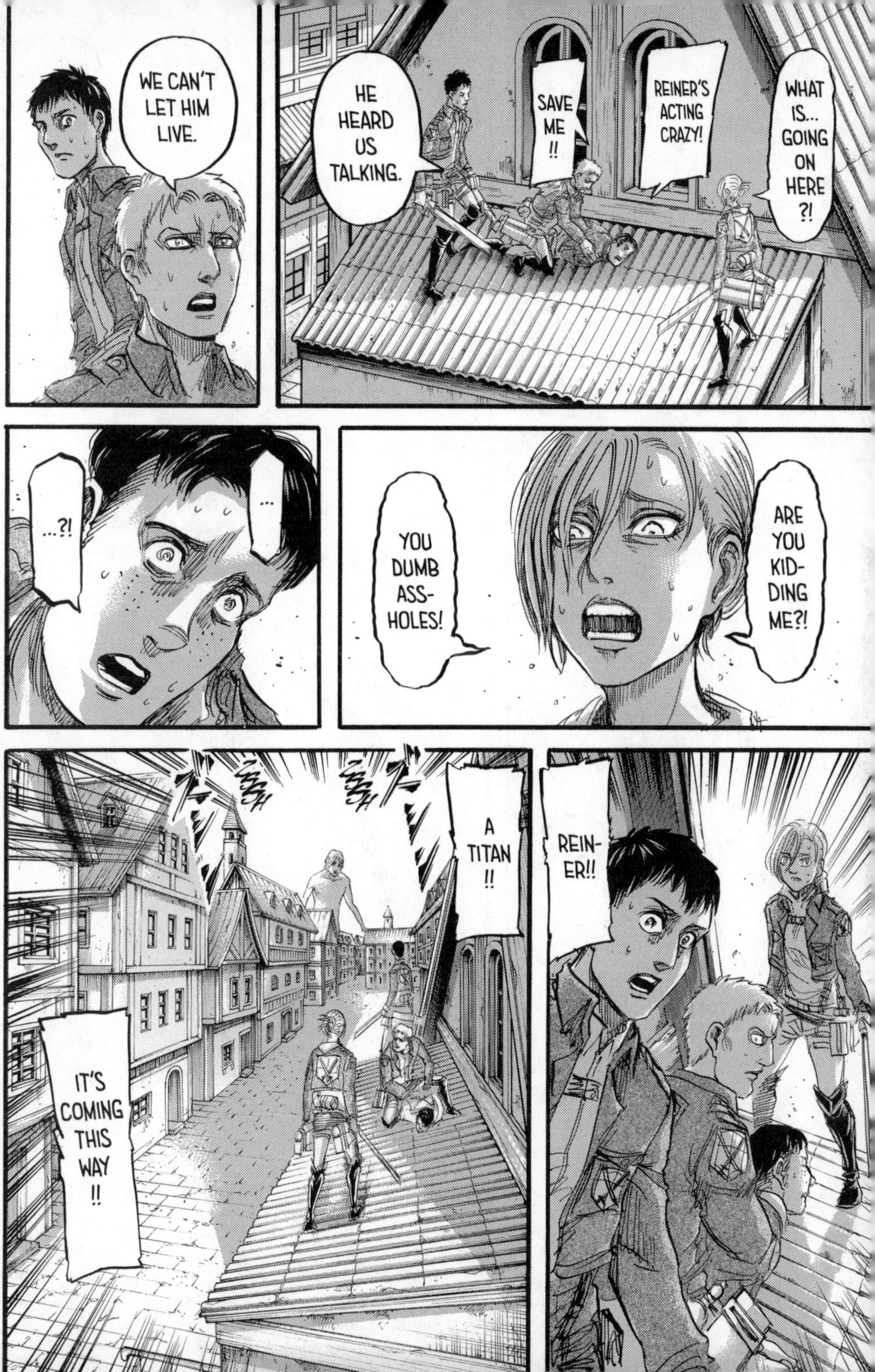
WHAT IS... GOING ON HERE?!
REINER'S ACTING CRAZY!
SAVE ME!!
HE HEARD US TALKING.
WE CAN'T LET HIM LIVE.
ARE YOU KID-DING ME?!
YOU DUMB ASS-HOLES!
...
...?!
REIN-ER!!
A TITAN!!
ZSSH
ZSSH
IT'S COMING THIS WAY!!

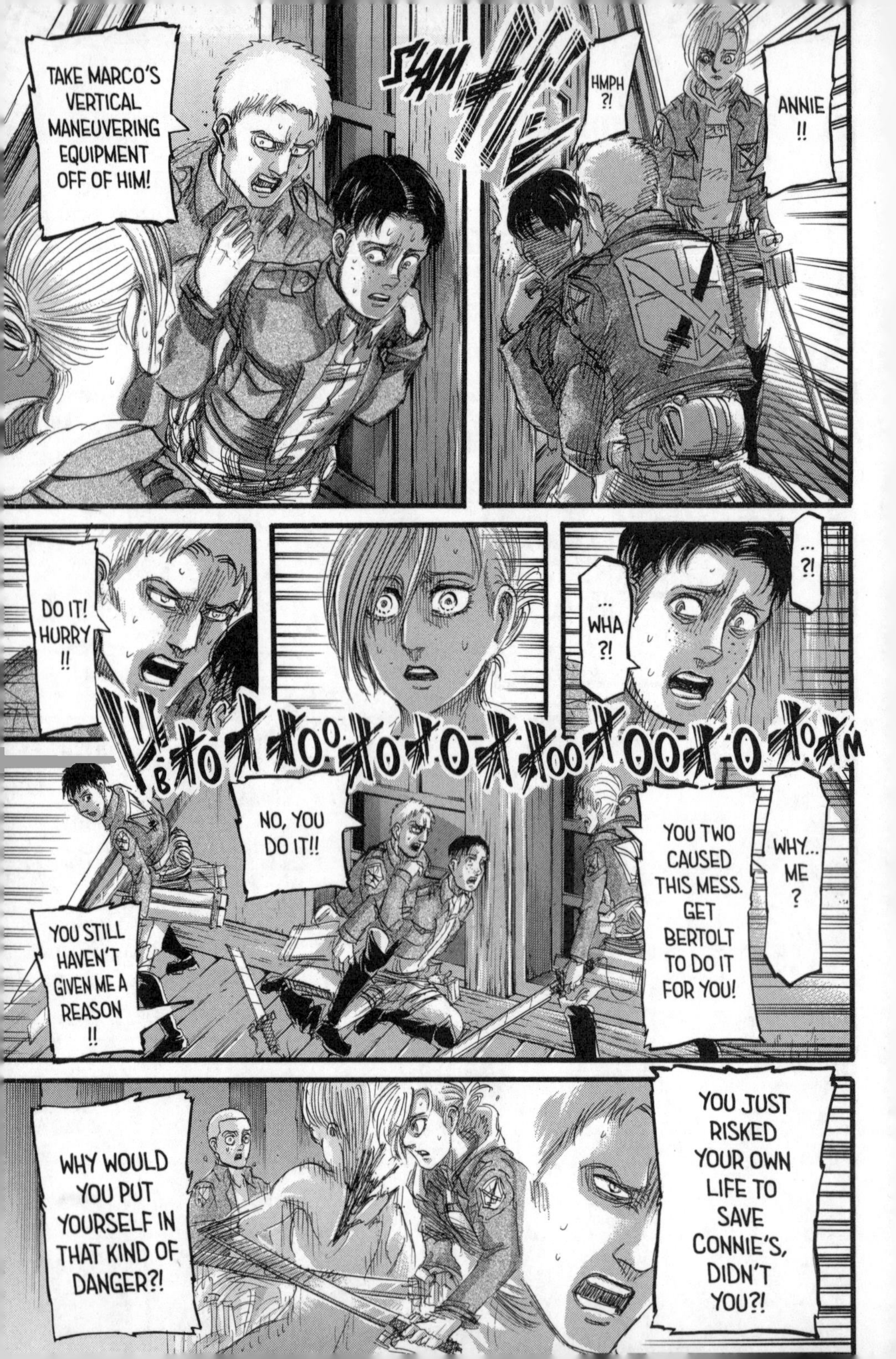
ANNIE !!
HMPH ?!
SLAM
TAKE MARCO'S VERTICAL MANEUVERING EQUIPMENT OFF OF HIM!
... ?!
... WHA ?!
DO IT! HURRY !!
BOOOOOOOOOOOOOOOM
WHY... ME ?
YOU TWO CAUSED THIS MESS. GET BERTOLT TO DO IT FOR YOU!
NO, YOU DO IT!!
YOU STILL HAVEN'T GIVEN ME A REASON !!
YOU JUST RISKED YOUR OWN LIFE TO SAVE CONNIE'S, DIDN'T YOU?!
WHY WOULD YOU PUT YOURSELF IN THAT KIND OF DANGER?!

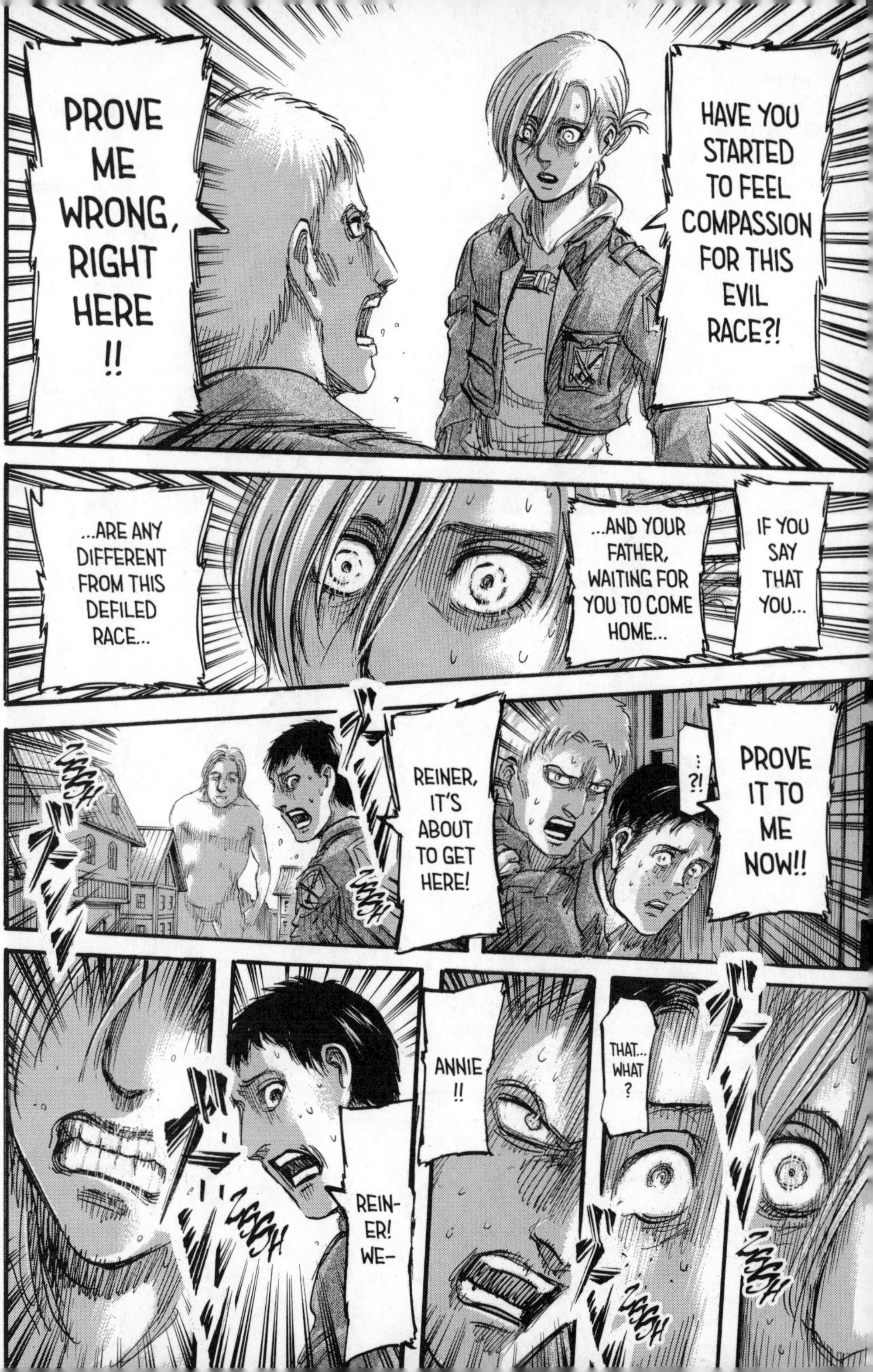
HAVE YOU STARTED TO FEEL COMPASSION FOR THIS EVIL RACE?!
PROVE ME WRONG, RIGHT HERE !!
IF YOU SAY THAT YOU...
...AND YOUR FATHER, WAITING FOR YOU TO COME HOME...
...ARE ANY DIFFERENT FROM THIS DEFILED RACE...
PROVE IT TO ME NOW!!
...?!
REINER, IT'S ABOUT TO GET HERE!
ZSSH
ZSSH
THAT... WHAT ?
ZSSH
ZSSH
ANNIE !!
REIN-ER! WE-
ZSSH

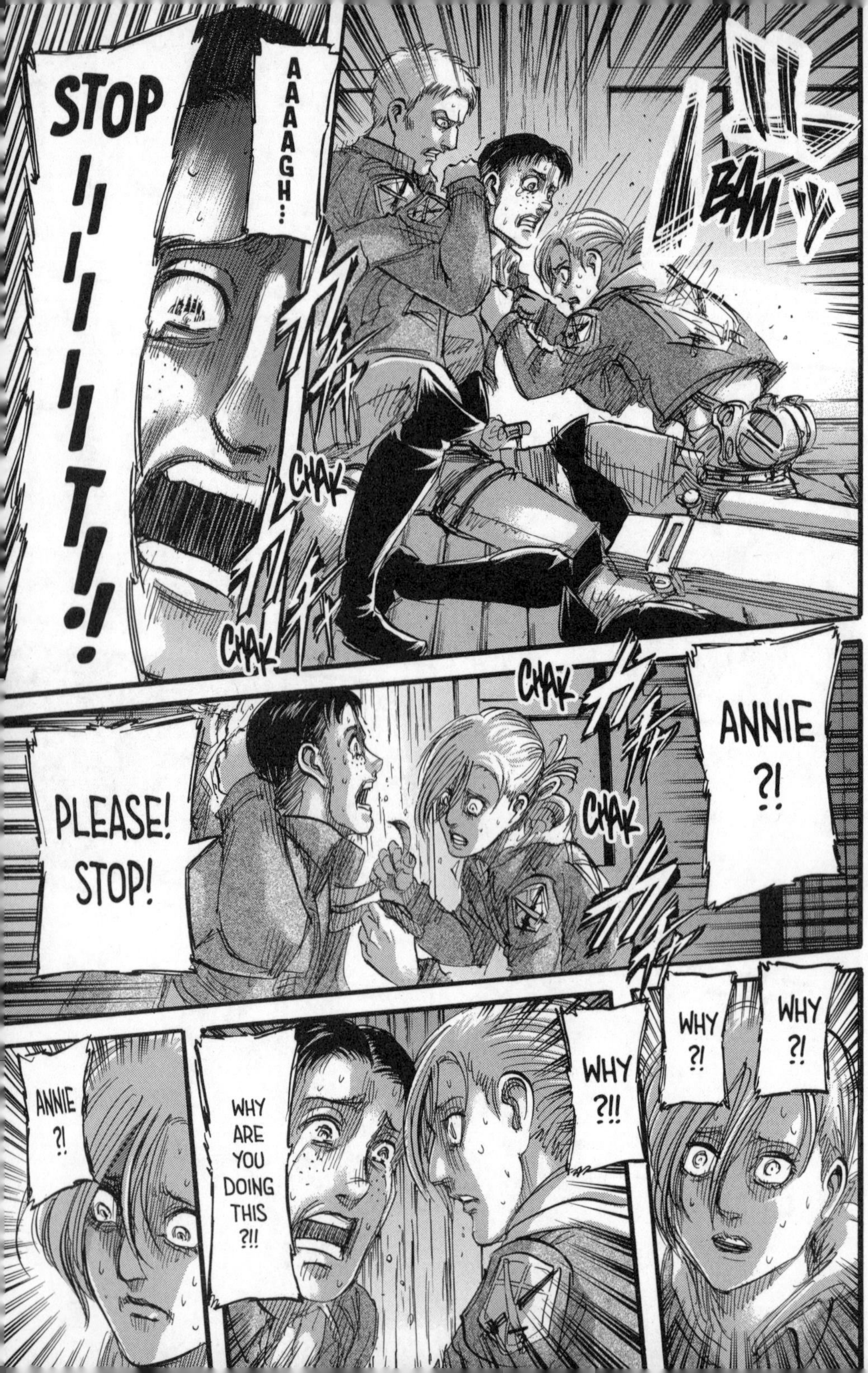

BAM
AAAAGH...
CHAK
CHAK
STOP IIIIIT!!
ANNIE ?!
CHAK
CHAK
PLEASE! STOP!
WHY ?!
WHY ?!
WHY ?!!
WHY ARE YOU DOING THIS ?!!
ANNIE ?!

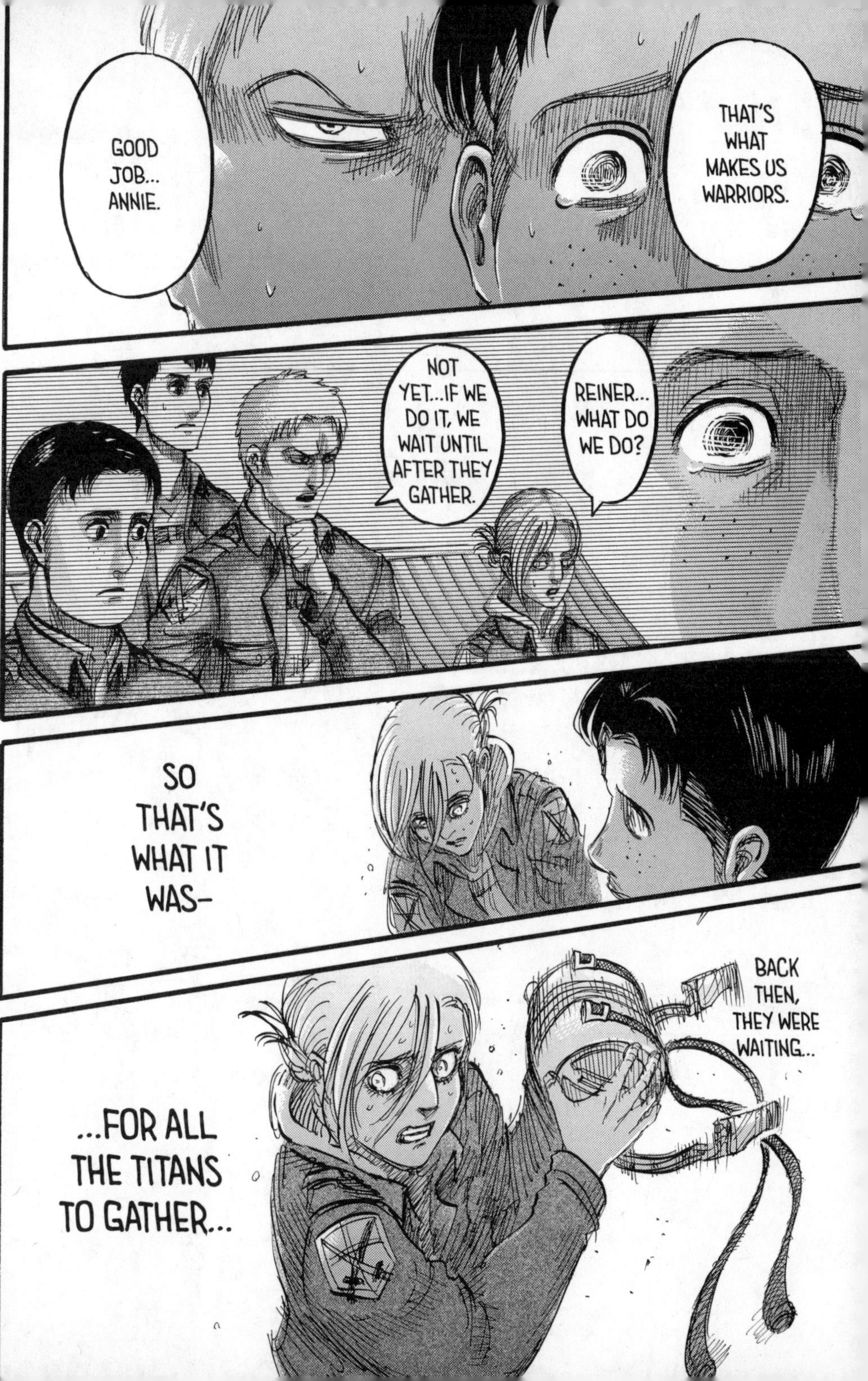
THAT'S WHAT MAKES US WARRIORS.
GOOD JOB... ANNIE.
REINER... WHAT DO WE DO?
NOT YET...IF WE DO IT, WE WAIT UNTIL AFTER THEY GATHER.
SO THAT'S WHAT IT WAS-
BACK THEN, THEY WERE WAITING...
...FOR ALL THE TITANS TO GATHER...

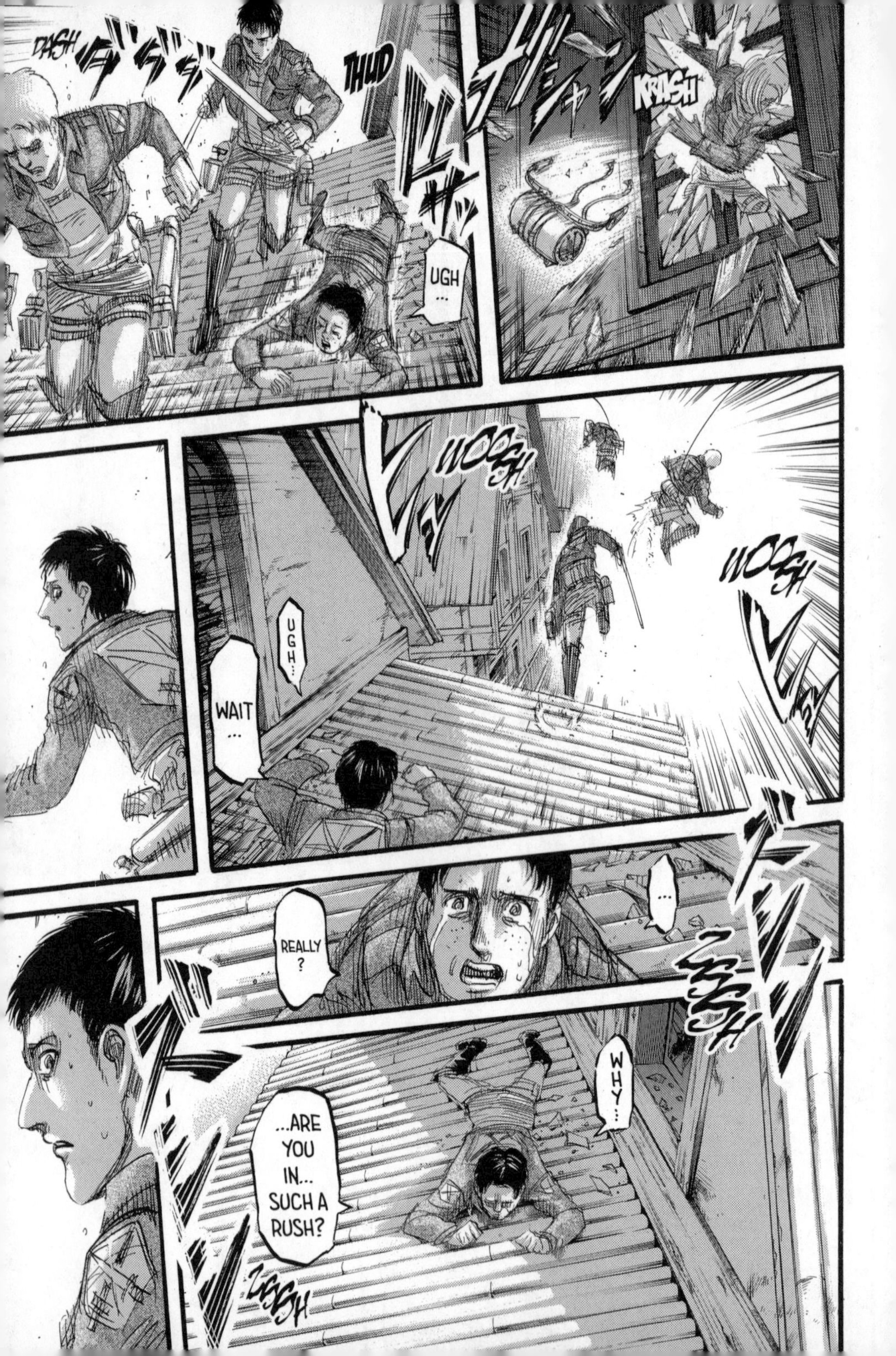
KRASH
THUD
DASH
UGH...
WOOSH
WOOSH
UGH...
WAIT...
...
REALLY?
ZASH
WHY...
...ARE YOU IN... SUCH A RUSH?
ZASH

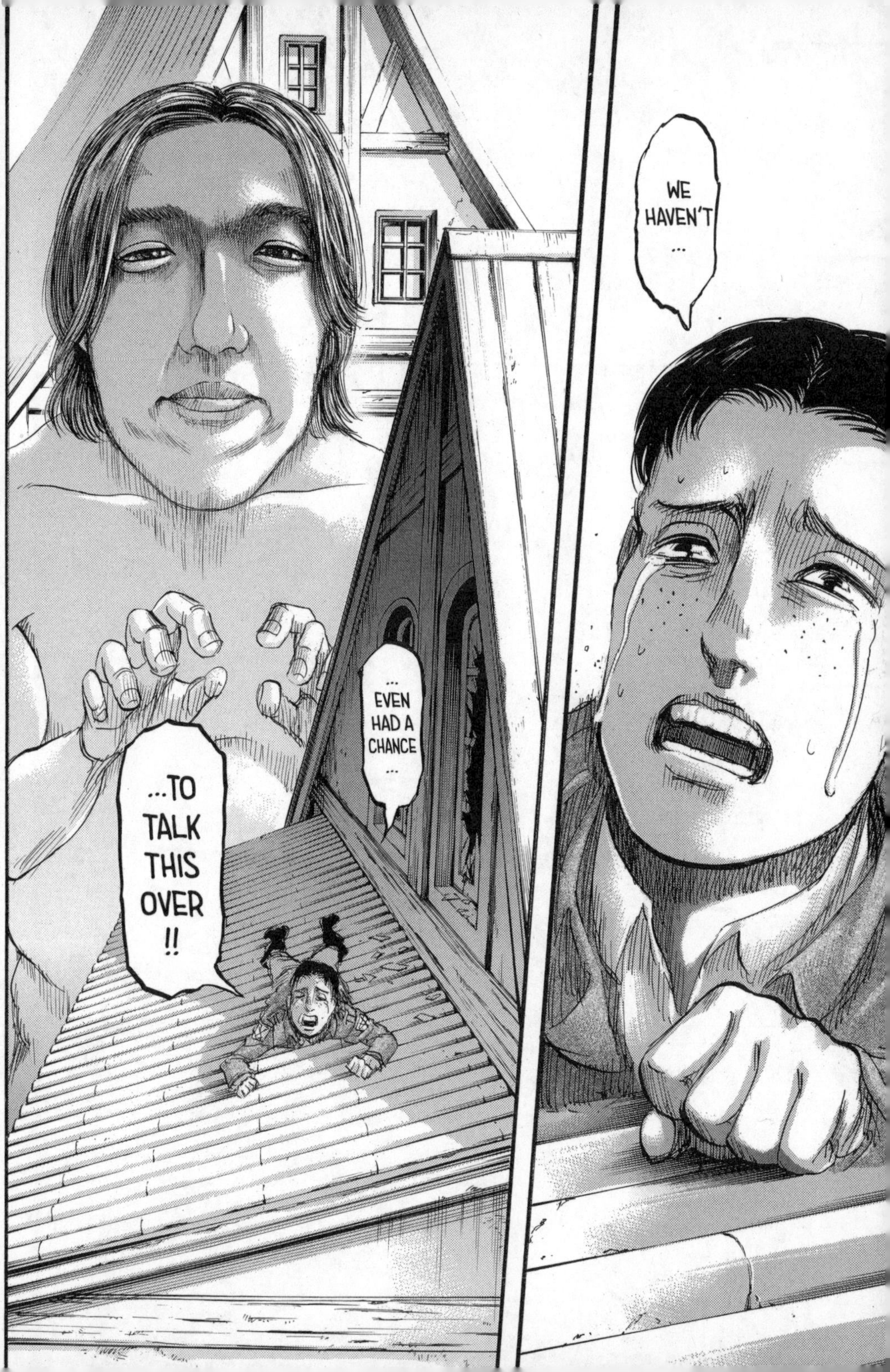
WE HAVEN'T ...
... EVEN HAD A CHANCE ...
...TO TALK THIS OVER !!

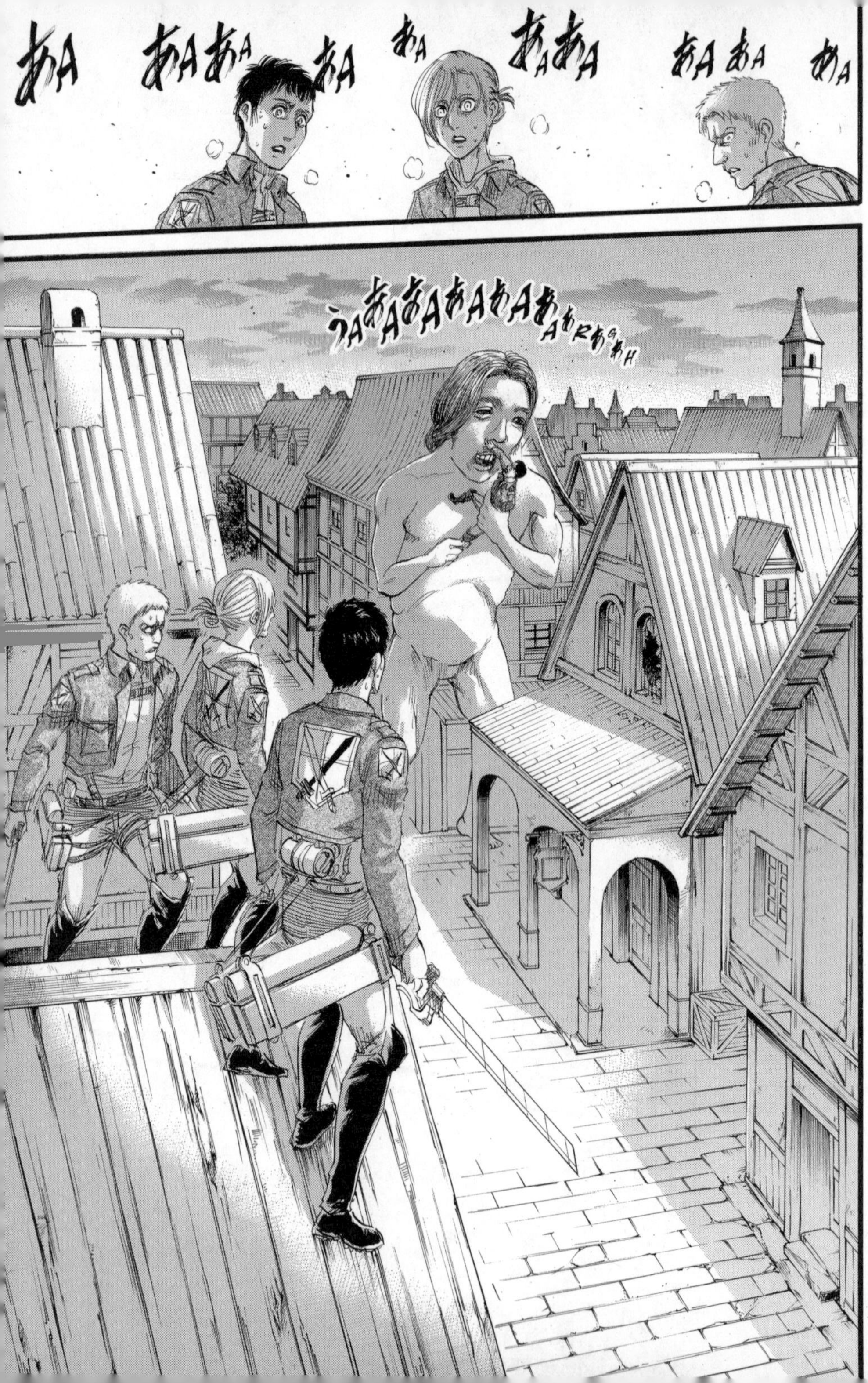

あA
あA あA
あA あA
あA
あA
あA あA
あA
うAあAあAあAあAあ

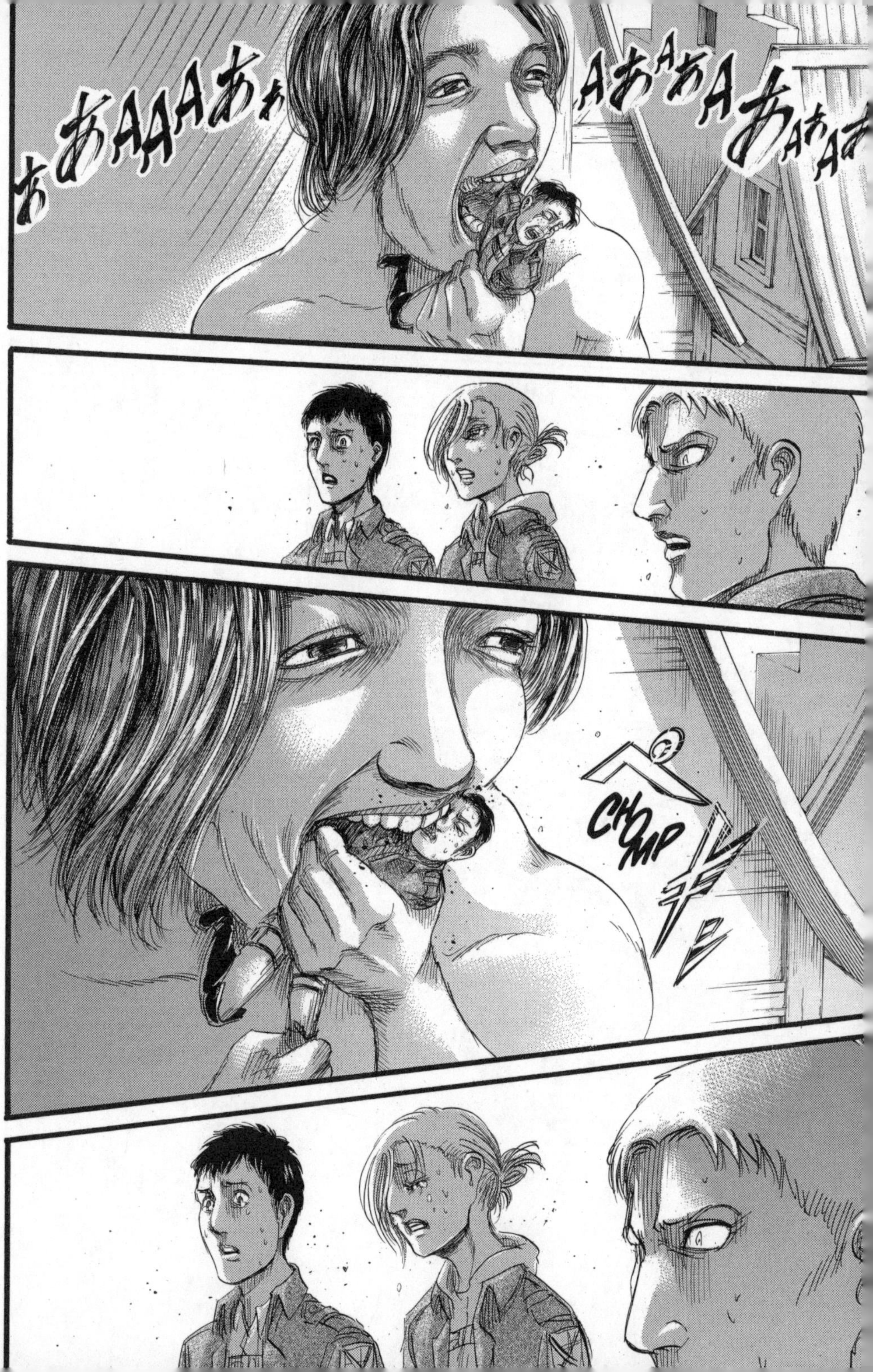

AあAあAあAあAあ
あああAAAあぁ
CHOMP

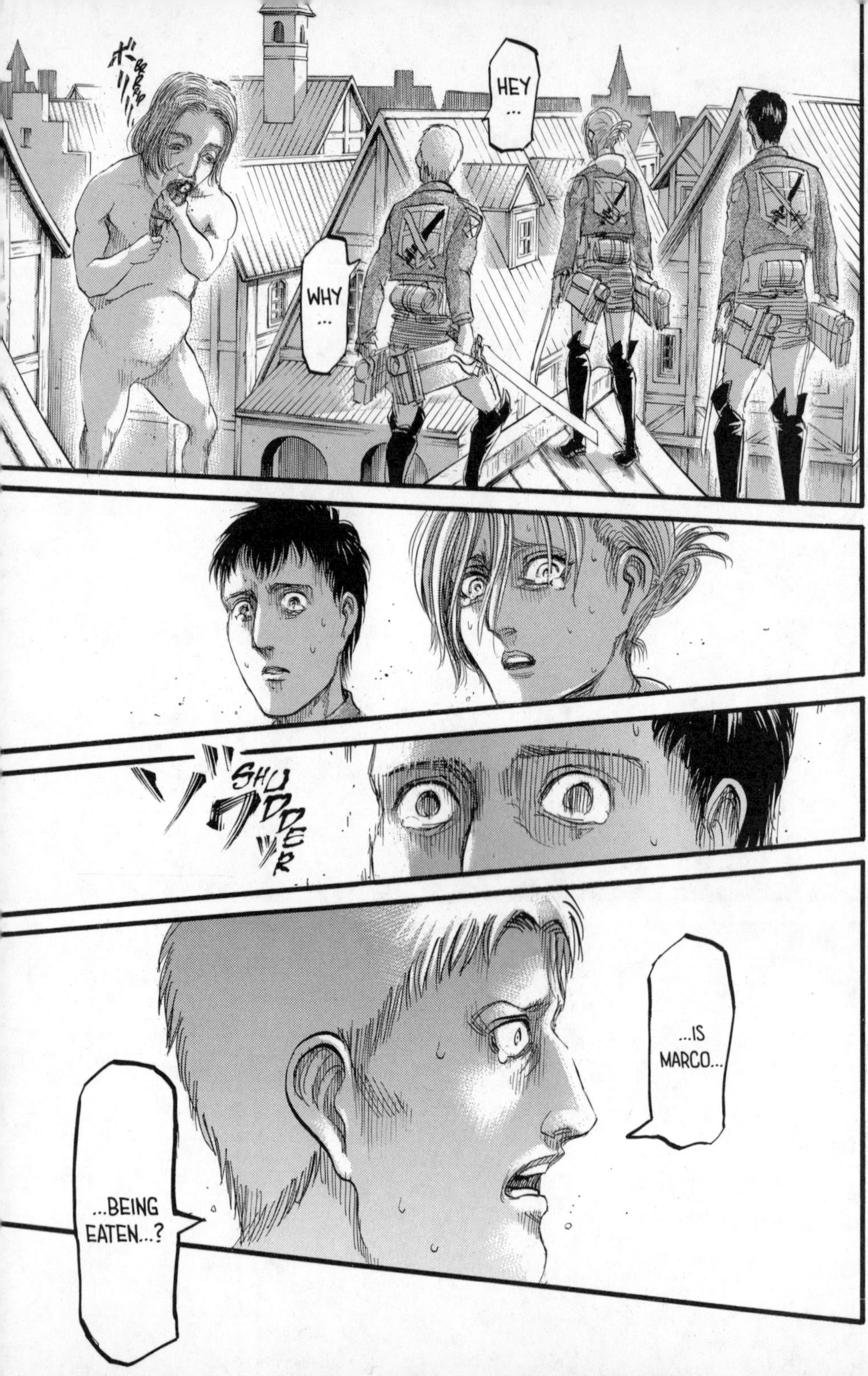
HEY ...
WHY ...
SHUDDER
...IS MARCO...
...BEING EATEN...?

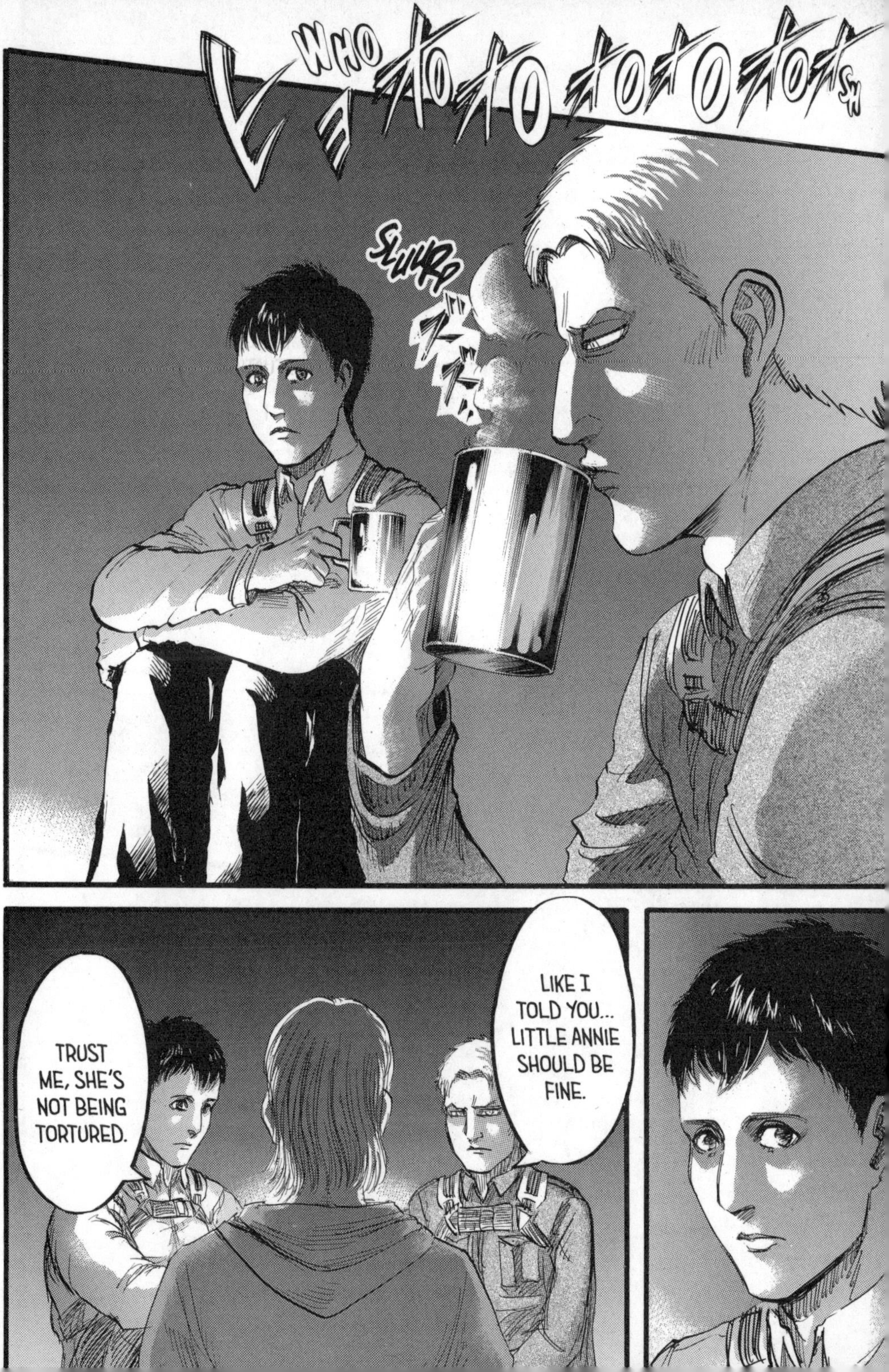

WHOOOOOOSH
SLURP
LIKE I TOLD YOU... LITTLE ANNIE SHOULD BE FINE.
TRUST ME, SHE'S NOT BEING TORTURED.

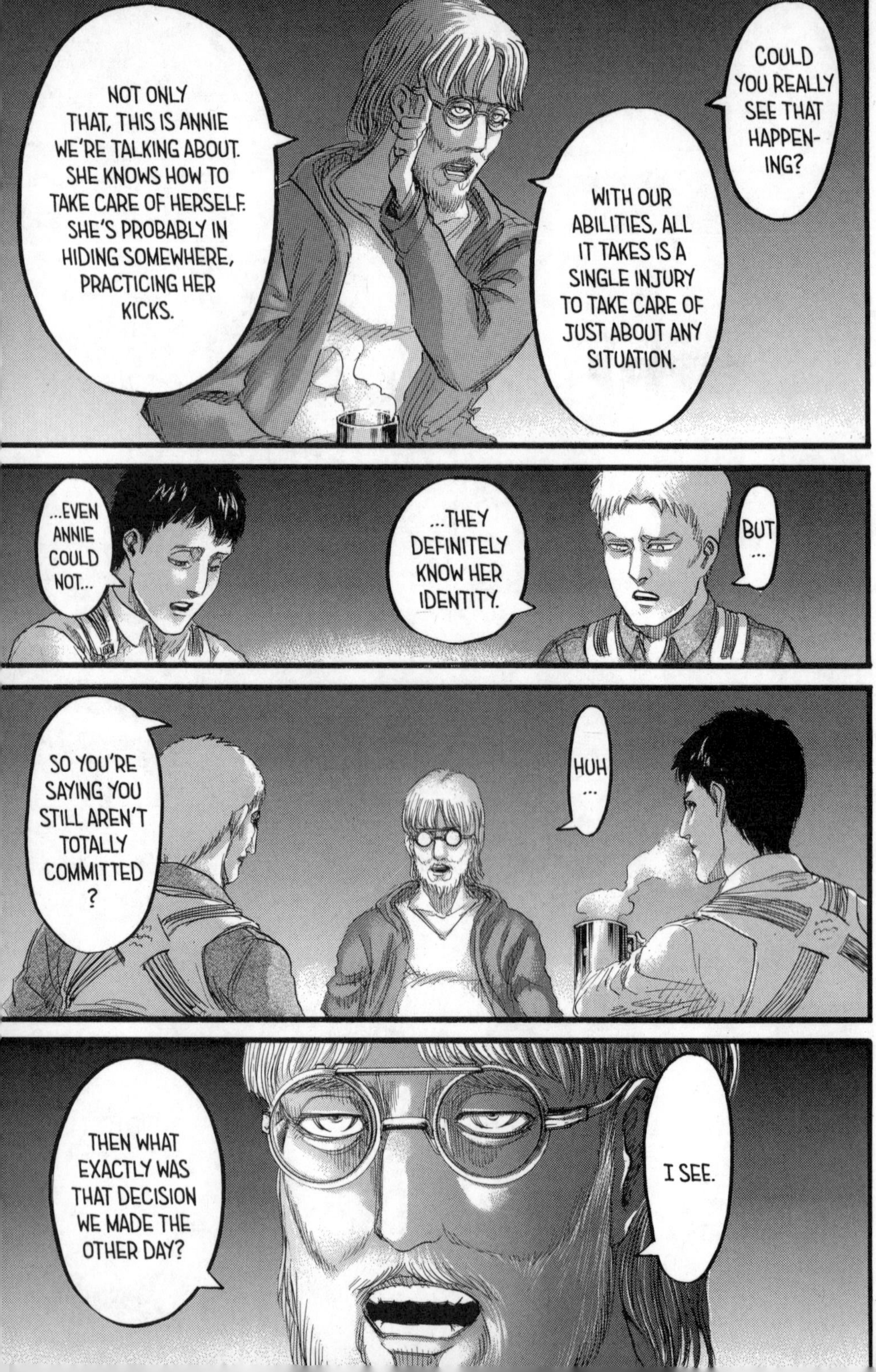
COULD YOU REALLY SEE THAT HAPPENING?
WITH OUR ABILITIES, ALL IT TAKES IS A SINGLE INJURY TO TAKE CARE OF JUST ABOUT ANY SITUATION.
NOT ONLY THAT, THIS IS ANNIE WE'RE TALKING ABOUT. SHE KNOWS HOW TO TAKE CARE OF HERSELF. SHE'S PROBABLY IN HIDING SOMEWHERE, PRACTICING HER KICKS.
BUT...
...THEY DEFINITELY KNOW HER IDENTITY.
...EVEN ANNIE COULD NOT...
HUH...
SO YOU'RE SAYING YOU STILL AREN'T TOTALLY COMMITTED?
I SEE.
THEN WHAT EXACTLY WAS THAT DECISION WE MADE THE OTHER DAY?

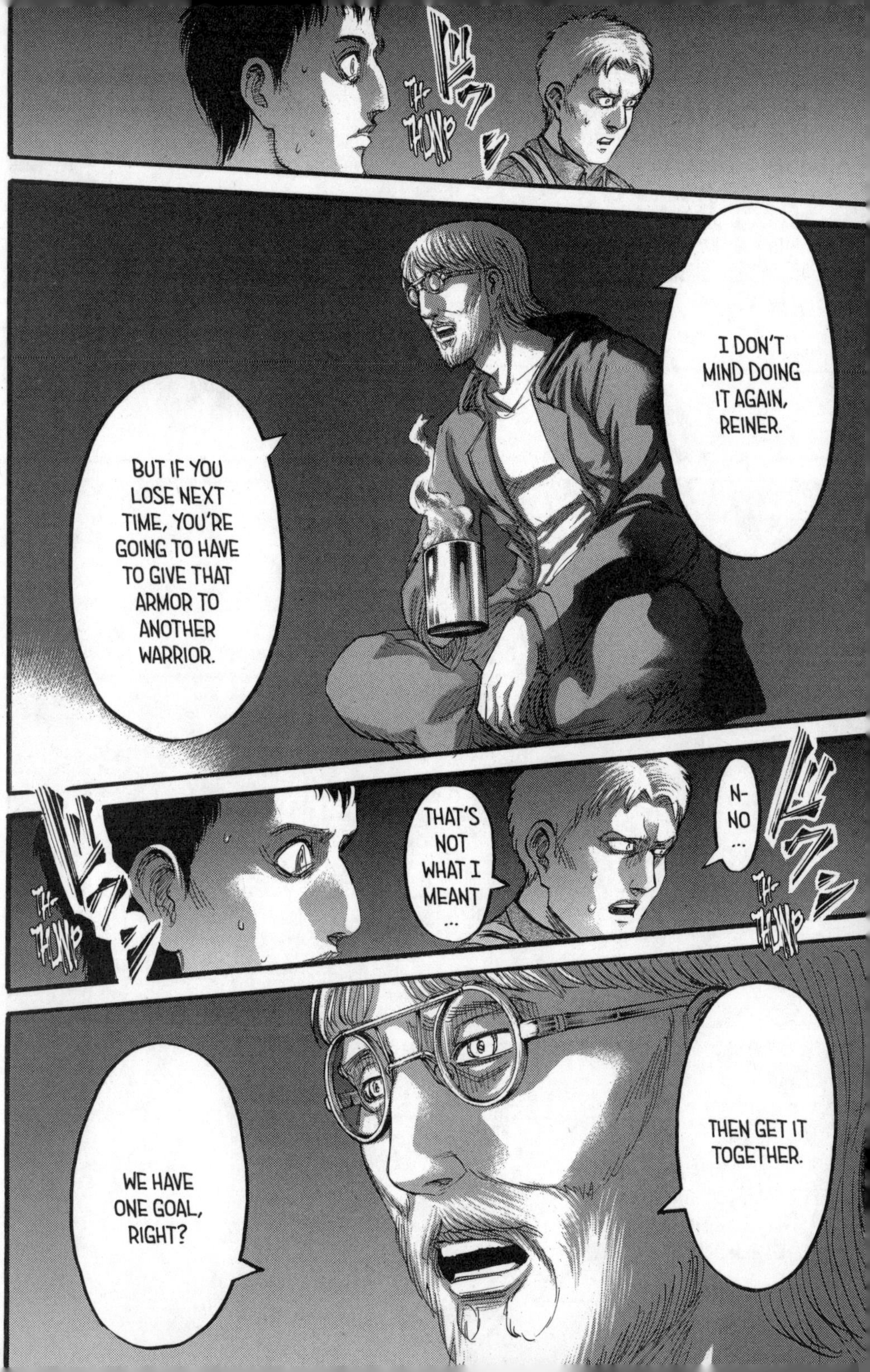
TH-THUMP
I DON'T MIND DOING IT AGAIN, REINER.
BUT IF YOU LOSE NEXT TIME, YOU'RE GOING TO HAVE TO GIVE THAT ARMOR TO ANOTHER WARRIOR.
TH-THUMP
N-NO ...
THAT'S NOT WHAT I MEANT ...
TH-THUMP
THEN GET IT TOGETHER.
WE HAVE ONE GOAL, RIGHT?

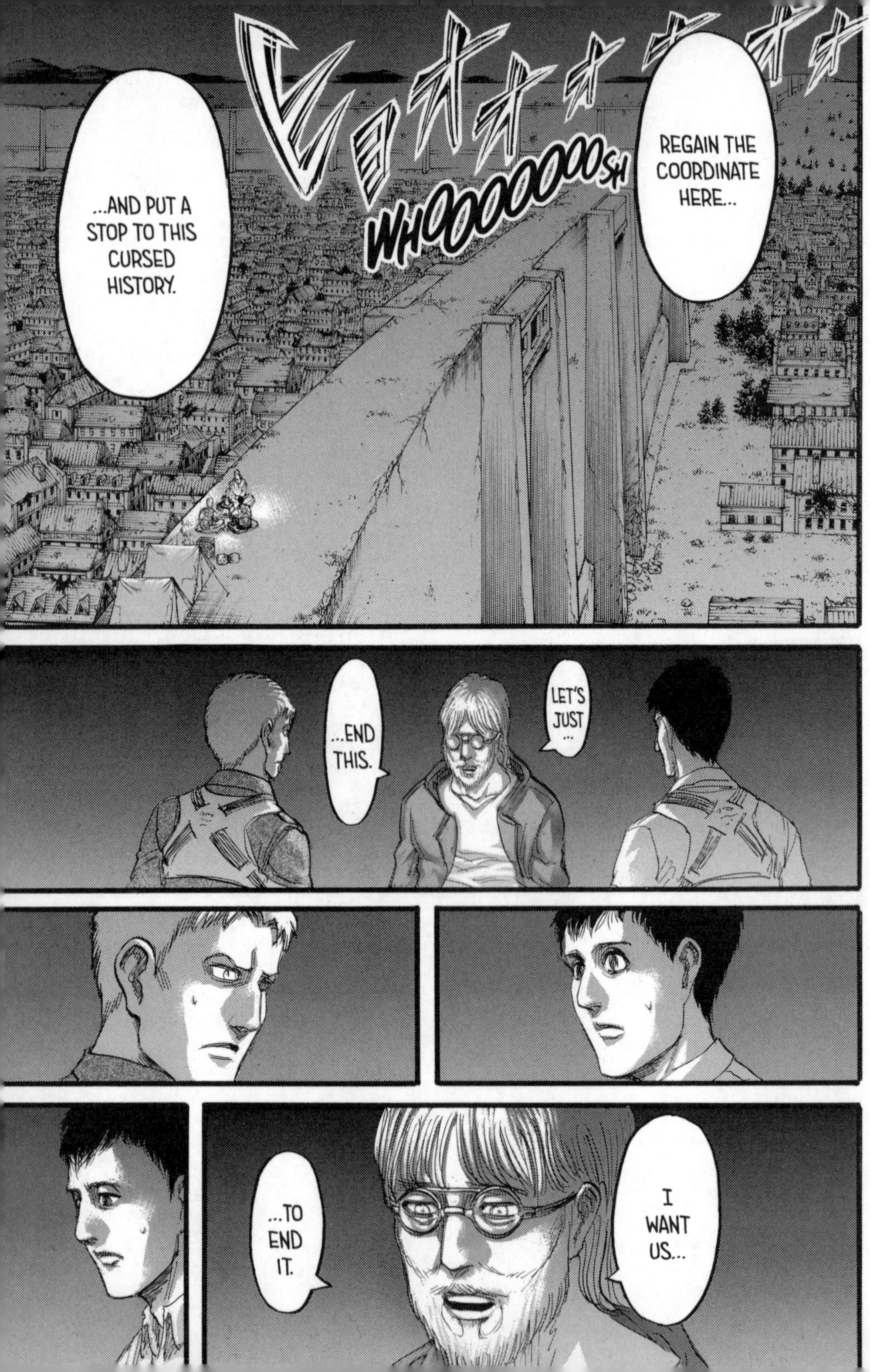
WHOOOOOOOSH
REGAIN THE COORDINATE HERE...
...AND PUT A STOP TO THIS CURSED HISTORY.
LET'S JUST ...
...END THIS.
I WANT US...
...TO END IT.

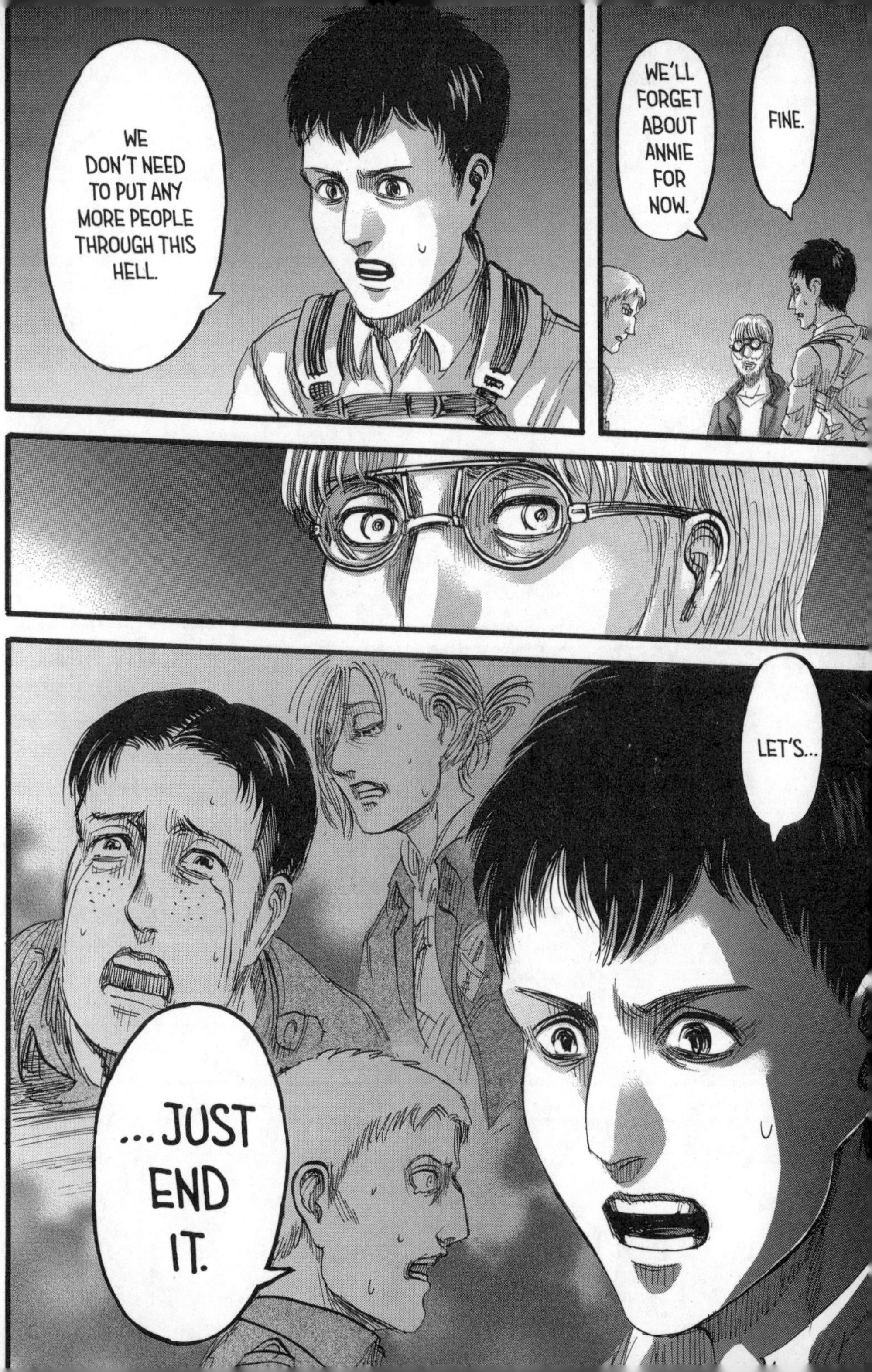
FINE.
WE'LL FORGET ABOUT ANNIE FOR NOW.
WE DON'T NEED TO PUT ANY MORE PEOPLE THROUGH THIS HELL.
LET'S...
...JUST END IT.

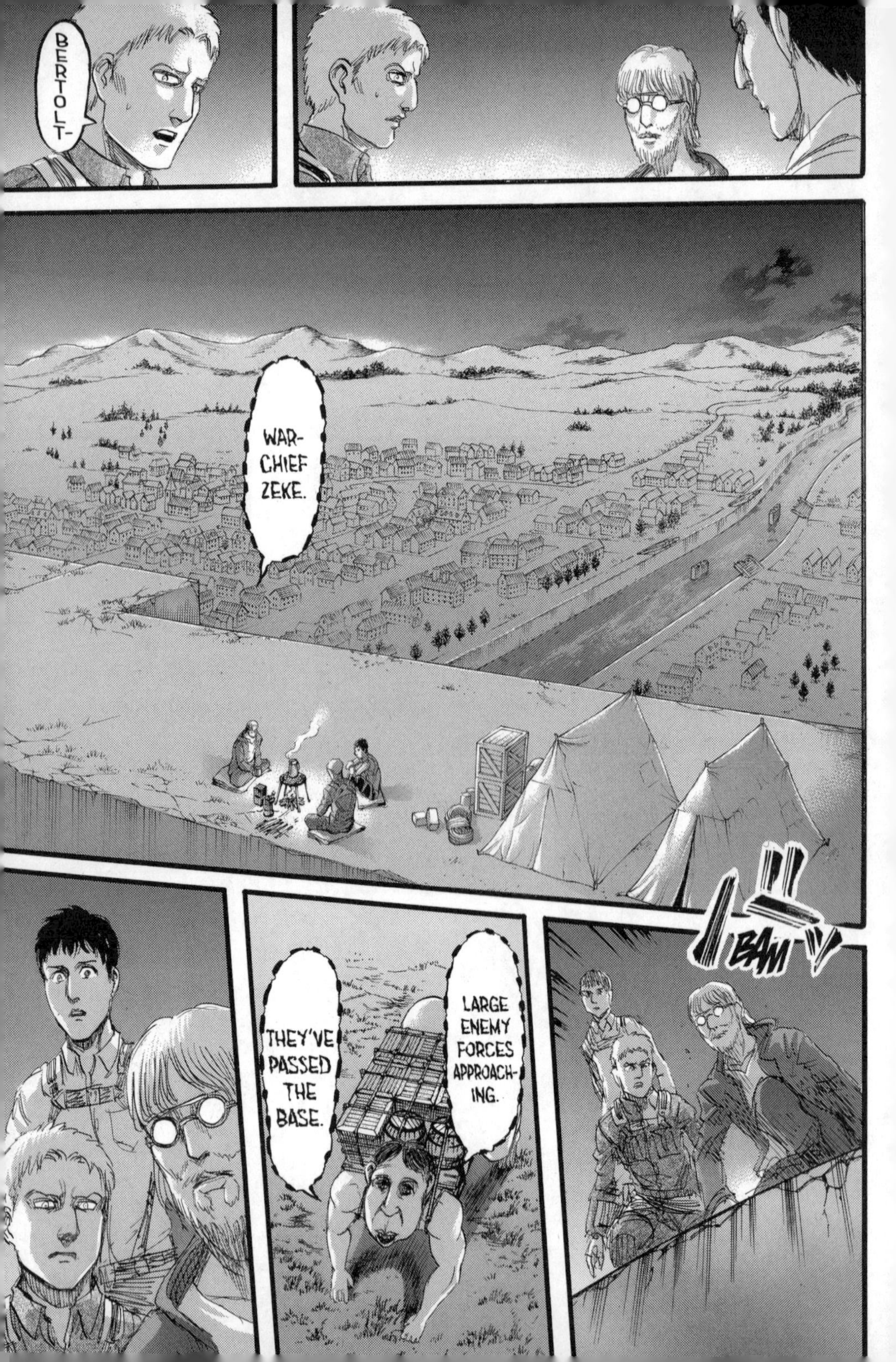
BERTOLT-
WAR-CHIEF ZEKE.
BAM
LARGE ENEMY FORCES APPROACHING.
THEY'VE PASSED THE BASE.

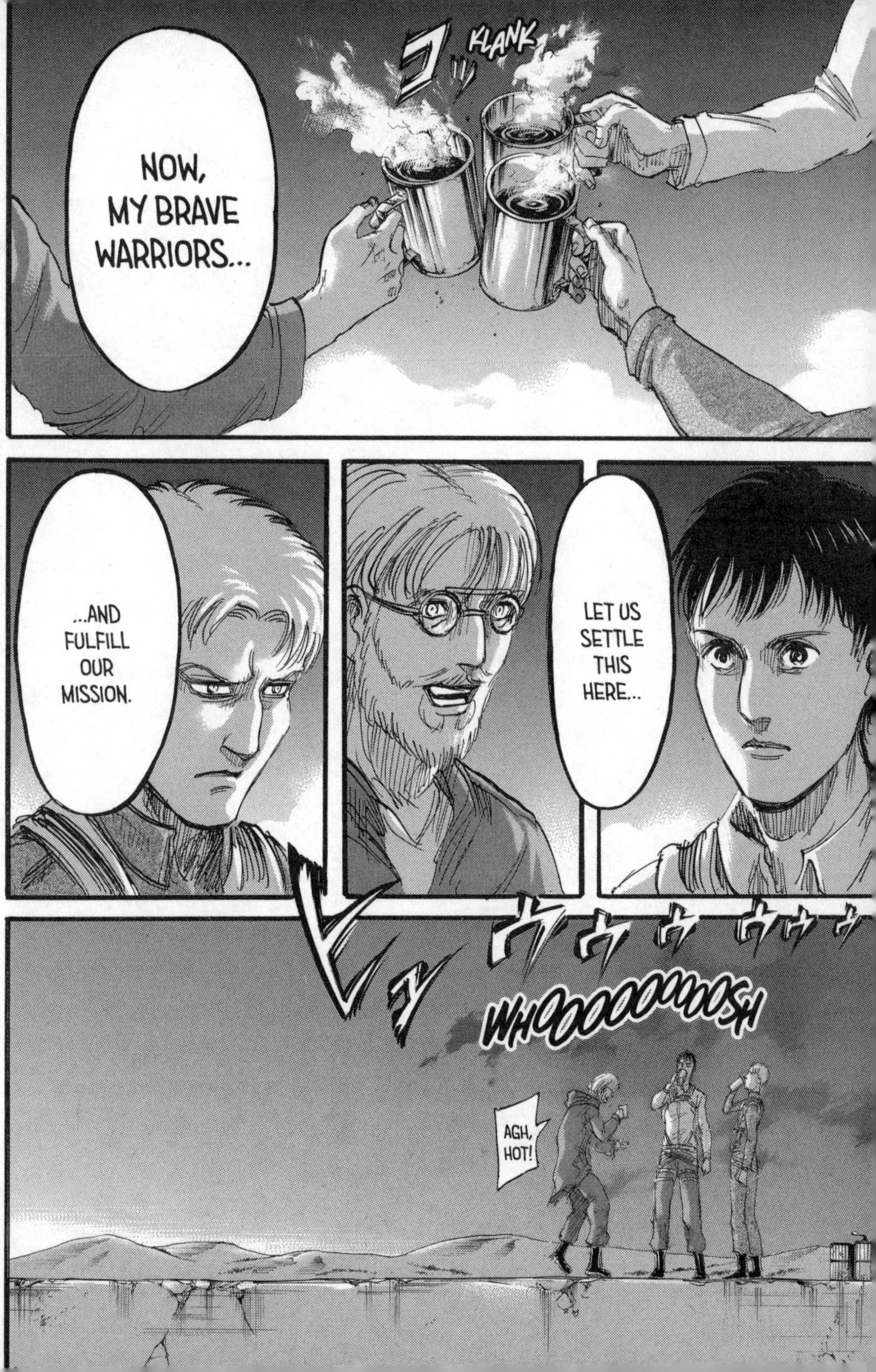
ゴッ
KLANK
NOW, MY BRAVE WARRIORS...
LET US SETTLE THIS HERE...
...AND FULFILL OUR MISSION.
ビュウウウ ウウウ
WHOOOOOOOOSH
AGH, HOT!

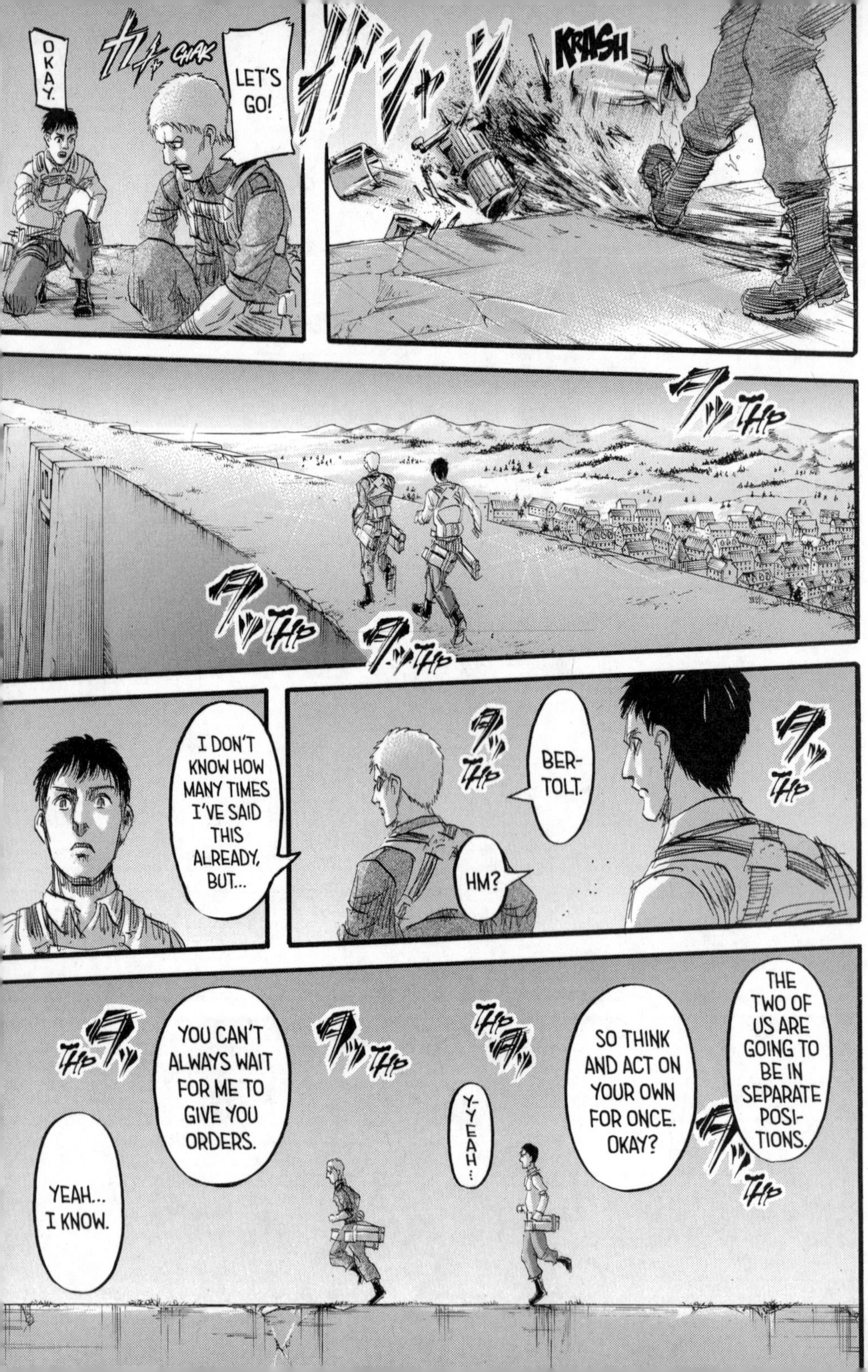
KRASH
LET'S GO!
CHAK
OKAY.
THP
THP
THP
THP
BER-TOLT.
HM?
THP
THP
I DON'T KNOW HOW MANY TIMES I'VE SAID THIS ALREADY, BUT...
THE TWO OF US ARE GOING TO BE IN SEPARATE POSI-TIONS.
THP
SO THINK AND ACT ON YOUR OWN FOR ONCE. OKAY?
THP
Y-YEAH...
THP
YOU CAN'T ALWAYS WAIT FOR ME TO GIVE YOU ORDERS.
THP
YEAH... I KNOW.

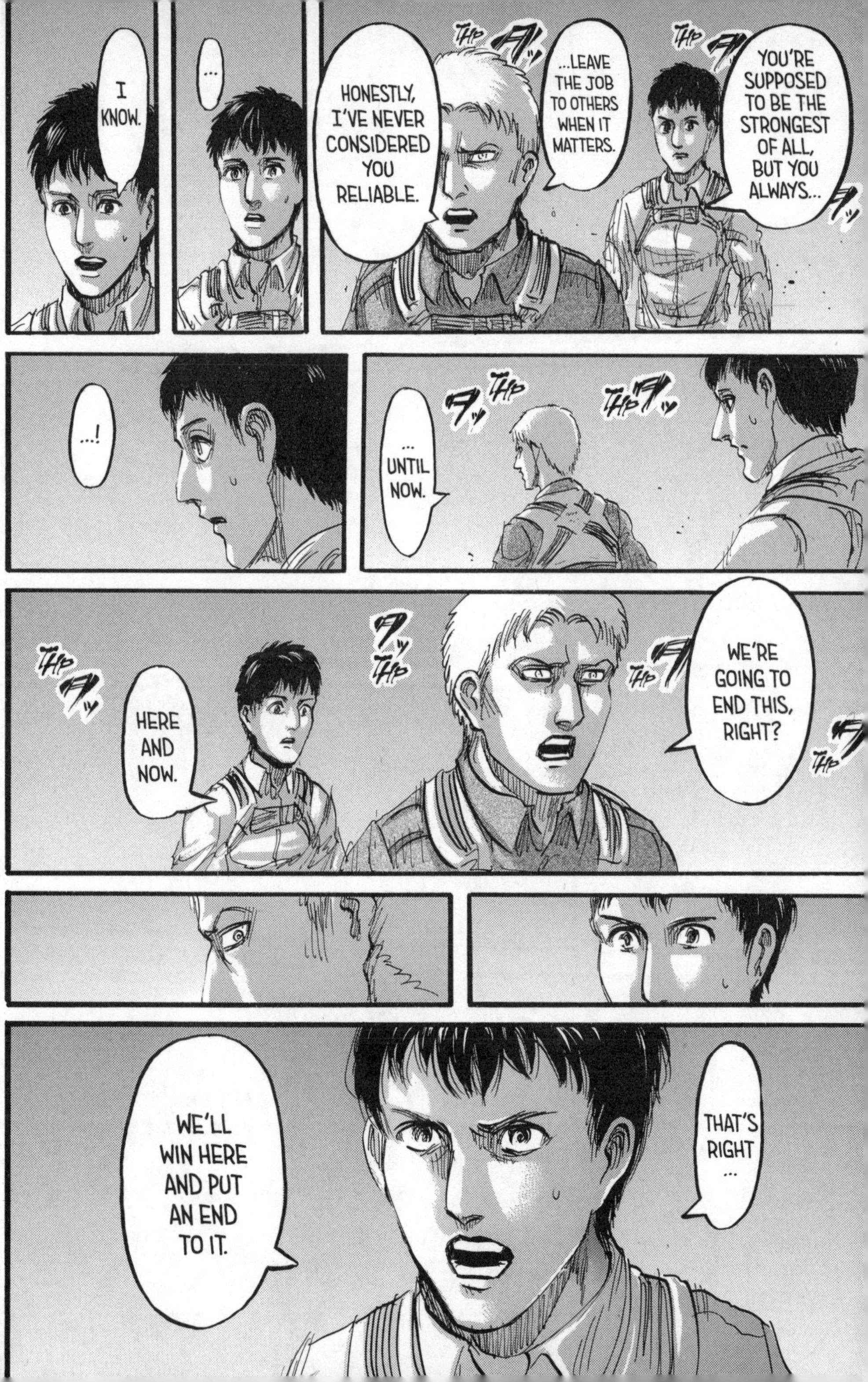
THP
YOU'RE SUPPOSED TO BE THE STRONGEST OF ALL, BUT YOU ALWAYS...
THP
...LEAVE THE JOB TO OTHERS WHEN IT MATTERS.
HONESTLY, I'VE NEVER CONSIDERED YOU RELIABLE.
...
I KNOW.
THP
THP
... UNTIL NOW.
...!
THP
WE'RE GOING TO END THIS, RIGHT?
THP
THP
HERE AND NOW.
THAT'S RIGHT...
WE'LL WIN HERE AND PUT AN END TO IT.

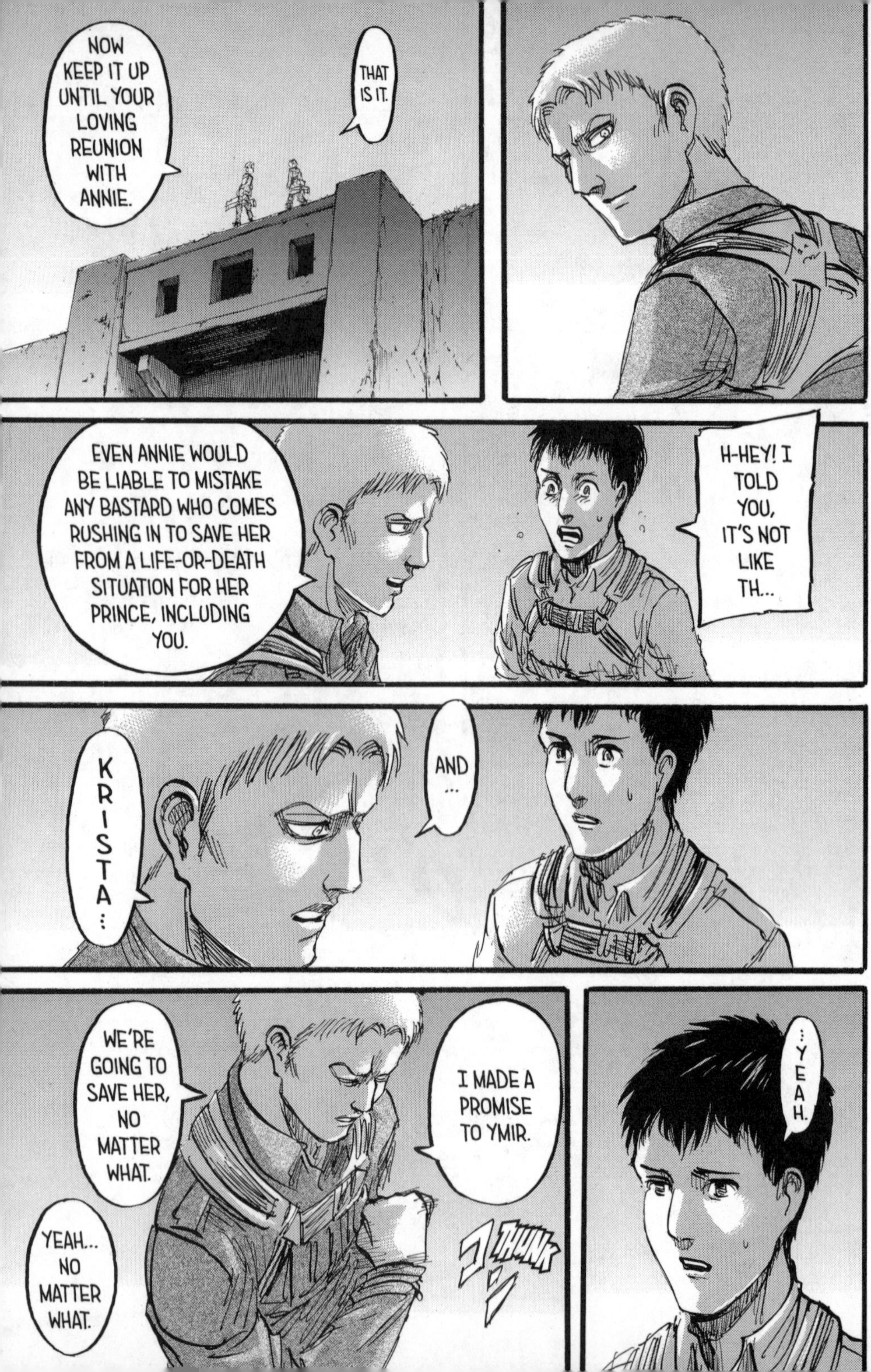
THAT IS IT.
NOW KEEP IT UP UNTIL YOUR LOVING REUNION WITH ANNIE.
H-HEY! I TOLD YOU, IT'S NOT LIKE TH...
EVEN ANNIE WOULD BE LIABLE TO MISTAKE ANY BASTARD WHO COMES RUSHING IN TO SAVE HER FROM A LIFE-OR-DEATH SITUATION FOR HER PRINCE, INCLUDING YOU.
AND ...
KRISTA...
...YEAH.
I MADE A PROMISE TO YMIR.
WE'RE GOING TO SAVE HER, NO MATTER WHAT.
THUNK
YEAH... NO MATTER WHAT.

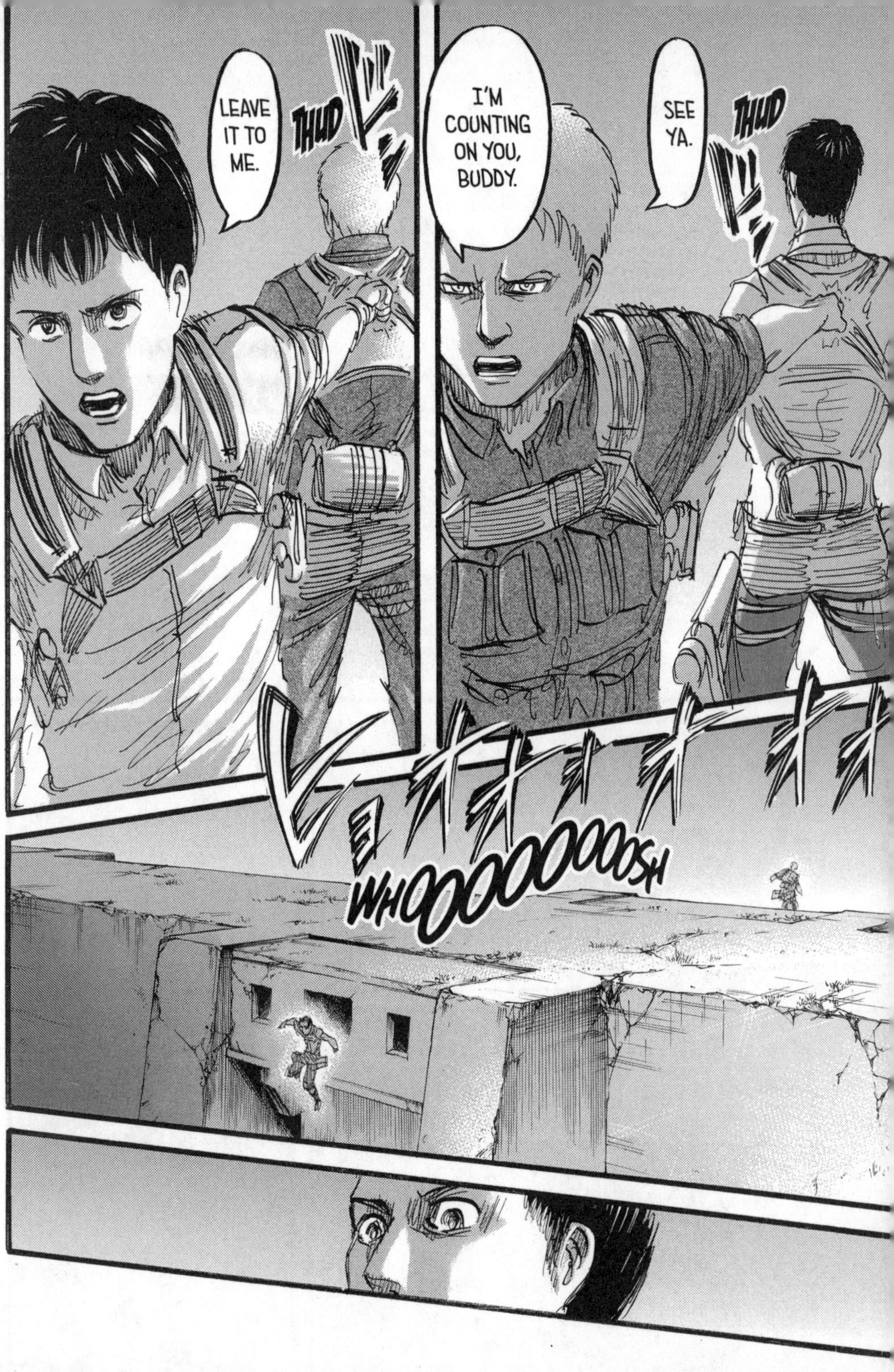
SEE YA.
THUD
I'M COUNTING ON YOU, BUDDY.
THUD
LEAVE IT TO ME.
WHOOOOOOOOOSH

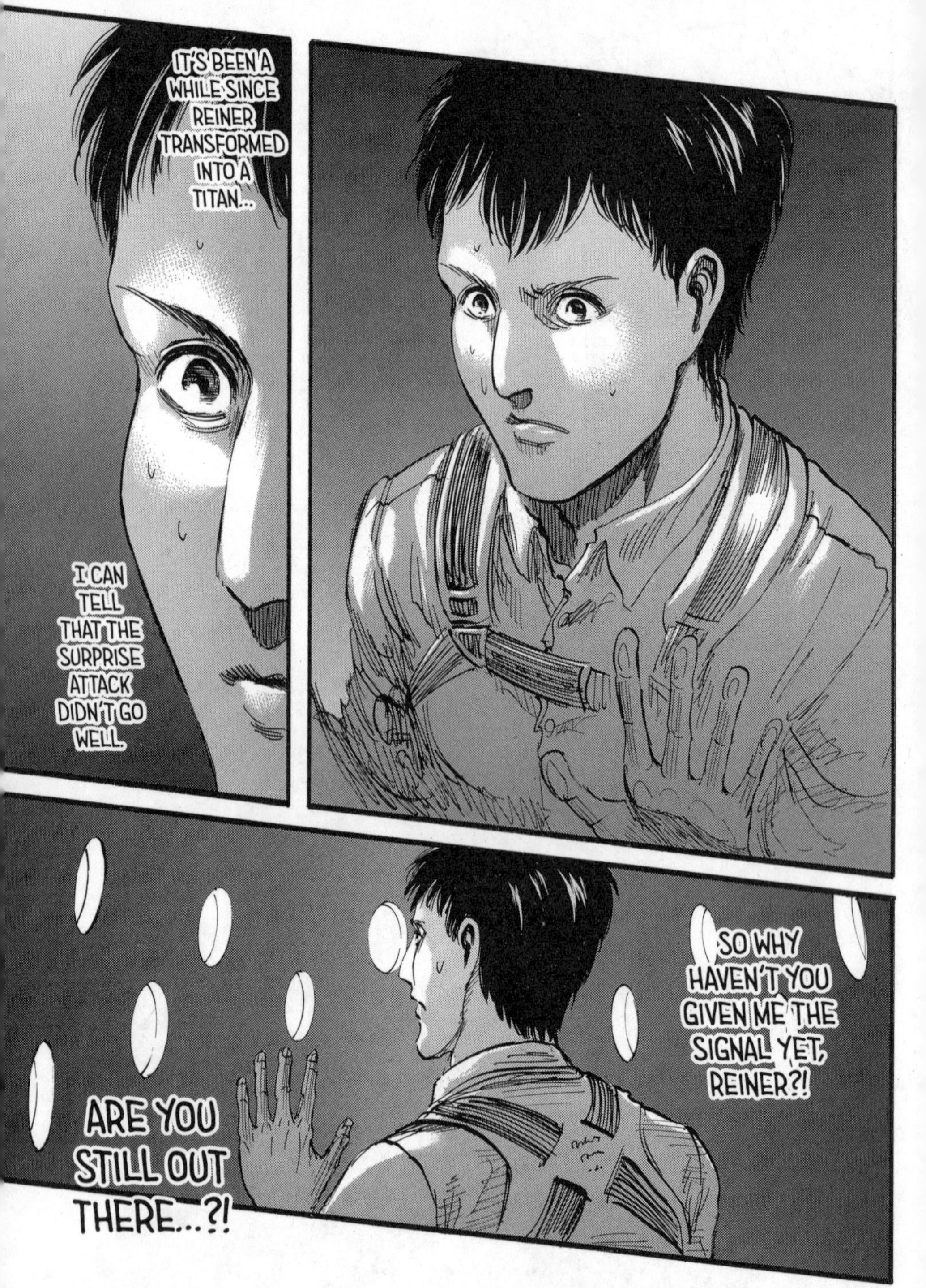
IT'S BEEN A WHILE SINCE REINER TRANSFORMED INTO A TITAN...
I CAN TELL THAT THE SURPRISE ATTACK DIDN'T GO WELL.
SO WHY HAVEN'T YOU GIVEN ME THE SIGNAL YET, REINER?!
ARE YOU STILL OUT THERE...?!

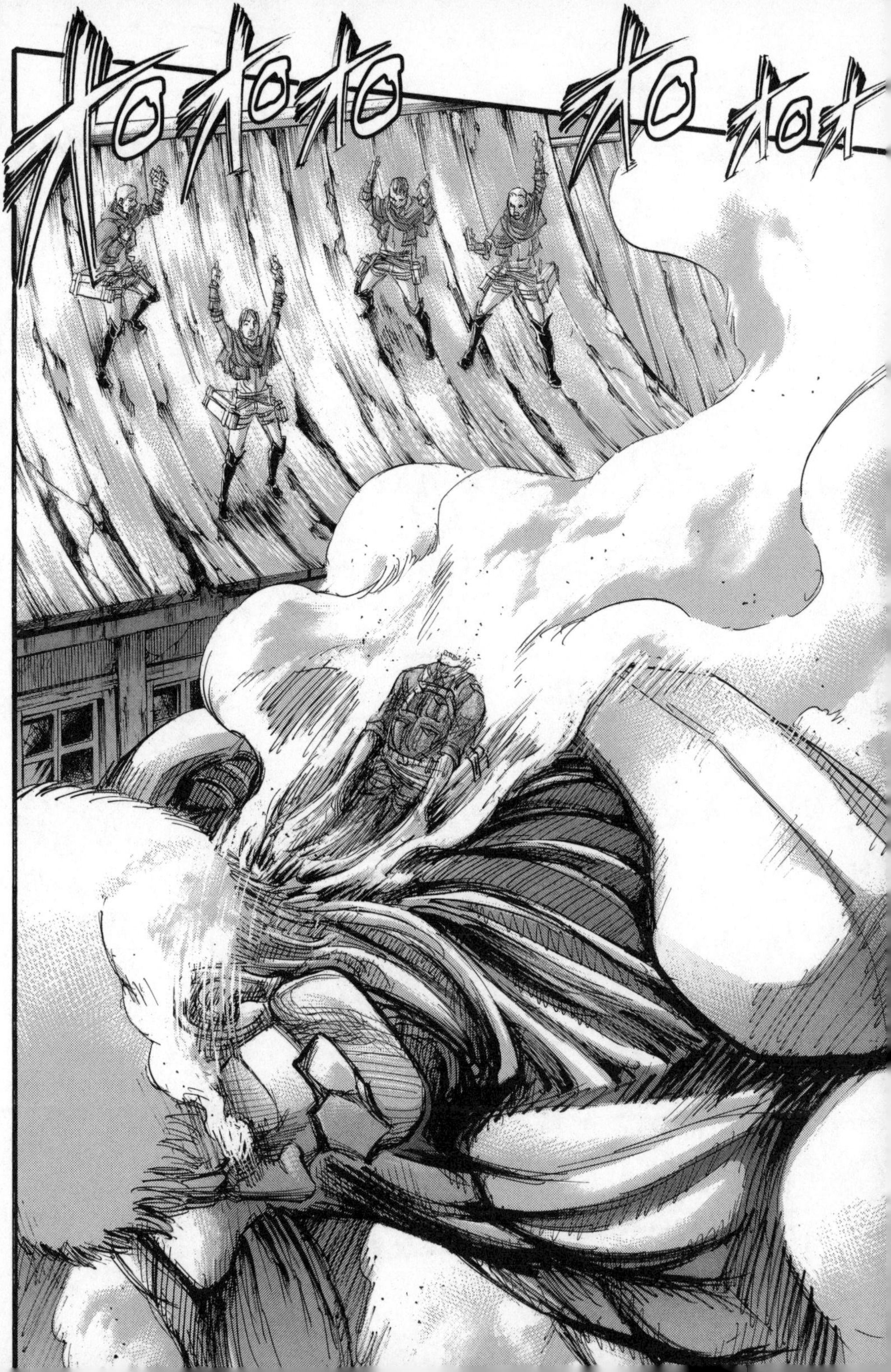

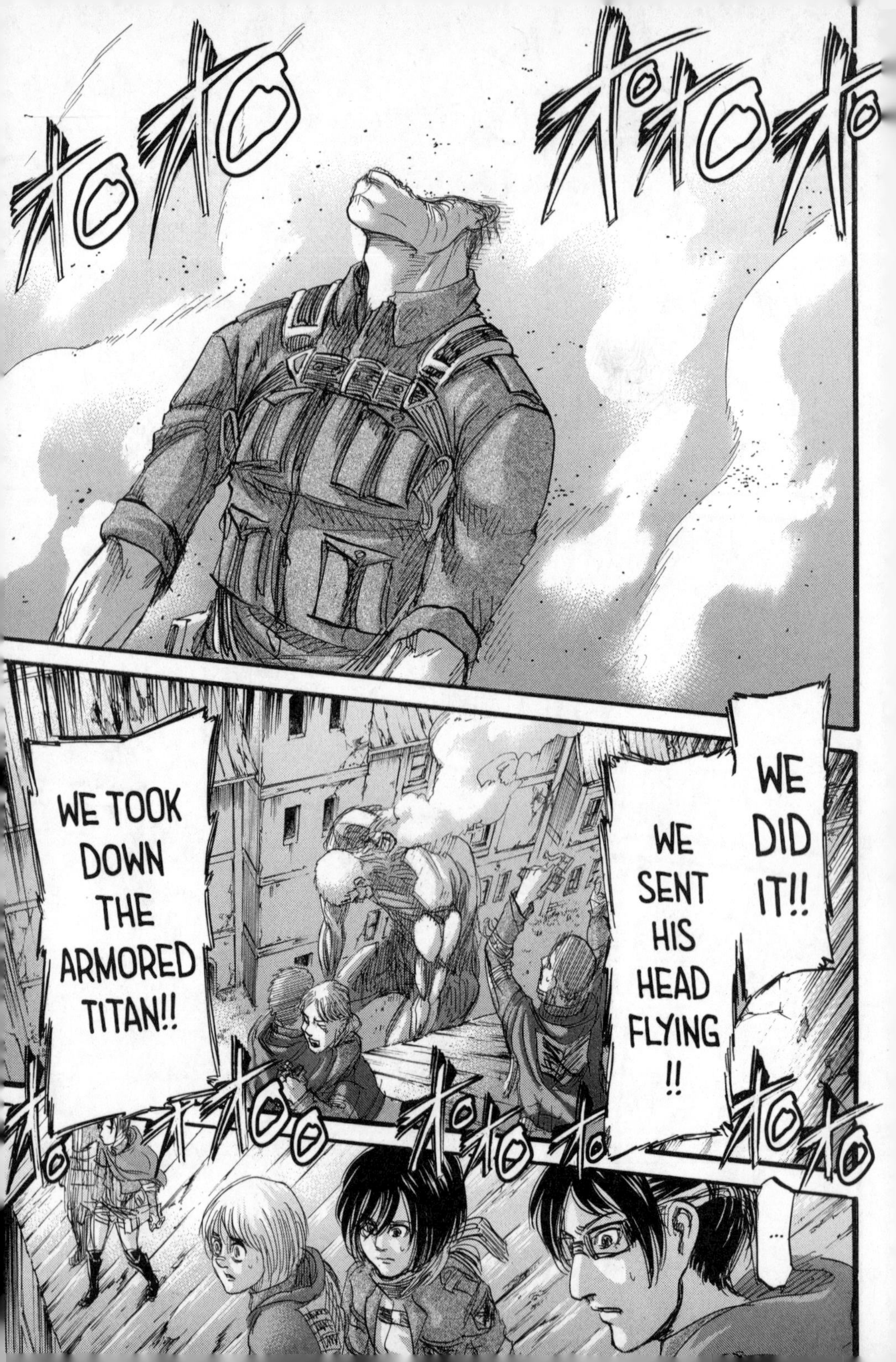
WE DID IT!!
WE SENT HIS HEAD FLYING!!
WE TOOK DOWN THE ARMORED TITAN!!
...

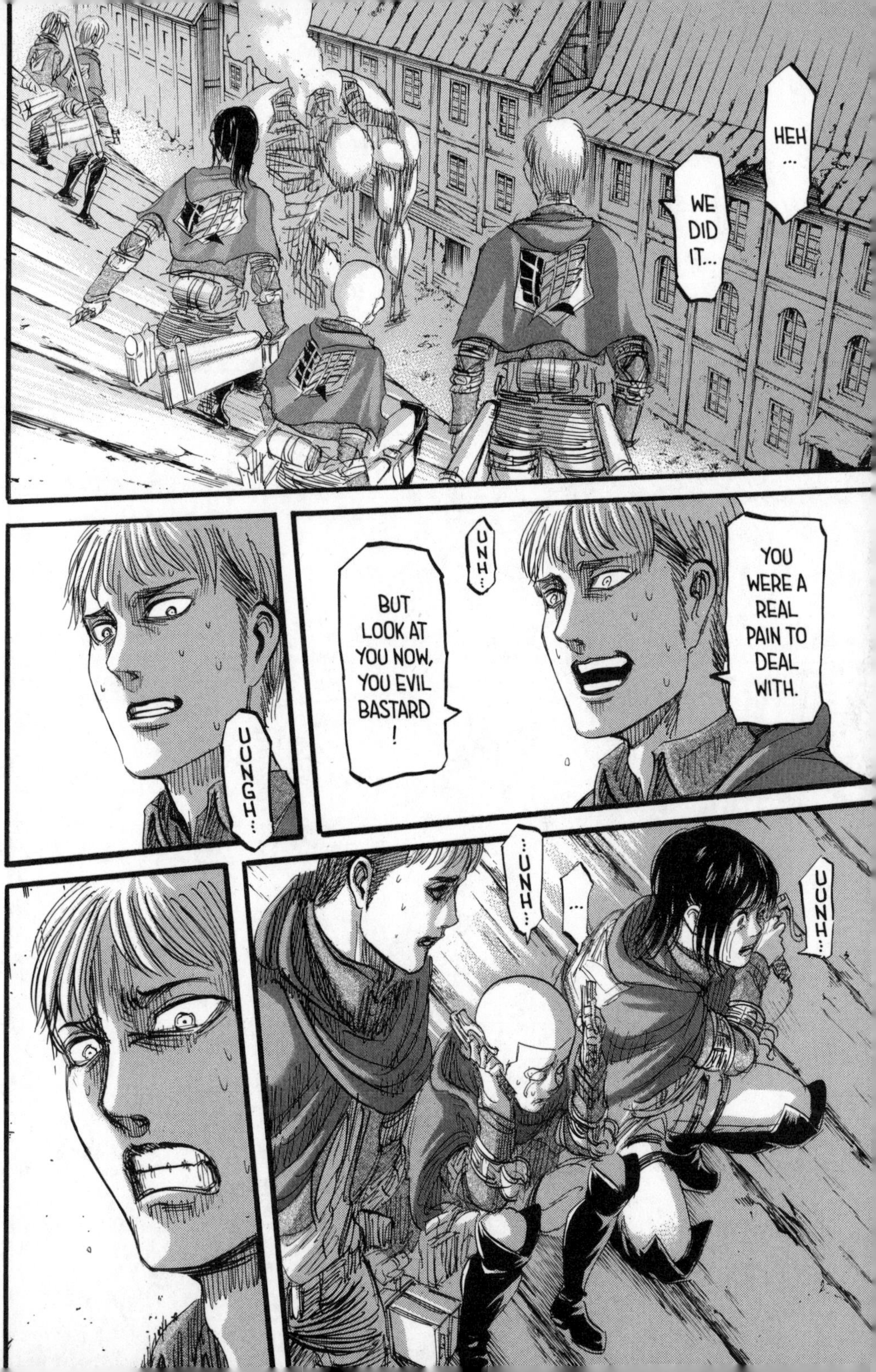

HEH...
WE DID IT...
YOU WERE A REAL PAIN TO DEAL WITH.
UNH...
BUT LOOK AT YOU NOW, YOU EVIL BASTARD!
UUNGH...
UUNH...
...
...UNH...

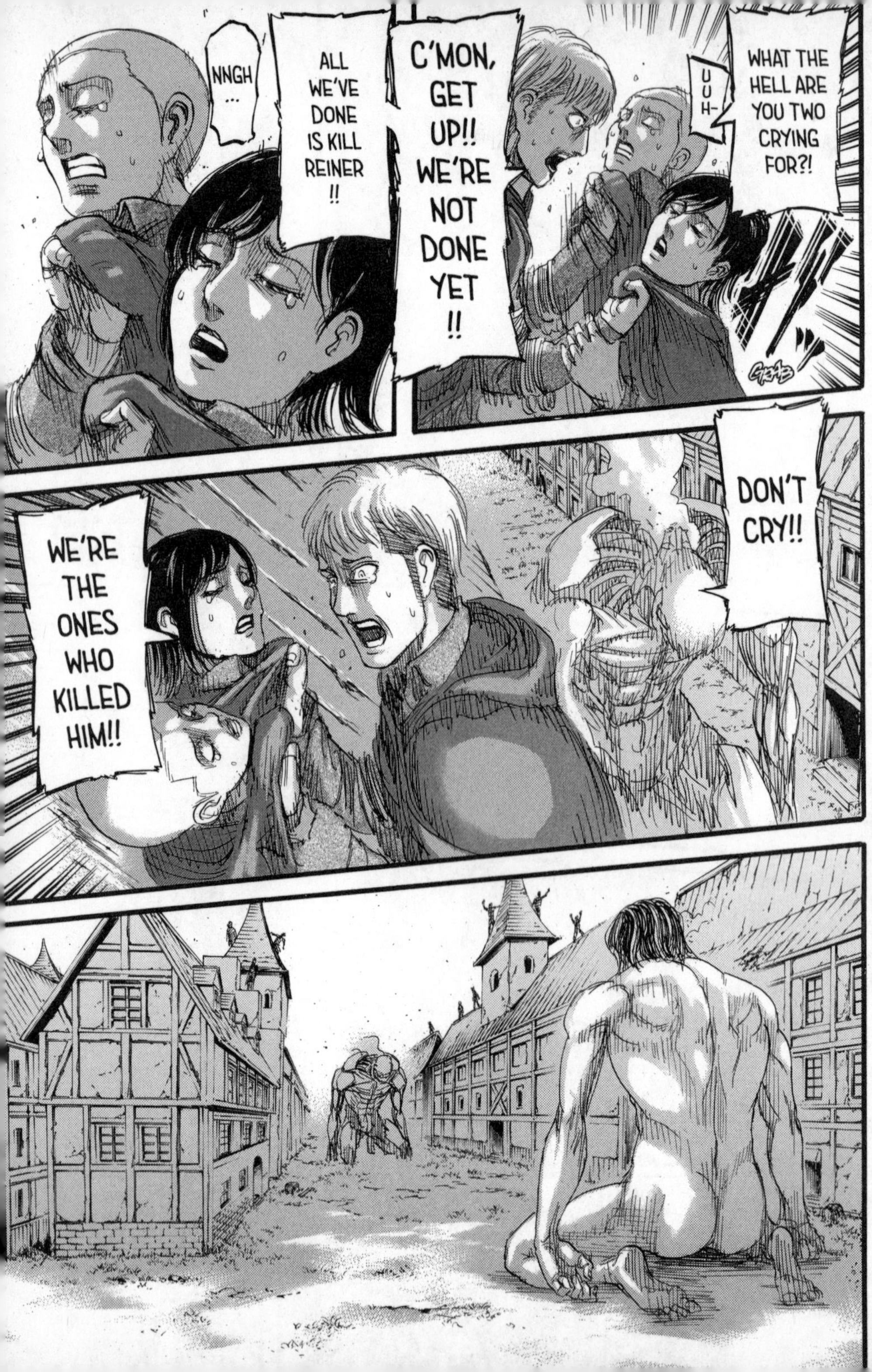
WHAT THE HELL ARE YOU TWO CRYING FOR?!
UUH-
GRAB
C'MON, GET UP!! WE'RE NOT DONE YET!!
ALL WE'VE DONE IS KILL REINER!!
NNGH...
DON'T CRY!!
WE'RE THE ONES WHO KILLED HIM!!

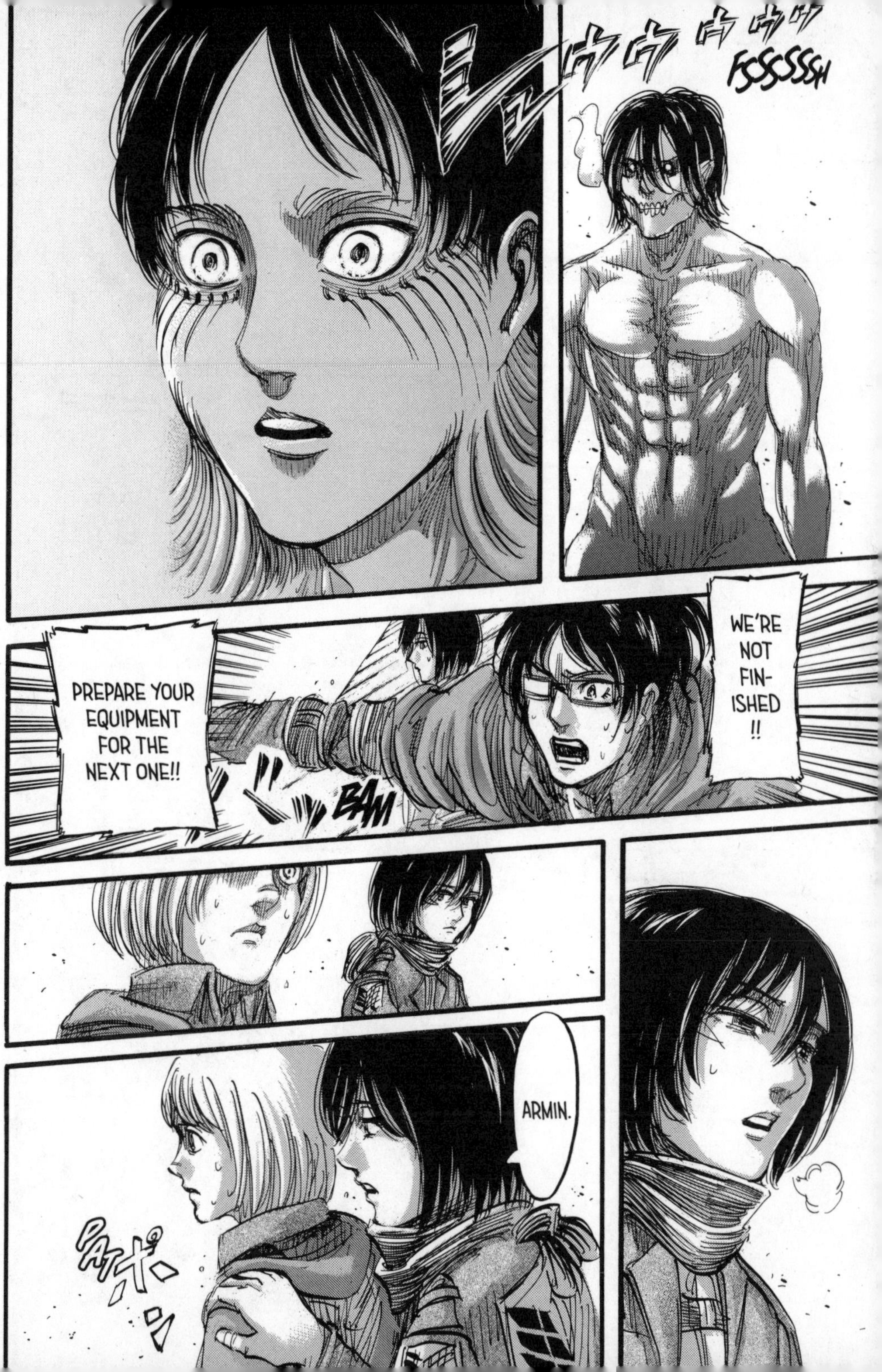
FSSSSSH
WE'RE NOT FIN-ISHED!!
PREPARE YOUR EQUIPMENT FOR THE NEXT ONE!!
BAM
ARMIN.
PAT

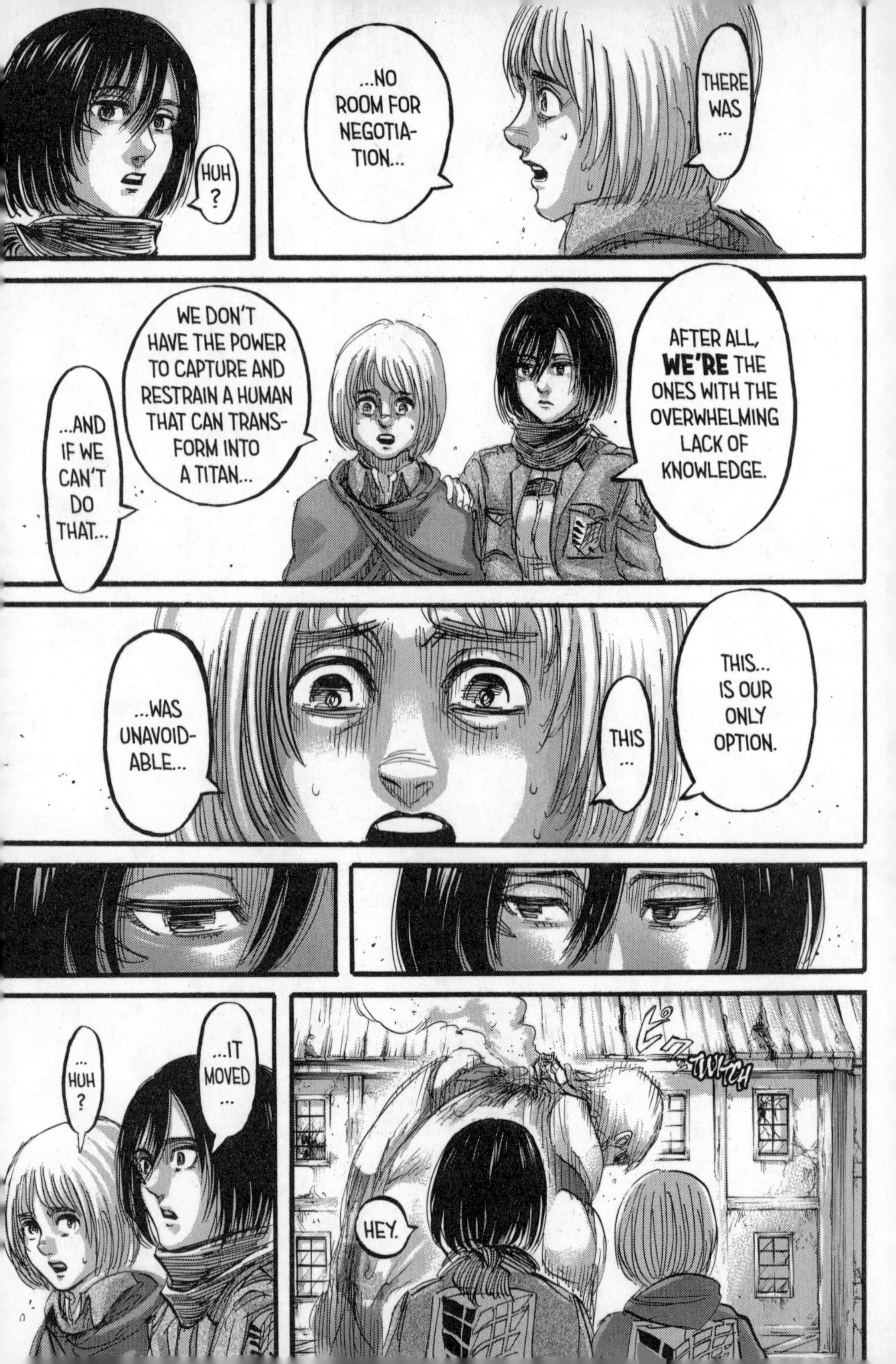
THERE WAS ...
...NO ROOM FOR NEGOTIA-TION...
HUH ?
AFTER ALL, **WE'RE** THE ONES WITH THE OVERWHELMING LACK OF KNOWLEDGE.
WE DON'T HAVE THE POWER TO CAPTURE AND RESTRAIN A HUMAN THAT CAN TRANS-FORM INTO A TITAN...
...AND IF WE CAN'T DO THAT...
THIS... IS OUR ONLY OPTION.
THIS ...
...WAS UNAVOID-ABLE...
ピク
TWITCH
HEY.
...IT MOVED ...
... HUH ?

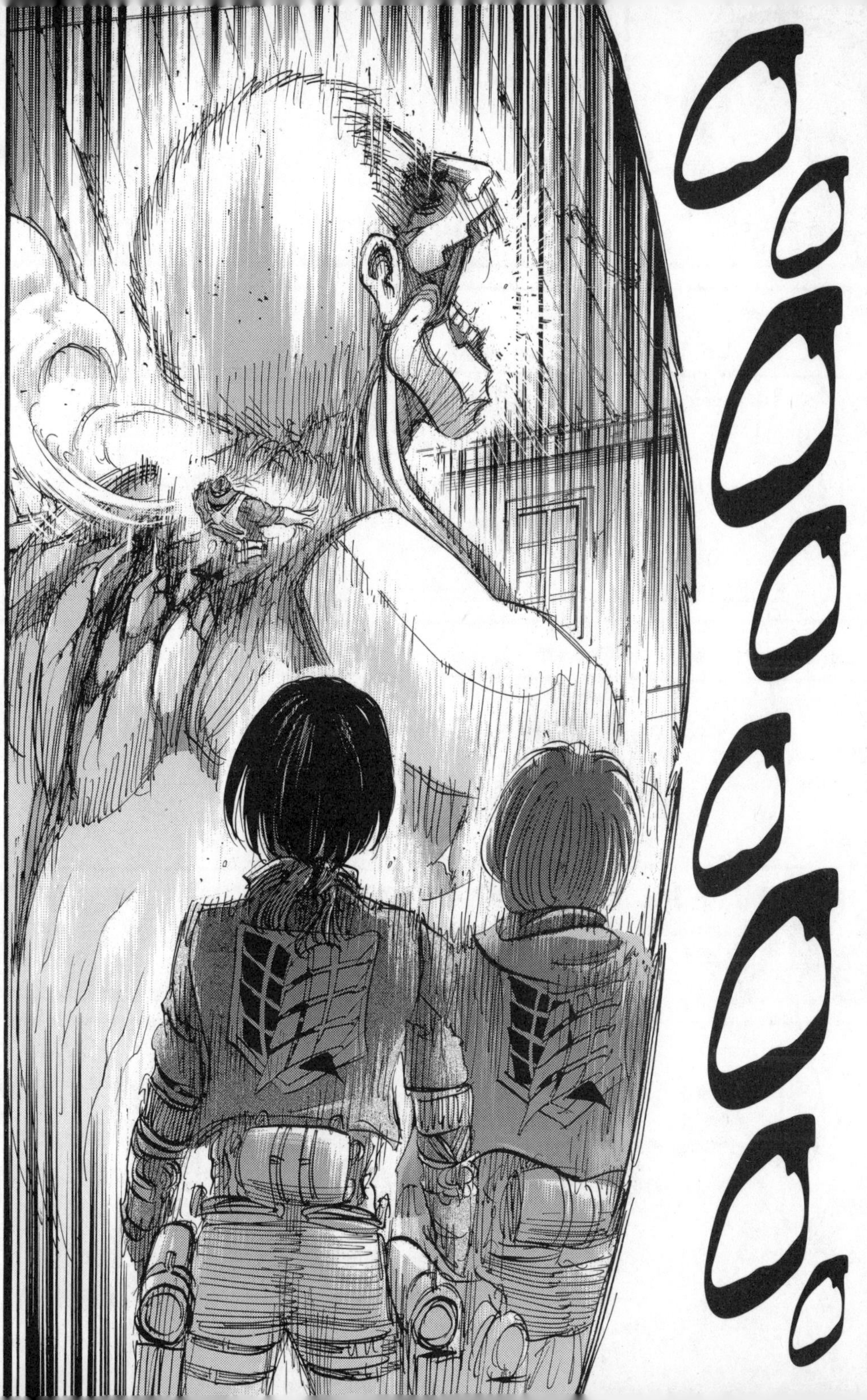
OOOOOOOO

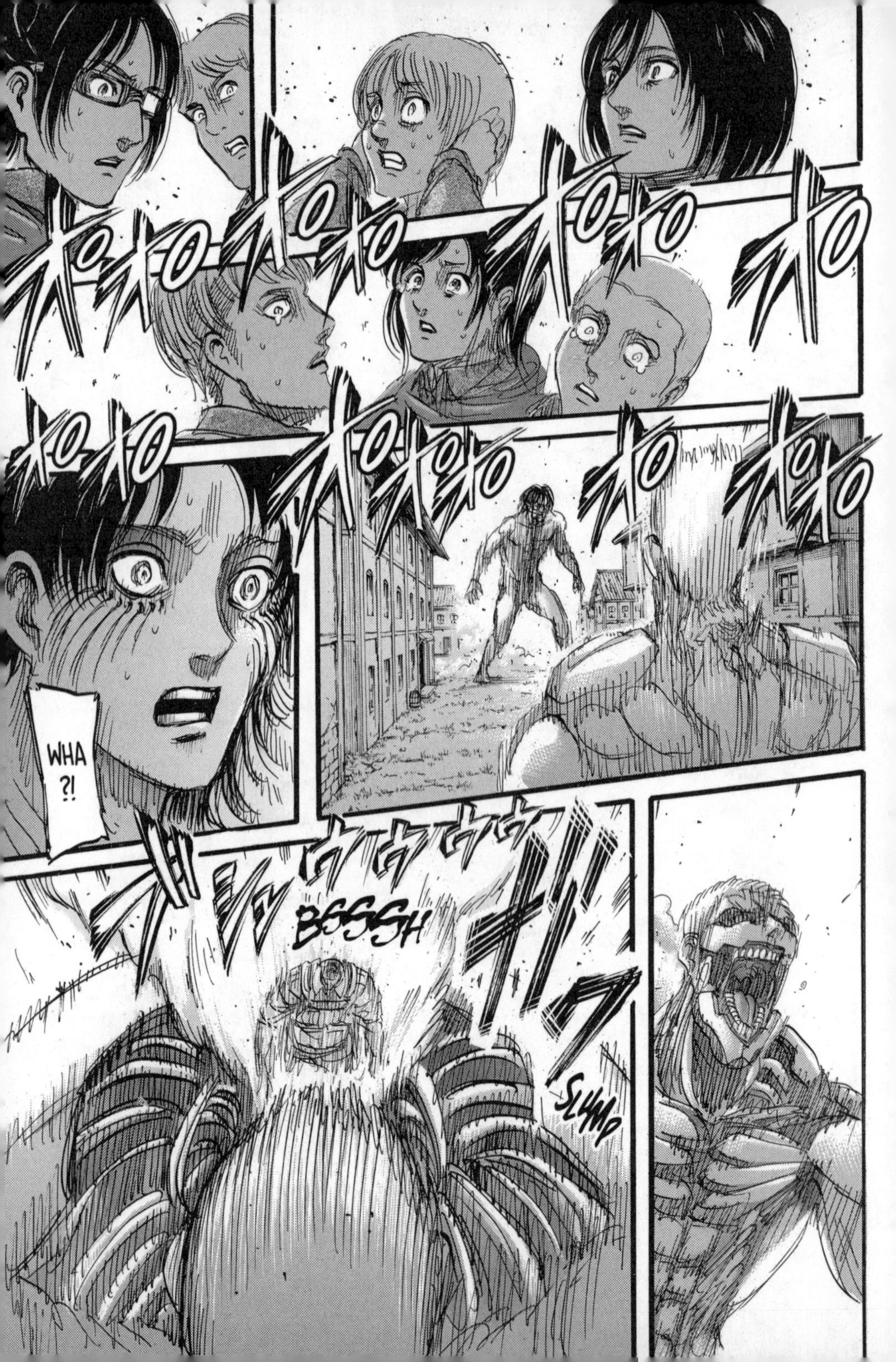
WHA ?!
BSSSH
SLUMP

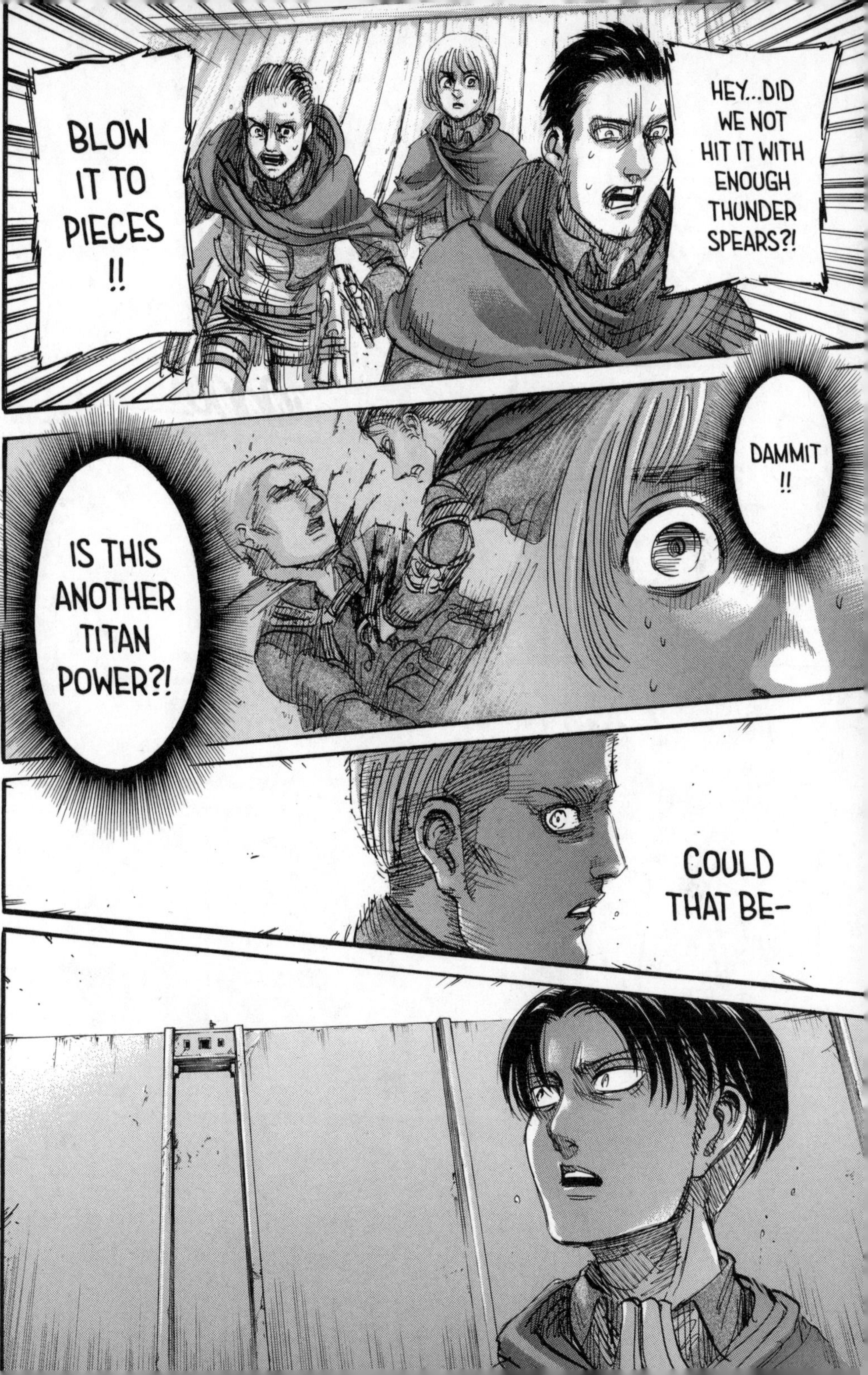
HEY...DID WE NOT HIT IT WITH ENOUGH THUNDER SPEARS?!
BLOW IT TO PIECES !!
DAMMIT !!
IS THIS ANOTHER TITAN POWER?!
COULD THAT BE-

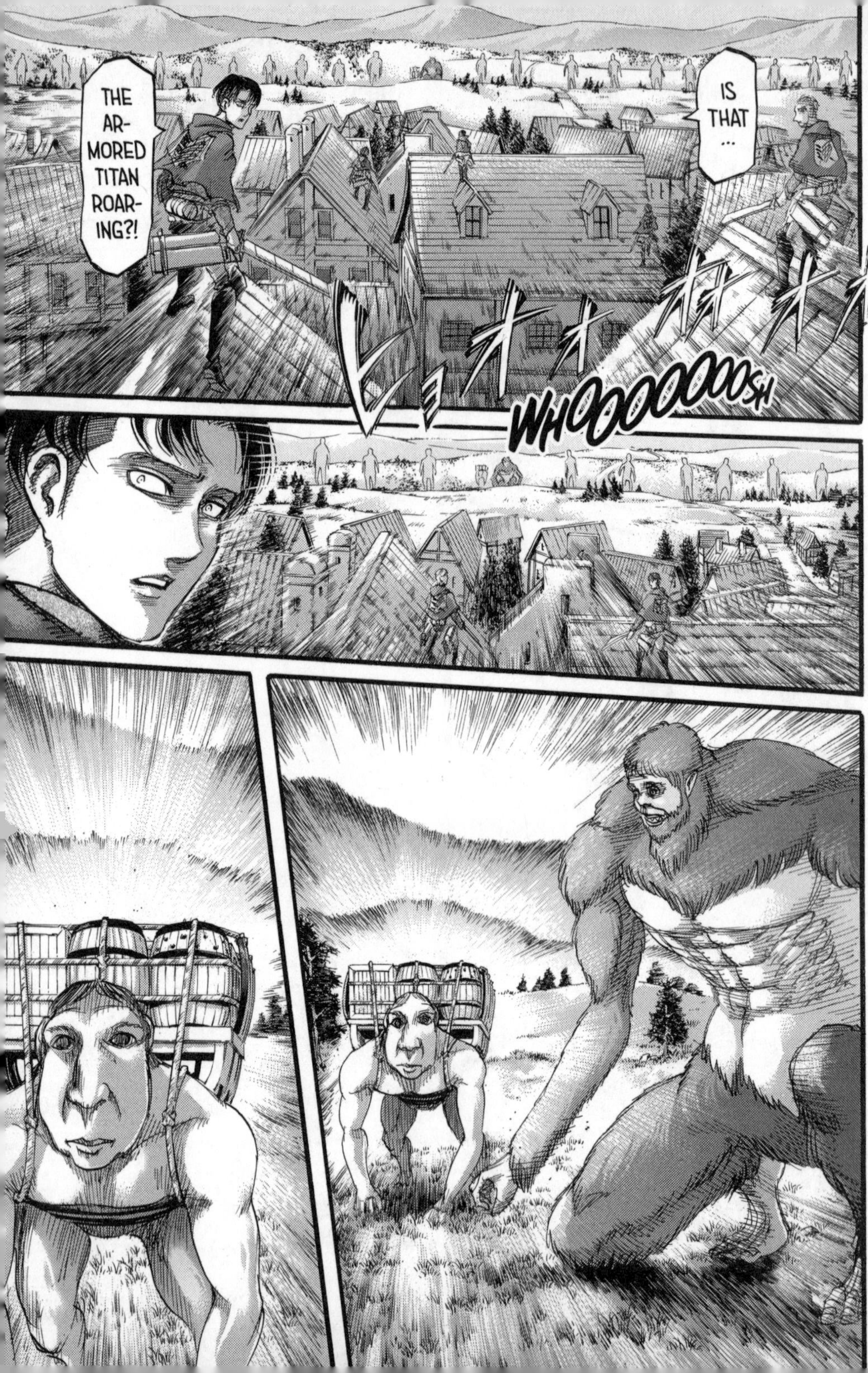

IS THAT ...
THE ARMORED TITAN ROARING?!
WHOOOOOOOSH

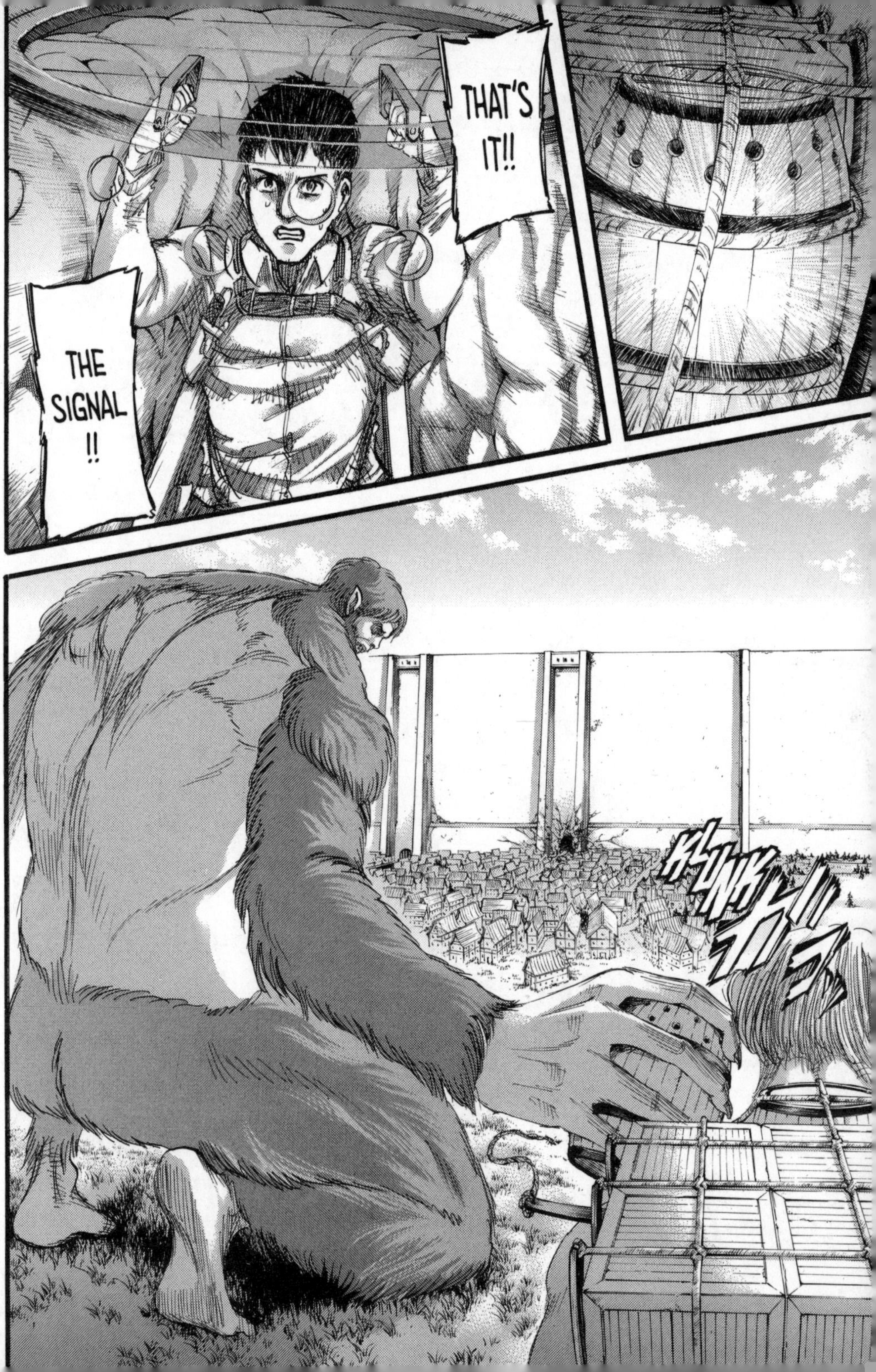
THAT'S IT!!
THE SIGNAL !!
KLUNK

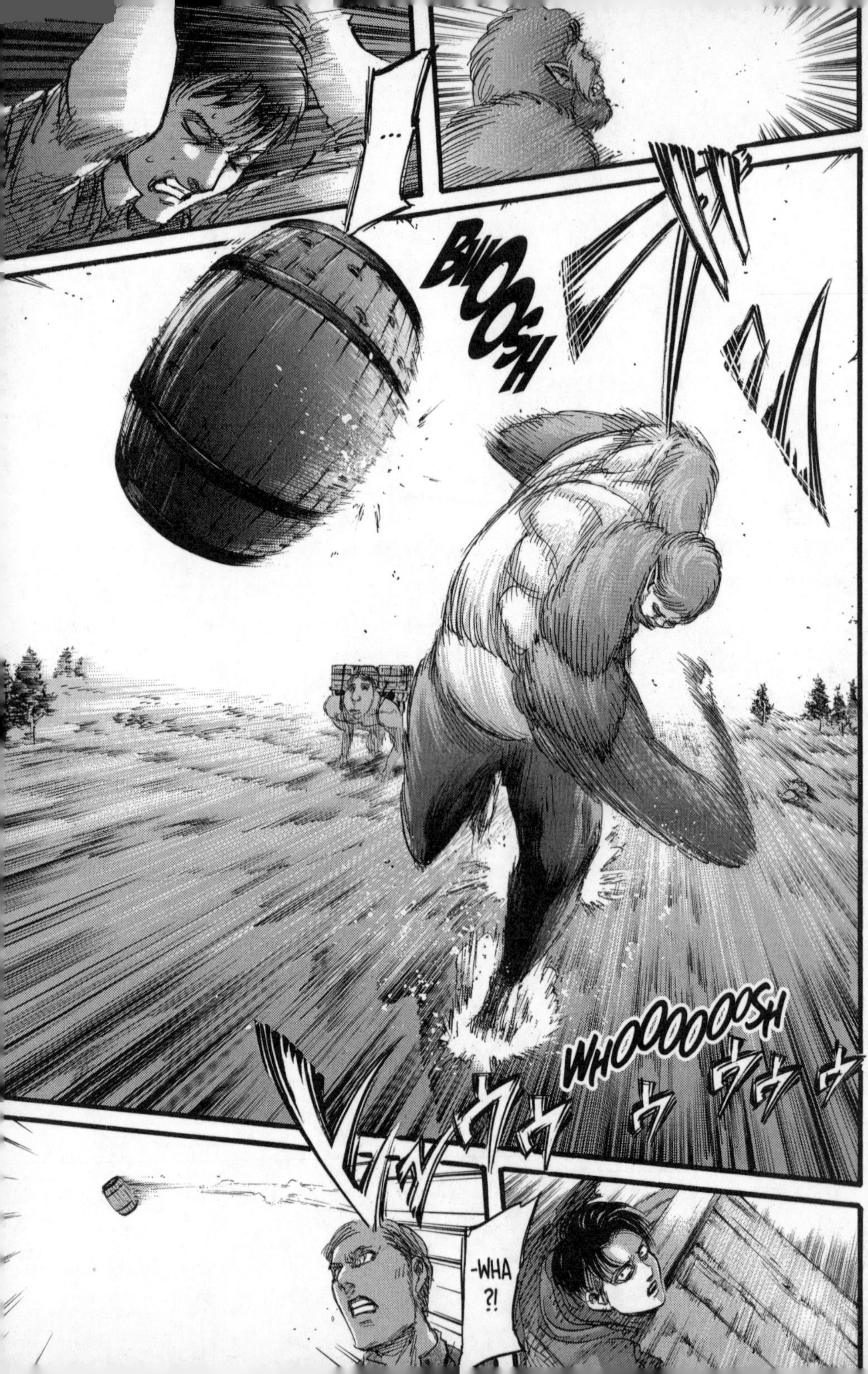
...
BWOOSH
WHOOOOOOOSH
-WHA ?!

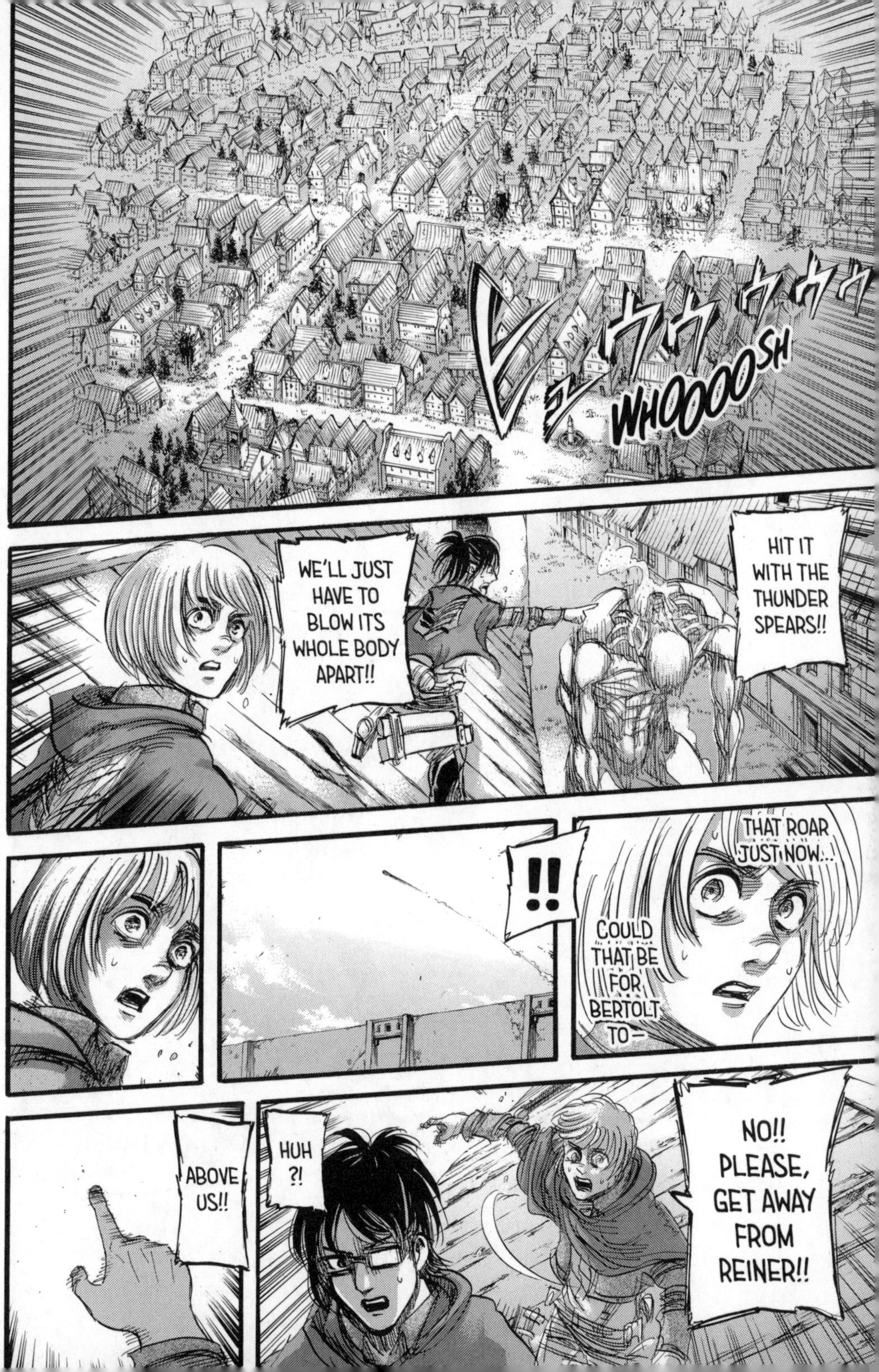
WHOOOOOSH
HIT IT WITH THE THUNDER SPEARS!!
WE'LL JUST HAVE TO BLOW ITS WHOLE BODY APART!!
THAT ROAR JUST NOW...
COULD THAT BE FOR BERTOLT TO—
!!
NO!! PLEASE, GET AWAY FROM REINER!!
HUH?!
ABOVE US!!

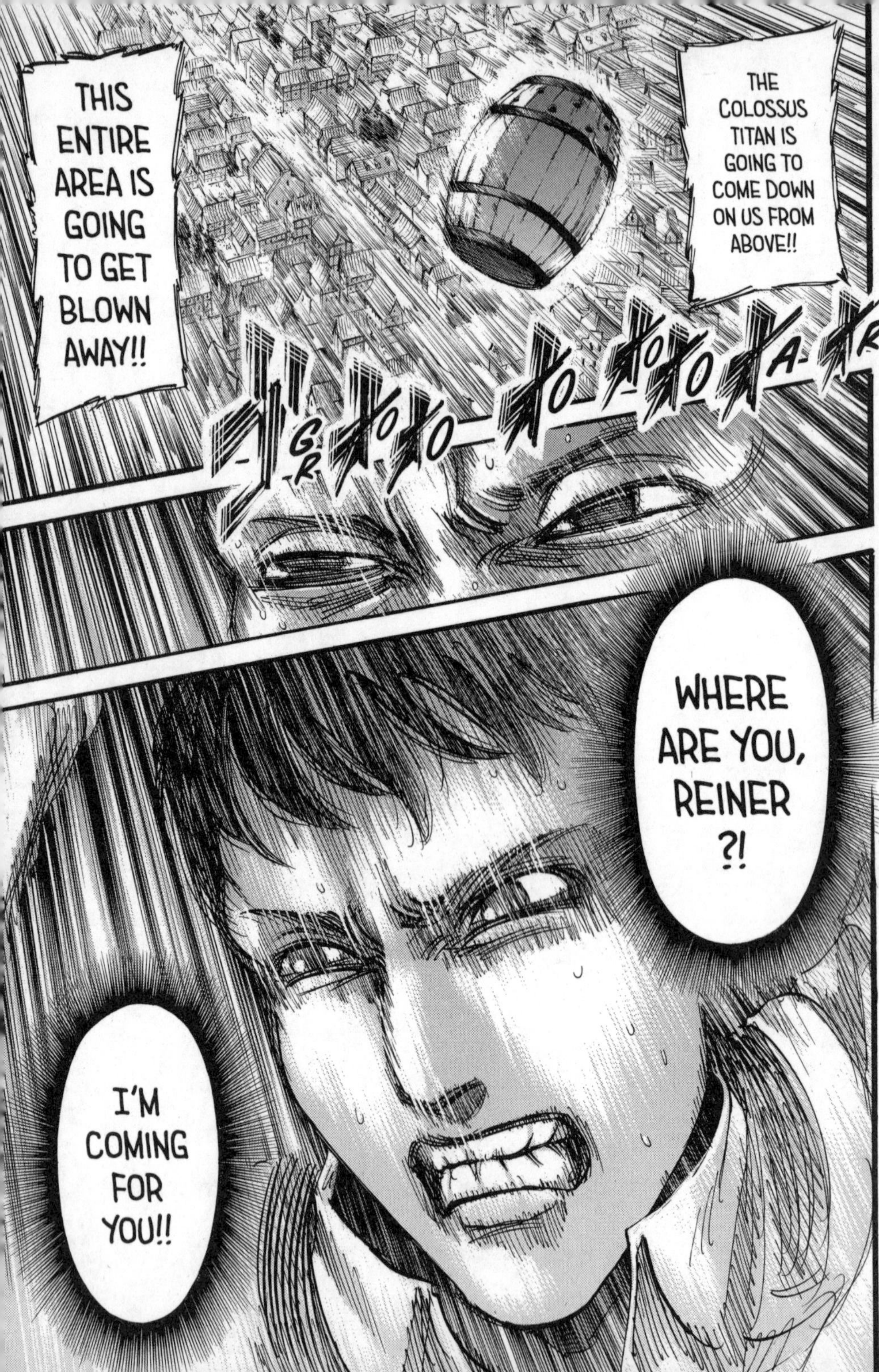
THE COLOSSUS TITAN IS GOING TO COME DOWN ON US FROM ABOVE!!
THIS ENTIRE AREA IS GOING TO GET BLOWN AWAY!!
WHERE ARE YOU, REINER ?!
I'M COMING FOR YOU!!

ATTACK on TITAN

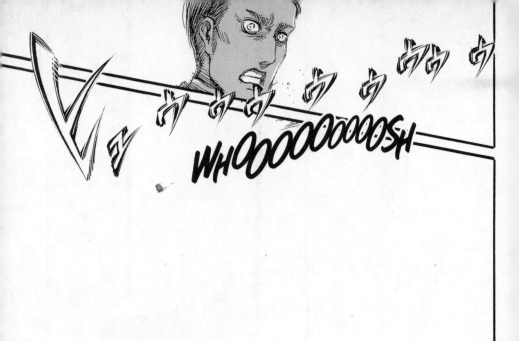

WHOOOOOOOOOSH

...AGH.

...THEY GOT US.

Episode 78: Descent

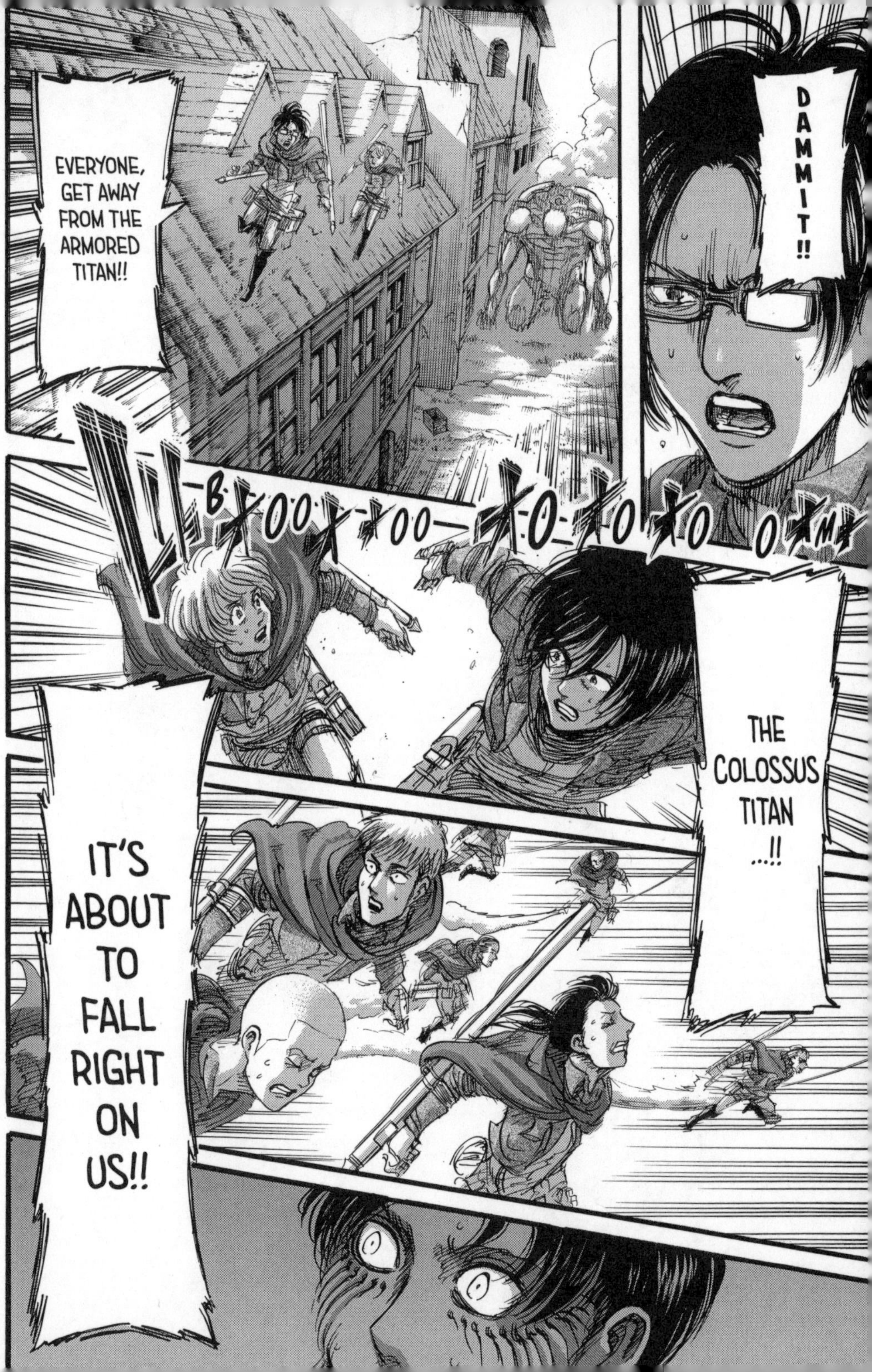
DAMMIT!!
EVERYONE, GET AWAY FROM THE ARMORED TITAN!!
THE COLOSSUS TITAN ...!!
IT'S ABOUT TO FALL RIGHT ON US!!

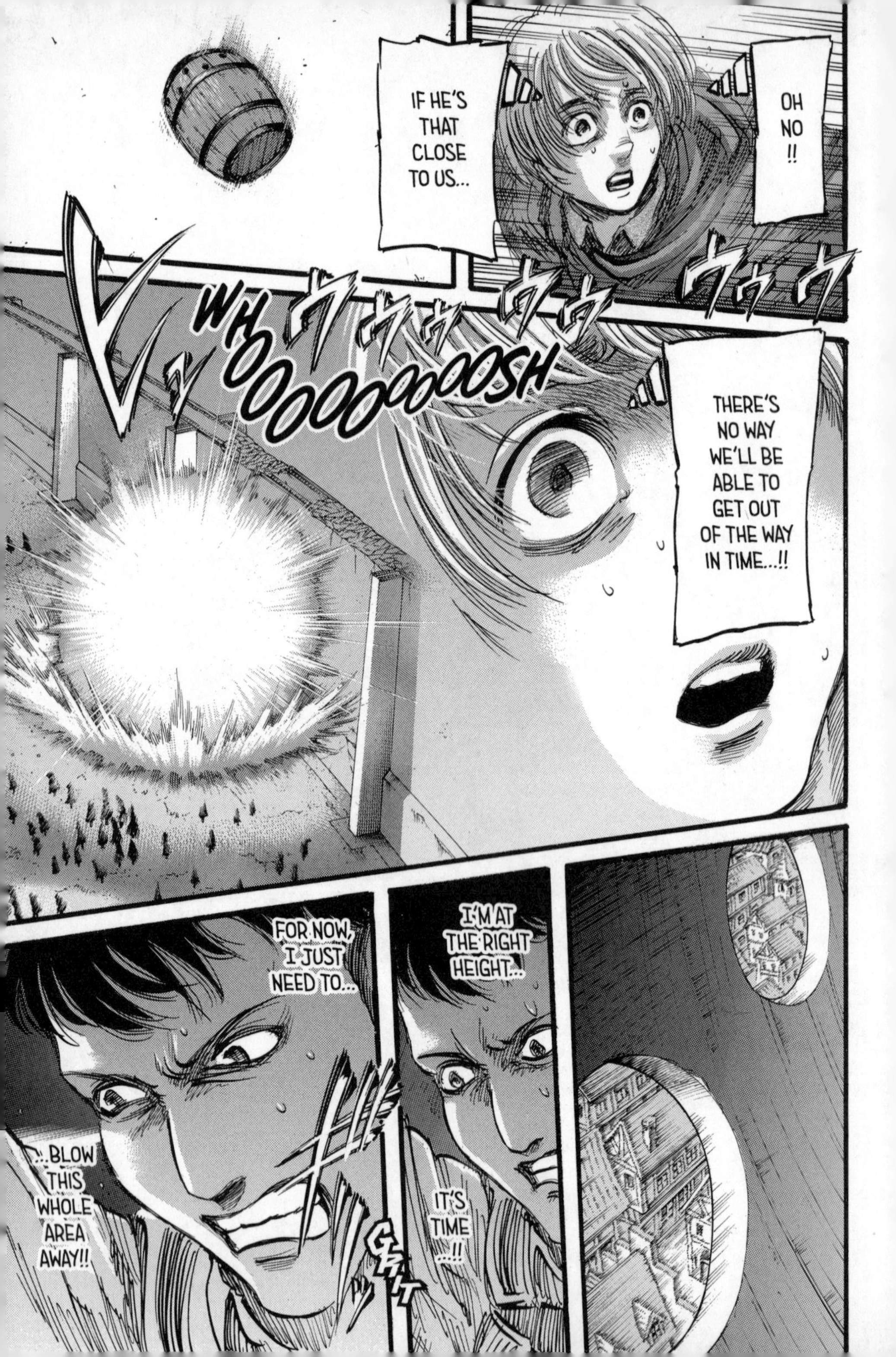
OH NO !!
IF HE'S THAT CLOSE TO US...
WHOOOOOOOOOOSH
ウウウ
THERE'S NO WAY WE'LL BE ABLE TO GET OUT OF THE WAY IN TIME...!!
I'M AT THE RIGHT HEIGHT...
IT'S TIME ...!!
FOR NOW, I JUST NEED TO...
...BLOW THIS WHOLE AREA AWAY!!
GRIT

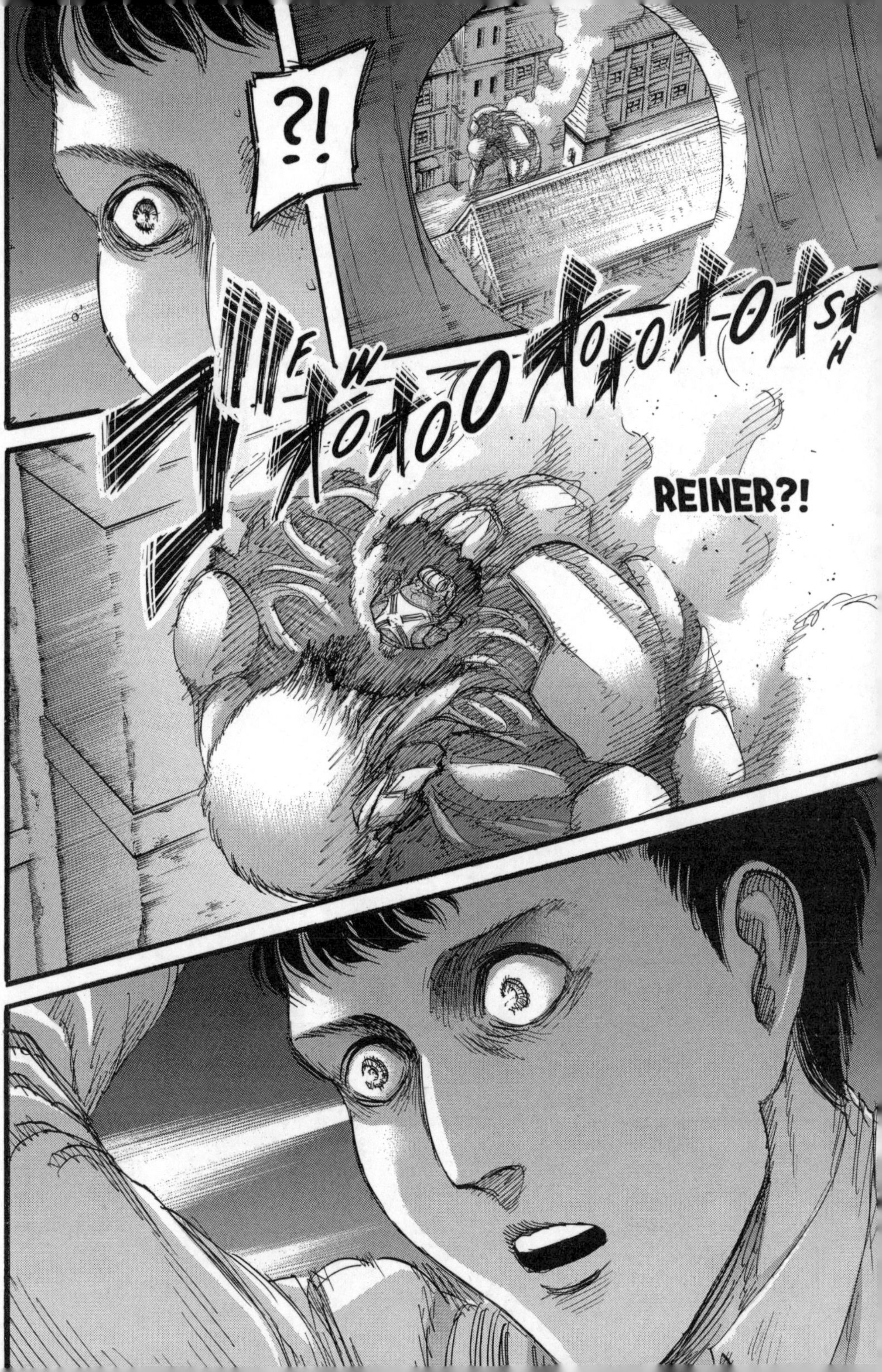
?!
FWOOOOOOOOOOSH
REINER?!

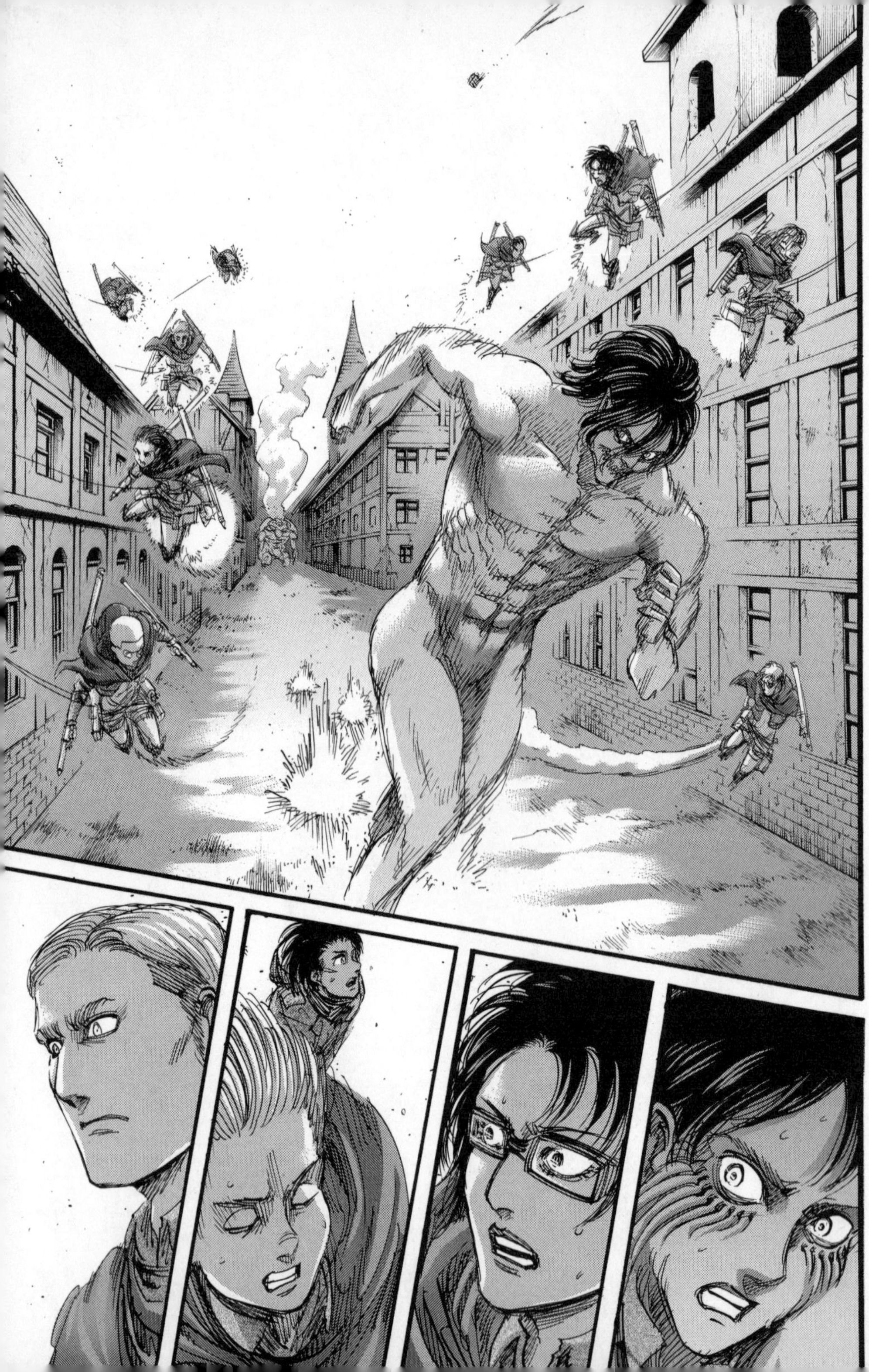

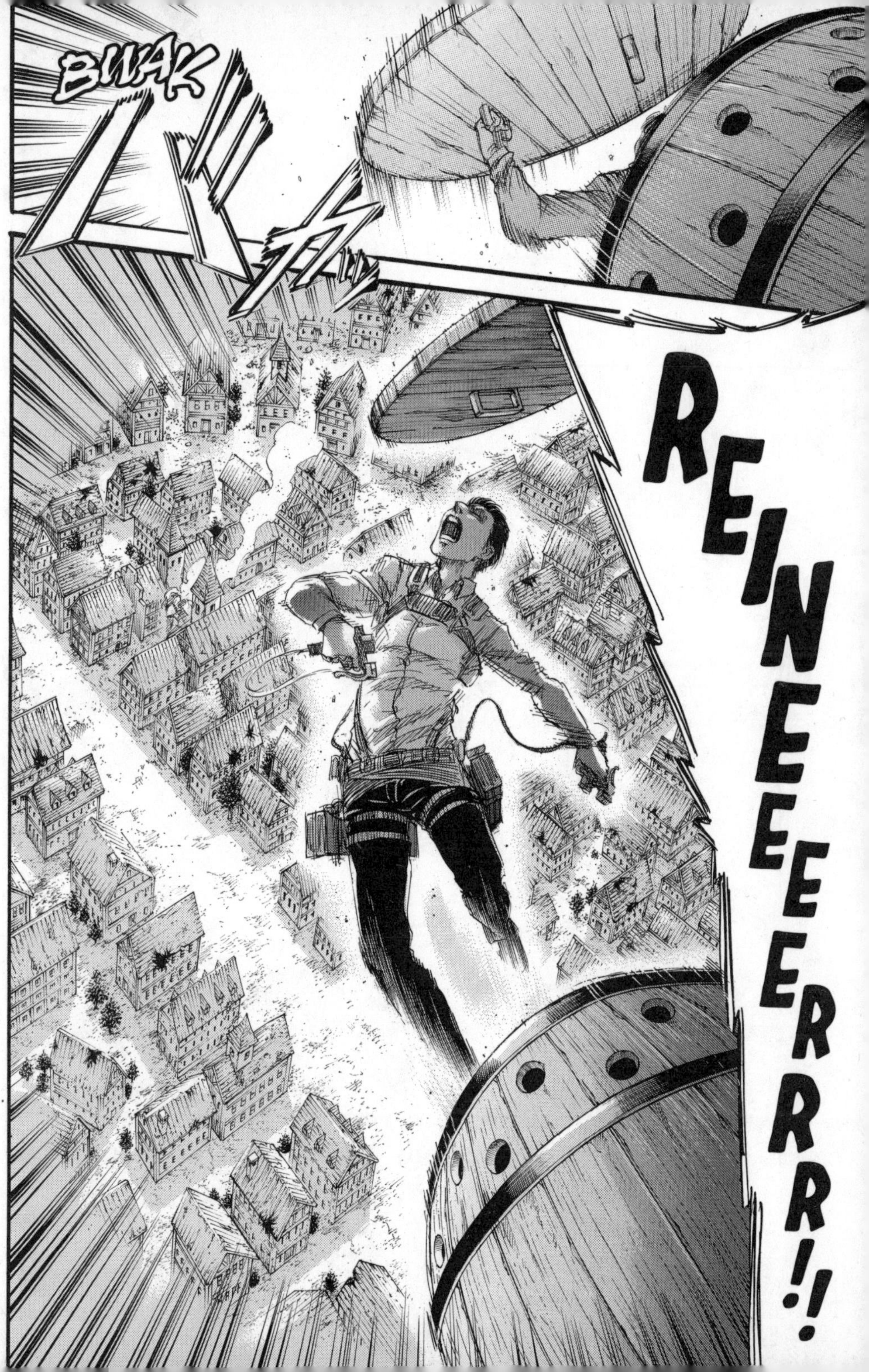
BWAK
REINEEEERRR!!

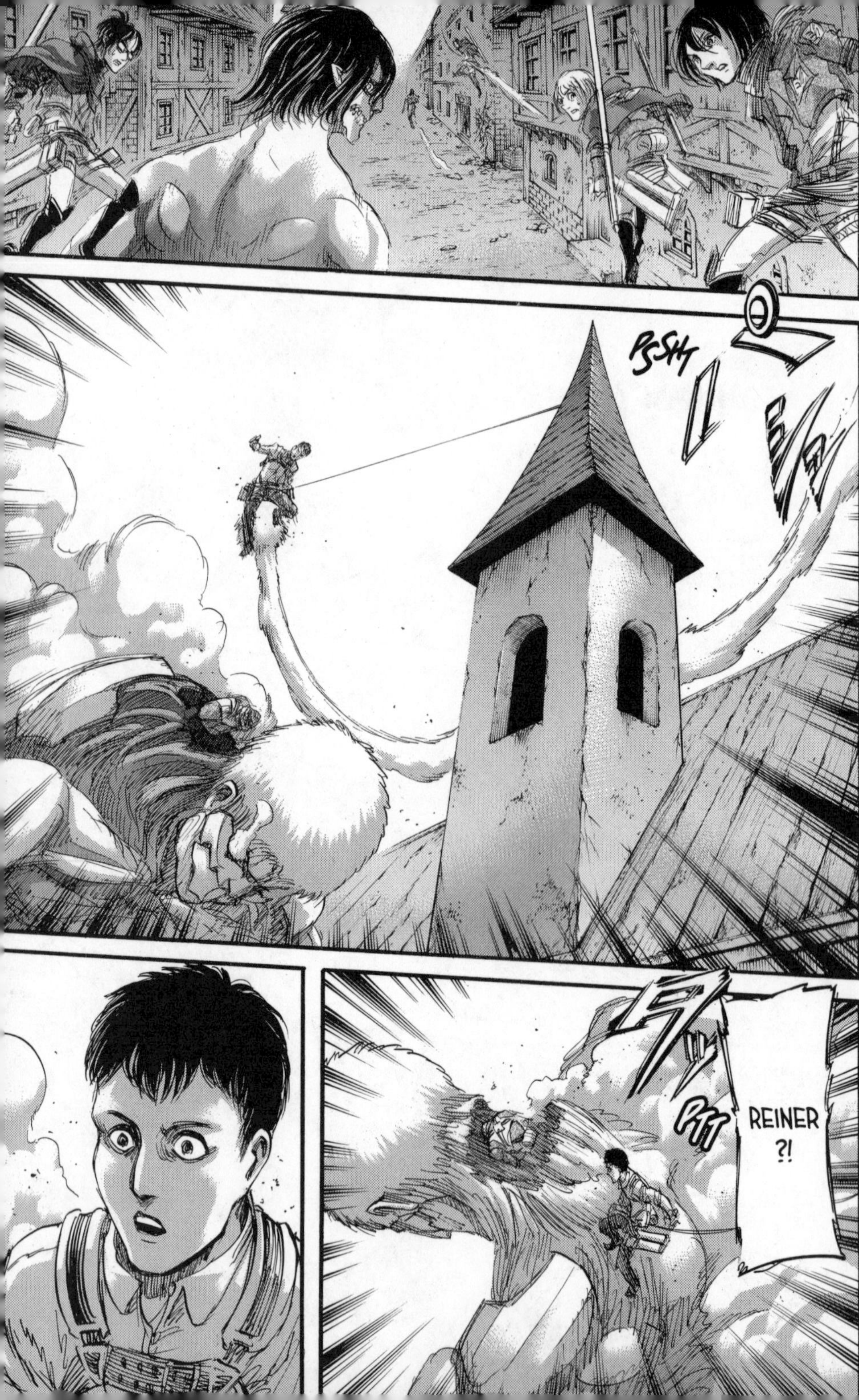
PSSH
REINER ?!
PTT

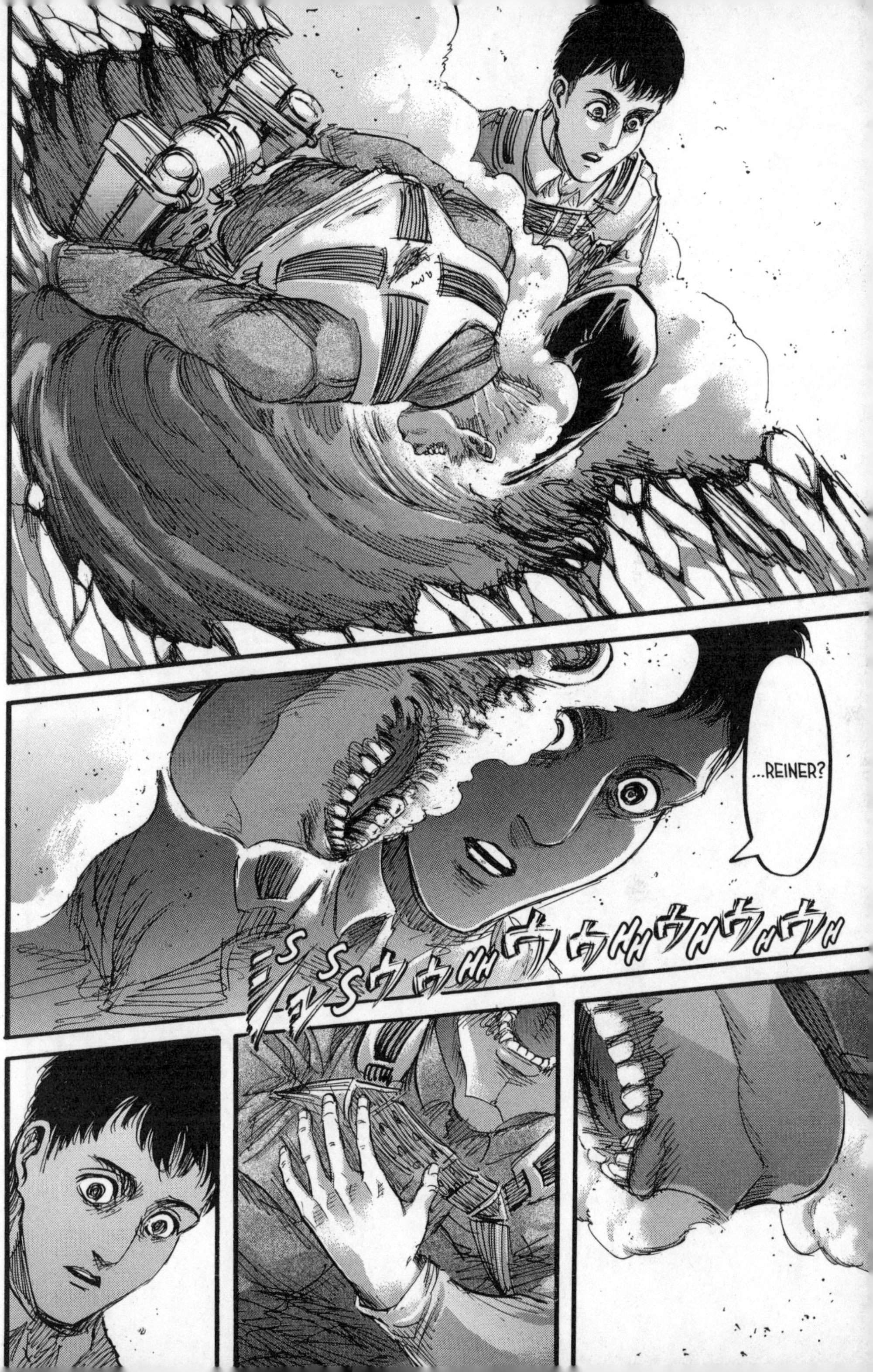
...REINER?

TH-THUMP
HE'S ALIVE.
TH-THUMP
SO ...
DOES THIS MEAN YOU WERE ABLE TO TRANSFER YOUR CONSCIOUSNESS ACROSS YOUR BODY'S NERVOUS SYSTEM?
TH-THUMP
...I SEE.
TH-THUMP
IF YOU USE YOUR NERVOUS SYSTEM WITH A TITAN'S BRAIN, YOU'LL EVEN BE ABLE TO RETAIN YOUR MEMORIES.
TH-THUMP
BUT... THAT'S A LAST RESORT.
I CAN'T BELIEVE YOU'D ACTUALLY DO IT...

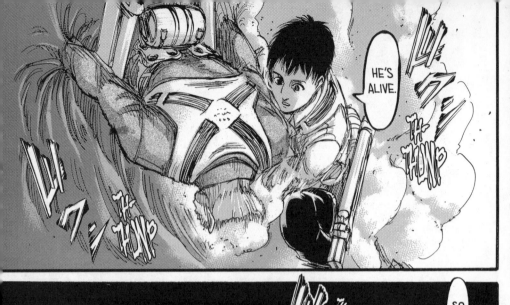

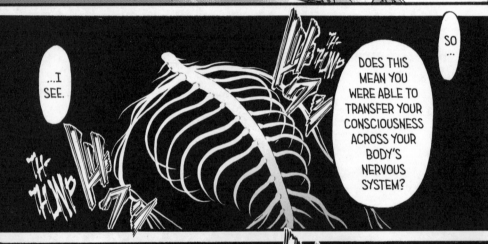

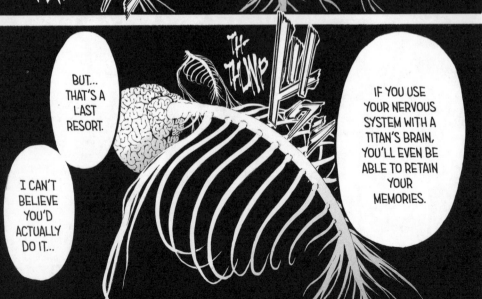

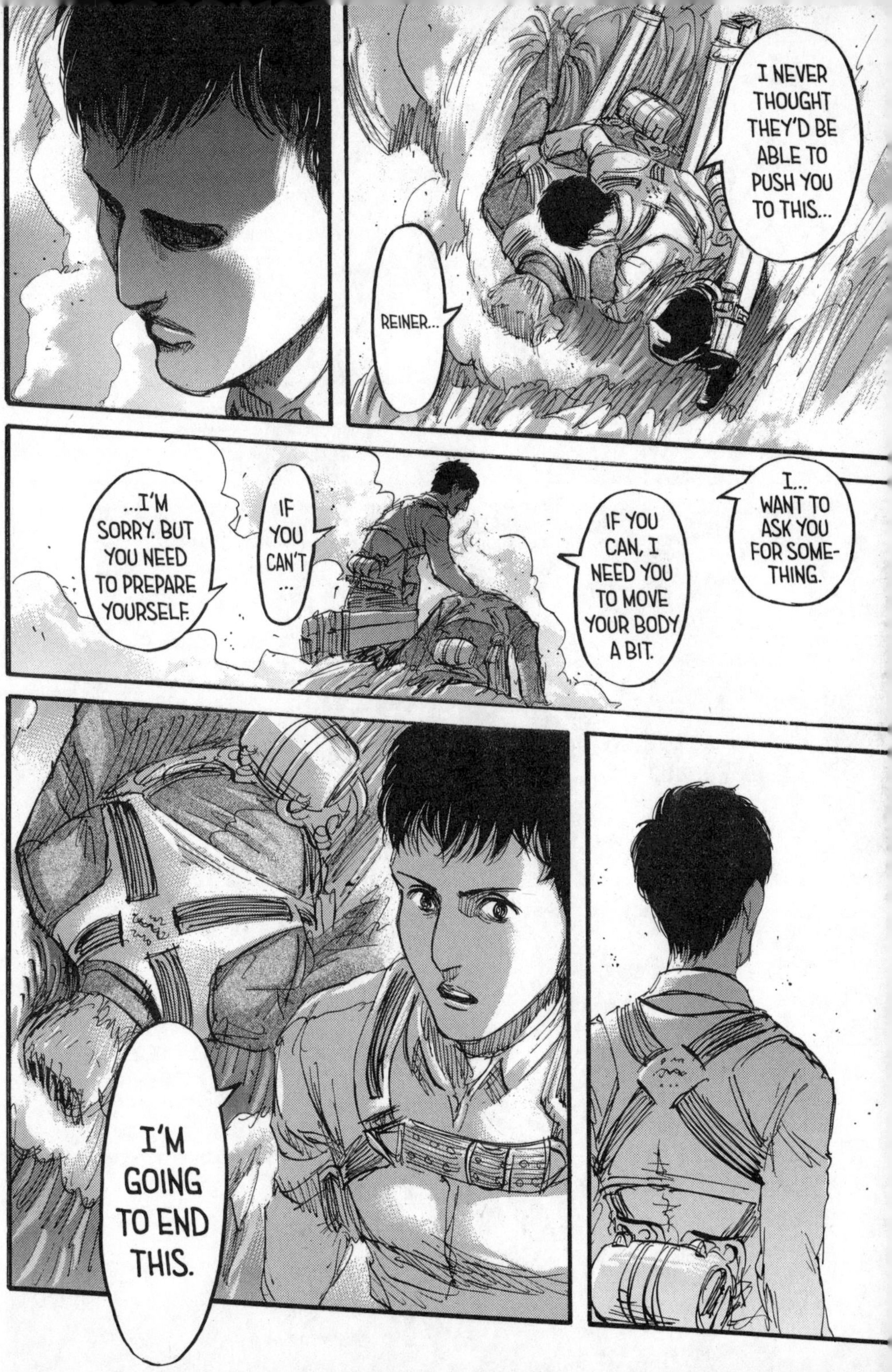
I NEVER THOUGHT THEY'D BE ABLE TO PUSH YOU TO THIS...
REINER...
I... WANT TO ASK YOU FOR SOME-THING.
IF YOU CAN, I NEED YOU TO MOVE YOUR BODY A BIT.
IF YOU CAN'T ...
...I'M SORRY. BUT YOU NEED TO PREPARE YOURSELF.
I'M GOING TO END THIS.

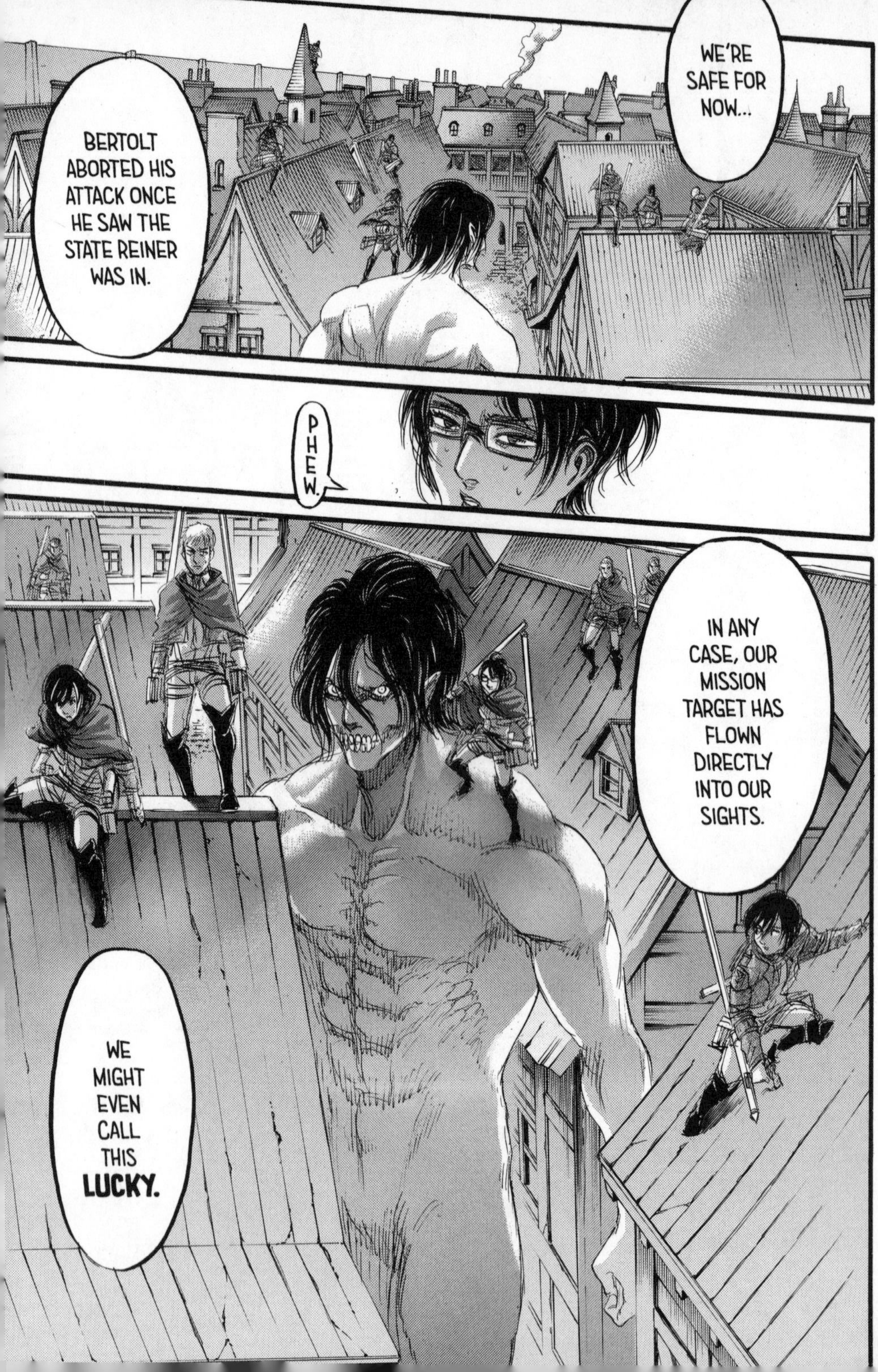
WE'RE SAFE FOR NOW...
BERTOLT ABORTED HIS ATTACK ONCE HE SAW THE STATE REINER WAS IN.
PHEW.
IN ANY CASE, OUR MISSION TARGET HAS FLOWN DIRECTLY INTO OUR SIGHTS.
WE MIGHT EVEN CALL THIS **LUCKY.**

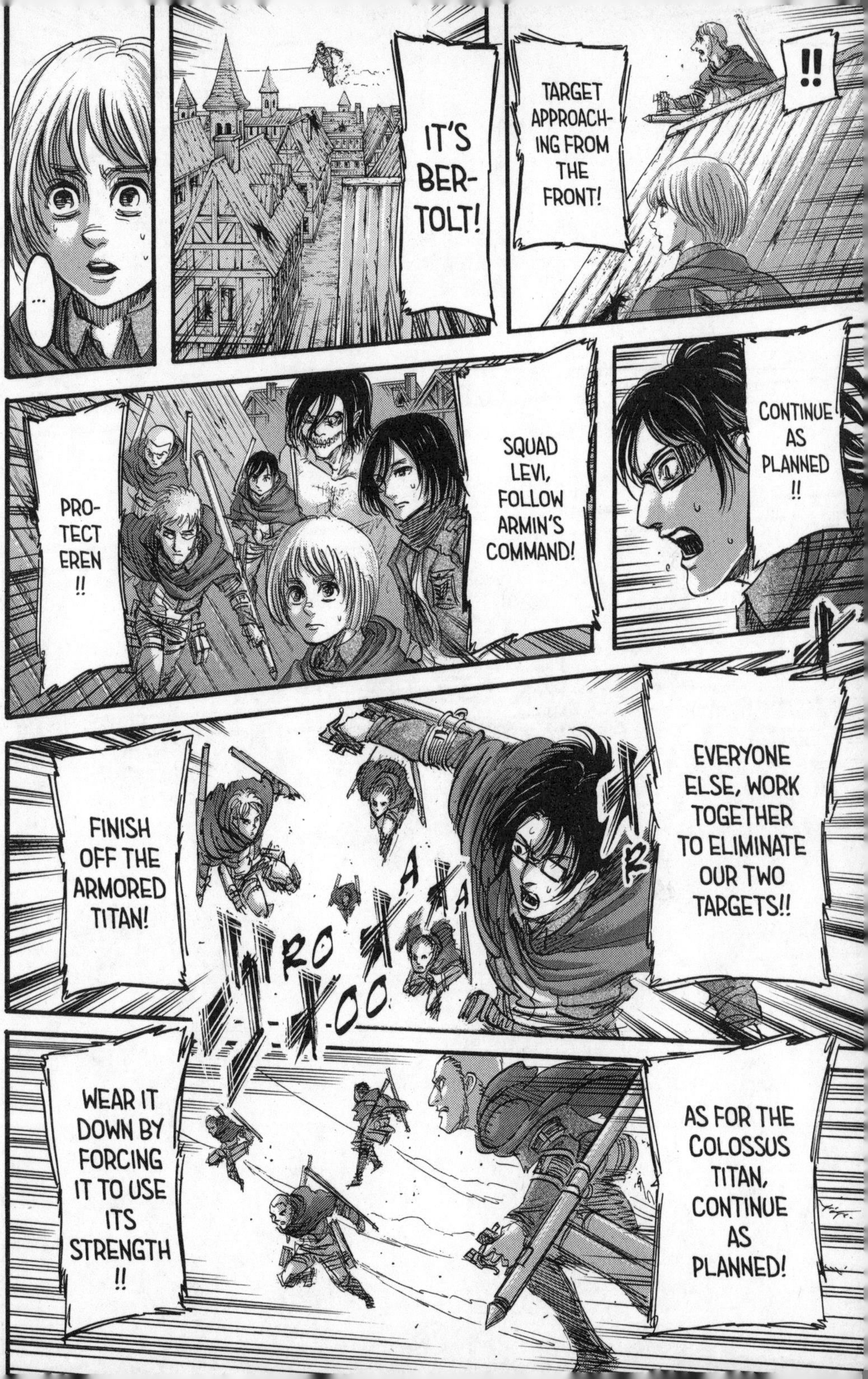
!!
TARGET APPROACHING FROM THE FRONT!
IT'S BERTOLT!
...
CONTINUE AS PLANNED!!
SQUAD LEVI, FOLLOW ARMIN'S COMMAND!
PROTECT EREN!!
EVERYONE ELSE, WORK TOGETHER TO ELIMINATE OUR TWO TARGETS!!
FINISH OFF THE ARMORED TITAN!
AS FOR THE COLOSSUS TITAN, CONTINUE AS PLANNED!
WEAR IT DOWN BY FORCING IT TO USE ITS STRENGTH!!

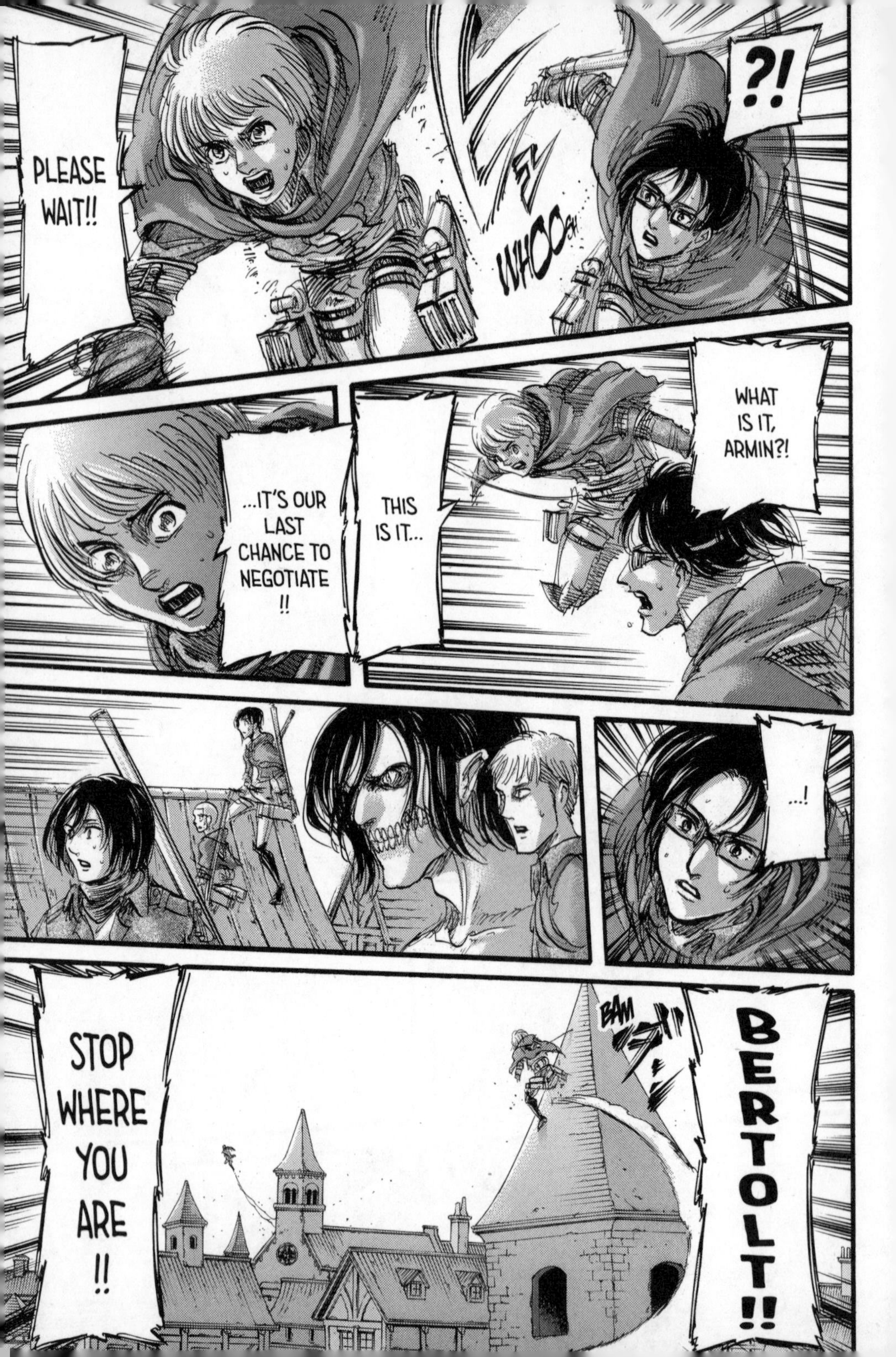
?!
WHOOSH
PLEASE WAIT!!
WHAT IS IT, ARMIN?!
THIS IS IT...
...IT'S OUR LAST CHANCE TO NEGOTIATE !!
...!
BERTOLT!!
BAM
STOP WHERE YOU ARE !!

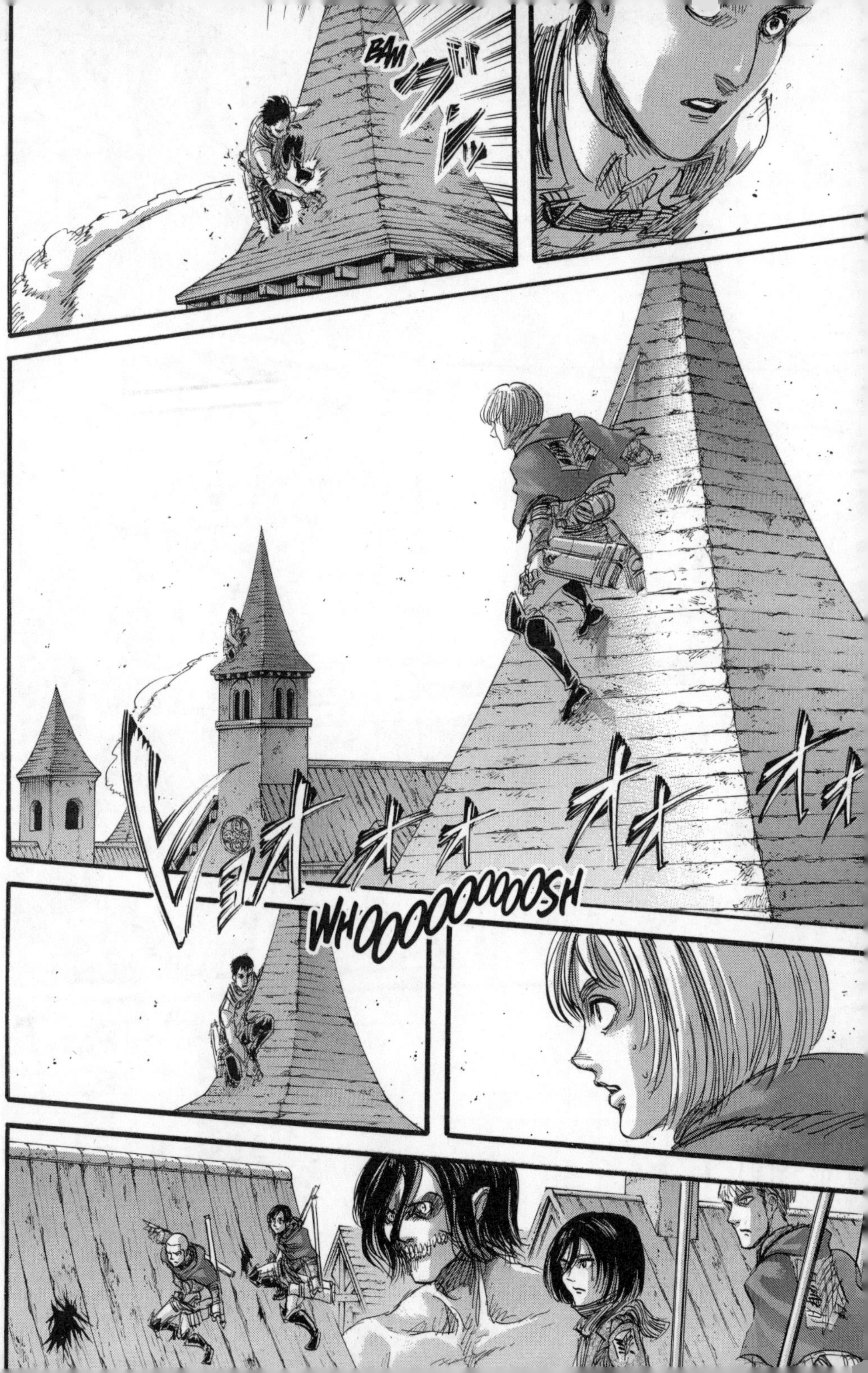
BAM
WHOOOOOOOOOSH

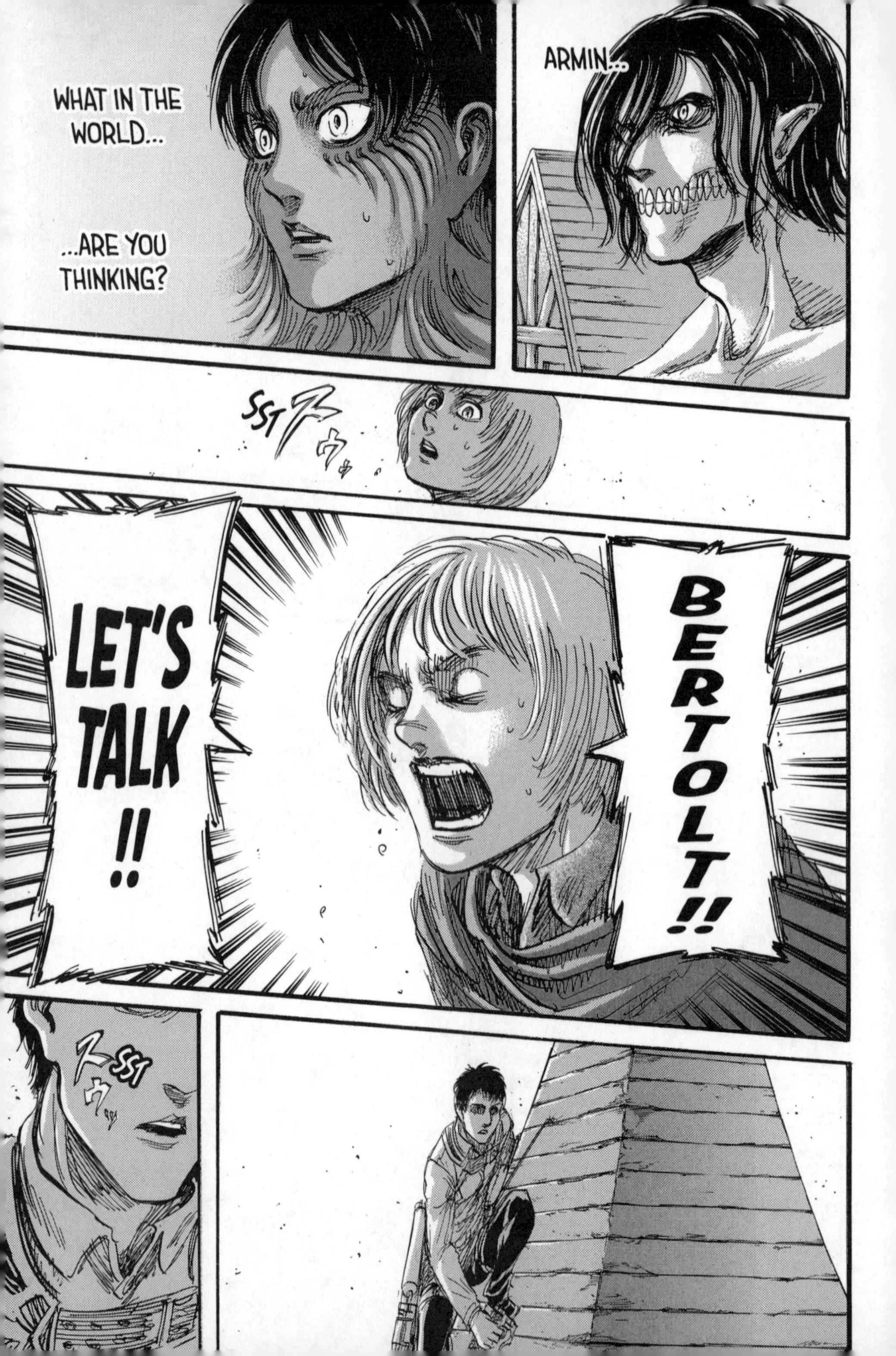
ARMIN...
WHAT IN THE WORLD...
...ARE YOU THINKING?
SST スゥ
BERTOLT!!
LET'S TALK!!
SST スゥ

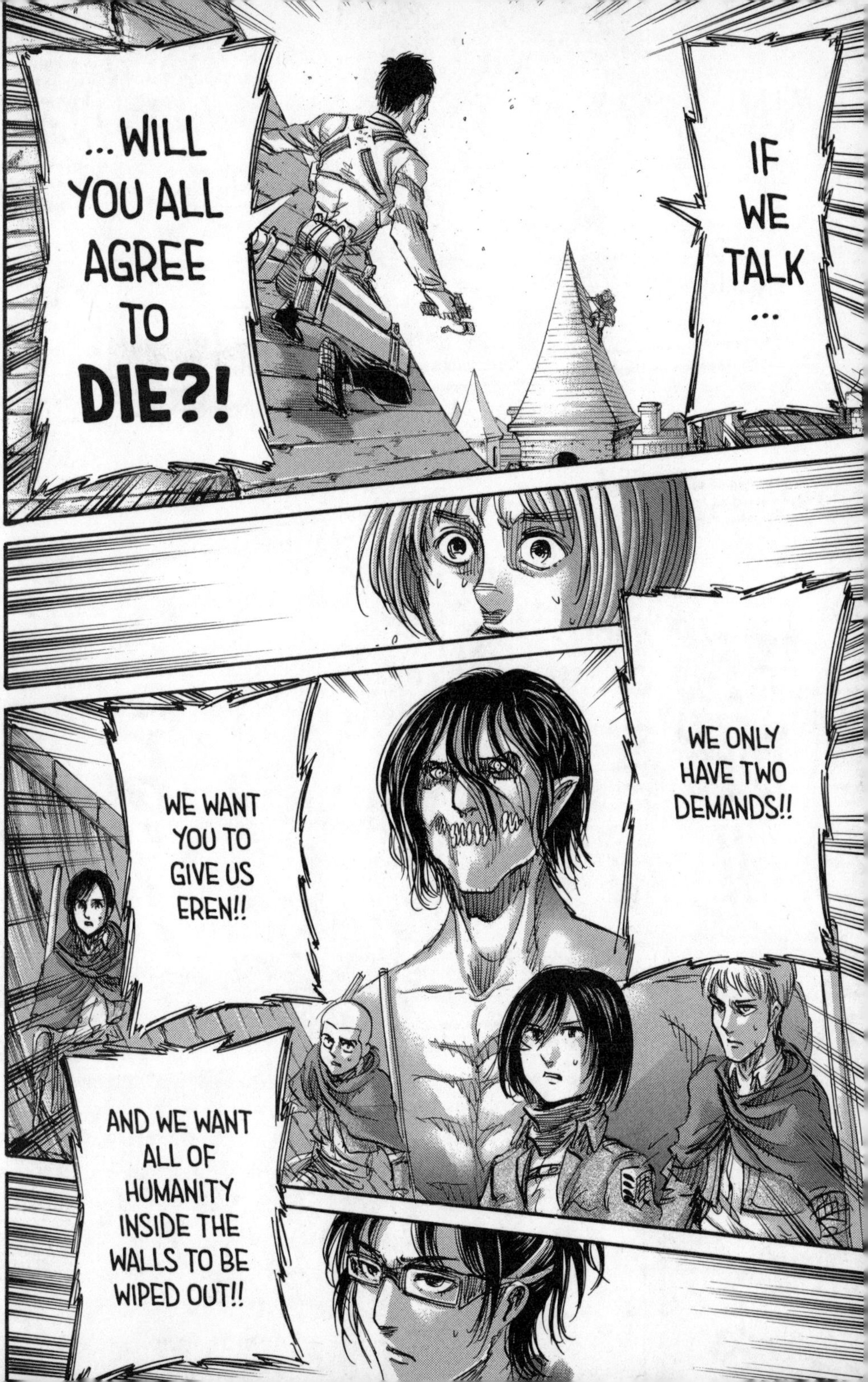
IF WE TALK ...
... WILL YOU ALL AGREE TO DIE?!
WE ONLY HAVE TWO DEMANDS!!
WE WANT YOU TO GIVE US EREN!!
AND WE WANT ALL OF HUMANITY INSIDE THE WALLS TO BE WIPED OUT!!

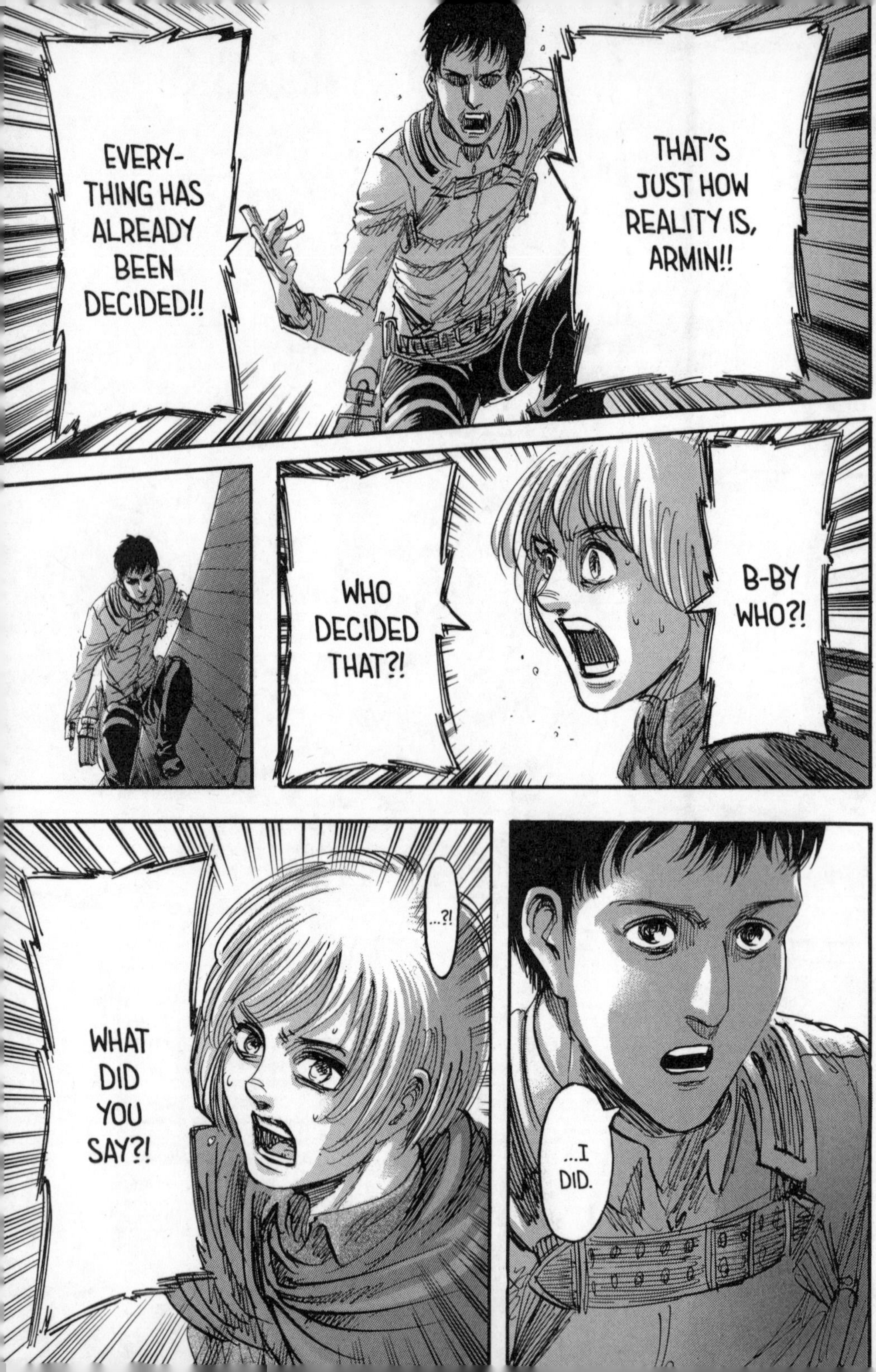
THAT'S JUST HOW REALITY IS, ARMIN!!
EVERY-THING HAS ALREADY BEEN DECIDED!!
B-BY WHO?!
WHO DECIDED THAT?!
...I DID.
...?!
WHAT DID YOU SAY?!

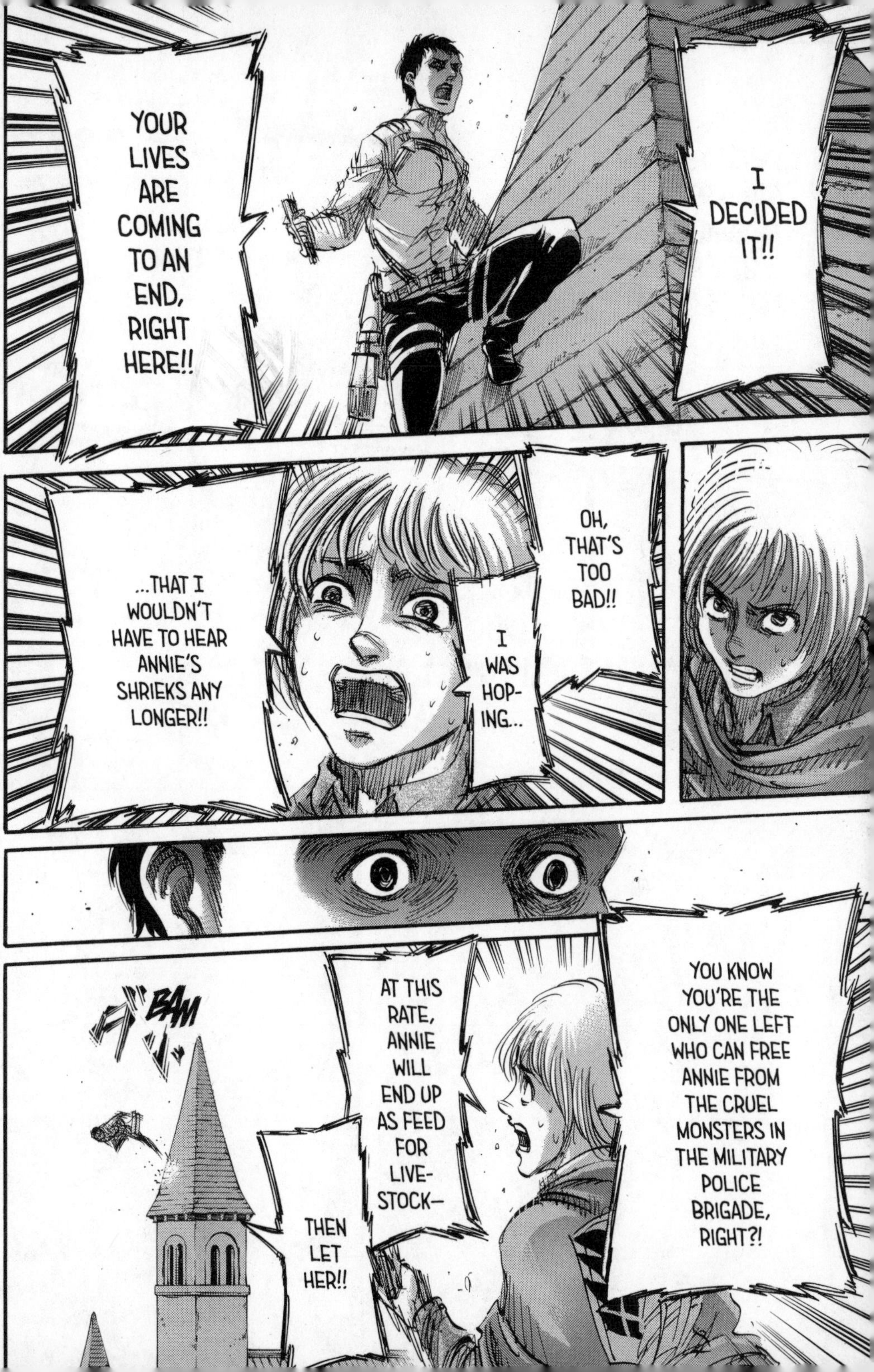
I DECIDED IT!!
YOUR LIVES ARE COMING TO AN END, RIGHT HERE!!
OH, THAT'S TOO BAD!!
I WAS HOP-ING...
...THAT I WOULDN'T HAVE TO HEAR ANNIE'S SHRIEKS ANY LONGER!!
YOU KNOW YOU'RE THE ONLY ONE LEFT WHO CAN FREE ANNIE FROM THE CRUEL MONSTERS IN THE MILITARY POLICE BRIGADE, RIGHT?!
AT THIS RATE, ANNIE WILL END UP AS FEED FOR LIVE-STOCK—
THEN LET HER!!
BAM

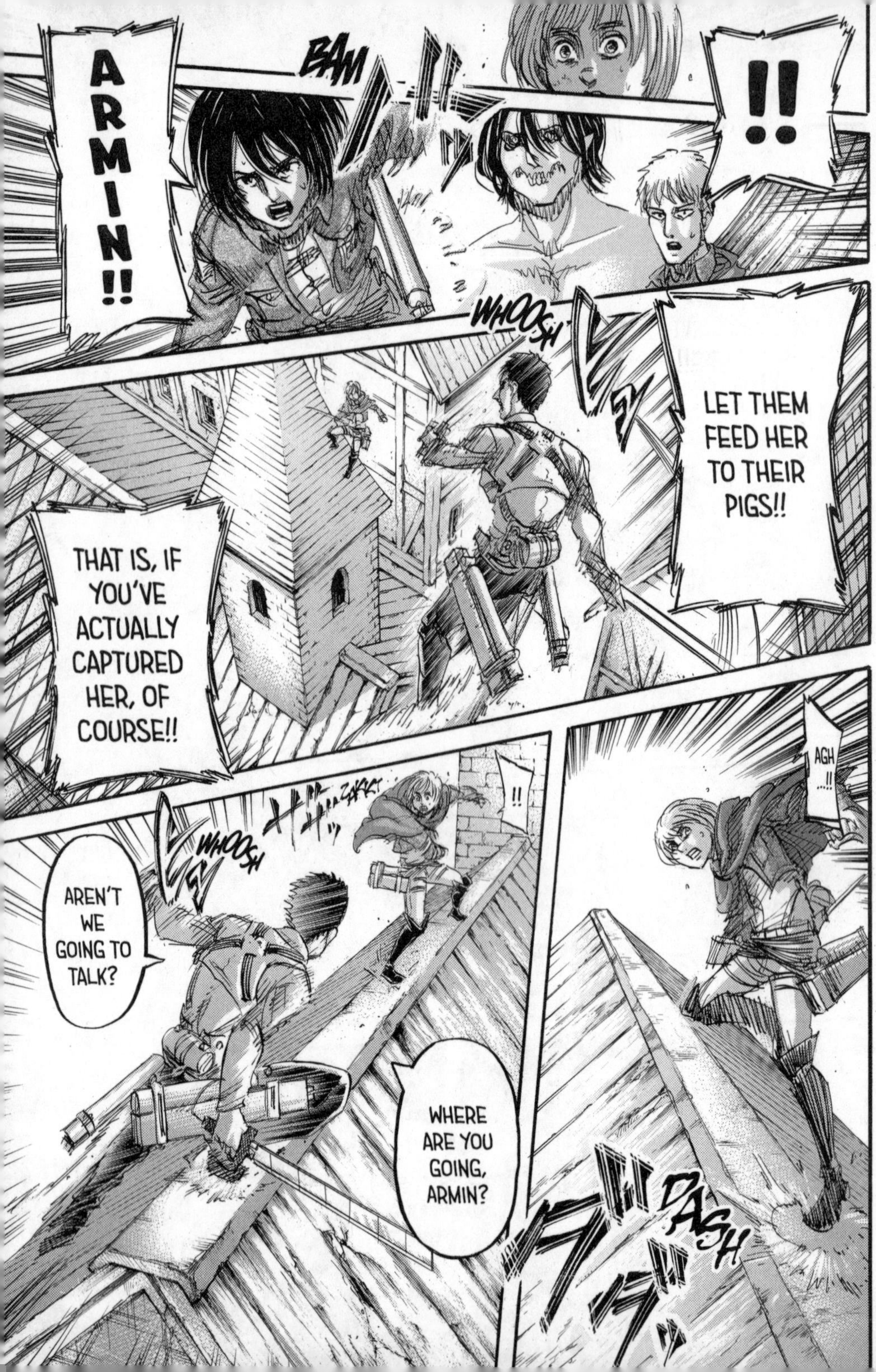
!!
BAM
ARMIN!!
LET THEM FEED HER TO THEIR PIGS!!
WHOOSH
THAT IS, IF YOU'VE ACTUALLY CAPTURED HER, OF COURSE!!
AGH ...!!
DASH
!!
WHOOSH
AREN'T WE GOING TO TALK?
WHERE ARE YOU GOING, ARMIN?

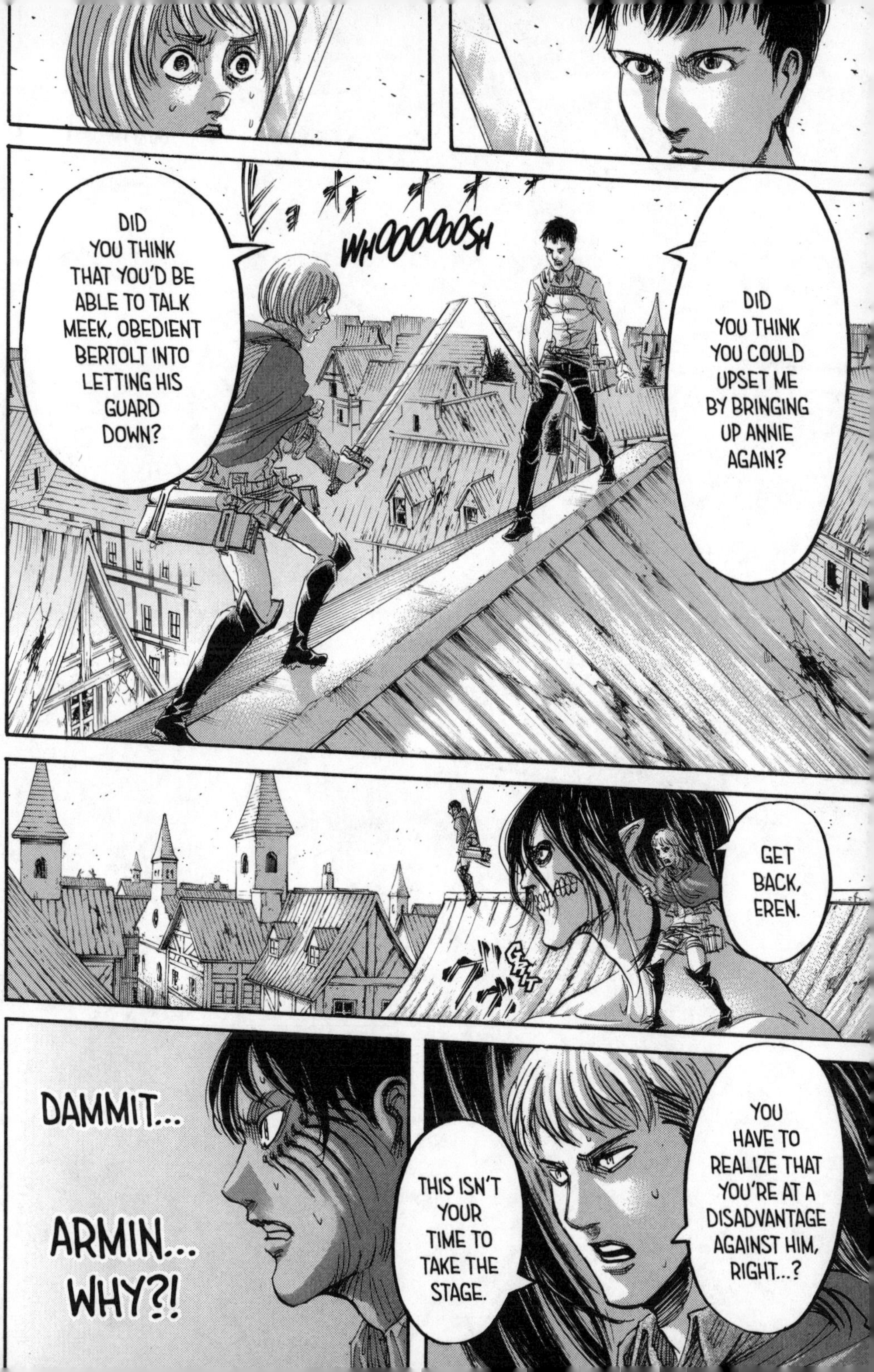
DID YOU THINK YOU COULD UPSET ME BY BRINGING UP ANNIE AGAIN?
WHOOOOOOSH
DID YOU THINK THAT YOU'D BE ABLE TO TALK MEEK, OBEDIENT BERTOLT INTO LETTING HIS GUARD DOWN?
GET BACK, EREN.
GRIT
YOU HAVE TO REALIZE THAT YOU'RE AT A DISADVANTAGE AGAINST HIM, RIGHT...?
THIS ISN'T YOUR TIME TO TAKE THE STAGE.
DAMMIT...
ARMIN... WHY?!

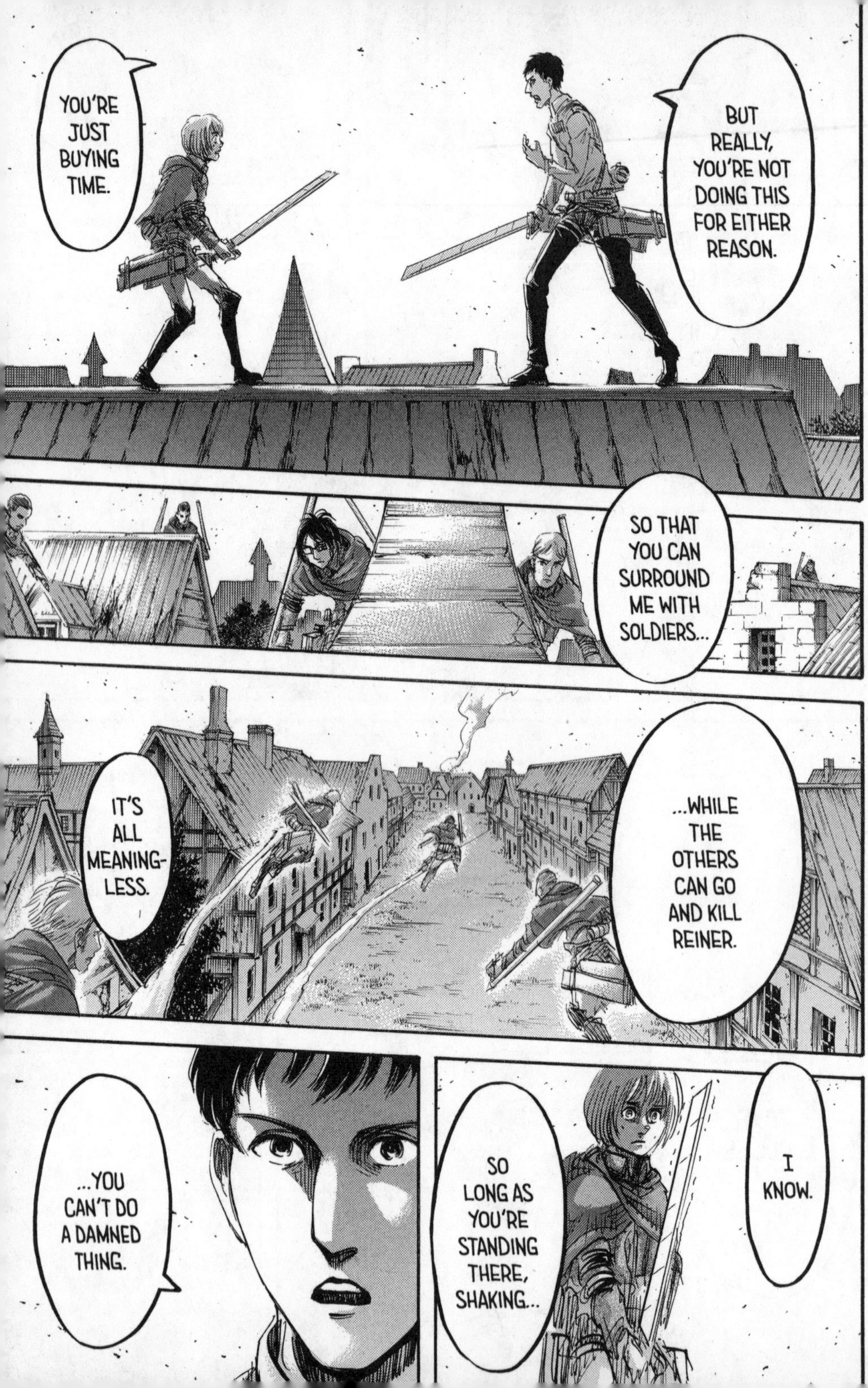
BUT REALLY, YOU'RE NOT DOING THIS FOR EITHER REASON.
YOU'RE JUST BUYING TIME.
SO THAT YOU CAN SURROUND ME WITH SOLDIERS...
...WHILE THE OTHERS CAN GO AND KILL REINER.
IT'S ALL MEANING-LESS.
I KNOW.
SO LONG AS YOU'RE STANDING THERE, SHAKING...
...YOU CAN'T DO A DAMNED THING.

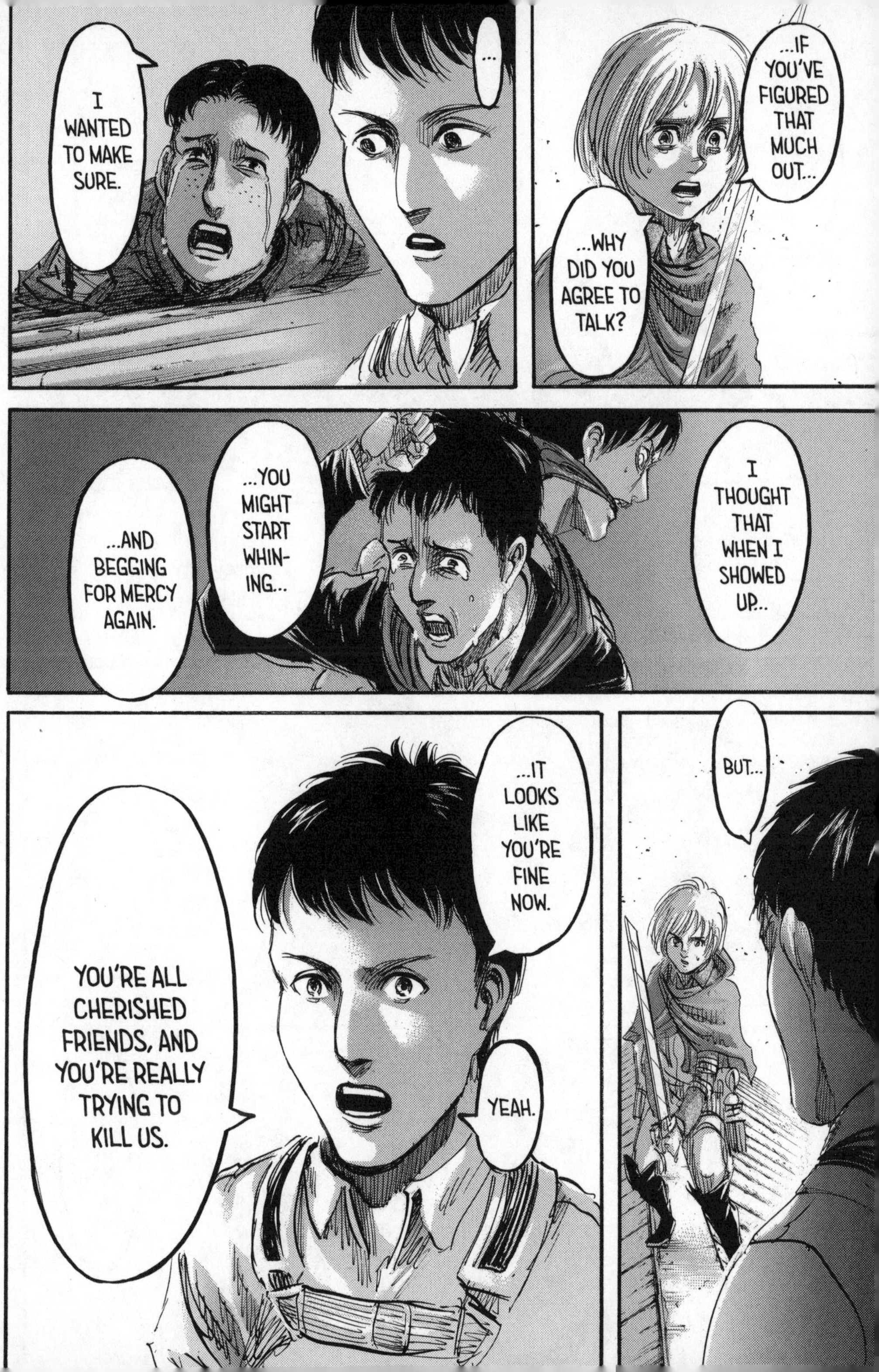
...IF YOU'VE FIGURED THAT MUCH OUT...
...WHY DID YOU AGREE TO TALK?
...
I WANTED TO MAKE SURE.
I THOUGHT THAT WHEN I SHOWED UP...
...YOU MIGHT START WHIN-ING...
...AND BEGGING FOR MERCY AGAIN.
BUT...
...IT LOOKS LIKE YOU'RE FINE NOW.
YEAH.
YOU'RE ALL CHERISHED FRIENDS, AND YOU'RE REALLY TRYING TO KILL US.

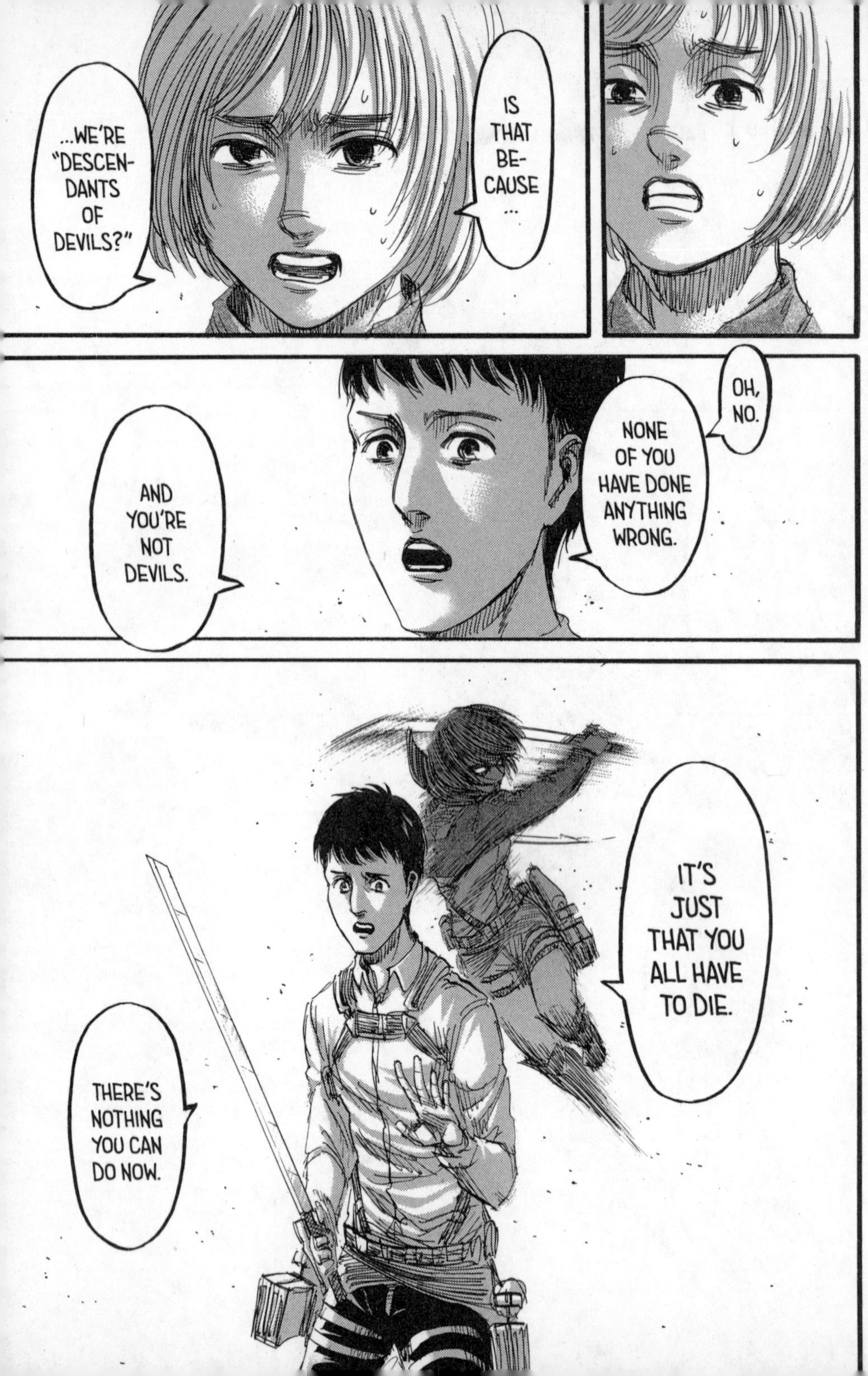
IS THAT BE-CAUSE ...
...WE'RE "DESCEN-DANTS OF DEVILS?"
OH, NO.
NONE OF YOU HAVE DONE ANYTHING WRONG.
AND YOU'RE NOT DEVILS.
IT'S JUST THAT YOU ALL HAVE TO DIE.
THERE'S NOTHING YOU CAN DO NOW.

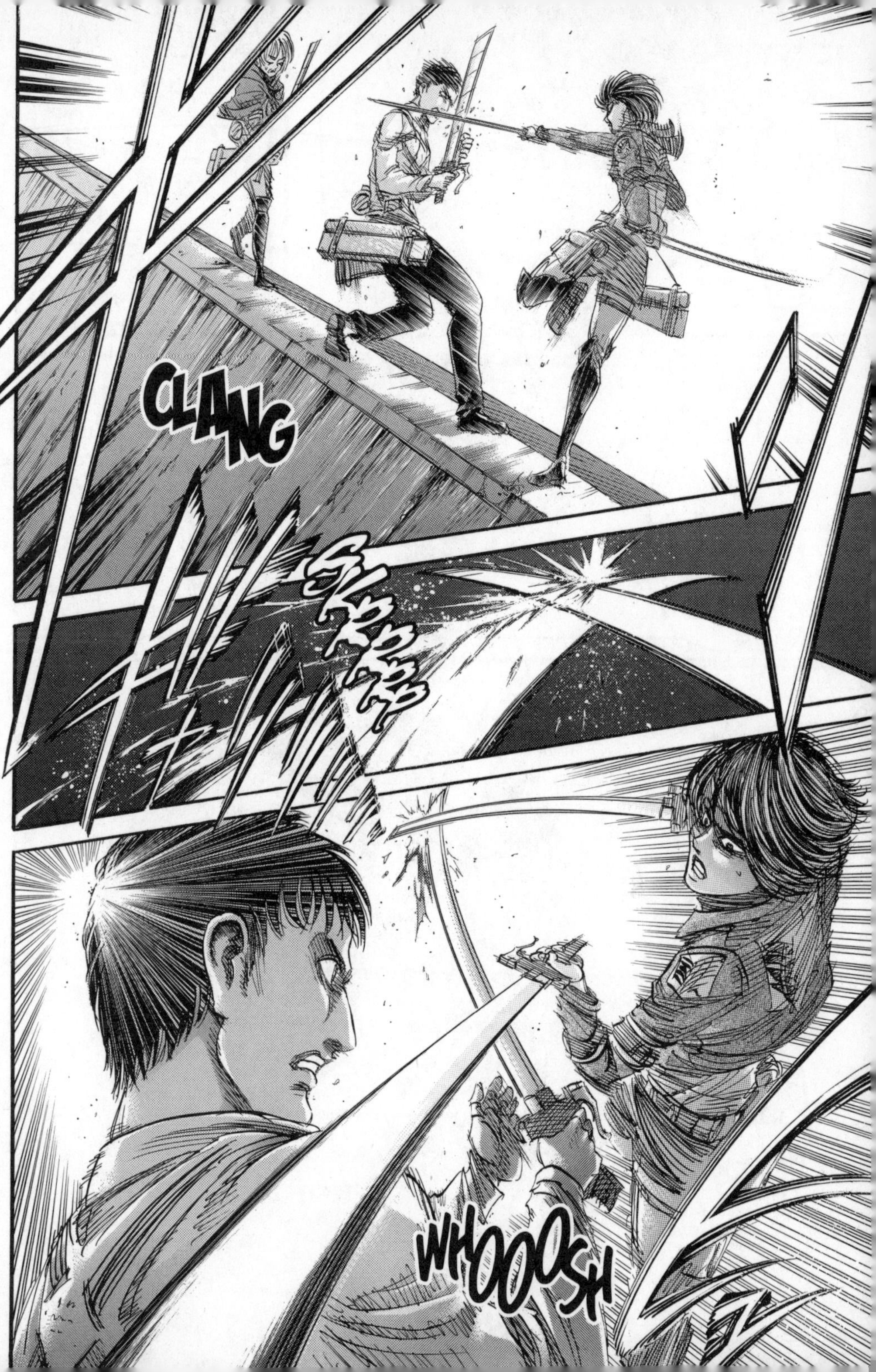
CLANG
WHOOOSH

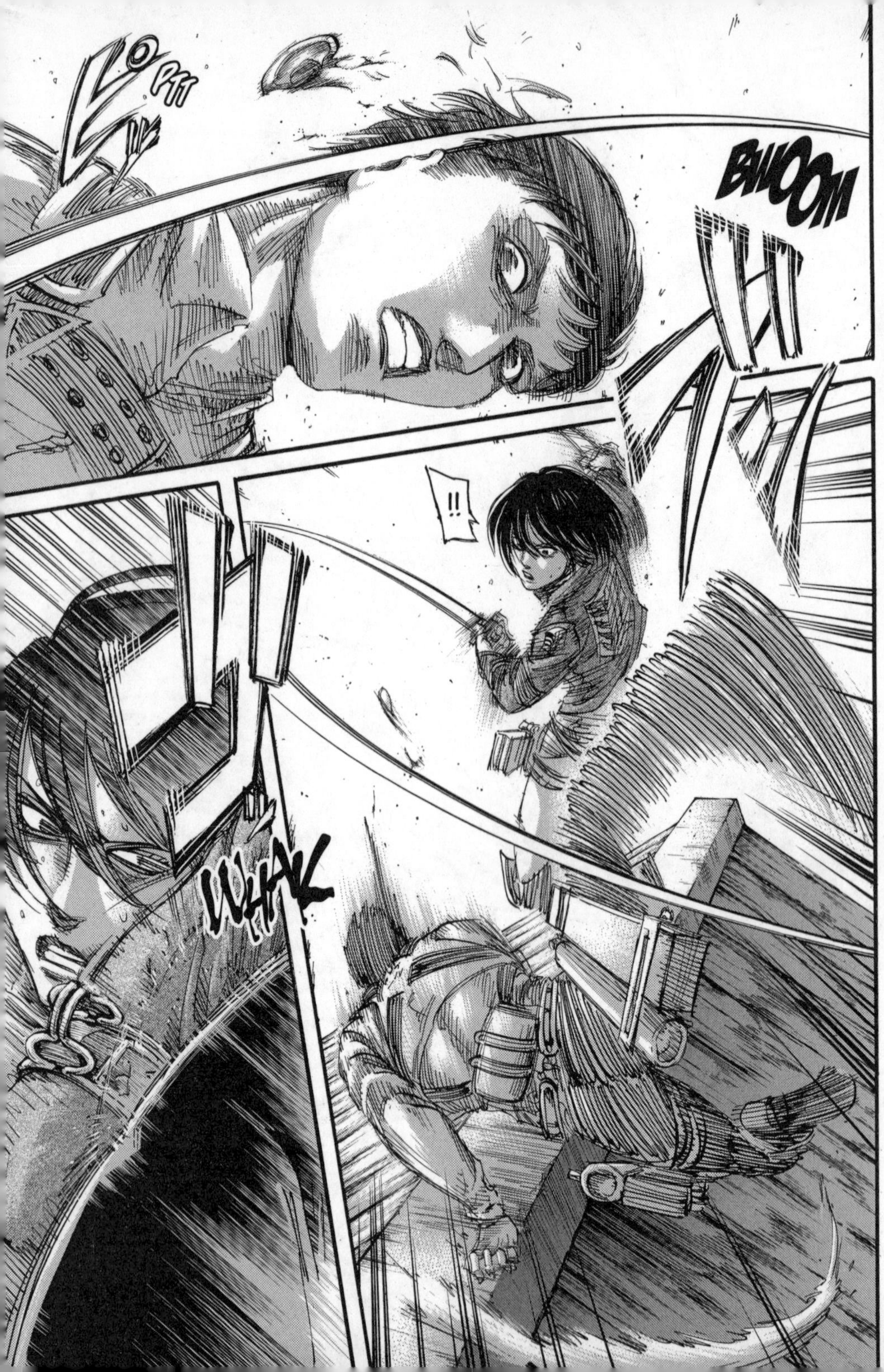
BWOOM
PTT
!!
WHAK

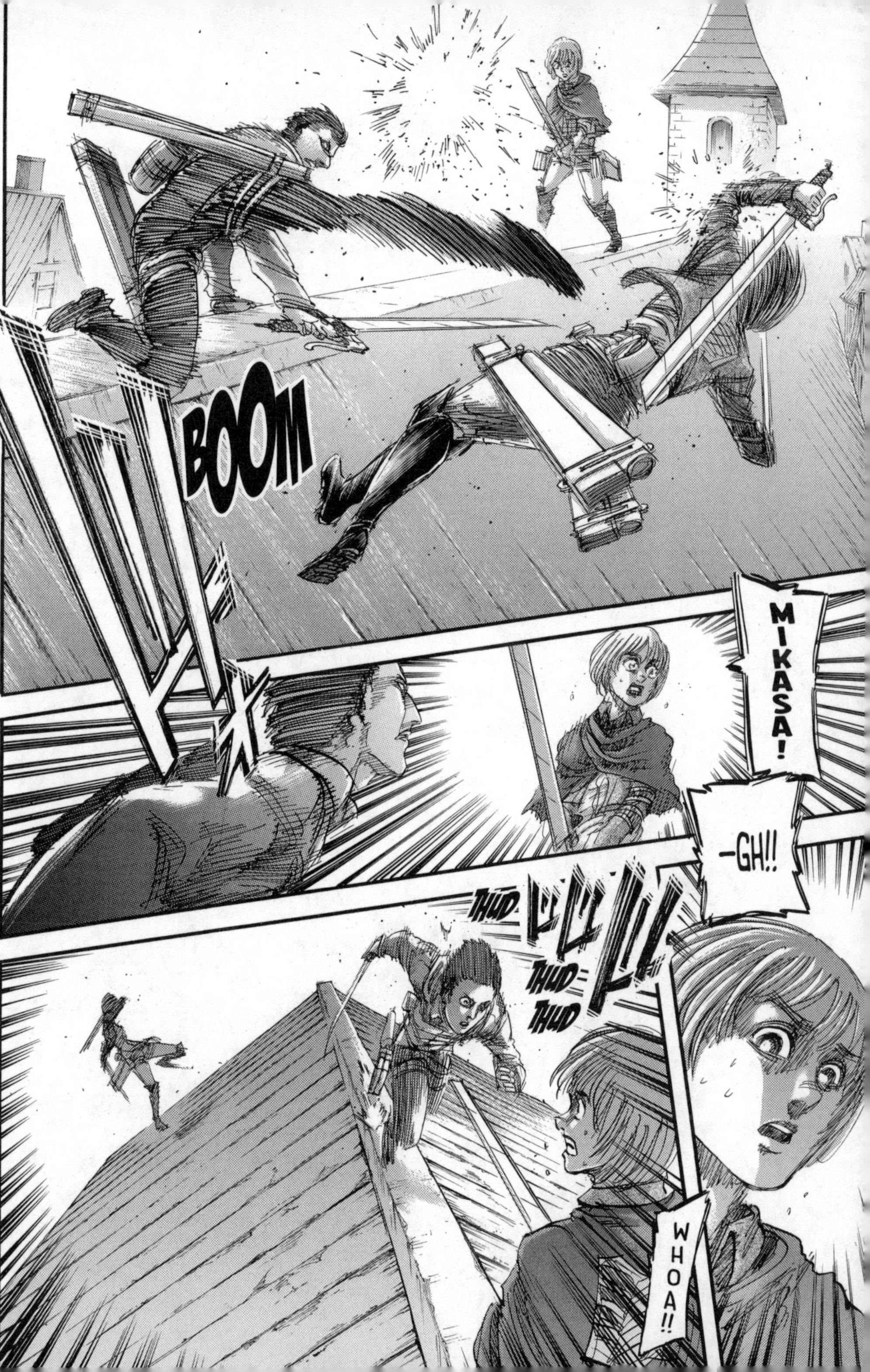
BOOM
MIKASA!
-GH!!
THUD
THUD
THUD
WHOA!!

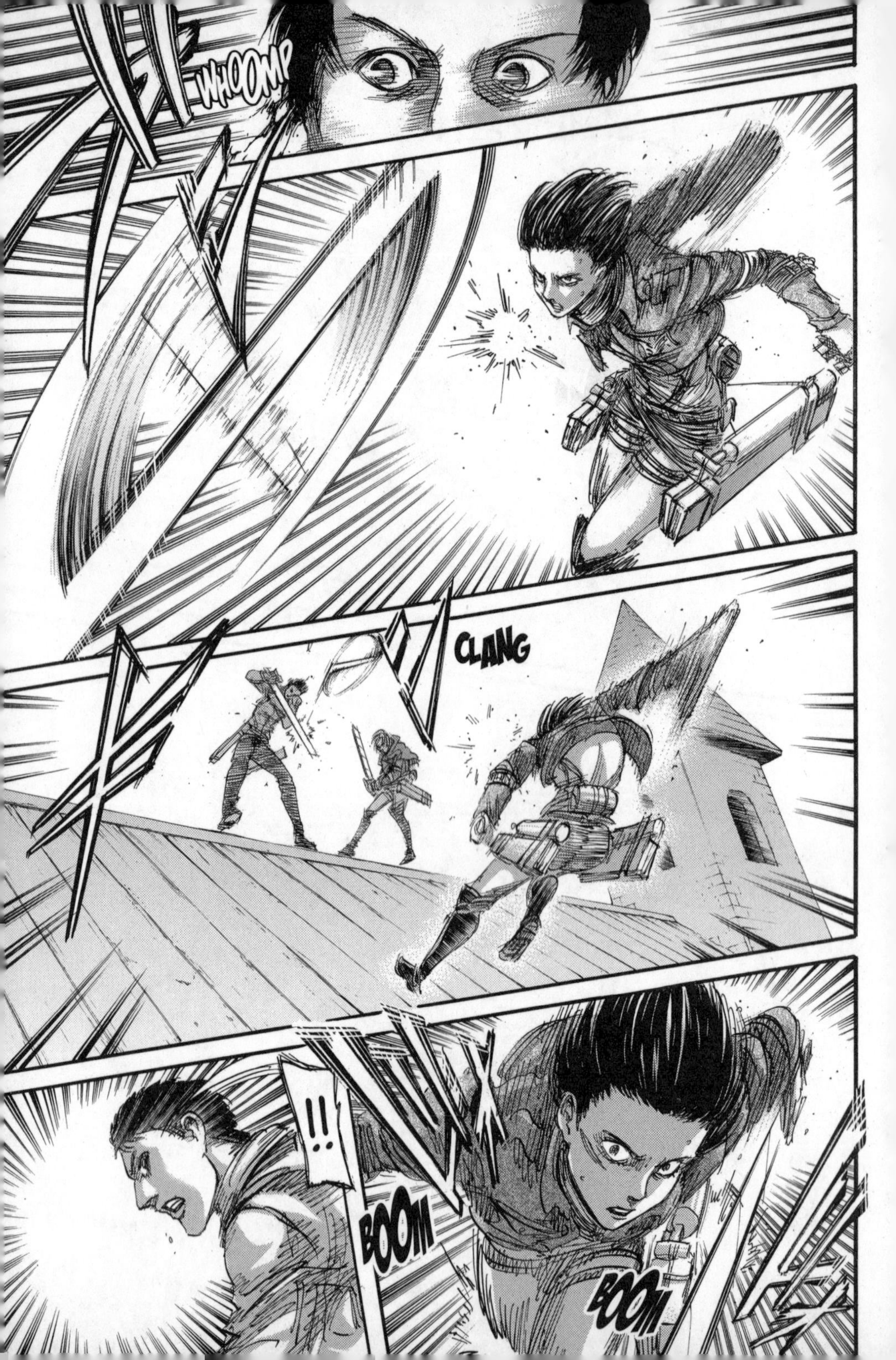
WHOOMP
CLANG
!!
BOOM
BOOM

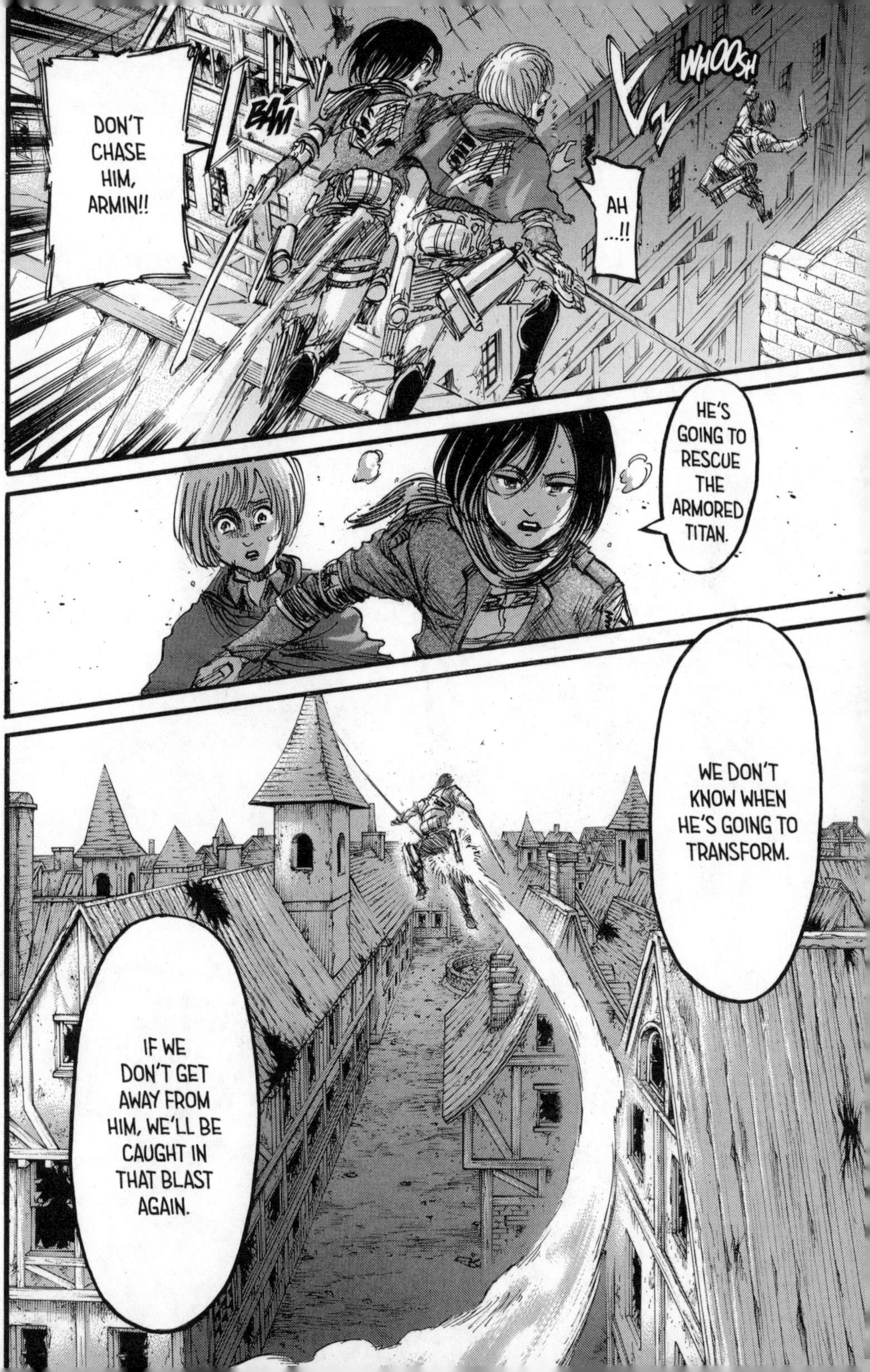
WHOOSH
AH ...!!
BAM
DON'T CHASE HIM, ARMIN!!
HE'S GOING TO RESCUE THE ARMORED TITAN.
WE DON'T KNOW WHEN HE'S GOING TO TRANSFORM.
IF WE DON'T GET AWAY FROM HIM, WE'LL BE CAUGHT IN THAT BLAST AGAIN.

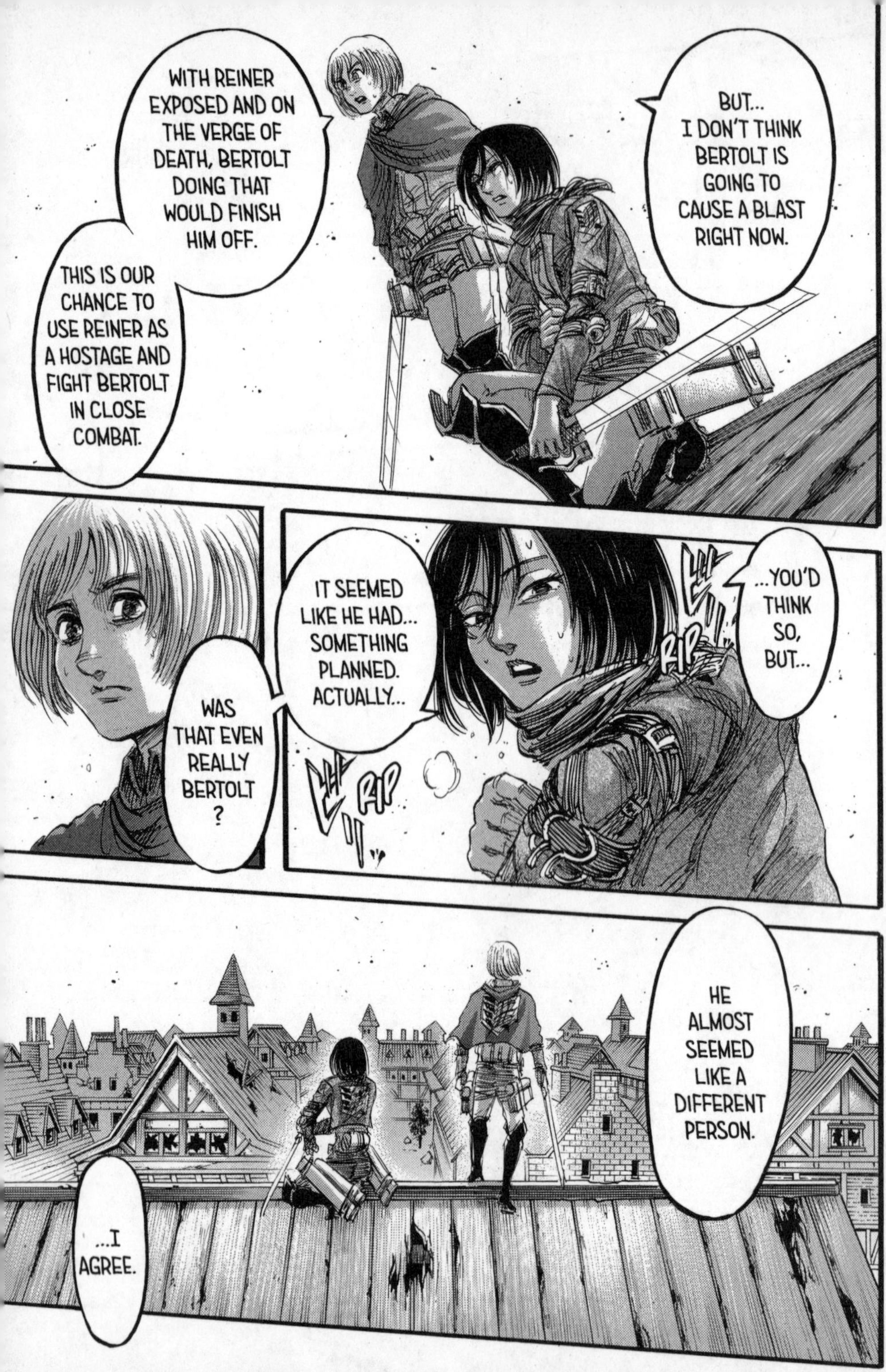
BUT... I DON'T THINK BERTOLT IS GOING TO CAUSE A BLAST RIGHT NOW.
WITH REINER EXPOSED AND ON THE VERGE OF DEATH, BERTOLT DOING THAT WOULD FINISH HIM OFF.
THIS IS OUR CHANCE TO USE REINER AS A HOSTAGE AND FIGHT BERTOLT IN CLOSE COMBAT.
...YOU'D THINK SO, BUT...
RIP
IT SEEMED LIKE HE HAD... SOMETHING PLANNED. ACTUALLY...
RIP
WAS THAT EVEN REALLY BERTOLT?
HE ALMOST SEEMED LIKE A DIFFERENT PERSON.
...I AGREE.

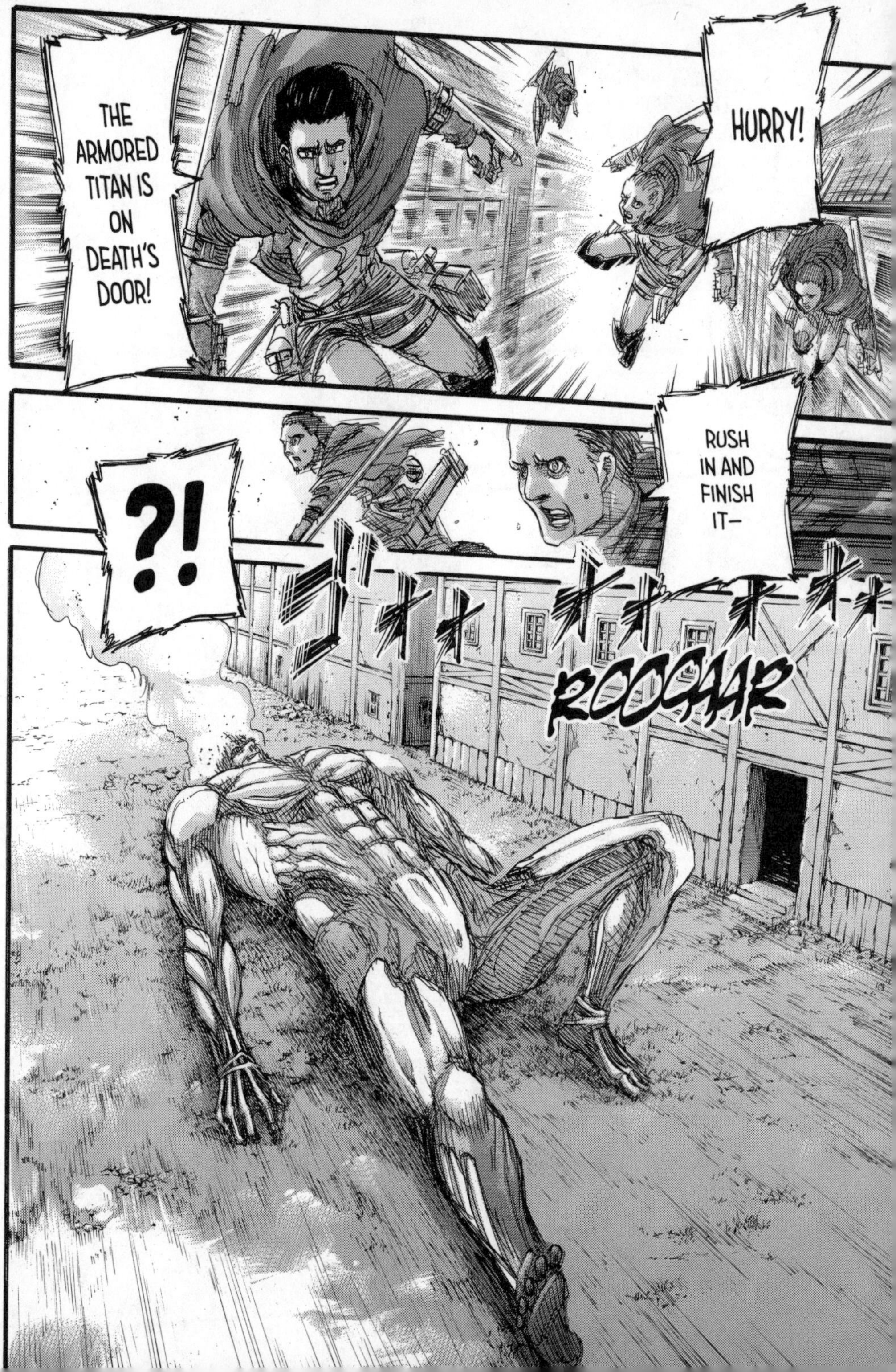
HURRY!
THE ARMORED TITAN IS ON DEATH'S DOOR!
RUSH IN AND FINISH IT—
?!
ROOOAAR

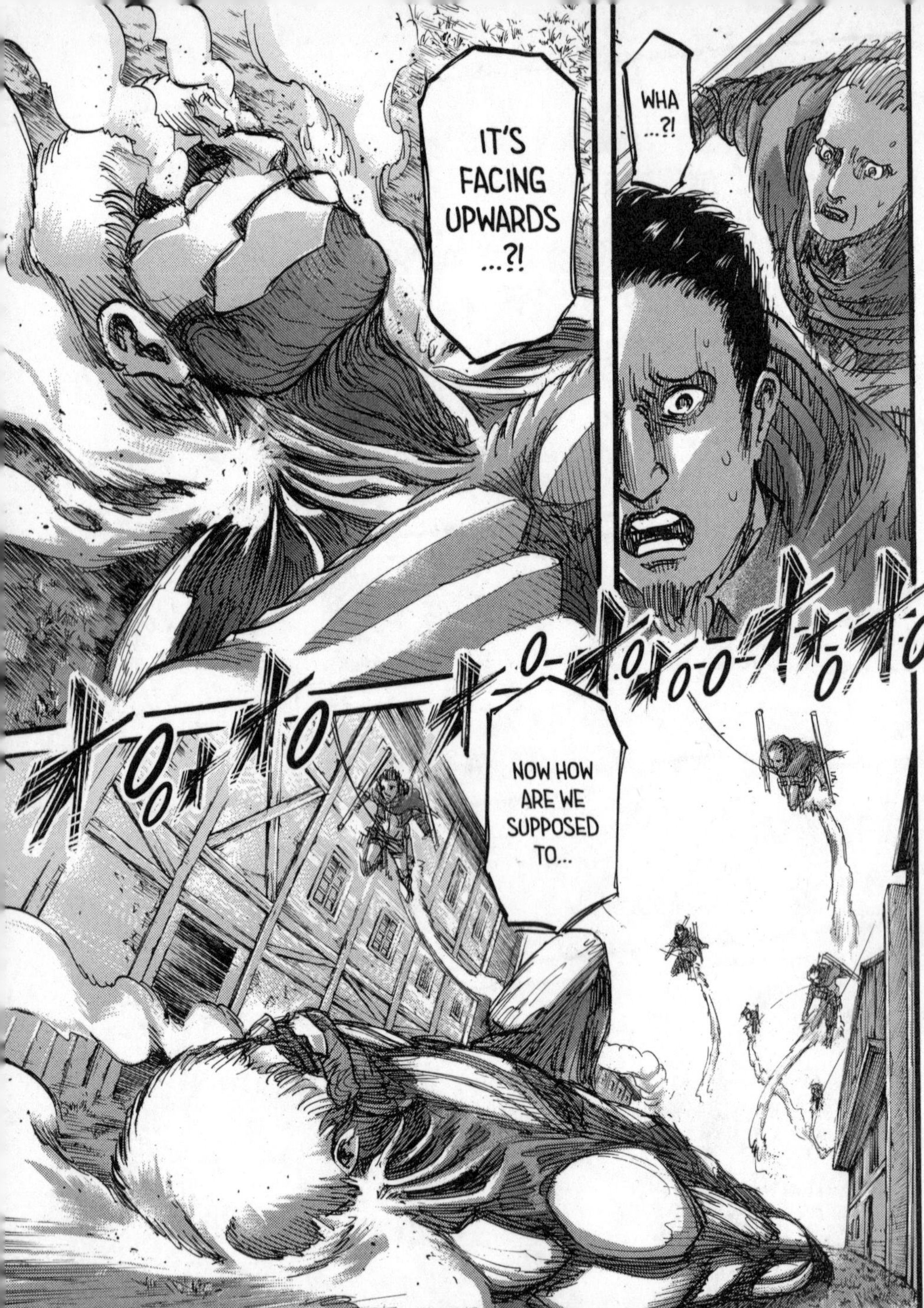
WHA ...?!
IT'S FACING UPWARDS ...?!
NOW HOW ARE WE SUPPOSED TO...

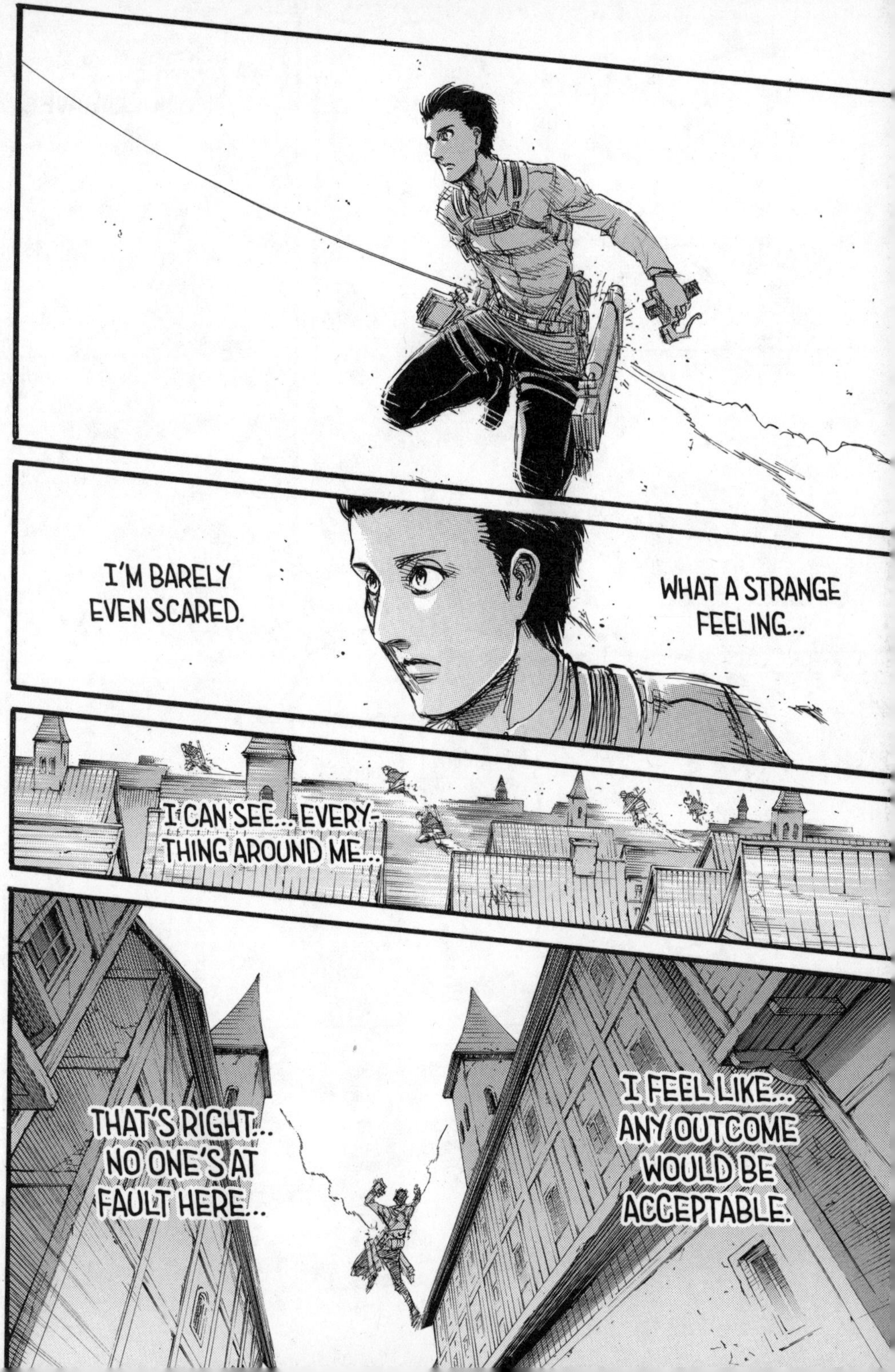
WHAT A STRANGE FEELING...
I'M BARELY EVEN SCARED.
I CAN SEE... EVERY-THING AROUND ME...
I FEEL LIKE... ANY OUTCOME WOULD BE ACCEPTABLE.
THAT'S RIGHT... NO ONE'S AT FAULT HERE...

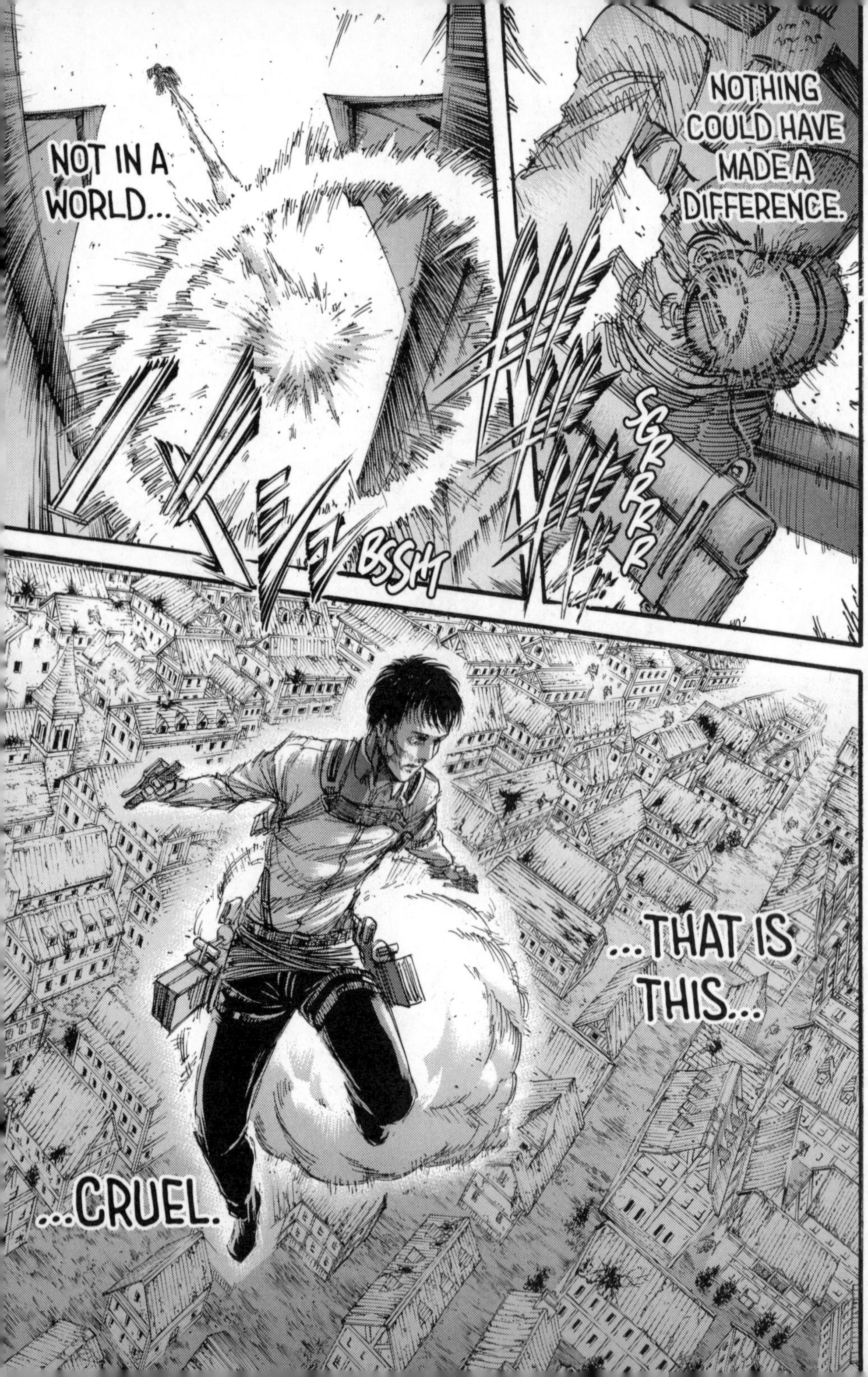
NOTHING COULD HAVE MADE A DIFFERENCE.
SGRRRR
NOT IN A WORLD...
BSSHT
...THAT IS THIS...
...CRUEL.

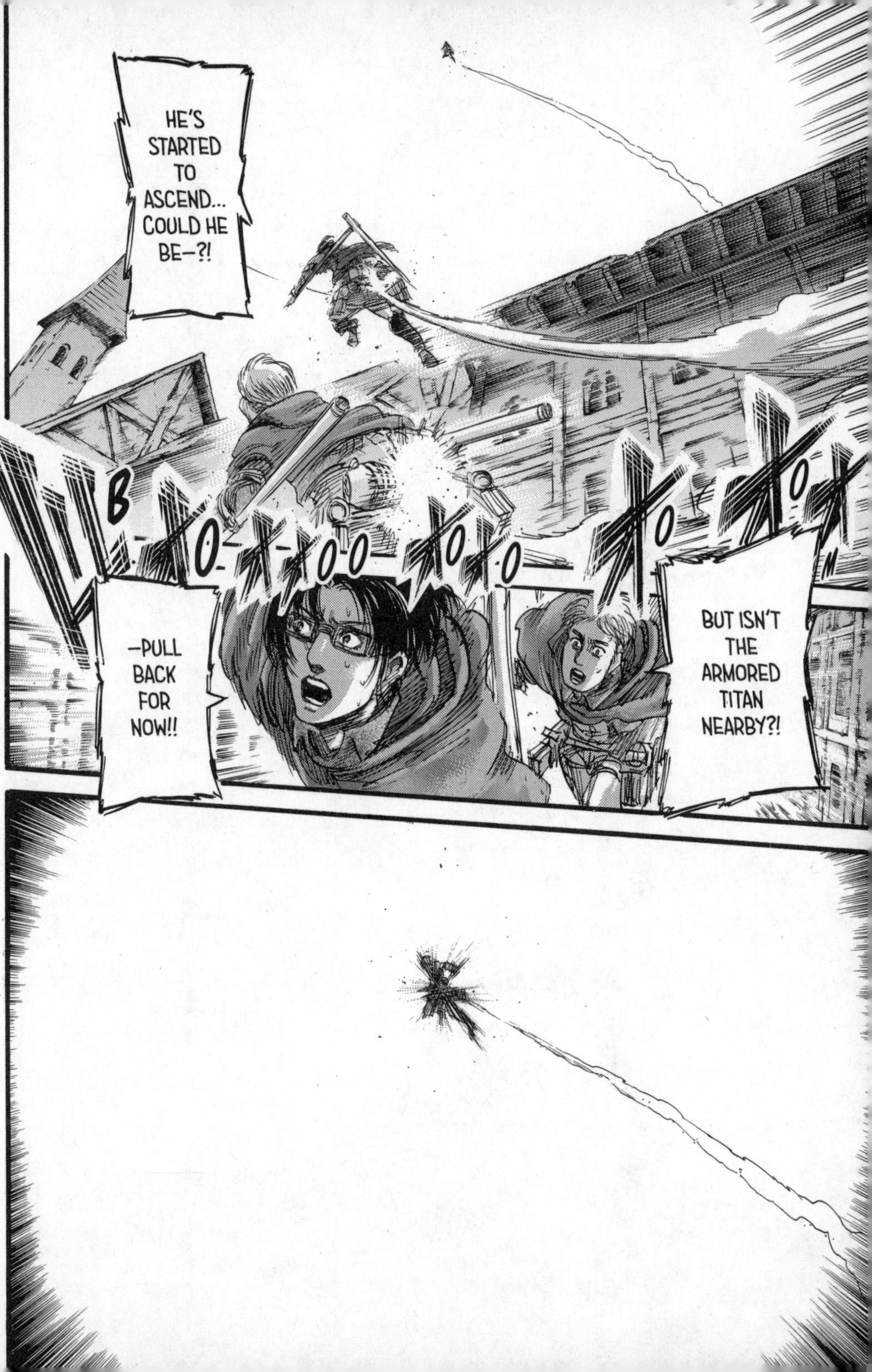
HE'S STARTED TO ASCEND... COULD HE BE—?!
BOOOOOOOM
BUT ISN'T THE ARMORED TITAN NEARBY?!
—PULL BACK FOR NOW!!

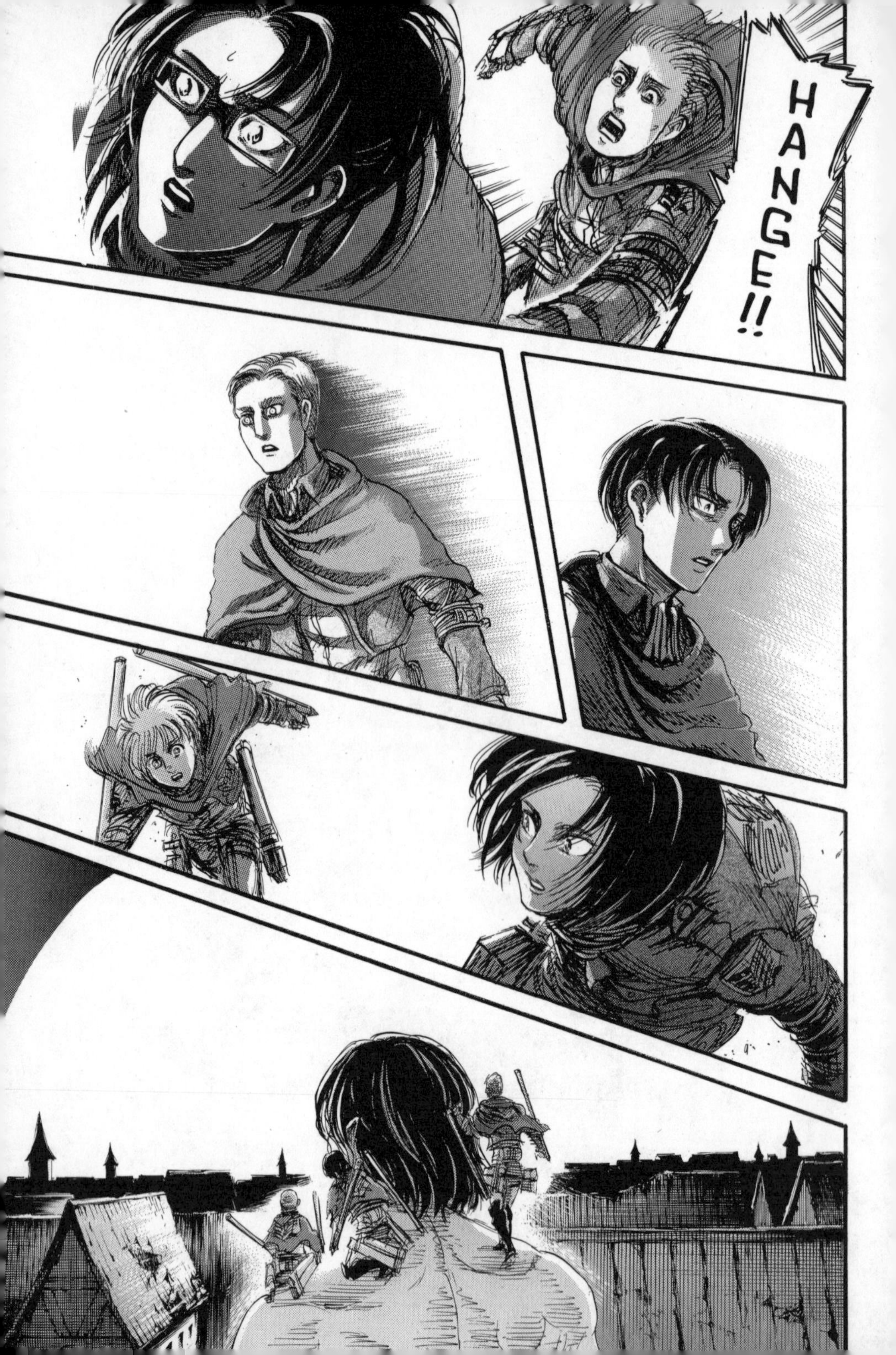
HANGE!!

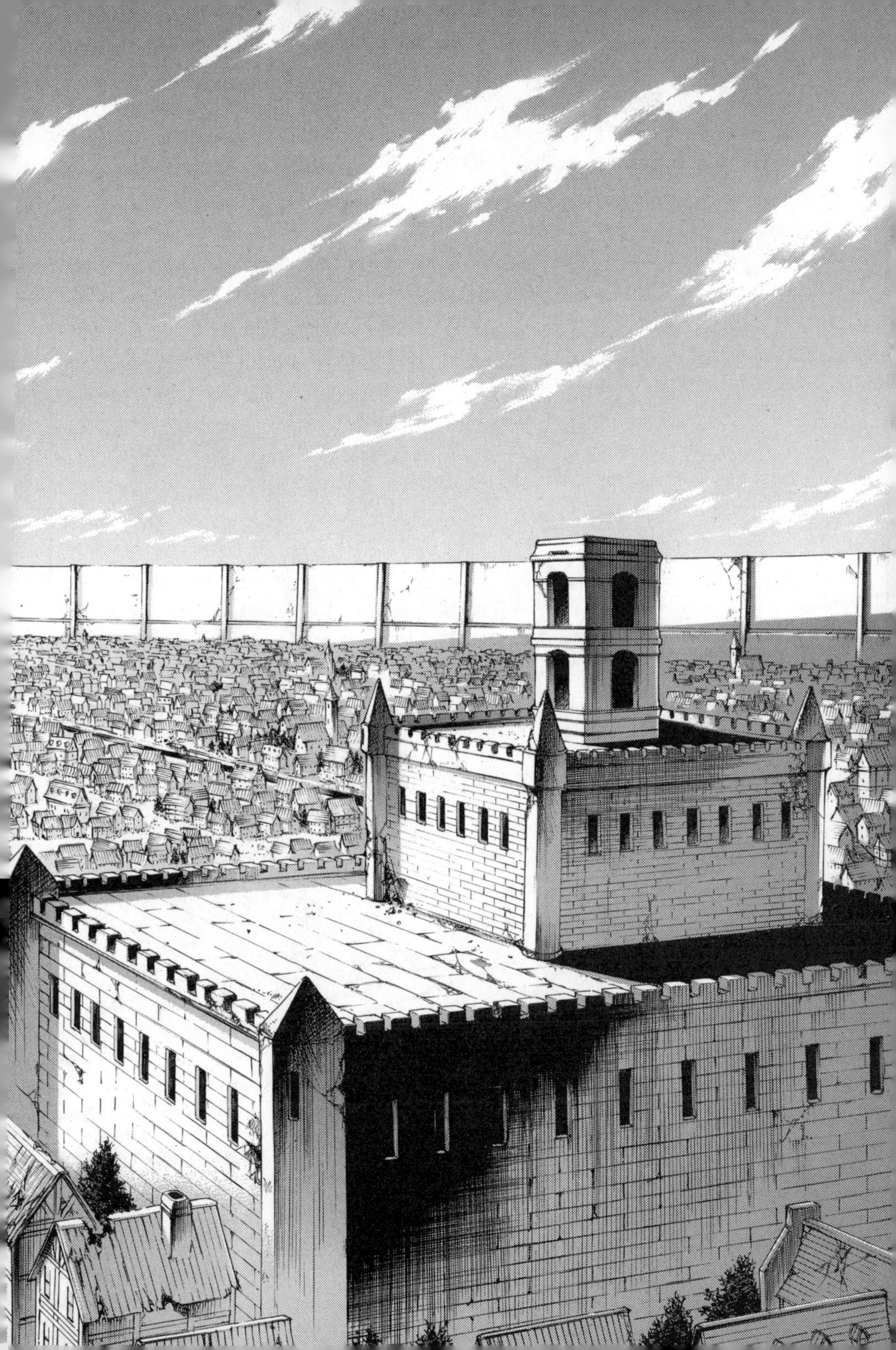

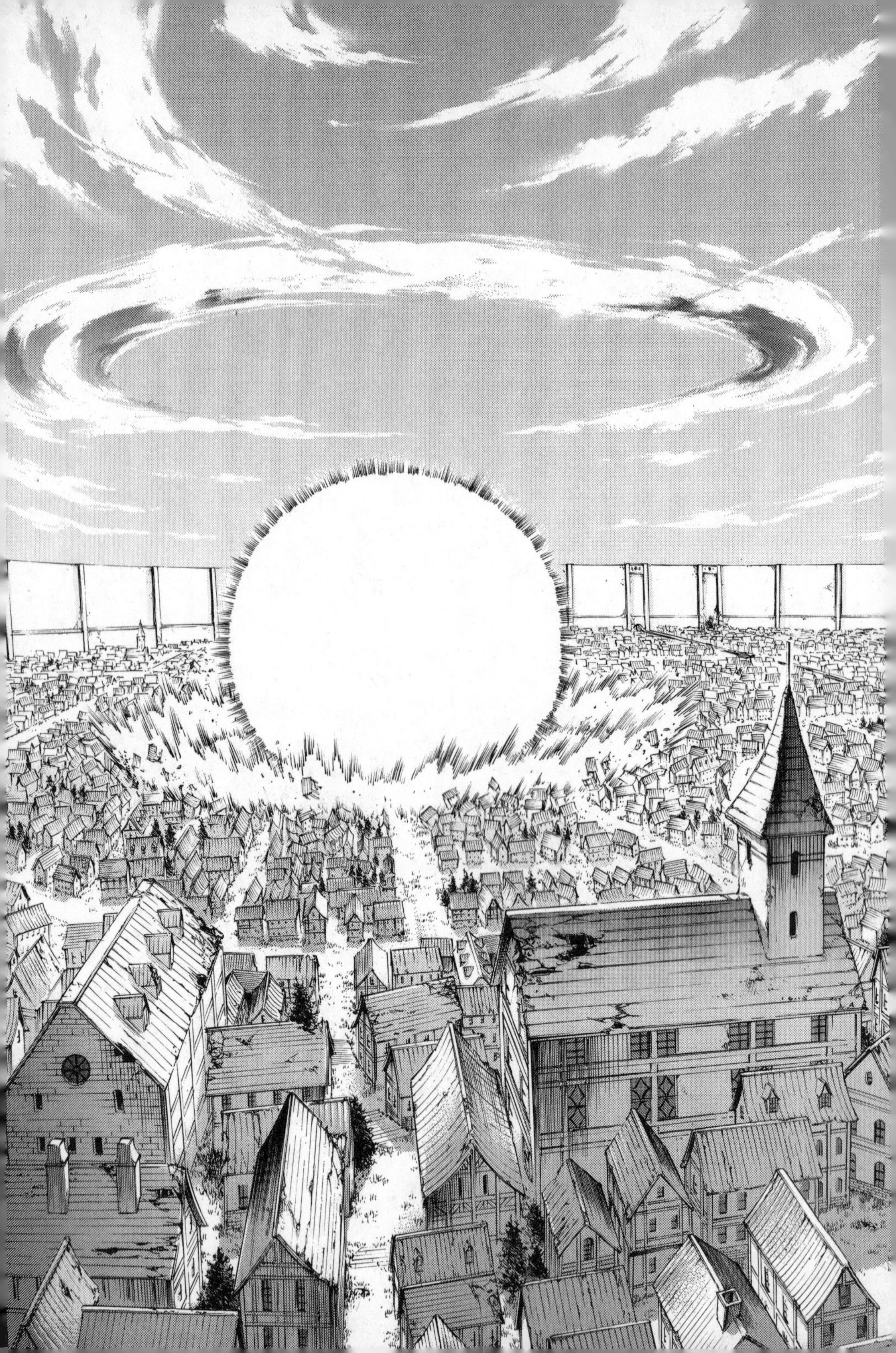

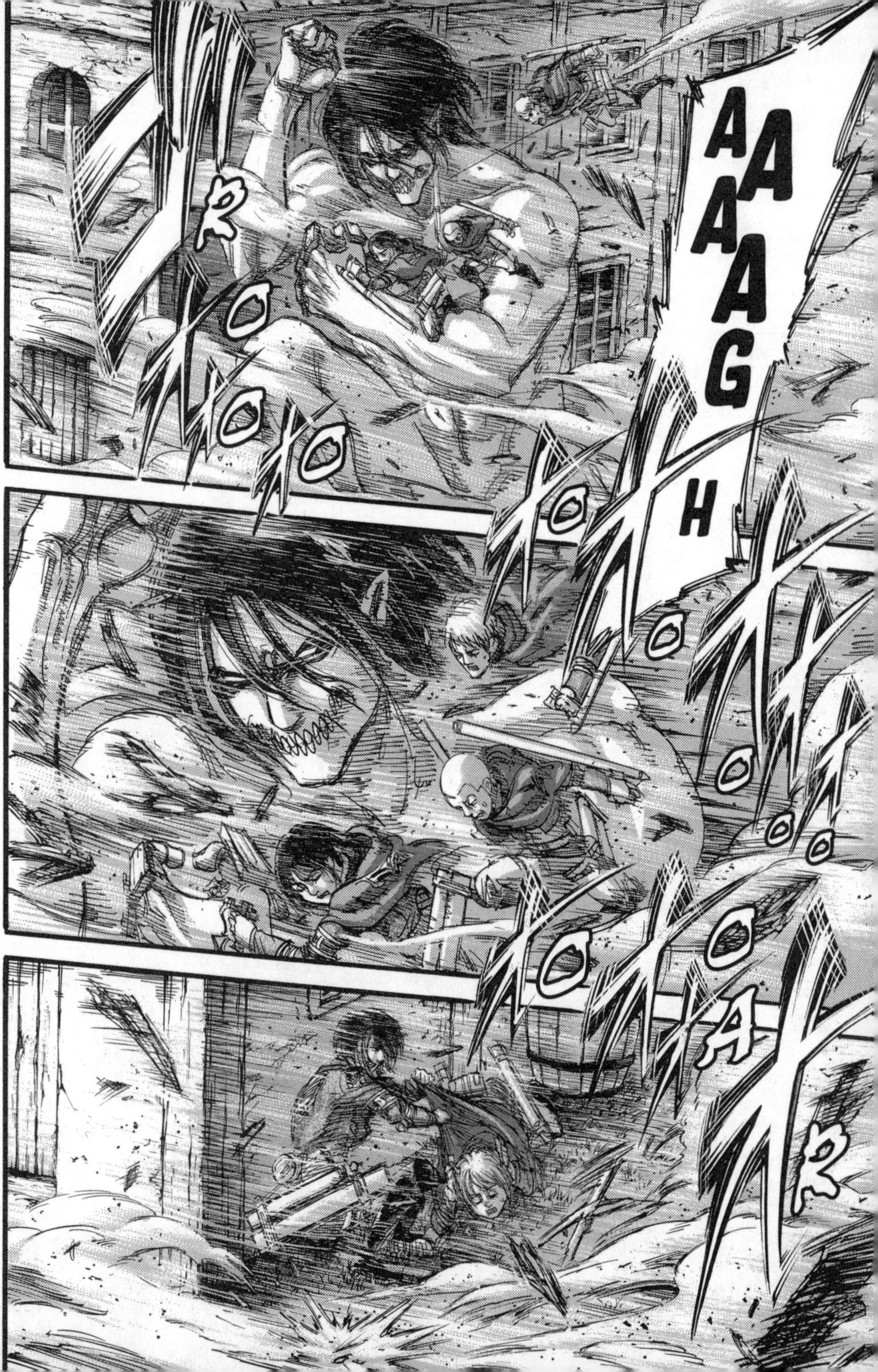
AAAAGH
ROOOO
OOOOOO...
OOOOAR

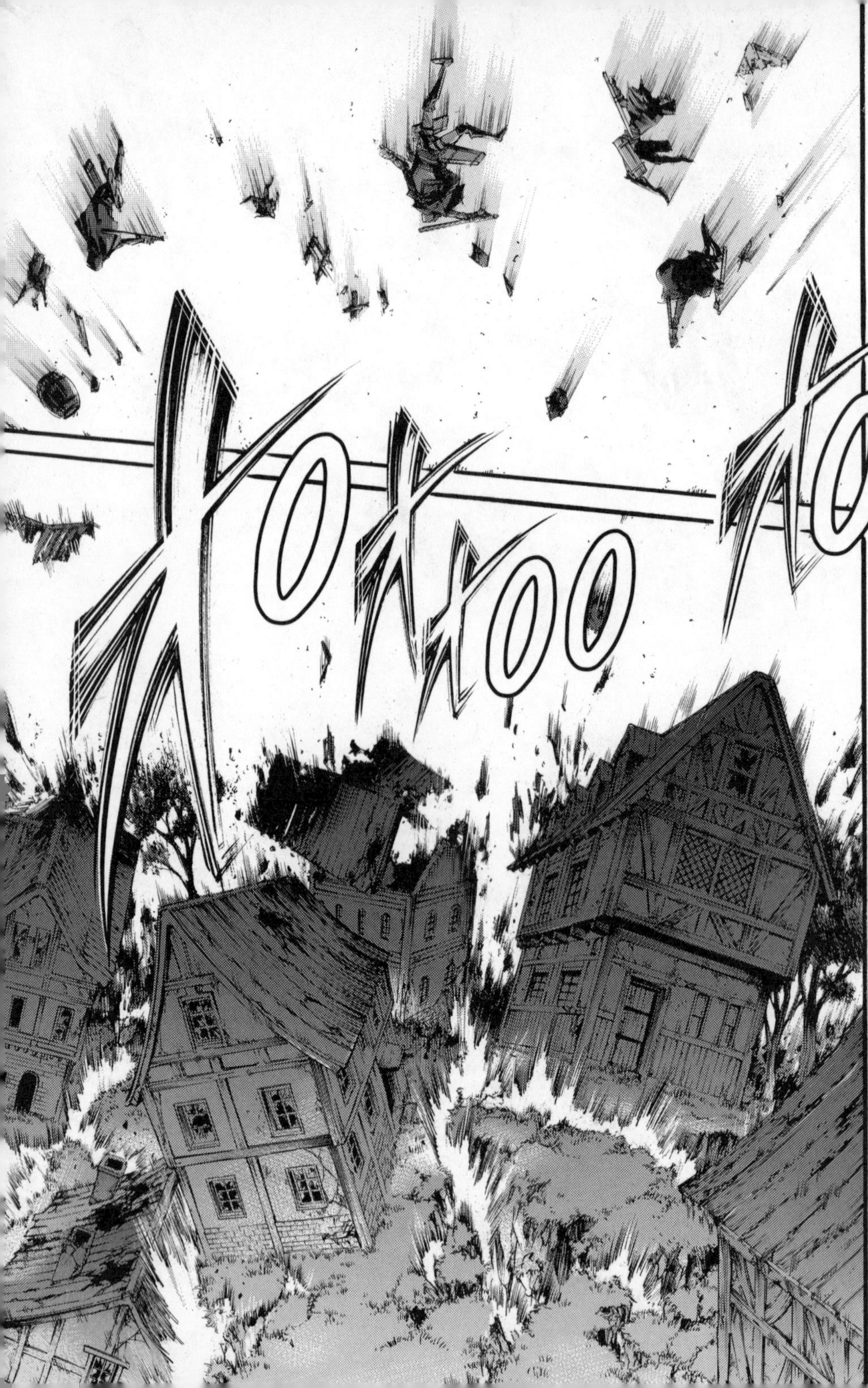

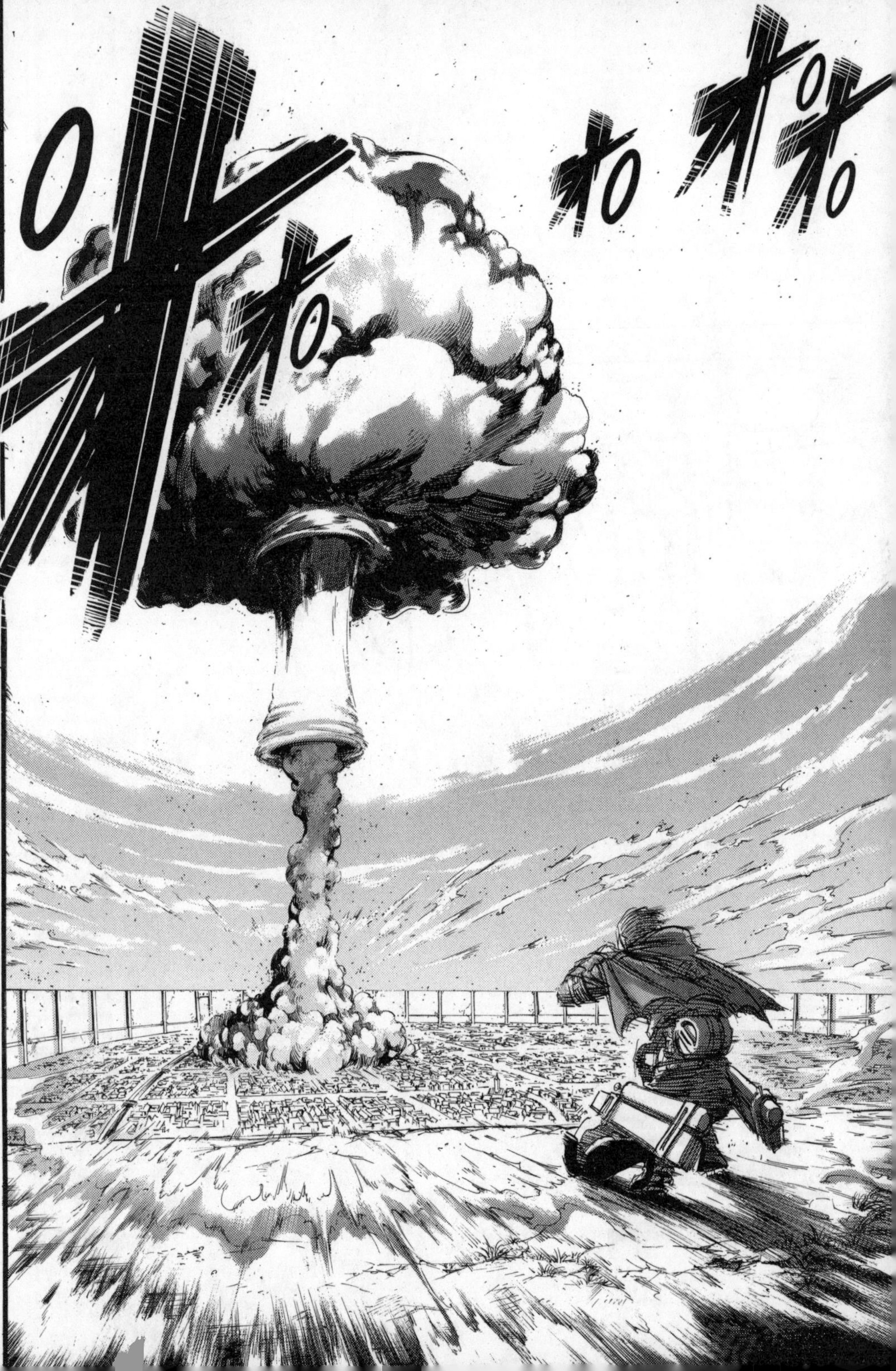

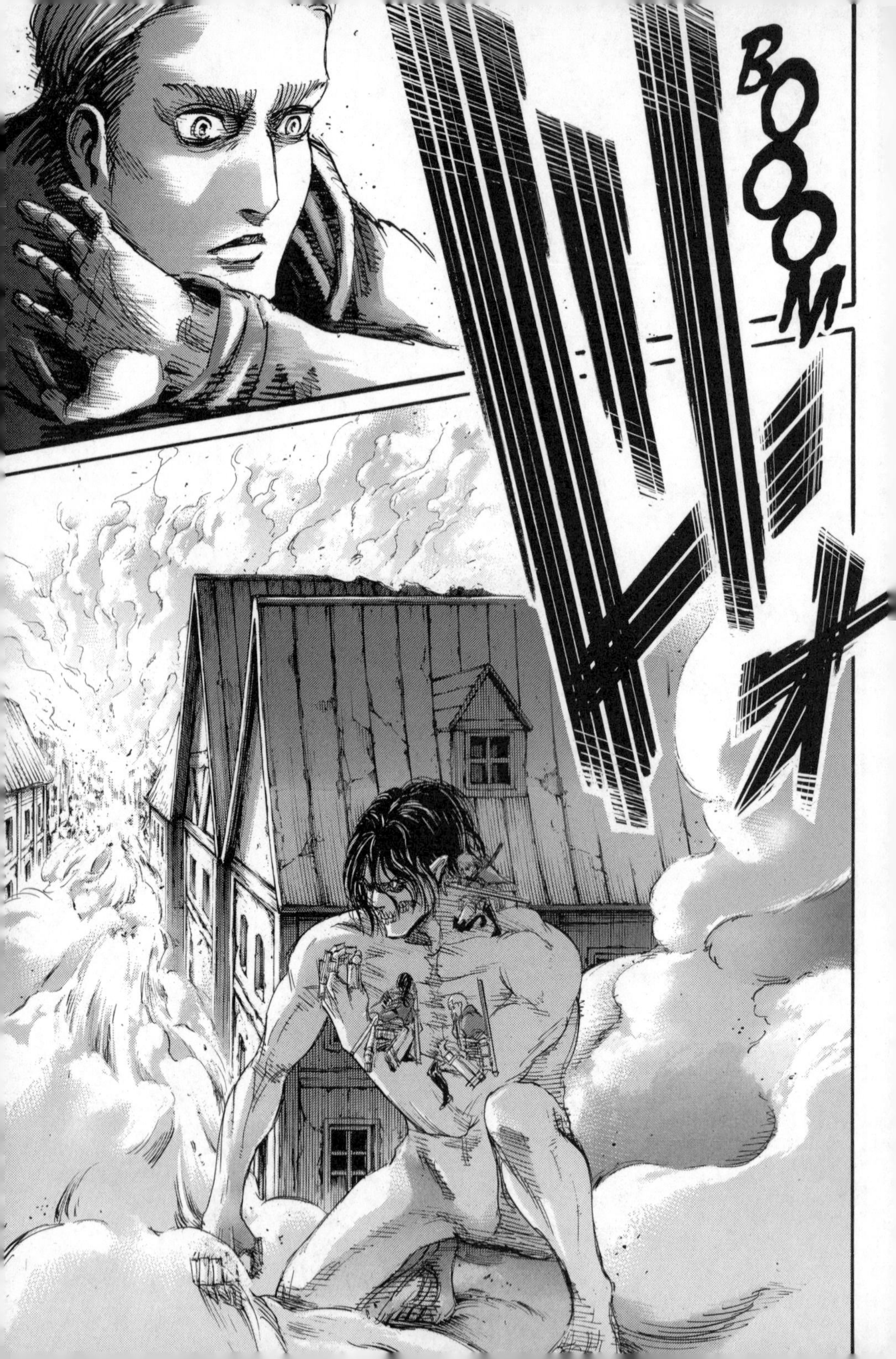
BOOOM

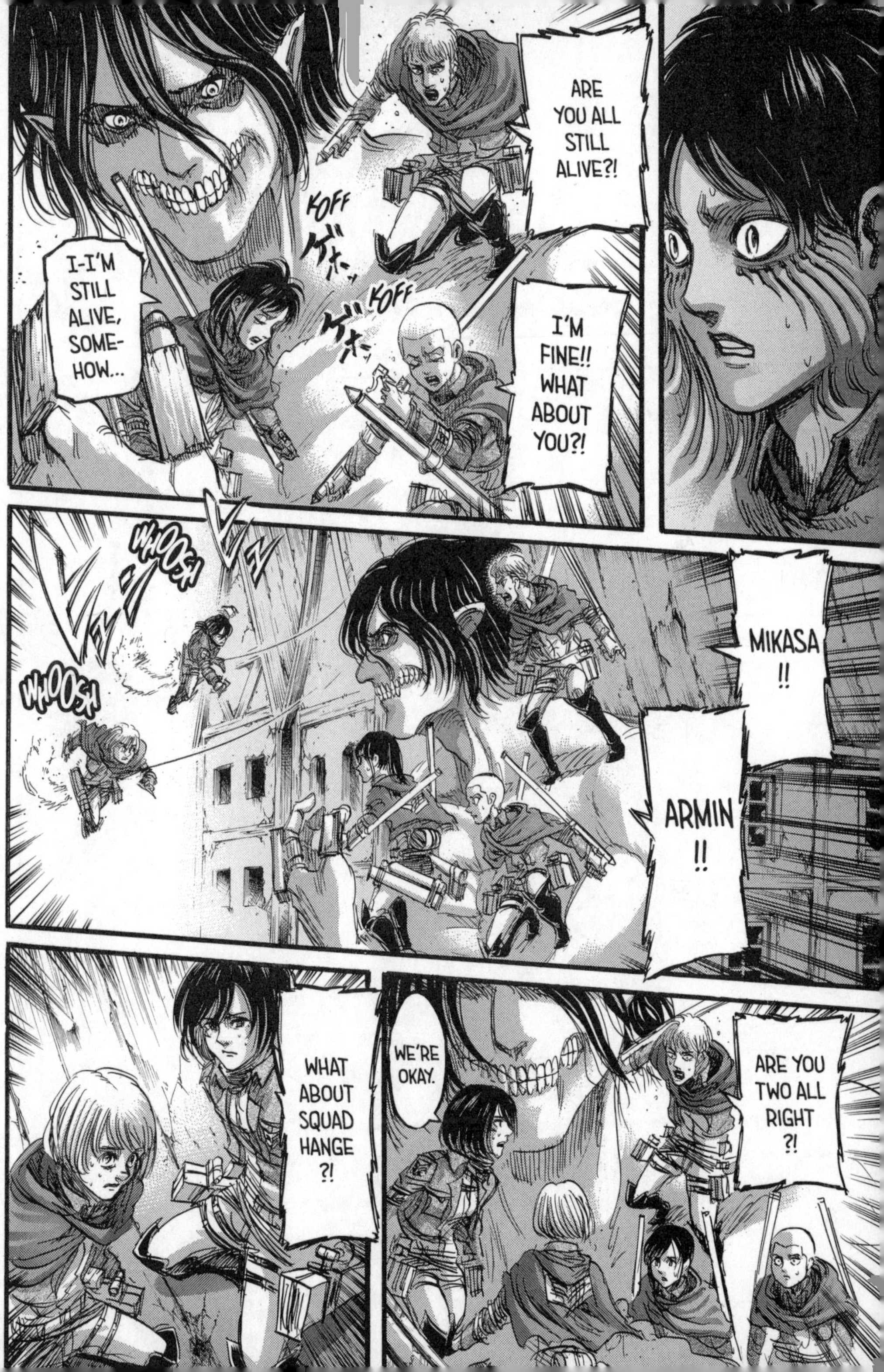

ARE YOU ALL STILL ALIVE?!
KOFF
ゲホッ
I'M FINE!! WHAT ABOUT YOU?!
KOFF
ゲホッ
I-I'M STILL ALIVE, SOME-HOW...
MIKASA!!
ARMIN!!
WHOOSH
WHOOSH
ARE YOU TWO ALL RIGHT?!
WE'RE OKAY.
WHAT ABOUT SQUAD HANGE?!

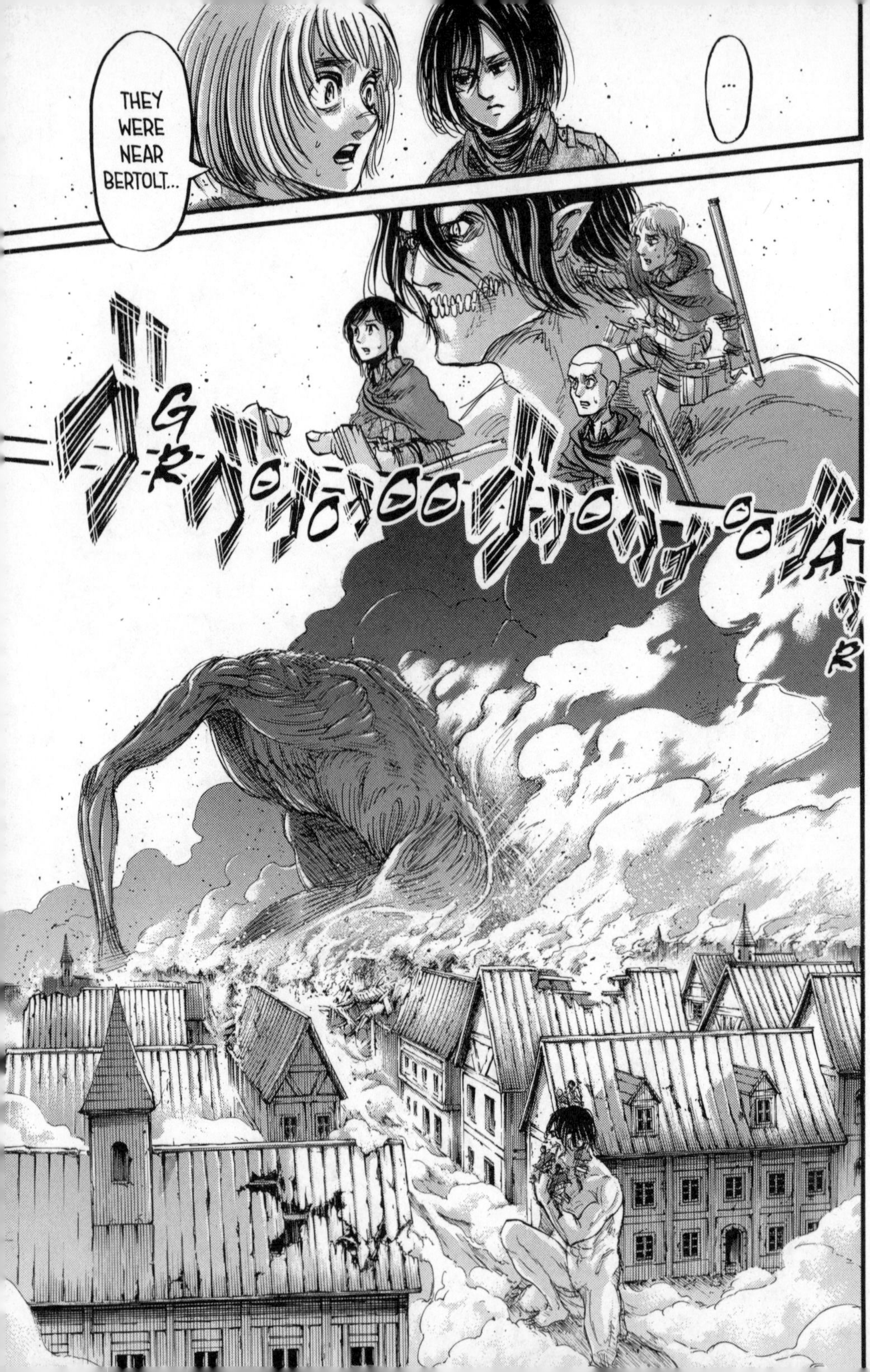
...
THEY WERE NEAR BERTOLT...
GROOOOOOOOAR

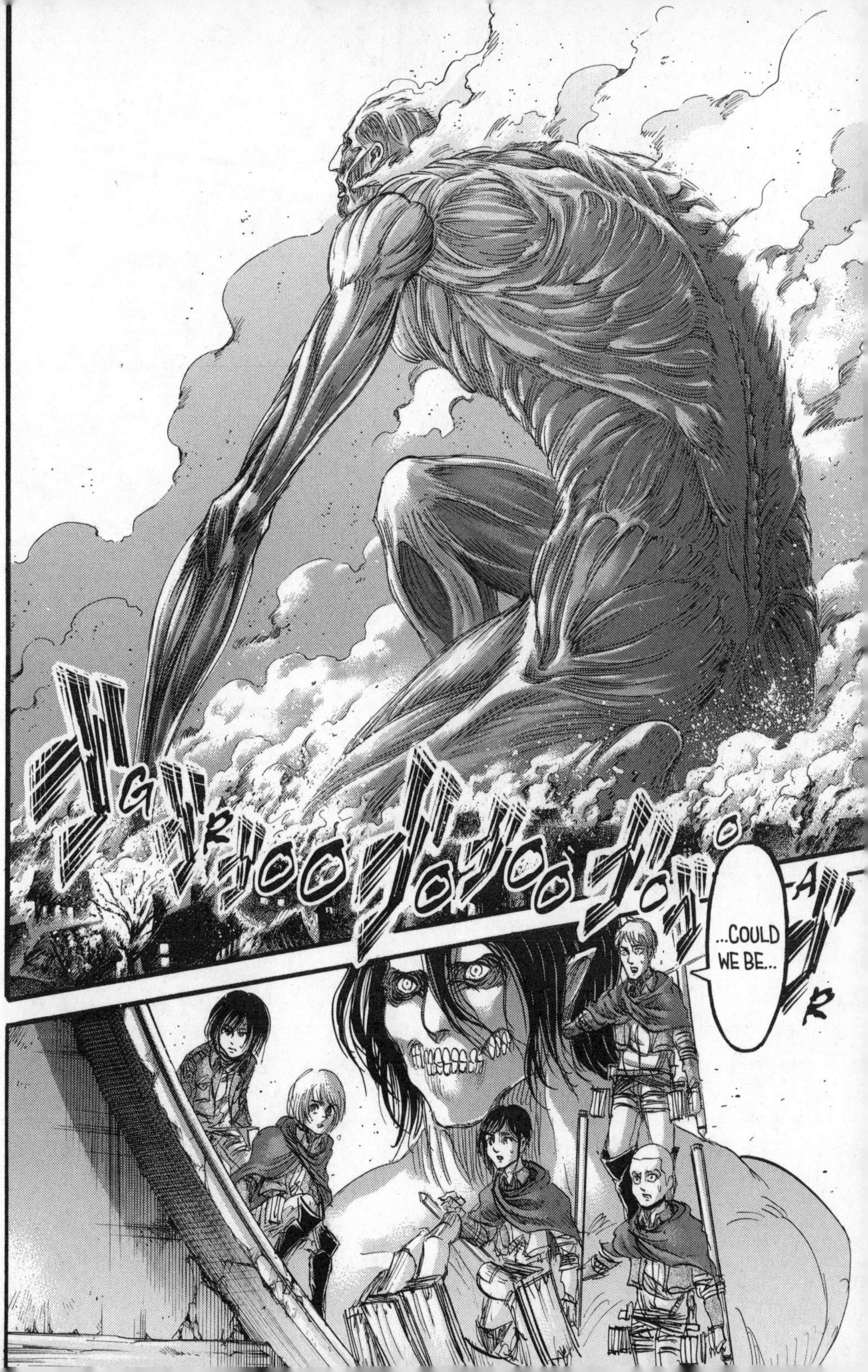
...COULD WE BE...

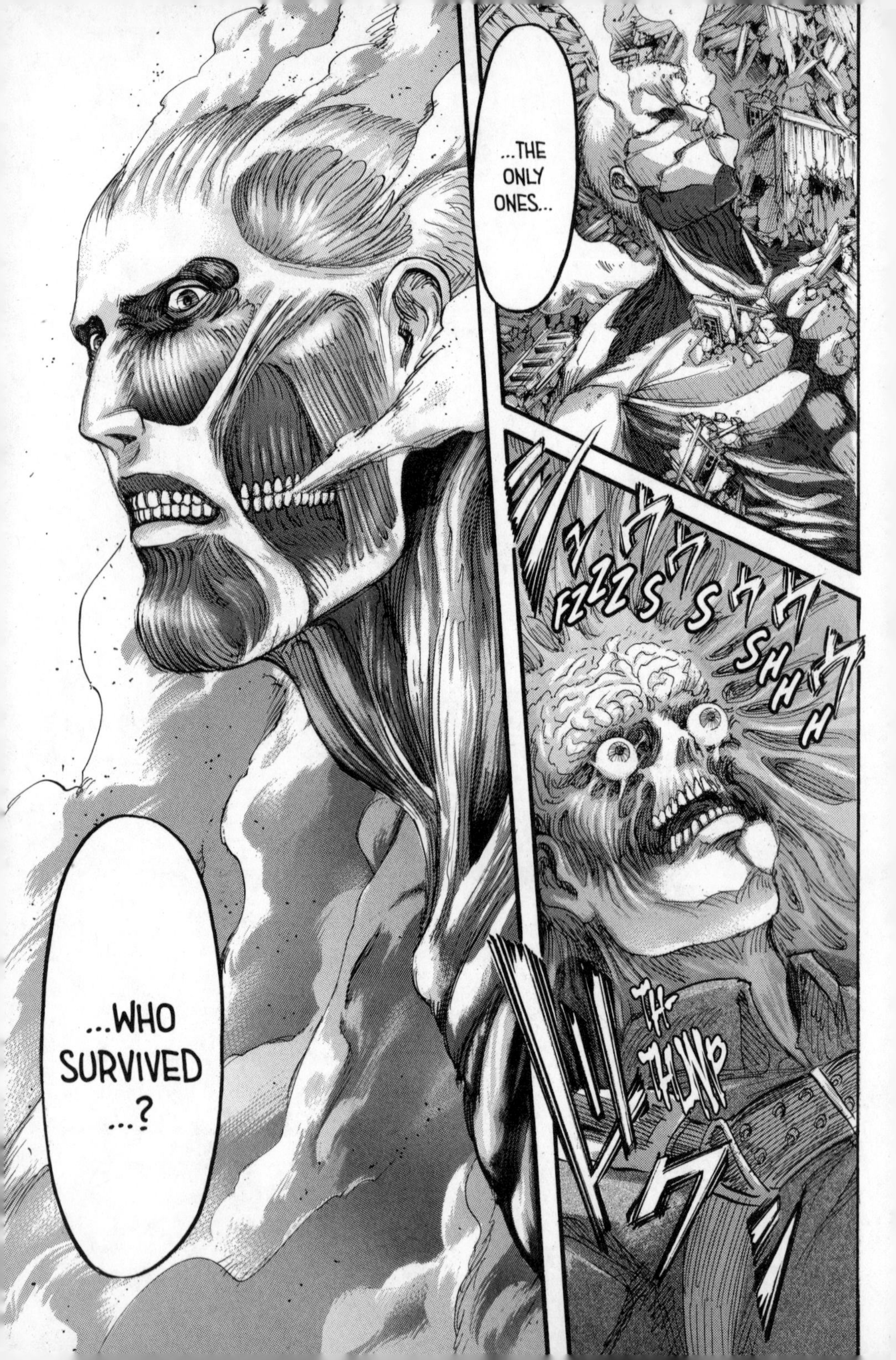
...THE ONLY ONES...
FZZZSSSHHH
TH-
THUMP
...WHO SURVIVED ...?

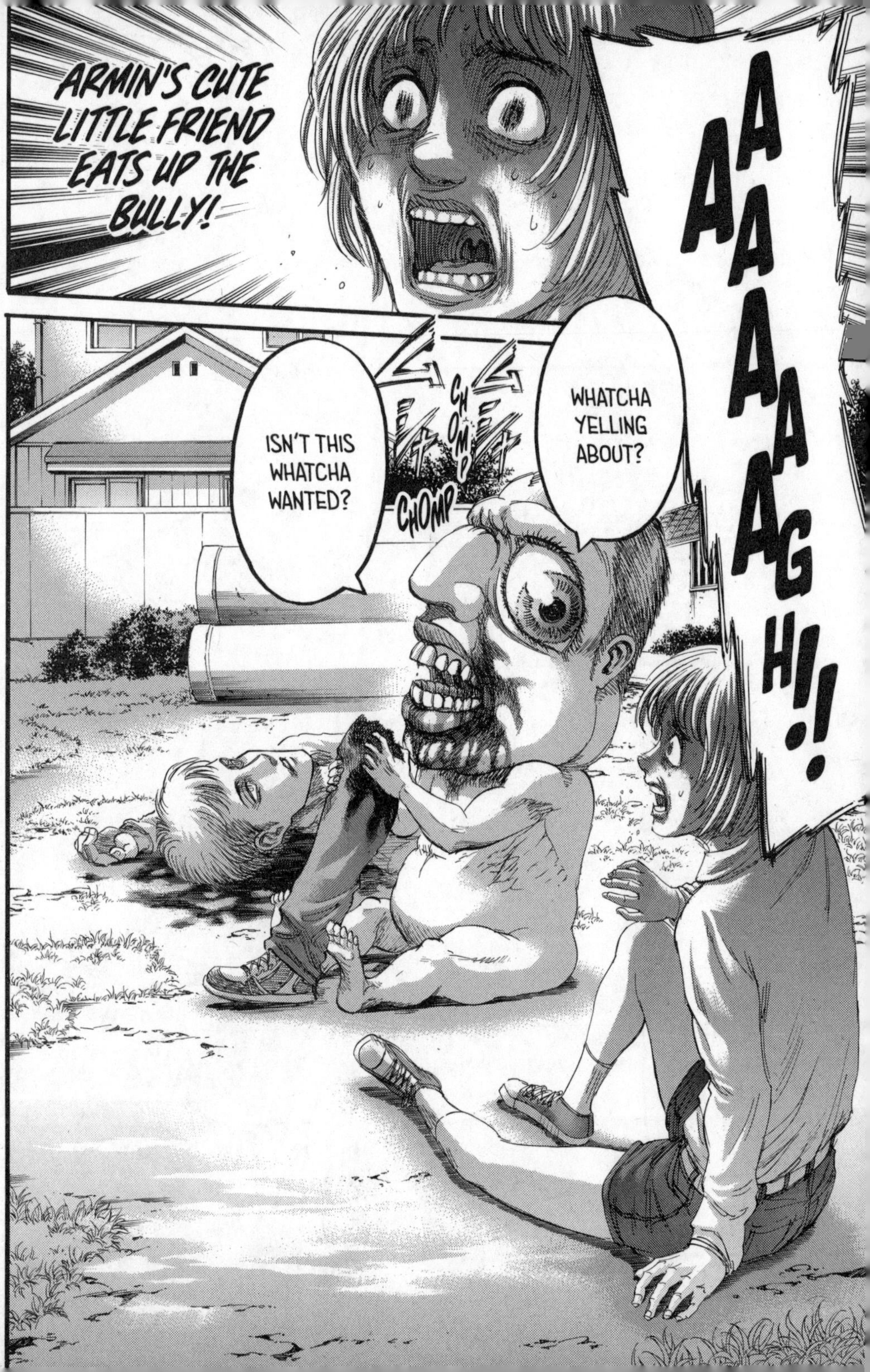
ARMIN'S CUTE LITTLE FRIEND EATS UP THE BULLY!
AAAAAAAAAGH!!
WHATCHA YELLING ABOUT?
ISN'T THIS WHATCHA WANTED?
CHOMP
CHOMP

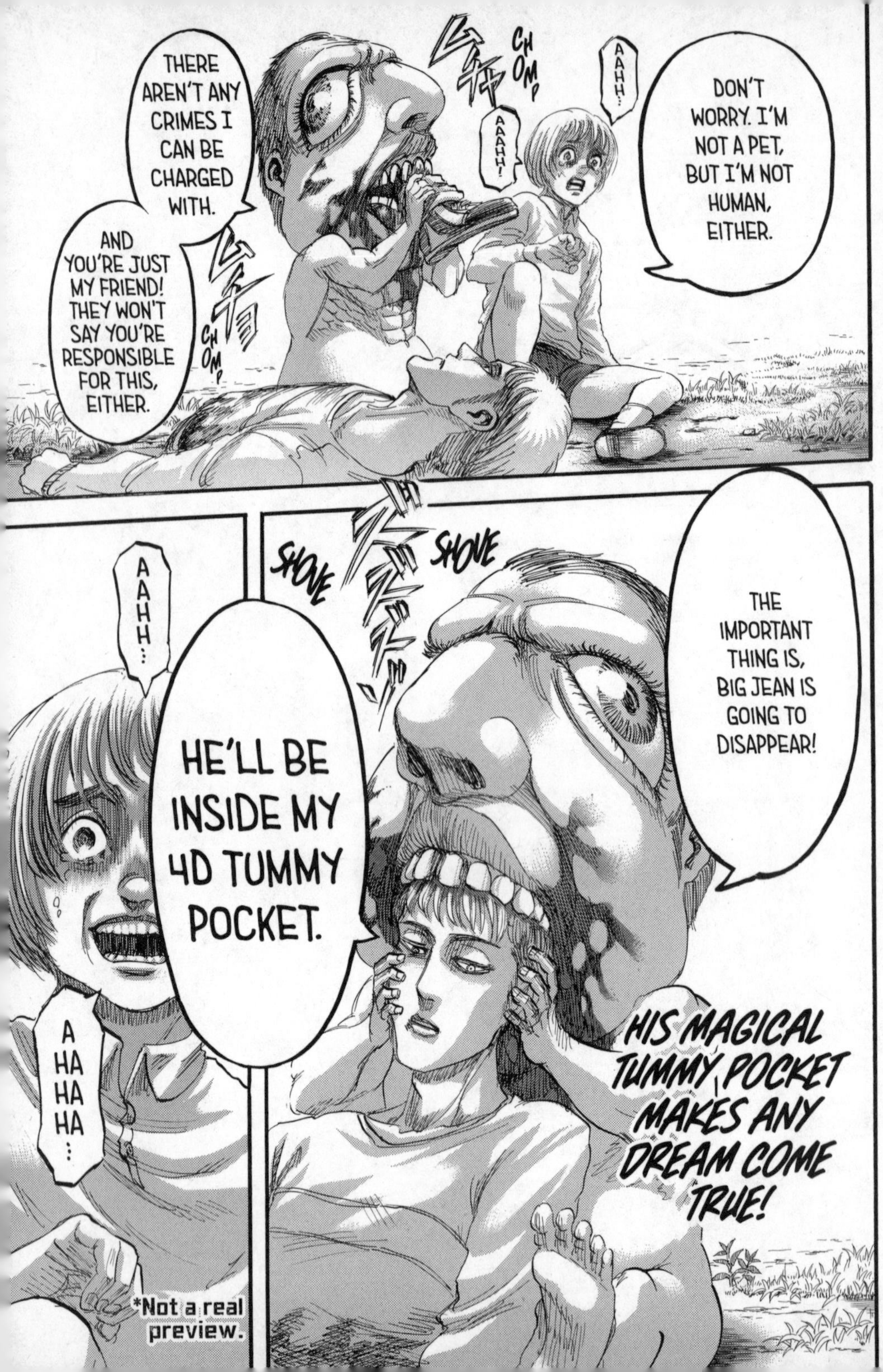
DON'T WORRY. I'M NOT A PET, BUT I'M NOT HUMAN, EITHER.
AAHH...
CHOMP
AAAHH!
THERE AREN'T ANY CRIMES I CAN BE CHARGED WITH.
AND YOU'RE JUST MY FRIEND! THEY WON'T SAY YOU'RE RESPONSIBLE FOR THIS, EITHER.
CHOMP
THE IMPORTANT THING IS, BIG JEAN IS GOING TO DISAPPEAR!
SHOVE
SHOVE
HE'LL BE INSIDE MY 4D TUMMY POCKET.
HIS MAGICAL TUMMY POCKET MAKES ANY DREAM COME TRUE!
*Not a real preview.
AAHH...
AHAHAHAHA...

ATTACK on TITAN

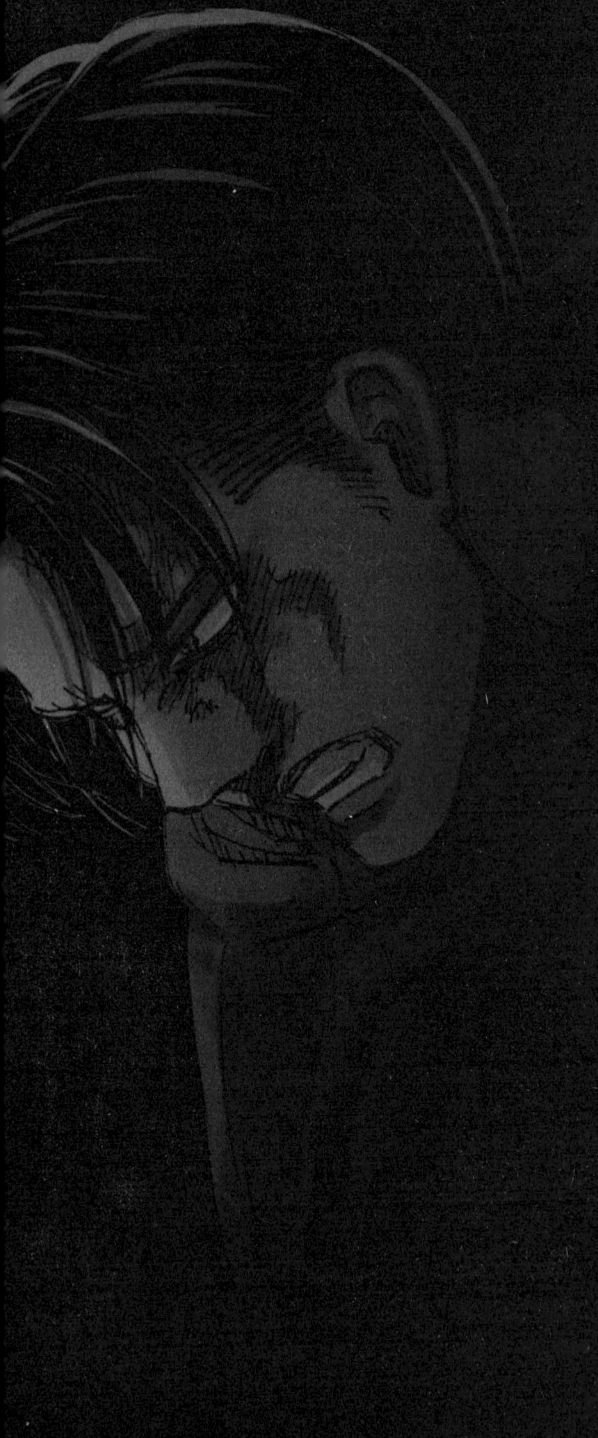

ATTACK ON TITAN 20

HAJIME ISAYAMA

"Attack on Titan" Character Introductions

104th Corps

raduated at
e top of her
raining corps,
ikasa is a
ighly talented
oldier. Her
arents were
urdered before
er eyes when
he was a child,
ut Eren saved
er life. Since
hen, she has
nade it her
nission to
rotect him.

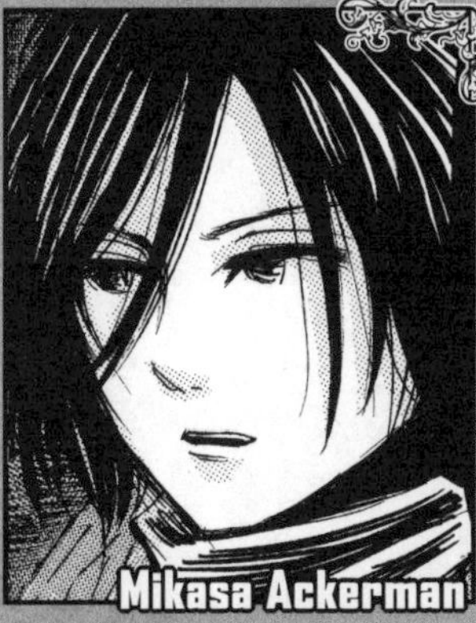

Mikasa Ackerman

Eren joined the Survey Corps out of his longing for the outside world and his hatred of the Titans. He has the power to turn himself into a Titan, but its origins are unknown.

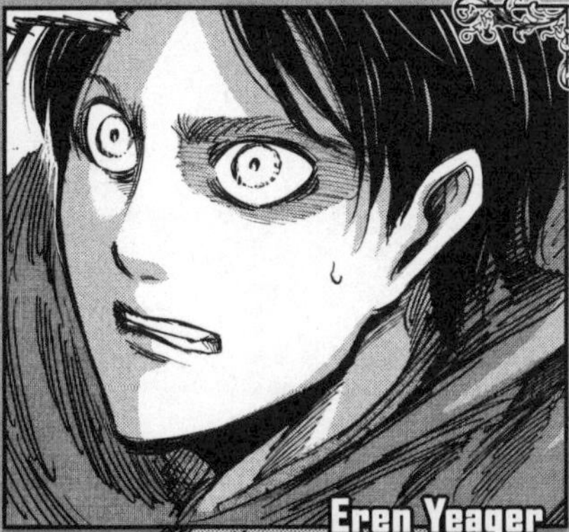

Eren Yeager

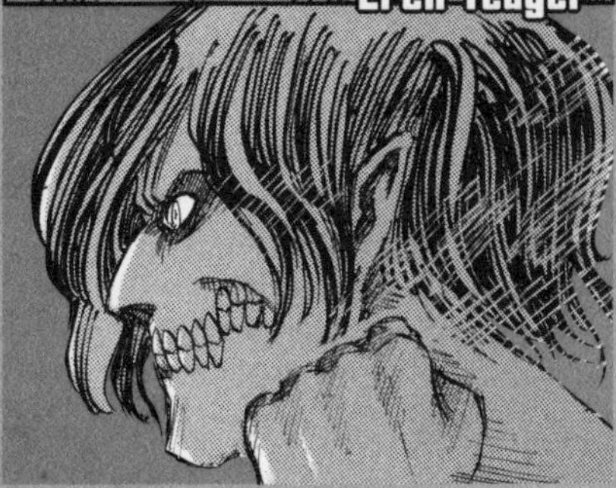

Eren and Mikasa's childhood friend. Though Armin isn't athletic in the least, he possesses both sharp observational powers and keen insight, and he exhibits an extraordinary ability to develop strategies.

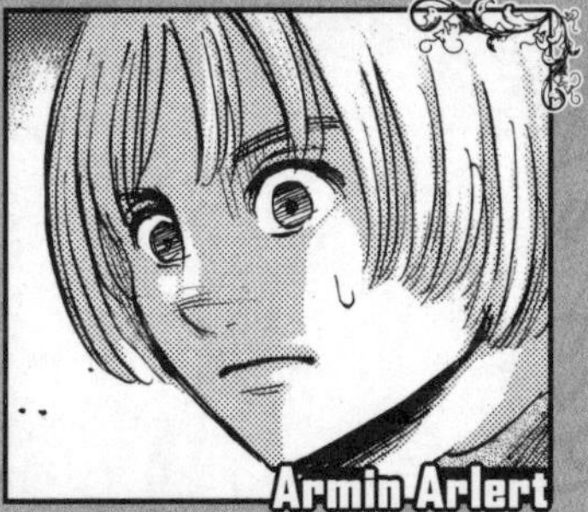

Armin Arlert

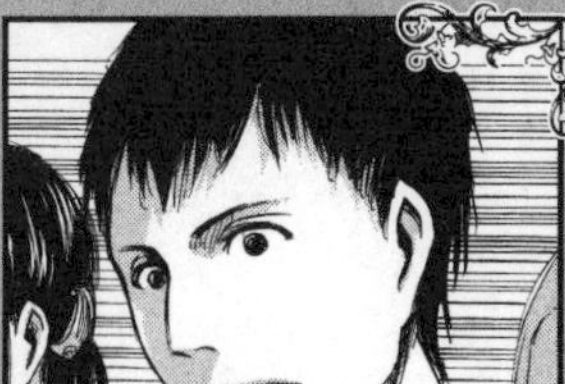

Bertolt Hoover

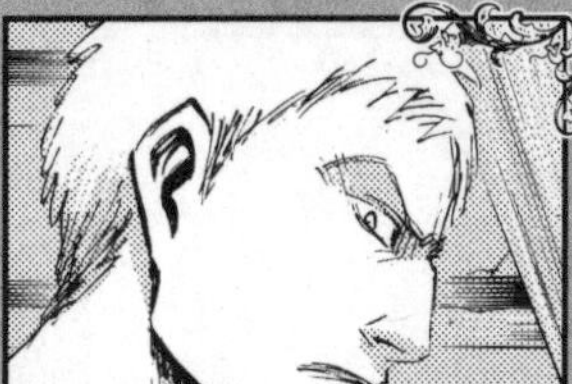

Reiner Braun

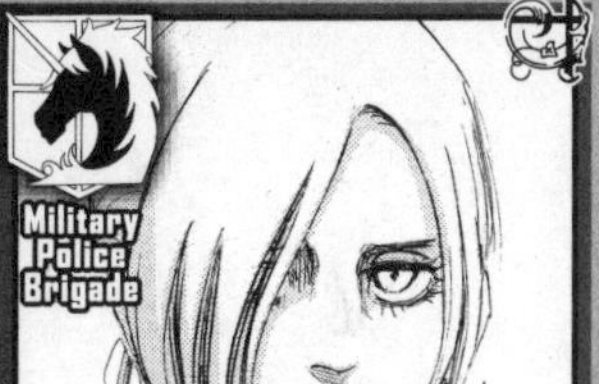
Military Police Brigade

Annie Leonhart

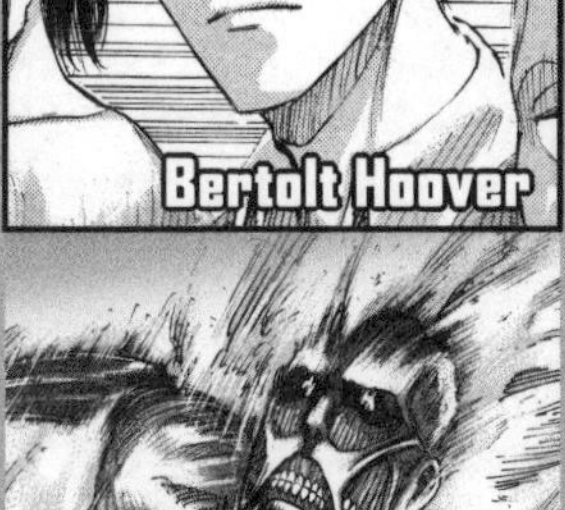

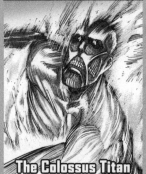

The Colossus Titan

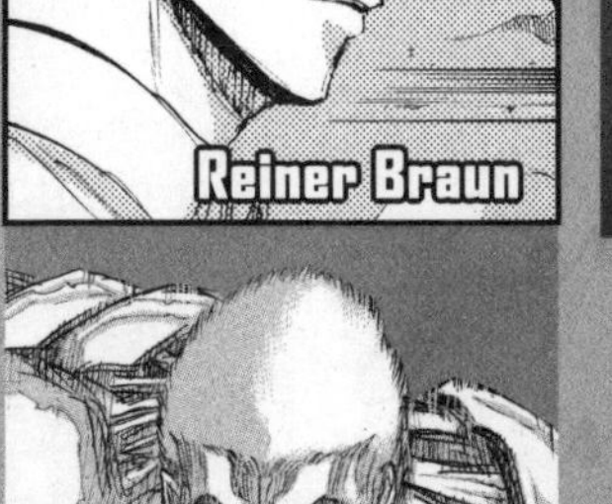

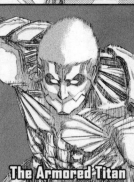

The Armored Titan

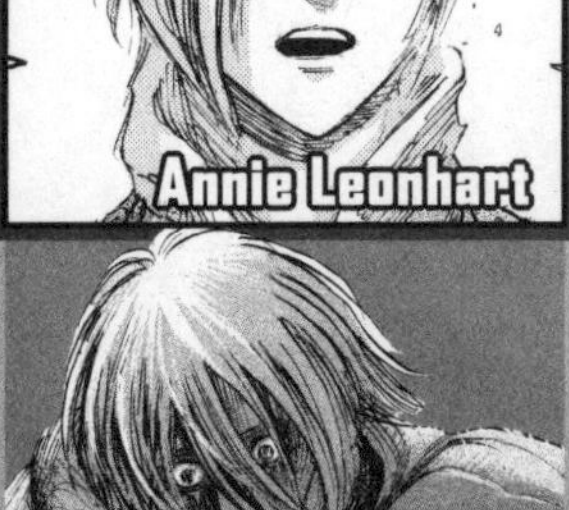

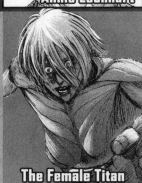

The Female Titan

Survey Corps

Soldiers who are prepared to sacrifice themselves as they brave the Titan territory outside the walls

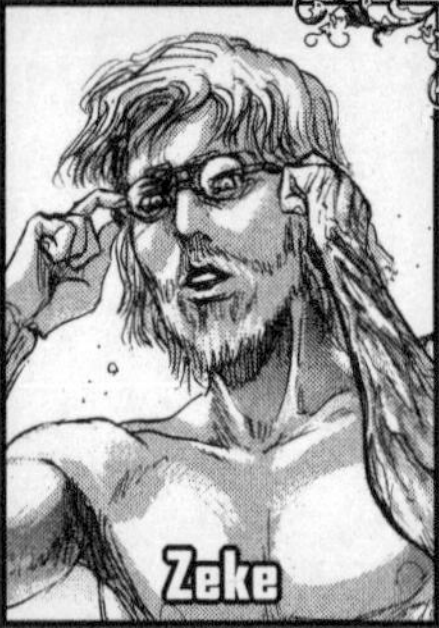
Zeke

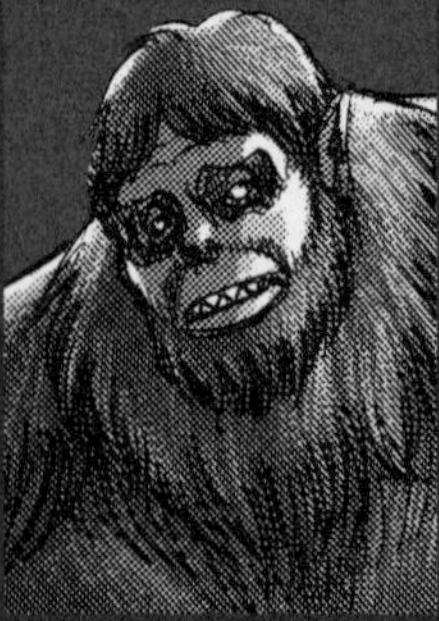

The Beast Titan

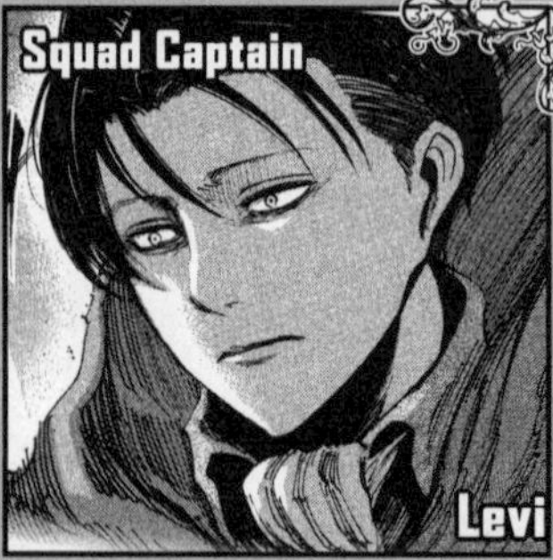
Squad Captain
Levi

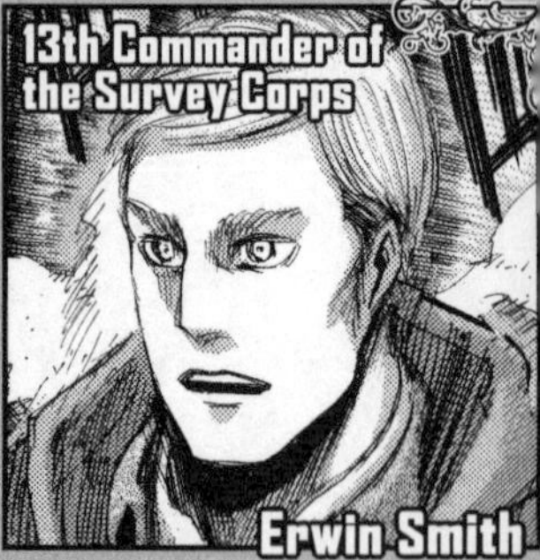
13th Commander of the Survey Corps
Erwin Smith

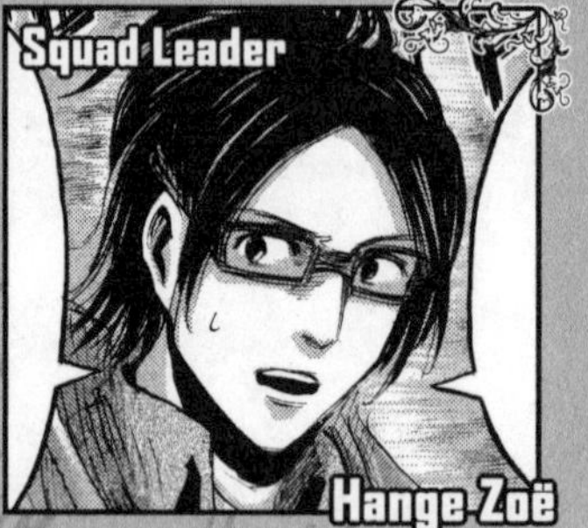
Squad Leader
Hange Zoë

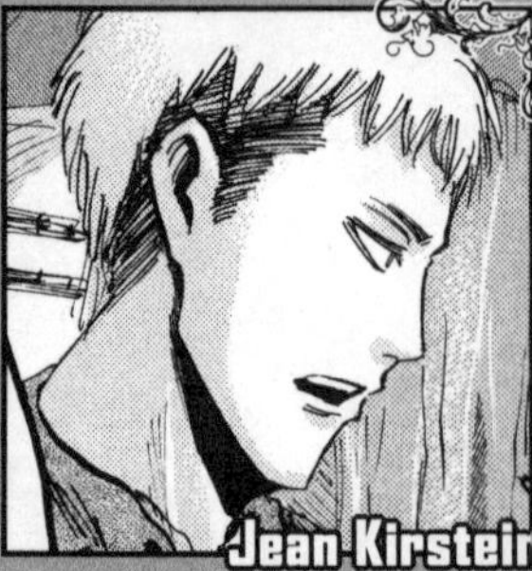
Jean Kirstein

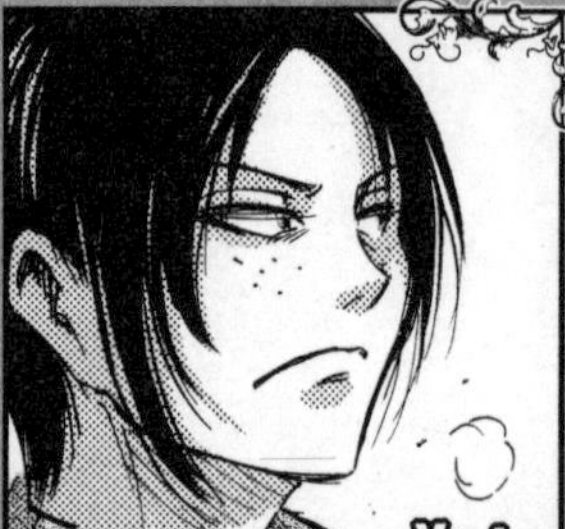
Ymir

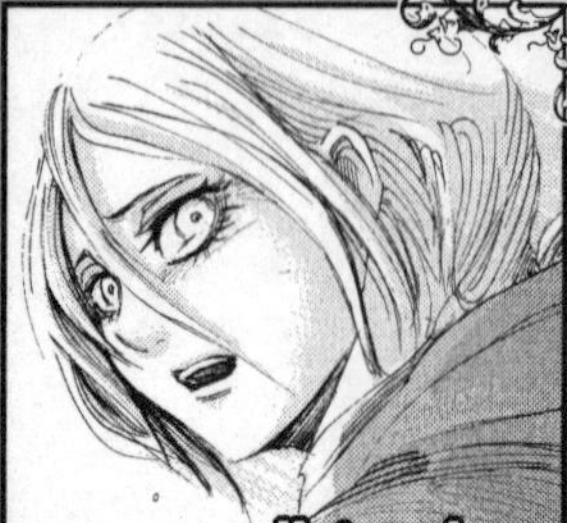
Krista Lenz

(Historia Reiss)

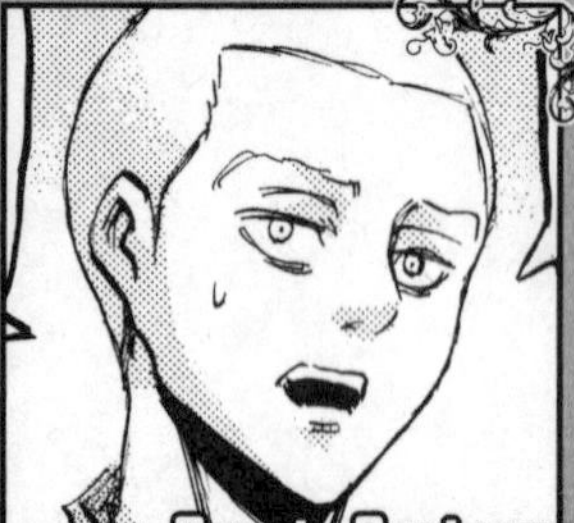
Connie Springer

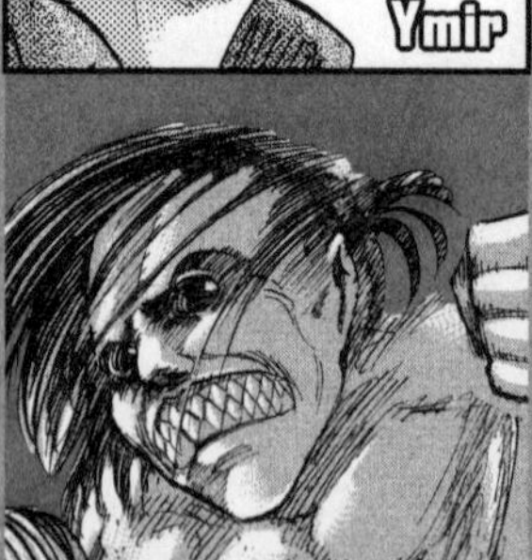

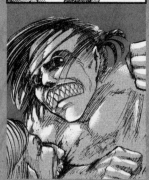

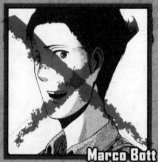

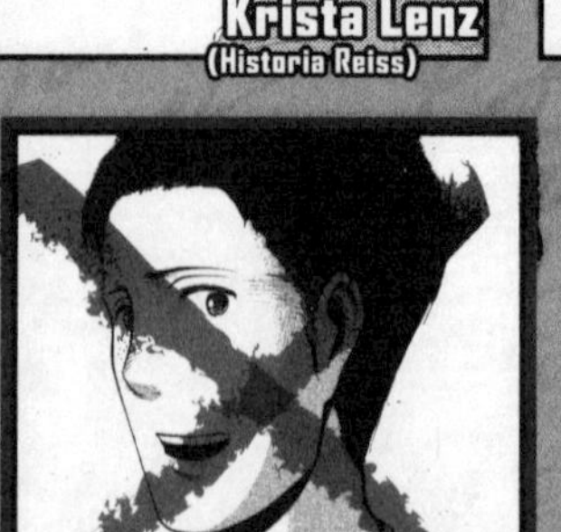
Marco Bott

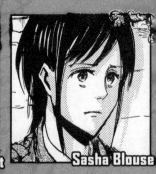

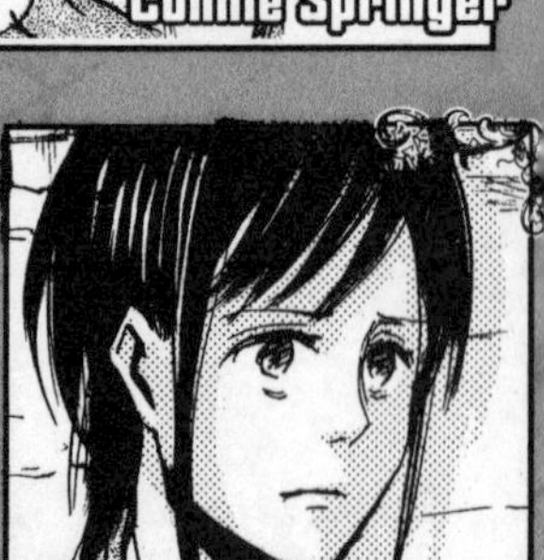
Sasha Blouse

ATTACK on TITAN

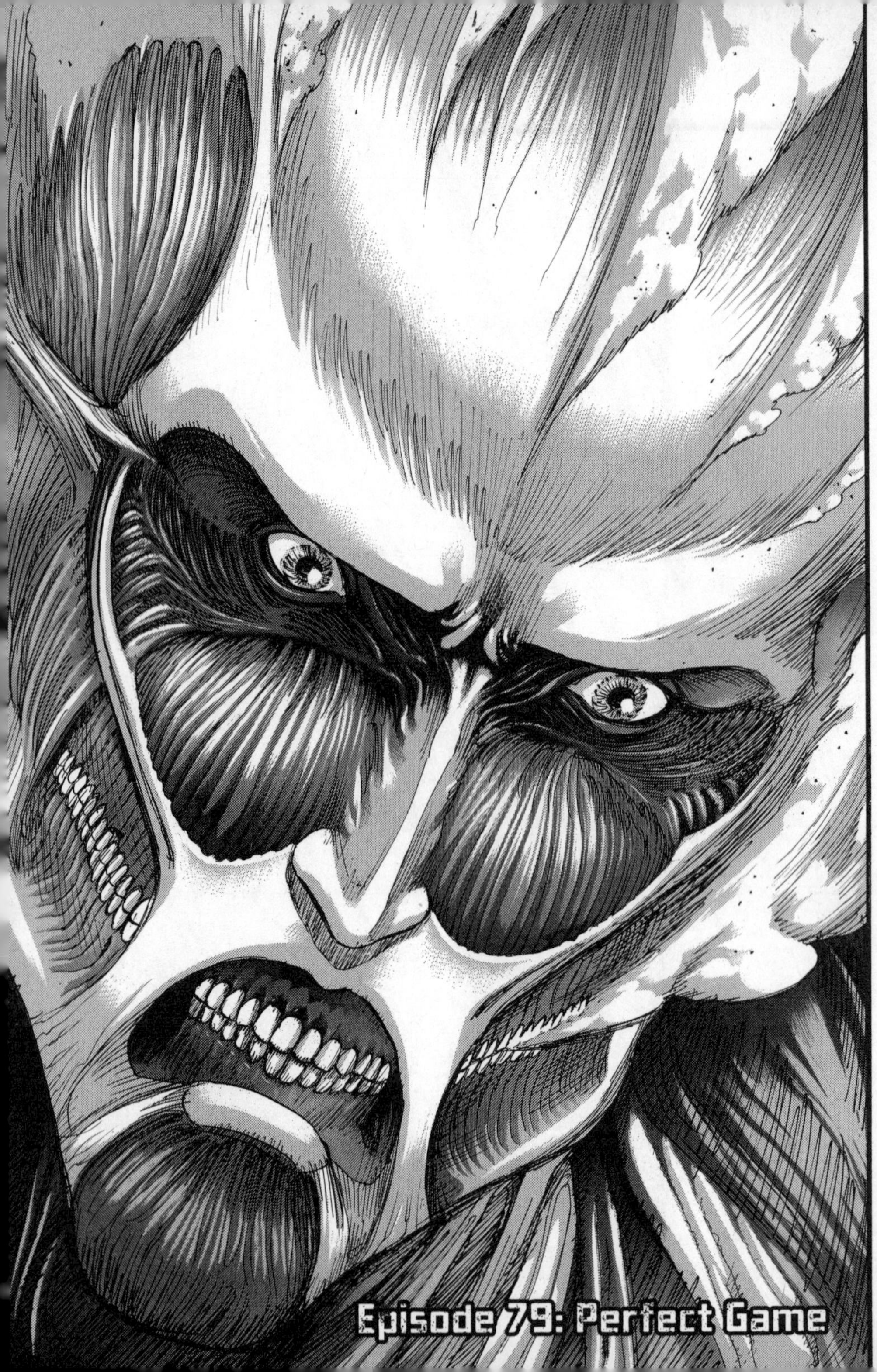
Episode 79: Perfect Game

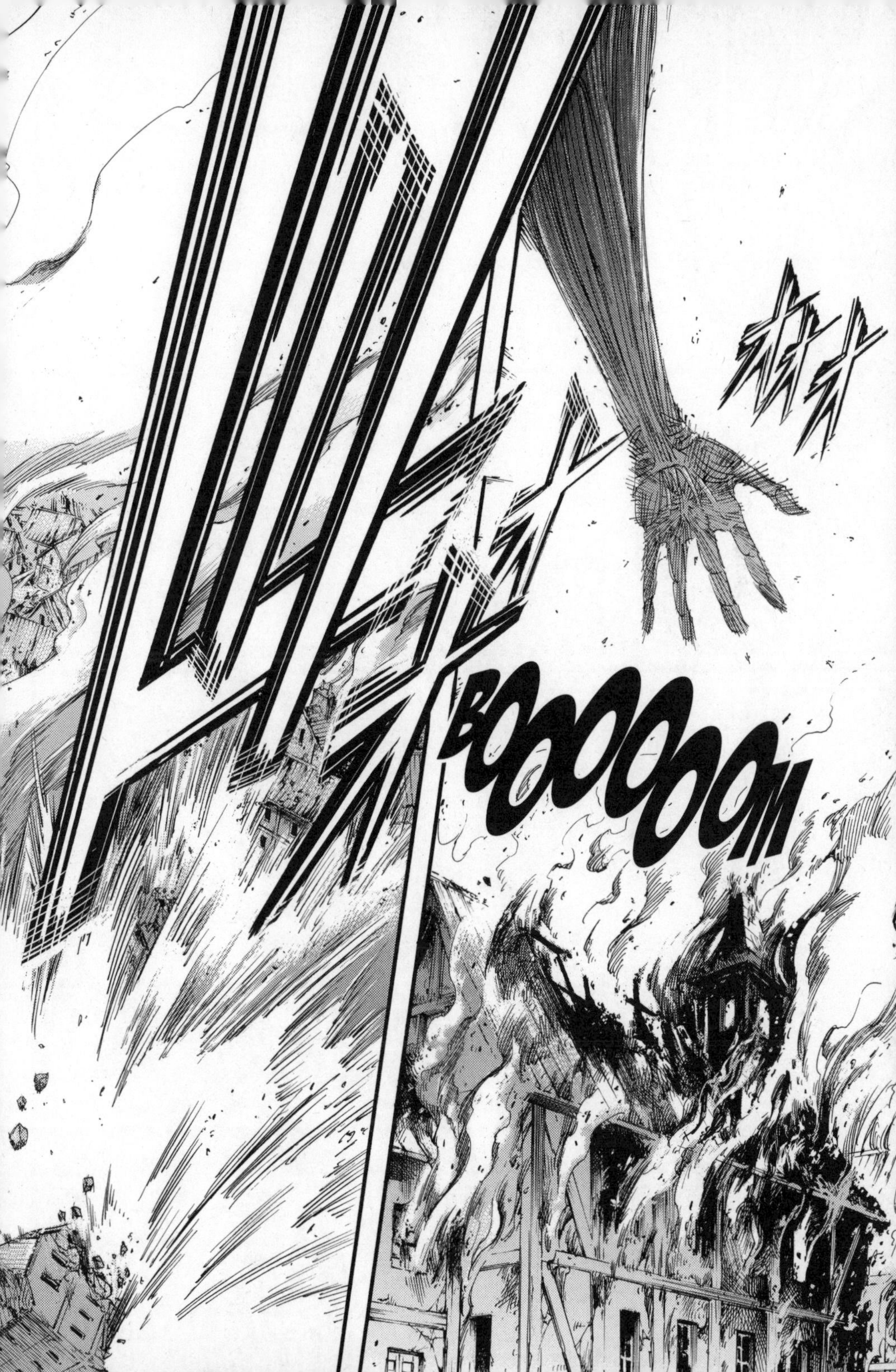
BOOOOOM

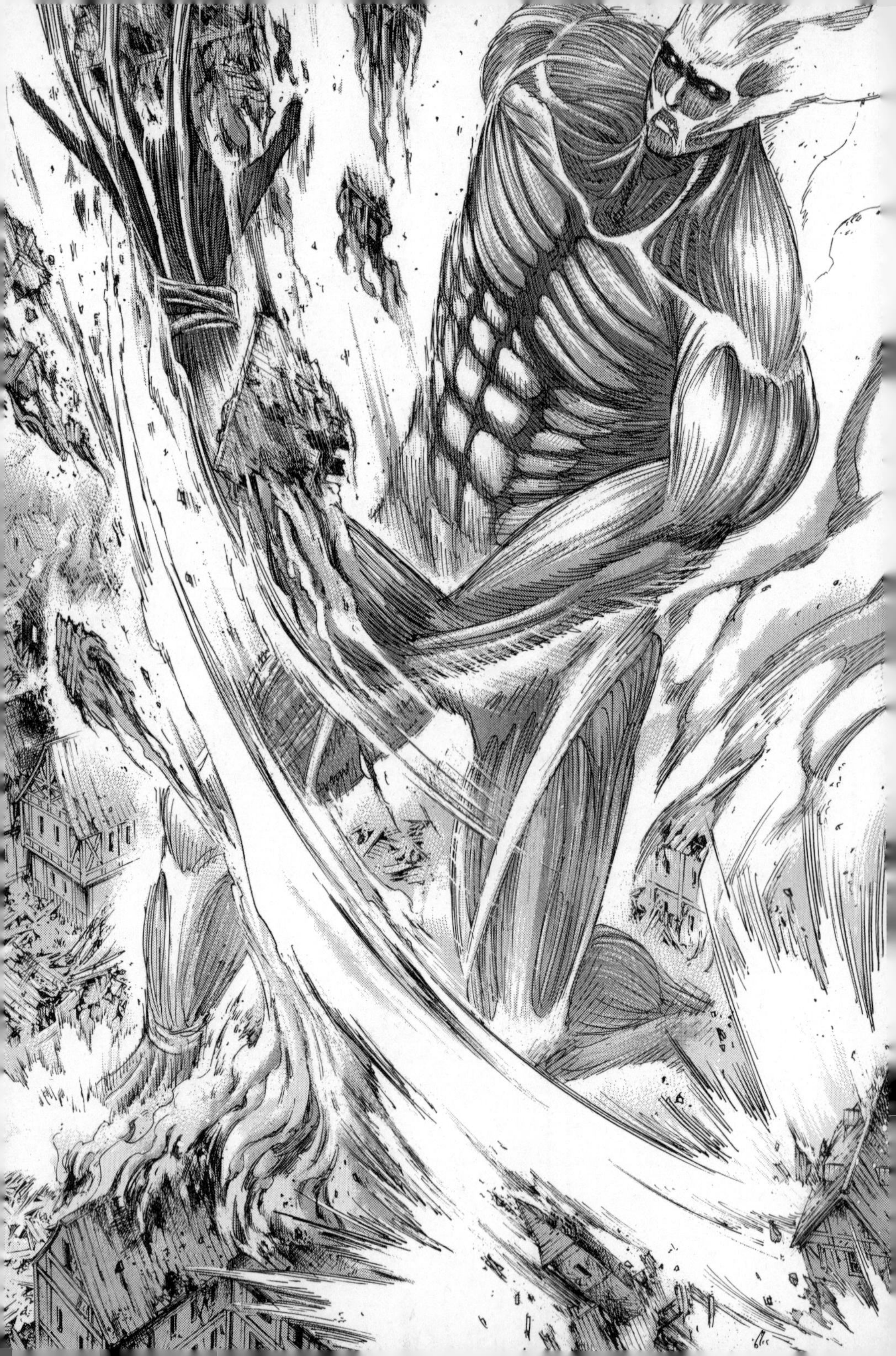

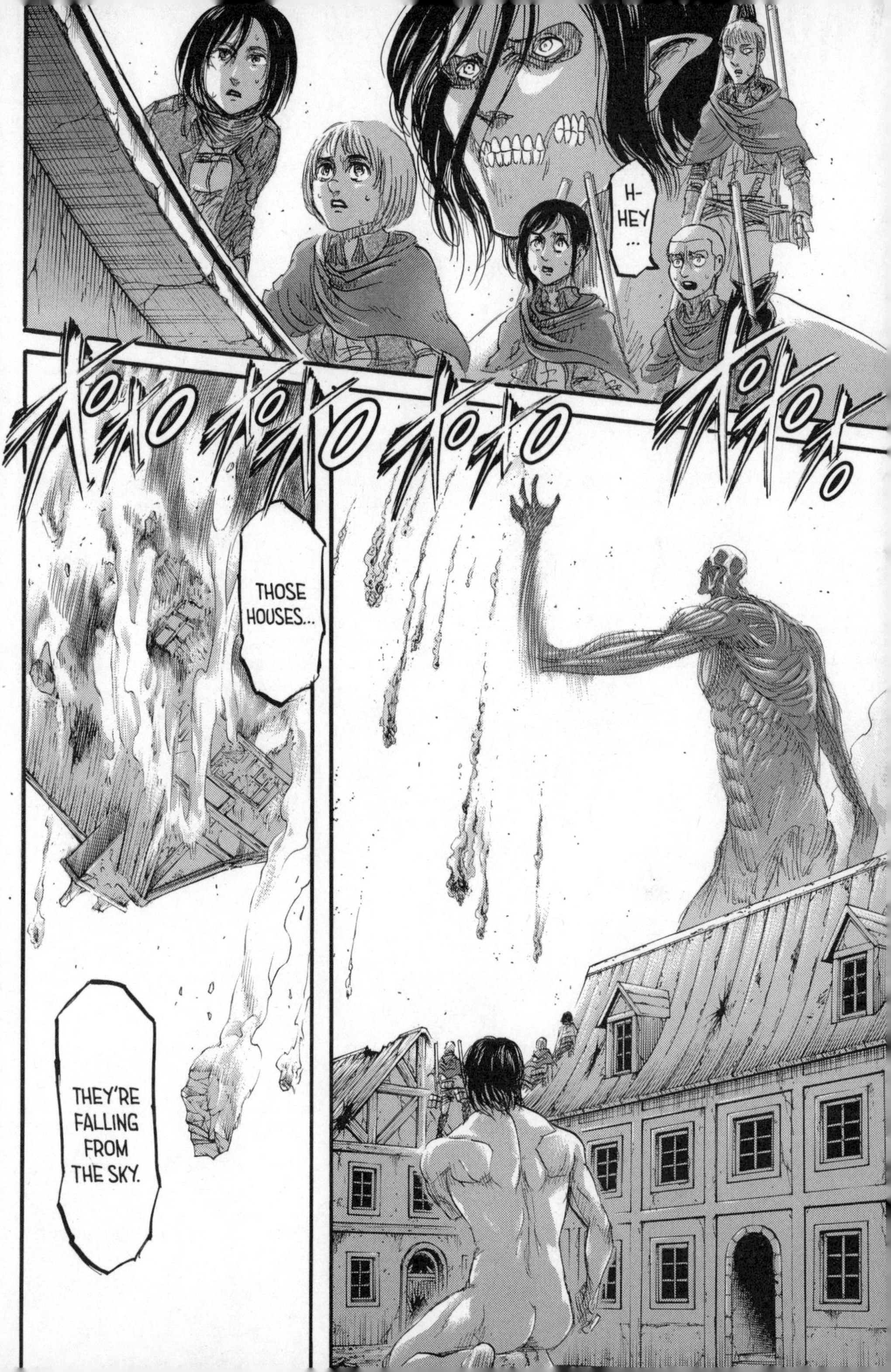
H-HEY ...
THOSE HOUSES...
THEY'RE FALLING FROM THE SKY.

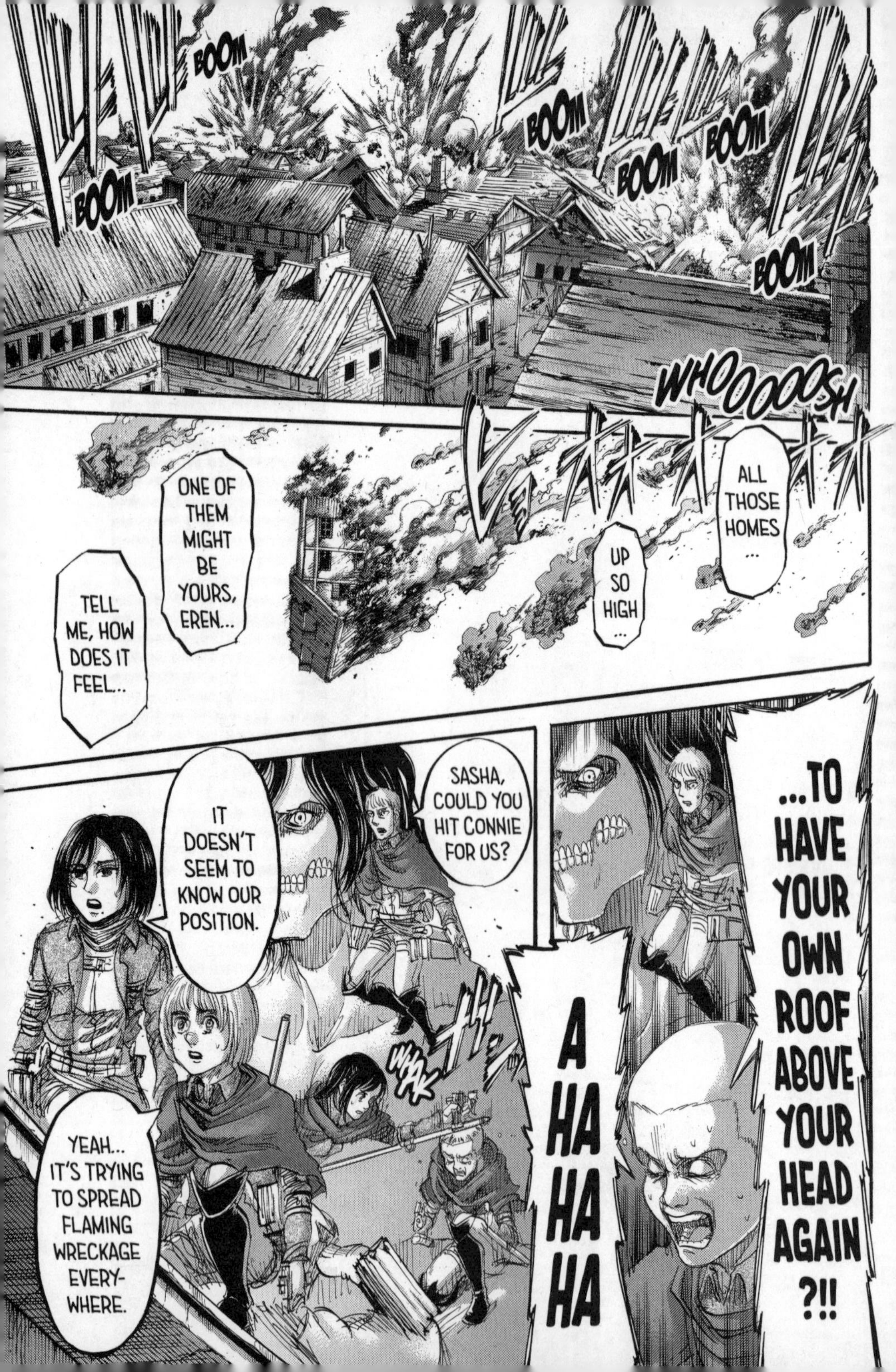
BOOM
BOOM
BOOM
BOOM
BOOM
BOOM
WHOOOOOOSH
ALL THOSE HOMES ...
UP SO HIGH ...
ONE OF THEM MIGHT BE YOURS, EREN...
TELL ME, HOW DOES IT FEEL..
...TO HAVE YOUR OWN ROOF ABOVE YOUR HEAD AGAIN?!!
A HA HA HA HA HA
SASHA, COULD YOU HIT CONNIE FOR US?
IT DOESN'T SEEM TO KNOW OUR POSITION.
WHAK
YEAH... IT'S TRYING TO SPREAD FLAMING WRECKAGE EVERY-WHERE.

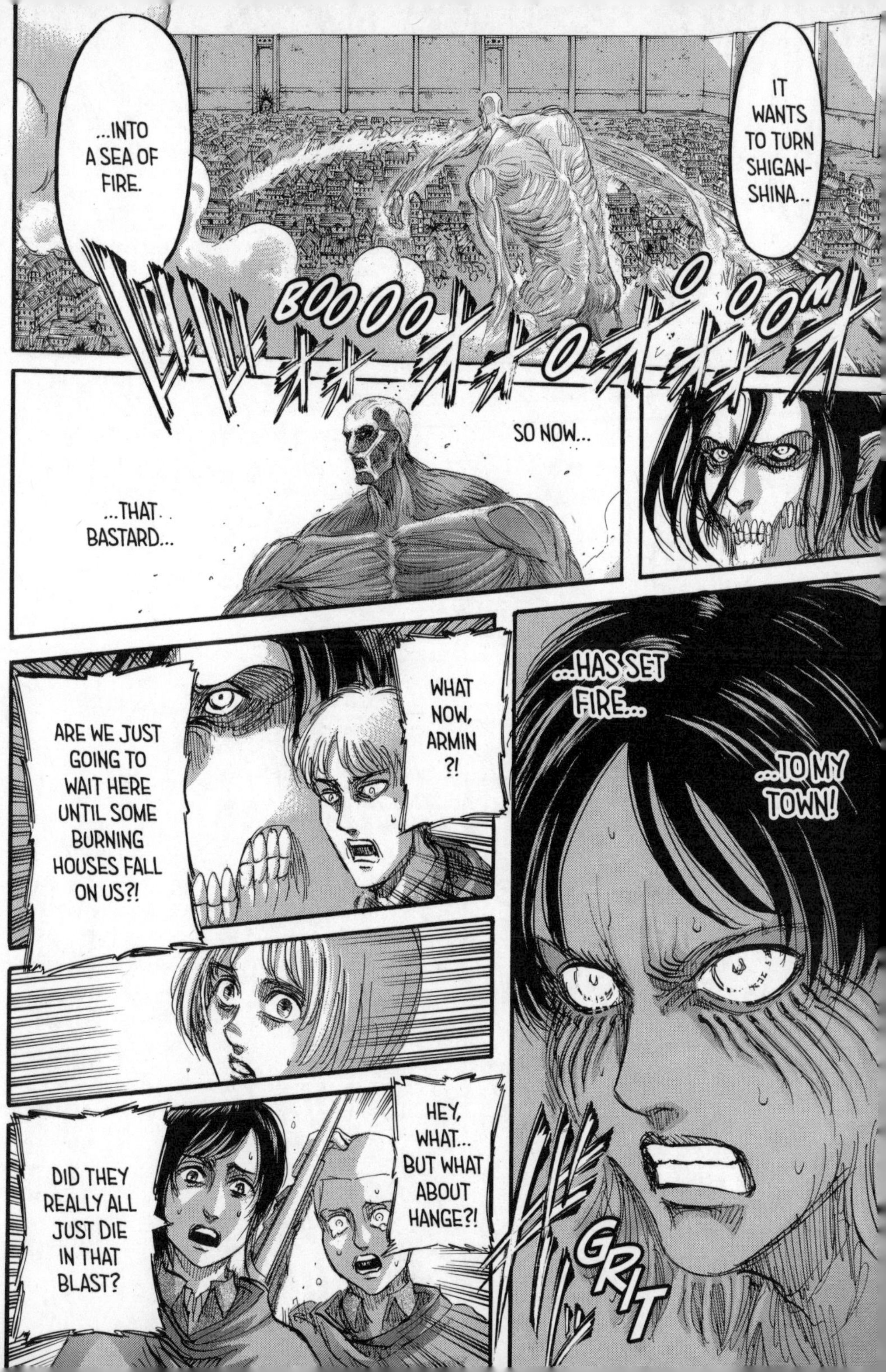

IT WANTS TO TURN SHIGAN-SHINA...
...INTO A SEA OF FIRE.
BOOOOOOOOM
SO NOW...
...THAT BASTARD...
...HAS SET FIRE...
...TO MY TOWN!
GRIT
WHAT NOW, ARMIN?!
ARE WE JUST GOING TO WAIT HERE UNTIL SOME BURNING HOUSES FALL ON US?!
HEY, WHAT... BUT WHAT ABOUT HANGE?!
DID THEY REALLY ALL JUST DIE IN THAT BLAST?

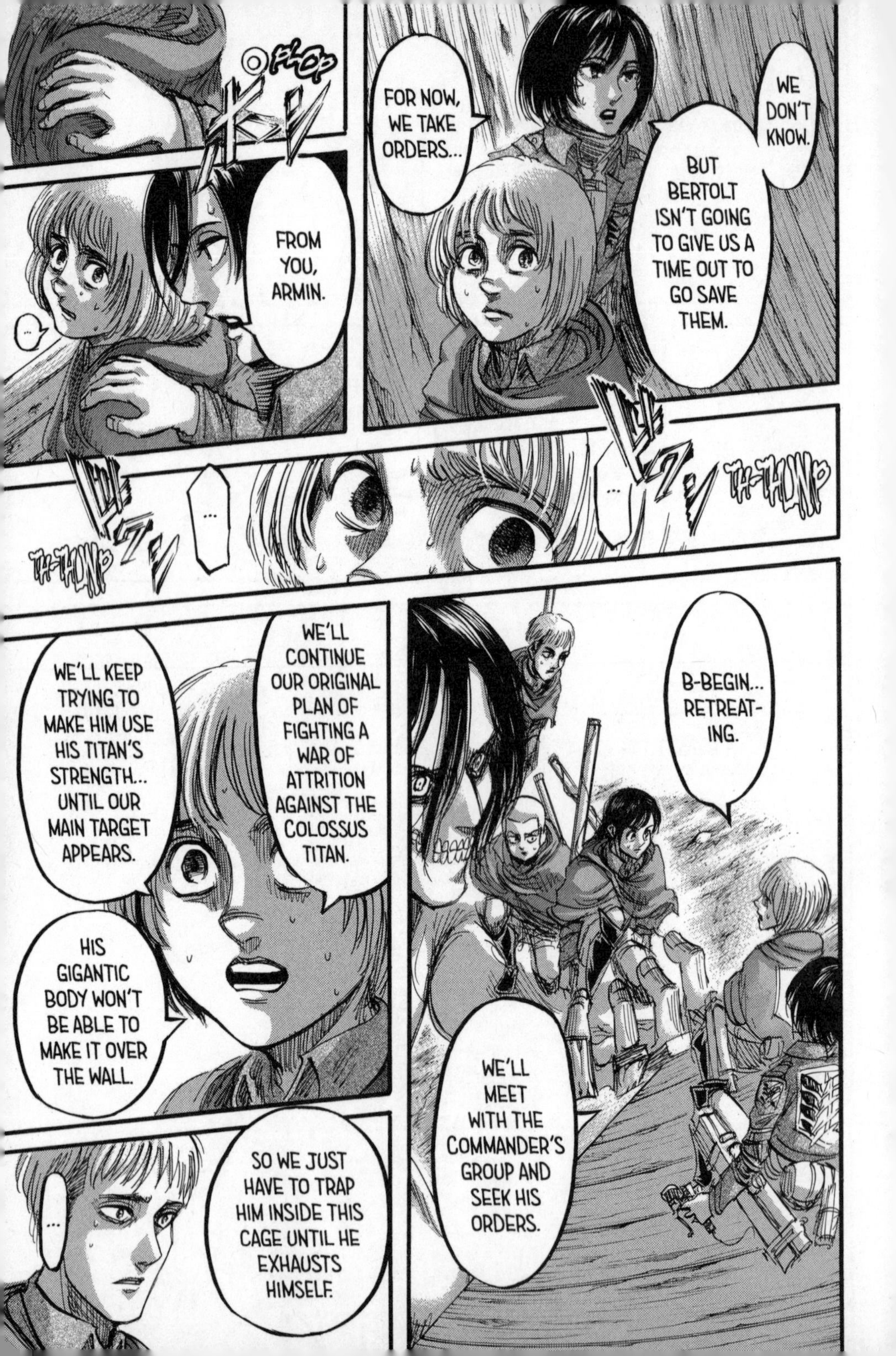
WE DON'T KNOW.
BUT BERTOLT ISN'T GOING TO GIVE US A TIME OUT TO GO SAVE THEM.
FOR NOW, WE TAKE ORDERS...
PLOP
FROM YOU, ARMIN.
...
TH-THUMP
...
...
TH-THUMP
B-BEGIN... RETREATING.
WE'LL MEET WITH THE COMMANDER'S GROUP AND SEEK HIS ORDERS.
WE'LL CONTINUE OUR ORIGINAL PLAN OF FIGHTING A WAR OF ATTRITION AGAINST THE COLOSSUS TITAN.
WE'LL KEEP TRYING TO MAKE HIM USE HIS TITAN'S STRENGTH... UNTIL OUR MAIN TARGET APPEARS.
HIS GIGANTIC BODY WON'T BE ABLE TO MAKE IT OVER THE WALL.
SO WE JUST HAVE TO TRAP HIM INSIDE THIS CAGE UNTIL HE EXHAUSTS HIMSELF.
...

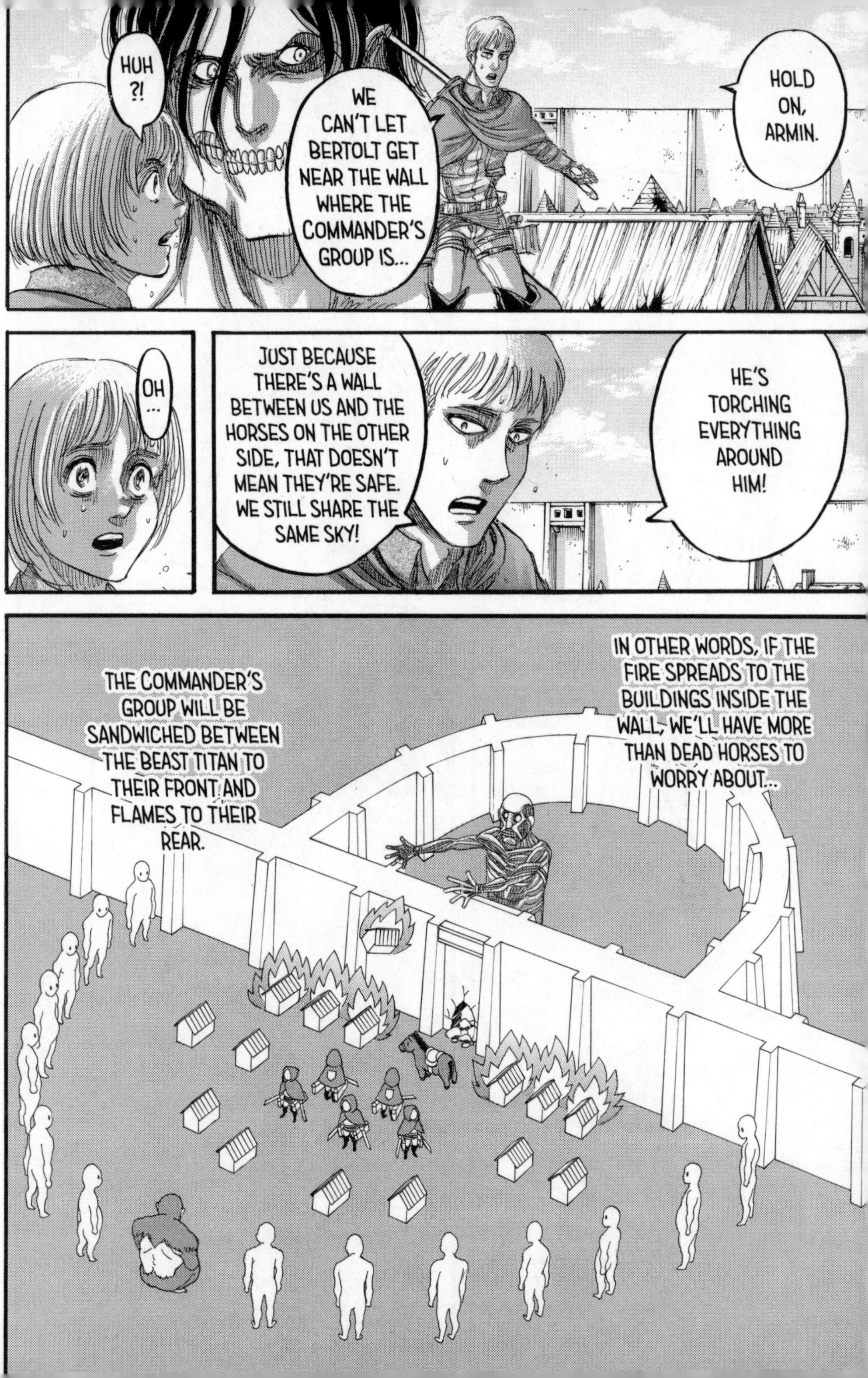
HOLD ON, ARMIN.
WE CAN'T LET BERTOLT GET NEAR THE WALL WHERE THE COMMANDER'S GROUP IS...
HUH ?!
HE'S TORCHING EVERYTHING AROUND HIM!
JUST BECAUSE THERE'S A WALL BETWEEN US AND THE HORSES ON THE OTHER SIDE, THAT DOESN'T MEAN THEY'RE SAFE. WE STILL SHARE THE SAME SKY!
OH ...
IN OTHER WORDS, IF THE FIRE SPREADS TO THE BUILDINGS INSIDE THE WALL, WE'LL HAVE MORE THAN DEAD HORSES TO WORRY ABOUT...
THE COMMANDER'S GROUP WILL BE SANDWICHED BETWEEN THE BEAST TITAN TO THEIR FRONT AND FLAMES TO THEIR REAR.

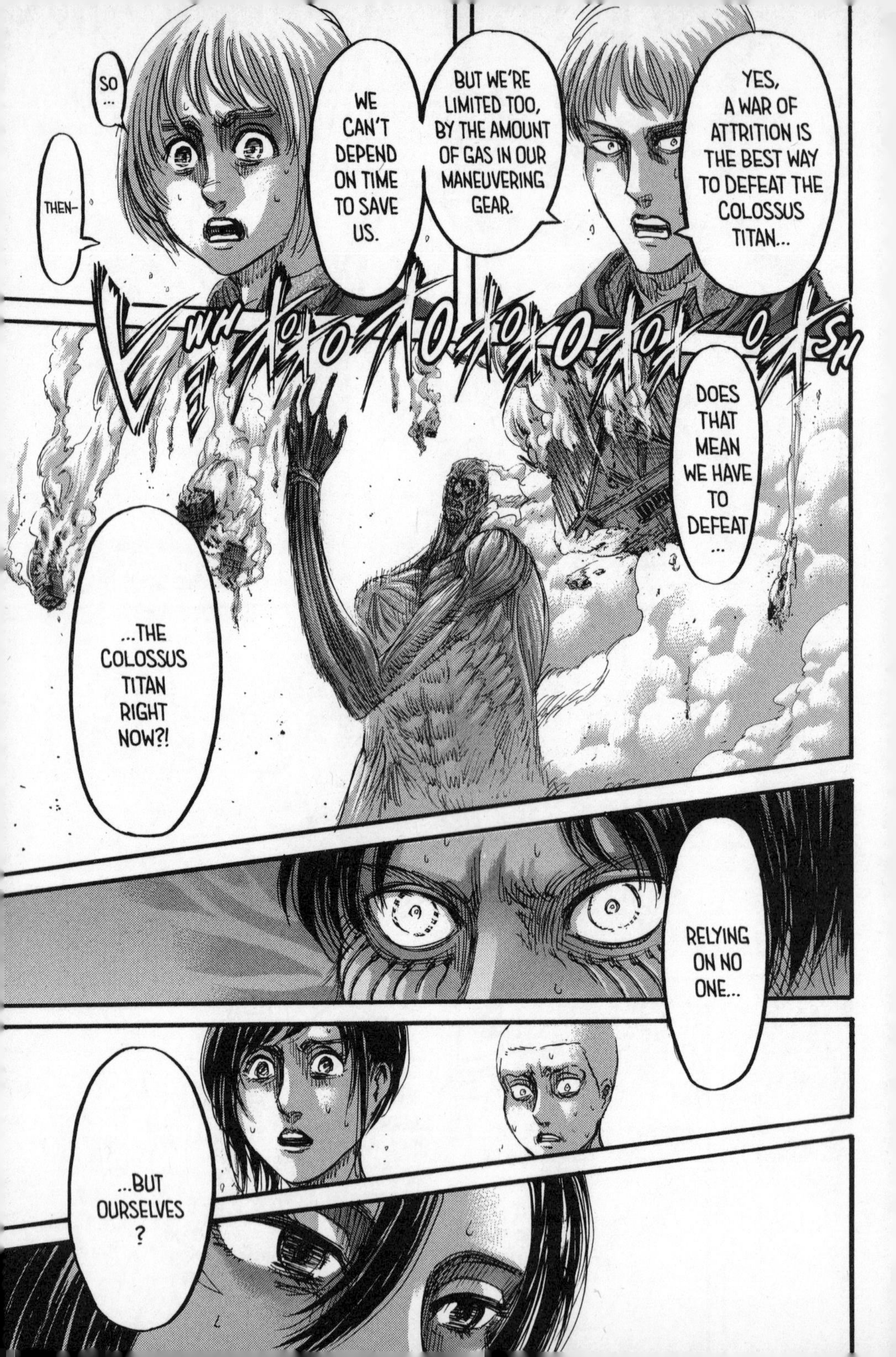
YES, A WAR OF ATTRITION IS THE BEST WAY TO DEFEAT THE COLOSSUS TITAN...
BUT WE'RE LIMITED TOO, BY THE AMOUNT OF GAS IN OUR MANEUVERING GEAR.
WE CAN'T DEPEND ON TIME TO SAVE US.
SO ...
THEN-
DOES THAT MEAN WE HAVE TO DEFEAT ...
...THE COLOSSUS TITAN RIGHT NOW?!
RELYING ON NO ONE...
...BUT OURSELVES ?

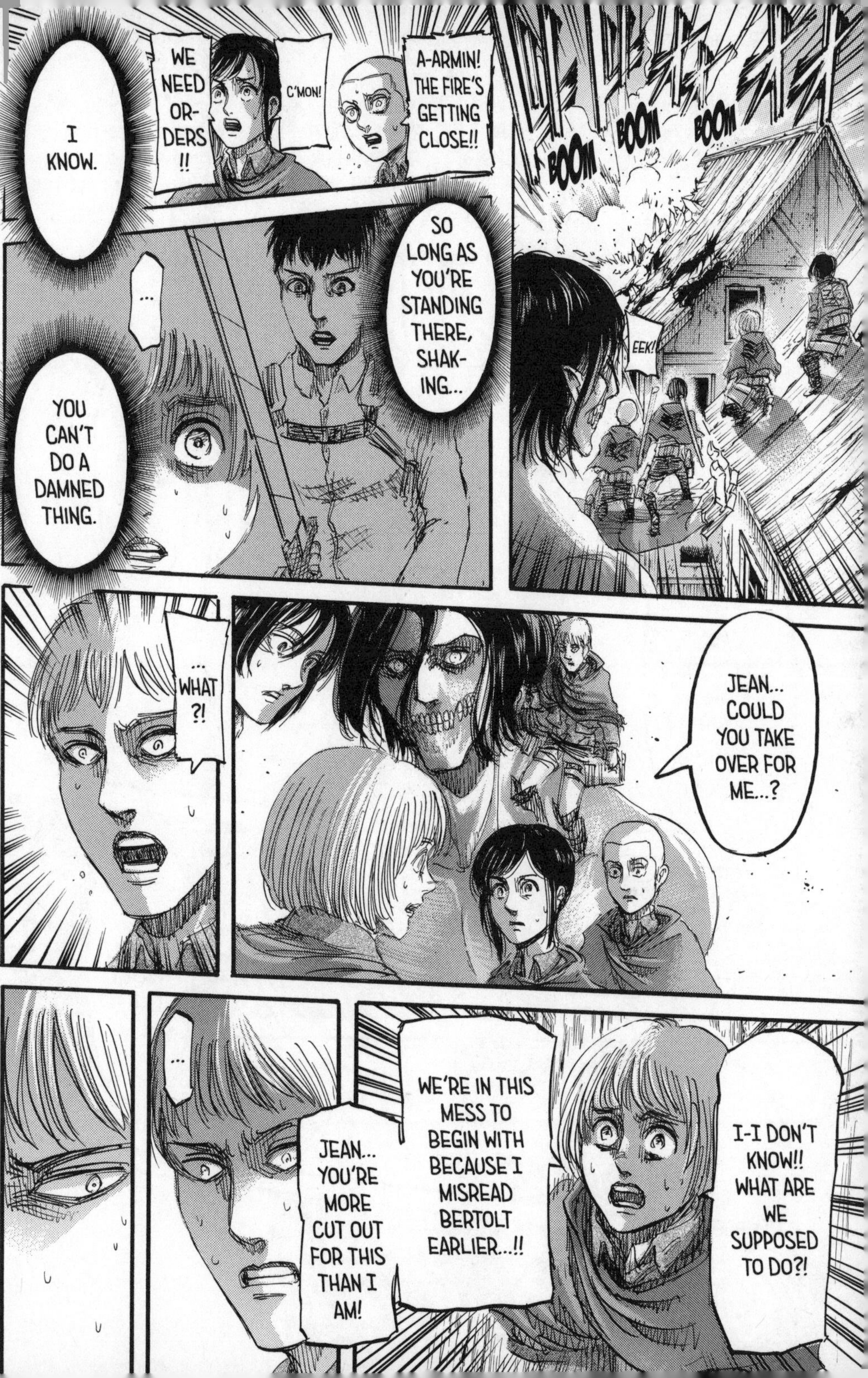
BOOM BOOM BOOM
EEK!
A-ARMIN! THE FIRE'S GETTING CLOSE!!
C'MON!
WE NEED ORDERS!!
I KNOW.
SO LONG AS YOU'RE STANDING THERE, SHAKING...
...
YOU CAN'T DO A DAMNED THING.
JEAN... COULD YOU TAKE OVER FOR ME...?
...WHAT?!
I-I DON'T KNOW!! WHAT ARE WE SUPPOSED TO DO?!
WE'RE IN THIS MESS TO BEGIN WITH BECAUSE I MISREAD BERTOLT EARLIER...!!
JEAN... YOU'RE MORE CUT OUT FOR THIS THAN I AM!
...

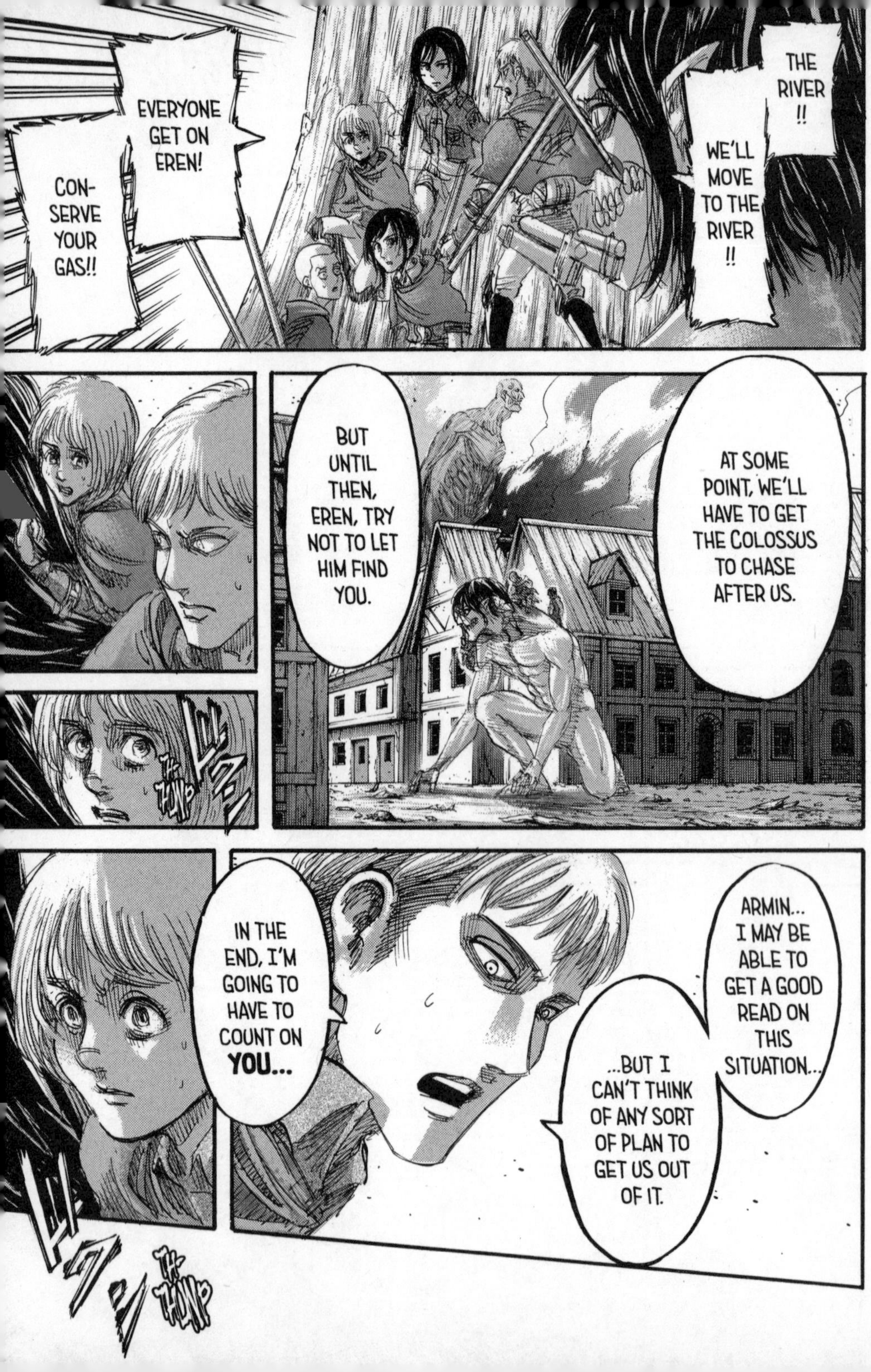
THE RIVER!!
WE'LL MOVE TO THE RIVER!!
EVERYONE GET ON EREN!
CON-SERVE YOUR GAS!!
AT SOME POINT, WE'LL HAVE TO GET THE COLOSSUS TO CHASE AFTER US.
BUT UNTIL THEN, EREN, TRY NOT TO LET HIM FIND YOU.
ARMIN... I MAY BE ABLE TO GET A GOOD READ ON THIS SITUATION...
...BUT I CAN'T THINK OF ANY SORT OF PLAN TO GET US OUT OF IT.
IN THE END, I'M GOING TO HAVE TO COUNT ON **YOU...**

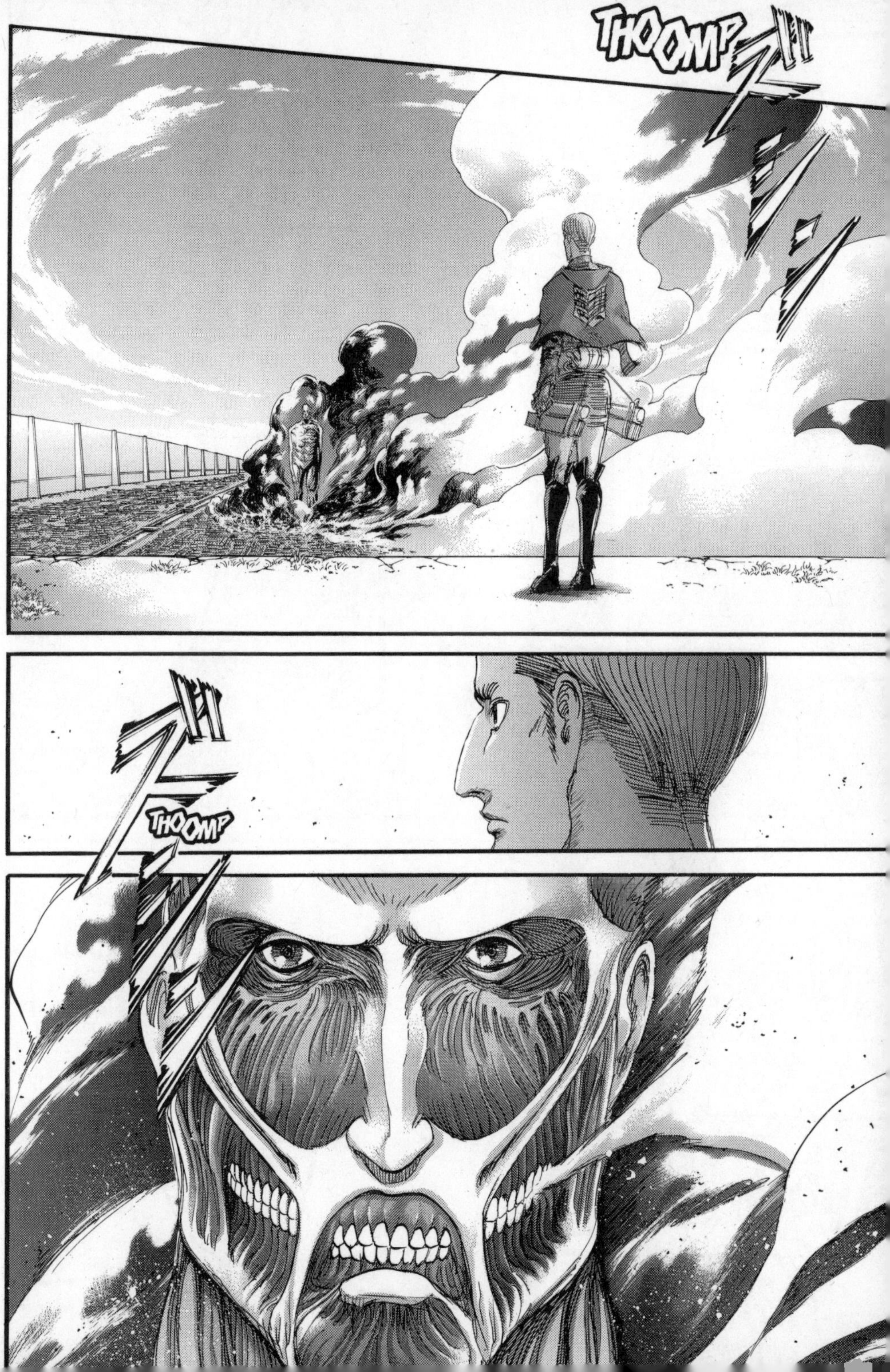
THOOMP
THOOMP

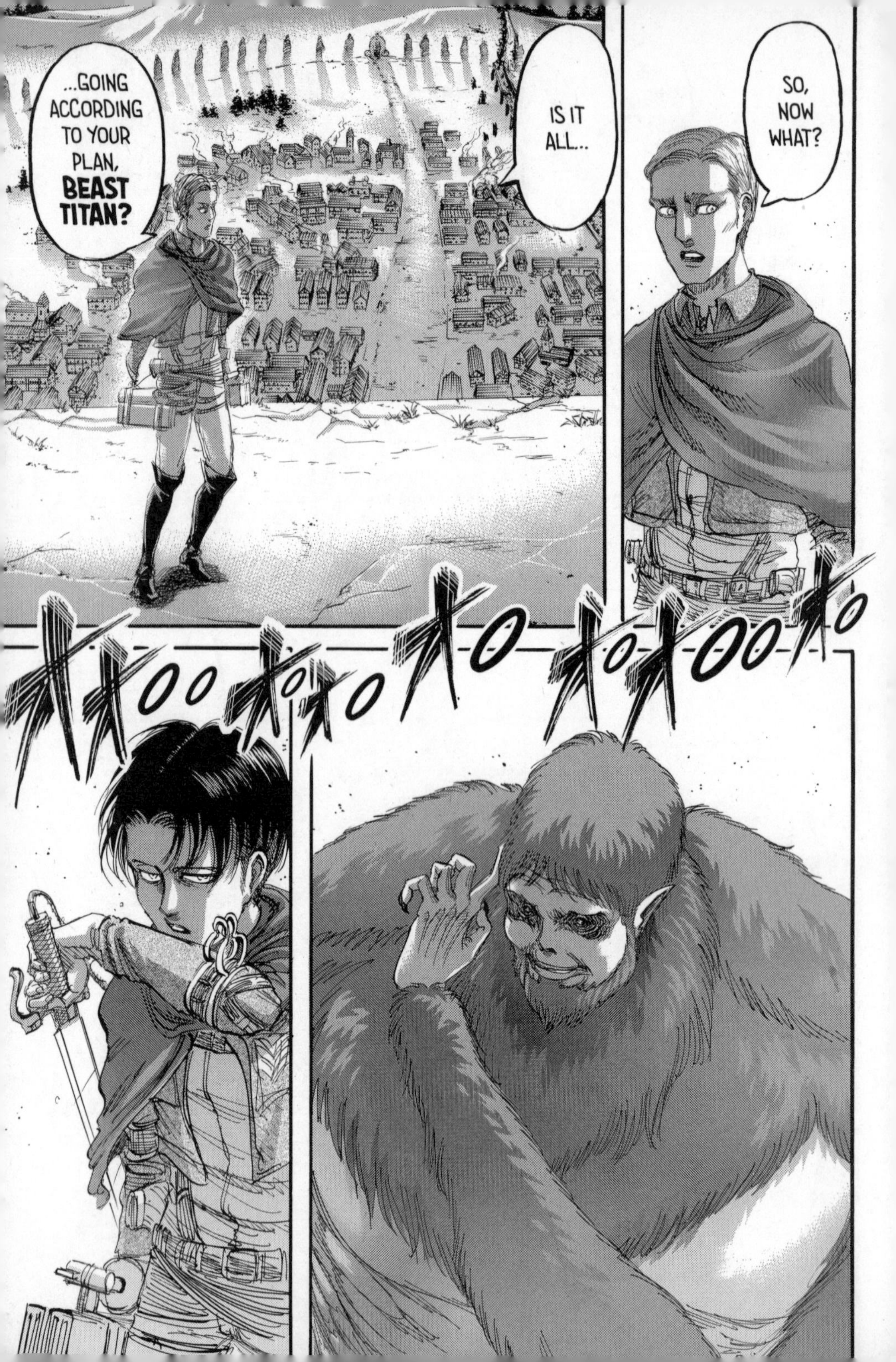
SO, NOW WHAT?
IS IT ALL...
...GOING ACCORDING TO YOUR PLAN, BEAST TITAN?

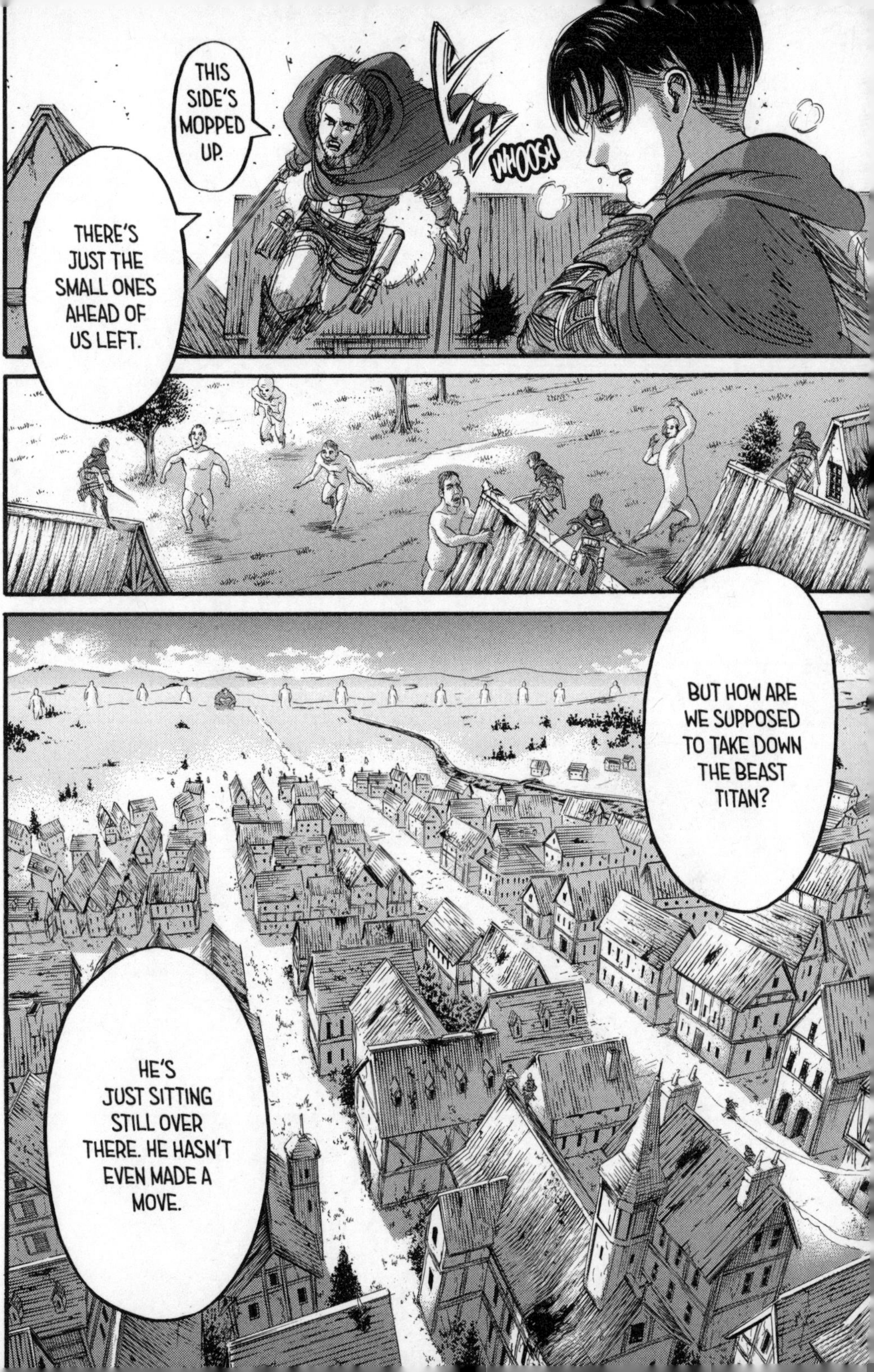
WHOOSH
THIS SIDE'S MOPPED UP.
THERE'S JUST THE SMALL ONES AHEAD OF US LEFT.
BUT HOW ARE WE SUPPOSED TO TAKE DOWN THE BEAST TITAN?
HE'S JUST SITTING STILL OVER THERE. HE HASN'T EVEN MADE A MOVE.

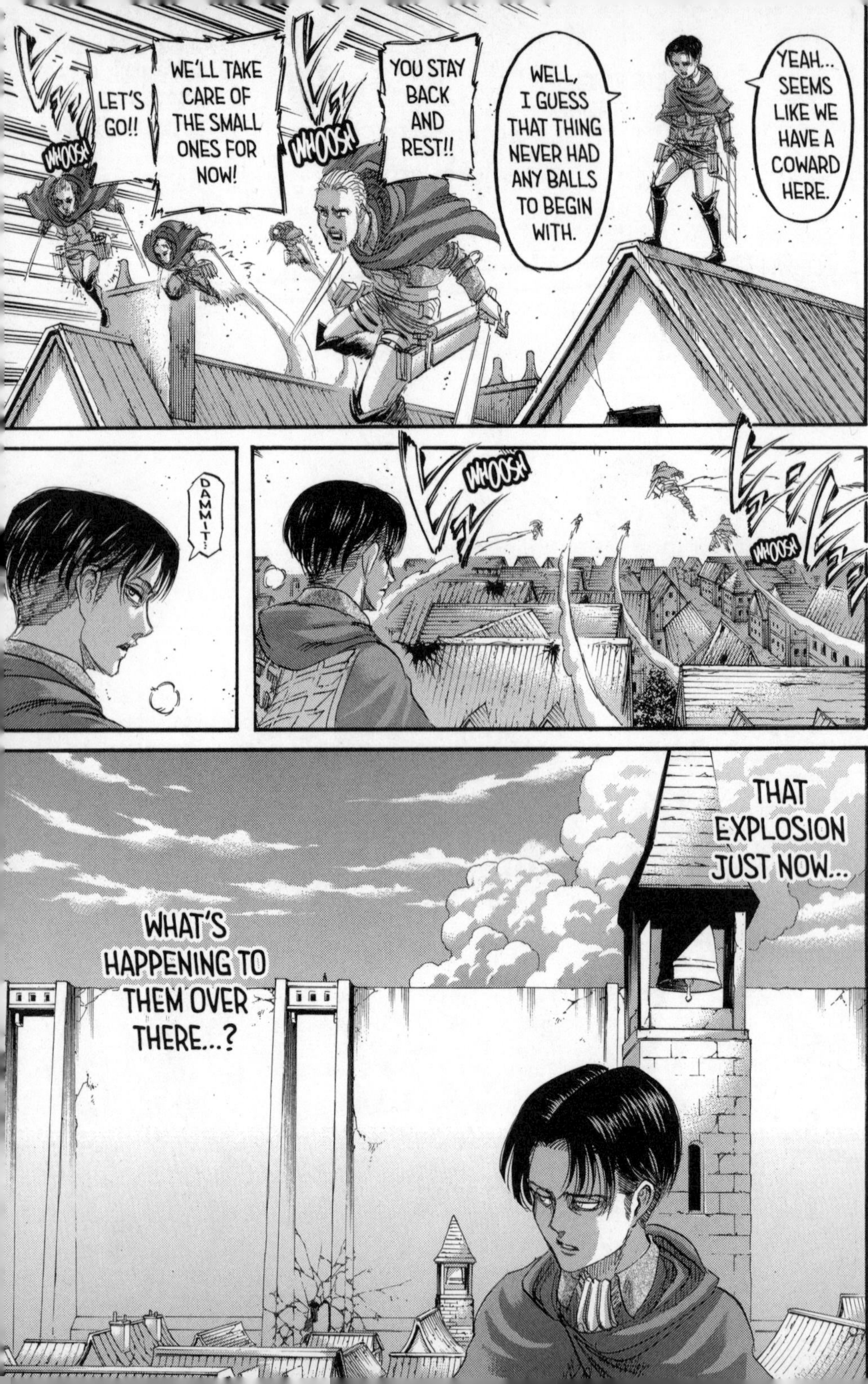
YEAH... SEEMS LIKE WE HAVE A COWARD HERE.
WELL, I GUESS THAT THING NEVER HAD ANY BALLS TO BEGIN WITH.
YOU STAY BACK AND REST!!
WHOOSH
WE'LL TAKE CARE OF THE SMALL ONES FOR NOW!
LET'S GO!!
WHOOSH
WHOOSH
WHOOSH
DAMMIT...!
THAT EXPLOSION JUST NOW...
WHAT'S HAPPENING TO THEM OVER THERE...?

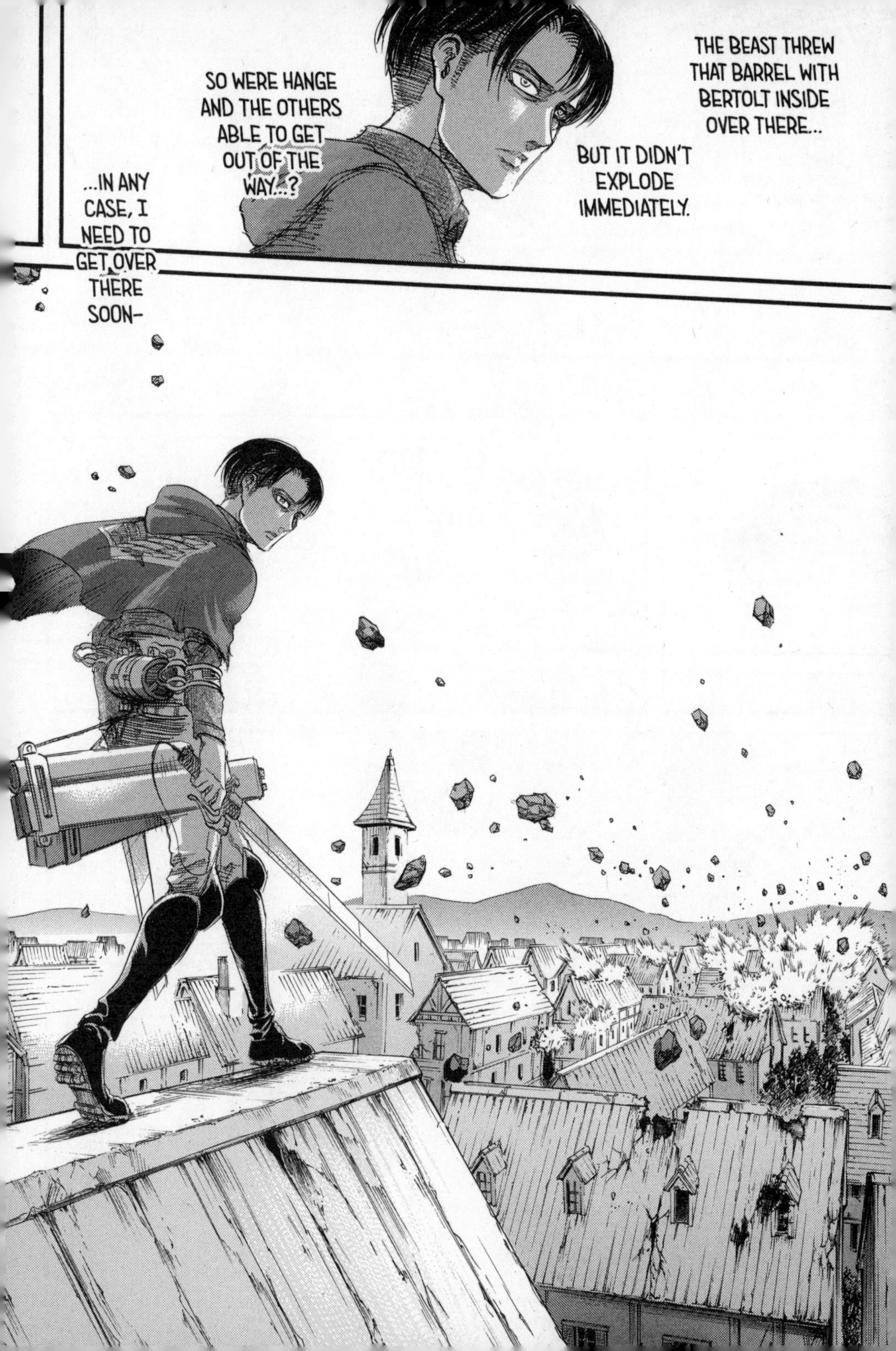
THE BEAST THREW THAT BARREL WITH BERTOLT INSIDE OVER THERE...
BUT IT DIDN'T EXPLODE IMMEDIATELY.
SO WERE HANGE AND THE OTHERS ABLE TO GET OUT OF THE WAY...?
...IN ANY CASE, I NEED TO GET OVER THERE SOON-

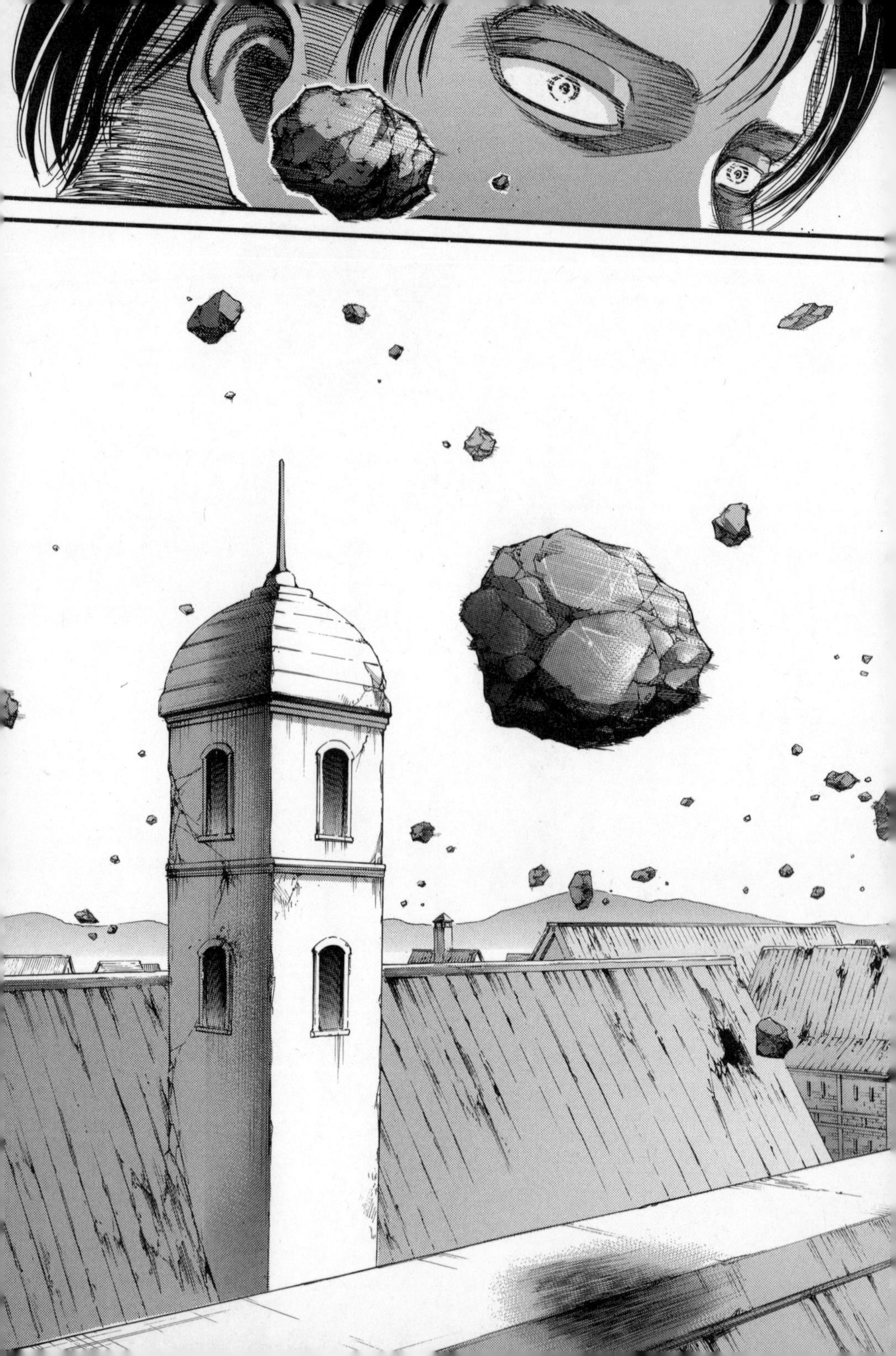

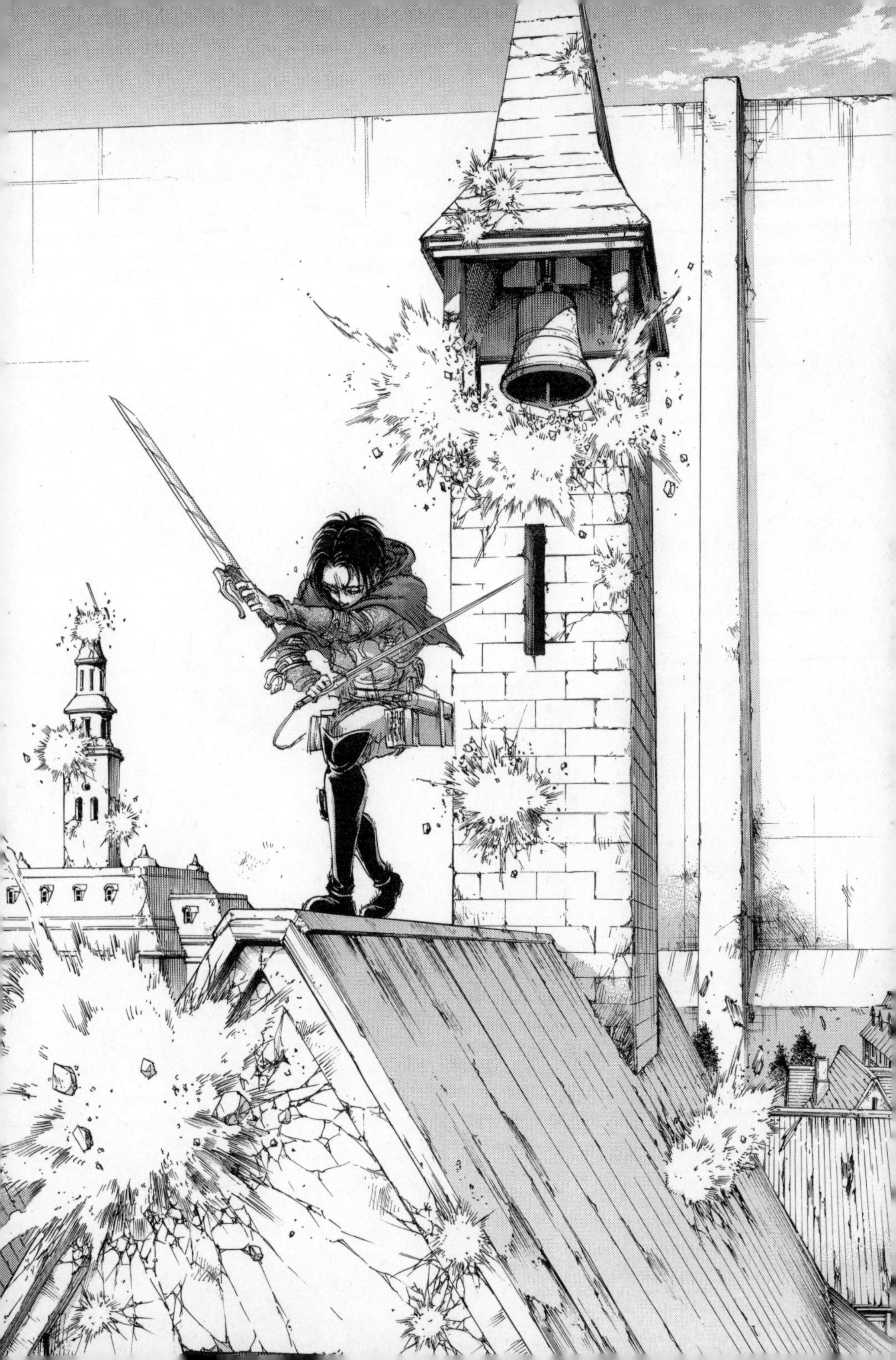

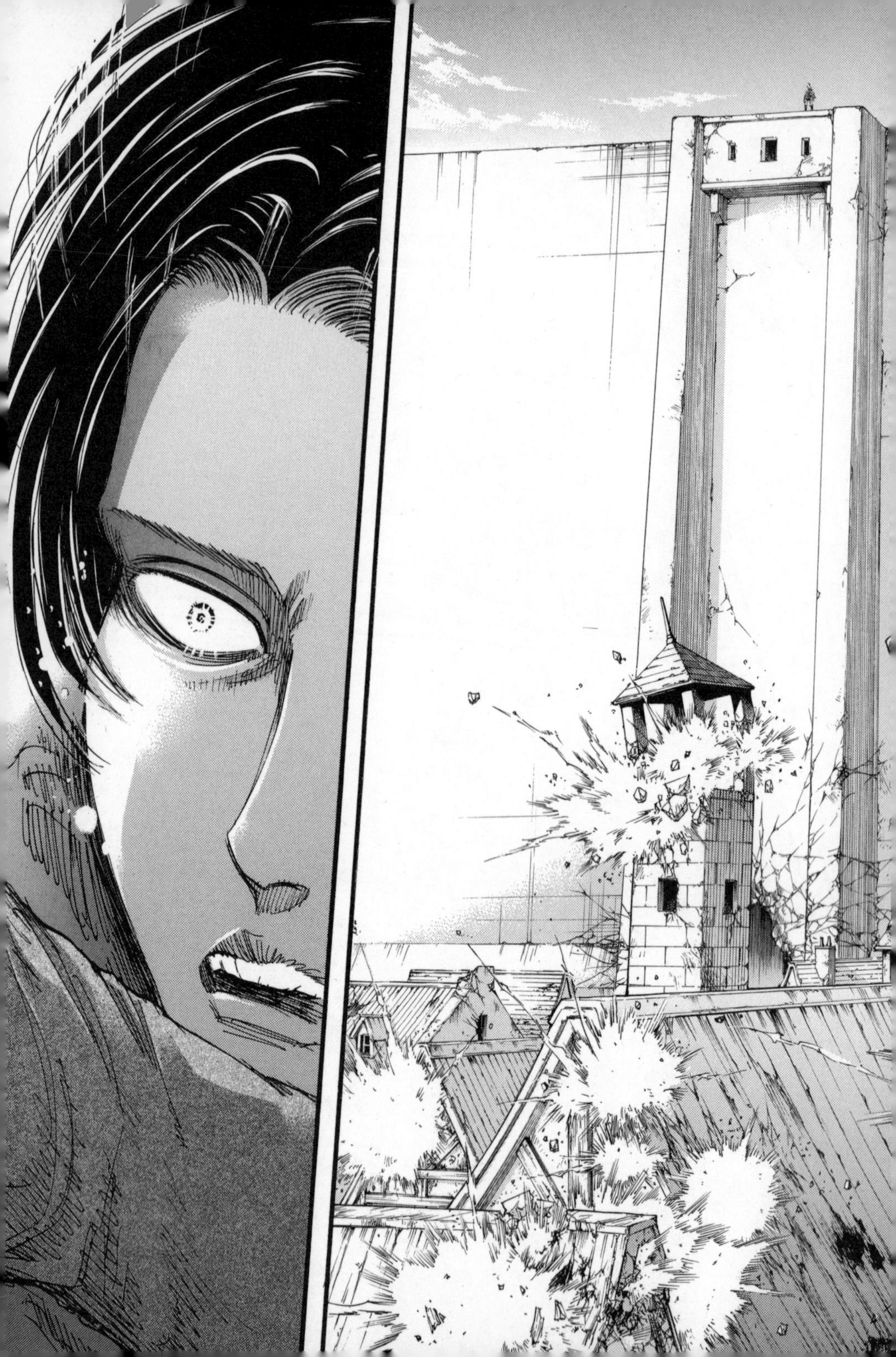

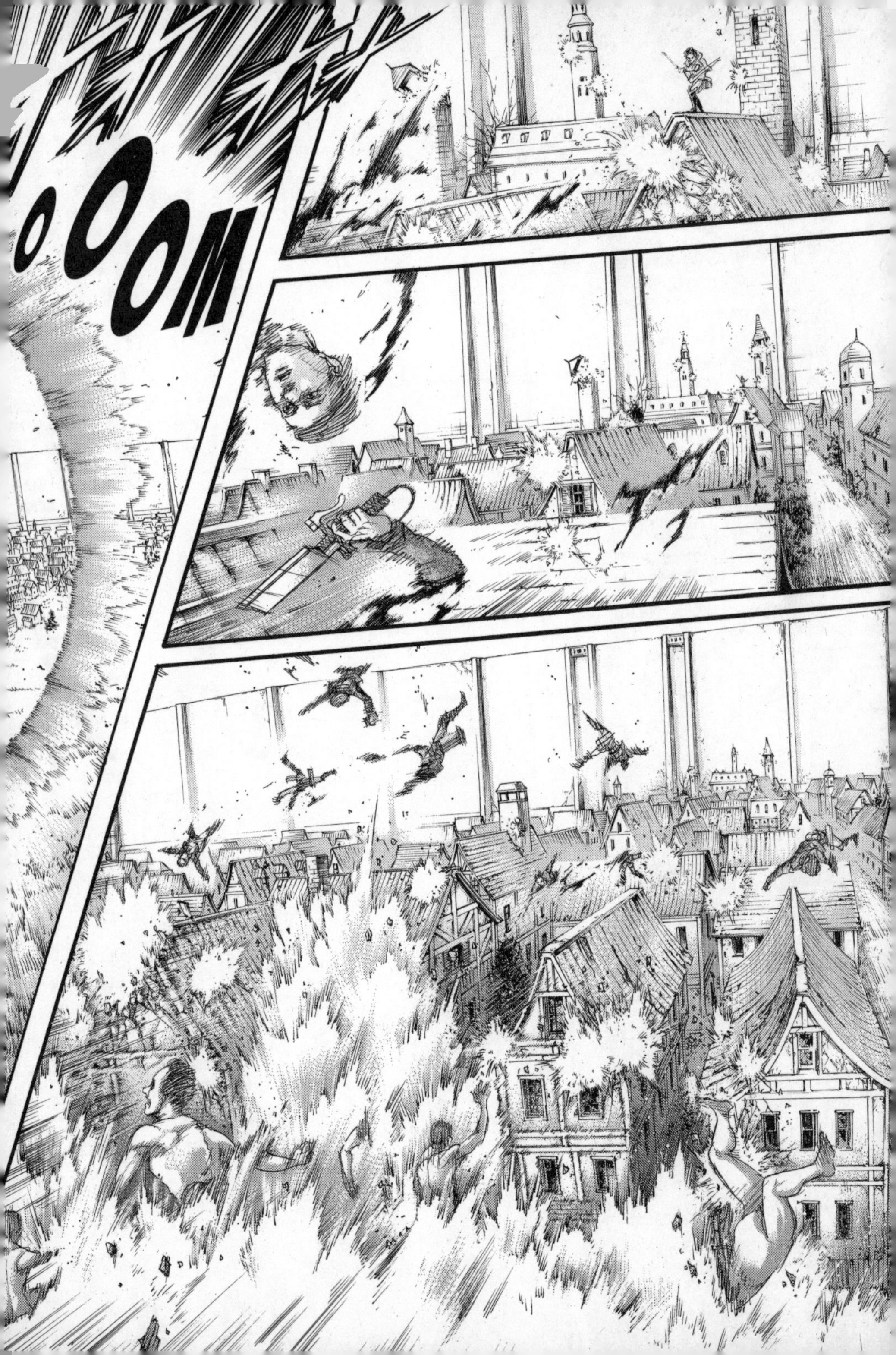
oOOM

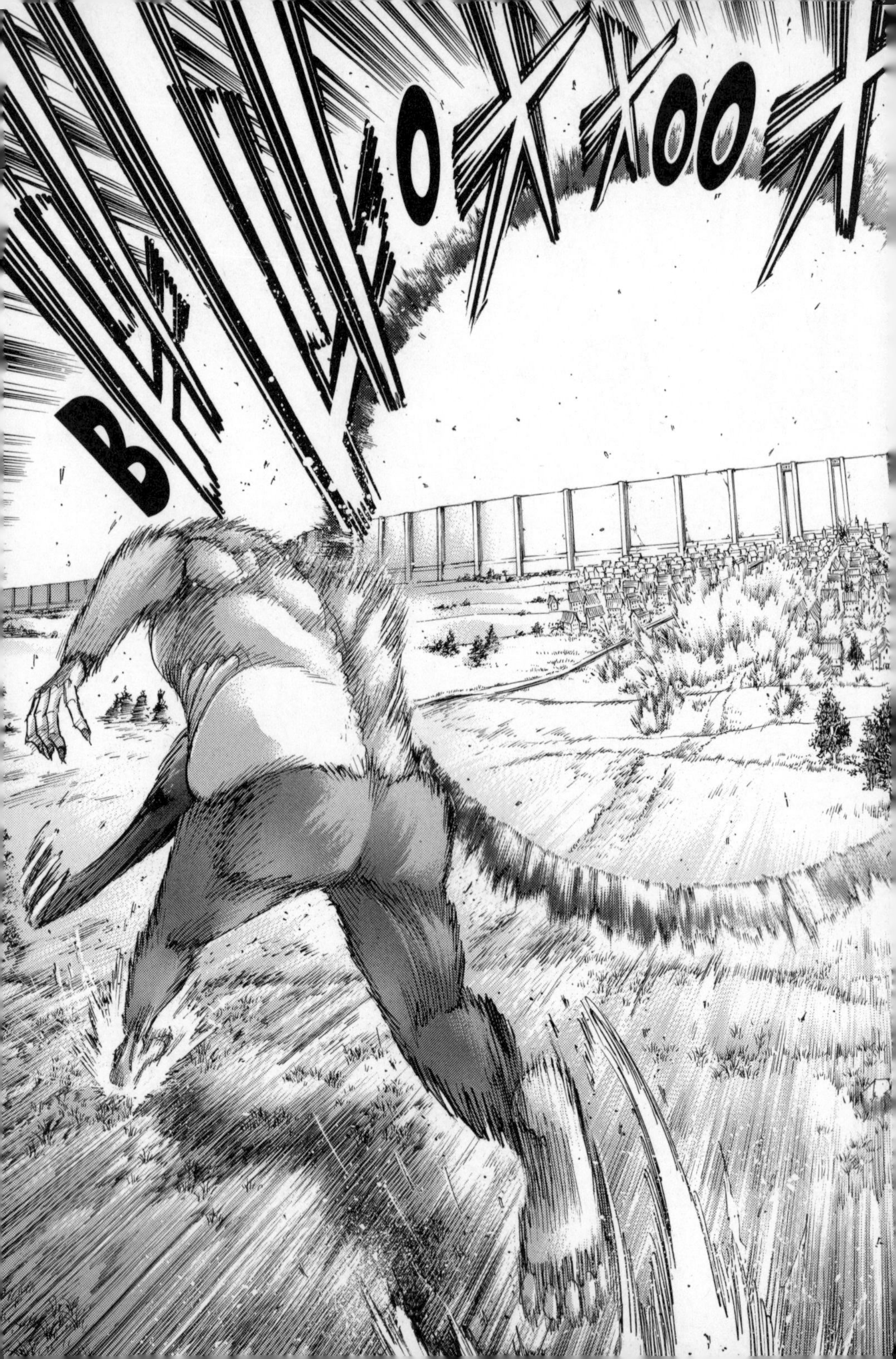

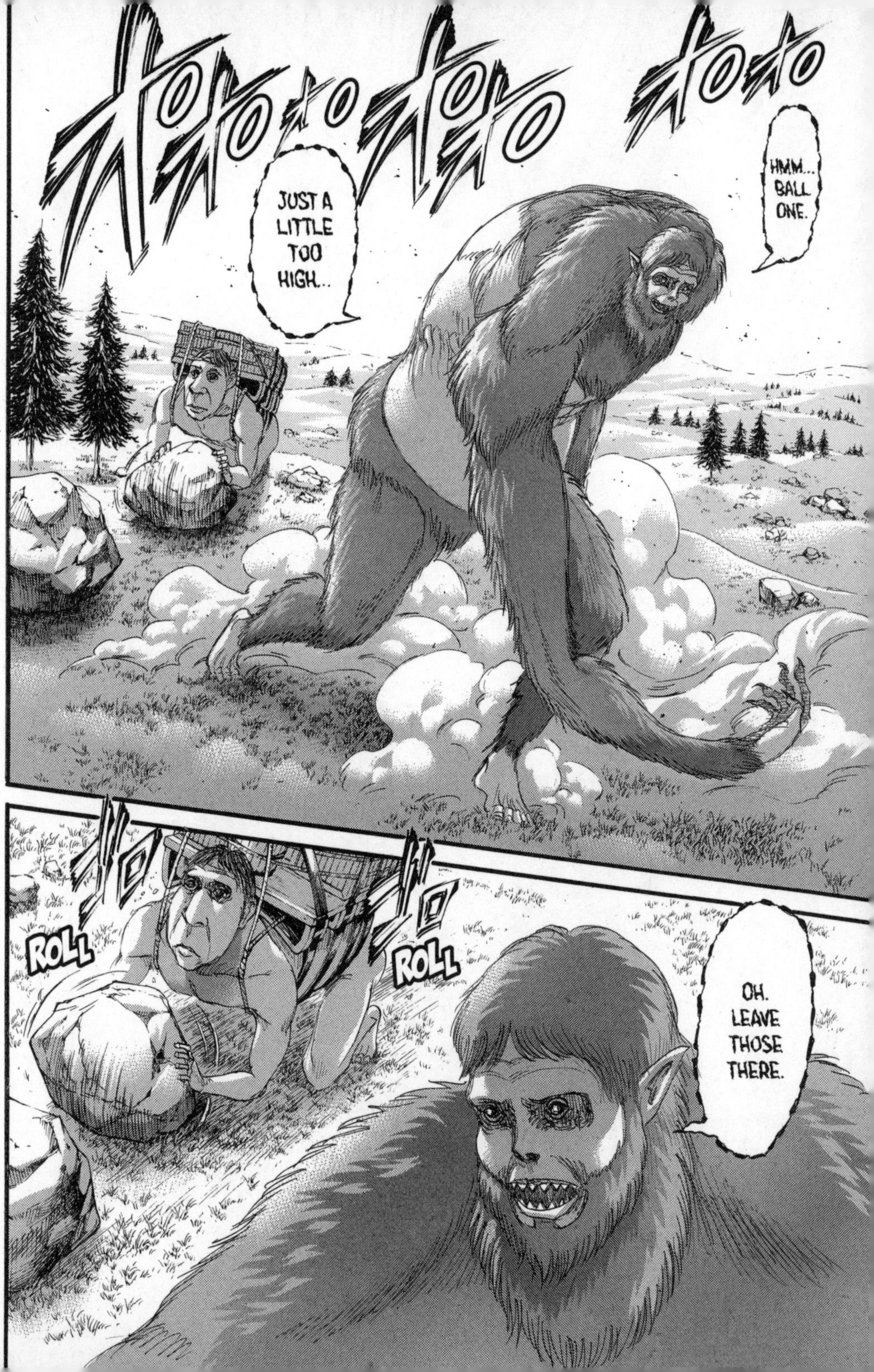
HMM... BALL ONE.
JUST A LITTLE TOO HIGH...
OH. LEAVE THOSE THERE.
ROLL
ROLL

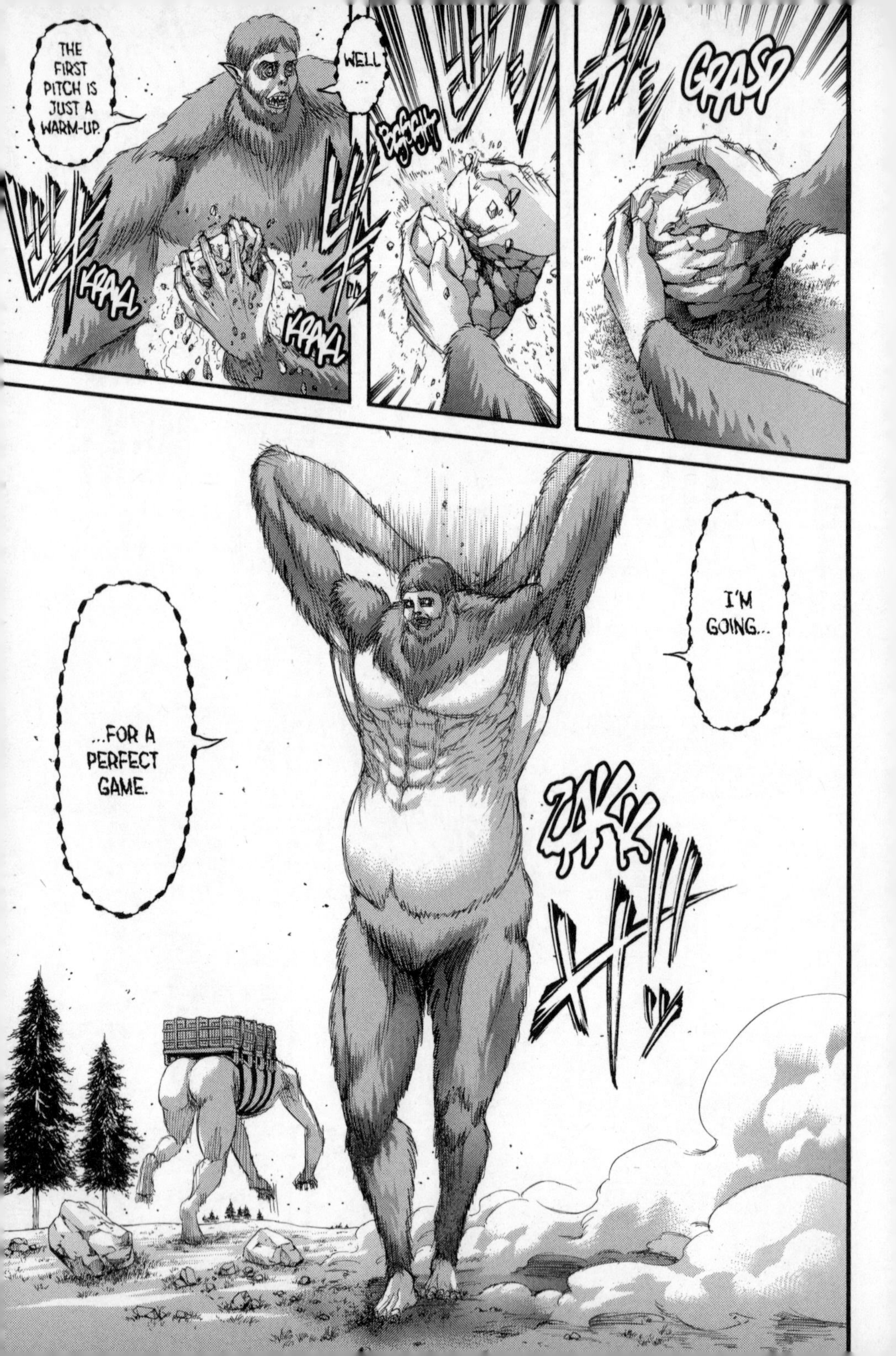
GRASP
WELL ...
THE FIRST PITCH IS JUST A WARM-UP.
KRAK
KRAK
I'M GOING...
...FOR A PERFECT GAME.
ZAK

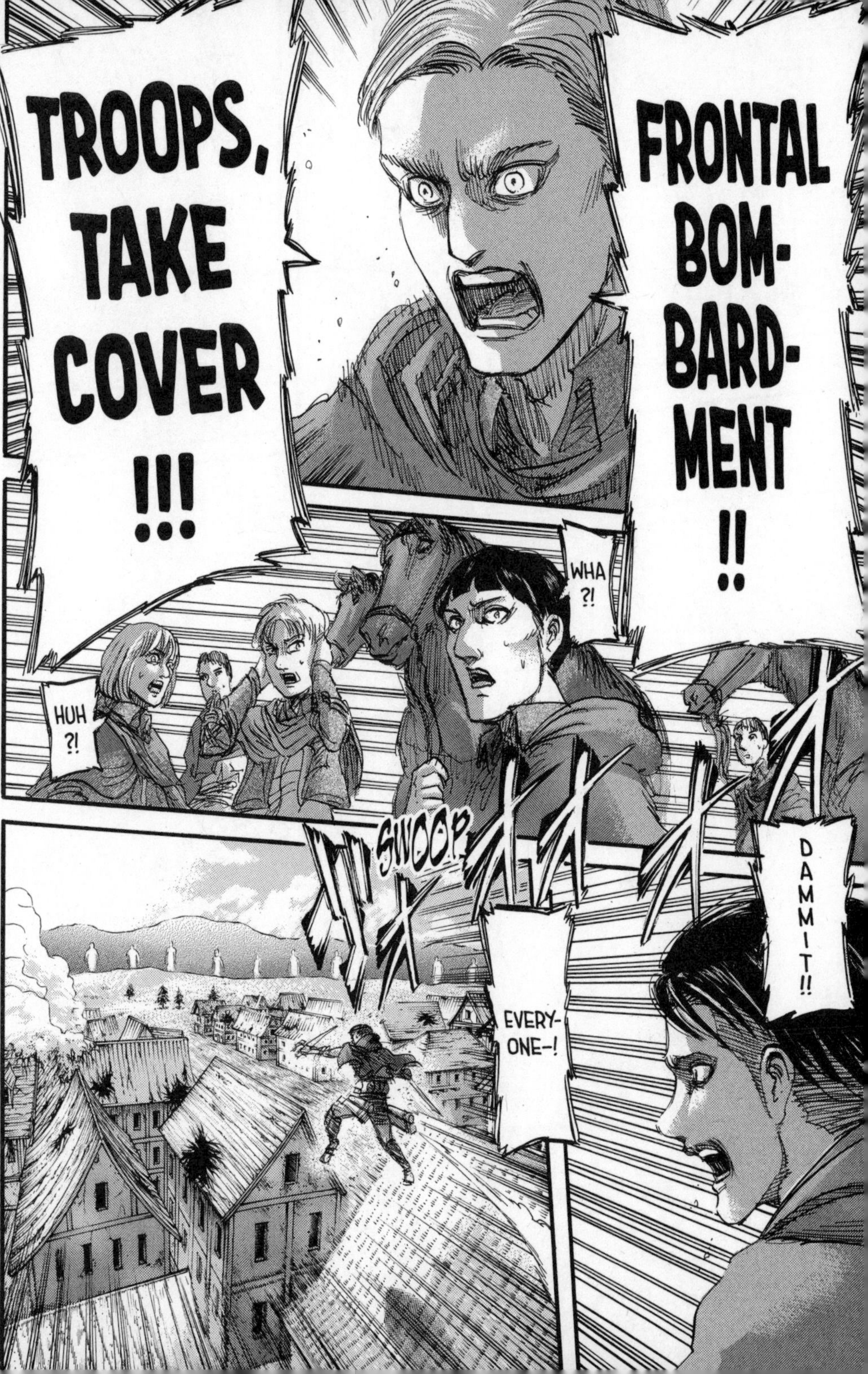
FRONTAL BOM-BARD-MENT!!
TROOPS, TAKE COVER!!!
WHA?!
HUH?!
DAMMIT!!
EVERY-ONE-!
SWOOP

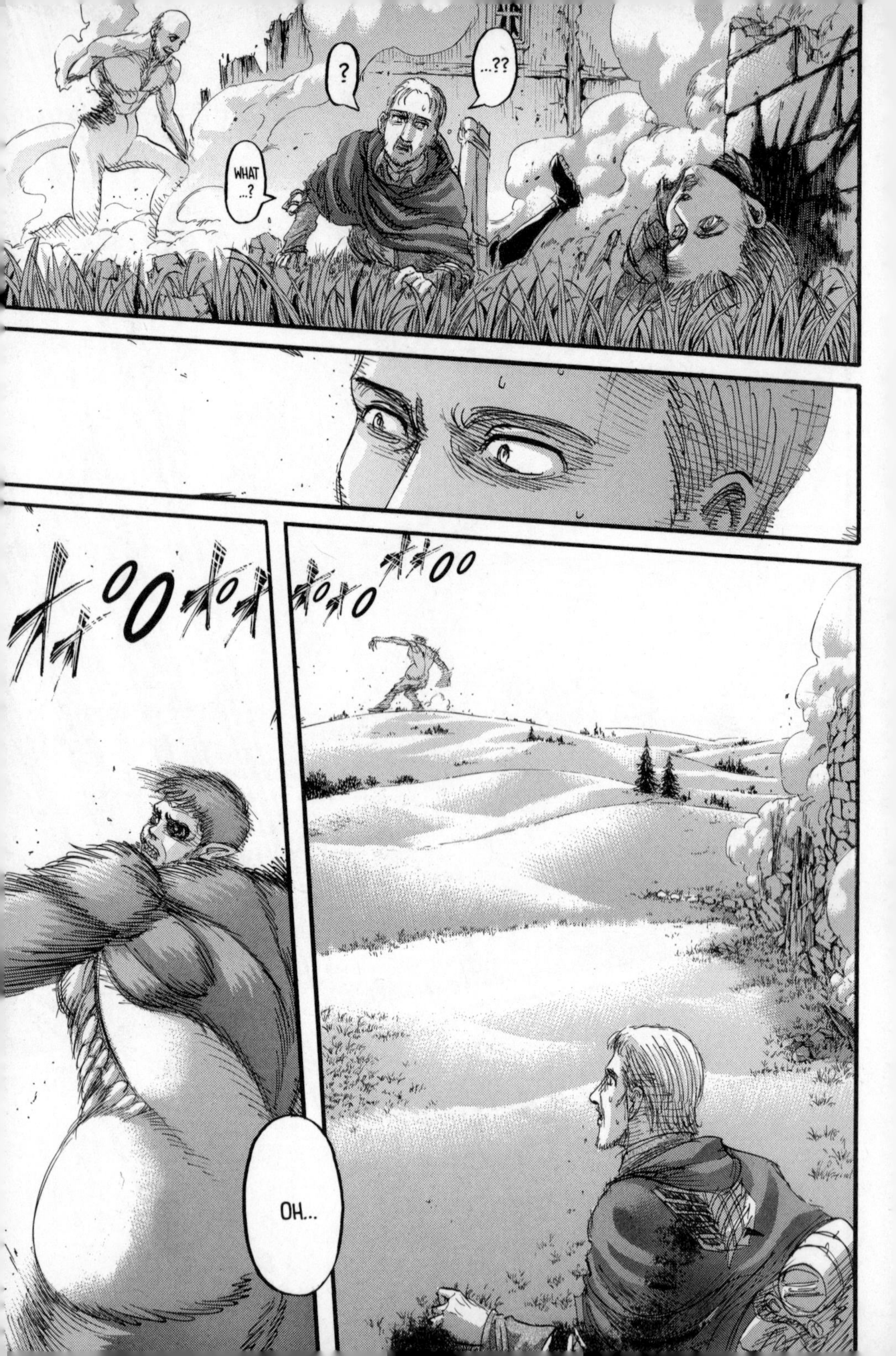
...??
?
WHAT ...?
OH...

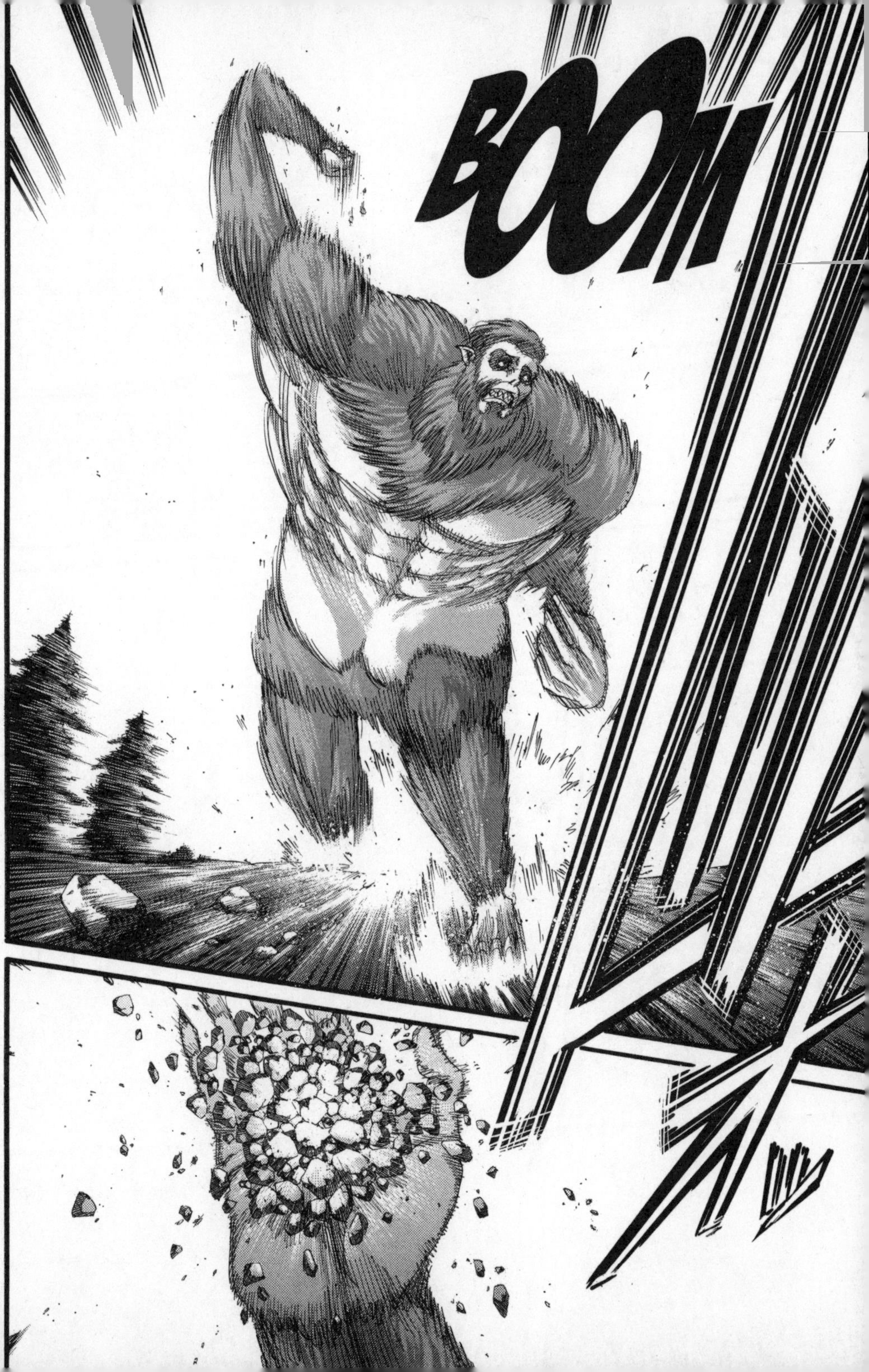
BOOM

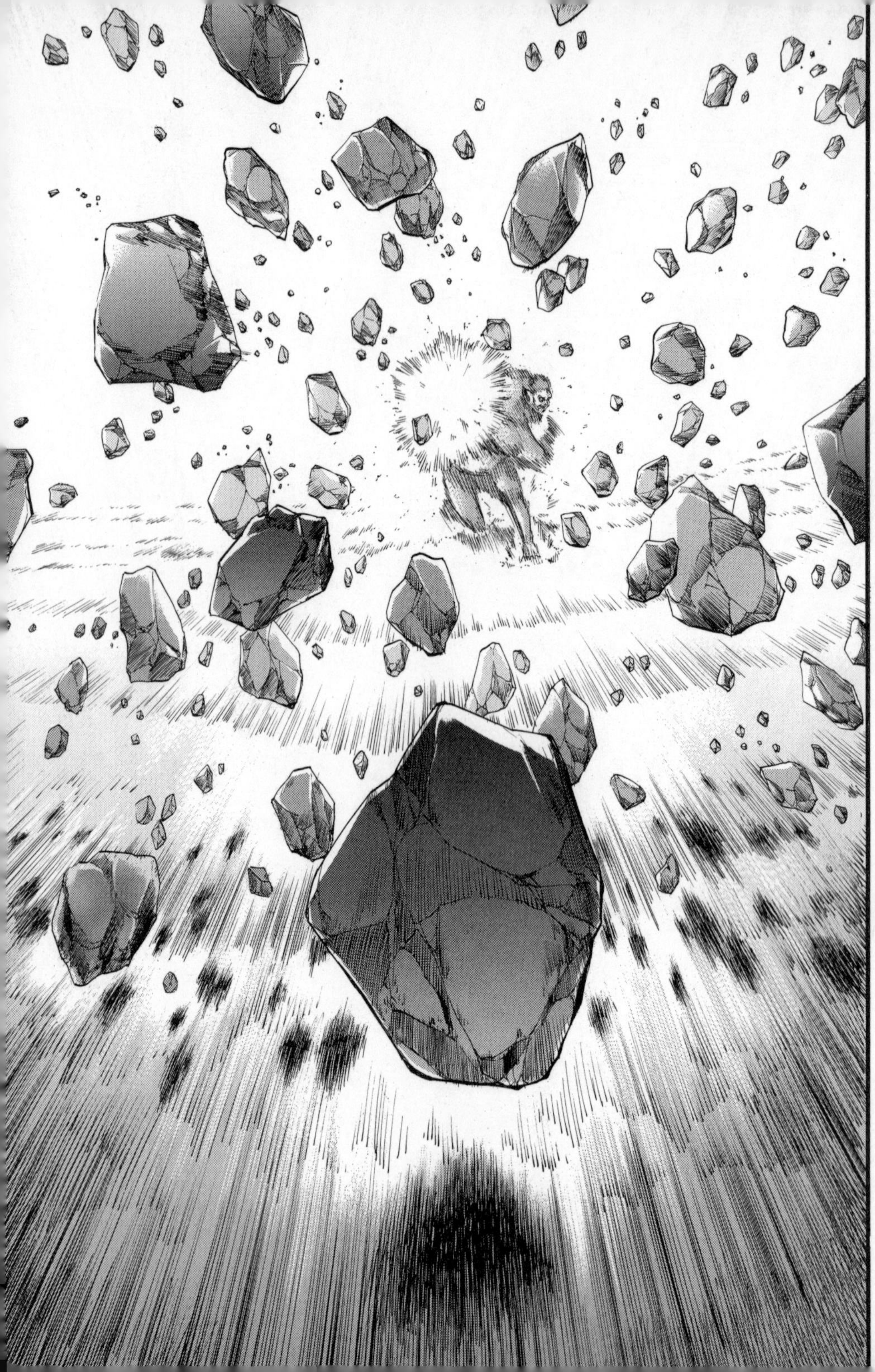

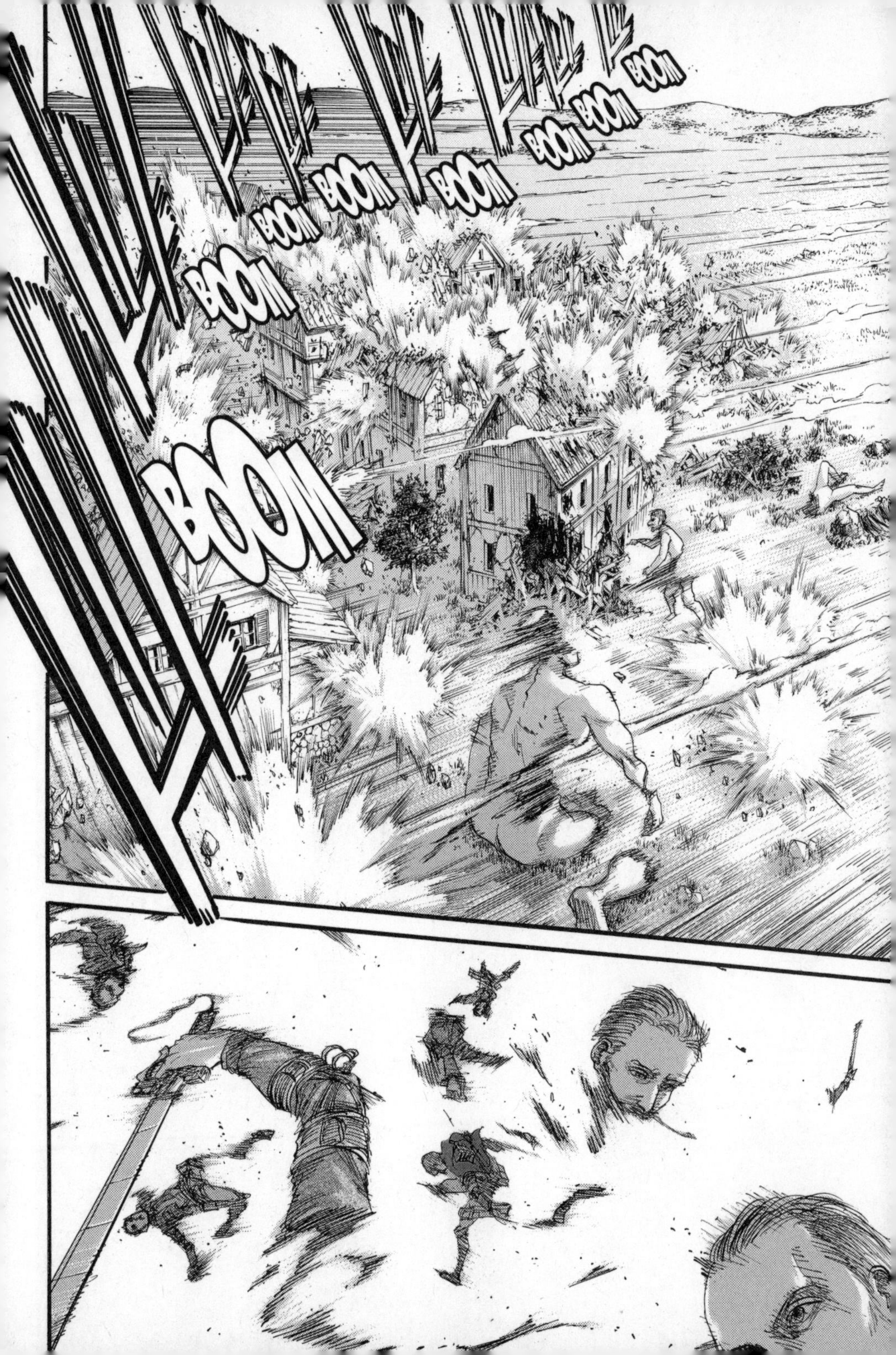
BOOM
BOOM
BOOM
BOOM
BOOM
BOOM
BOOM
BOOM

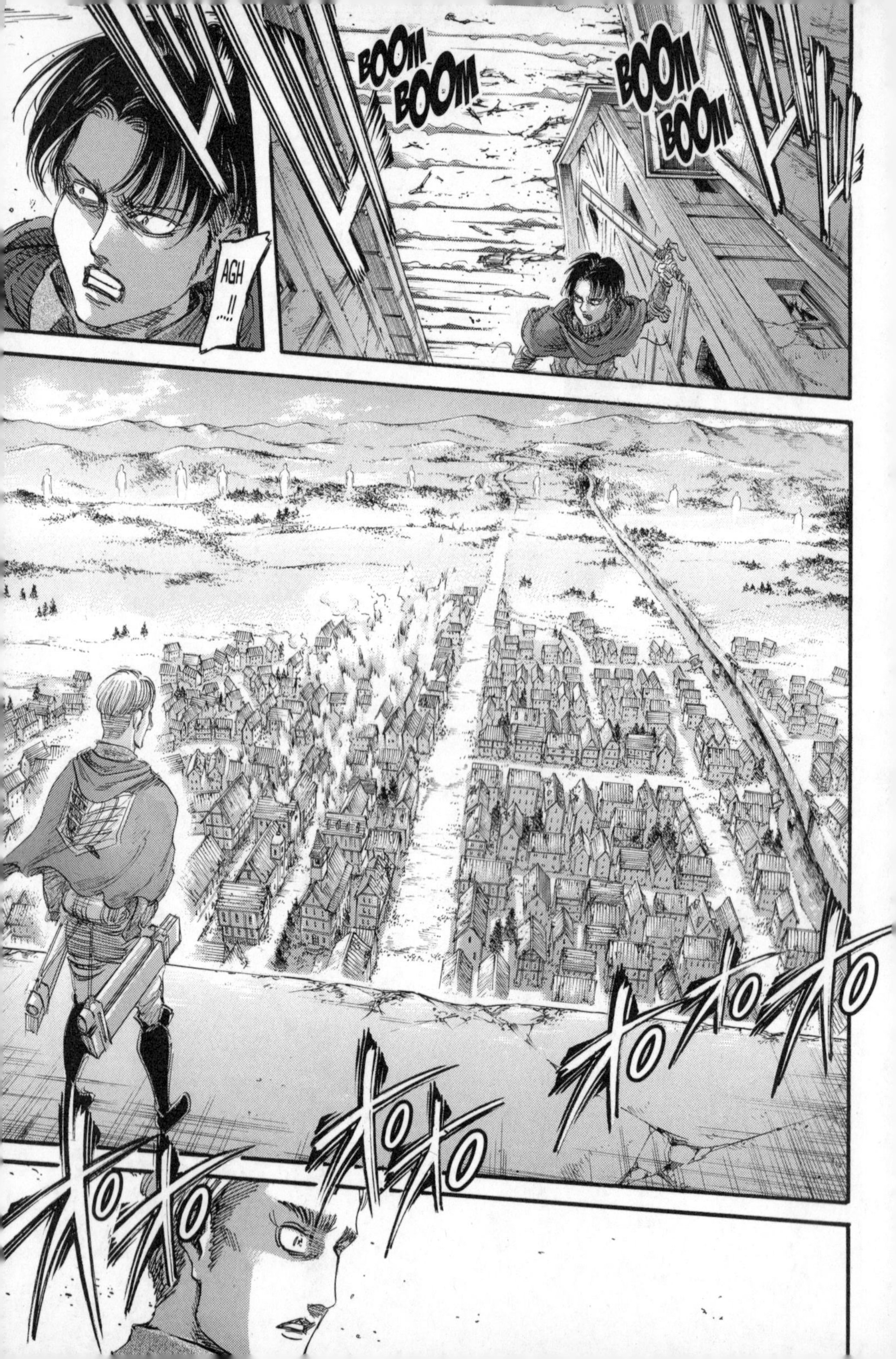
BOOM BOOM
BOOM BOOM
AGH ...!!

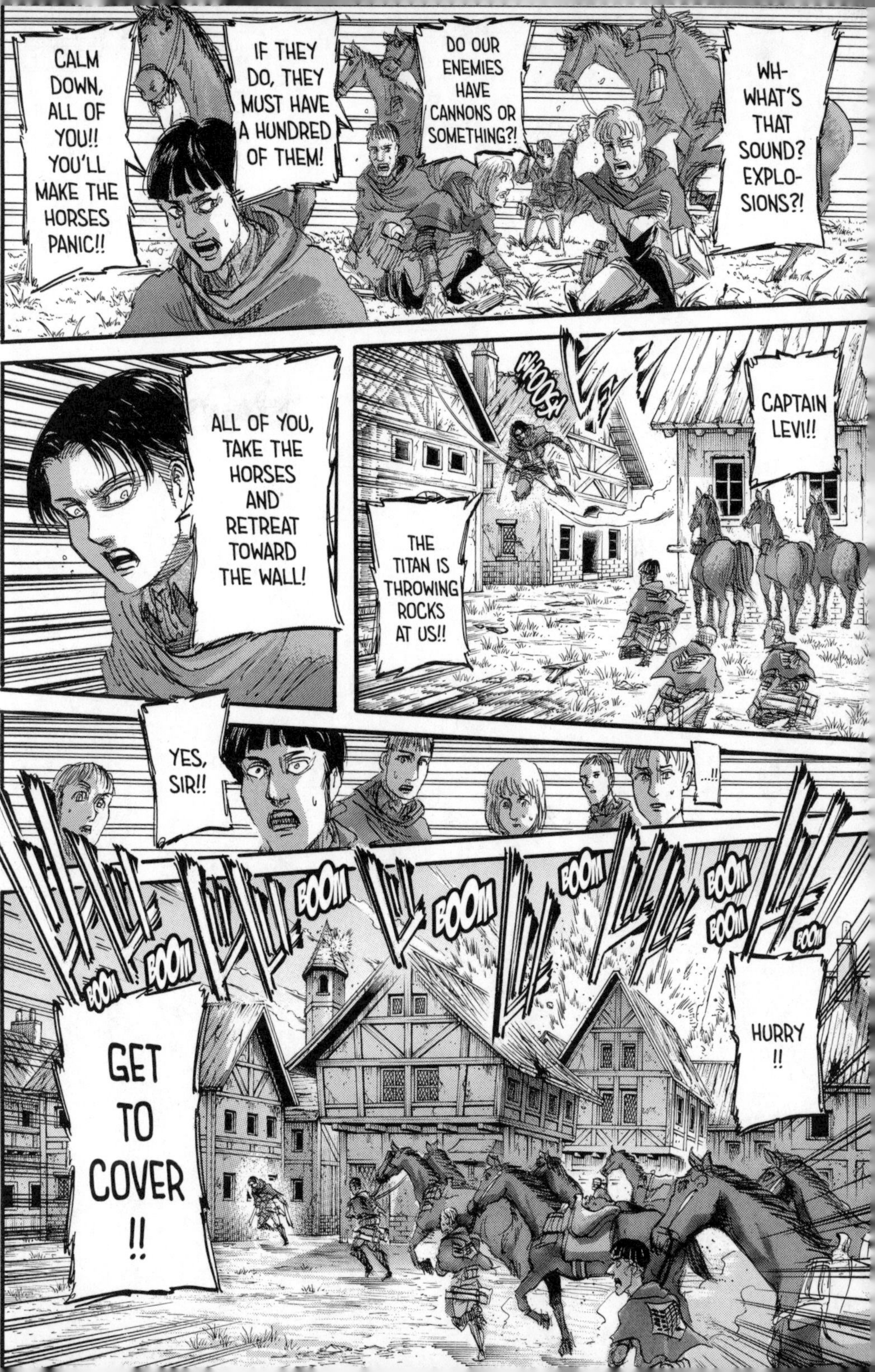
WH- WHAT'S THAT SOUND? EXPLOSIONS?!
DO OUR ENEMIES HAVE CANNONS OR SOMETHING?!
IF THEY DO, THEY MUST HAVE A HUNDRED OF THEM!
CALM DOWN, ALL OF YOU!! YOU'LL MAKE THE HORSES PANIC!!
WHOOSH
CAPTAIN LEVI!!
THE TITAN IS THROWING ROCKS AT US!!
ALL OF YOU, TAKE THE HORSES AND RETREAT TOWARD THE WALL!
...!!
YES, SIR!!
BOOM
BOOM BOOM
BOOM
BOOM
BOOM
BOOM
BOOM
BOOM
HURRY!!
GET TO COVER!!

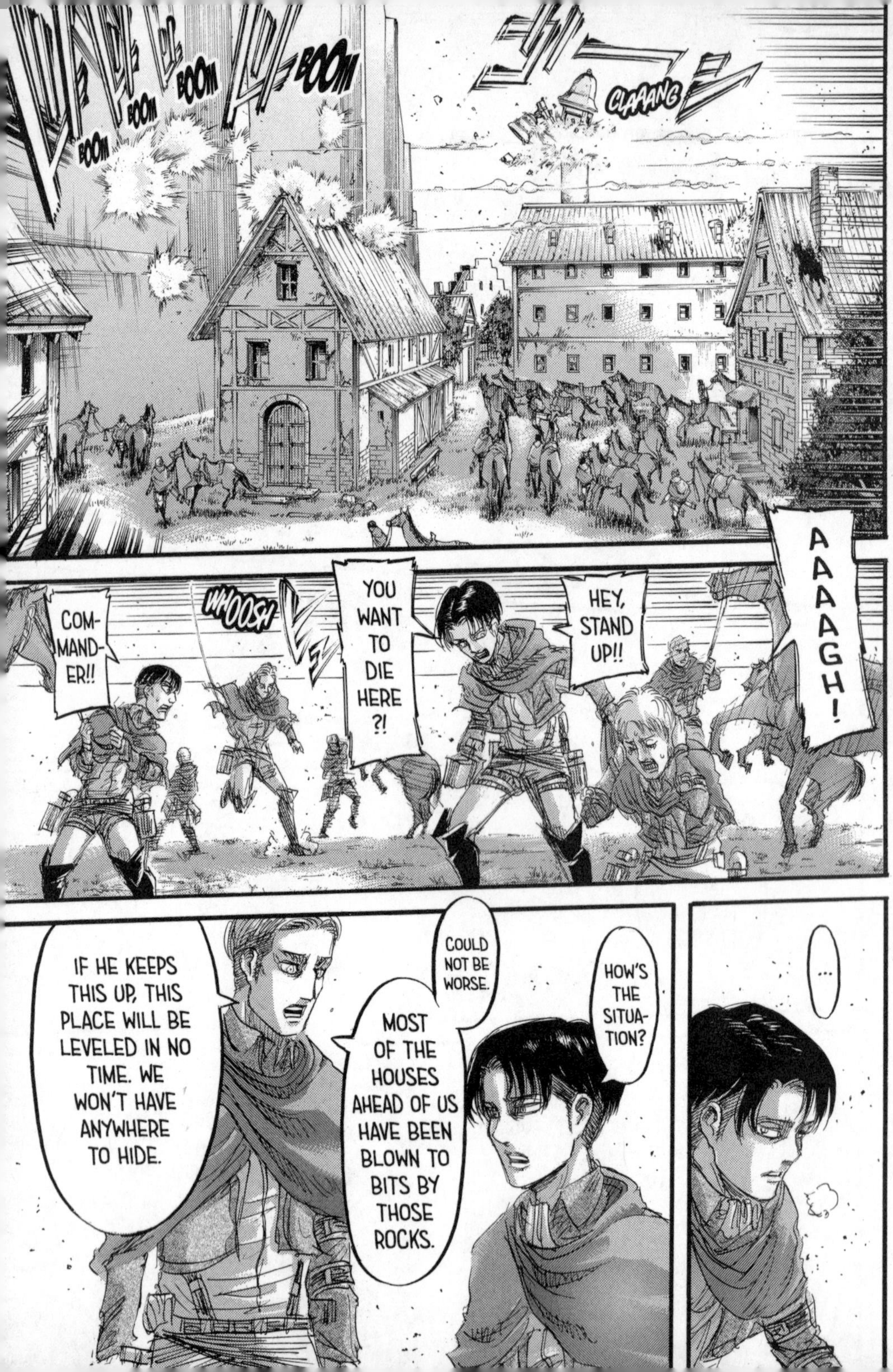
CLAAANG
BOOM
BOOM
BOOM
BOOM
AAAAGH!
HEY, STAND UP!!
YOU WANT TO DIE HERE?!
WHOOSH
COMMANDER!!
...
HOW'S THE SITUATION?
COULD NOT BE WORSE.
MOST OF THE HOUSES AHEAD OF US HAVE BEEN BLOWN TO BITS BY THOSE ROCKS.
IF HE KEEPS THIS UP, THIS PLACE WILL BE LEVELED IN NO TIME. WE WON'T HAVE ANYWHERE TO HIDE.

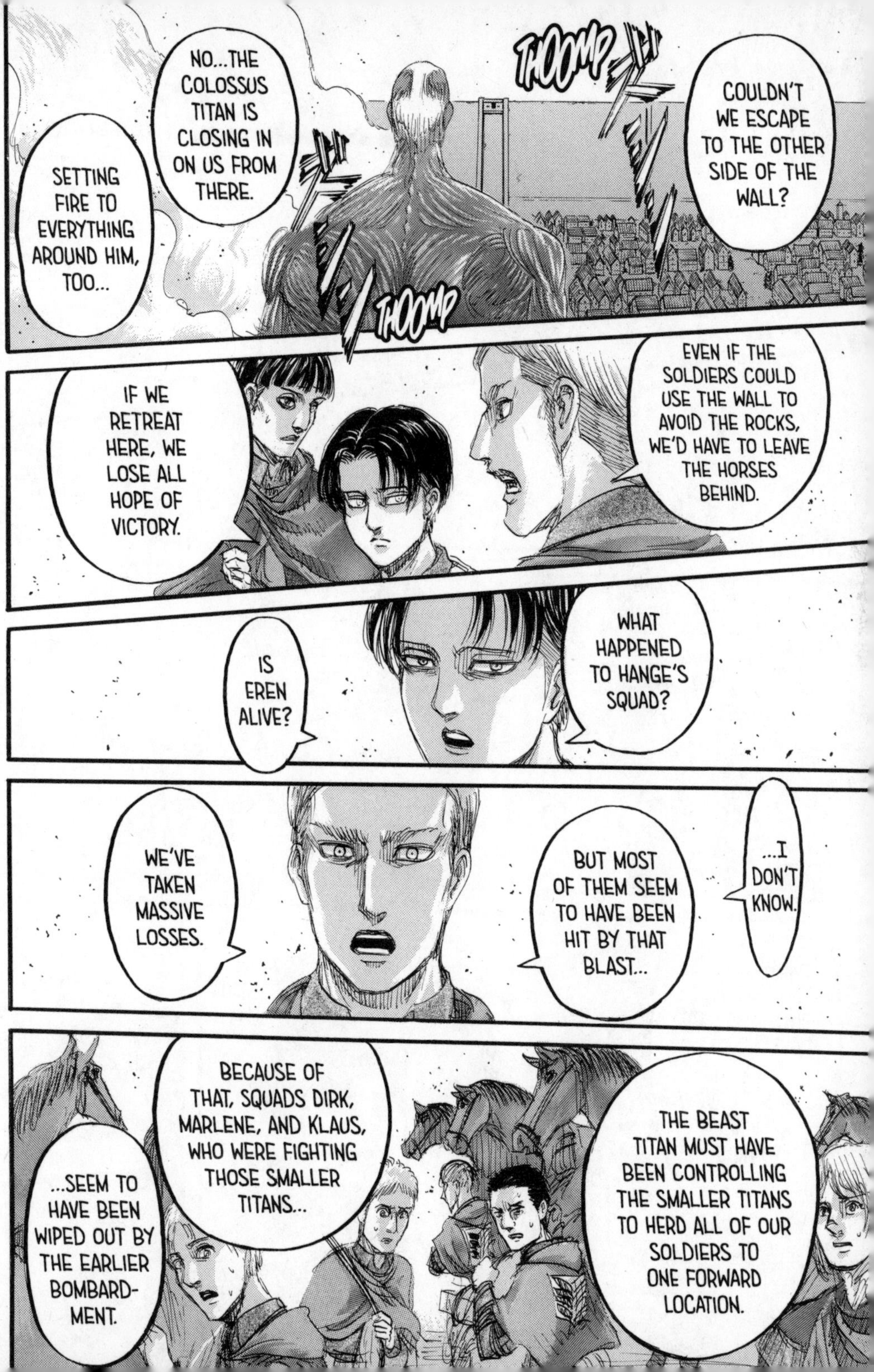
THOOMP
COULDN'T WE ESCAPE TO THE OTHER SIDE OF THE WALL?
NO...THE COLOSSUS TITAN IS CLOSING IN ON US FROM THERE.
SETTING FIRE TO EVERYTHING AROUND HIM, TOO...
THOOMP
EVEN IF THE SOLDIERS COULD USE THE WALL TO AVOID THE ROCKS, WE'D HAVE TO LEAVE THE HORSES BEHIND.
IF WE RETREAT HERE, WE LOSE ALL HOPE OF VICTORY.
WHAT HAPPENED TO HANGE'S SQUAD?
IS EREN ALIVE?
...I DON'T KNOW.
BUT MOST OF THEM SEEM TO HAVE BEEN HIT BY THAT BLAST...
WE'VE TAKEN MASSIVE LOSSES.
THE BEAST TITAN MUST HAVE BEEN CONTROLLING THE SMALLER TITANS TO HERD ALL OF OUR SOLDIERS TO ONE FORWARD LOCATION.
BECAUSE OF THAT, SQUADS DIRK, MARLENE, AND KLAUS, WHO WERE FIGHTING THOSE SMALLER TITANS...
...SEEM TO HAVE BEEN WIPED OUT BY THE EARLIER BOMBARD-MENT.

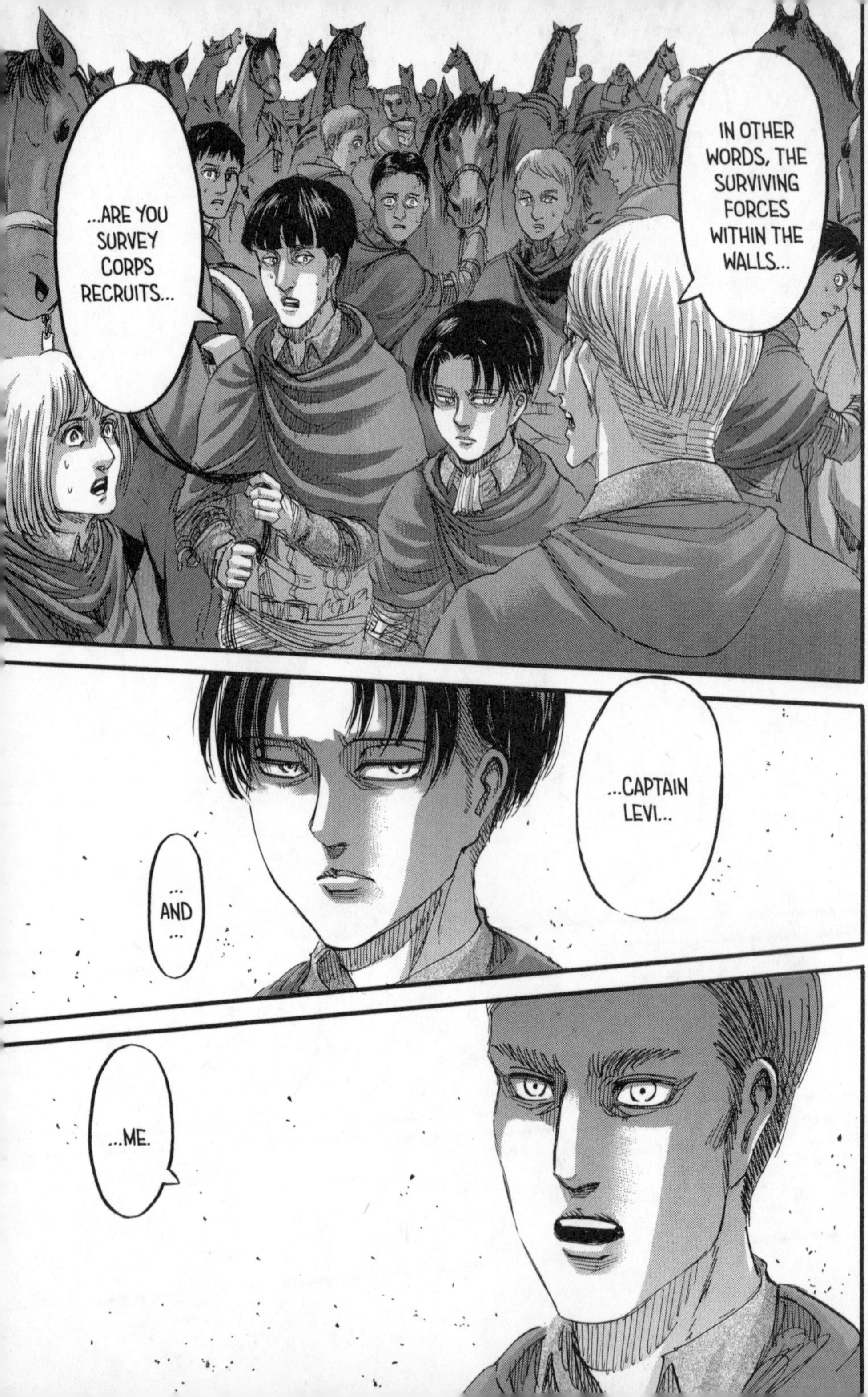
IN OTHER WORDS, THE SURVIVING FORCES WITHIN THE WALLS...
...ARE YOU SURVEY CORPS RECRUITS...
...CAPTAIN LEVI...
...AND...
...ME.

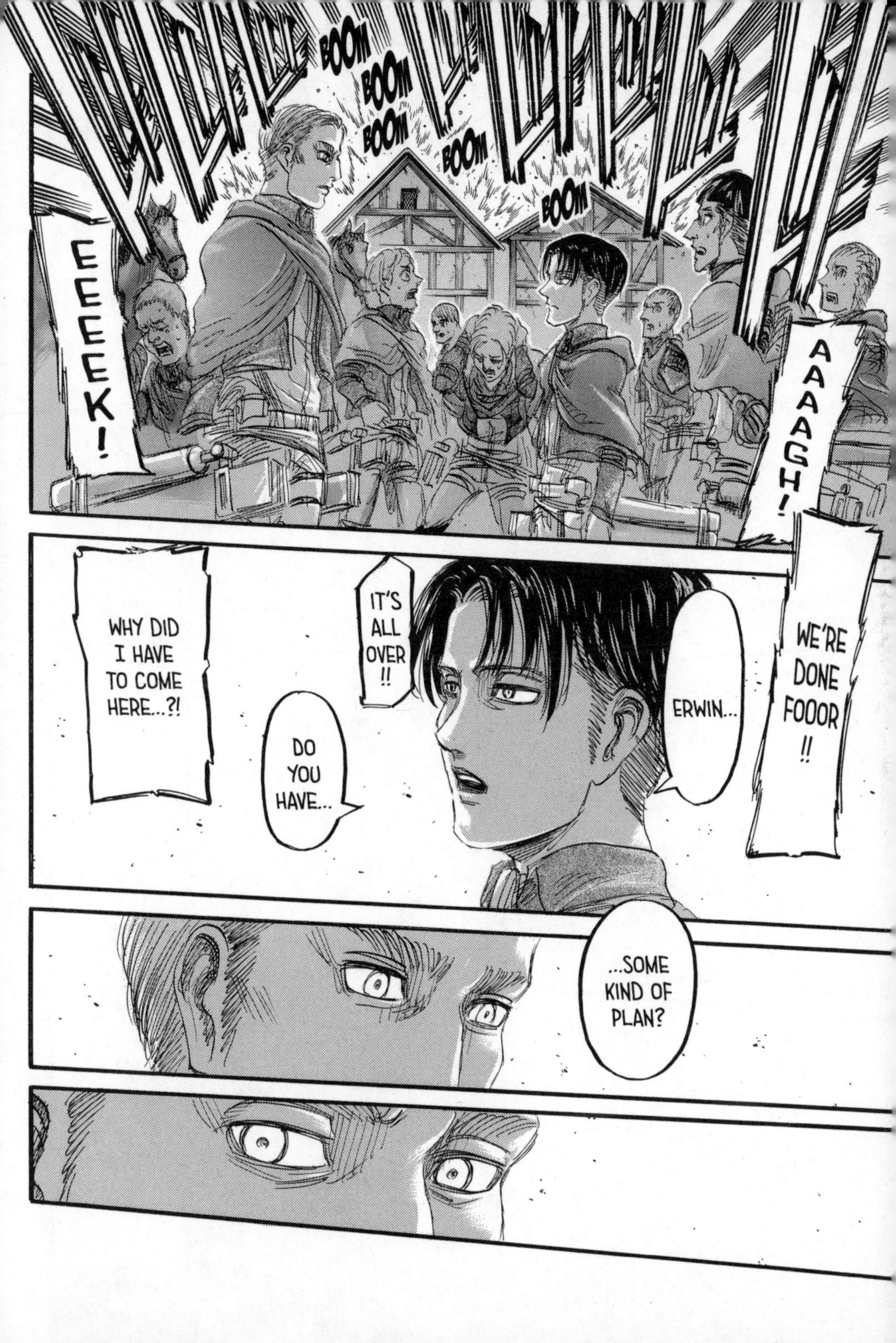
AAAAGH!
BOOM
BOOM
BOOM
BOOM
BOOM
EEEEK!
WE'RE DONE FOOOR!!
ERWIN...
IT'S ALL OVER!!
DO YOU HAVE...
WHY DID I HAVE TO COME HERE...?!
...SOME KIND OF PLAN?

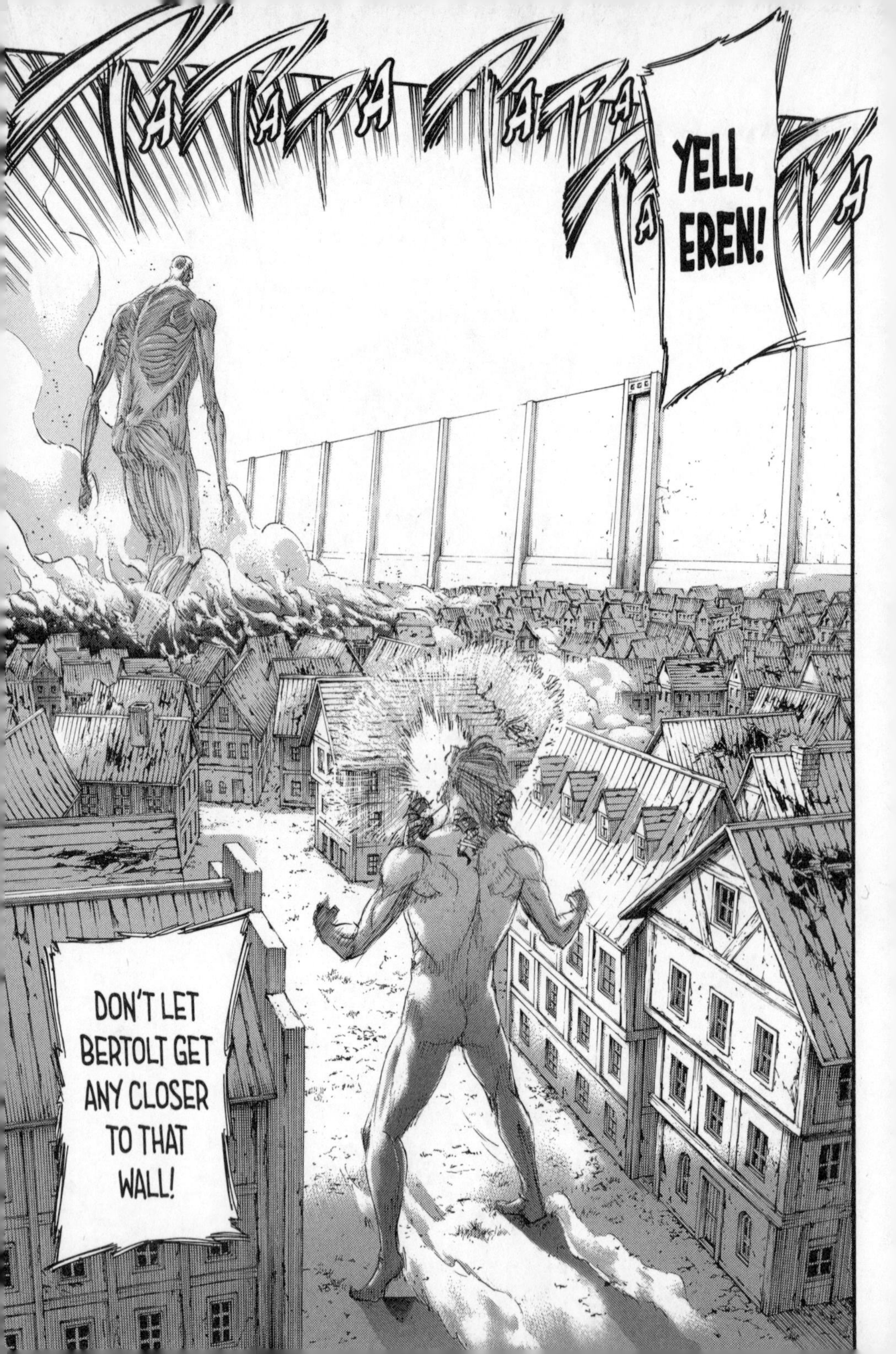
YELL, EREN!
DON'T LET BERTOLT GET ANY CLOSER TO THAT WALL!

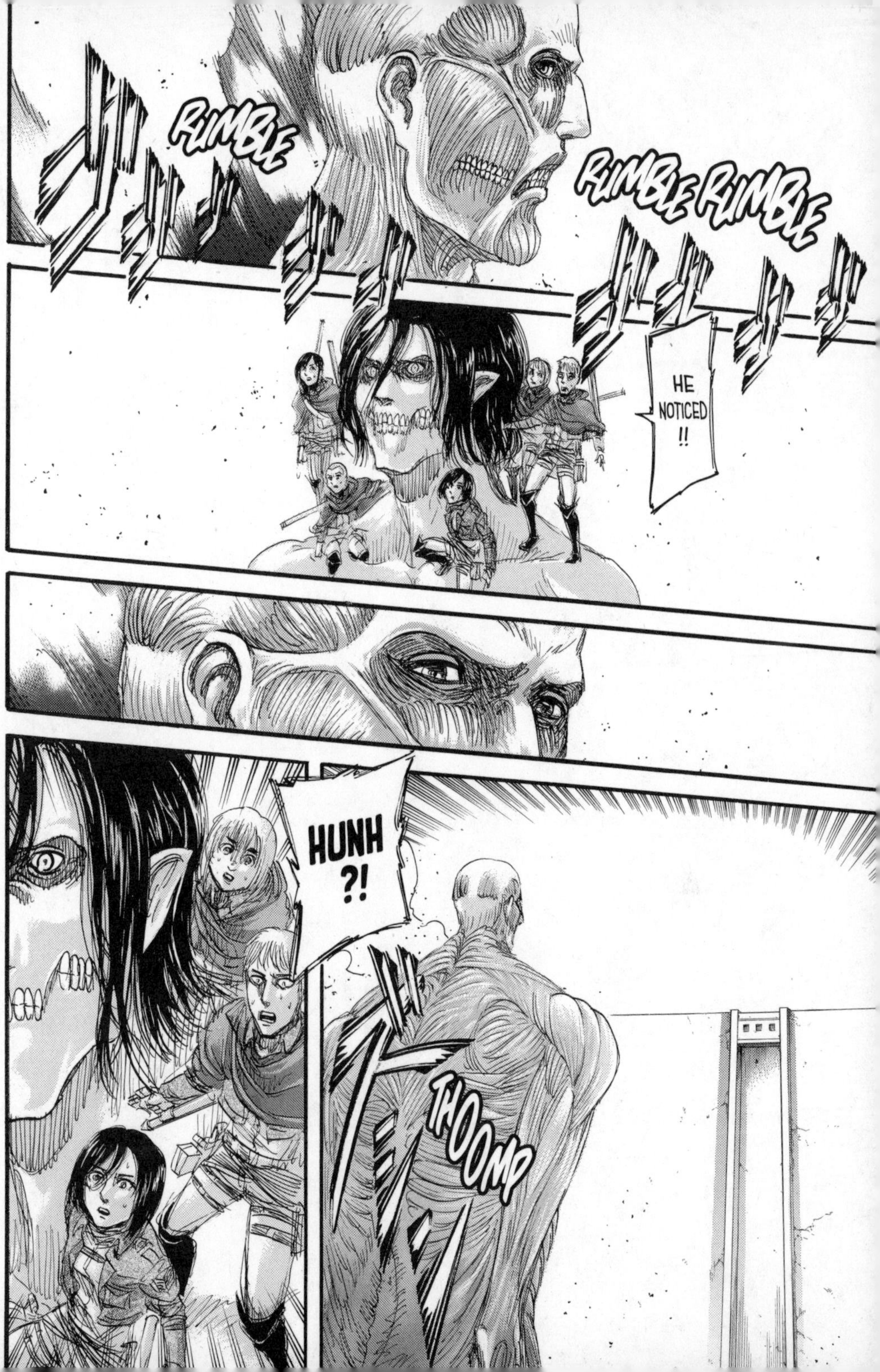
RUMBLE
RUMBLE RUMBLE
HE NOTICED !!
HUNH ?!
THOOMP

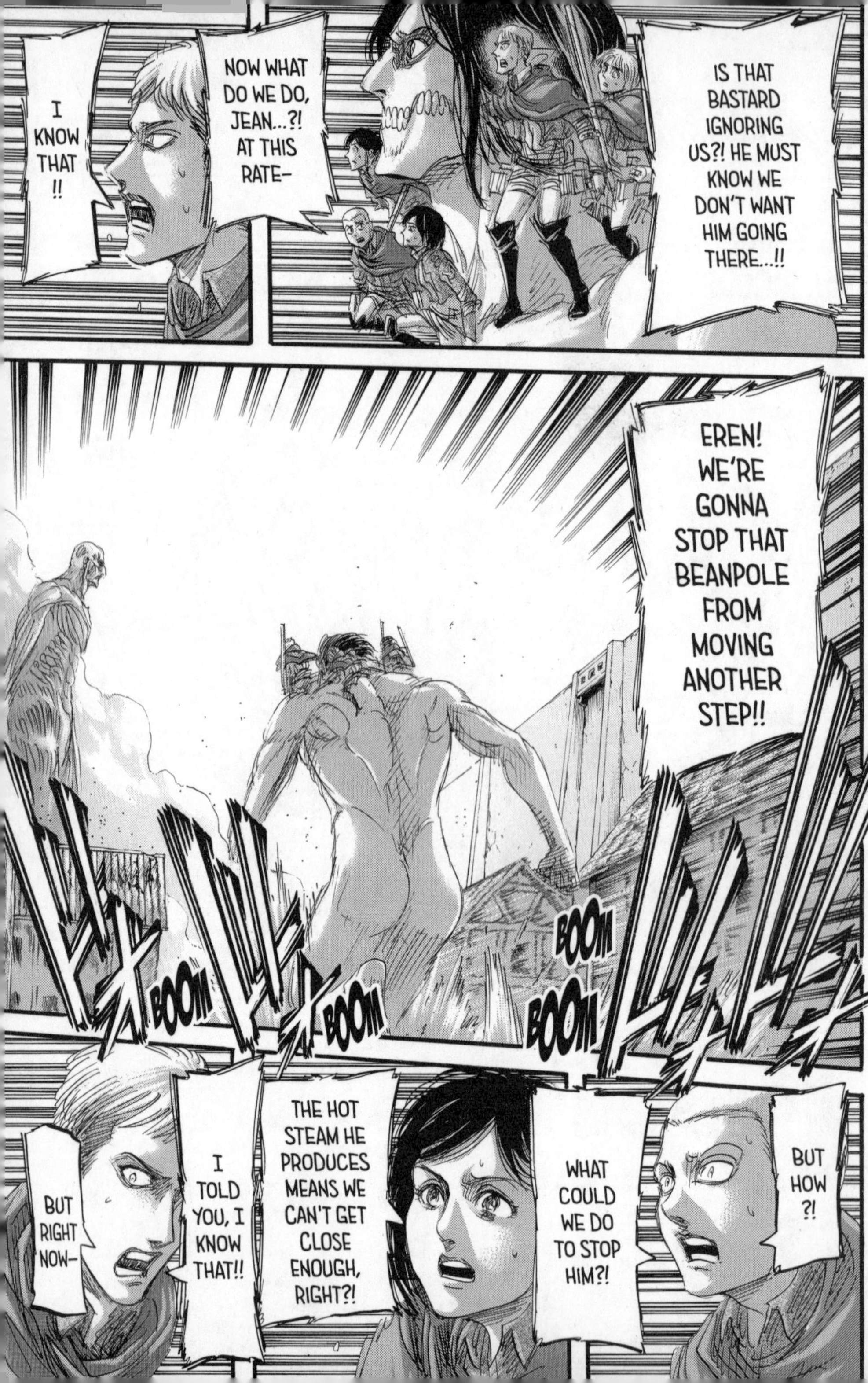
IS THAT BASTARD IGNORING US?! HE MUST KNOW WE DON'T WANT HIM GOING THERE...!!
NOW WHAT DO WE DO, JEAN...?! AT THIS RATE-
I KNOW THAT!!
EREN! WE'RE GONNA STOP THAT BEANPOLE FROM MOVING ANOTHER STEP!!
BOOM
BOOM
BOOM
BOOM
BUT HOW?!
WHAT COULD WE DO TO STOP HIM?!
THE HOT STEAM HE PRODUCES MEANS WE CAN'T GET CLOSE ENOUGH, RIGHT?!
I TOLD YOU, I KNOW THAT!!
BUT RIGHT NOW-

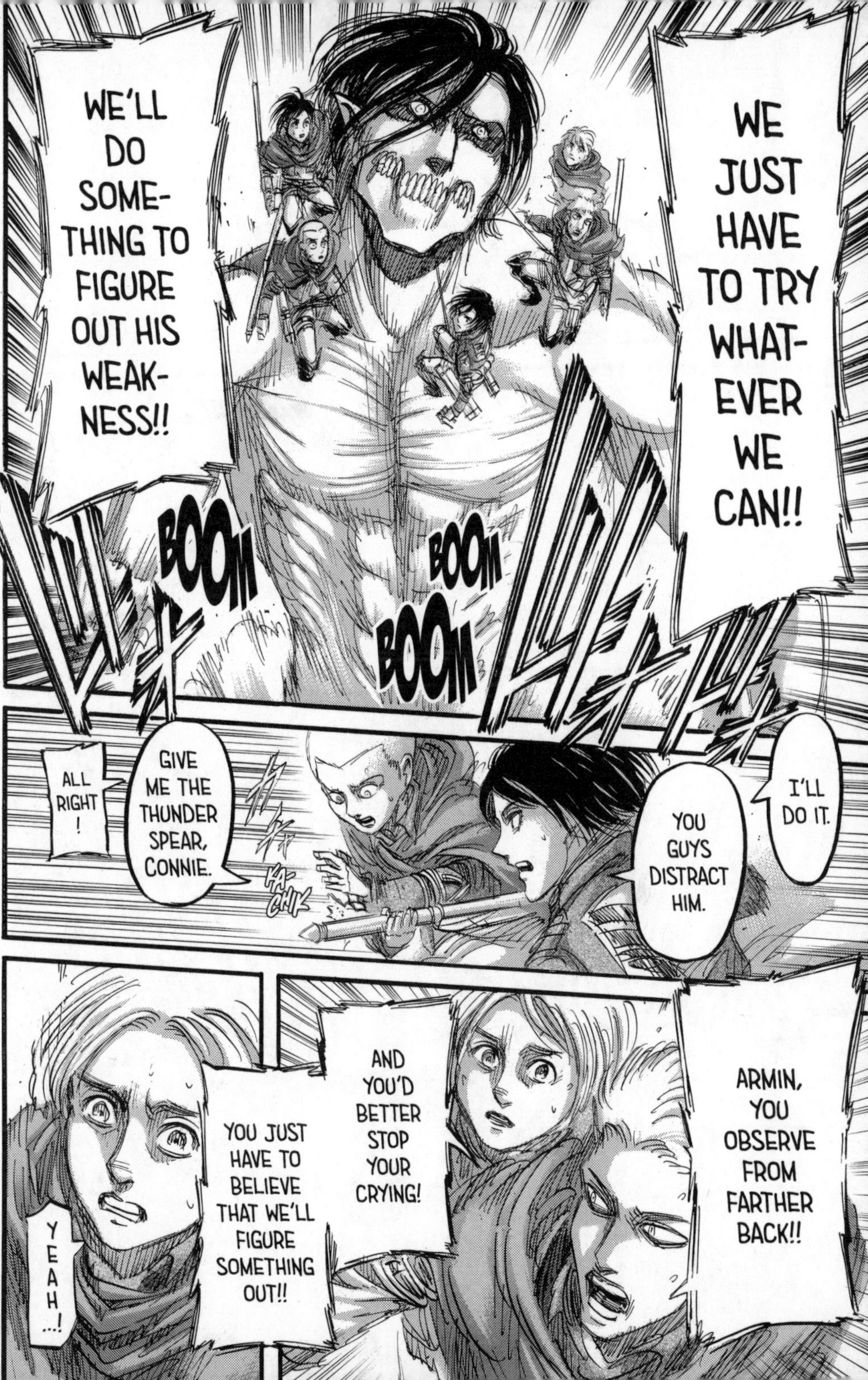

WE JUST HAVE TO TRY WHATEVER WE CAN!!
WE'LL DO SOMETHING TO FIGURE OUT HIS WEAKNESS!!
BOOM
BOOM
BOOM
I'LL DO IT.
YOU GUYS DISTRACT HIM.
GIVE ME THE THUNDER SPEAR, CONNIE.
ALL RIGHT!
KA-CHIK
ARMIN, YOU OBSERVE FROM FARTHER BACK!!
AND YOU'D BETTER STOP YOUR CRYING!
YOU JUST HAVE TO BELIEVE THAT WE'LL FIGURE SOMETHING OUT!!
YEAH...!

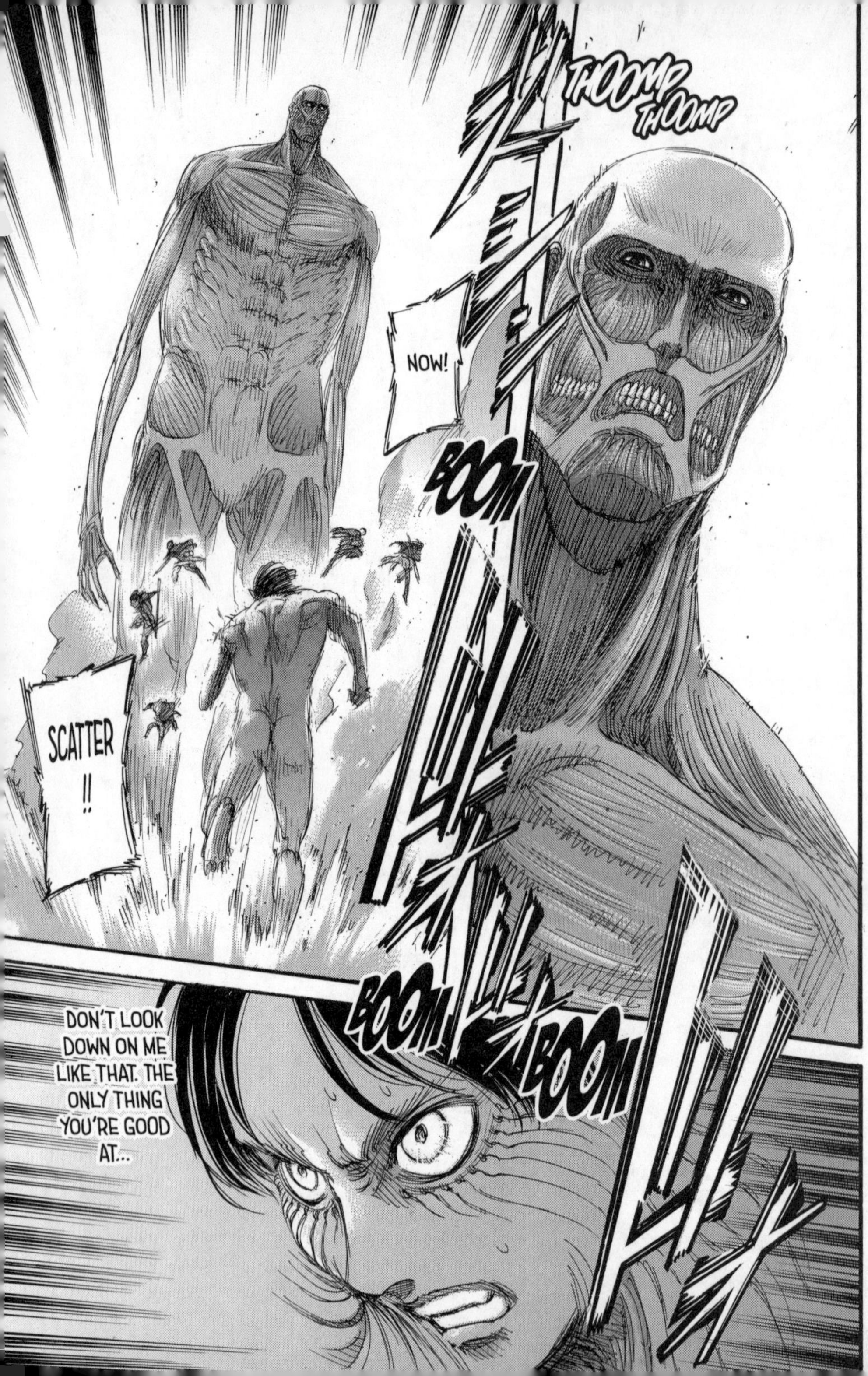
THOOMP THOOMP
NOW!
BOOM
SCATTER !!
BOOM
BOOM!
DON'T LOOK DOWN ON ME LIKE THAT. THE ONLY THING YOU'RE GOOD AT...

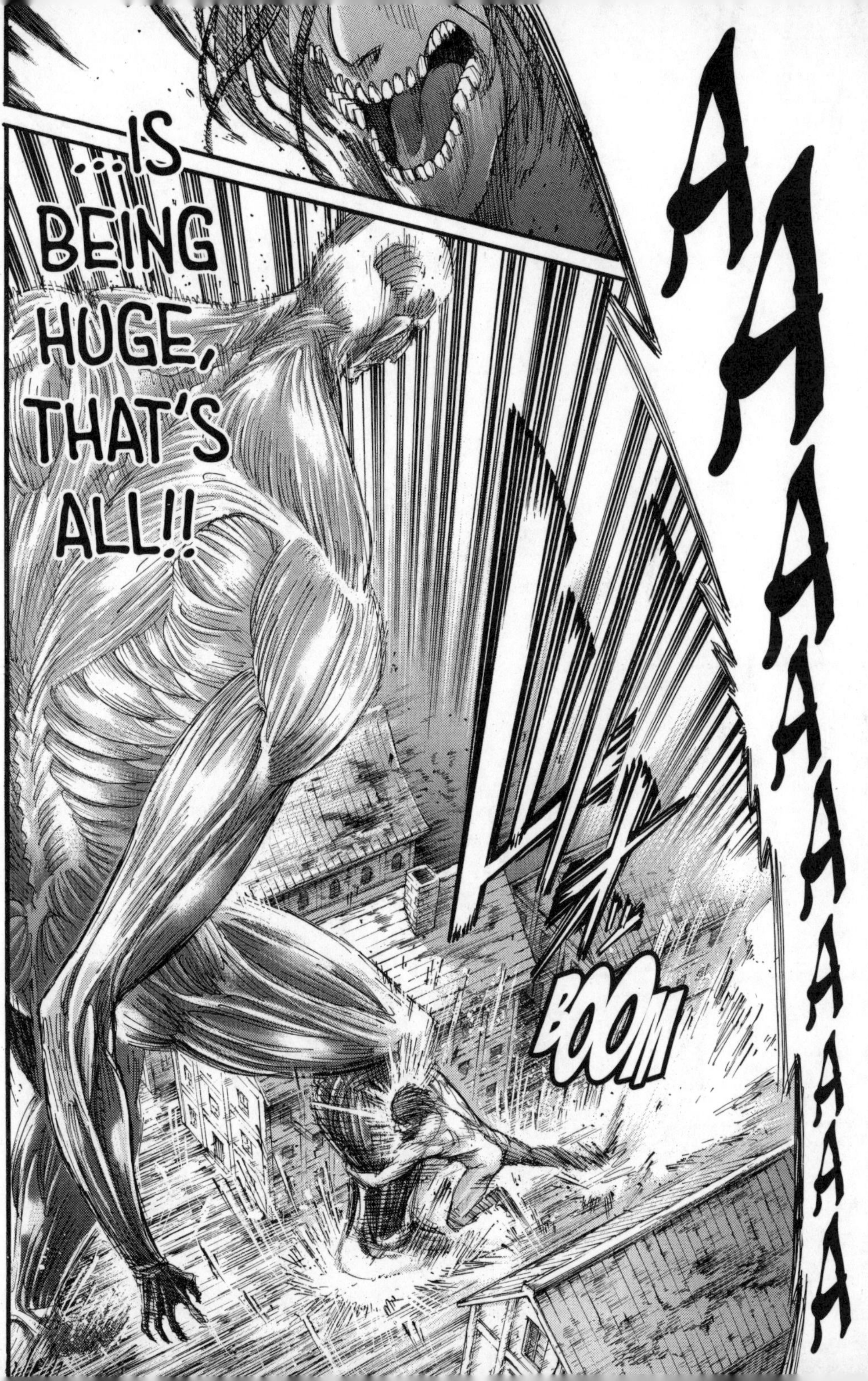
AAAAAAAAAAAAAA
...IS BEING HUGE, THAT'S ALL!!
BOOM

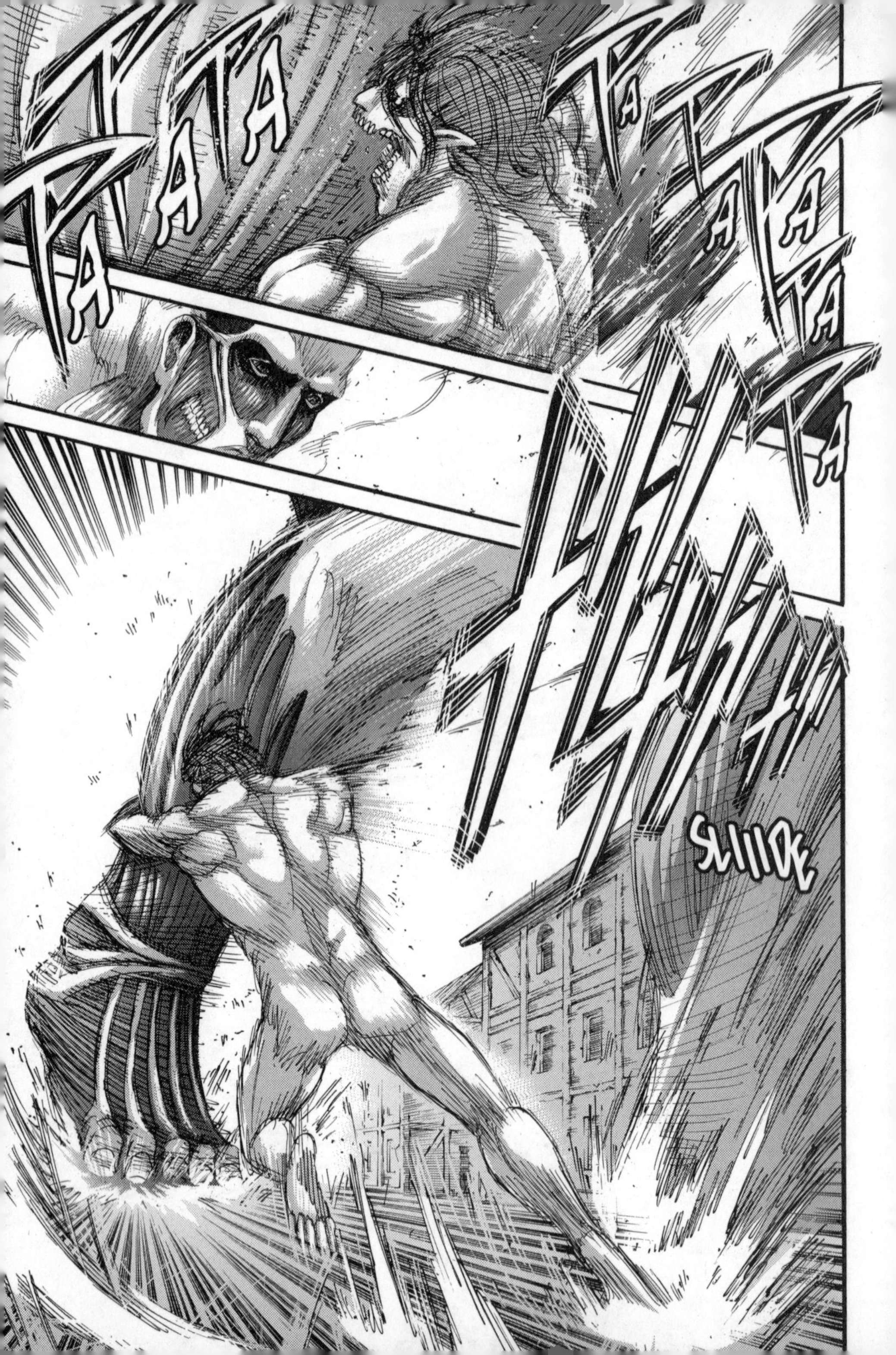
SLIIIDE

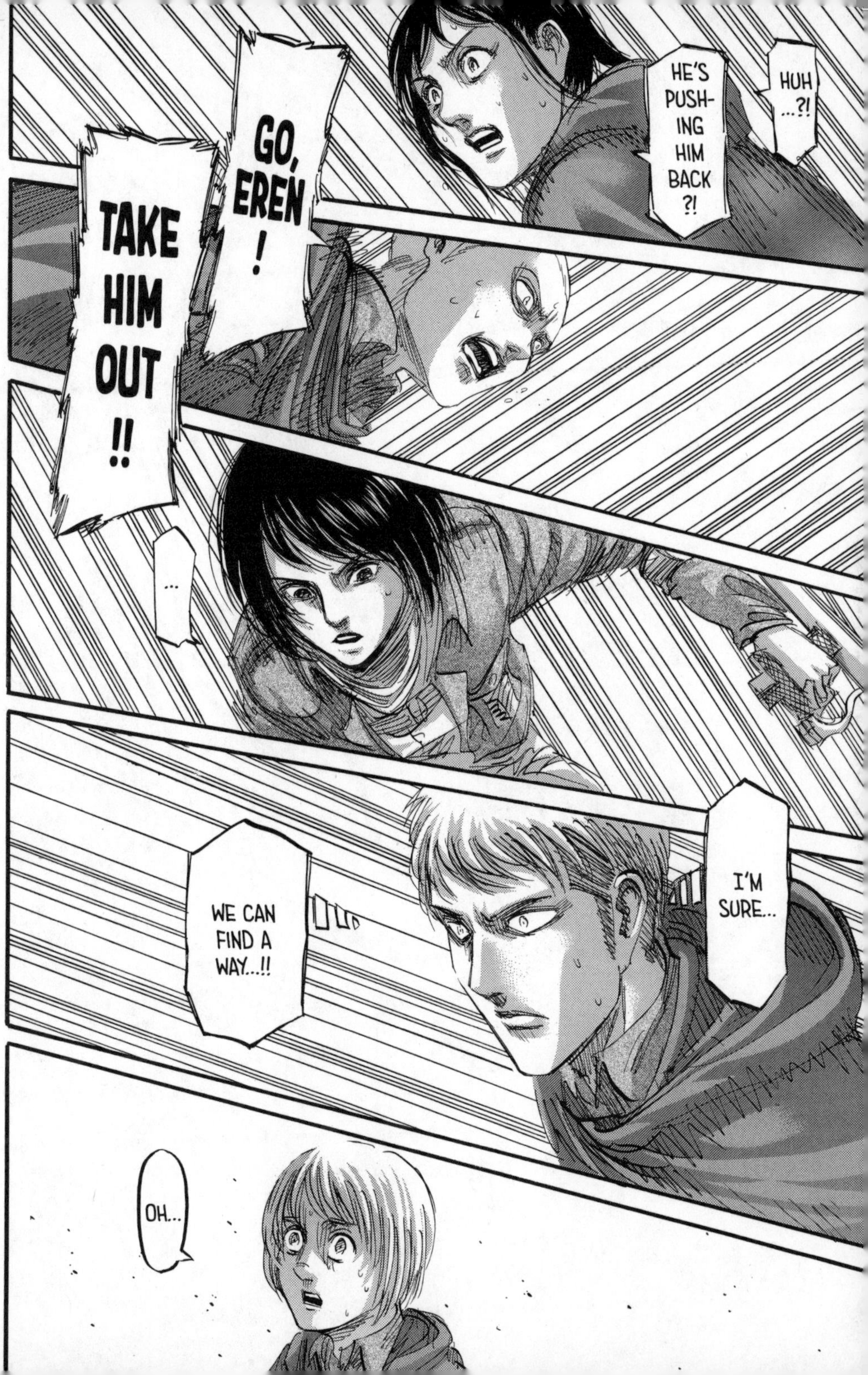
HUH ...?!
HE'S PUSHING HIM BACK ?!
GO, EREN !
TAKE HIM OUT !!
...
I'M SURE...
WE CAN FIND A WAY...!!
OH...

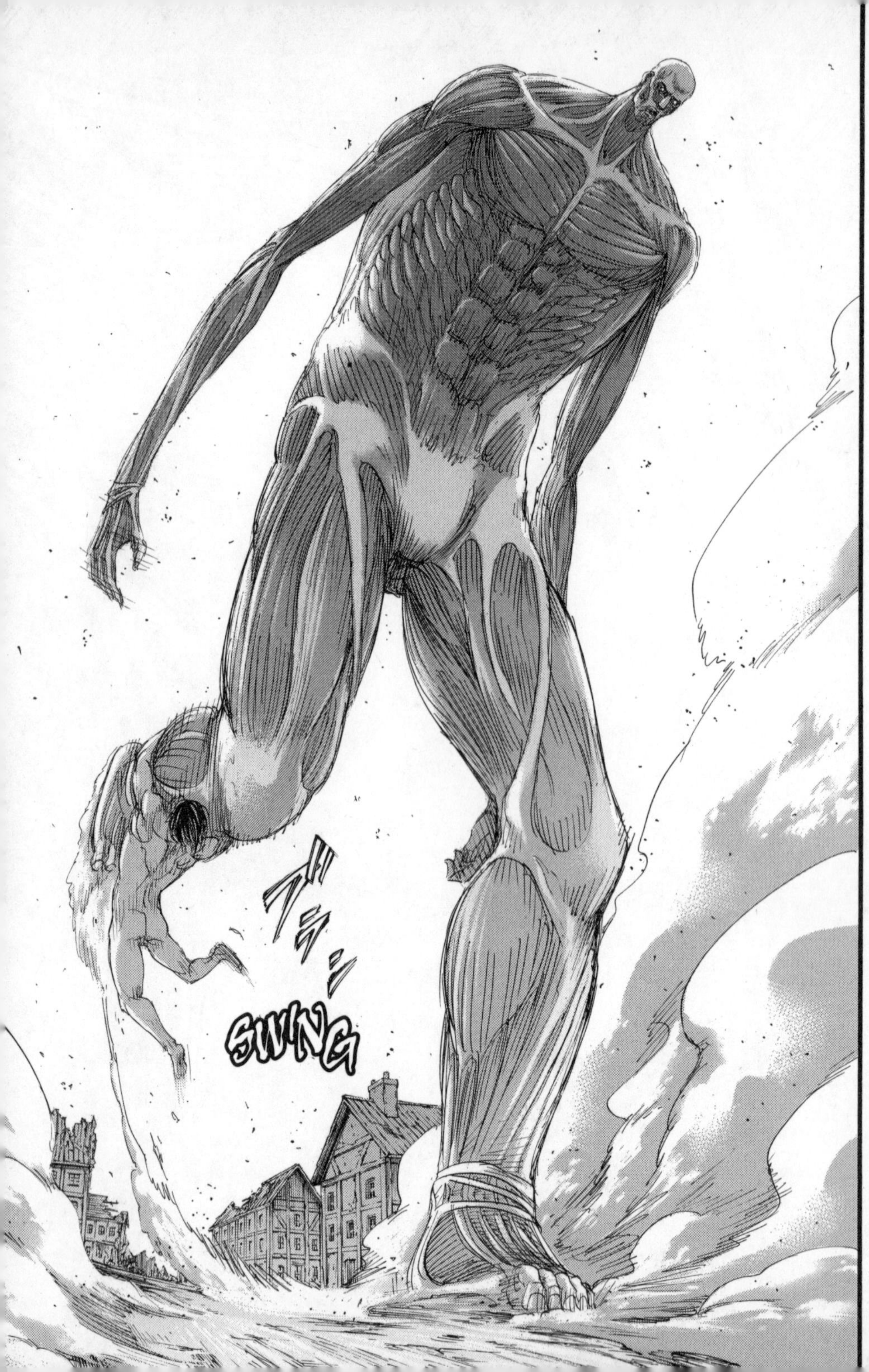
SWING

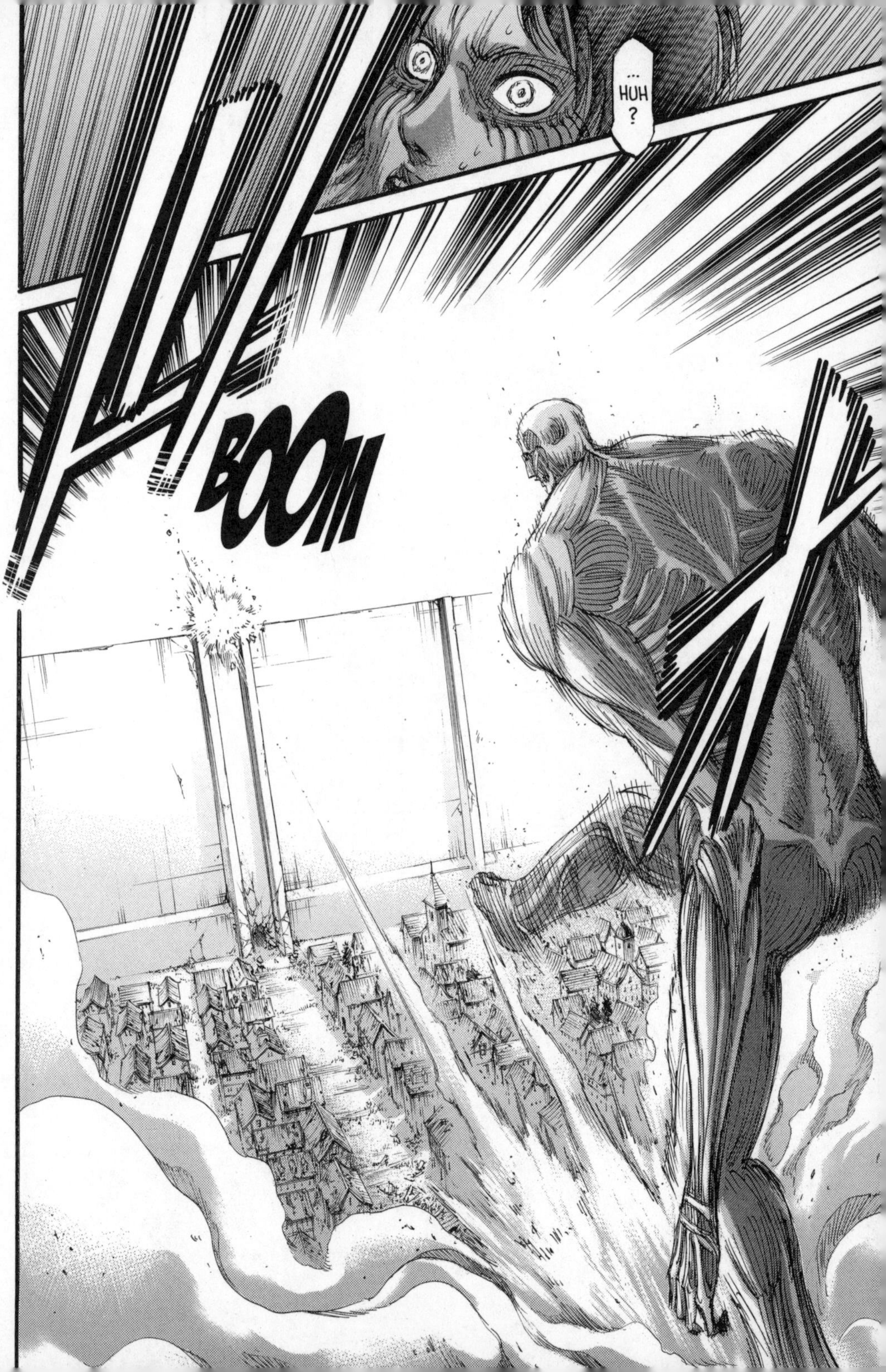
... HUH ?
BOOM

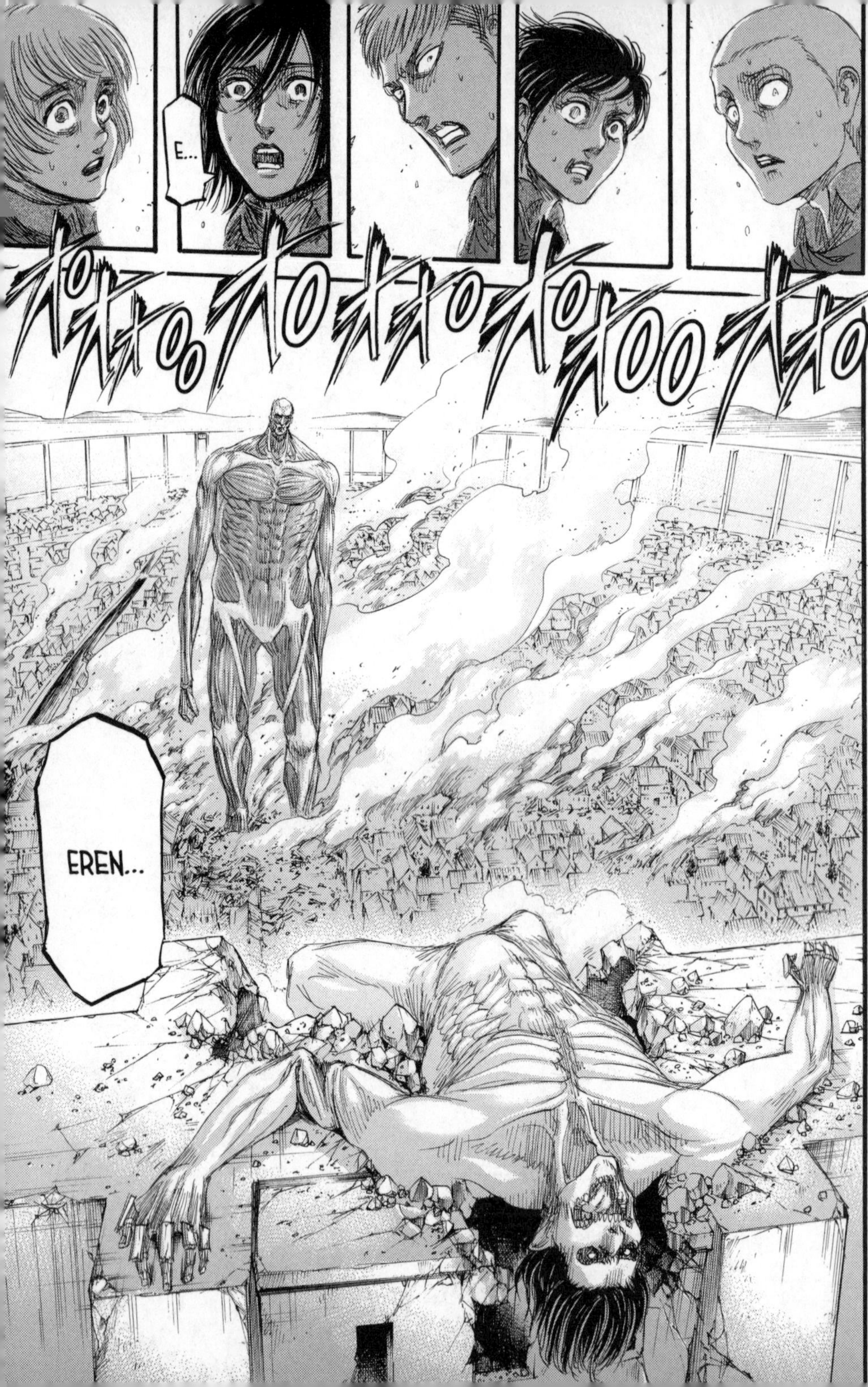
E...
EREN...

ATTACK on TITAN

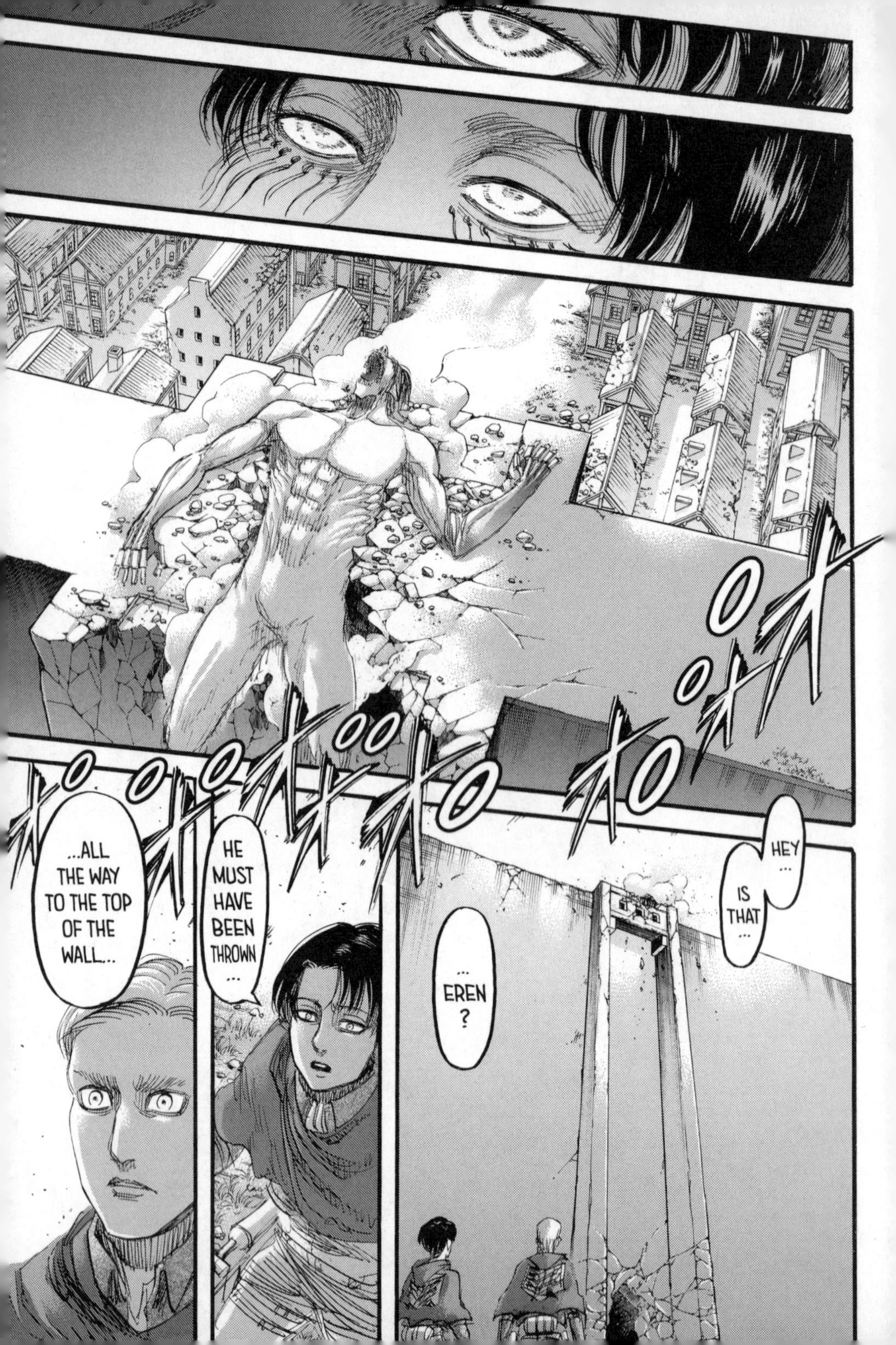
HEY... IS THAT...
...EREN?
HE MUST HAVE BEEN THROWN...
...ALL THE WAY TO THE TOP OF THE WALL...

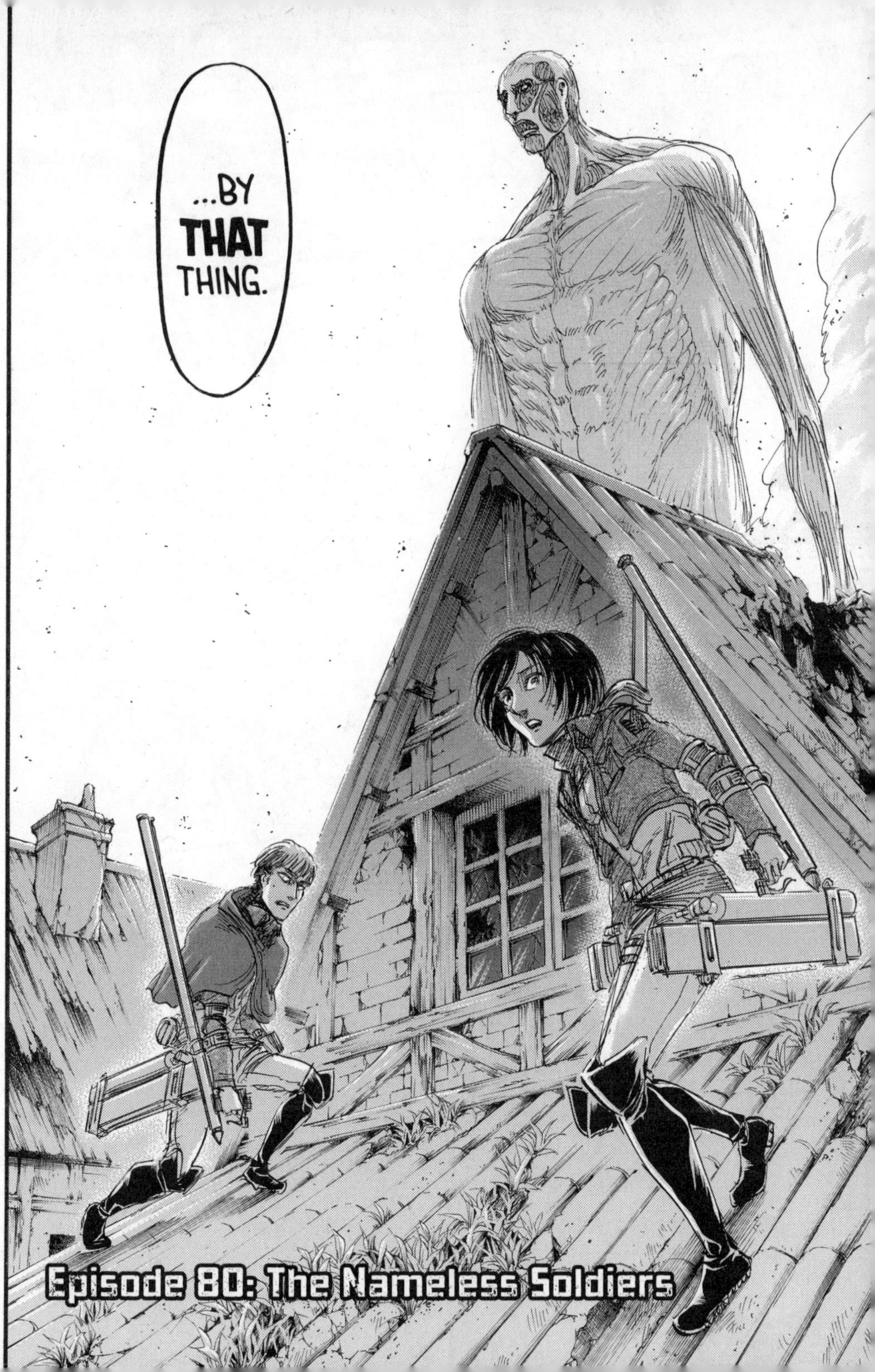
...BY THAT THING.
Episode 80: The Nameless Soldiers

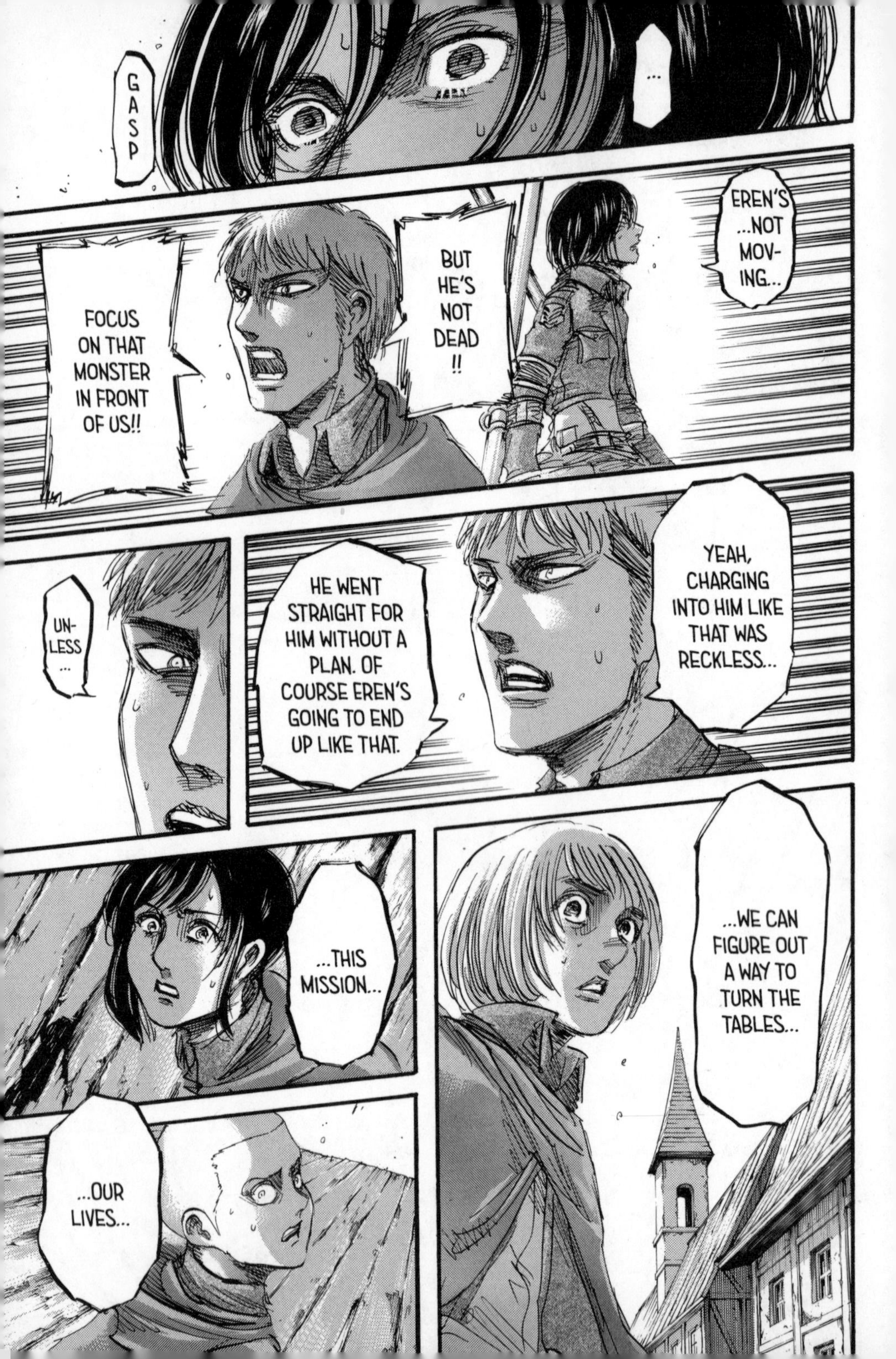
...
GASP
EREN'S ...NOT MOVING...
BUT HE'S NOT DEAD!!
FOCUS ON THAT MONSTER IN FRONT OF US!!
YEAH, CHARGING INTO HIM LIKE THAT WAS RECKLESS...
HE WENT STRAIGHT FOR HIM WITHOUT A PLAN. OF COURSE EREN'S GOING TO END UP LIKE THAT.
UN-LESS ...
...WE CAN FIGURE OUT A WAY TO TURN THE TABLES...
...THIS MISSION...
...OUR LIVES...

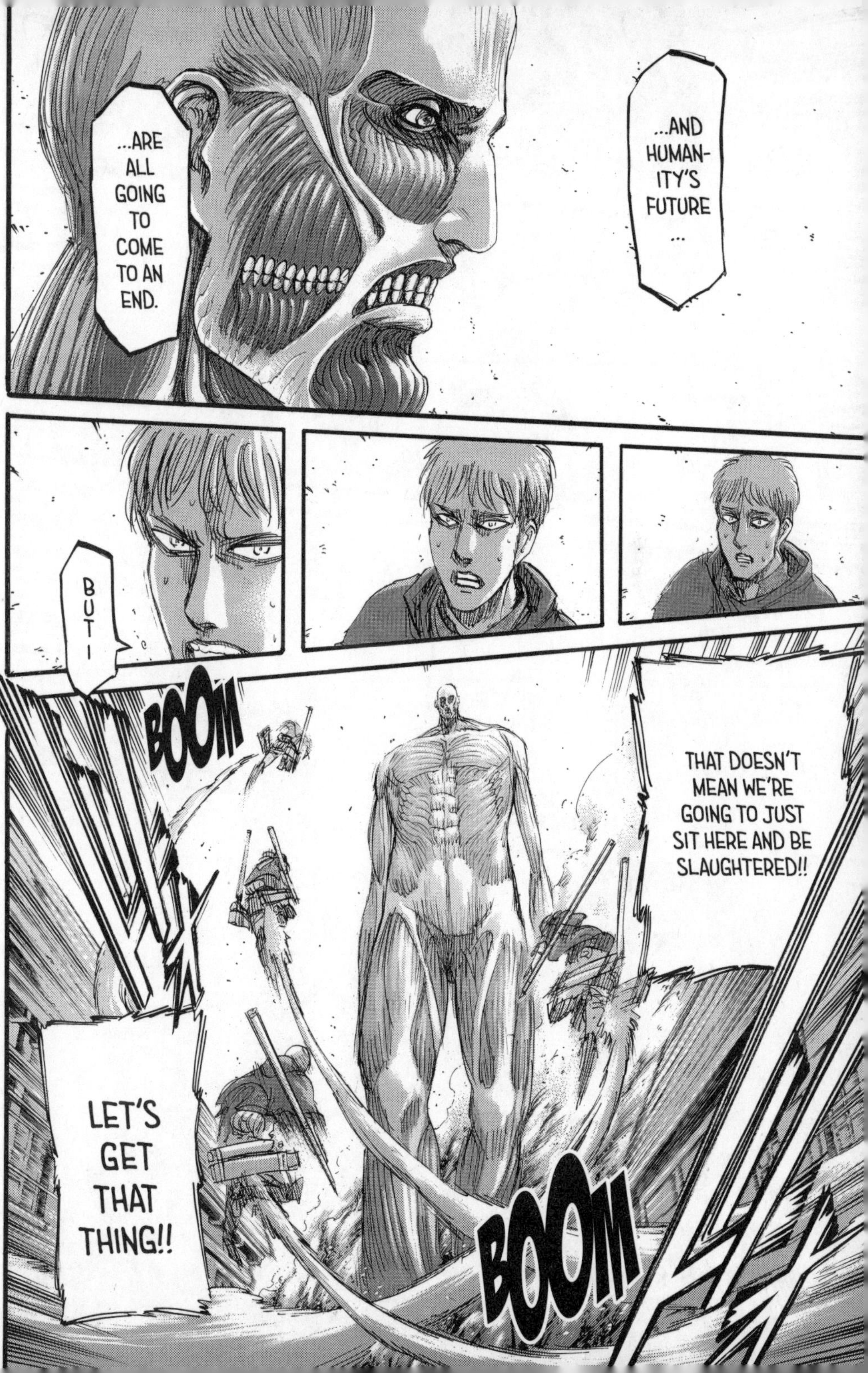
...AND HUMAN-ITY'S FUTURE ...
...ARE ALL GOING TO COME TO AN END.
BUT I
THAT DOESN'T MEAN WE'RE GOING TO JUST SIT HERE AND BE SLAUGHTERED!!
BOOM
LET'S GET THAT THING!!
BOOM

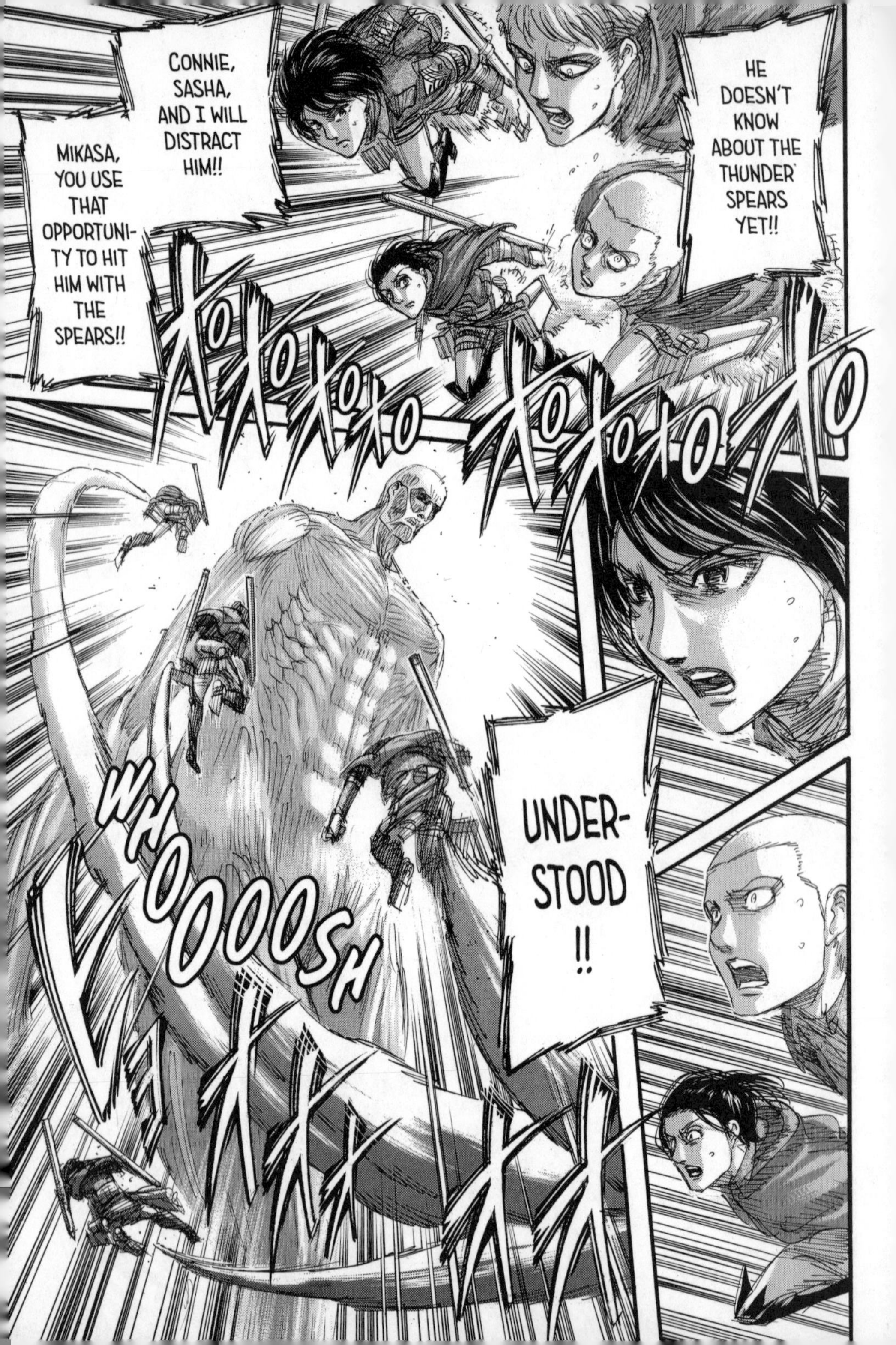
HE DOESN'T KNOW ABOUT THE THUNDER SPEARS YET!!
CONNIE, SASHA, AND I WILL DISTRACT HIM!!
MIKASA, YOU USE THAT OPPORTUNITY TO HIT HIM WITH THE SPEARS!!
UNDER-STOOD !!
WHOOOOOSH

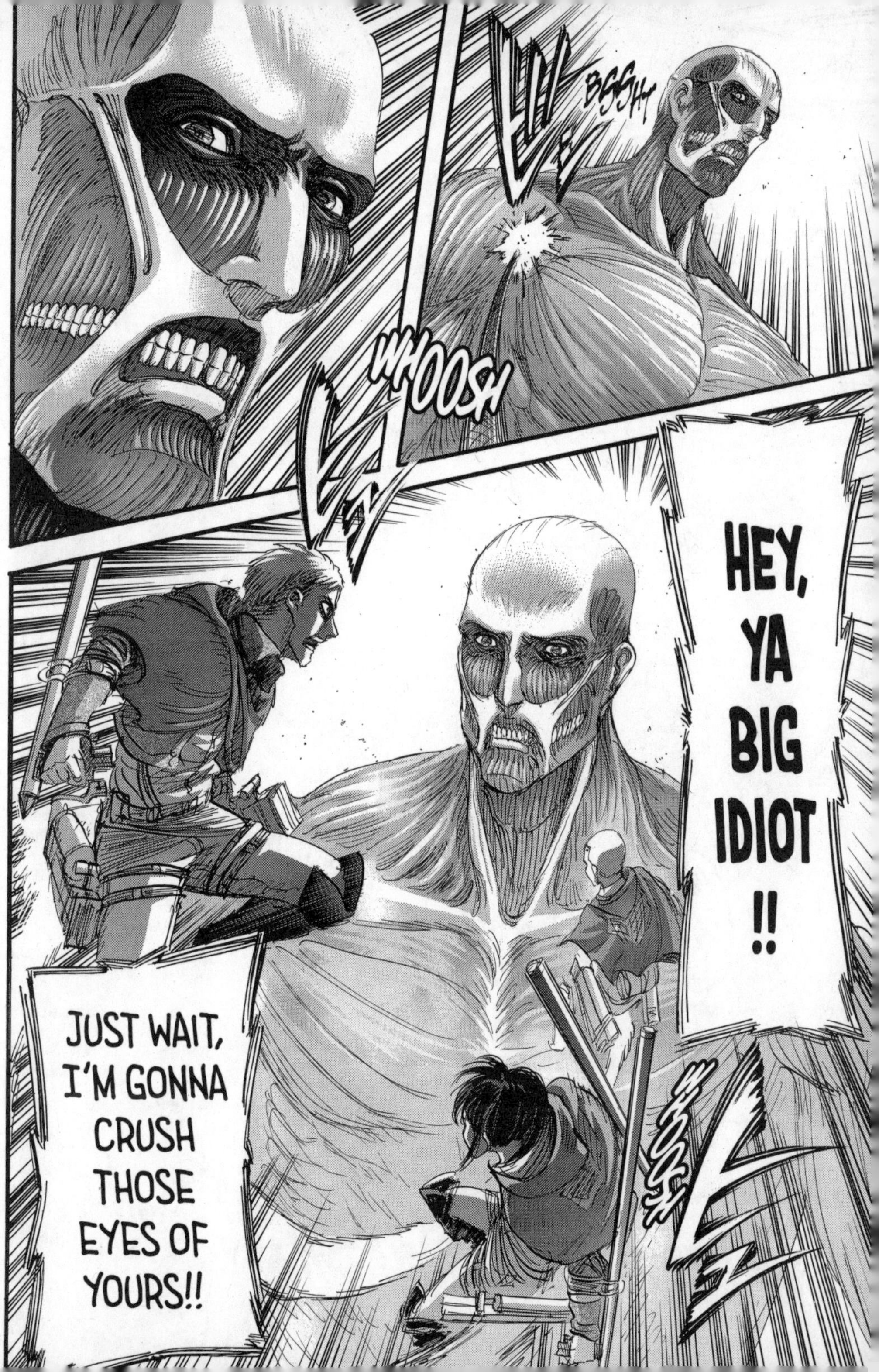
BSSH
WHOOSH
HEY, YA BIG IDIOT!!
JUST WAIT, I'M GONNA CRUSH THOSE EYES OF YOURS!!
WHOOSH

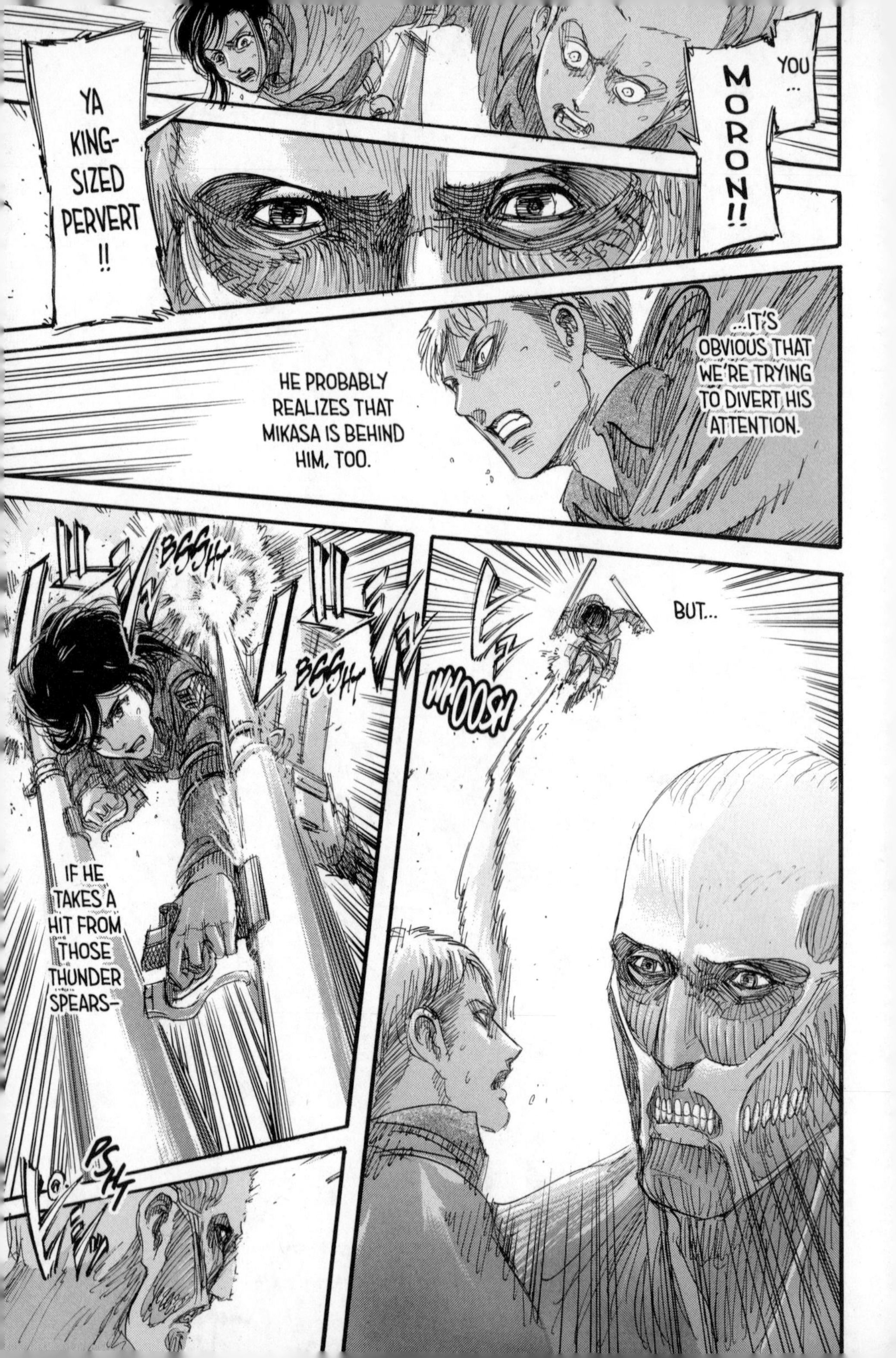
YOU... MORON!!
YA KING-SIZED PERVERT!!
...IT'S OBVIOUS THAT WE'RE TRYING TO DIVERT HIS ATTENTION.
HE PROBABLY REALIZES THAT MIKASA IS BEHIND HIM, TOO.
BUT...
WHOOSH
BSSSH
BSSSH
IF HE TAKES A HIT FROM THOSE THUNDER SPEARS-
PSSH

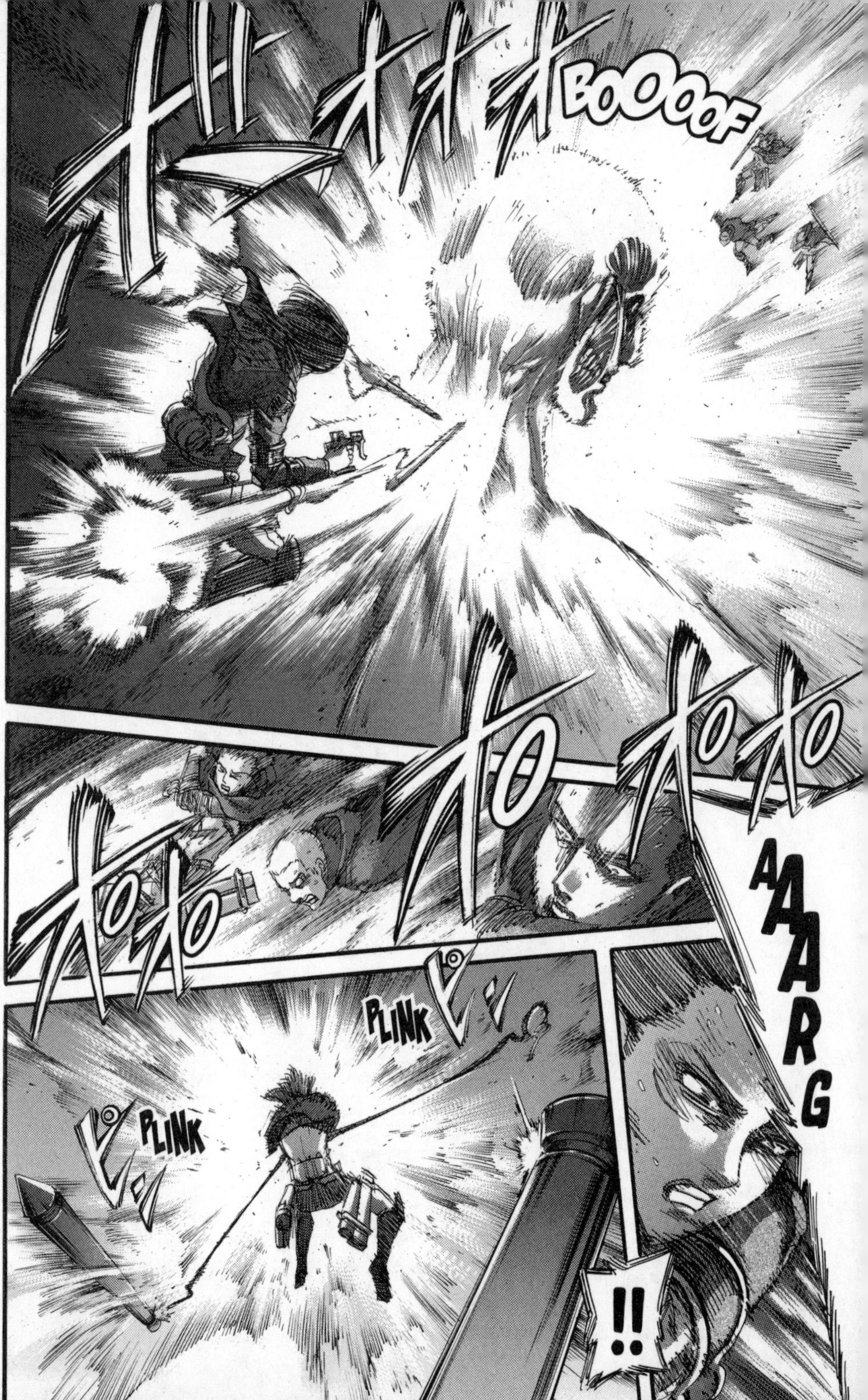

BOOOOF
AAAARG
!!
PLINK
PLINK

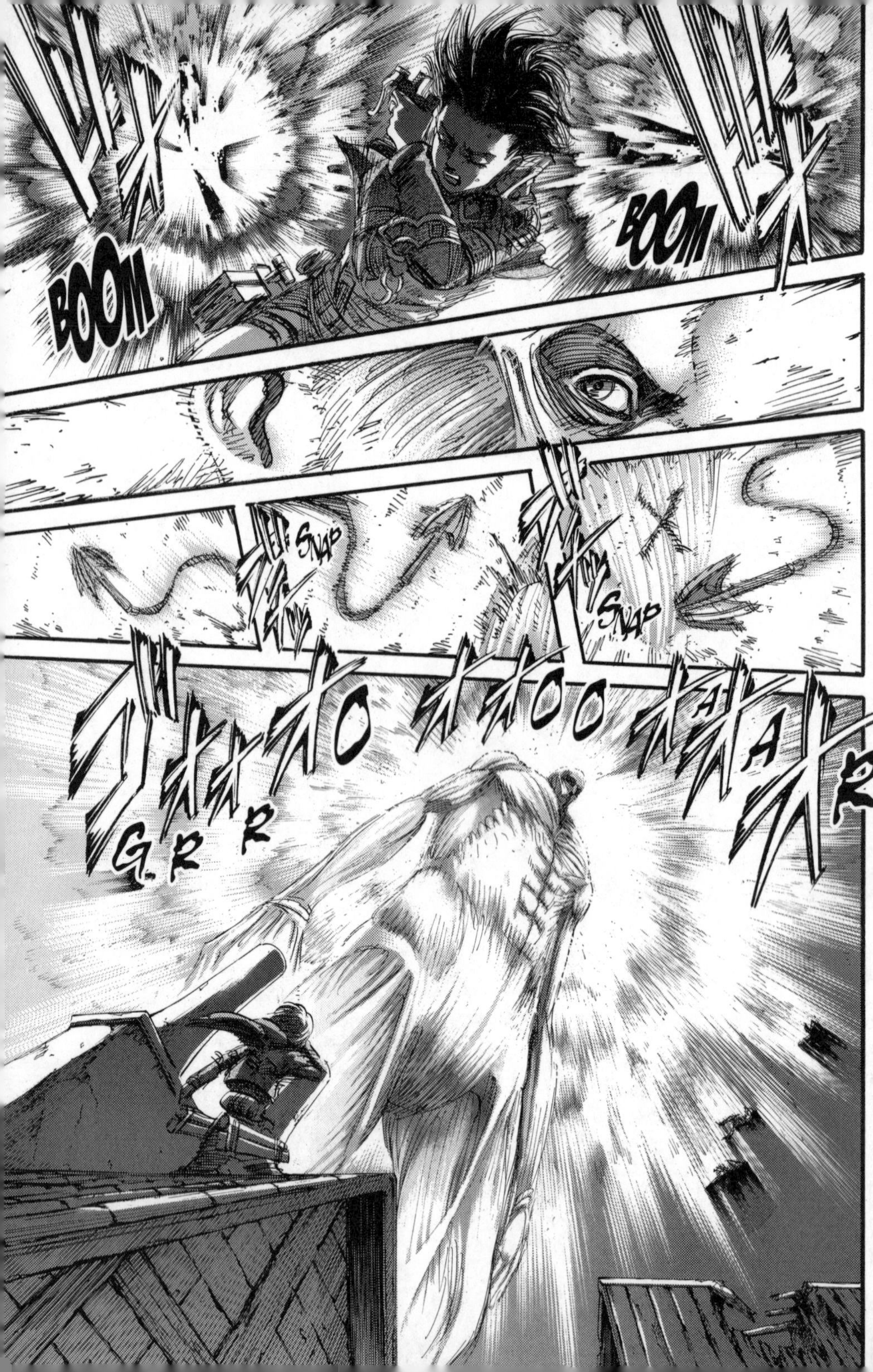
BOOM
BOOM
SNAP
SNAP
GRR
AAR

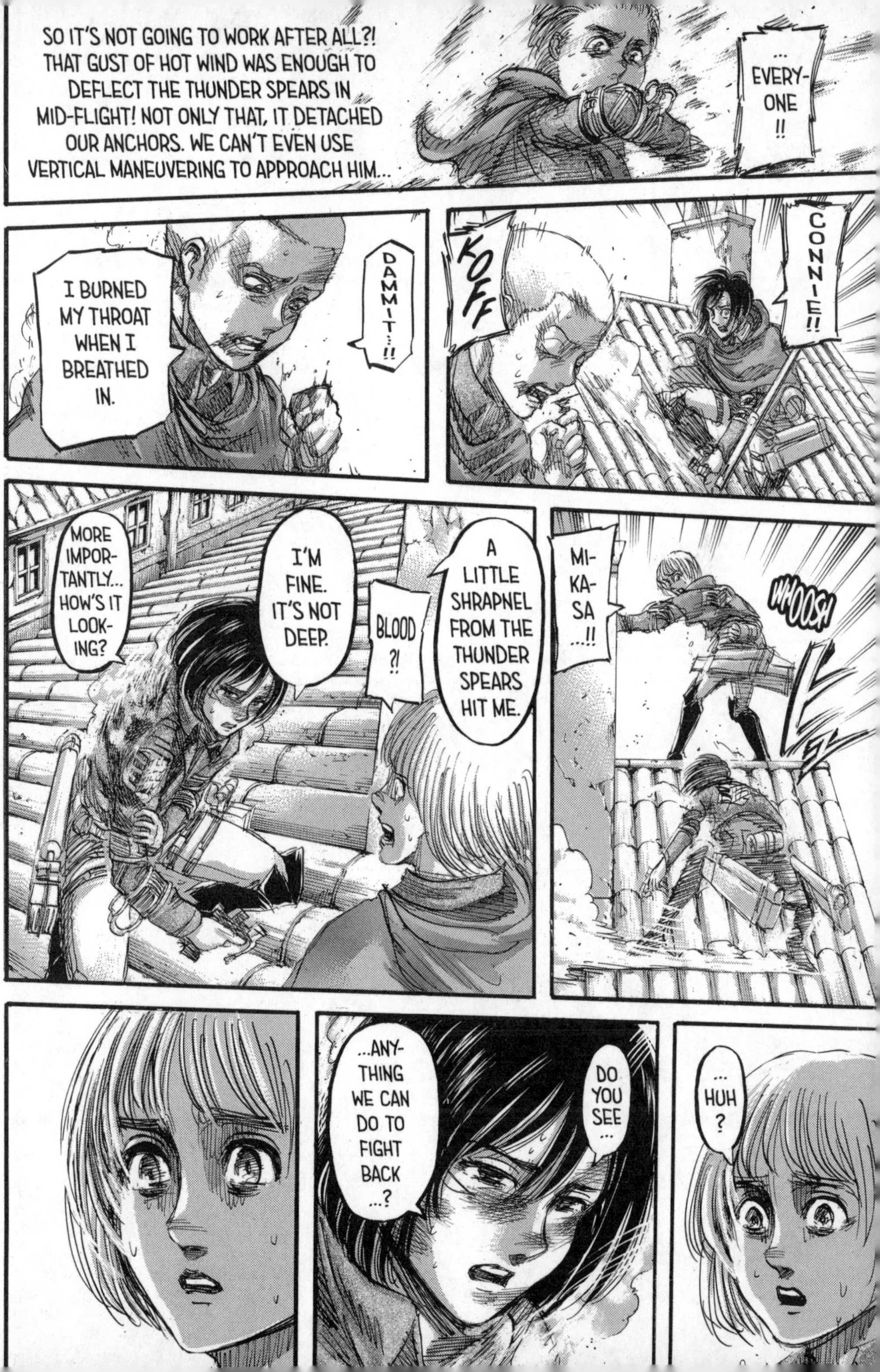
...EVERYONE!!
SO IT'S NOT GOING TO WORK AFTER ALL?! THAT GUST OF HOT WIND WAS ENOUGH TO DEFLECT THE THUNDER SPEARS IN MID-FLIGHT! NOT ONLY THAT, IT DETACHED OUR ANCHORS. WE CAN'T EVEN USE VERTICAL MANEUVERING TO APPROACH HIM...
CONNIE!!
KOFF
DAMMIT...!!
I BURNED MY THROAT WHEN I BREATHED IN.
MIKASA...!!
WHOOSH
A LITTLE SHRAPNEL FROM THE THUNDER SPEARS HIT ME.
BLOOD?!
I'M FINE. IT'S NOT DEEP.
MORE IMPORTANTLY... HOW'S IT LOOKING?
...HUH?
DO YOU SEE...
...ANYTHING WE CAN DO TO FIGHT BACK...?

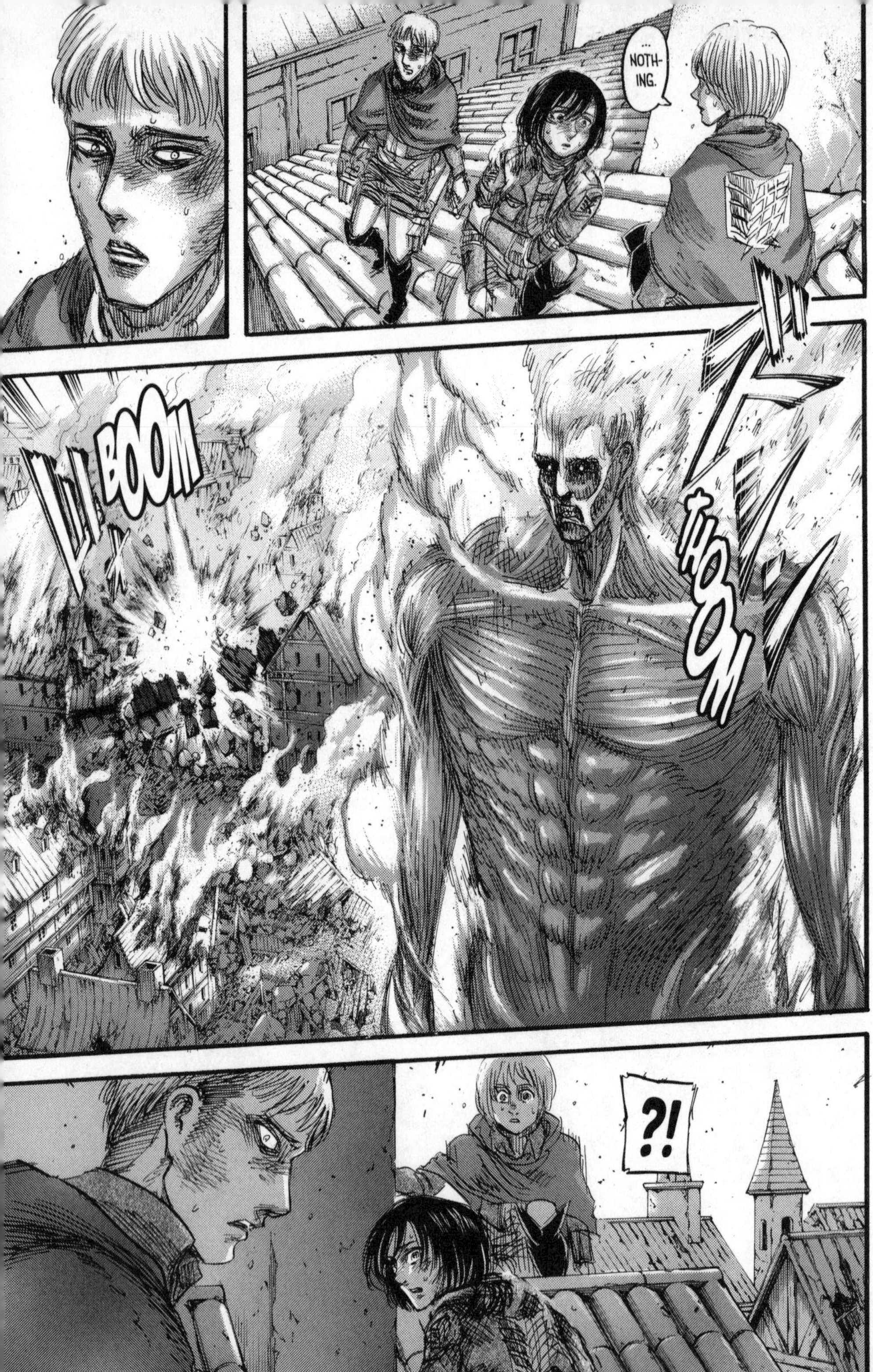

... NOTH-ING.
THOOM
BOOM
?!

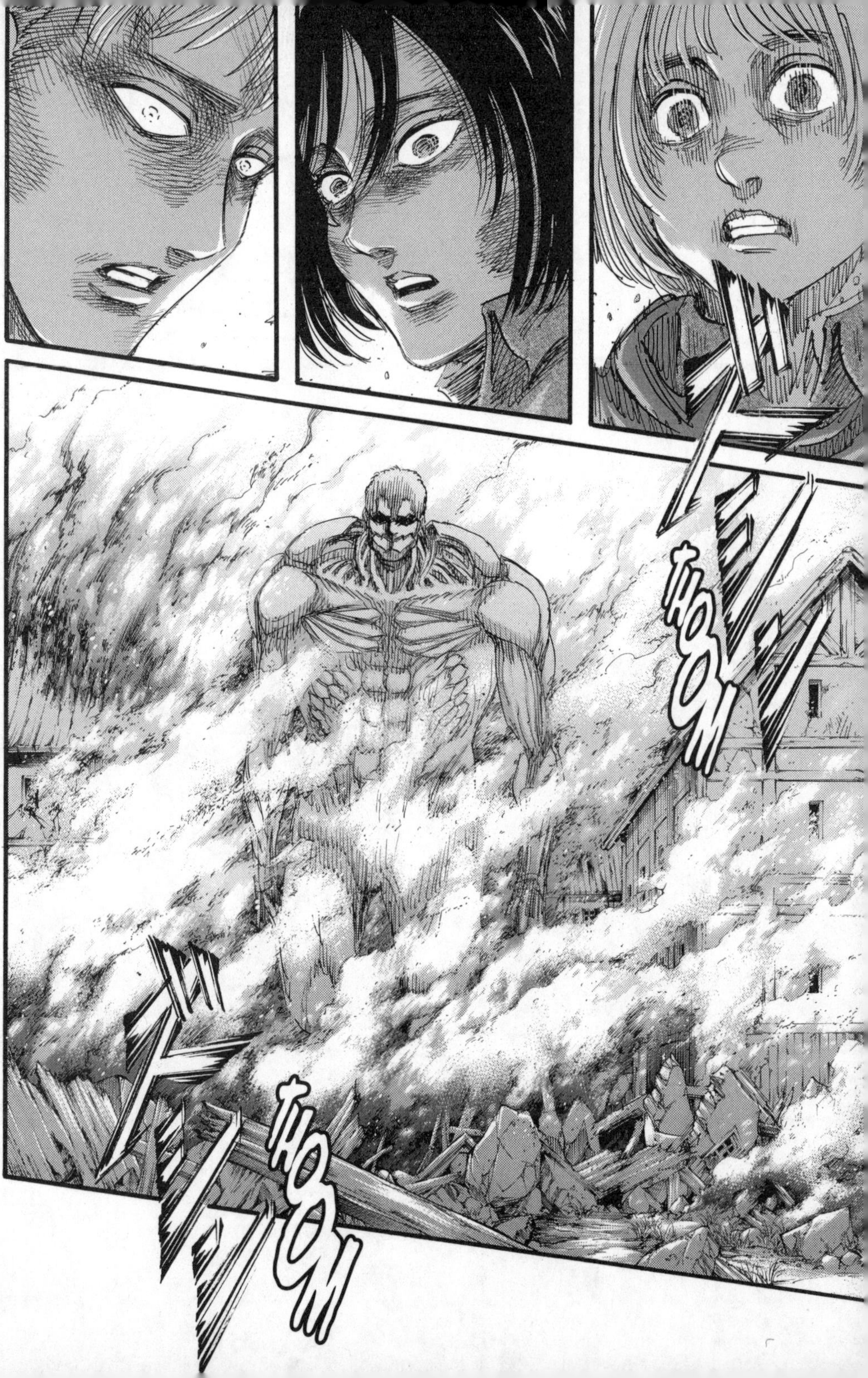
THOOM
THOOM

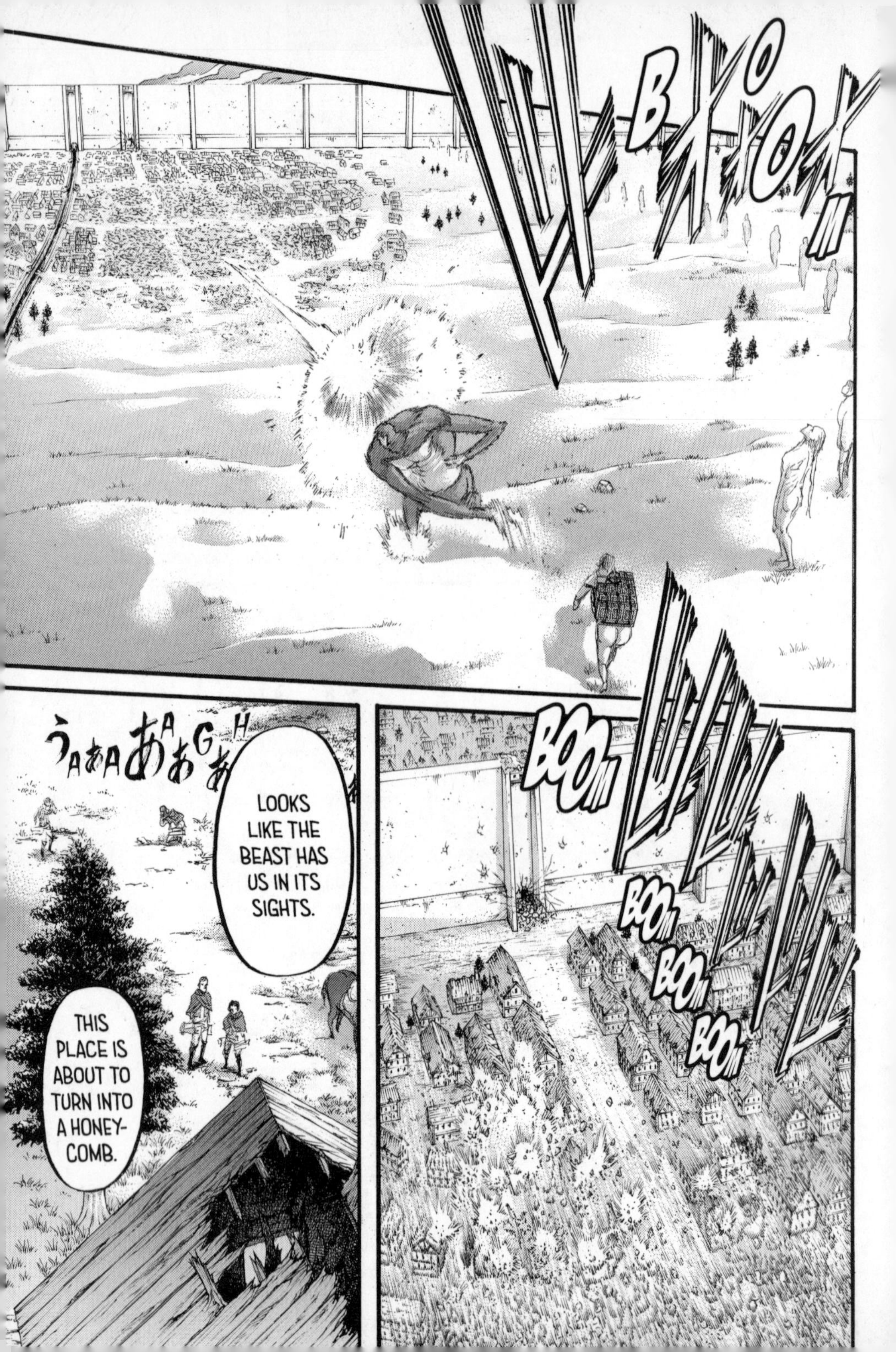
B
BOOM
BOOM
BOOM
BOOM
AAAGH
LOOKS LIKE THE BEAST HAS US IN ITS SIGHTS.
THIS PLACE IS ABOUT TO TURN INTO A HONEY-COMB.

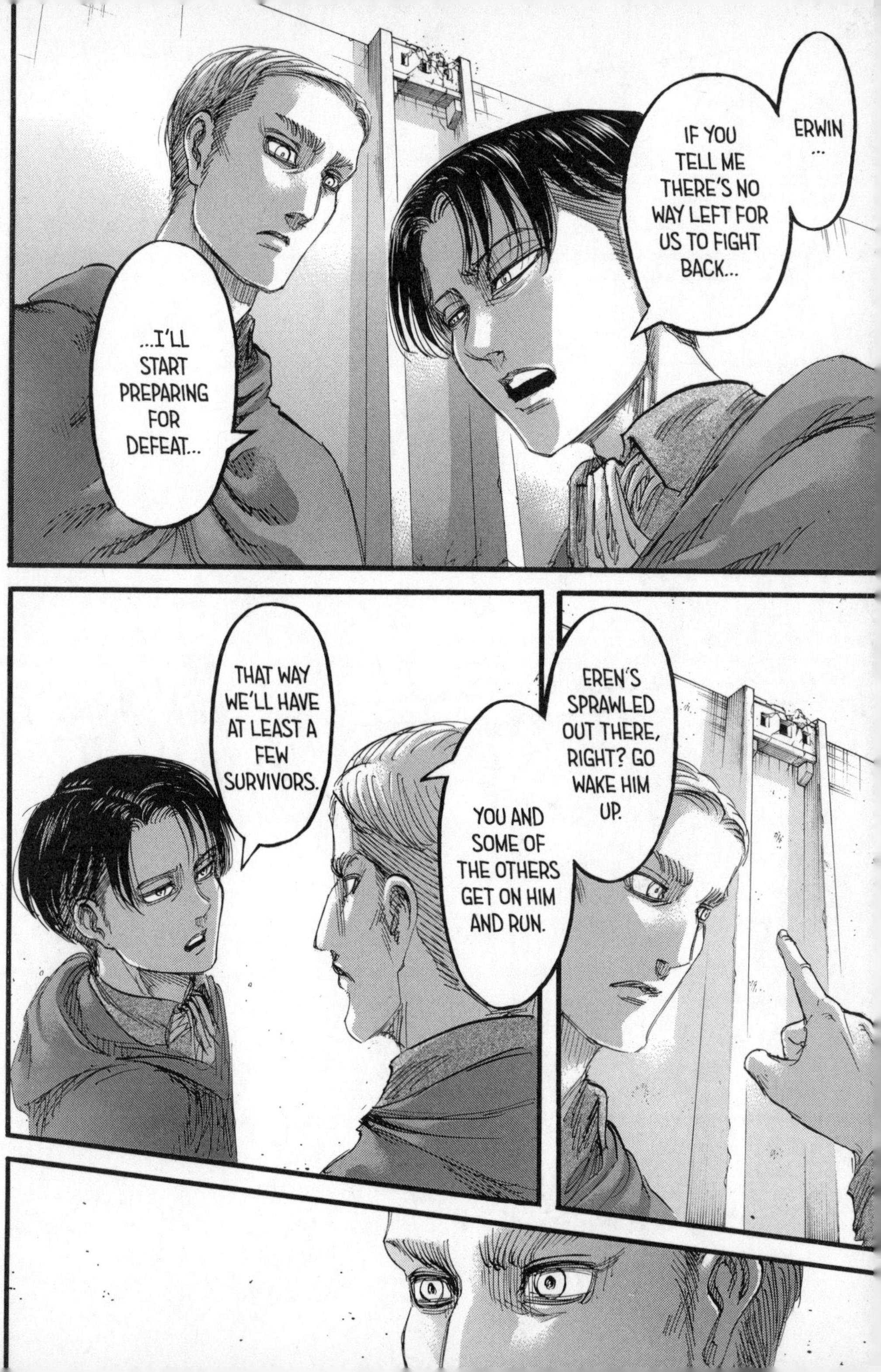
ERWIN ...
IF YOU TELL ME THERE'S NO WAY LEFT FOR US TO FIGHT BACK...
...I'LL START PREPARING FOR DEFEAT...
EREN'S SPRAWLED OUT THERE, RIGHT? GO WAKE HIM UP.
YOU AND SOME OF THE OTHERS GET ON HIM AND RUN.
THAT WAY WE'LL HAVE AT LEAST A FEW SURVIVORS.

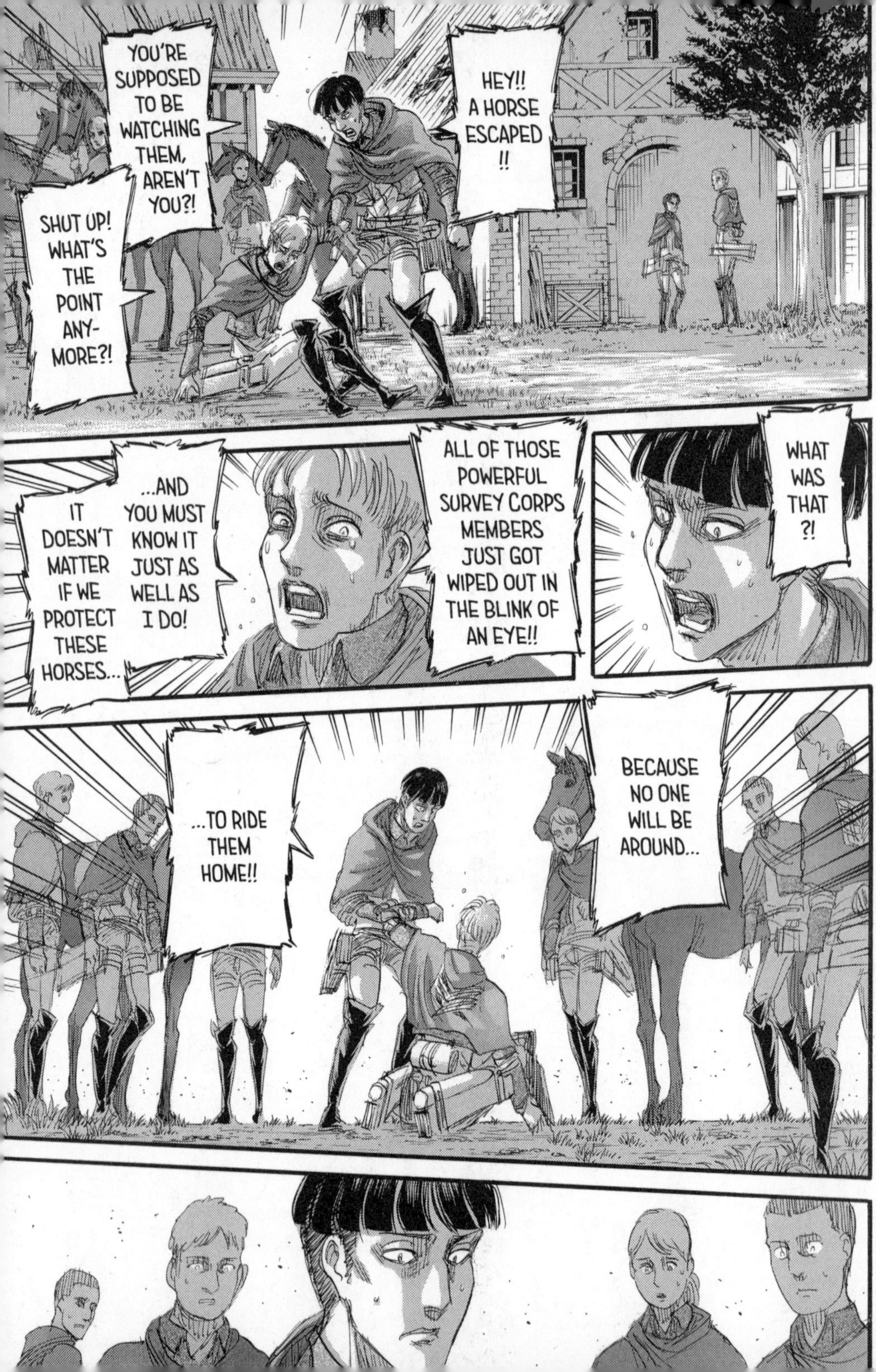
HEY!! A HORSE ESCAPED!!
YOU'RE SUPPOSED TO BE WATCHING THEM, AREN'T YOU?!
SHUT UP! WHAT'S THE POINT ANY-MORE?!
WHAT WAS THAT?!
ALL OF THOSE POWERFUL SURVEY CORPS MEMBERS JUST GOT WIPED OUT IN THE BLINK OF AN EYE!!
...AND YOU MUST KNOW IT JUST AS WELL AS I DO!
IT DOESN'T MATTER IF WE PROTECT THESE HORSES...
BECAUSE NO ONE WILL BE AROUND...
...TO RIDE THEM HOME!!

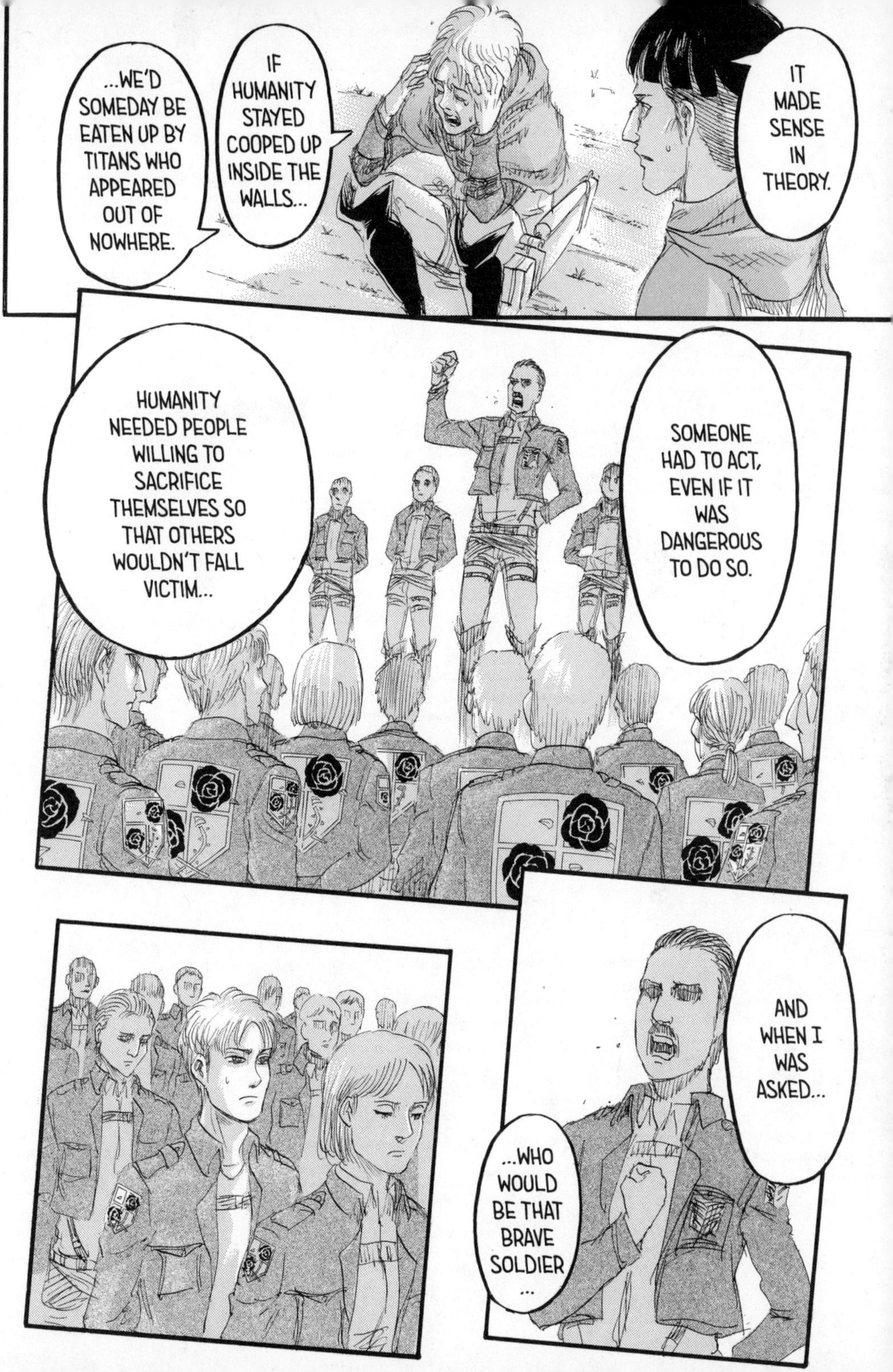
IT MADE SENSE IN THEORY.
IF HUMANITY STAYED COOPED UP INSIDE THE WALLS...
...WE'D SOMEDAY BE EATEN UP BY TITANS WHO APPEARED OUT OF NOWHERE.
SOMEONE HAD TO ACT, EVEN IF IT WAS DANGEROUS TO DO SO.
HUMANITY NEEDED PEOPLE WILLING TO SACRIFICE THEMSELVES SO THAT OTHERS WOULDN'T FALL VICTIM...
AND WHEN I WAS ASKED...
...WHO WOULD BE THAT BRAVE SOLDIER ...

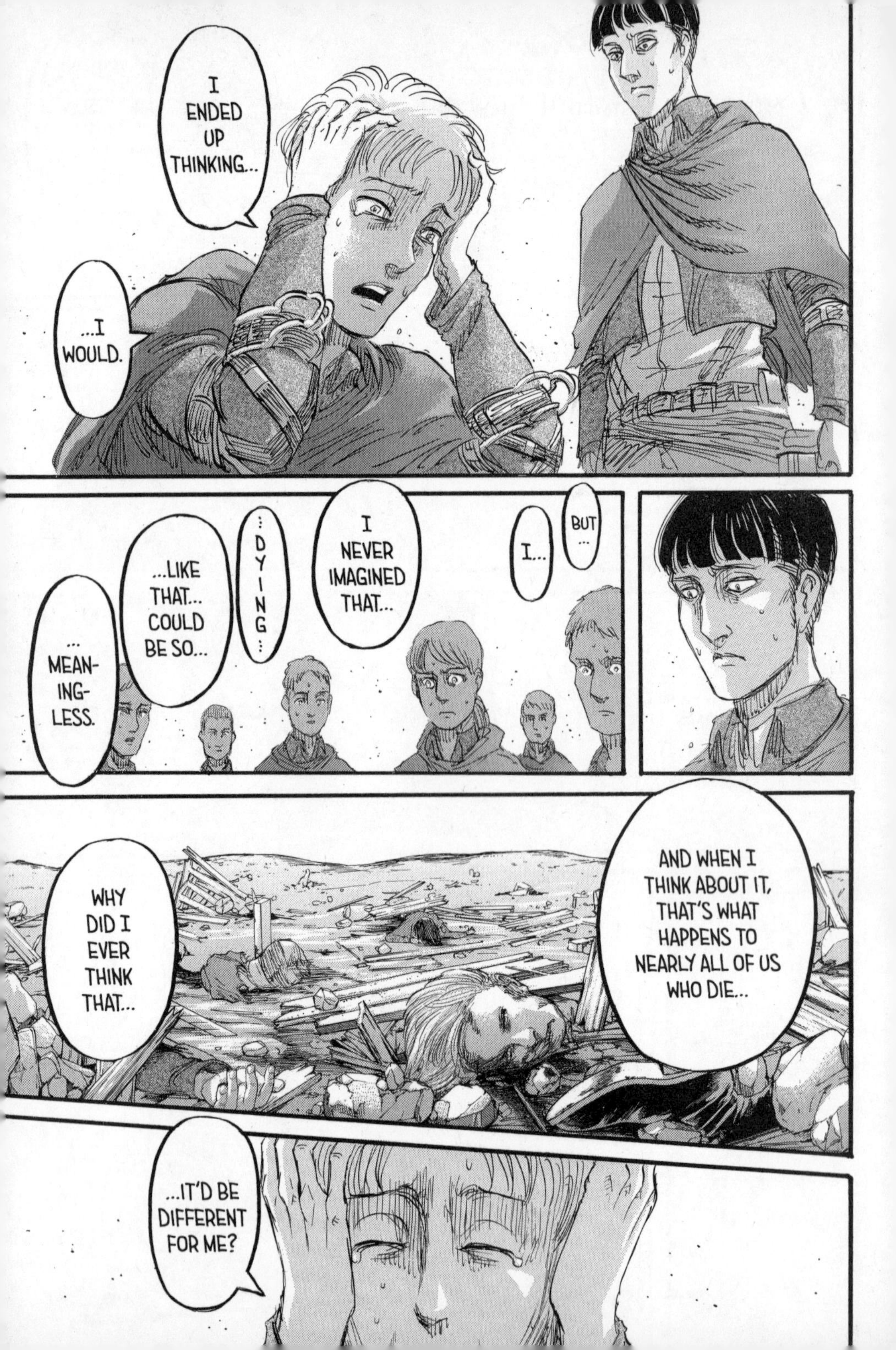
I ENDED UP THINKING...
...I WOULD.
BUT...
I...
I NEVER IMAGINED THAT...
...DYING...
...LIKE THAT... COULD BE SO...
...MEAN-ING-LESS.
AND WHEN I THINK ABOUT IT, THAT'S WHAT HAPPENS TO NEARLY ALL OF US WHO DIE...
WHY DID I EVER THINK THAT...
...IT'D BE DIFFERENT FOR ME?

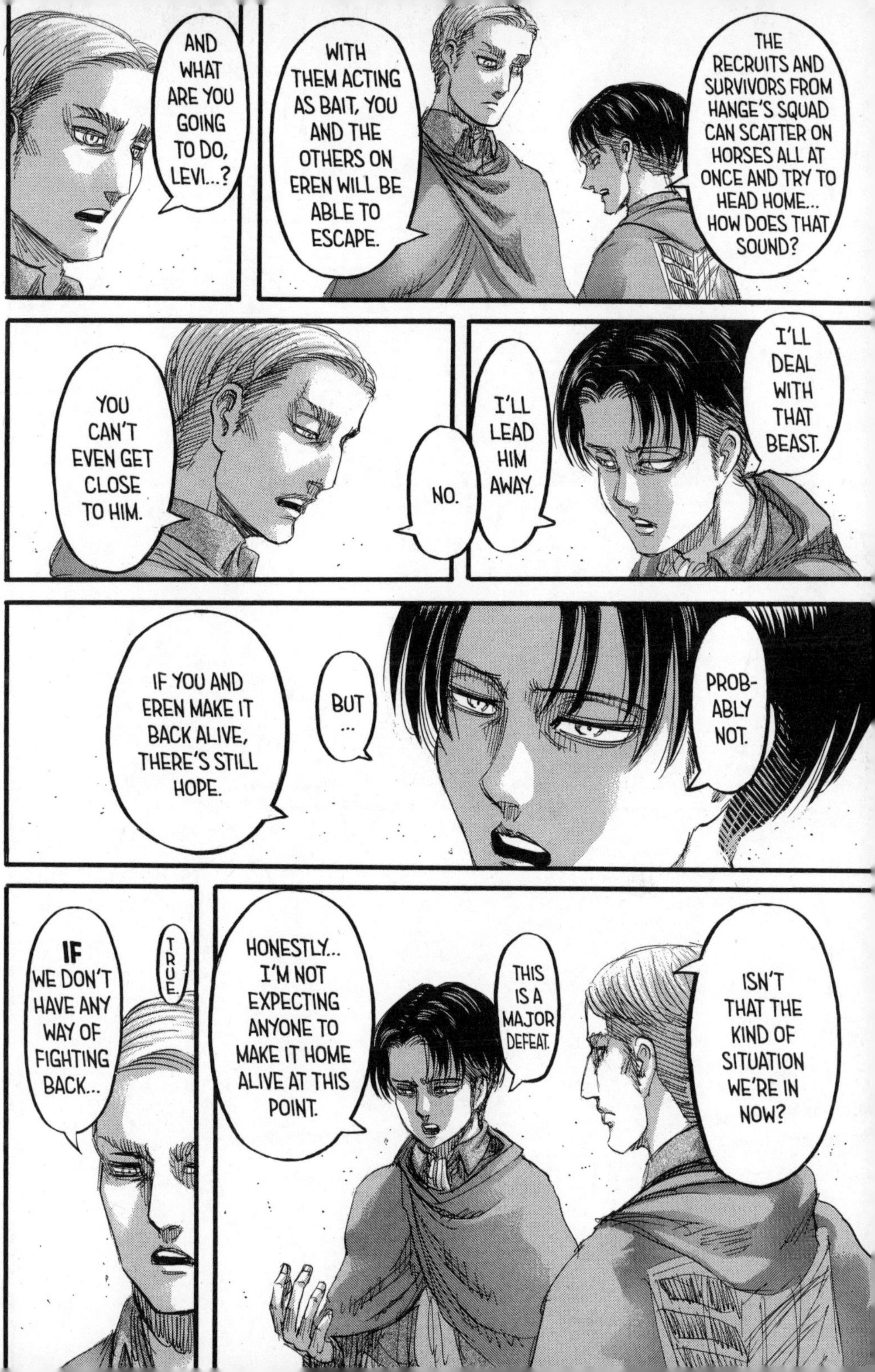
THE RECRUITS AND SURVIVORS FROM HANGE'S SQUAD CAN SCATTER ON HORSES ALL AT ONCE AND TRY TO HEAD HOME... HOW DOES THAT SOUND?
WITH THEM ACTING AS BAIT, YOU AND THE OTHERS ON EREN WILL BE ABLE TO ESCAPE.
AND WHAT ARE YOU GOING TO DO, LEVI...?
I'LL DEAL WITH THAT BEAST.
I'LL LEAD HIM AWAY.
NO.
YOU CAN'T EVEN GET CLOSE TO HIM.
PROB-ABLY NOT.
BUT ...
IF YOU AND EREN MAKE IT BACK ALIVE, THERE'S STILL HOPE.
ISN'T THAT THE KIND OF SITUATION WE'RE IN NOW?
THIS IS A MAJOR DEFEAT.
HONESTLY... I'M NOT EXPECTING ANYONE TO MAKE IT HOME ALIVE AT THIS POINT.
TRUE.
IF WE DON'T HAVE ANY WAY OF FIGHTING BACK...

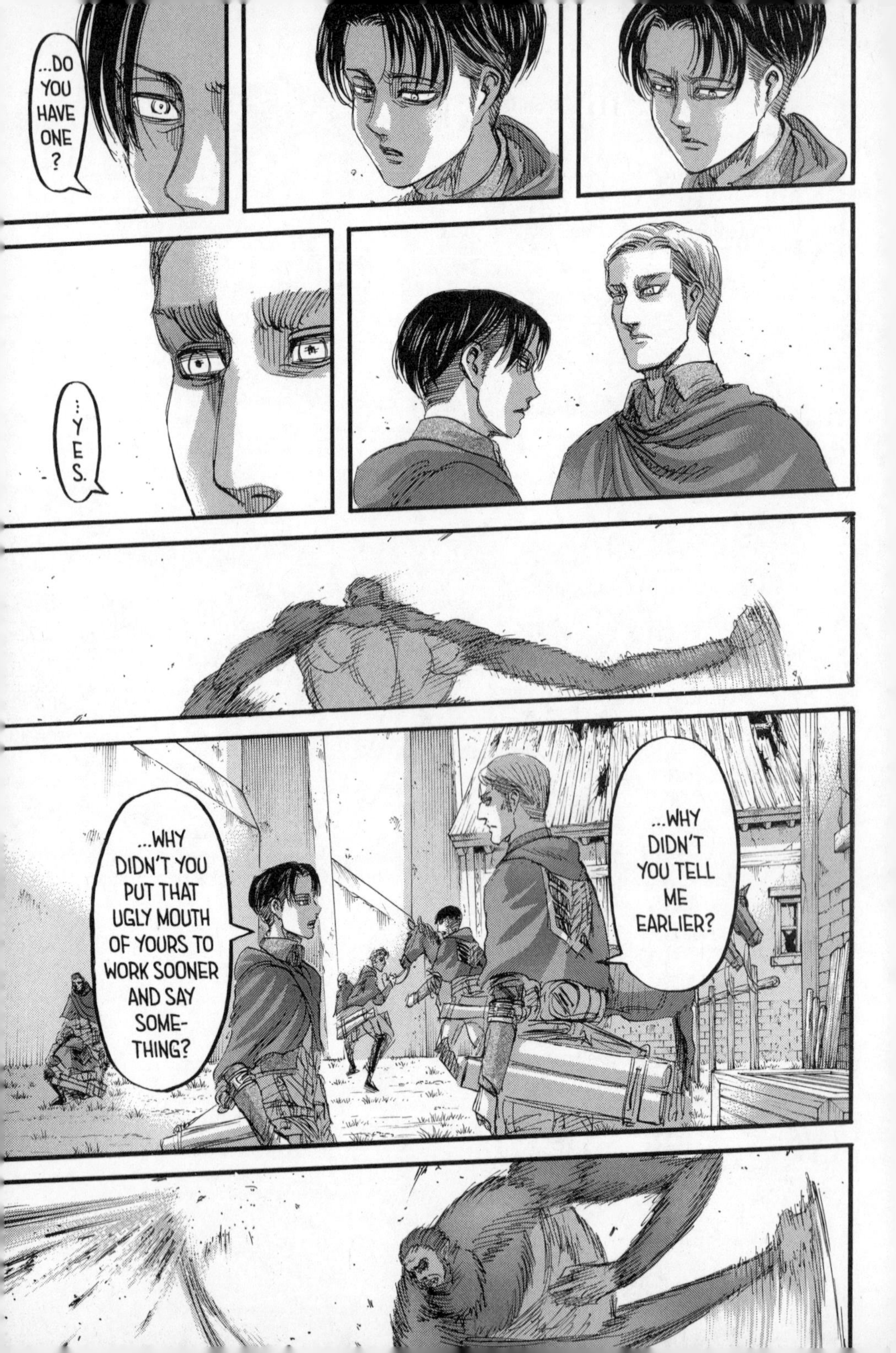
...DO YOU HAVE ONE?
...YES.
...WHY DIDN'T YOU TELL ME EARLIER?
...WHY DIDN'T YOU PUT THAT UGLY MOUTH OF YOURS TO WORK SOONER AND SAY SOMETHING?

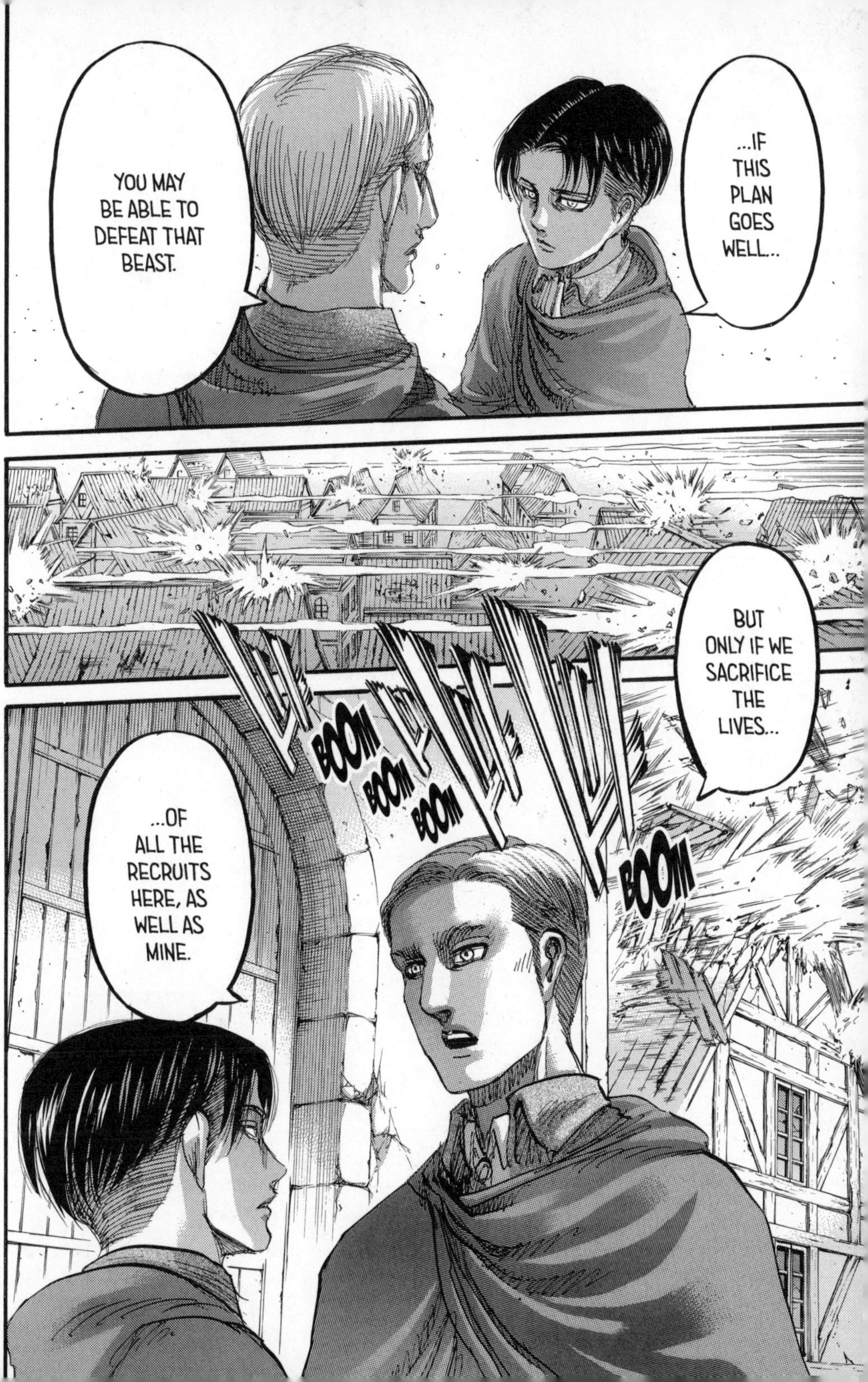
...IF THIS PLAN GOES WELL...
YOU MAY BE ABLE TO DEFEAT THAT BEAST.
BUT ONLY IF WE SACRIFICE THE LIVES...
BOOM
BOOM
BOOM
BOOM
...OF ALL THE RECRUITS HERE, AS WELL AS MINE.

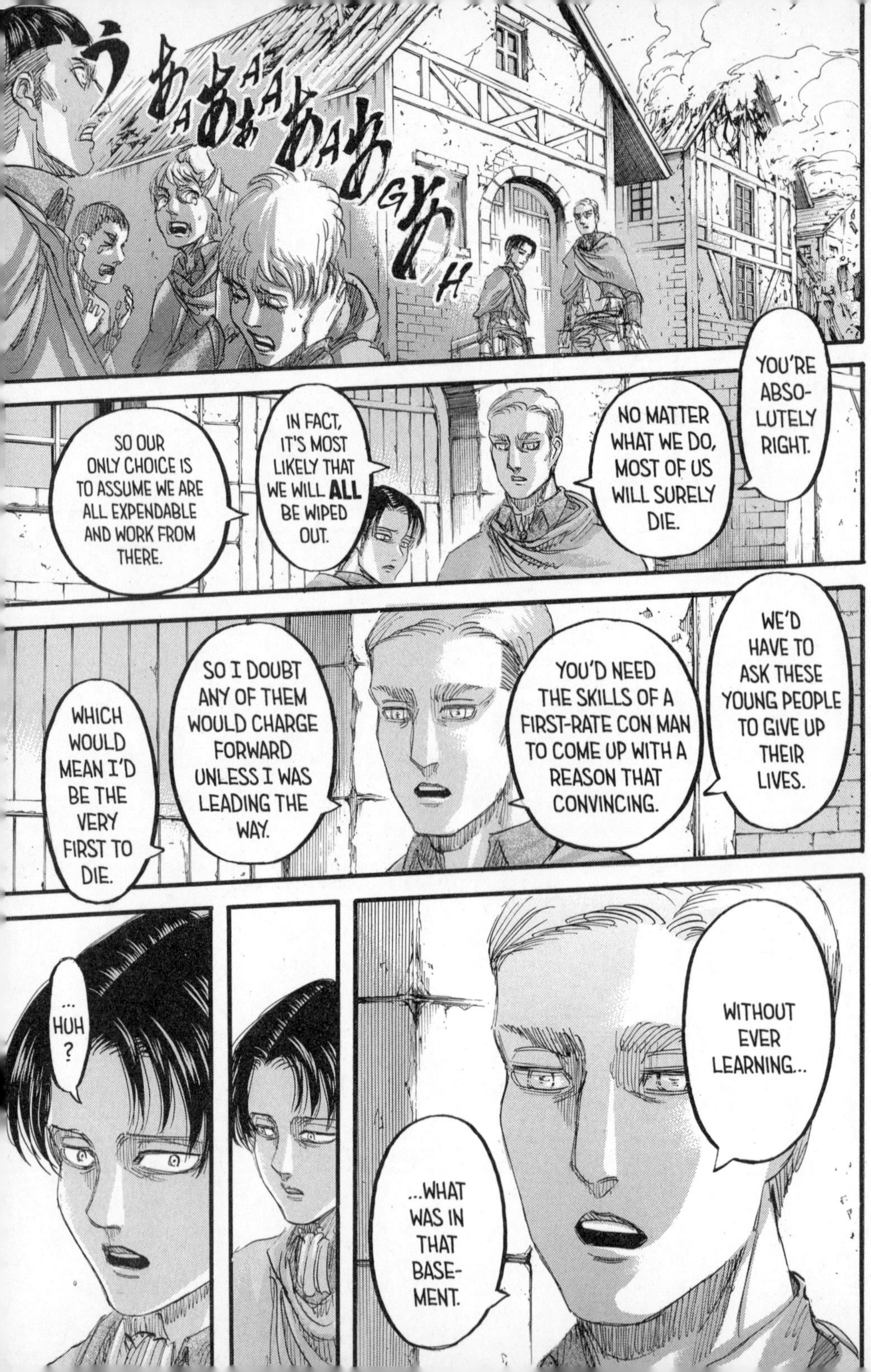

うあああああ
AAAAAGH
YOU'RE ABSOLUTELY RIGHT.
NO MATTER WHAT WE DO, MOST OF US WILL SURELY DIE.
IN FACT, IT'S MOST LIKELY THAT WE WILL **ALL** BE WIPED OUT.
SO OUR ONLY CHOICE IS TO ASSUME WE ARE ALL EXPENDABLE AND WORK FROM THERE.
WE'D HAVE TO ASK THESE YOUNG PEOPLE TO GIVE UP THEIR LIVES.
YOU'D NEED THE SKILLS OF A FIRST-RATE CON MAN TO COME UP WITH A REASON THAT CONVINCING.
SO I DOUBT ANY OF THEM WOULD CHARGE FORWARD UNLESS I WAS LEADING THE WAY.
WHICH WOULD MEAN I'D BE THE VERY FIRST TO DIE.
WITHOUT EVER LEARNING...
...WHAT WAS IN THAT BASEMENT.
...HUH?

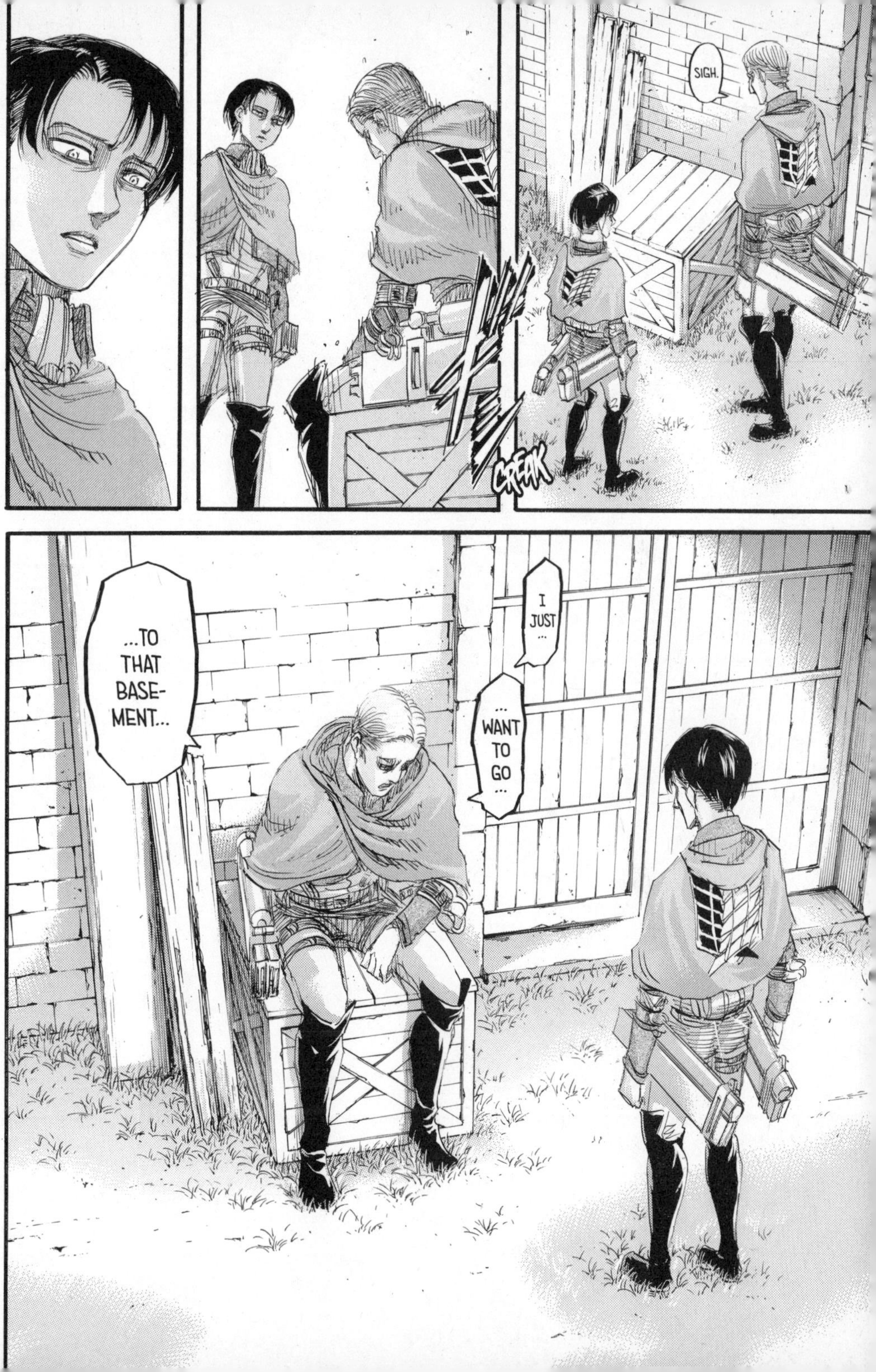
SIGH.
CREAK
I JUST ...
... WANT TO GO ...
...TO THAT BASEMENT...

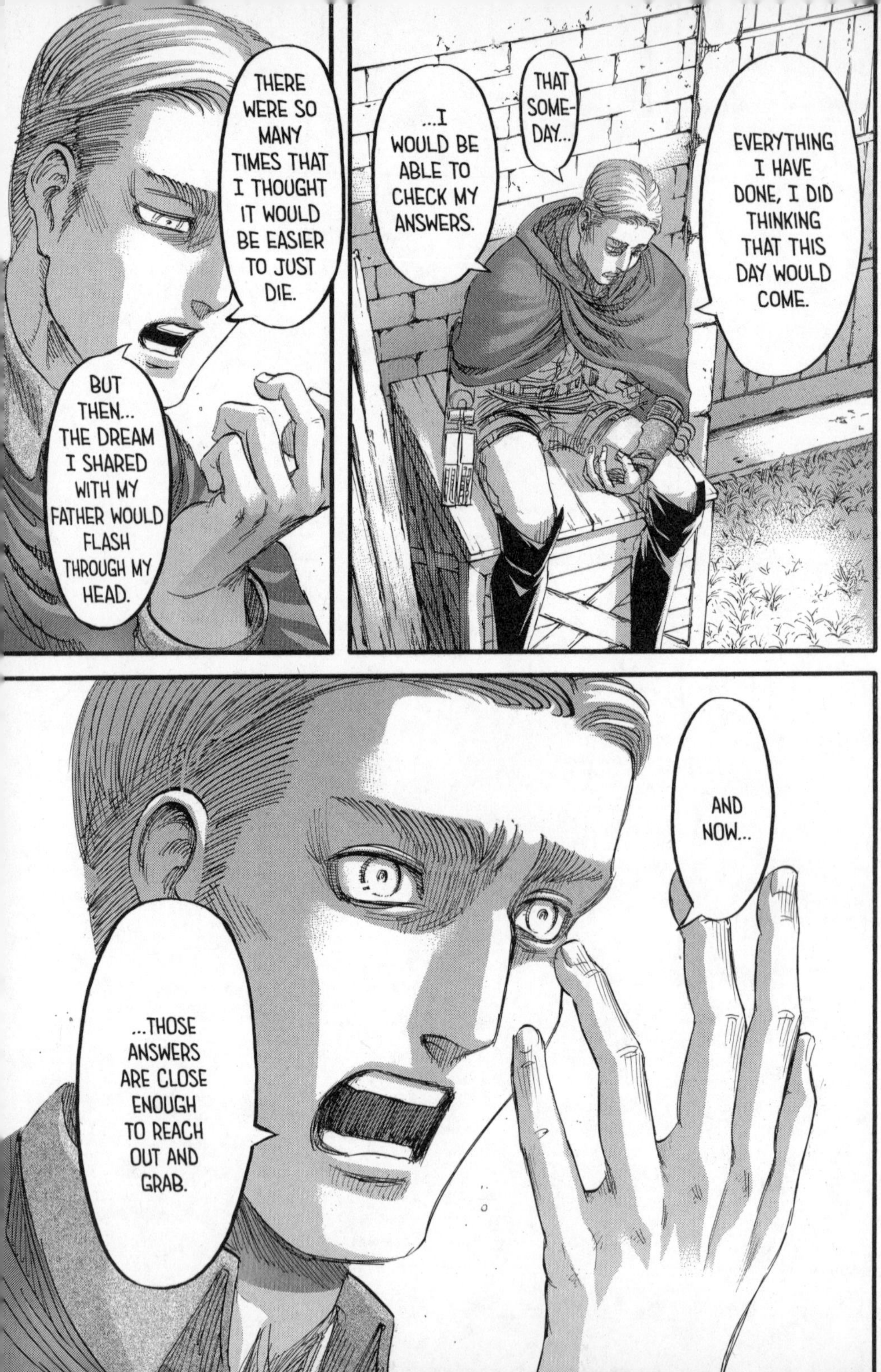
EVERYTHING I HAVE DONE, I DID THINKING THAT THIS DAY WOULD COME.
THAT SOME-DAY...
...I WOULD BE ABLE TO CHECK MY ANSWERS.
THERE WERE SO MANY TIMES THAT I THOUGHT IT WOULD BE EASIER TO JUST DIE.
BUT THEN... THE DREAM I SHARED WITH MY FATHER WOULD FLASH THROUGH MY HEAD.
AND NOW...
...THOSE ANSWERS ARE CLOSE ENOUGH TO REACH OUT AND GRAB.

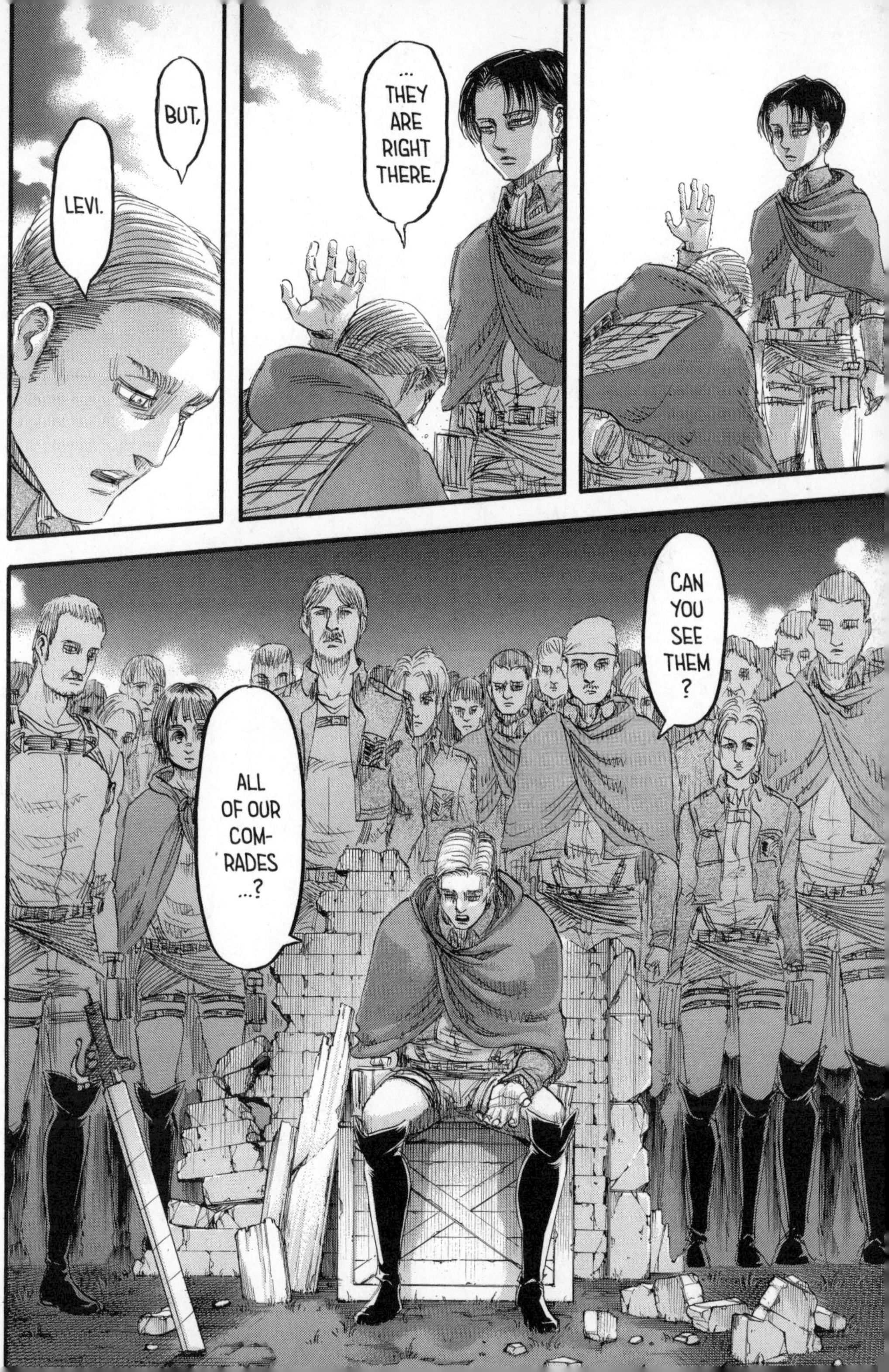
... THEY ARE RIGHT THERE.
BUT,
LEVI.
CAN YOU SEE THEM?
ALL OF OUR COM-RADES ...?

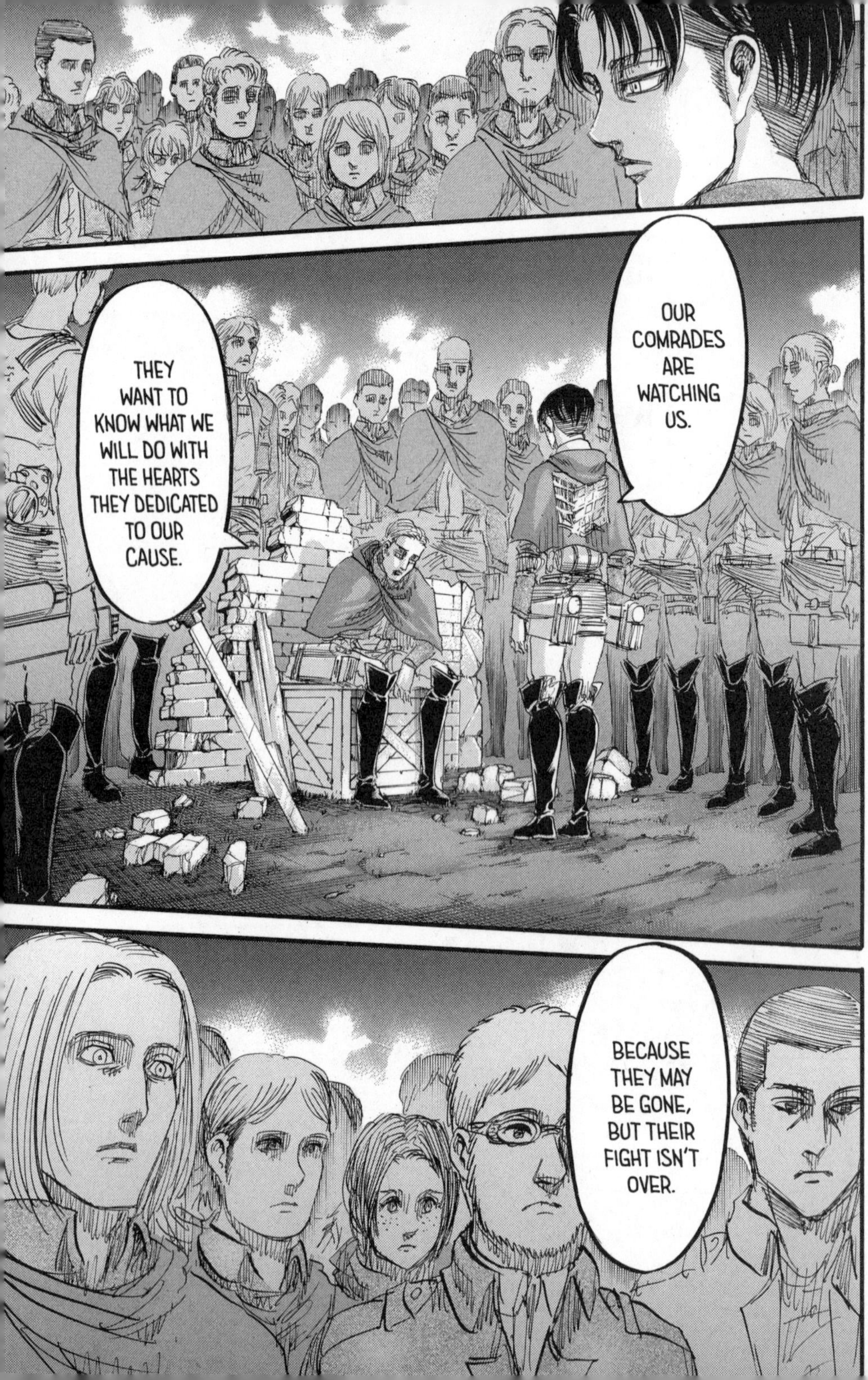
OUR COMRADES ARE WATCHING US.
THEY WANT TO KNOW WHAT WE WILL DO WITH THE HEARTS THEY DEDICATED TO OUR CAUSE.
BECAUSE THEY MAY BE GONE, BUT THEIR FIGHT ISN'T OVER.

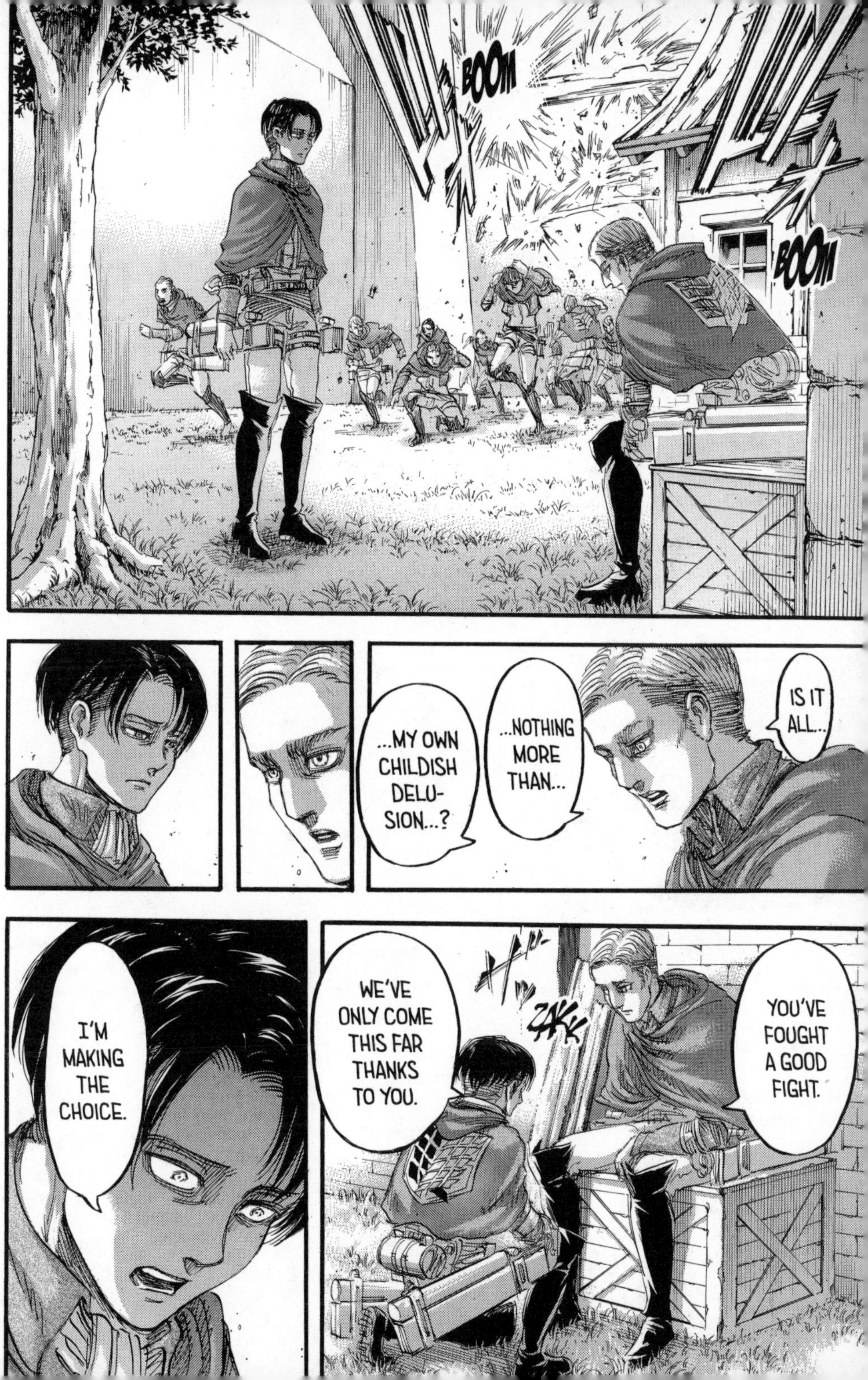
BOOM
BOOM
IS IT ALL...
...NOTHING MORE THAN...
...MY OWN CHILDISH DELUSION...?
YOU'VE FOUGHT A GOOD FIGHT.
WE'VE ONLY COME THIS FAR THANKS TO YOU.
ZAKK
I'M MAKING THE CHOICE.

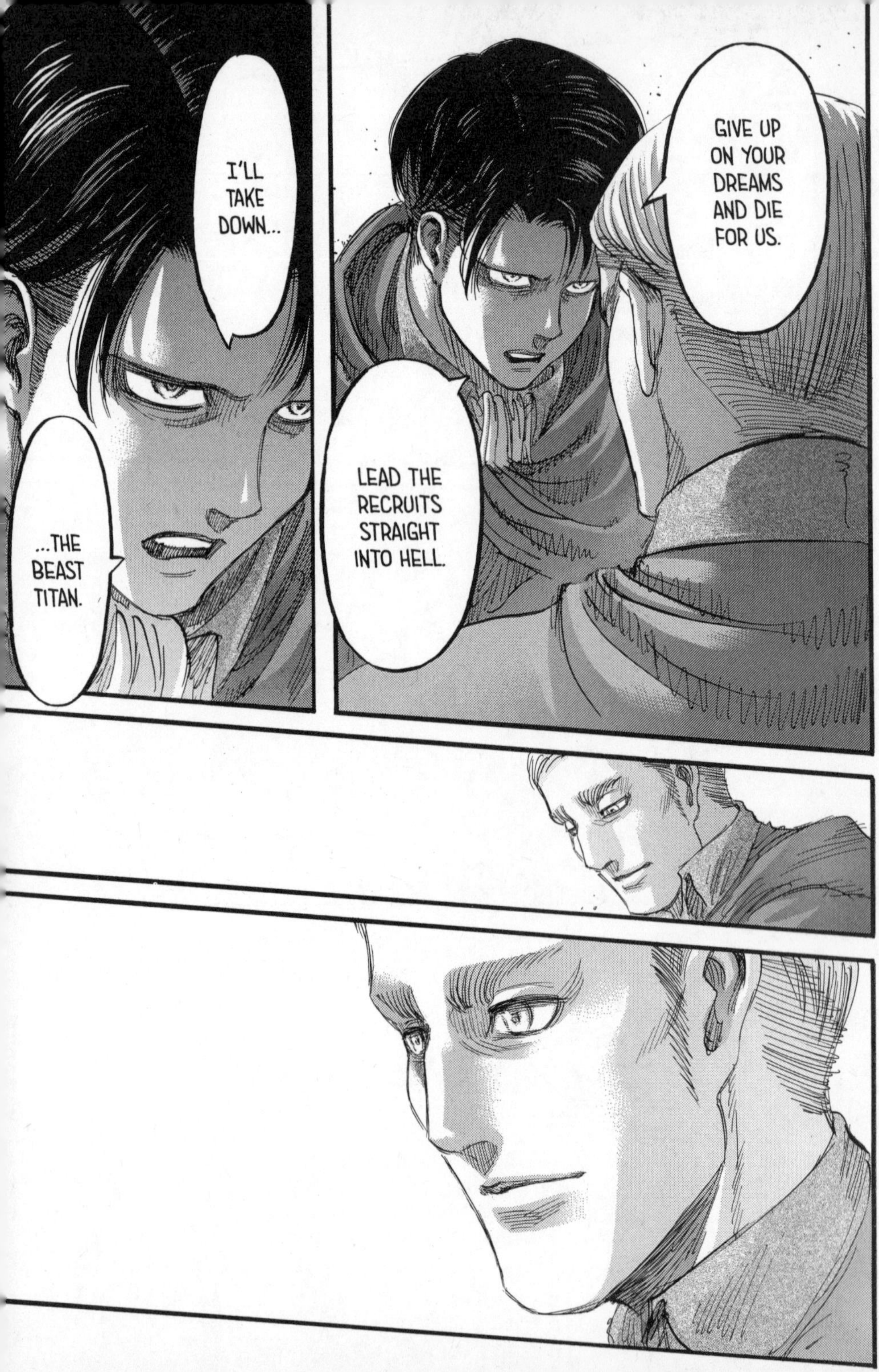
GIVE UP ON YOUR DREAMS AND DIE FOR US.
LEAD THE RECRUITS STRAIGHT INTO HELL.
I'LL TAKE DOWN...
...THE BEAST TITAN.

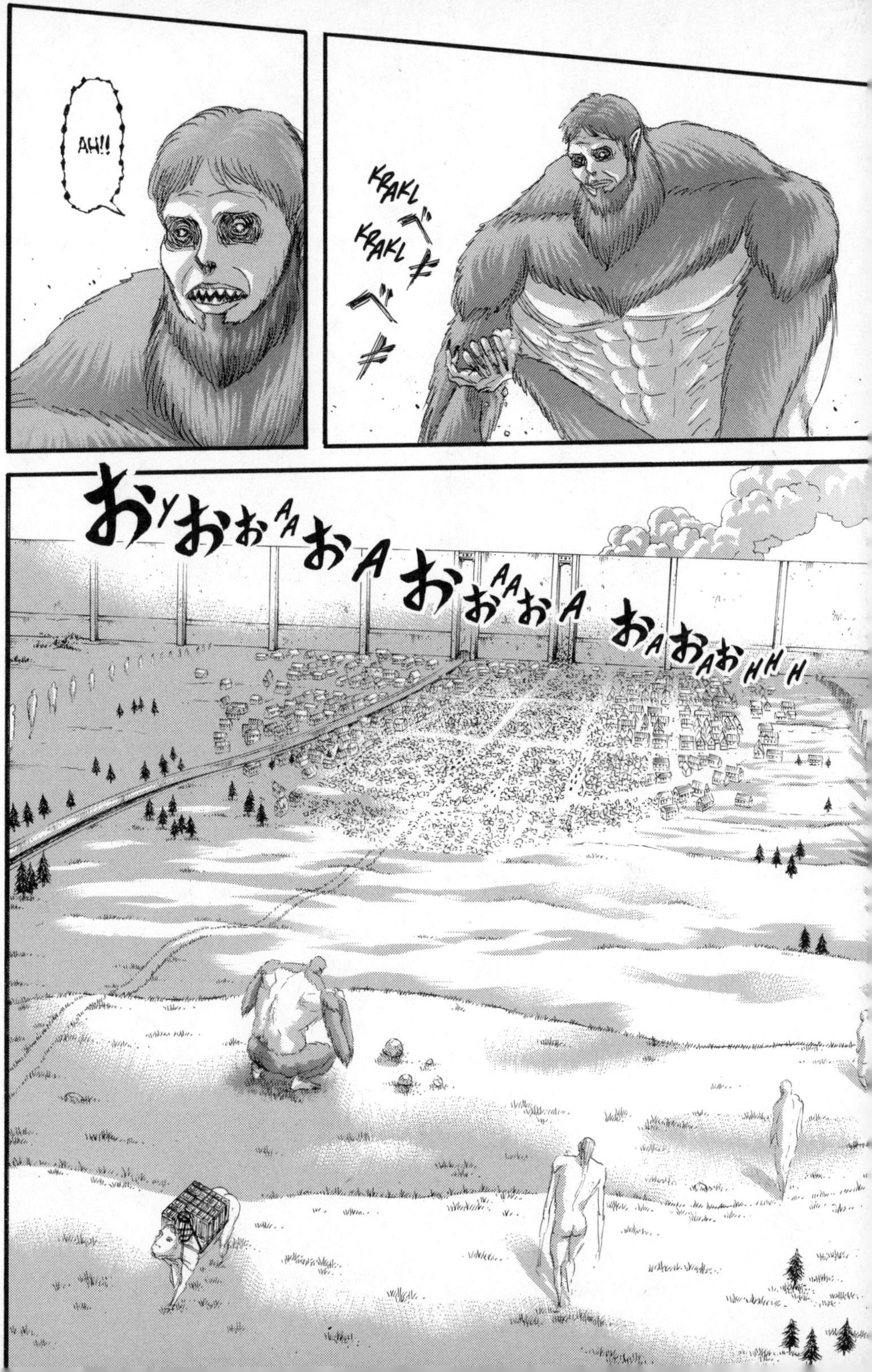

KRAKL ベキ
KRAKL ベキ
AH!!
おYおぉAAおAおおAAおA おAおAおHHH

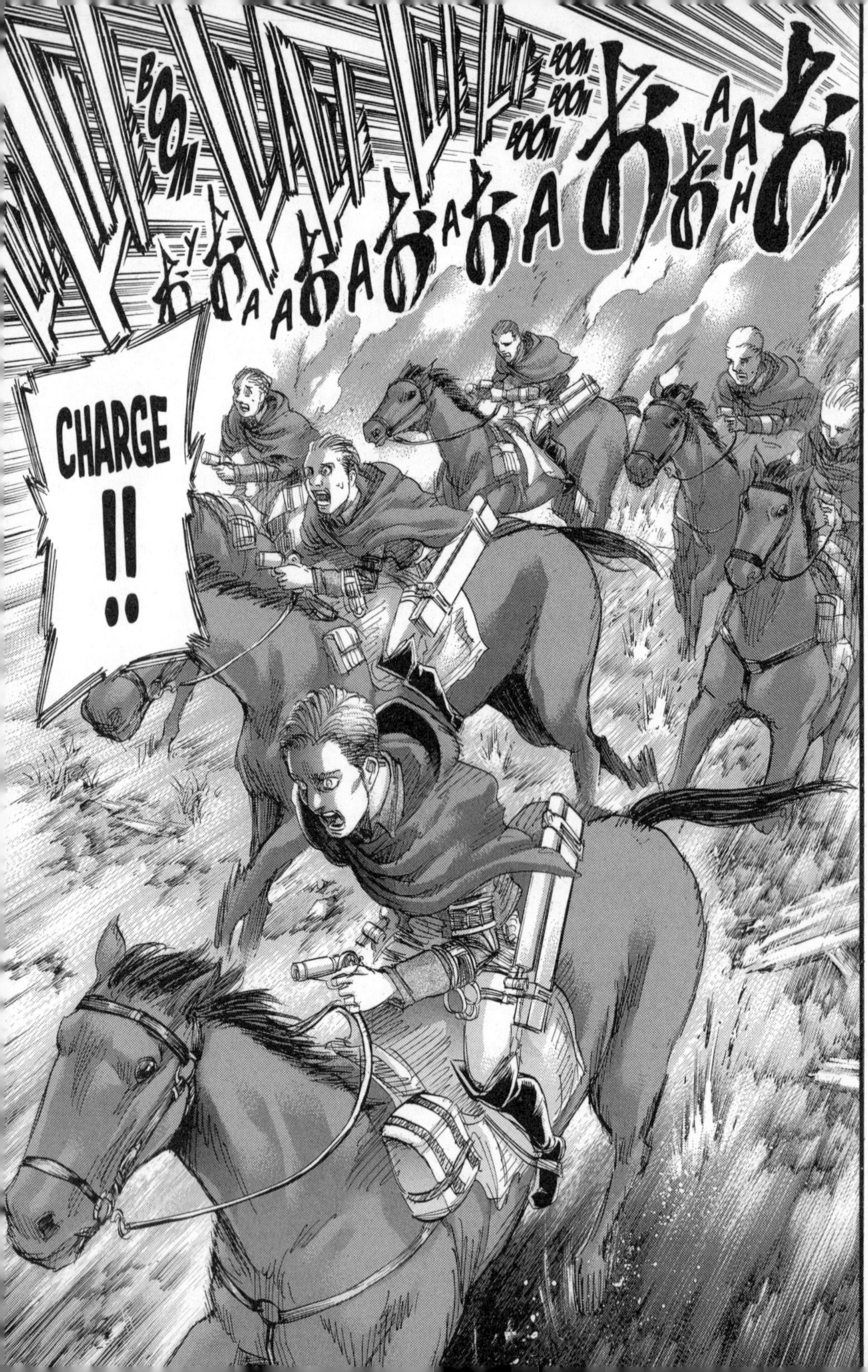
BOOM
BOOM BOOM BOOM
YAAAAAAAAH
おおおおおおお
CHARGE !!

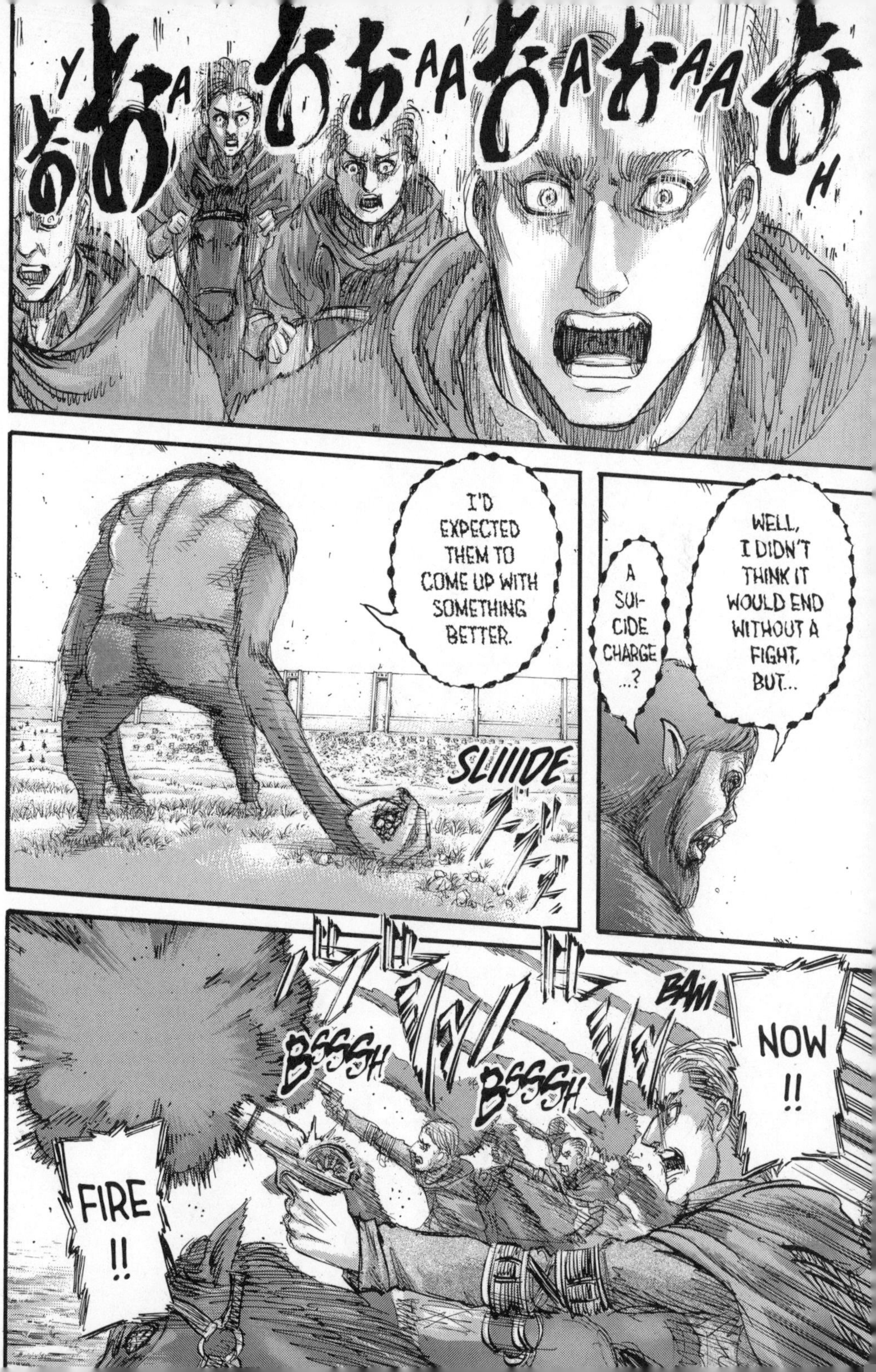
YAAAAAAH
WELL, I DIDN'T THINK IT WOULD END WITHOUT A FIGHT, BUT...
A SUI-CIDE CHARGE ...?
I'D EXPECTED THEM TO COME UP WITH SOMETHING BETTER.
SLIIIDE
NOW !!
BAM
BSSSH
BSSSH
FIRE !!

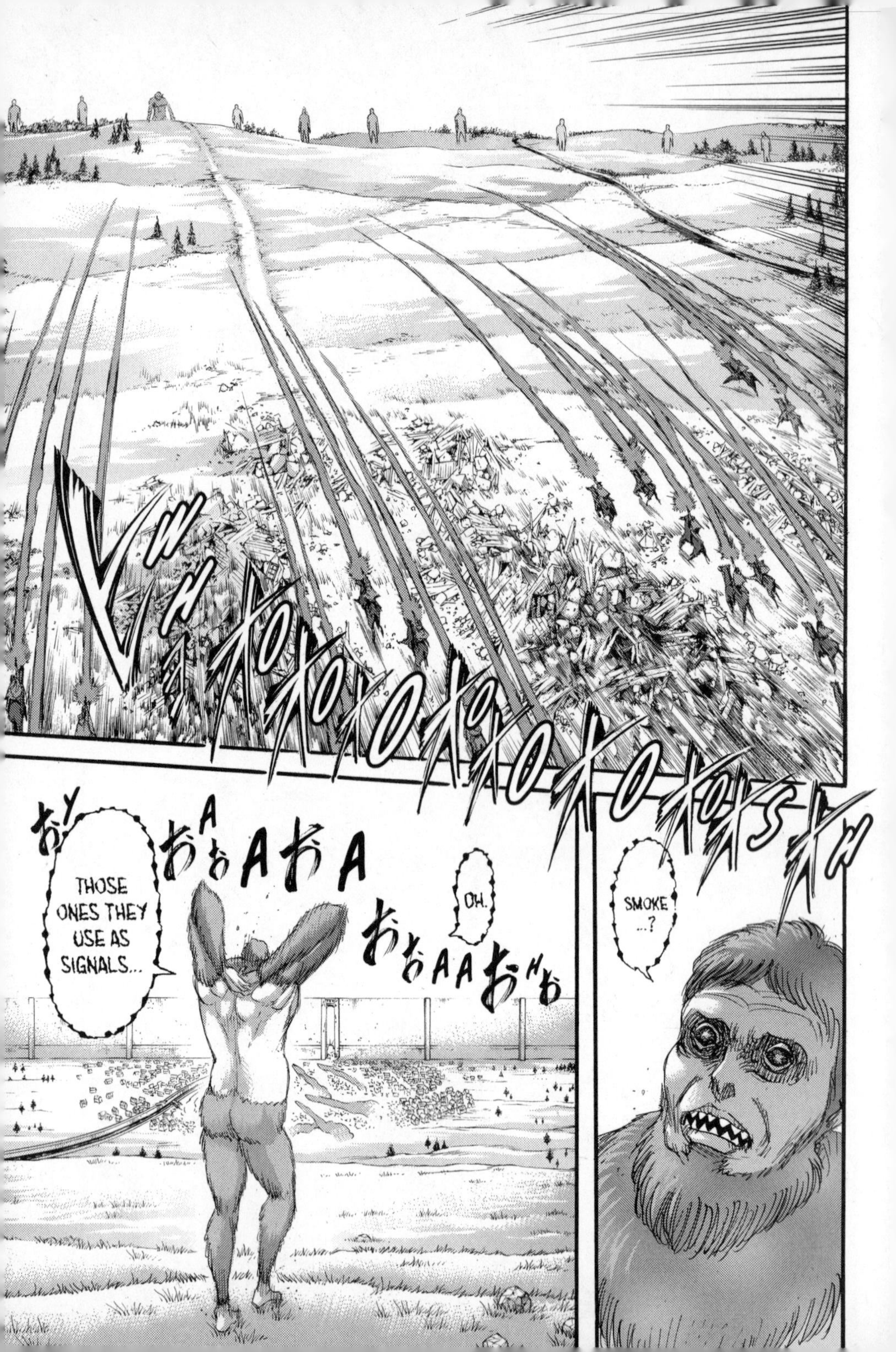
SMOKE ...?
OH.
THOSE ONES THEY USE AS SIGNALS...

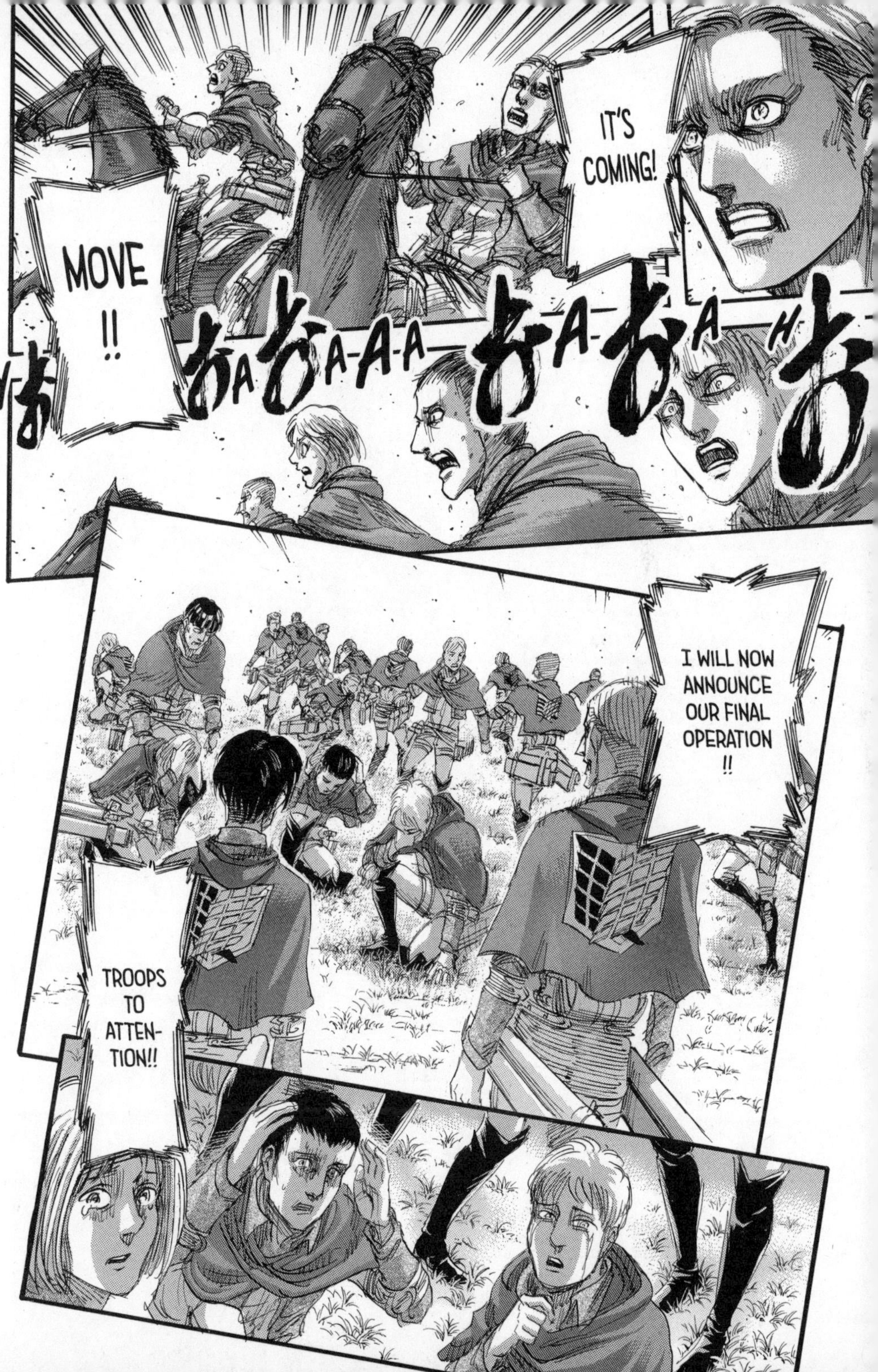
IT'S COMING!
MOVE !!
I WILL NOW ANNOUNCE OUR FINAL OPERATION !!
TROOPS TO ATTEN- TION!!

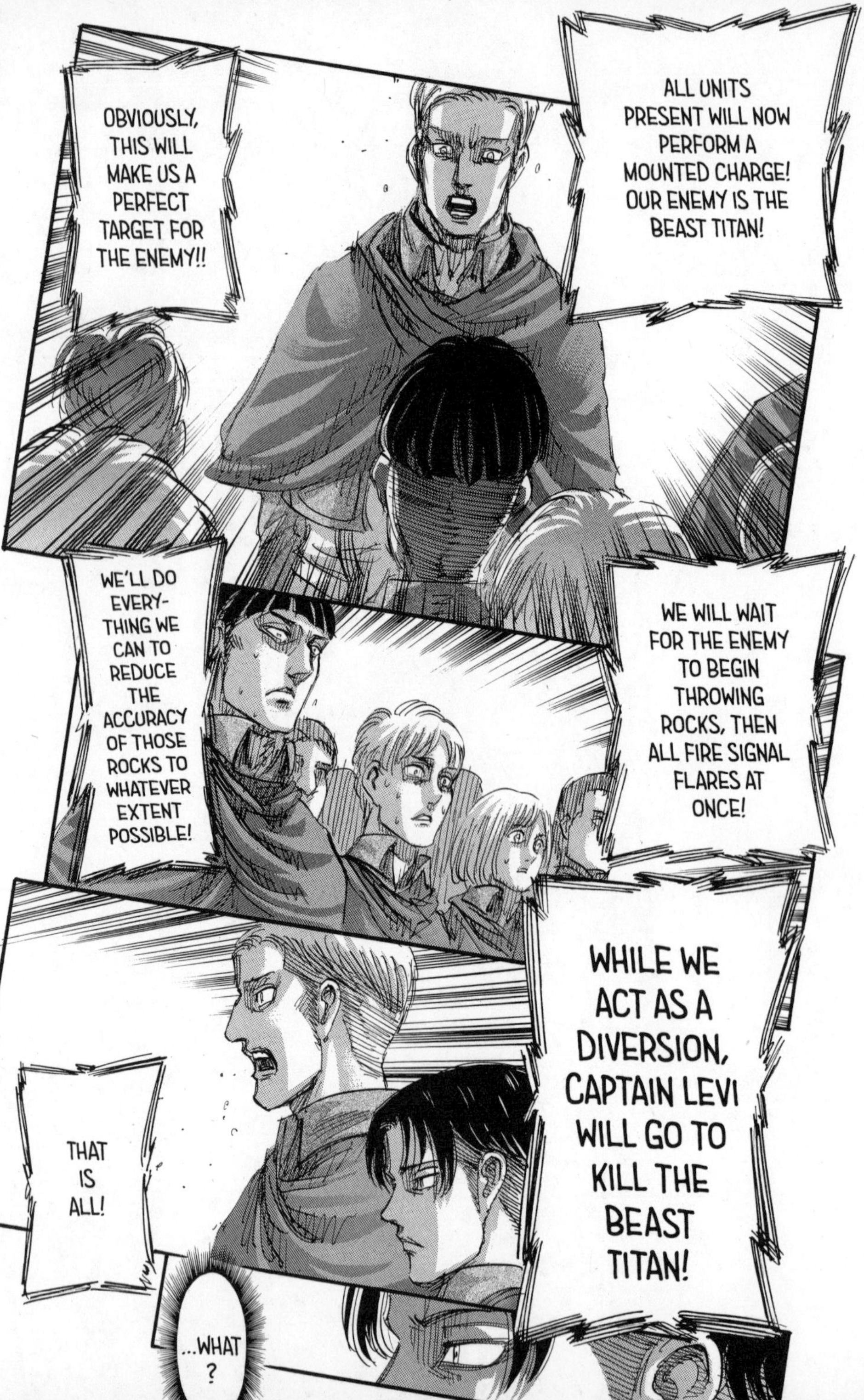
ALL UNITS PRESENT WILL NOW PERFORM A MOUNTED CHARGE! OUR ENEMY IS THE BEAST TITAN!
OBVIOUSLY, THIS WILL MAKE US A PERFECT TARGET FOR THE ENEMY!!
WE WILL WAIT FOR THE ENEMY TO BEGIN THROWING ROCKS, THEN ALL FIRE SIGNAL FLARES AT ONCE!
WE'LL DO EVERY-THING WE CAN TO REDUCE THE ACCURACY OF THOSE ROCKS TO WHATEVER EXTENT POSSIBLE!
WHILE WE ACT AS A DIVERSION, CAPTAIN LEVI WILL GO TO KILL THE BEAST TITAN!
THAT IS ALL!
...WHAT ?

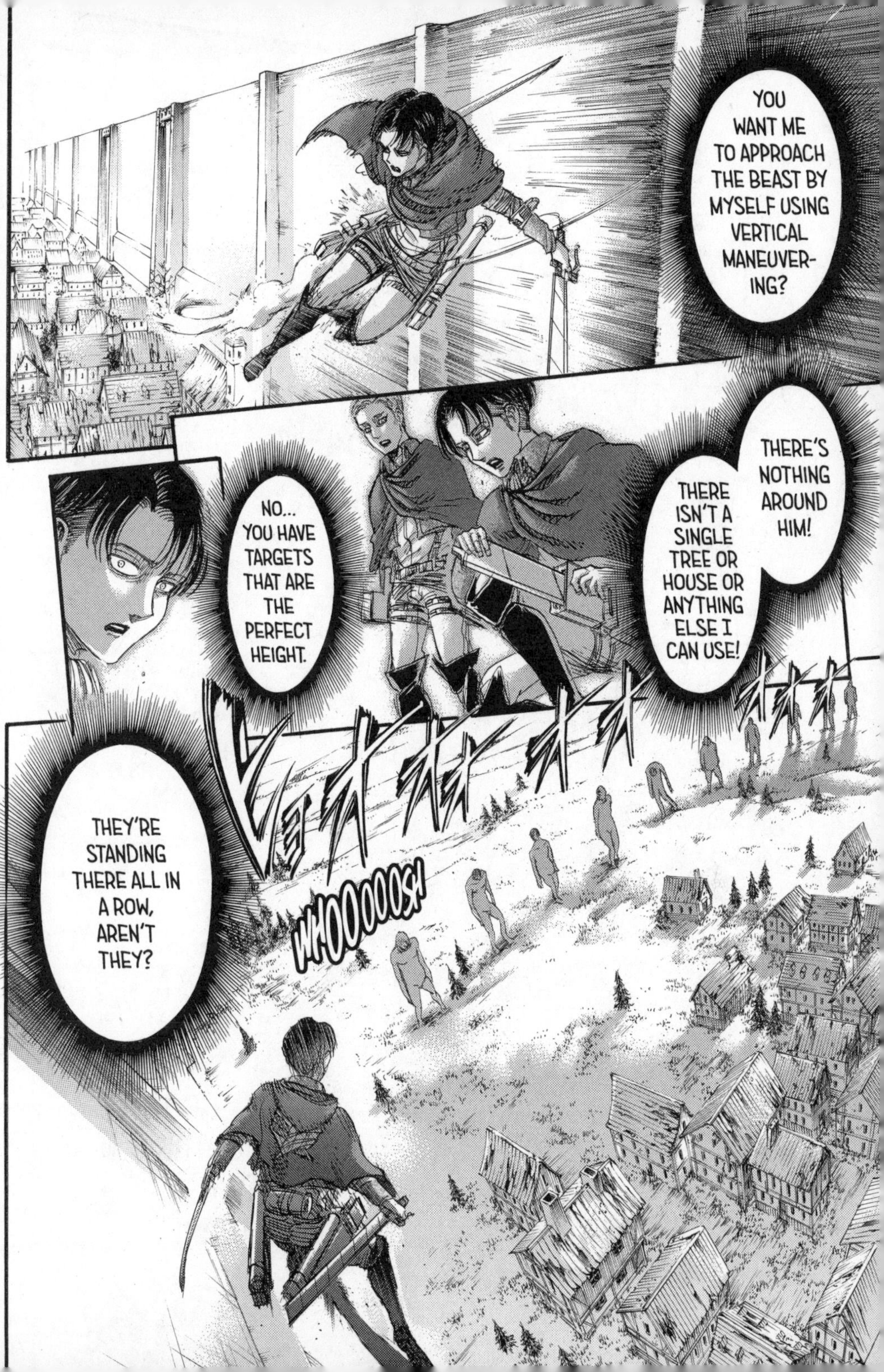
YOU WANT ME TO APPROACH THE BEAST BY MYSELF USING VERTICAL MANEUVER-ING?
THERE'S NOTHING AROUND HIM!
THERE ISN'T A SINGLE TREE OR HOUSE OR ANYTHING ELSE I CAN USE!
NO... YOU HAVE TARGETS THAT ARE THE PERFECT HEIGHT.
WHOOOOOSH!
THEY'RE STANDING THERE ALL IN A ROW, AREN'T THEY?

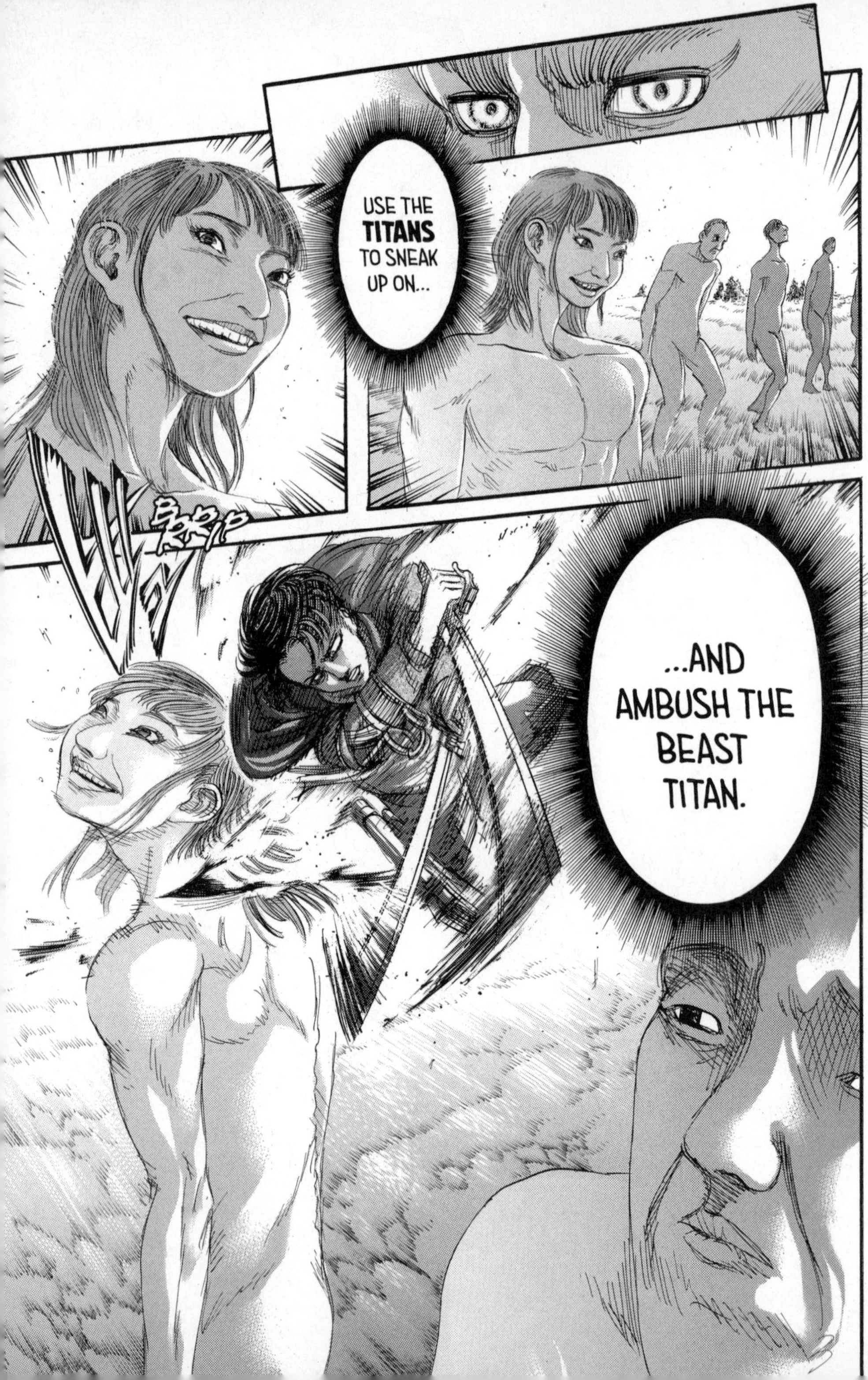
USE THE **TITANS** TO SNEAK UP ON...
...AND AMBUSH THE BEAST TITAN.

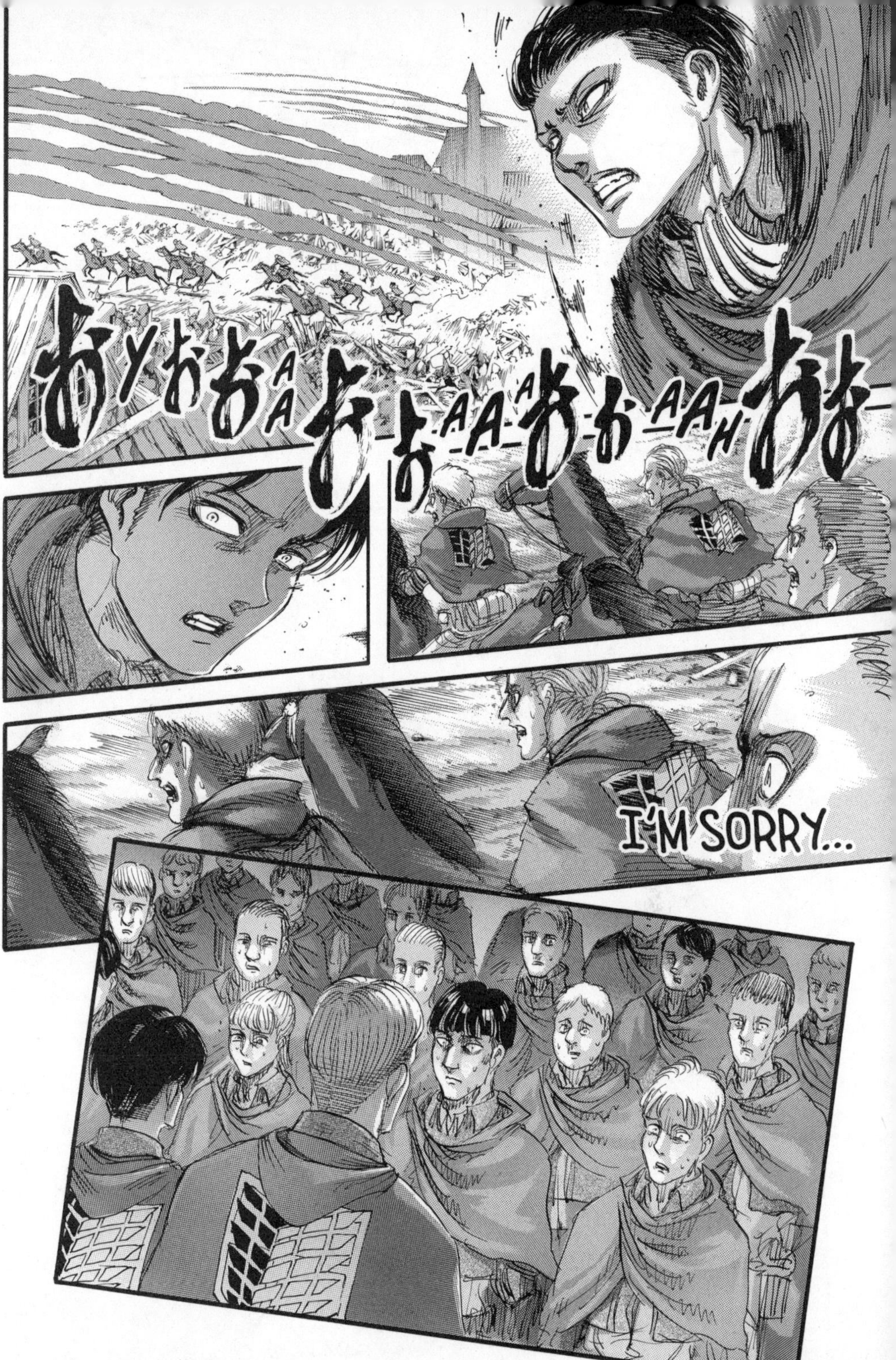
I'M SORRY...

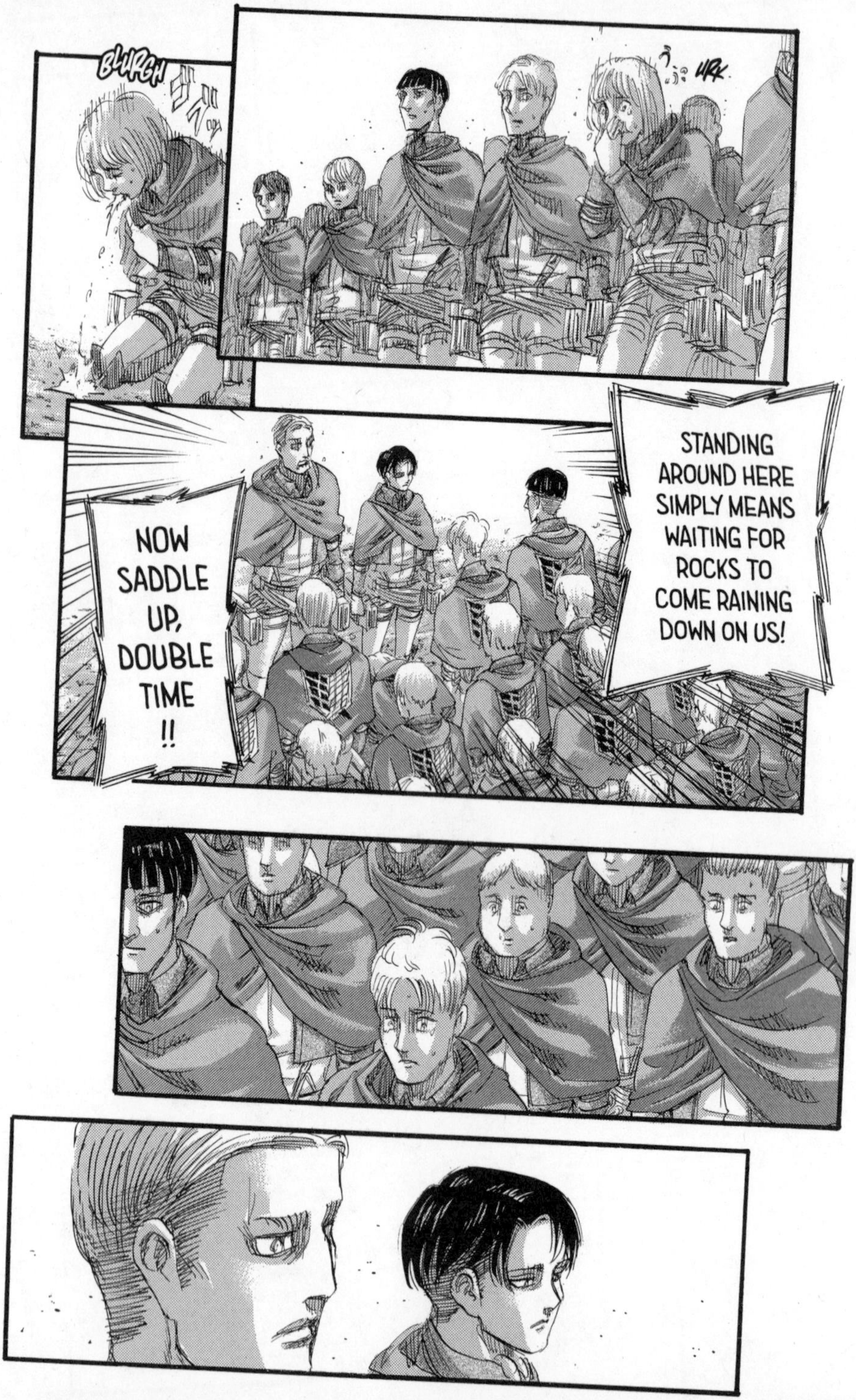
URK
BLURGH
STANDING AROUND HERE SIMPLY MEANS WAITING FOR ROCKS TO COME RAINING DOWN ON US!
NOW SADDLE UP, DOUBLE TIME !!

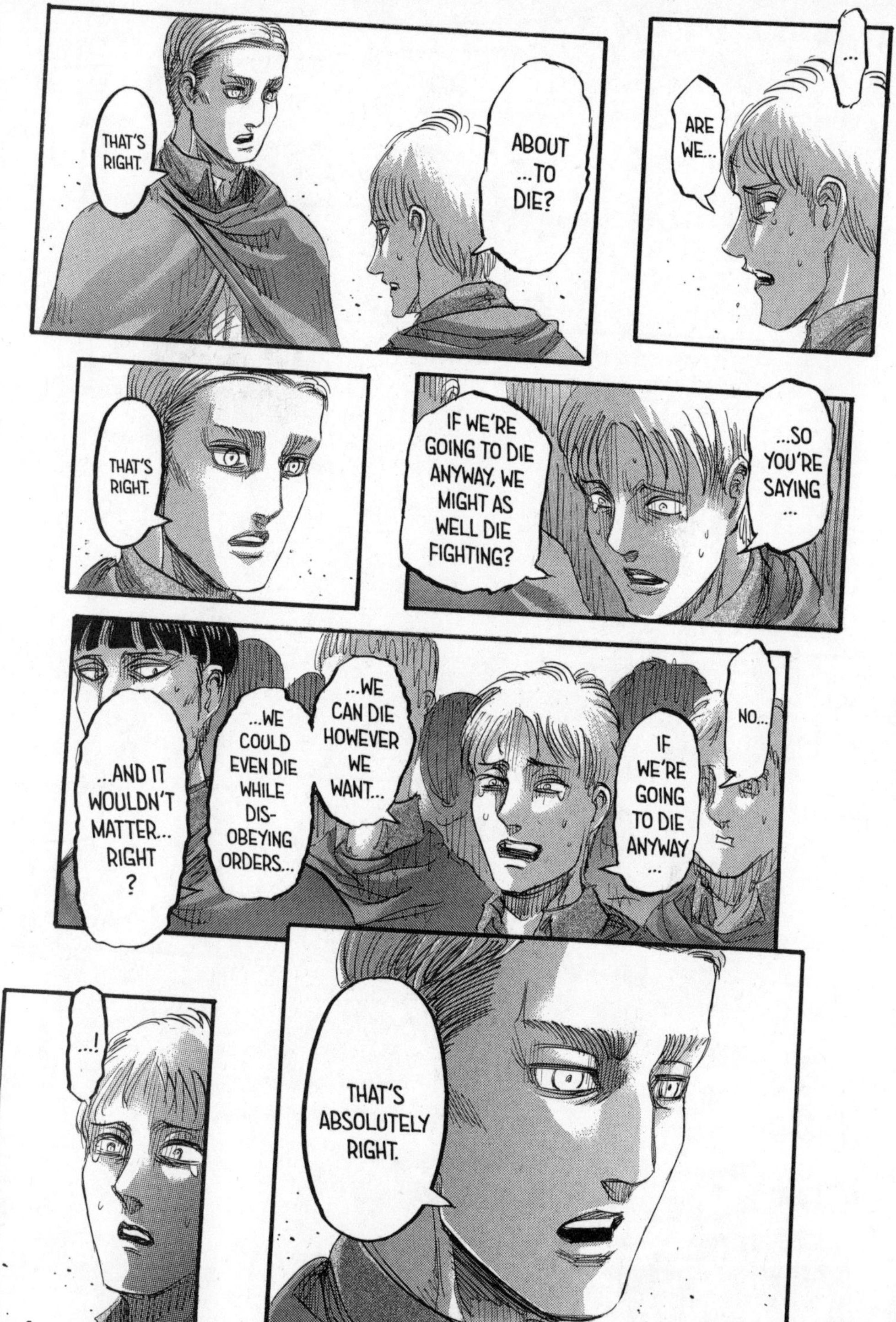
...
ARE WE...
ABOUT ...TO DIE?
THAT'S RIGHT.
...SO YOU'RE SAYING ...
IF WE'RE GOING TO DIE ANYWAY, WE MIGHT AS WELL DIE FIGHTING?
THAT'S RIGHT.
NO...
IF WE'RE GOING TO DIE ANYWAY ...
...WE CAN DIE HOWEVER WE WANT...
...WE COULD EVEN DIE WHILE DIS-OBEYING ORDERS...
...AND IT WOULDN'T MATTER... RIGHT ?
THAT'S ABSOLUTELY RIGHT.
...!

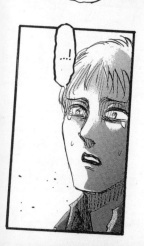

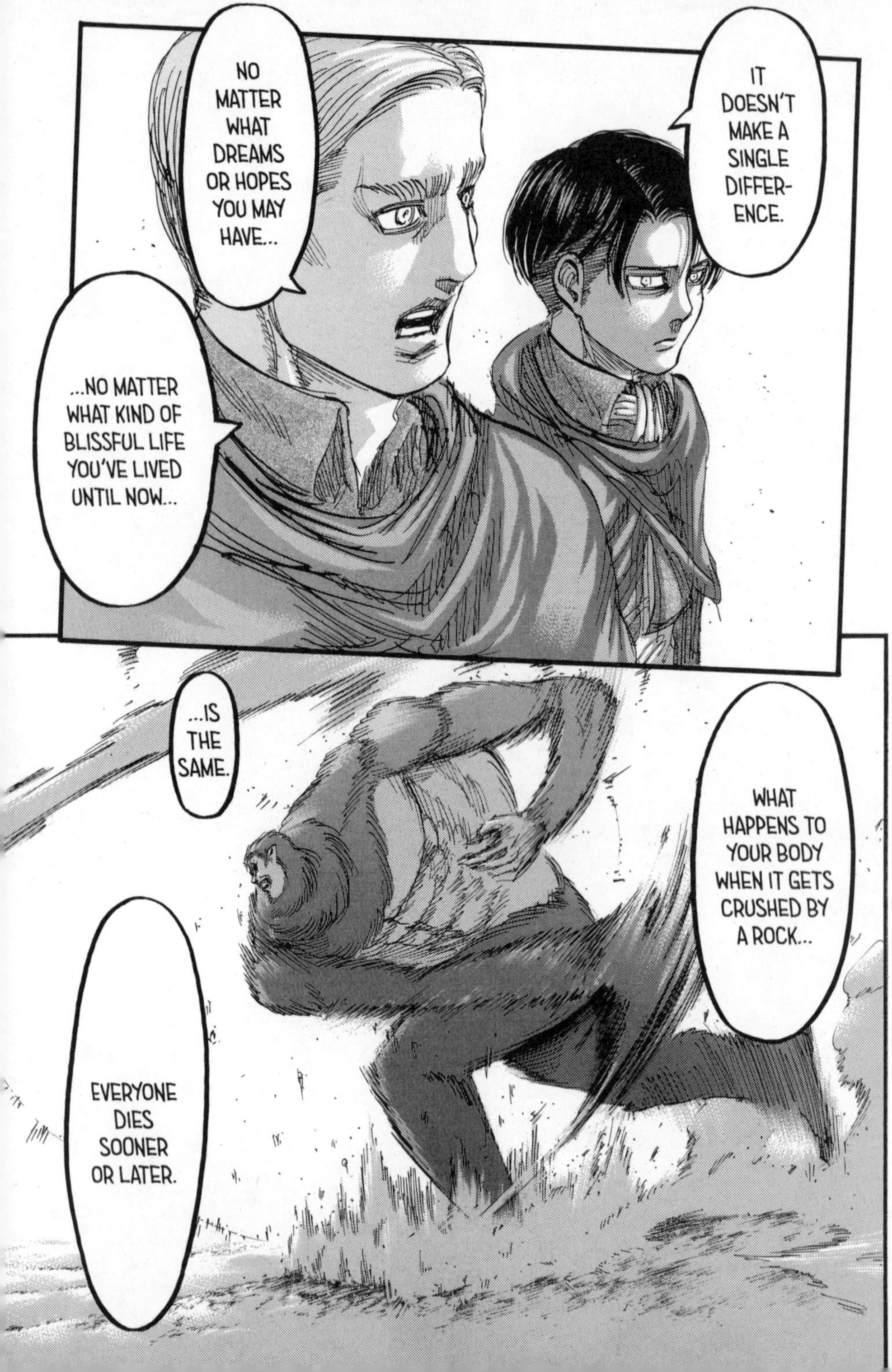
IT DOESN'T MAKE A SINGLE DIFFER-ENCE.
NO MATTER WHAT DREAMS OR HOPES YOU MAY HAVE...
...NO MATTER WHAT KIND OF BLISSFUL LIFE YOU'VE LIVED UNTIL NOW...
WHAT HAPPENS TO YOUR BODY WHEN IT GETS CRUSHED BY A ROCK...
...IS THE SAME.
EVERYONE DIES SOONER OR LATER.

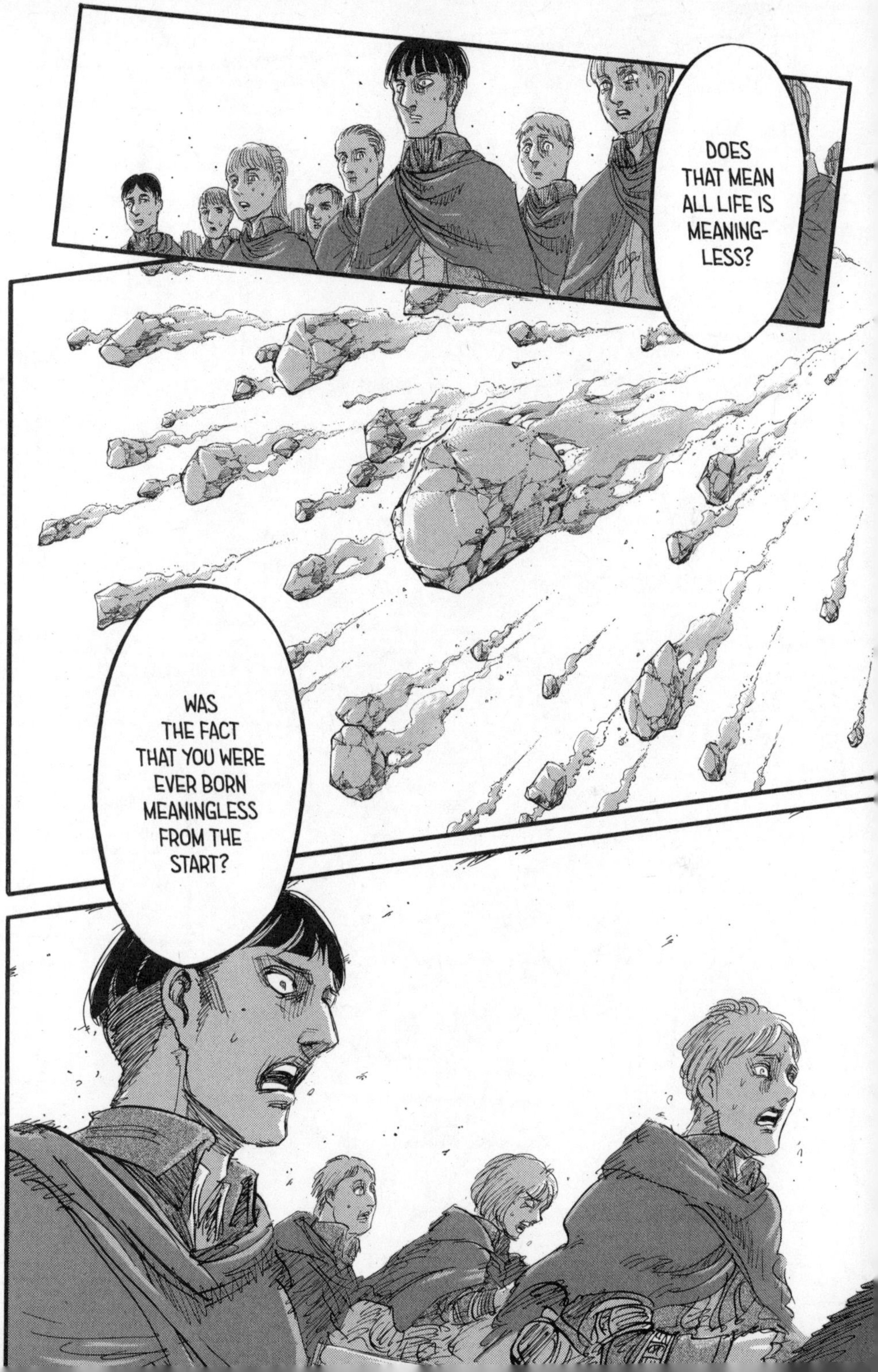
DOES THAT MEAN ALL LIFE IS MEANING-LESS?
WAS THE FACT THAT YOU WERE EVER BORN MEANINGLESS FROM THE START?

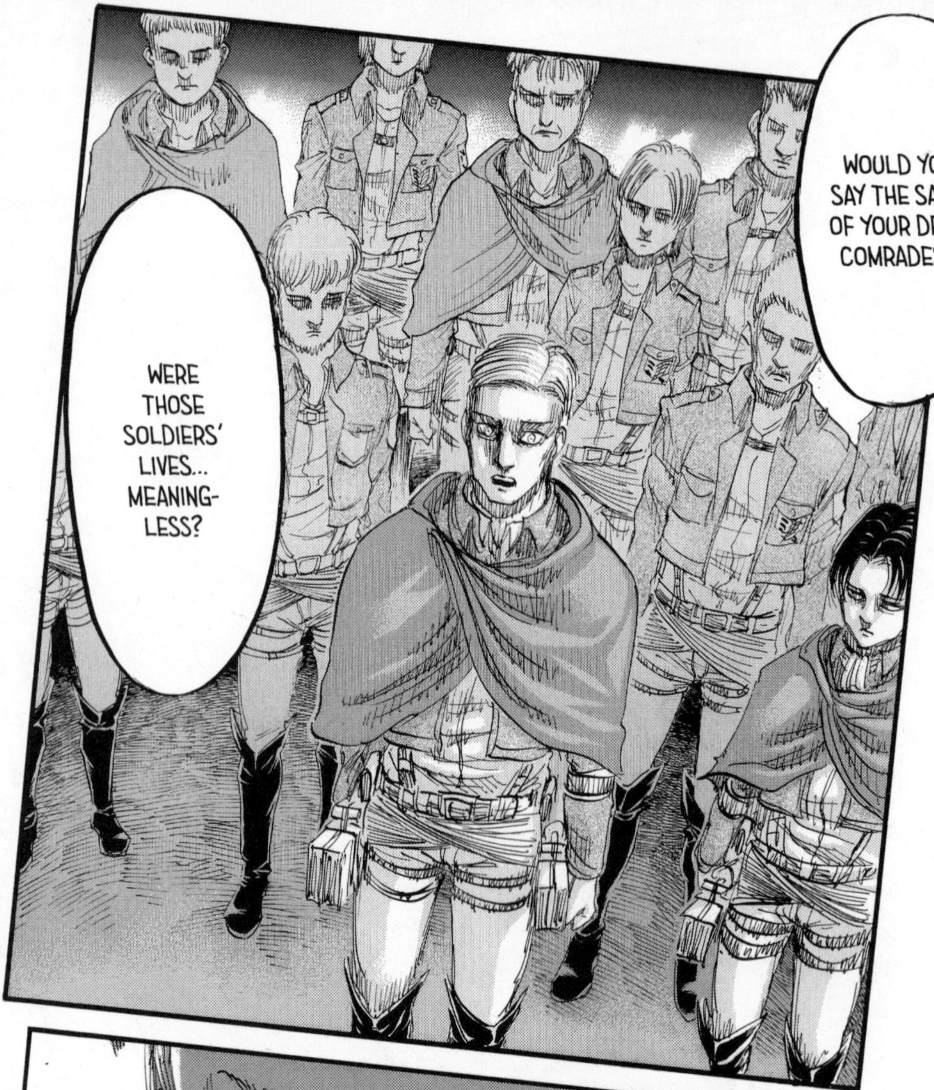
WOULD YOU SAY THE SAME OF YOUR DEAD COMRADES?
WERE THOSE SOLDIERS' LIVES... MEANING-LESS?
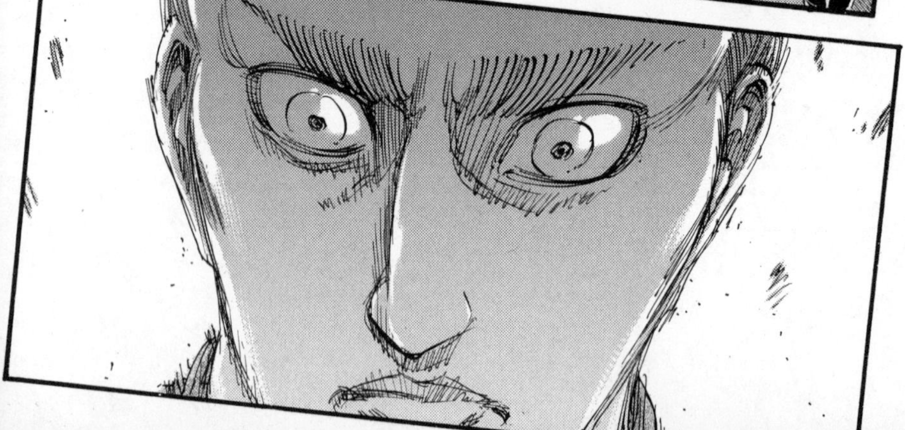

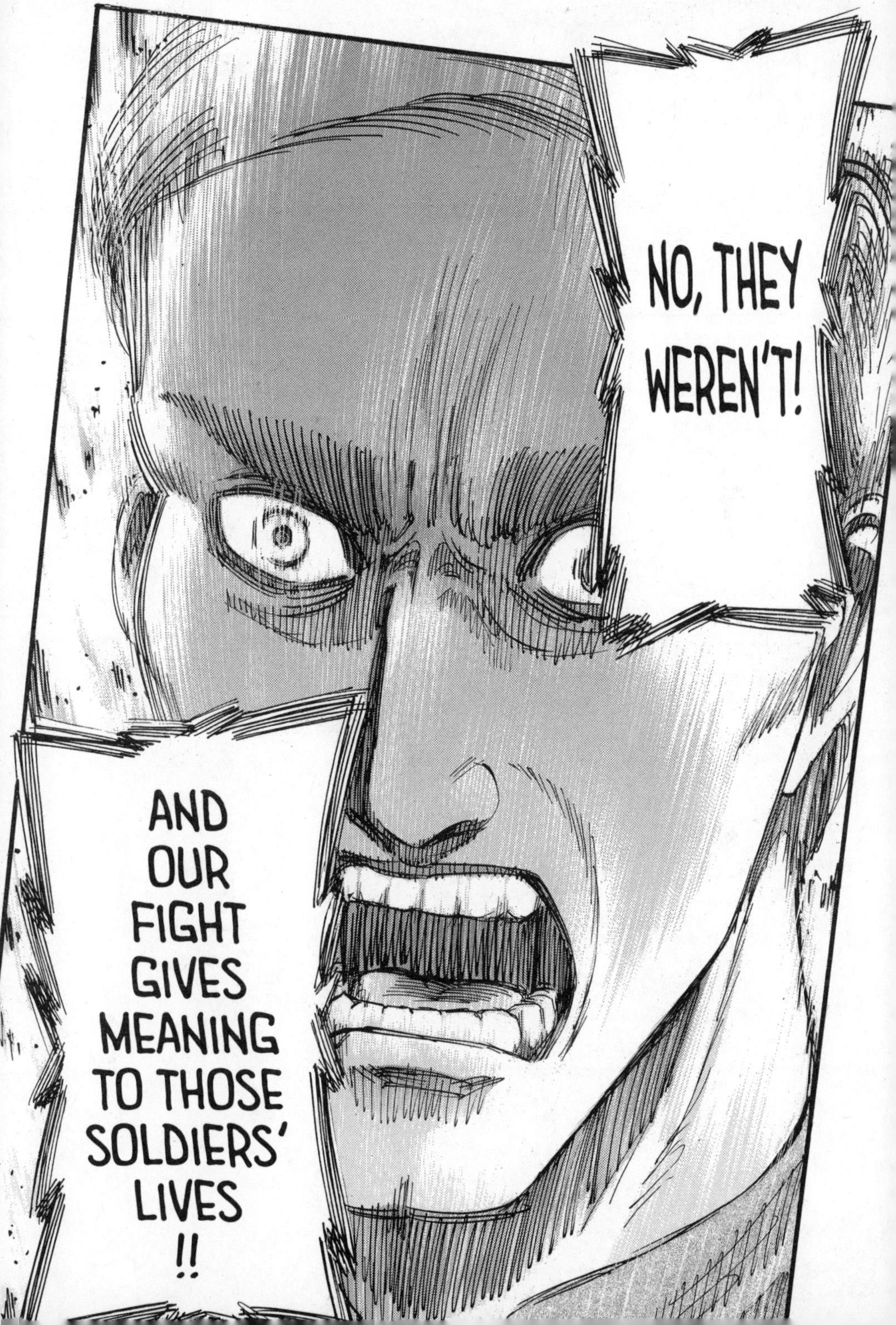
NO, THEY WEREN'T!
AND OUR FIGHT GIVES MEANING TO THOSE SOLDIERS' LIVES !!

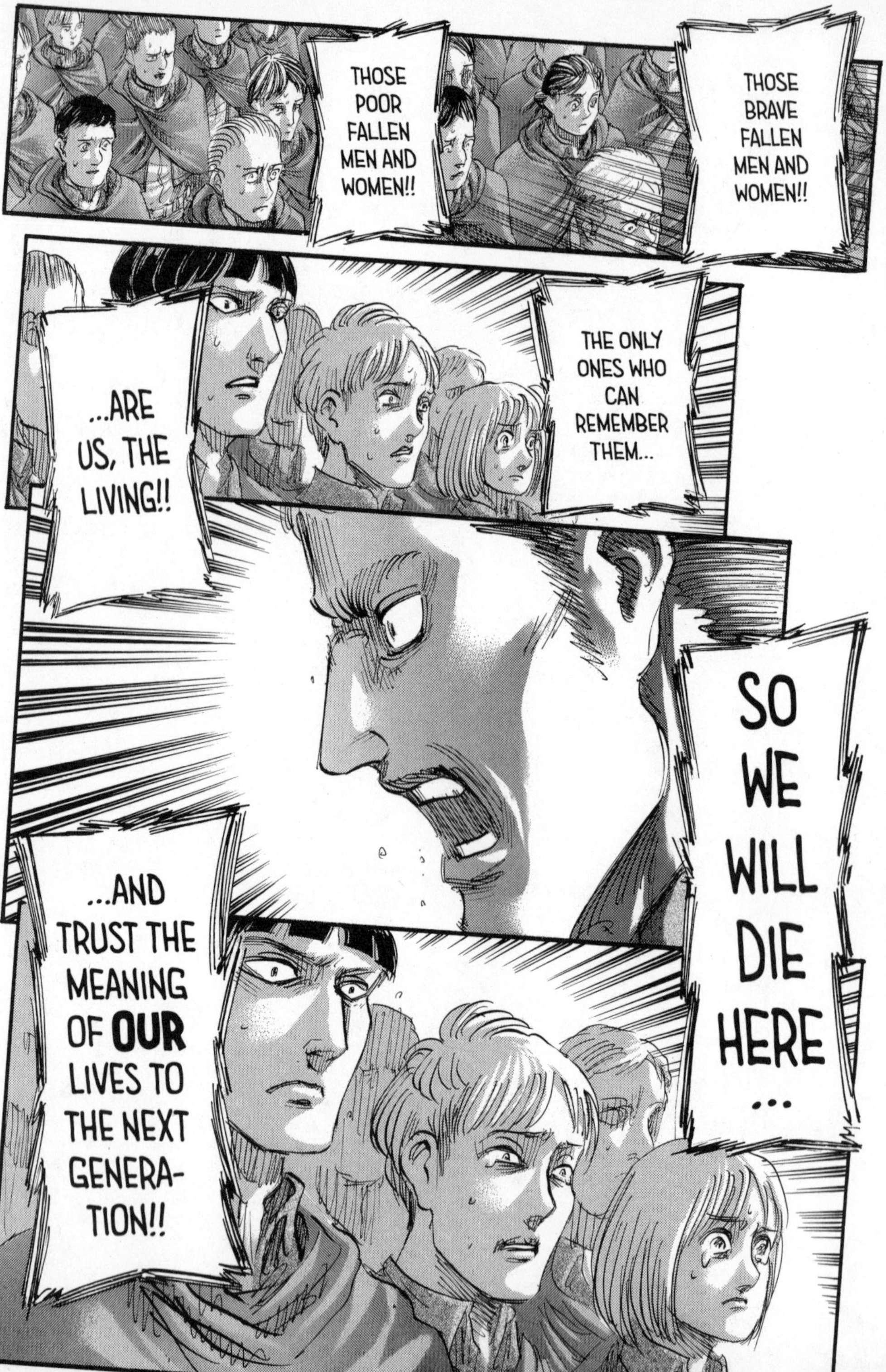
THOSE BRAVE FALLEN MEN AND WOMEN!!
THOSE POOR FALLEN MEN AND WOMEN!!
THE ONLY ONES WHO CAN REMEMBER THEM...
...ARE US, THE LIVING!!
SO WE WILL DIE HERE...
...AND TRUST THE MEANING OF **OUR** LIVES TO THE NEXT GENERA-TION!!

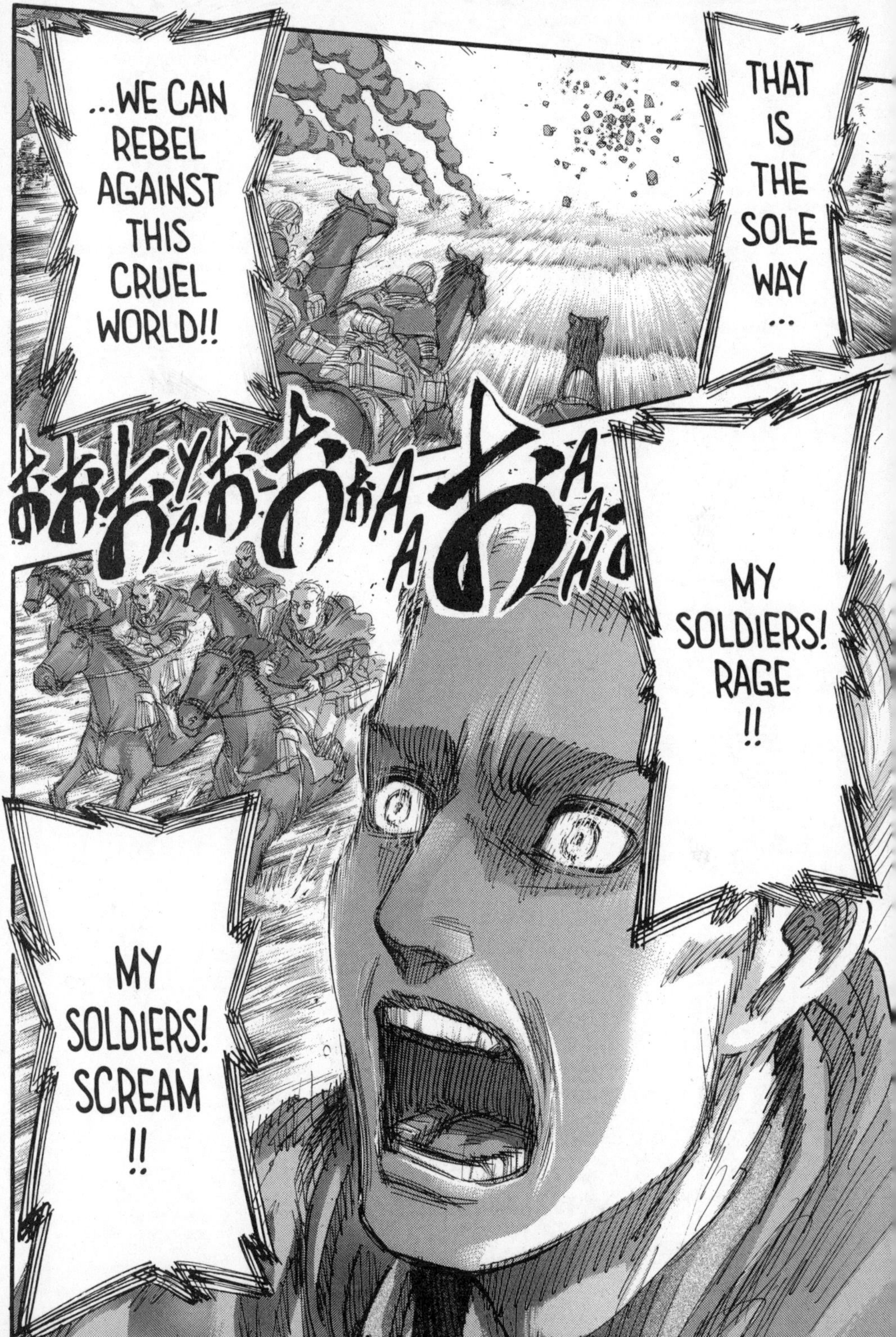
THAT IS THE SOLE WAY ...
...WE CAN REBEL AGAINST THIS CRUEL WORLD!!
MY SOLDIERS! RAGE !!
MY SOLDIERS! SCREAM !!

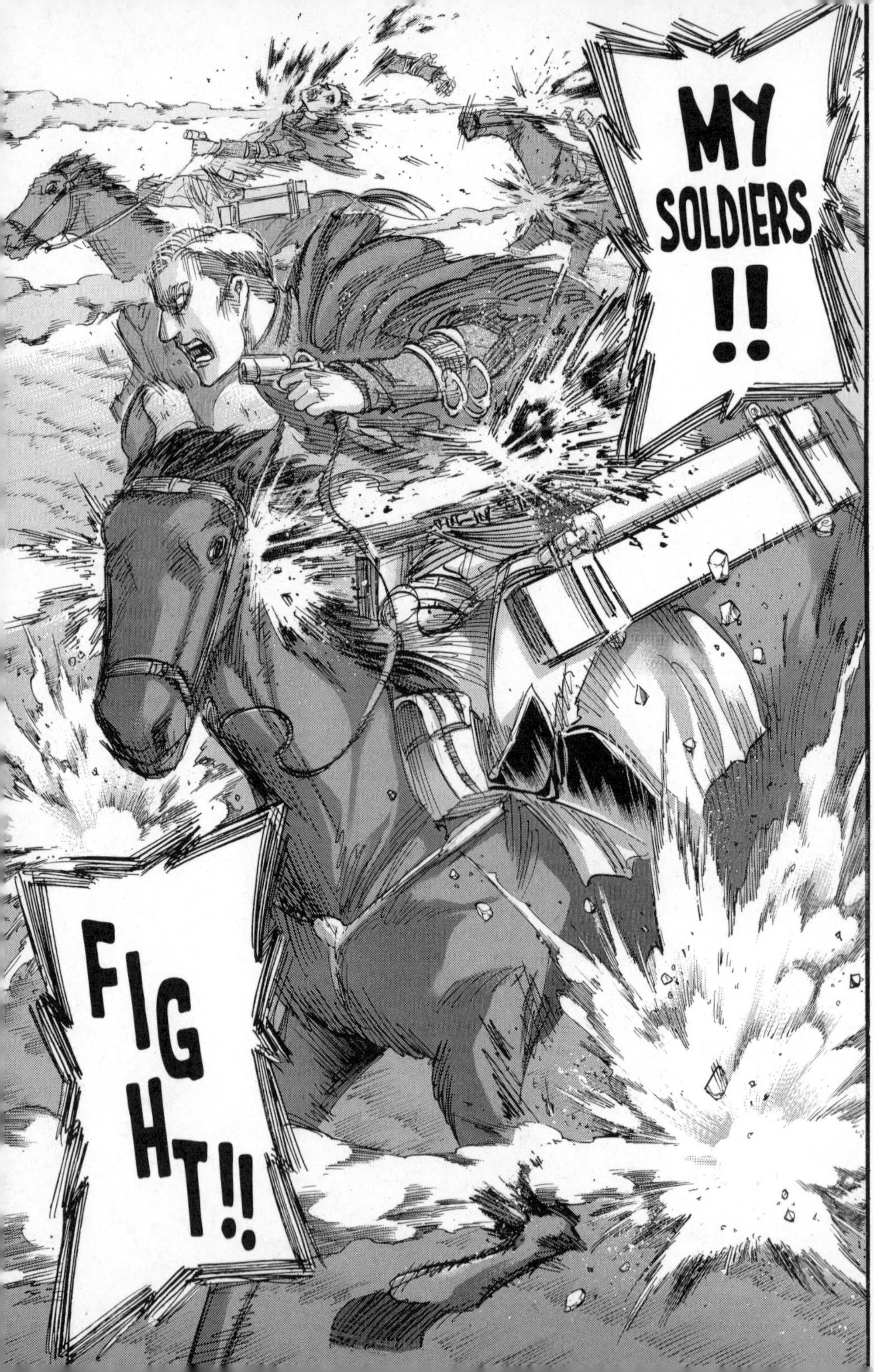
MY SOLDIERS!!
FIGHT!!

ATTACK on TITAN

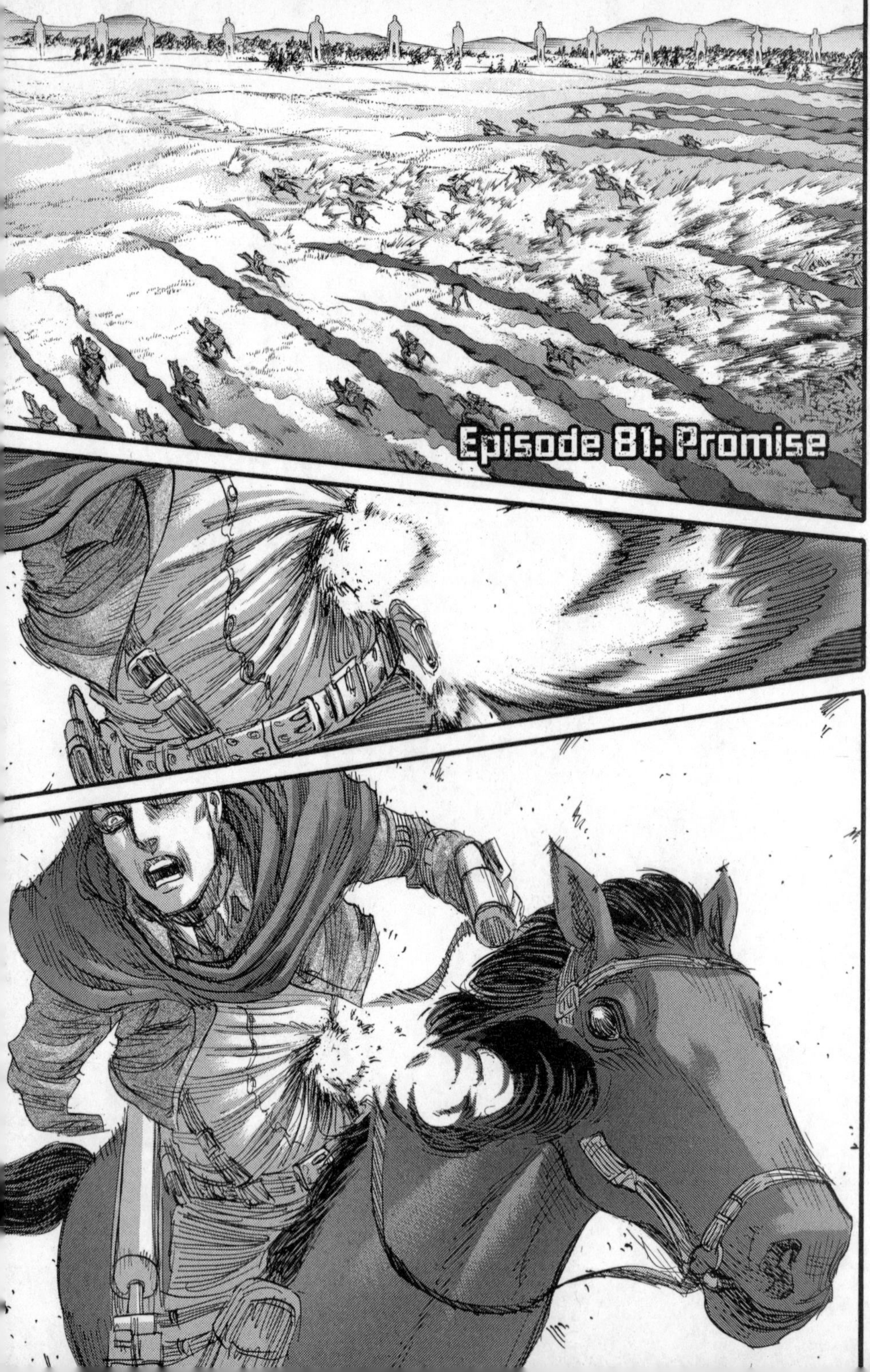
Episode 81: Promise

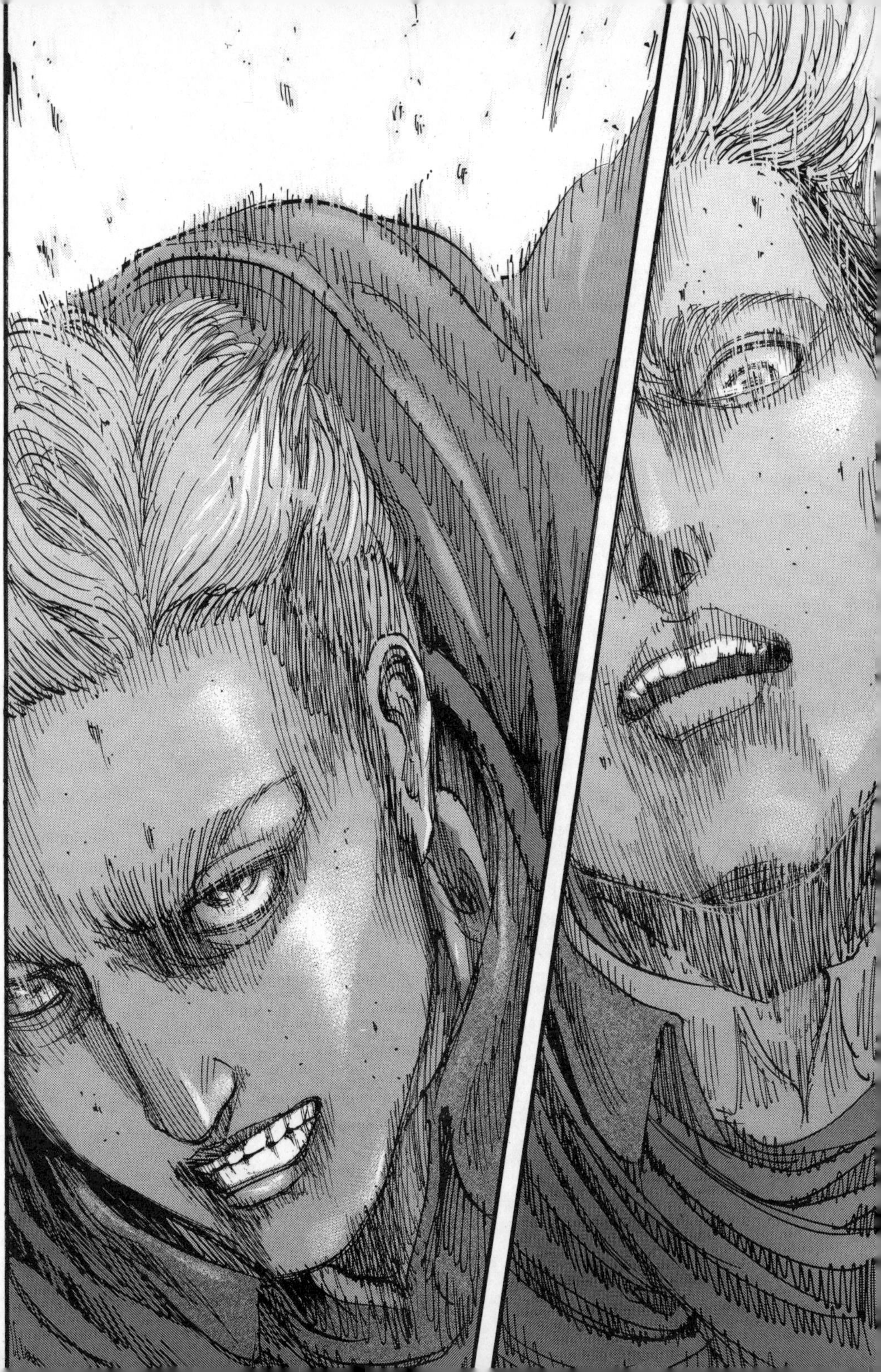

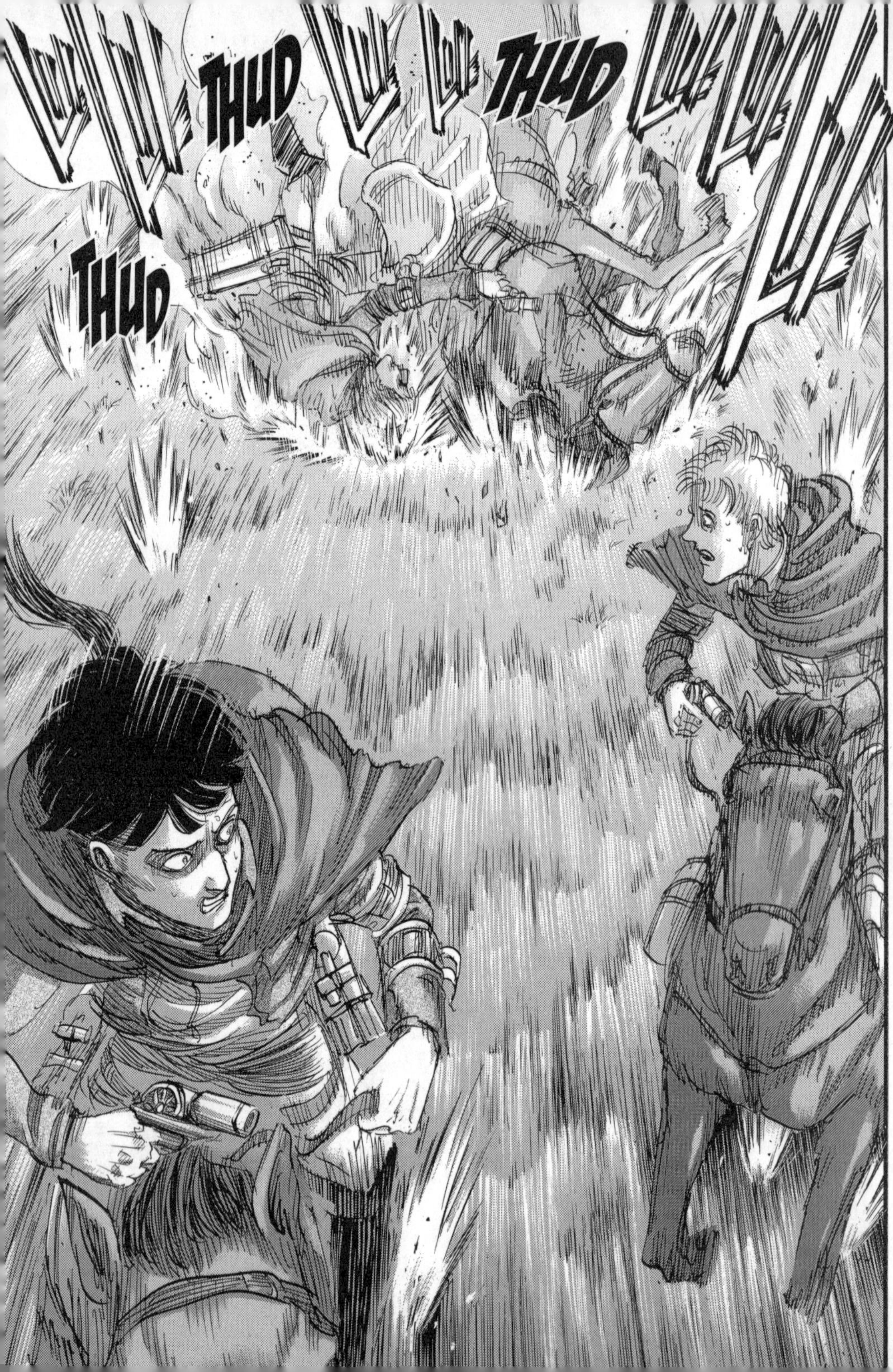

THUD
THUD
THUD

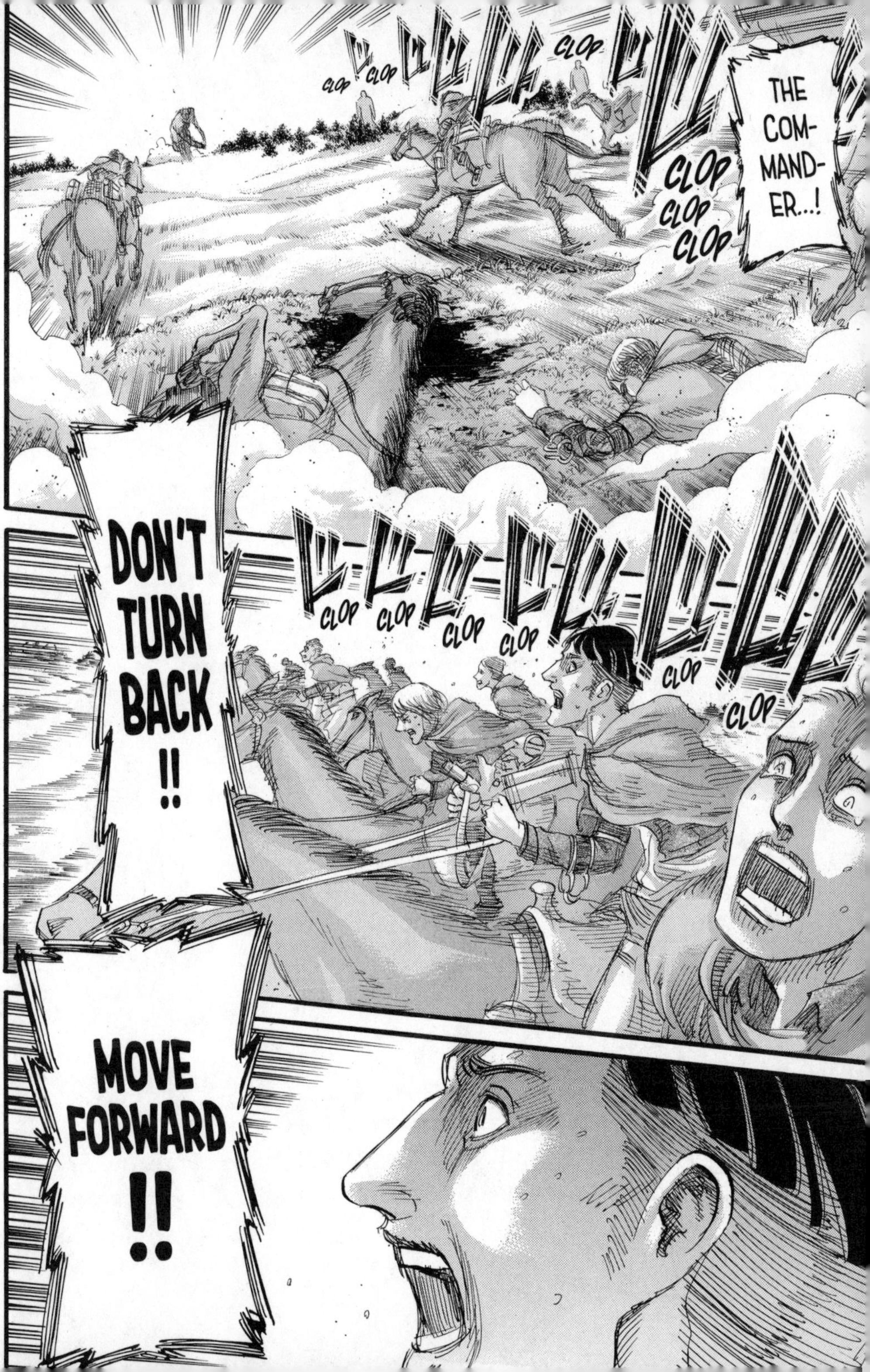

THE COMMANDER...!
CLOP CLOP CLOP
CLOP CLOP CLOP CLOP
CLOP CLOP CLOP CLOP CLOP CLOP
DON'T TURN BACK !!
MOVE FORWARD !!

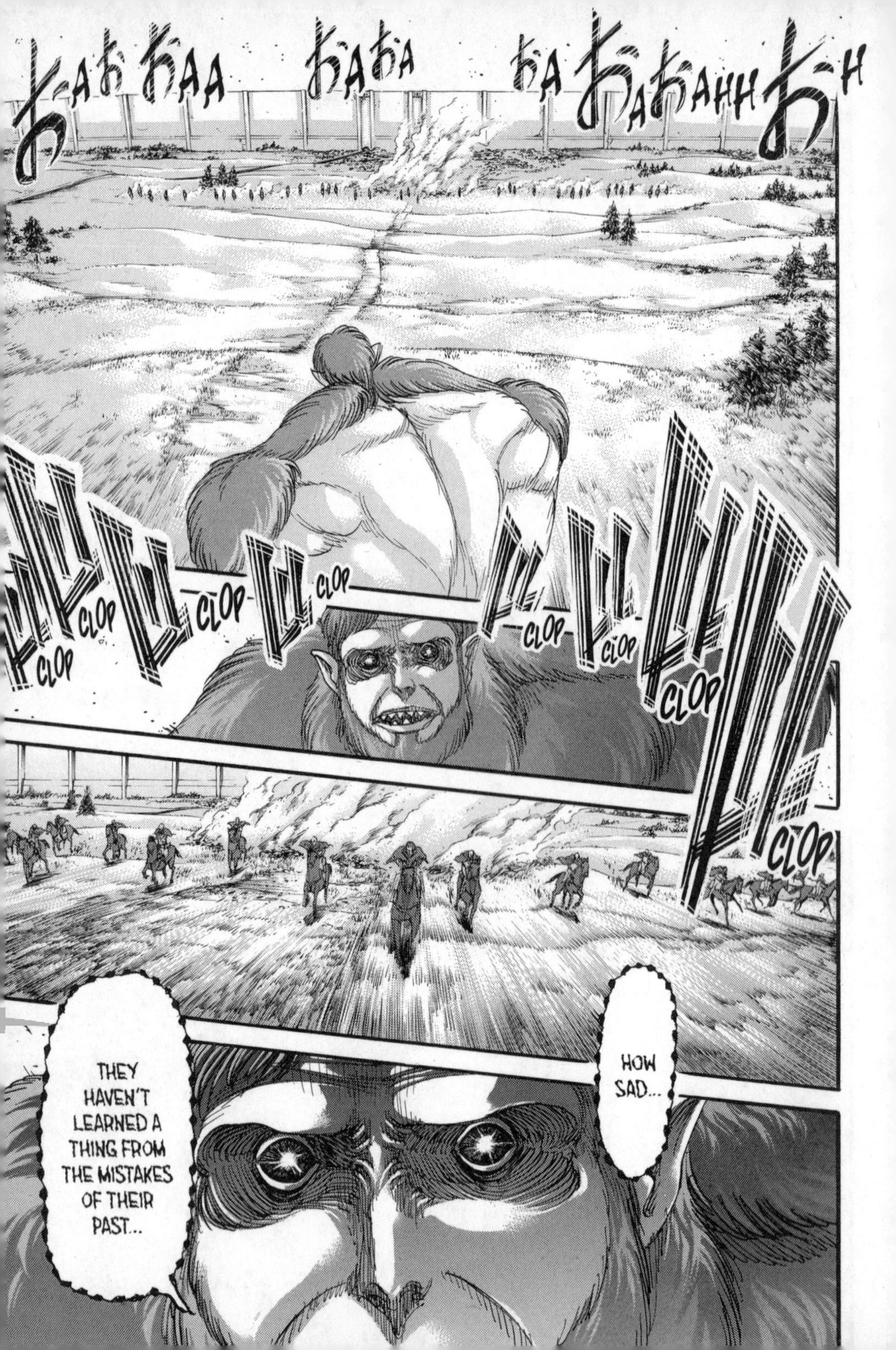
おAおおAA おAおA おAおAおAAHHおH
CLOP
CLOP
CLOP
CLOP
CLOP
CLOP
CLOP
CLOP
CLOP
HOW SAD...
THEY HAVEN'T LEARNED A THING FROM THE MISTAKES OF THEIR PAST...

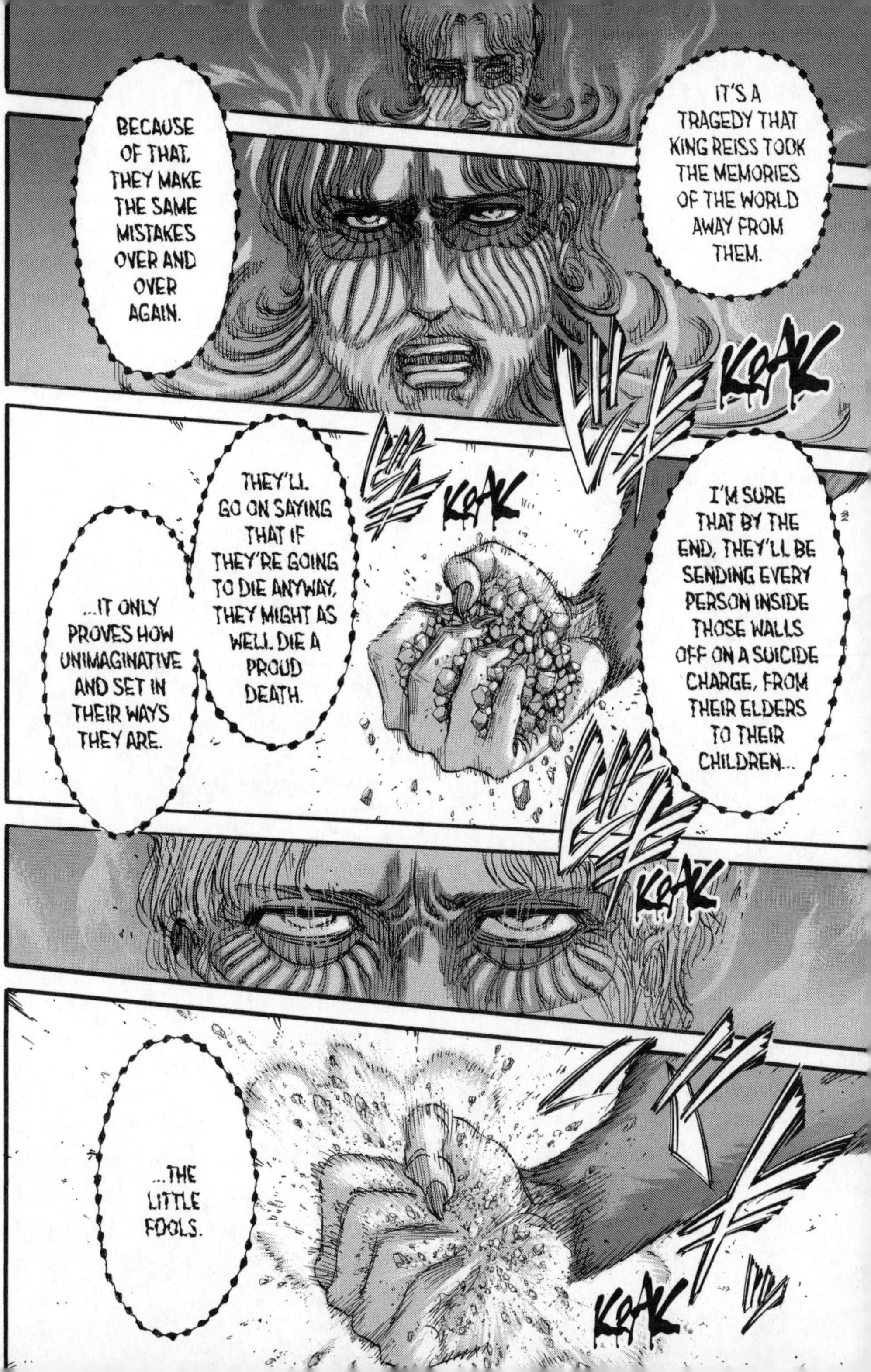
IT'S A TRAGEDY THAT KING REISS TOOK THE MEMORIES OF THE WORLD AWAY FROM THEM.
BECAUSE OF THAT, THEY MAKE THE SAME MISTAKES OVER AND OVER AGAIN.
KRAK
I'M SURE THAT BY THE END, THEY'LL BE SENDING EVERY PERSON INSIDE THOSE WALLS OFF ON A SUICIDE CHARGE, FROM THEIR ELDERS TO THEIR CHILDREN...
KRAK
THEY'LL GO ON SAYING THAT IF THEY'RE GOING TO DIE ANYWAY, THEY MIGHT AS WELL DIE A PROUD DEATH.
...IT ONLY PROVES HOW UNIMAGINATIVE AND SET IN THEIR WAYS THEY ARE.
KRAK
...THE LITTLE FOOLS.
KRAK

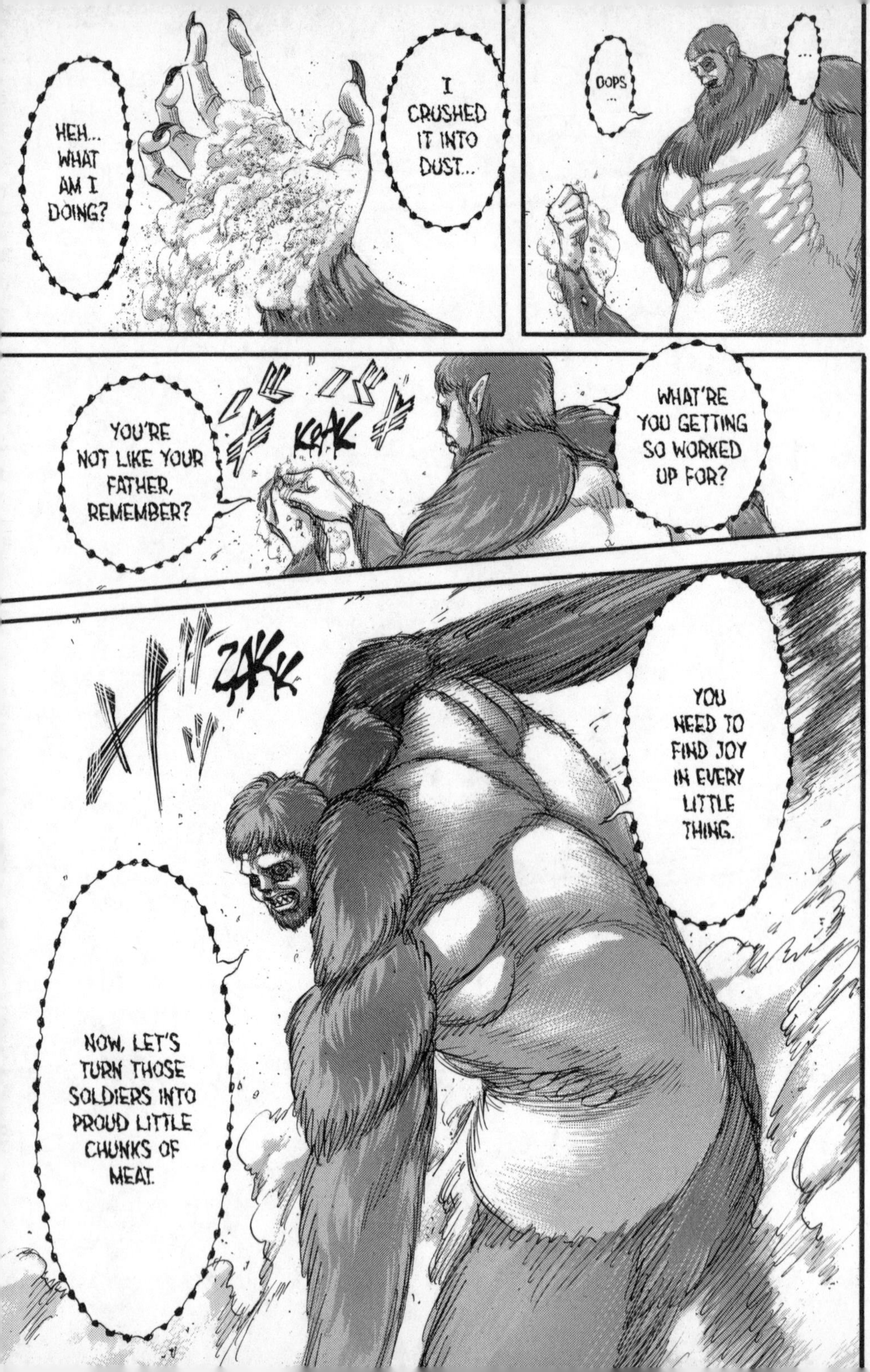
...
OOPS ...
I CRUSHED IT INTO DUST...
HEH... WHAT AM I DOING?
WHAT'RE YOU GETTING SO WORKED UP FOR?
KRAK
YOU'RE NOT LIKE YOUR FATHER, REMEMBER?
YOU NEED TO FIND JOY IN EVERY LITTLE THING.
ZAKK
NOW, LET'S TURN THOSE SOLDIERS INTO PROUD LITTLE CHUNKS OF MEAT.

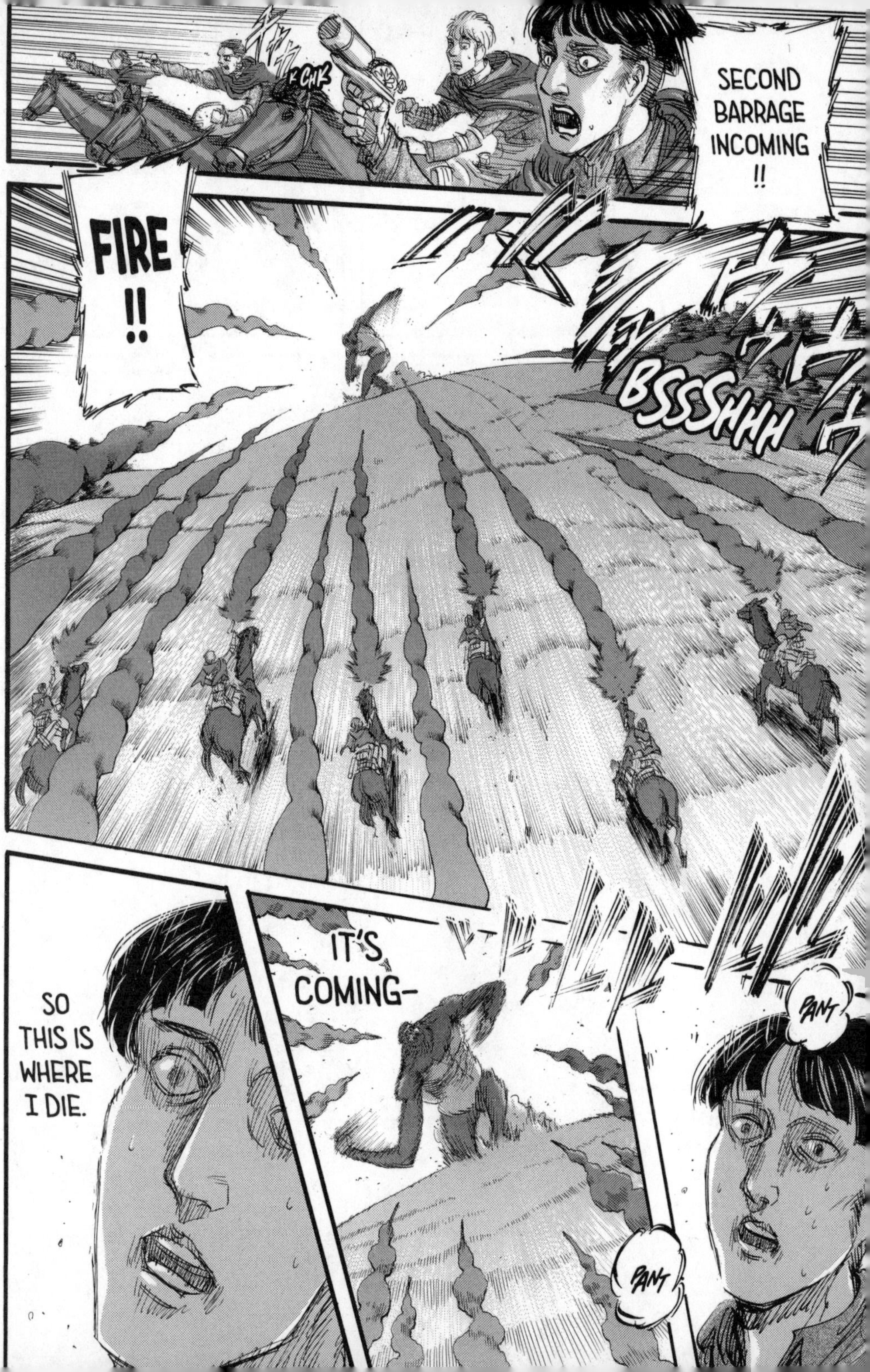
SECOND BARRAGE INCOMING !!
K CHK
FIRE !!
BSSSHHH
PANT
PANT
IT'S COMING-
SO THIS IS WHERE I DIE.

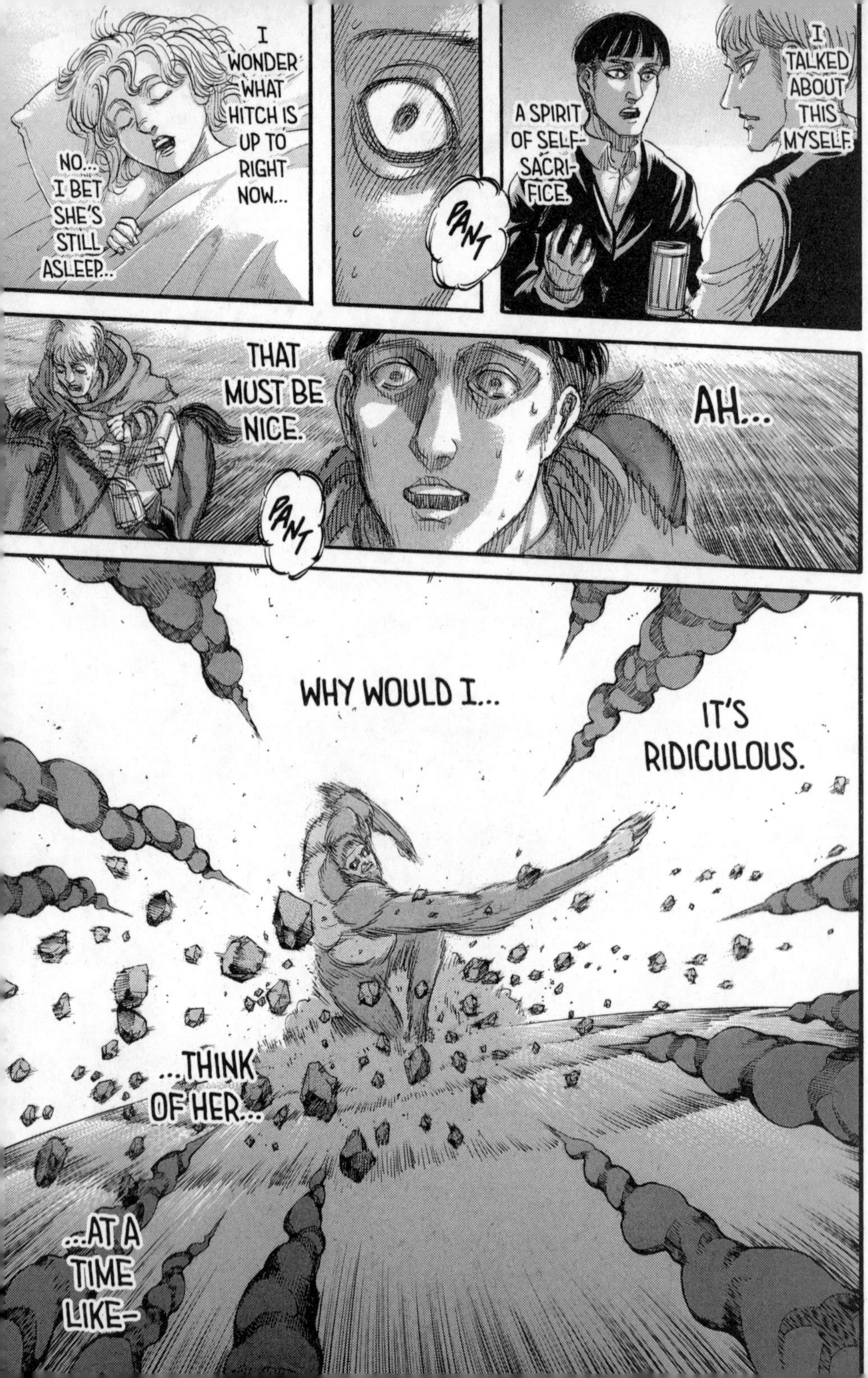
I TALKED ABOUT THIS MYSELF
A SPIRIT OF SELF-SACRIFICE.
PANT
I WONDER WHAT HITCH IS UP TO RIGHT NOW...
NO... I BET SHE'S STILL ASLEEP...
AH...
THAT MUST BE NICE.
PANT
IT'S RIDICULOUS.
WHY WOULD I...
...THINK OF HER...
...AT A TIME LIKE-

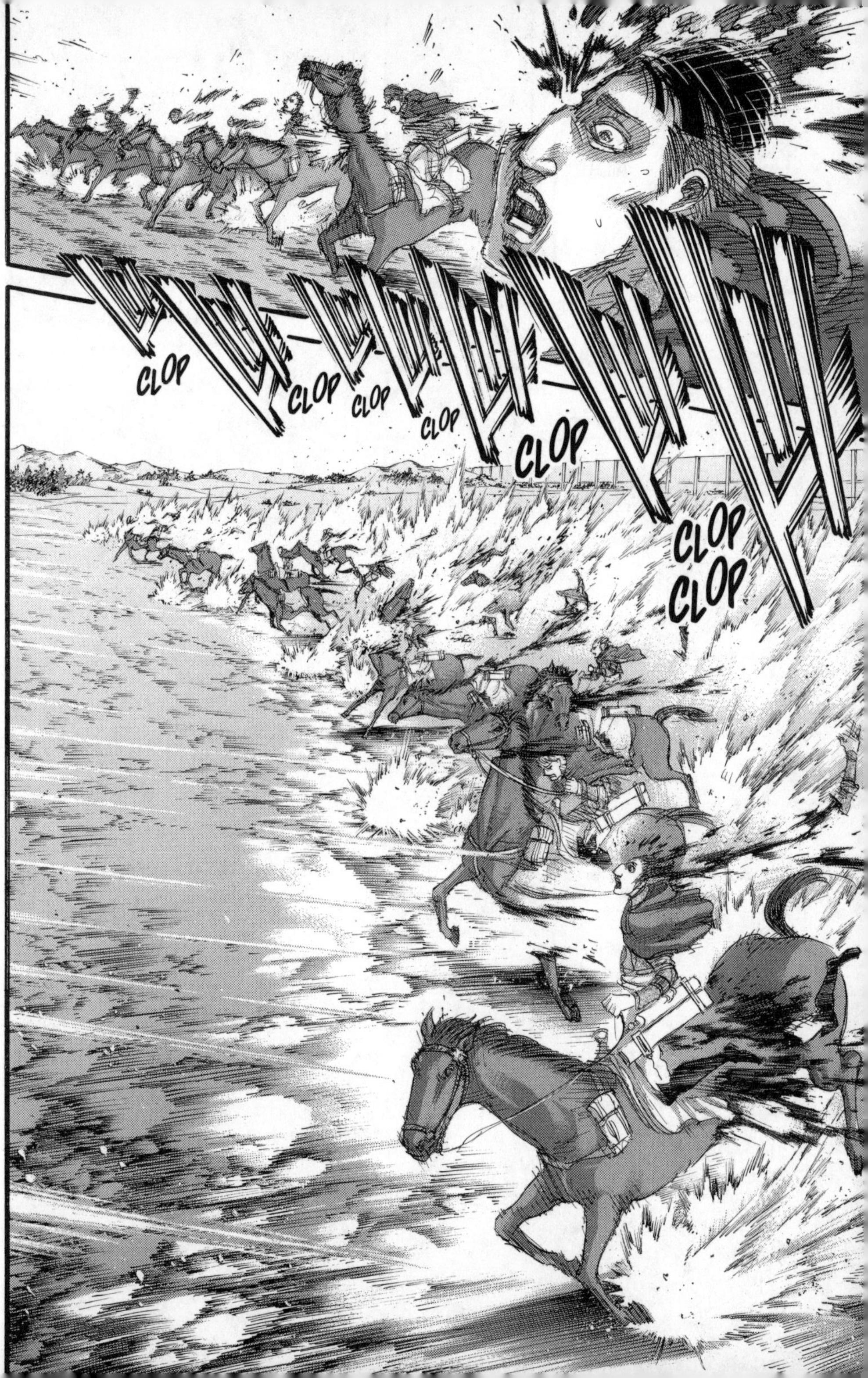
CLOP
CLOP
CLOP
CLOP
CLOP
CLOP
CLOP

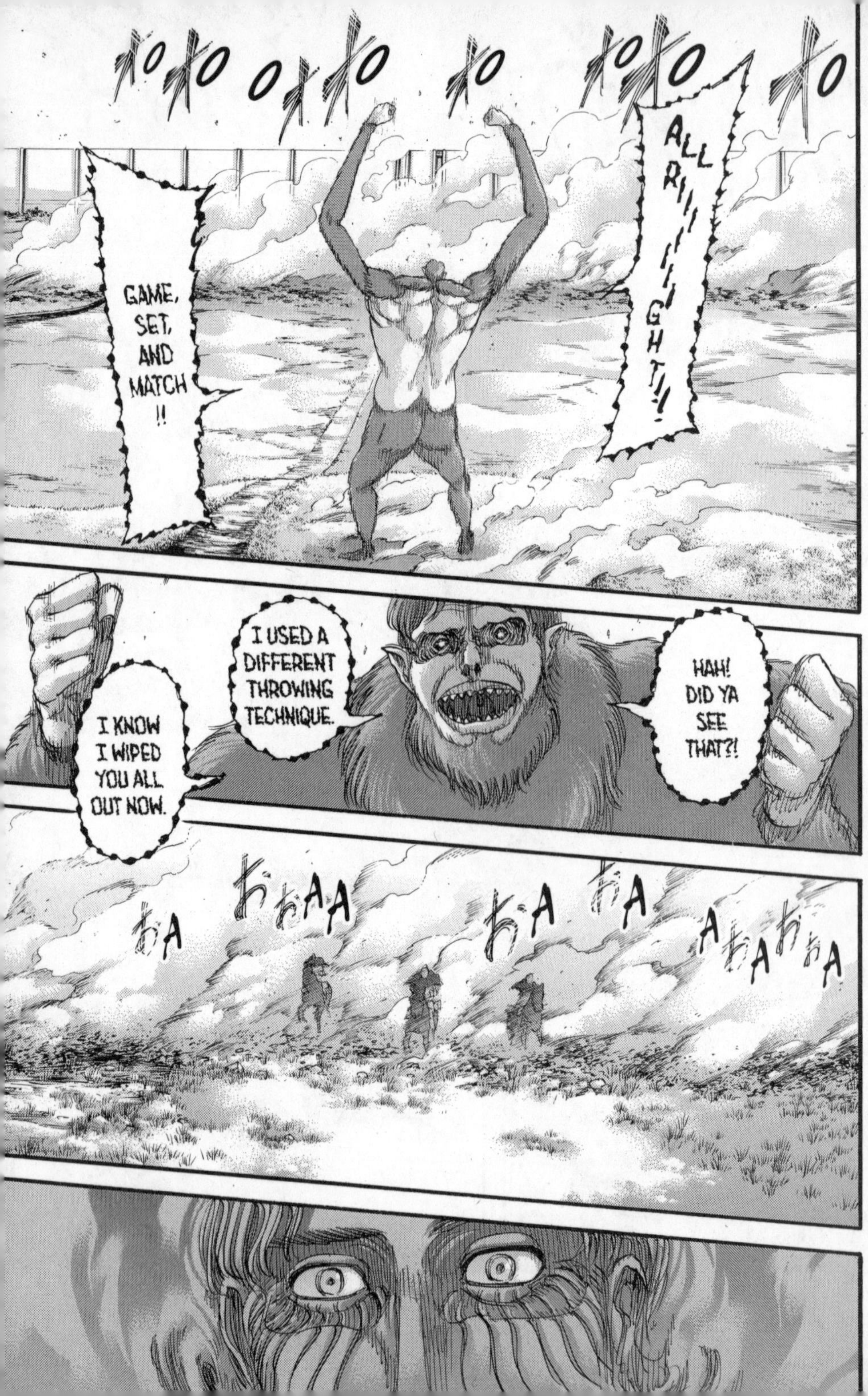
ALL RIIIIIIIGHT!!
GAME, SET, AND MATCH!!
HAH! DID YA SEE THAT?!
I USED A DIFFERENT THROWING TECHNIQUE.
I KNOW I WIPED YOU ALL OUT NOW.

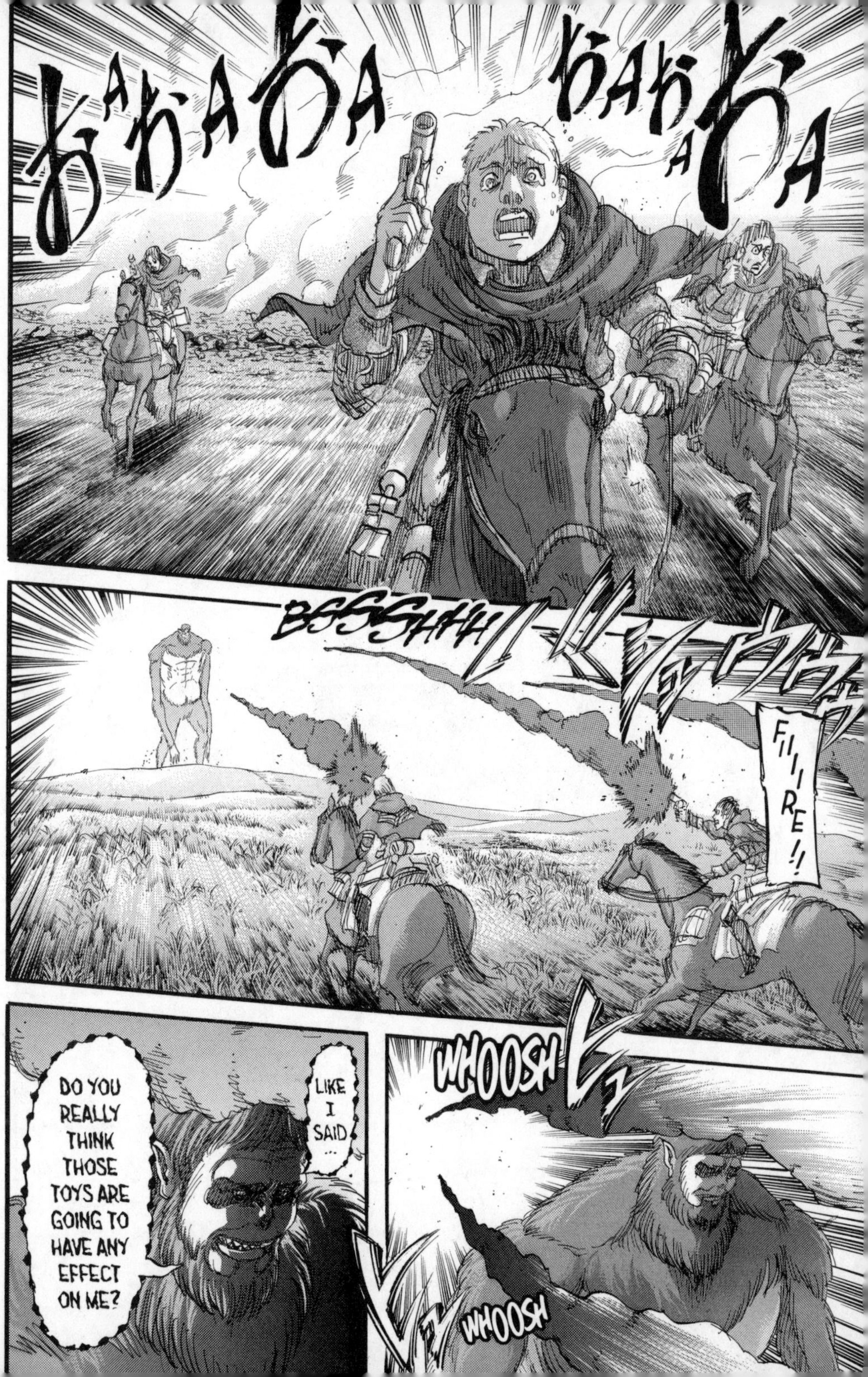
FIIIIRE!!
BSSSHHH
WHOOSH
WHOOSH
LIKE I SAID...
DO YOU REALLY THINK THOSE TOYS ARE GOING TO HAVE ANY EFFECT ON ME?

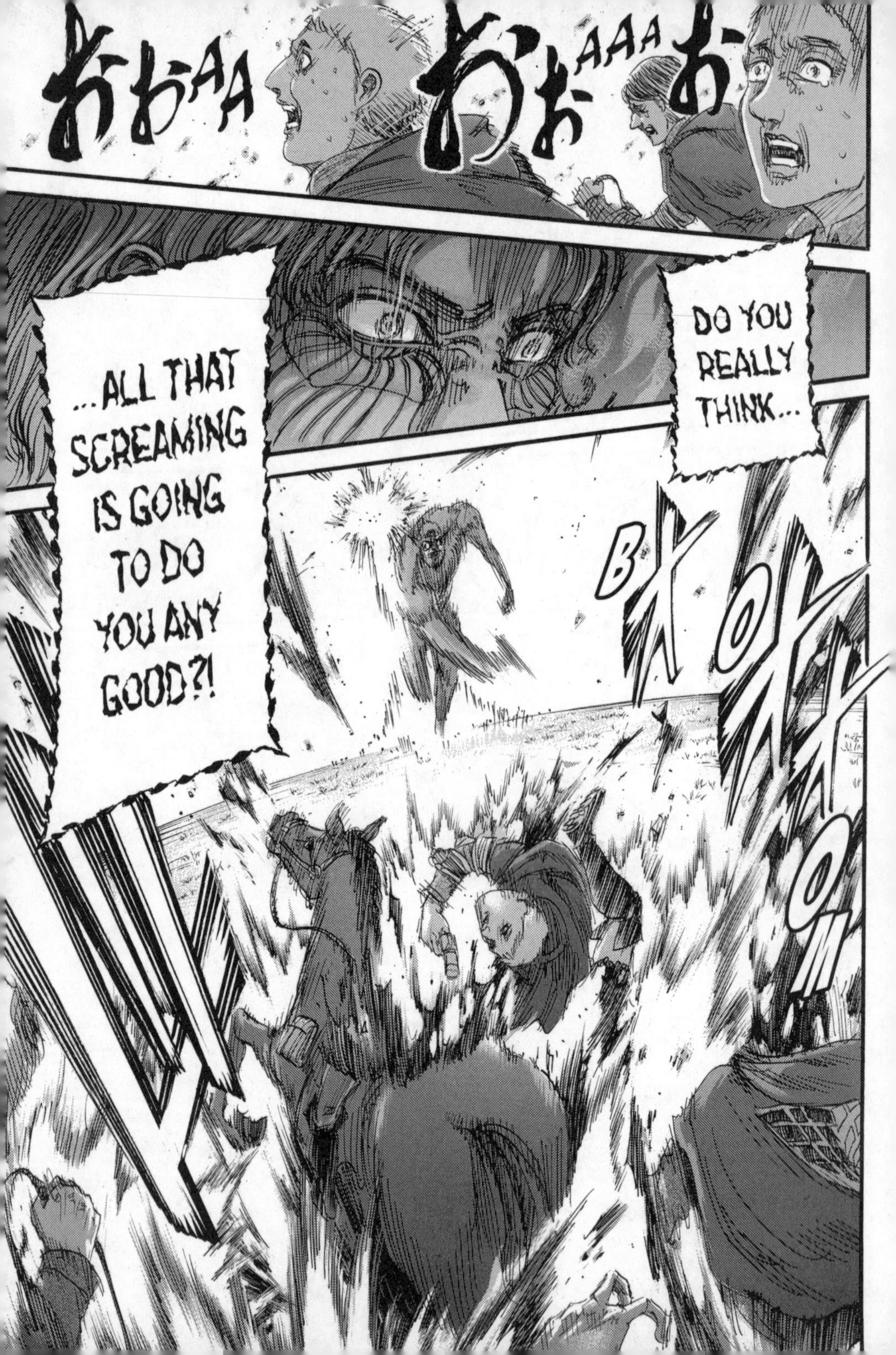
おおAA
おぉAAA
おー
DO YOU REALLY THINK...
...ALL THAT SCREAMING IS GOING TO DO YOU ANY GOOD?!
B

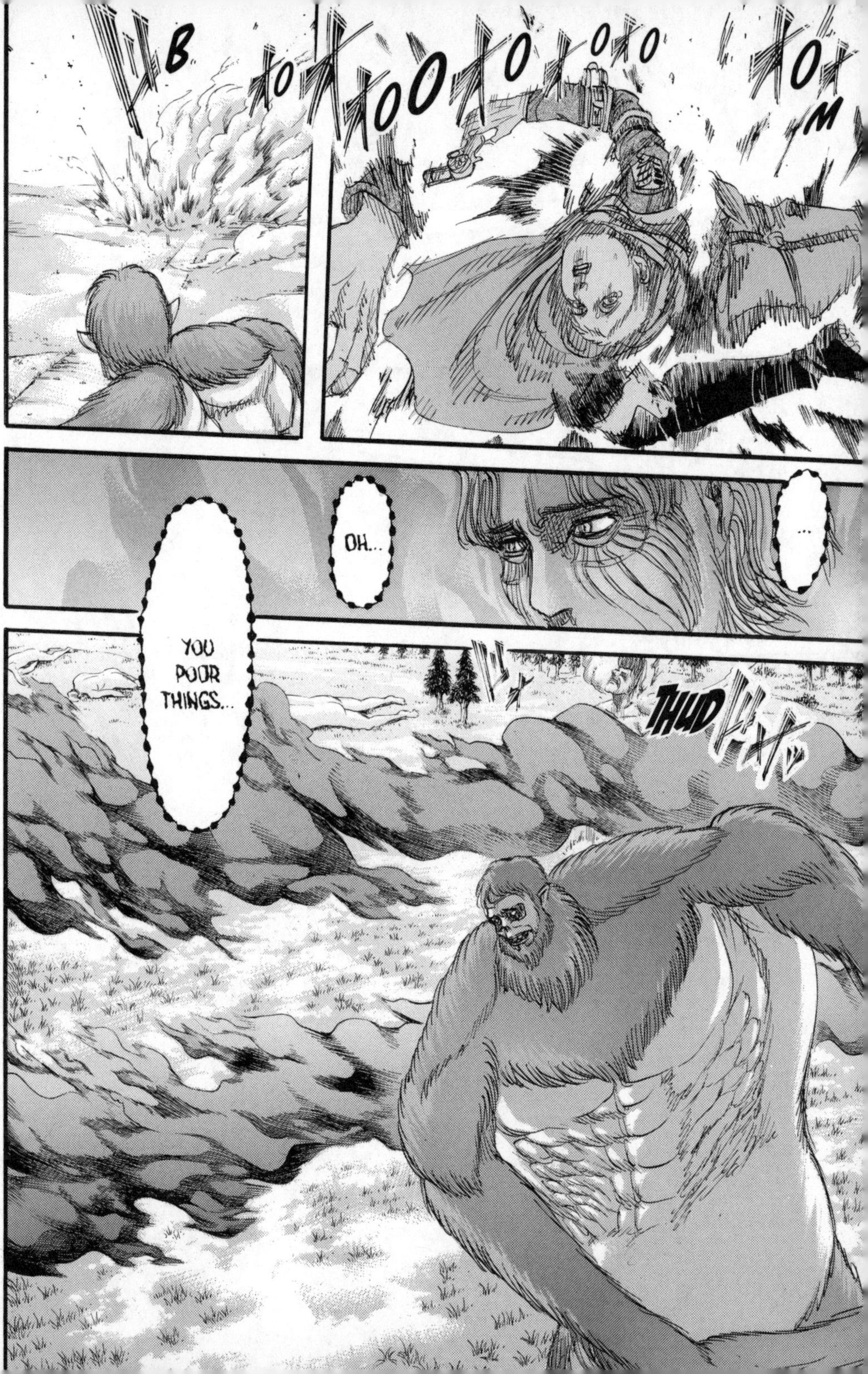
BOOOOOOOOM
...
OH...
YOU POOR THINGS...
THUD

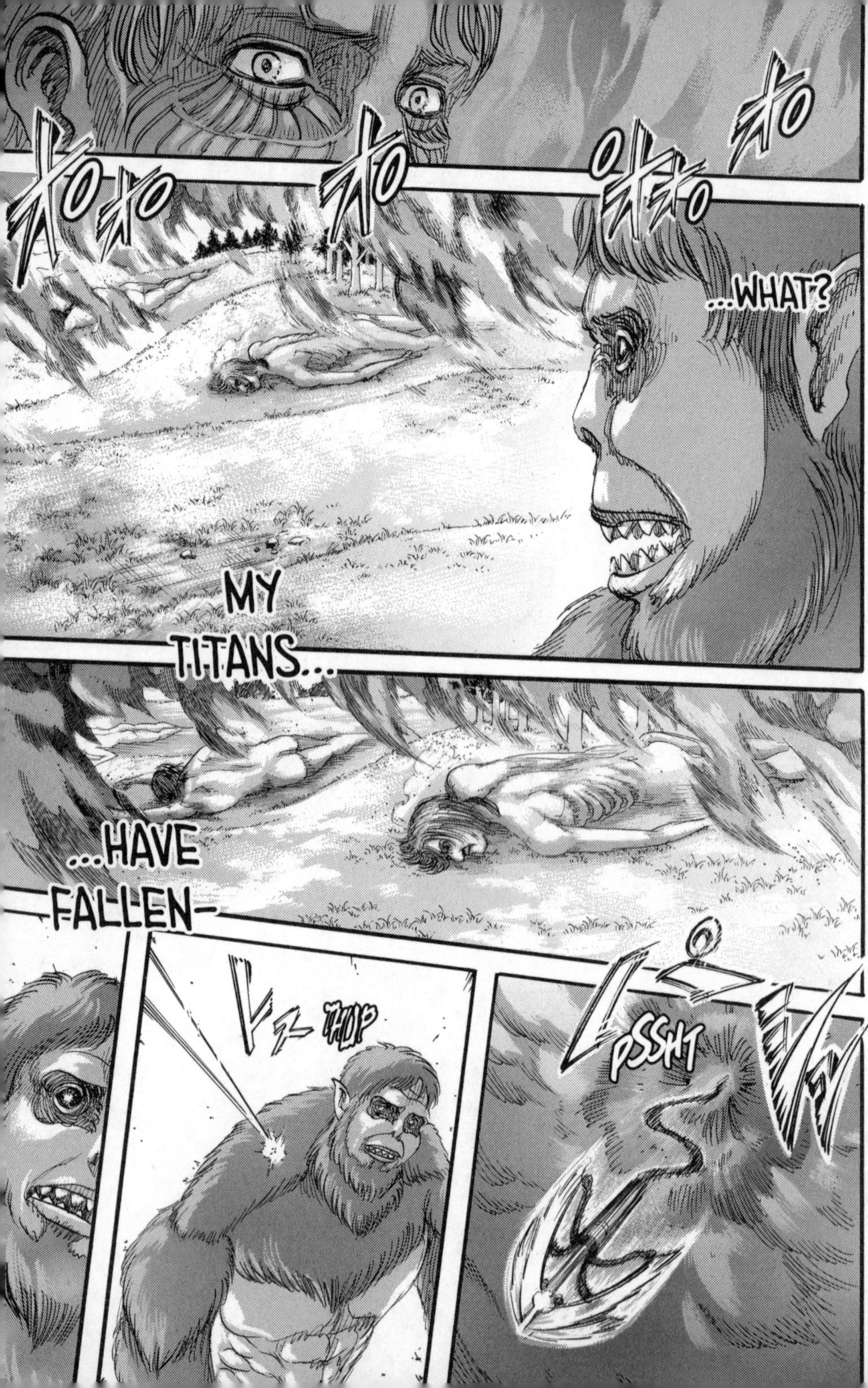
...WHAT?
MY TITANS...
...HAVE FALLEN—
PSSHT
THUP

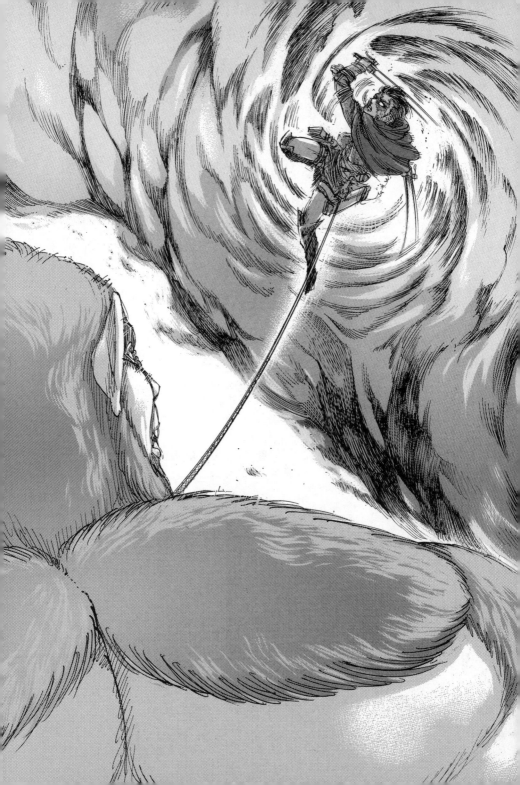

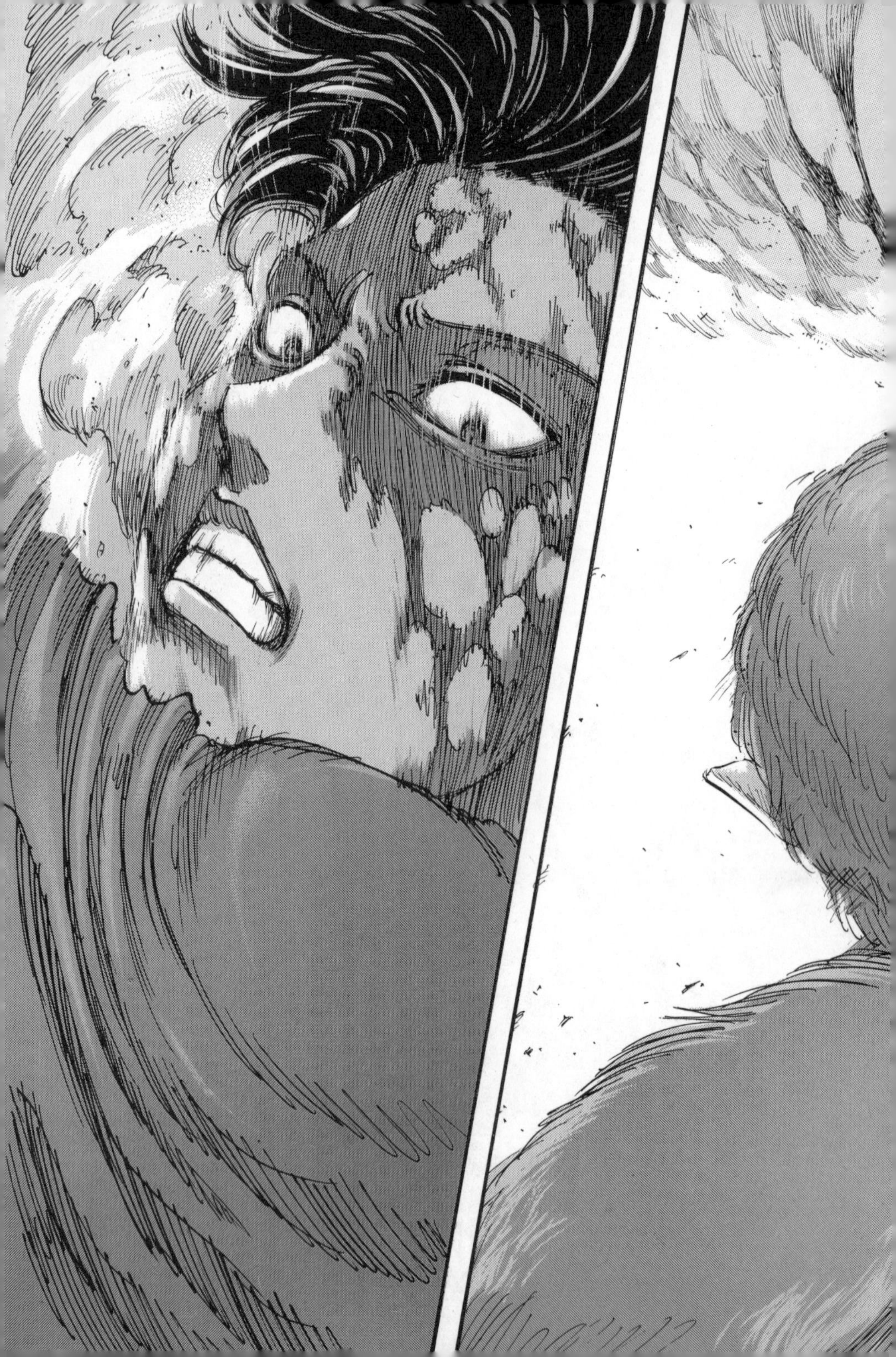

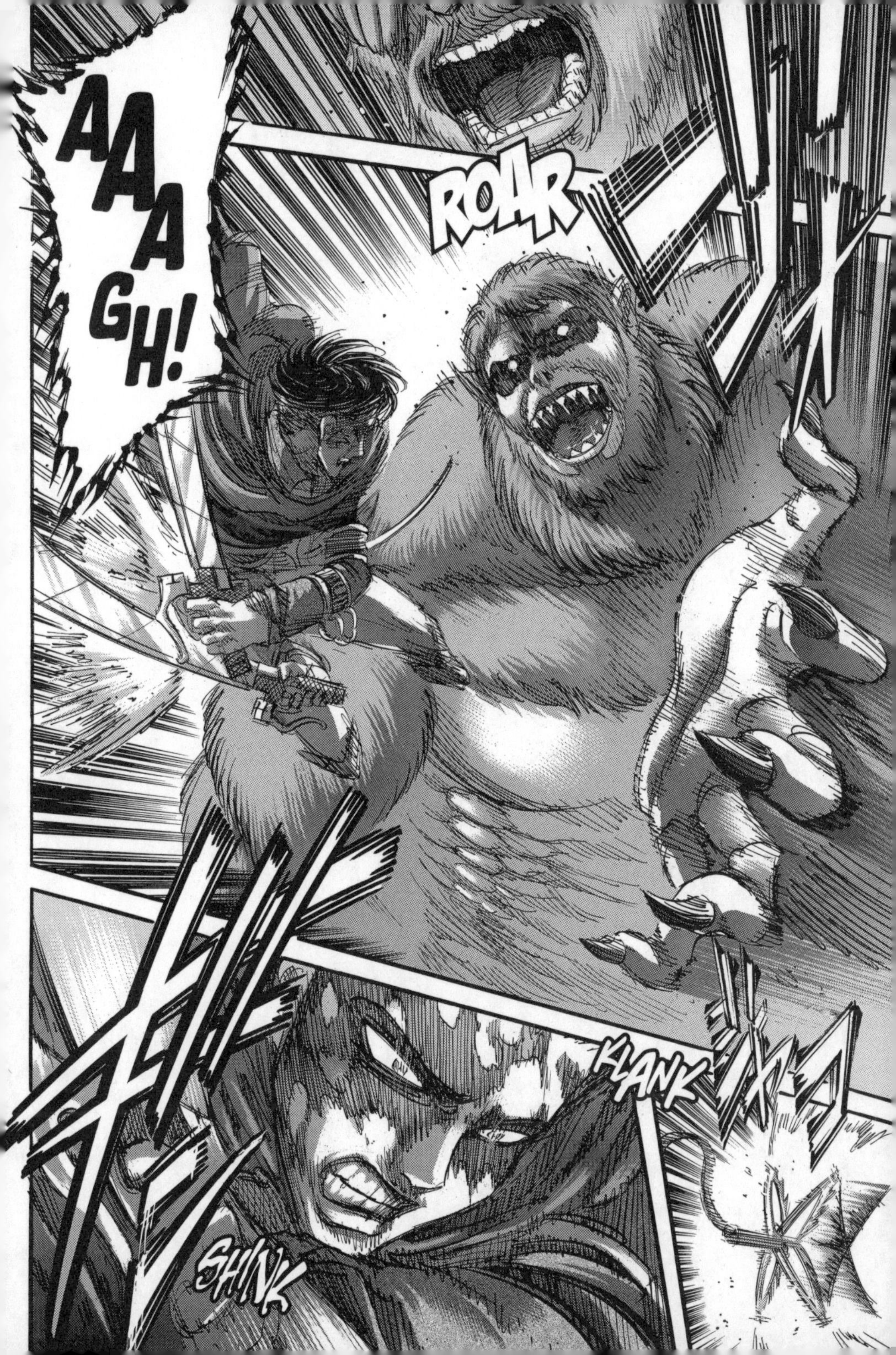
ROAR
AAAGH!
KLANK
SHINK

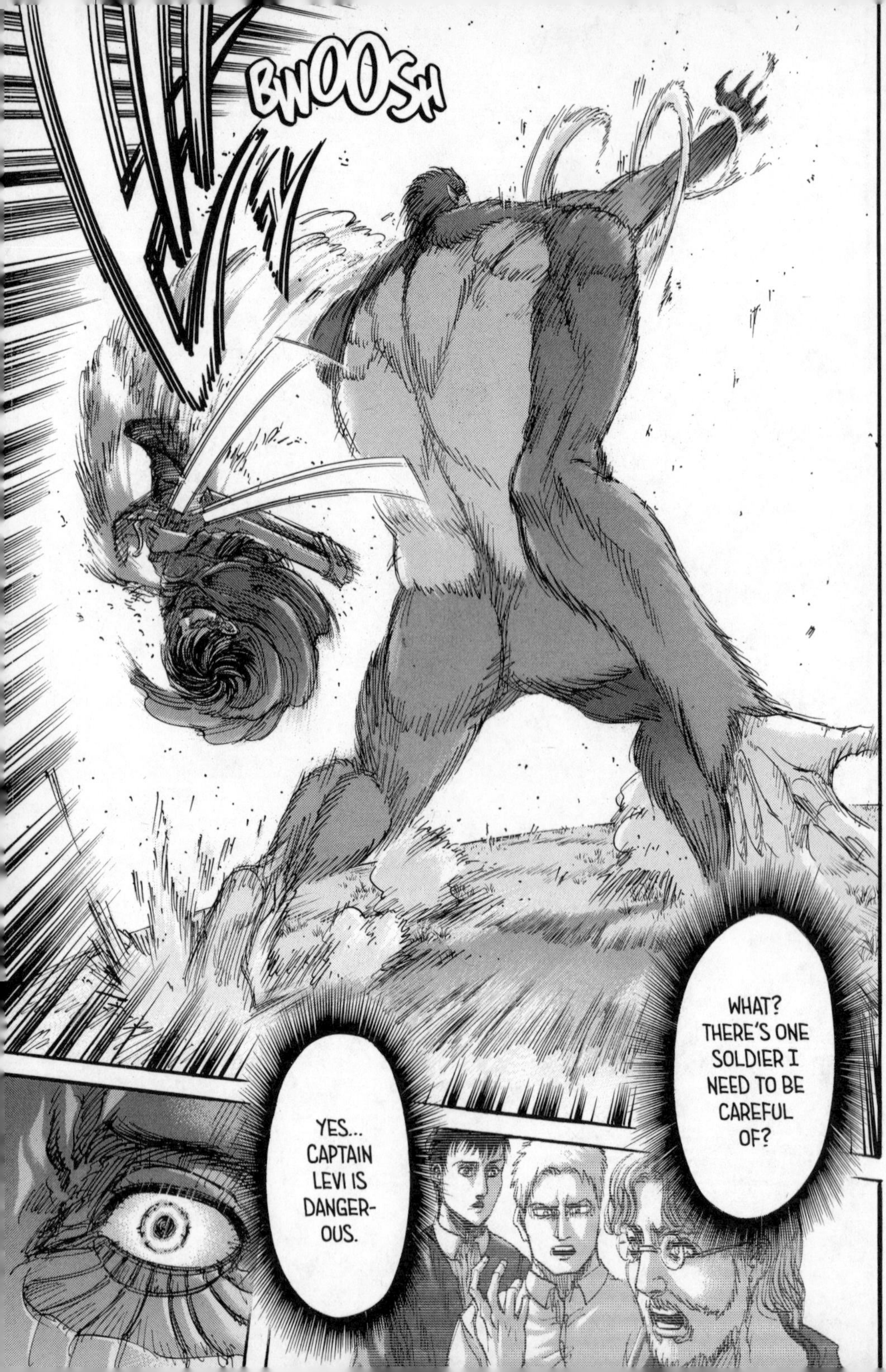
BWOOSH
WHAT? THERE'S ONE SOLDIER I NEED TO BE CAREFUL OF?
YES... CAPTAIN LEVI IS DANGER-OUS.

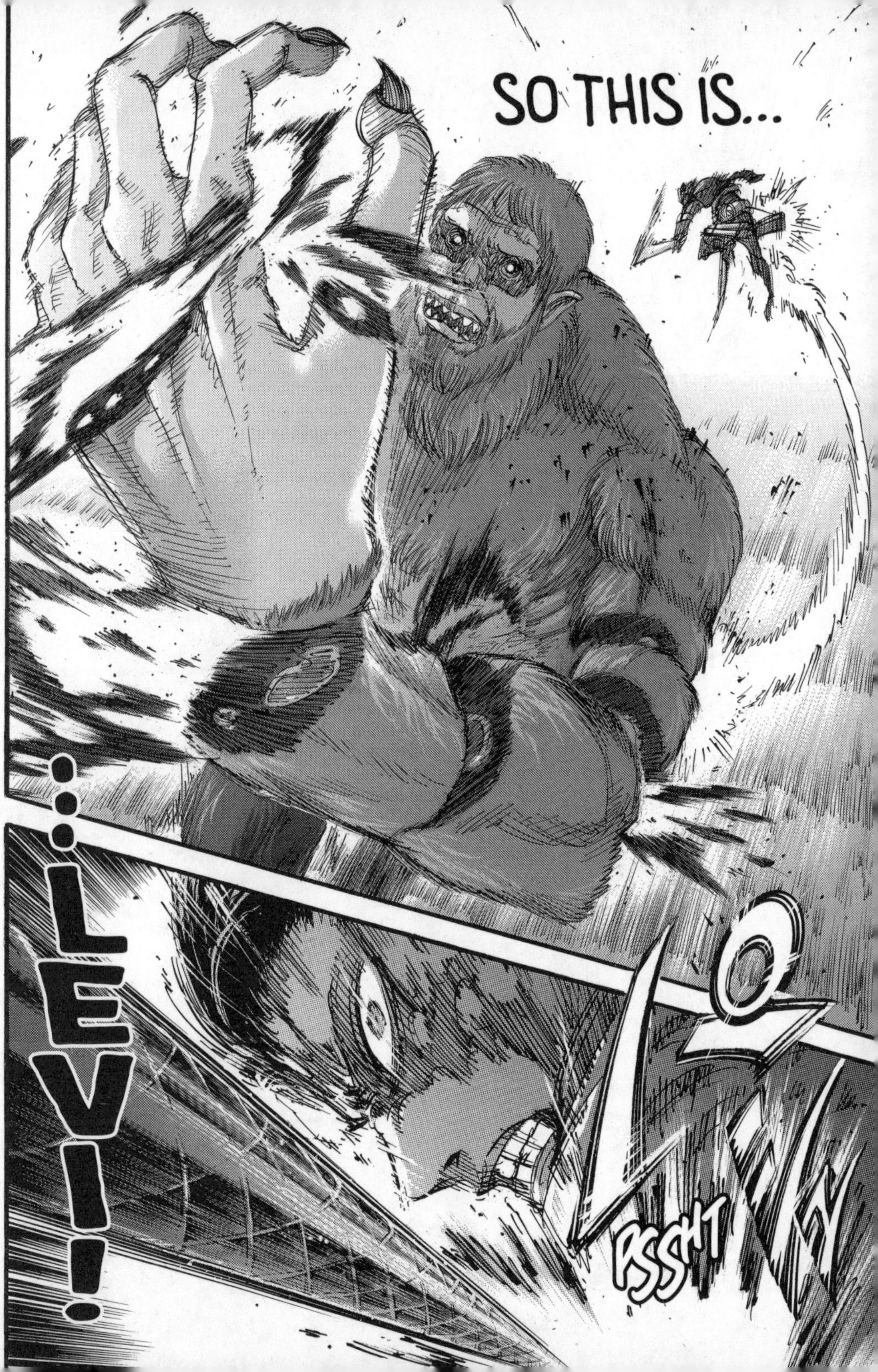
SO THIS IS...
...LEVI!
PSSHT

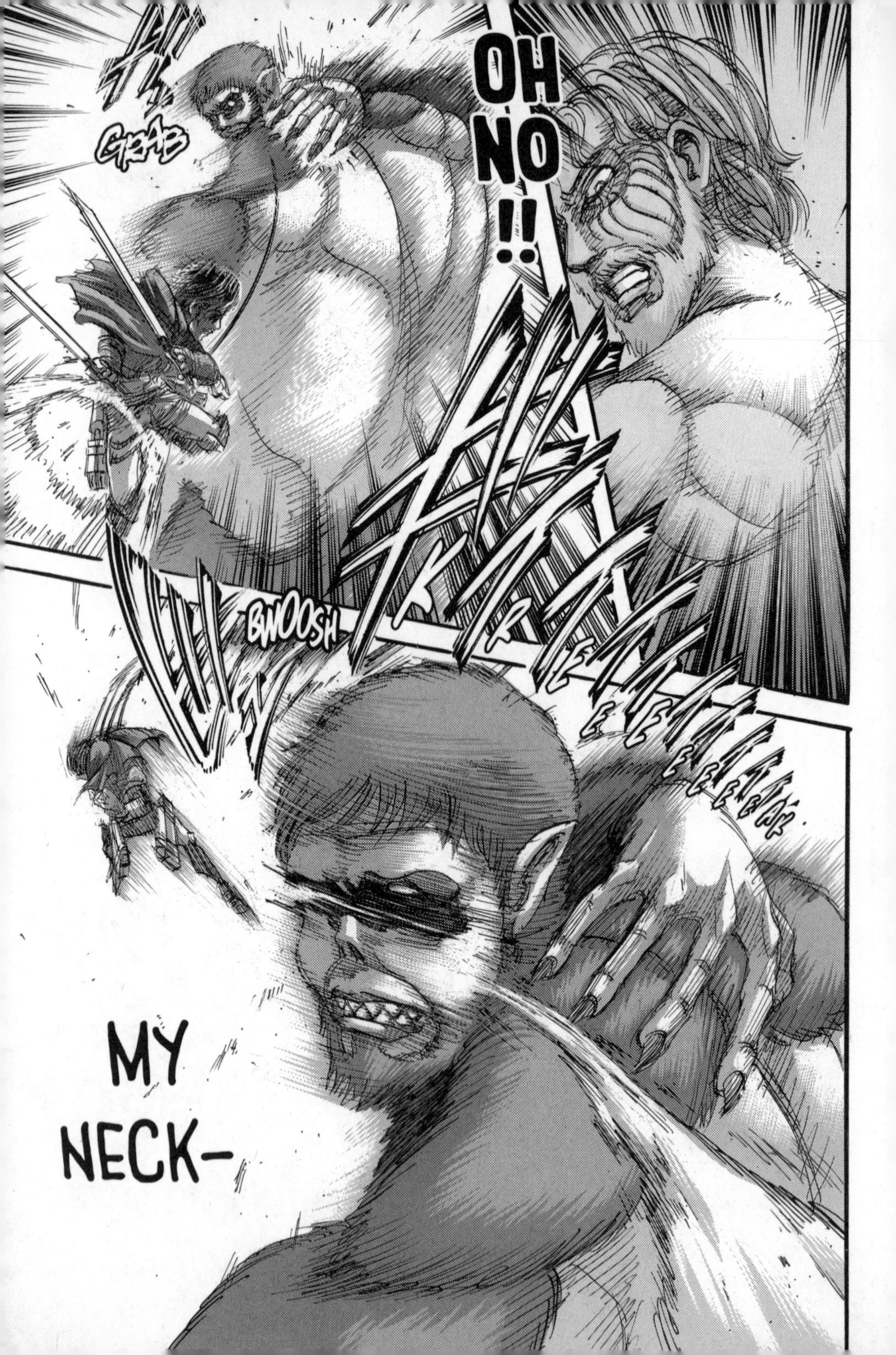

OH NO!!
GRAB
BWOOSH
MY NECK-

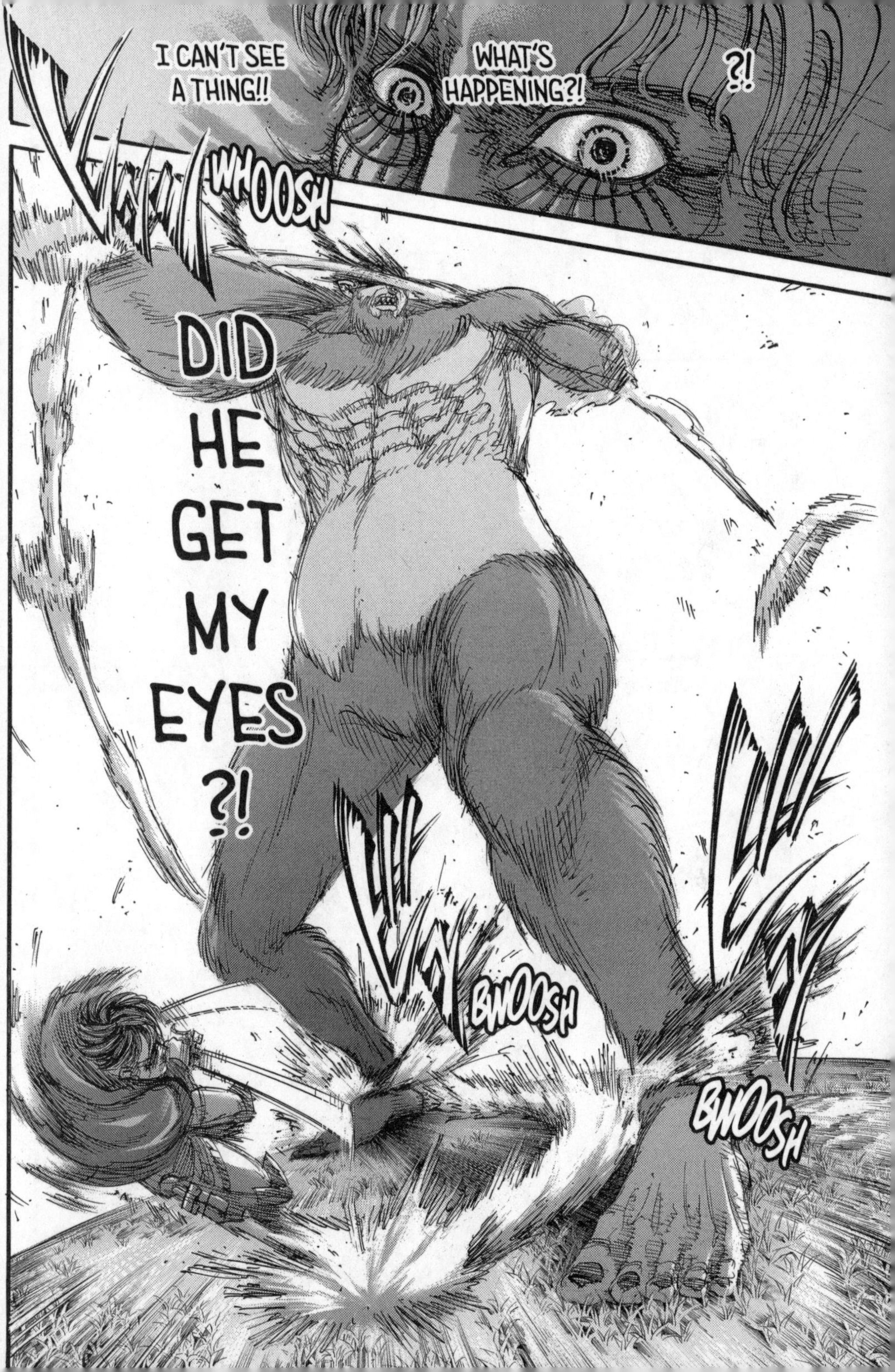

?!
WHAT'S HAPPENING?!
I CAN'T SEE A THING!!
WHOOSH
DID HE GET MY EYES ?!
BWOOSH
BWOOSH

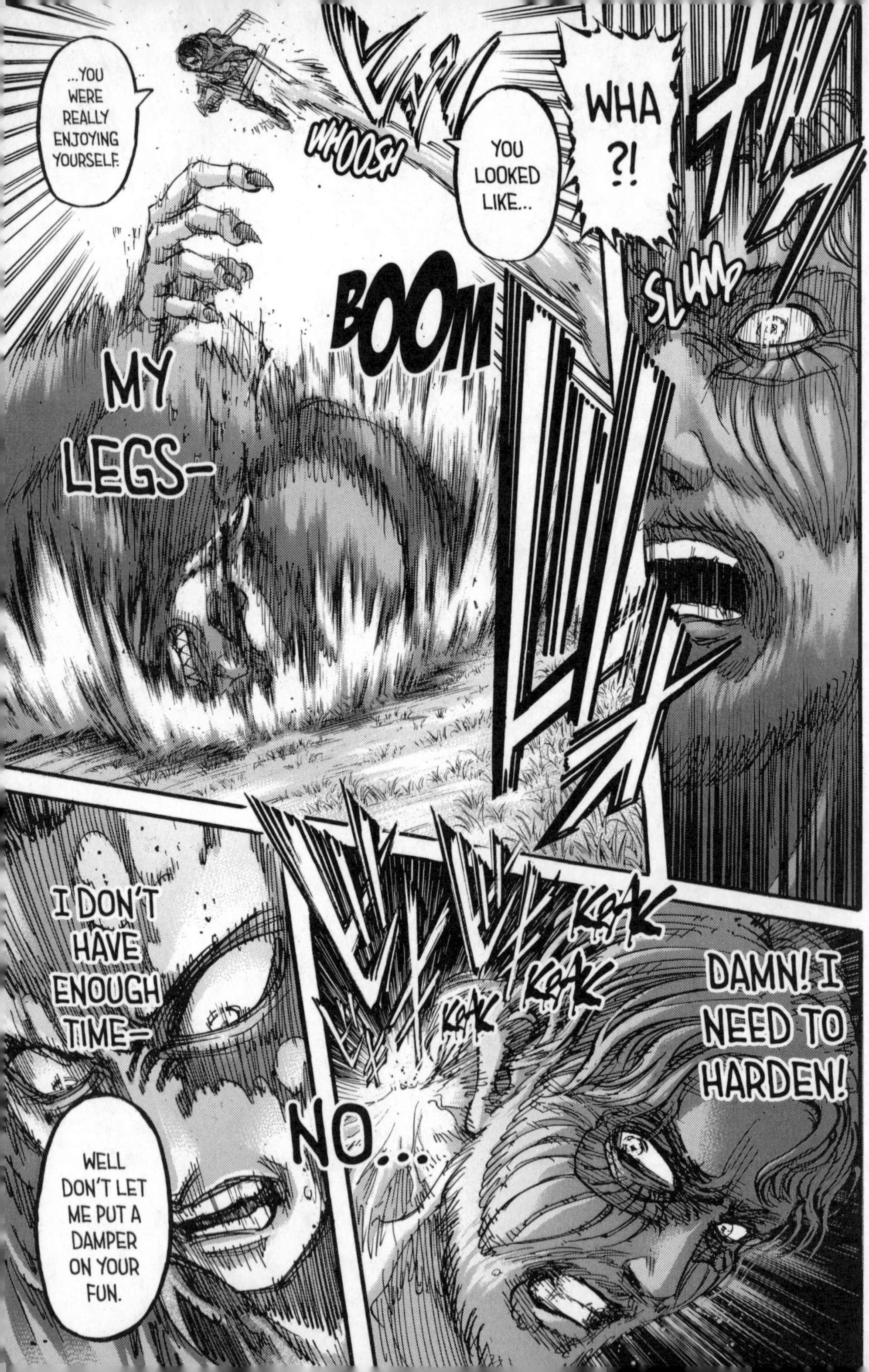
WHA ?!
SLUMP
YOU LOOKED LIKE...
WHOOSH
...YOU WERE REALLY ENJOYING YOURSELF.
BOOM
MY LEGS-
DAMN! I NEED TO HARDEN!
KRAK
KRAK
KRAK
NO...
I DON'T HAVE ENOUGH TIME-
WELL DON'T LET ME PUT A DAMPER ON YOUR FUN.

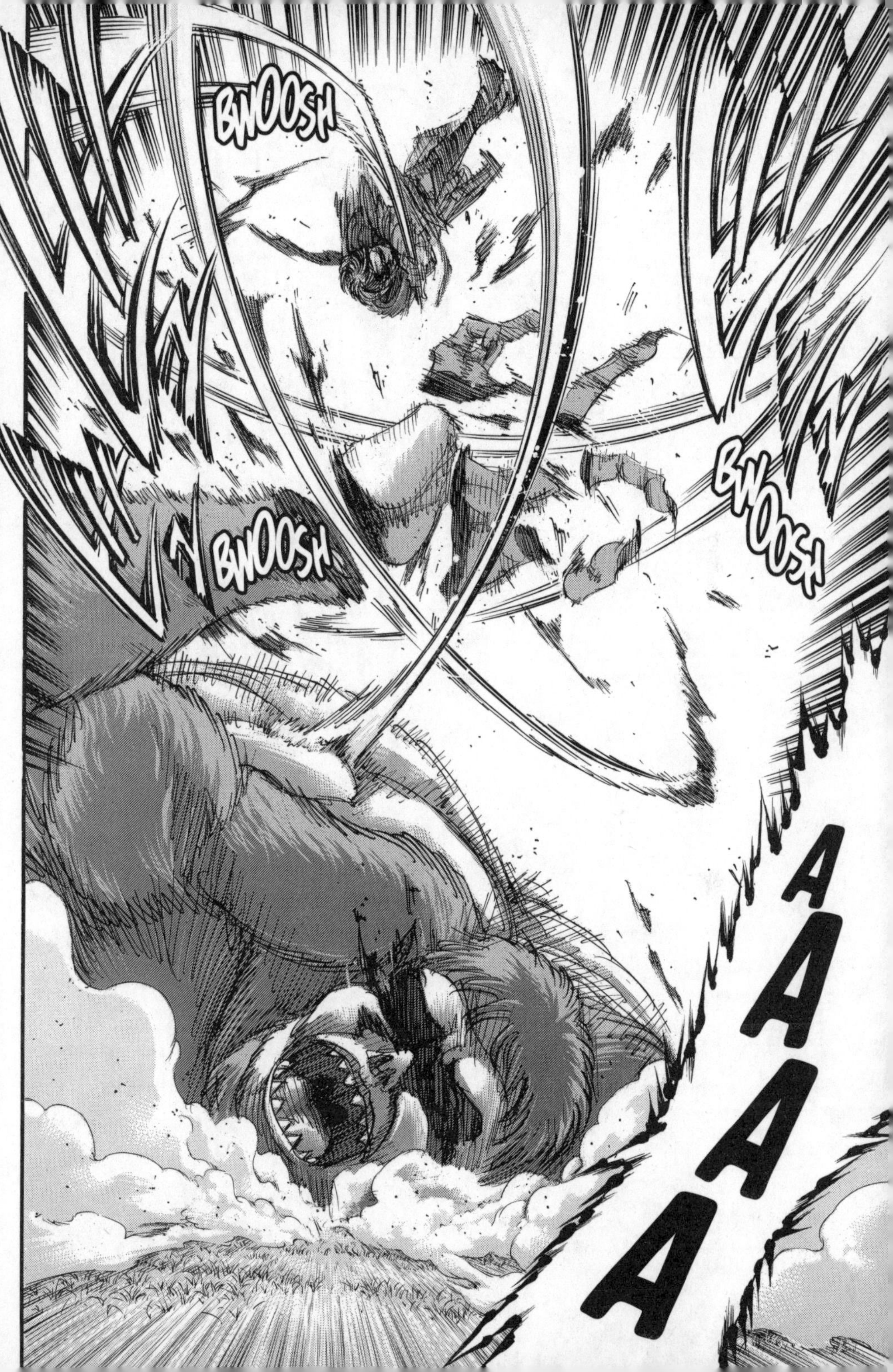
BWOOSH
BWOOSH
BWOOSH
AAAAA

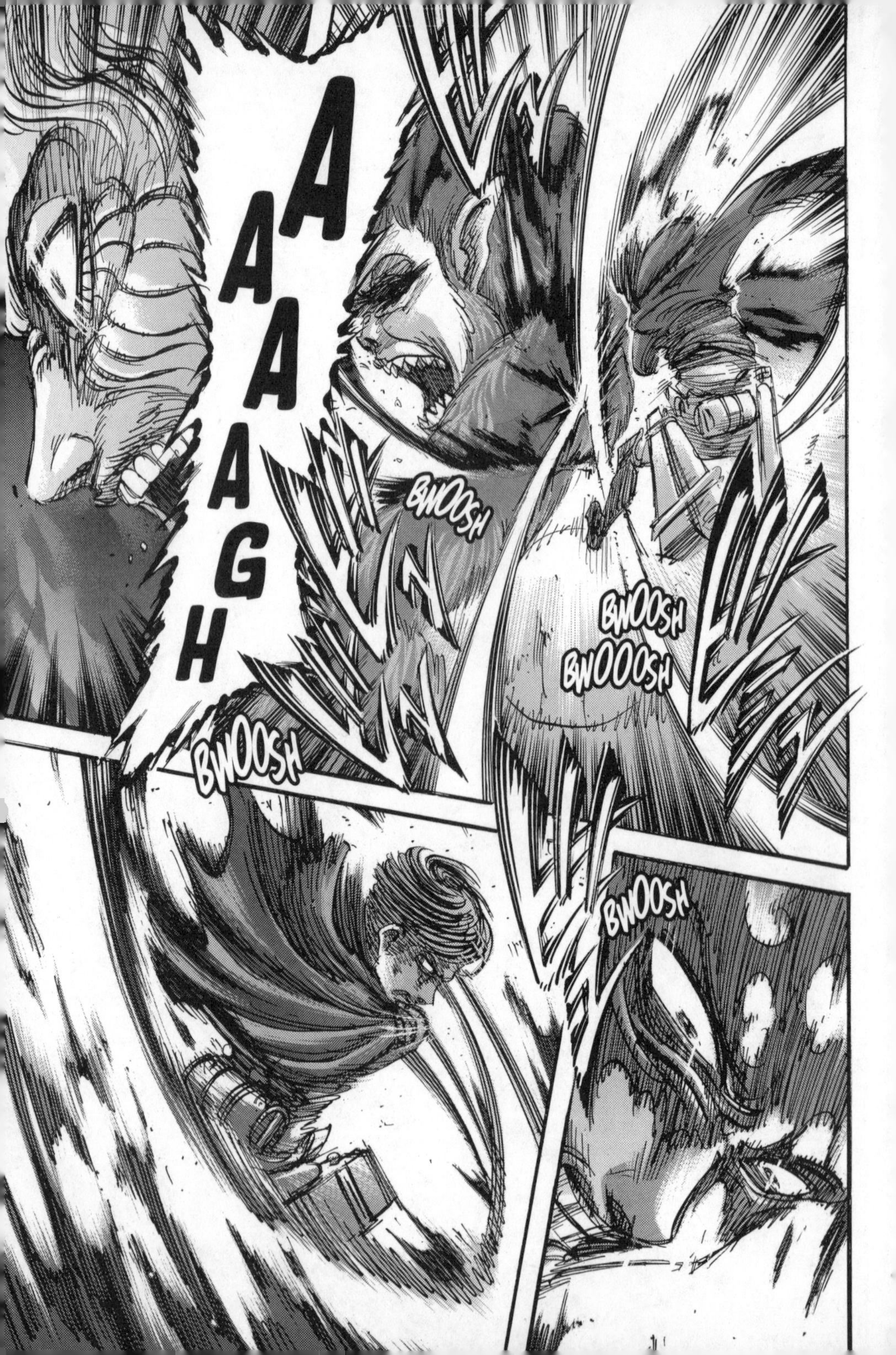
BWOOSH
BWOOOSH
BWOOSH
AAAAAGH
BWOOSH
BWOOSH

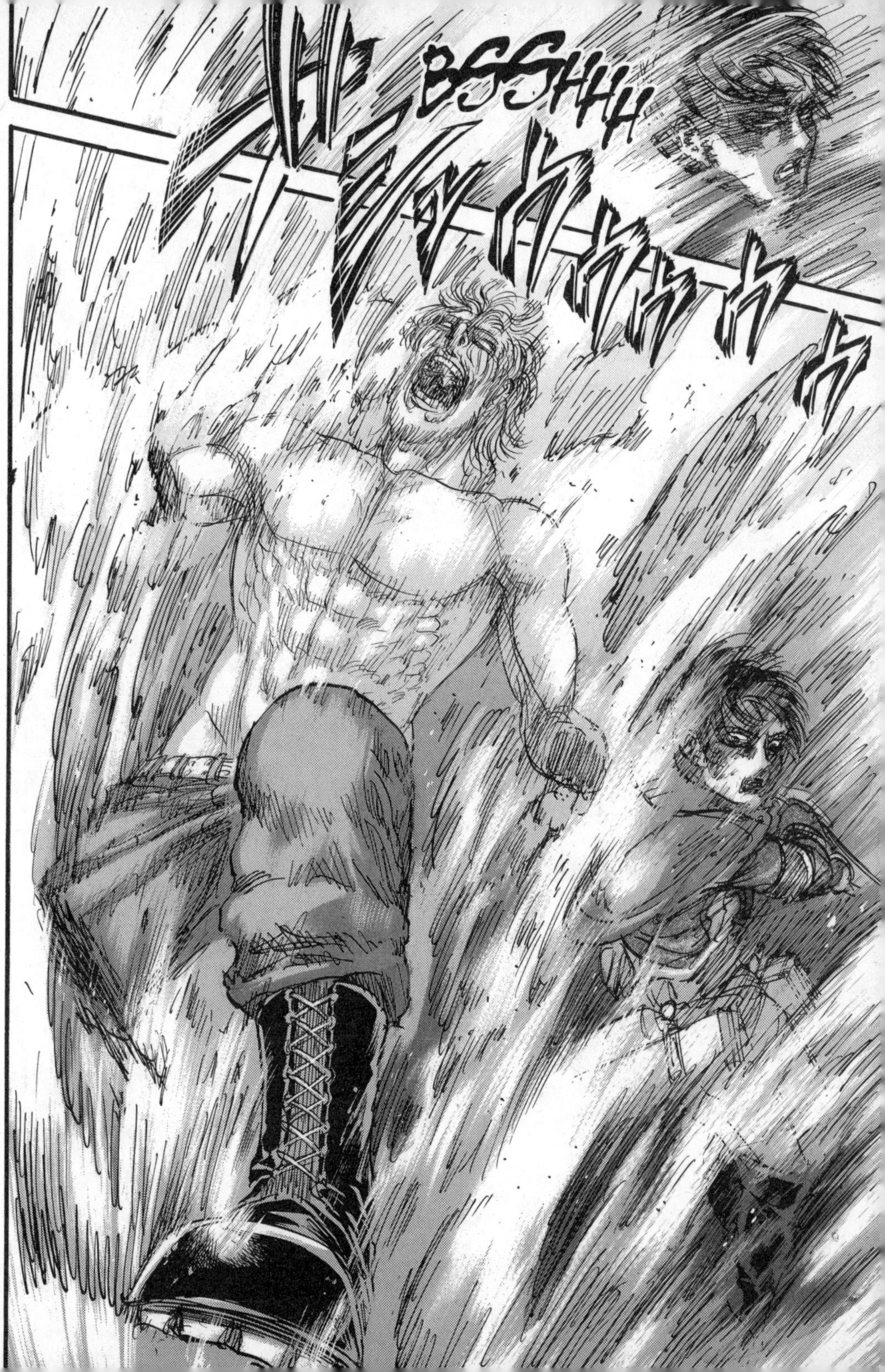

BSSHHH

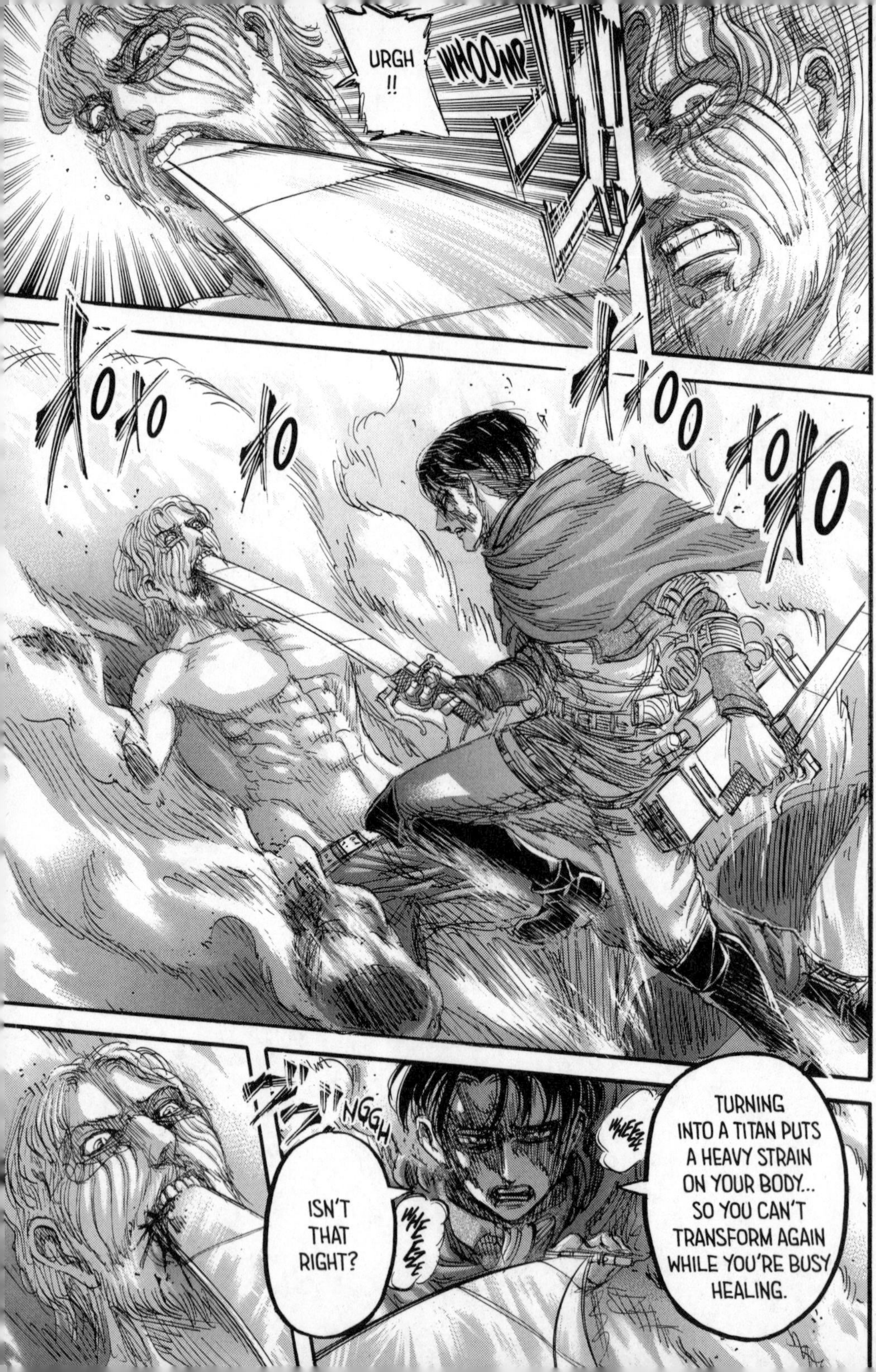
WHOOMP
URGH !!
TURNING INTO A TITAN PUTS A HEAVY STRAIN ON YOUR BODY... SO YOU CAN'T TRANSFORM AGAIN WHILE YOU'RE BUSY HEALING.
ISN'T THAT RIGHT?
NGGH

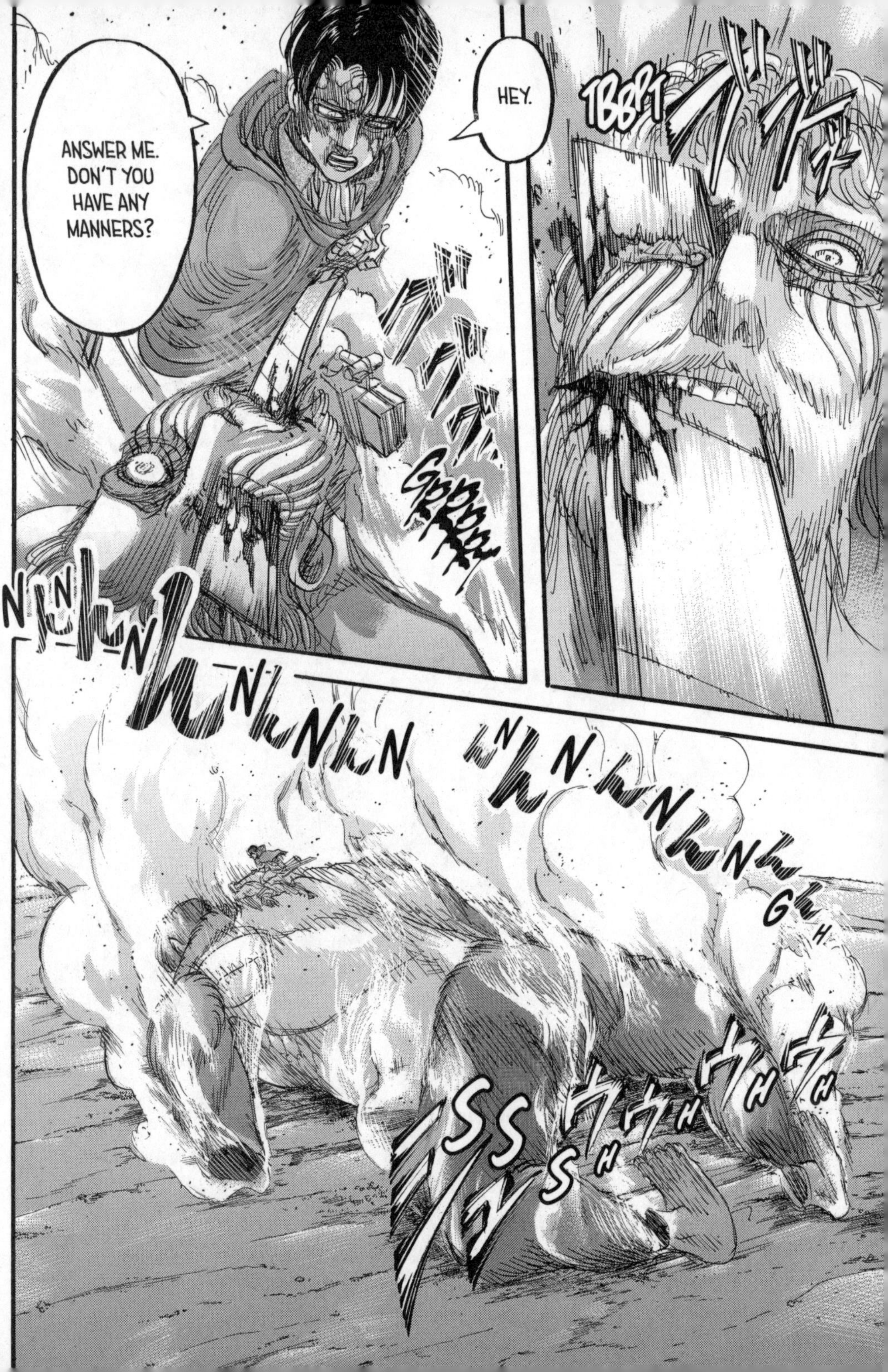
TBBPT
HEY.
ANSWER ME. DON'T YOU HAVE ANY MANNERS?
GRRRR
NNNNNNNNNNNNNNNNNNGH
SSSHH

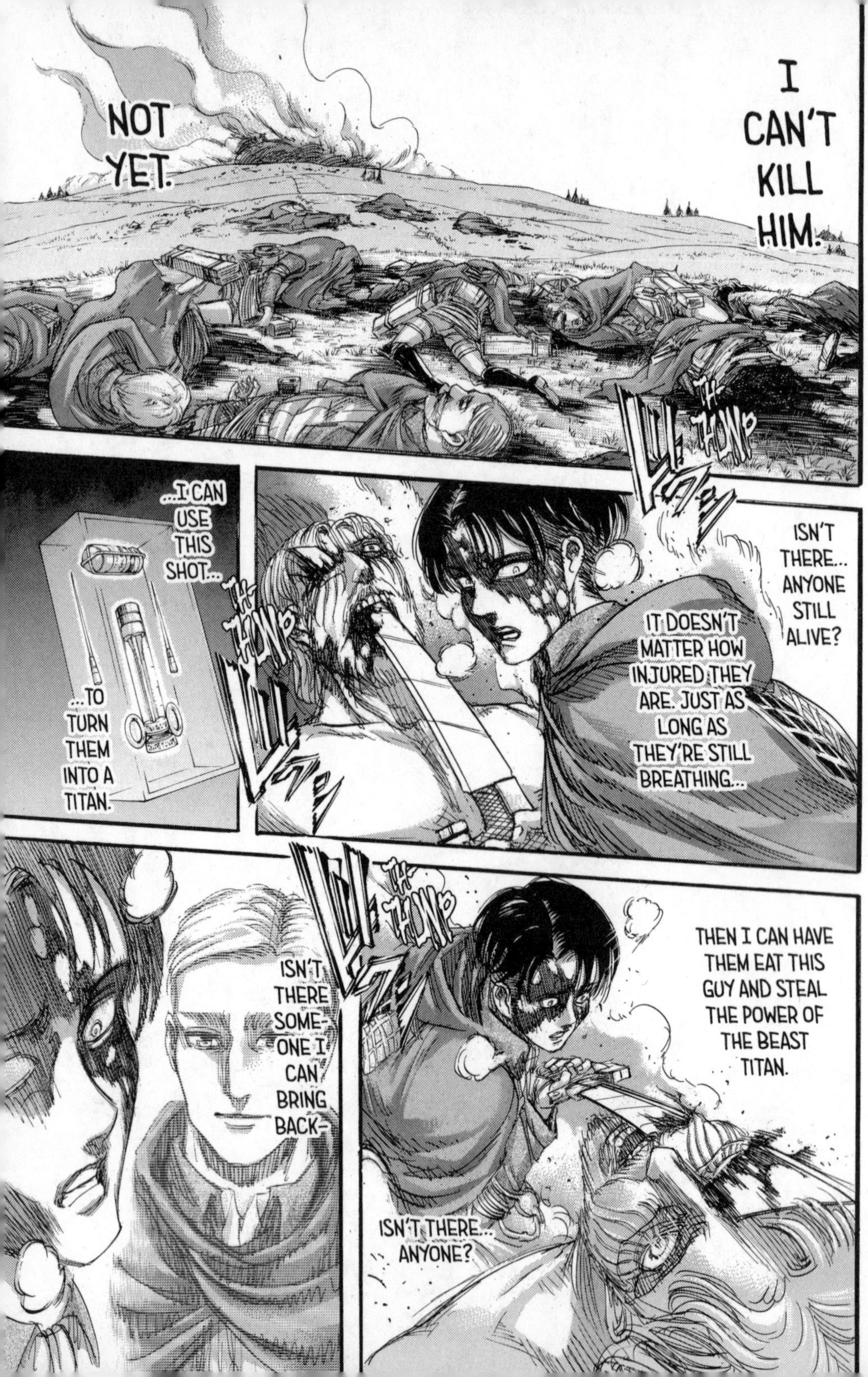
I CAN'T KILL HIM.
NOT YET.
TH-THUNK
ISN'T THERE... ANYONE STILL ALIVE?
IT DOESN'T MATTER HOW INJURED THEY ARE. JUST AS LONG AS THEY'RE STILL BREATHING...
TH-THUNK
...I CAN USE THIS SHOT...
...TO TURN THEM INTO A TITAN.
TH-THUNK
THEN I CAN HAVE THEM EAT THIS GUY AND STEAL THE POWER OF THE BEAST TITAN.
ISN'T THERE... ANYONE?
ISN'T THERE SOMEONE I CAN BRING BACK-

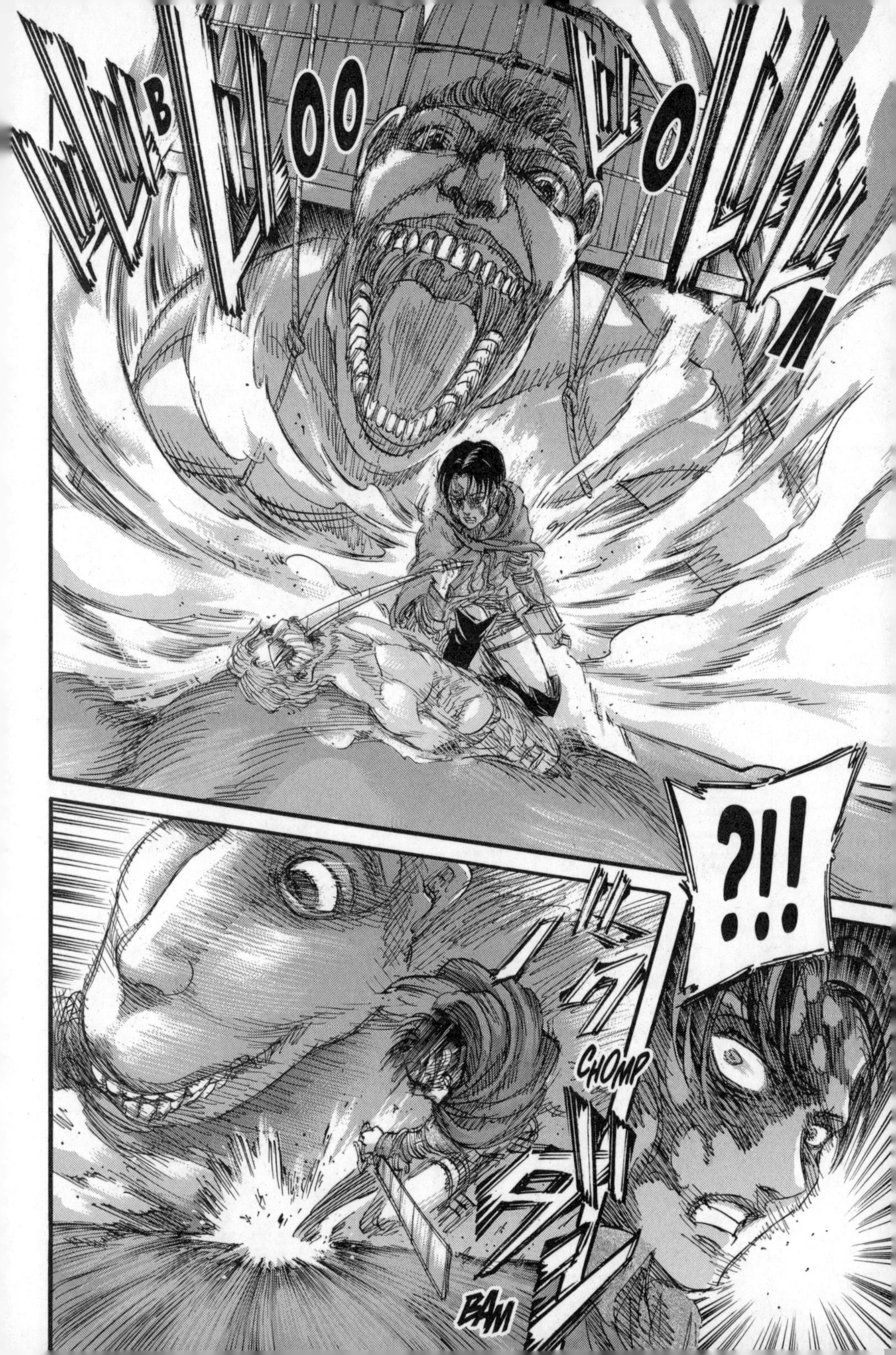
?!!
CHOMP
BAM

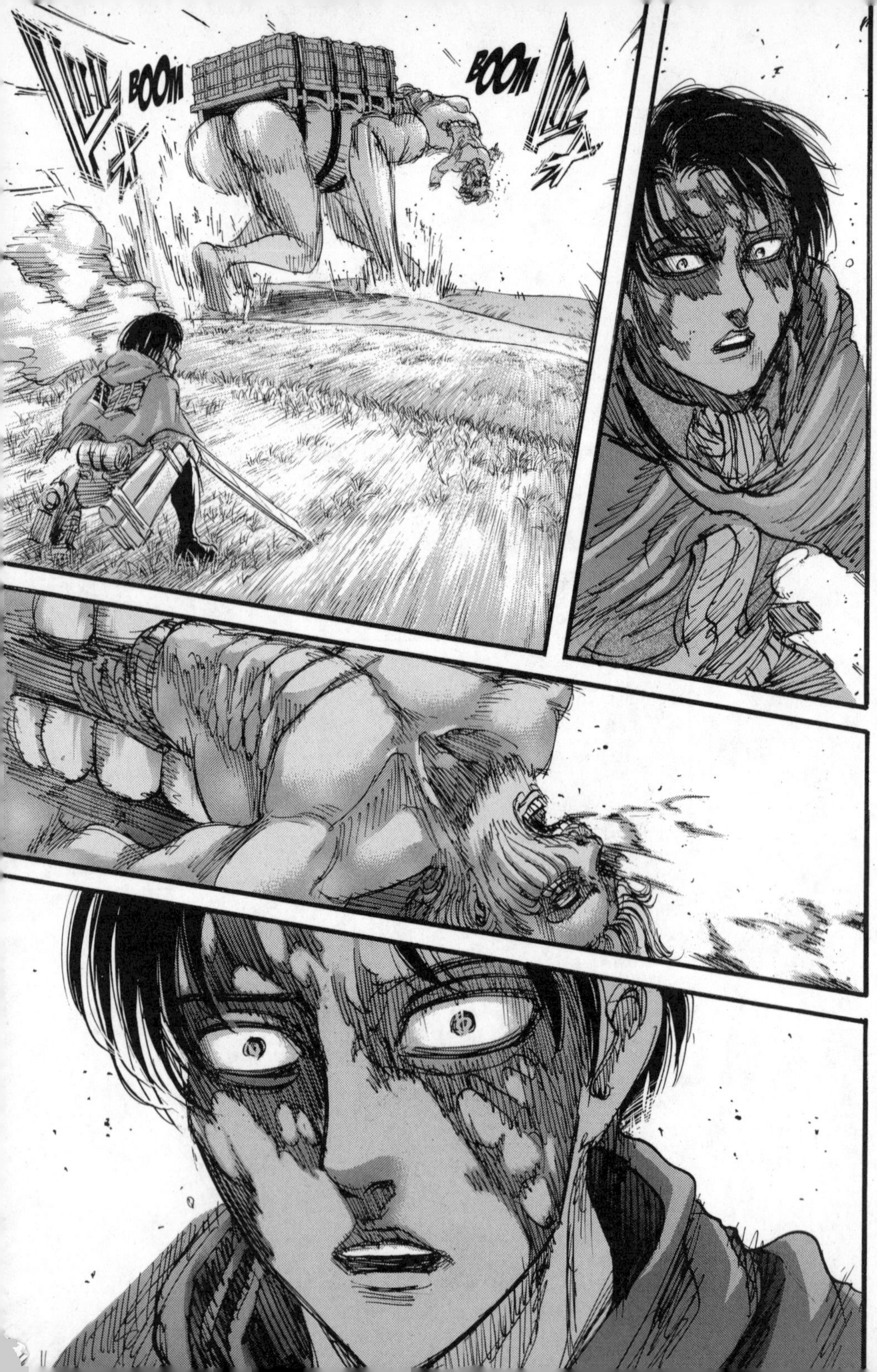
BOOM
BOOM

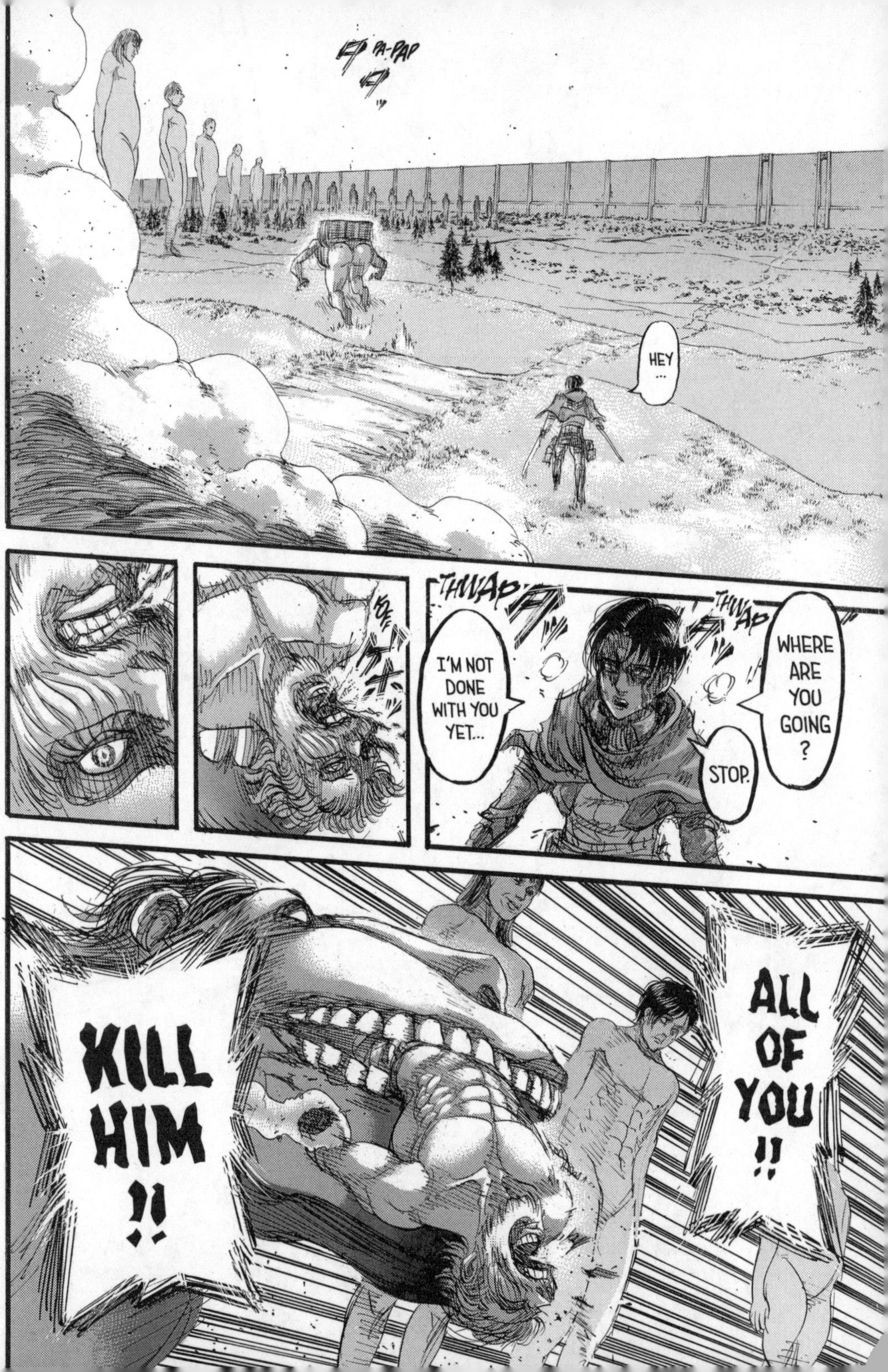
PA-PAP
HEY ...
THWAP
THWAP
WHERE ARE YOU GOING ?
STOP.
I'M NOT DONE WITH YOU YET...
KOFF
ALL OF YOU !!
KILL HIM !!

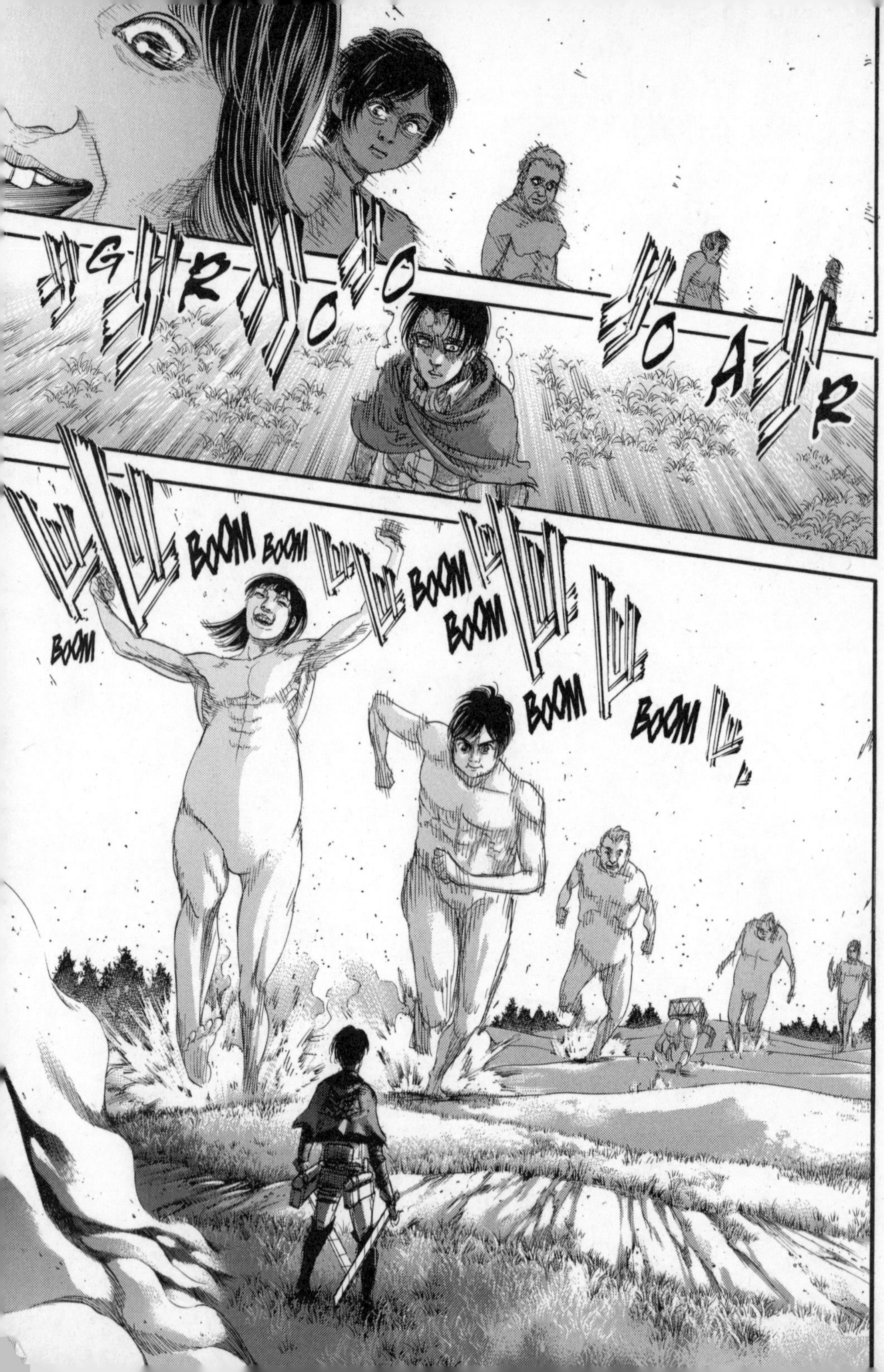

GROOOAR
BOOM
BOOM
BOOM
BOOM
BOOM
BOOM
BOOM

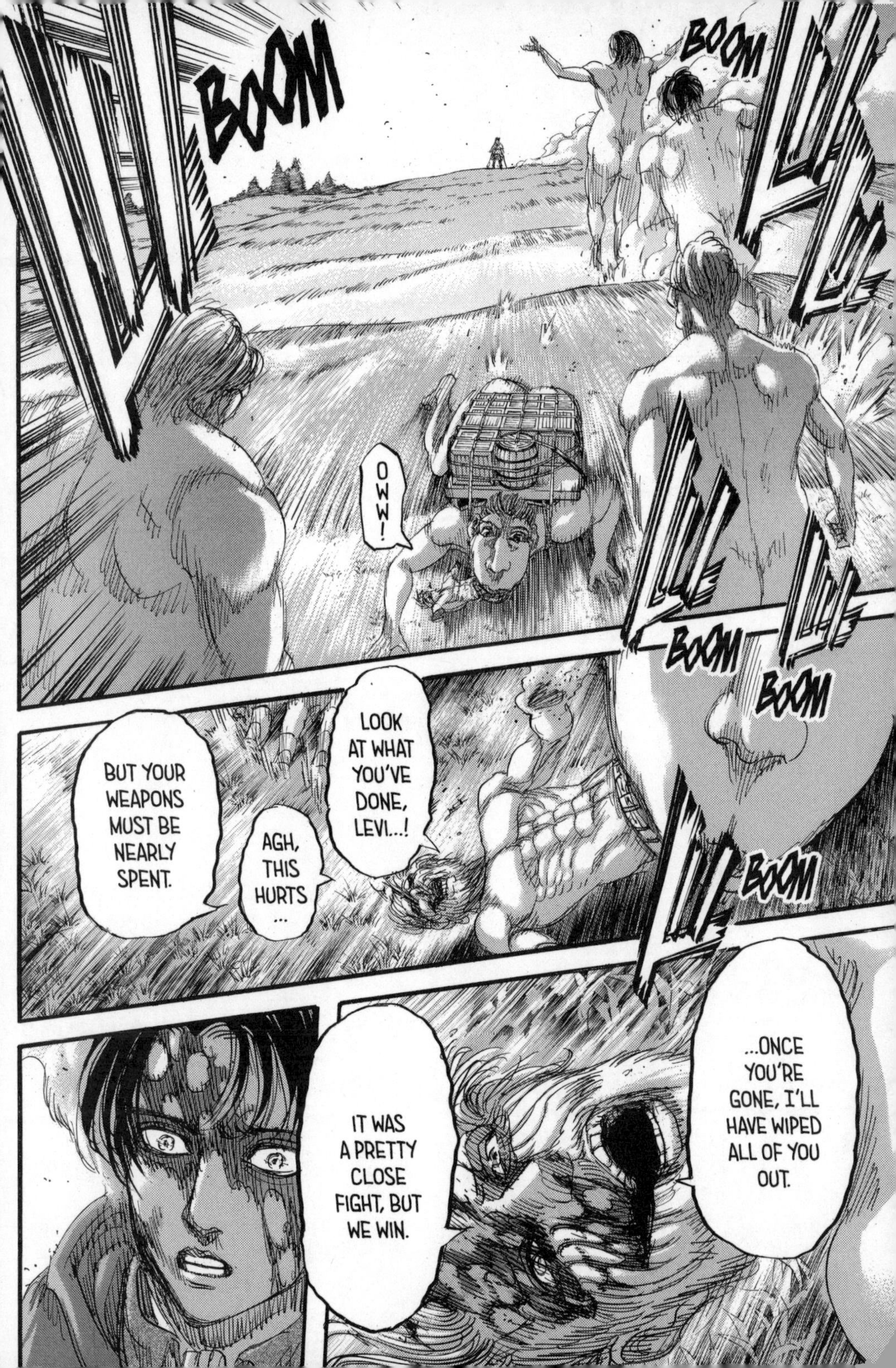
BOOM
BOOM
OWW!
BOOM
BOOM
BOOM
LOOK AT WHAT YOU'VE DONE, LEVI...!
AGH, THIS HURTS ...
BUT YOUR WEAPONS MUST BE NEARLY SPENT.
...ONCE YOU'RE GONE, I'LL HAVE WIPED ALL OF YOU OUT.
IT WAS A PRETTY CLOSE FIGHT, BUT WE WIN.

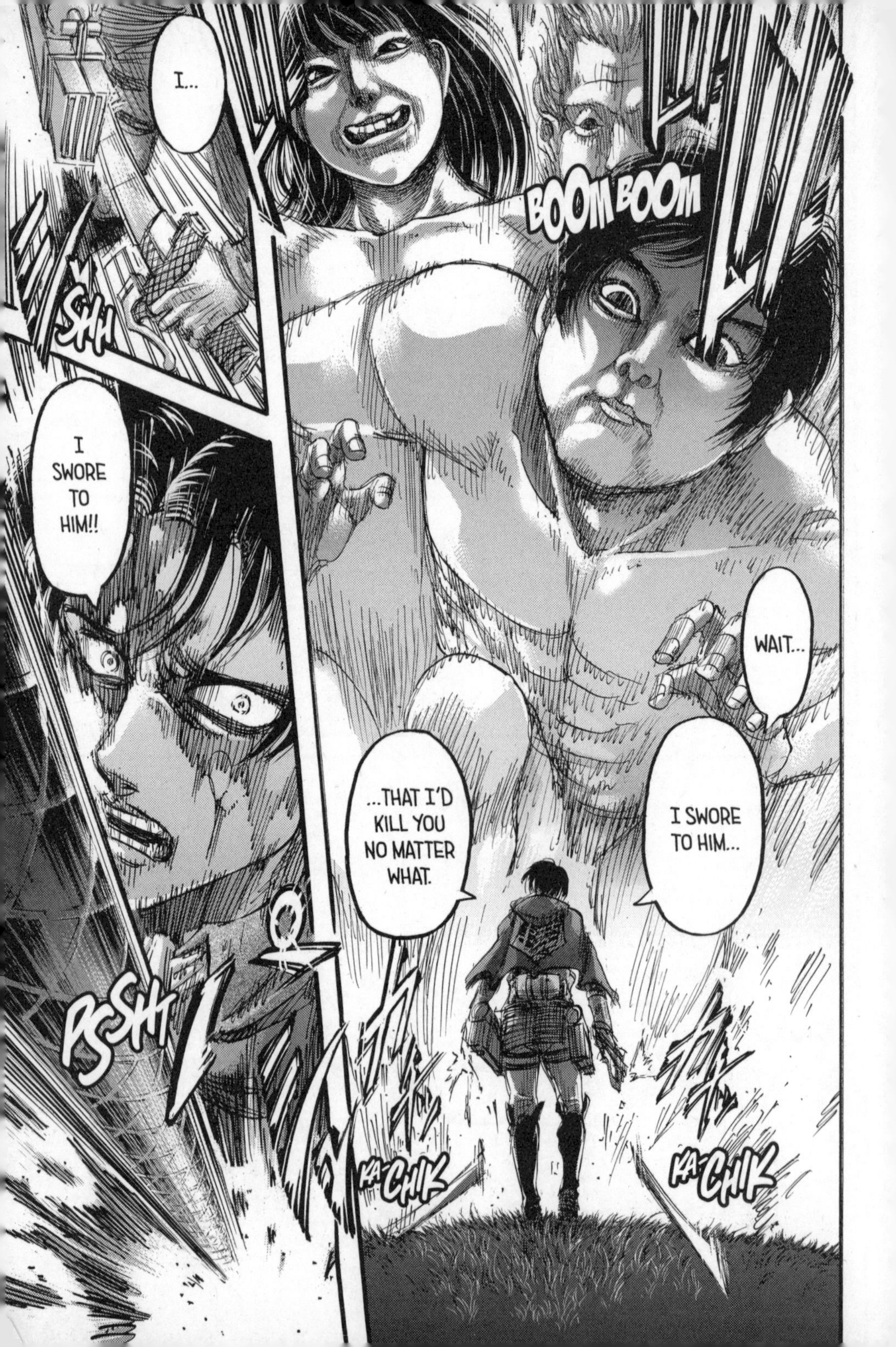
BOOM BOOM
WAIT...
I SWORE TO HIM...
...THAT I'D KILL YOU NO MATTER WHAT.
KA-CHIK
KA-CHIK
I...
SHH
I SWORE TO HIM!!
PSSHT

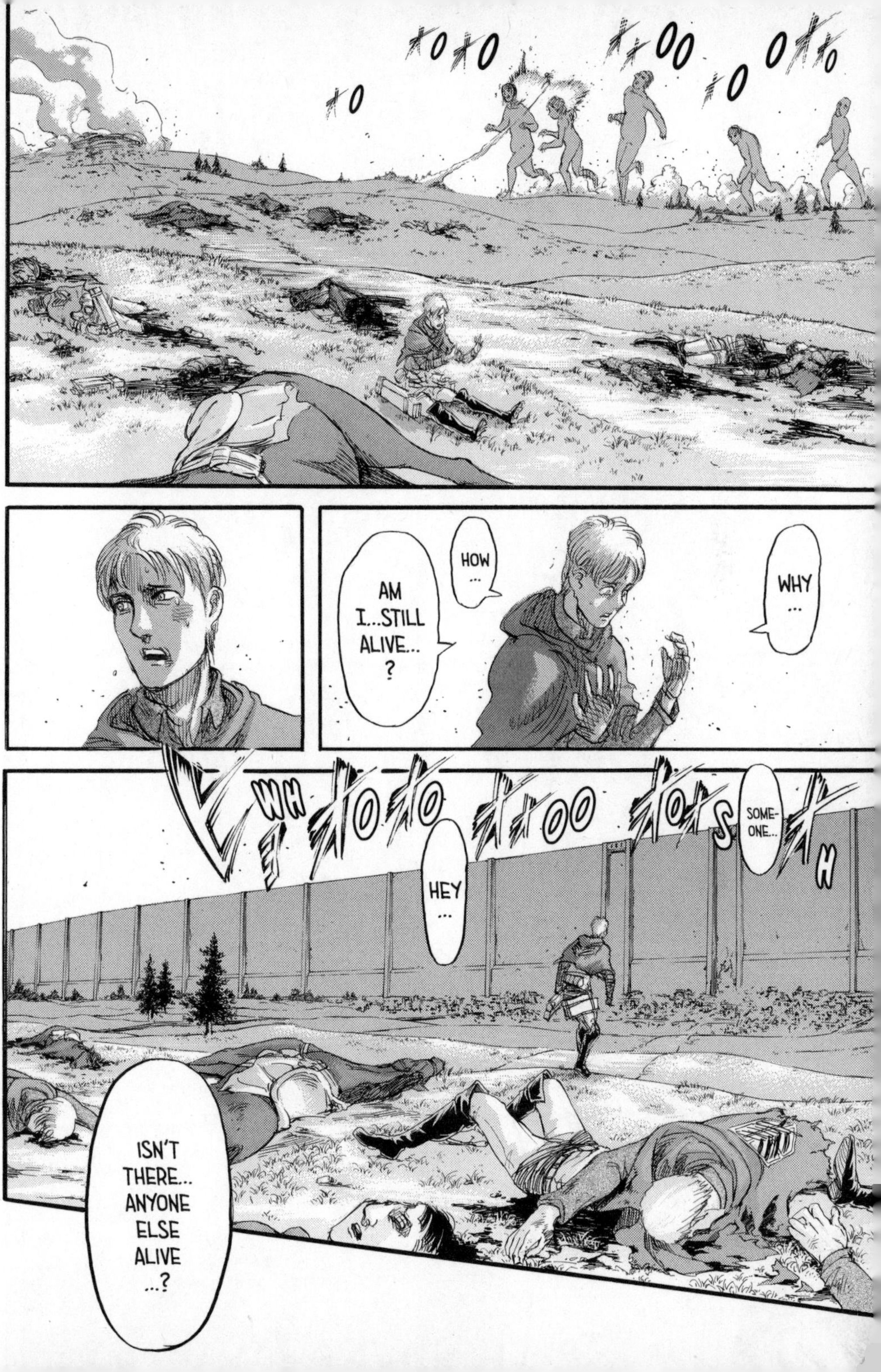
WHY ...
HOW ...
AM I...STILL ALIVE... ?
SOME-ONE...
HEY ...
ISN'T THERE... ANYONE ELSE ALIVE ...?

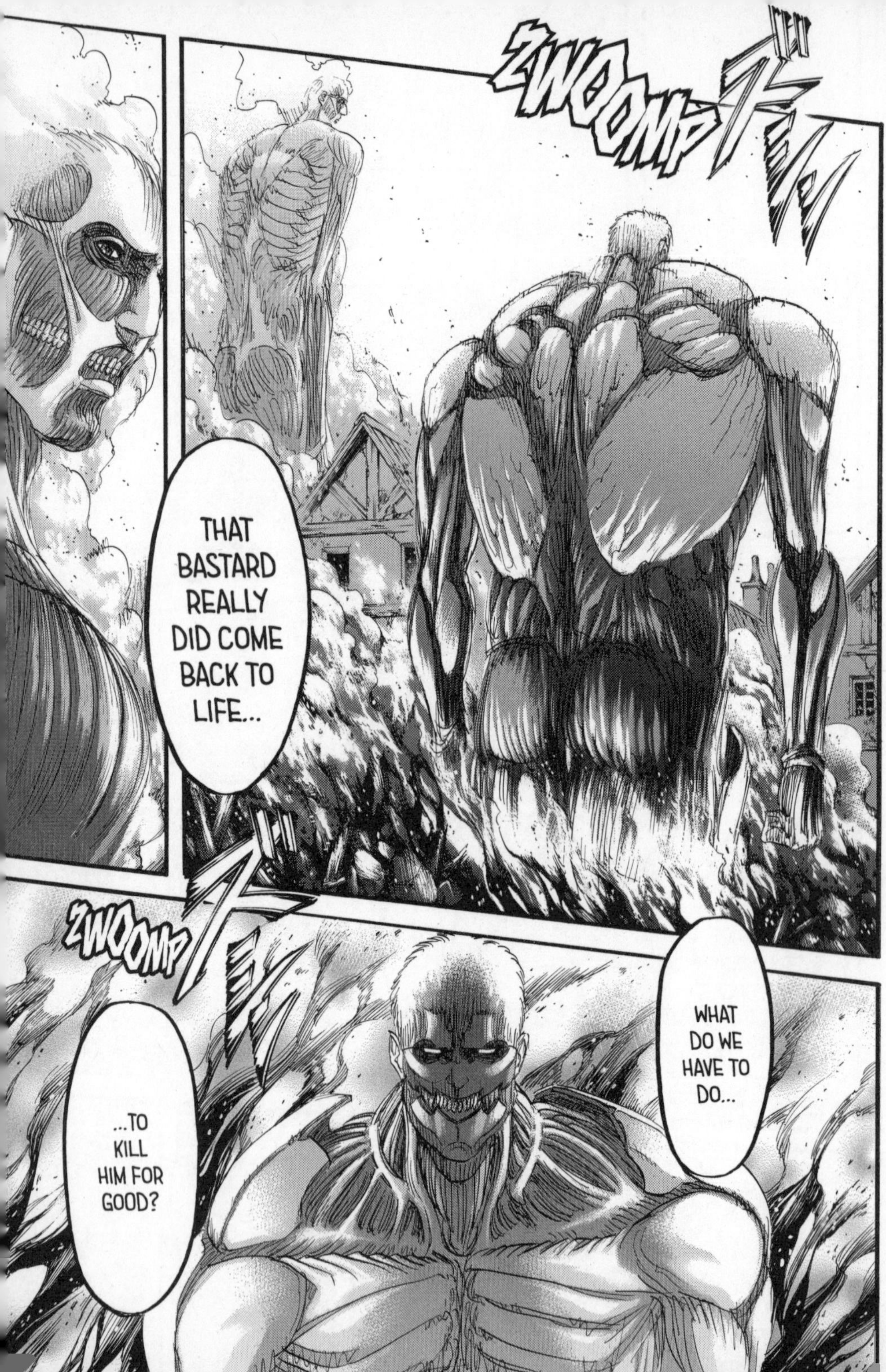
ZWOOMP
THAT BASTARD REALLY DID COME BACK TO LIFE...
ZWOOMP
WHAT DO WE HAVE TO DO...
...TO KILL HIM FOR GOOD?

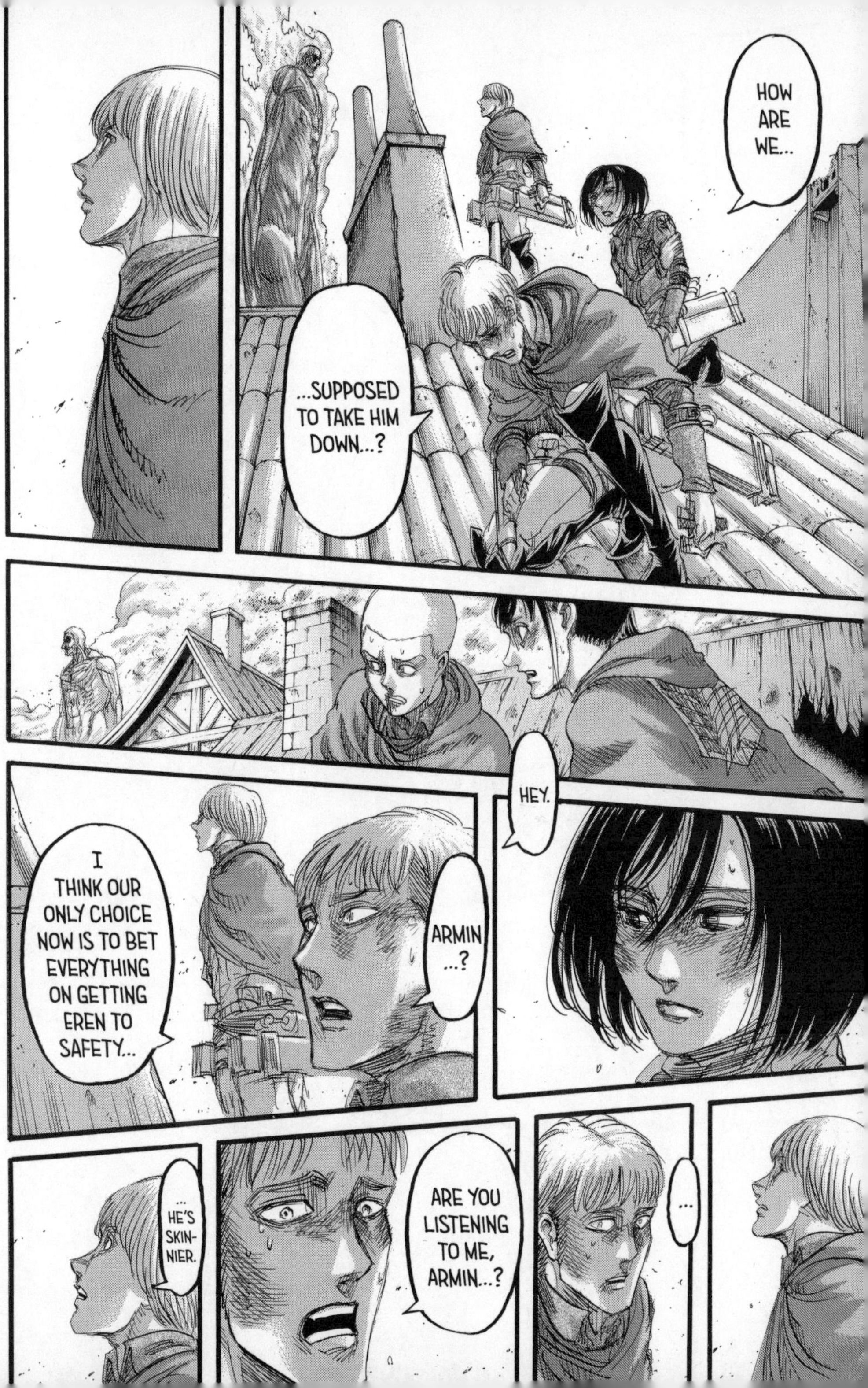
HOW ARE WE...
...SUPPOSED TO TAKE HIM DOWN...?
HEY.
ARMIN ...?
I THINK OUR ONLY CHOICE NOW IS TO BET EVERYTHING ON GETTING EREN TO SAFETY...
...
ARE YOU LISTENING TO ME, ARMIN...?
... HE'S SKIN-NIER.

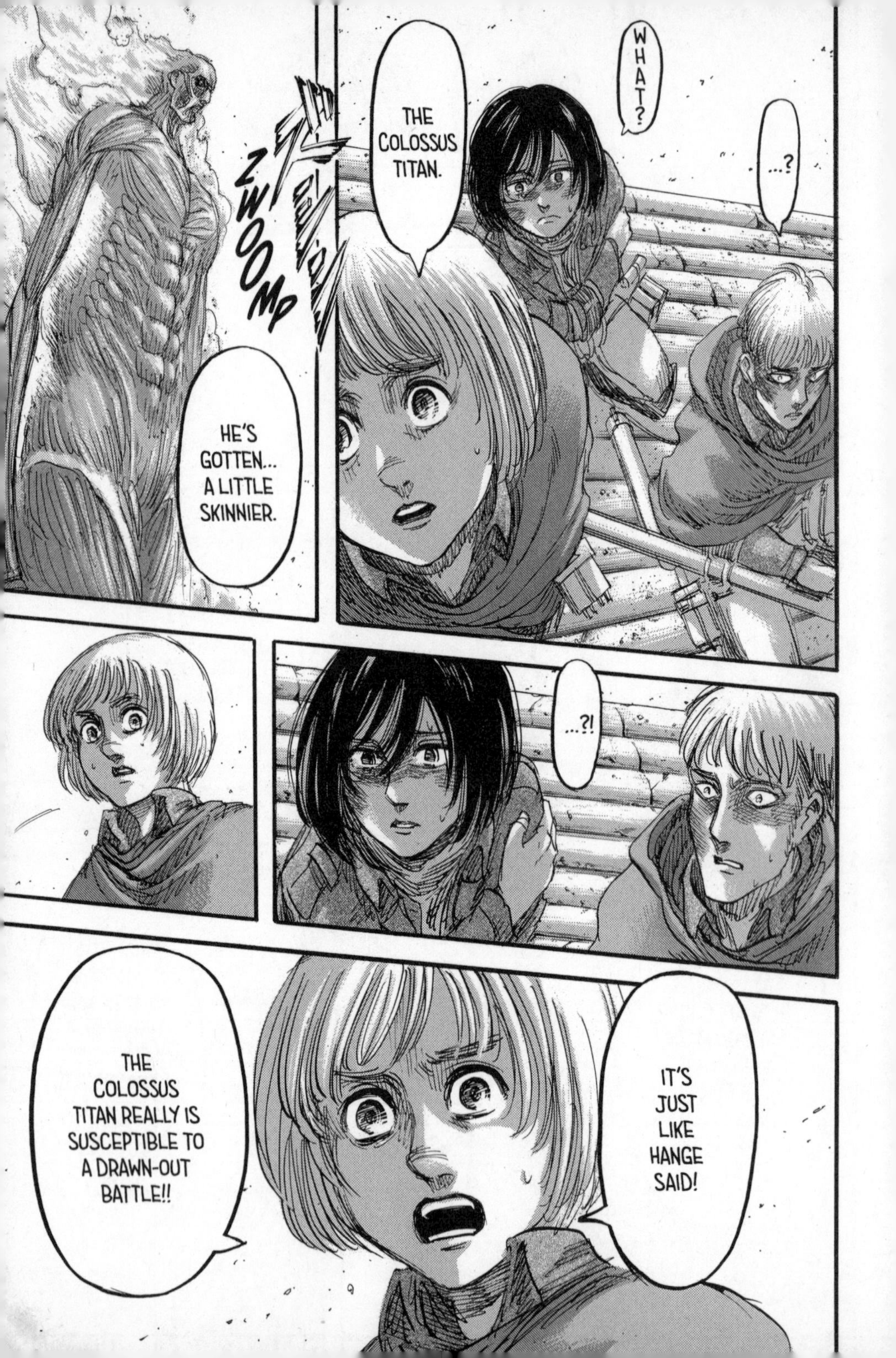
WHAT?
...?
THE COLOSSUS TITAN.
ZWOOOM
HE'S GOTTEN... A LITTLE SKINNIER.
...?!
IT'S JUST LIKE HANGE SAID!
THE COLOSSUS TITAN REALLY IS SUSCEPTIBLE TO A DRAWN-OUT BATTLE!!

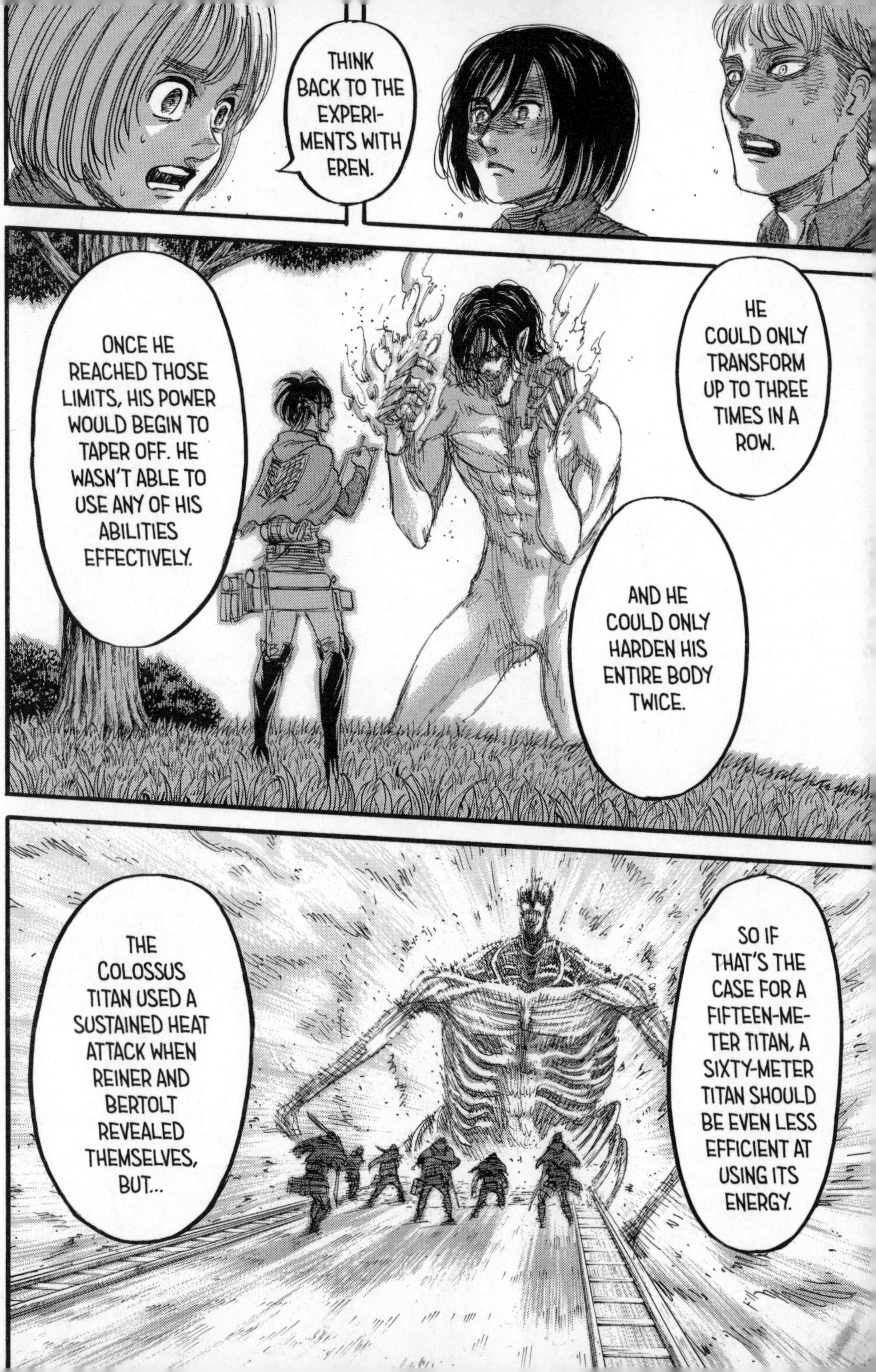
THINK BACK TO THE EXPERI-MENTS WITH EREN.
HE COULD ONLY TRANSFORM UP TO THREE TIMES IN A ROW.
AND HE COULD ONLY HARDEN HIS ENTIRE BODY TWICE.
ONCE HE REACHED THOSE LIMITS, HIS POWER WOULD BEGIN TO TAPER OFF. HE WASN'T ABLE TO USE ANY OF HIS ABILITIES EFFECTIVELY.
SO IF THAT'S THE CASE FOR A FIFTEEN-ME-TER TITAN, A SIXTY-METER TITAN SHOULD BE EVEN LESS EFFICIENT AT USING ITS ENERGY.
THE COLOSSUS TITAN USED A SUSTAINED HEAT ATTACK WHEN REINER AND BERTOLT REVEALED THEMSELVES, BUT...

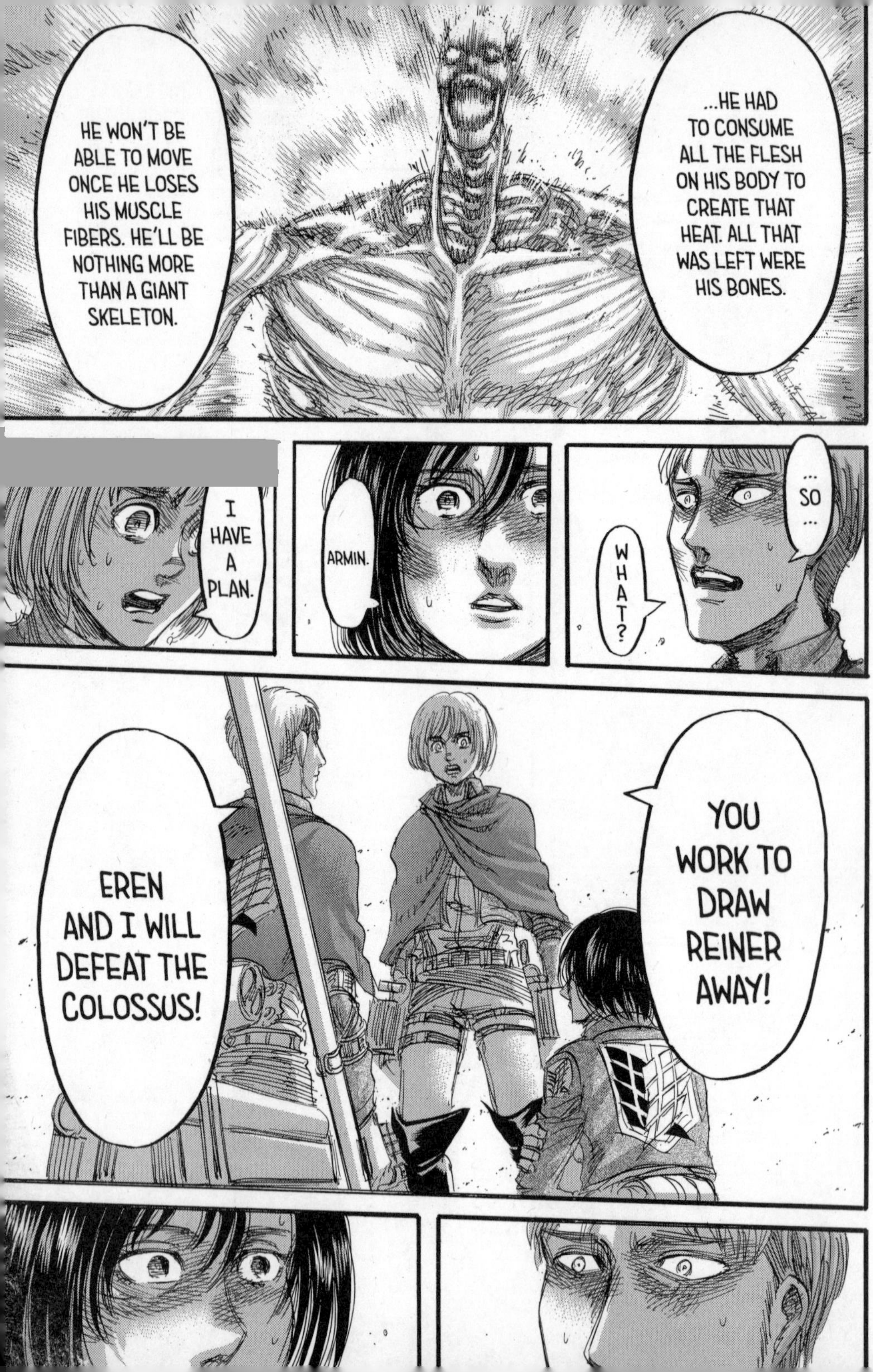
...HE HAD TO CONSUME ALL THE FLESH ON HIS BODY TO CREATE THAT HEAT. ALL THAT WAS LEFT WERE HIS BONES.
HE WON'T BE ABLE TO MOVE ONCE HE LOSES HIS MUSCLE FIBERS. HE'LL BE NOTHING MORE THAN A GIANT SKELETON.
... SO ...
WHAT?
ARMIN.
I HAVE A PLAN.
YOU WORK TO DRAW REINER AWAY!
EREN AND I WILL DEFEAT THE COLOSSUS!

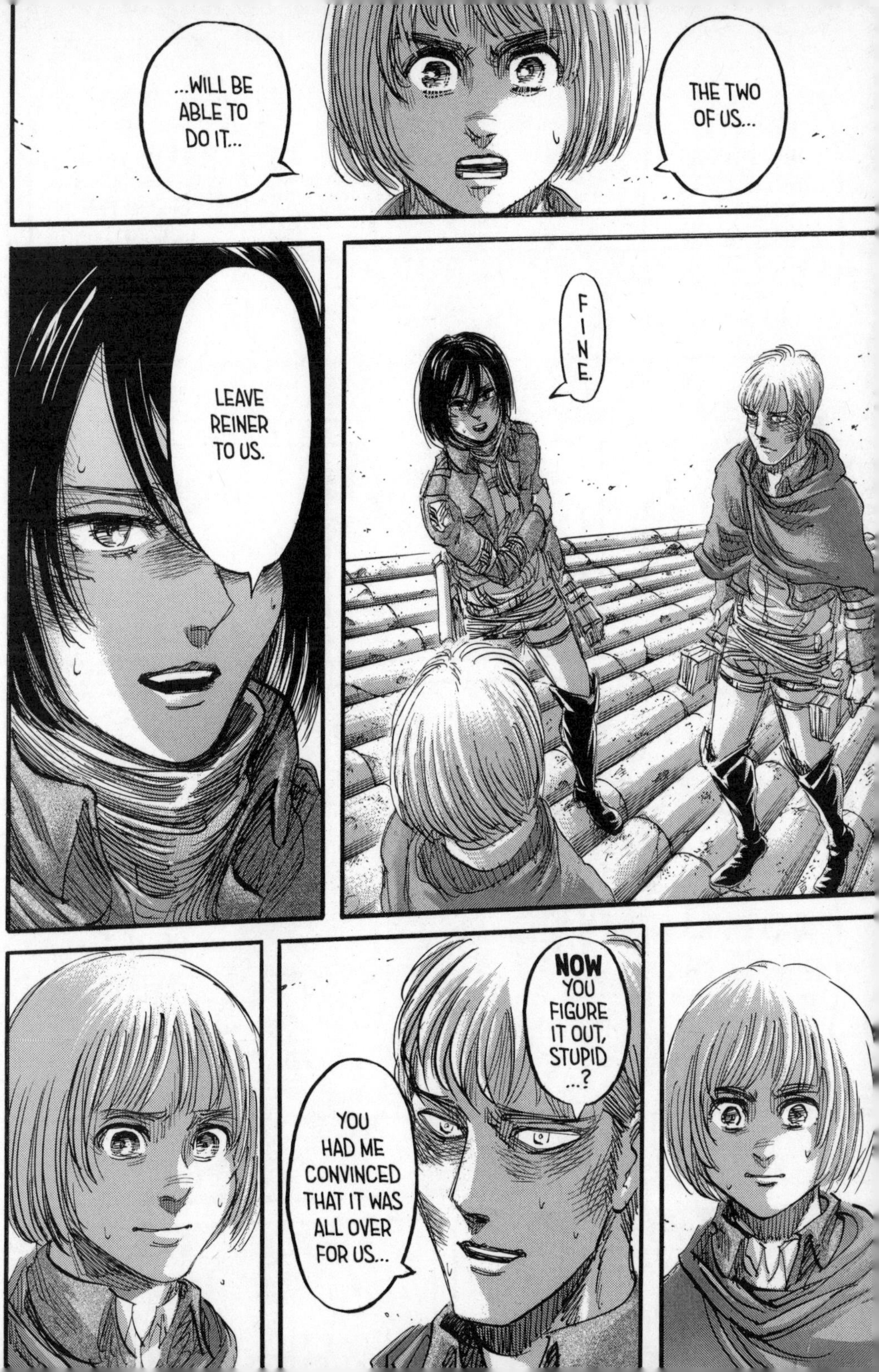
THE TWO OF US...
...WILL BE ABLE TO DO IT...
FINE.
LEAVE REINER TO US.
NOW YOU FIGURE IT OUT, STUPID ...?
YOU HAD ME CONVINCED THAT IT WAS ALL OVER FOR US...

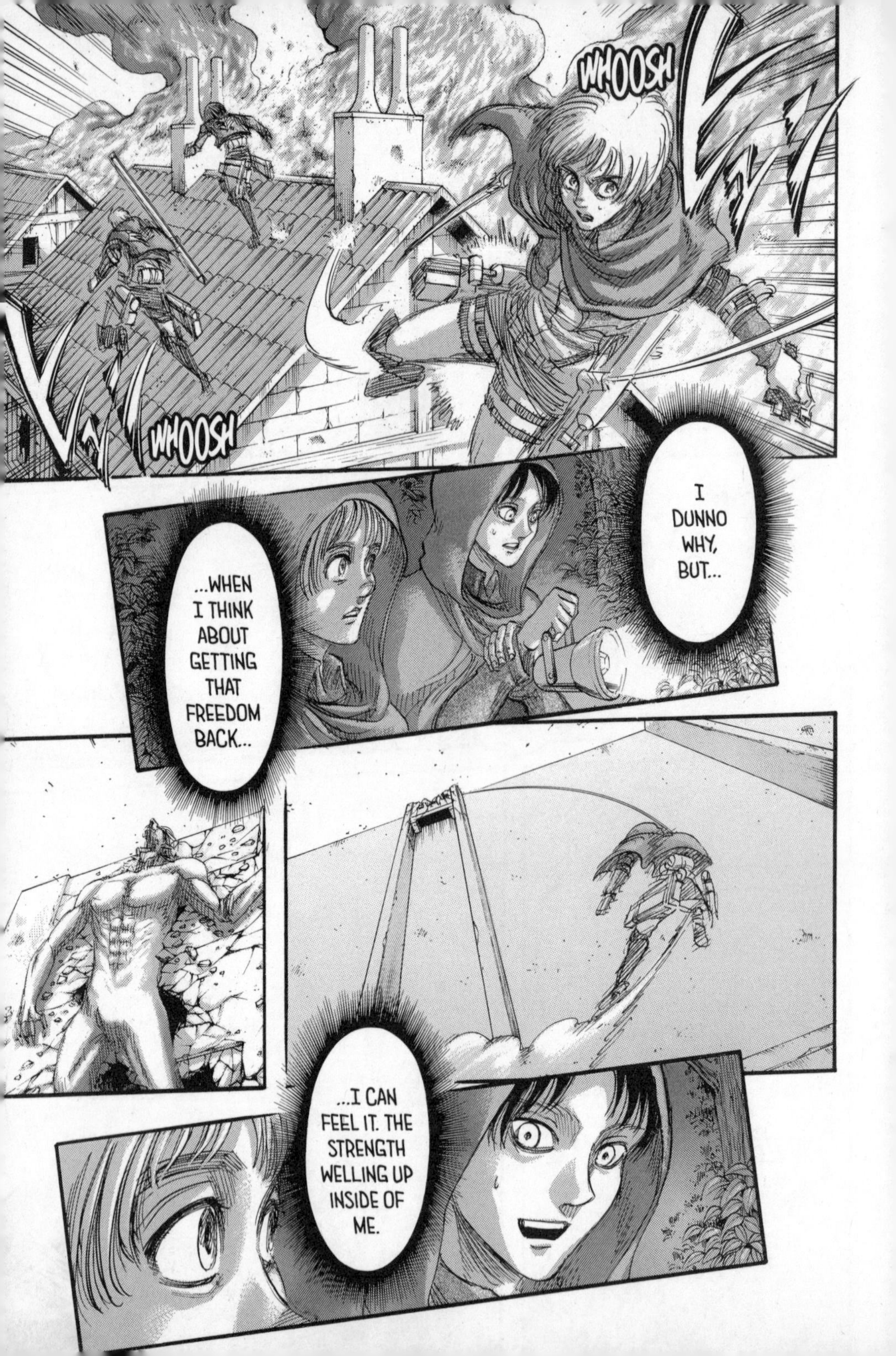
WHOOSH
WHOOSH
I DUNNO WHY, BUT...
...WHEN I THINK ABOUT GETTING THAT FREEDOM BACK...
...I CAN FEEL IT. THE STRENGTH WELLING UP INSIDE OF ME.

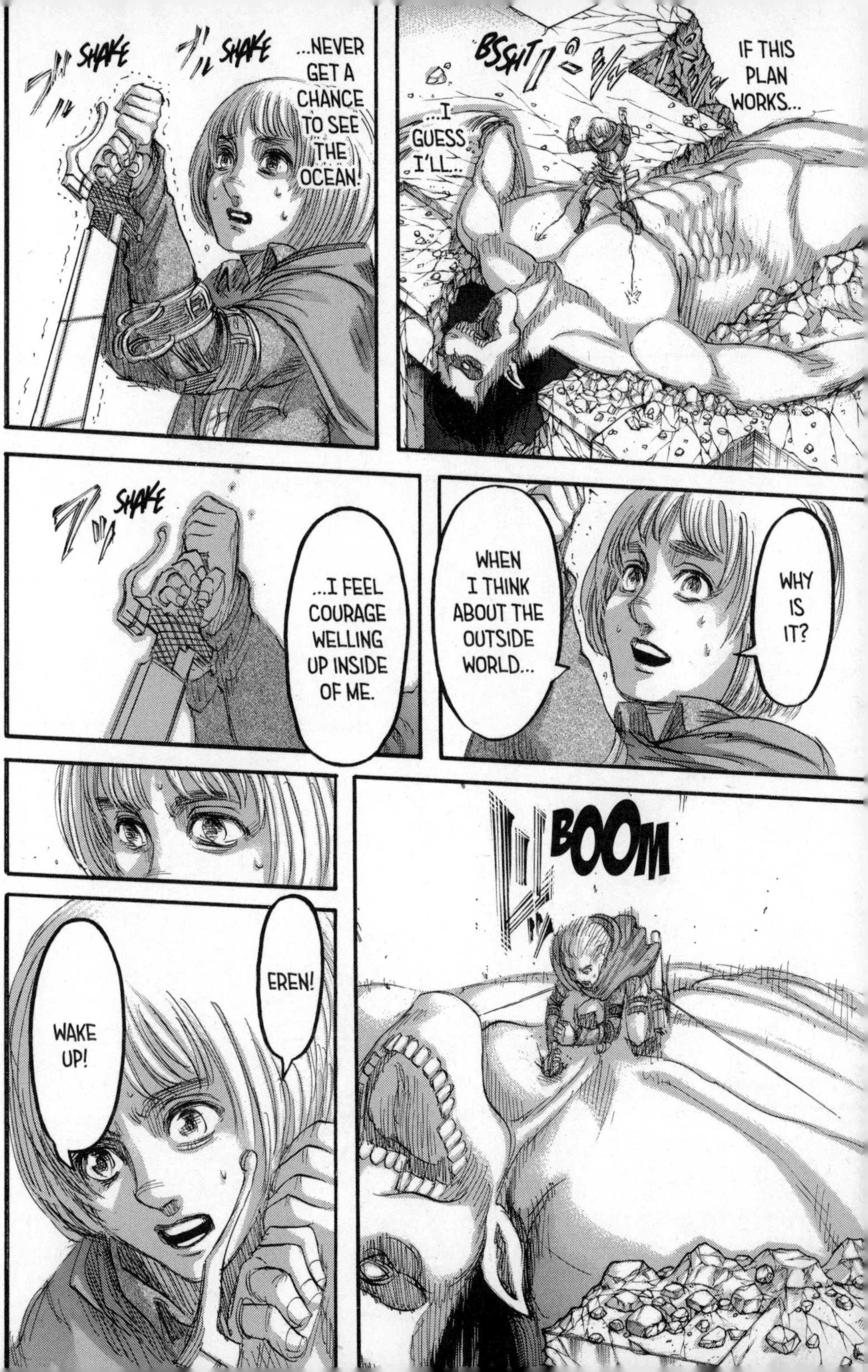
IF THIS PLAN WORKS...
BSSHT
...I GUESS I'LL...
...NEVER GET A CHANCE TO SEE THE OCEAN.
SHAKE
SHAKE
WHY IS IT?
WHEN I THINK ABOUT THE OUTSIDE WORLD...
...I FEEL COURAGE WELLING UP INSIDE OF ME.
SHAKE
BOOM
EREN!
WAKE UP!

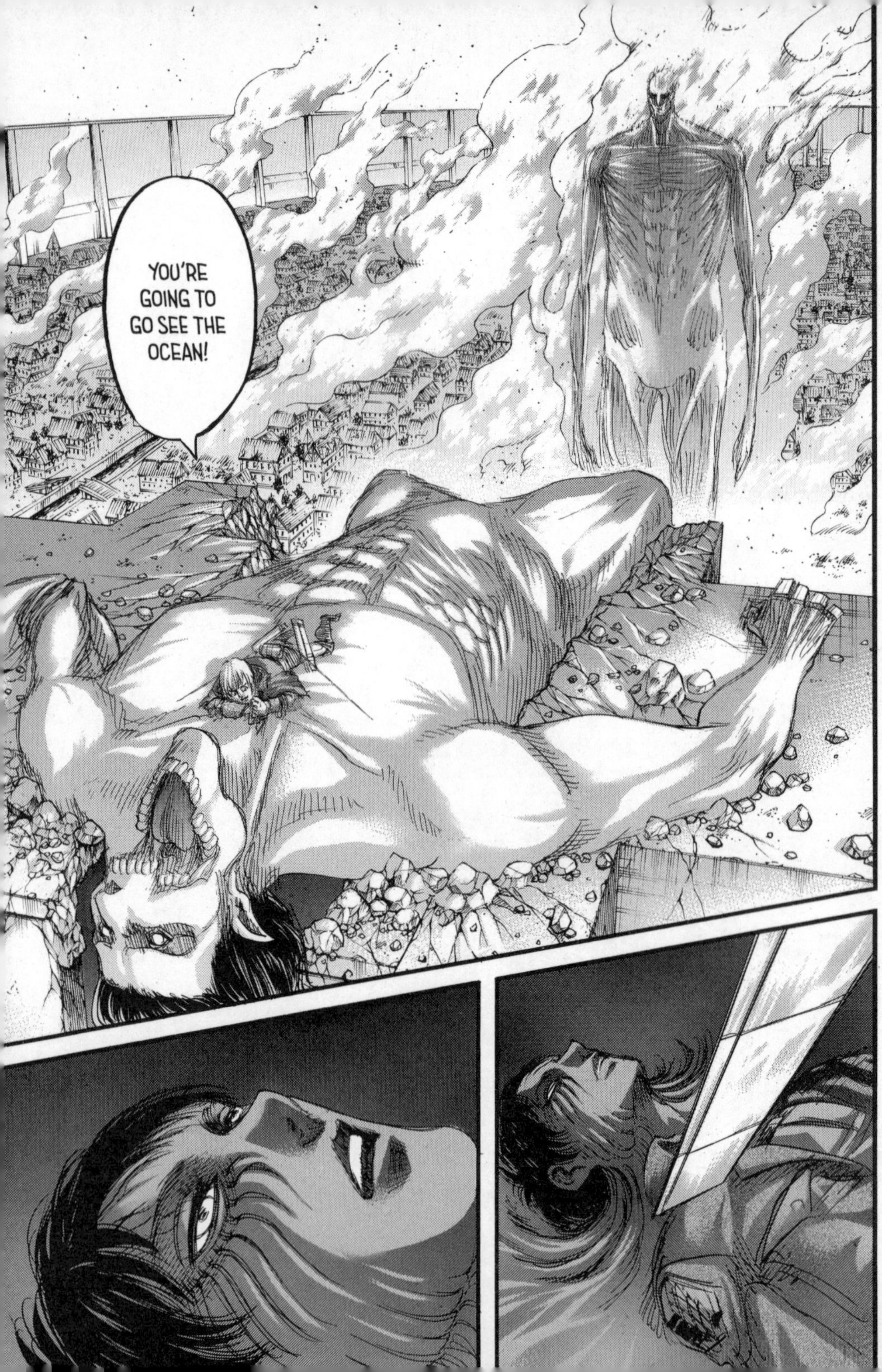
YOU'RE GOING TO GO SEE THE OCEAN!

ATTACK on TITAN

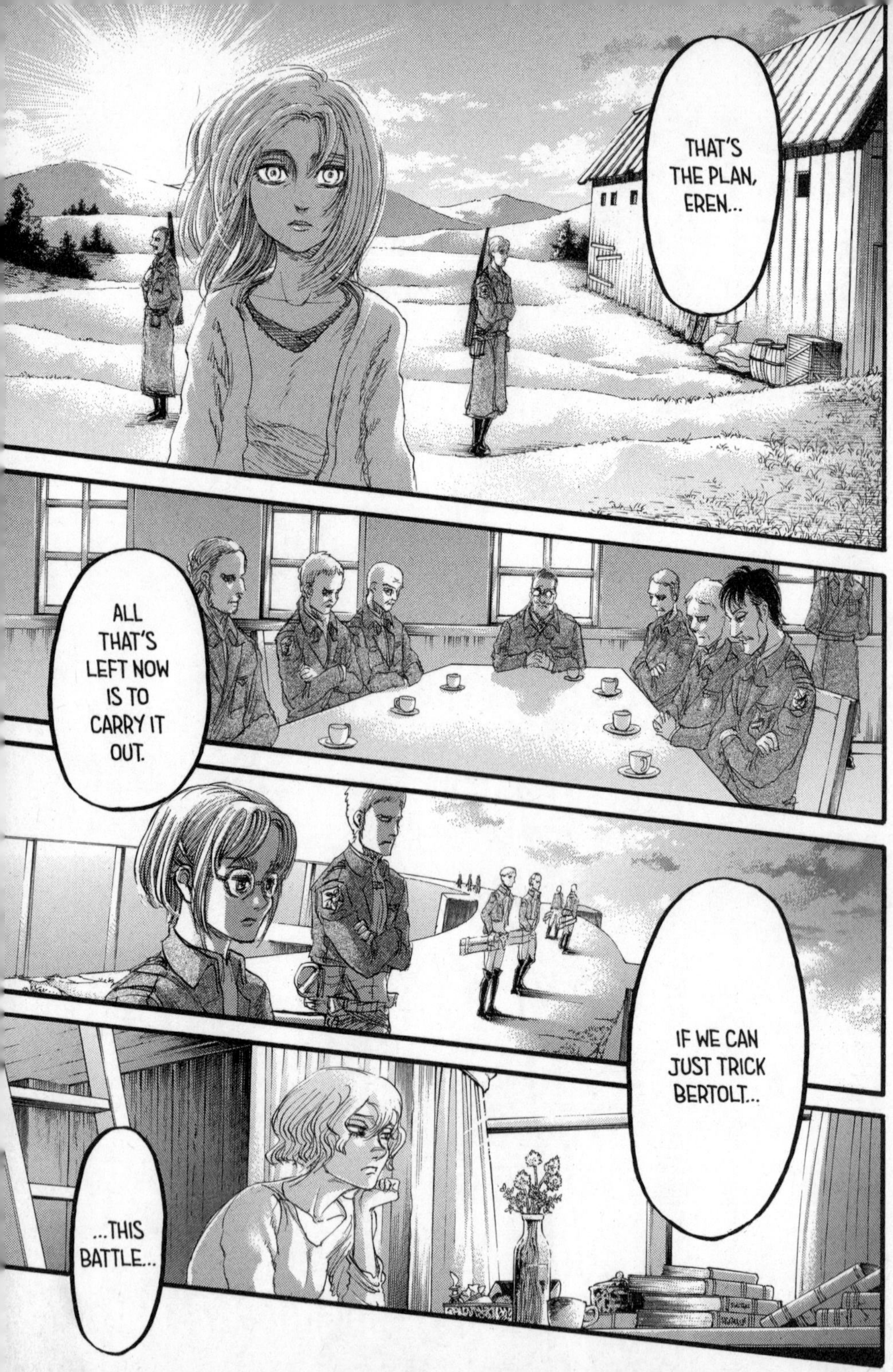
THAT'S THE PLAN, EREN...
ALL THAT'S LEFT NOW IS TO CARRY IT OUT.
IF WE CAN JUST TRICK BERTOLT...
...THIS BATTLE...

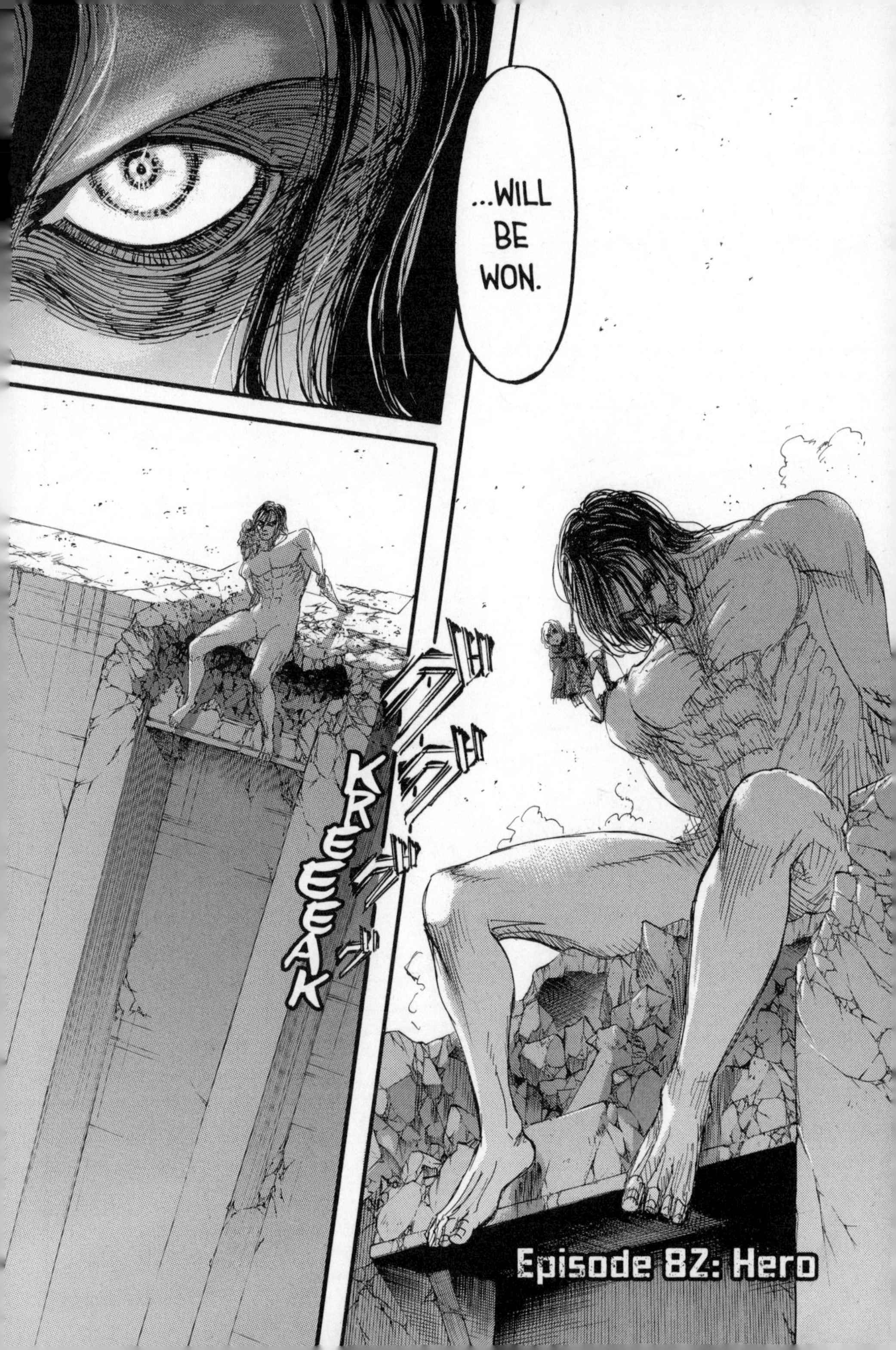
...WILL BE WON.
KREEEEAK

Episode 82: Hero

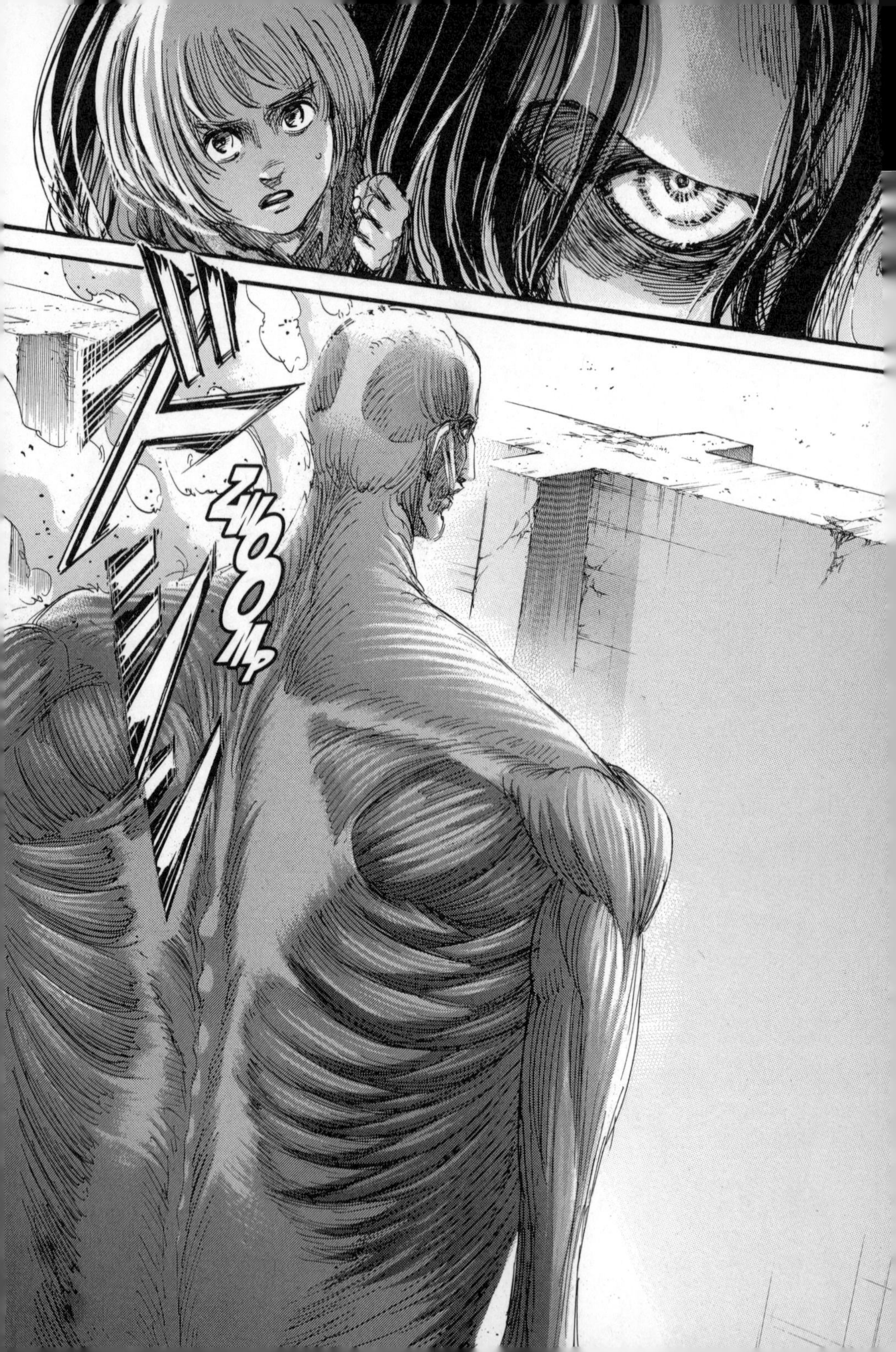
ZWOOOMP

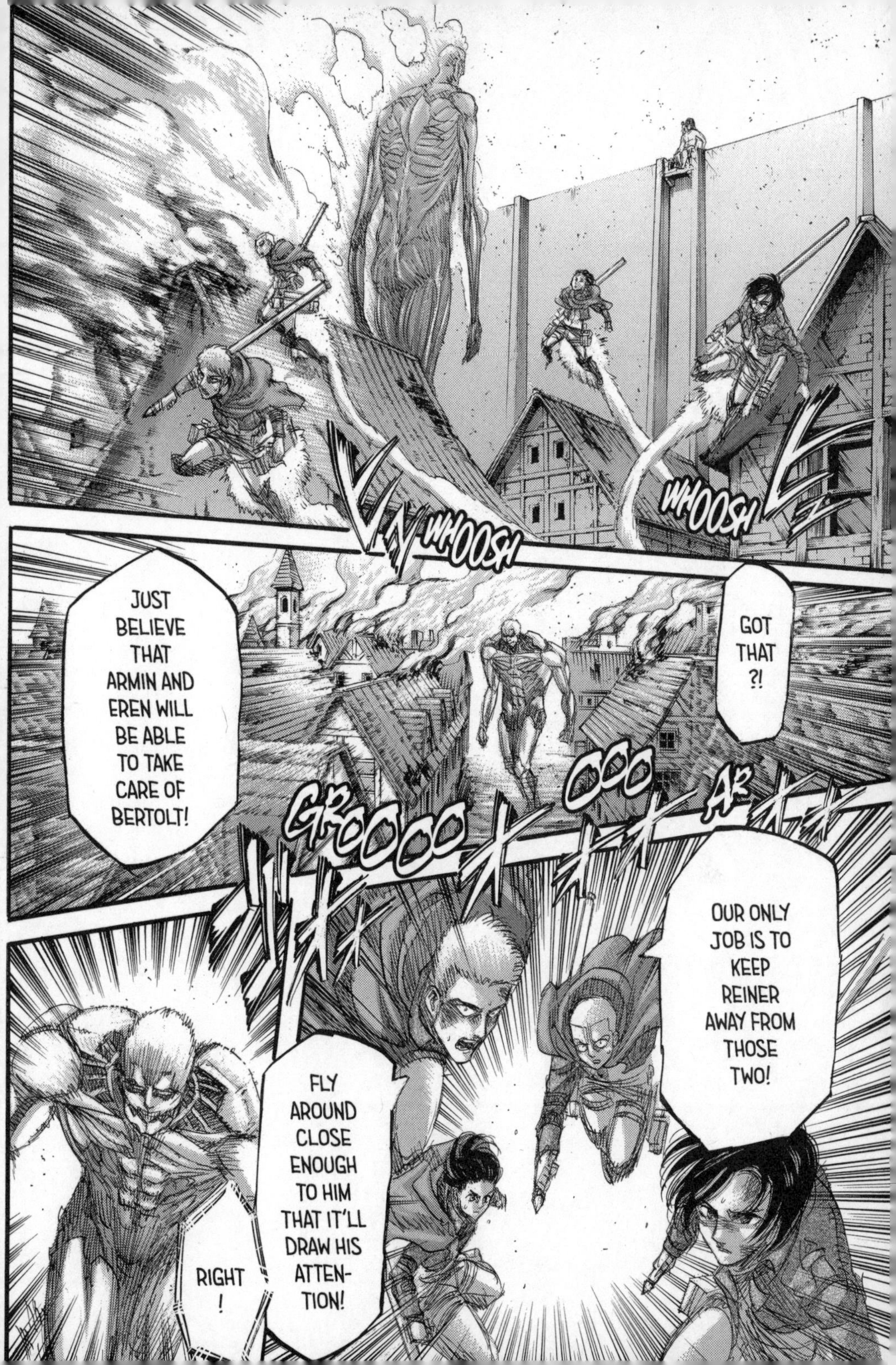

WHOOSH
WHOOSH
GOT THAT?!
JUST BELIEVE THAT ARMIN AND EREN WILL BE ABLE TO TAKE CARE OF BERTOLT!
GROOOOOOOOAR
OUR ONLY JOB IS TO KEEP REINER AWAY FROM THOSE TWO!
FLY AROUND CLOSE ENOUGH TO HIM THAT IT'LL DRAW HIS ATTENTION!
RIGHT!

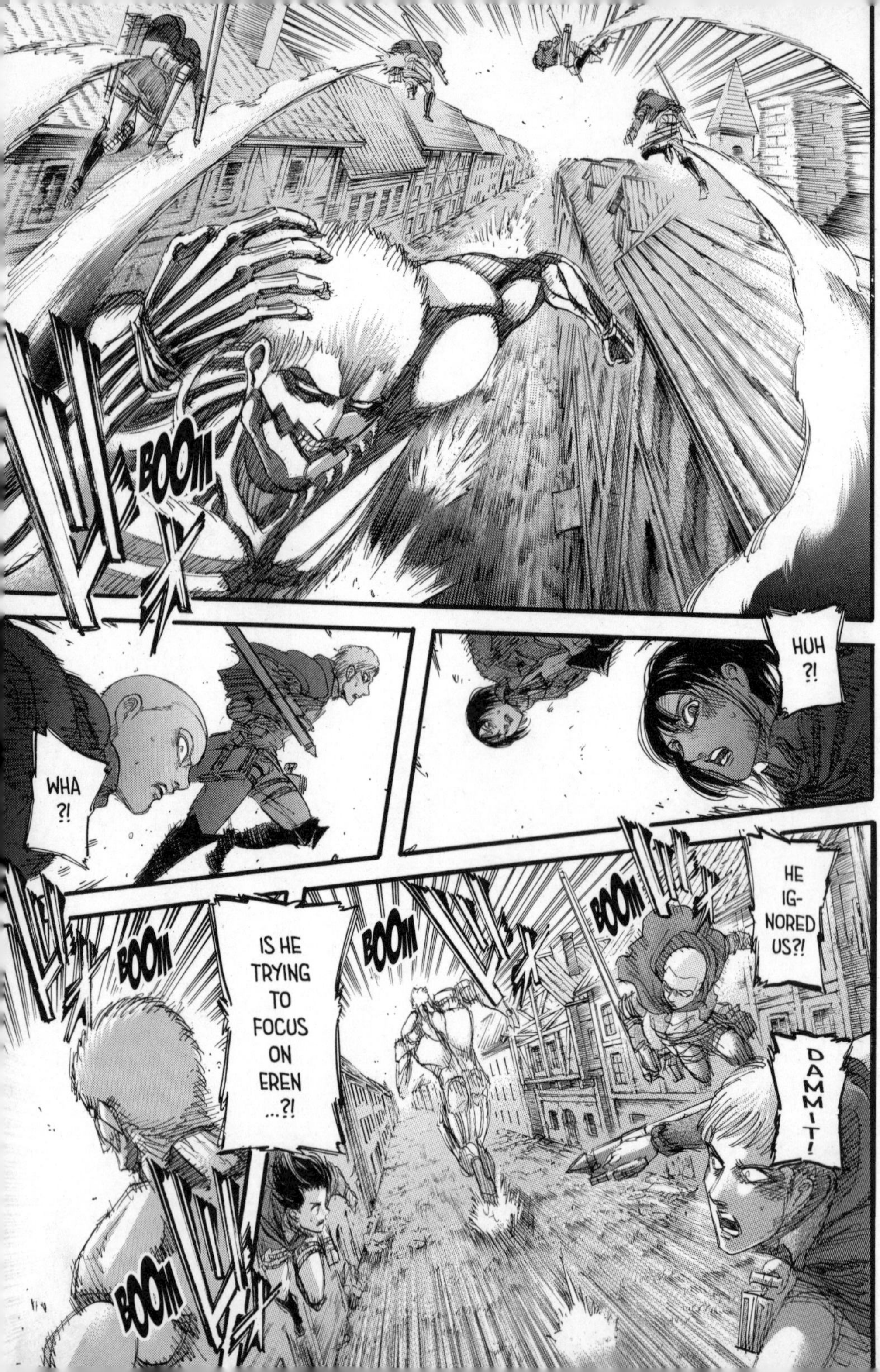
BOOM
HUH ?!
WHA ?!
HE IG-NORED US?!
BOOM
DAMMIT!
BOOM
IS HE TRYING TO FOCUS ON EREN ...?!
BOOM
BOOM

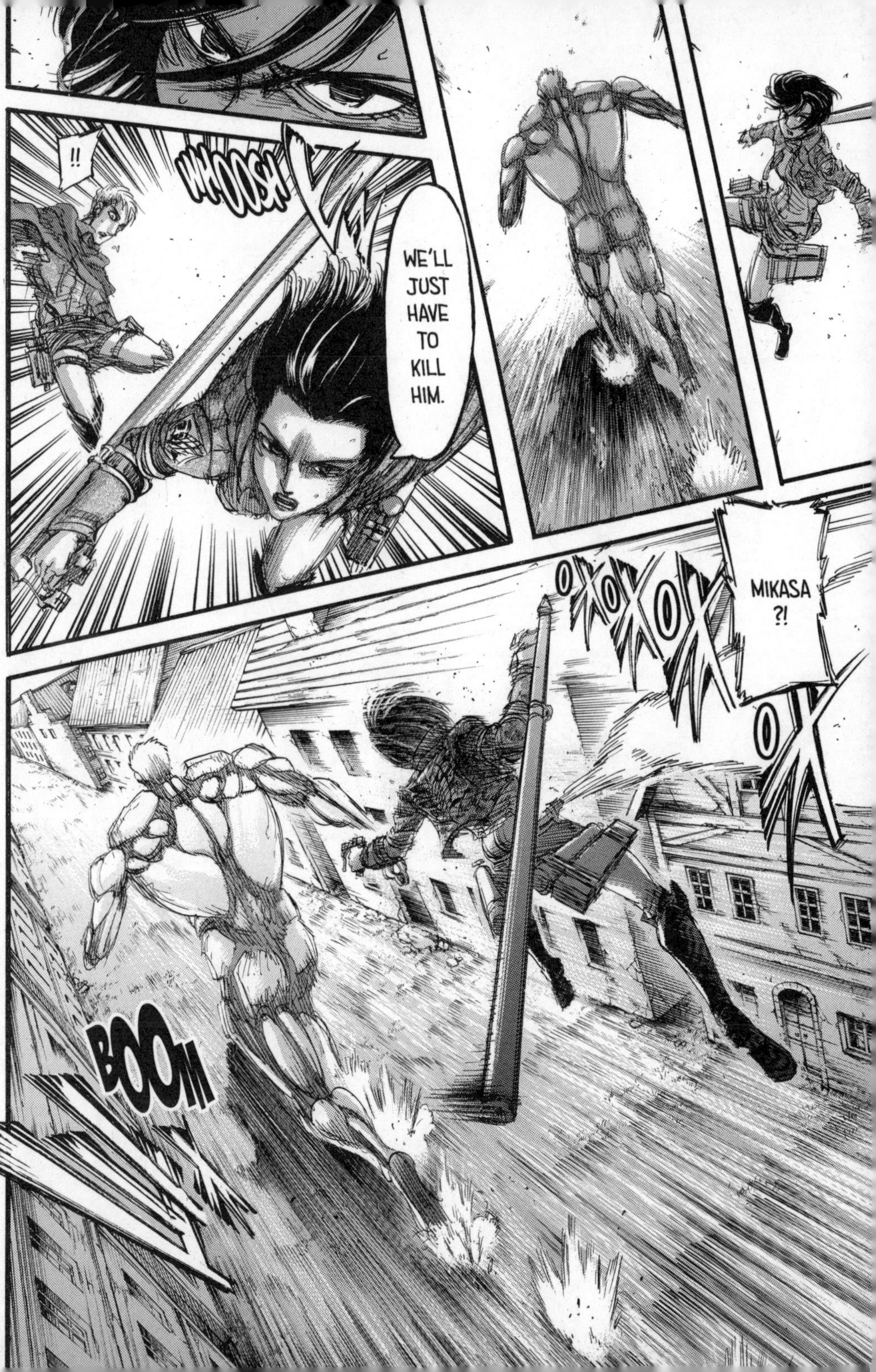

WHOOSH
WE'LL JUST HAVE TO KILL HIM.
!!
MIKASA ?!
OXOXOXOX
OX
BOOM

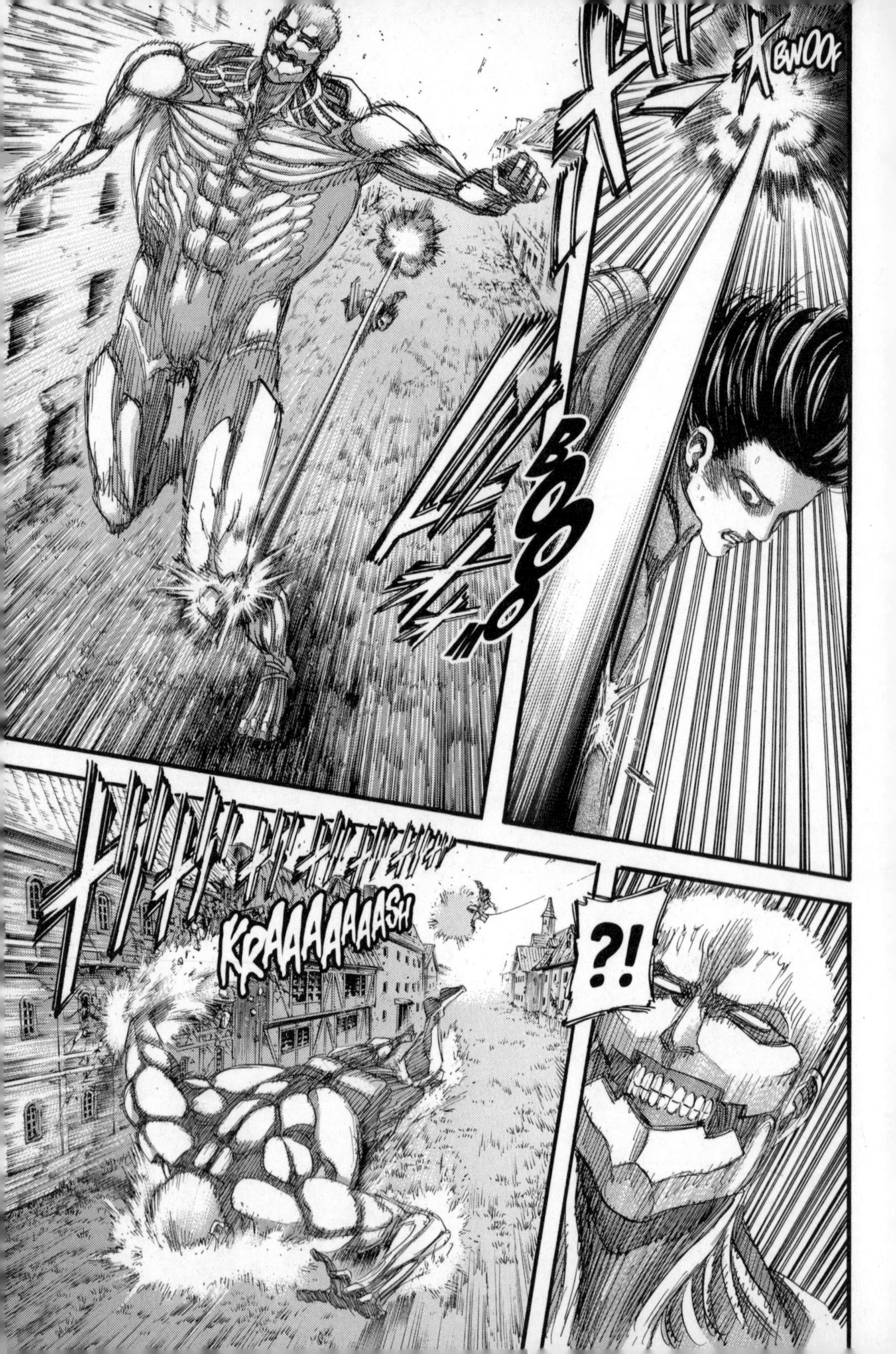
BWOOF
BOOOOM
?!
KRAAAAAAASH

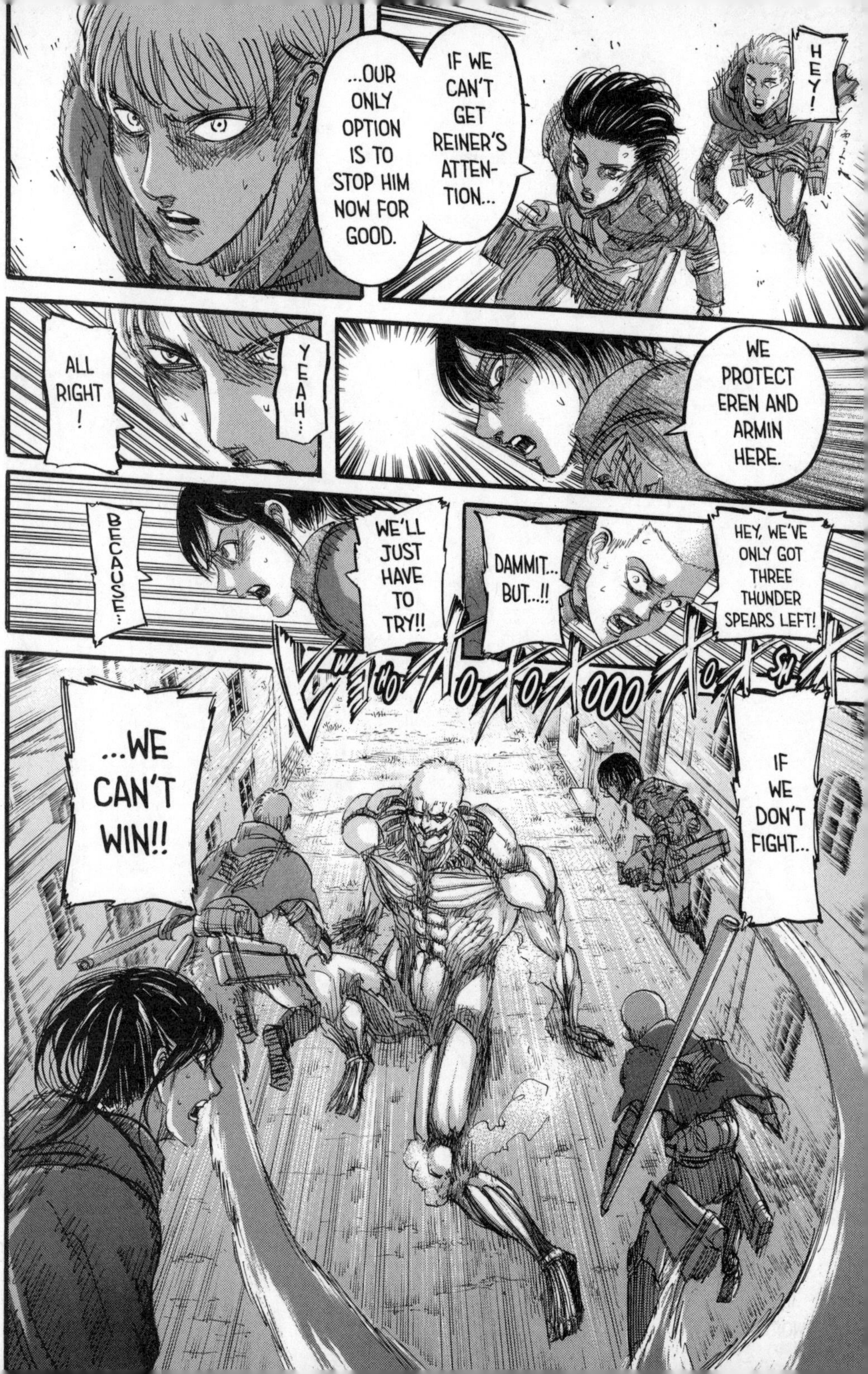
HEY!
IF WE CAN'T GET REINER'S ATTENTION...
...OUR ONLY OPTION IS TO STOP HIM NOW FOR GOOD.
WE PROTECT EREN AND ARMIN HERE.
YEAH...
ALL RIGHT!
HEY, WE'VE ONLY GOT THREE THUNDER SPEARS LEFT!
DAMMIT... BUT...!!
WE'LL JUST HAVE TO TRY!!
BECAUSE...
IF WE DON'T FIGHT...
...WE CAN'T WIN!!

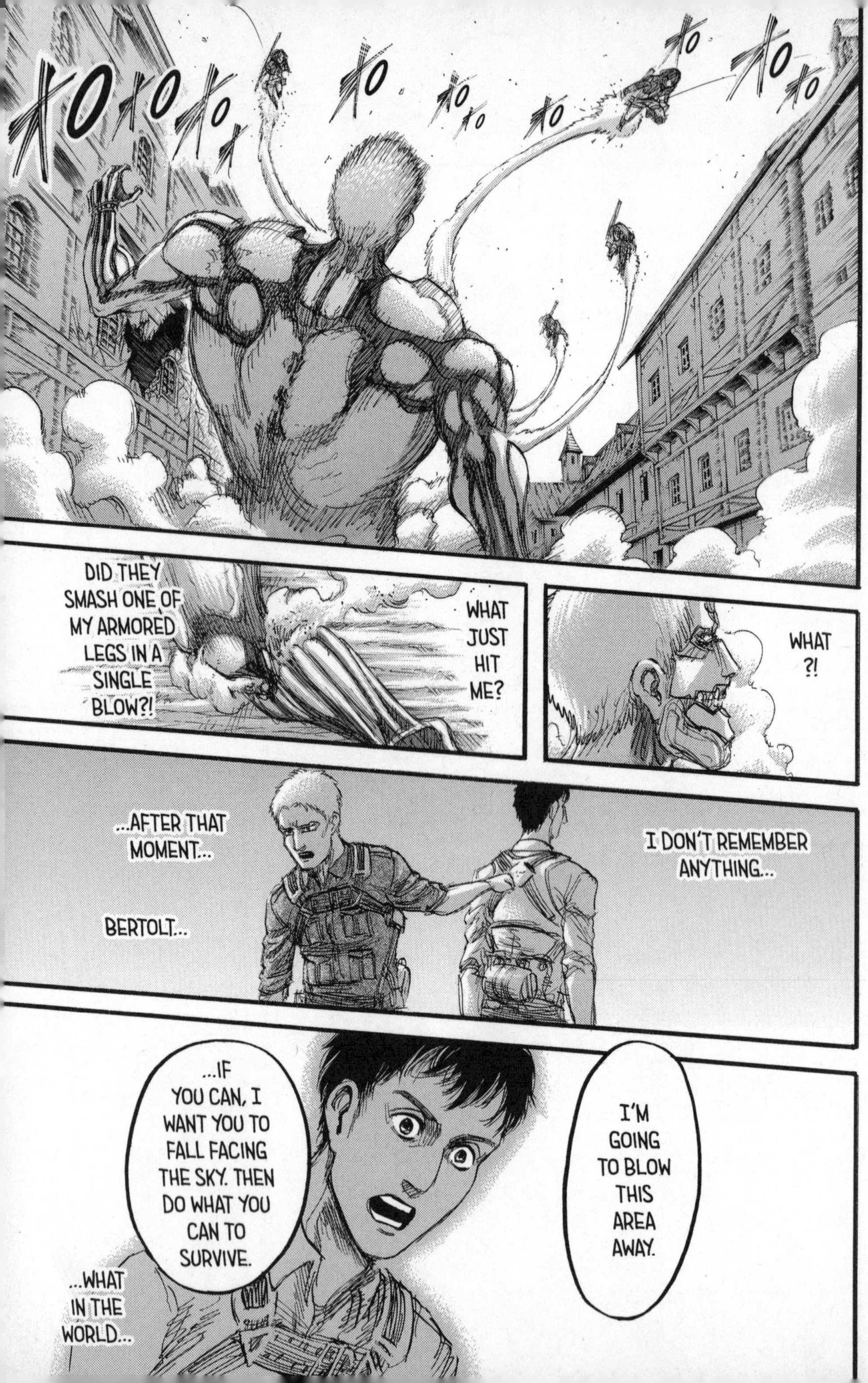
WHAT ?!
WHAT JUST HIT ME?
DID THEY SMASH ONE OF MY ARMORED LEGS IN A SINGLE BLOW?!
I DON'T REMEMBER ANYTHING...
...AFTER THAT MOMENT...
BERTOLT...
I'M GOING TO BLOW THIS AREA AWAY.
...IF YOU CAN, I WANT YOU TO FALL FACING THE SKY. THEN DO WHAT YOU CAN TO SURVIVE.
...WHAT IN THE WORLD...

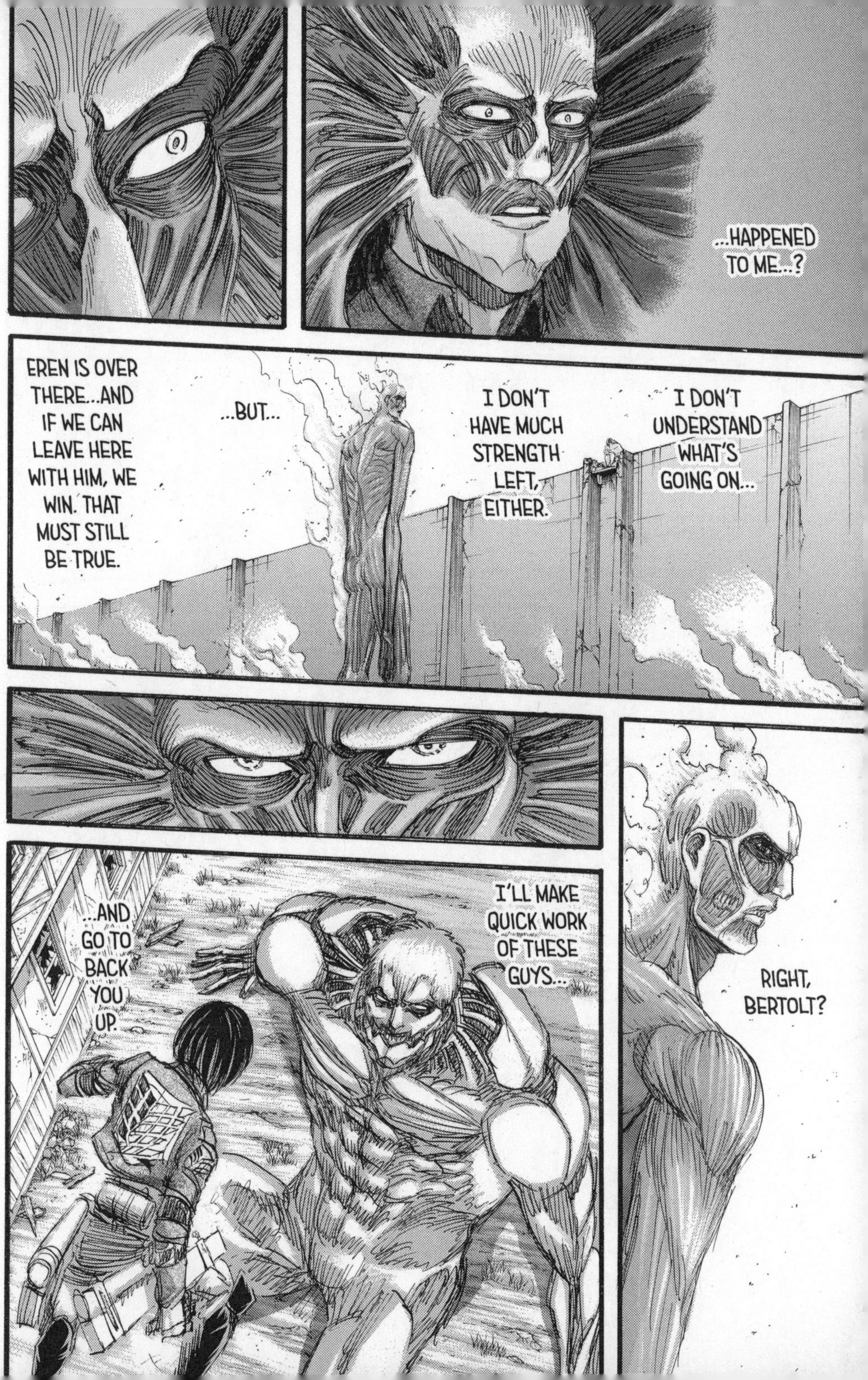
...HAPPENED TO ME...?
I DON'T UNDERSTAND WHAT'S GOING ON...
I DON'T HAVE MUCH STRENGTH LEFT, EITHER.
...BUT...
EREN IS OVER THERE...AND IF WE CAN LEAVE HERE WITH HIM, WE WIN. THAT MUST STILL BE TRUE.
RIGHT, BERTOLT?
I'LL MAKE QUICK WORK OF THESE GUYS...
...AND GO TO BACK YOU UP.

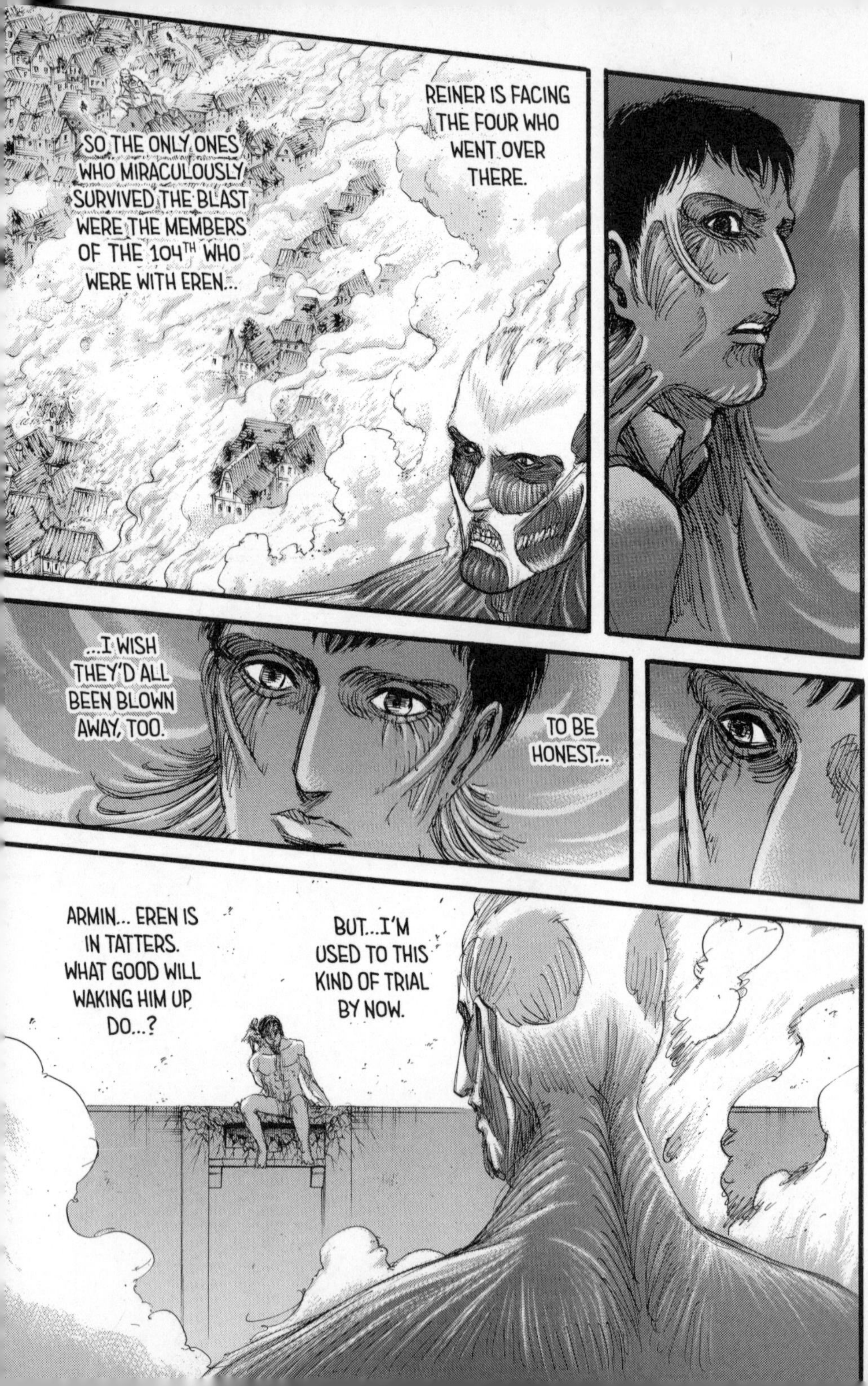
REINER IS FACING THE FOUR WHO WENT OVER THERE.
SO THE ONLY ONES WHO MIRACULOUSLY SURVIVED THE BLAST WERE THE MEMBERS OF THE 104TH WHO WERE WITH EREN...
TO BE HONEST...
...I WISH THEY'D ALL BEEN BLOWN AWAY, TOO.
BUT...I'M USED TO THIS KIND OF TRIAL BY NOW.
ARMIN... EREN IS IN TATTERS. WHAT GOOD WILL WAKING HIM UP DO...?

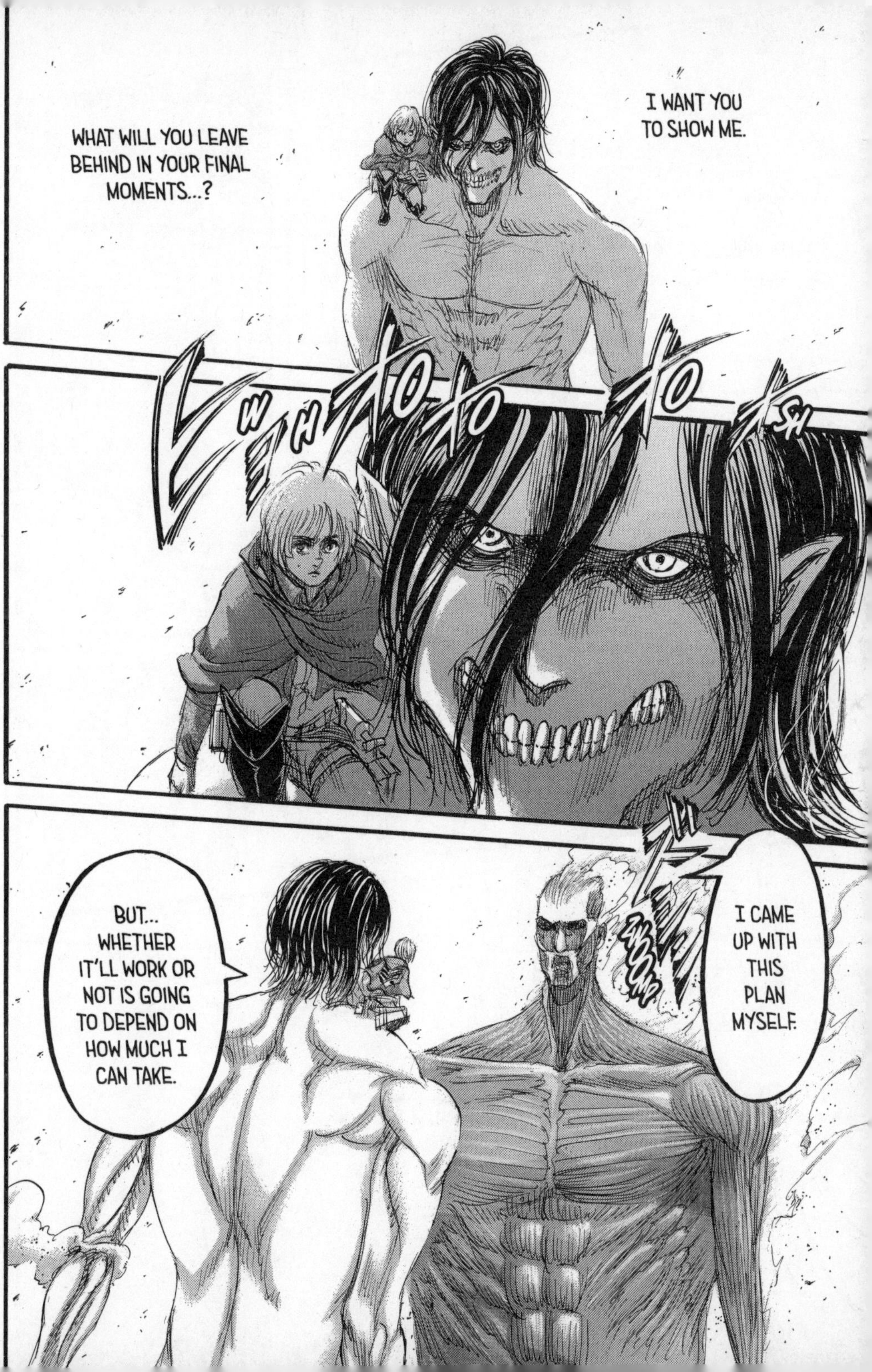
I WANT YOU TO SHOW ME.
WHAT WILL YOU LEAVE BEHIND IN YOUR FINAL MOMENTS...?
I CAME UP WITH THIS PLAN MYSELF.
BUT... WHETHER IT'LL WORK OR NOT IS GOING TO DEPEND ON HOW MUCH I CAN TAKE.

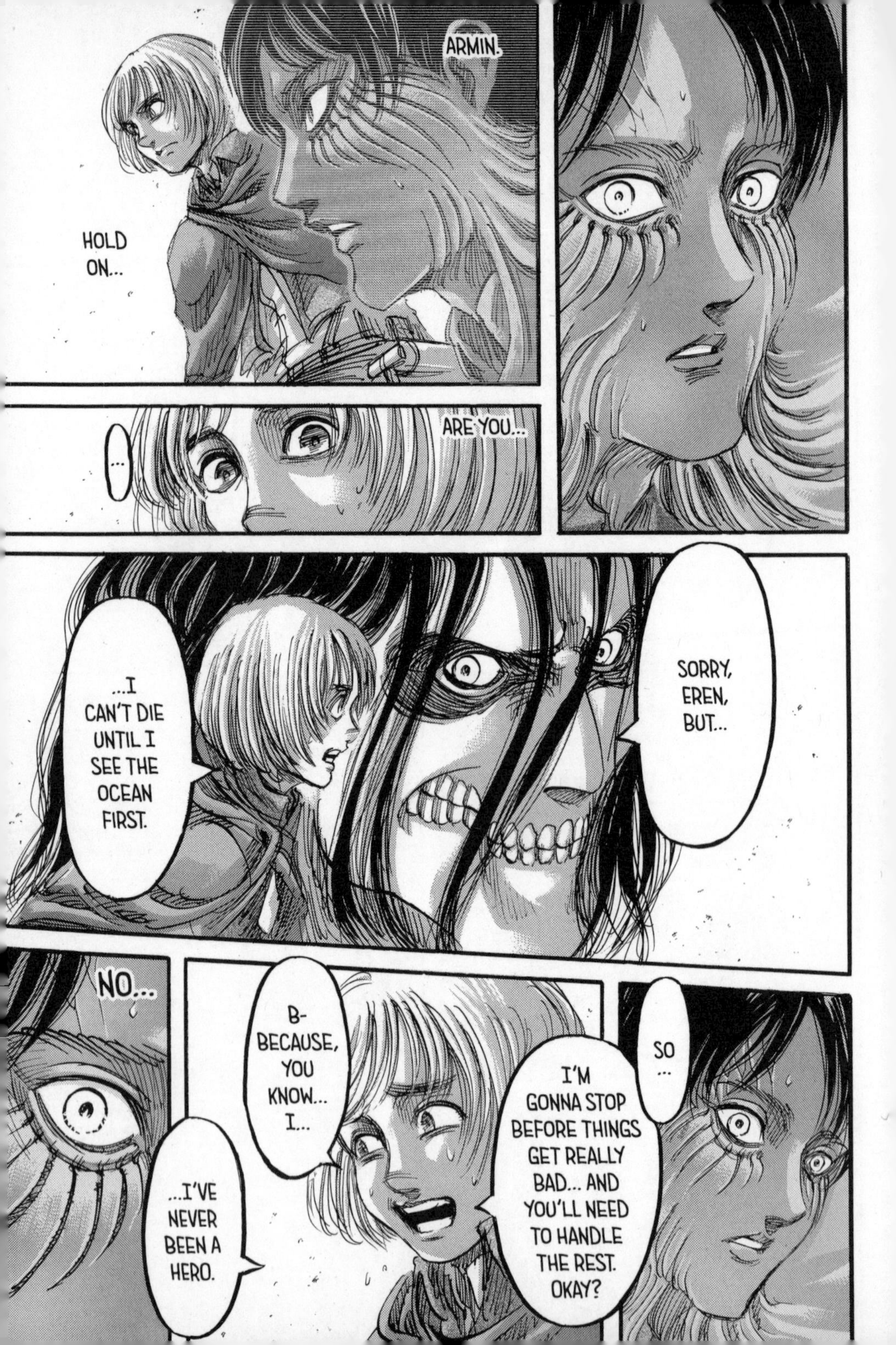

ARMIN.
HOLD ON...
ARE YOU...
...
SORRY, EREN, BUT...
...I CAN'T DIE UNTIL I SEE THE OCEAN FIRST.
SO ...
B- BECAUSE, YOU KNOW... I...
I'M GONNA STOP BEFORE THINGS GET REALLY BAD... AND YOU'LL NEED TO HANDLE THE REST. OKAY?
NO...
...I'VE NEVER BEEN A HERO.

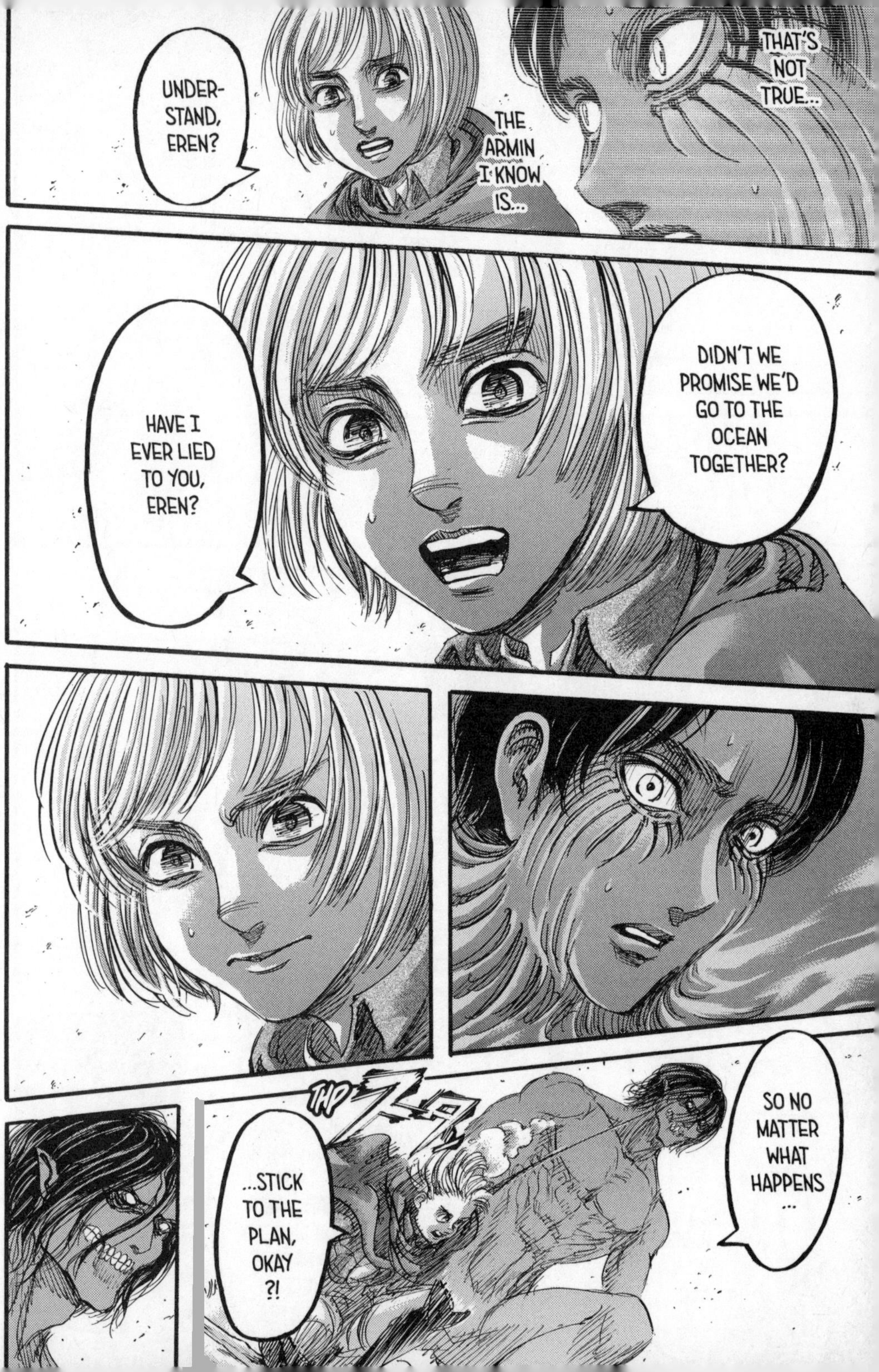
THAT'S NOT TRUE...
THE ARMIN I KNOW IS...
UNDER-STAND, EREN?
DIDN'T WE PROMISE WE'D GO TO THE OCEAN TOGETHER?
HAVE I EVER LIED TO YOU, EREN?
SO NO MATTER WHAT HAPPENS...
THP
...STICK TO THE PLAN, OKAY?!

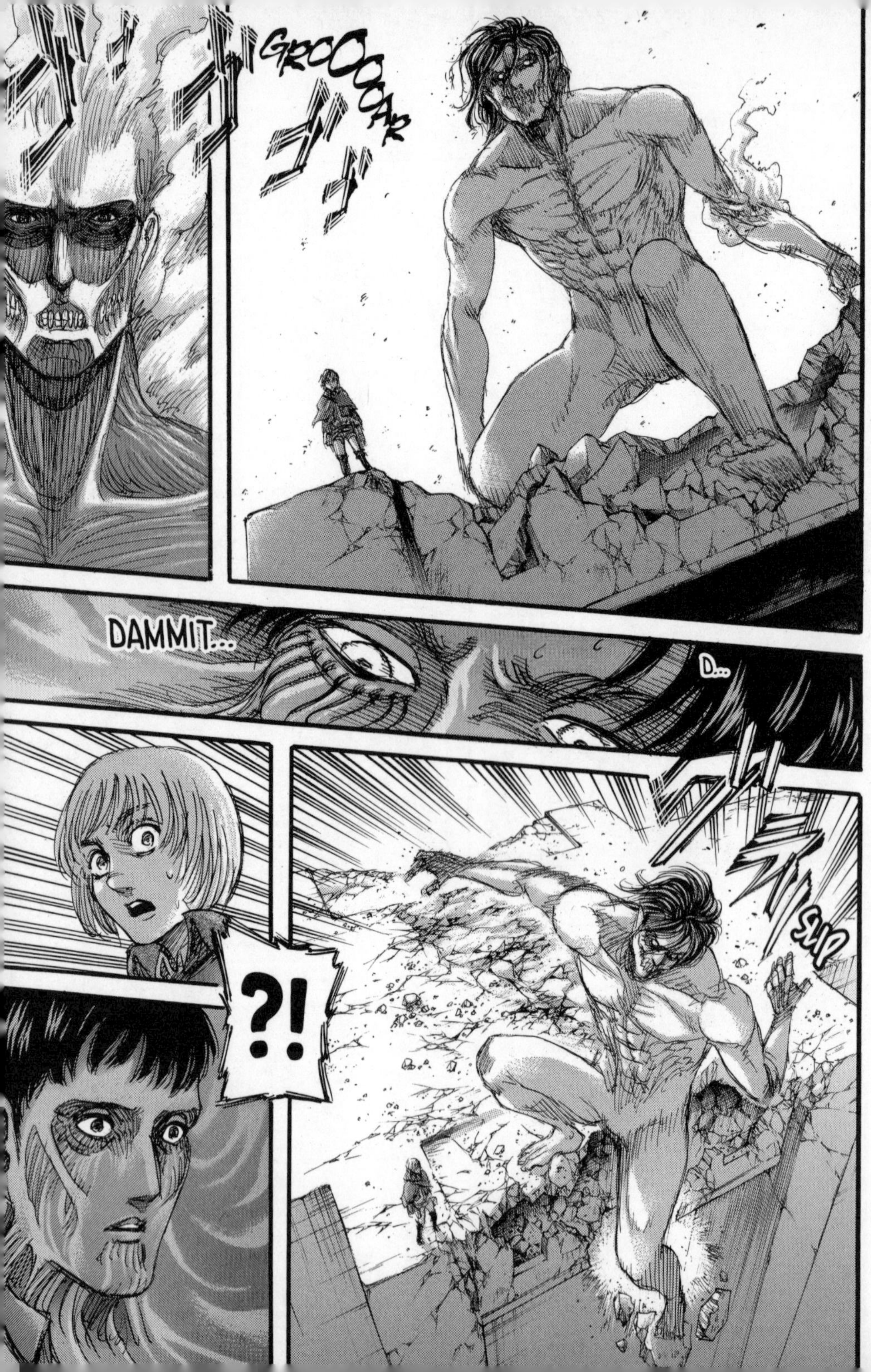
GROOOOAR
D...
DAMMIT...
SHP
?!

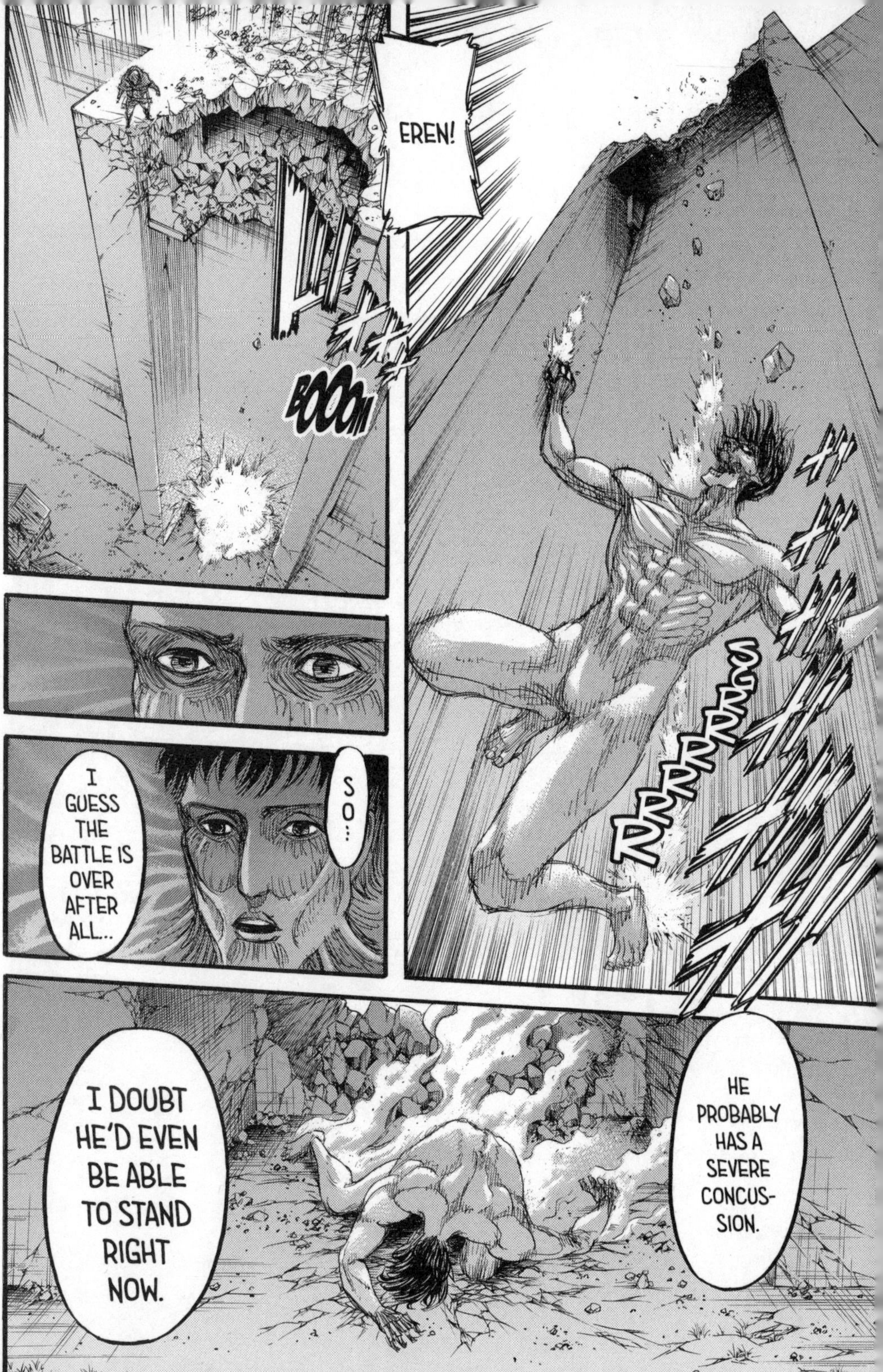

EREN!
BOOOM
SO...
I GUESS THE BATTLE IS OVER AFTER ALL...
HE PROBABLY HAS A SEVERE CONCUS-SION.
I DOUBT HE'D EVEN BE ABLE TO STAND RIGHT NOW.

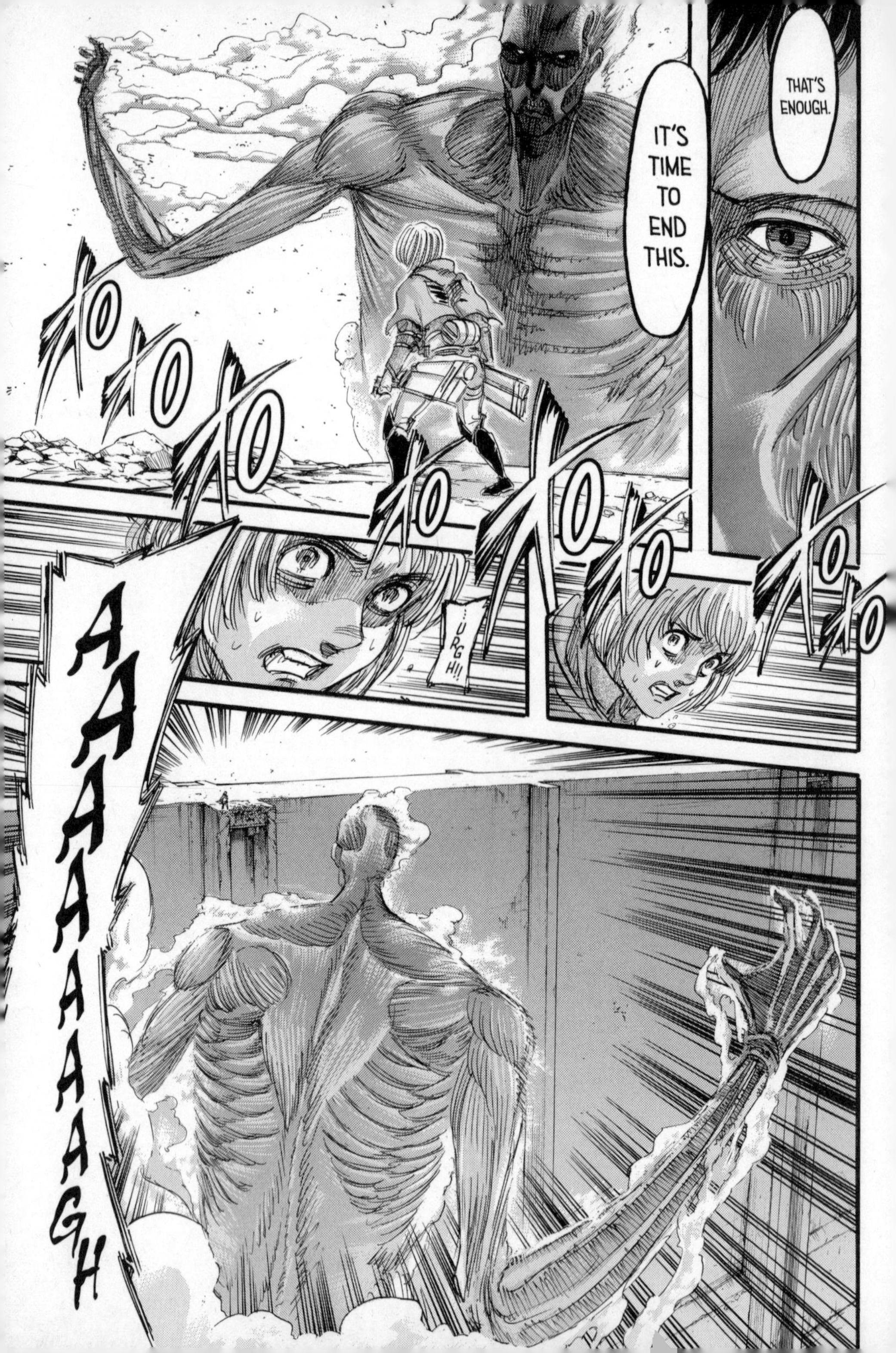
THAT'S ENOUGH.
IT'S TIME TO END THIS.
...URGH!!
AAAAAAAAGH

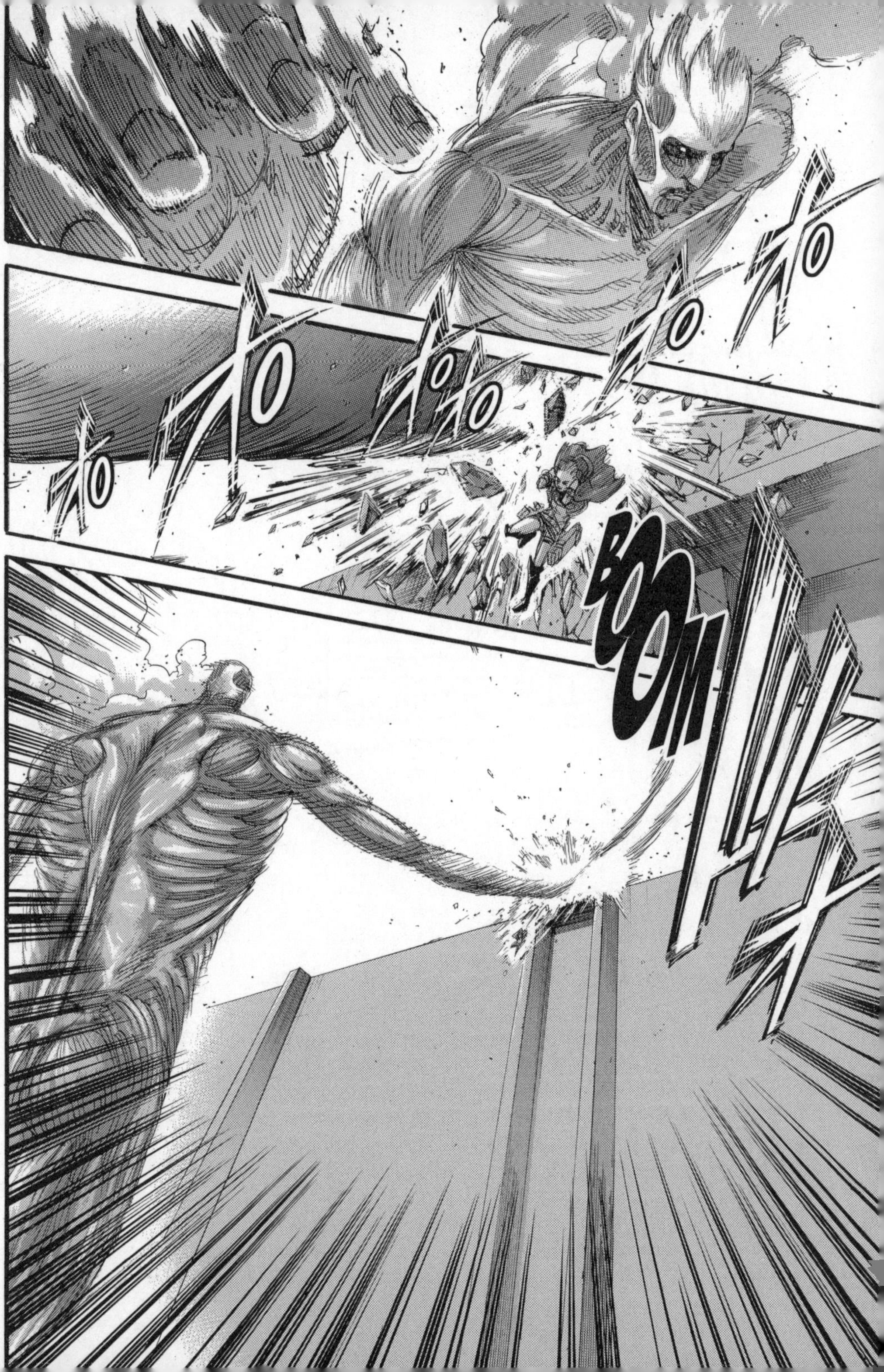
BOOM

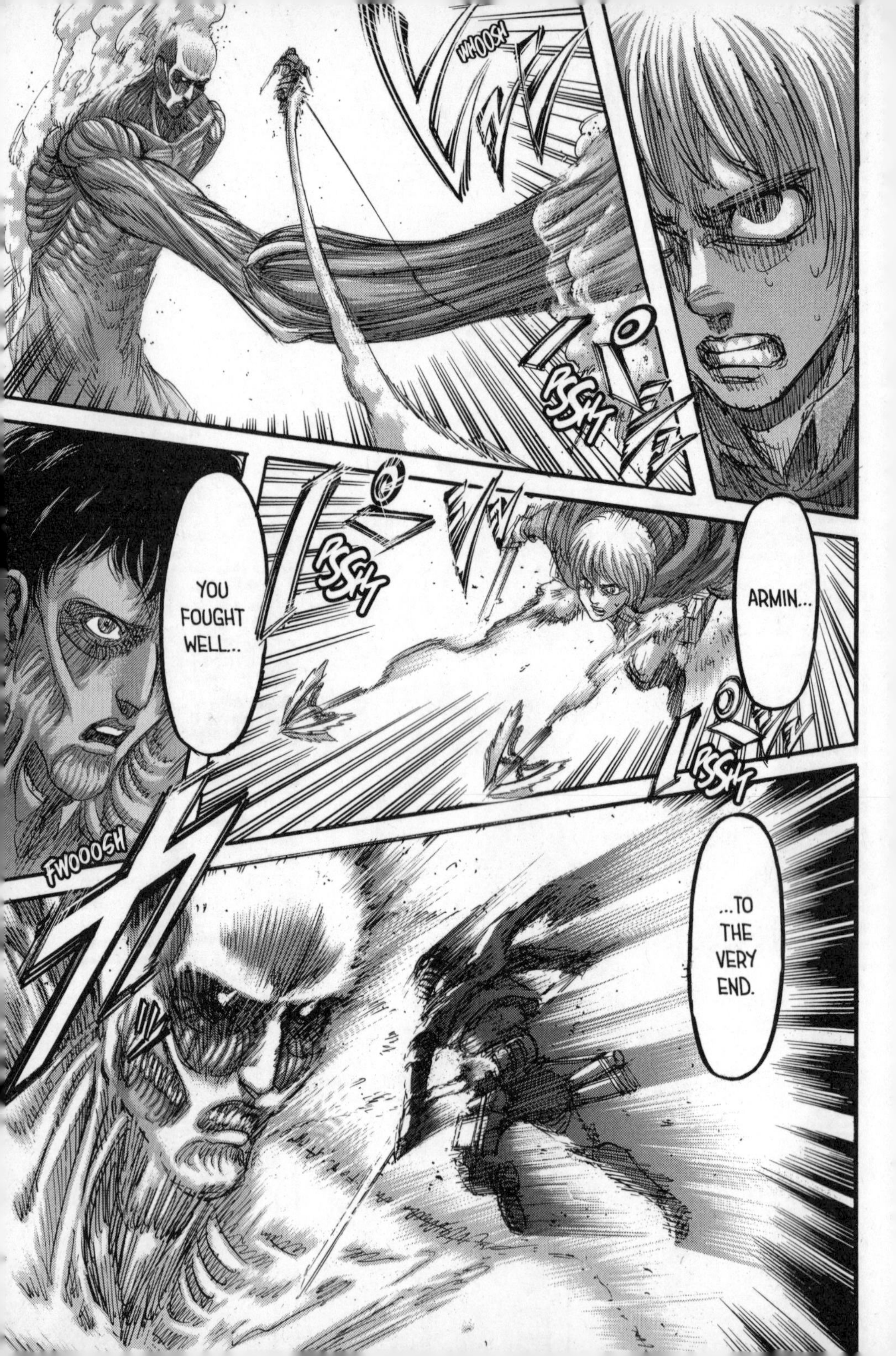
PSSH
WHOOSH
ARMIN...
PSSH
PSSH
YOU FOUGHT WELL...
...TO THE VERY END.
FWOOOSH

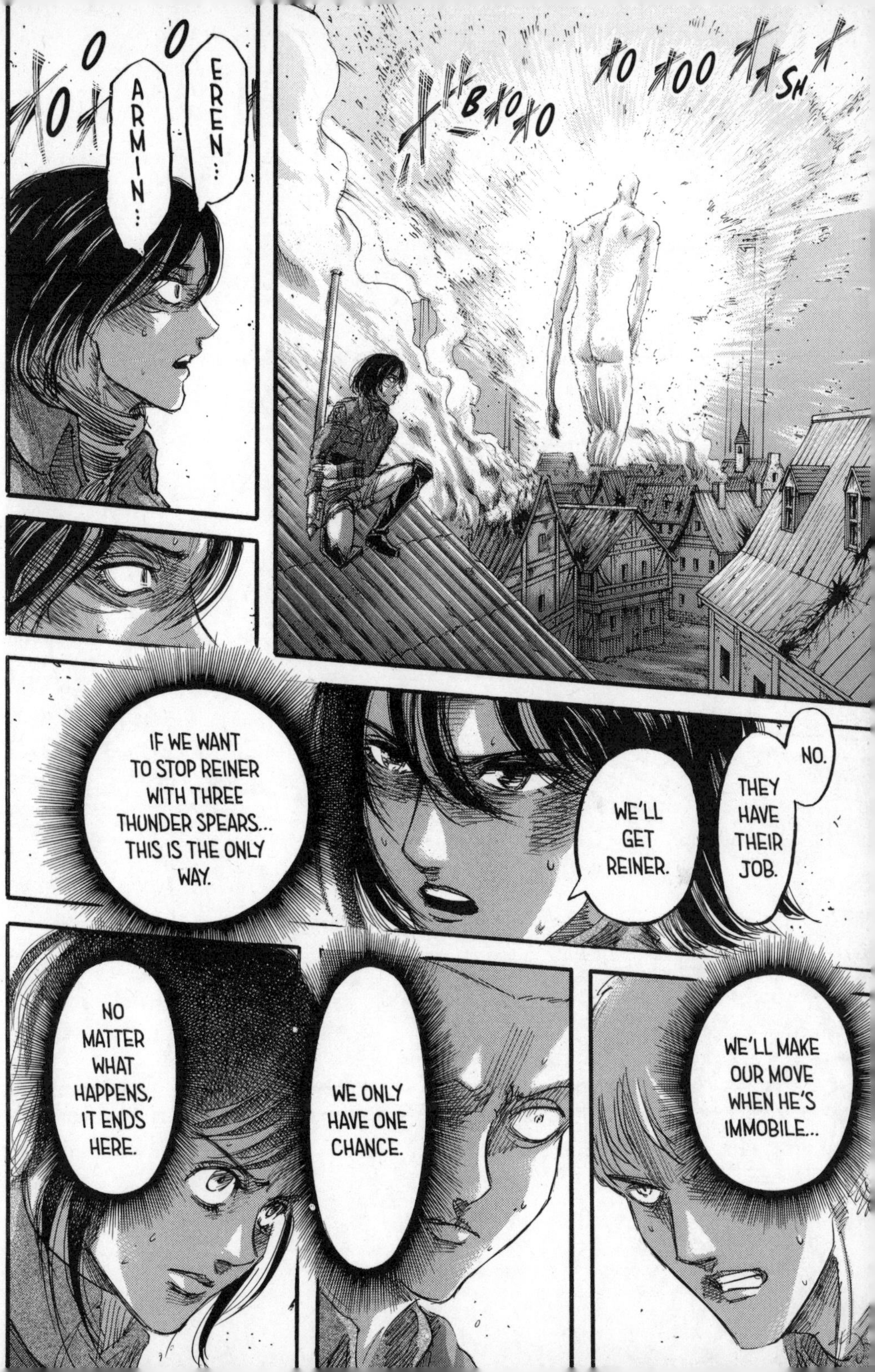
EREN...
ARMIN...
NO.
THEY HAVE THEIR JOB.
WE'LL GET REINER.
IF WE WANT TO STOP REINER WITH THREE THUNDER SPEARS... THIS IS THE ONLY WAY.
WE'LL MAKE OUR MOVE WHEN HE'S IMMOBILE...
WE ONLY HAVE ONE CHANCE.
NO MATTER WHAT HAPPENS, IT ENDS HERE.

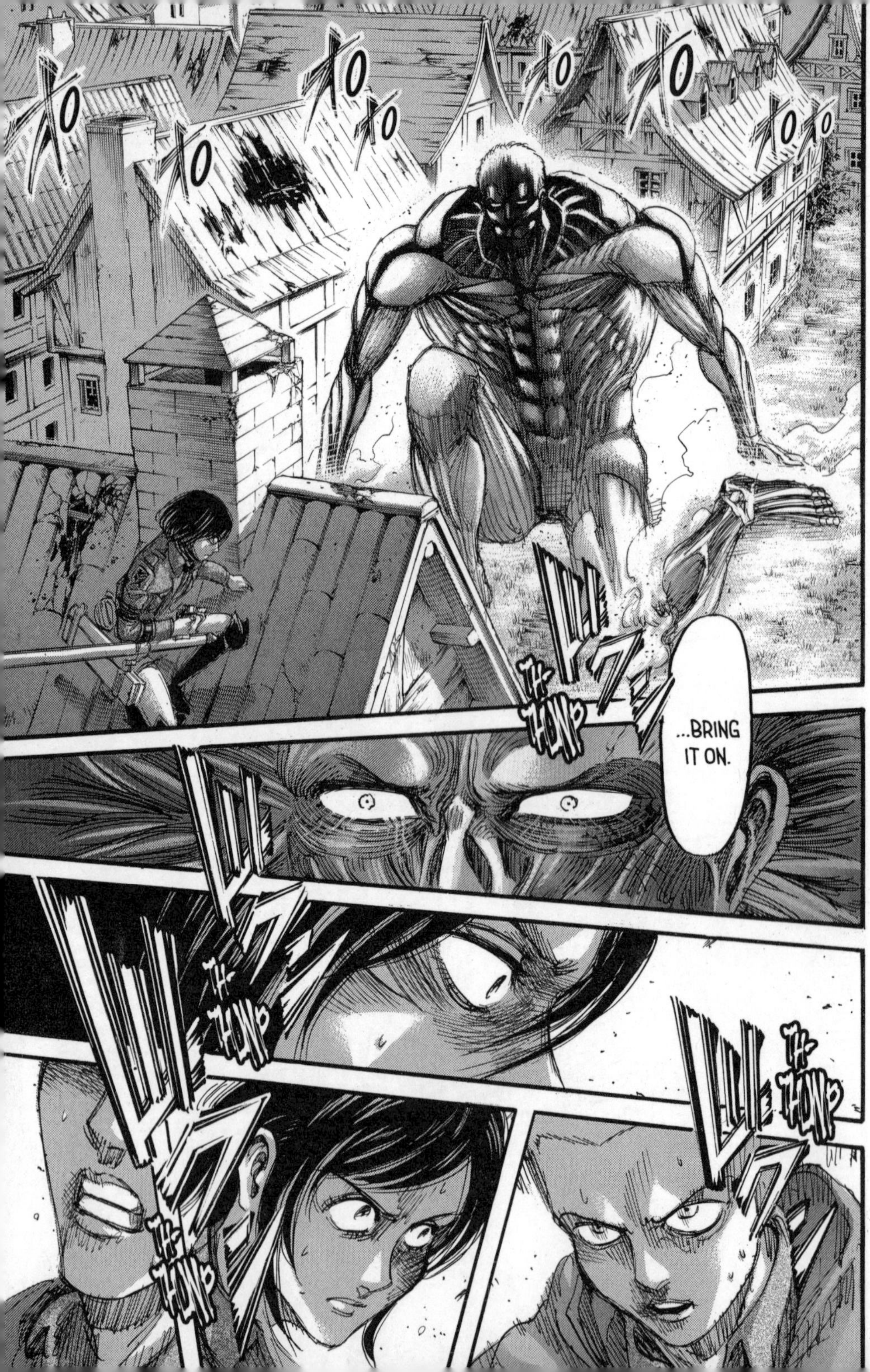
...BRING IT ON.
TH-THOMP
TH-THOMP
TH-THOMP
TH-THOMP

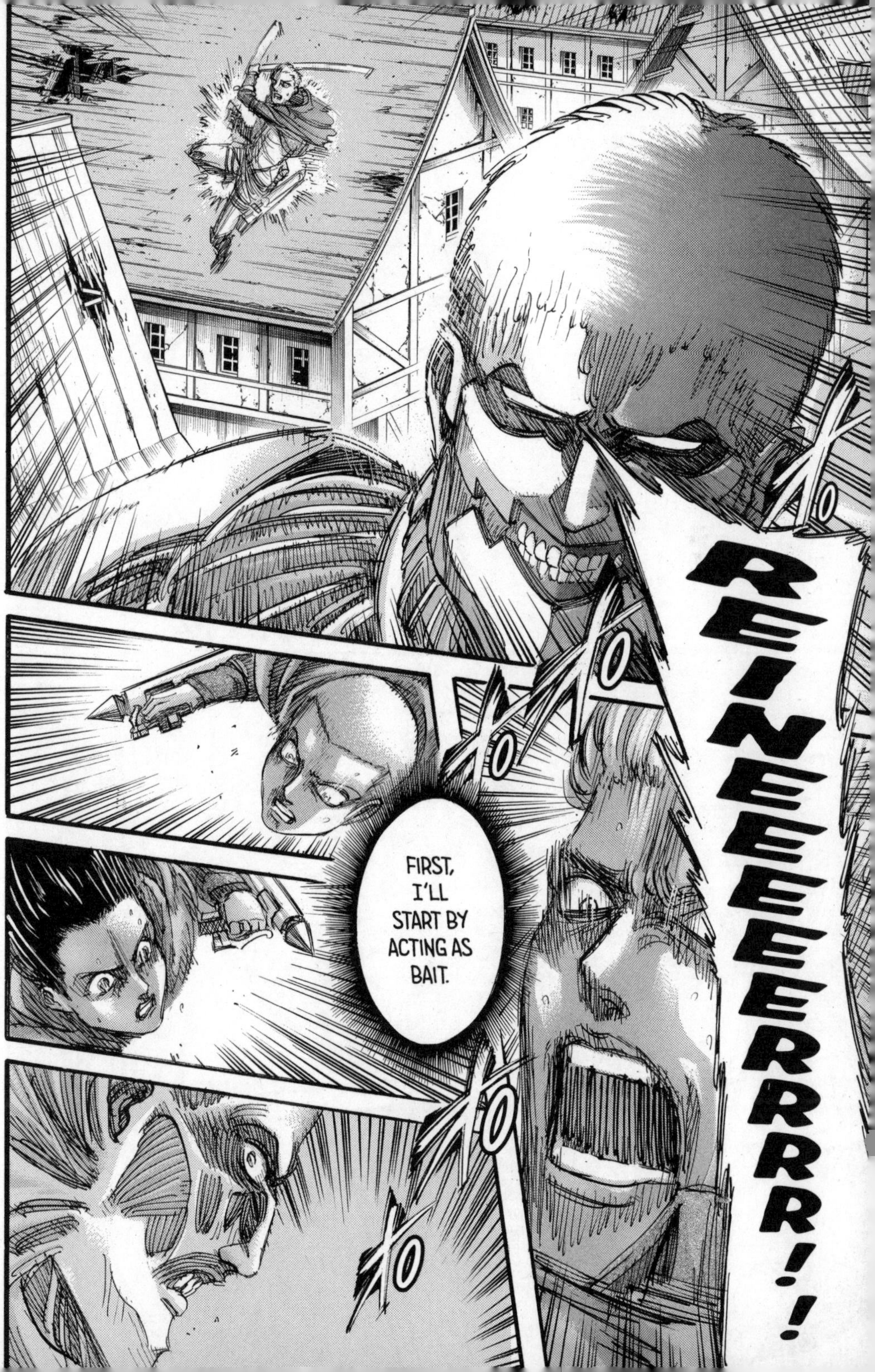
REINEEEERRRR!!
FIRST, I'LL START BY ACTING AS BAIT.

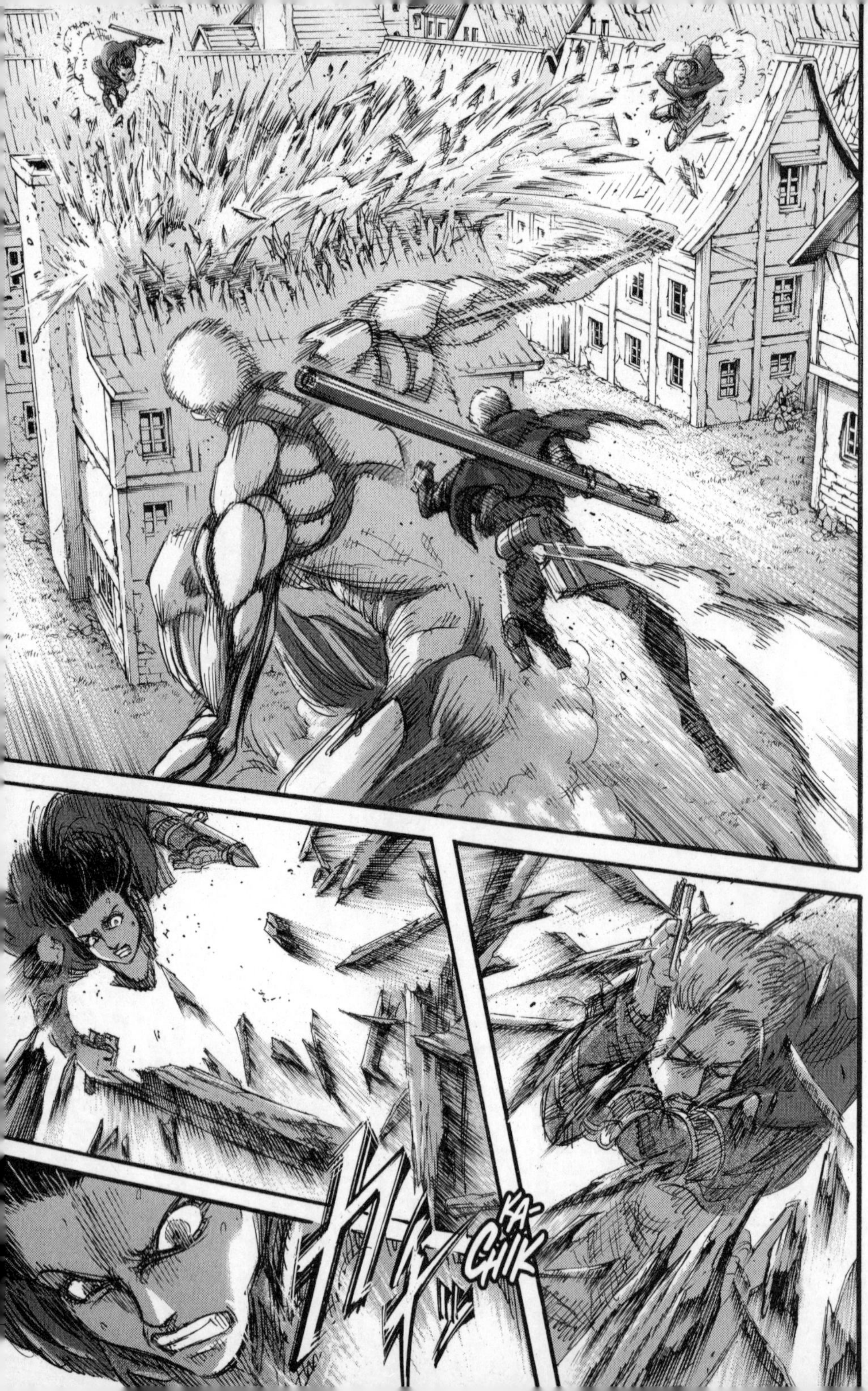
KA-
CHIK

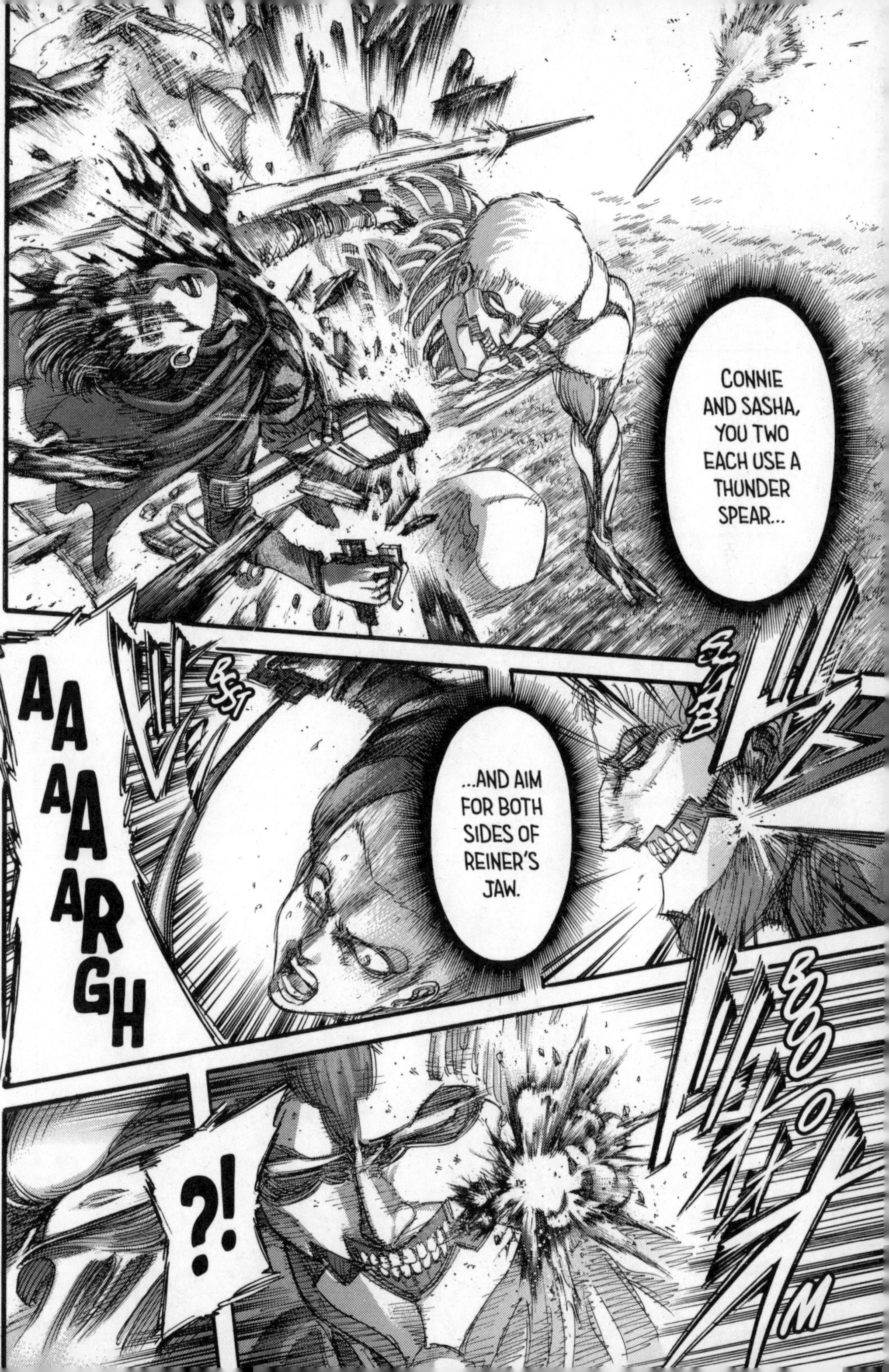

CONNIE AND SASHA, YOU TWO EACH USE A THUNDER SPEAR...
GRAB
...AND AIM FOR BOTH SIDES OF REINER'S JAW.
AAAAARGH
BOOOOM
?!

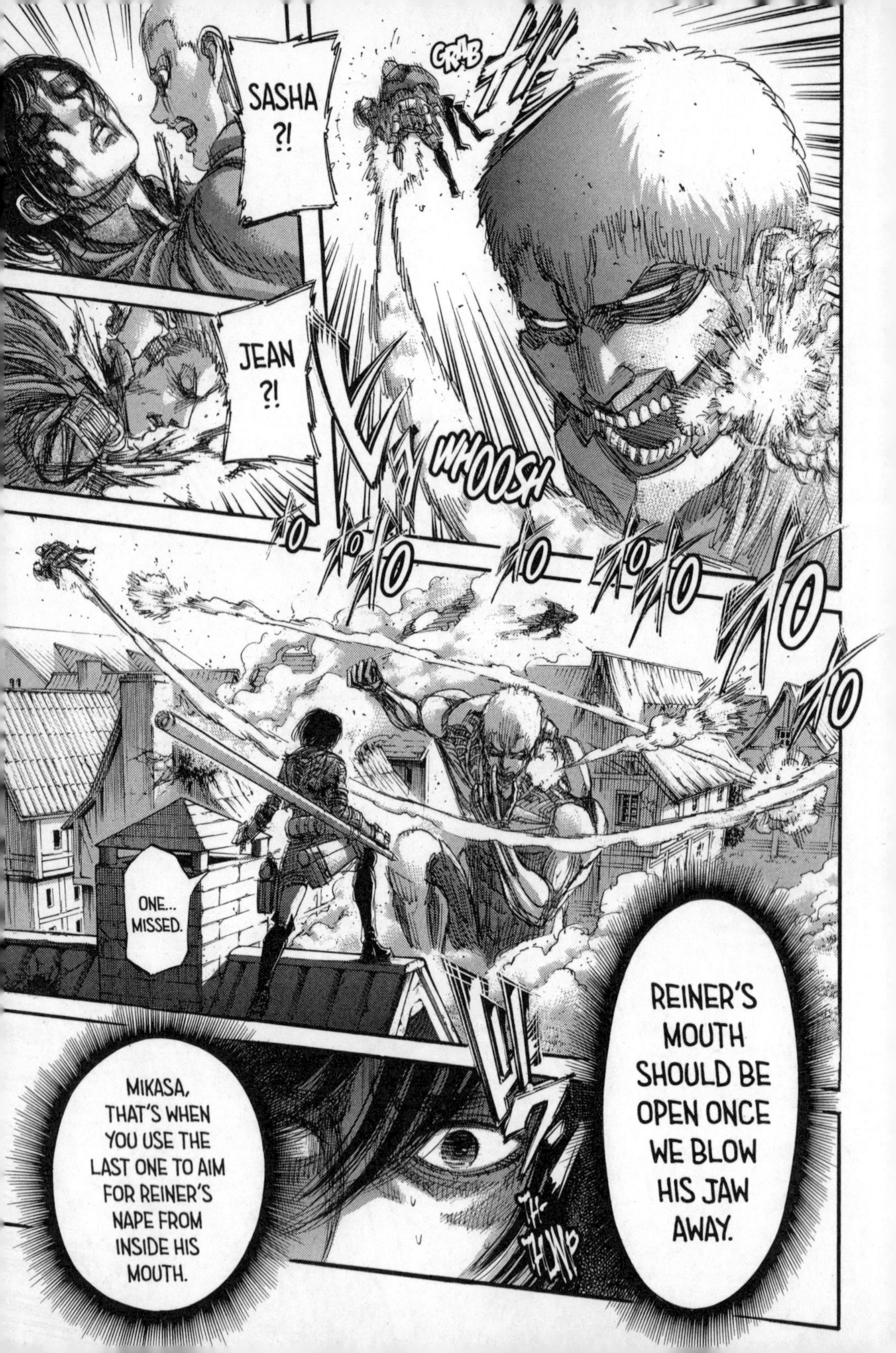
GRAB
WHOOSH
SASHA ?!
JEAN ?!
ONE... MISSED.
REINER'S MOUTH SHOULD BE OPEN ONCE WE BLOW HIS JAW AWAY.
MIKASA, THAT'S WHEN YOU USE THE LAST ONE TO AIM FOR REINER'S NAPE FROM INSIDE HIS MOUTH.

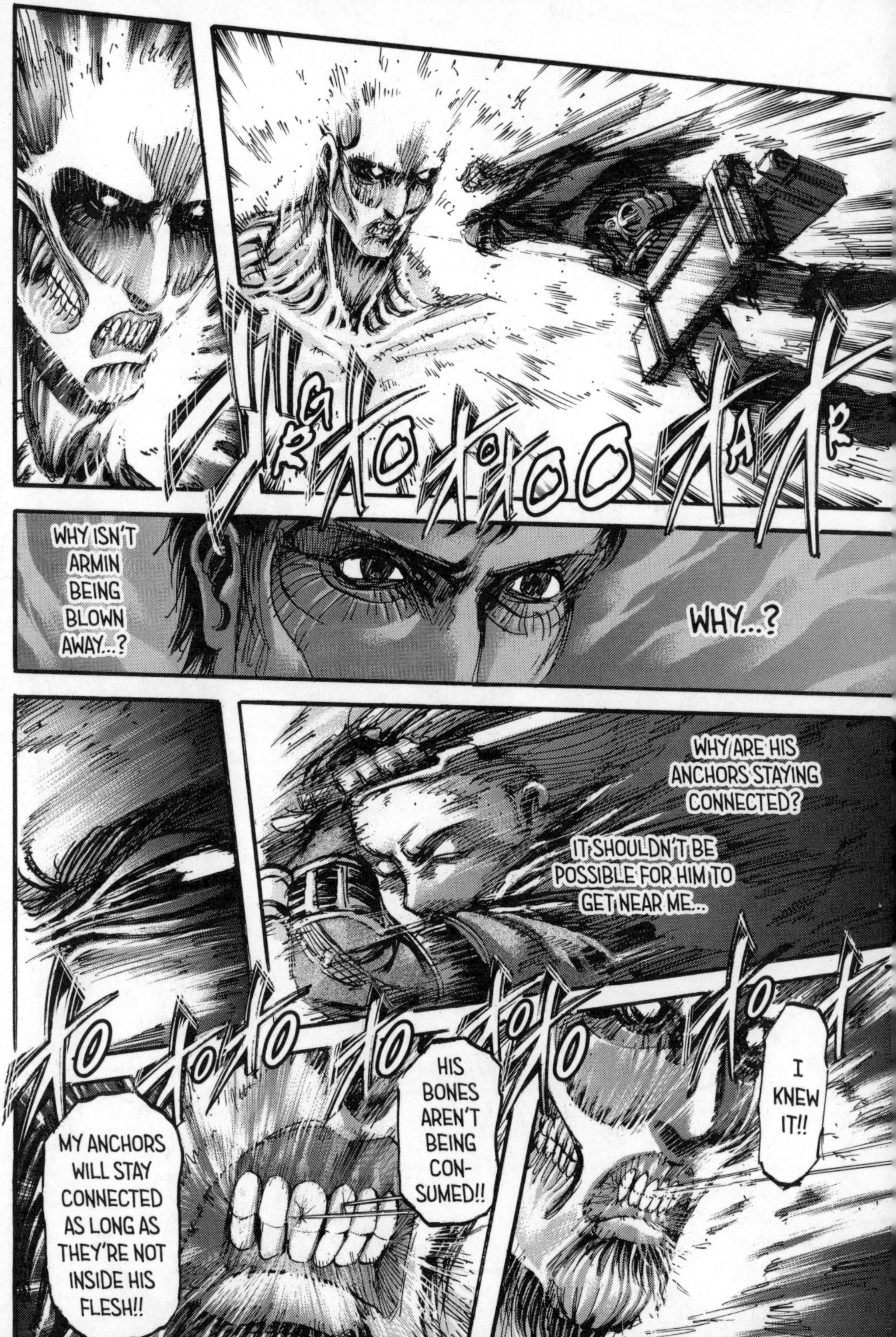
WHY...?
WHY ISN'T ARMIN BEING BLOWN AWAY...?
WHY ARE HIS ANCHORS STAYING CONNECTED?
IT SHOULDN'T BE POSSIBLE FOR HIM TO GET NEAR ME...
I KNEW IT!!
HIS BONES AREN'T BEING CONSUMED!!
MY ANCHORS WILL STAY CONNECTED AS LONG AS THEY'RE NOT INSIDE HIS FLESH!!

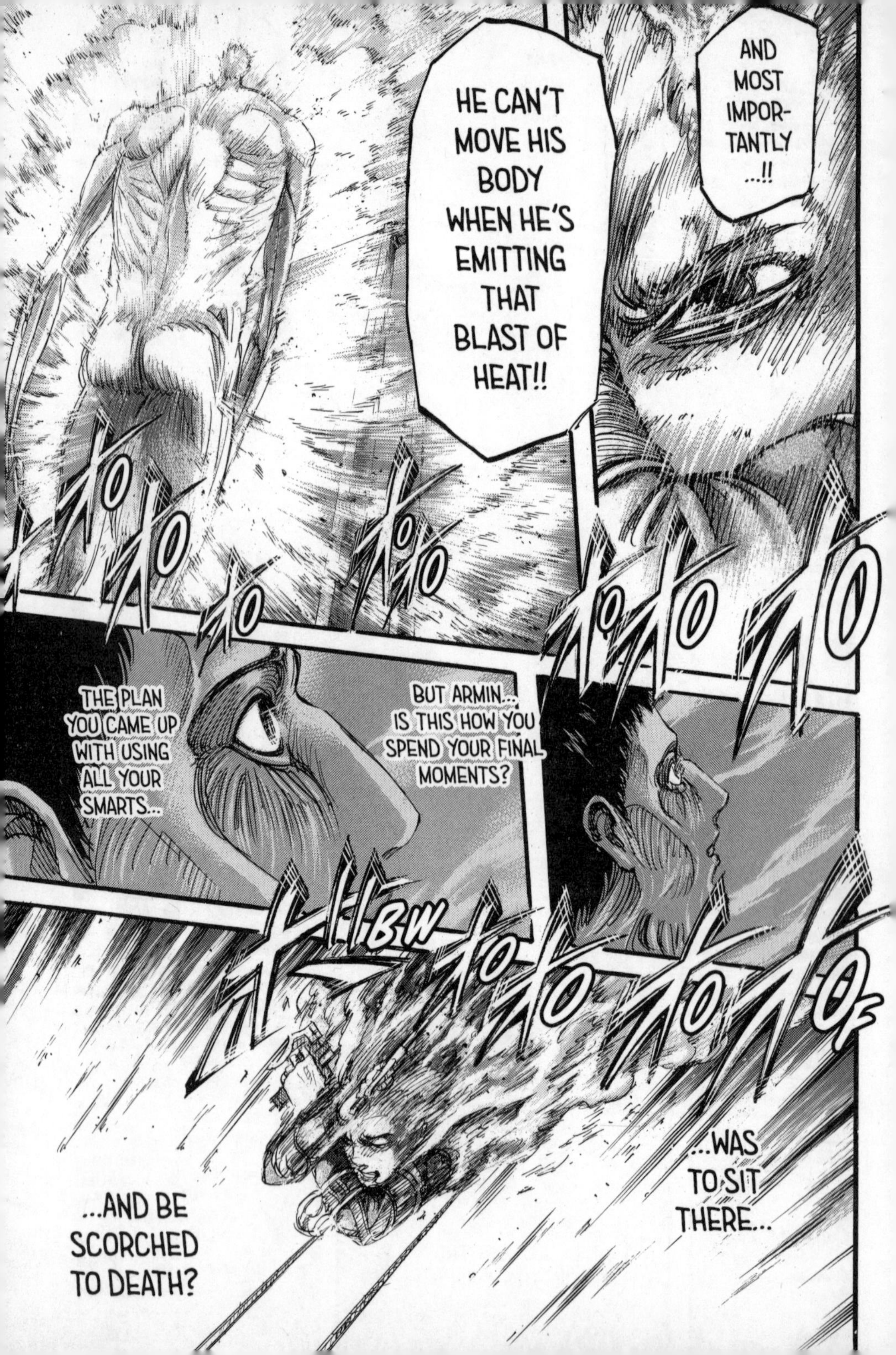
HE CAN'T MOVE HIS BODY WHEN HE'S EMITTING THAT BLAST OF HEAT!!
AND MOST IMPORTANTLY ...!!
BUT ARMIN... IS THIS HOW YOU SPEND YOUR FINAL MOMENTS?
THE PLAN YOU CAME UP WITH USING ALL YOUR SMARTS...
...WAS TO SIT THERE...
...AND BE SCORCHED TO DEATH?

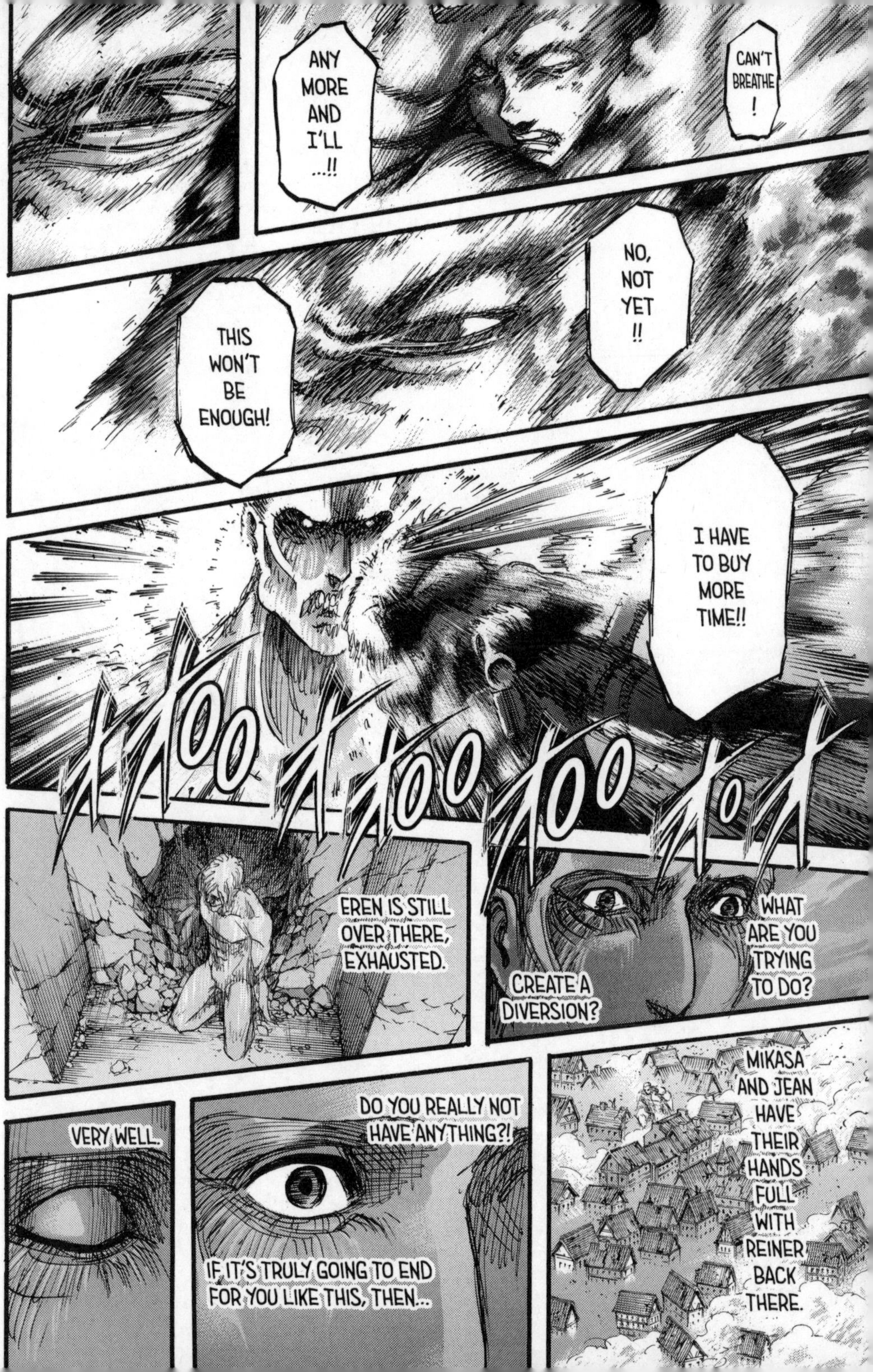
CAN'T BREATHE !
ANY MORE AND I'LL ...!!
NO, NOT YET !!
THIS WON'T BE ENOUGH!
I HAVE TO BUY MORE TIME!!
WHAT ARE YOU TRYING TO DO?
CREATE A DIVERSION?
EREN IS STILL OVER THERE, EXHAUSTED.
MIKASA AND JEAN HAVE THEIR HANDS FULL WITH REINER BACK THERE.
DO YOU REALLY NOT HAVE ANYTHING?!
IF IT'S TRULY GOING TO END FOR YOU LIKE THIS, THEN...
VERY WELL.

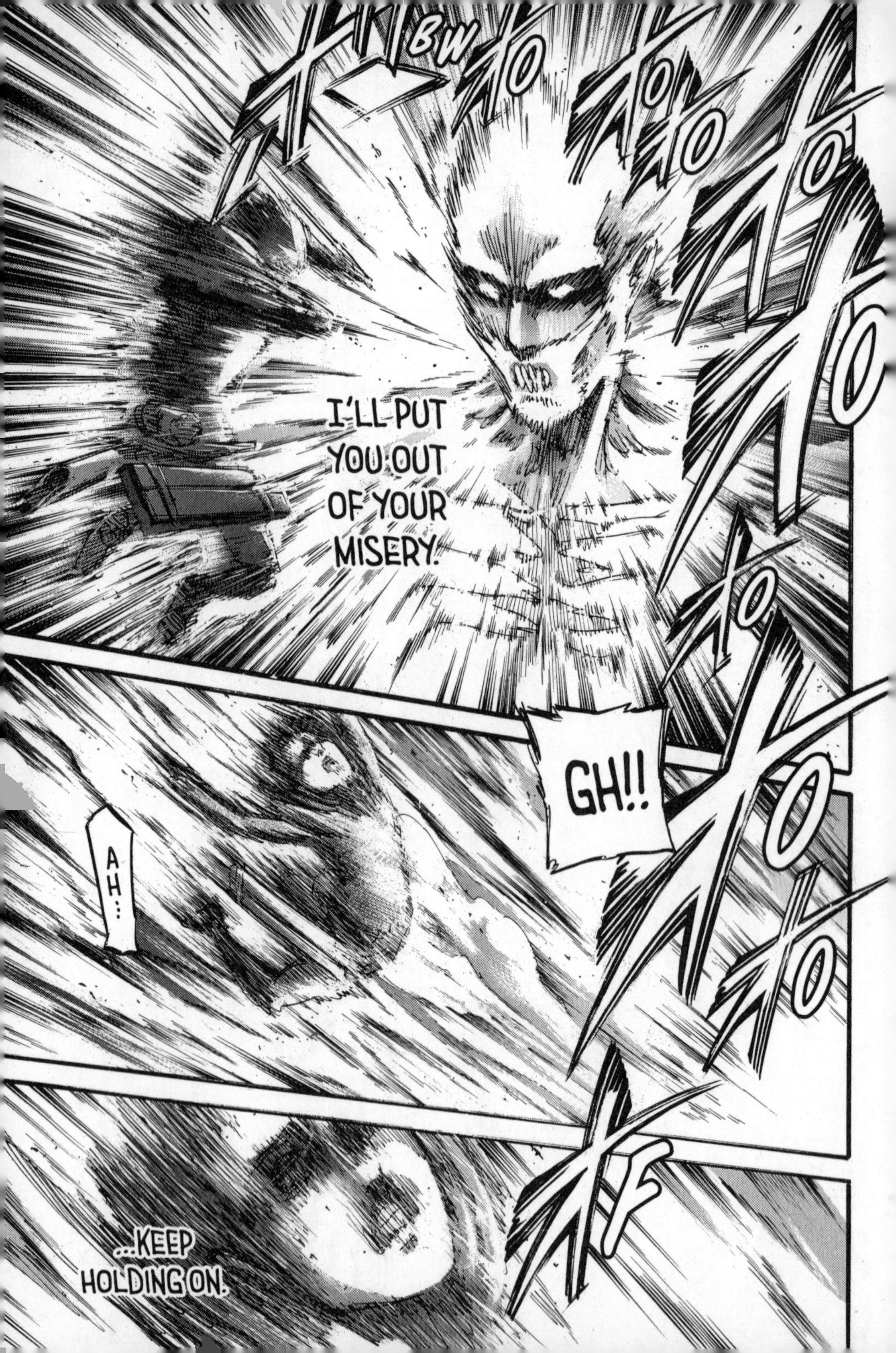
BW
I'LL PUT YOU OUT OF YOUR MISERY.
GH!!
AH...
...KEEP HOLDING ON.

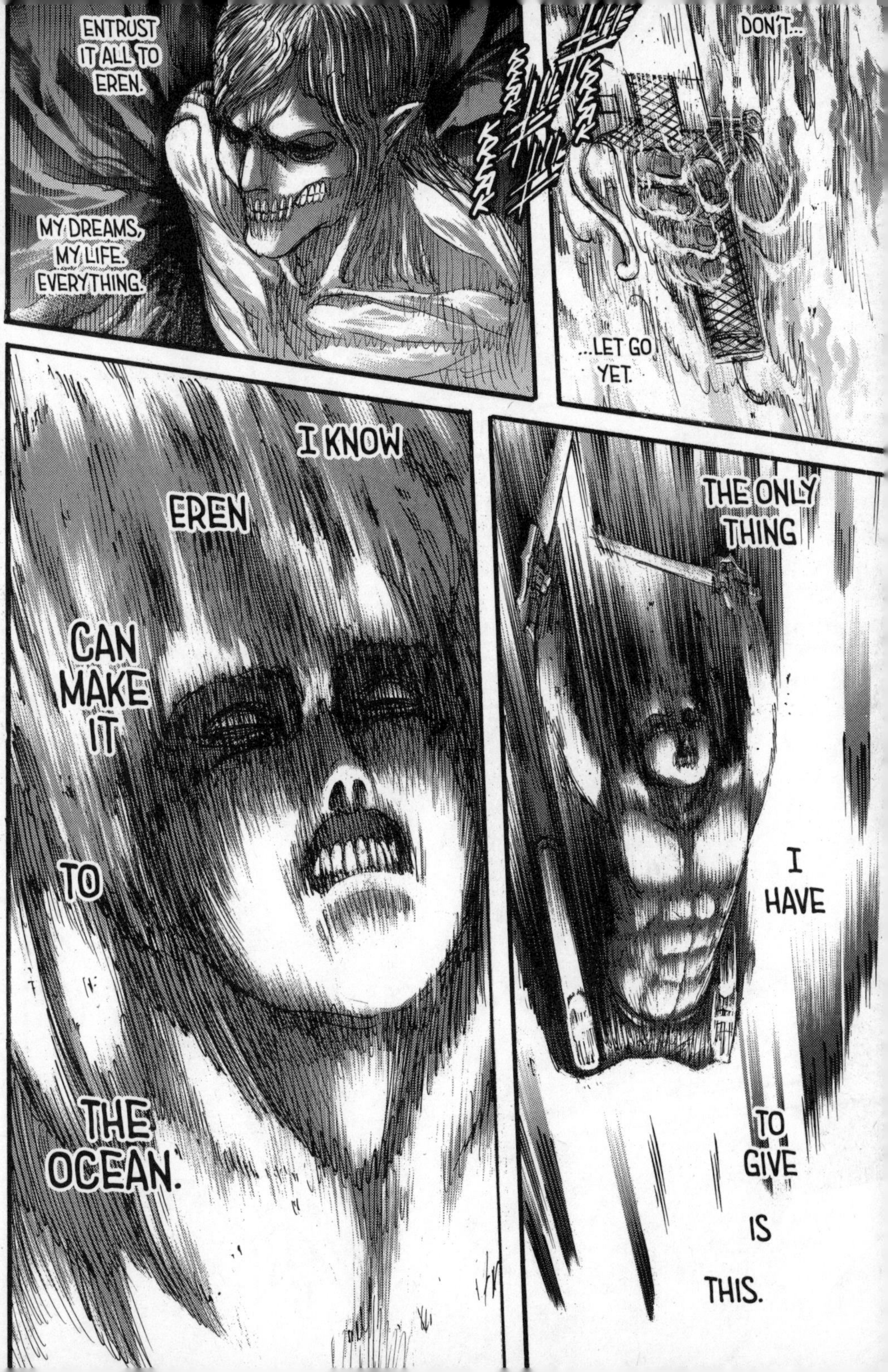
DON'T...
...LET GO YET.
KREAK
ENTRUST IT ALL TO EREN.
MY DREAMS, MY LIFE. EVERYTHING.
THE ONLY THING
I HAVE
TO GIVE
IS
THIS.
I KNOW
EREN
CAN MAKE IT
TO
THE OCEAN.

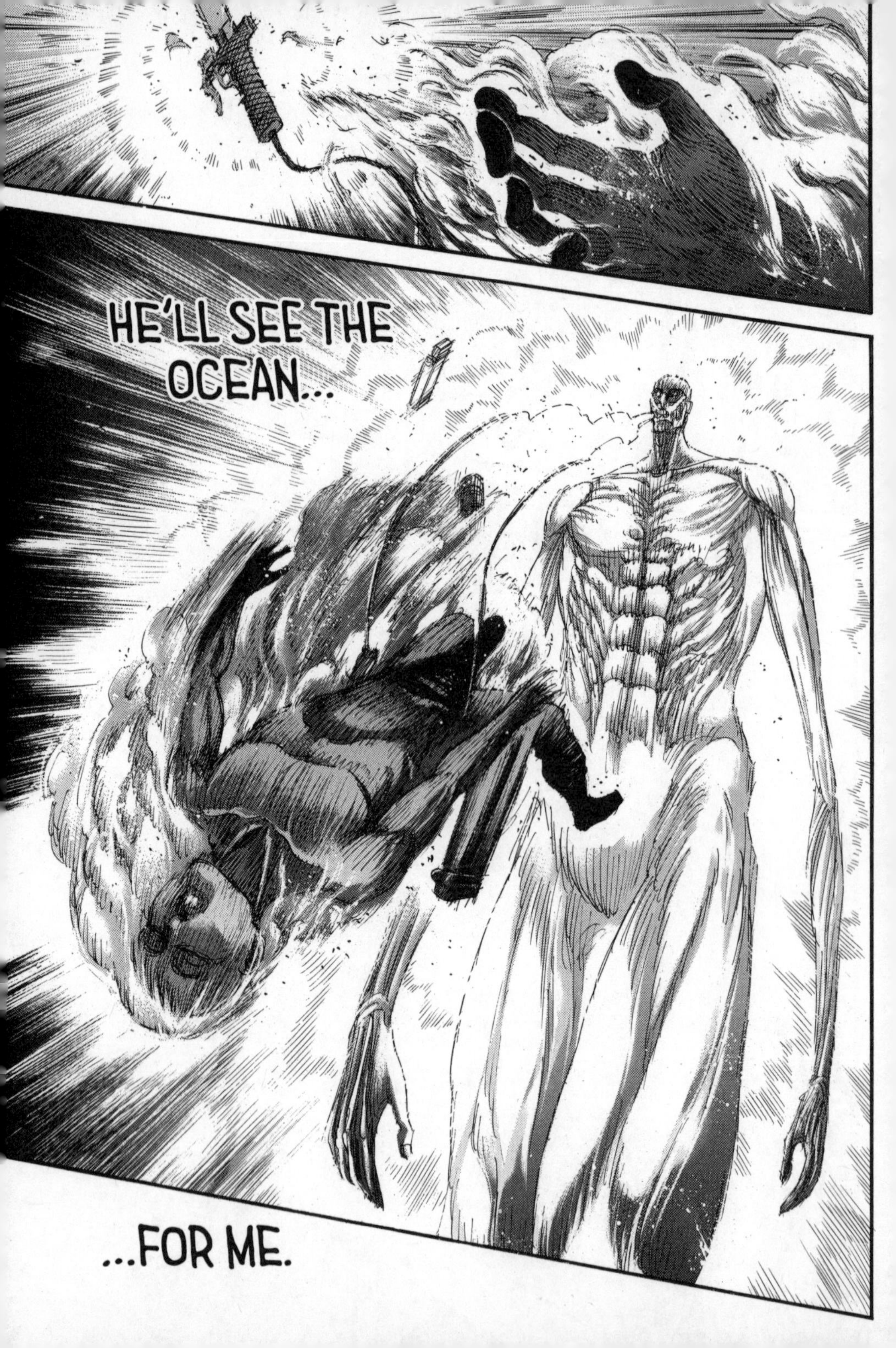
HE'LL SEE THE OCEAN...
...FOR ME.

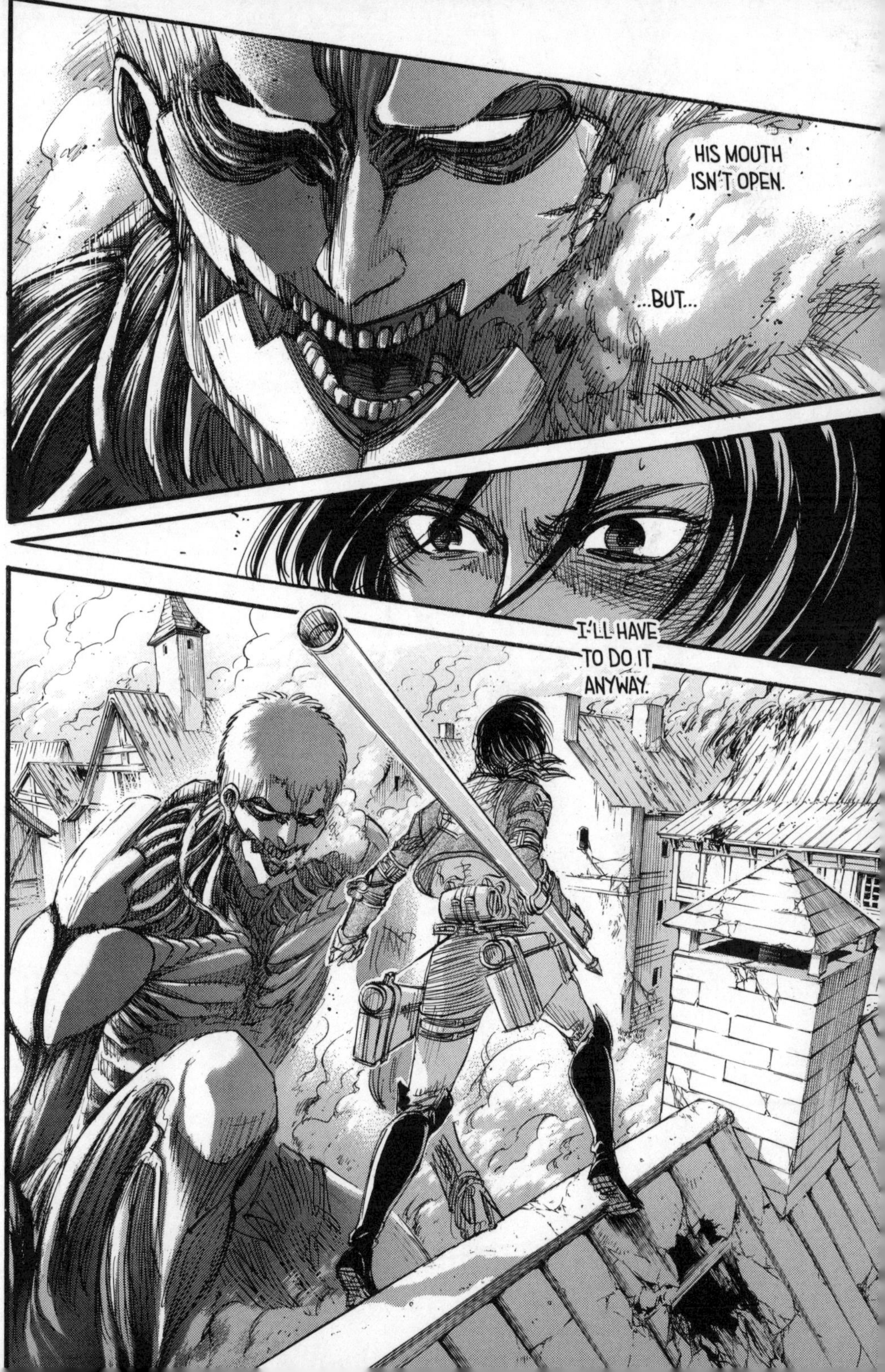
HIS MOUTH ISN'T OPEN.
...BUT...
I'LL HAVE TO DO IT ANYWAY.

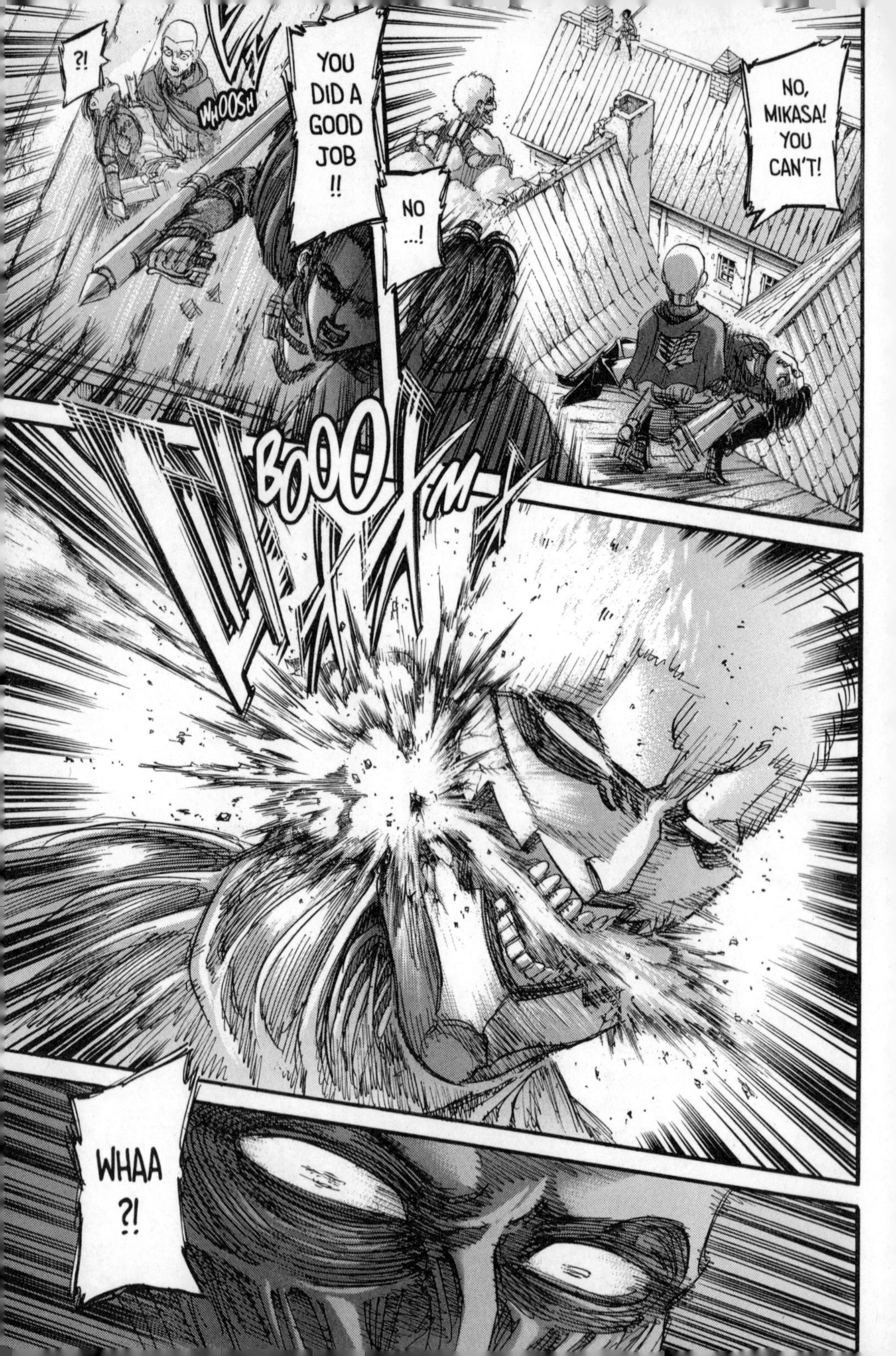
NO, MIKASA! YOU CAN'T!
NO ...!
YOU DID A GOOD JOB !!
WHOOSH
?!
BOOOM
WHAA ?!

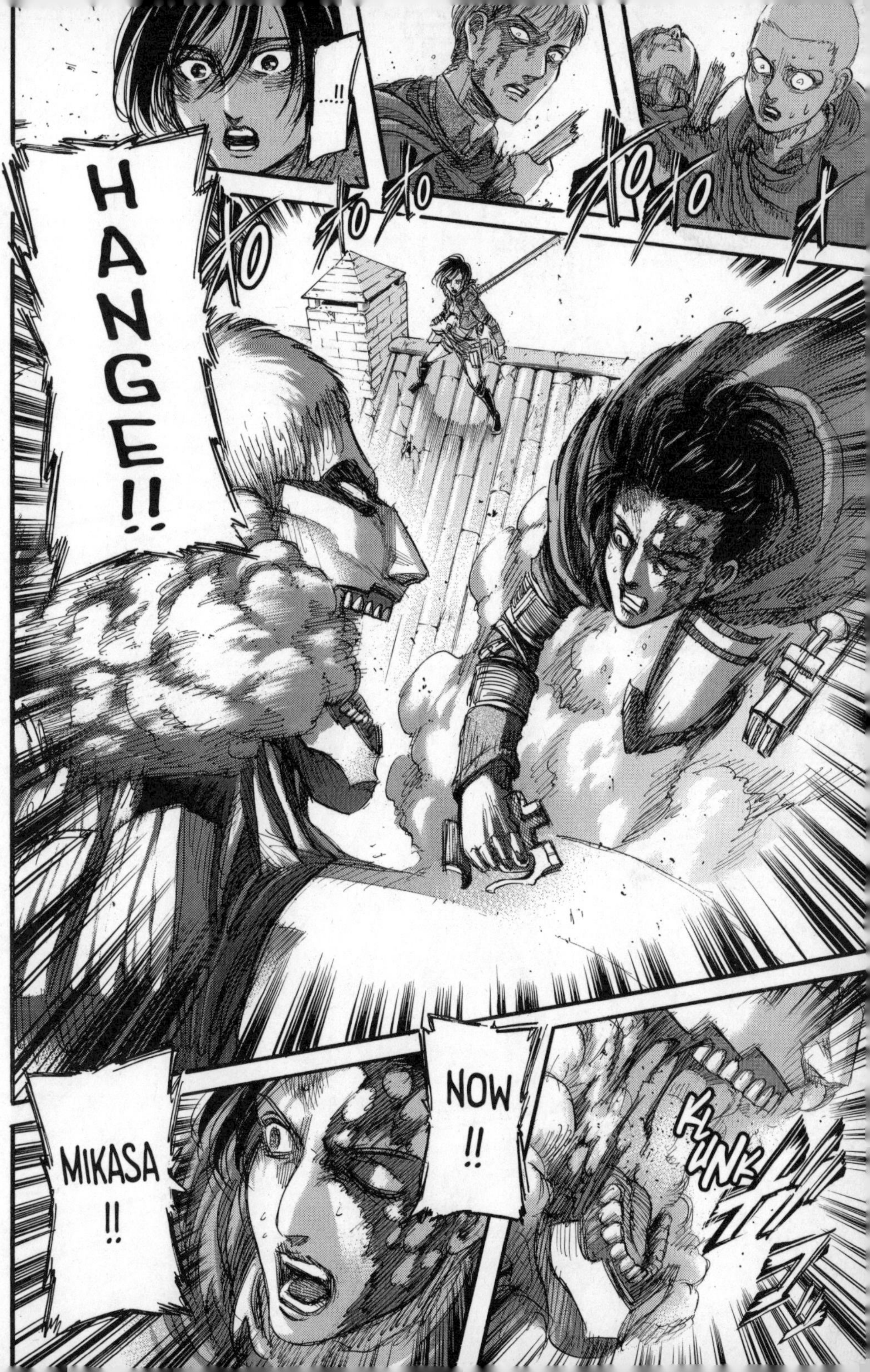

...!!
HANGE!!
KLUNK
NOW!!
MIKASA!!

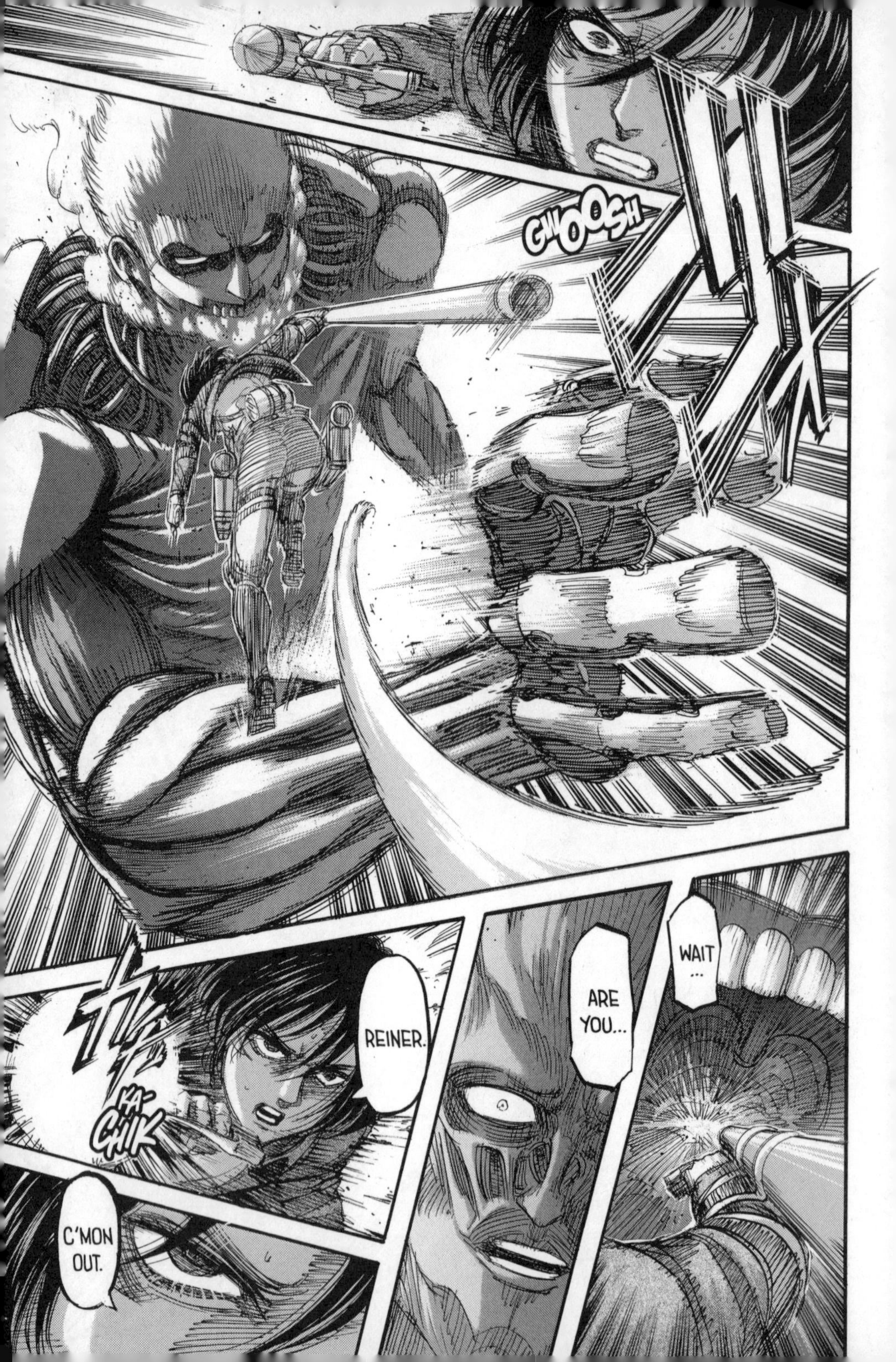
GWOOSH
WAIT ...
ARE YOU...
REINER.
KA-CHIK
C'MON OUT.

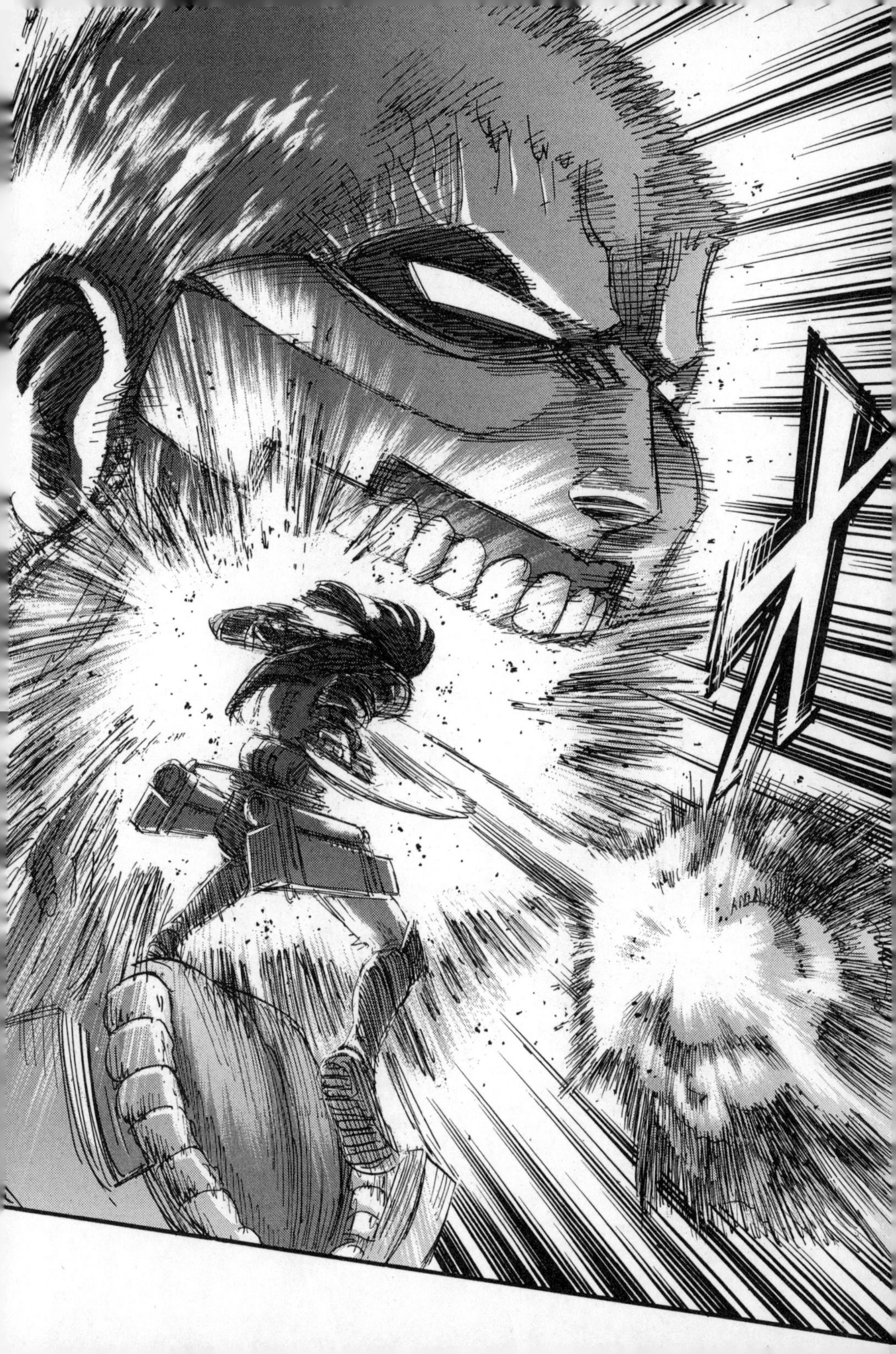

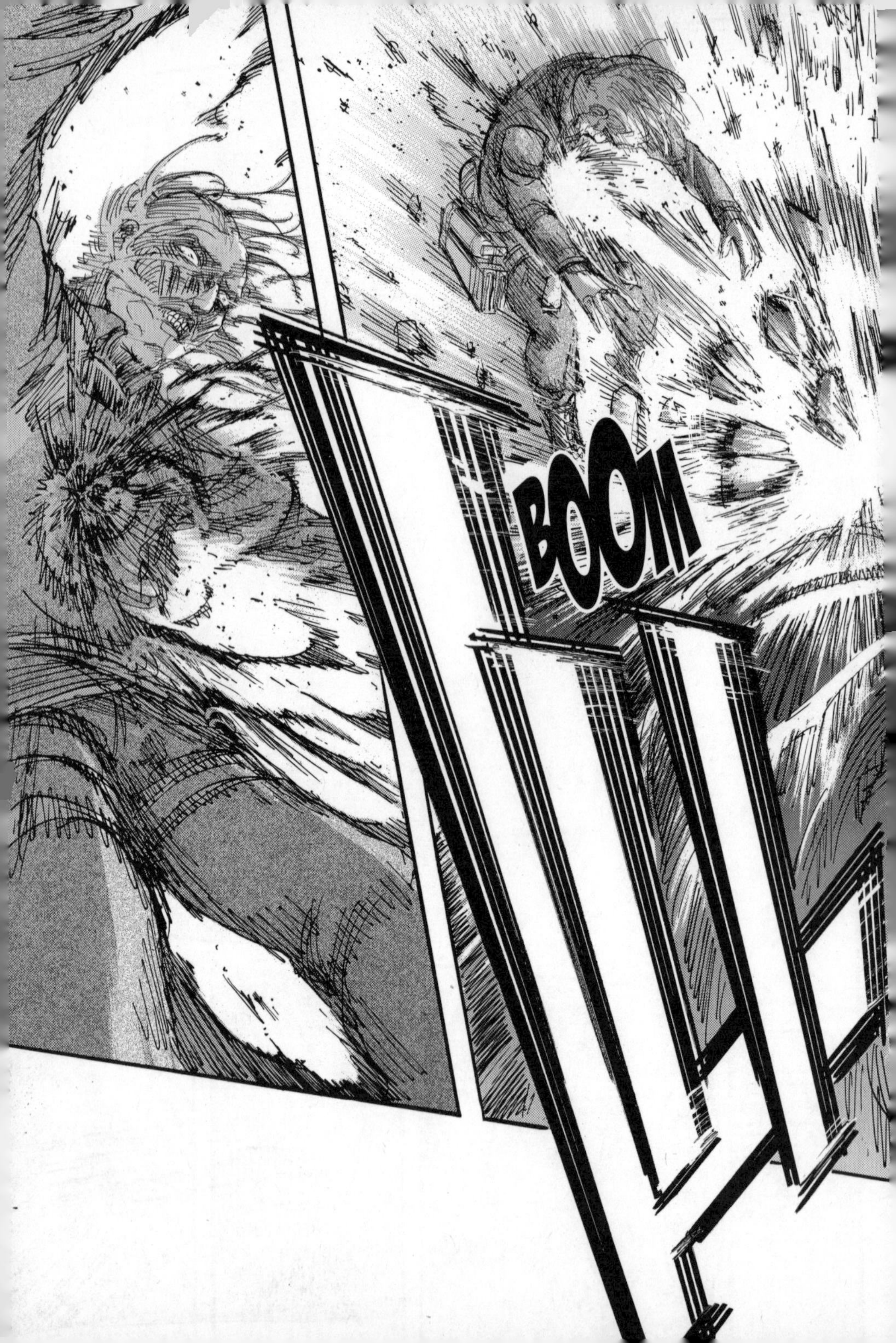
BOOM

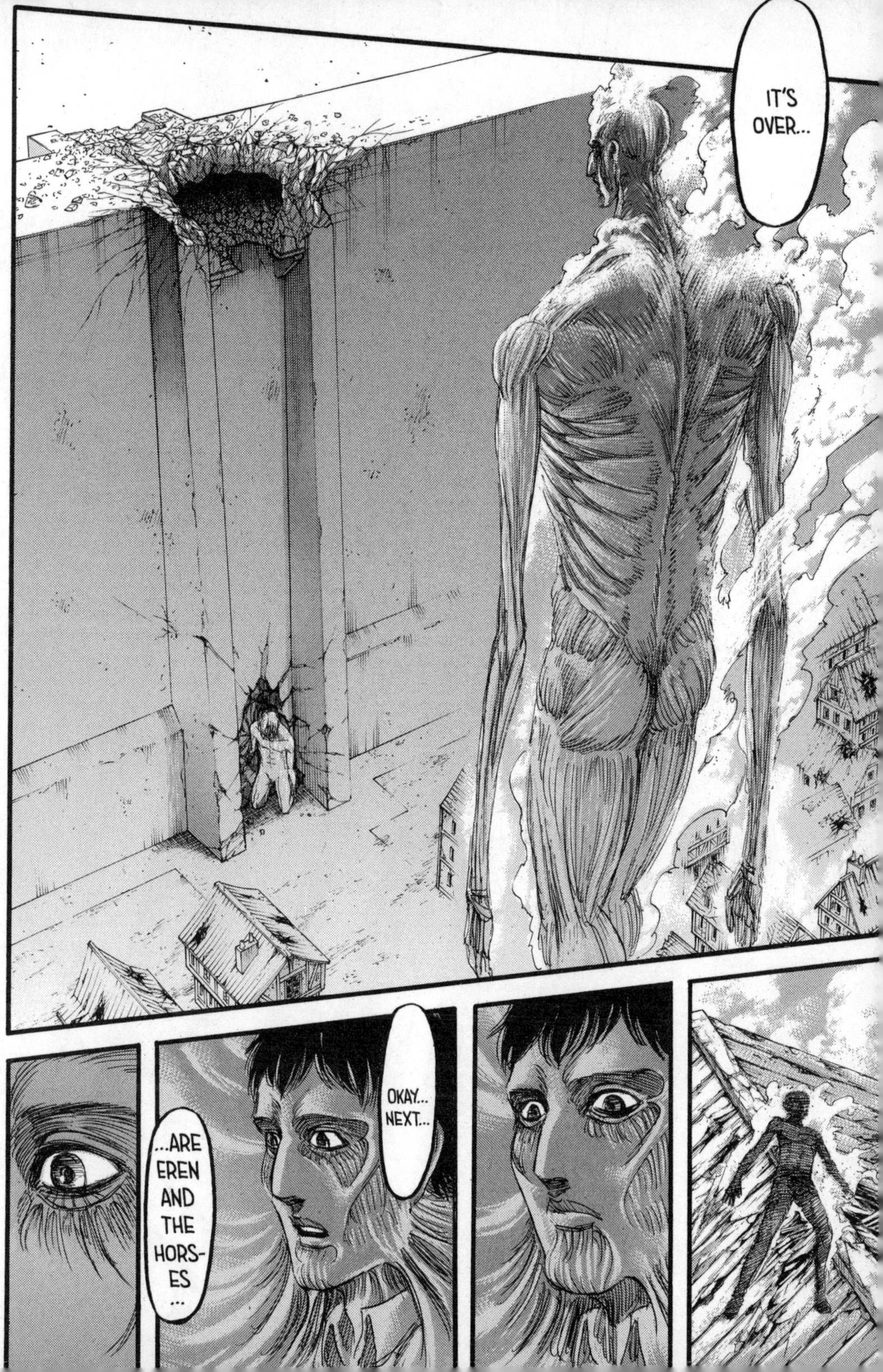
IT'S OVER...
OKAY... NEXT...
...ARE EREN AND THE HORS-ES ...

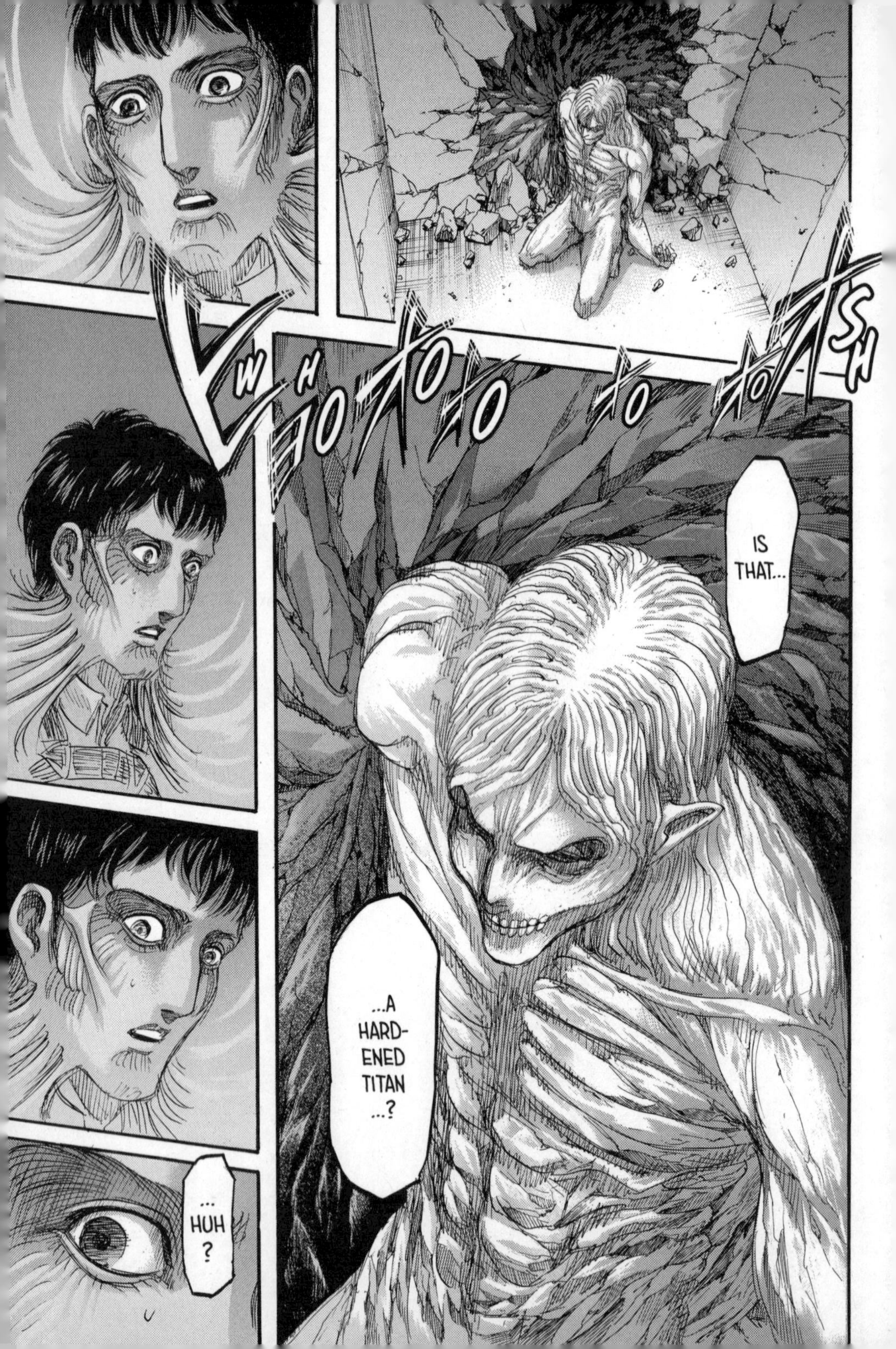
VWHOOOOSH
IS THAT...
...A HARDENED TITAN...?
...HUH?

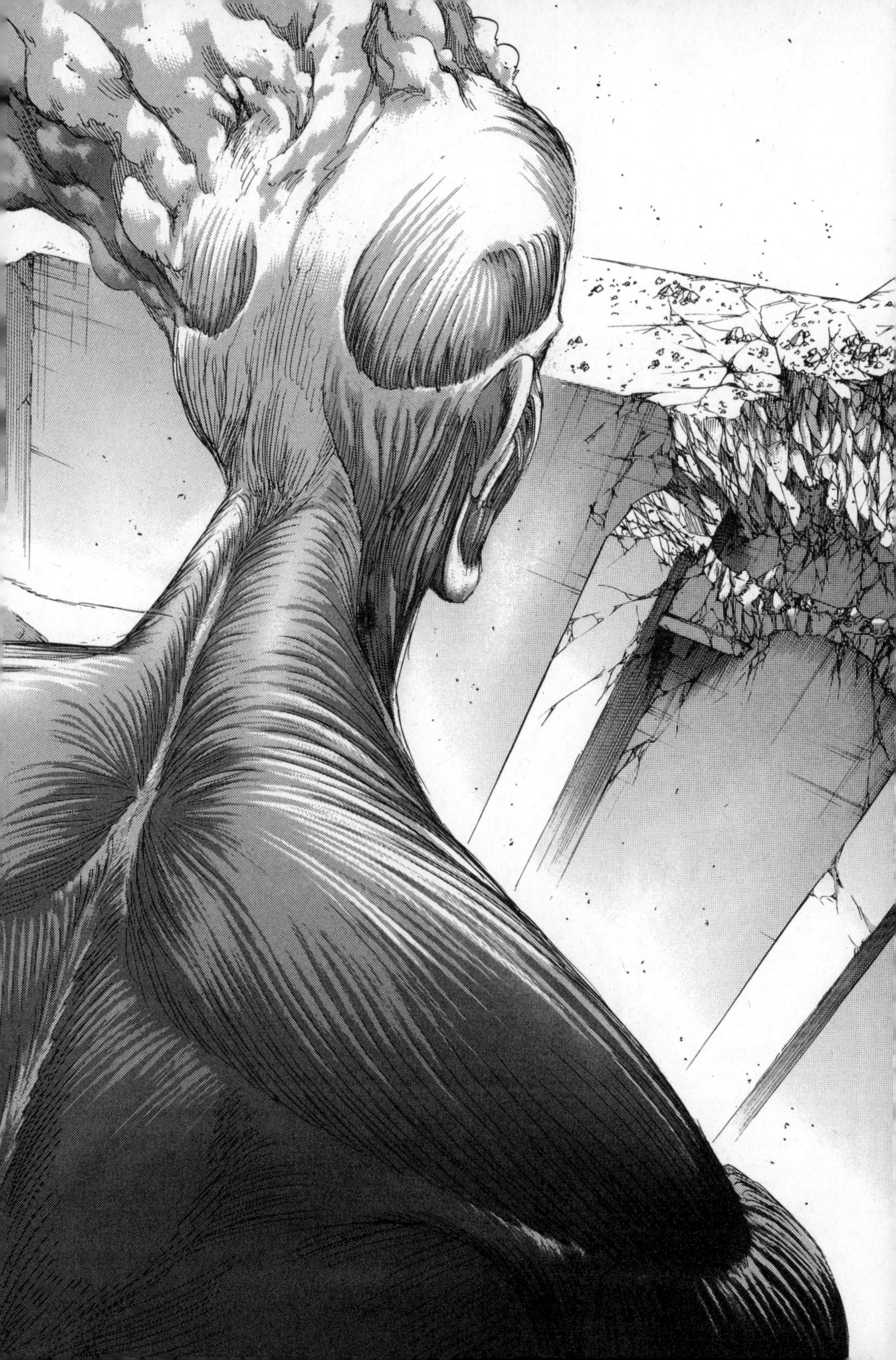

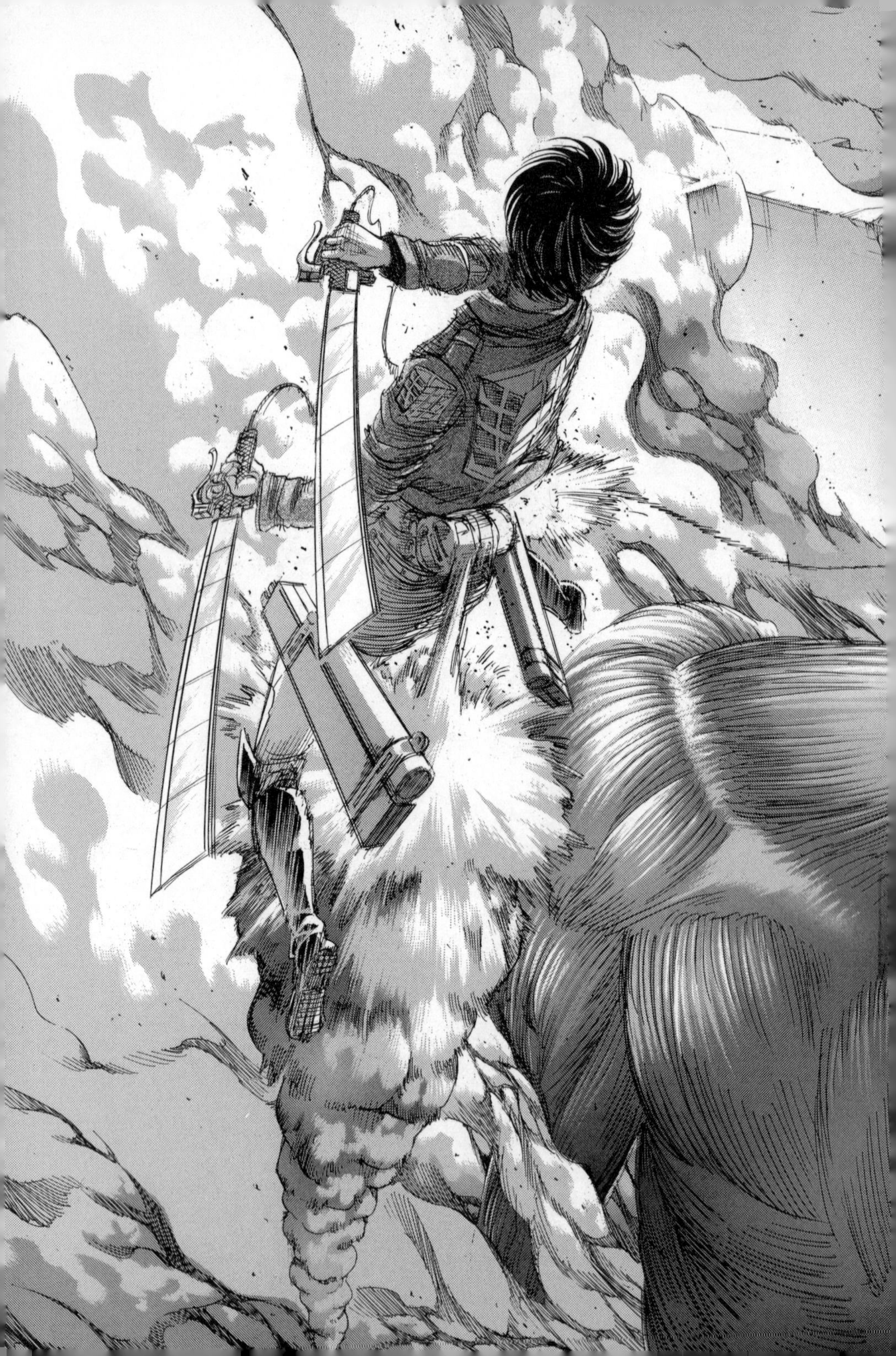

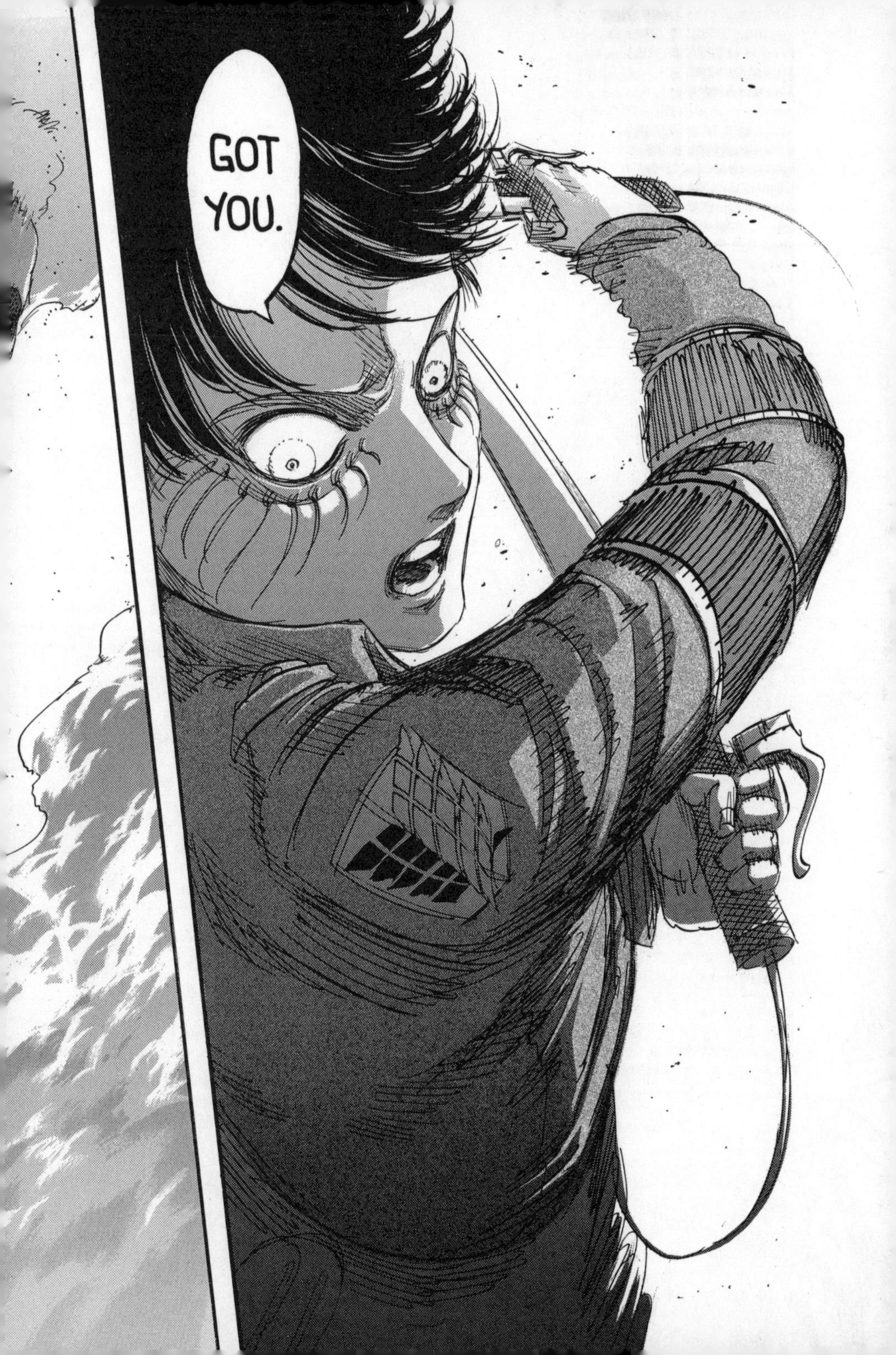
GOT YOU.

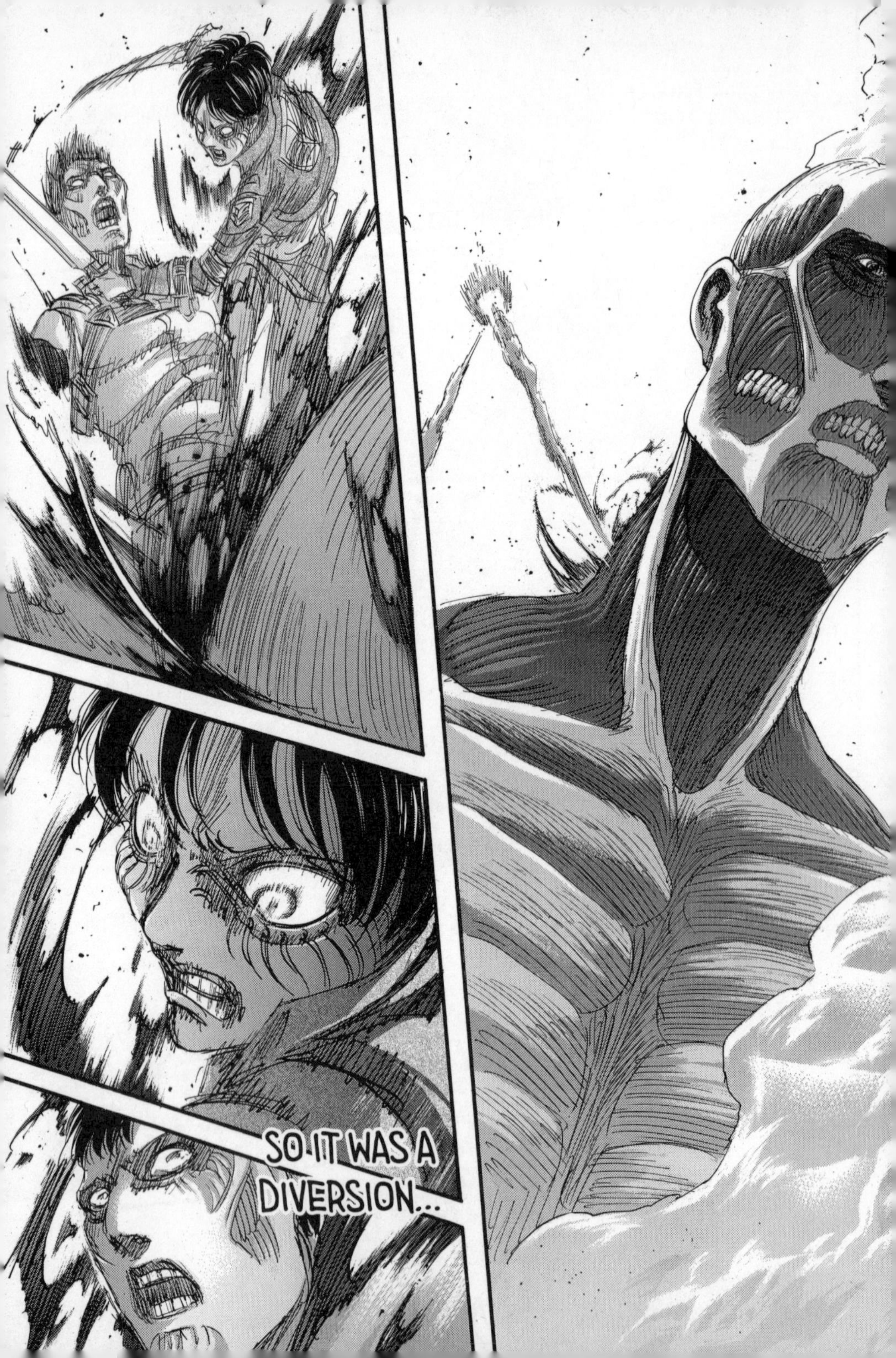
SO IT WAS A DIVERSION...

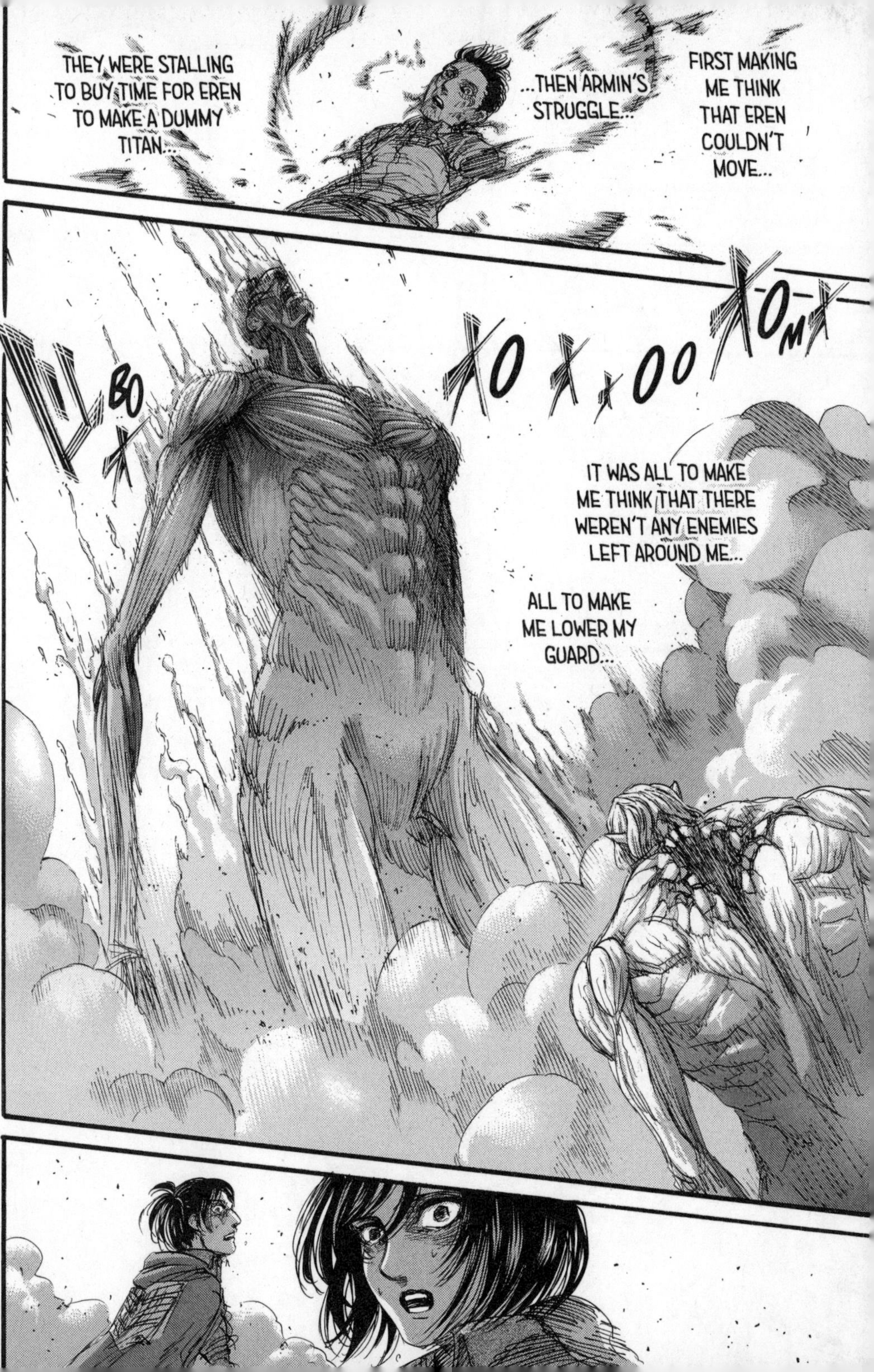
FIRST MAKING ME THINK THAT EREN COULDN'T MOVE...
...THEN ARMIN'S STRUGGLE...
THEY WERE STALLING TO BUY TIME FOR EREN TO MAKE A DUMMY TITAN...
IT WAS ALL TO MAKE ME THINK THAT THERE WEREN'T ANY ENEMIES LEFT AROUND ME...
ALL TO MAKE ME LOWER MY GUARD...

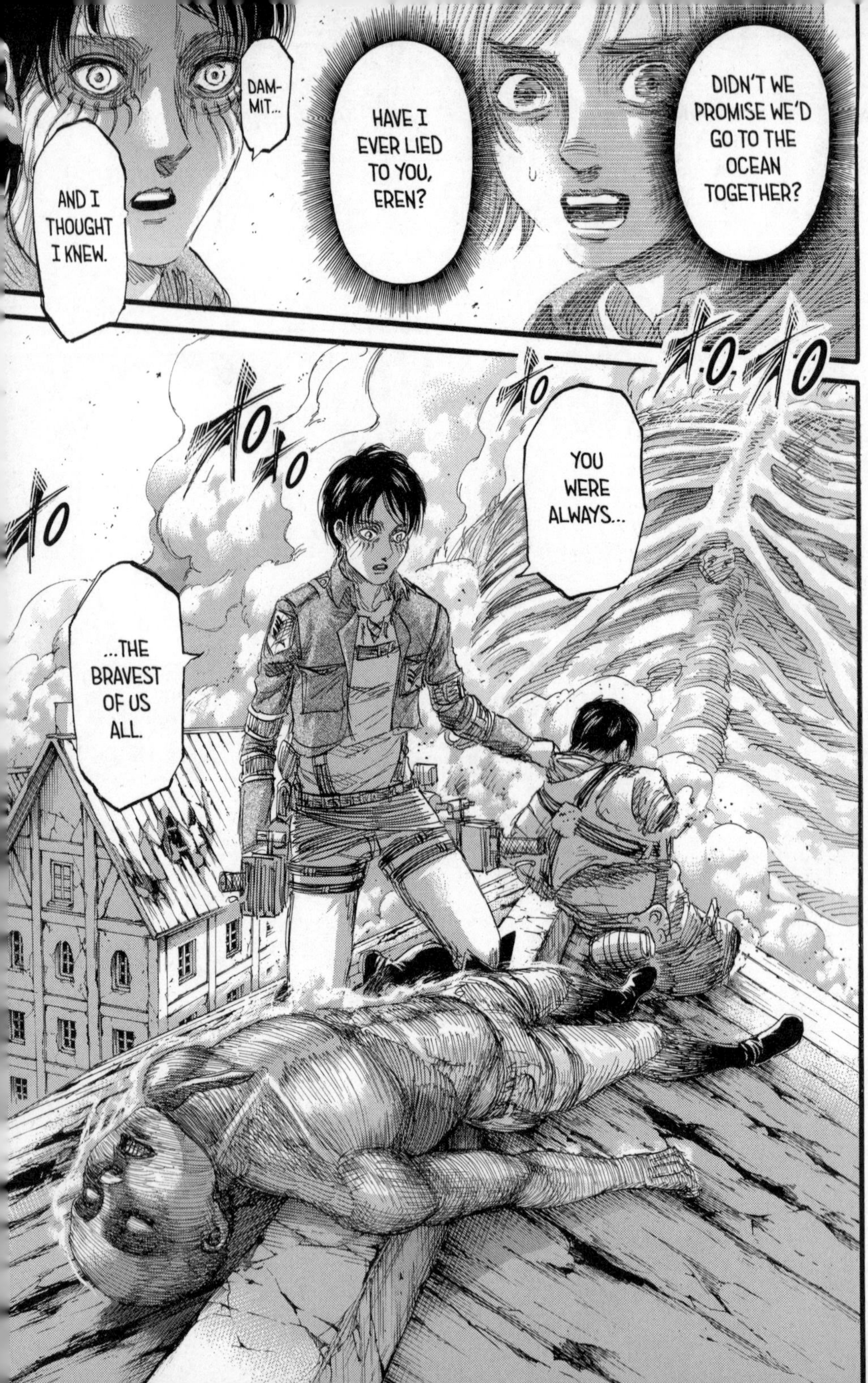
DIDN'T WE PROMISE WE'D GO TO THE OCEAN TOGETHER?
HAVE I EVER LIED TO YOU, EREN?
DAM-MIT...
AND I THOUGHT I KNEW.
YOU WERE ALWAYS...
...THE BRAVEST OF US ALL.

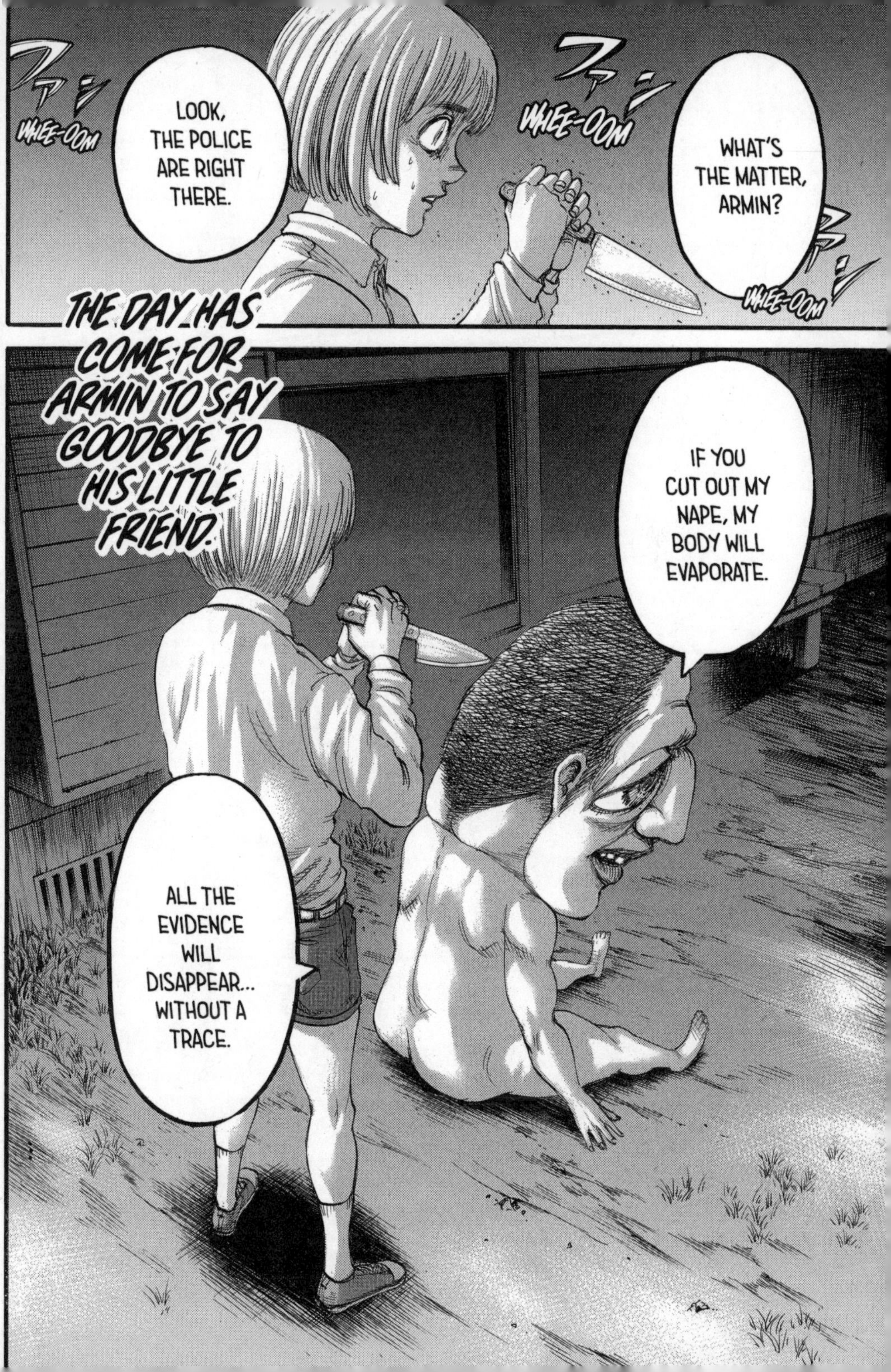
ファシ
WHEE-OOM
WHAT'S THE MATTER, ARMIN?
ファシ
WHEE-OOM
LOOK, THE POLICE ARE RIGHT THERE.
ファシ
WHEE-OOM
THE DAY HAS COME FOR ARMIN TO SAY GOODBYE TO HIS LITTLE FRIEND.
IF YOU CUT OUT MY NAPE, MY BODY WILL EVAPORATE.
ALL THE EVIDENCE WILL DISAPPEAR... WITHOUT A TRACE.

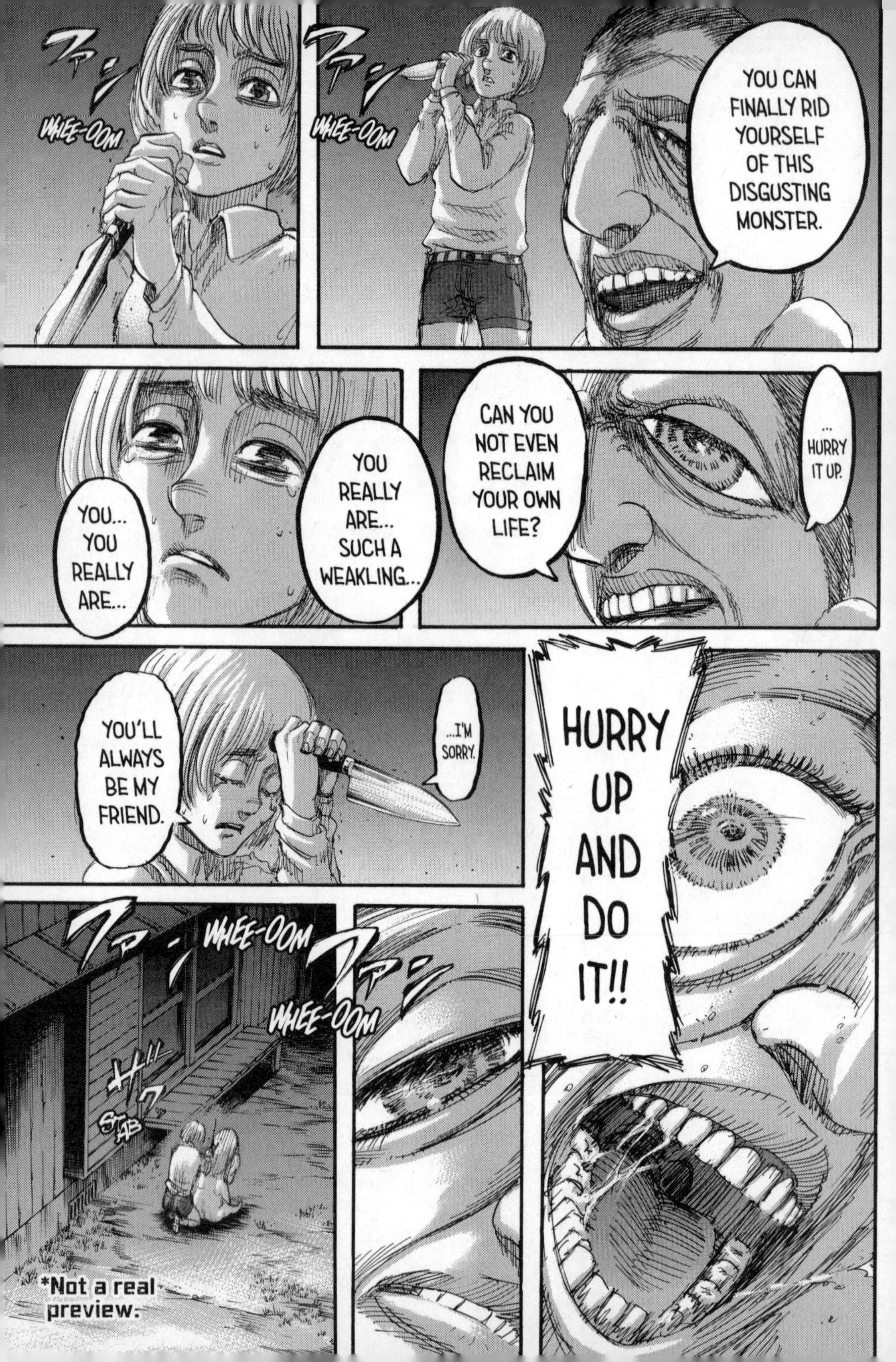
YOU CAN FINALLY RID YOURSELF OF THIS DISGUSTING MONSTER.
WHEE-OOM
WHEE-OOM
... HURRY IT UP.
CAN YOU NOT EVEN RECLAIM YOUR OWN LIFE?
YOU REALLY ARE... SUCH A WEAKLING...
YOU... YOU REALLY ARE...
HURRY UP AND DO IT!!
...I'M SORRY.
YOU'LL ALWAYS BE MY FRIEND.
WHEE-OOM
WHEE-OOM
STAB
*Not a real preview.

ATTACK on TITAN

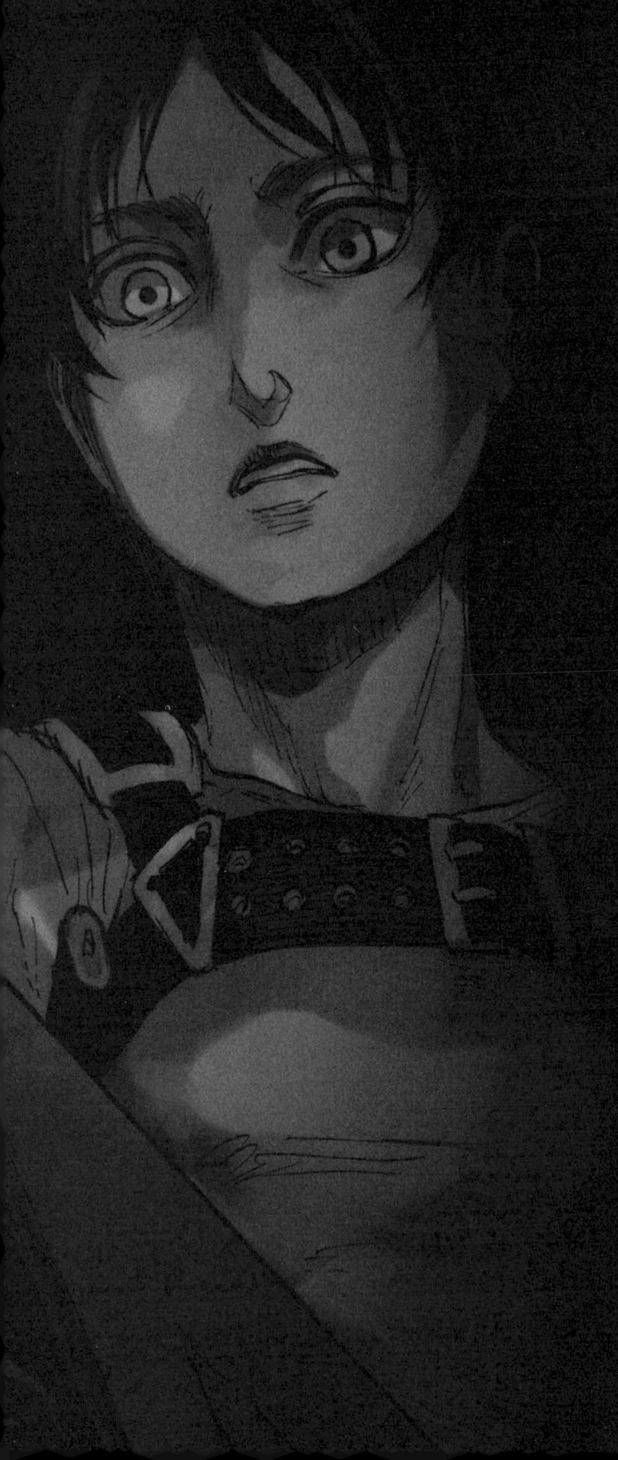

ATTACK ON TITAN 21

HAJIME ISAYAMA

"Attack on Titan" Character Introductions

104th Corps

Graduated at the top of her training corps, Mikasa is a highly talented soldier. Her parents were murdered before her eyes when she was a child, but Eren saved her life. Since then, she has made it her mission to protect him.

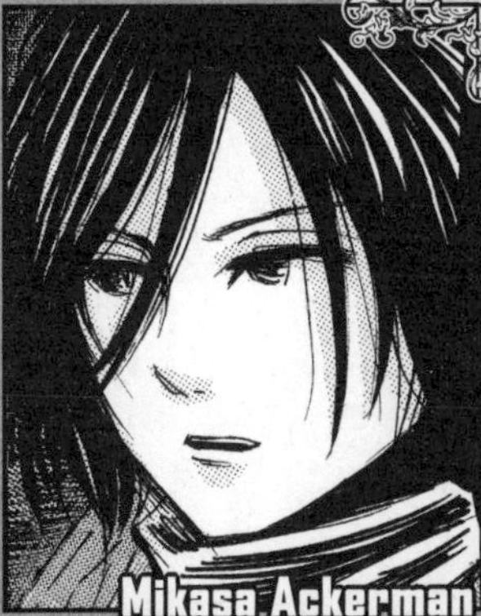
Mikasa Ackerman

Eren joined the Survey Corps out of his longing for the outside world and his hatred of the Titans. He has the power to turn himself into a Titan, but its origins are unknown.

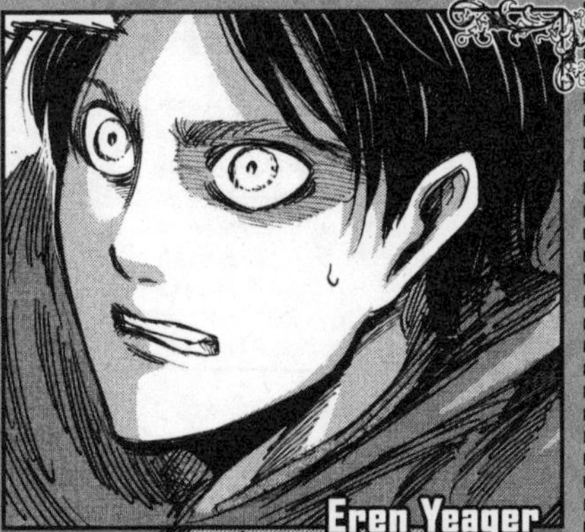
Eren Yeager

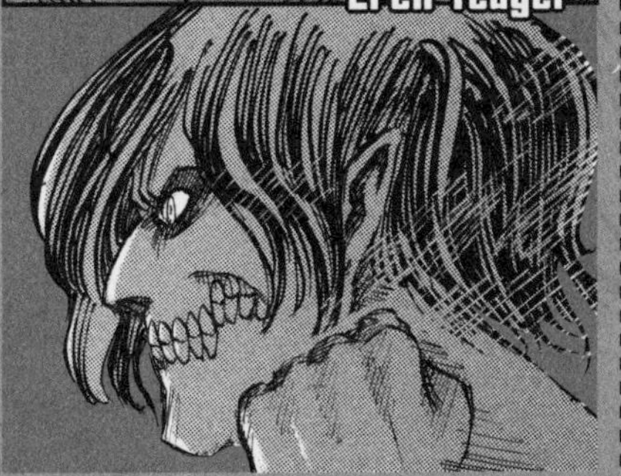

Eren and Mikasa's childhood friend. Though Armin isn't athletic in the least, he possesses both sharp observational powers and keen insight, and he exhibits an extraordinary ability to develop strategies.

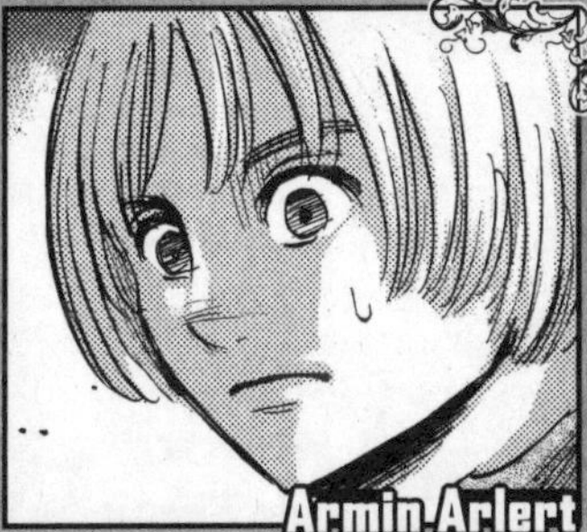
Armin Arlert

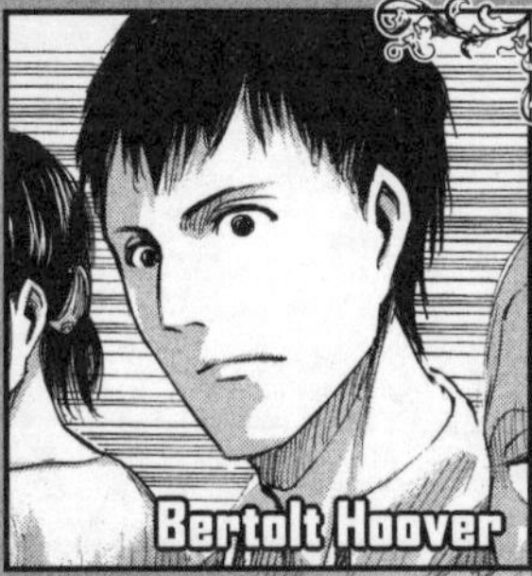
Bertolt Hoover

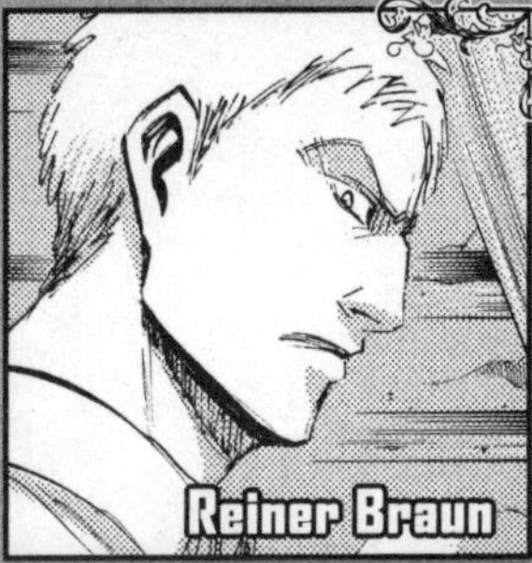
Reiner Braun

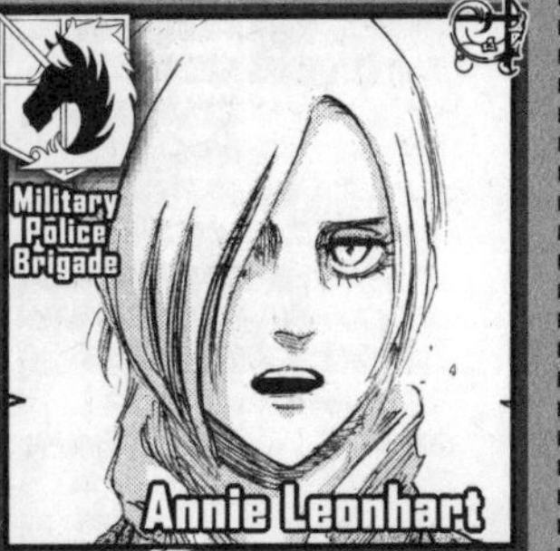
Military Police Brigade
Annie Leonhart

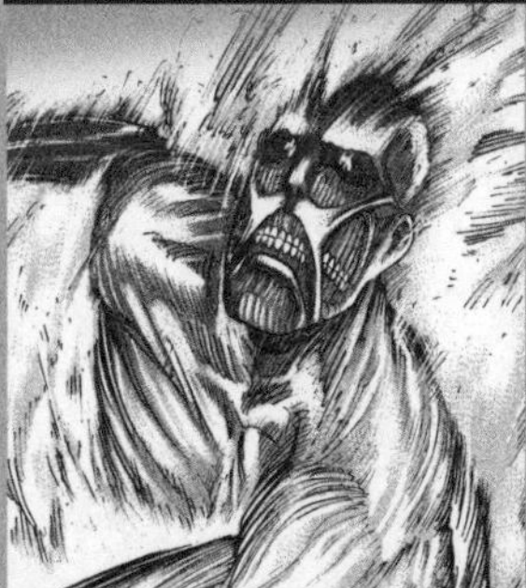
The Colossus Titan

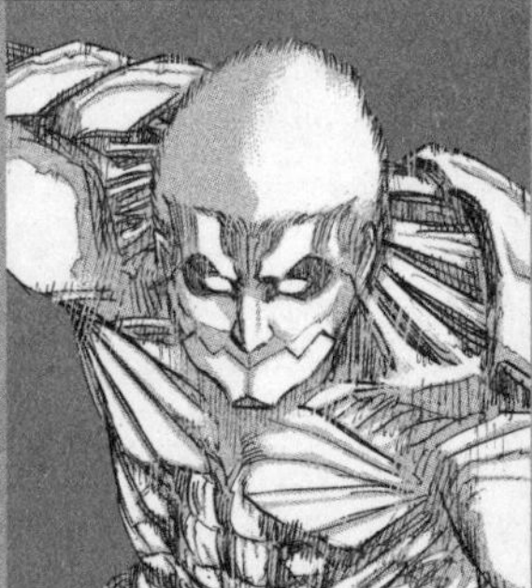
The Armored Titan

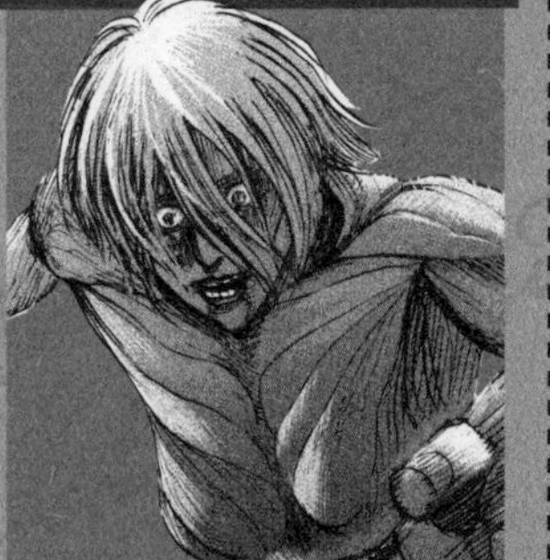
The Female Titan

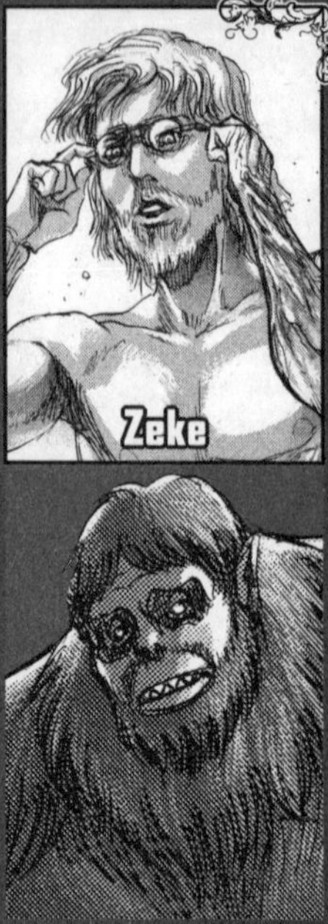
Zeke

The Beast Titan

Survey Corps

Soldiers who are prepared to sacrifice themselve
as they brave the Titan territory outside the wall

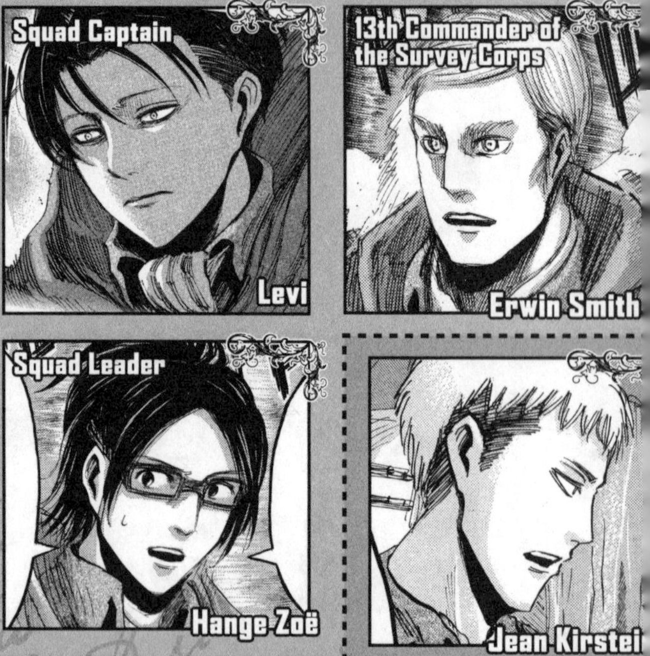
13th Commander of the Survey Corps
Erwin Smith
Squad Captain
Levi
Jean Kirstei
Squad Leader
Hange Zoë

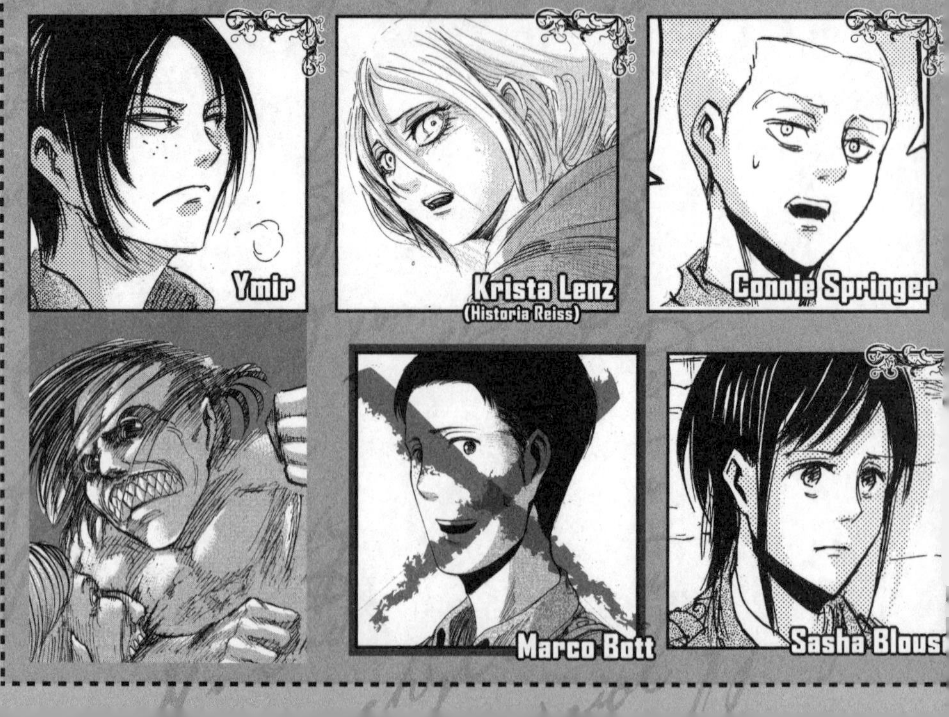
Connie Springer
Krista Lenz
(Historia Reiss)
Ymir
Sasha Blous
Marco Bott

ATTACK on TITAN

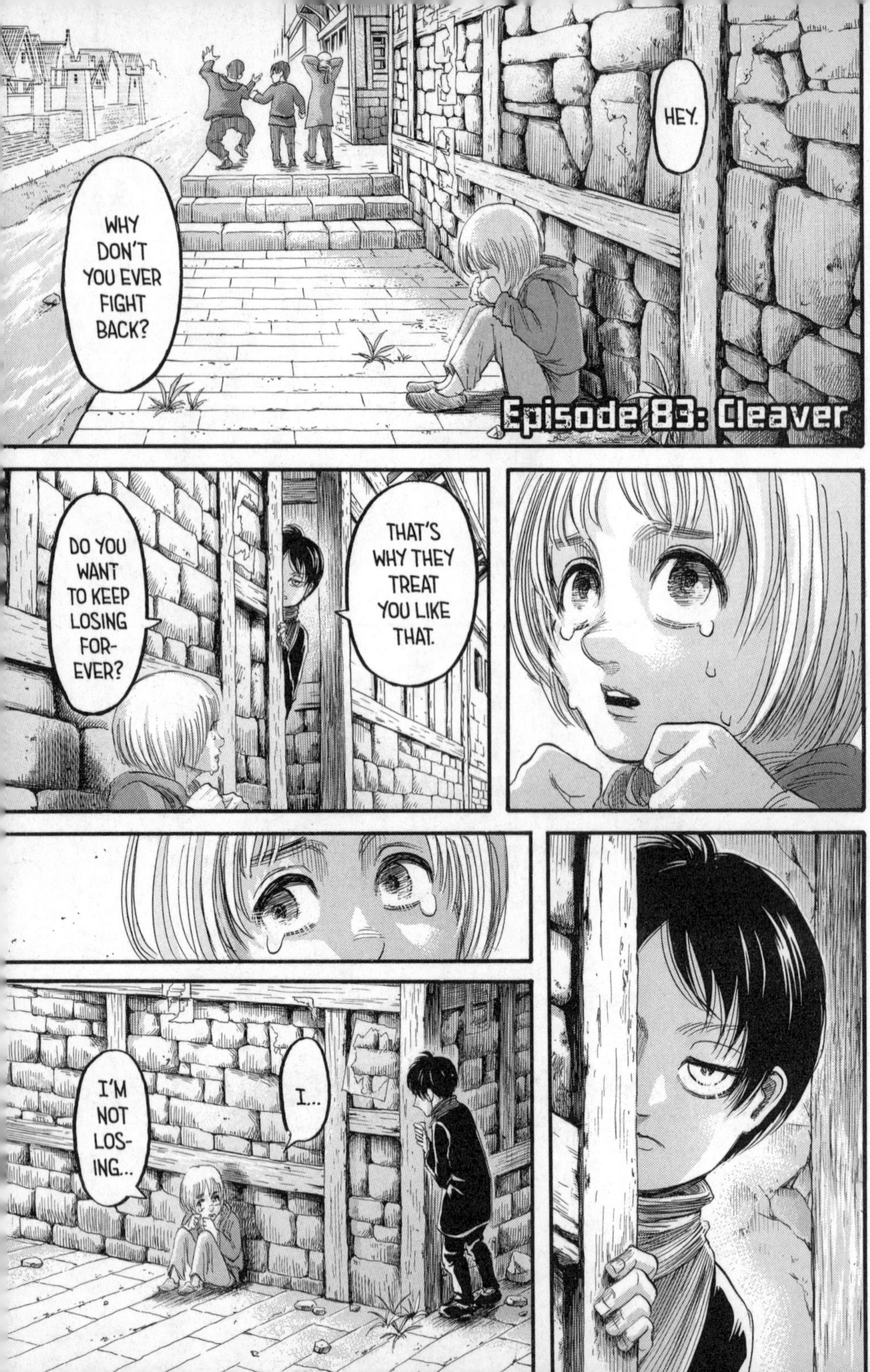
HEY.
WHY DON'T YOU EVER FIGHT BACK?
Episode 83: Cleaver
THAT'S WHY THEY TREAT YOU LIKE THAT.
DO YOU WANT TO KEEP LOSING FOR-EVER?
I...
I'M NOT LOS-ING...

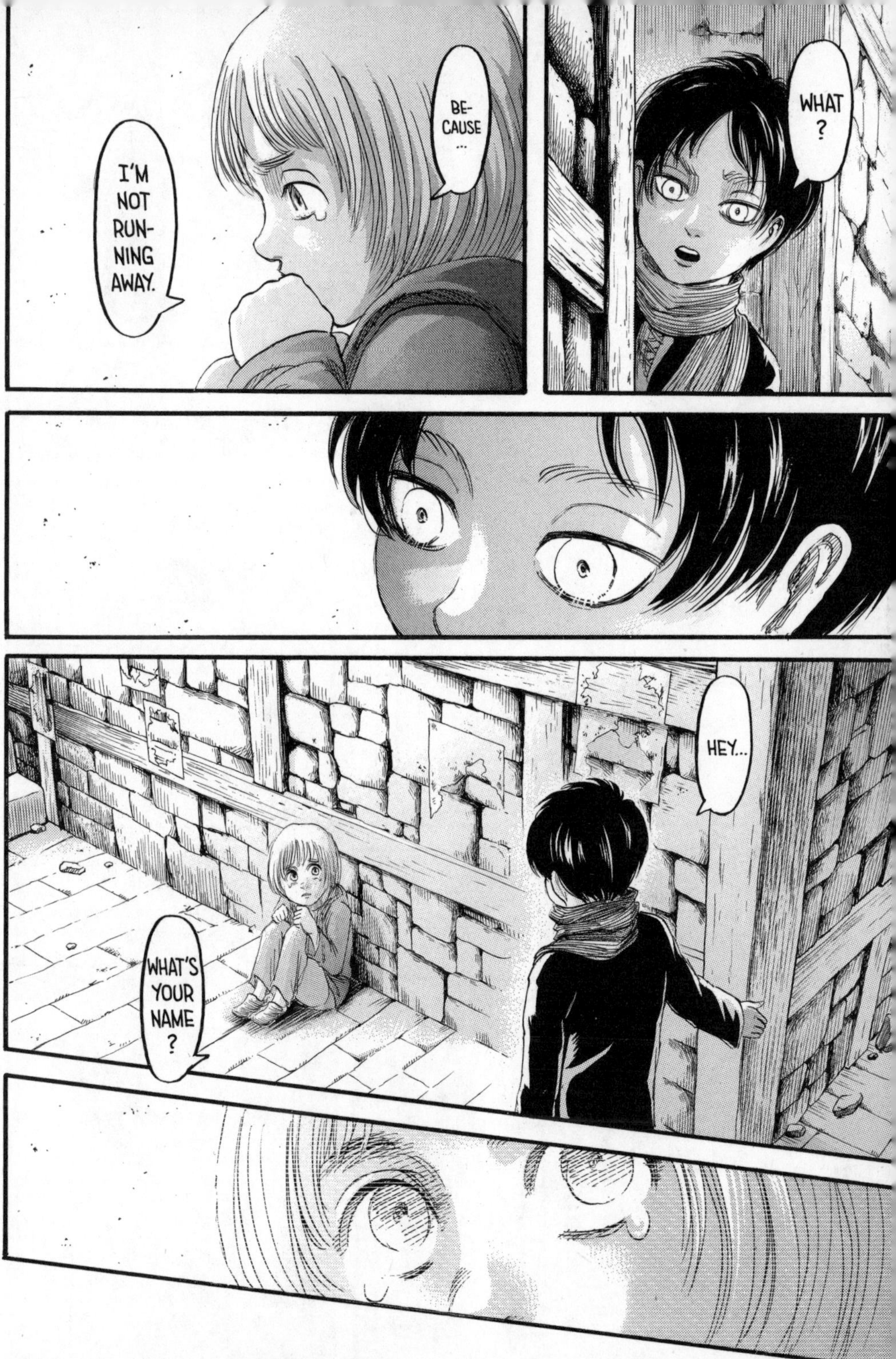
WHAT ?
BE-CAUSE ...
I'M NOT RUN-NING AWAY.
HEY...
WHAT'S YOUR NAME ?

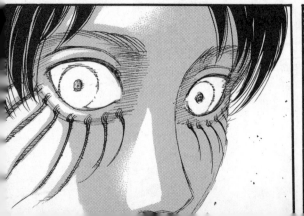

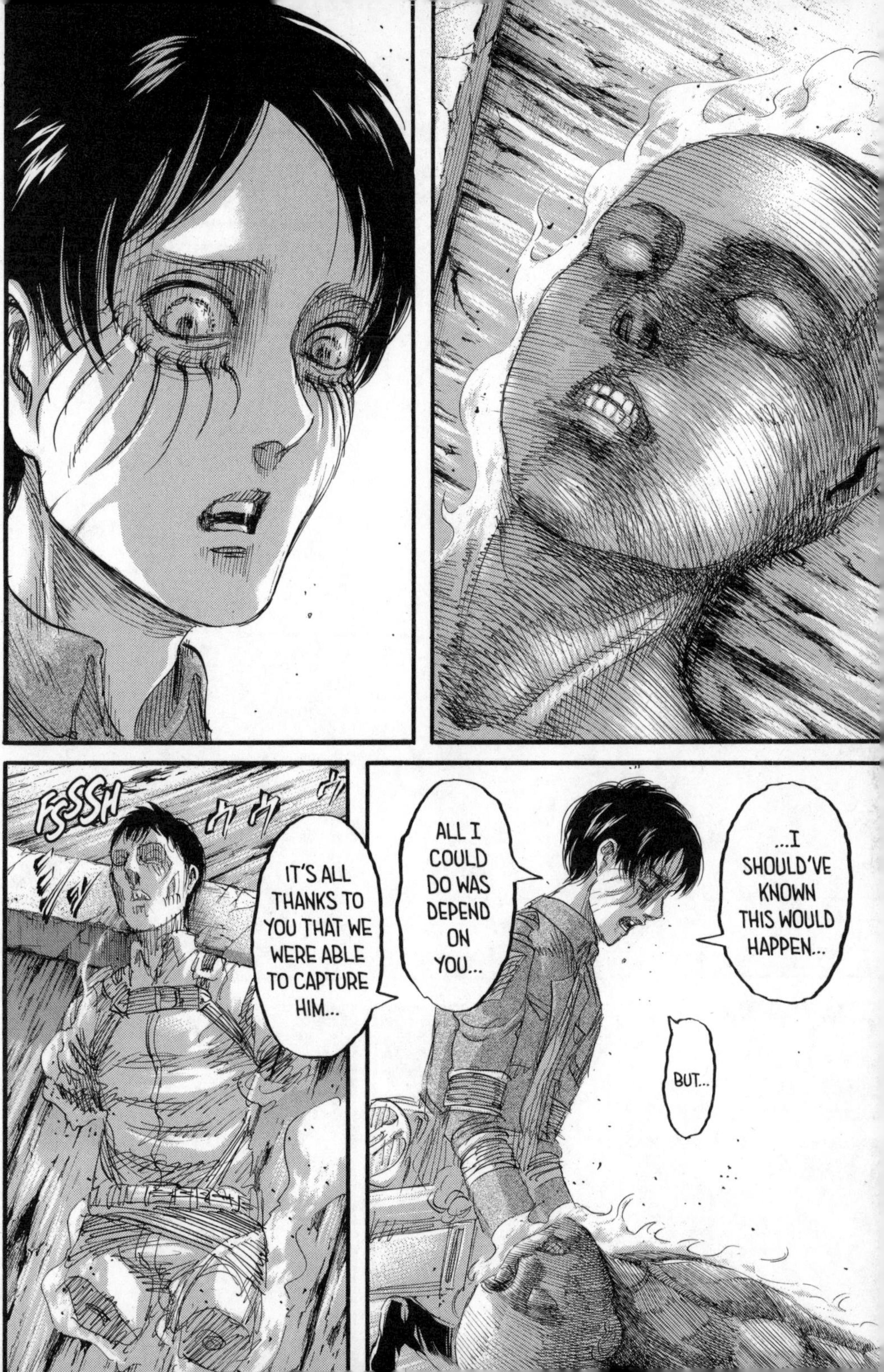
...I SHOULD'VE KNOWN THIS WOULD HAPPEN...
ALL I COULD DO WAS DEPEND ON YOU...
BUT...
FSSSH
IT'S ALL THANKS TO YOU THAT WE WERE ABLE TO CAPTURE HIM...

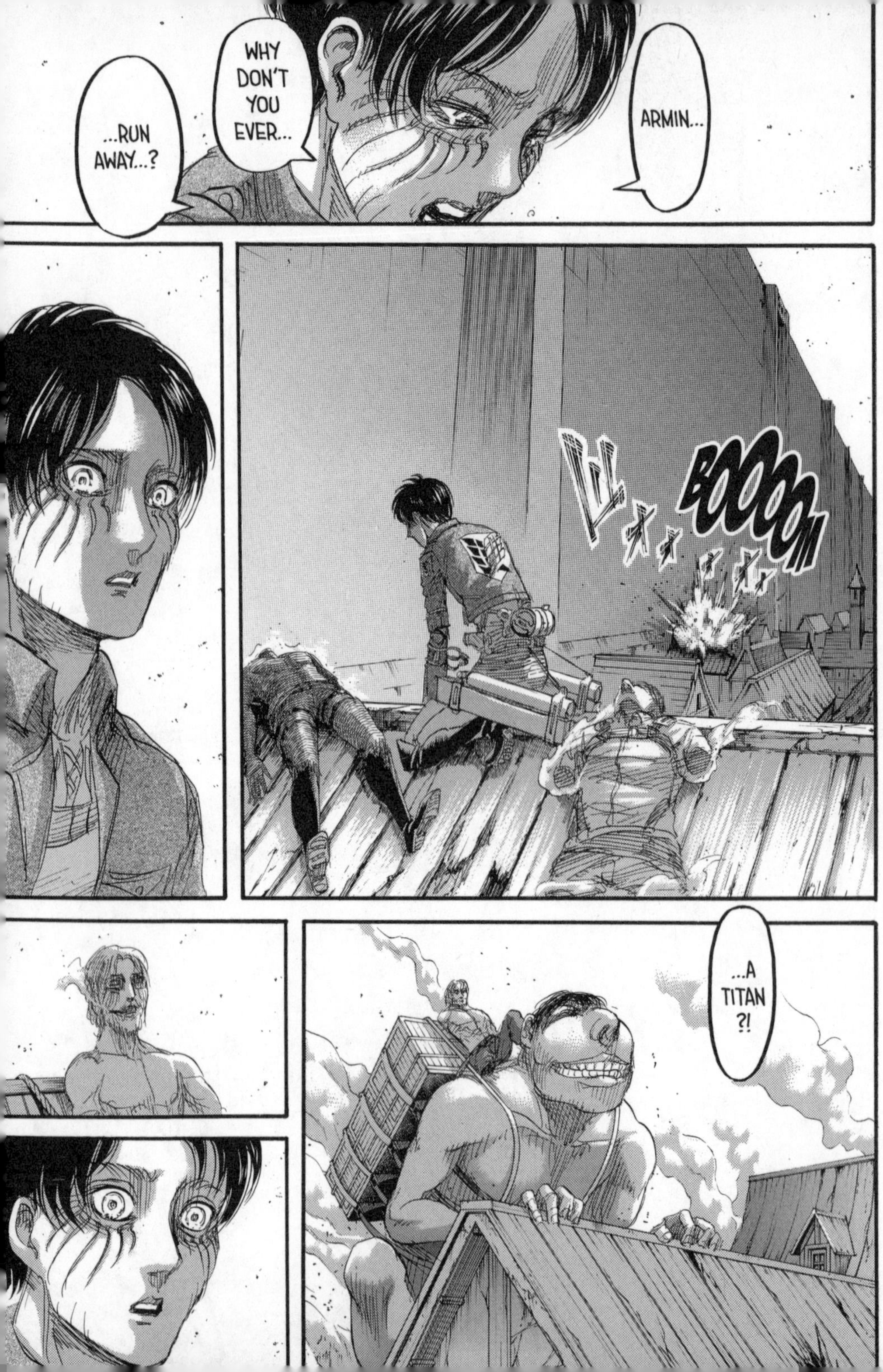
ARMIN...
WHY DON'T YOU EVER...
...RUN AWAY...?
BOOOOM
...A TITAN ?!

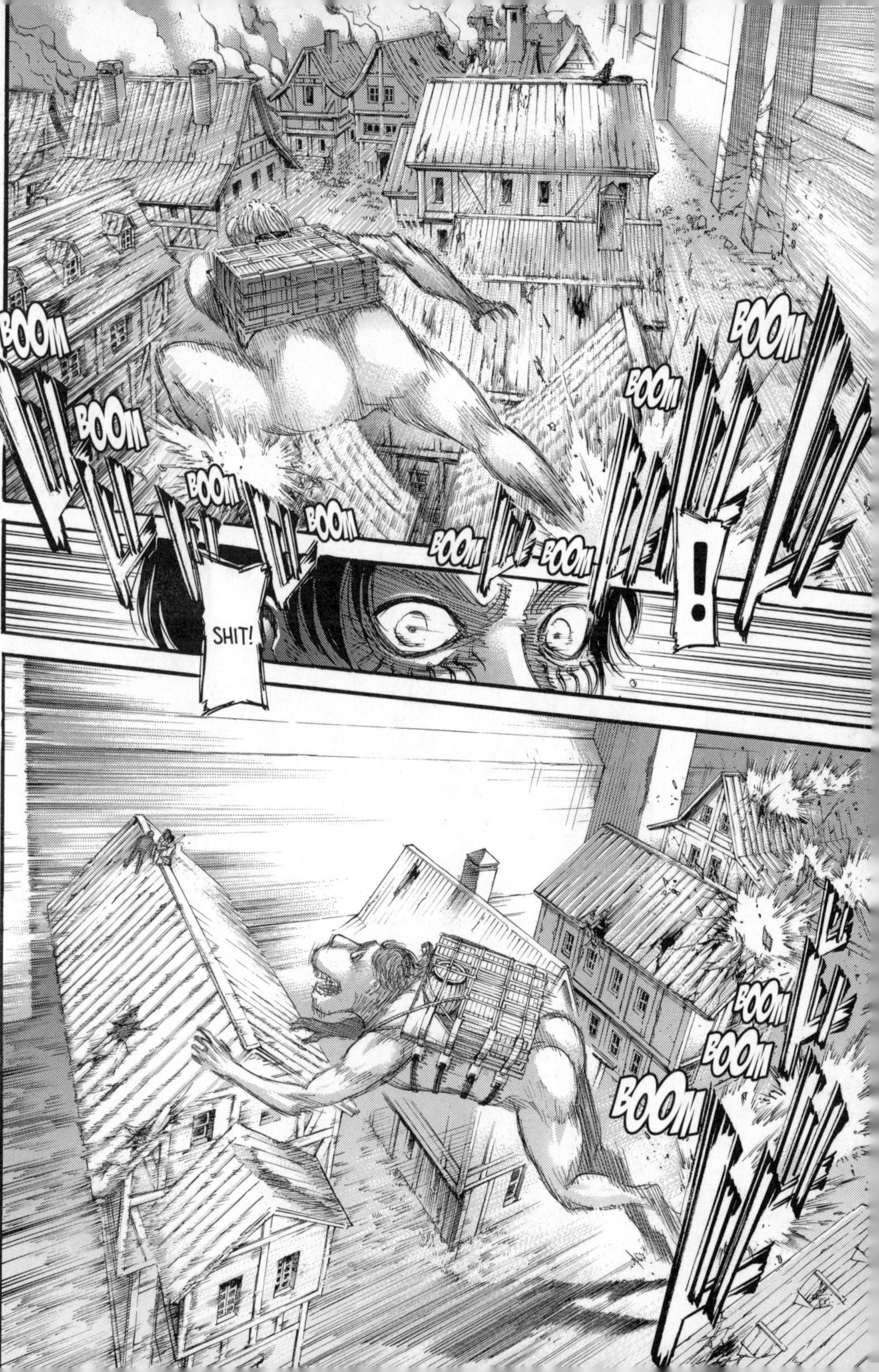
BOOM
BOOM
BOOM
BOOM
BOOM
BOOM
BOOM
BOOM
!
SHIT!
BOOM
BOOM
BOOM

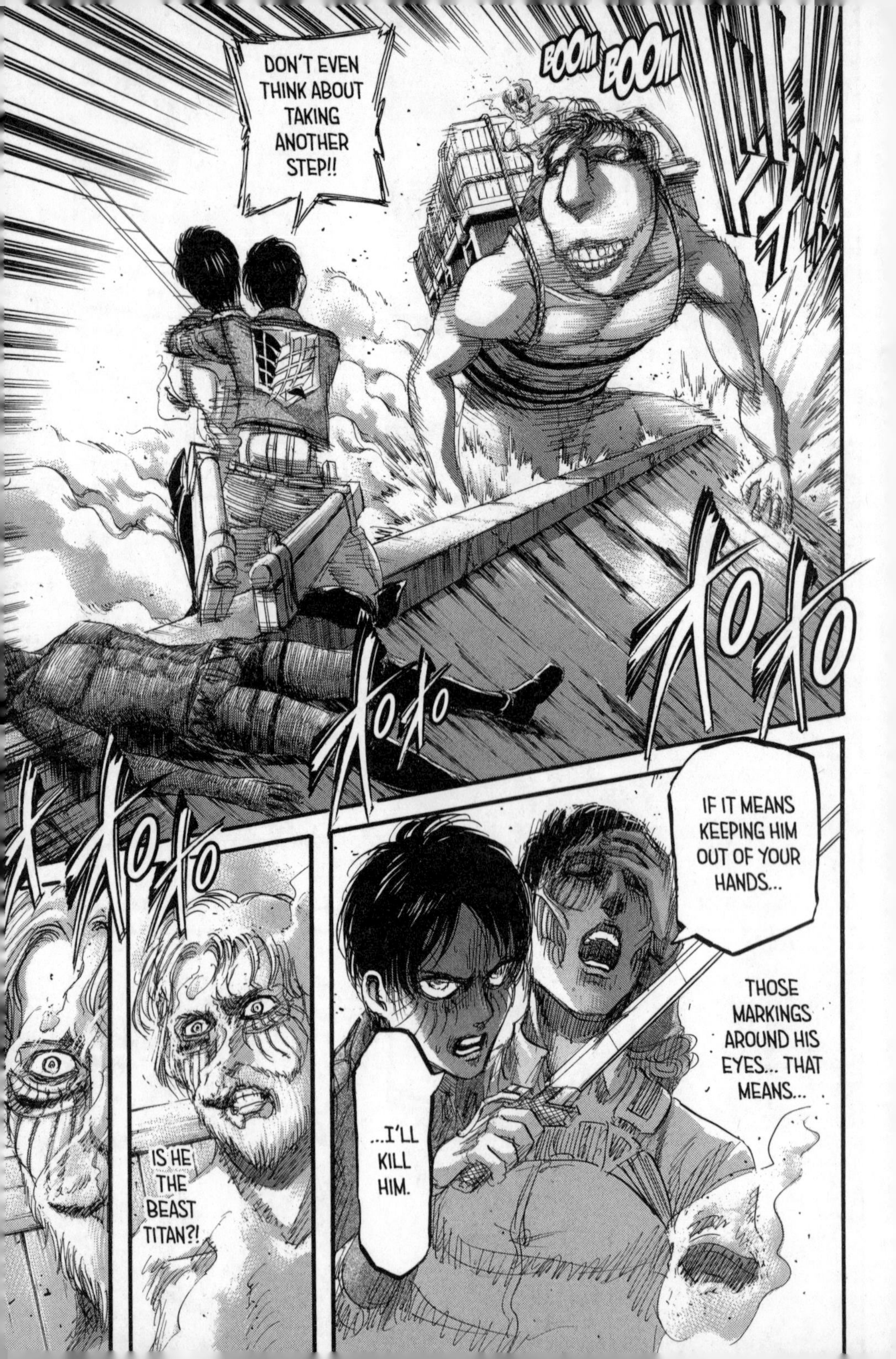
BOOM BOOM
DON'T EVEN THINK ABOUT TAKING ANOTHER STEP!!
IF IT MEANS KEEPING HIM OUT OF YOUR HANDS...
...I'LL KILL HIM.
THOSE MARKINGS AROUND HIS EYES... THAT MEANS...
IS HE THE BEAST TITAN?!

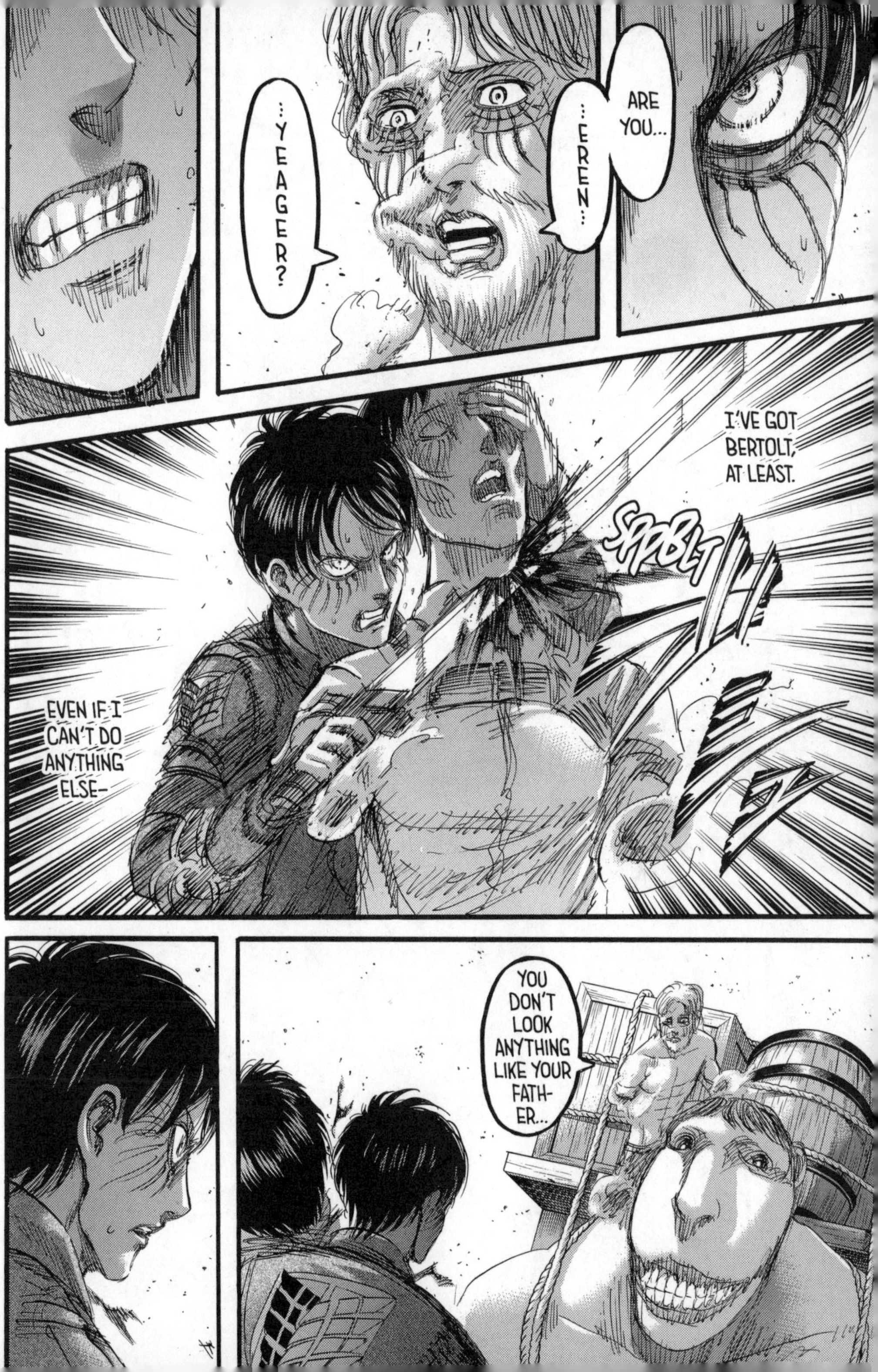
ARE YOU...
...EREN...
...YEAGER?
I'VE GOT BERTOLT, AT LEAST.
SPBLT
EVEN IF I CAN'T DO ANYTHING ELSE-
YOU DON'T LOOK ANYTHING LIKE YOUR FATH-ER...

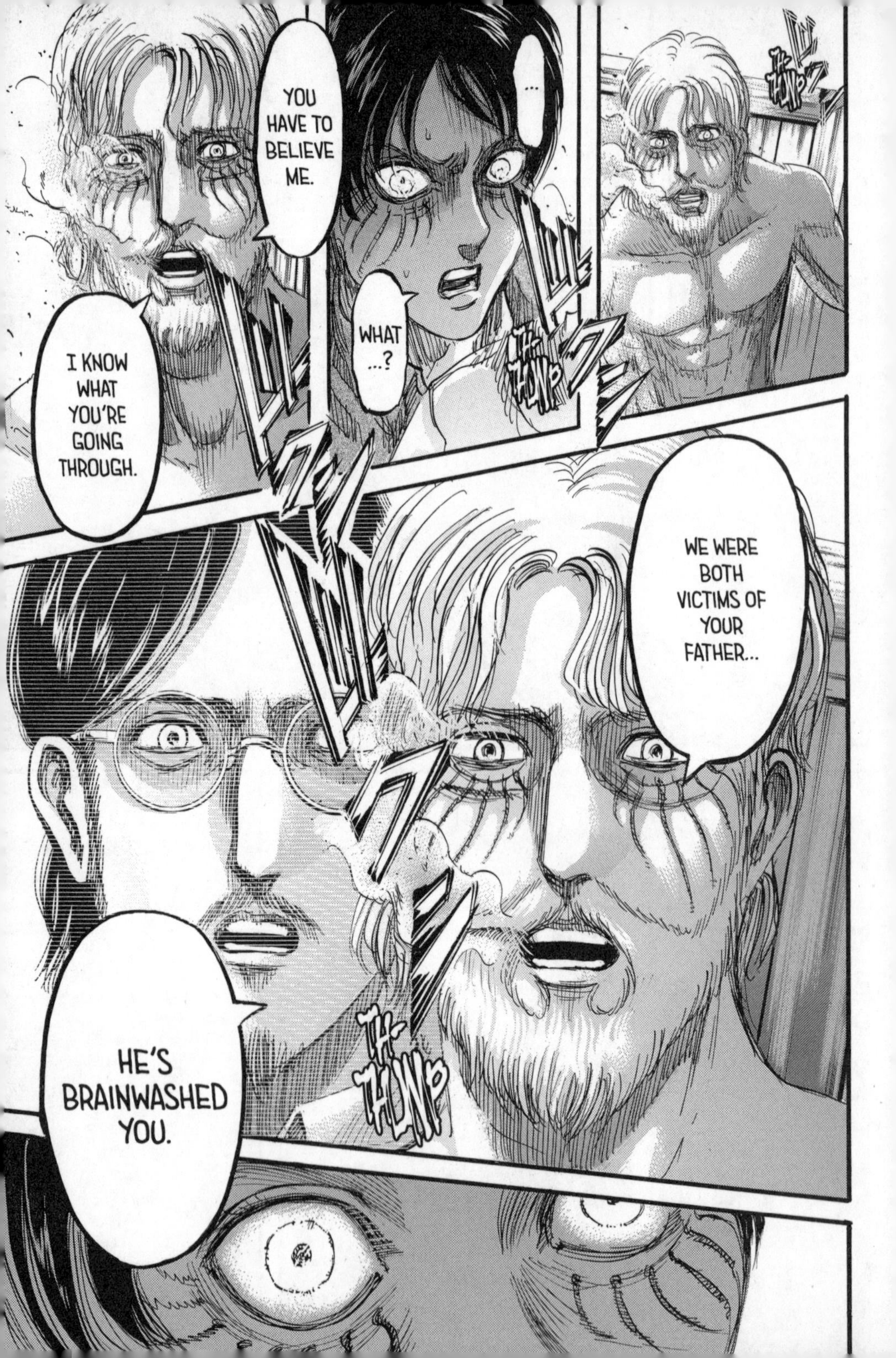
TH-THUMP
...
WHAT ...?
TH-THUMP
YOU HAVE TO BELIEVE ME.
I KNOW WHAT YOU'RE GOING THROUGH.
WE WERE BOTH VICTIMS OF YOUR FATHER...
TH-THUMP
HE'S BRAINWASHED YOU.

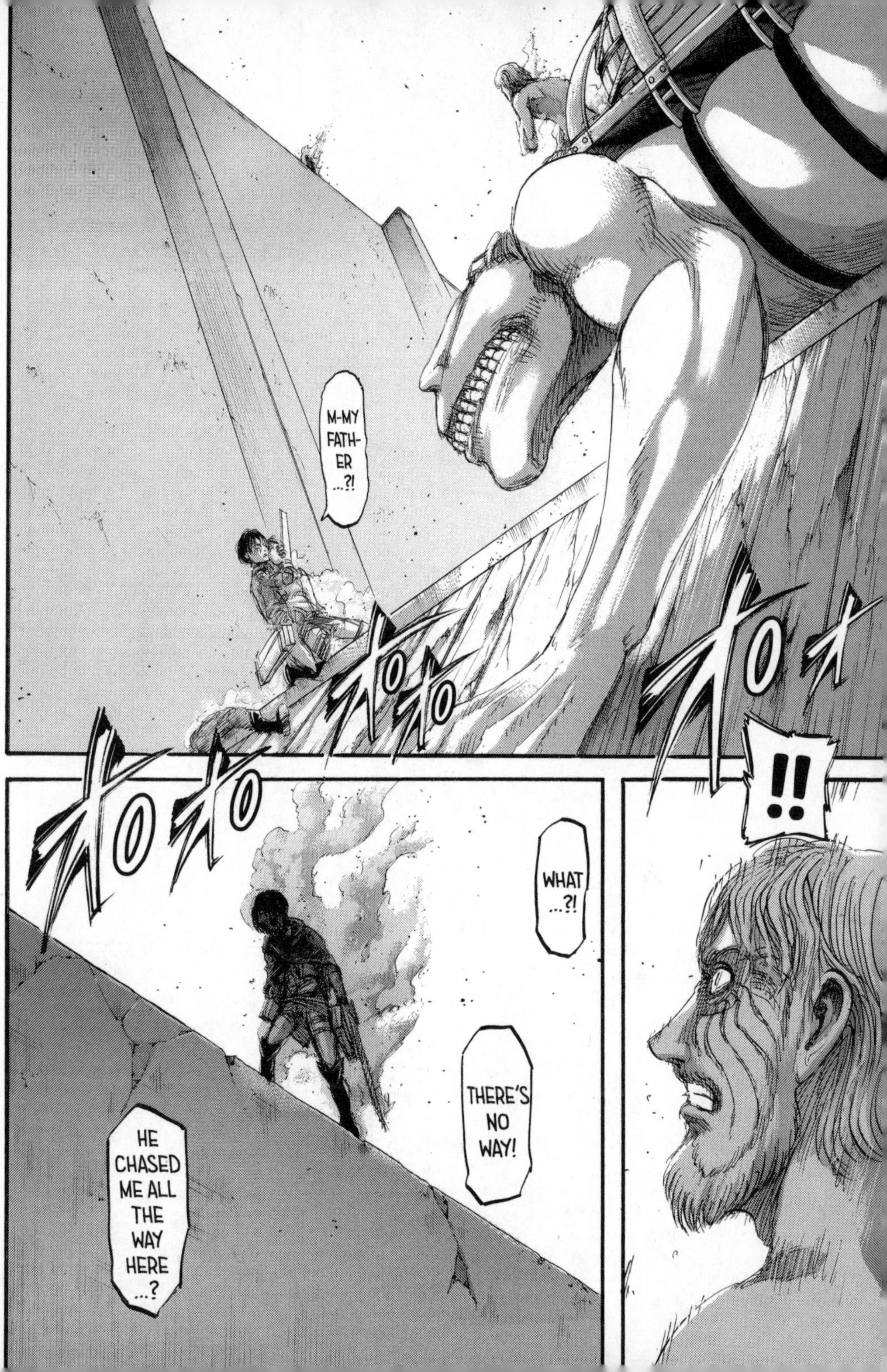
M-MY FATHER-ER ...?!
!!
WHAT ...?!
THERE'S NO WAY!
HE CHASED ME ALL THE WAY HERE ...?

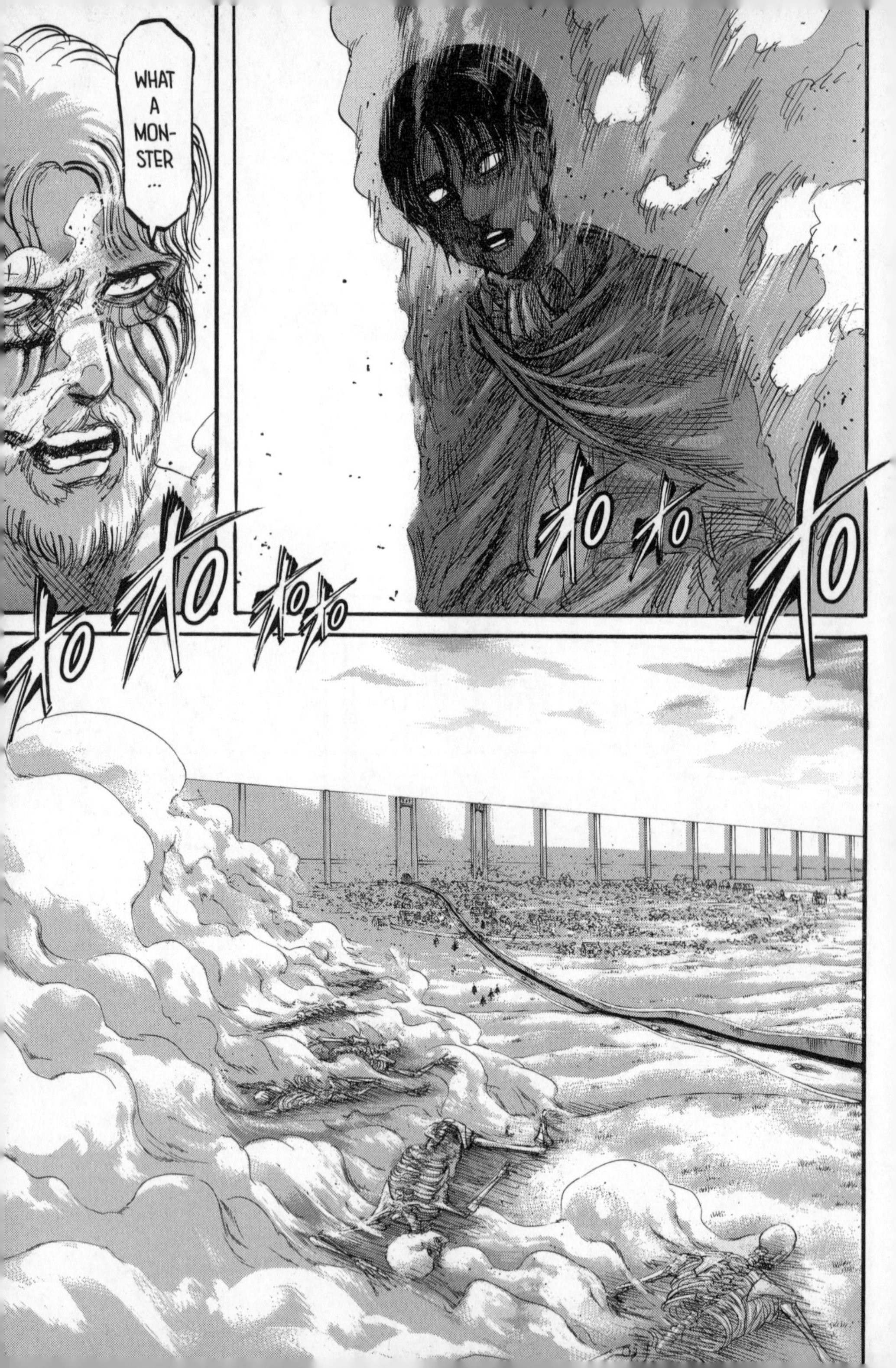
WHAT A MONSTER ...

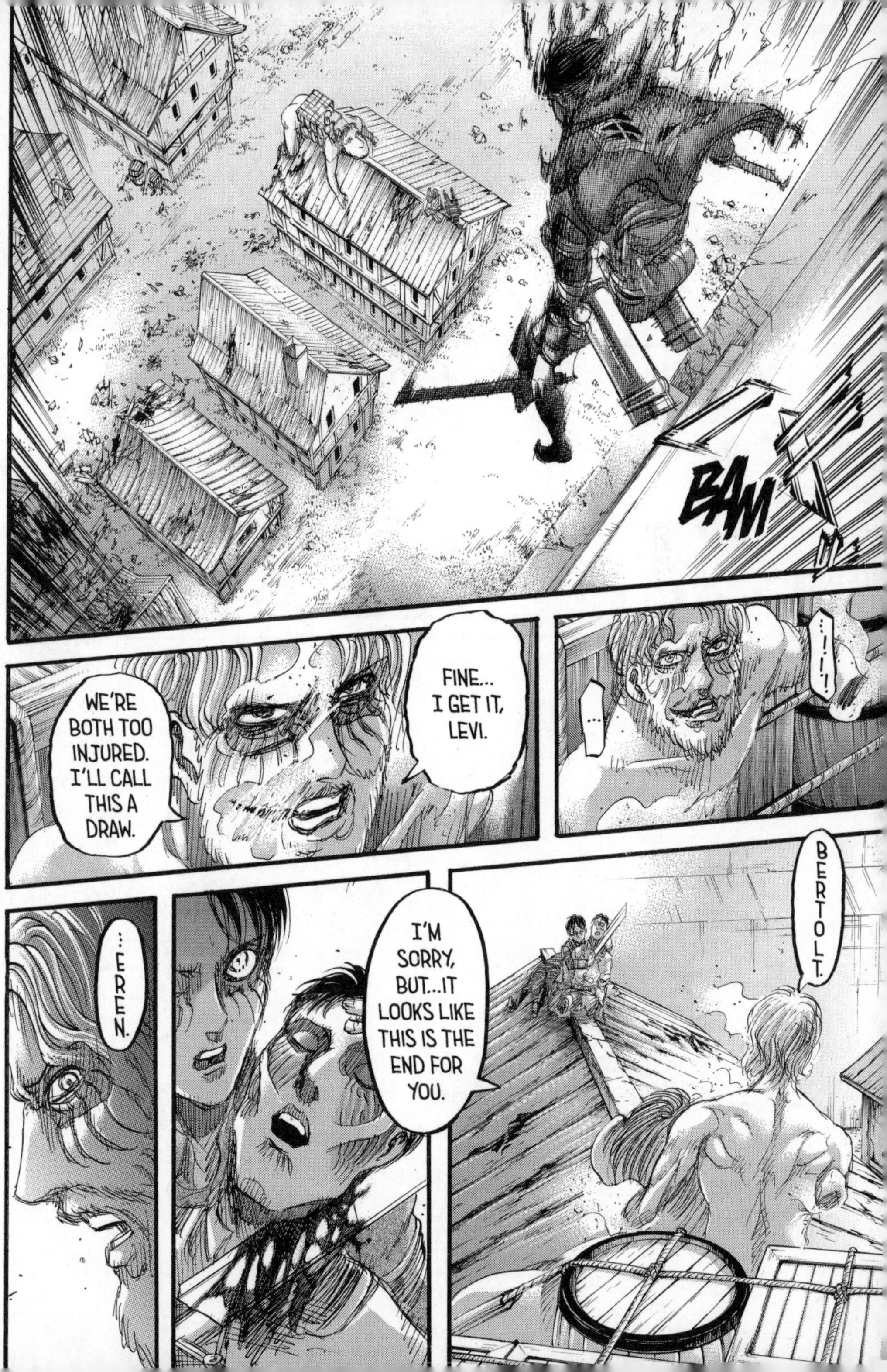
BAM
...!!
...
FINE... I GET IT, LEVI.
WE'RE BOTH TOO INJURED. I'LL CALL THIS A DRAW.
BERTOLT.
I'M SORRY, BUT...IT LOOKS LIKE THIS IS THE END FOR YOU.
...EREN.

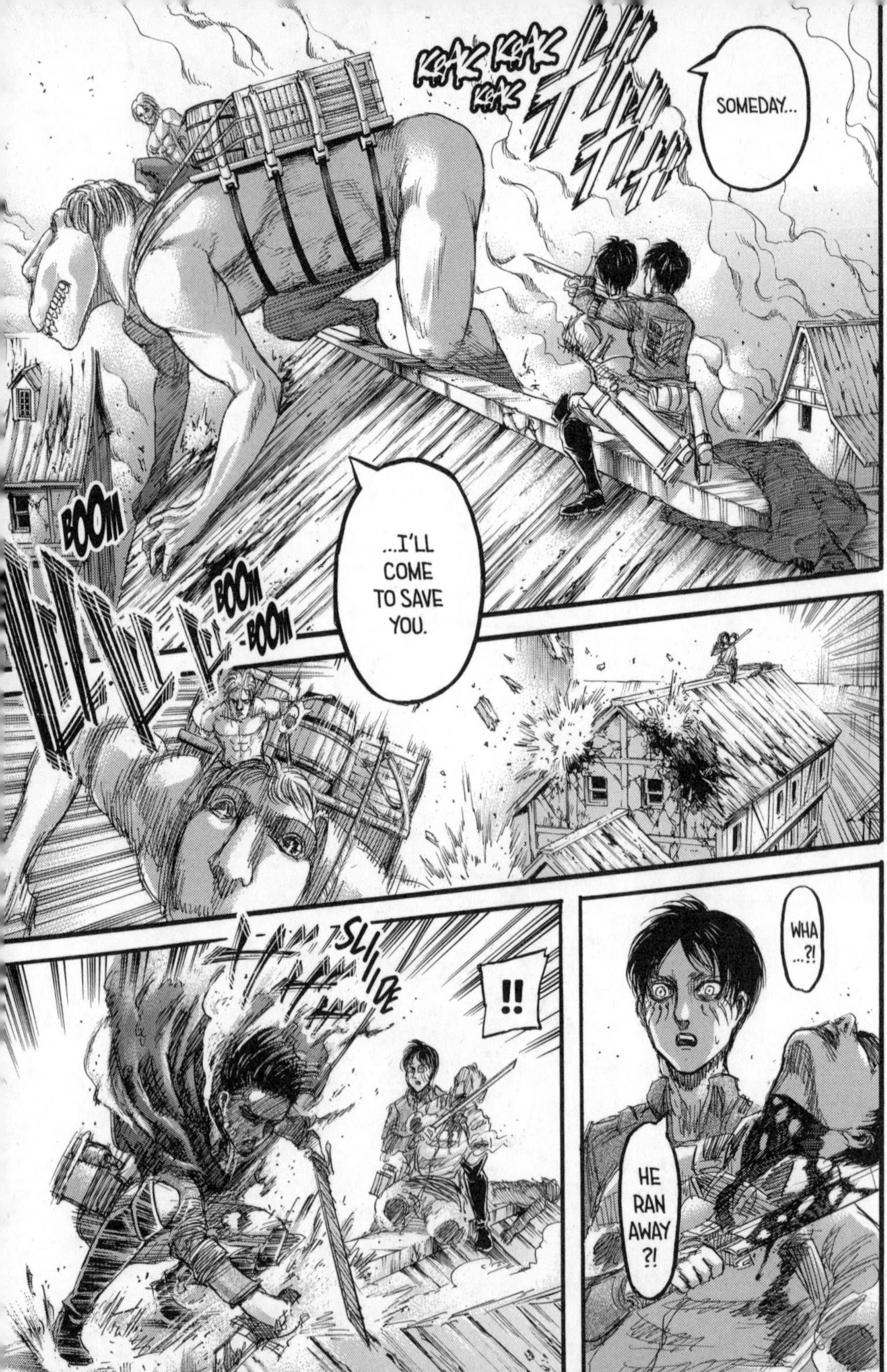

SOMEDAY...
KRAK KRAK KRAK
...I'LL COME TO SAVE YOU.
BOOM
BOOM BOOM-BOOM
WHA...?!
HE RAN AWAY?!
!!
SLIIIDE

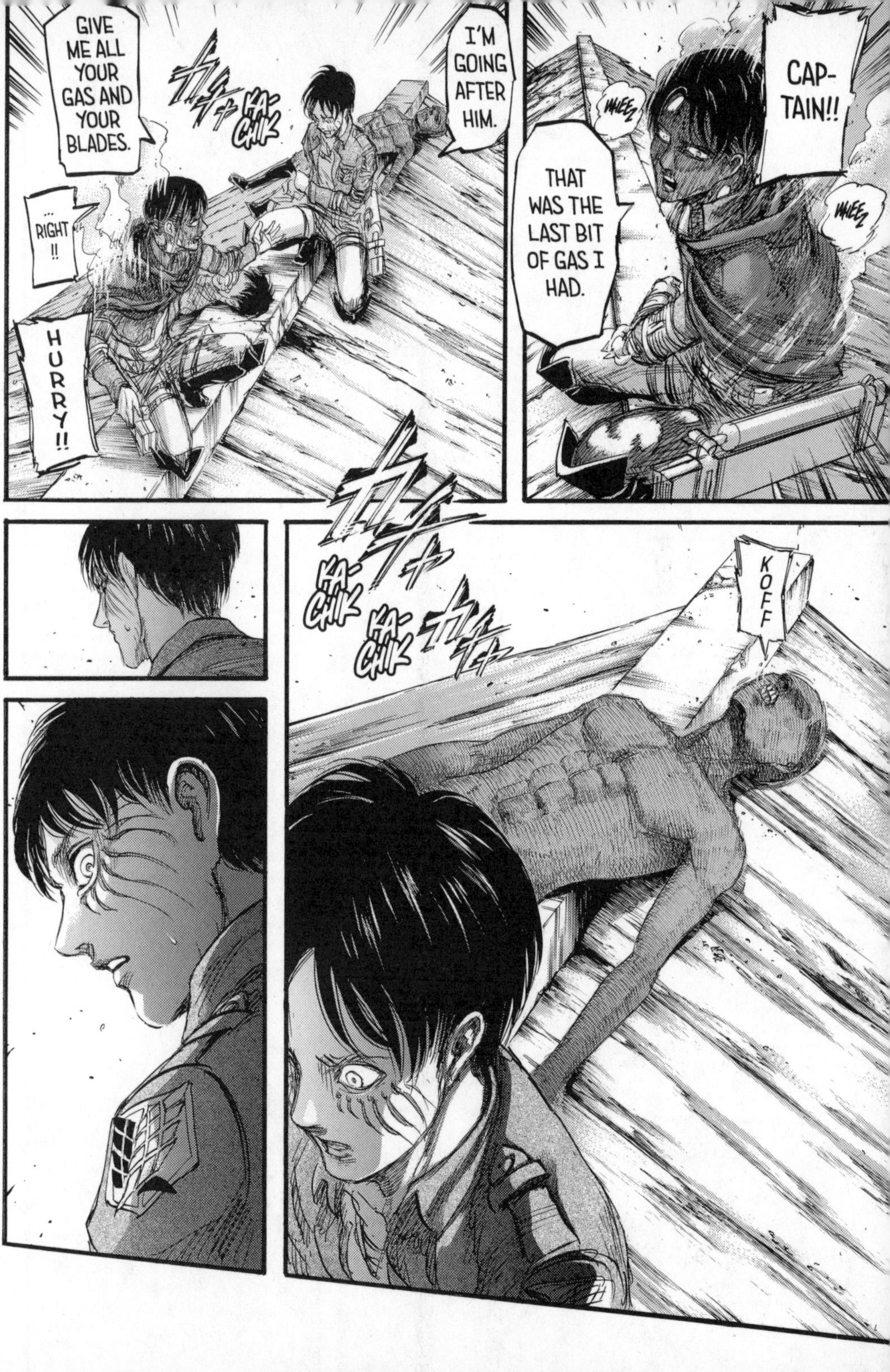

CAP-TAIN!!
WHEEZ
THAT WAS THE LAST BIT OF GAS I HAD.
WHEEZ
I'M GOING AFTER HIM.
KA-CHIK
GIVE ME ALL YOUR GAS AND YOUR BLADES.
...RIGHT!!
HURRY!!
KOFF
KA-CHIK
KA-CHIK

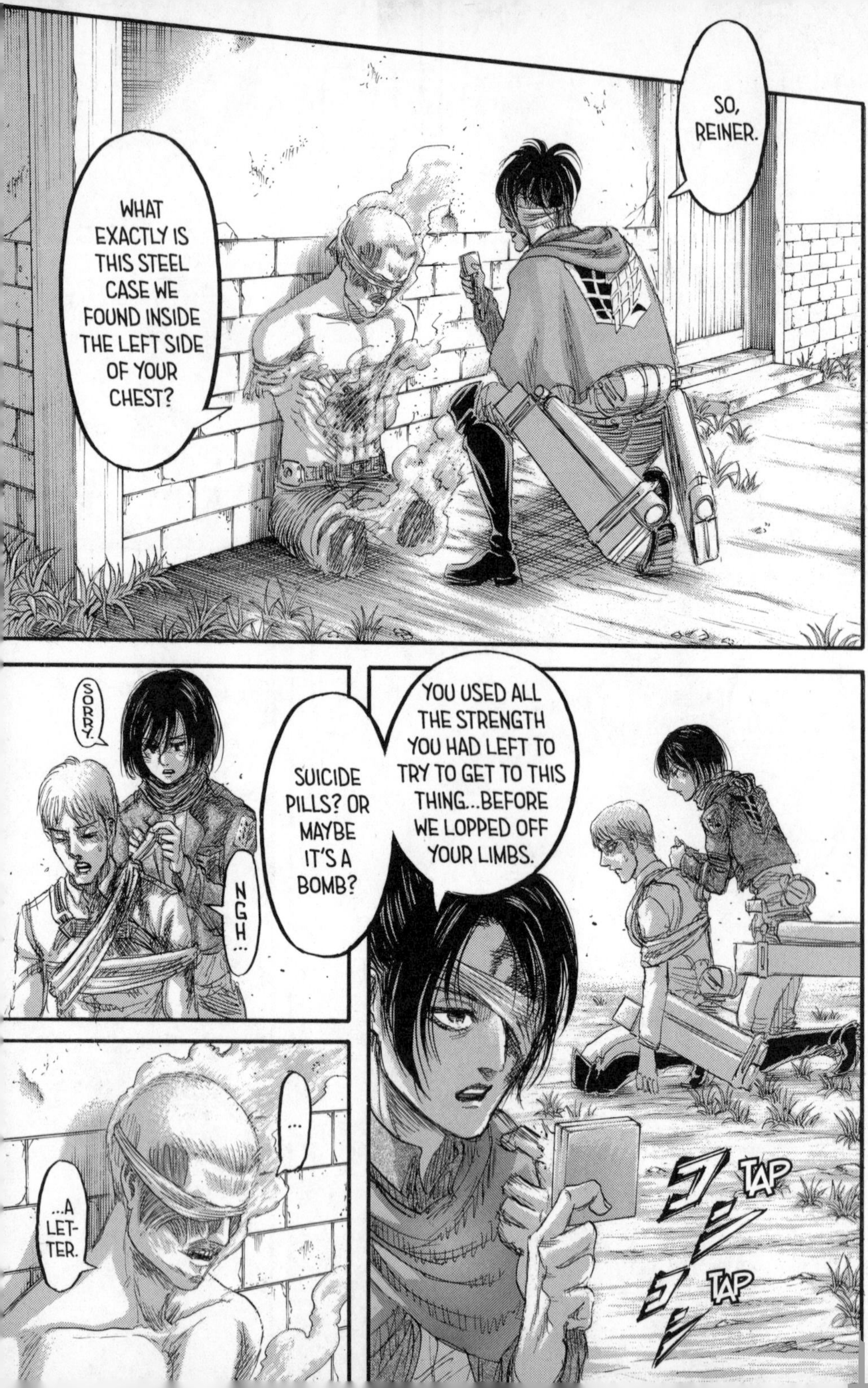
SO, REINER.
WHAT EXACTLY IS THIS STEEL CASE WE FOUND INSIDE THE LEFT SIDE OF YOUR CHEST?
YOU USED ALL THE STRENGTH YOU HAD LEFT TO TRY TO GET TO THIS THING...BEFORE WE LOPPED OFF YOUR LIMBS.
SUICIDE PILLS? OR MAYBE IT'S A BOMB?
TAP
TAP
NGH...
SORRY.
...
...A LETTER.

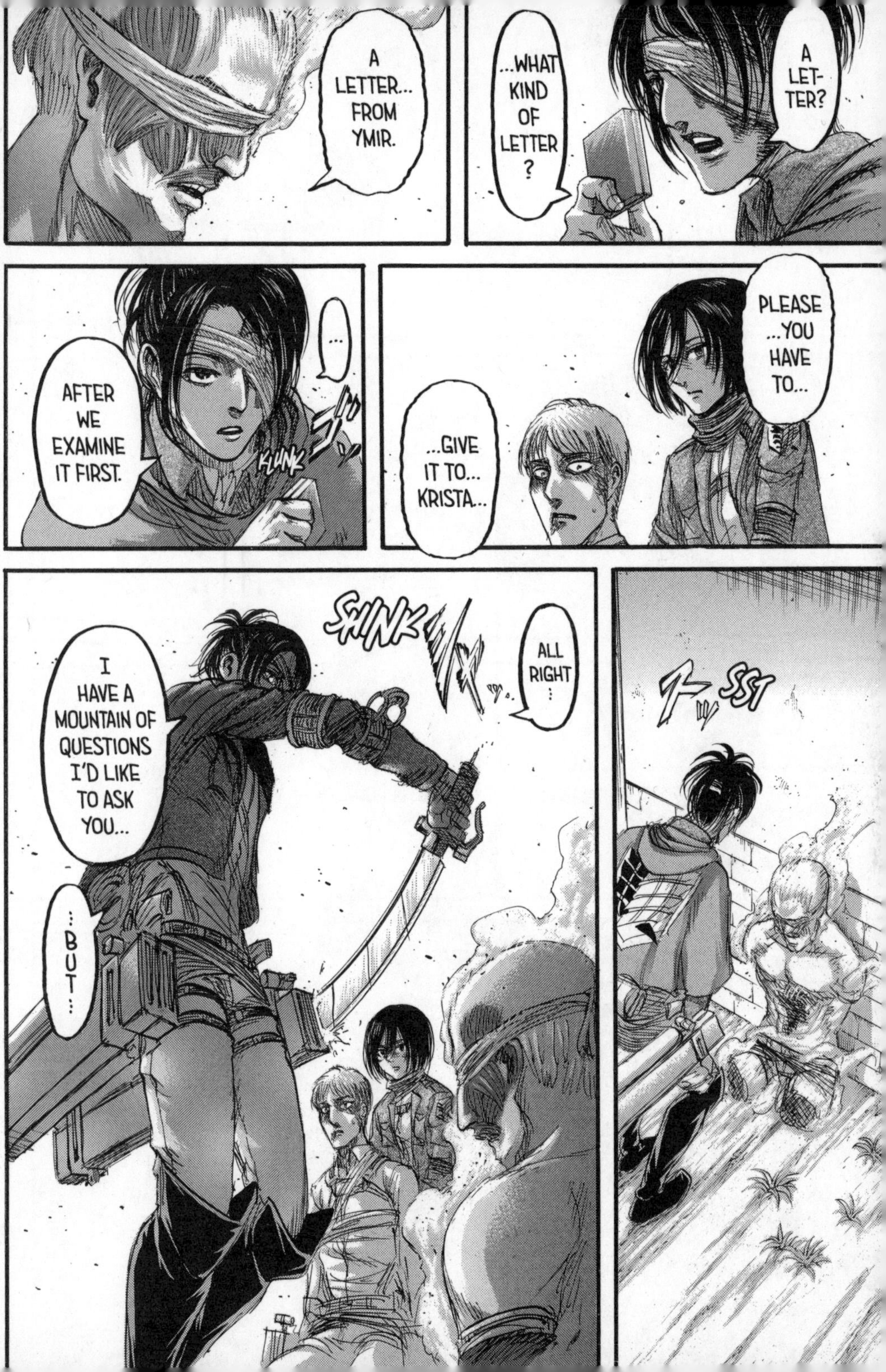
A LETTER?
...WHAT KIND OF LETTER?
A LETTER... FROM YMIR.
PLEASE ...YOU HAVE TO...
...GIVE IT TO... KRISTA...
...
KLUNK
AFTER WE EXAMINE IT FIRST.
SSST
ALL RIGHT...
SHINK
I HAVE A MOUNTAIN OF QUESTIONS I'D LIKE TO ASK YOU...
...BUT...

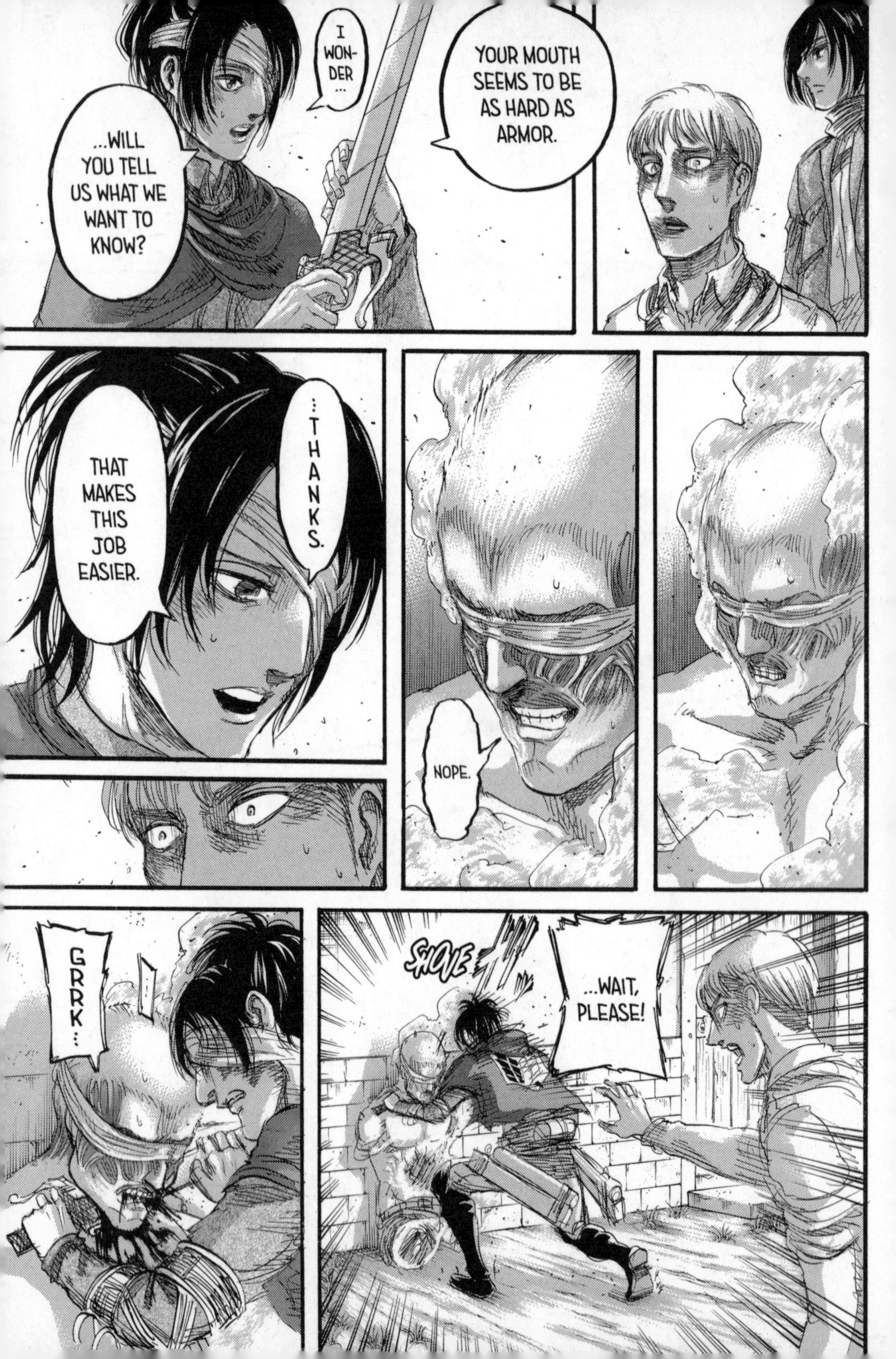
YOUR MOUTH SEEMS TO BE AS HARD AS ARMOR.
I WONDER...
...WILL YOU TELL US WHAT WE WANT TO KNOW?
NOPE.
...THANKS.
THAT MAKES THIS JOB EASIER.
...WAIT, PLEASE!
SHOVE
!
GRRK...

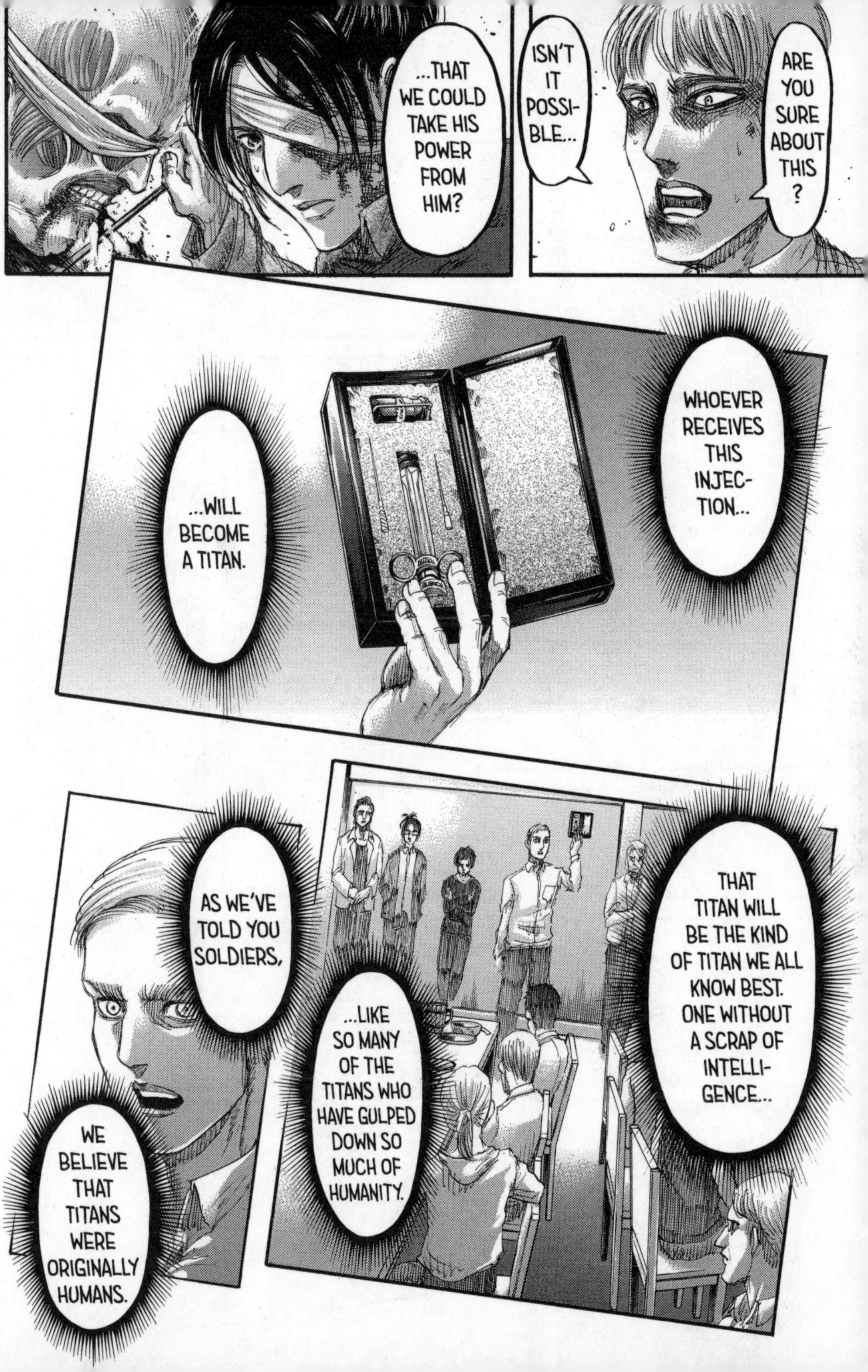
ARE YOU SURE ABOUT THIS?
ISN'T IT POSSIBLE...
...THAT WE COULD TAKE HIS POWER FROM HIM?
WHOEVER RECEIVES THIS INJECTION...
...WILL BECOME A TITAN.
THAT TITAN WILL BE THE KIND OF TITAN WE ALL KNOW BEST. ONE WITHOUT A SCRAP OF INTELLIGENCE...
...LIKE SO MANY OF THE TITANS WHO HAVE GULPED DOWN SO MUCH OF HUMANITY.
AS WE'VE TOLD YOU SOLDIERS,
WE BELIEVE THAT TITANS WERE ORIGINALLY HUMANS.

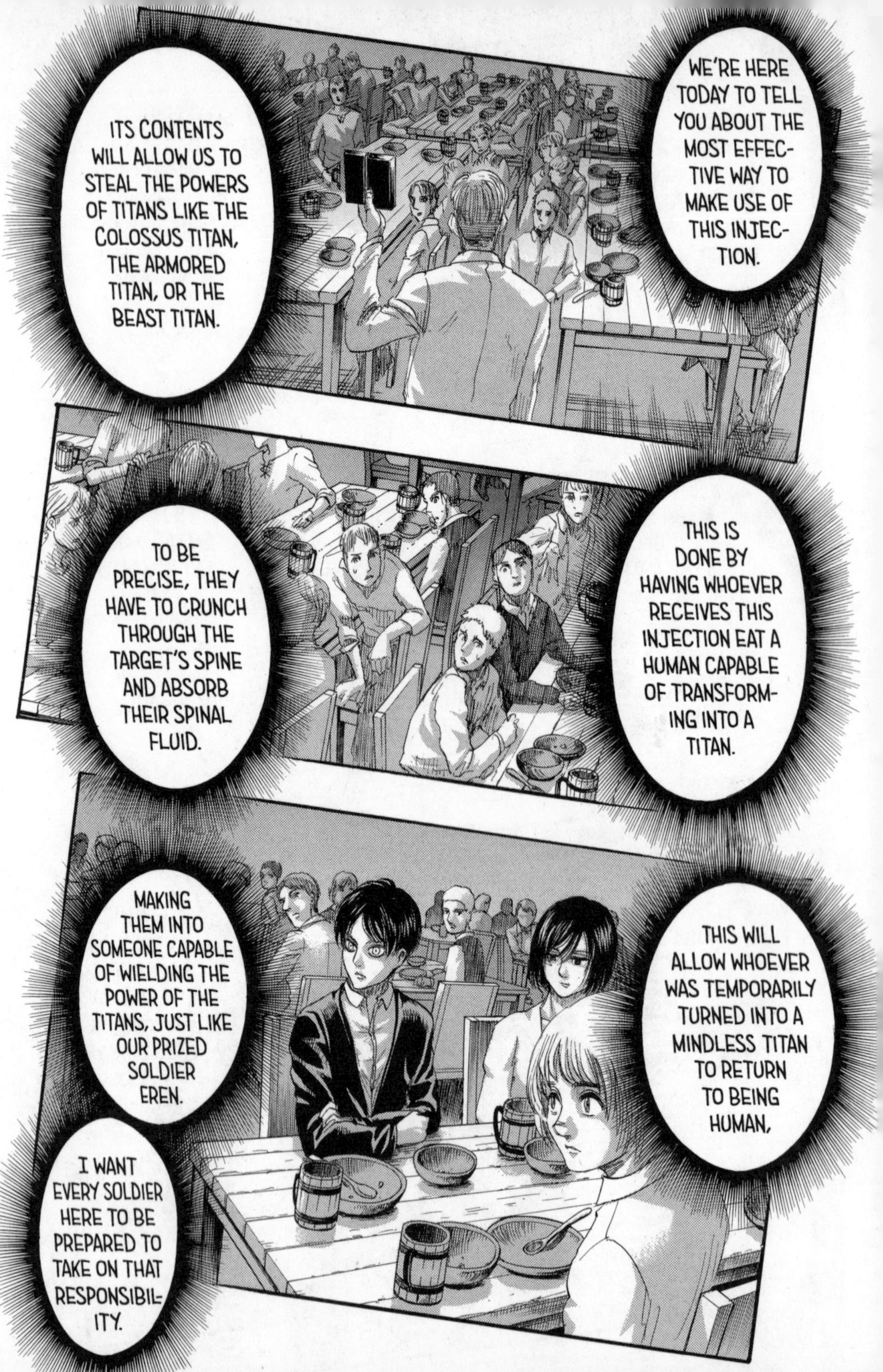
WE'RE HERE TODAY TO TELL YOU ABOUT THE MOST EFFECTIVE WAY TO MAKE USE OF THIS INJECTION.
ITS CONTENTS WILL ALLOW US TO STEAL THE POWERS OF TITANS LIKE THE COLOSSUS TITAN, THE ARMORED TITAN, OR THE BEAST TITAN.
THIS IS DONE BY HAVING WHOEVER RECEIVES THIS INJECTION EAT A HUMAN CAPABLE OF TRANSFORMING INTO A TITAN.
TO BE PRECISE, THEY HAVE TO CRUNCH THROUGH THE TARGET'S SPINE AND ABSORB THEIR SPINAL FLUID.
THIS WILL ALLOW WHOEVER WAS TEMPORARILY TURNED INTO A MINDLESS TITAN TO RETURN TO BEING HUMAN,
MAKING THEM INTO SOMEONE CAPABLE OF WIELDING THE POWER OF THE TITANS, JUST LIKE OUR PRIZED SOLDIER EREN.
I WANT EVERY SOLDIER HERE TO BE PREPARED TO TAKE ON THAT RESPONSIBILITY.

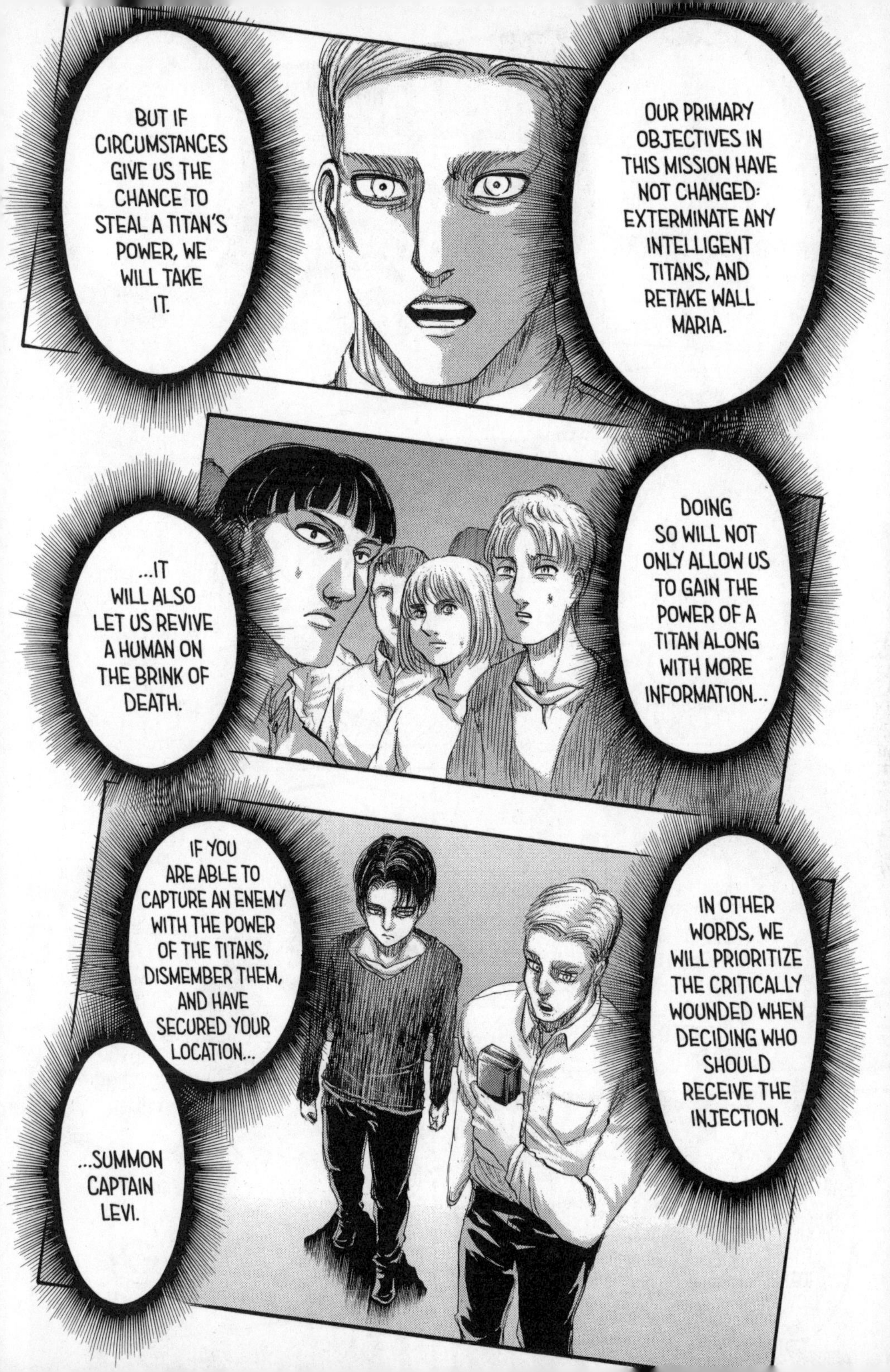
OUR PRIMARY OBJECTIVES IN THIS MISSION HAVE NOT CHANGED: EXTERMINATE ANY INTELLIGENT TITANS, AND RETAKE WALL MARIA.
BUT IF CIRCUMSTANCES GIVE US THE CHANCE TO STEAL A TITAN'S POWER, WE WILL TAKE IT.
DOING SO WILL NOT ONLY ALLOW US TO GAIN THE POWER OF A TITAN ALONG WITH MORE INFORMATION...
...IT WILL ALSO LET US REVIVE A HUMAN ON THE BRINK OF DEATH.
IN OTHER WORDS, WE WILL PRIORITIZE THE CRITICALLY WOUNDED WHEN DECIDING WHO SHOULD RECEIVE THE INJECTION.
IF YOU ARE ABLE TO CAPTURE AN ENEMY WITH THE POWER OF THE TITANS, DISMEMBER THEM, AND HAVE SECURED YOUR LOCATION...
...SUMMON CAPTAIN LEVI.

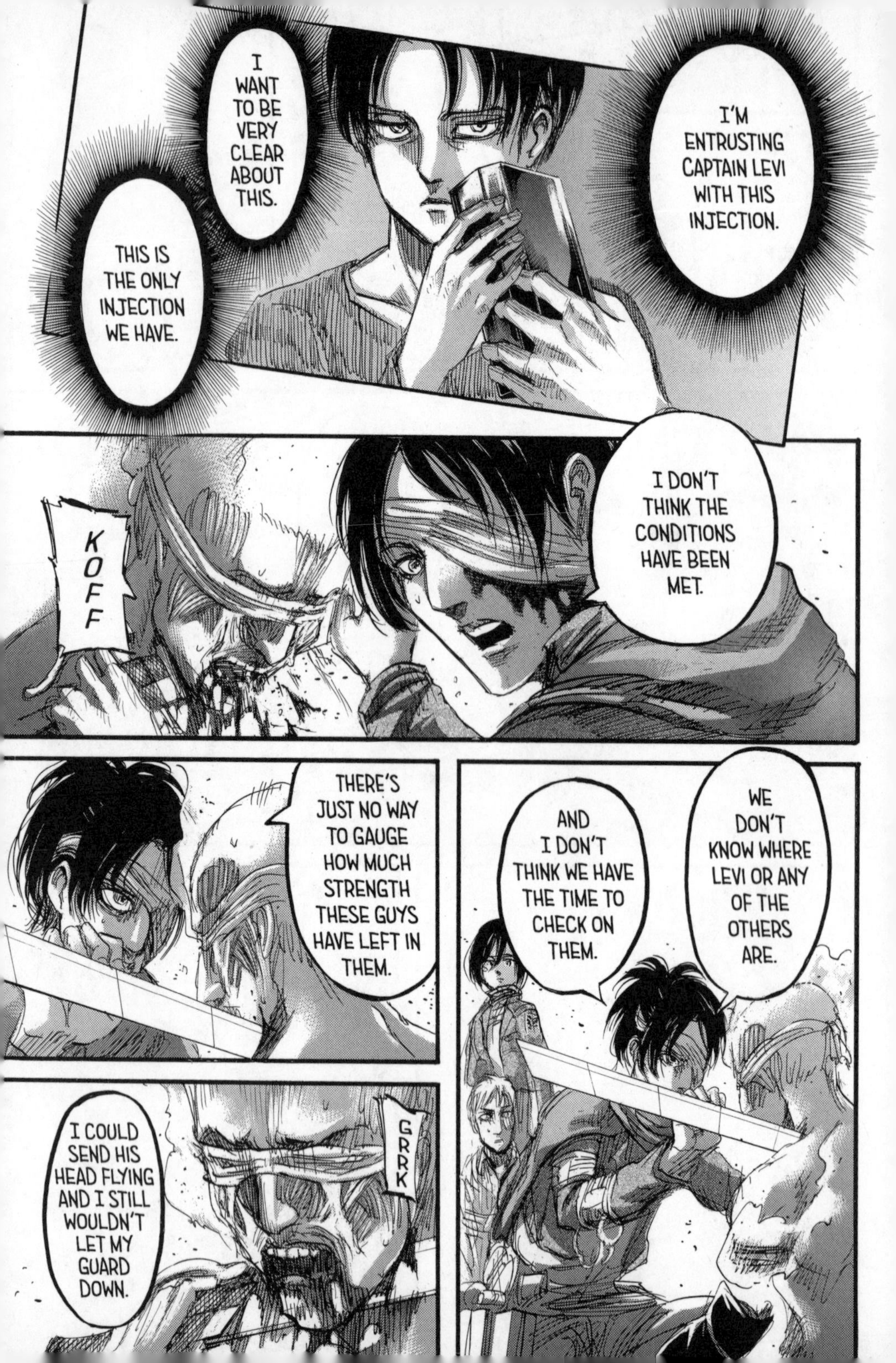
I'M ENTRUSTING CAPTAIN LEVI WITH THIS INJECTION.
I WANT TO BE VERY CLEAR ABOUT THIS.
THIS IS THE ONLY INJECTION WE HAVE.
I DON'T THINK THE CONDITIONS HAVE BEEN MET.
KOFF
WE DON'T KNOW WHERE LEVI OR ANY OF THE OTHERS ARE.
AND I DON'T THINK WE HAVE THE TIME TO CHECK ON THEM.
THERE'S JUST NO WAY TO GAUGE HOW MUCH STRENGTH THESE GUYS HAVE LEFT IN THEM.
GRRK
I COULD SEND HIS HEAD FLYING AND I STILL WOULDN'T LET MY GUARD DOWN.

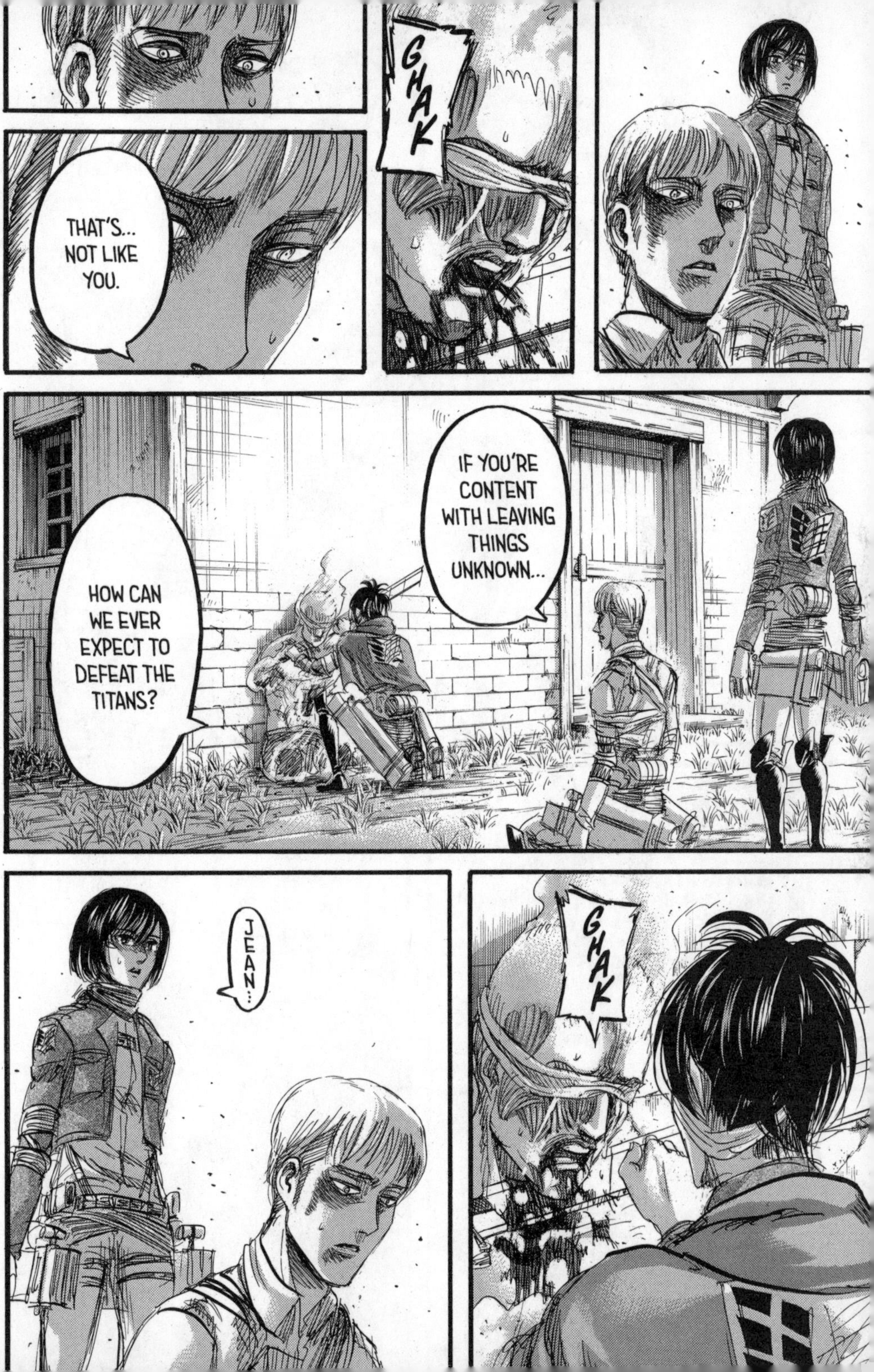
GHAK
THAT'S... NOT LIKE YOU.
IF YOU'RE CONTENT WITH LEAVING THINGS UNKNOWN...
HOW CAN WE EVER EXPECT TO DEFEAT THE TITANS?
GHAK
JEAN...

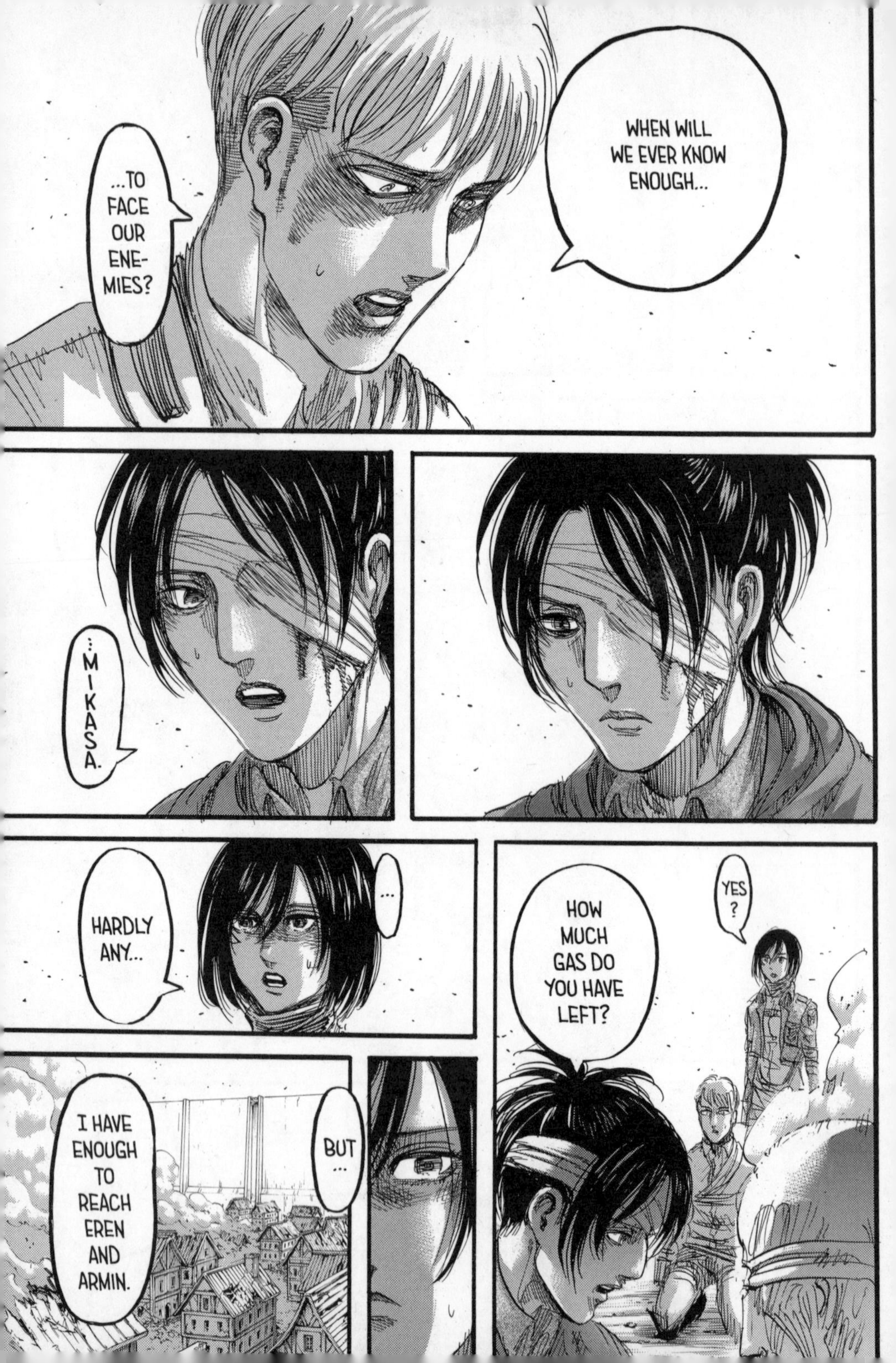
WHEN WILL WE EVER KNOW ENOUGH...
...TO FACE OUR ENE-MIES?
...MIKASA.
YES?
HOW MUCH GAS DO YOU HAVE LEFT?
...
HARDLY ANY...
BUT ...
I HAVE ENOUGH TO REACH EREN AND ARMIN.

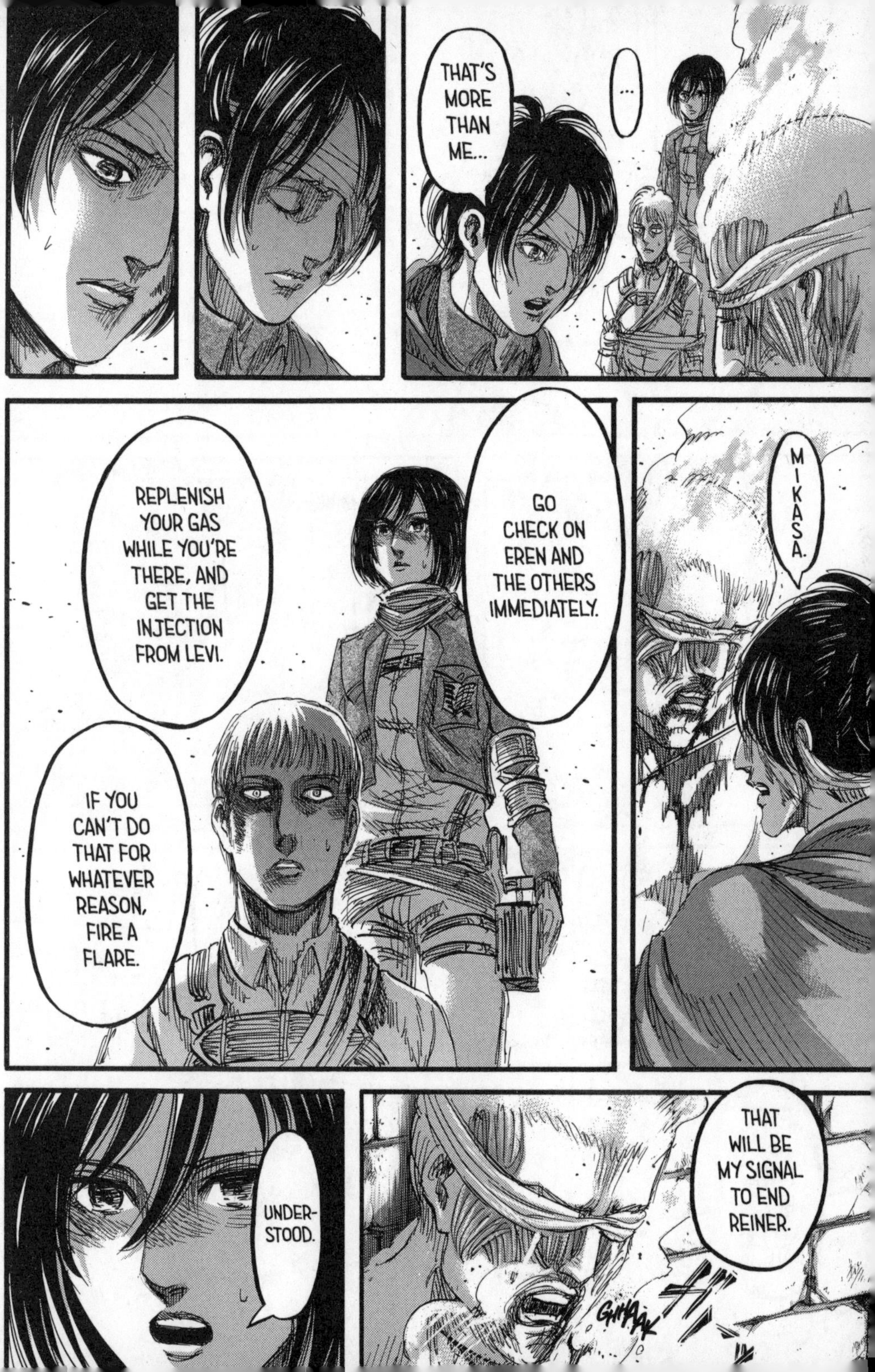
...
THAT'S MORE THAN ME...
MIKASA.
GO CHECK ON EREN AND THE OTHERS IMMEDIATELY.
REPLENISH YOUR GAS WHILE YOU'RE THERE, AND GET THE INJECTION FROM LEVI.
IF YOU CAN'T DO THAT FOR WHATEVER REASON, FIRE A FLARE.
THAT WILL BE MY SIGNAL TO END REINER.
GHHAAK
UNDER-STOOD.

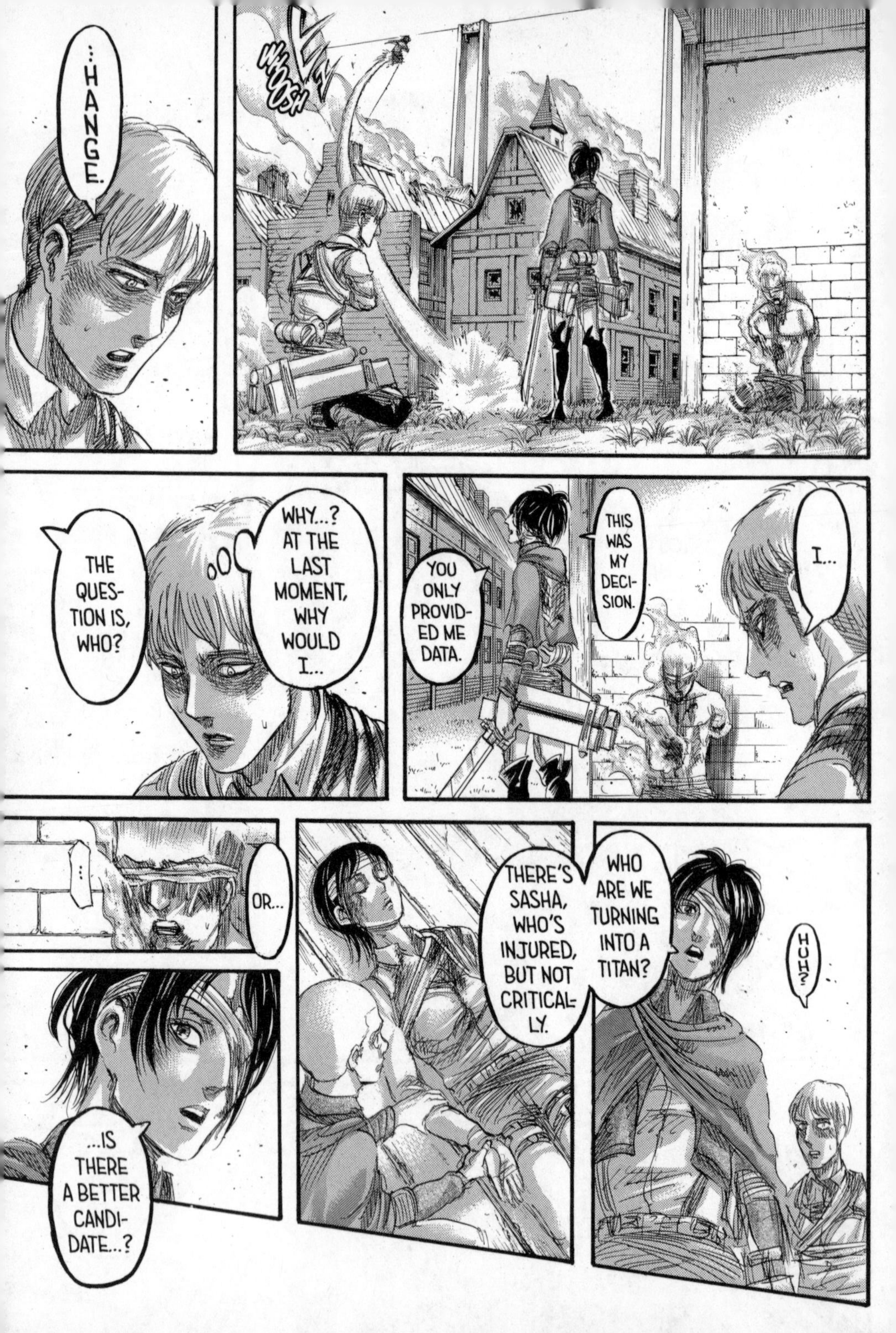
WHOOSH
...HANGE.
I...
THIS WAS MY DECISION.
YOU ONLY PROVIDED ME DATA.
WHY...? AT THE LAST MOMENT, WHY WOULD I...
THE QUESTION IS, WHO?
HUH?
WHO ARE WE TURNING INTO A TITAN?
THERE'S SASHA, WHO'S INJURED, BUT NOT CRITICALLY.
OR...
...
...IS THERE A BETTER CANDIDATE...?

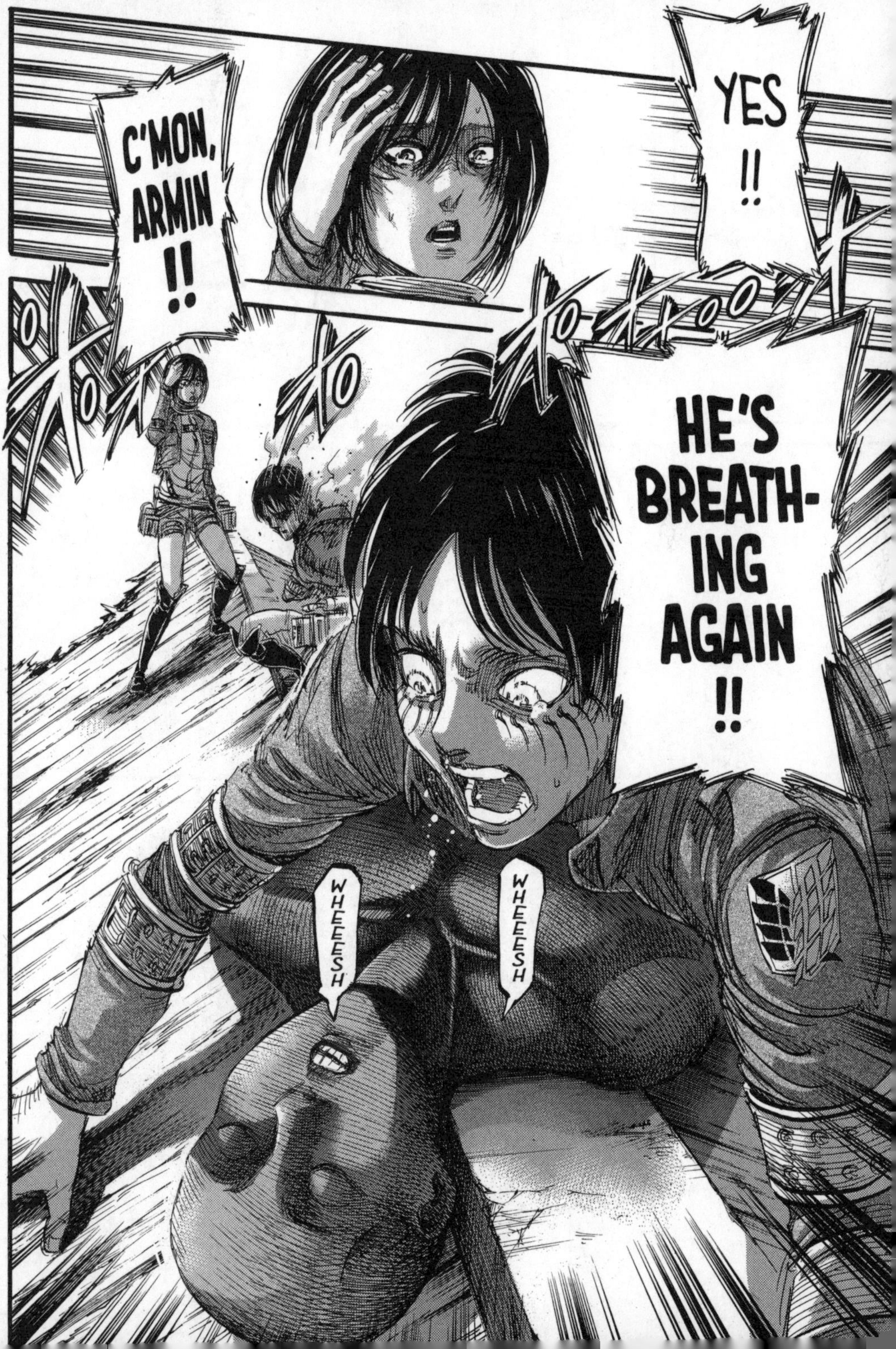
YES !!
C'MON, ARMIN !!
HE'S BREATH-ING AGAIN !!
WHEEEESH
WHEEEESH

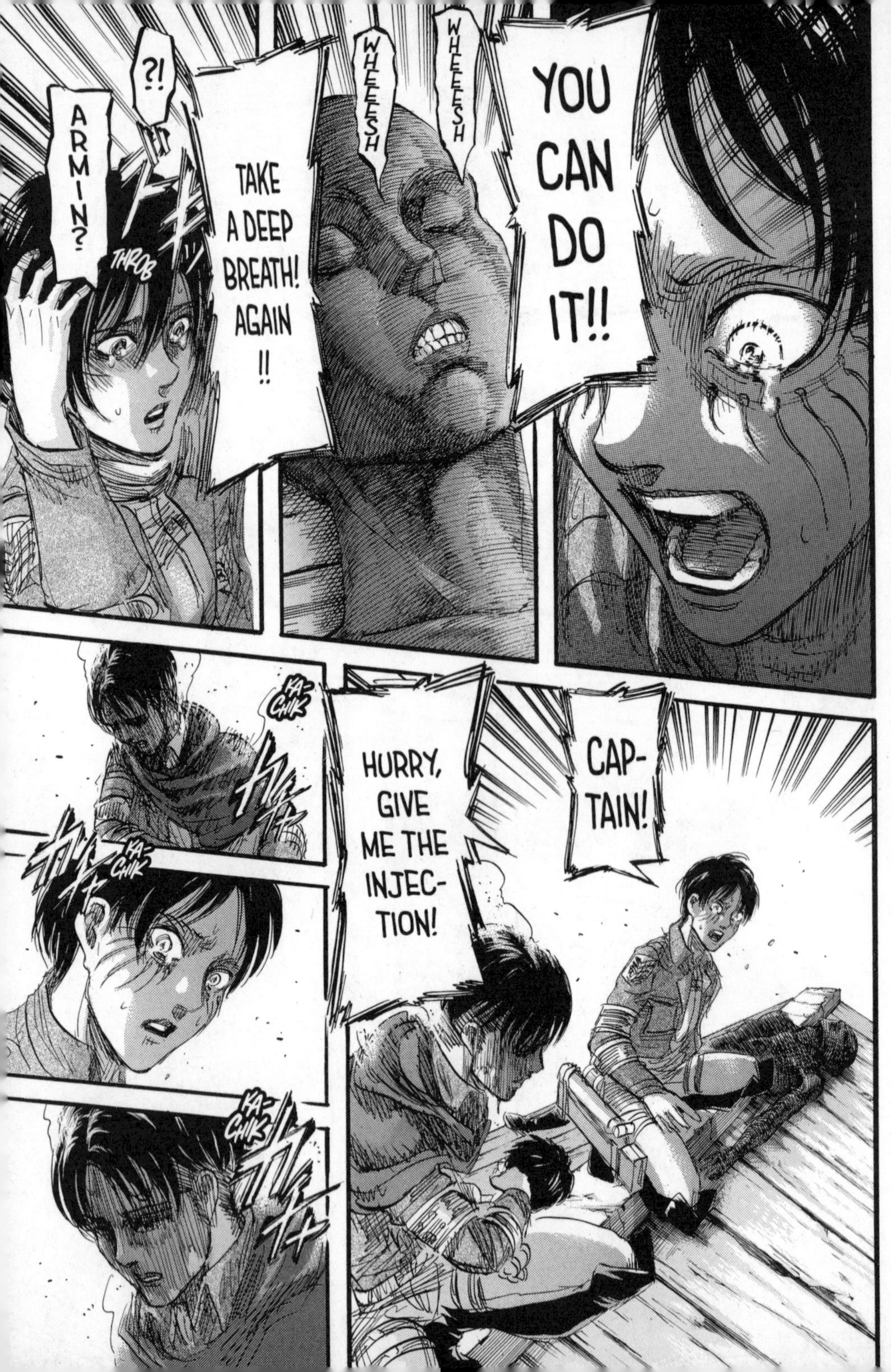
YOU CAN DO IT!!
WHEEEESH
WHEEEESH
TAKE A DEEP BREATH! AGAIN !!
?!
ARMIN?
THROB
CAP-TAIN!
HURRY, GIVE ME THE INJEC-TION!
KA-CHIK
KA-CHIK
KA-CHIK

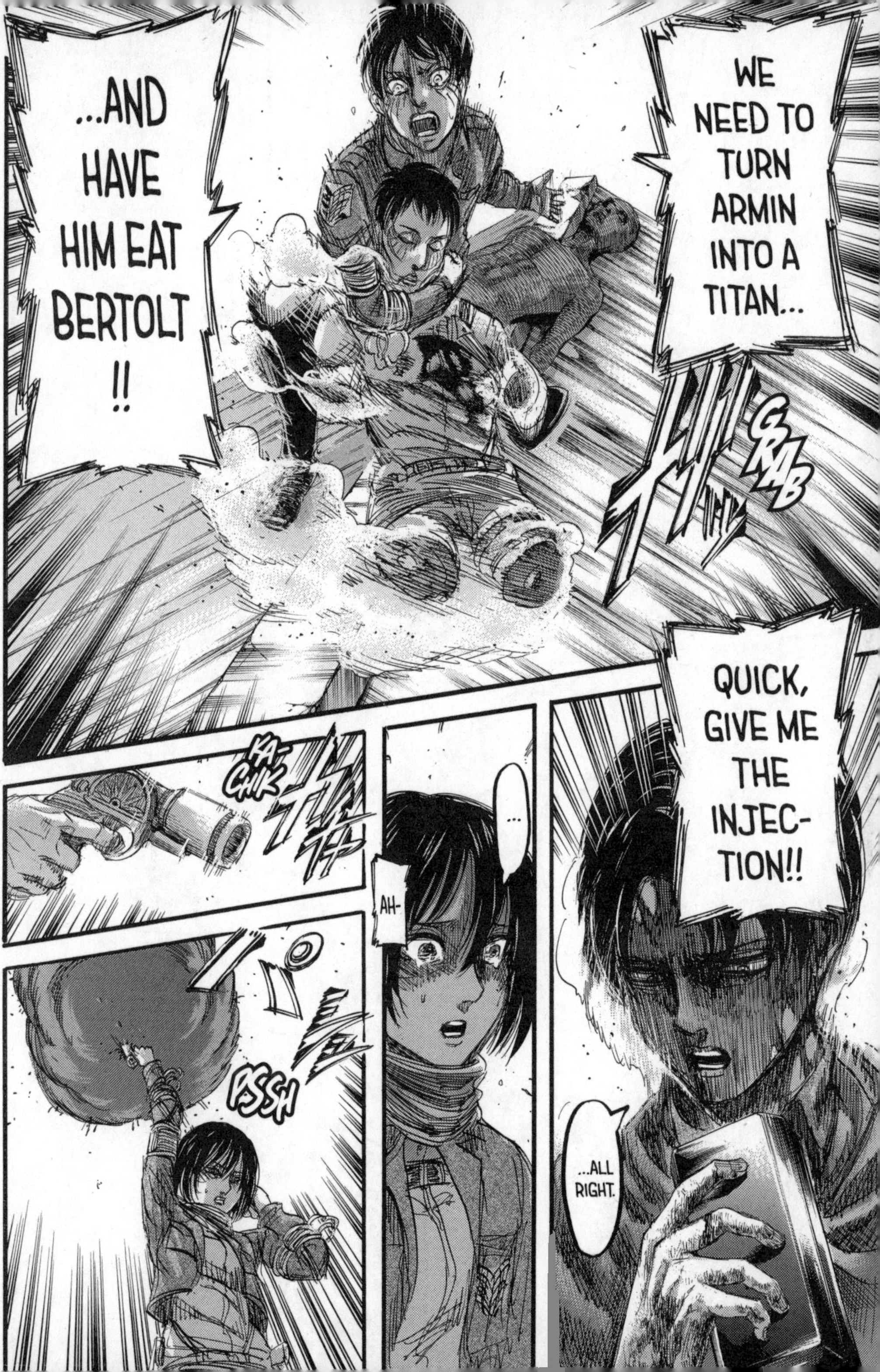
WE NEED TO TURN ARMIN INTO A TITAN...
...AND HAVE HIM EAT BERTOLT !!
GRAB
QUICK, GIVE ME THE INJECTION!!
...ALL RIGHT.
...
AH-
KA-CHIK
PSSH

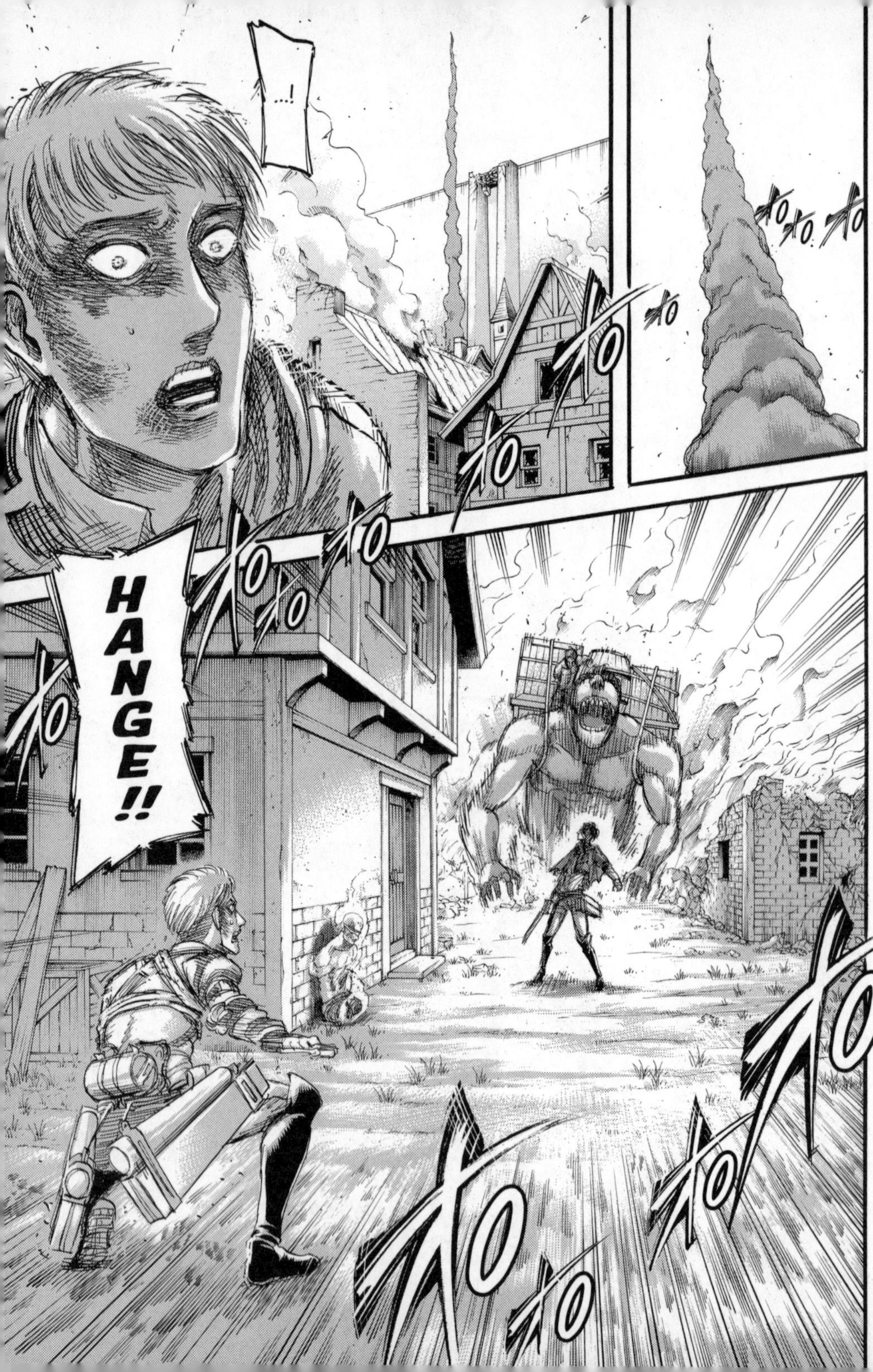
…!
HANGE!!

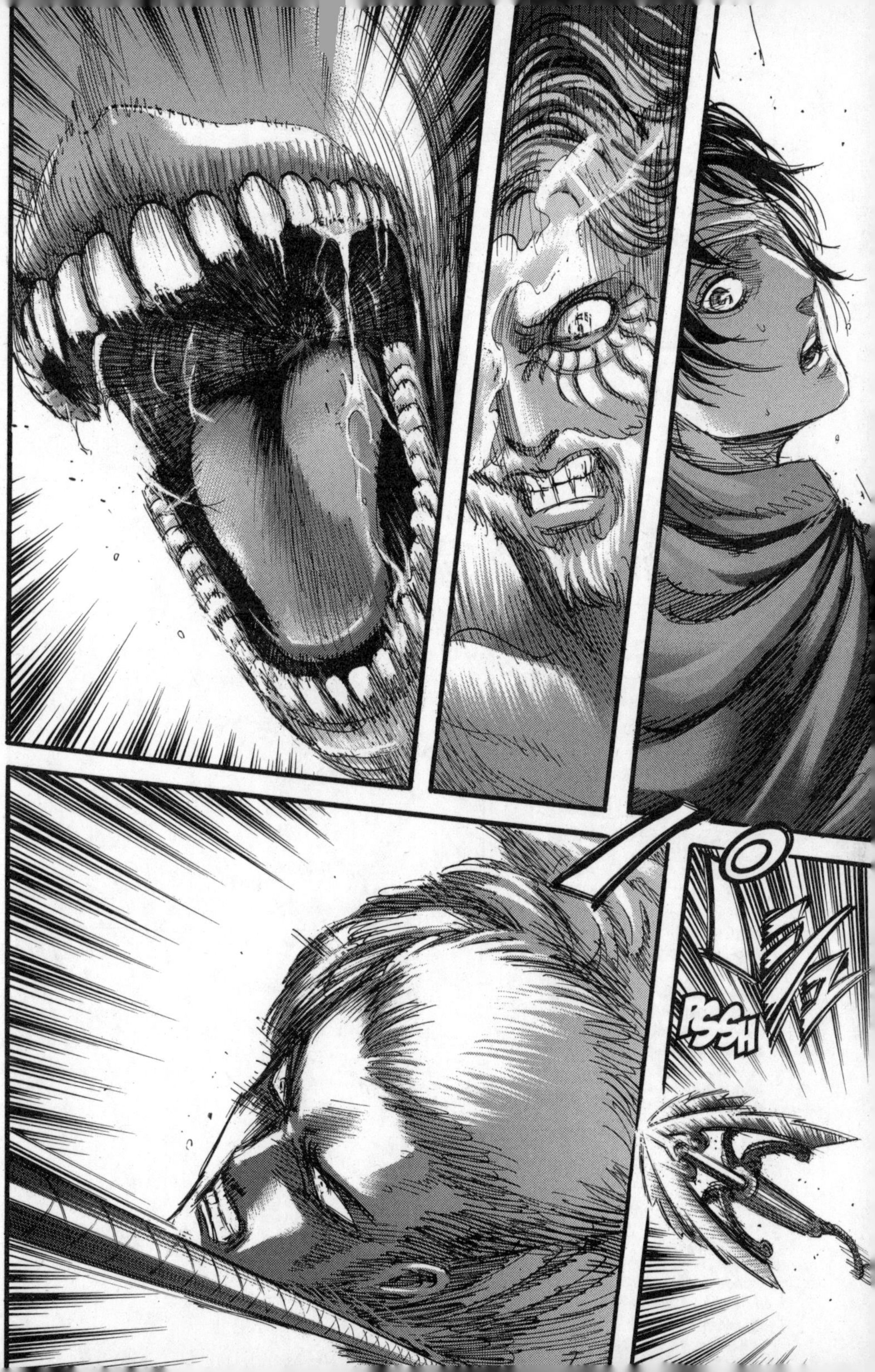
PSSH

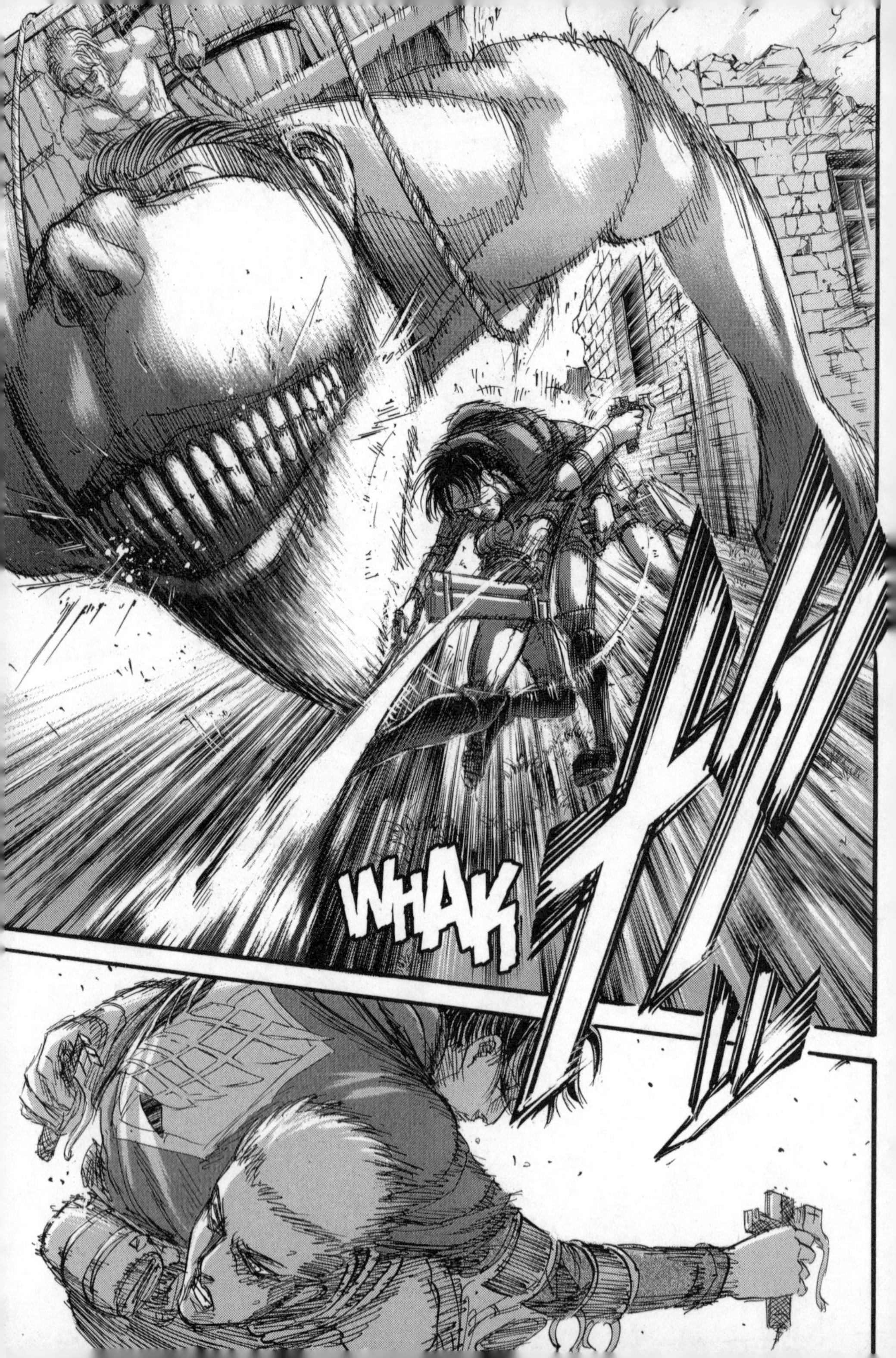
WHAK

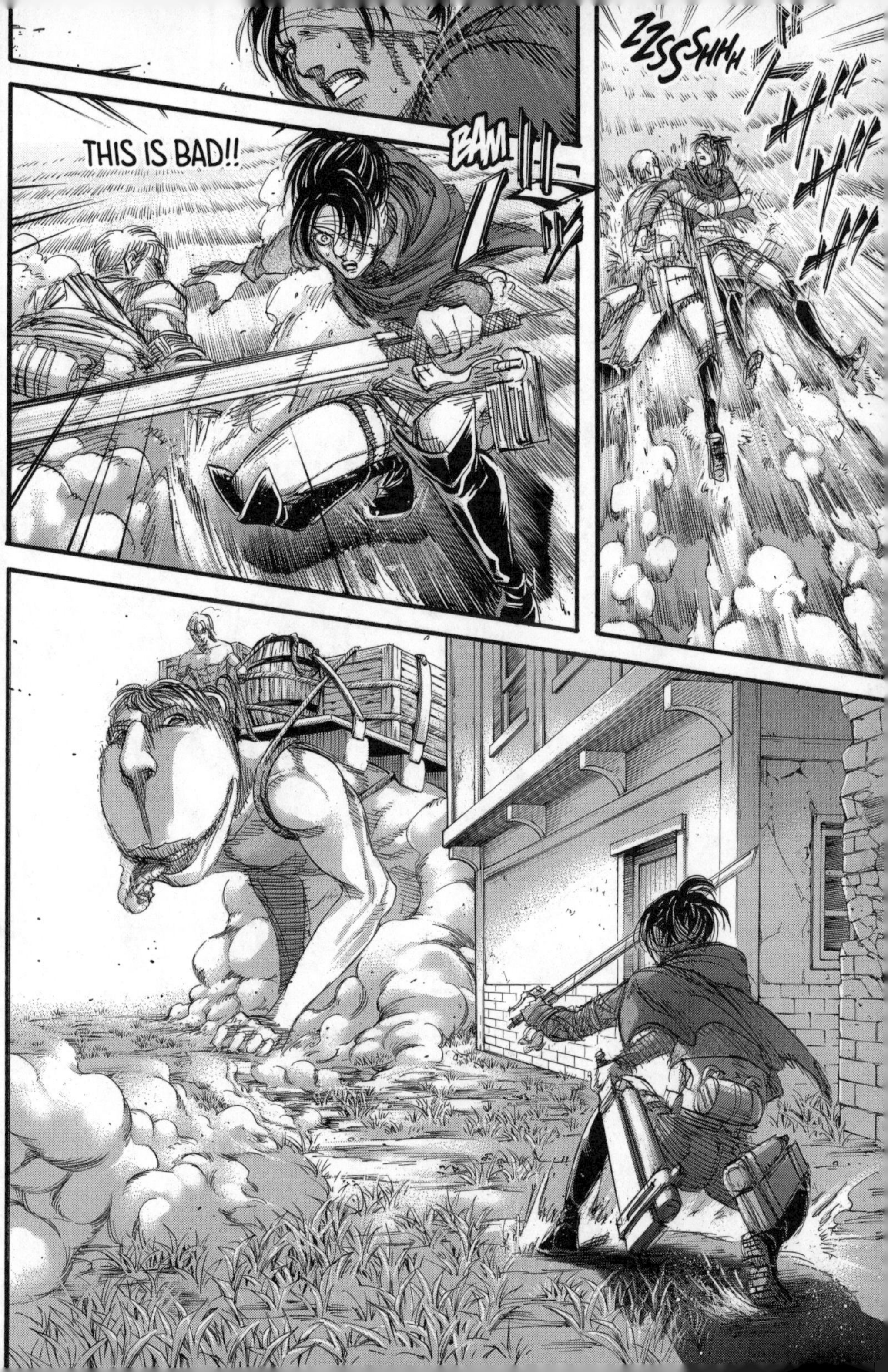
ZZSSSHHH
BAM
THIS IS BAD!!

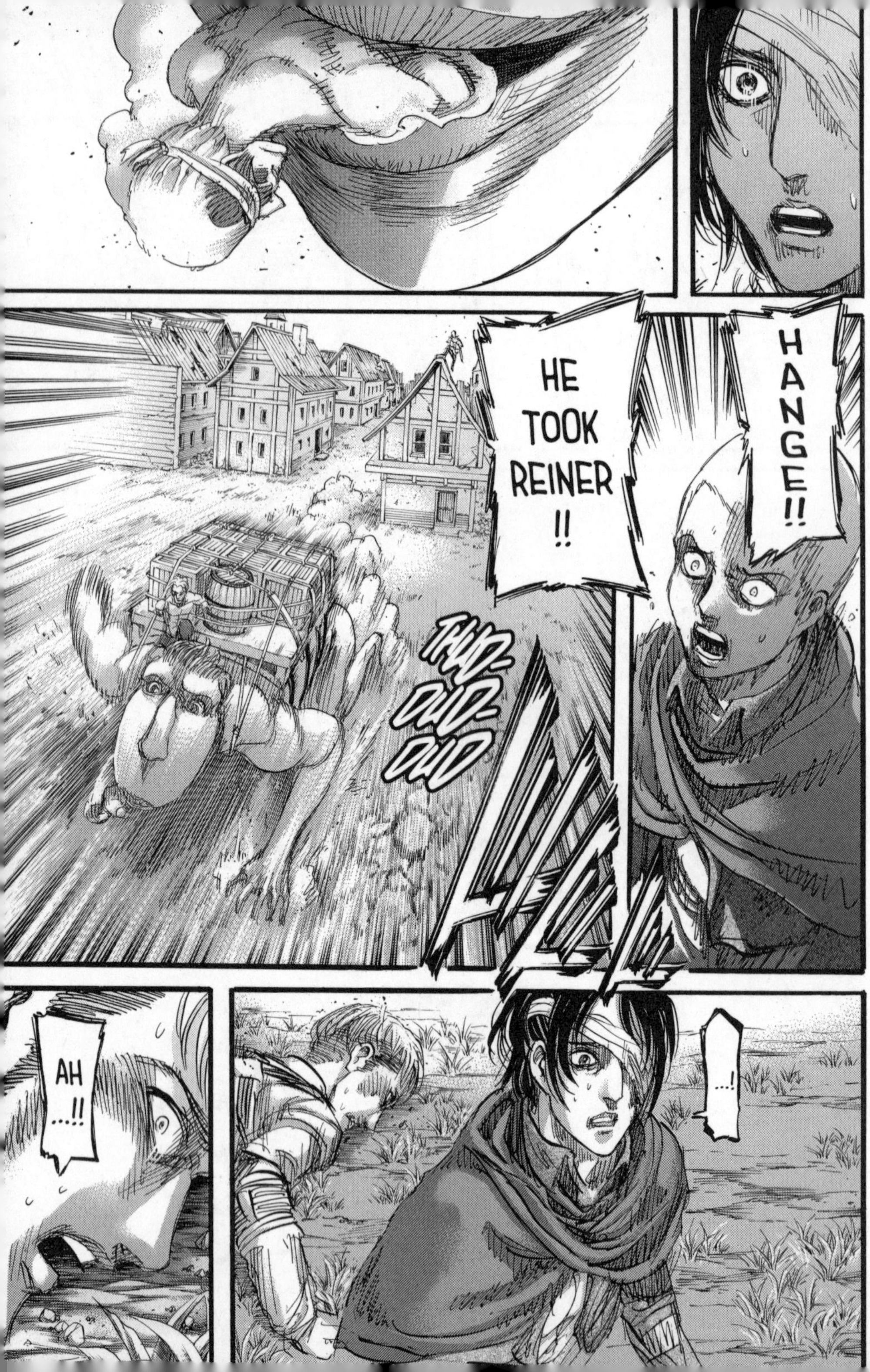
HANGE!!
HE TOOK REINER !!
THUD-DUD-DUD
...!
AH ...!!

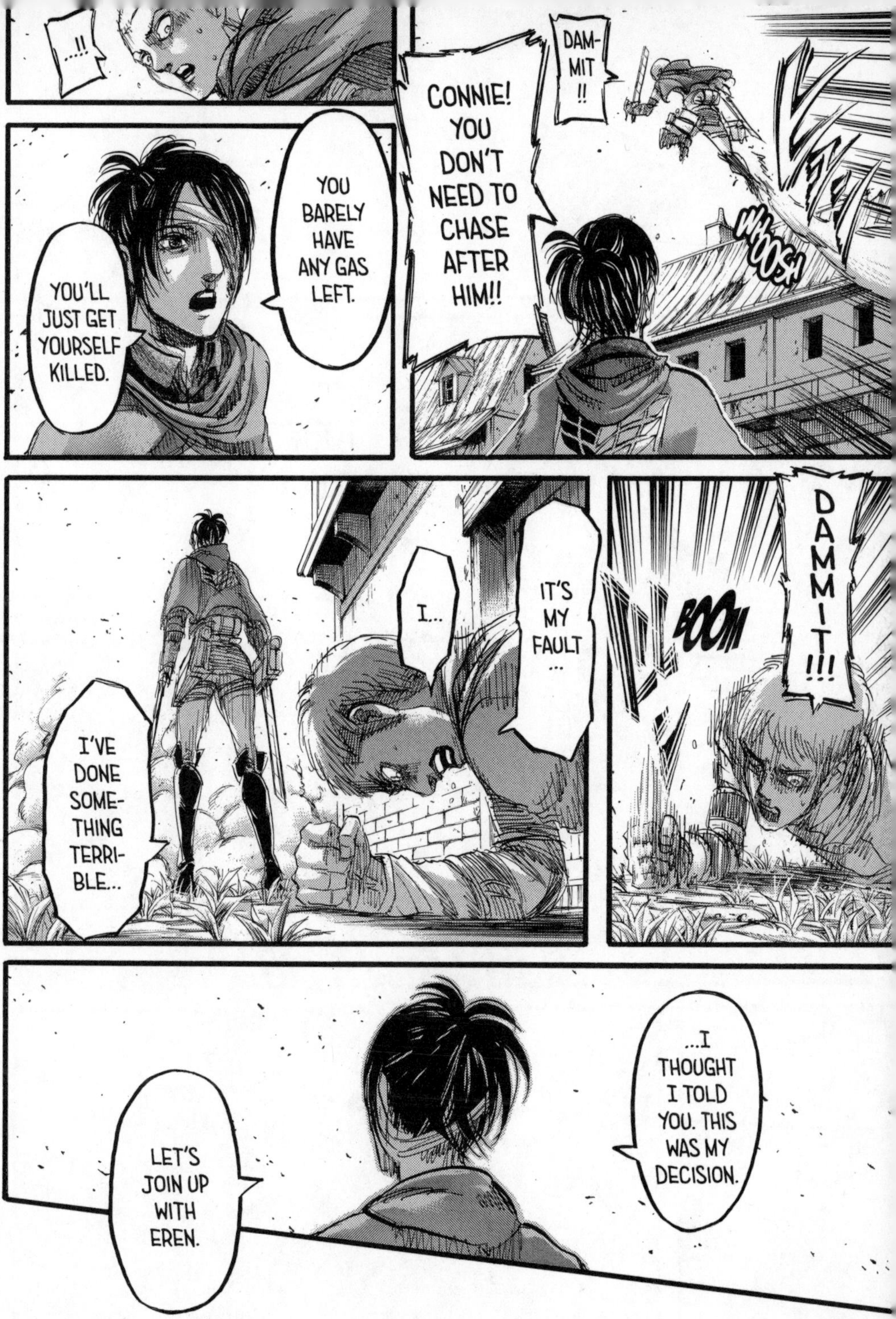
DAM-MIT !!
CONNIE! YOU DON'T NEED TO CHASE AFTER HIM!!
WHOOSH
...!!
YOU BARELY HAVE ANY GAS LEFT.
YOU'LL JUST GET YOURSELF KILLED.
DAMMIT!!!
BOOM
IT'S MY FAULT...
I...
I'VE DONE SOMETHING TERRIBLE...
...I THOUGHT I TOLD YOU. THIS WAS MY DECISION.
LET'S JOIN UP WITH EREN.

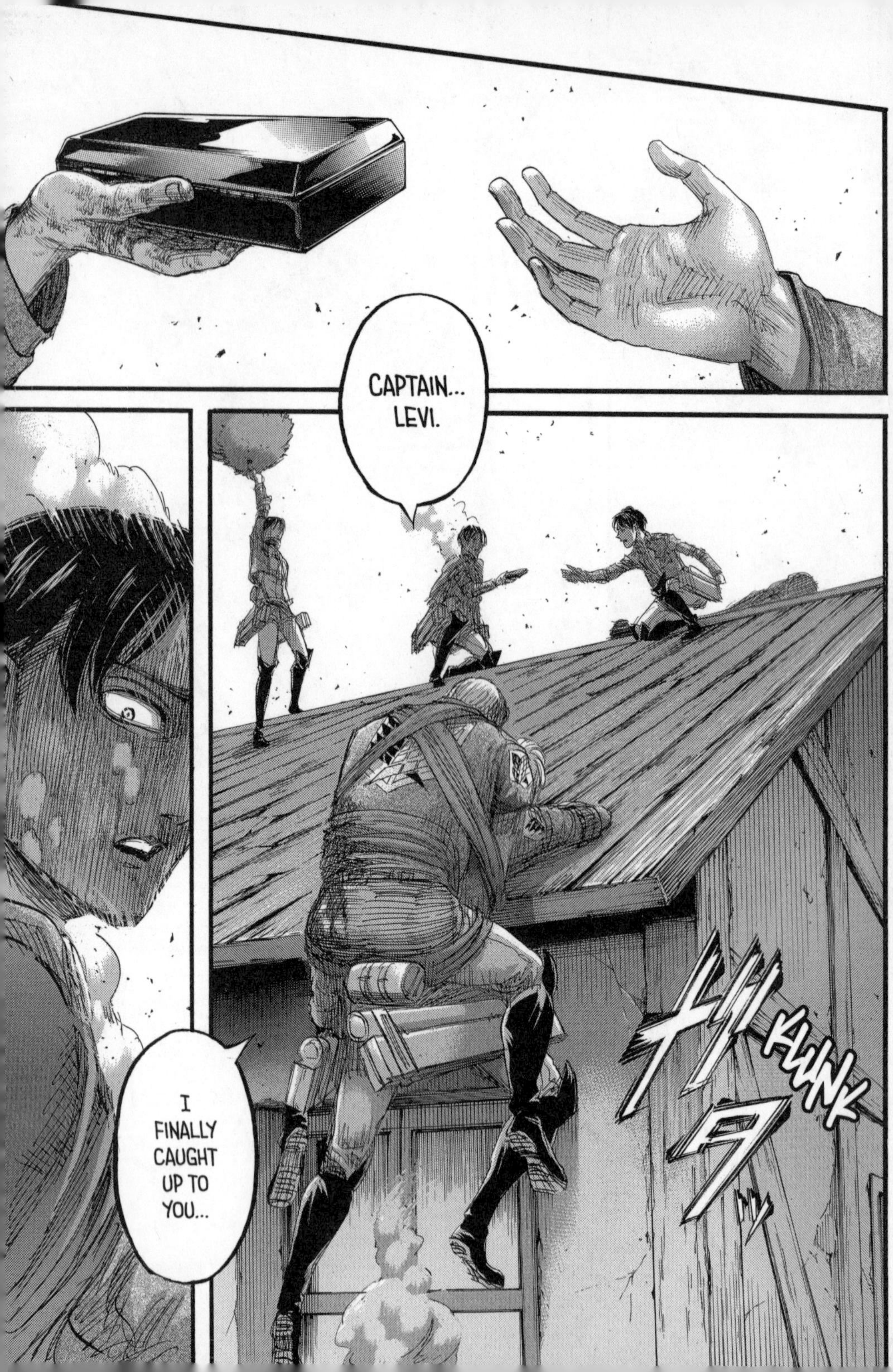
CAPTAIN... LEVI.
KLUNK
I FINALLY CAUGHT UP TO YOU...

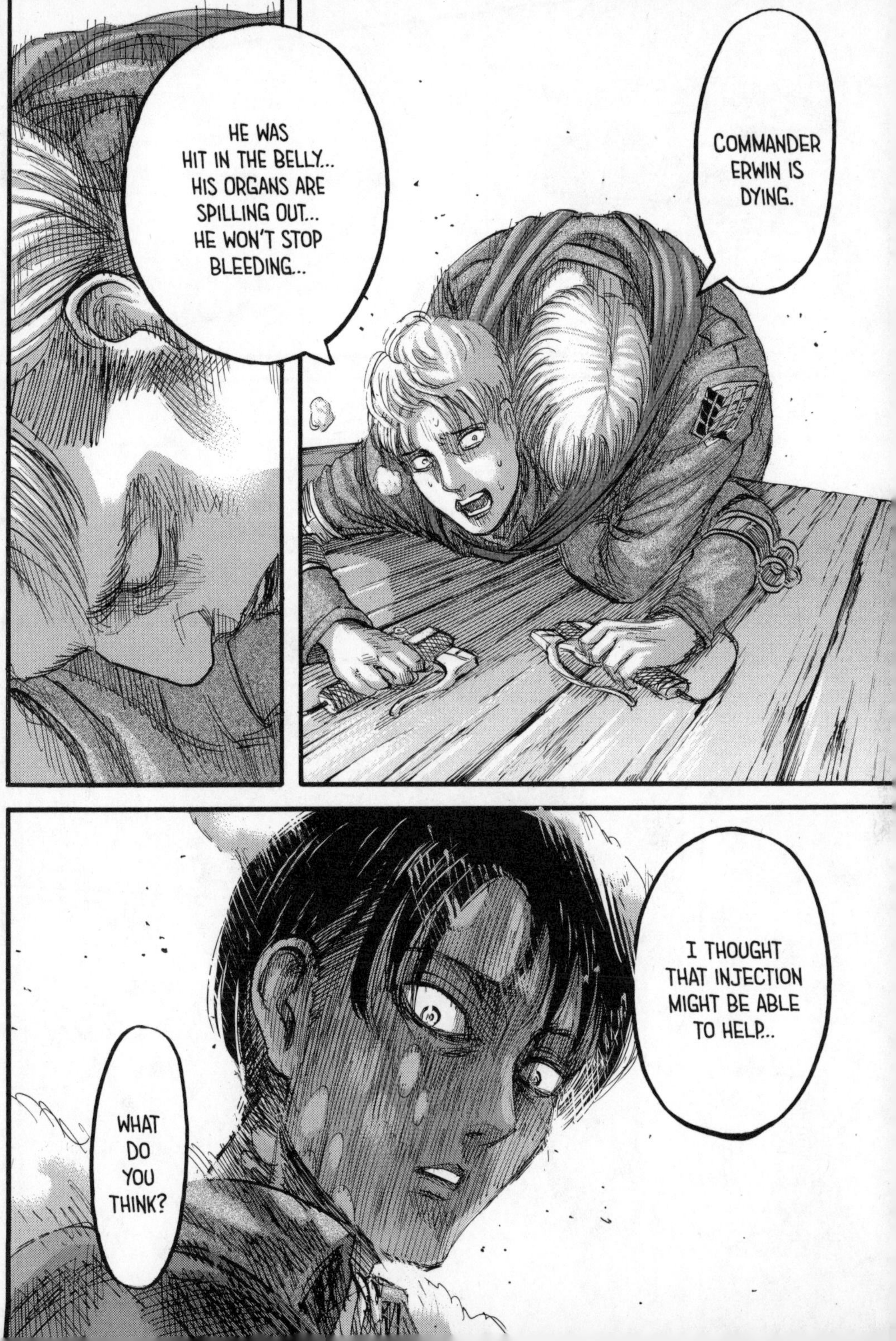
COMMANDER ERWIN IS DYING.
HE WAS HIT IN THE BELLY... HIS ORGANS ARE SPILLING OUT... HE WON'T STOP BLEEDING...
I THOUGHT THAT INJECTION MIGHT BE ABLE TO HELP...
WHAT DO YOU THINK?

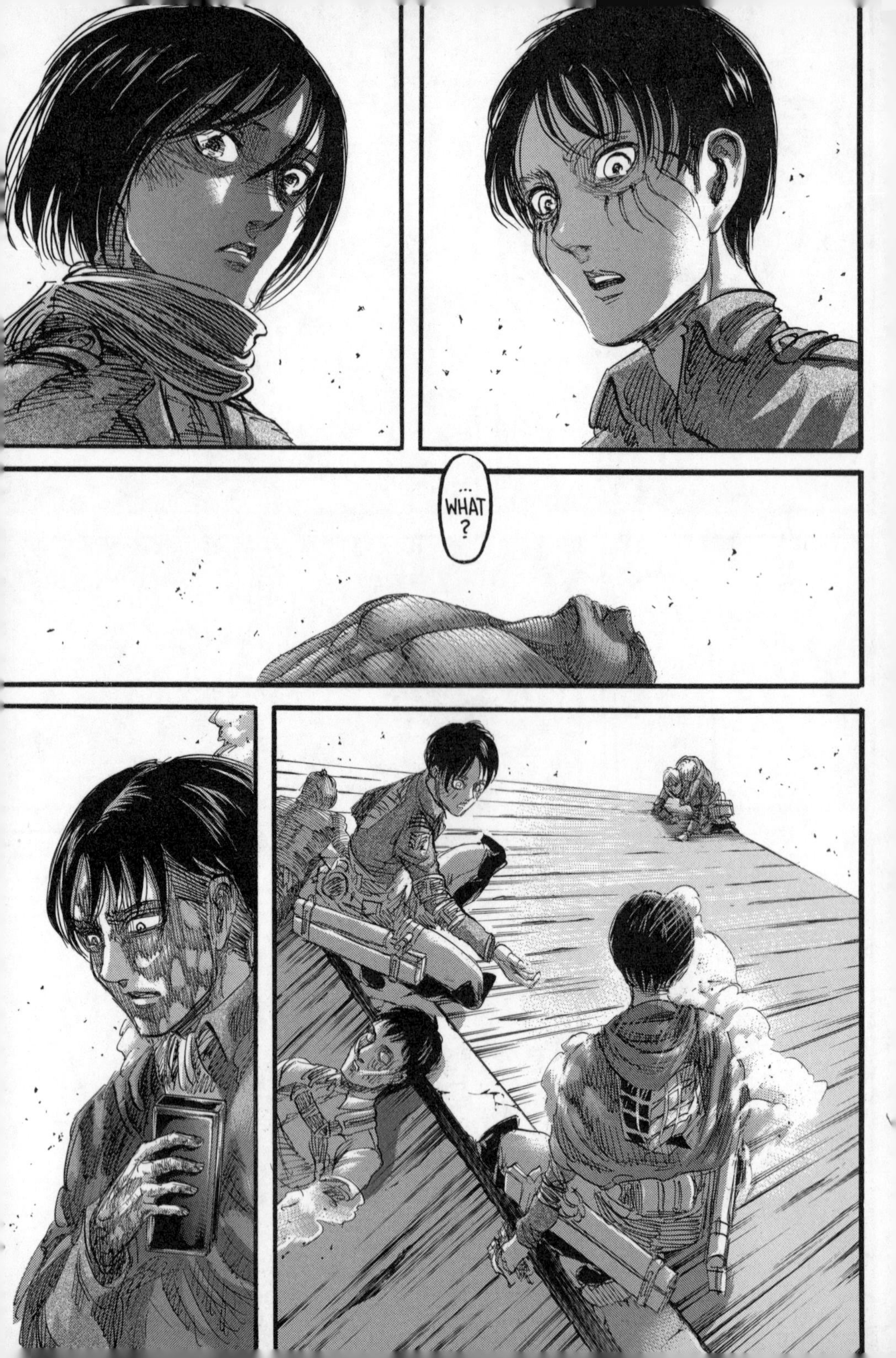
... WHAT ?

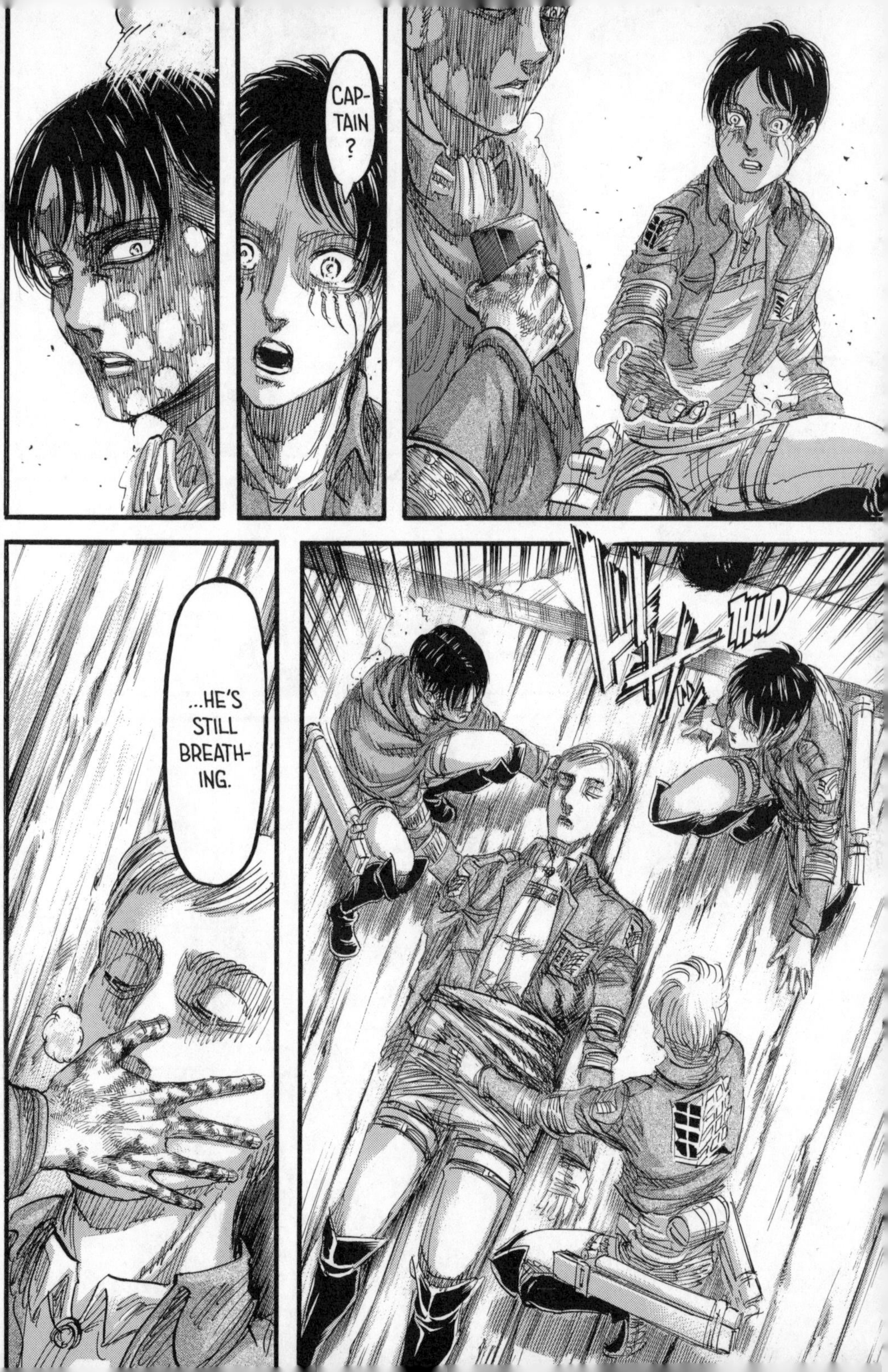
CAP-TAIN ?
THUD
...HE'S STILL BREATH-ING.

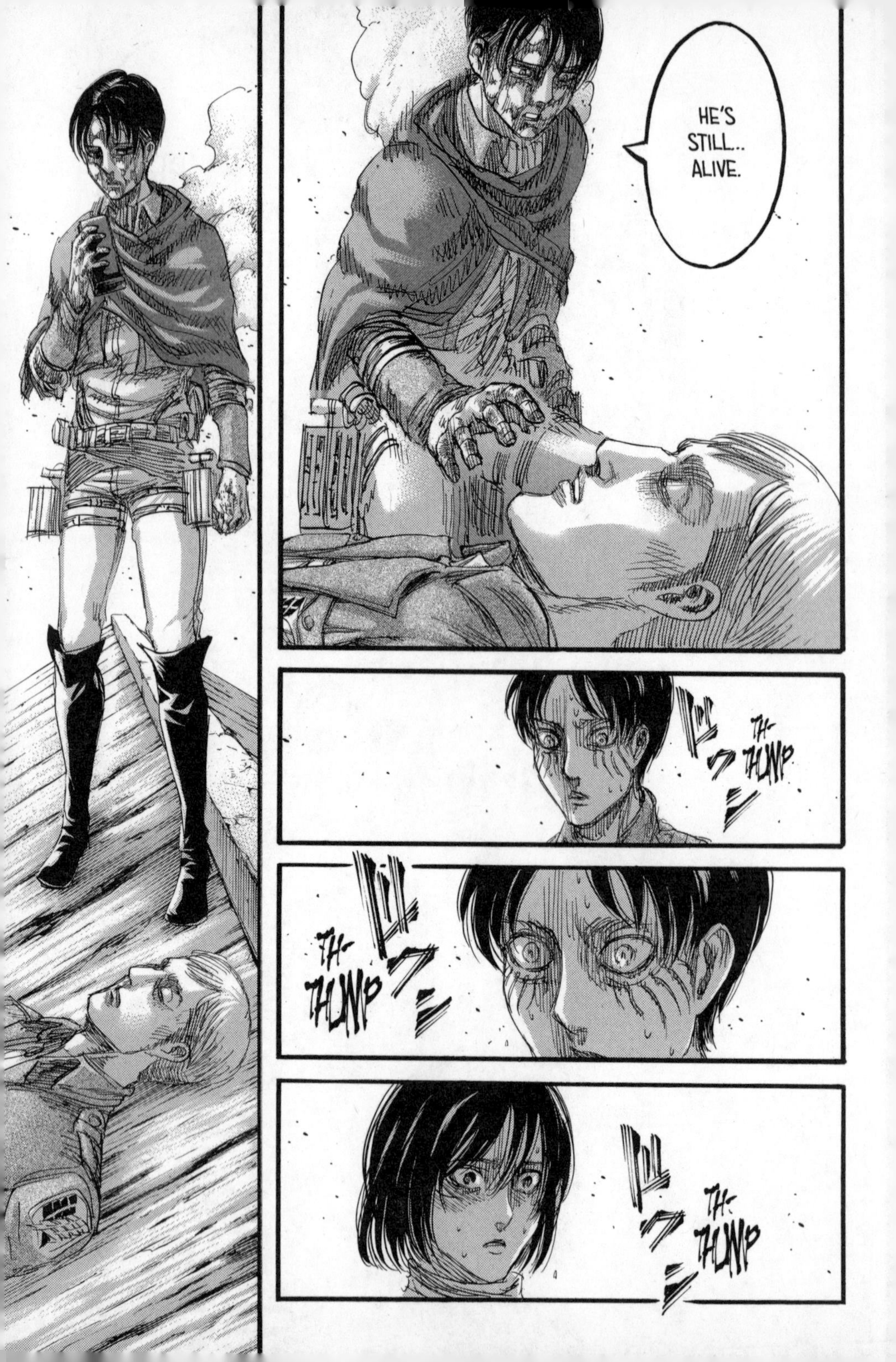
HE'S STILL... ALIVE.
TH-THUMP
TH-THUMP
TH-THUMP

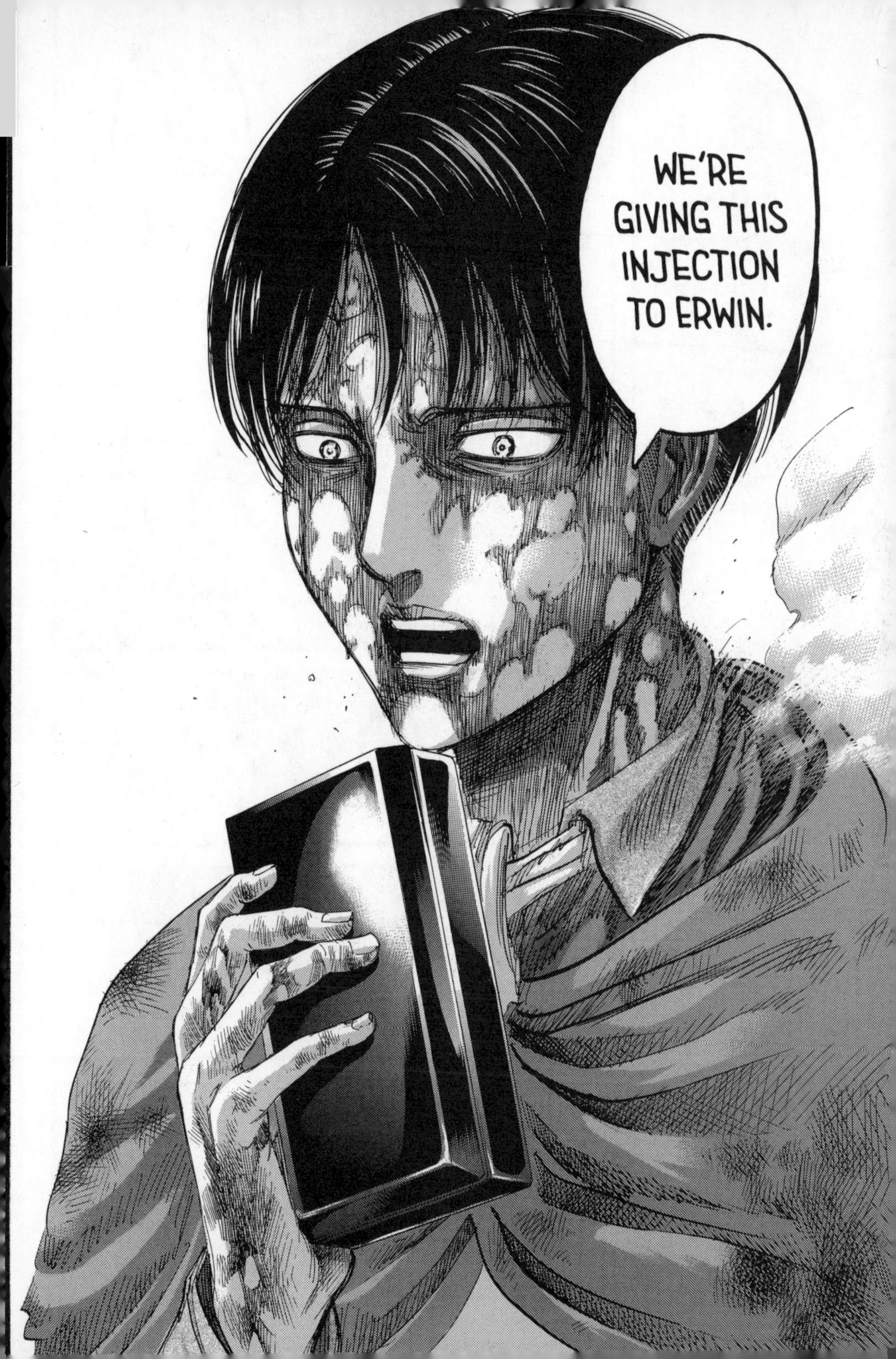
WE'RE GIVING THIS INJECTION TO ERWIN.

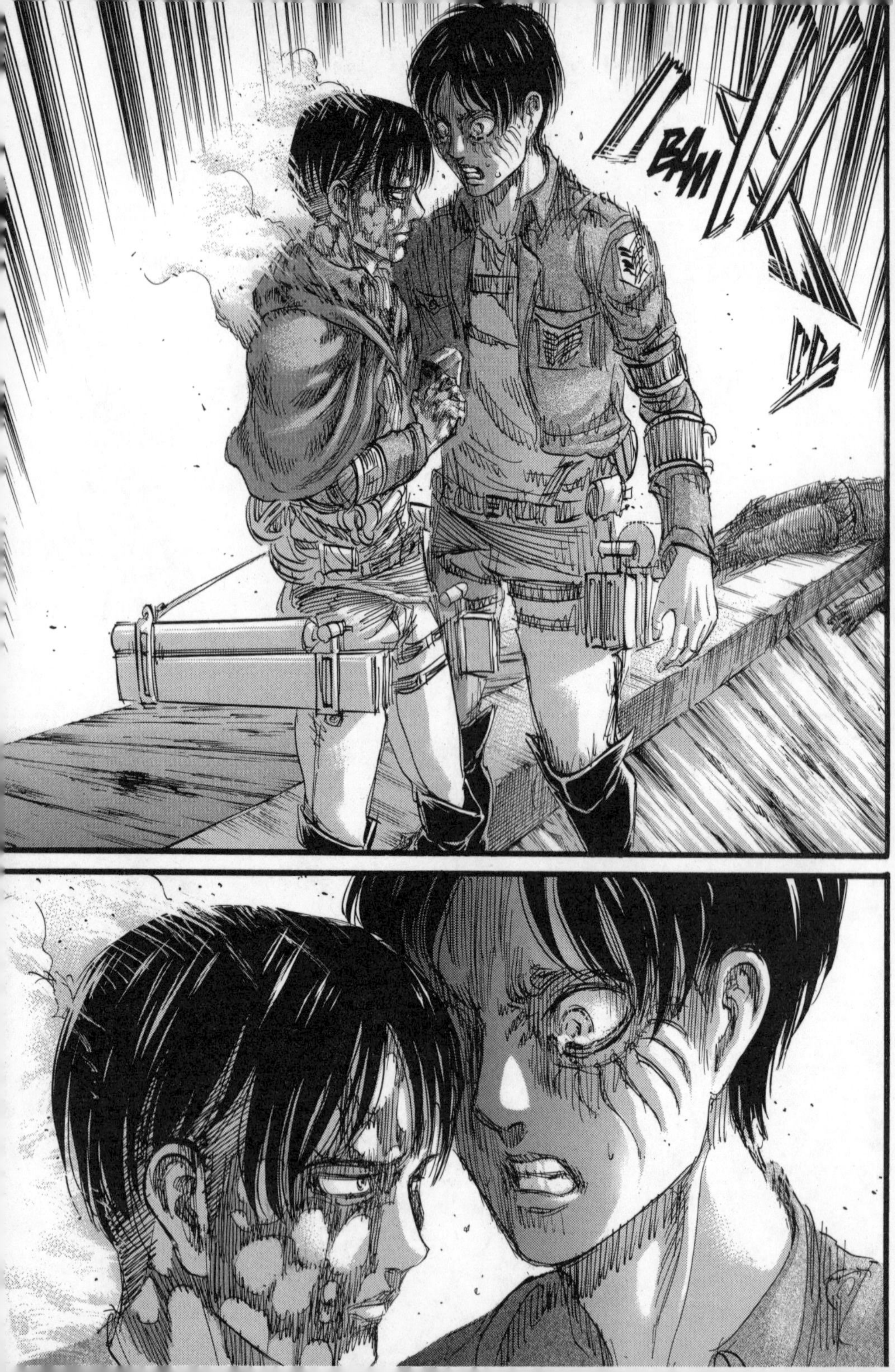
BAM

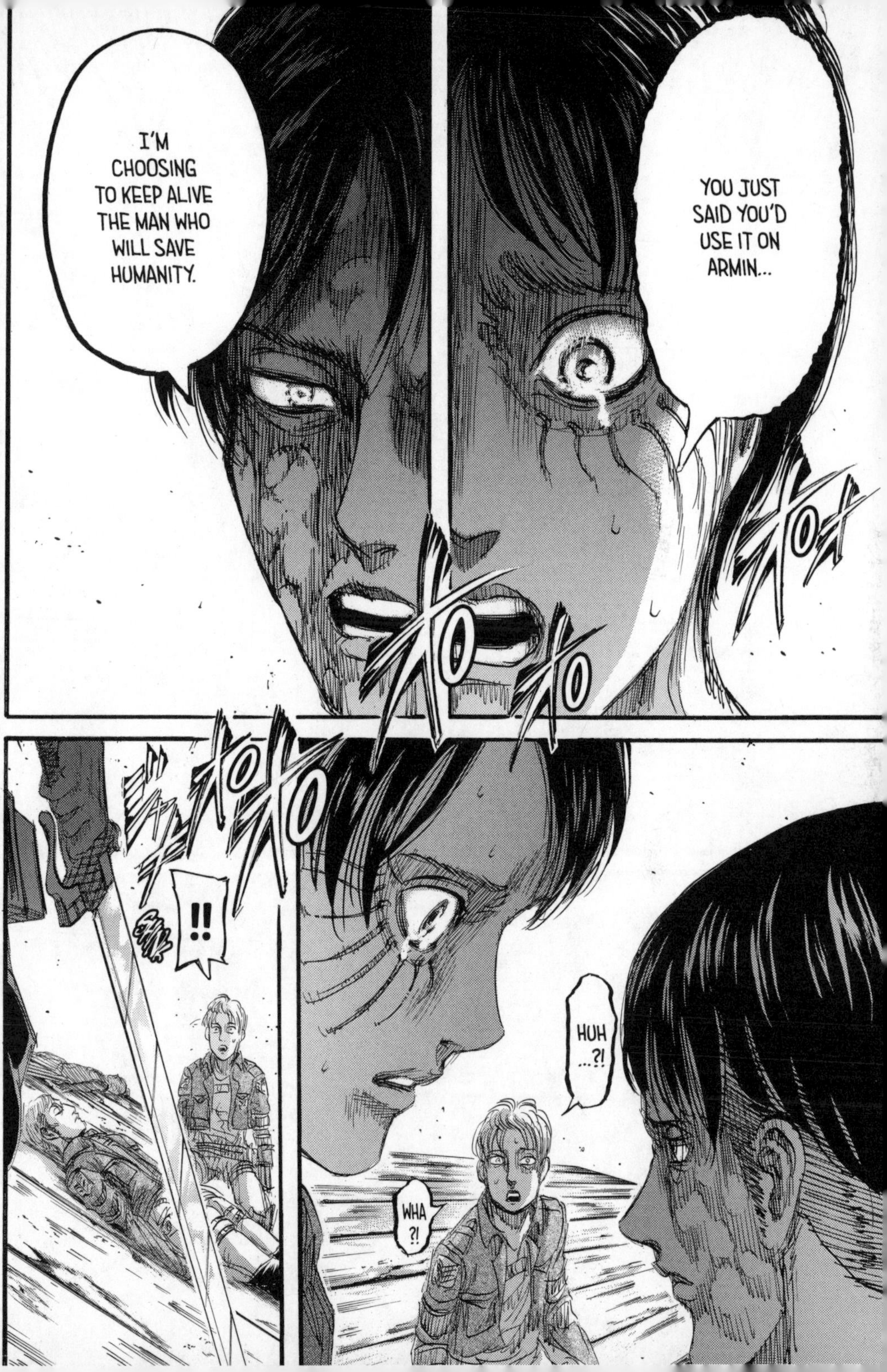
YOU JUST SAID YOU'D USE IT ON ARMIN...
I'M CHOOSING TO KEEP ALIVE THE MAN WHO WILL SAVE HUMANITY.
HUH ...?!
WHA ?!
!!

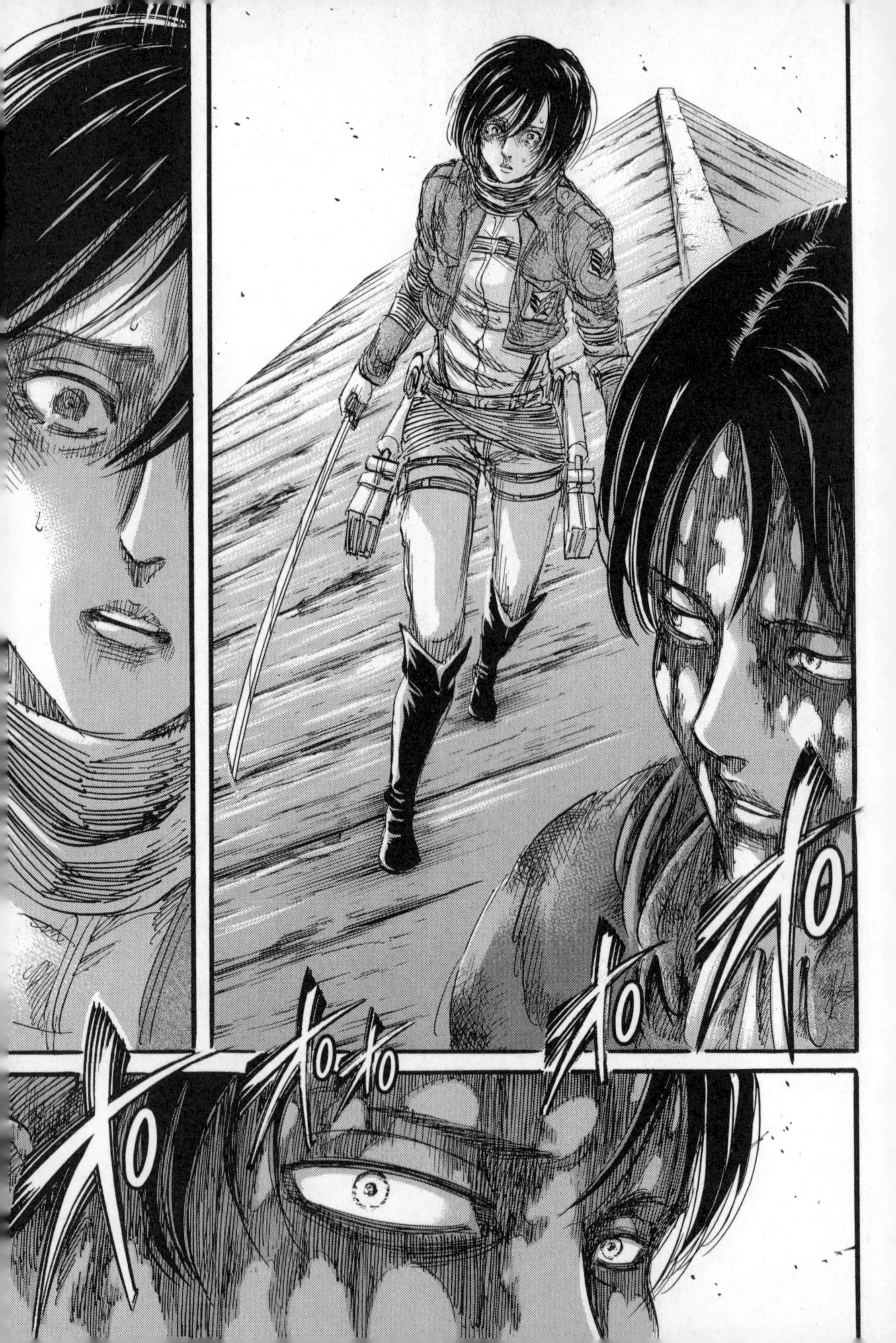

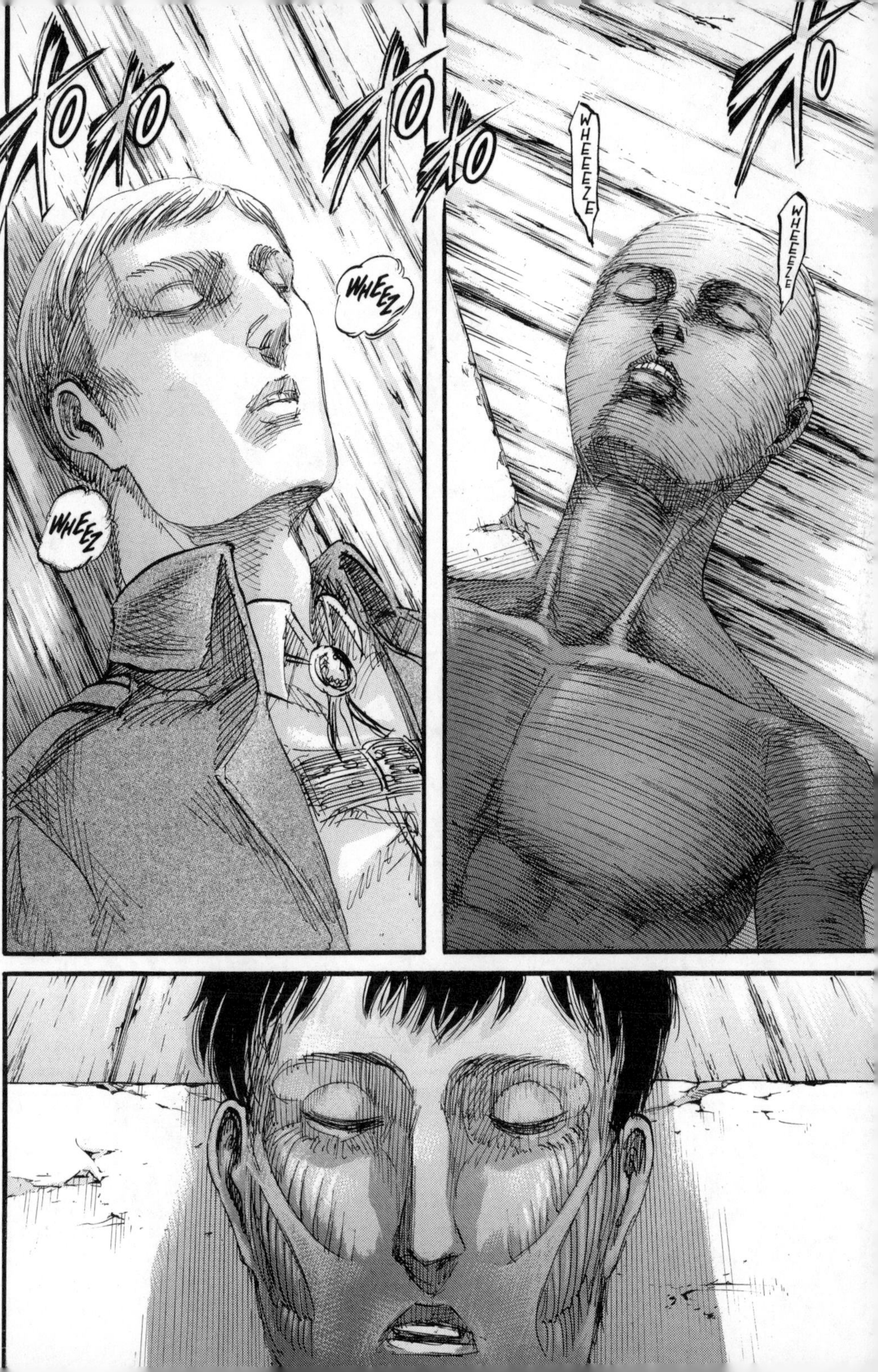

WHEEEEZE
WHEEEEZE
WHEEZ
WHEEZ

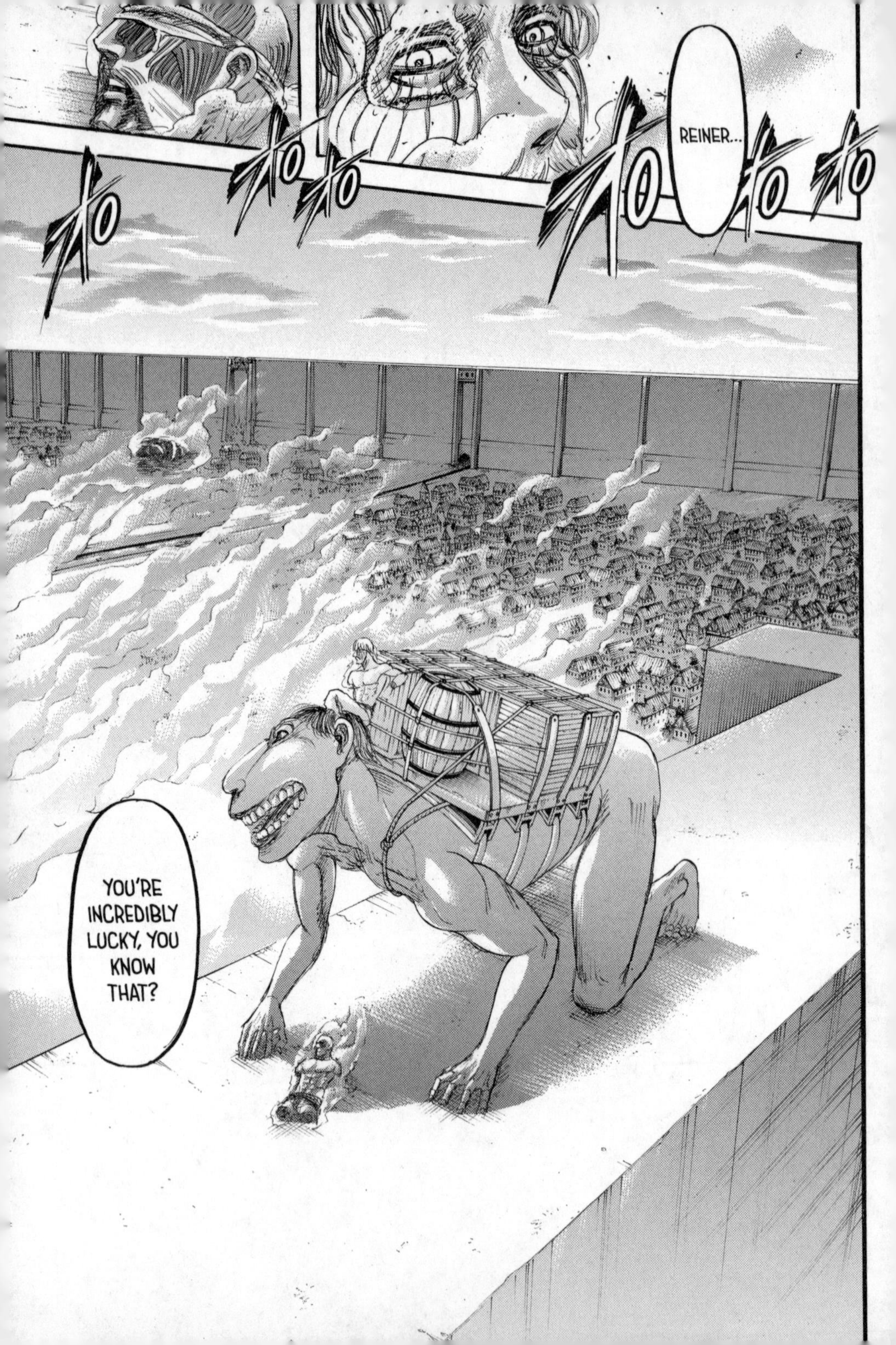
REINER...
YOU'RE INCREDIBLY LUCKY, YOU KNOW THAT?

ATTACK on TITAN

Episode 84: Midnight Sun

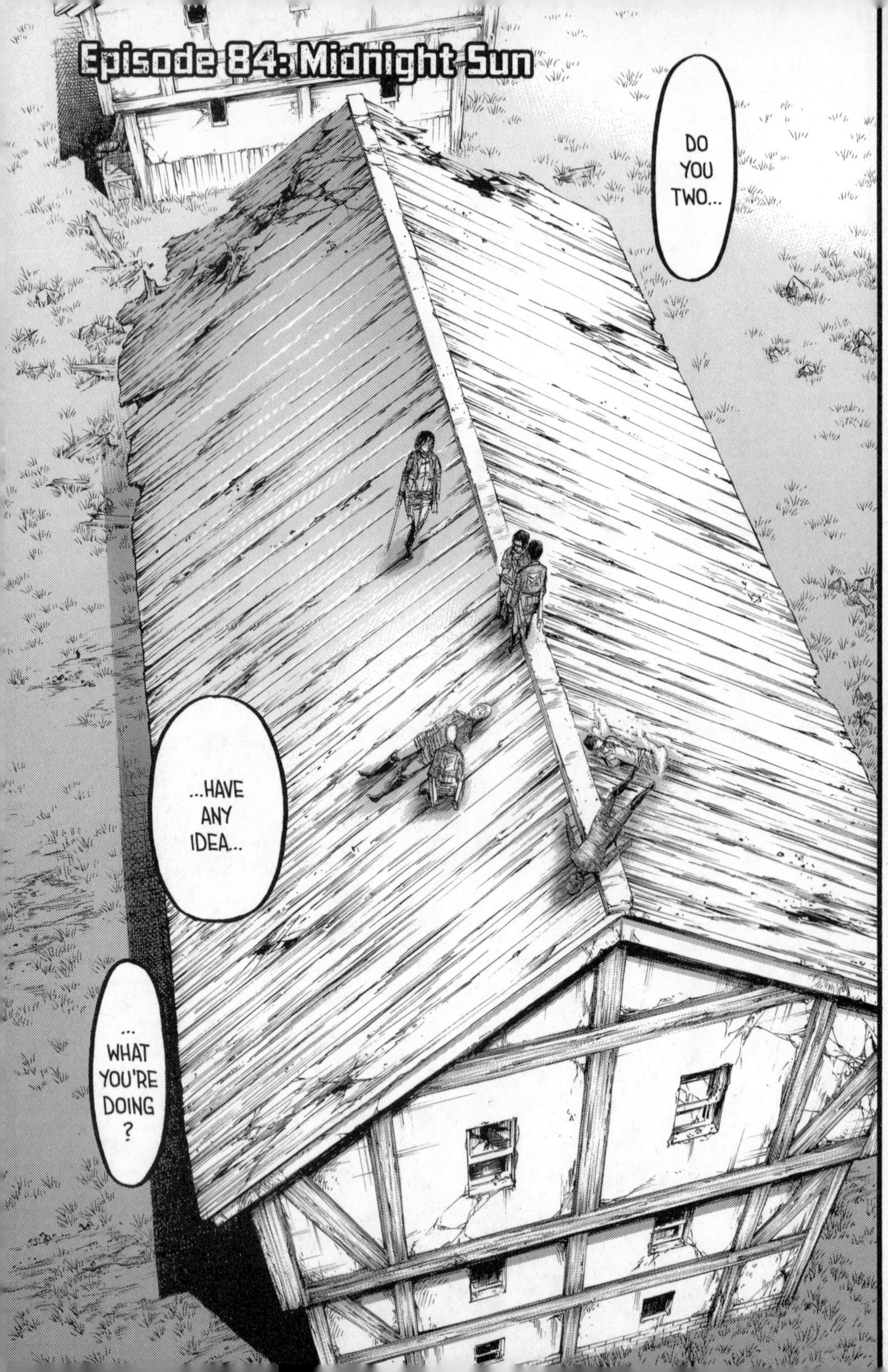
DO YOU TWO...
...HAVE ANY IDEA...
... WHAT YOU'RE DOING?

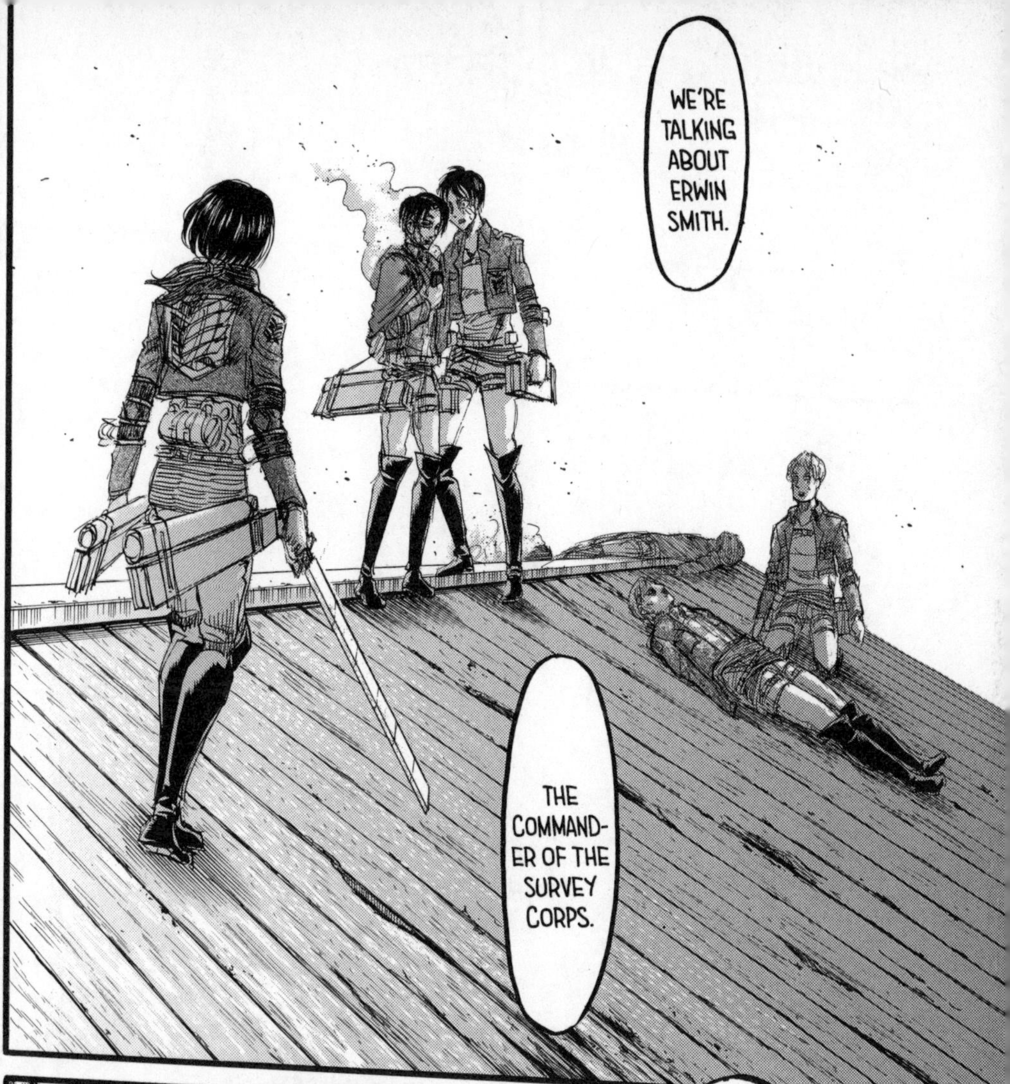
WE'RE TALKING ABOUT ERWIN SMITH.
THE COMMANDER OF THE SURVEY CORPS.

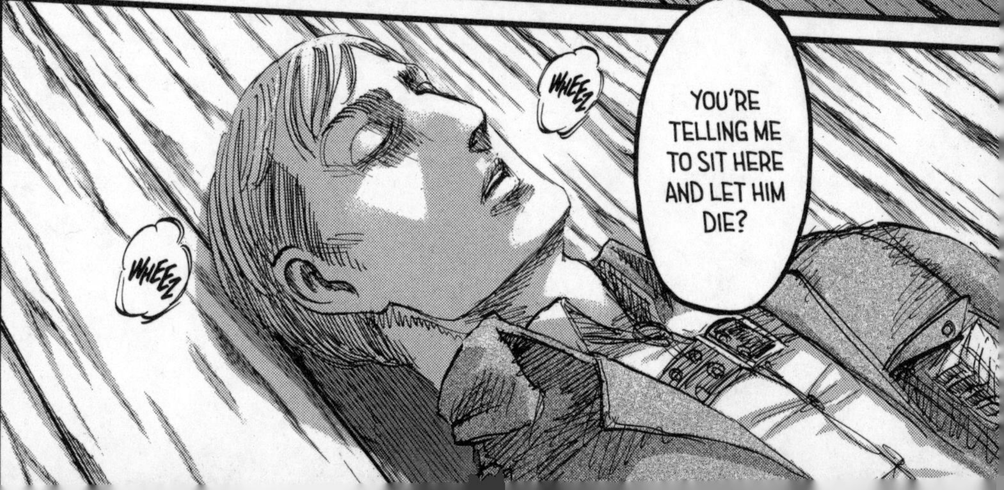
YOU'RE TELLING ME TO SIT HERE AND LET HIM DIE?
WHEEZ
WHEEZ

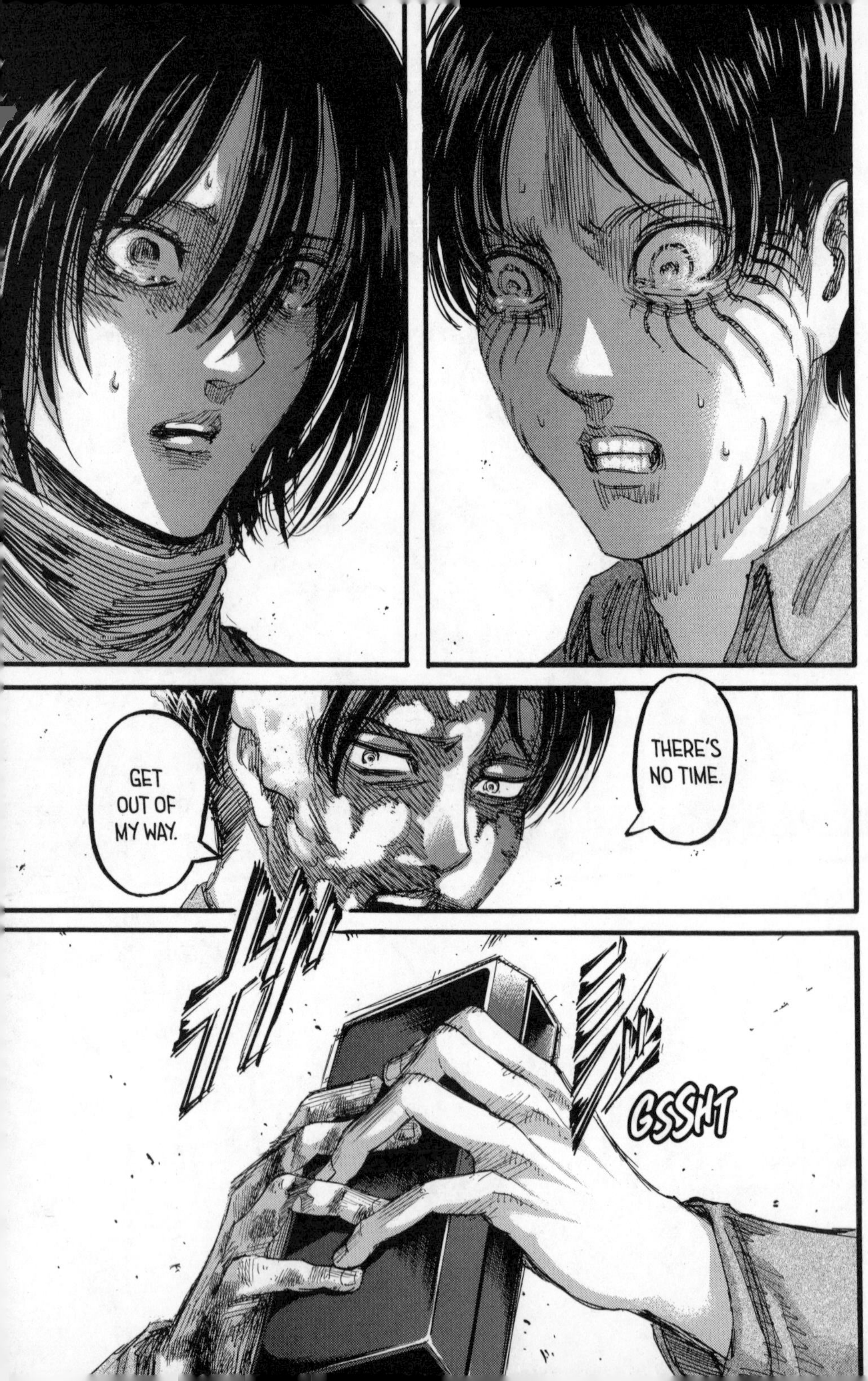
THERE'S NO TIME.
GET OUT OF MY WAY.
GSSHT

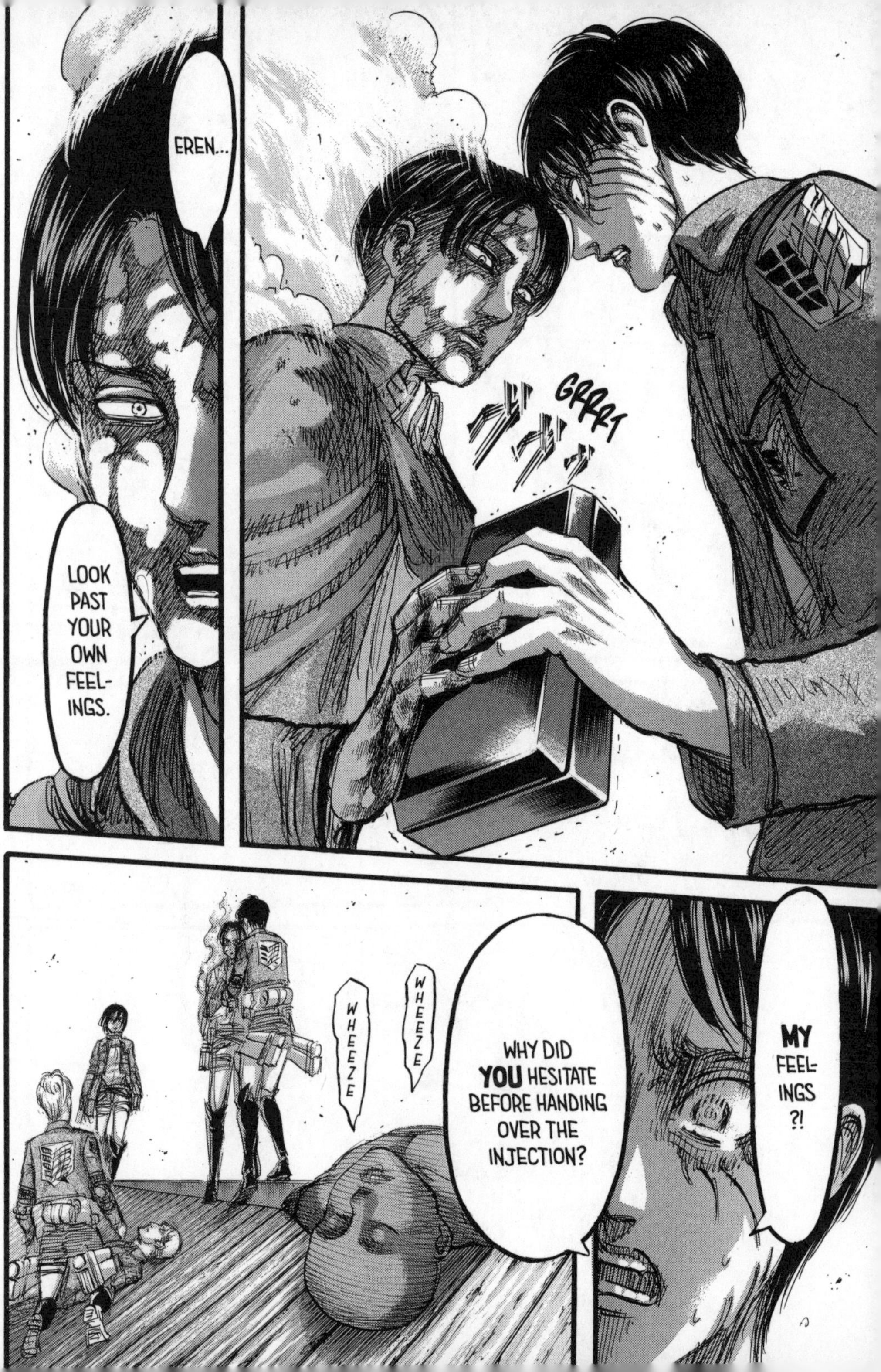
GRRR1
EREN...
LOOK PAST YOUR OWN FEELINGS.
MY FEELINGS?!
WHY DID **YOU** HESITATE BEFORE HANDING OVER THE INJECTION?
WHEEZE
WHEEZE

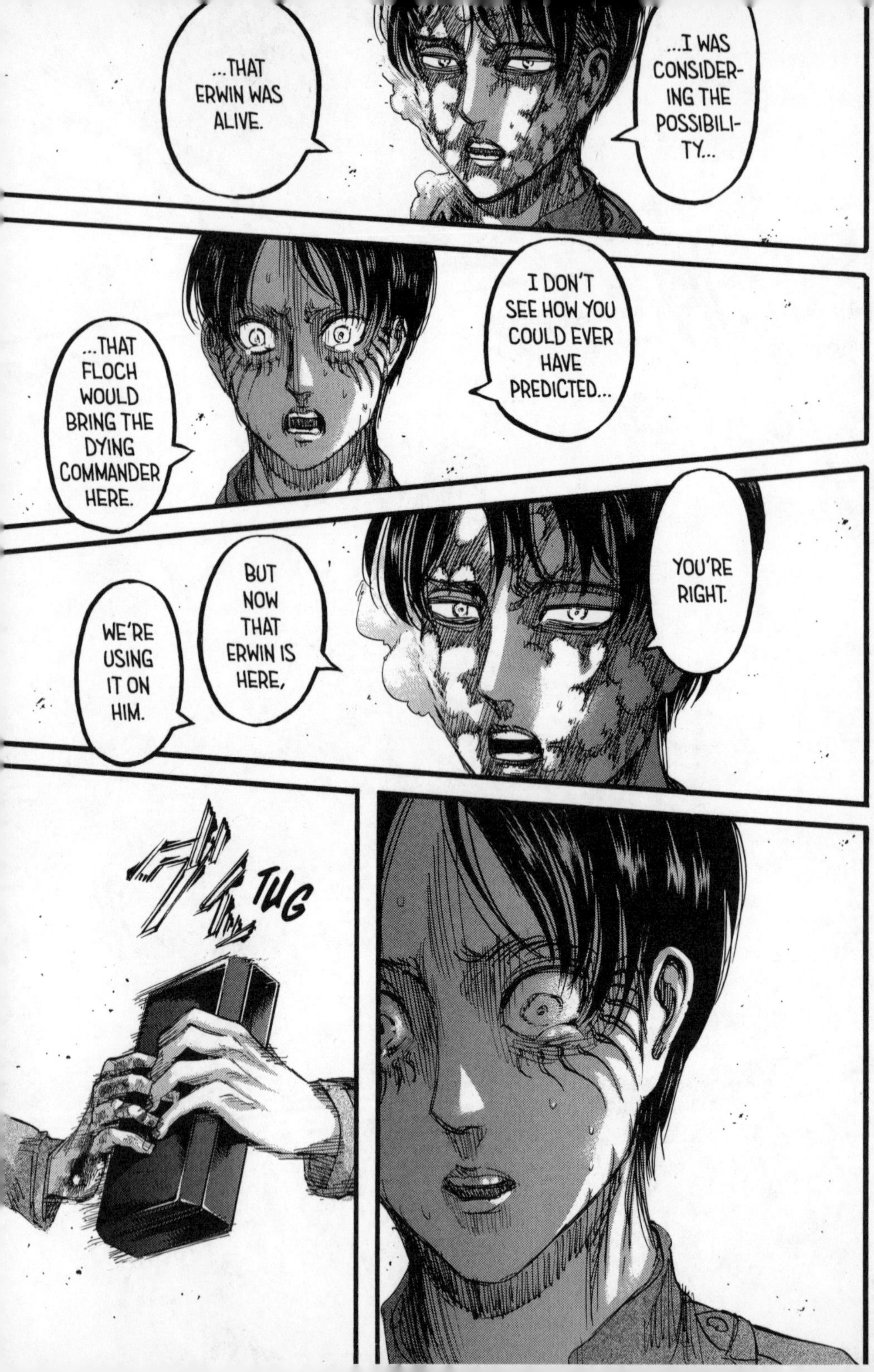
...I WAS CONSIDERING THE POSSIBILITY...
...THAT ERWIN WAS ALIVE.
I DON'T SEE HOW YOU COULD EVER HAVE PREDICTED...
...THAT FLOCH WOULD BRING THE DYING COMMANDER HERE.
YOU'RE RIGHT.
BUT NOW THAT ERWIN IS HERE,
WE'RE USING IT ON HIM.
TUG

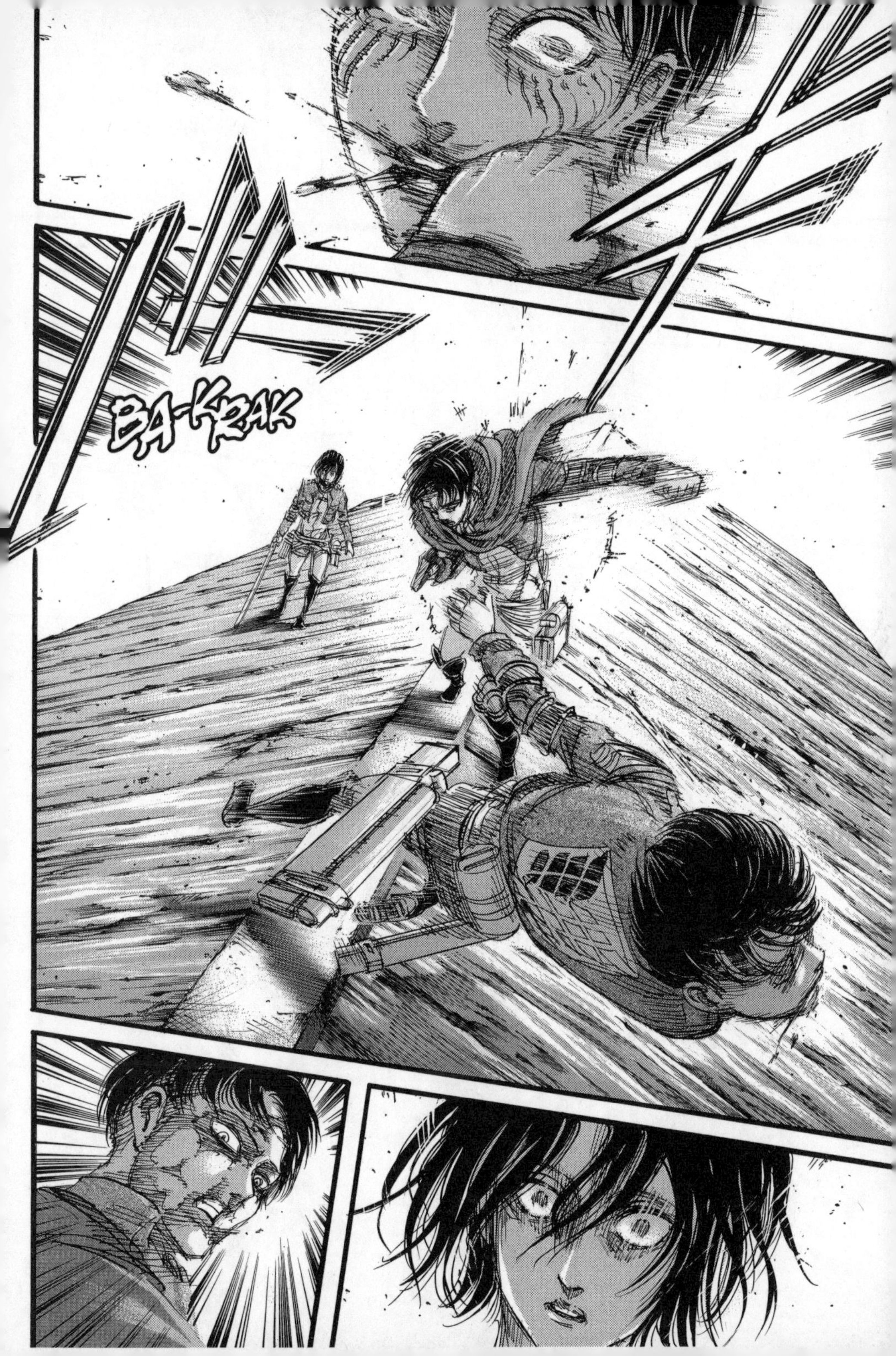
BA-KRAK

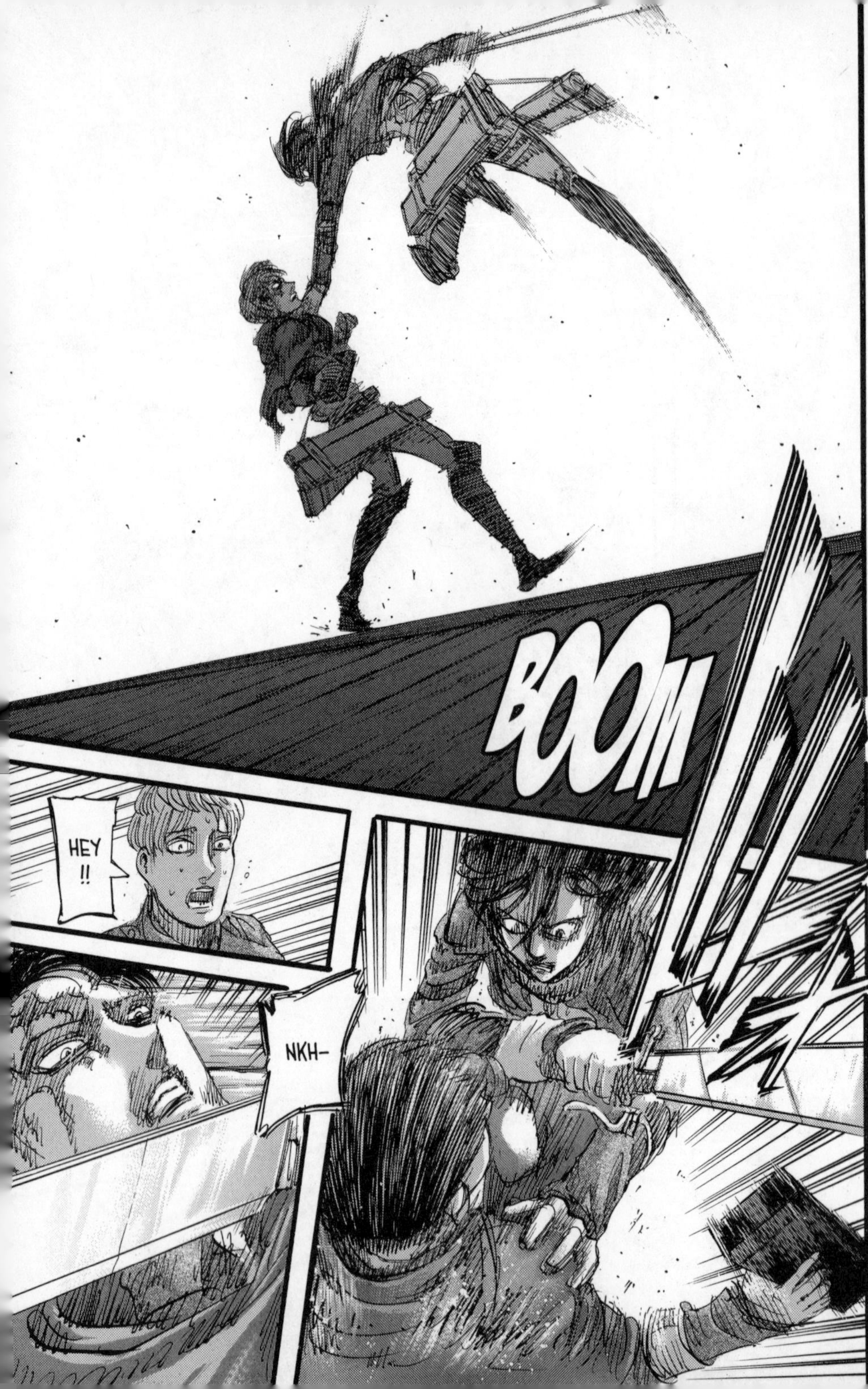
BOOM
HEY !!
NKH-

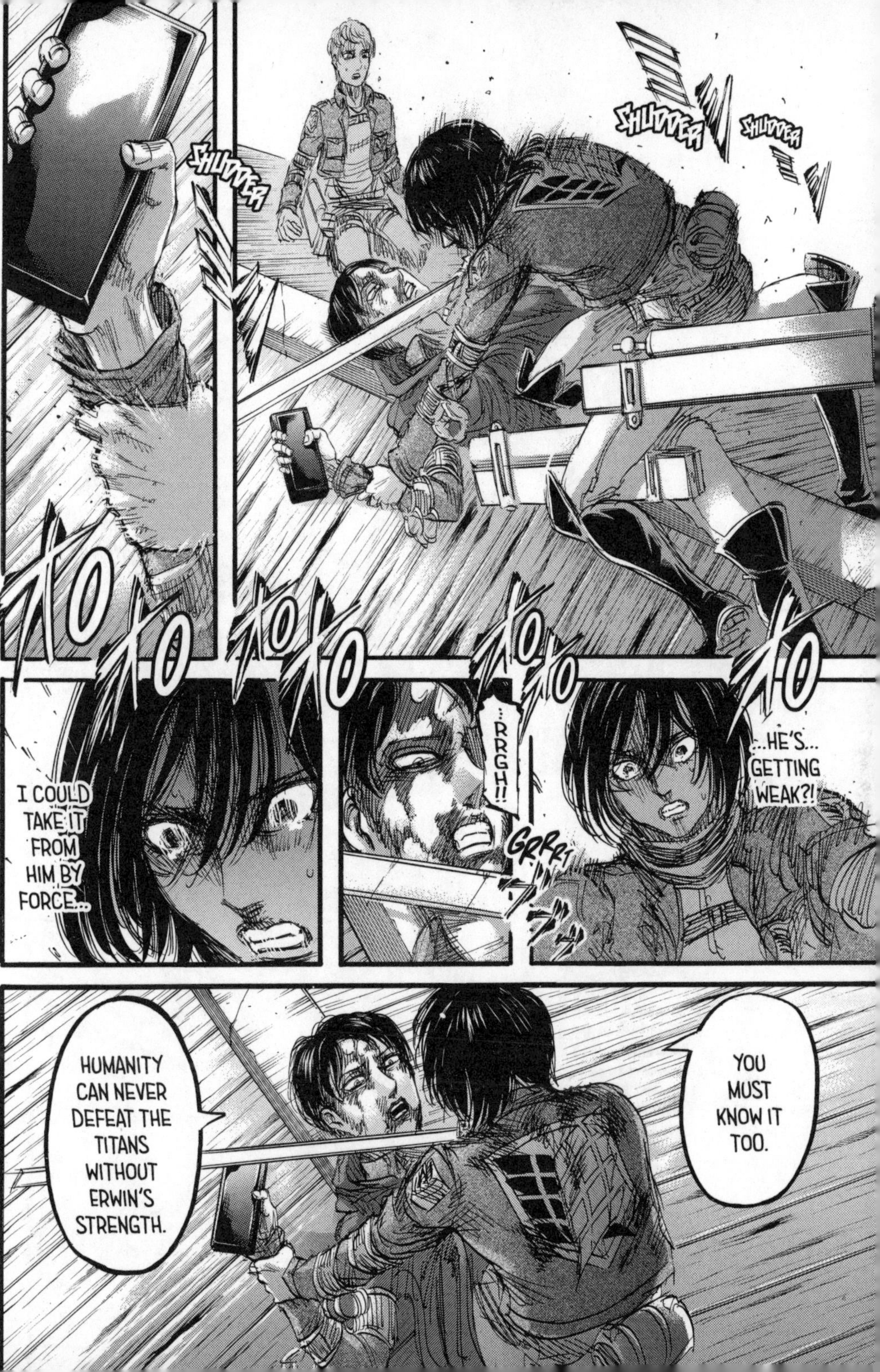
SHUDDER
SHUDDER
SHUDDER
...HE'S... GETTING WEAK?!
...RRGH!!
GRRR
I COULD TAKE IT FROM HIM BY FORCE...
YOU MUST KNOW IT TOO.
HUMANITY CAN NEVER DEFEAT THE TITANS WITHOUT ERWIN'S STRENGTH.

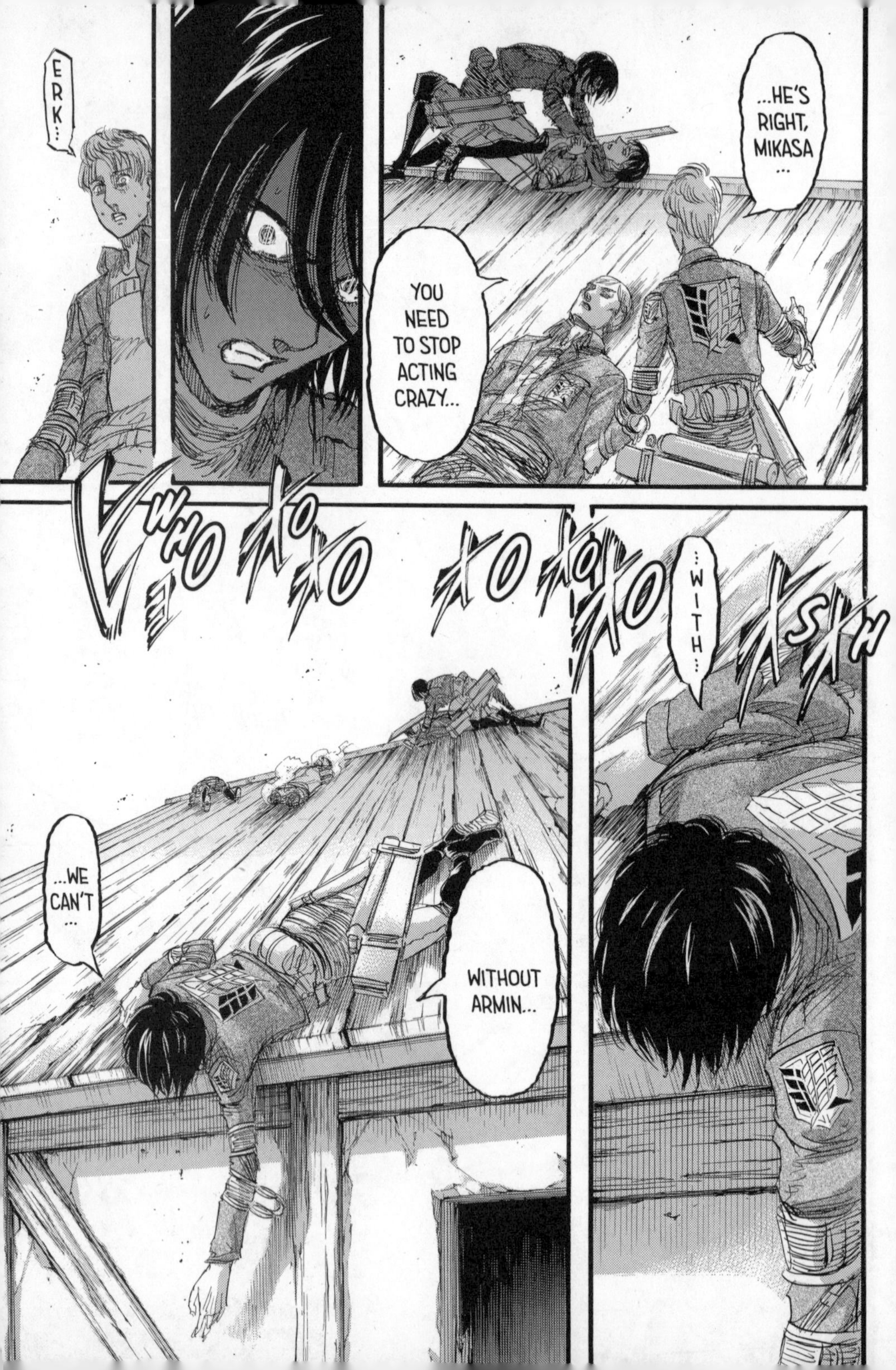
...HE'S RIGHT, MIKASA...
YOU NEED TO STOP ACTING CRAZY...
ERK...
...WITH...
...WE CAN'T...
WITHOUT ARMIN...

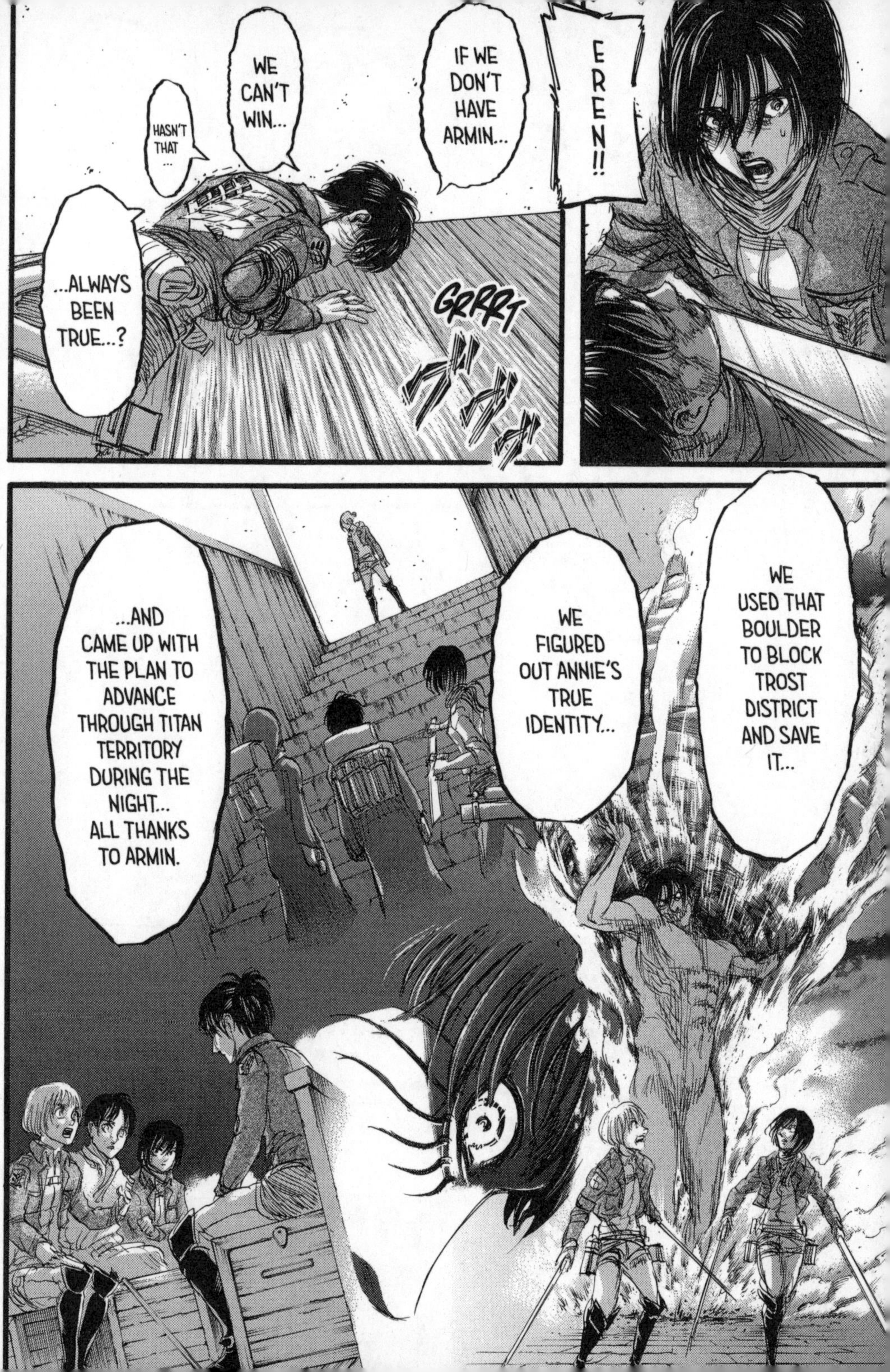
EREN!!
IF WE DON'T HAVE ARMIN...
WE CAN'T WIN...
HASN'T THAT ...
...ALWAYS BEEN TRUE...?
GRRRT
WE USED THAT BOULDER TO BLOCK TROST DISTRICT AND SAVE IT...
WE FIGURED OUT ANNIE'S TRUE IDENTITY...
...AND CAME UP WITH THE PLAN TO ADVANCE THROUGH TITAN TERRITORY DURING THE NIGHT... ALL THANKS TO ARMIN.

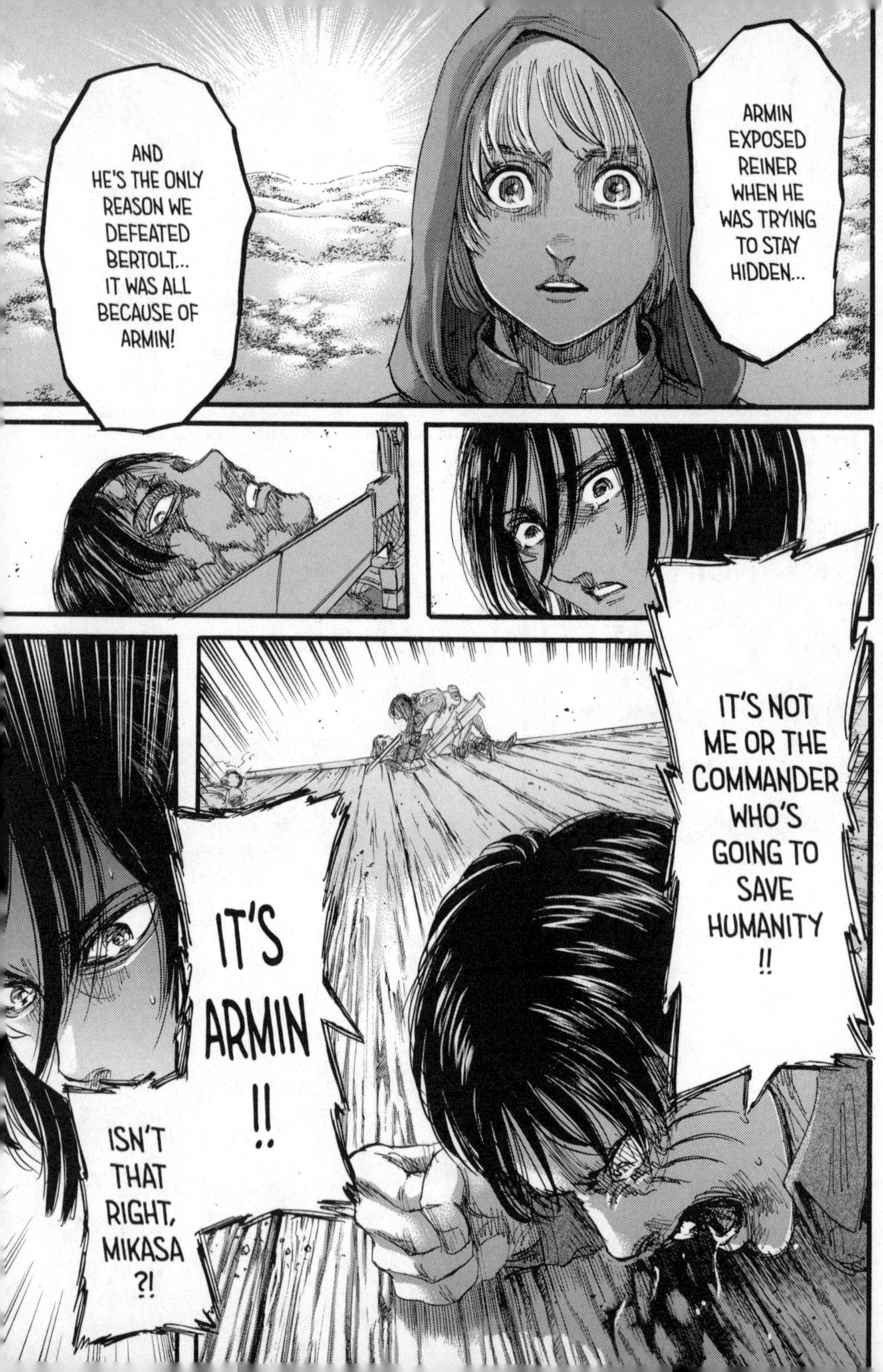
ARMIN EXPOSED REINER WHEN HE WAS TRYING TO STAY HIDDEN...
AND HE'S THE ONLY REASON WE DEFEATED BERTOLT... IT WAS ALL BECAUSE OF ARMIN!
IT'S NOT ME OR THE COMMANDER WHO'S GOING TO SAVE HUMANITY !!
IT'S ARMIN !!
ISN'T THAT RIGHT, MIKASA ?!

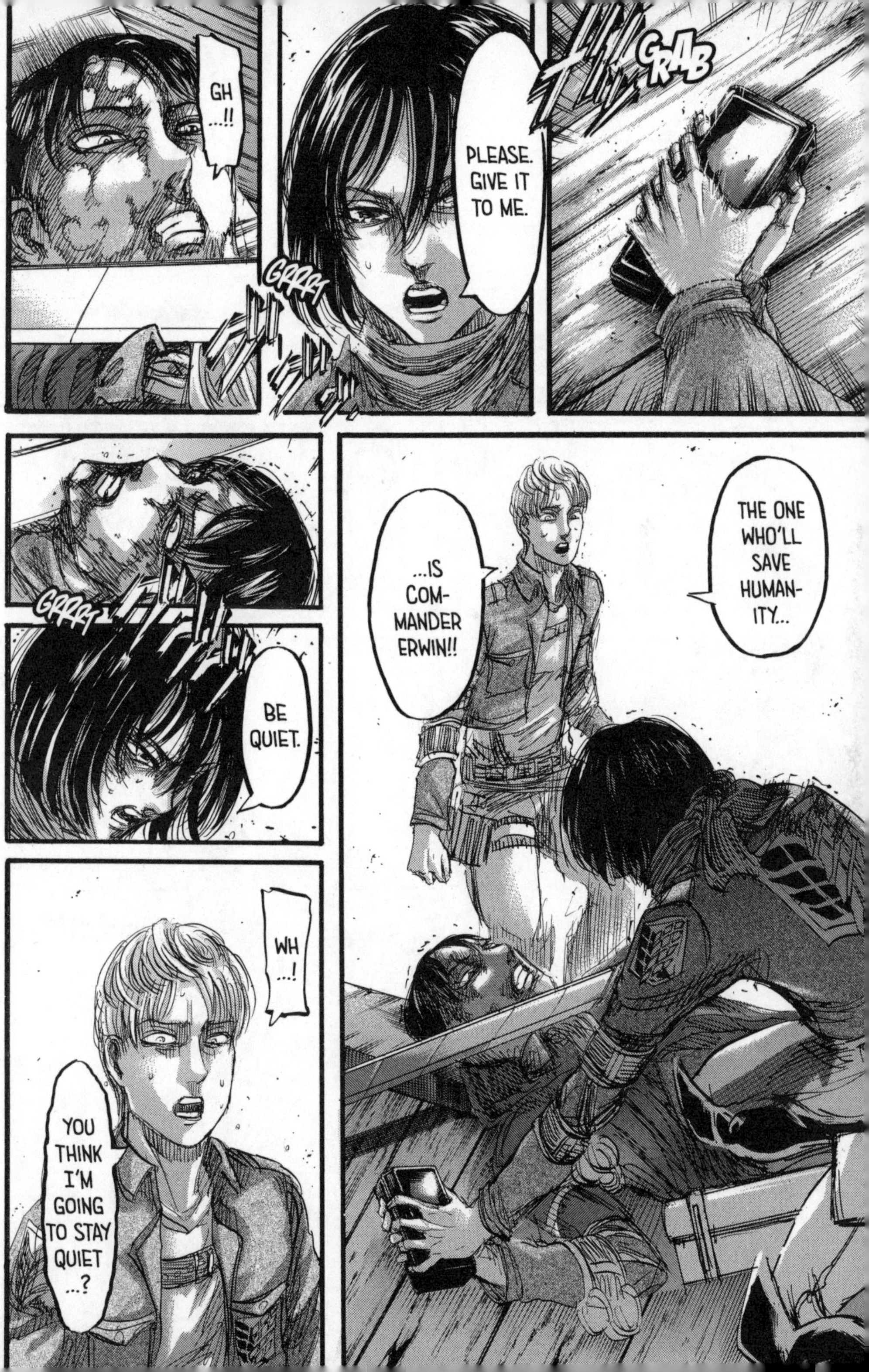
GRAB
PLEASE. GIVE IT TO ME.
GRRRT
GH ...!!
THE ONE WHO'LL SAVE HUMAN-ITY...
...IS COM-MANDER ERWIN!!
GRRRT
BE QUIET.
WH ...!
YOU THINK I'M GOING TO STAY QUIET ...?

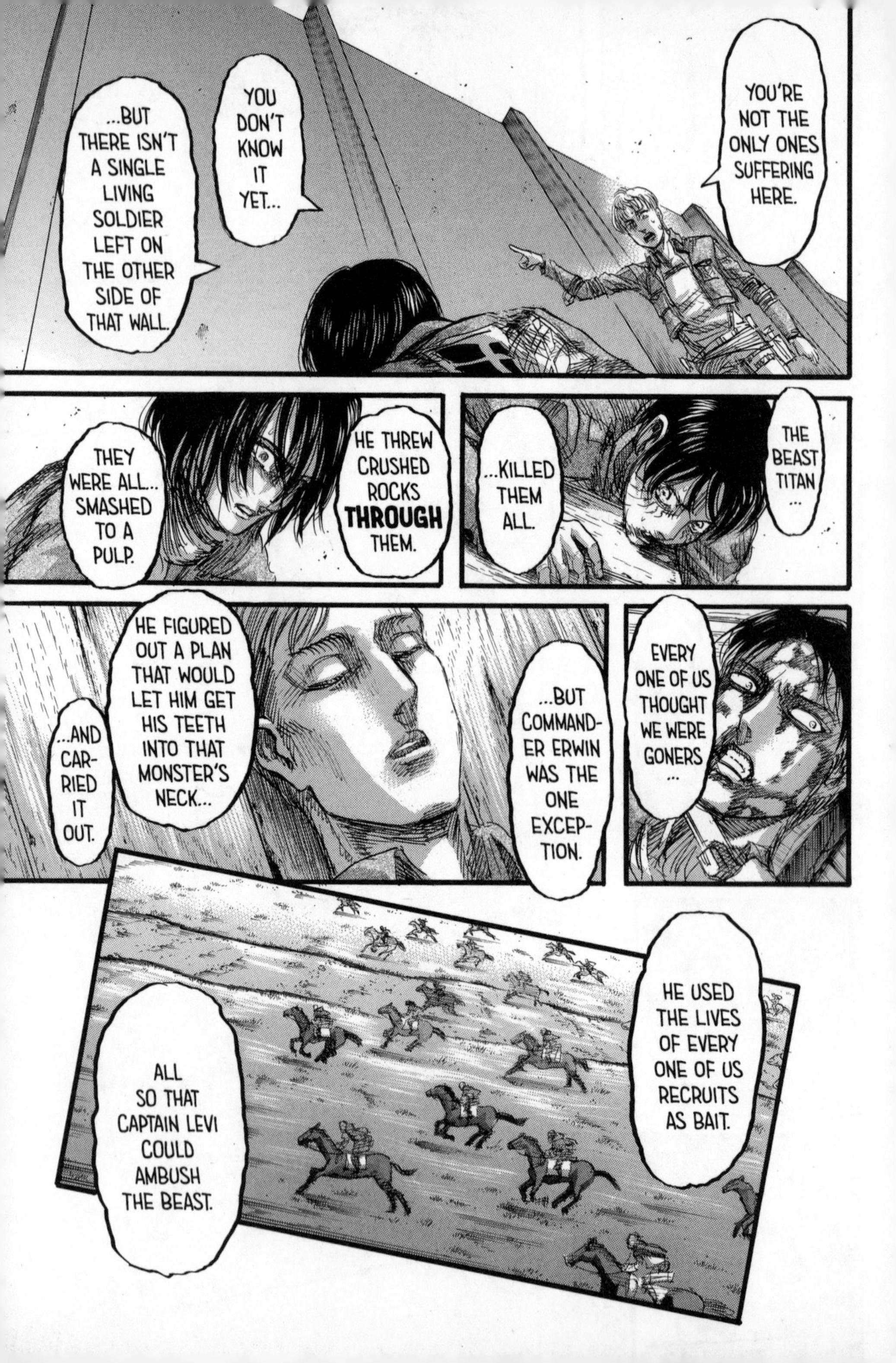
YOU'RE NOT THE ONLY ONES SUFFERING HERE.
YOU DON'T KNOW IT YET...
...BUT THERE ISN'T A SINGLE LIVING SOLDIER LEFT ON THE OTHER SIDE OF THAT WALL.
THE BEAST TITAN...
...KILLED THEM ALL.
HE THREW CRUSHED ROCKS **THROUGH** THEM.
THEY WERE ALL... SMASHED TO A PULP.
EVERY ONE OF US THOUGHT WE WERE GONERS...
...BUT COMMAND-ER ERWIN WAS THE ONE EXCEP-TION.
HE FIGURED OUT A PLAN THAT WOULD LET HIM GET HIS TEETH INTO THAT MONSTER'S NECK...
...AND CAR-RIED IT OUT.
HE USED THE LIVES OF EVERY ONE OF US RECRUITS AS BAIT.
ALL SO THAT CAPTAIN LEVI COULD AMBUSH THE BEAST.

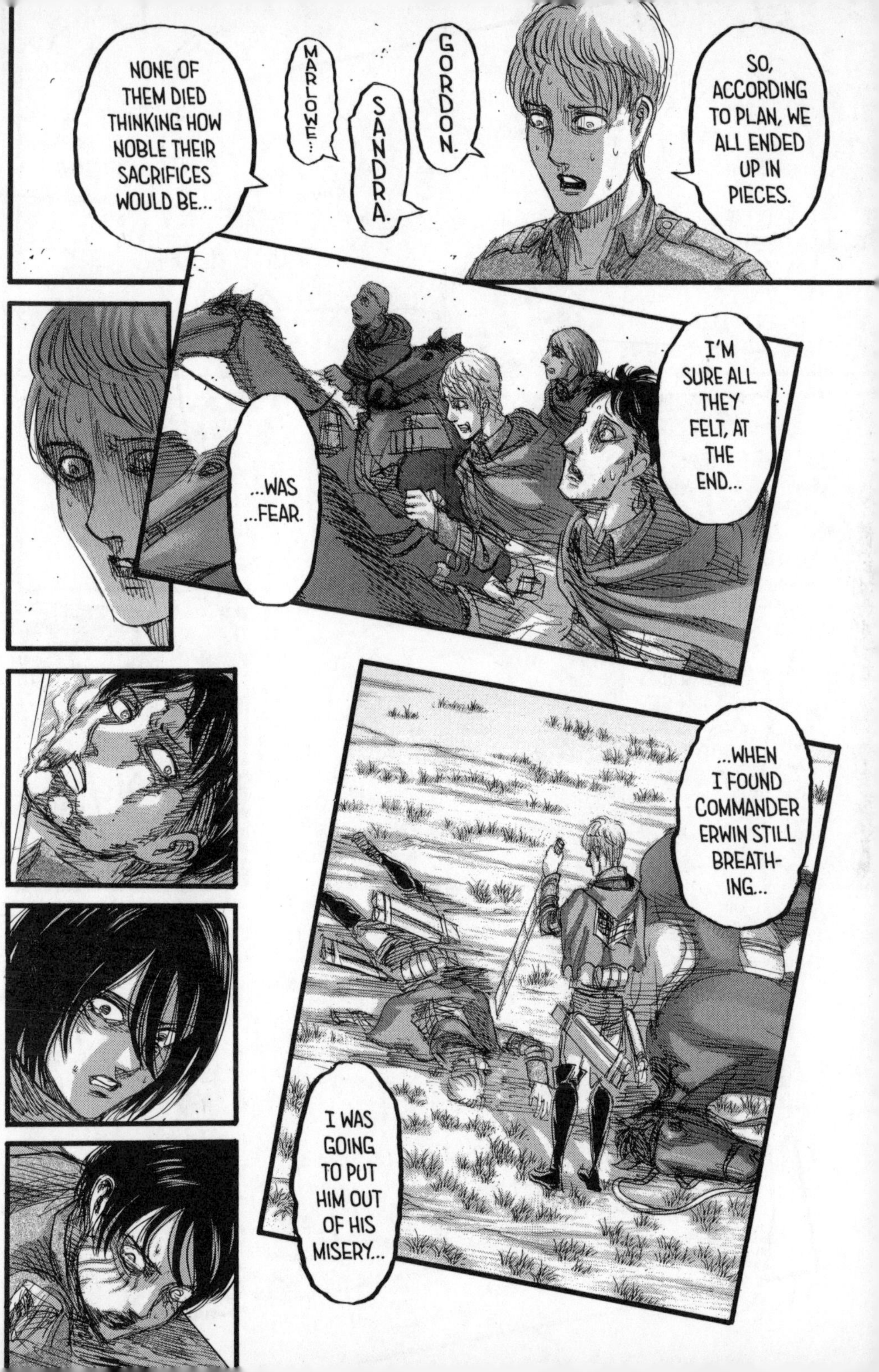
SO, ACCORDING TO PLAN, WE ALL ENDED UP IN PIECES.
GORDON.
SANDRA.
MARLOWE...
NONE OF THEM DIED THINKING HOW NOBLE THEIR SACRIFICES WOULD BE...
I'M SURE ALL THEY FELT, AT THE END...
...WAS ...FEAR.
...WHEN I FOUND COMMANDER ERWIN STILL BREATH-ING...
I WAS GOING TO PUT HIM OUT OF HIS MISERY...

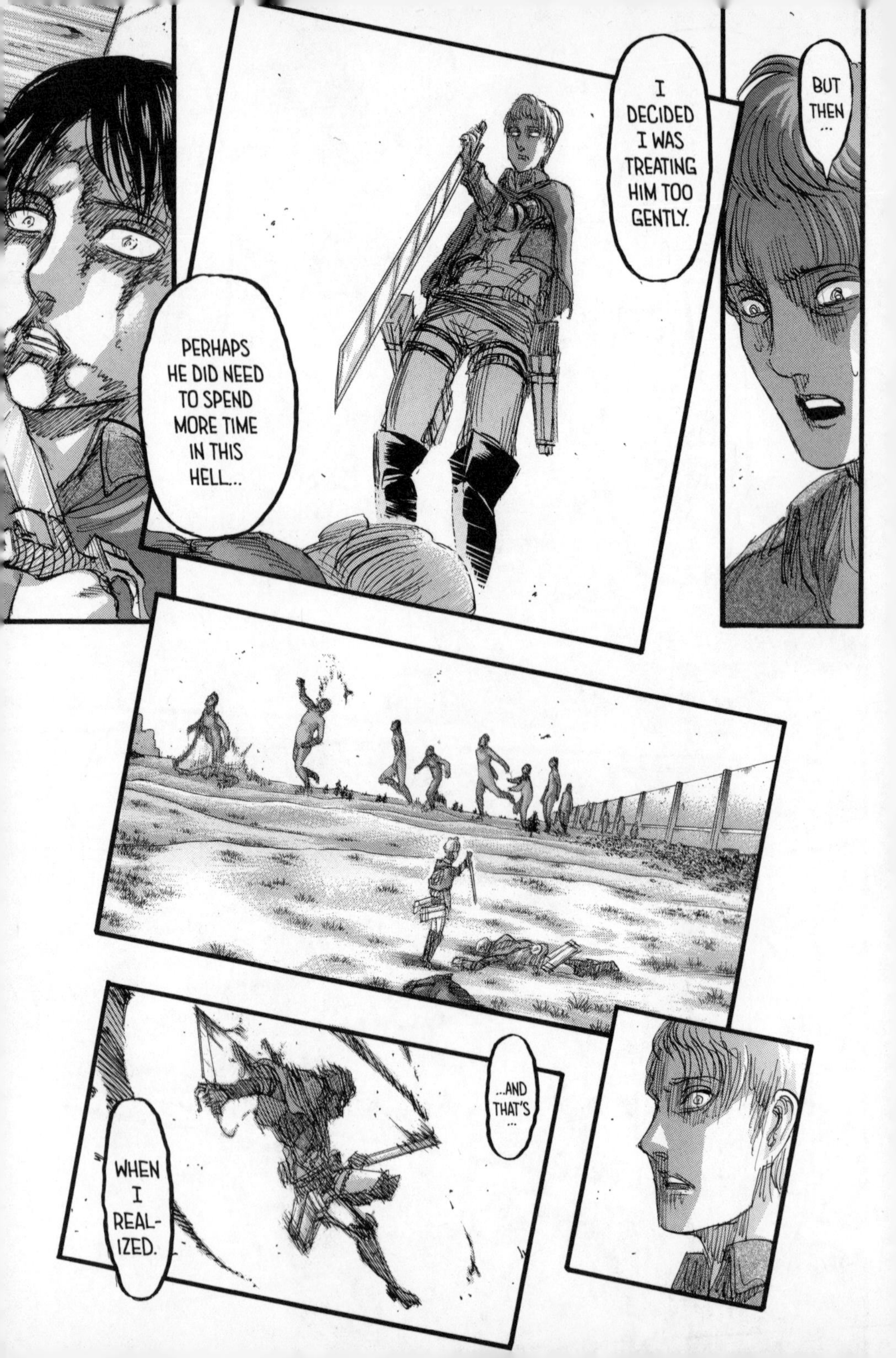
BUT THEN...
I DECIDED I WAS TREATING HIM TOO GENTLY.
PERHAPS HE DID NEED TO SPEND MORE TIME IN THIS HELL...
...AND THAT'S...
WHEN I REALIZED.

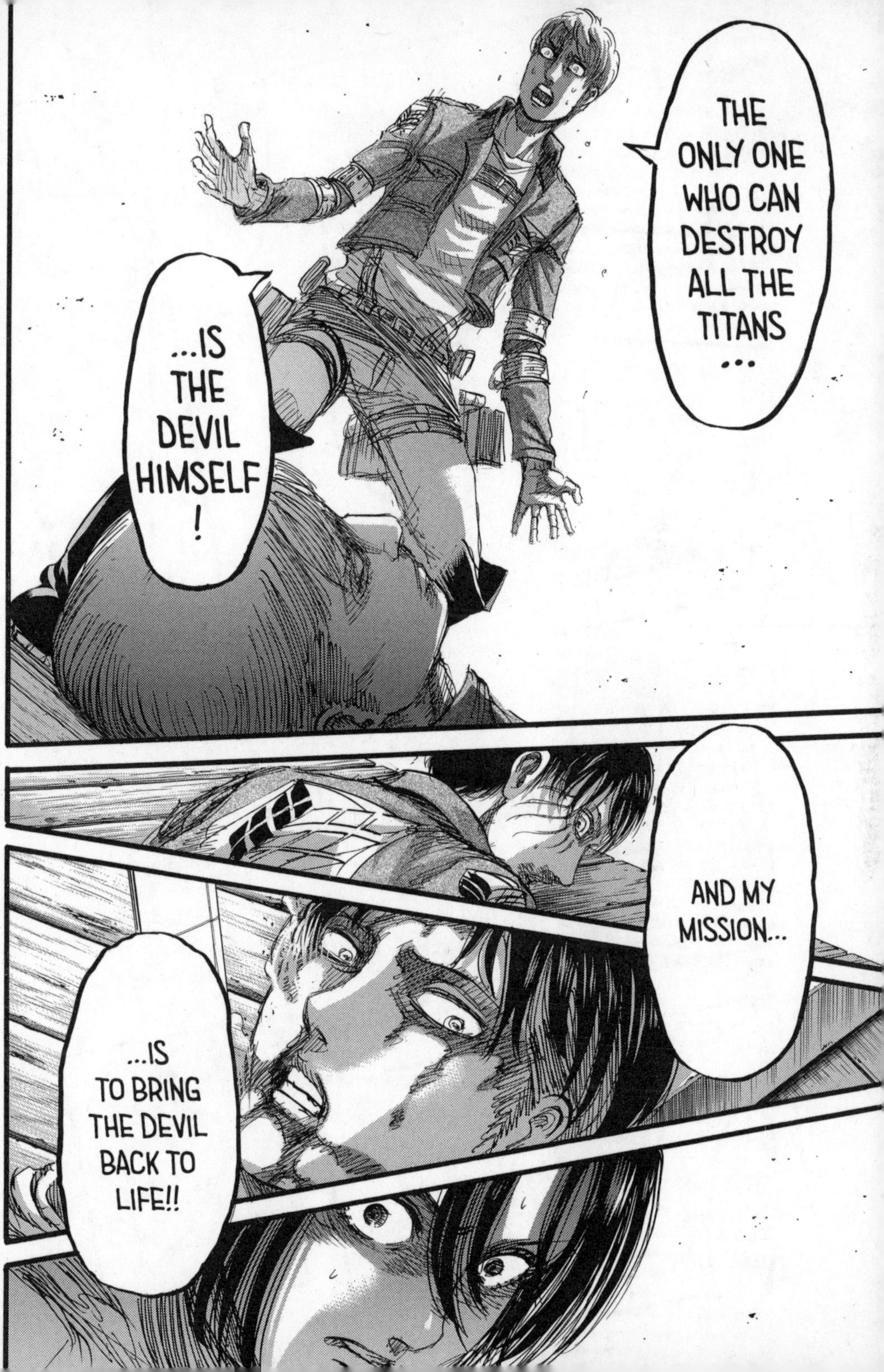
THE ONLY ONE WHO CAN DESTROY ALL THE TITANS...
...IS THE DEVIL HIMSELF!
AND MY MISSION...
...IS TO BRING THE DEVIL BACK TO LIFE!!

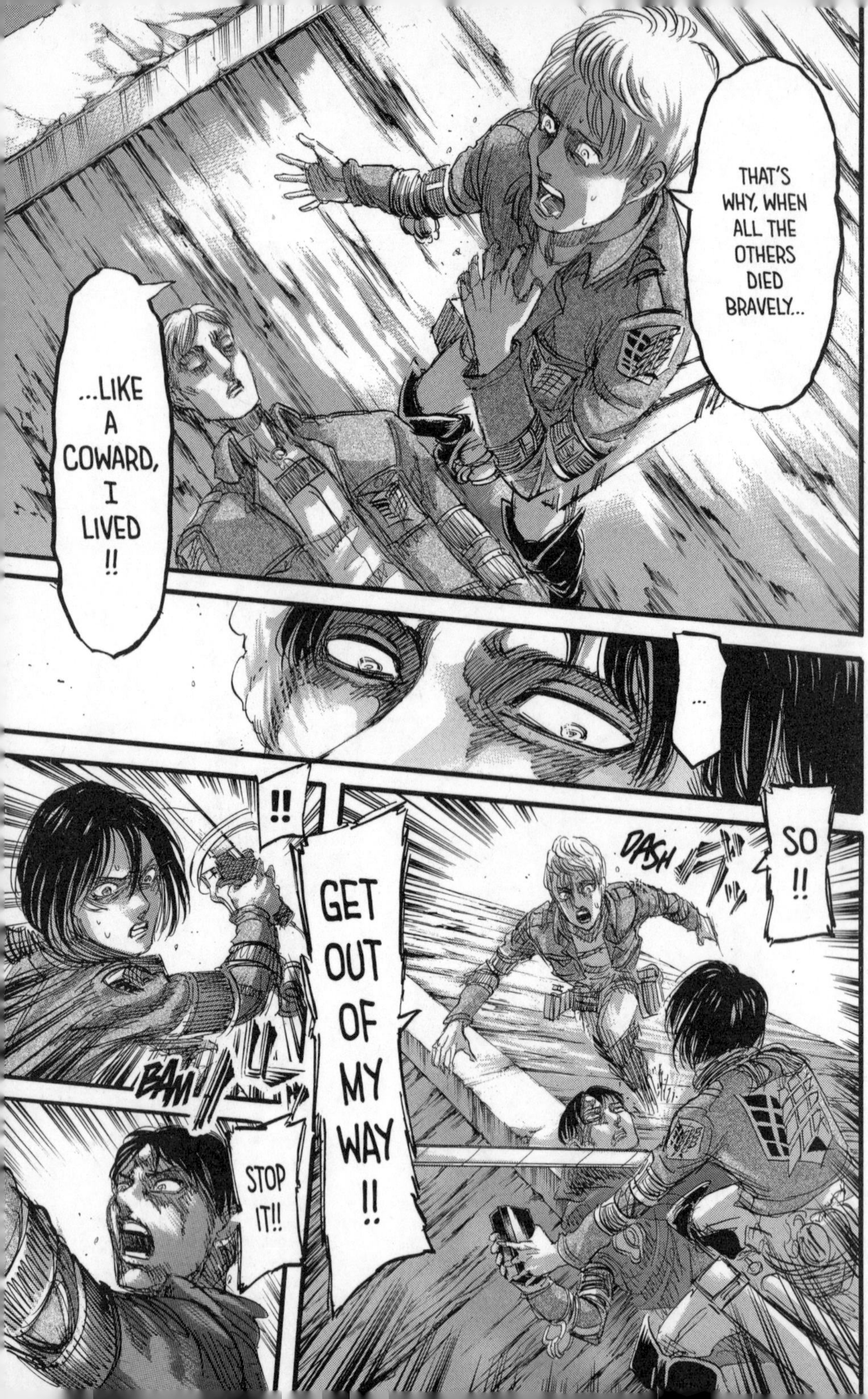
THAT'S WHY, WHEN ALL THE OTHERS DIED BRAVELY...
...LIKE A COWARD, I LIVED !!
...
SO !!
DASH
!!
GET OUT OF MY WAY !!
BAM
STOP IT!!

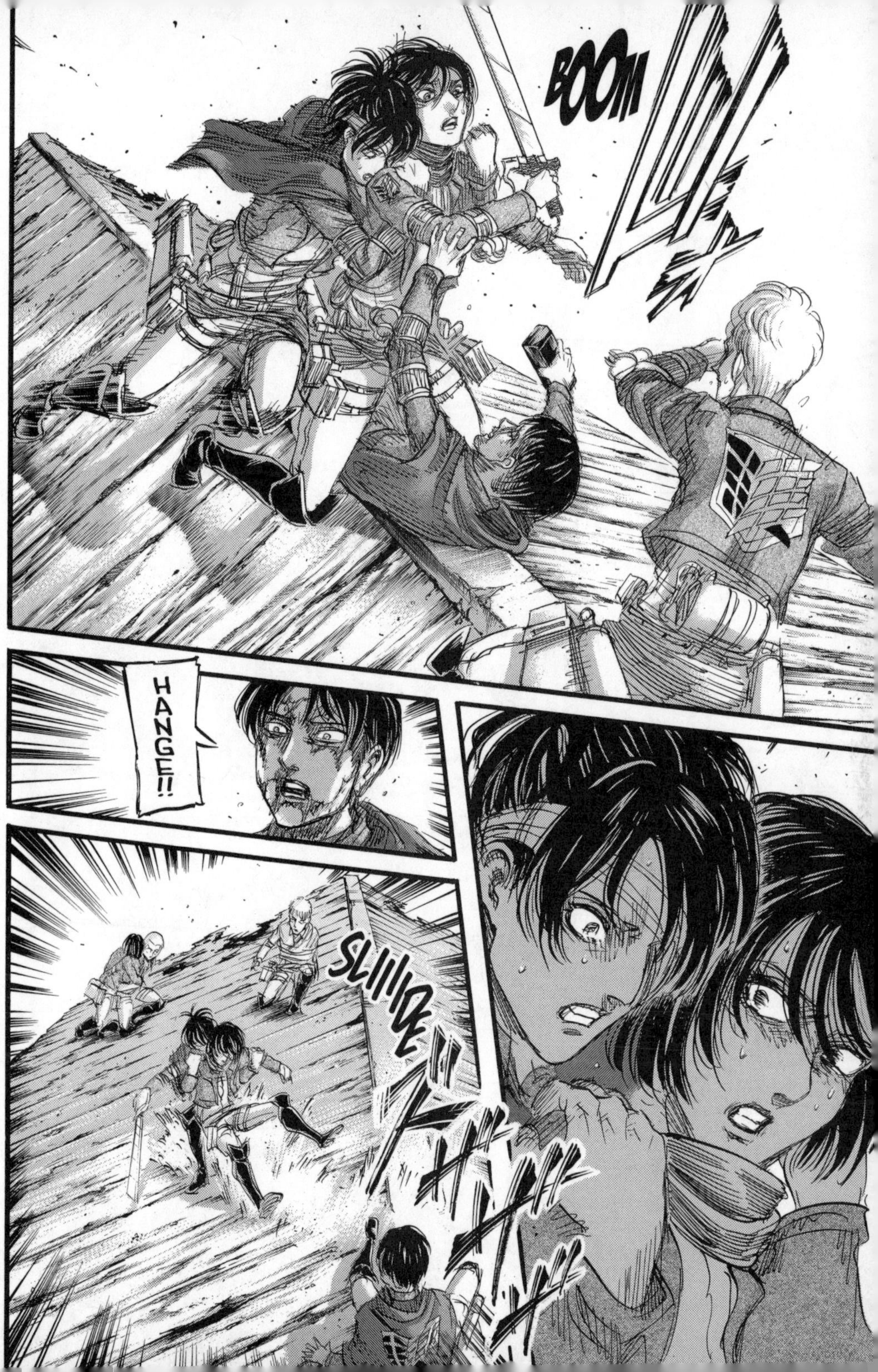
BOOM
HANGE!!
SLIIIDE

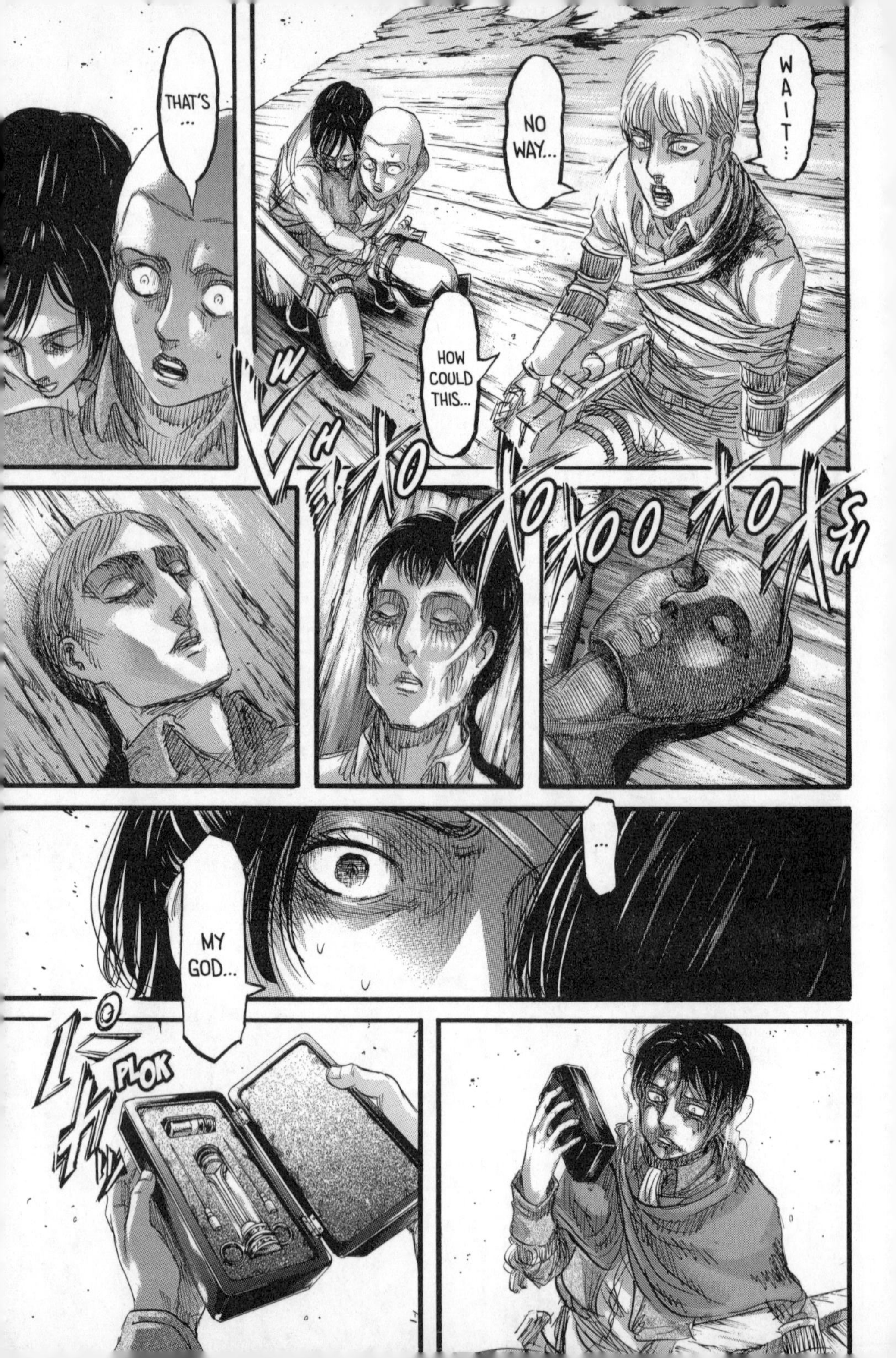

WAIT...
NO WAY...
HOW COULD THIS...
THAT'S ...
...
MY GOD...
PLOK

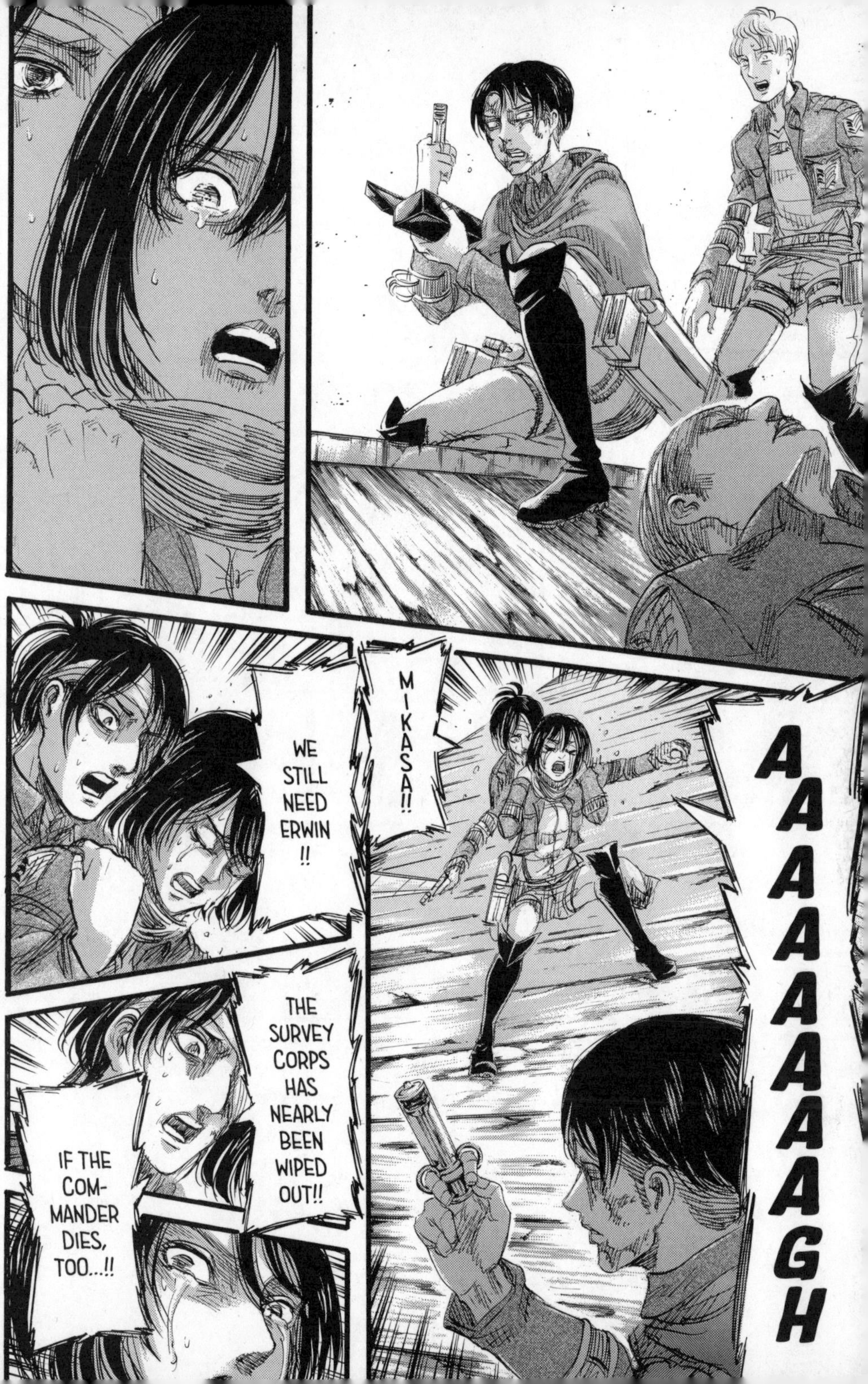
AAAAAAAAGH
MIKASA!!
WE STILL NEED ERWIN!!
THE SURVEY CORPS HAS NEARLY BEEN WIPED OUT!!
IF THE COM-MANDER DIES, TOO...!!

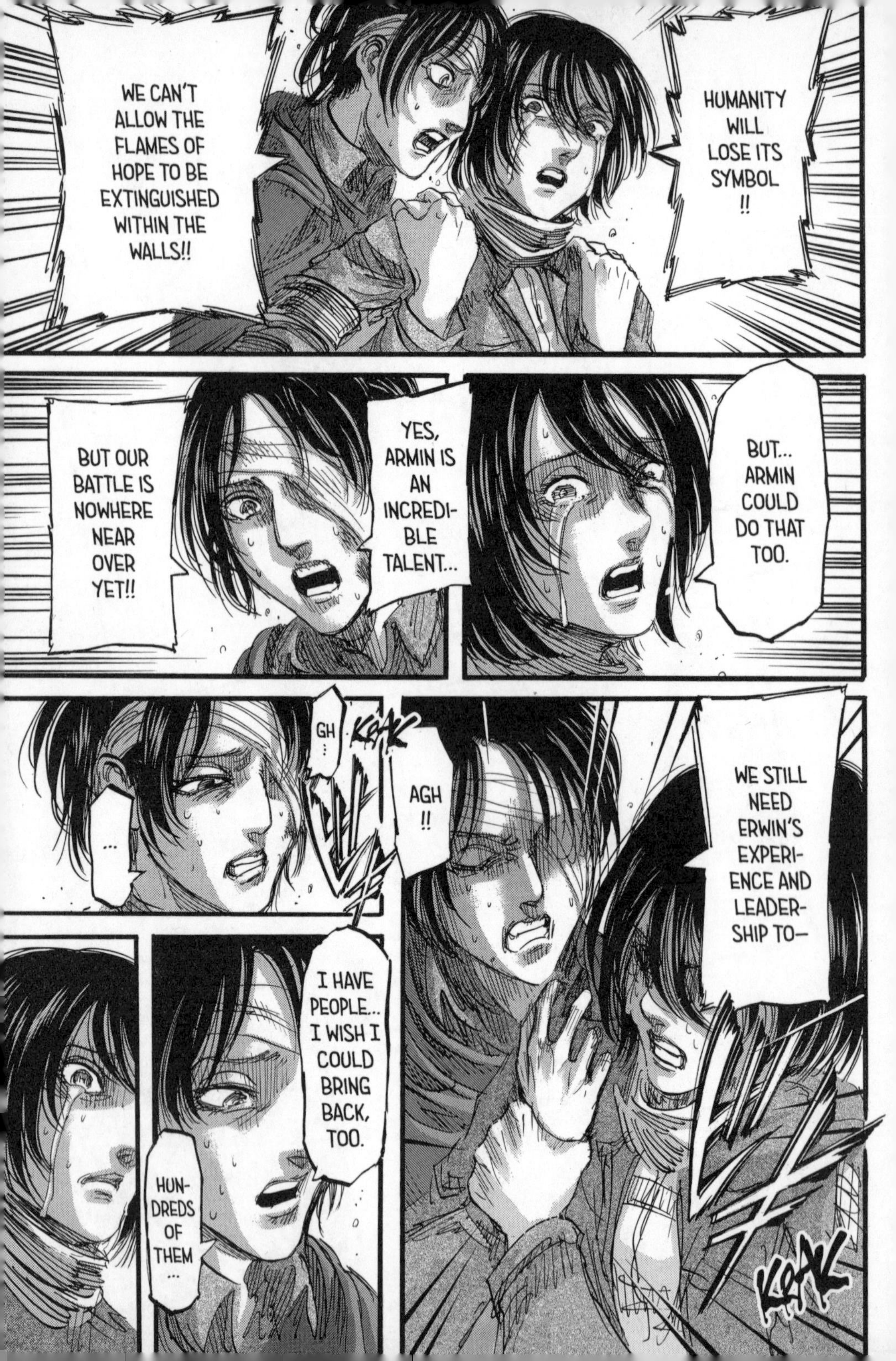
HUMANITY WILL LOSE ITS SYMBOL !!
WE CAN'T ALLOW THE FLAMES OF HOPE TO BE EXTINGUISHED WITHIN THE WALLS!!
BUT... ARMIN COULD DO THAT TOO.
YES, ARMIN IS AN INCREDI-BLE TALENT...
BUT OUR BATTLE IS NOWHERE NEAR OVER YET!!
WE STILL NEED ERWIN'S EXPERI-ENCE AND LEADER-SHIP TO—
AGH !!
KRAK
KRAK
GH ...
...
I HAVE PEOPLE... I WISH I COULD BRING BACK, TOO.
HUN-DREDS OF THEM ...

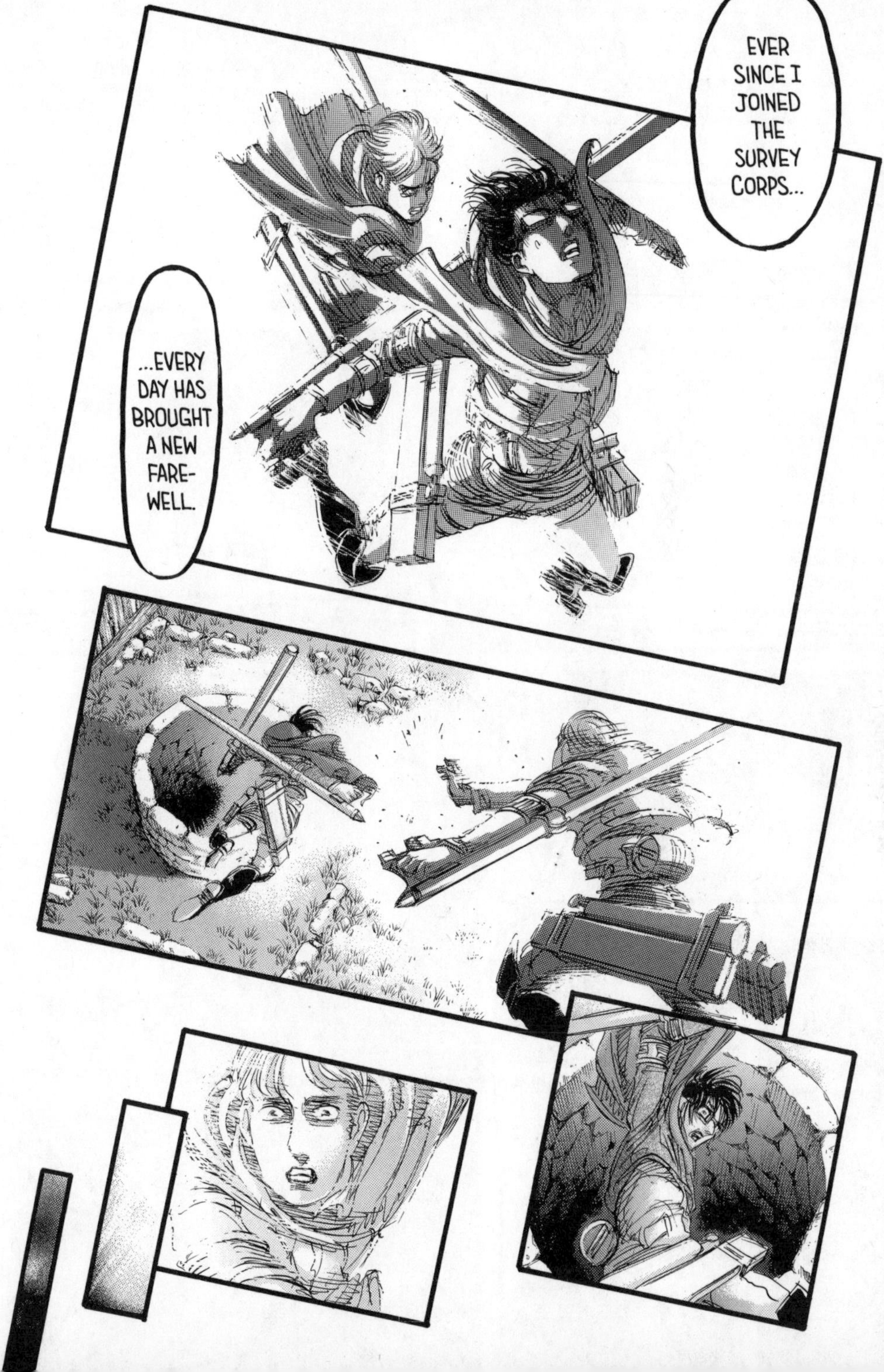
EVER SINCE I JOINED THE SURVEY CORPS...
...EVERY DAY HAS BROUGHT A NEW FARE-WELL.

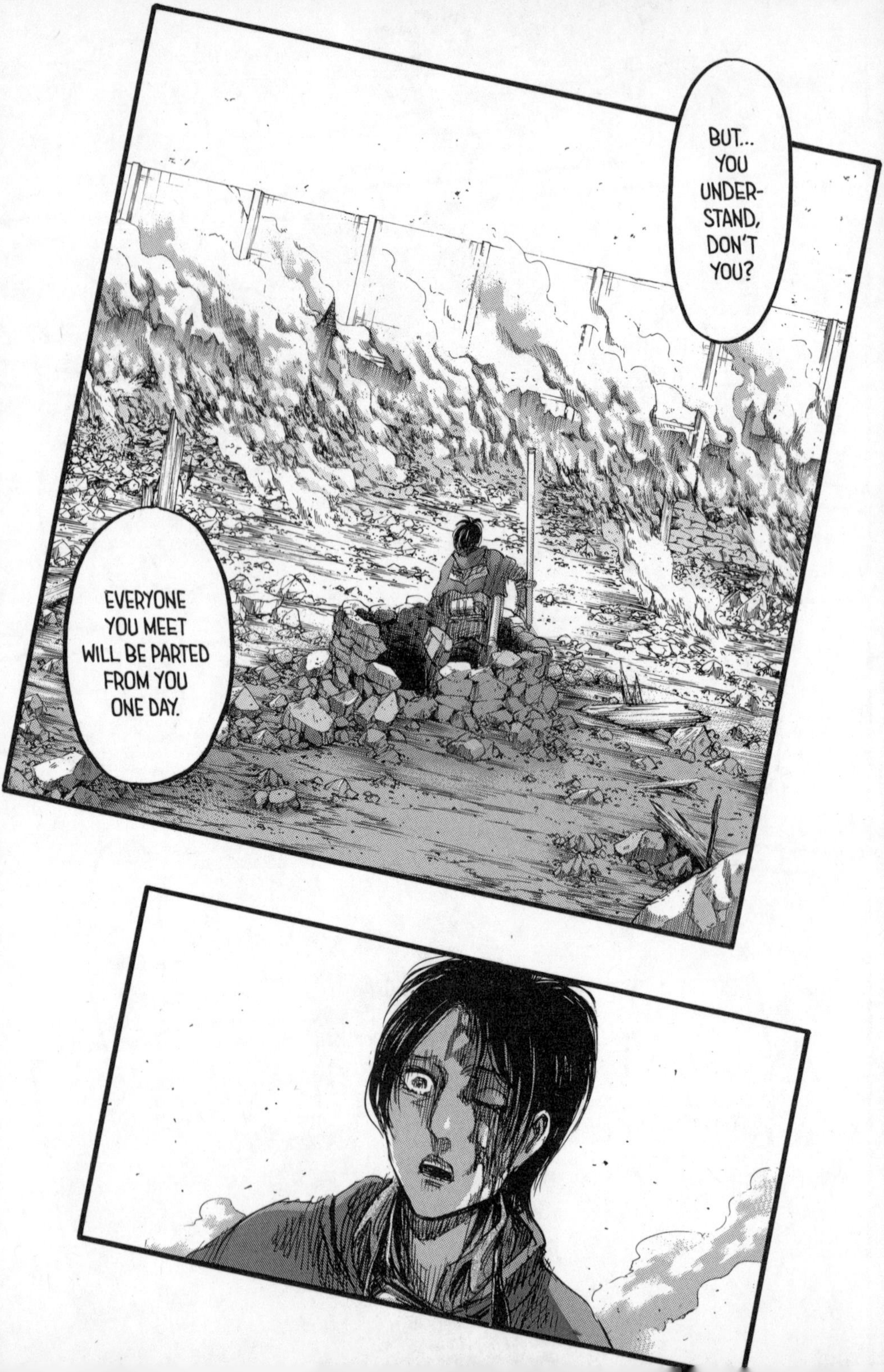
BUT... YOU UNDER-STAND, DON'T YOU?
EVERYONE YOU MEET WILL BE PARTED FROM YOU ONE DAY.

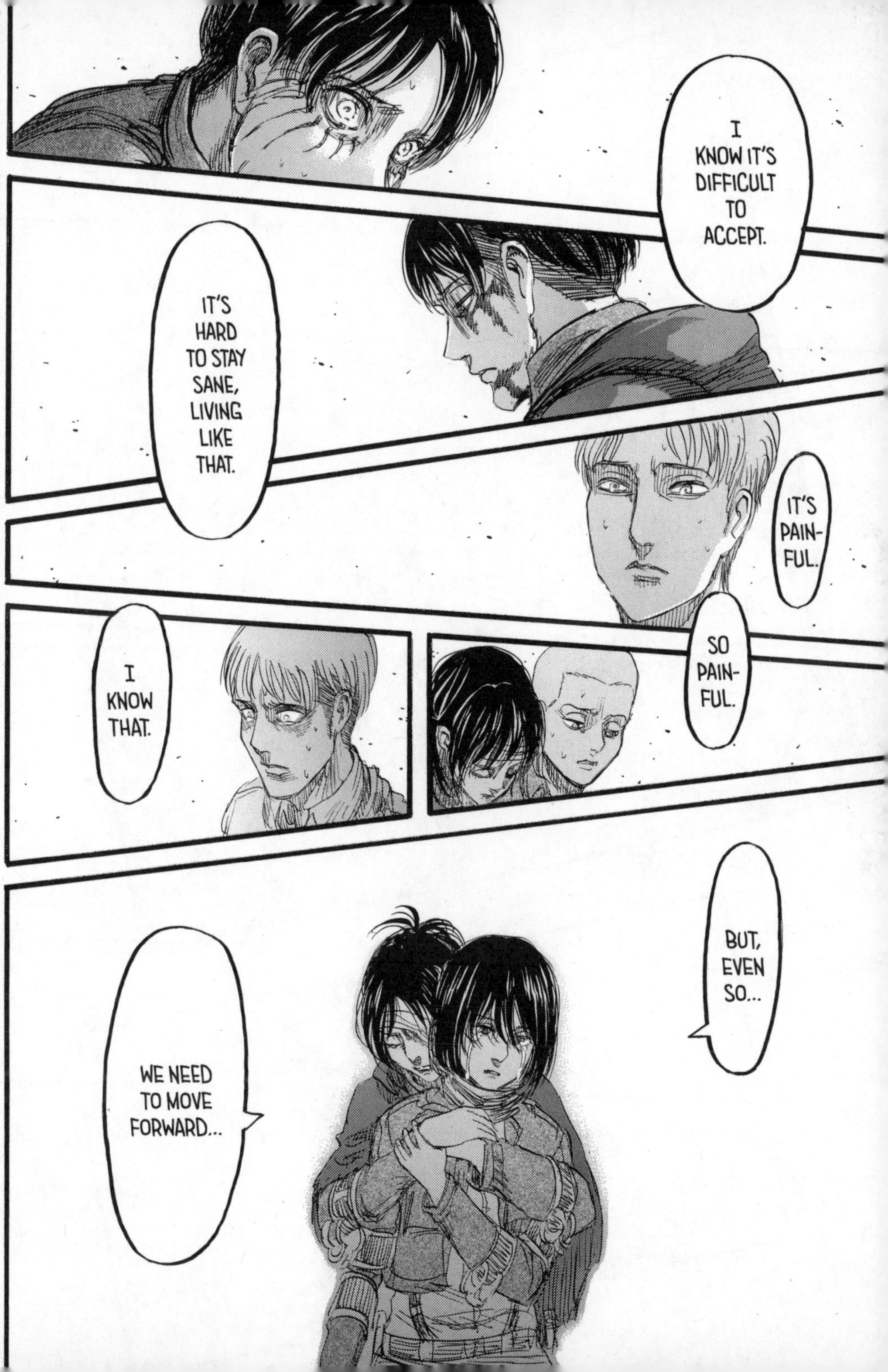
I KNOW IT'S DIFFICULT TO ACCEPT.
IT'S HARD TO STAY SANE, LIVING LIKE THAT.
IT'S PAIN-FUL.
SO PAIN-FUL.
I KNOW THAT.
BUT, EVEN SO...
WE NEED TO MOVE FORWARD...

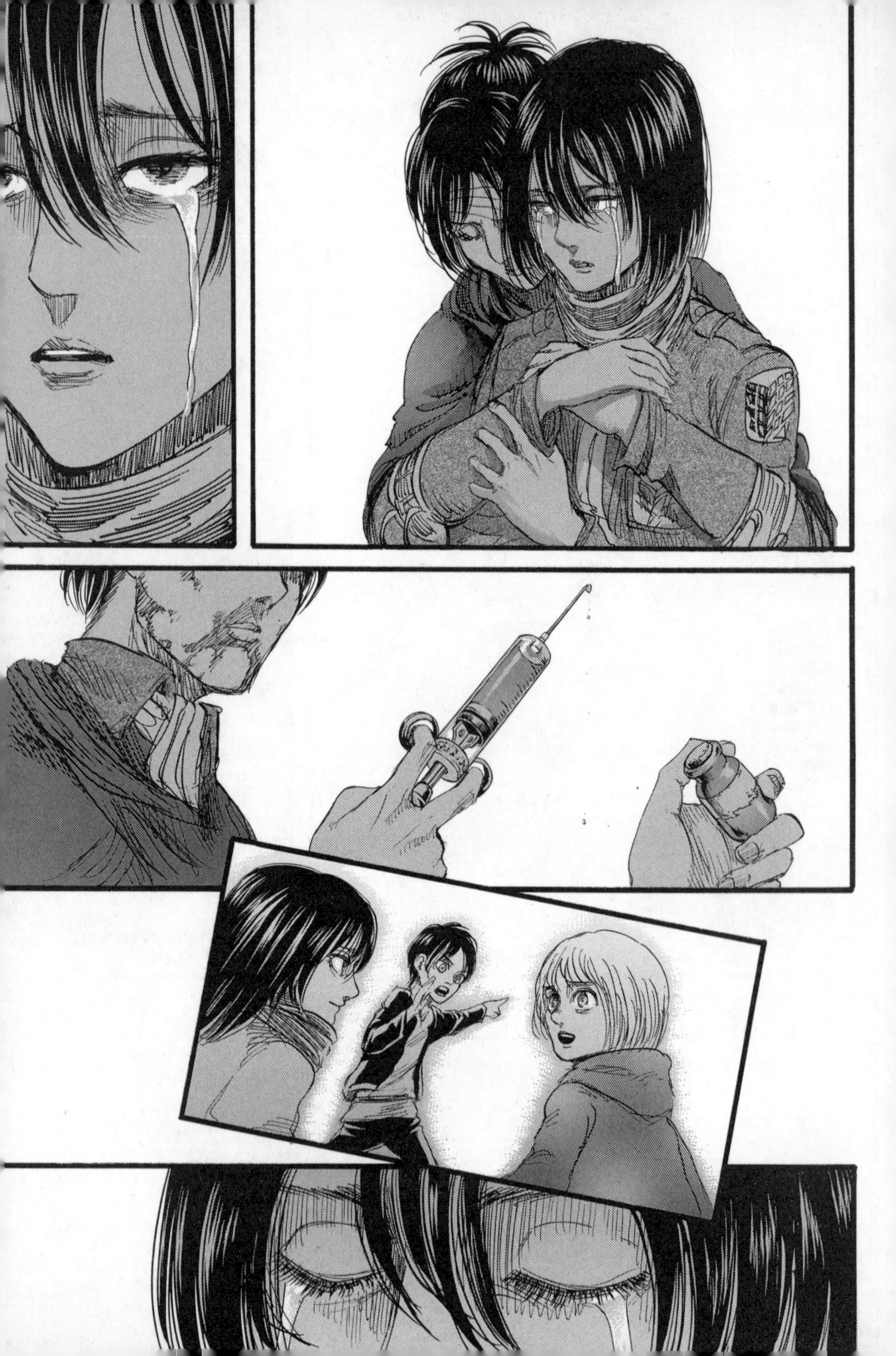

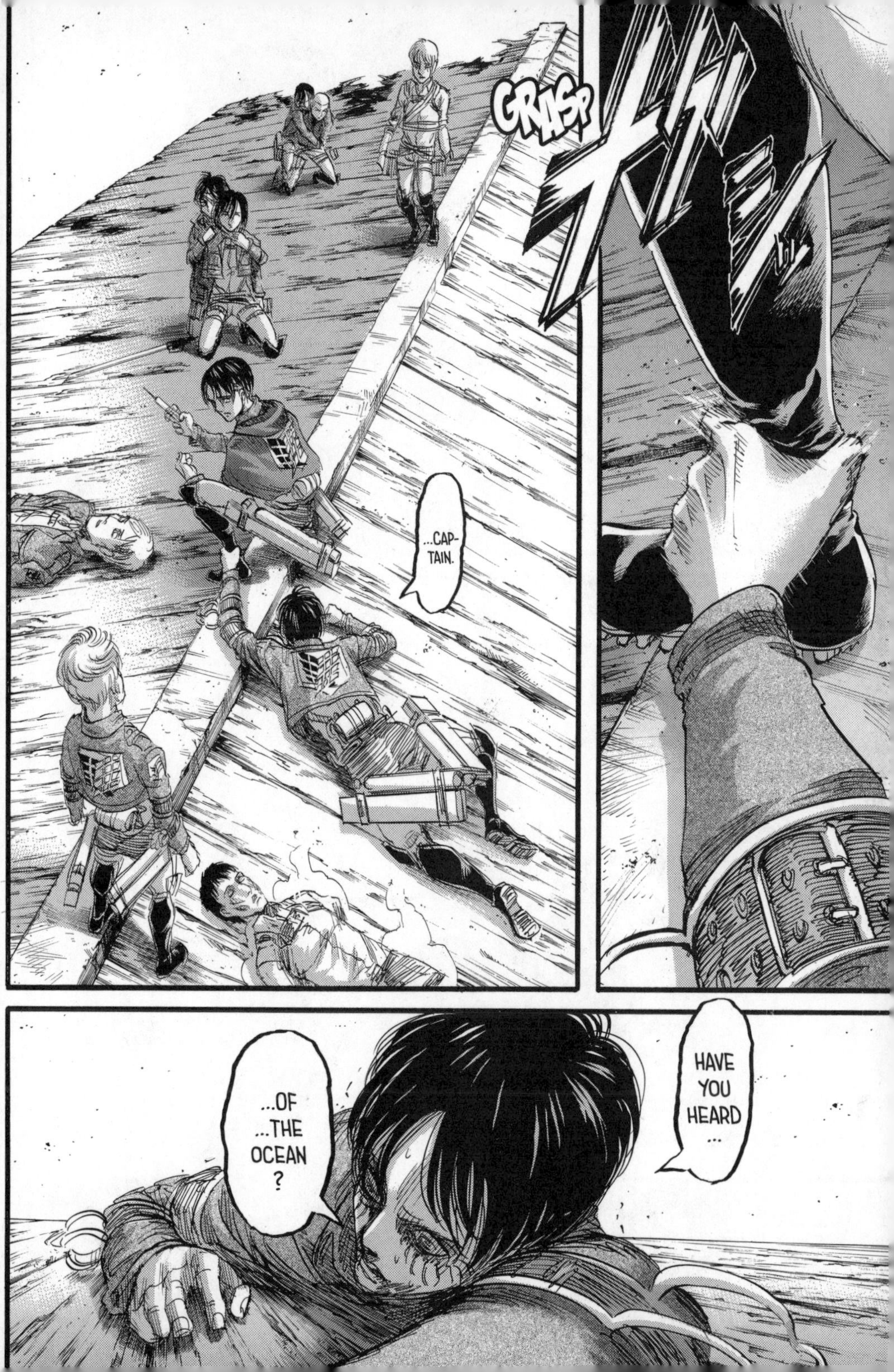
GRASP
...CAP-
TAIN.
HAVE
YOU
HEARD
...
...OF
...THE
OCEAN
?

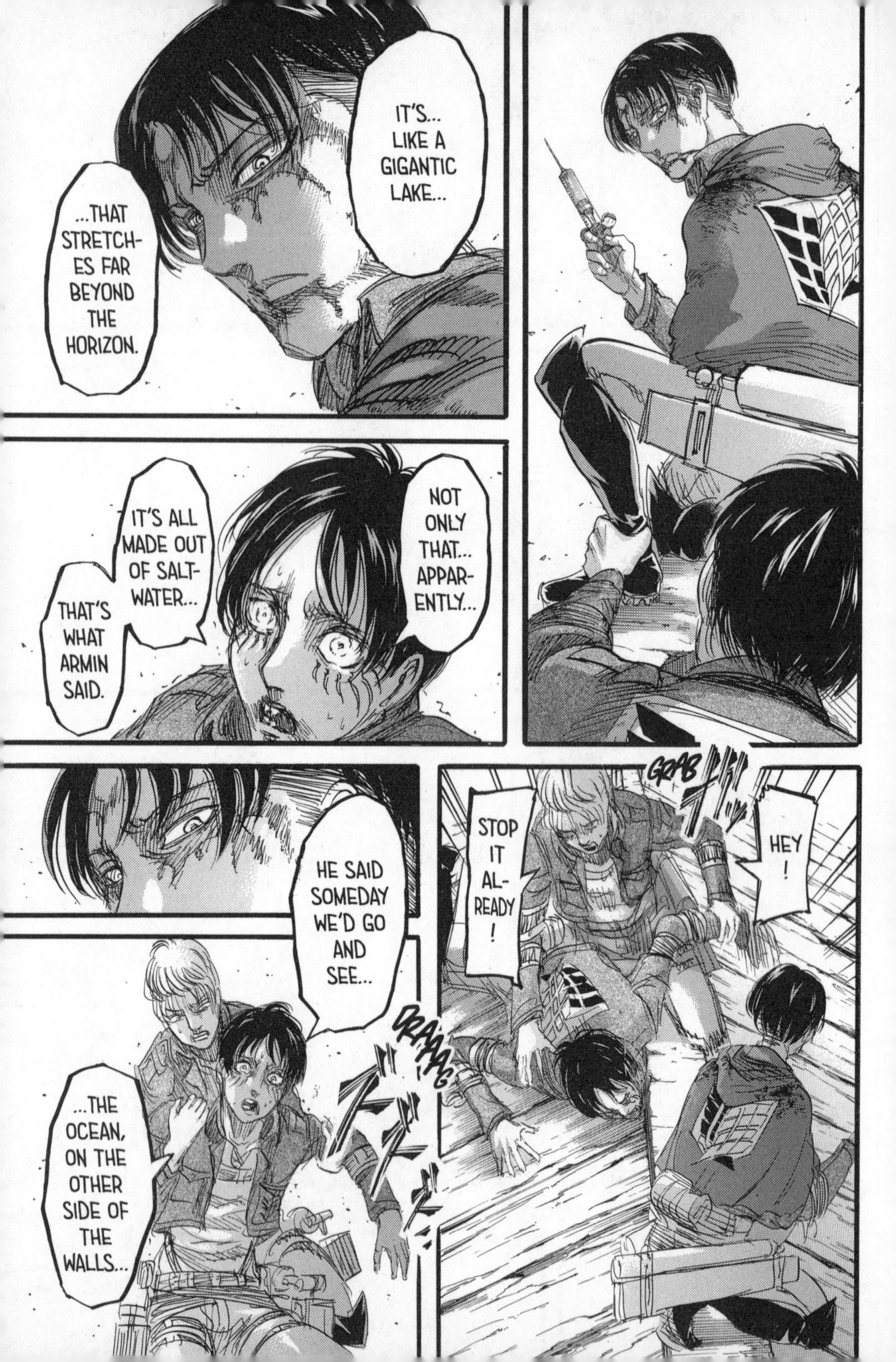
IT'S... LIKE A GIGANTIC LAKE...
...THAT STRETCH-ES FAR BEYOND THE HORIZON.
NOT ONLY THAT... APPAR-ENTLY...
IT'S ALL MADE OUT OF SALT-WATER...
THAT'S WHAT ARMIN SAID.
GRAB
HEY!
STOP IT AL-READY!
HE SAID SOMEDAY WE'D GO AND SEE...
DRAAAG
...THE OCEAN, ON THE OTHER SIDE OF THE WALLS...

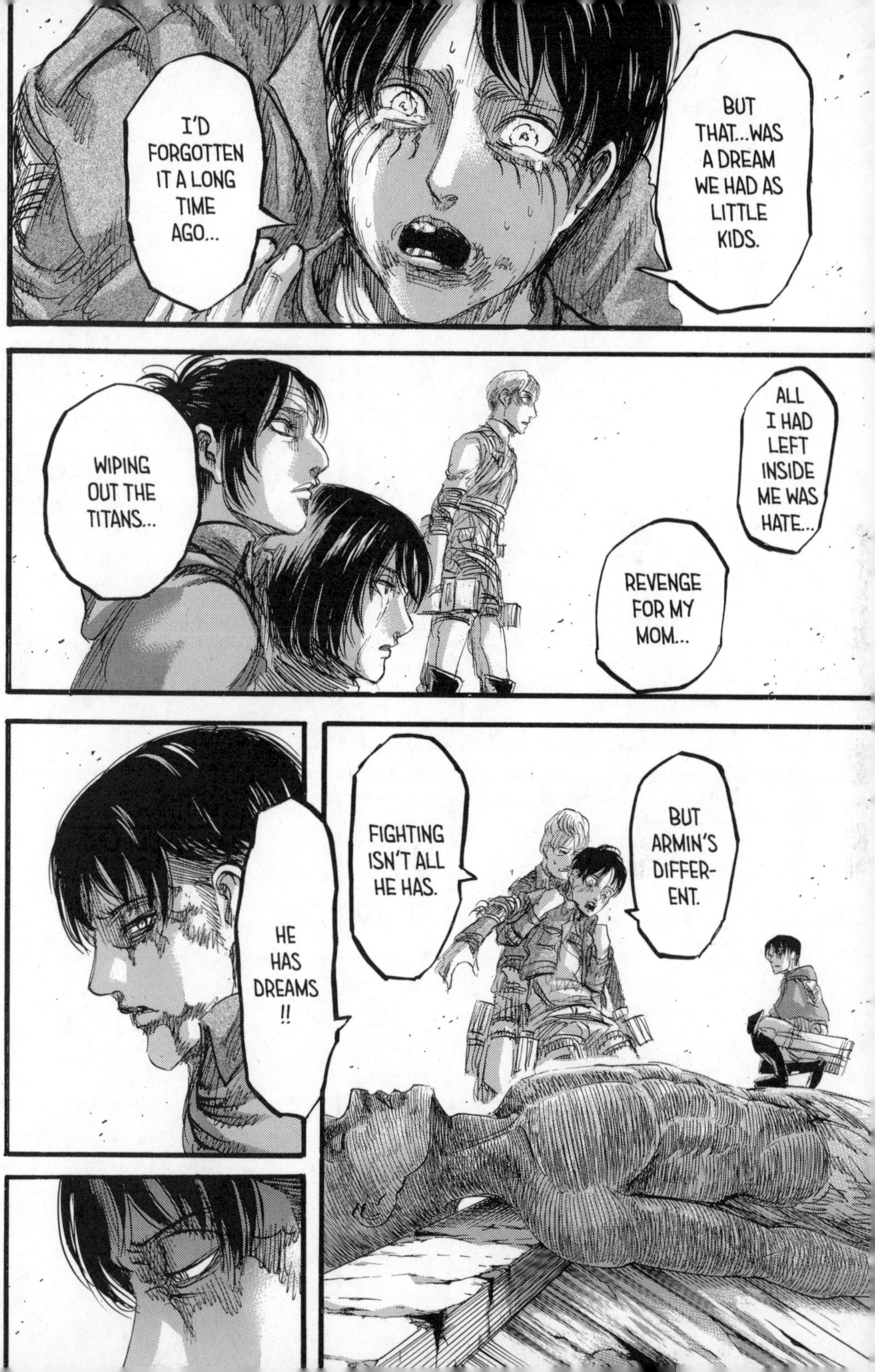
BUT THAT...WAS A DREAM WE HAD AS LITTLE KIDS.
I'D FORGOTTEN IT A LONG TIME AGO...
ALL I HAD LEFT INSIDE ME WAS HATE...
REVENGE FOR MY MOM...
WIPING OUT THE TITANS...
BUT ARMIN'S DIFFER-ENT.
FIGHTING ISN'T ALL HE HAS.
HE HAS DREAMS !!

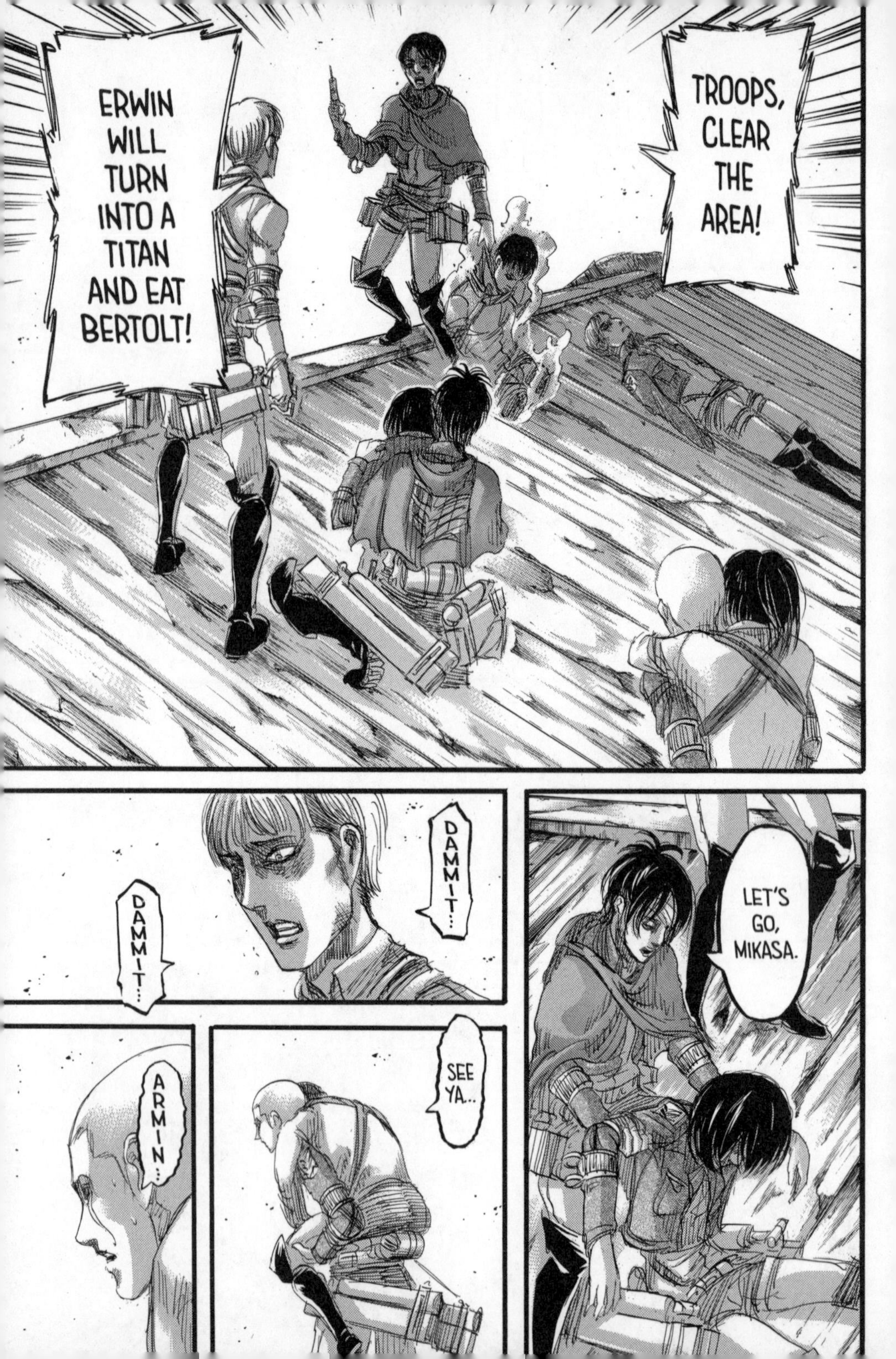
TROOPS, CLEAR THE AREA!
ERWIN WILL TURN INTO A TITAN AND EAT BERTOLT!
LET'S GO, MIKASA.
DAMMIT...
DAMMIT...
SEE YA...
ARMIN...

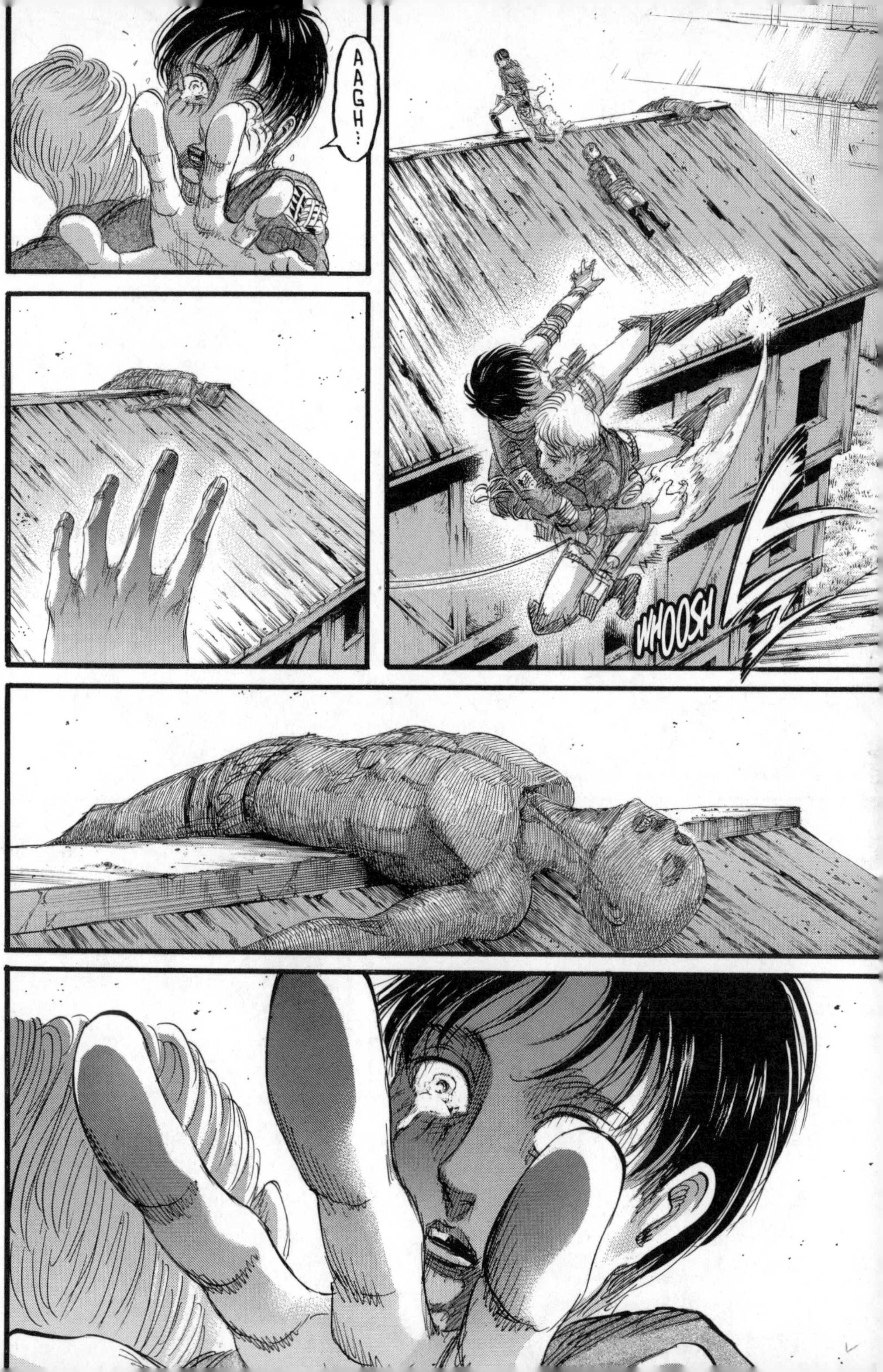
WHOOSH
AAGH...

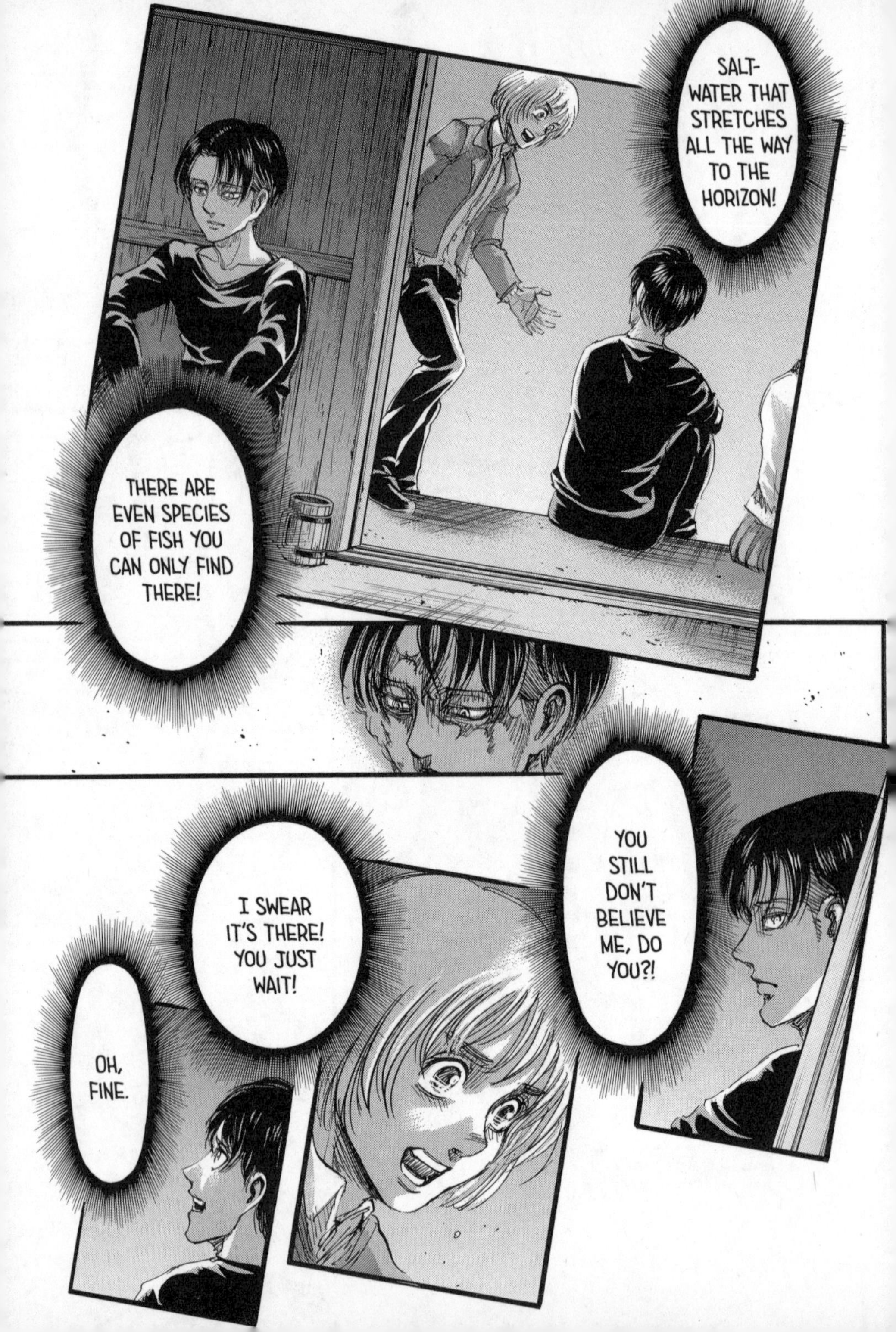
SALT-WATER THAT STRETCHES ALL THE WAY TO THE HORIZON!
THERE ARE EVEN SPECIES OF FISH YOU CAN ONLY FIND THERE!
YOU STILL DON'T BELIEVE ME, DO YOU?!
I SWEAR IT'S THERE! YOU JUST WAIT!
OH, FINE.

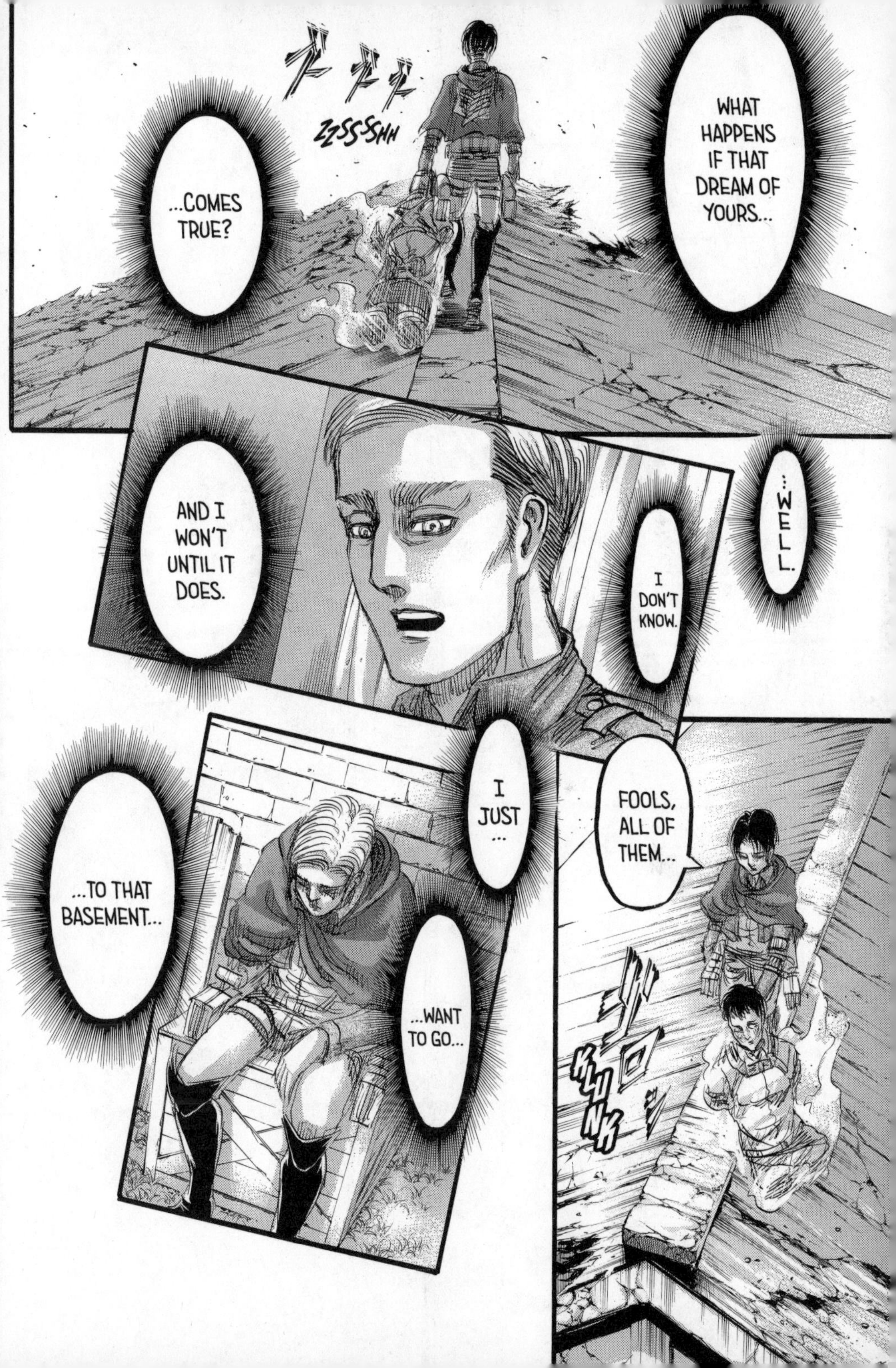
WHAT HAPPENS IF THAT DREAM OF YOURS...
ZZSS-SSHH
...COMES TRUE?
...WELL.
I DON'T KNOW.
AND I WON'T UNTIL IT DOES.
FOOLS, ALL OF THEM...
KLUNK
I JUST ...
...WANT TO GO...
...TO THAT BASEMENT...

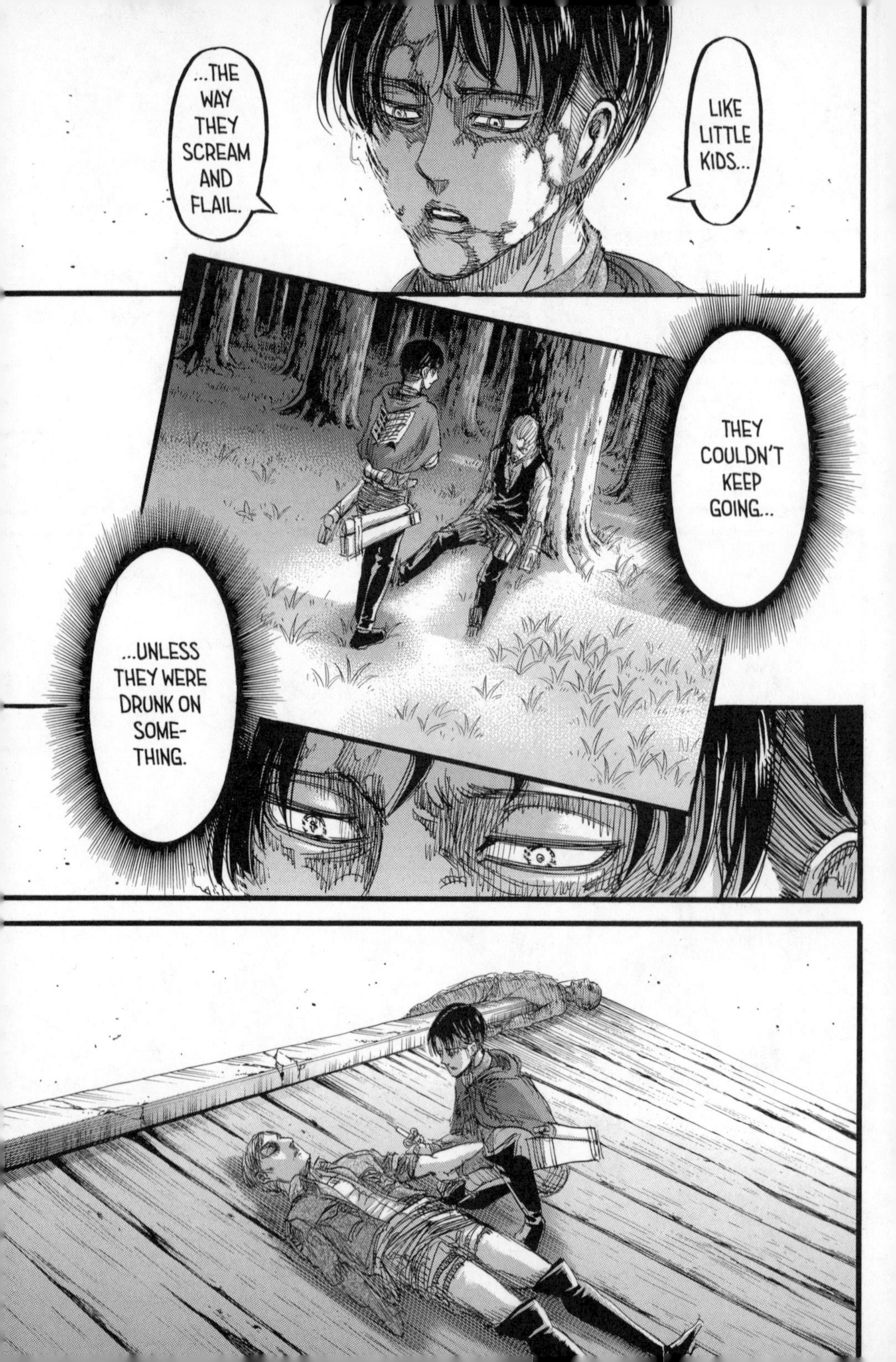
LIKE LITTLE KIDS...
...THE WAY THEY SCREAM AND FLAIL.
THEY COULDN'T KEEP GOING...
...UNLESS THEY WERE DRUNK ON SOME-THING.

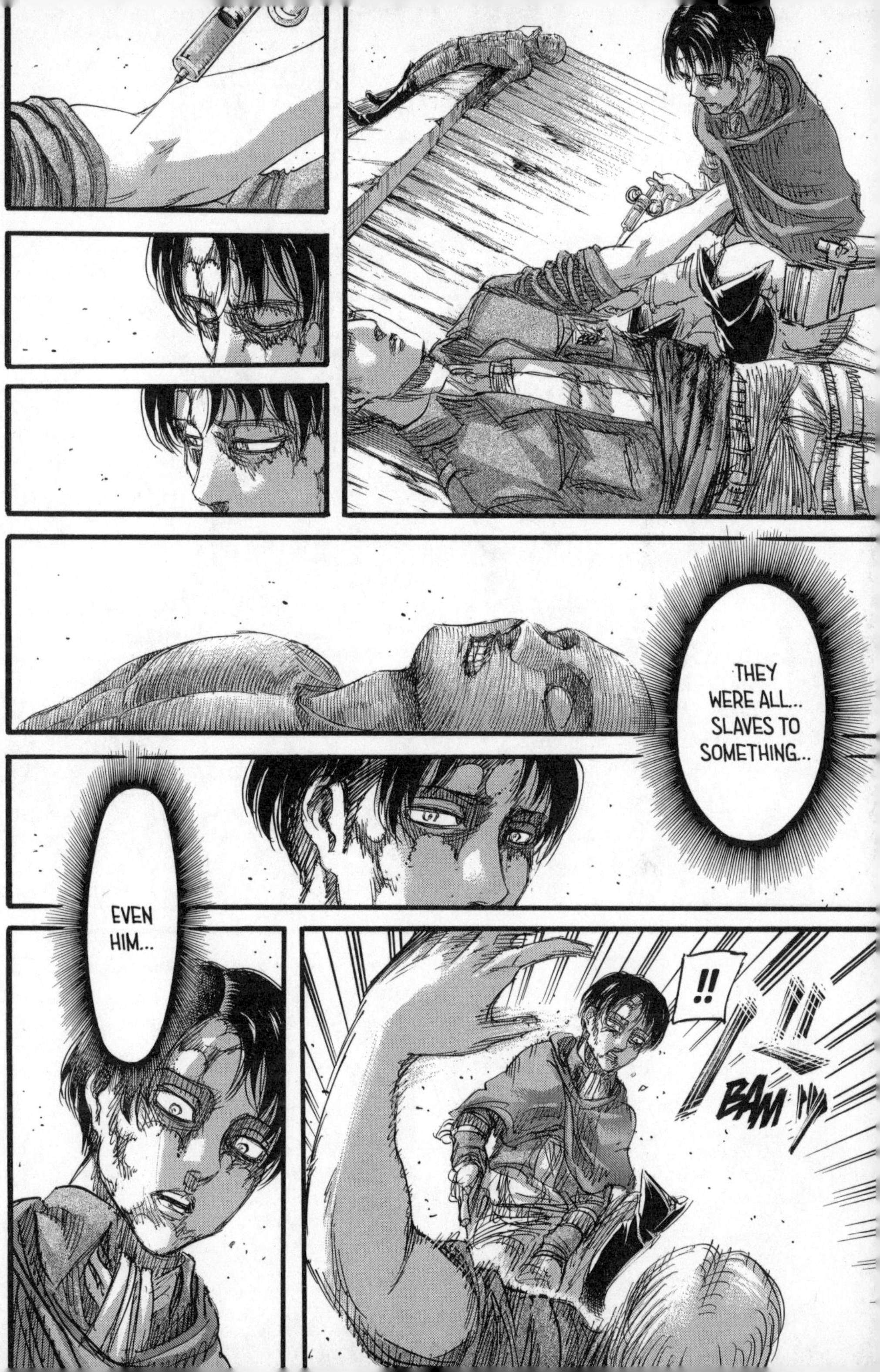
THEY WERE ALL... SLAVES TO SOMETHING...
EVEN HIM...
!!
BAM

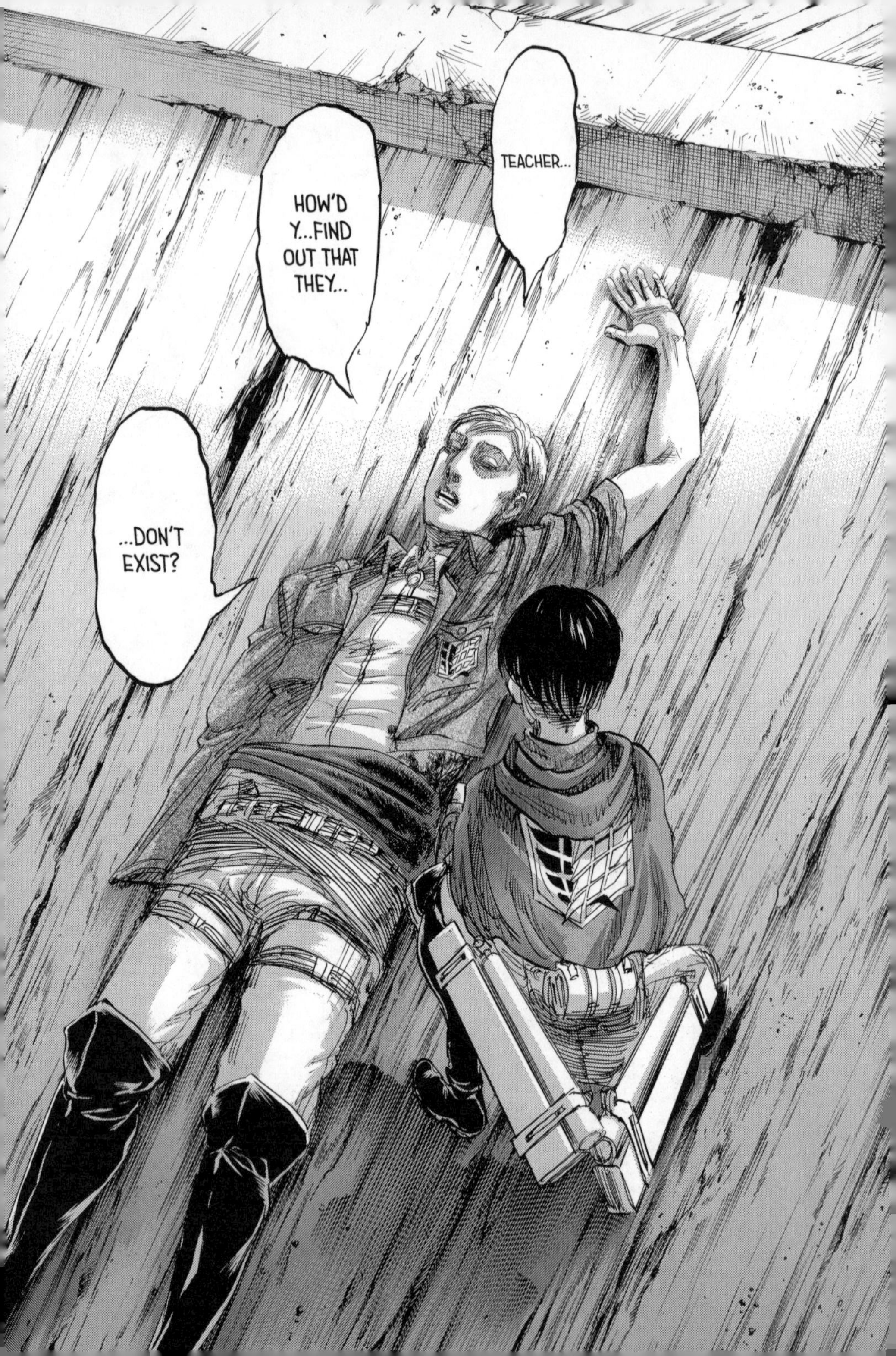
TEACHER...
HOW'D Y...FIND OUT THAT THEY...
...DON'T EXIST?

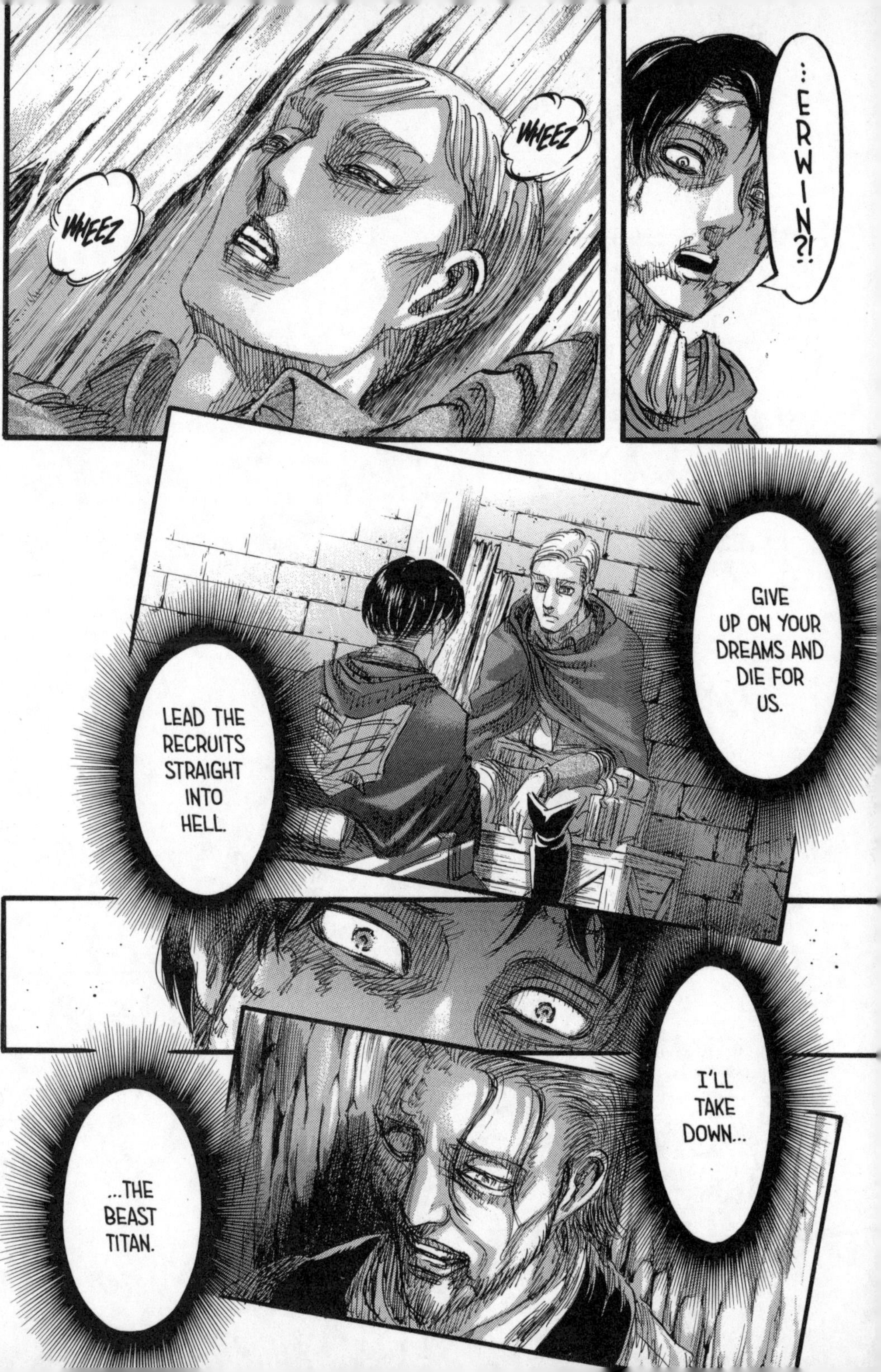
...ERWIN?!
WHEEZ
WHEEZ
GIVE UP ON YOUR DREAMS AND DIE FOR US.
LEAD THE RECRUITS STRAIGHT INTO HELL.
I'LL TAKE DOWN...
...THE BEAST TITAN.

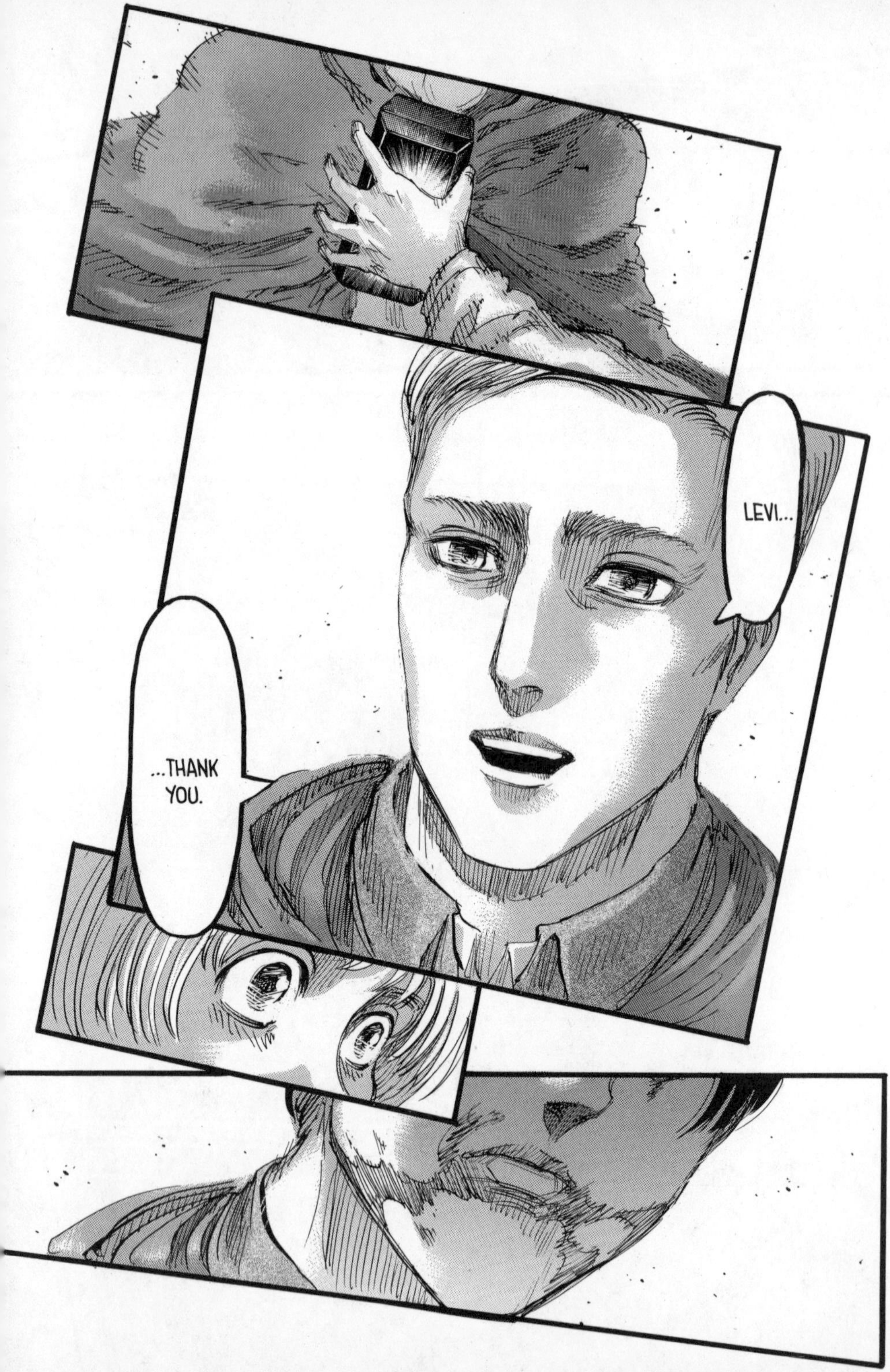
LEVI...
...THANK YOU.

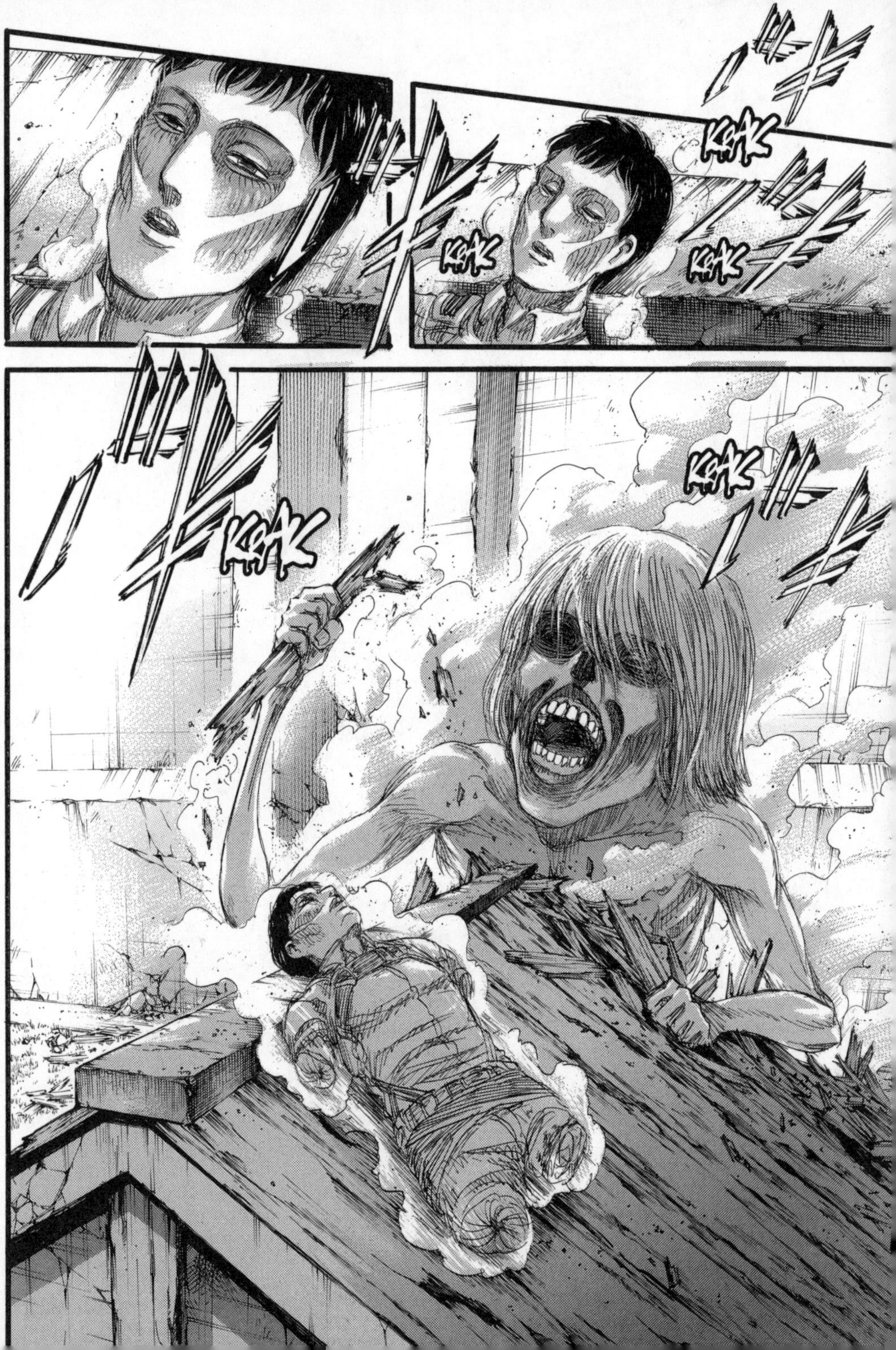
KRAK
KRAK
KRAK
KRAK
KRAK

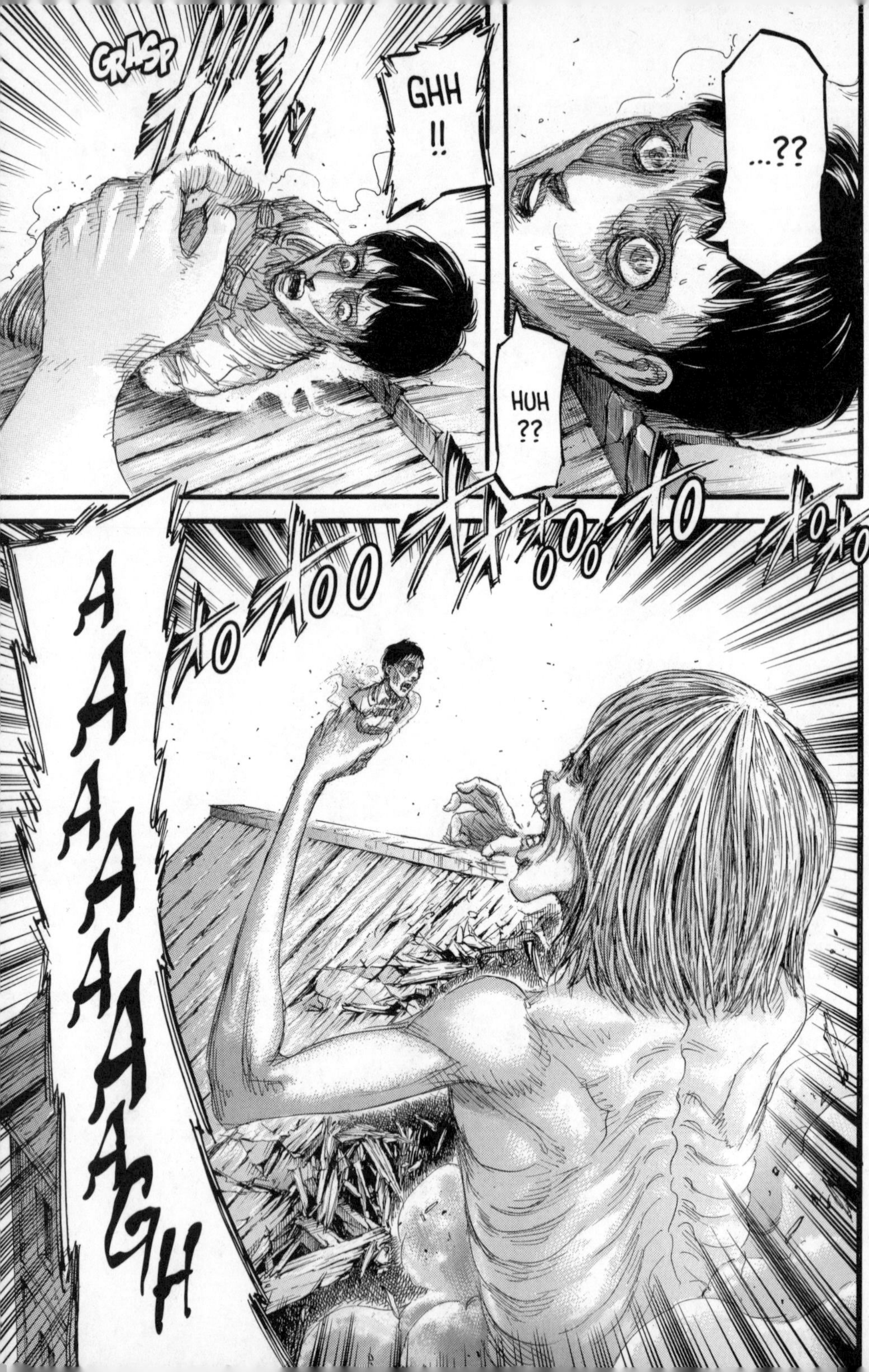
...??
HUH ??
GRASP
GHH !!
AAAAAAAGH

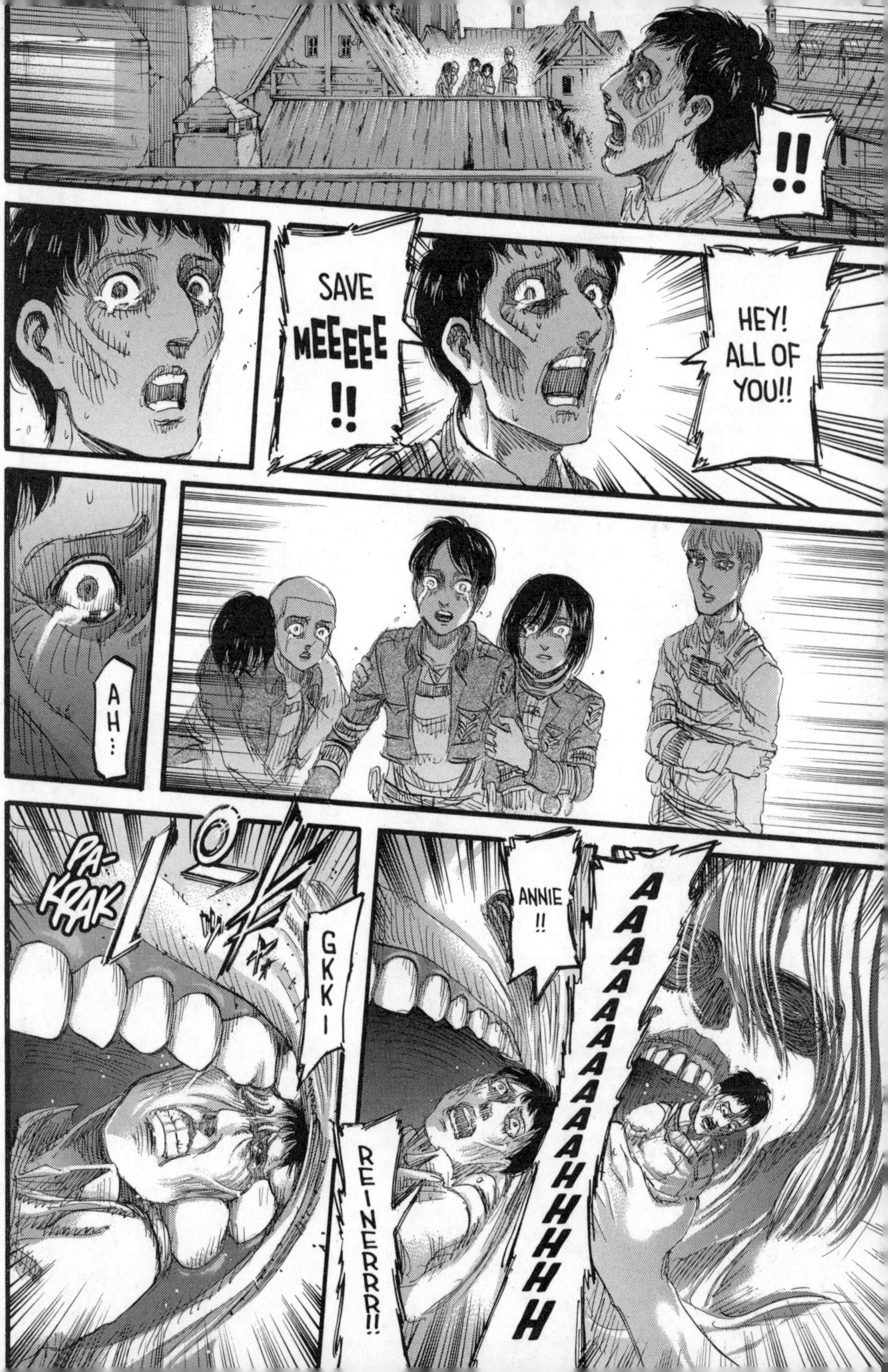
!!
HEY! ALL OF YOU!!
SAVE MEEEEE!!
AH...
ANNIE!!
AAAAAAAAAAAAAHHHHHHHH
REINERRR!!
GKKI
PA-KRAK

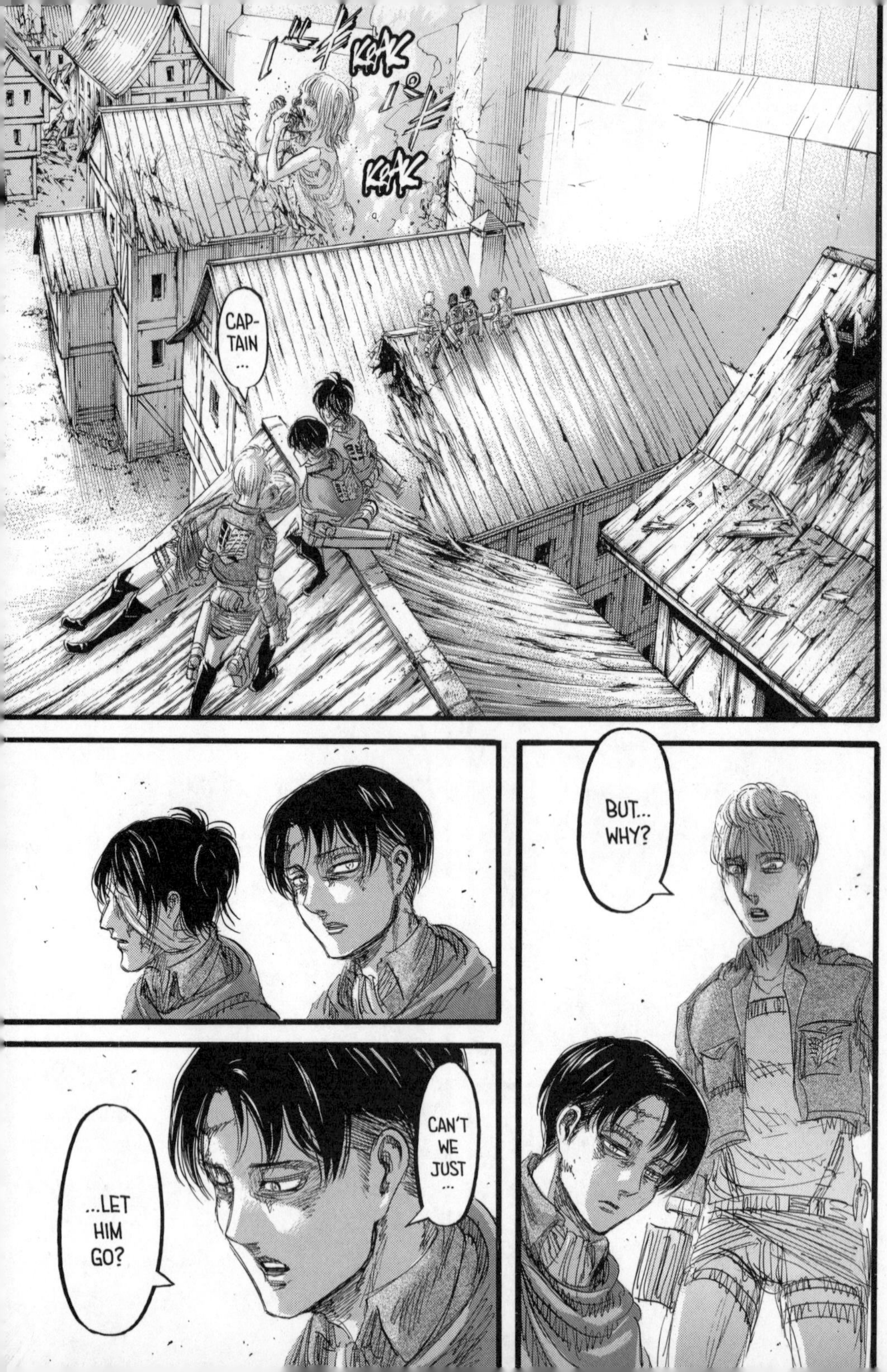
KRAK
KRAK
CAP-TAIN ...
BUT... WHY?
CAN'T WE JUST ...
...LET HIM GO?

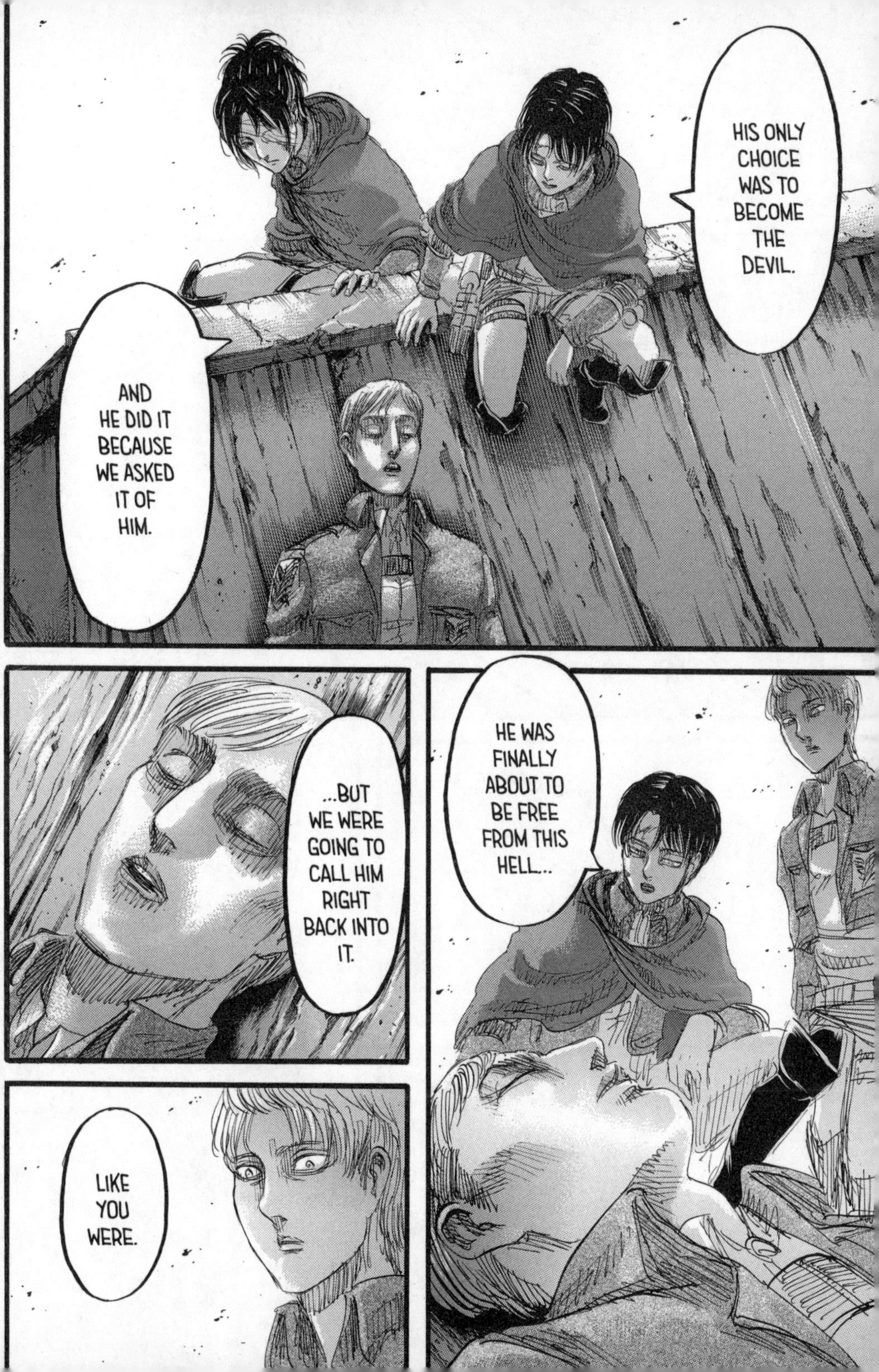
HIS ONLY CHOICE WAS TO BECOME THE DEVIL.
AND HE DID IT BECAUSE WE ASKED IT OF HIM.
HE WAS FINALLY ABOUT TO BE FREE FROM THIS HELL...
...BUT WE WERE GOING TO CALL HIM RIGHT BACK INTO IT.
LIKE YOU WERE.

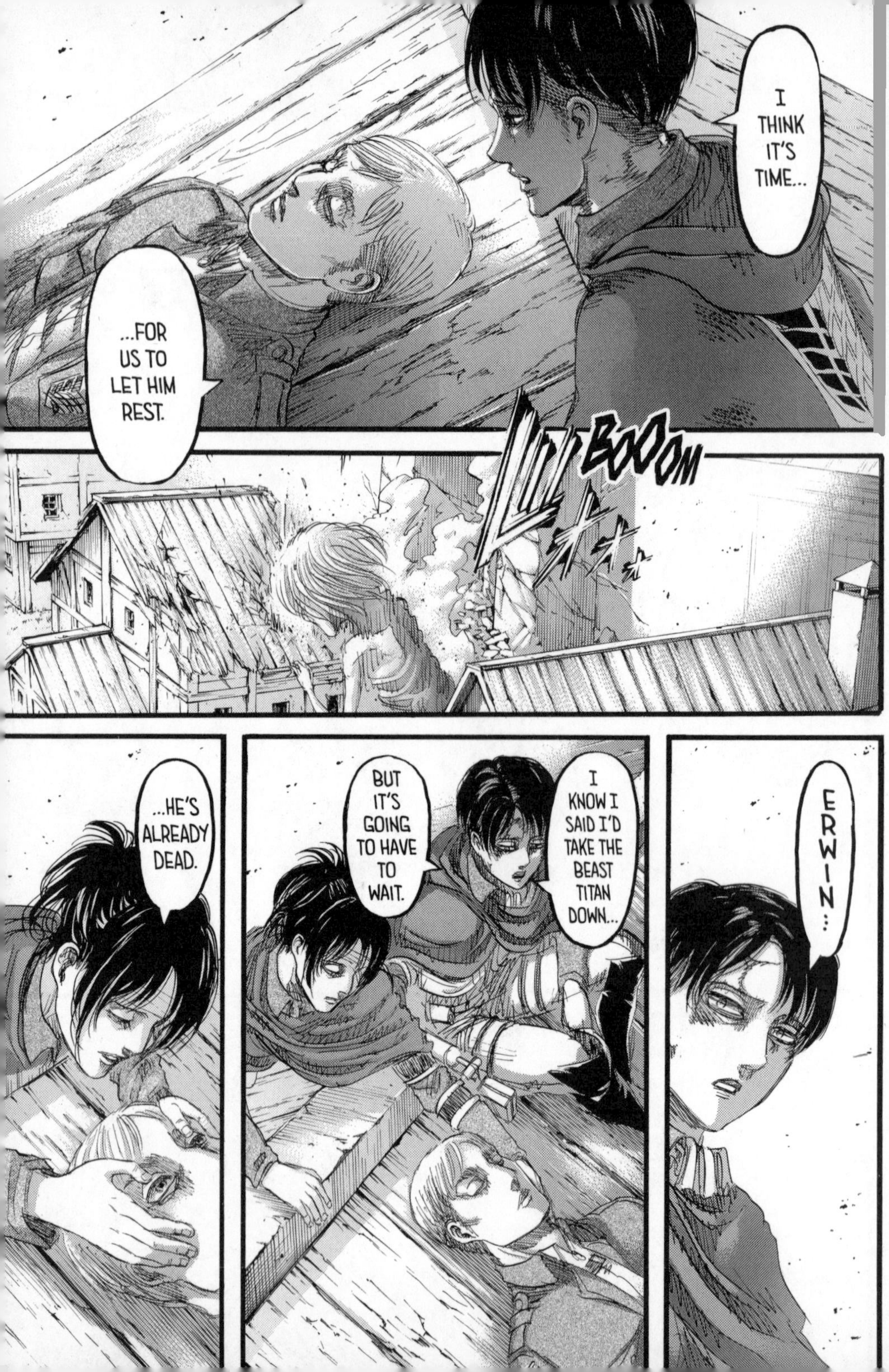
I THINK IT'S TIME...
...FOR US TO LET HIM REST.
BOOOM
ERWIN...
I KNOW I SAID I'D TAKE THE BEAST TITAN DOWN...
BUT IT'S GOING TO HAVE TO WAIT.
...HE'S ALREADY DEAD.

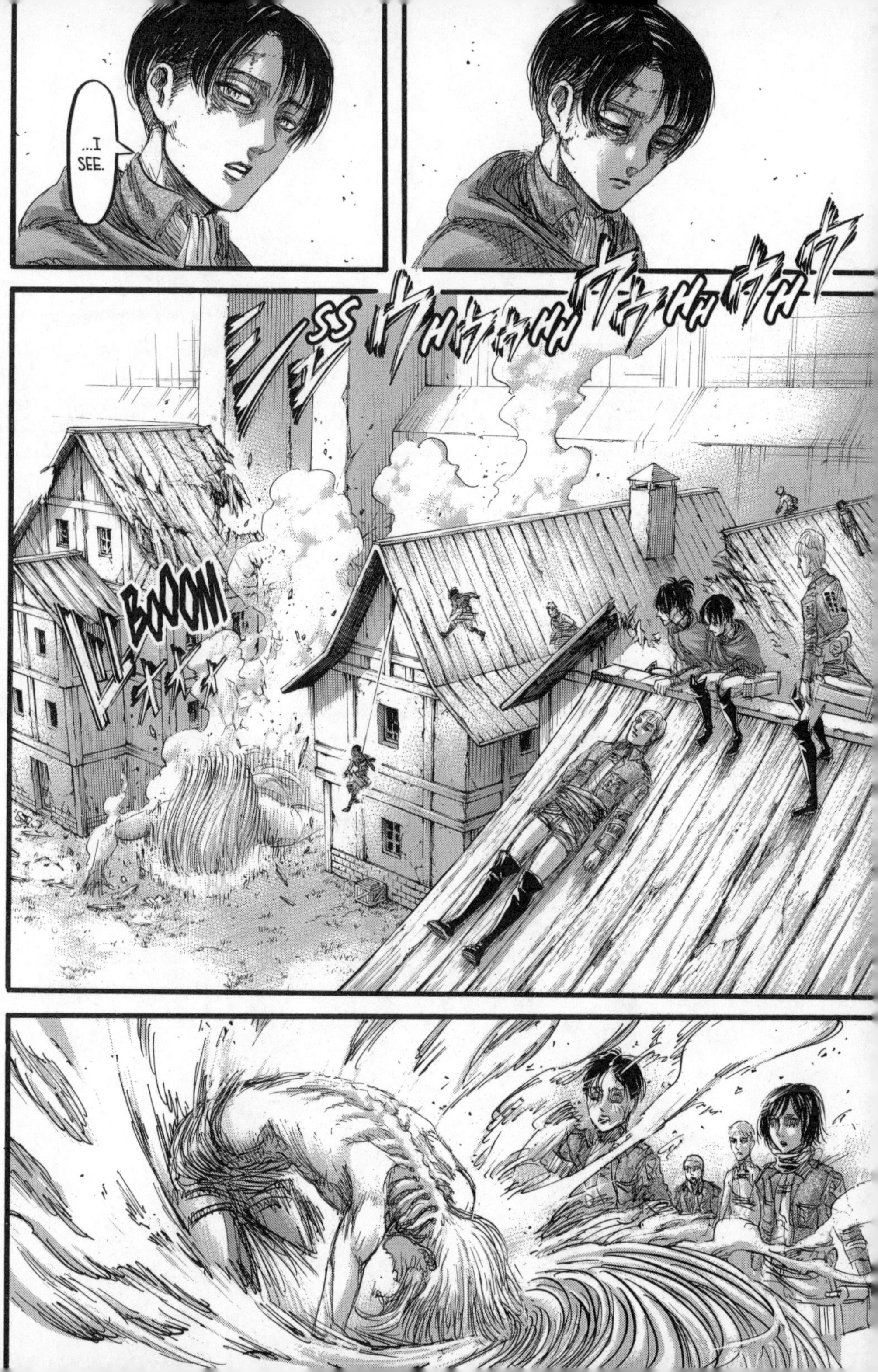
...I SEE.
SS
BOOOM

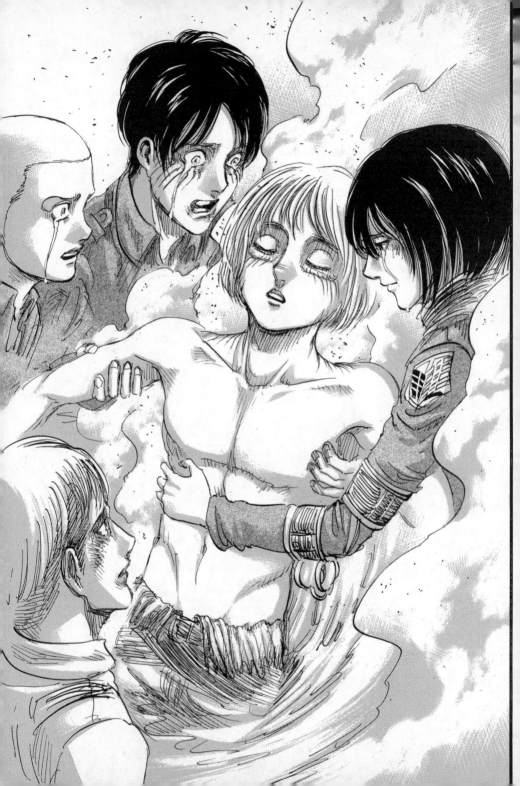

ATTACK on TITAN

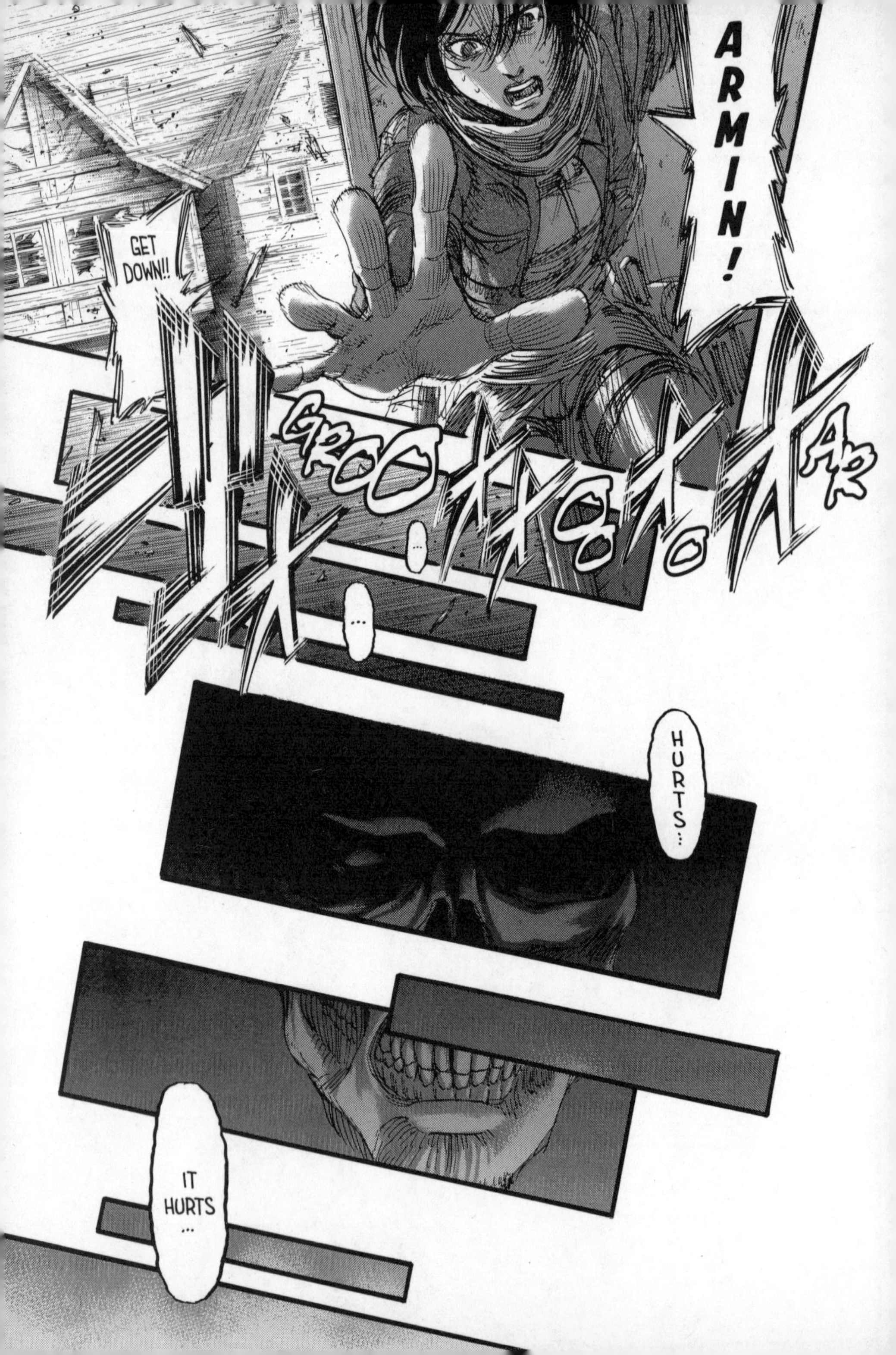
ARMIN!
GET DOWN!!
GROOOOOAR
...
...
HURTS...
IT HURTS...

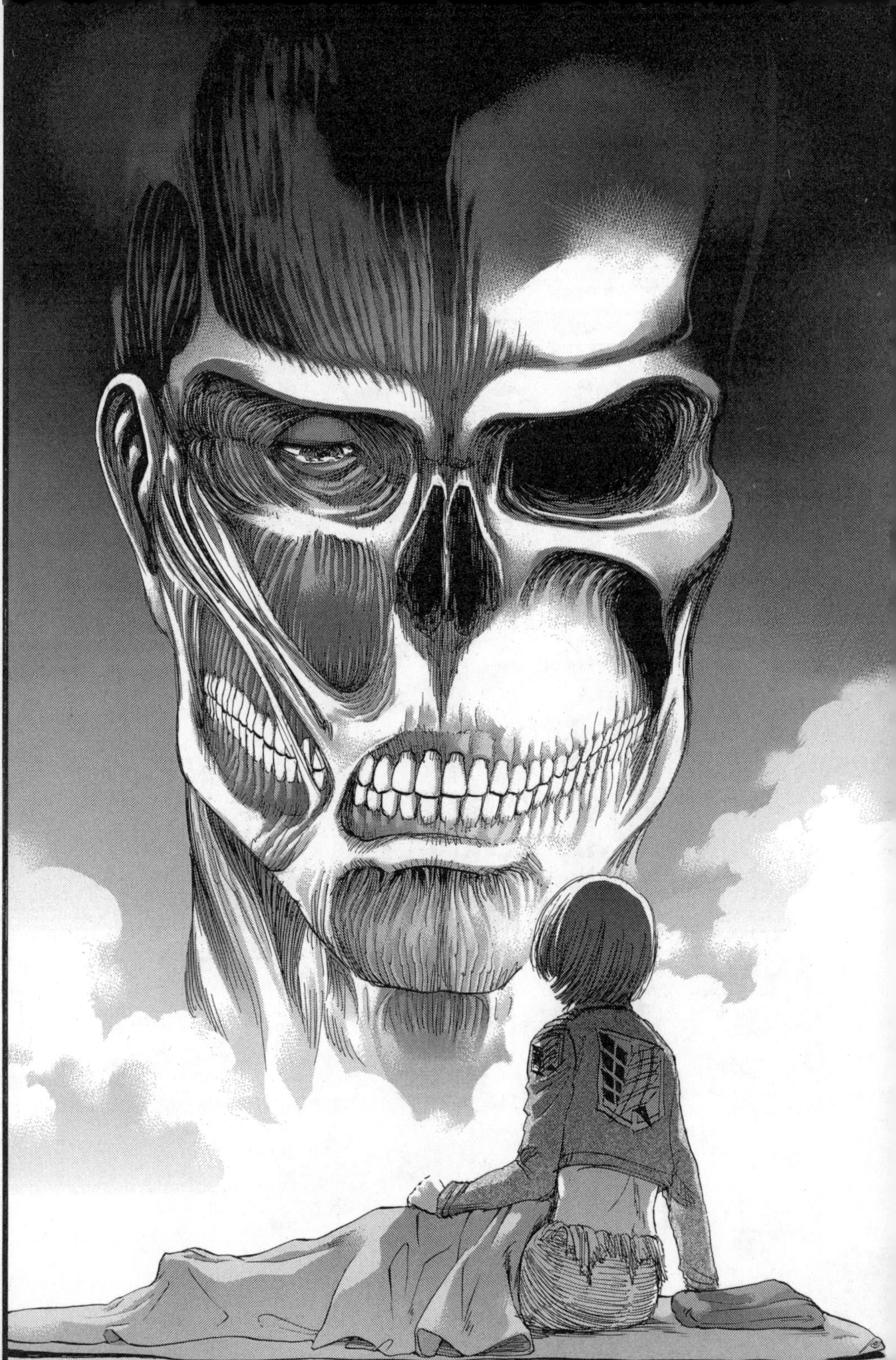

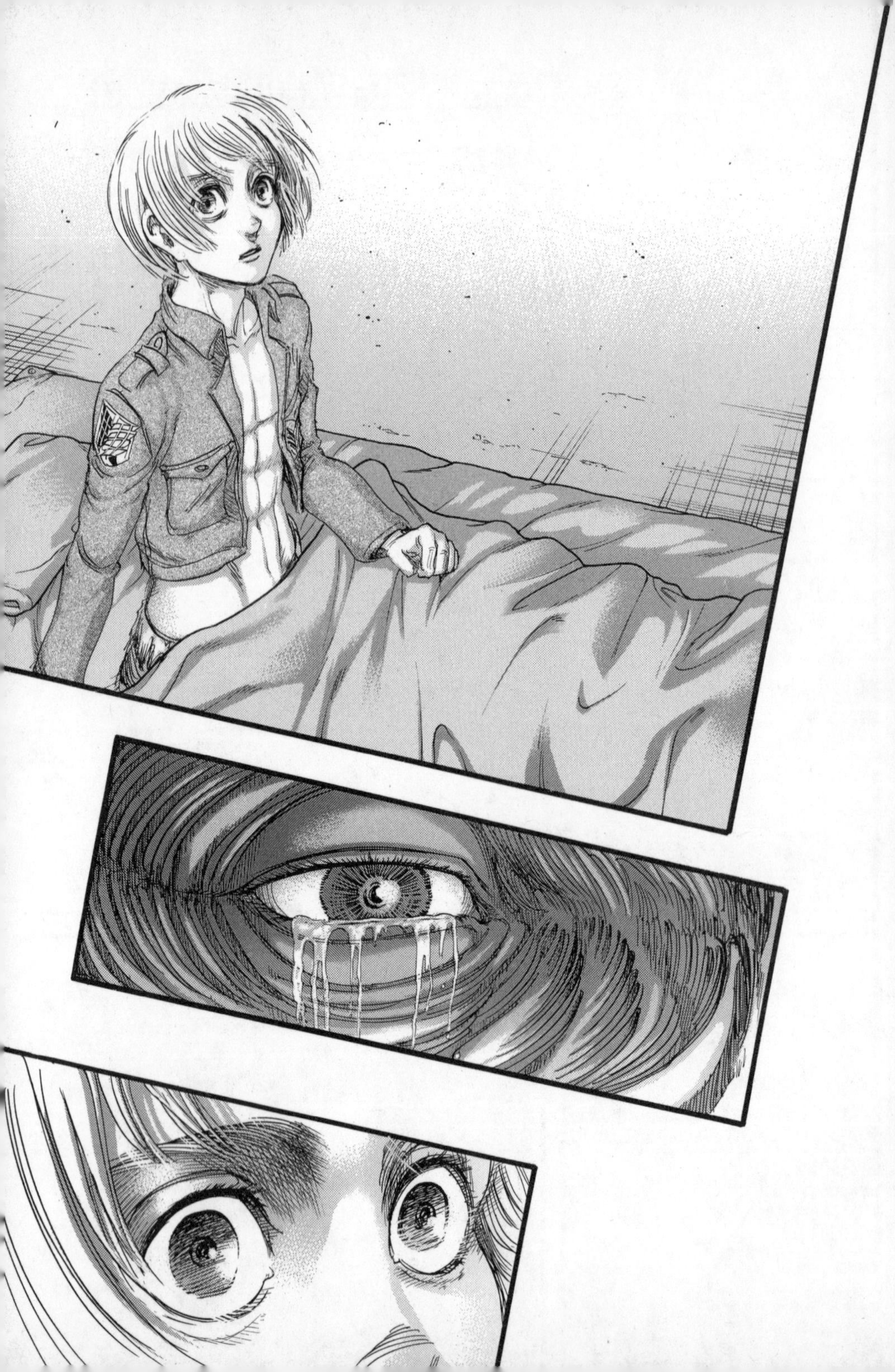

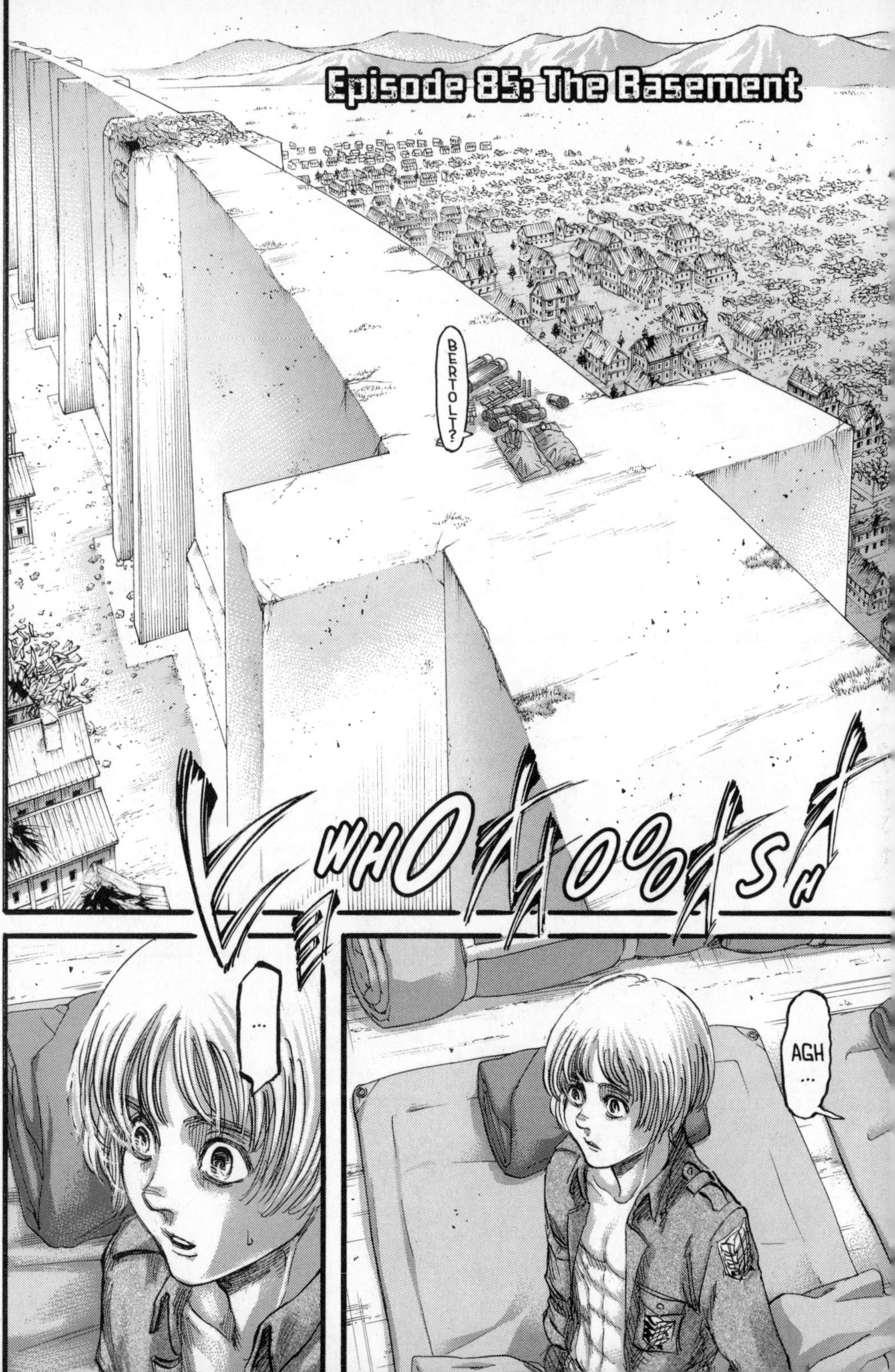
Episode 85: The Basement
BERTOLT?
WHOOOOSH
AGH ...
...

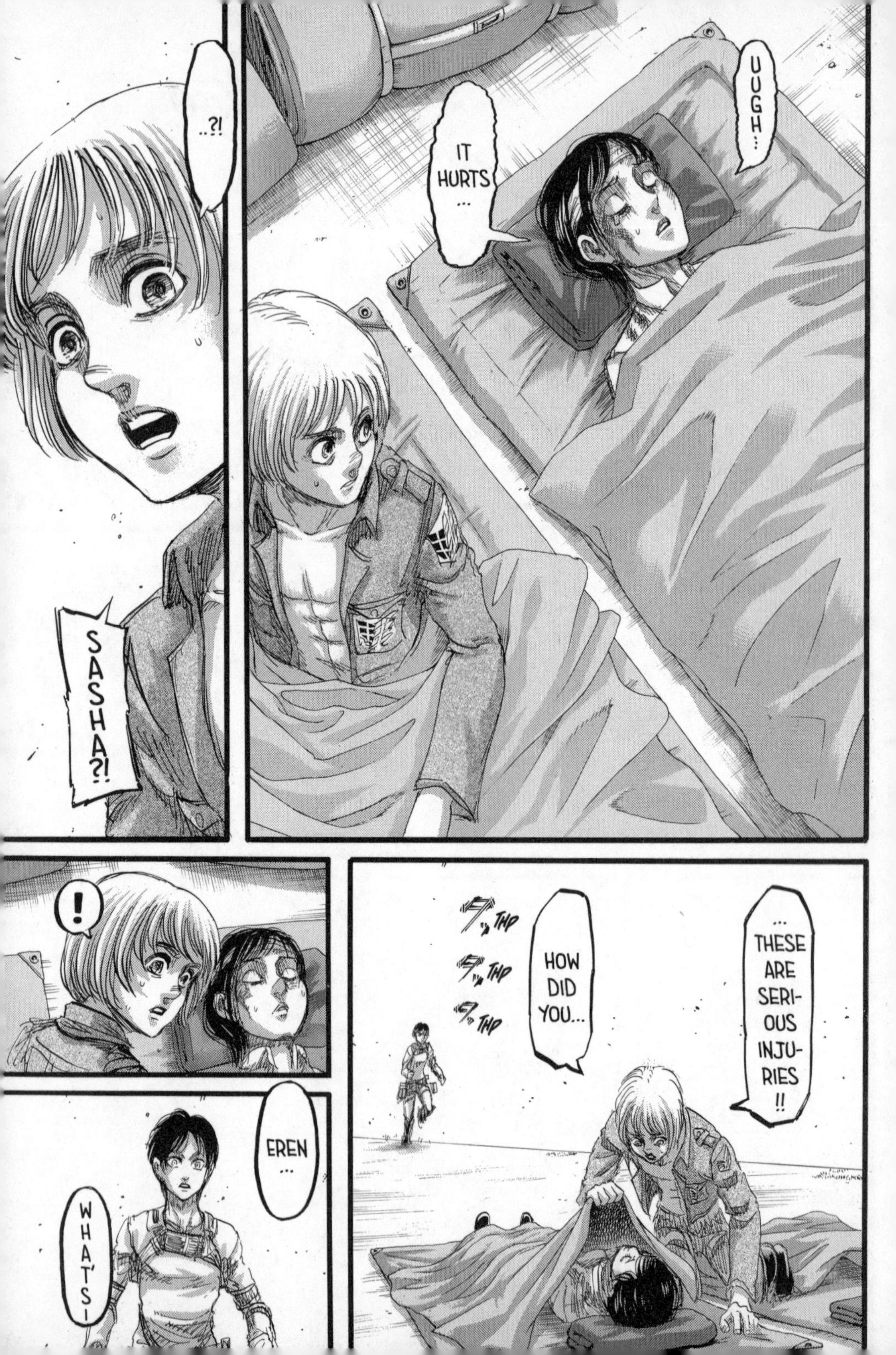
UUGH...
IT HURTS ...
...?!
SASHA?!
... THESE ARE SERI- OUS INJU- RIES !!
HOW DID YOU...
THP
THP
THP
!
EREN ...
WHAT'S I

HUH
?

WEL-
COME...
BACK.

CAP-
TAIN.

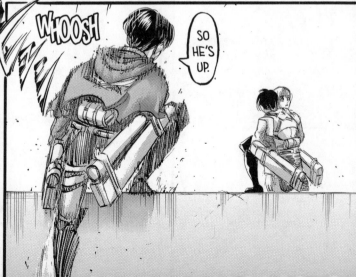

WHOOSH

SO
HE'S
UP.

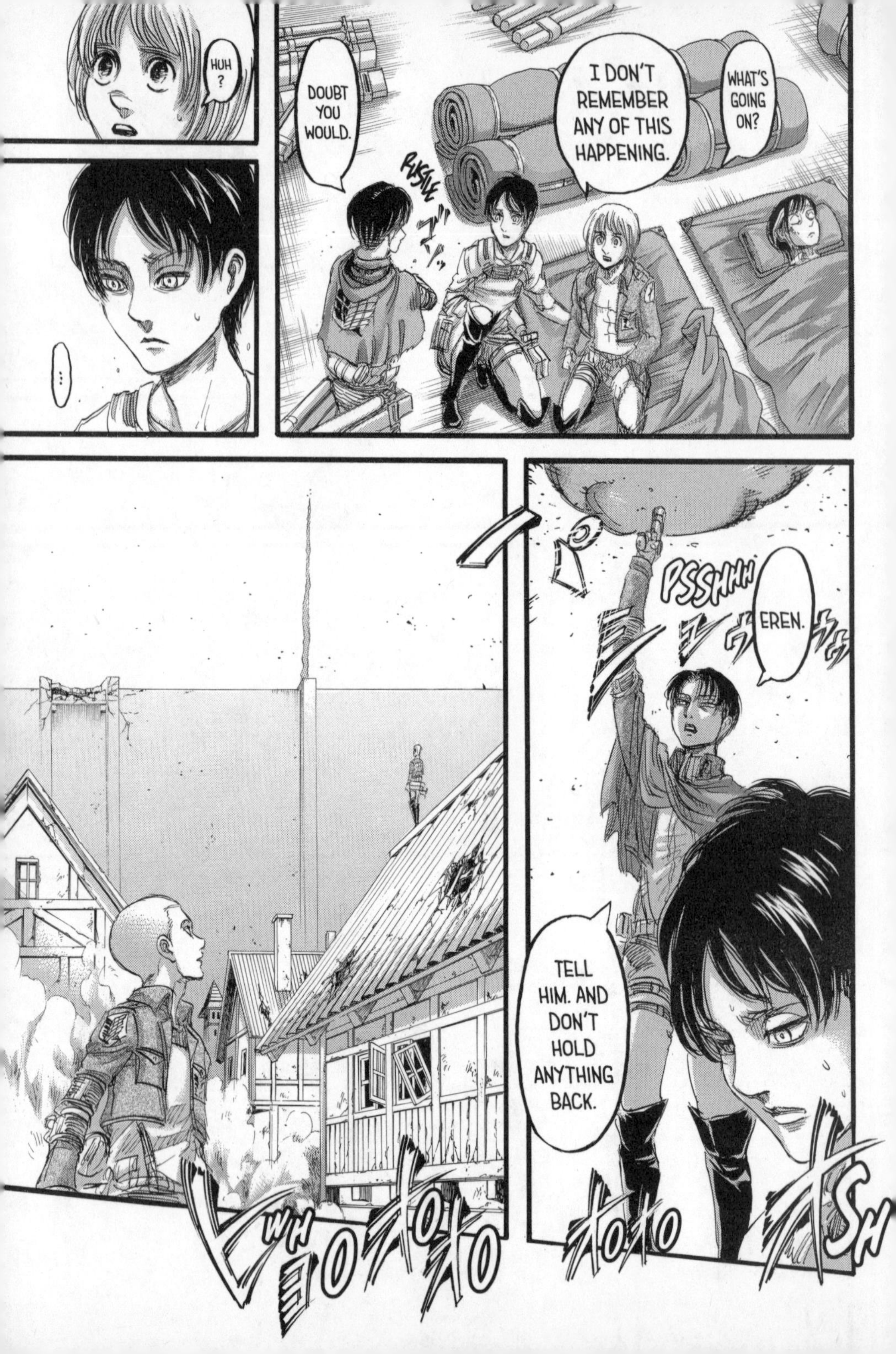
WHAT'S GOING ON?
I DON'T REMEMBER ANY OF THIS HAPPENING.
DOUBT YOU WOULD.
RUSTLE
HUH ?
...
PSSHHH
EREN.
TELL HIM. AND DON'T HOLD ANYTHING BACK.
SH
WH

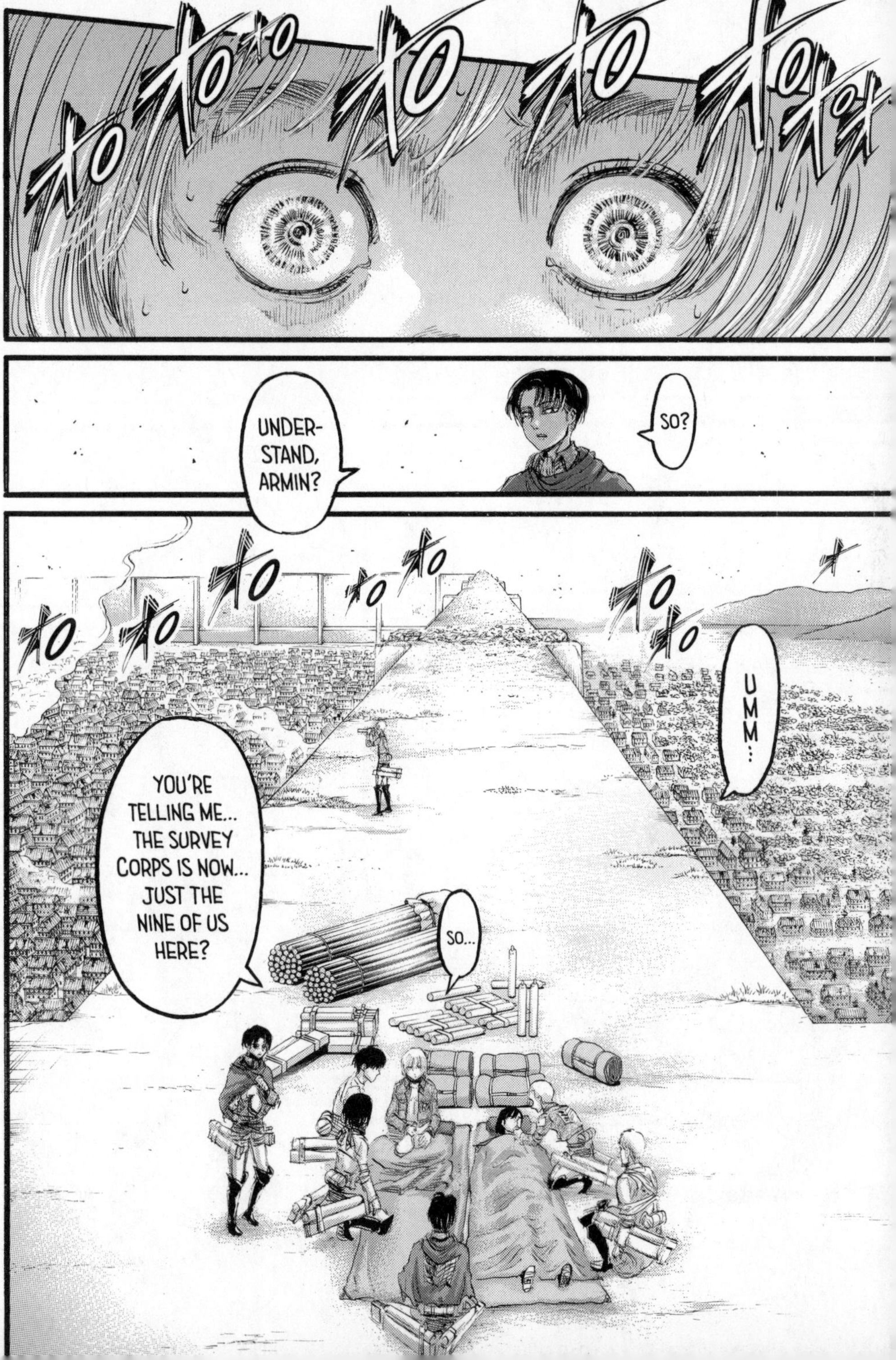
SO?
UNDER-STAND, ARMIN?
UMM...
SO...
YOU'RE TELLING ME... THE SURVEY CORPS IS NOW... JUST THE NINE OF US HERE?

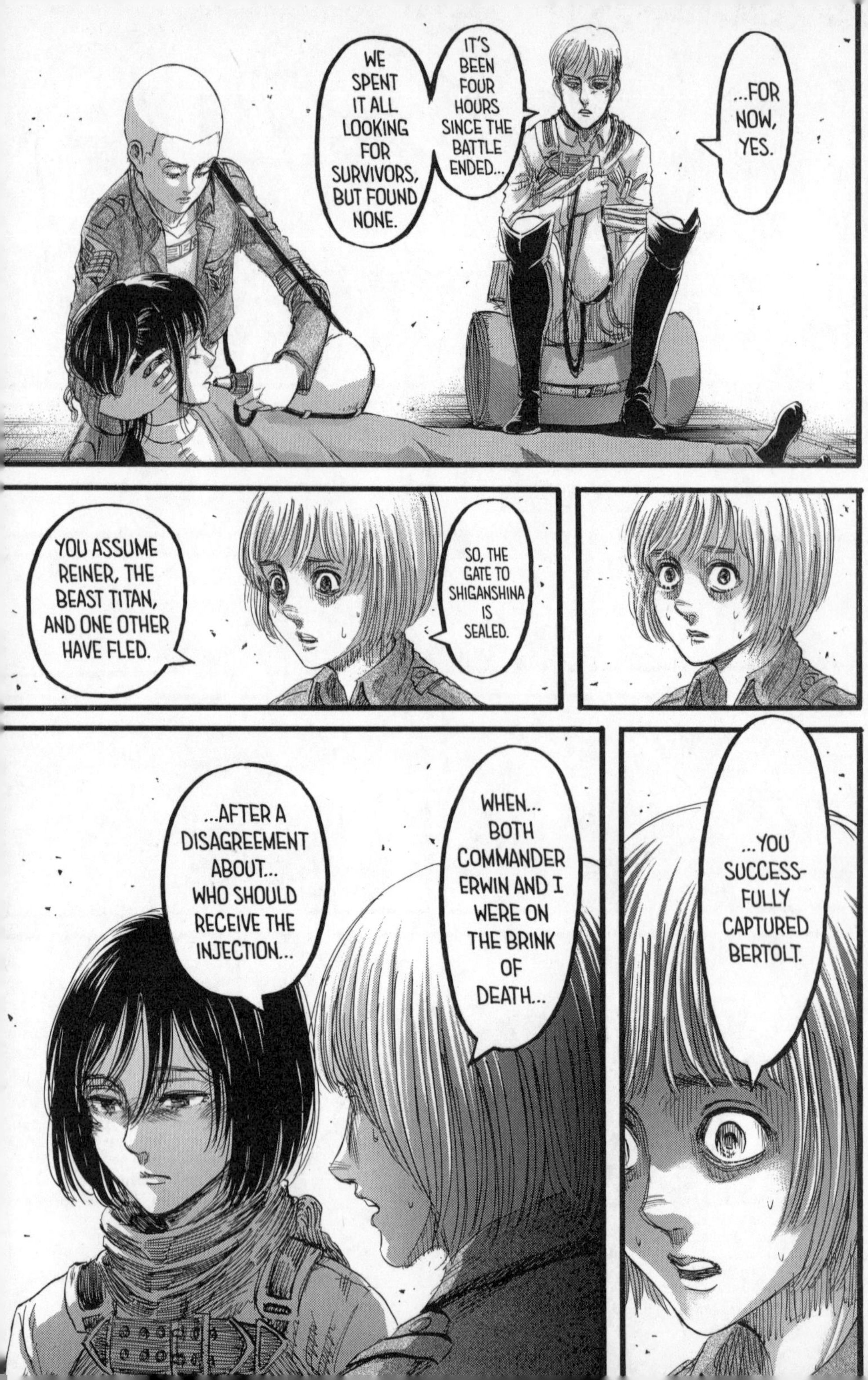
...FOR NOW, YES.
IT'S BEEN FOUR HOURS SINCE THE BATTLE ENDED...
WE SPENT IT ALL LOOKING FOR SURVIVORS, BUT FOUND NONE.
SO, THE GATE TO SHIGANSHINA IS SEALED.
YOU ASSUME REINER, THE BEAST TITAN, AND ONE OTHER HAVE FLED.
...YOU SUCCESS-FULLY CAPTURED BERTOLT.
WHEN... BOTH COMMANDER ERWIN AND I WERE ON THE BRINK OF DEATH...
...AFTER A DISAGREEMENT ABOUT... WHO SHOULD RECEIVE THE INJECTION...

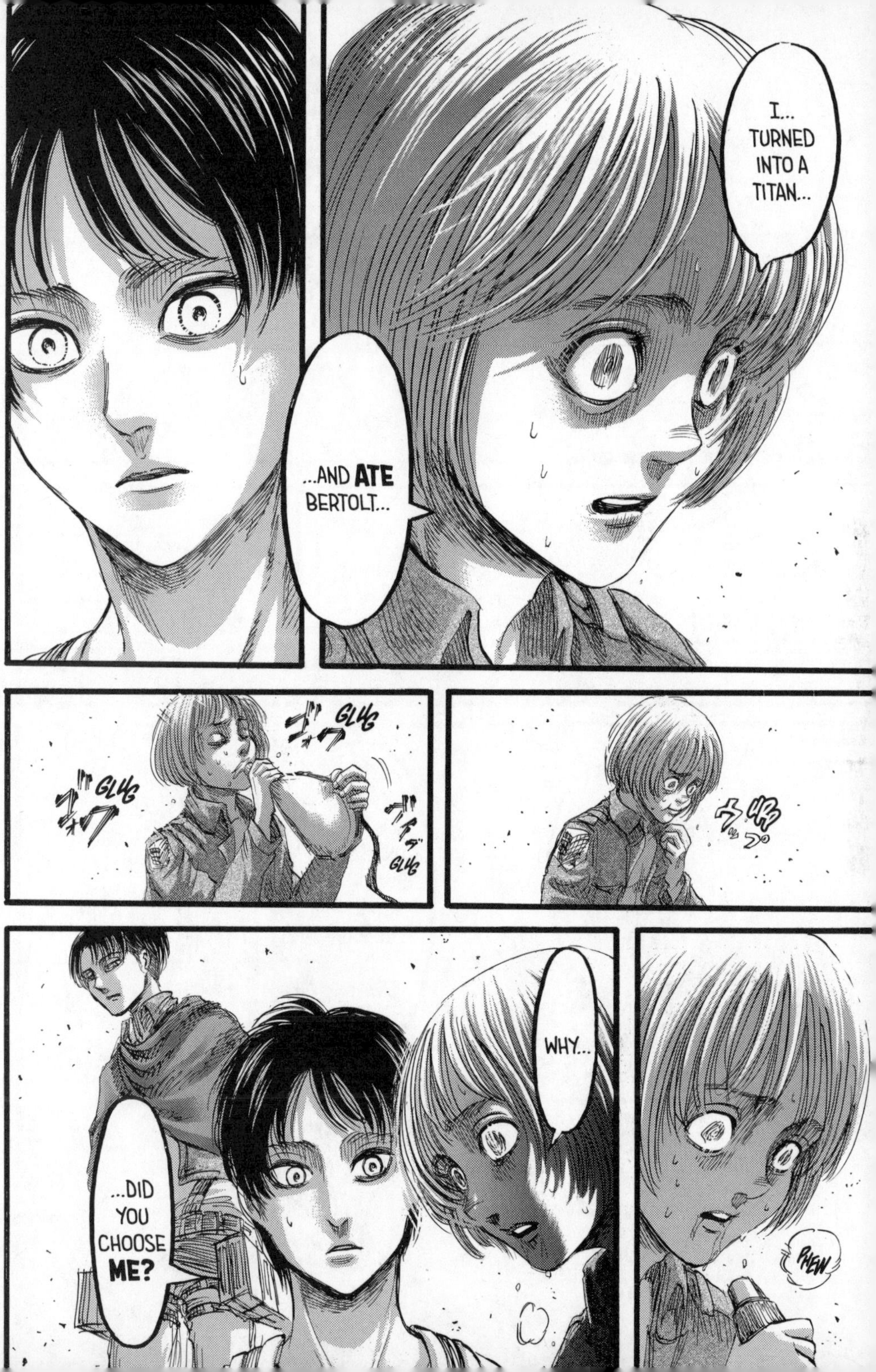
I... TURNED INTO A TITAN...
...AND ATE BERTOLT...
ウップ
GLUG
GLUG
GLUG
PHEW
WHY...
...DID YOU CHOOSE ME?

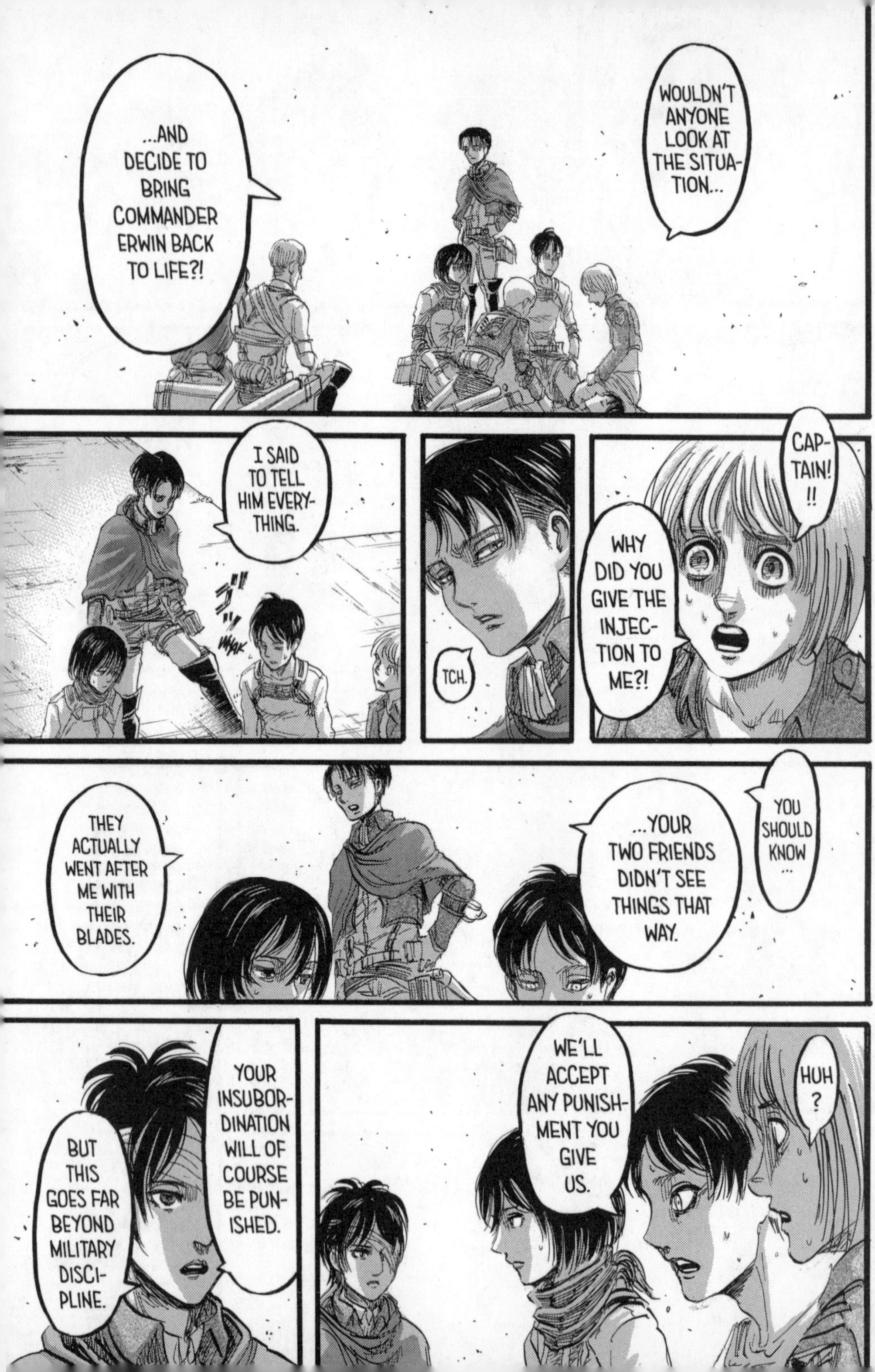
WOULDN'T ANYONE LOOK AT THE SITUATION...
...AND DECIDE TO BRING COMMANDER ERWIN BACK TO LIFE?!
CAPTAIN! !!
WHY DID YOU GIVE THE INJECTION TO ME?!
TCH.
I SAID TO TELL HIM EVERYTHING.
WHAK
YOU SHOULD KNOW ...
...YOUR TWO FRIENDS DIDN'T SEE THINGS THAT WAY.
THEY ACTUALLY WENT AFTER ME WITH THEIR BLADES.
HUH ?
WE'LL ACCEPT ANY PUNISHMENT YOU GIVE US.
YOUR INSUBORDINATION WILL OF COURSE BE PUNISHED.
BUT THIS GOES FAR BEYOND MILITARY DISCIPLINE.

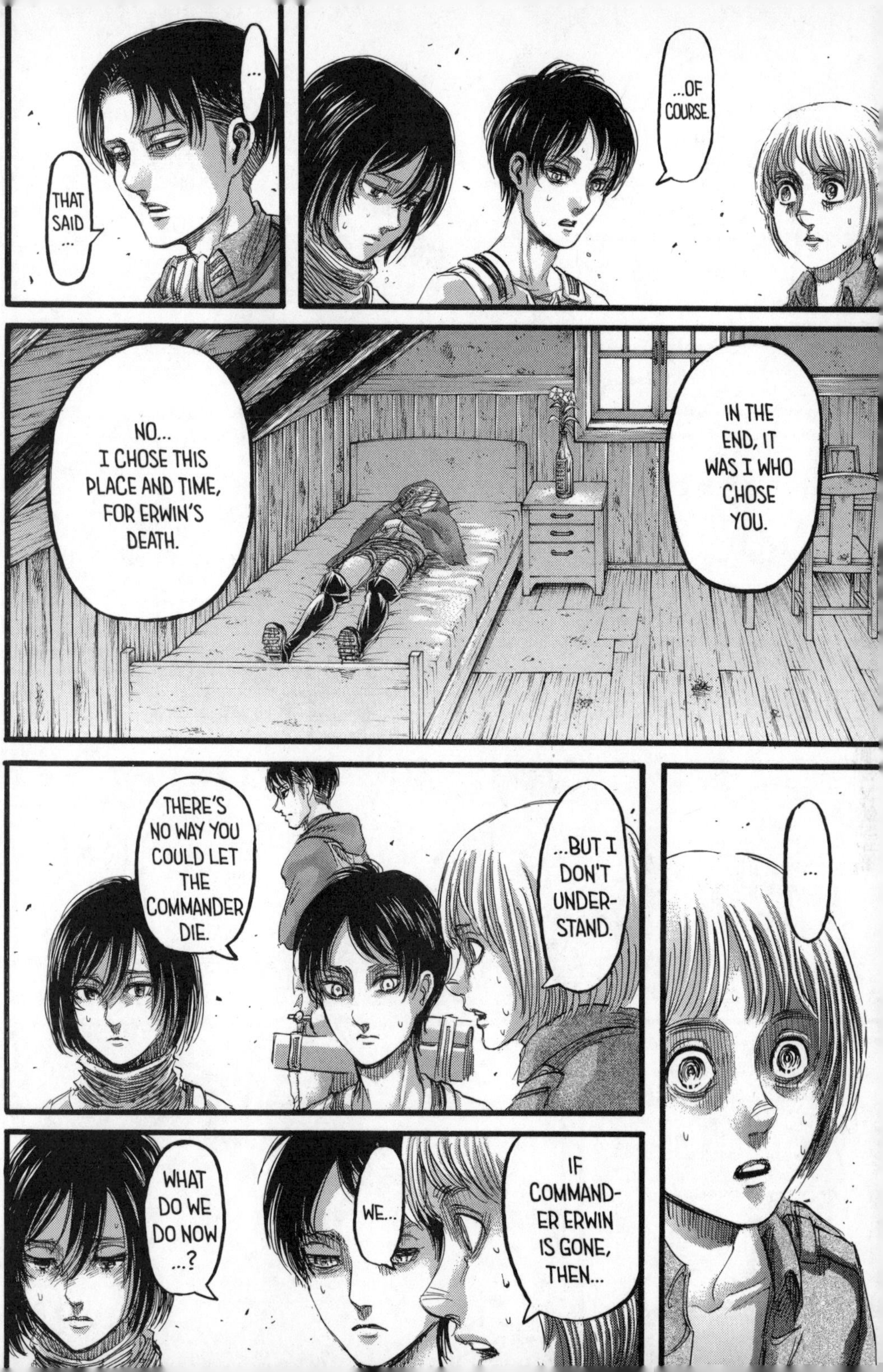

...OF COURSE.
...
THAT SAID ...
IN THE END, IT WAS I WHO CHOSE YOU.
NO... I CHOSE THIS PLACE AND TIME, FOR ERWIN'S DEATH.
...
...BUT I DON'T UNDER-STAND.
THERE'S NO WAY YOU COULD LET THE COMMANDER DIE.
IF COMMAND-ER ERWIN IS GONE, THEN...
WE...
WHAT DO WE DO NOW ...?

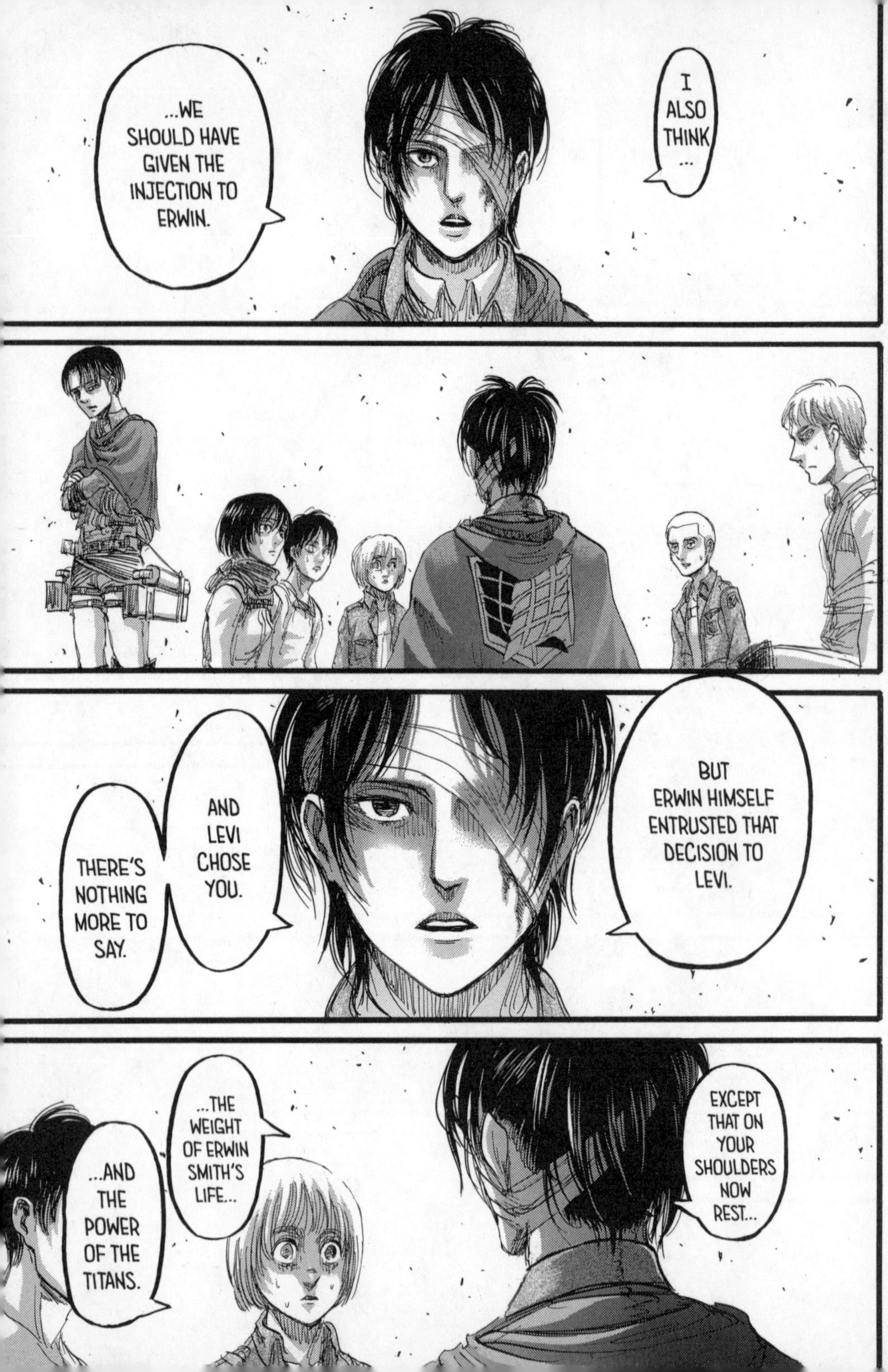
I ALSO THINK...
...WE SHOULD HAVE GIVEN THE INJECTION TO ERWIN.
BUT ERWIN HIMSELF ENTRUSTED THAT DECISION TO LEVI.
AND LEVI CHOSE YOU.
THERE'S NOTHING MORE TO SAY.
EXCEPT THAT ON YOUR SHOULDERS NOW REST...
...THE WEIGHT OF ERWIN SMITH'S LIFE...
...AND THE POWER OF THE TITANS.

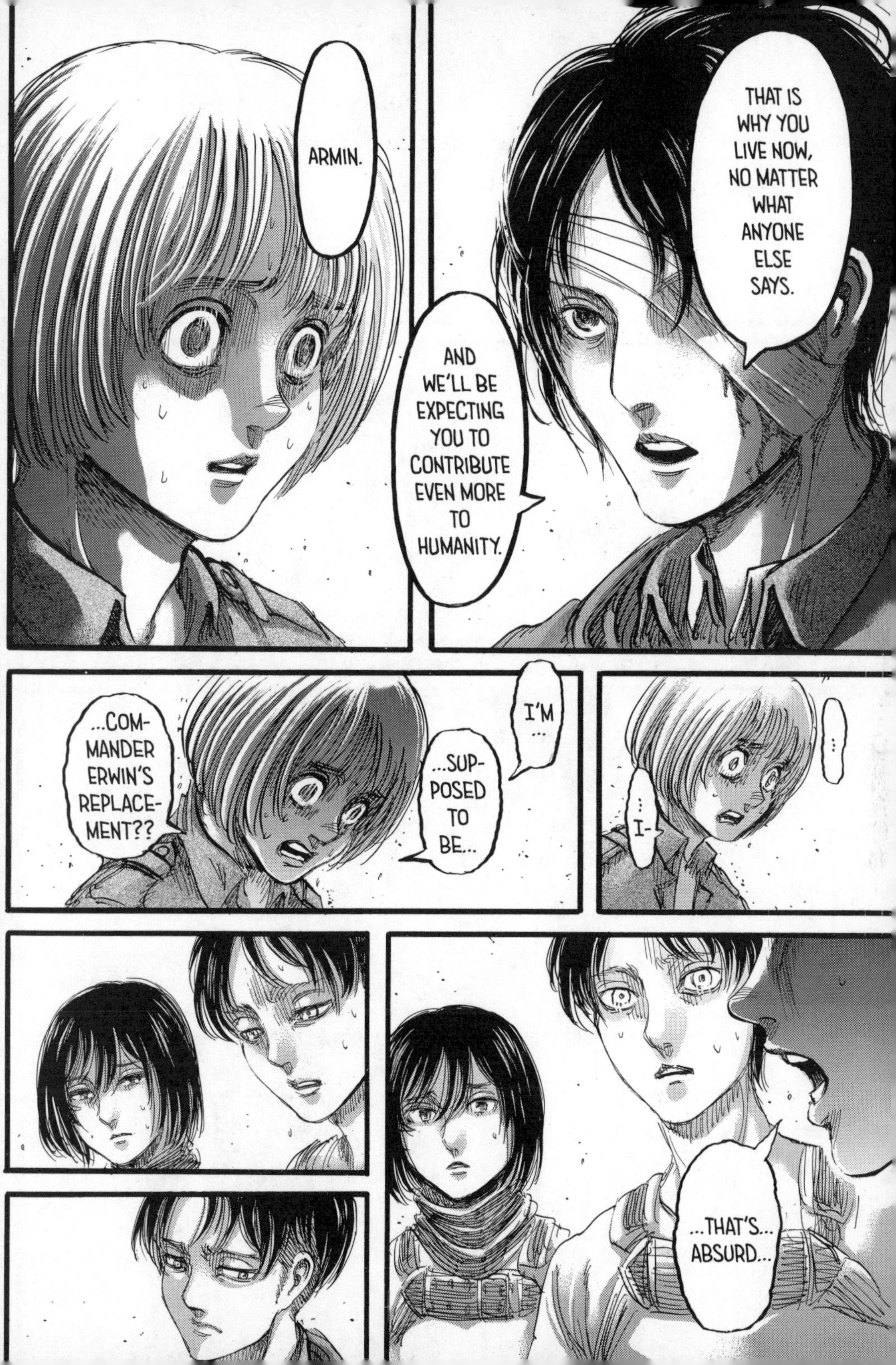
THAT IS WHY YOU LIVE NOW, NO MATTER WHAT ANYONE ELSE SAYS.
AND WE'LL BE EXPECTING YOU TO CONTRIBUTE EVEN MORE TO HUMANITY.
ARMIN.
...
...I-
I'M ...
...SUP-POSED TO BE...
...COM-MANDER ERWIN'S REPLACE-MENT??
...THAT'S... ABSURD...

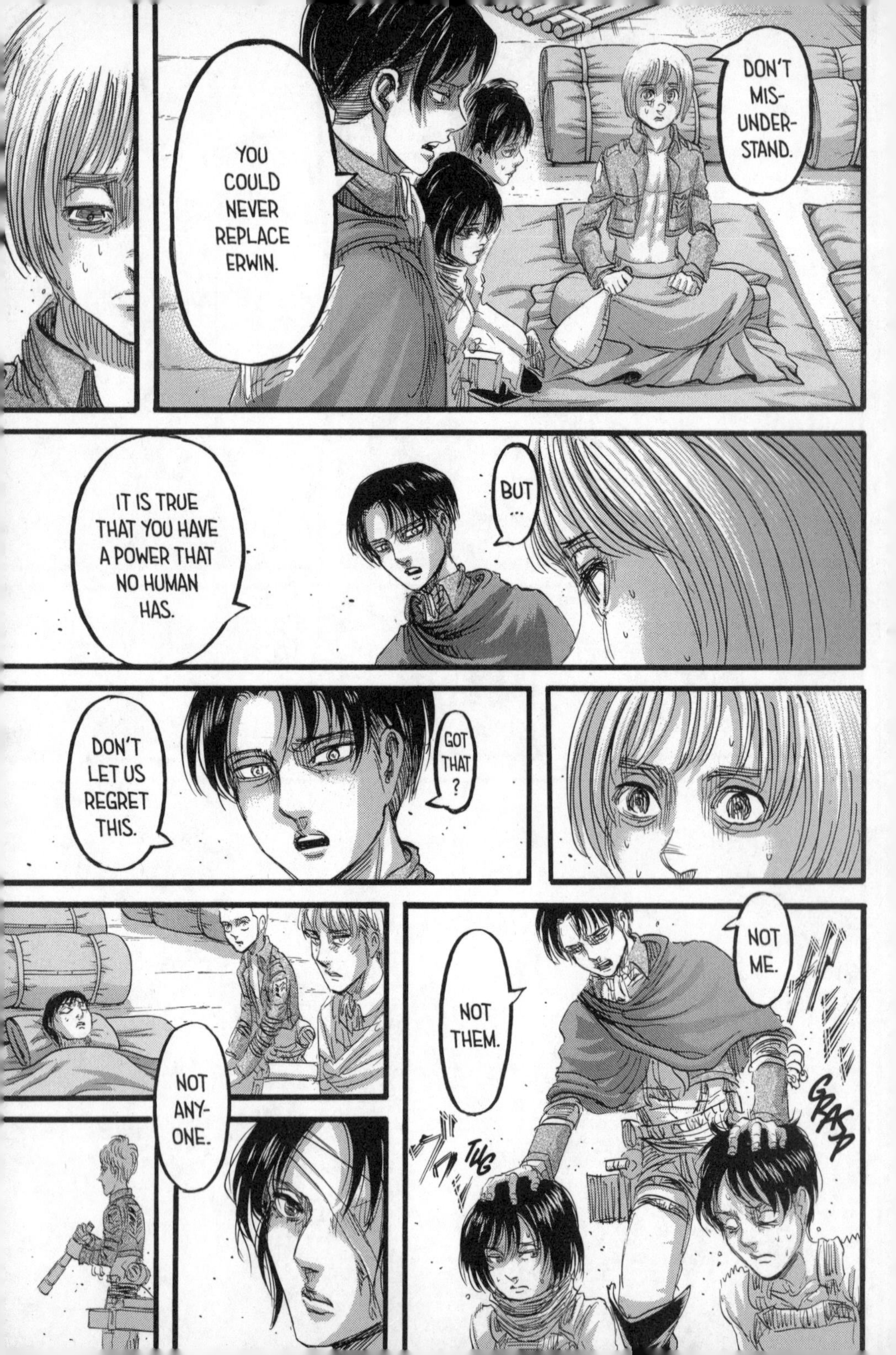
DON'T MIS-UNDER-STAND.
YOU COULD NEVER REPLACE ERWIN.
BUT ...
IT IS TRUE THAT YOU HAVE A POWER THAT NO HUMAN HAS.
GOT THAT ?
DON'T LET US REGRET THIS.
NOT ME.
NOT THEM.
GRASP
TUG
NOT ANY-ONE.

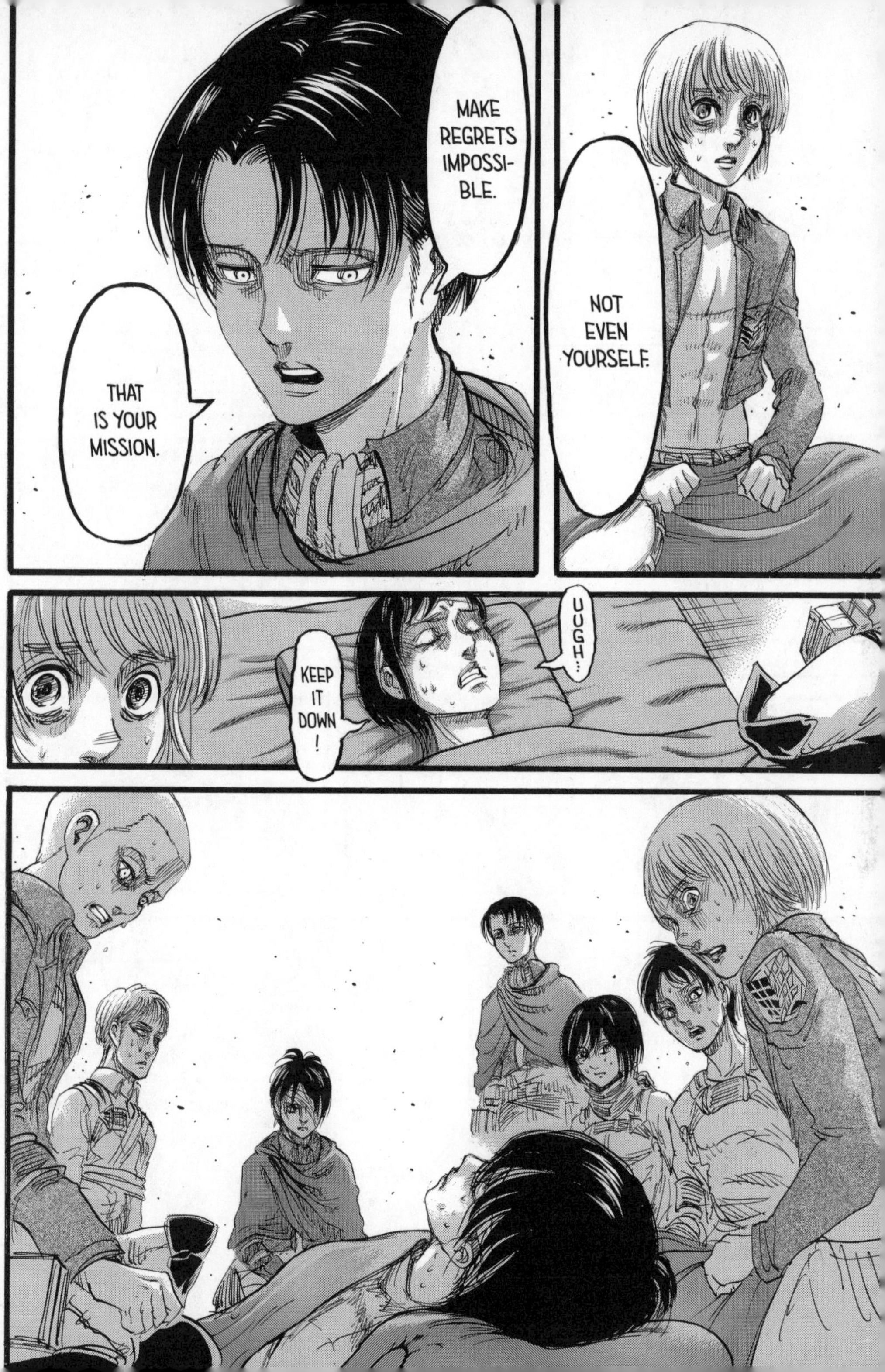
NOT EVEN YOURSELF.
MAKE REGRETS IMPOSSI-BLE.
THAT IS YOUR MISSION.
UUGH...
KEEP IT DOWN!

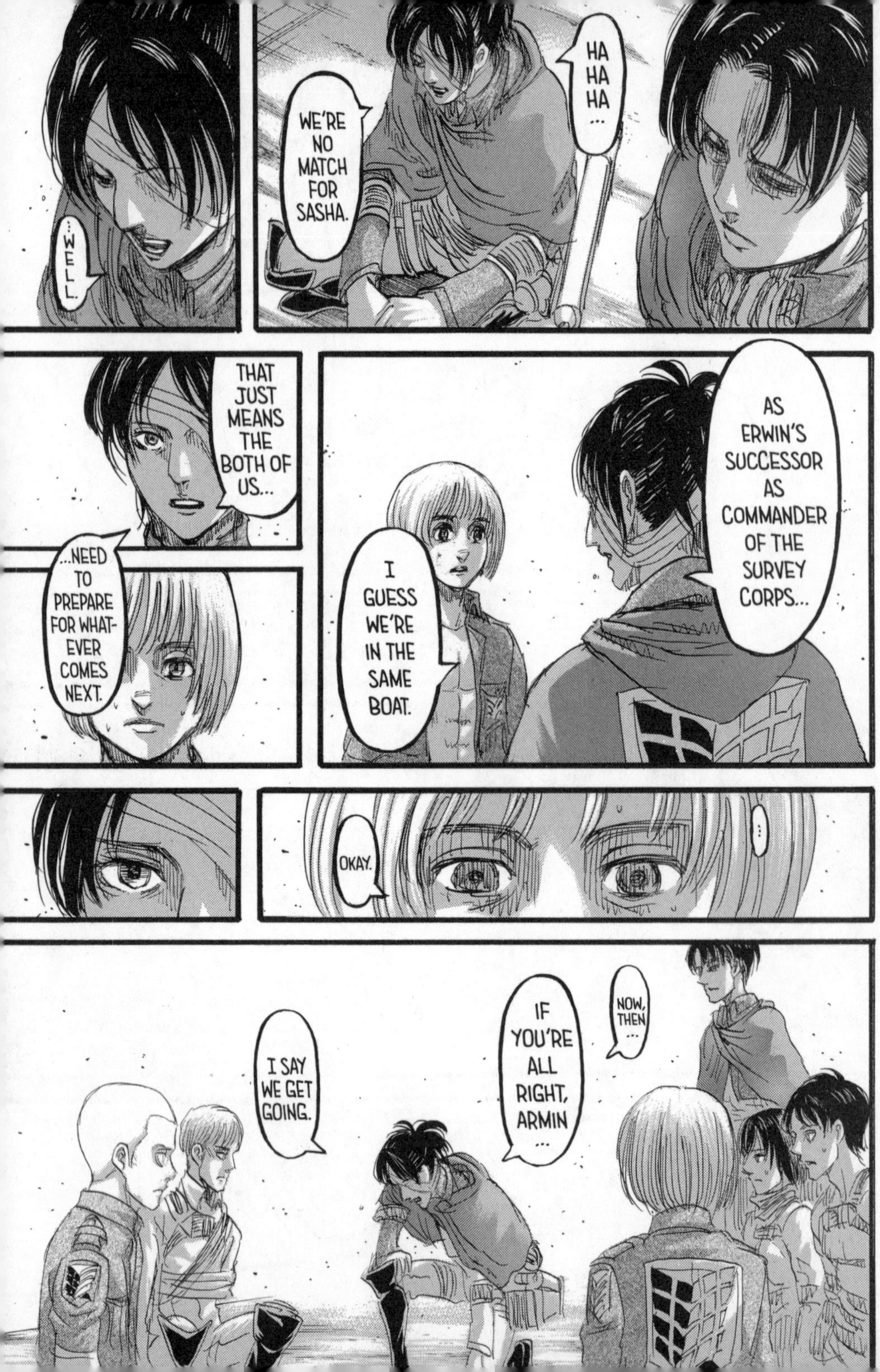
HA HA HA ...
WE'RE NO MATCH FOR SASHA.
...WELL.
AS ERWIN'S SUCCESSOR AS COMMANDER OF THE SURVEY CORPS...
I GUESS WE'RE IN THE SAME BOAT.
THAT JUST MEANS THE BOTH OF US...
...NEED TO PREPARE FOR WHATEVER COMES NEXT.
...
OKAY.
NOW, THEN...
IF YOU'RE ALL RIGHT, ARMIN...
I SAY WE GET GOING.

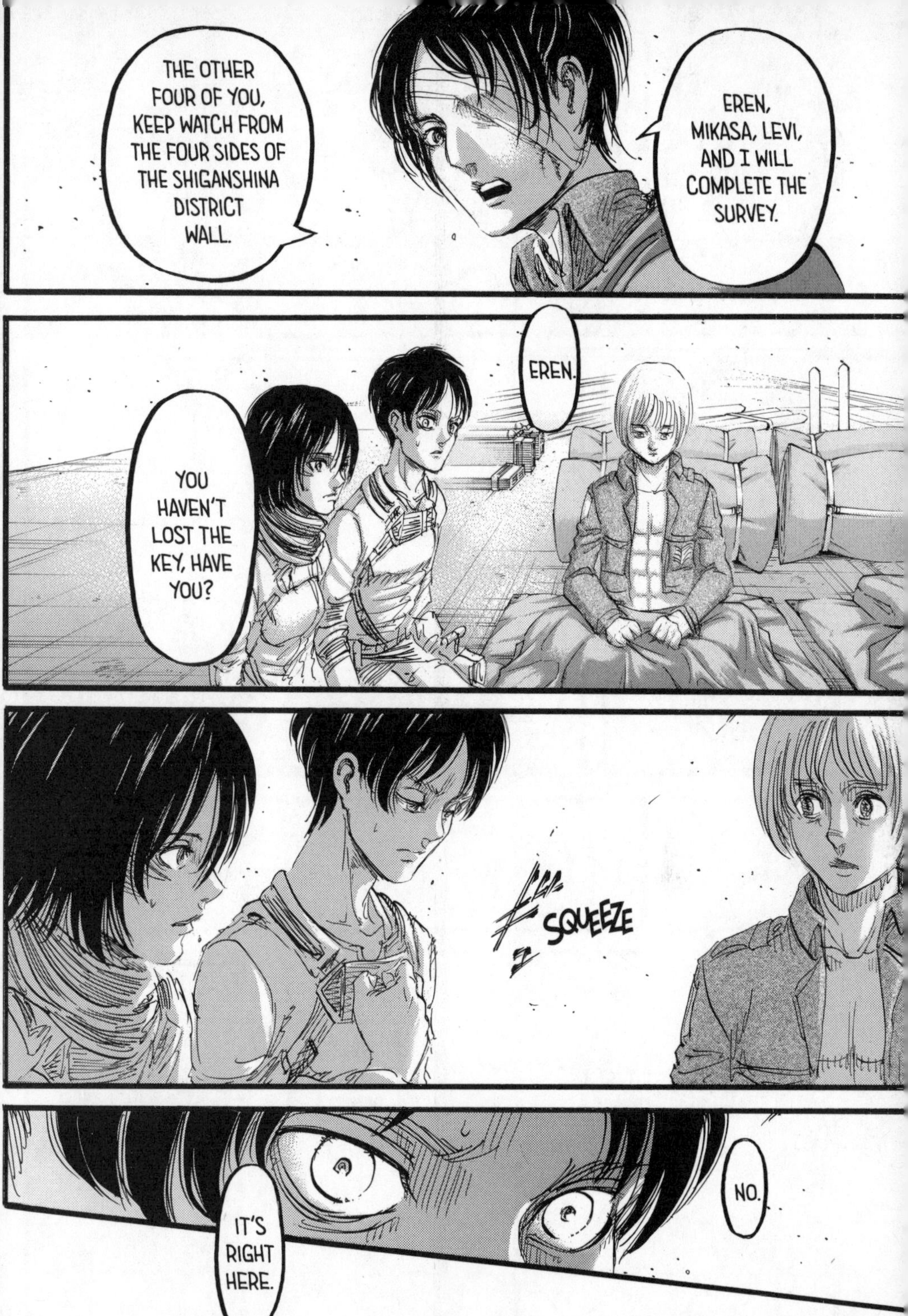
EREN, MIKASA, LEVI, AND I WILL COMPLETE THE SURVEY.
THE OTHER FOUR OF YOU, KEEP WATCH FROM THE FOUR SIDES OF THE SHIGANSHINA DISTRICT WALL.
EREN.
YOU HAVEN'T LOST THE KEY, HAVE YOU?
SQUEEZE
NO.
IT'S RIGHT HERE.

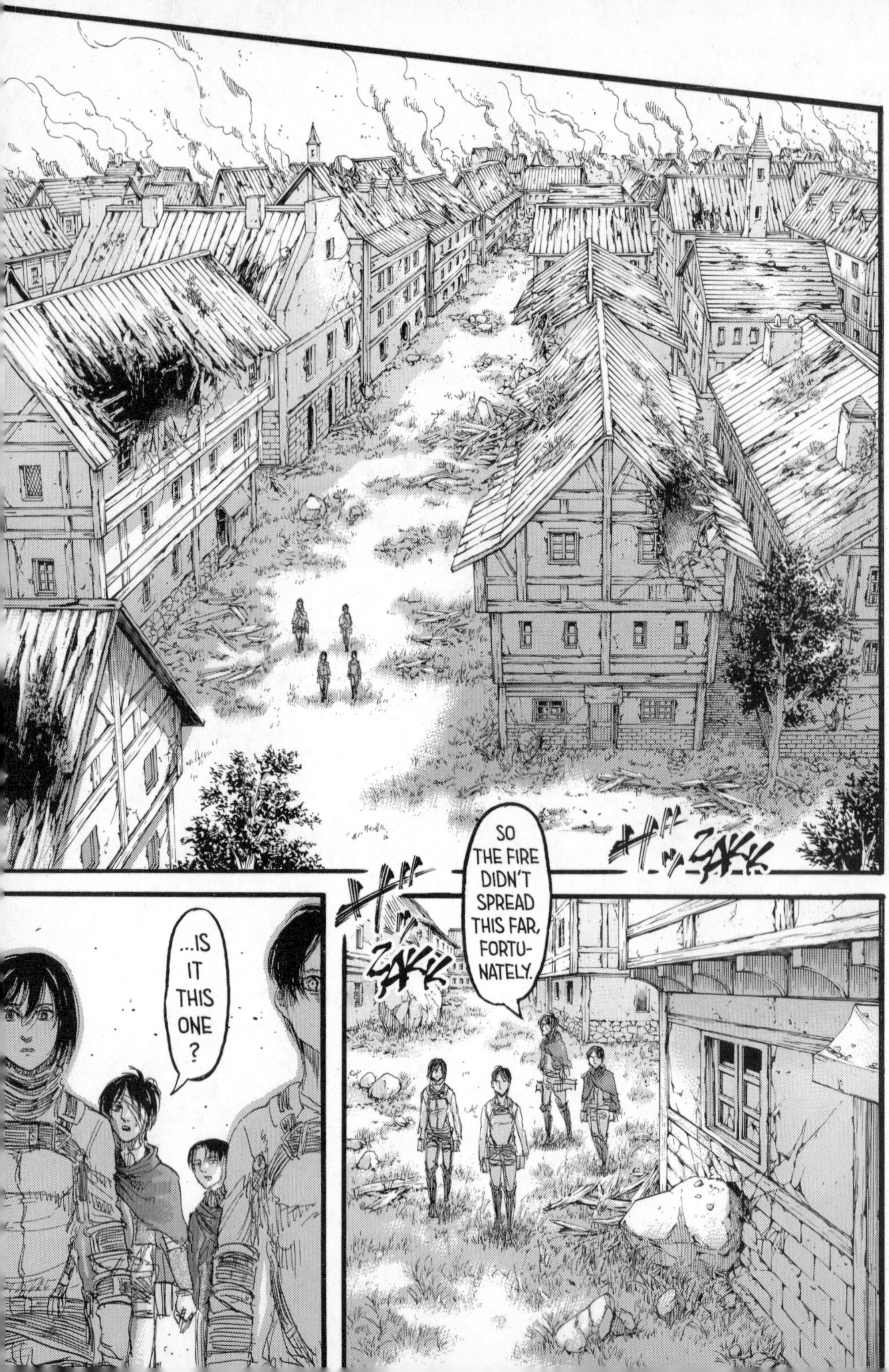
SO THE FIRE DIDN'T SPREAD THIS FAR, FORTUNATELY.
ZAKK
ZAKK
...IS IT THIS ONE?

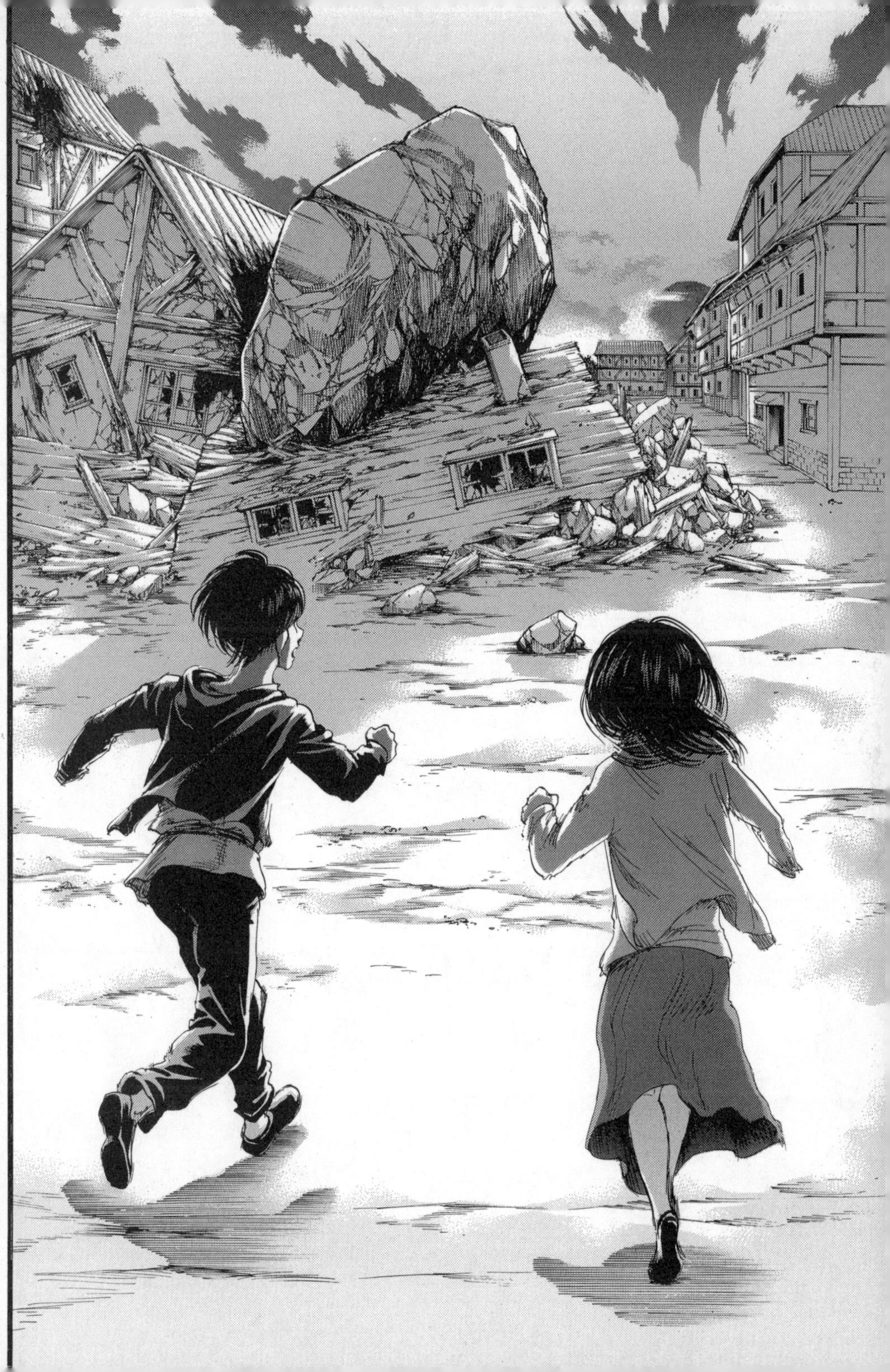

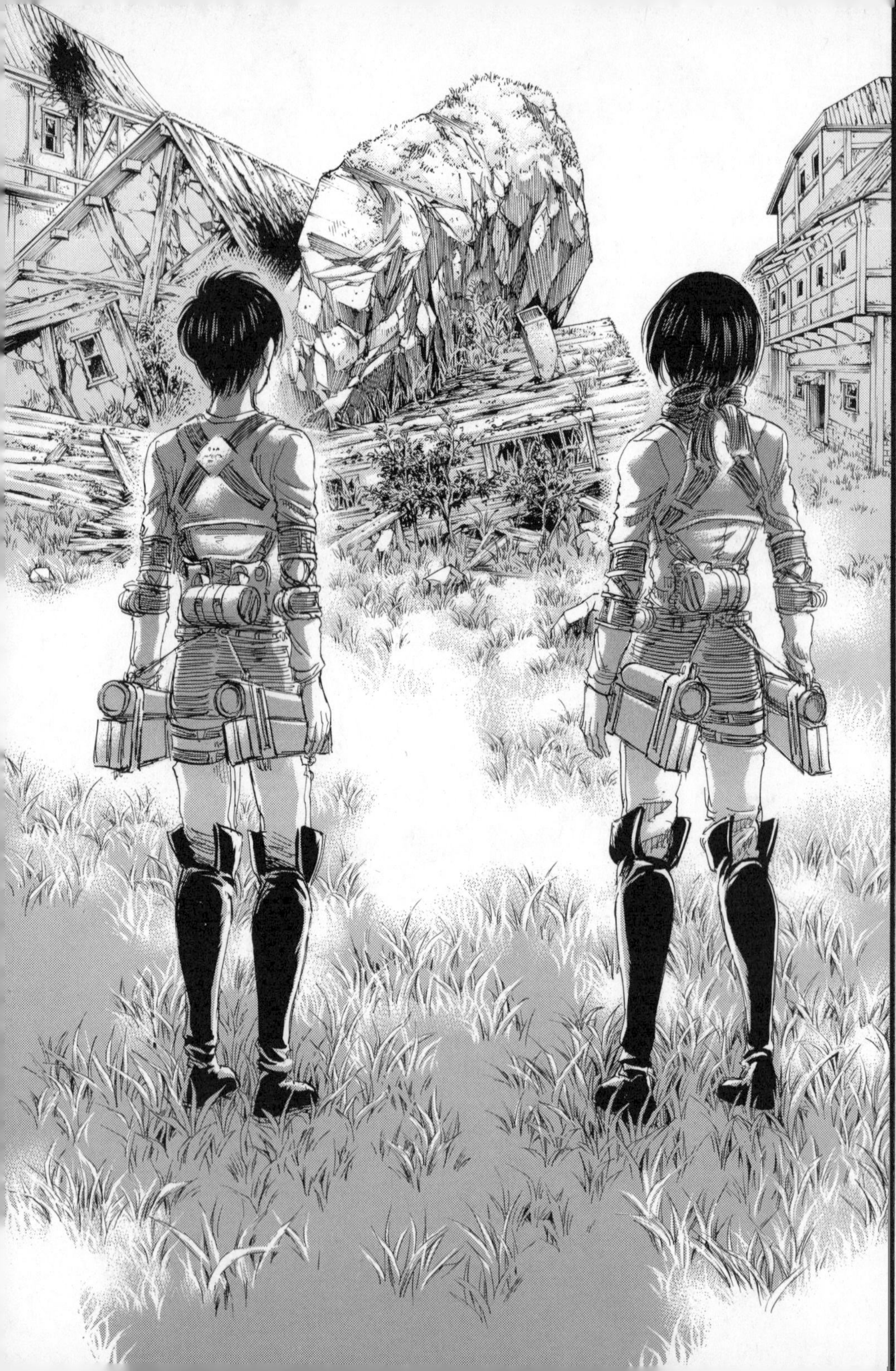

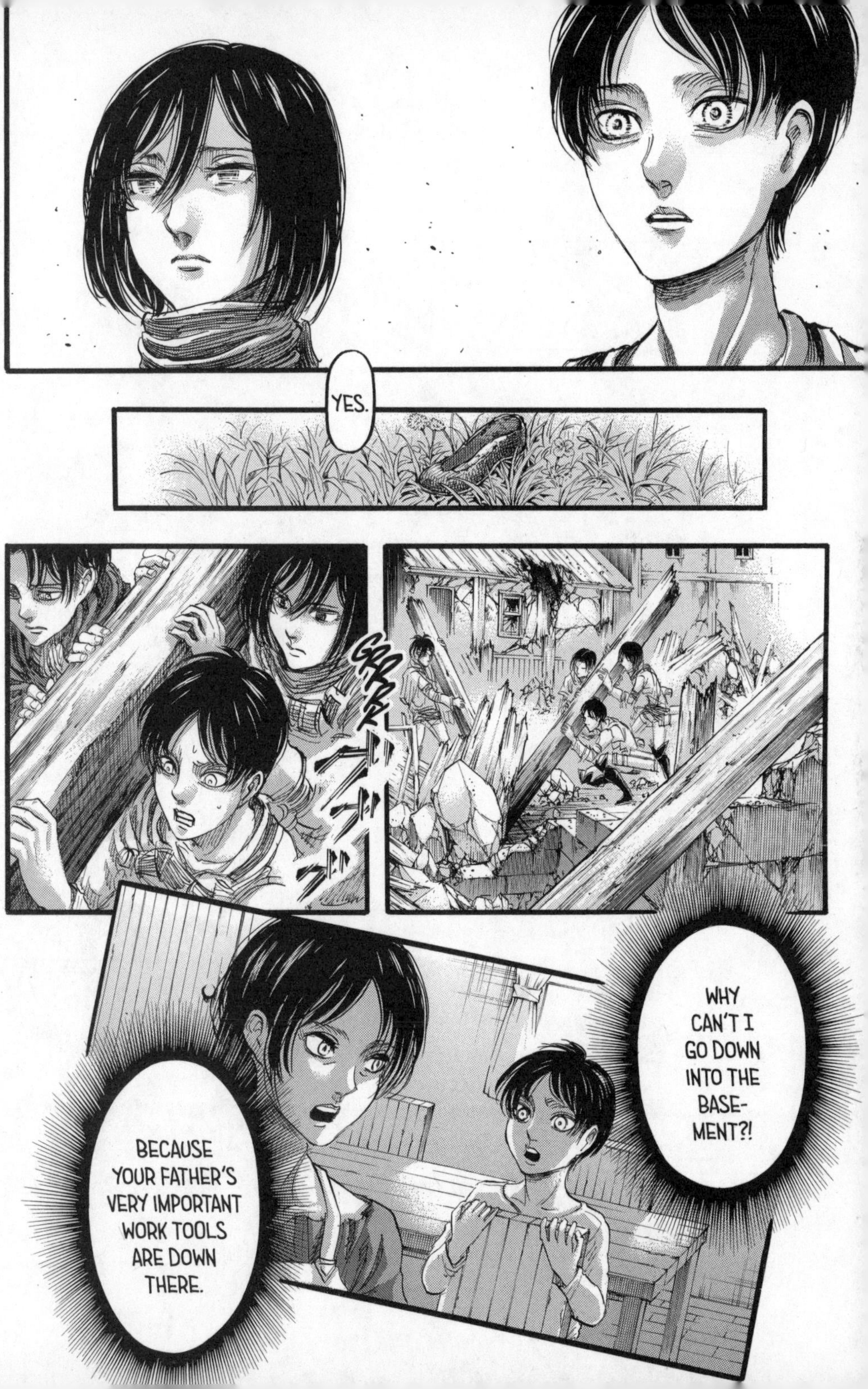
YES.
GRRRR
WHY CAN'T I GO DOWN INTO THE BASEMENT?!
BECAUSE YOUR FATHER'S VERY IMPORTANT WORK TOOLS ARE DOWN THERE.

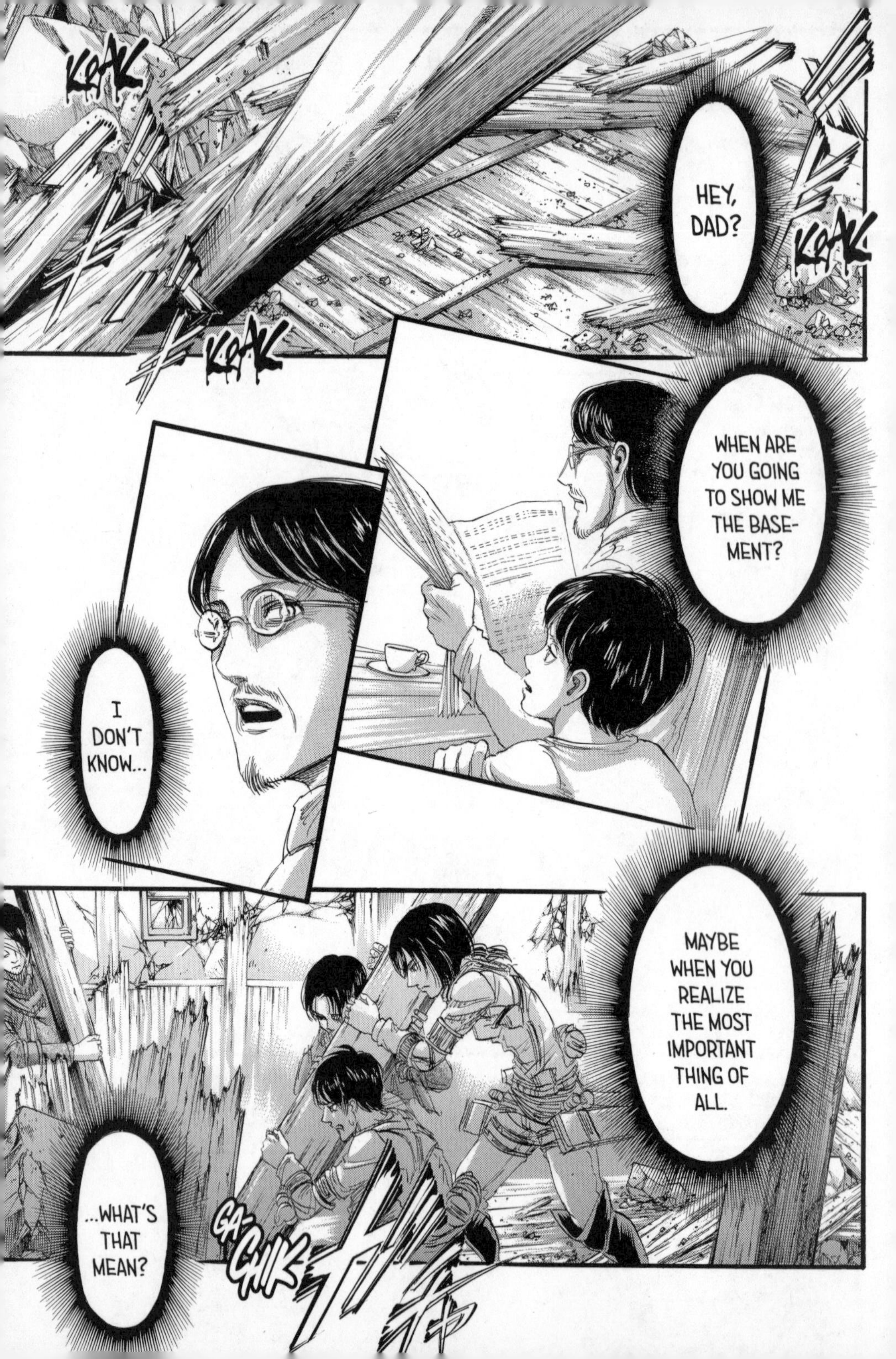
HEY, DAD?
KRAK
KRAK
KRAK
WHEN ARE YOU GOING TO SHOW ME THE BASE-MENT?
I DON'T KNOW...
MAYBE WHEN YOU REALIZE THE MOST IMPORTANT THING OF ALL.
GA-CHIK
...WHAT'S THAT MEAN?

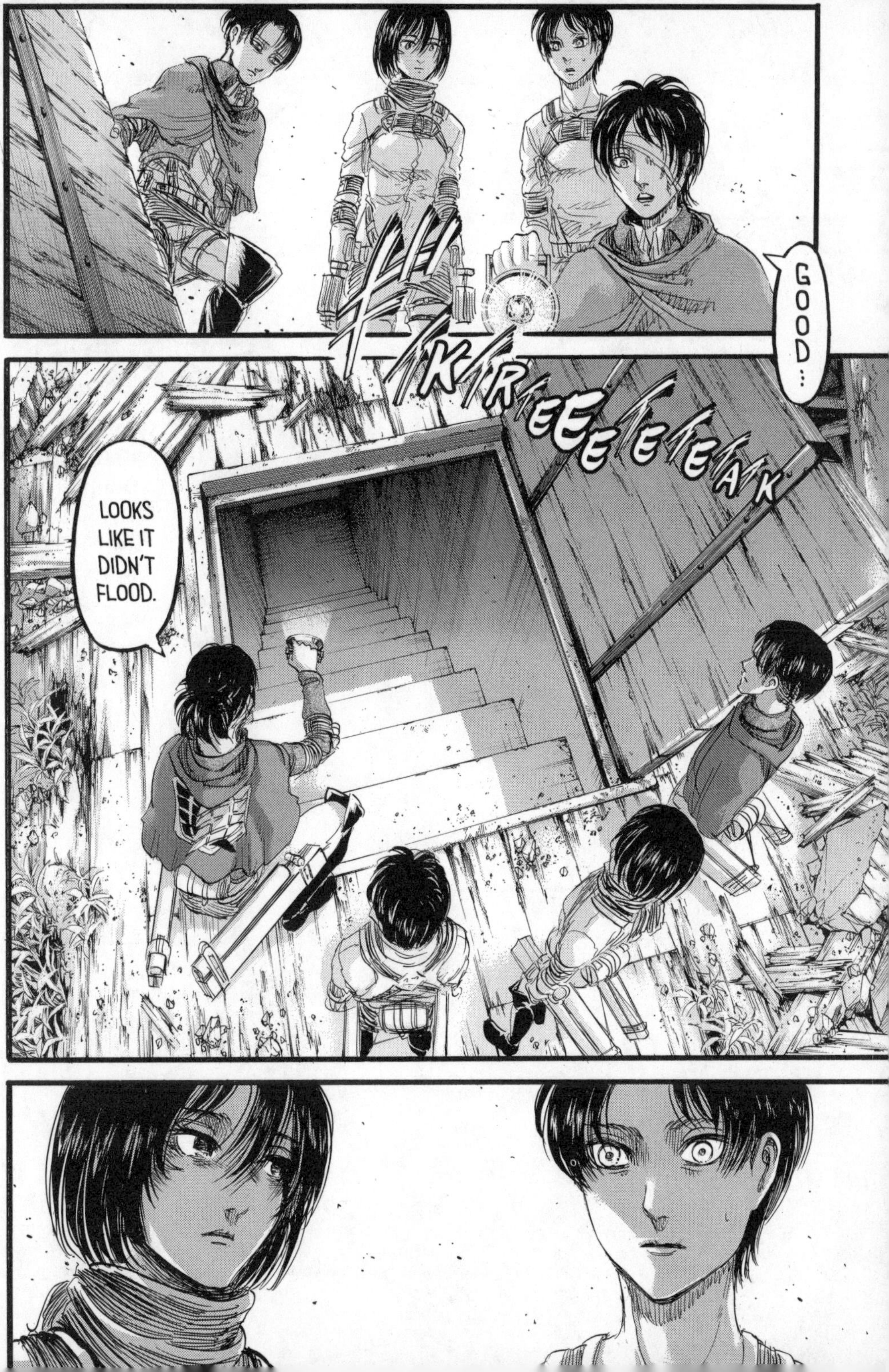
GOOD...
KREEEEEAK
LOOKS LIKE IT DIDN'T FLOOD.

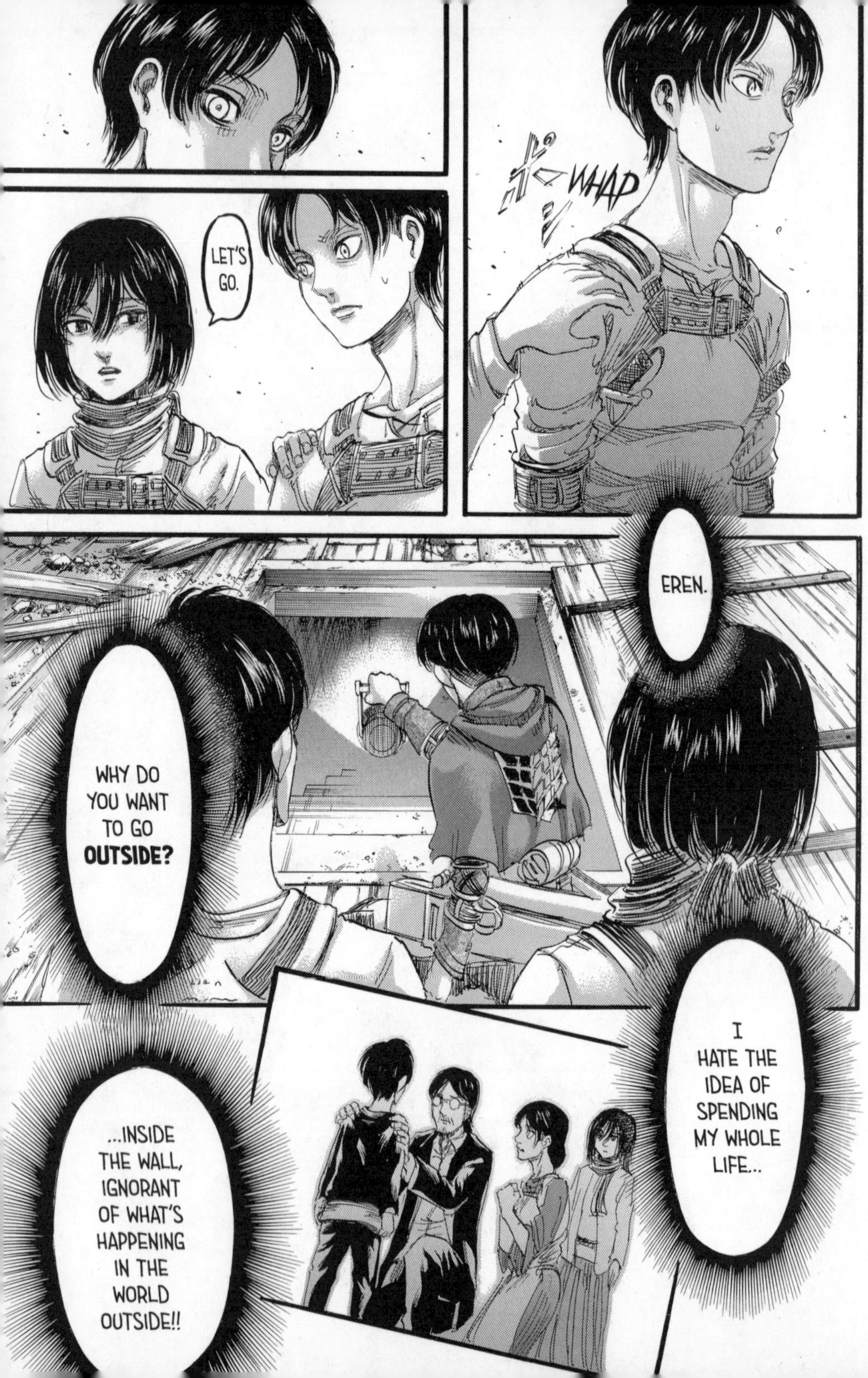
WHAP
LET'S GO.
EREN.
WHY DO YOU WANT TO GO **OUTSIDE?**
I HATE THE IDEA OF SPENDING MY WHOLE LIFE...
...INSIDE THE WALL, IGNORANT OF WHAT'S HAPPENING IN THE WORLD OUTSIDE!!

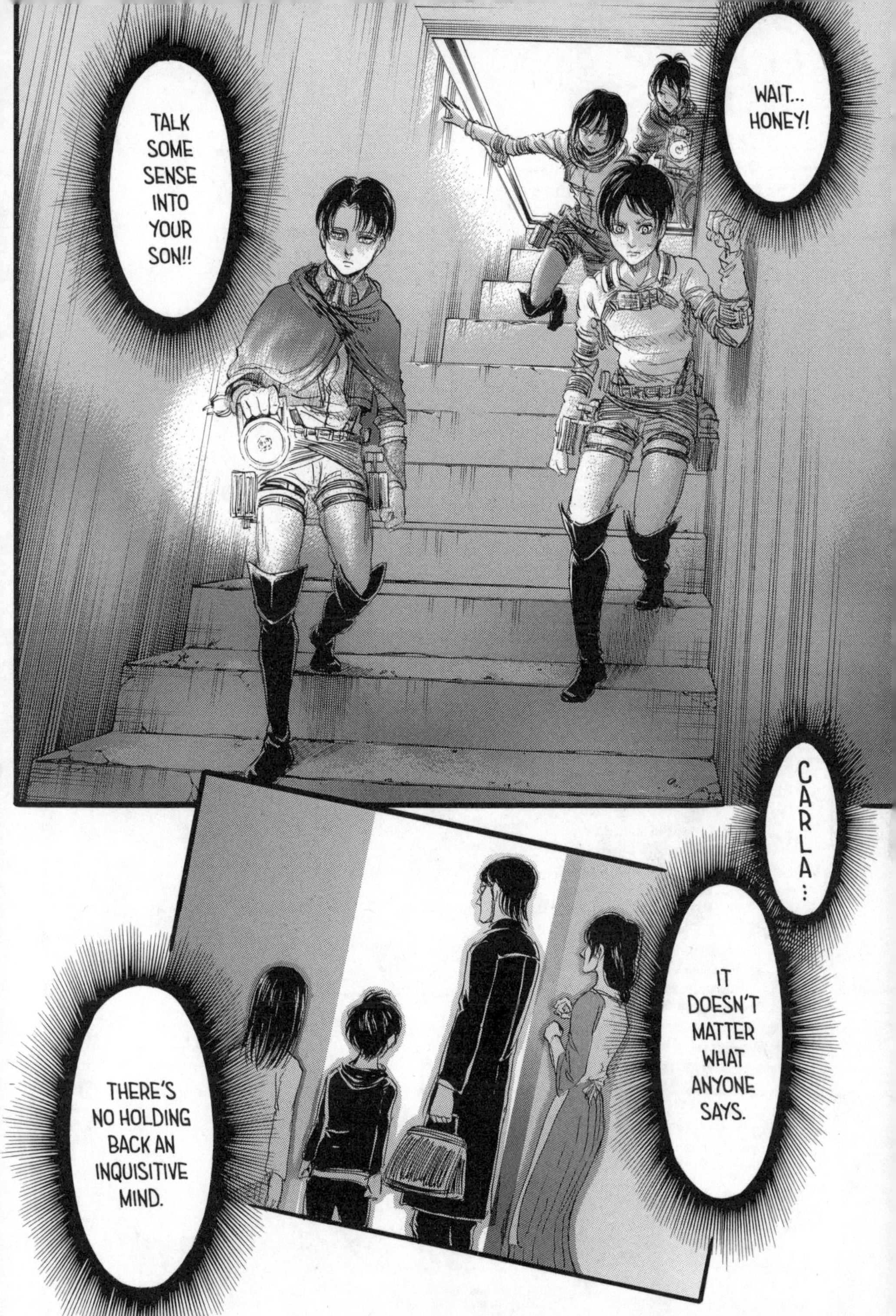
WAIT... HONEY!
TALK SOME SENSE INTO YOUR SON!!
CARLA...
IT DOESN'T MATTER WHAT ANYONE SAYS.
THERE'S NO HOLDING BACK AN INQUISITIVE MIND.

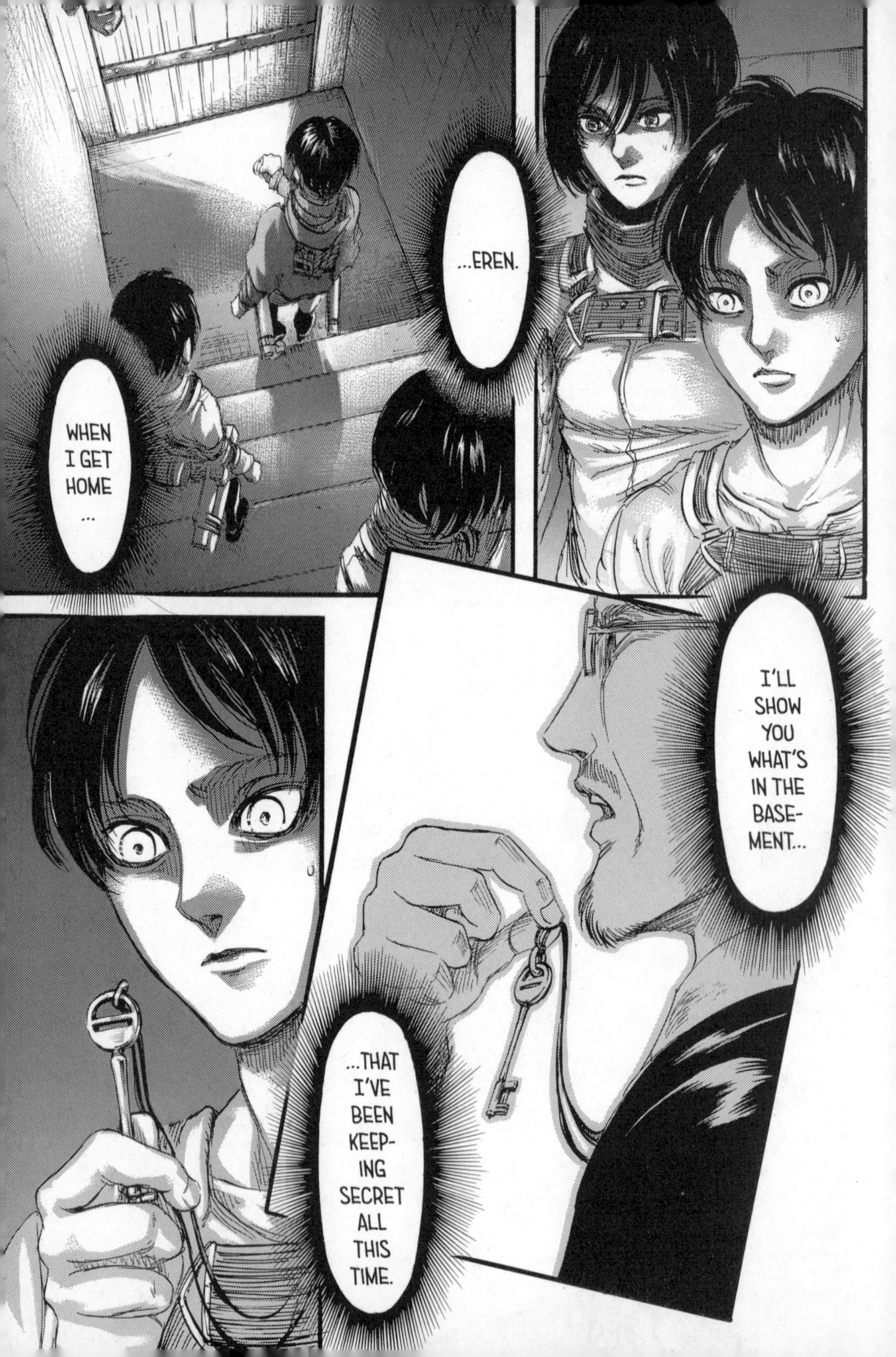
...EREN.
WHEN I GET HOME ...
I'LL SHOW YOU WHAT'S IN THE BASEMENT...
...THAT I'VE BEEN KEEPING SECRET ALL THIS TIME.

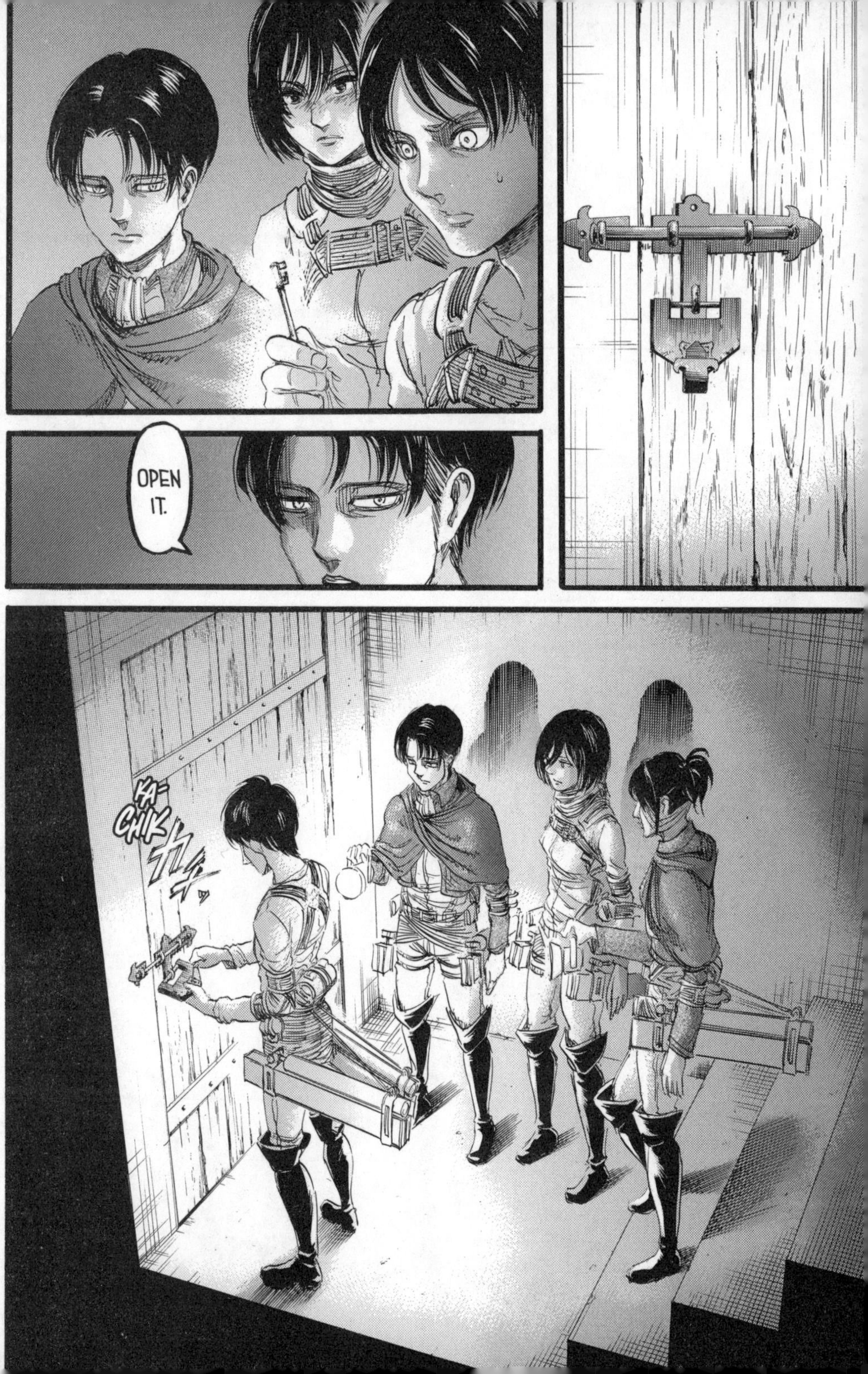
OPEN IT.
KA-CHIK

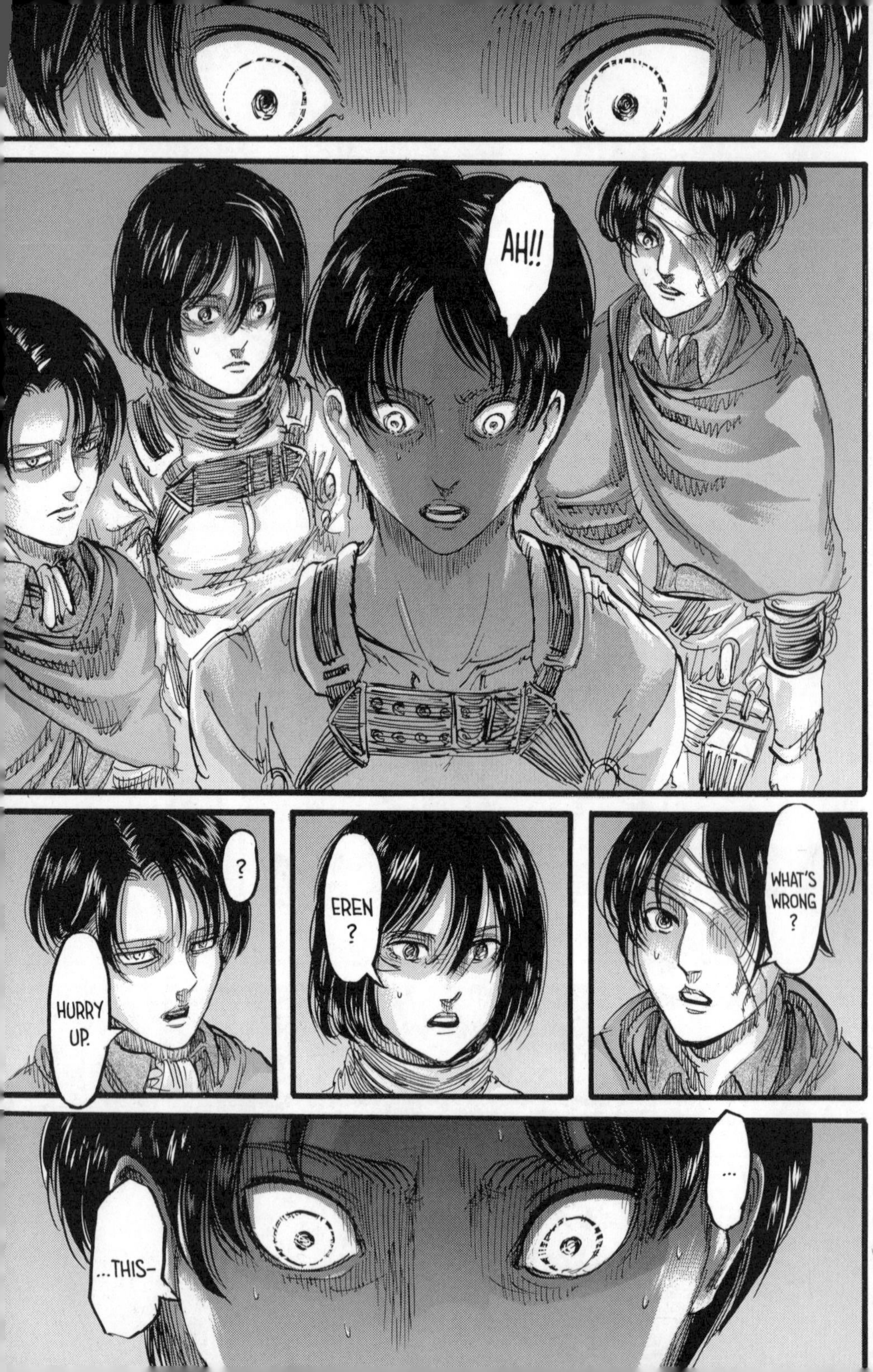
AH!!
WHAT'S WRONG?
EREN?
?
HURRY UP.
...
...THIS-

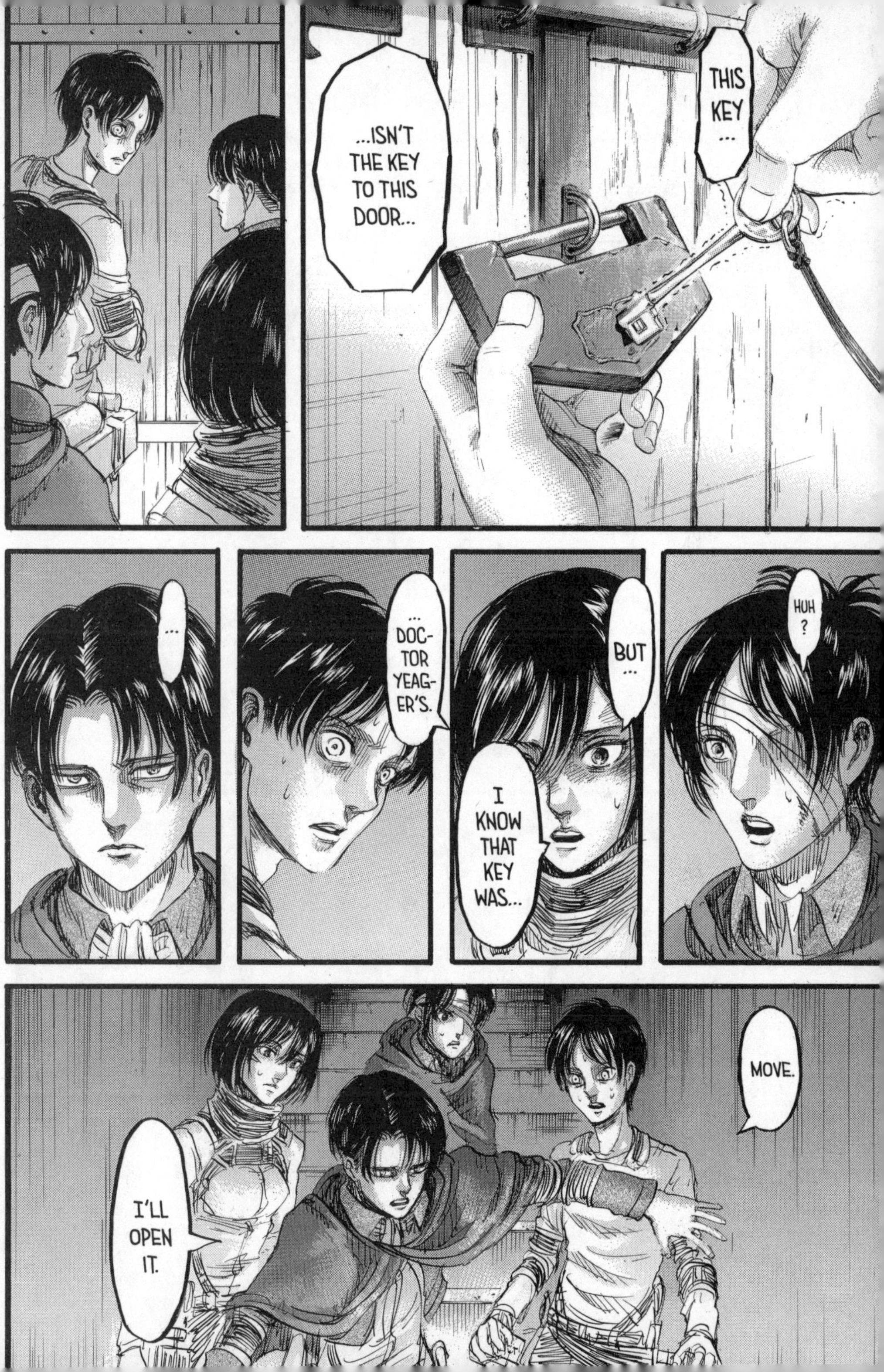
THIS KEY ...
...ISN'T THE KEY TO THIS DOOR...
HUH ?
BUT ...
I KNOW THAT KEY WAS...
... DOC-TOR YEAG-ER'S.
...
MOVE.
I'LL OPEN IT.

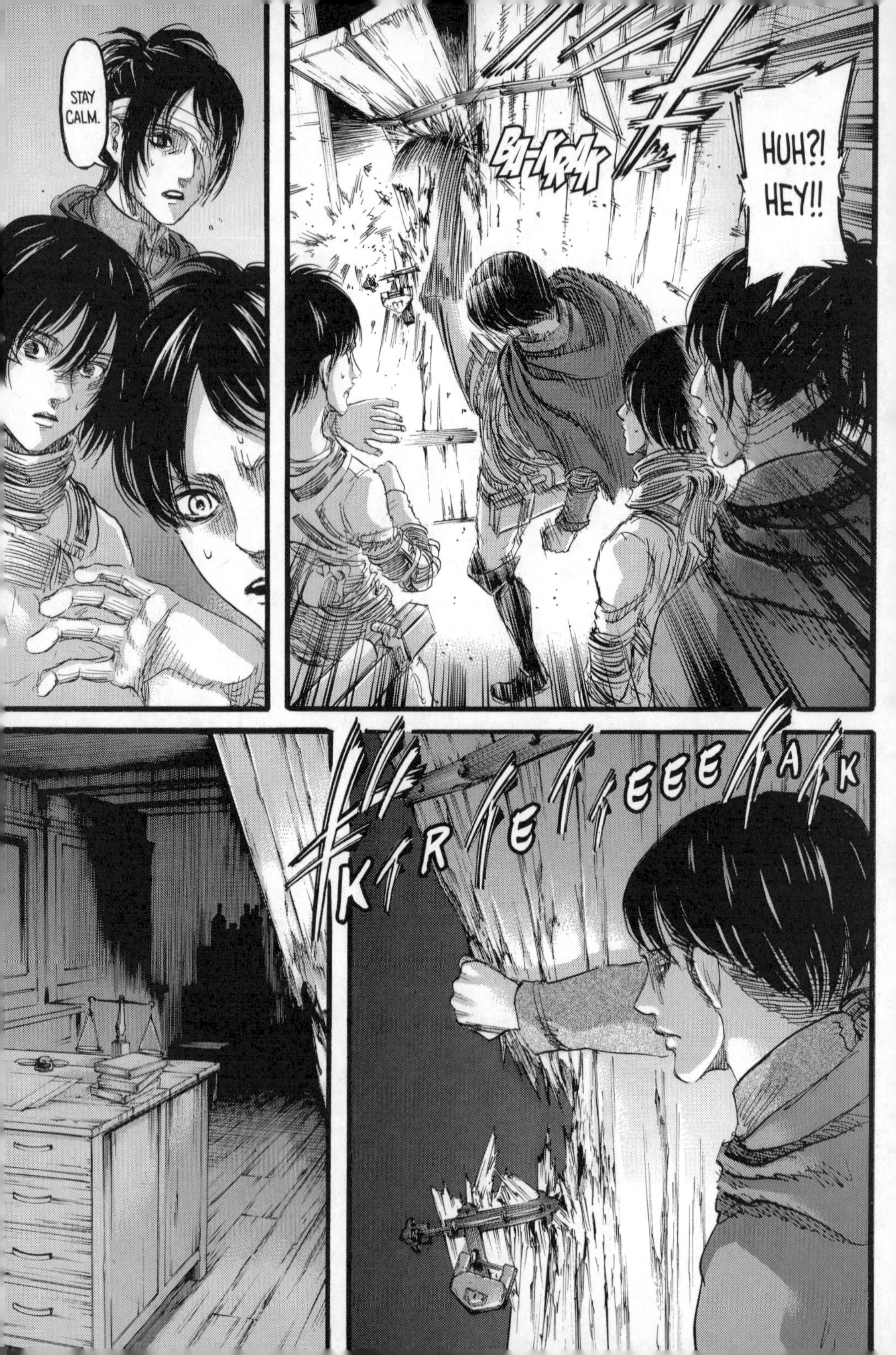
BA-KRAK
HUH?! HEY!!
STAY CALM.
KREEEEAK

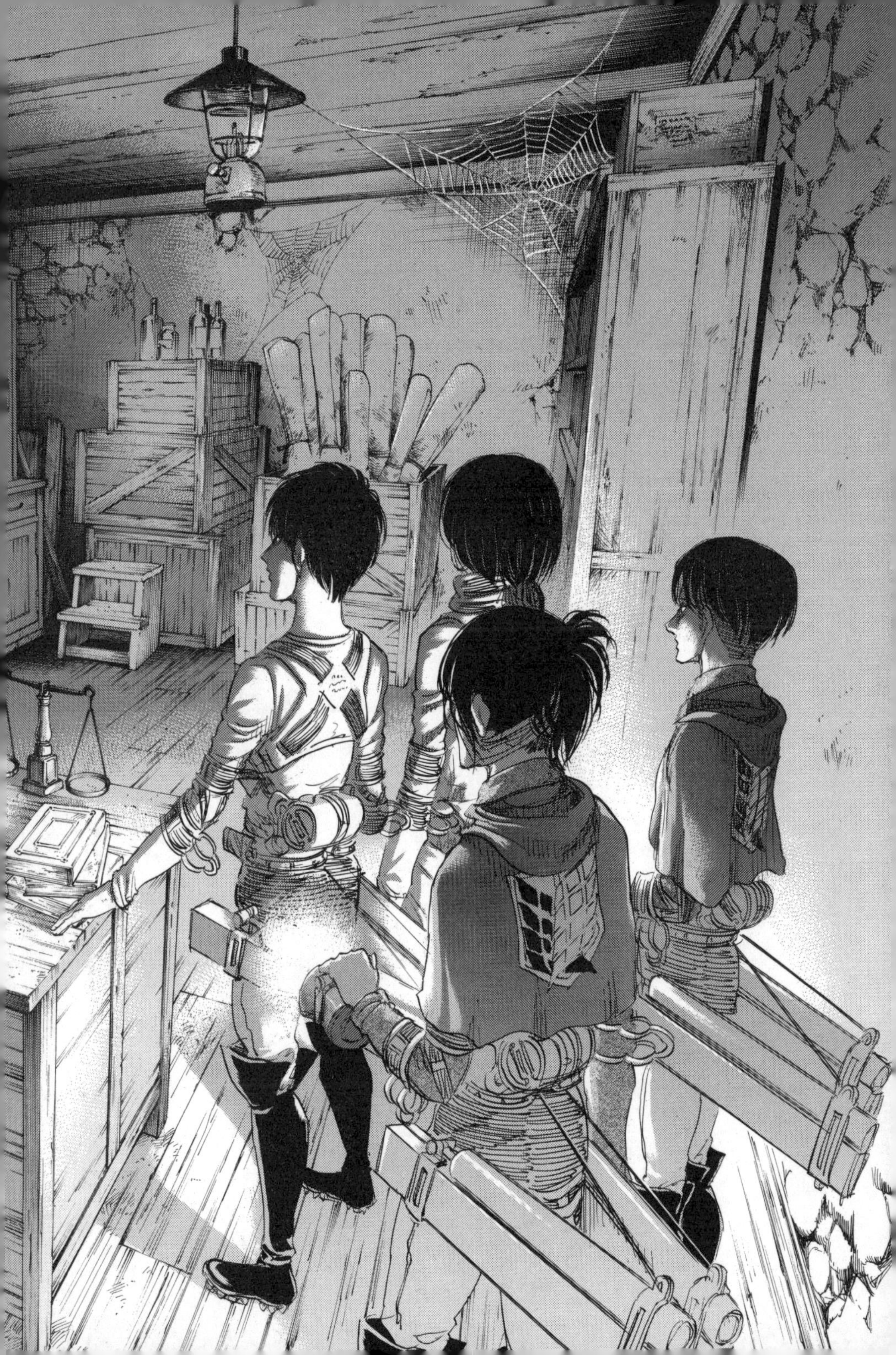

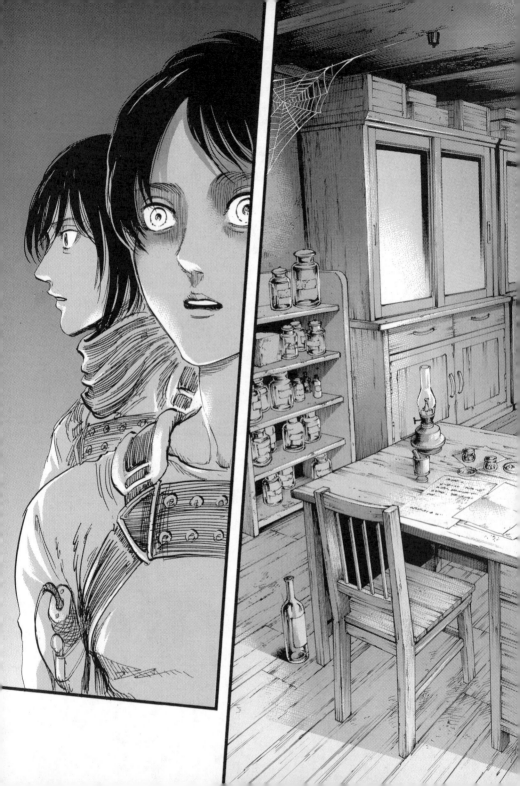

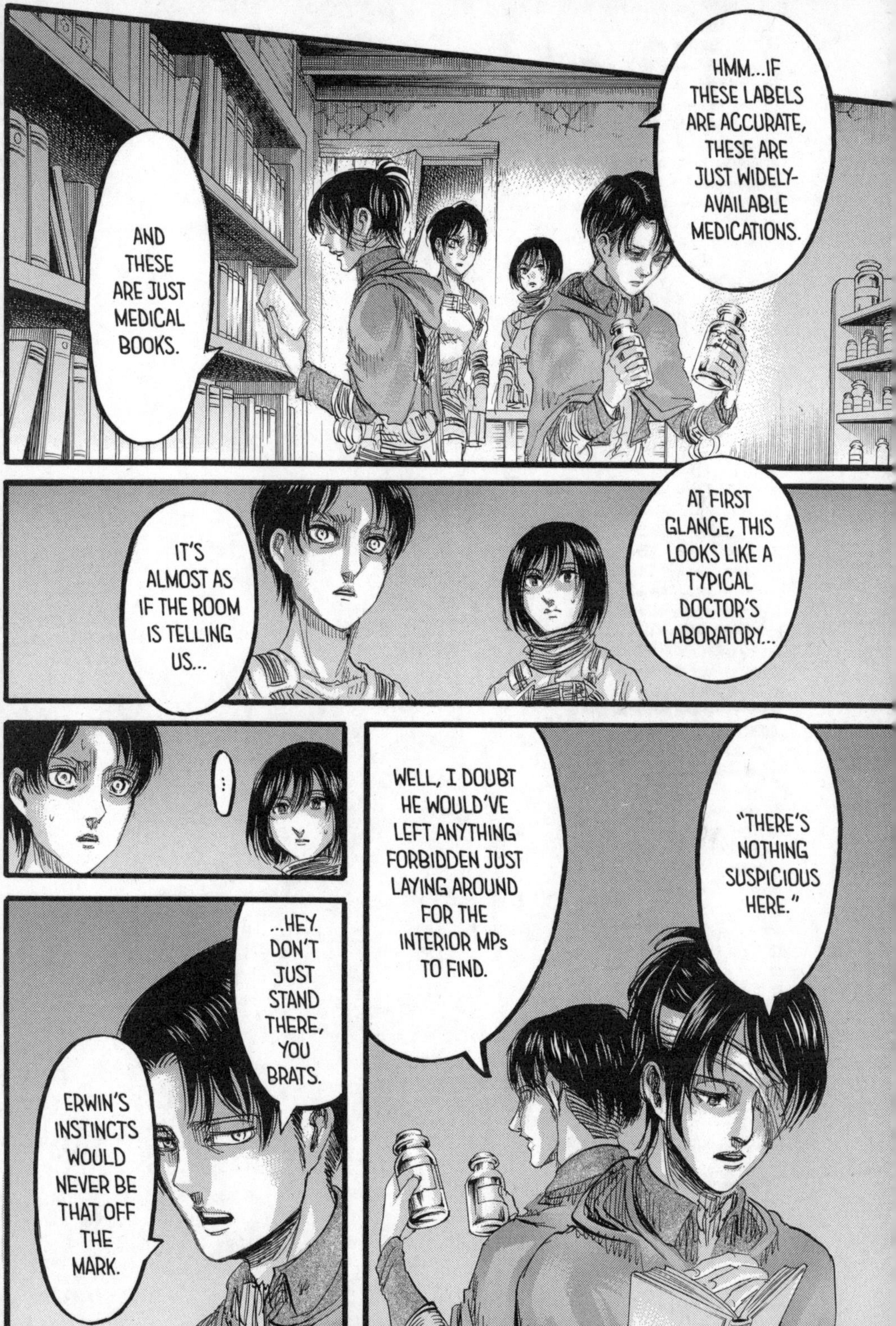
HMM...IF THESE LABELS ARE ACCURATE, THESE ARE JUST WIDELY-AVAILABLE MEDICATIONS.
AND THESE ARE JUST MEDICAL BOOKS.
AT FIRST GLANCE, THIS LOOKS LIKE A TYPICAL DOCTOR'S LABORATORY...
IT'S ALMOST AS IF THE ROOM IS TELLING US...
"THERE'S NOTHING SUSPICIOUS HERE."
WELL, I DOUBT HE WOULD'VE LEFT ANYTHING FORBIDDEN JUST LAYING AROUND FOR THE INTERIOR MPs TO FIND.
...
...HEY. DON'T JUST STAND THERE, YOU BRATS.
ERWIN'S INSTINCTS WOULD NEVER BE THAT OFF THE MARK.

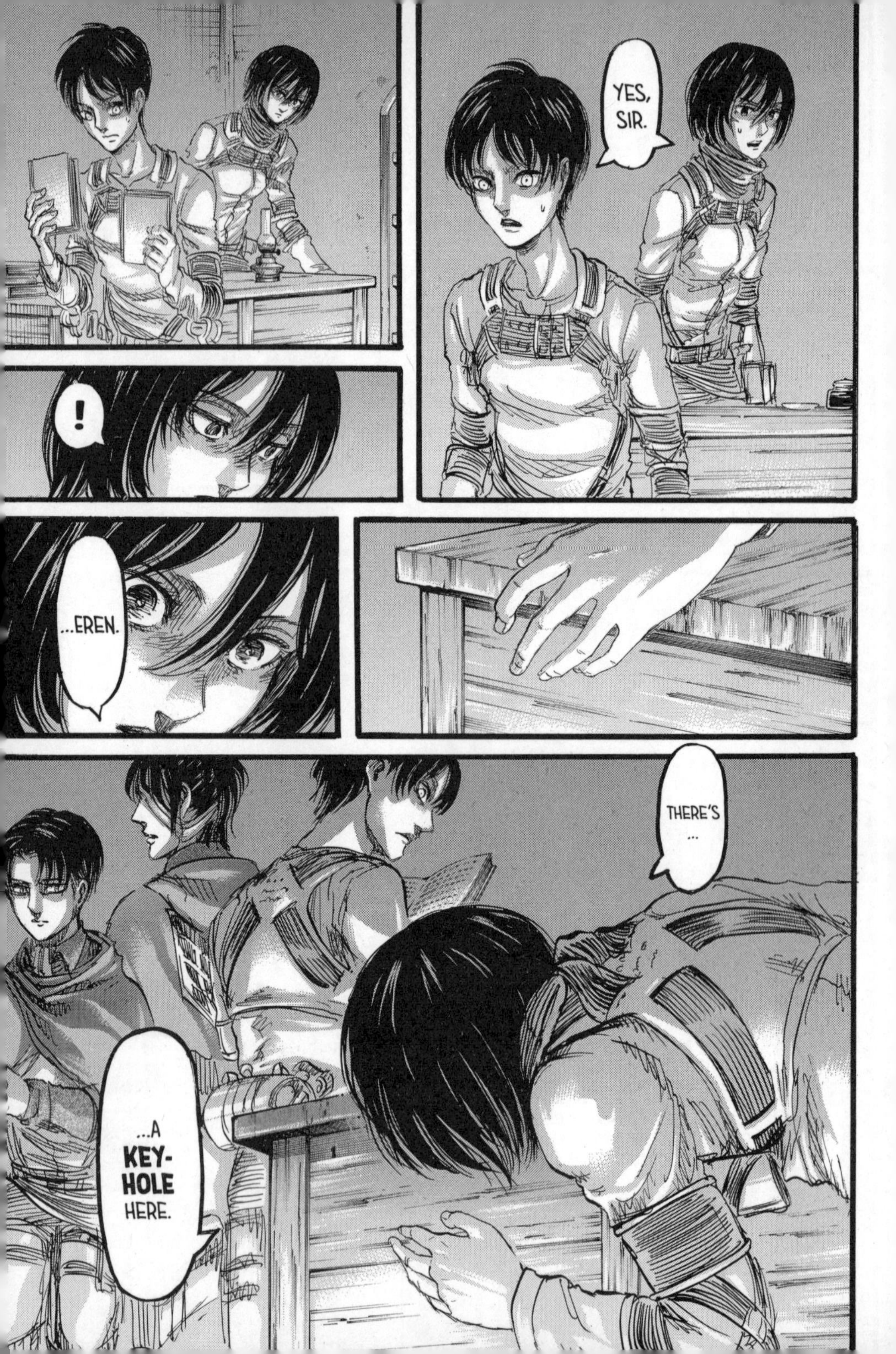
YES, SIR.
!
...EREN.
THERE'S ...
...A KEY-HOLE HERE.

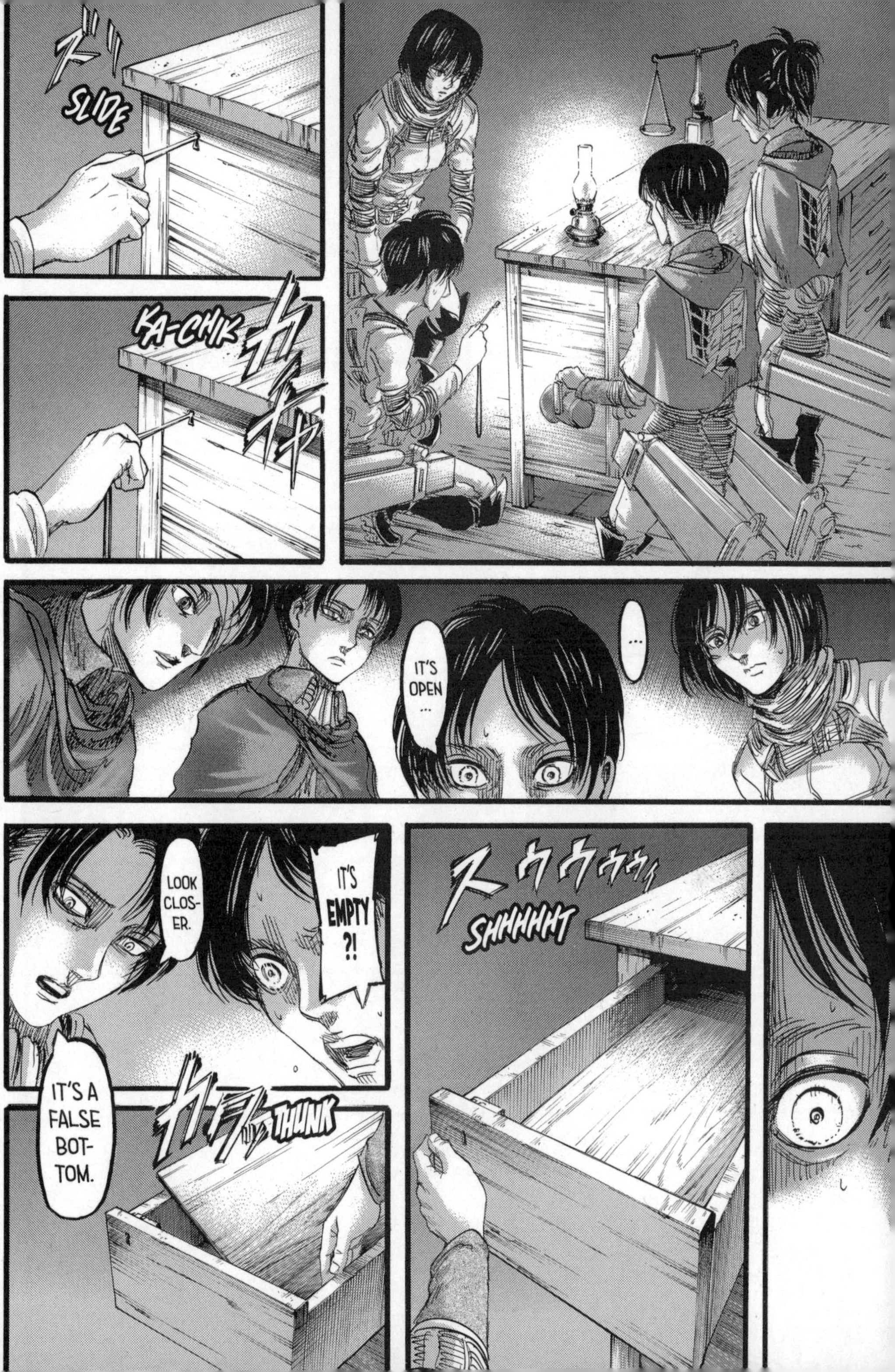

ズリ
SLIDE
KA-CHIK
カチャ
...
IT'S OPEN ...
スゥゥゥゥ
SHHHHHT
IT'S EMPTY?!
LOOK CLOSER.
IT'S A FALSE BOTTOM.
ガコッ
THUNK

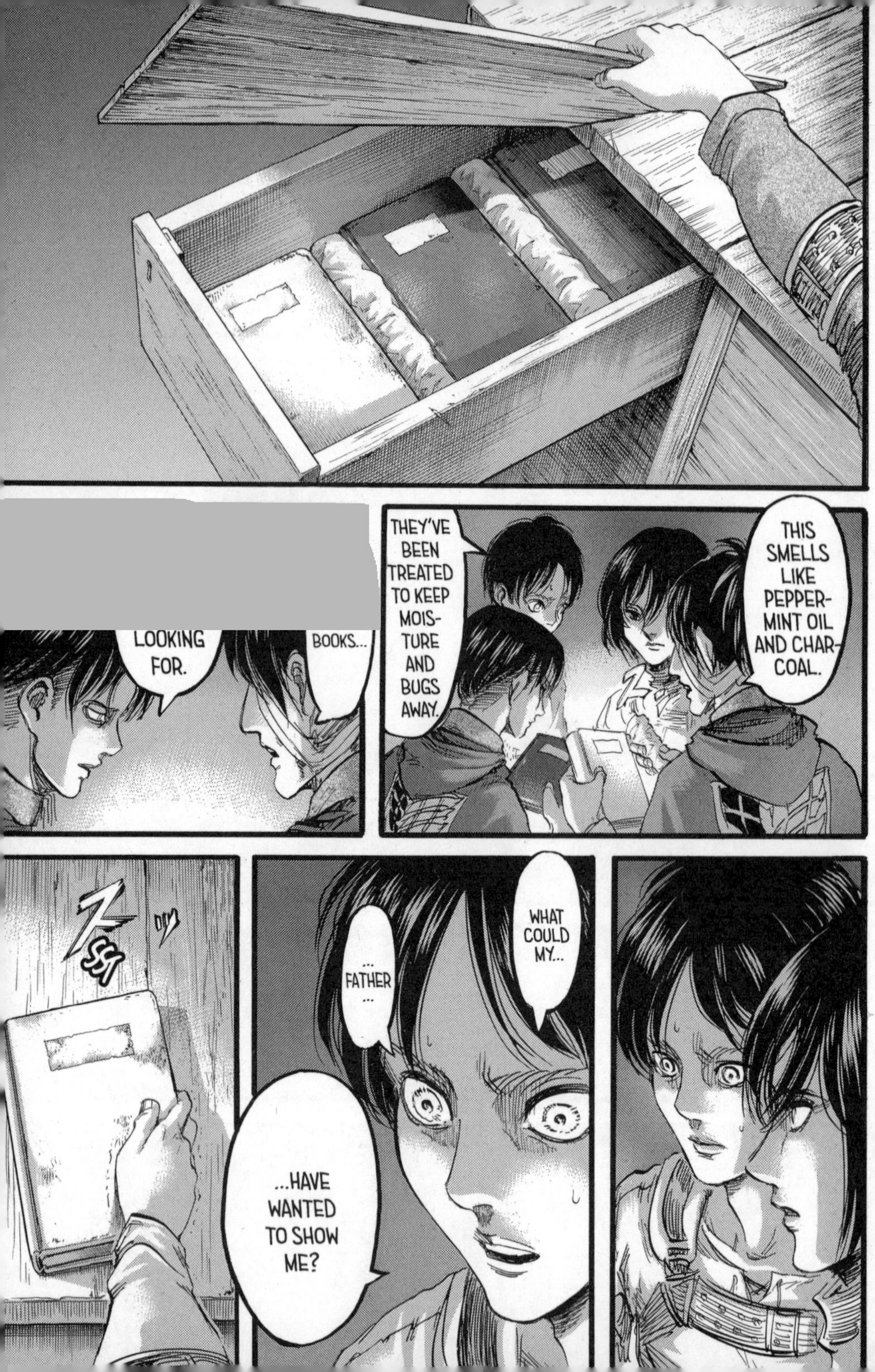
THIS SMELLS LIKE PEPPERMINT OIL AND CHARCOAL.
THEY'VE BEEN TREATED TO KEEP MOISTURE AND BUGS AWAY.
BOOKS...
LOOKING FOR.
WHAT COULD MY...
... FATHER ...
...HAVE WANTED TO SHOW ME?

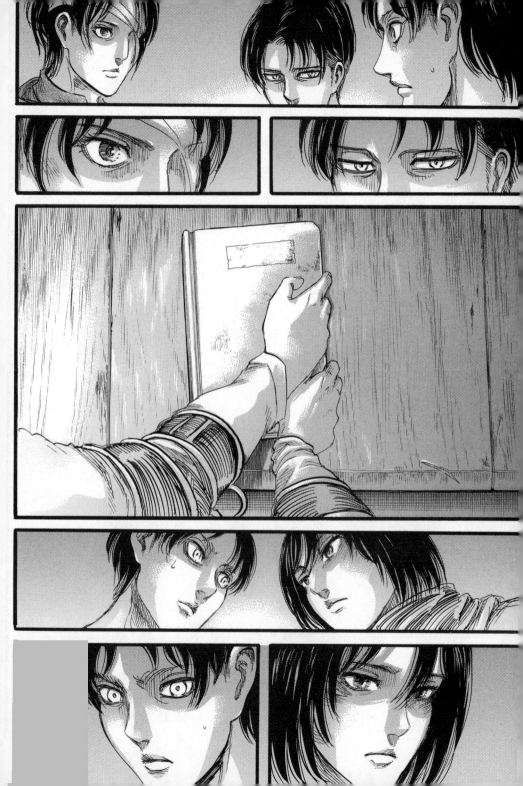

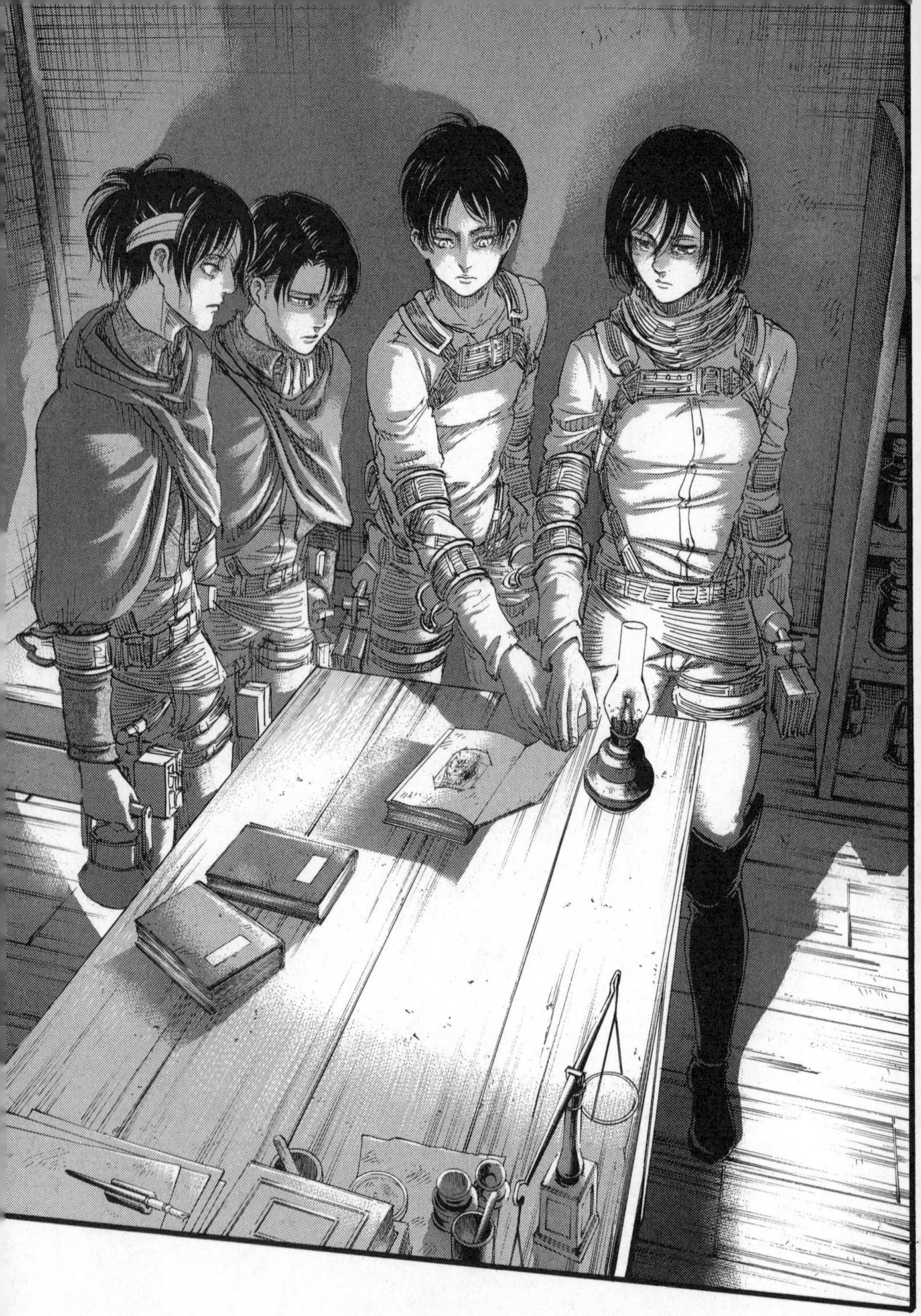

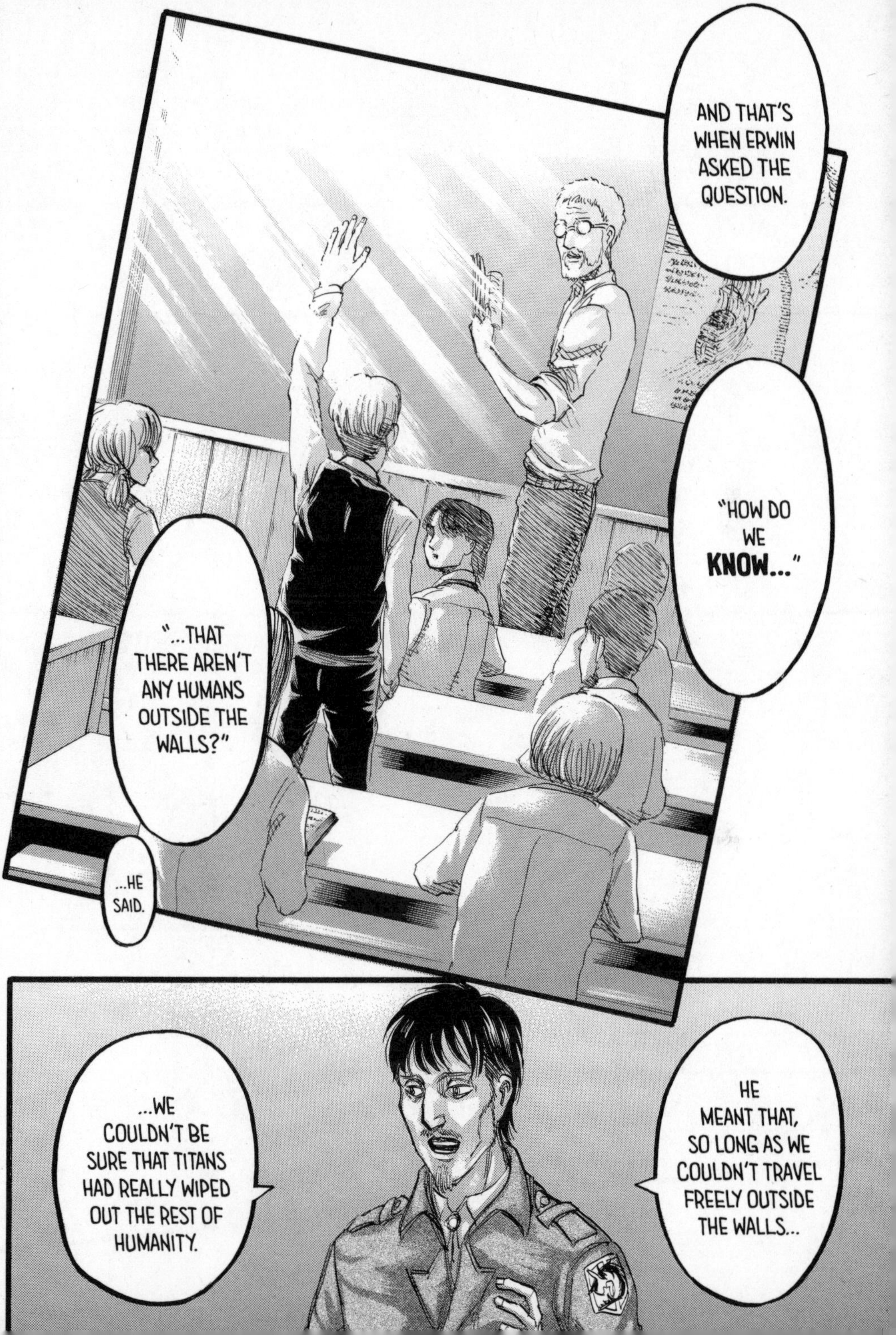
AND THAT'S WHEN ERWIN ASKED THE QUESTION.
"HOW DO WE **KNOW...**"
"...THAT THERE AREN'T ANY HUMANS OUTSIDE THE WALLS?"
...HE SAID.
HE MEANT THAT, SO LONG AS WE COULDN'T TRAVEL FREELY OUTSIDE THE WALLS...
...WE COULDN'T BE SURE THAT TITANS HAD REALLY WIPED OUT THE REST OF HUMANITY.

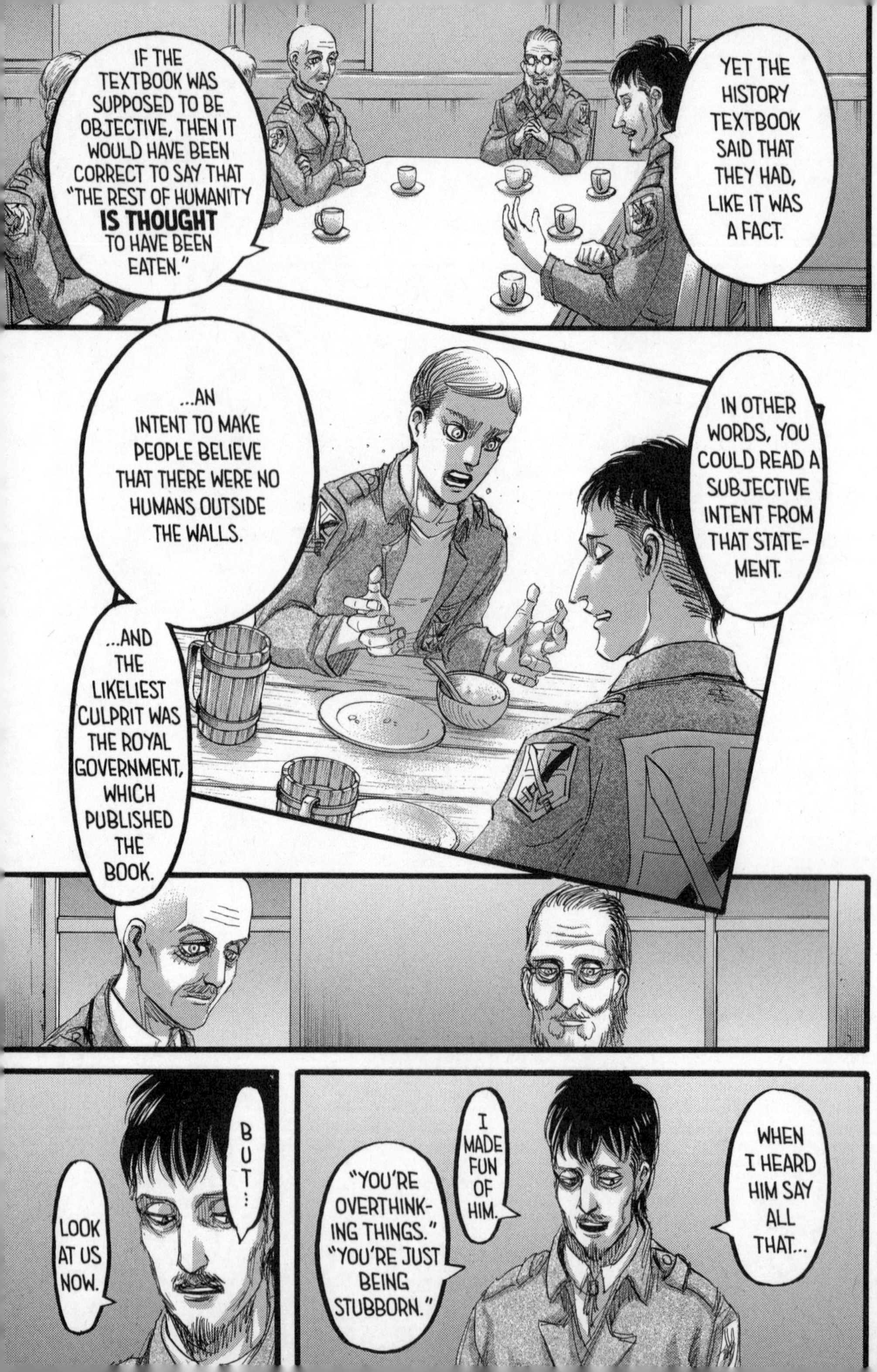
YET THE HISTORY TEXTBOOK SAID THAT THEY HAD, LIKE IT WAS A FACT.
IF THE TEXTBOOK WAS SUPPOSED TO BE OBJECTIVE, THEN IT WOULD HAVE BEEN CORRECT TO SAY THAT "THE REST OF HUMANITY **IS THOUGHT** TO HAVE BEEN EATEN."
IN OTHER WORDS, YOU COULD READ A SUBJECTIVE INTENT FROM THAT STATEMENT.
...AN INTENT TO MAKE PEOPLE BELIEVE THAT THERE WERE NO HUMANS OUTSIDE THE WALLS.
...AND THE LIKELIEST CULPRIT WAS THE ROYAL GOVERNMENT, WHICH PUBLISHED THE BOOK.
WHEN I HEARD HIM SAY ALL THAT...
I MADE FUN OF HIM.
"YOU'RE OVERTHINKING THINGS." "YOU'RE JUST BEING STUBBORN."
BUT...
LOOK AT US NOW.

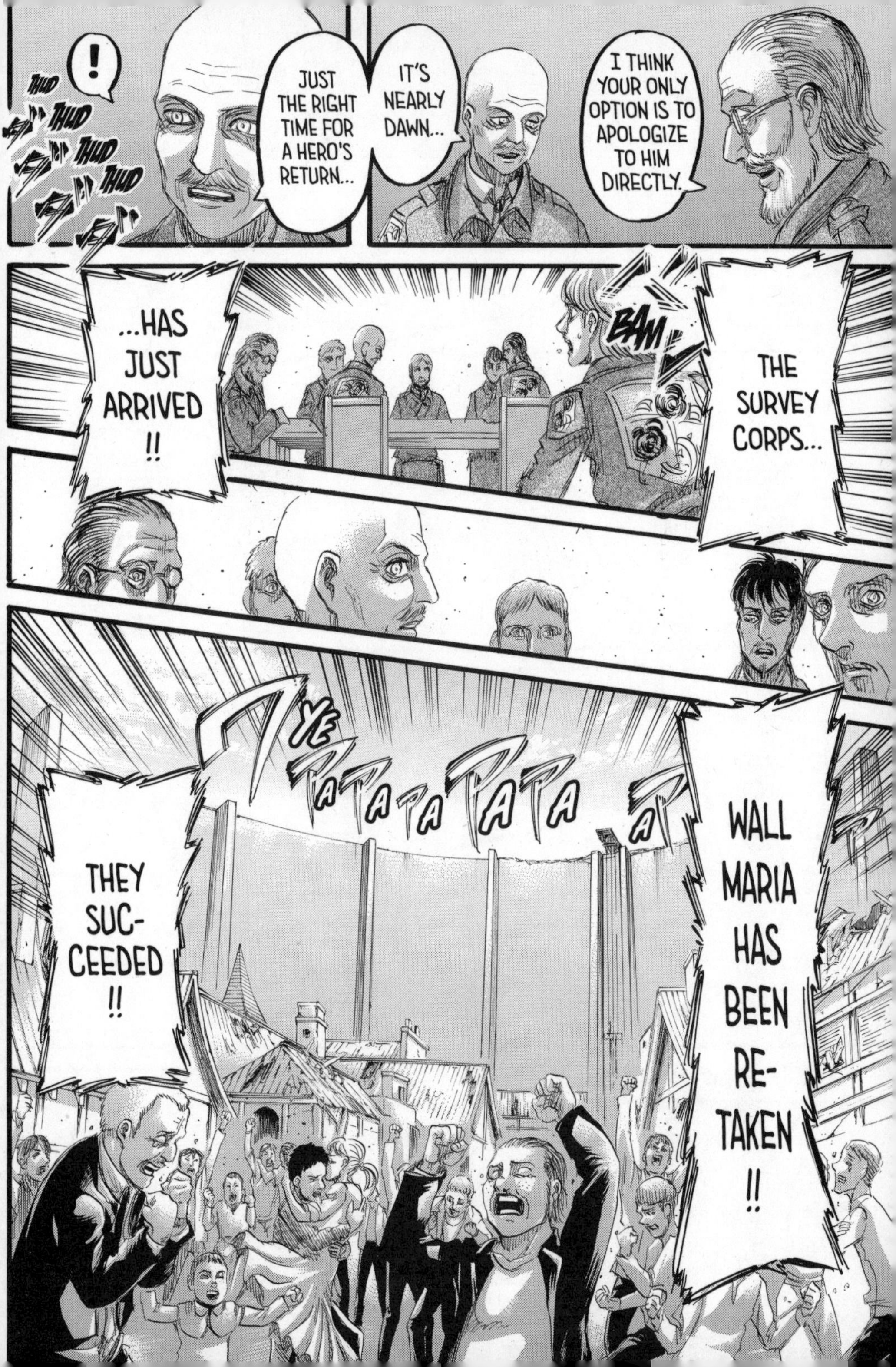
I THINK YOUR ONLY OPTION IS TO APOLOGIZE TO HIM DIRECTLY.
IT'S NEARLY DAWN...
JUST THE RIGHT TIME FOR A HERO'S RETURN...
!
THUD THUD THUD THUD
THE SURVEY CORPS...
BAM
...HAS JUST ARRIVED!!
YEAAAAAAAA
WALL MARIA HAS BEEN RE-TAKEN!!
THEY SUC-CEEDED!!

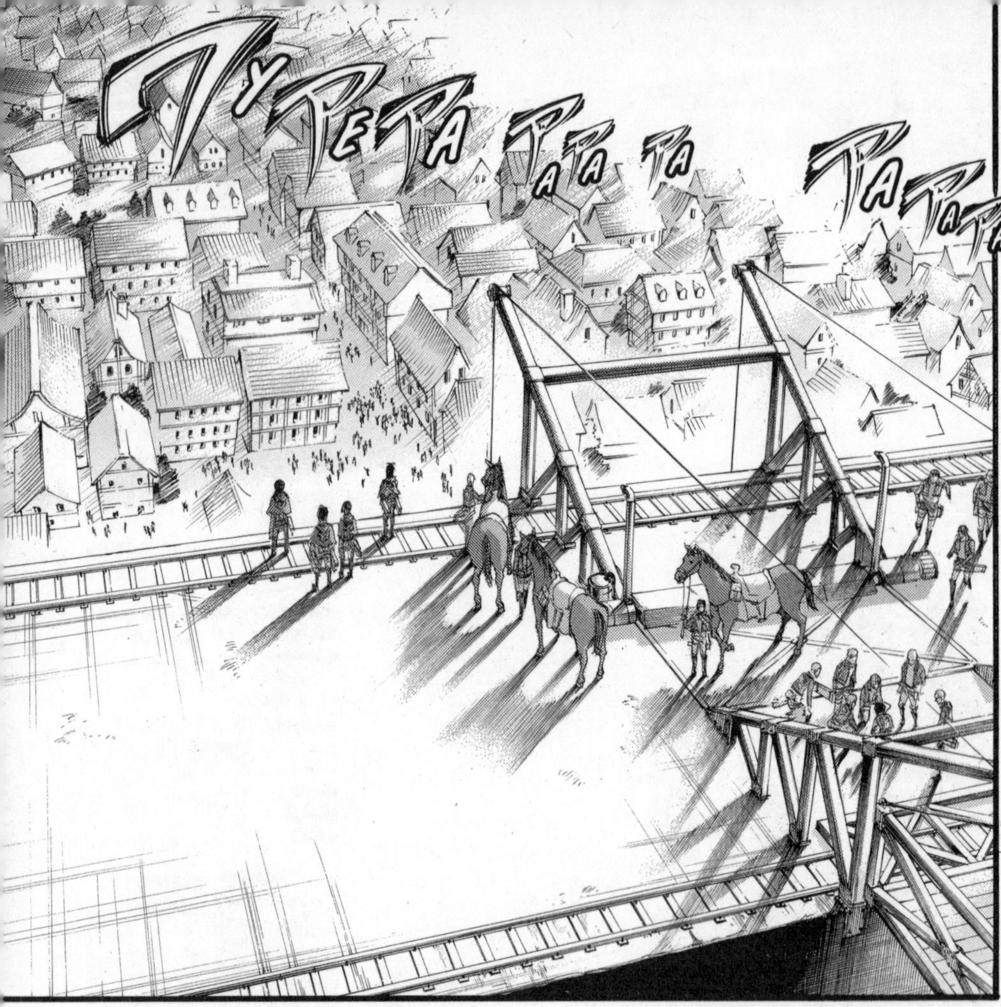
PEPA PAPA PA PAPAPA
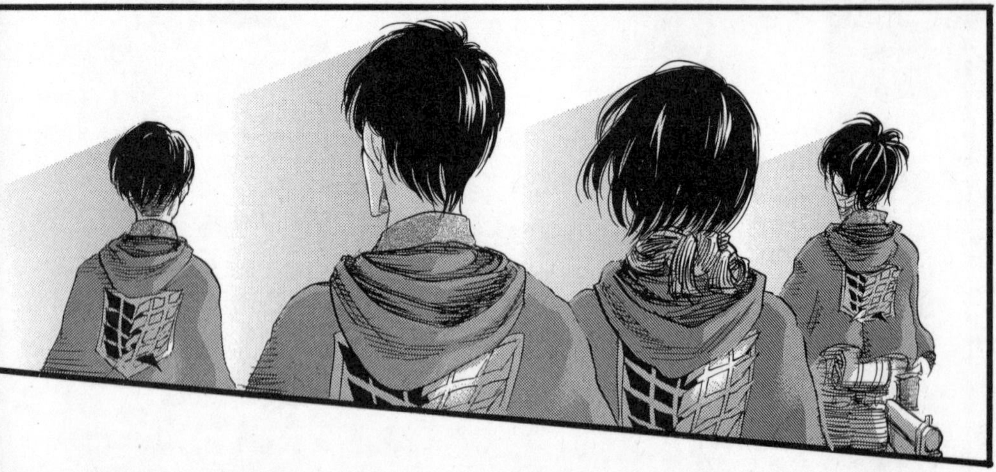

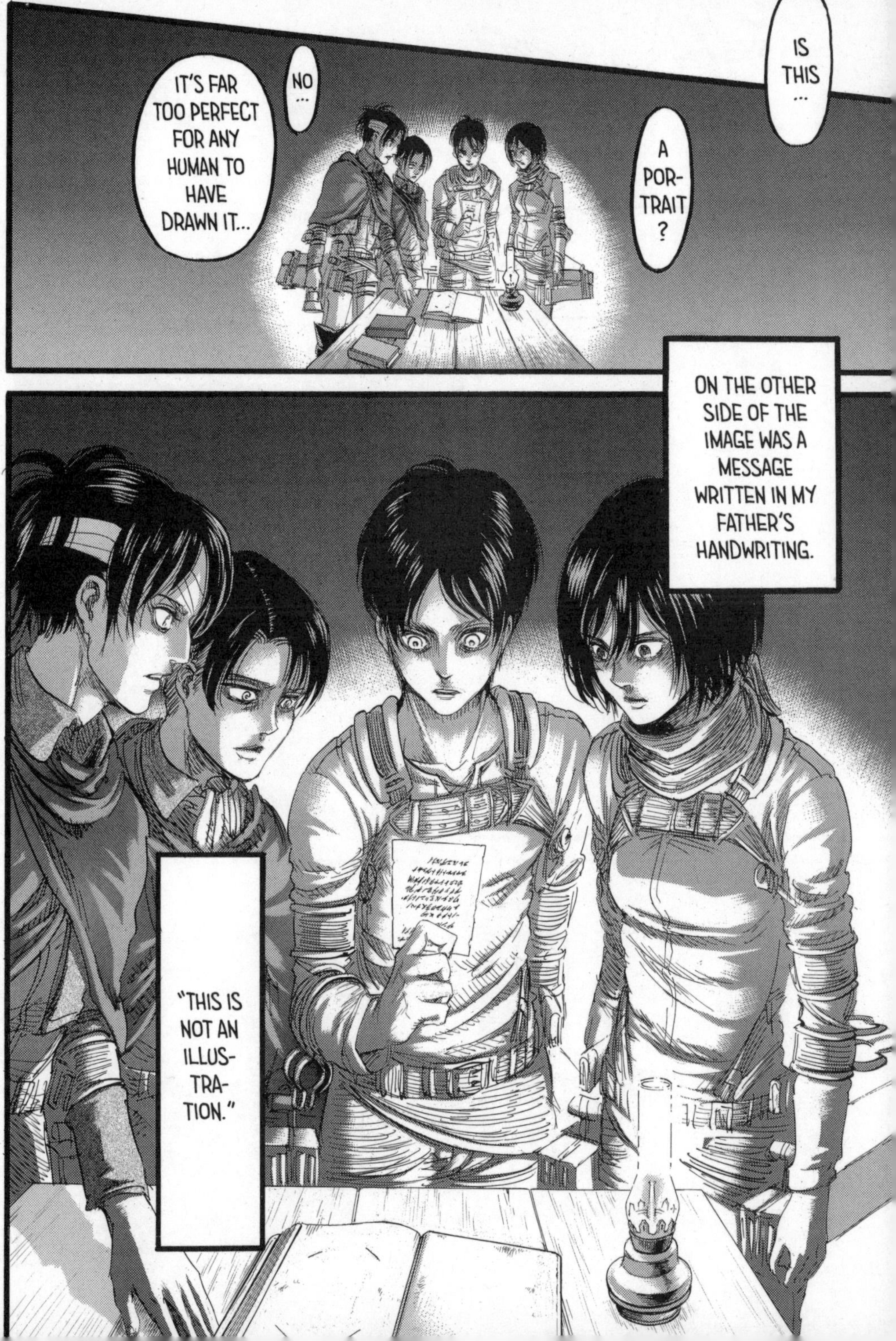
IS THIS ...
A POR-TRAIT?
NO ...
IT'S FAR TOO PERFECT FOR ANY HUMAN TO HAVE DRAWN IT...
ON THE OTHER SIDE OF THE IMAGE WAS A MESSAGE WRITTEN IN MY FATHER'S HANDWRITING.
"THIS IS NOT AN ILLUS-TRA-TION."

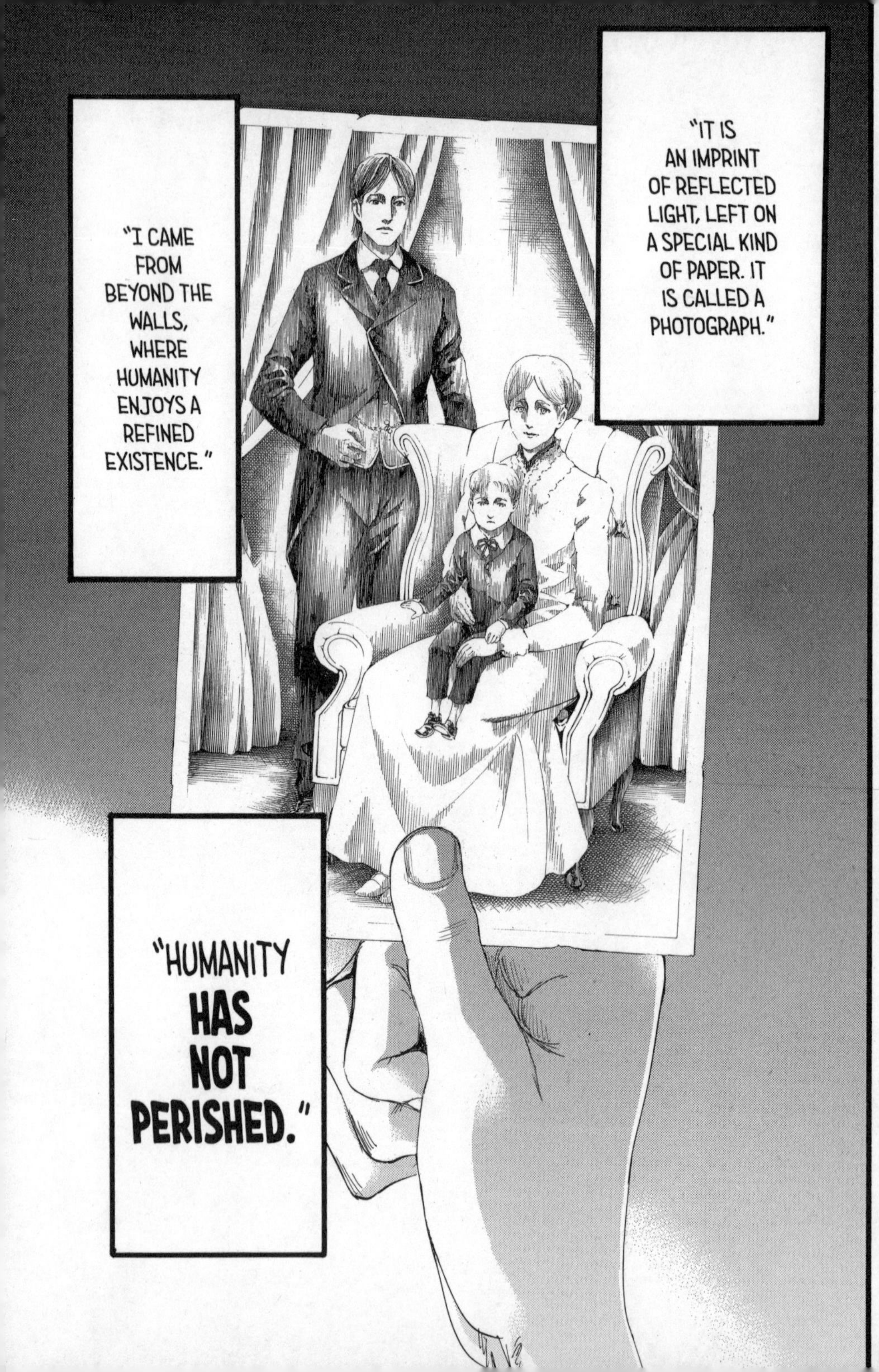
"IT IS AN IMPRINT OF REFLECTED LIGHT, LEFT ON A SPECIAL KIND OF PAPER. IT IS CALLED A PHOTOGRAPH."
"I CAME FROM BEYOND THE WALLS, WHERE HUMANITY ENJOYS A REFINED EXISTENCE."
"HUMANITY HAS NOT PERISHED."

ATTACK ON TITAN

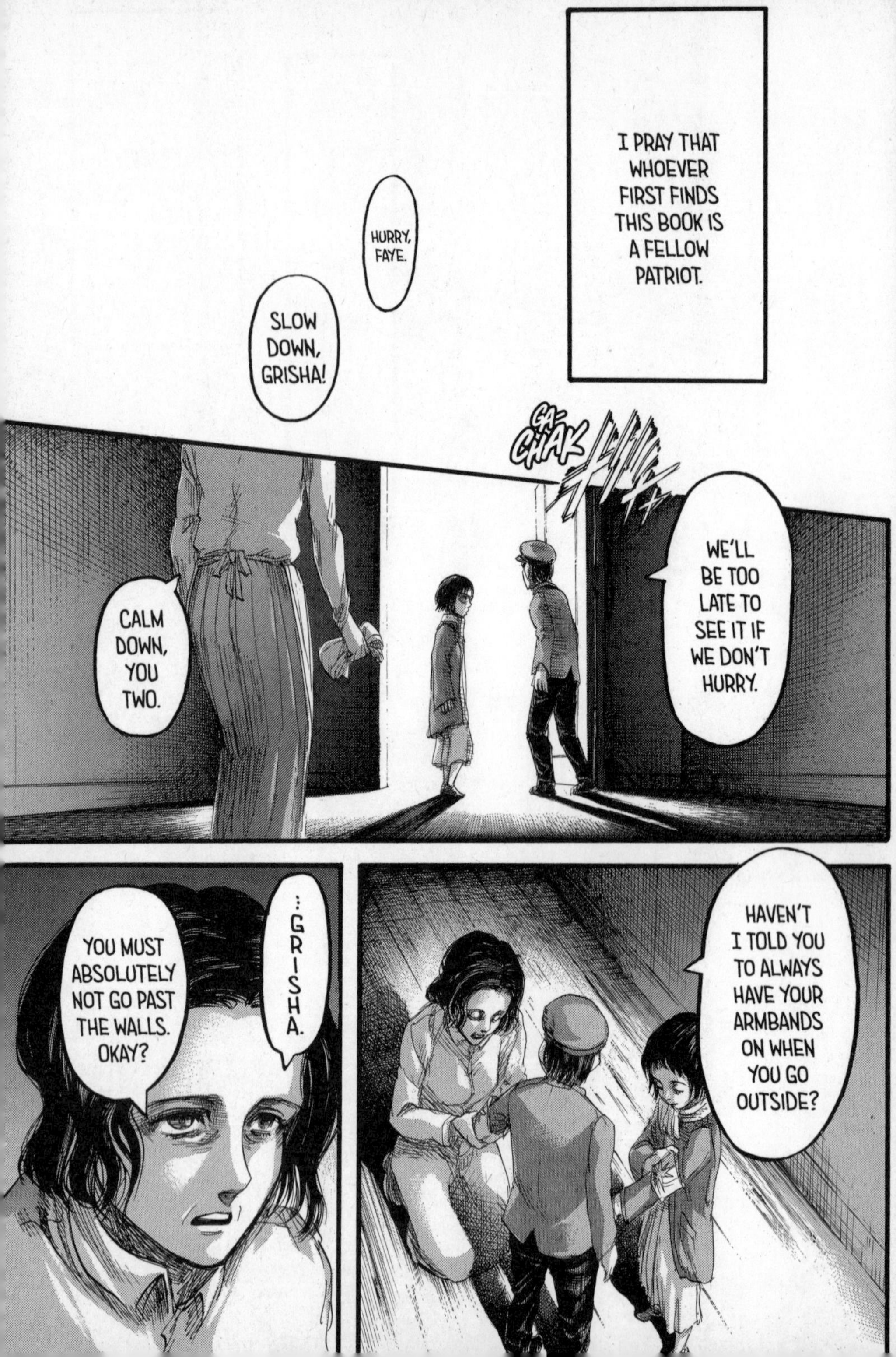
I PRAY THAT WHOEVER FIRST FINDS THIS BOOK IS A FELLOW PATRIOT.
HURRY, FAYE.
SLOW DOWN, GRISHA!
GA-CHAK
WE'LL BE TOO LATE TO SEE IT IF WE DON'T HURRY.
CALM DOWN, YOU TWO.
HAVEN'T I TOLD YOU TO ALWAYS HAVE YOUR ARMBANDS ON WHEN YOU GO OUTSIDE?
...GRISHA.
YOU MUST ABSOLUTELY NOT GO PAST THE WALLS. OKAY?

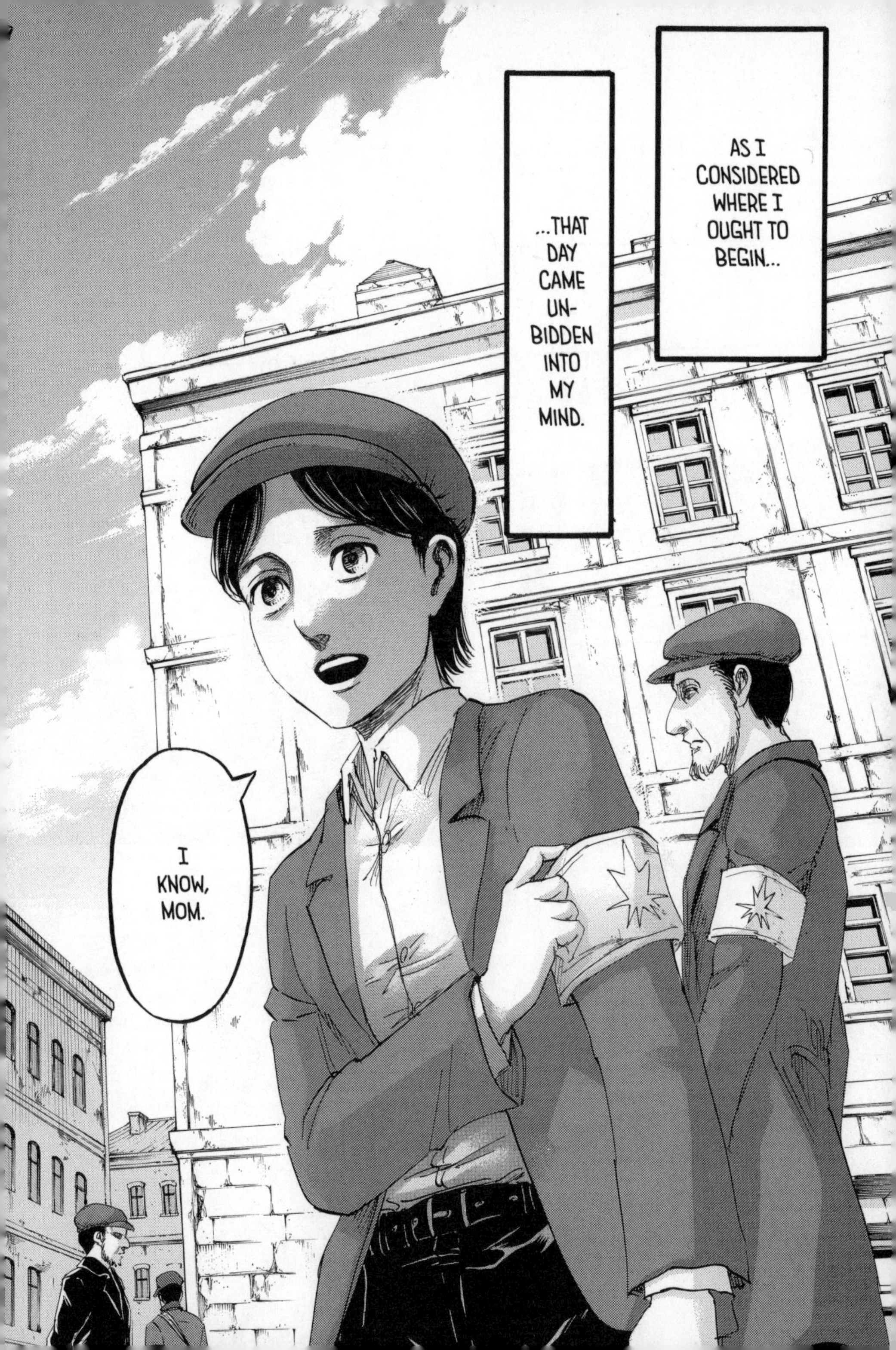
AS I CONSIDERED WHERE I OUGHT TO BEGIN...
...THAT DAY CAME UN-BIDDEN INTO MY MIND.
I KNOW, MOM.

Episode 86: That Day

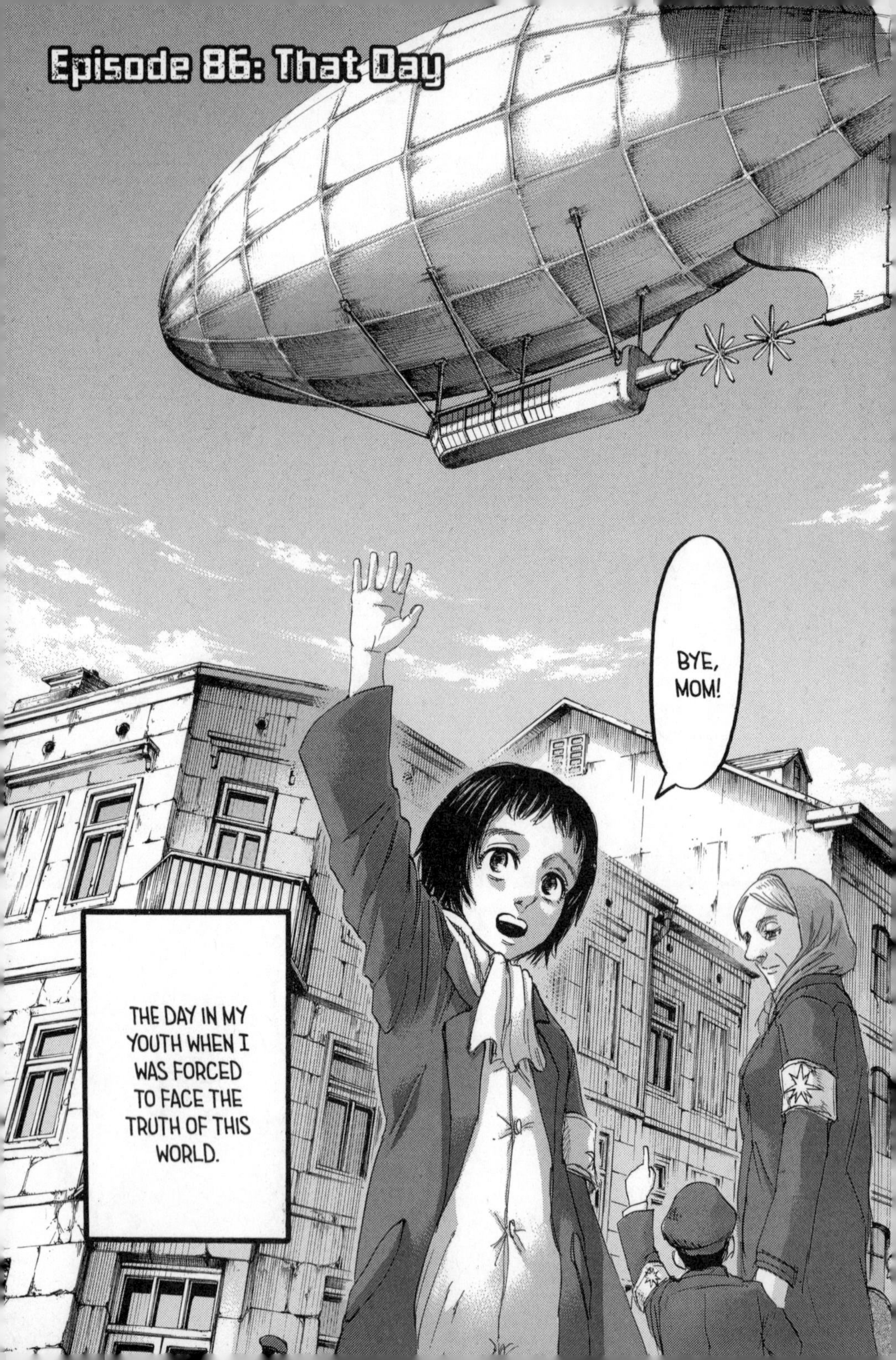
BYE, MOM!
THE DAY IN MY YOUTH WHEN I WAS FORCED TO FACE THE TRUTH OF THIS WORLD.

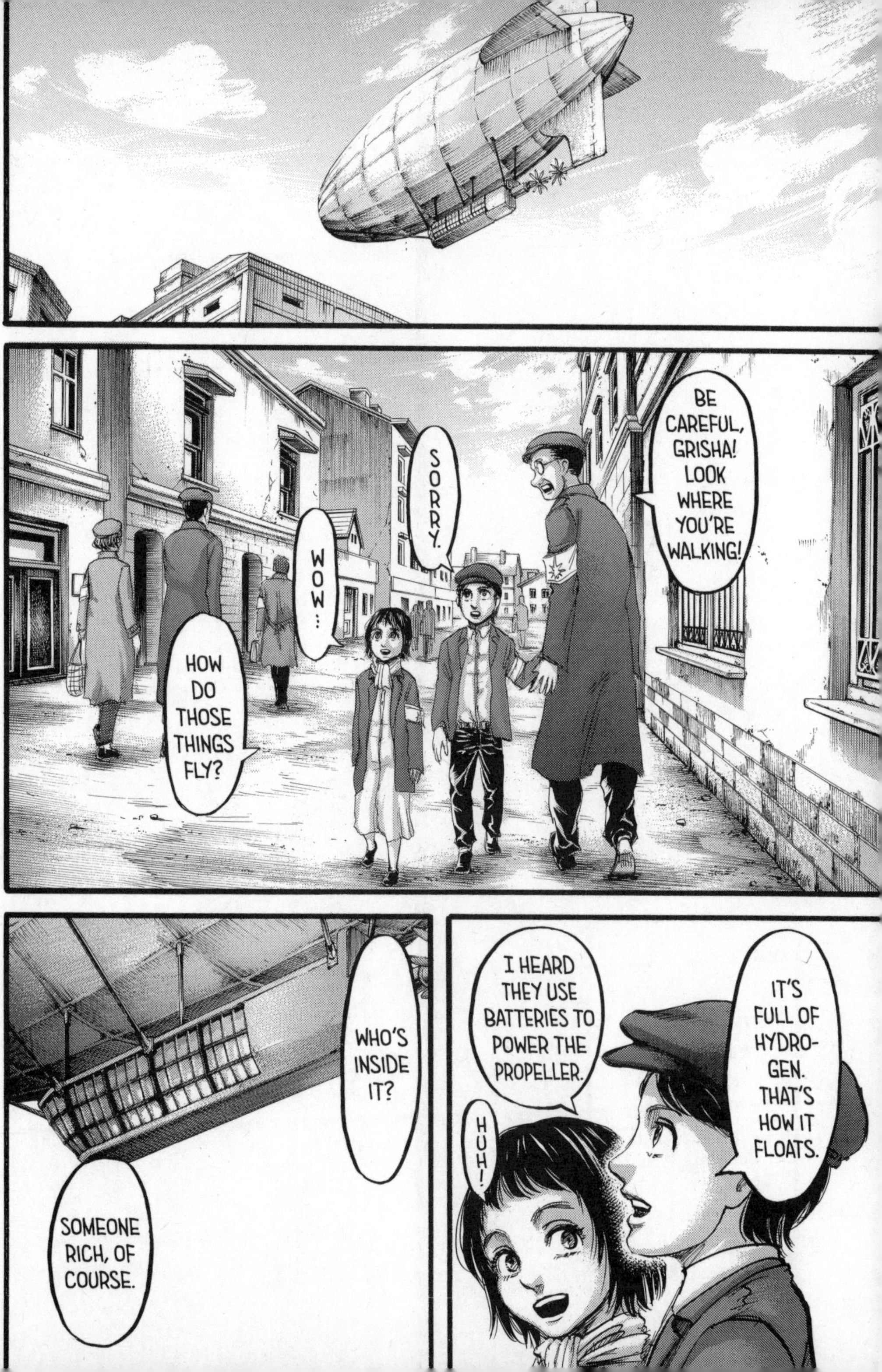
BE CAREFUL, GRISHA! LOOK WHERE YOU'RE WALKING!
SORRY.
WOW...
HOW DO THOSE THINGS FLY?
IT'S FULL OF HYDRO-GEN. THAT'S HOW IT FLOATS.
I HEARD THEY USE BATTERIES TO POWER THE PROPELLER.
HUH!
WHO'S INSIDE IT?
SOMEONE RICH, OF COURSE.

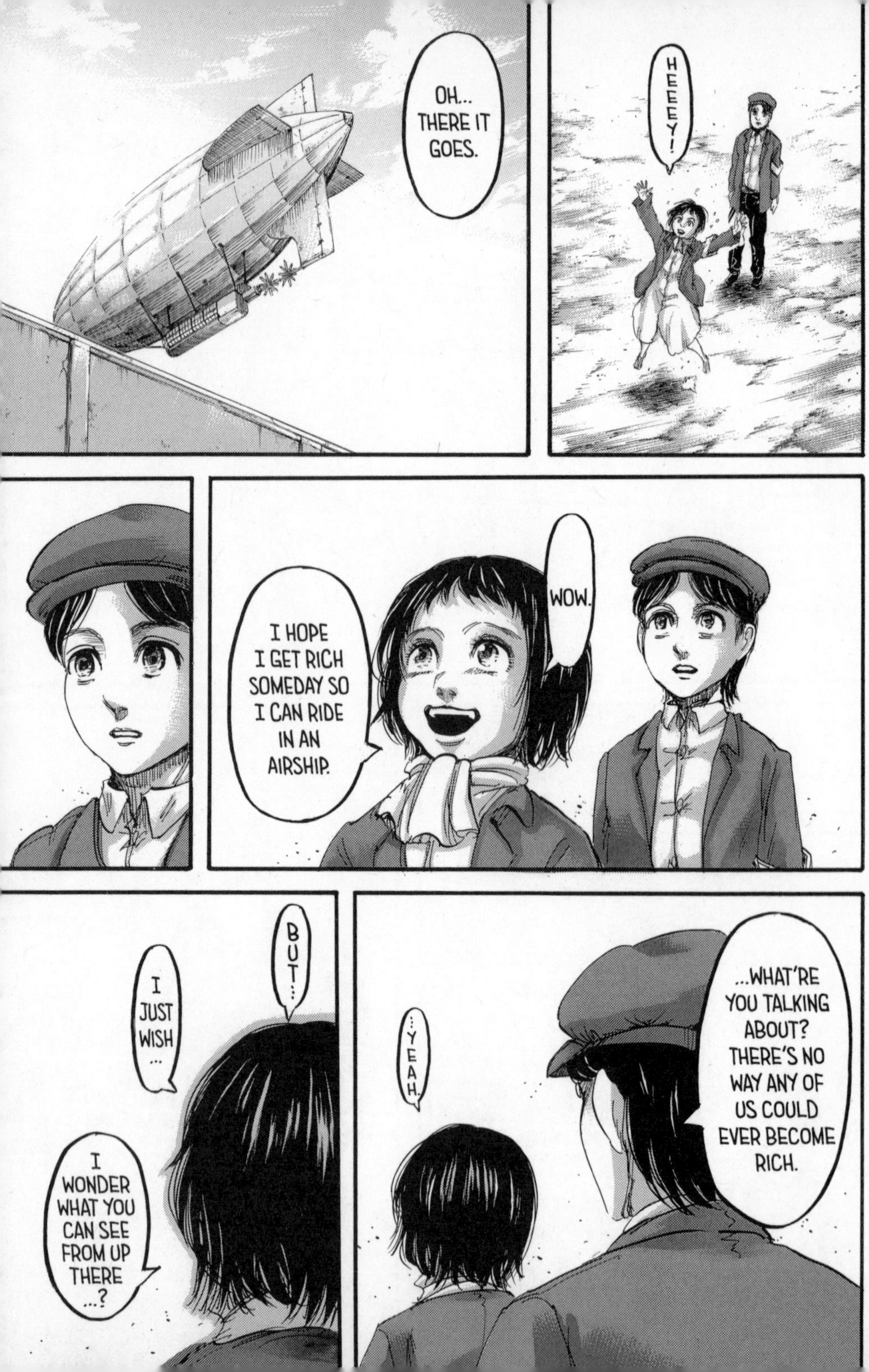
HEEEY!
OH... THERE IT GOES.
WOW.
I HOPE I GET RICH SOMEDAY SO I CAN RIDE IN AN AIRSHIP.
...WHAT'RE YOU TALKING ABOUT? THERE'S NO WAY ANY OF US COULD EVER BECOME RICH.
...YEAH.
BUT...
I JUST WISH...
I WONDER WHAT YOU CAN SEE FROM UP THERE...?

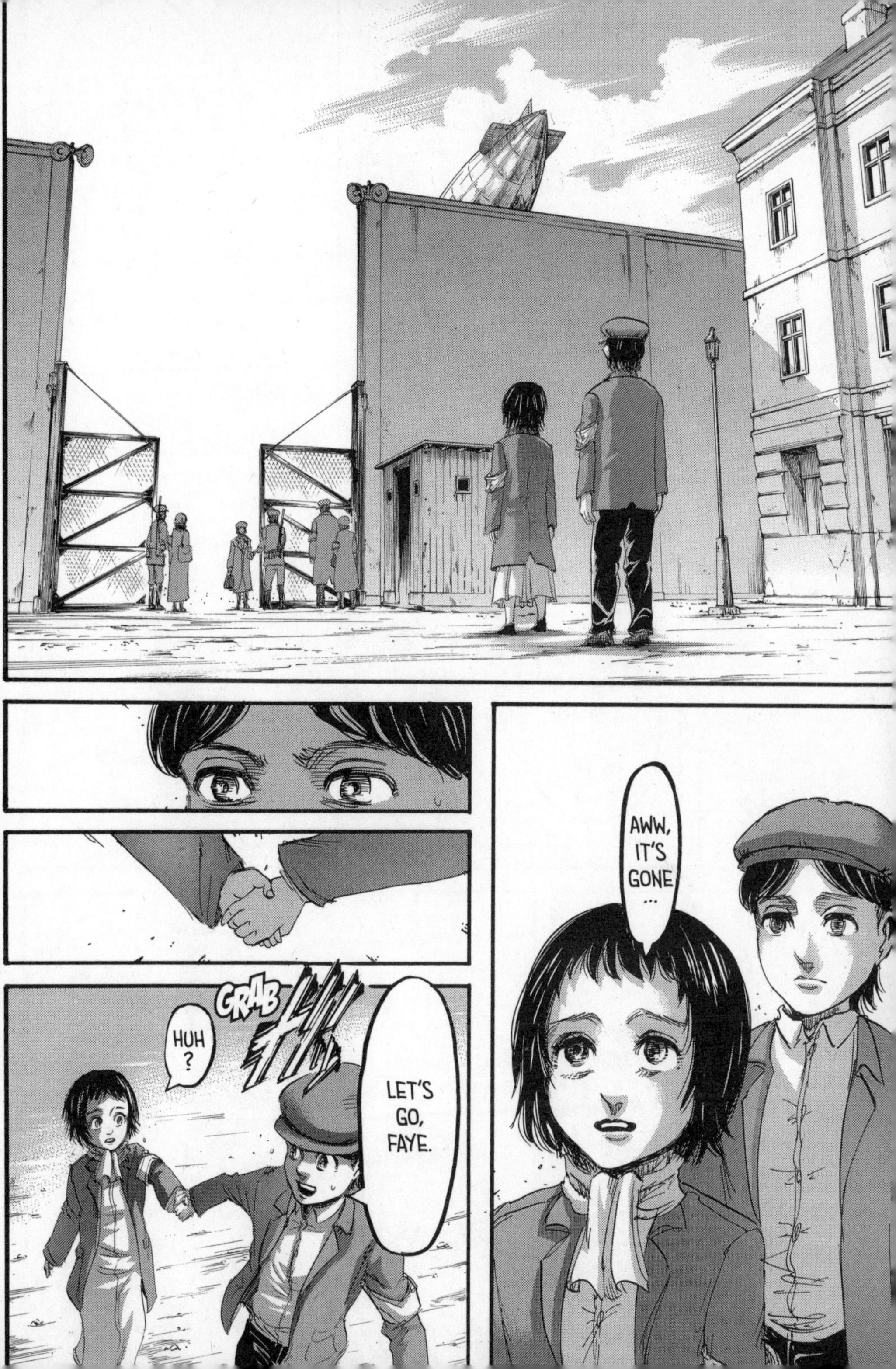
AWW, IT'S GONE ...
LET'S GO, FAYE.
GRAB
HUH ?

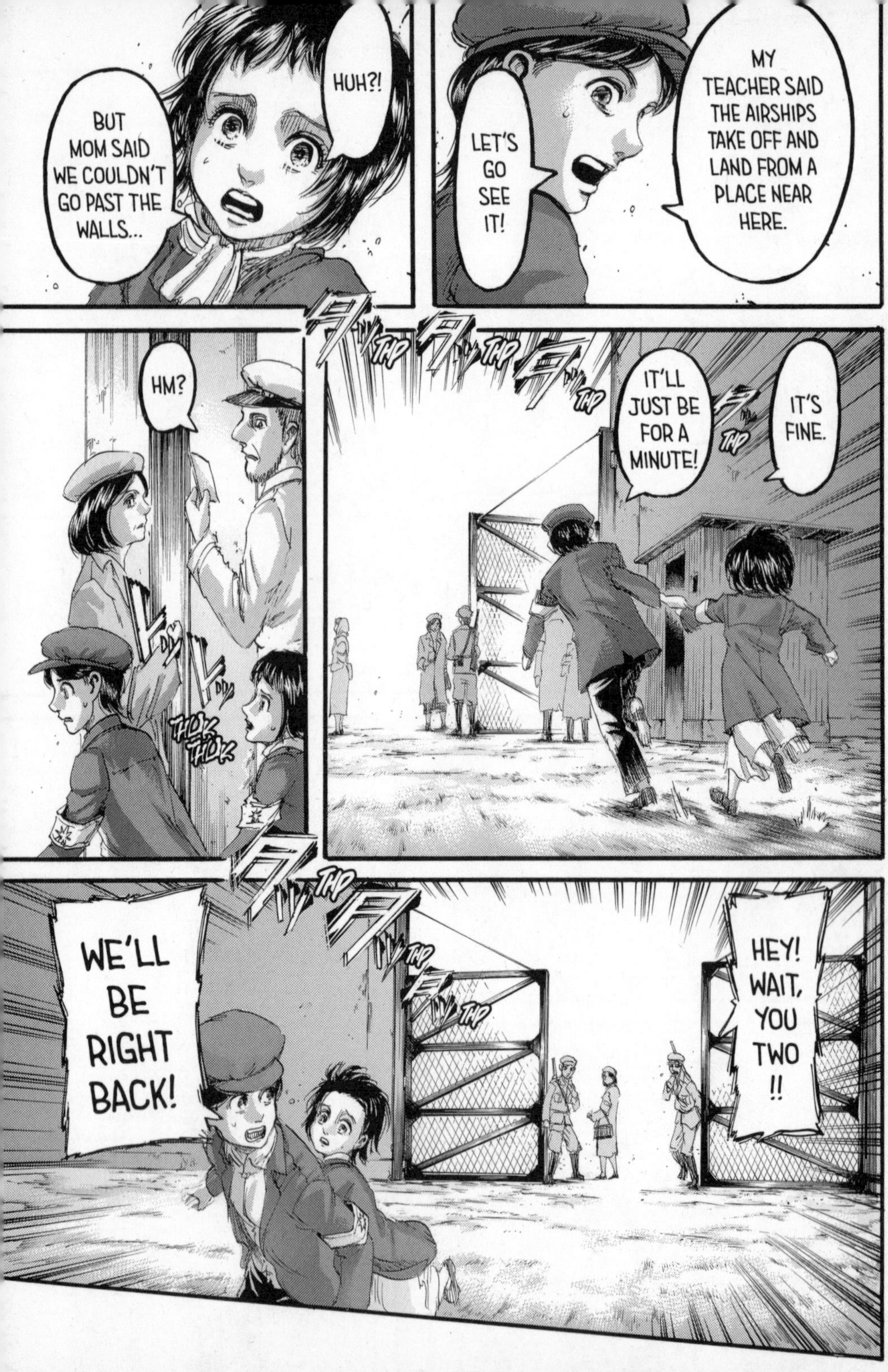
MY TEACHER SAID THE AIRSHIPS TAKE OFF AND LAND FROM A PLACE NEAR HERE.
LET'S GO SEE IT!
HUH?!
BUT MOM SAID WE COULDN'T GO PAST THE WALLS...
THP THP THP THP
IT'S FINE.
IT'LL JUST BE FOR A MINUTE!
HM?
THOK THOK
HEY! WAIT, YOU TWO!!
THP THP THP
WE'LL BE RIGHT BACK!

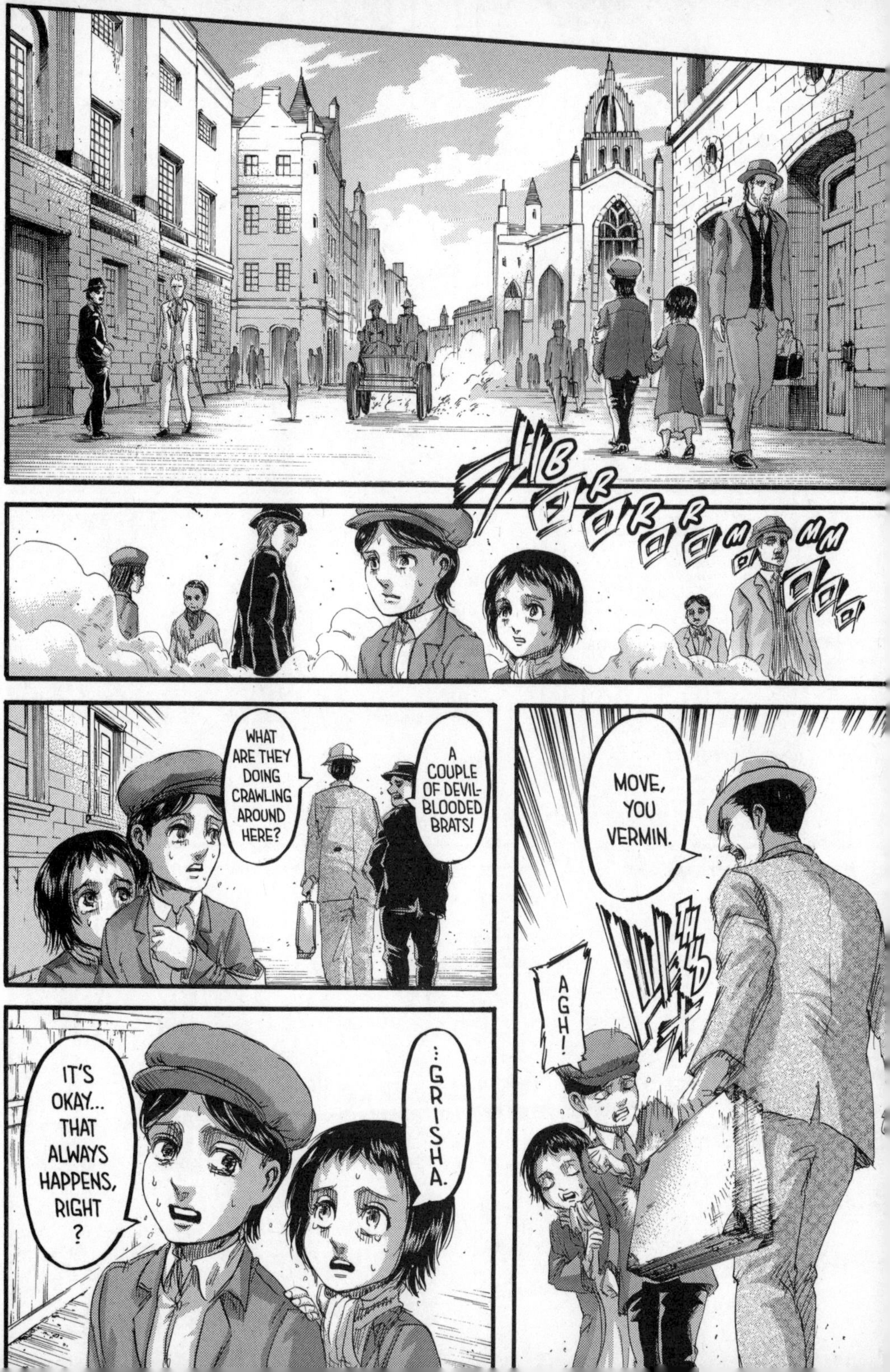
BRRROOOMMM
MOVE, YOU VERMIN.
THUD
AGH!
A COUPLE OF DEVIL-BLOODED BRATS!
WHAT ARE THEY DOING CRAWLING AROUND HERE?
...GRISHA.
IT'S OKAY... THAT ALWAYS HAPPENS, RIGHT?

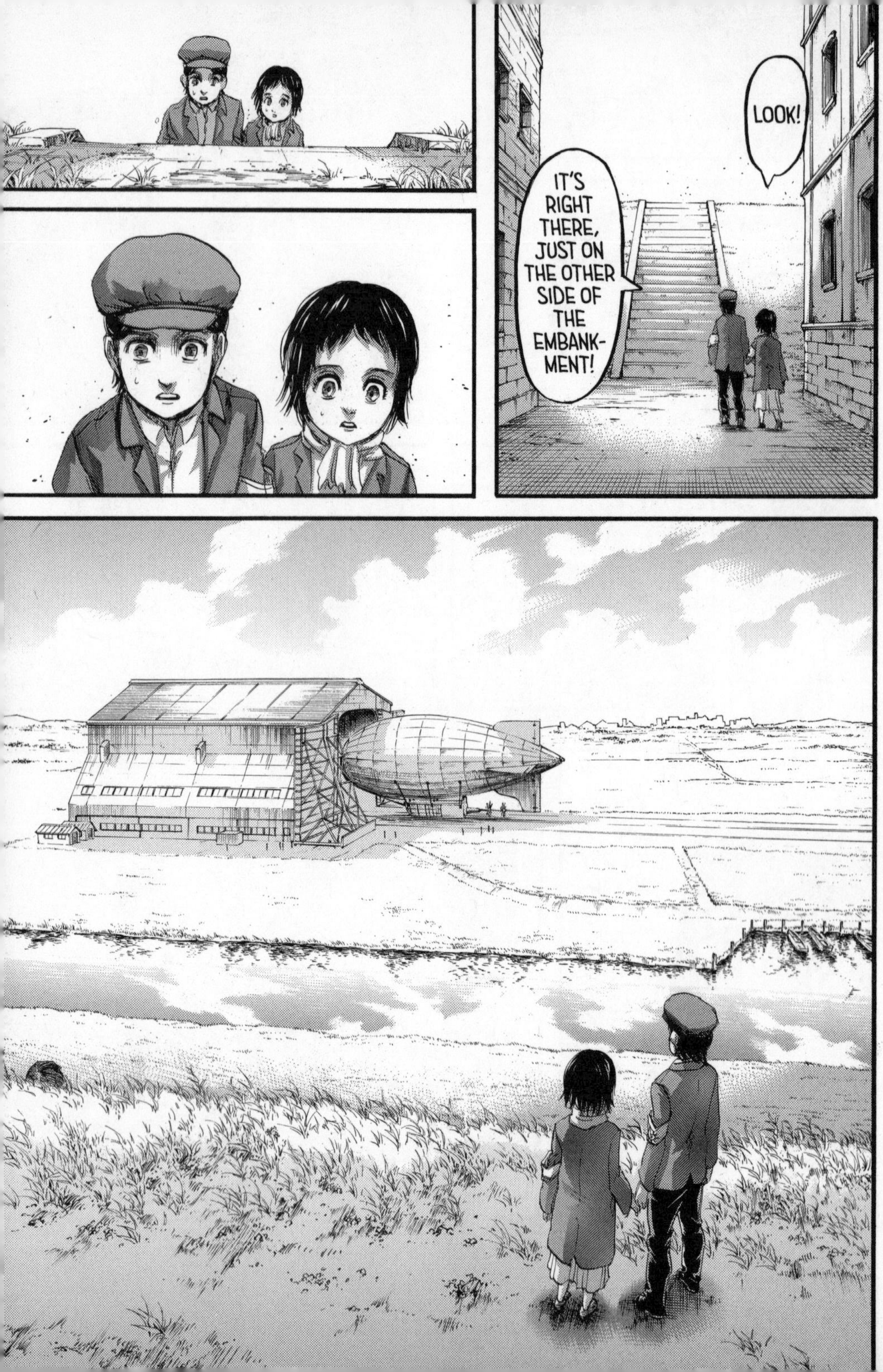
LOOK!
IT'S RIGHT THERE, JUST ON THE OTHER SIDE OF THE EMBANKMENT!

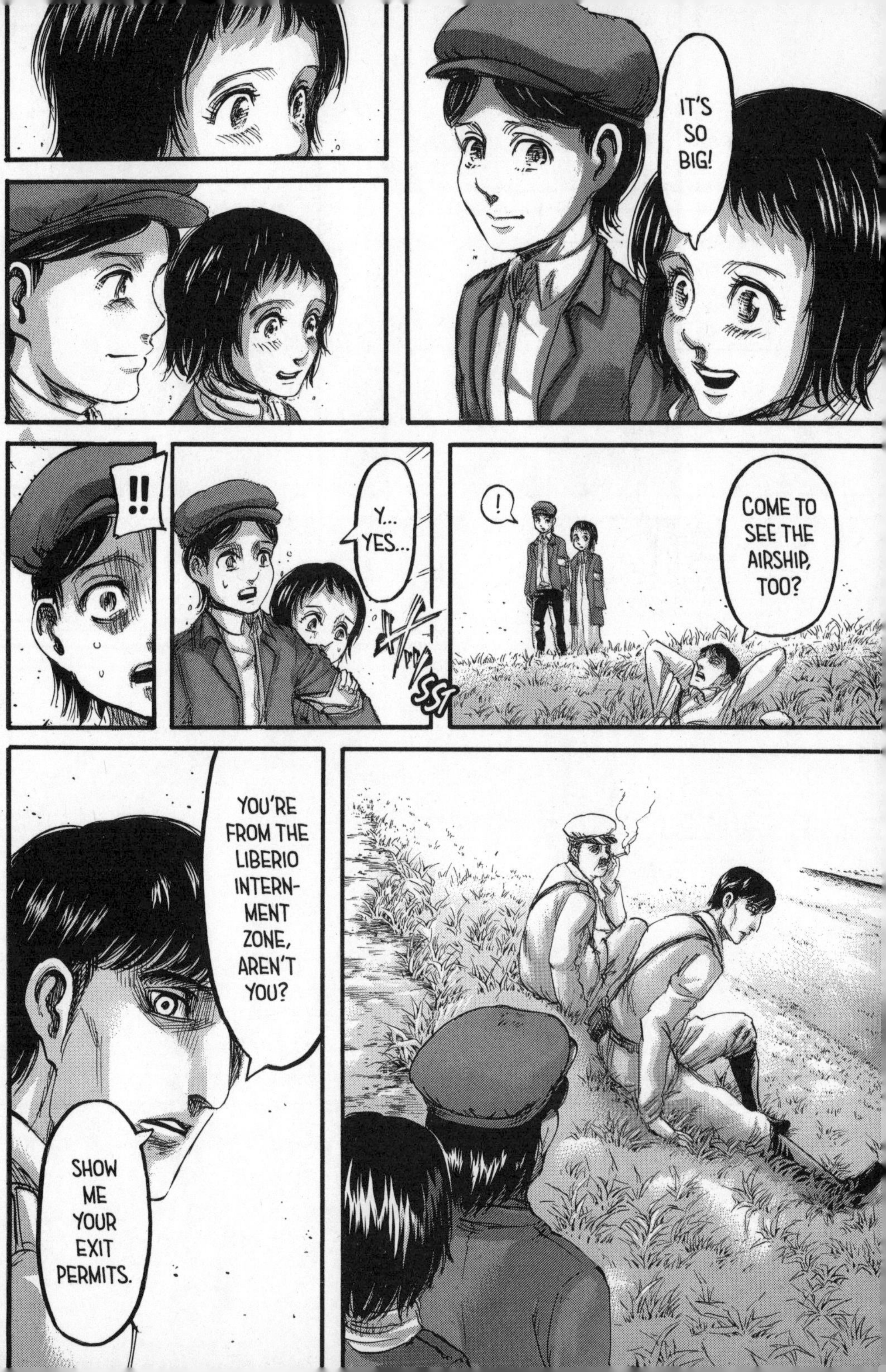
IT'S SO BIG!
COME TO SEE THE AIRSHIP, TOO?
!
Y... YES...
!!
YOU'RE FROM THE LIBERIO INTERN-MENT ZONE, AREN'T YOU?
SHOW ME YOUR EXIT PERMITS.

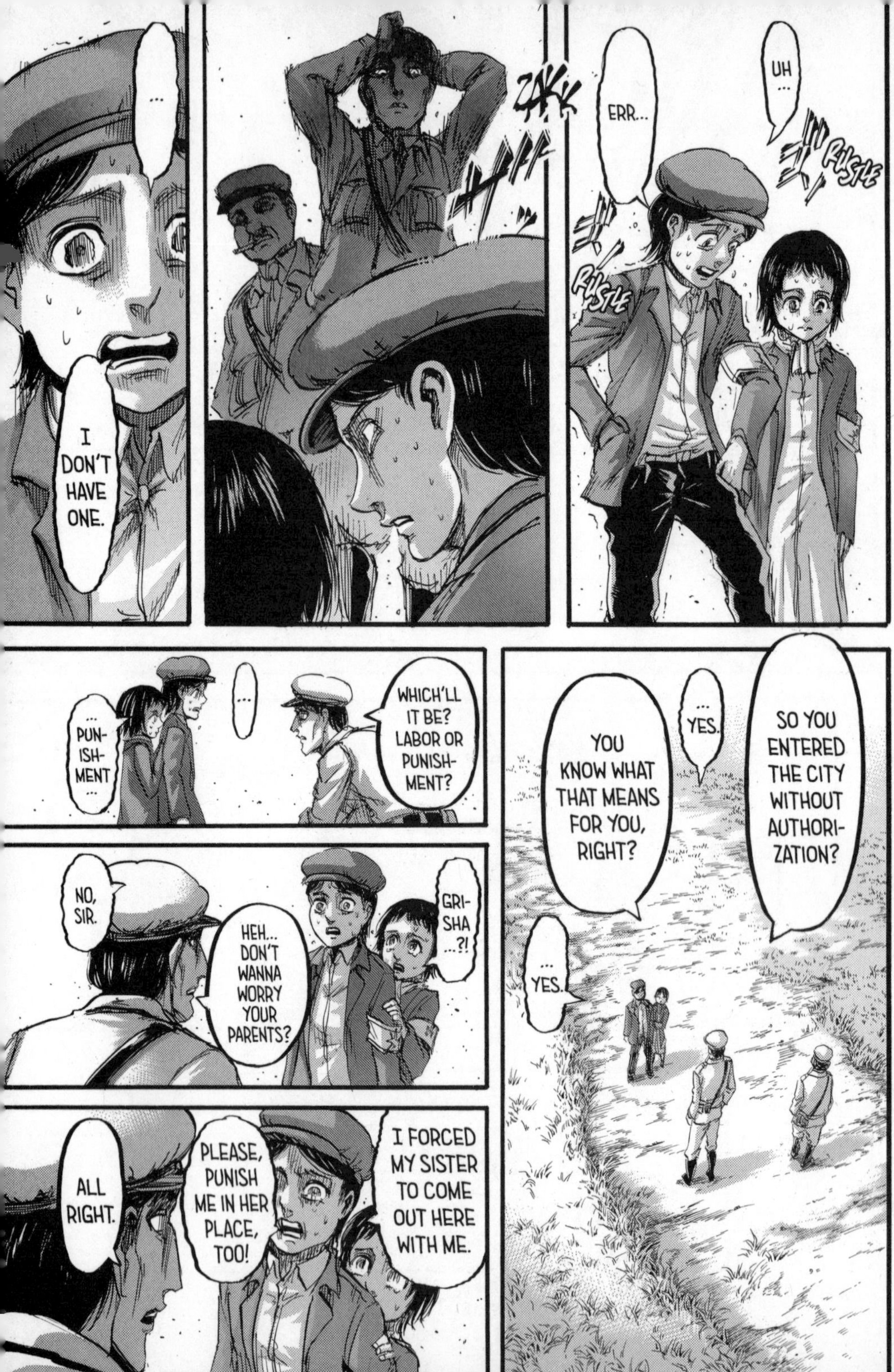
UH ...
RUSTLE
ERR...
RUSTLE
ZAKK
...
I DON'T HAVE ONE.
SO YOU ENTERED THE CITY WITHOUT AUTHORIZATION?
... YES.
YOU KNOW WHAT THAT MEANS FOR YOU, RIGHT?
... YES.
WHICH'LL IT BE? LABOR OR PUNISHMENT?
...
... PUNISHMENT ...
GRISHA ...?!
HEH... DON'T WANNA WORRY YOUR PARENTS?
NO, SIR.
I FORCED MY SISTER TO COME OUT HERE WITH ME.
PLEASE, PUNISH ME IN HER PLACE, TOO!
ALL RIGHT.

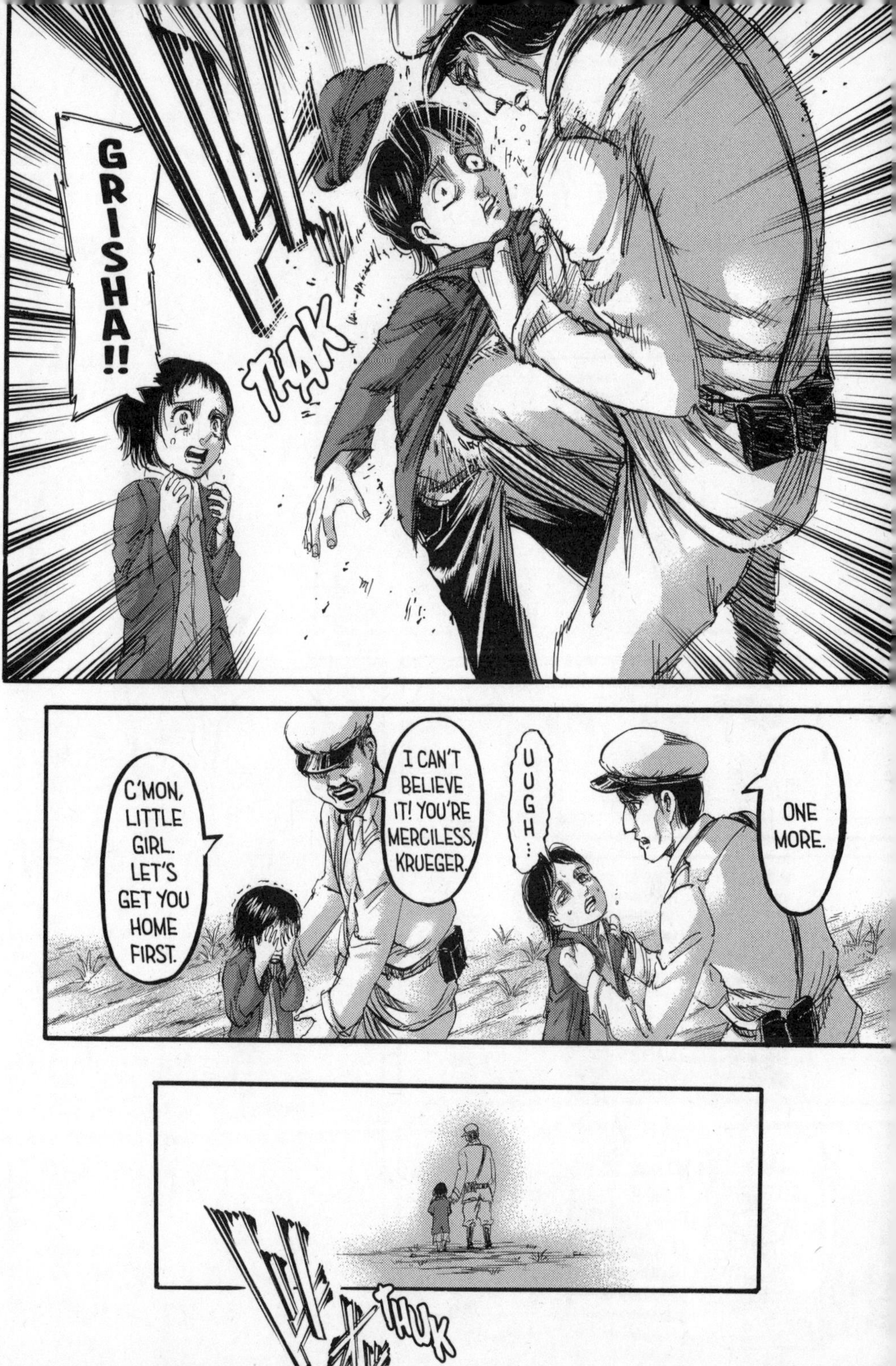
THAK
GRISHA!!
ONE MORE.
UUGH...
I CAN'T BELIEVE IT! YOU'RE MERCILESS, KRUEGER.
C'MON, LITTLE GIRL. LET'S GET YOU HOME FIRST.
THUK

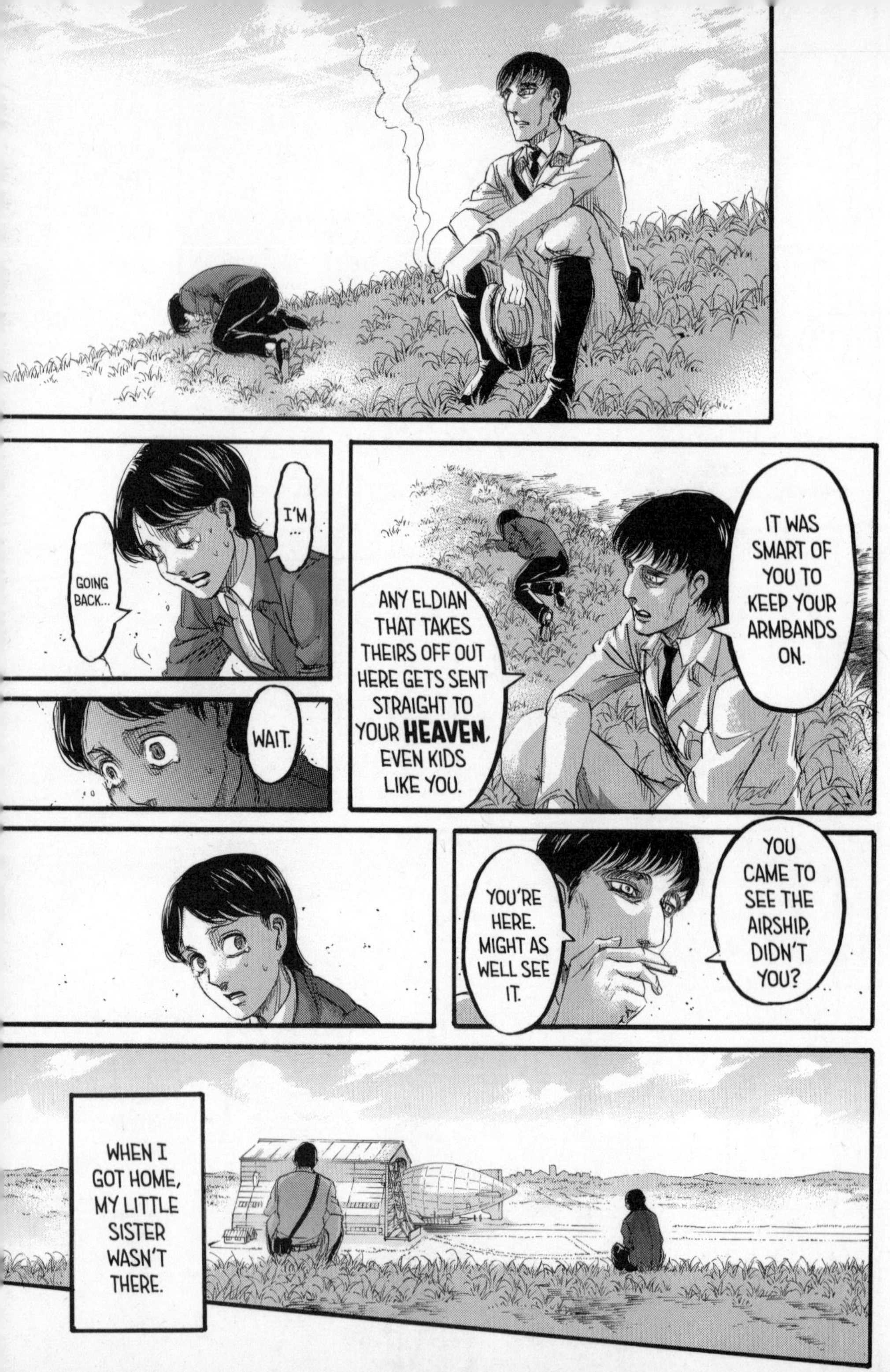
IT WAS SMART OF YOU TO KEEP YOUR ARMBANDS ON.
ANY ELDIAN THAT TAKES THEIRS OFF OUT HERE GETS SENT STRAIGHT TO YOUR **HEAVEN**, EVEN KIDS LIKE YOU.
I'M ...
GOING BACK...
WAIT.
YOU CAME TO SEE THE AIRSHIP, DIDN'T YOU?
YOU'RE HERE. MIGHT AS WELL SEE IT.
WHEN I GOT HOME, MY LITTLE SISTER WASN'T THERE.

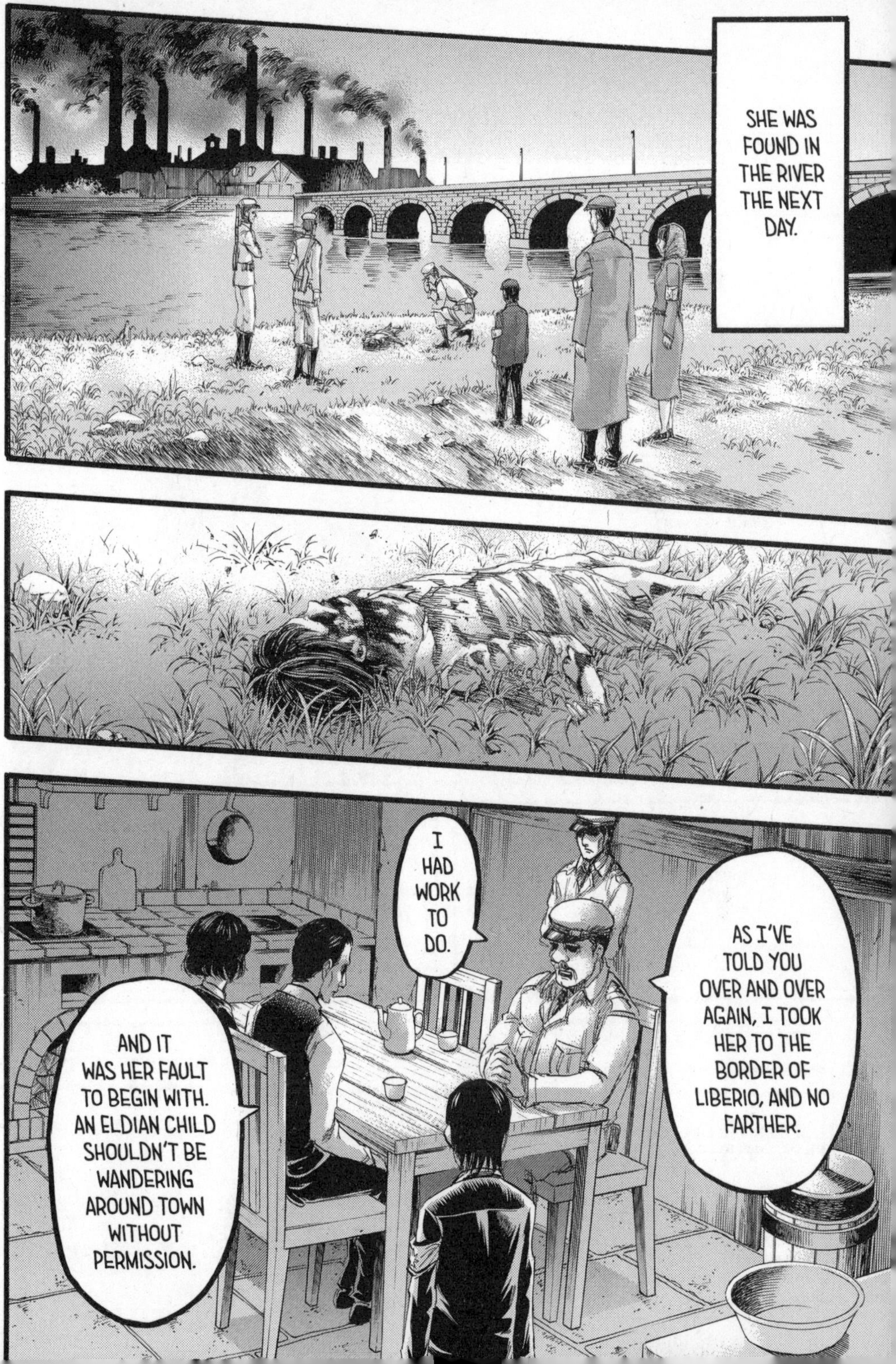
SHE WAS FOUND IN THE RIVER THE NEXT DAY.
AS I'VE TOLD YOU OVER AND OVER AGAIN, I TOOK HER TO THE BORDER OF LIBERIO, AND NO FARTHER.
I HAD WORK TO DO.
AND IT WAS HER FAULT TO BEGIN WITH. AN ELDIAN CHILD SHOULDN'T BE WANDERING AROUND TOWN WITHOUT PERMISSION.

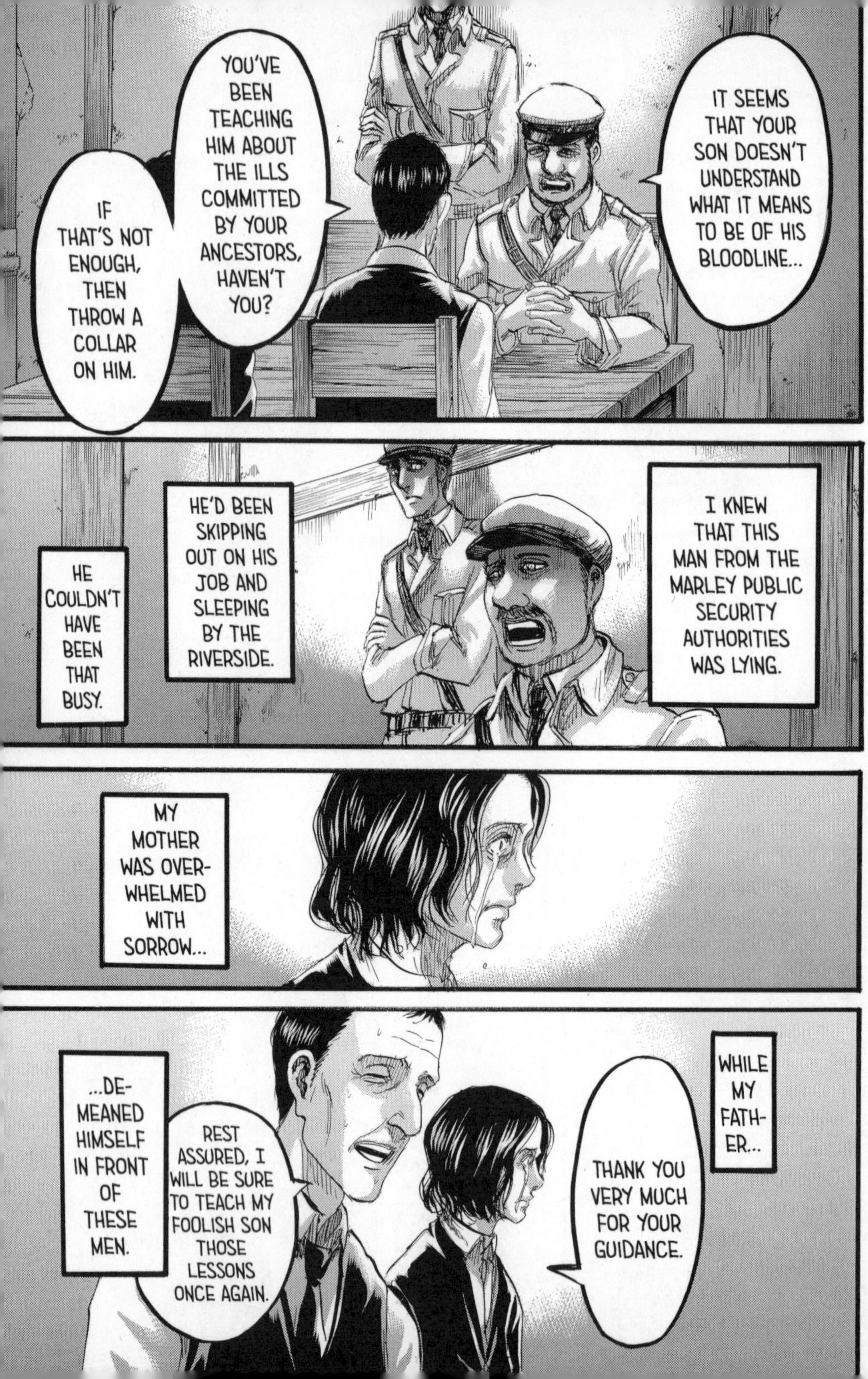
IT SEEMS THAT YOUR SON DOESN'T UNDERSTAND WHAT IT MEANS TO BE OF HIS BLOODLINE...
YOU'VE BEEN TEACHING HIM ABOUT THE ILLS COMMITTED BY YOUR ANCESTORS, HAVEN'T YOU?
IF THAT'S NOT ENOUGH, THEN THROW A COLLAR ON HIM.
I KNEW THAT THIS MAN FROM THE MARLEY PUBLIC SECURITY AUTHORITIES WAS LYING.
HE'D BEEN SKIPPING OUT ON HIS JOB AND SLEEPING BY THE RIVERSIDE.
HE COULDN'T HAVE BEEN THAT BUSY.
MY MOTHER WAS OVER-WHELMED WITH SORROW...
WHILE MY FATH-ER...
THANK YOU VERY MUCH FOR YOUR GUIDANCE.
REST ASSURED, I WILL BE SURE TO TEACH MY FOOLISH SON THOSE LESSONS ONCE AGAIN.
...DE-MEANED HIMSELF IN FRONT OF THESE MEN.

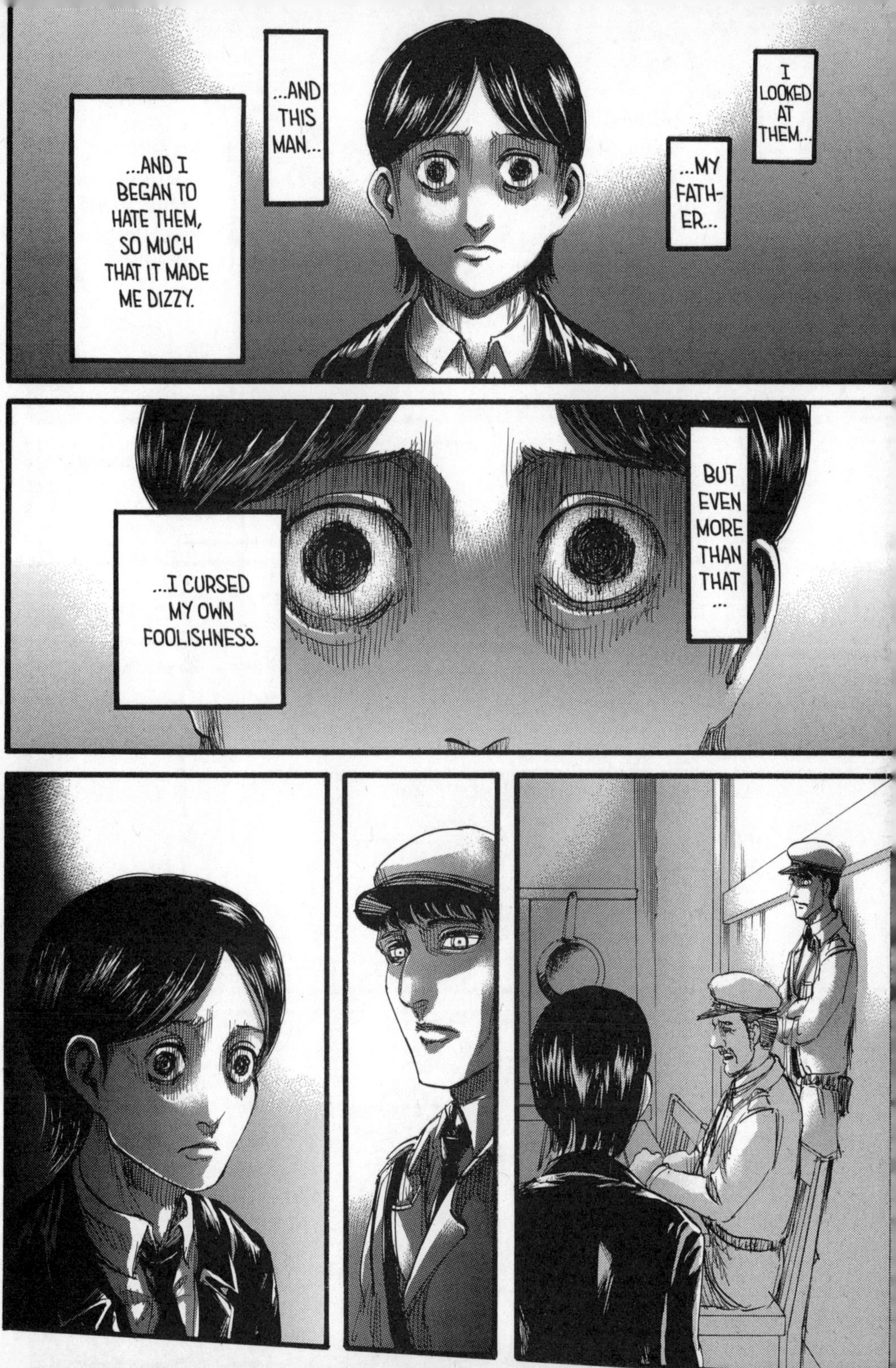
I LOOKED AT THEM...
...MY FATH-ER...
...AND THIS MAN...
...AND I BEGAN TO HATE THEM, SO MUCH THAT IT MADE ME DIZZY.
BUT EVEN MORE THAN THAT ...
...I CURSED MY OWN FOOLISHNESS.

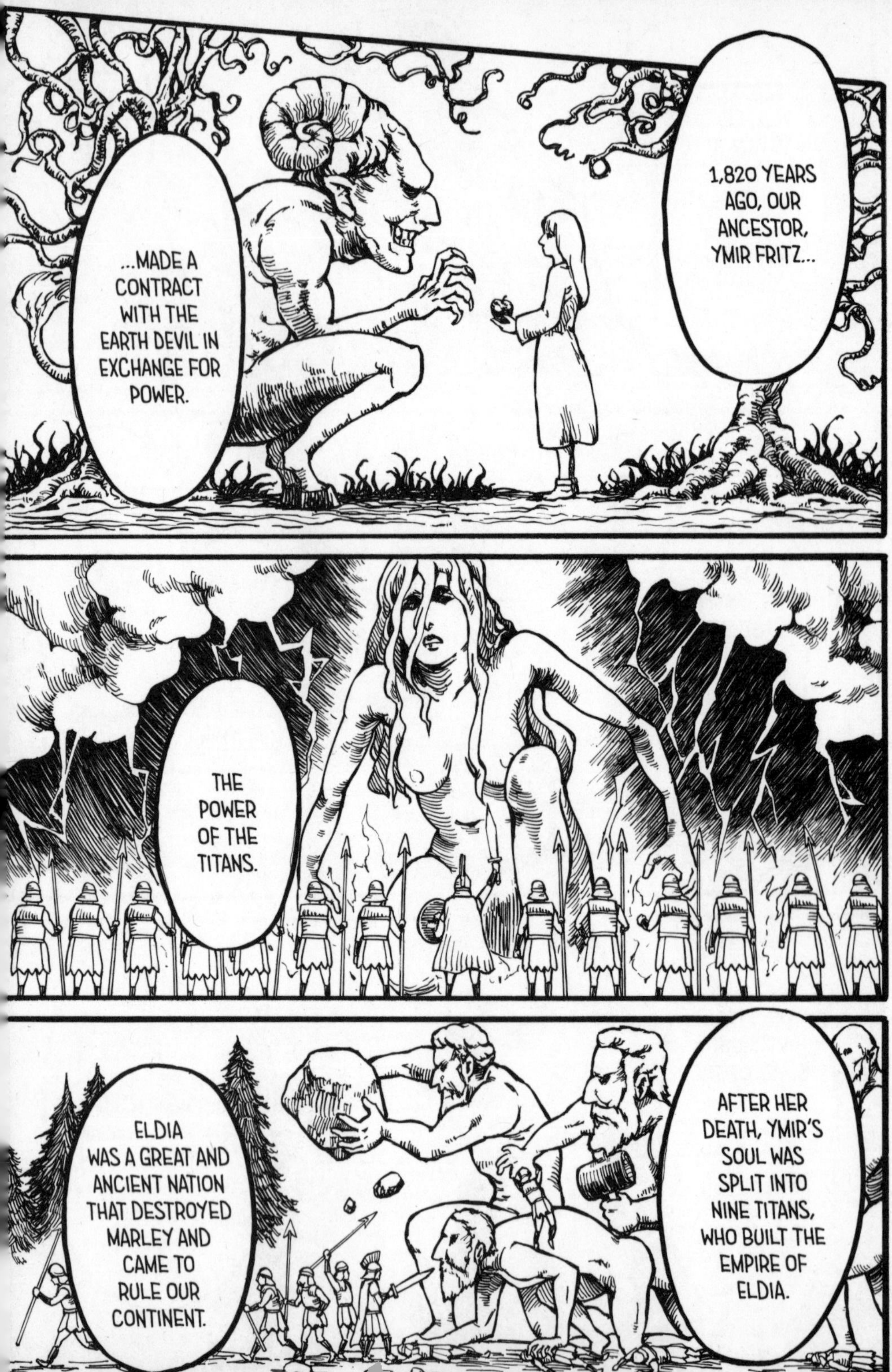
1,820 YEARS AGO, OUR ANCESTOR, YMIR FRITZ...
...MADE A CONTRACT WITH THE EARTH DEVIL IN EXCHANGE FOR POWER.
THE POWER OF THE TITANS.
AFTER HER DEATH, YMIR'S SOUL WAS SPLIT INTO NINE TITANS, WHO BUILT THE EMPIRE OF ELDIA.
ELDIA WAS A GREAT AND ANCIENT NATION THAT DESTROYED MARLEY AND CAME TO RULE OUR CONTINENT.

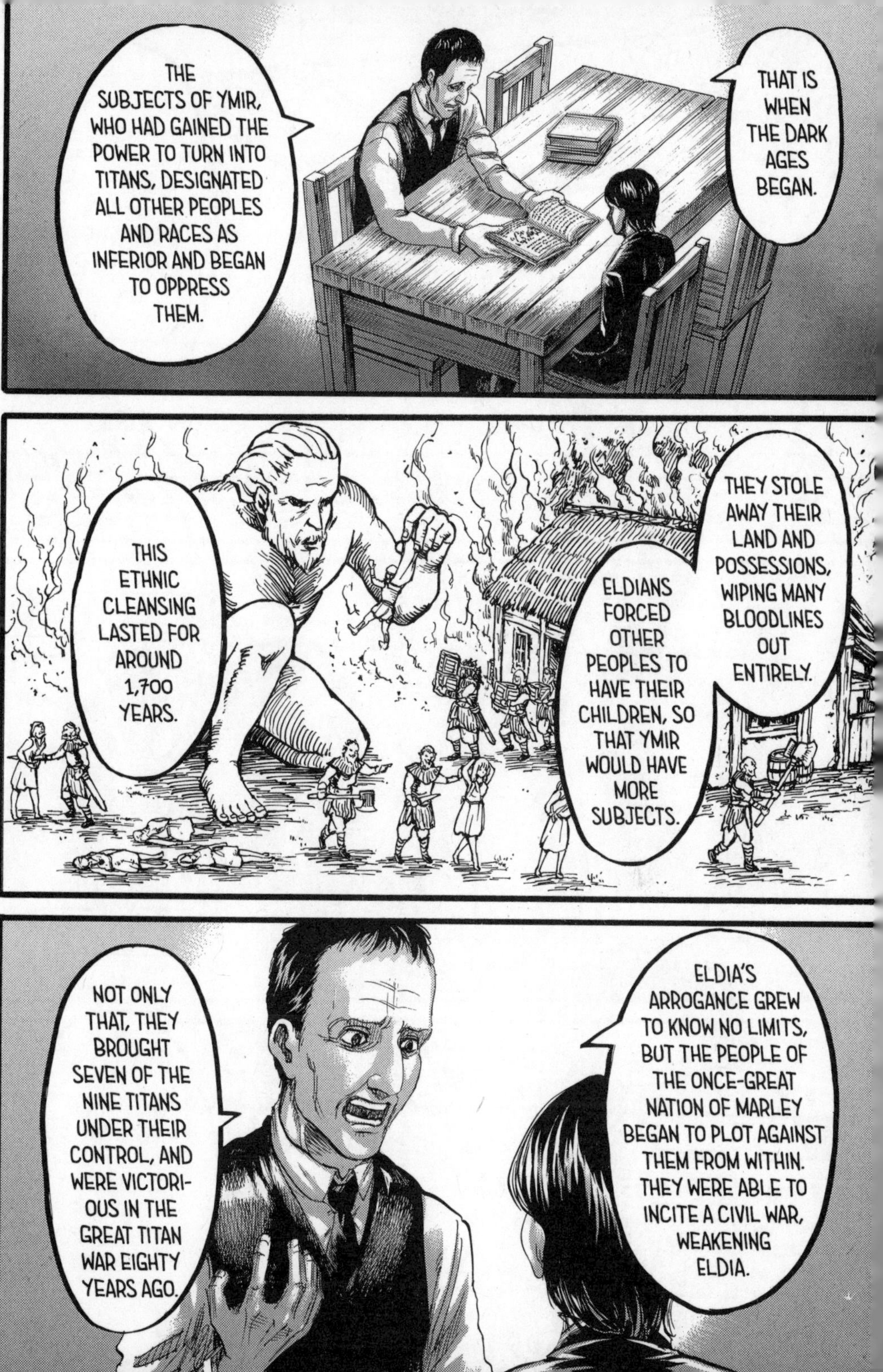
THAT IS WHEN THE DARK AGES BEGAN.
THE SUBJECTS OF YMIR, WHO HAD GAINED THE POWER TO TURN INTO TITANS, DESIGNATED ALL OTHER PEOPLES AND RACES AS INFERIOR AND BEGAN TO OPPRESS THEM.
THEY STOLE AWAY THEIR LAND AND POSSESSIONS, WIPING MANY BLOODLINES OUT ENTIRELY.
ELDIANS FORCED OTHER PEOPLES TO HAVE THEIR CHILDREN, SO THAT YMIR WOULD HAVE MORE SUBJECTS.
THIS ETHNIC CLEANSING LASTED FOR AROUND 1,700 YEARS.
ELDIA'S ARROGANCE GREW TO KNOW NO LIMITS, BUT THE PEOPLE OF THE ONCE-GREAT NATION OF MARLEY BEGAN TO PLOT AGAINST THEM FROM WITHIN. THEY WERE ABLE TO INCITE A CIVIL WAR, WEAKENING ELDIA.
NOT ONLY THAT, THEY BROUGHT SEVEN OF THE NINE TITANS UNDER THEIR CONTROL, AND WERE VICTORIOUS IN THE GREAT TITAN WAR EIGHTY YEARS AGO.

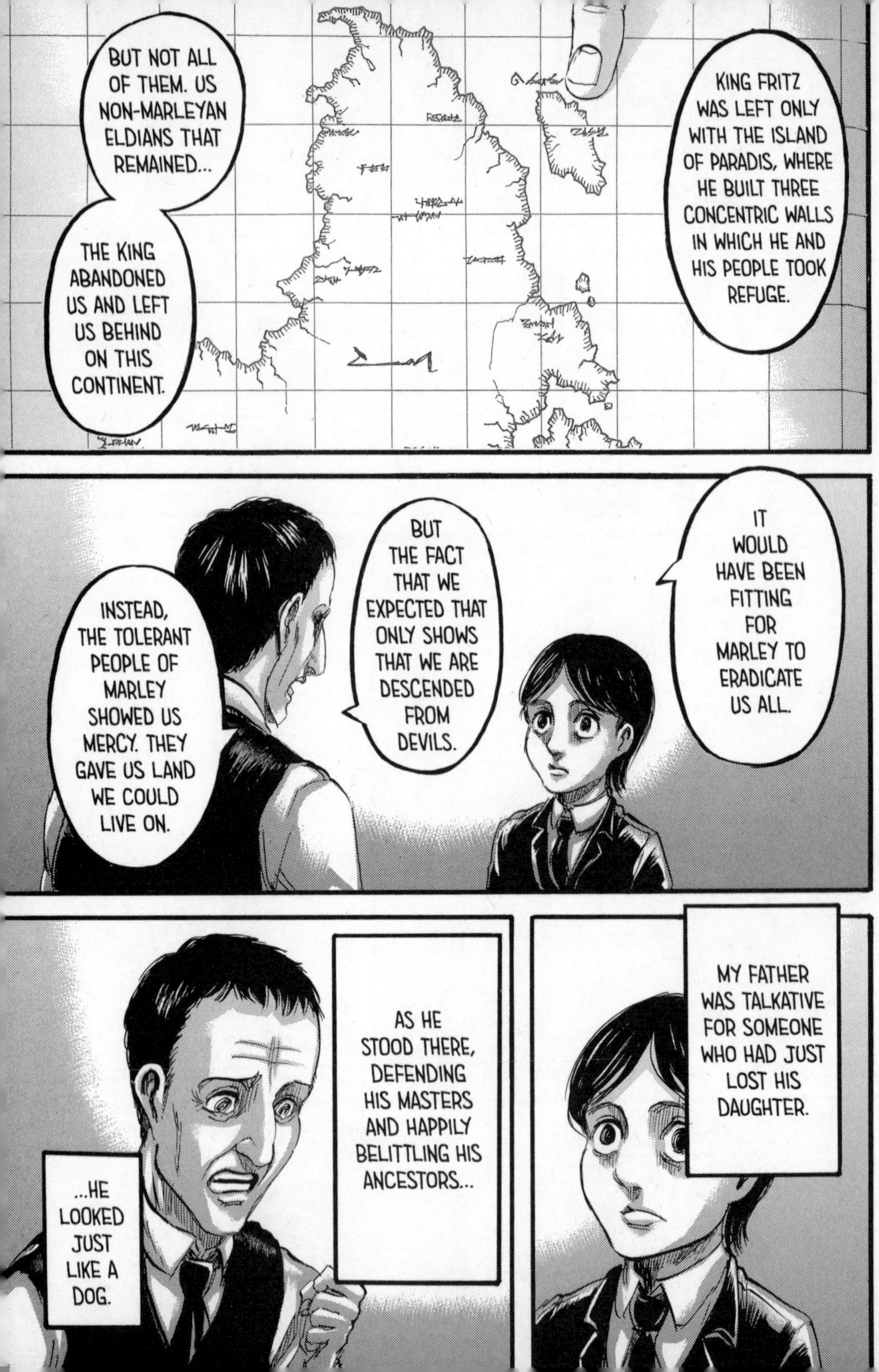
KING FRITZ WAS LEFT ONLY WITH THE ISLAND OF PARADIS, WHERE HE BUILT THREE CONCENTRIC WALLS IN WHICH HE AND HIS PEOPLE TOOK REFUGE.
BUT NOT ALL OF THEM. US NON-MARLEYAN ELDIANS THAT REMAINED...
THE KING ABANDONED US AND LEFT US BEHIND ON THIS CONTINENT.
IT WOULD HAVE BEEN FITTING FOR MARLEY TO ERADICATE US ALL.
BUT THE FACT THAT WE EXPECTED THAT ONLY SHOWS THAT WE ARE DESCENDED FROM DEVILS.
INSTEAD, THE TOLERANT PEOPLE OF MARLEY SHOWED US MERCY. THEY GAVE US LAND WE COULD LIVE ON.
MY FATHER WAS TALKATIVE FOR SOMEONE WHO HAD JUST LOST HIS DAUGHTER.
AS HE STOOD THERE, DEFENDING HIS MASTERS AND HAPPILY BELITTLING HIS ANCESTORS...
...HE LOOKED JUST LIKE A DOG.

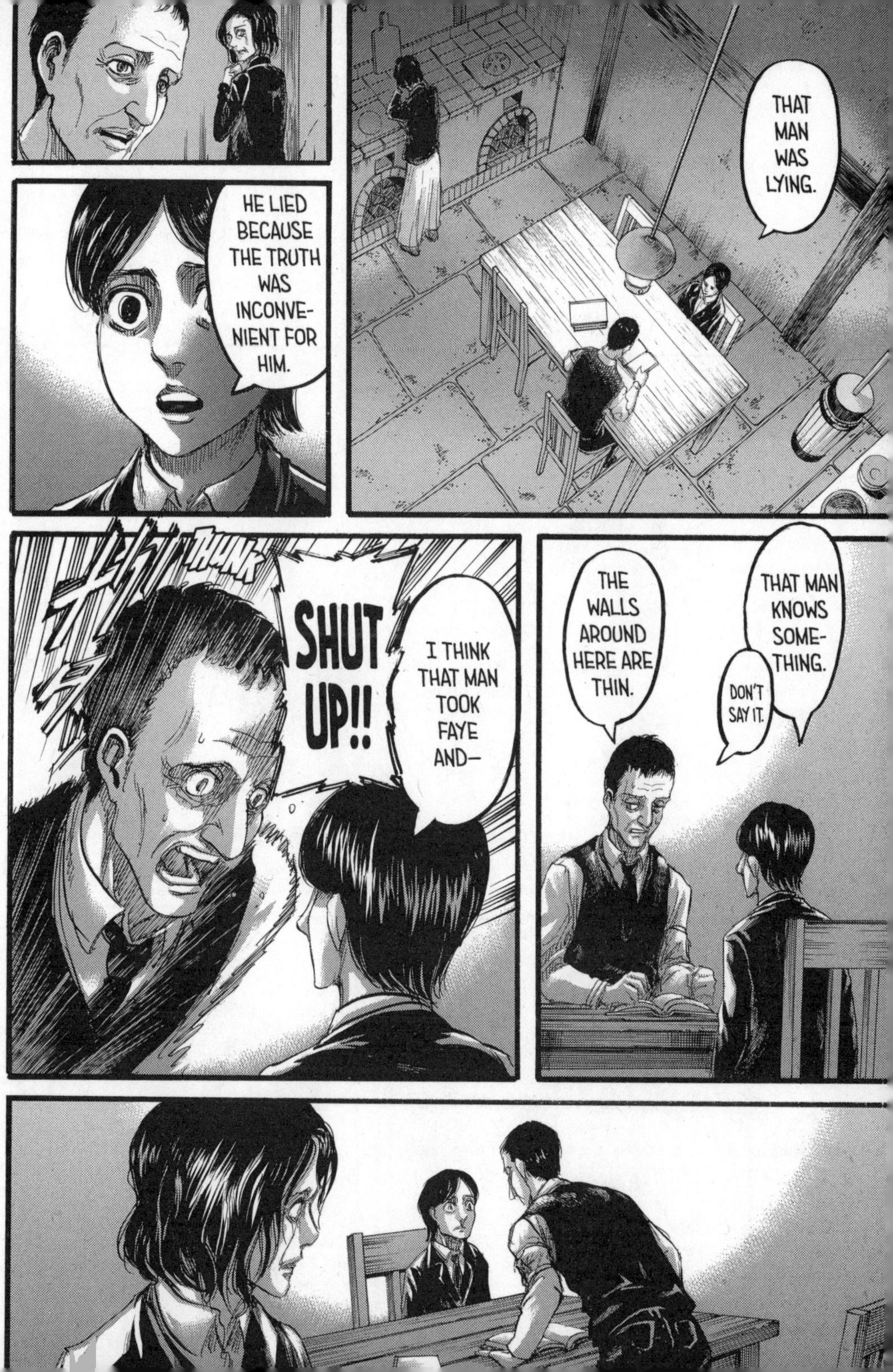
THAT MAN WAS LYING.
HE LIED BECAUSE THE TRUTH WAS INCONVENIENT FOR HIM.
THAT MAN KNOWS SOMETHING.
DON'T SAY IT.
THE WALLS AROUND HERE ARE THIN.
I THINK THAT MAN TOOK FAYE AND—
THUNK
SHUT UP!!

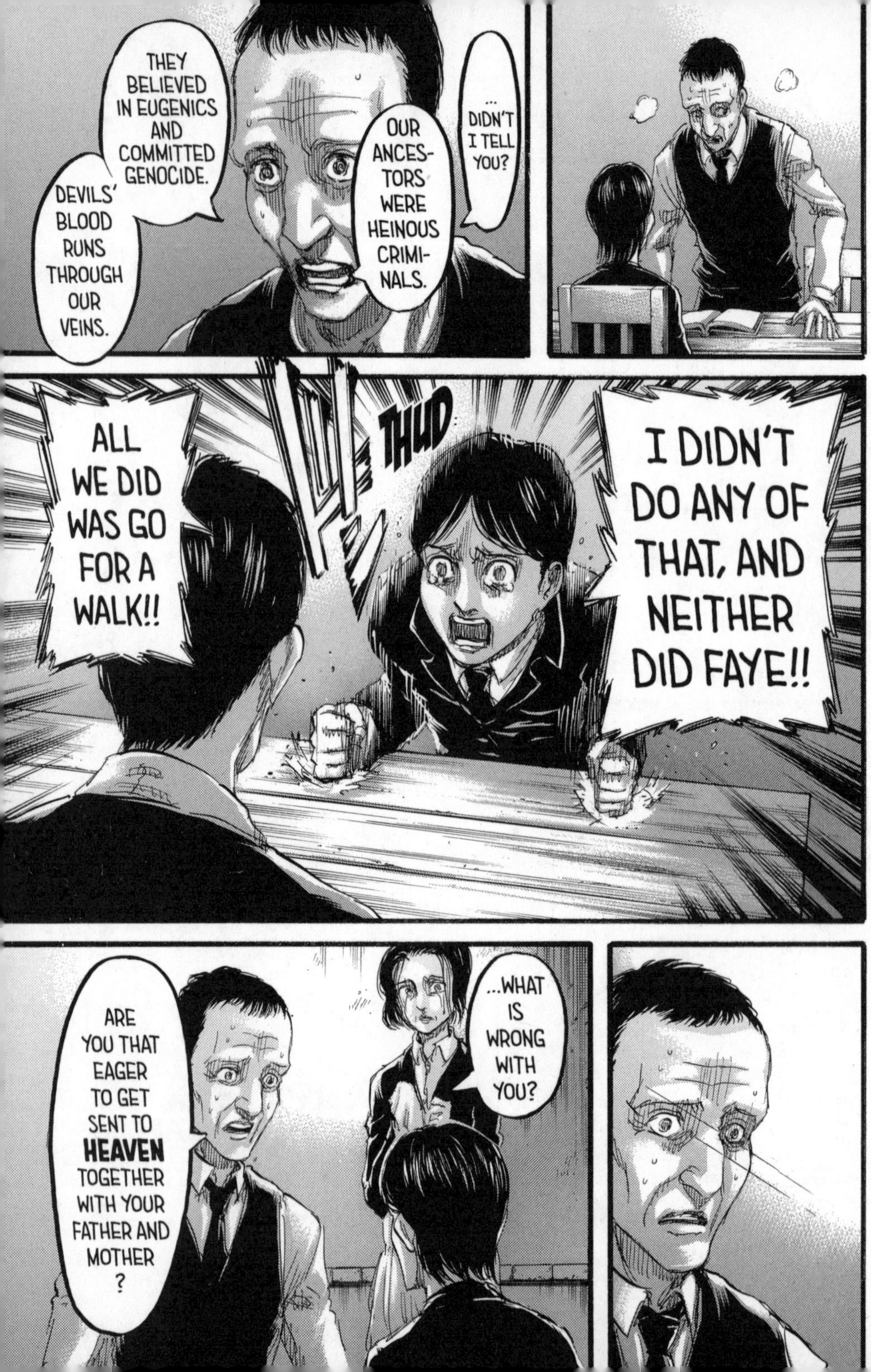
... DIDN'T I TELL YOU?
OUR ANCESTORS WERE HEINOUS CRIMINALS.
THEY BELIEVED IN EUGENICS AND COMMITTED GENOCIDE.
DEVILS' BLOOD RUNS THROUGH OUR VEINS.
I DIDN'T DO ANY OF THAT, AND NEITHER DID FAYE!!
THUD
ALL WE DID WAS GO FOR A WALK!!
...WHAT IS WRONG WITH YOU?
ARE YOU THAT EAGER TO GET SENT TO **HEAVEN** TOGETHER WITH YOUR FATHER AND MOTHER?

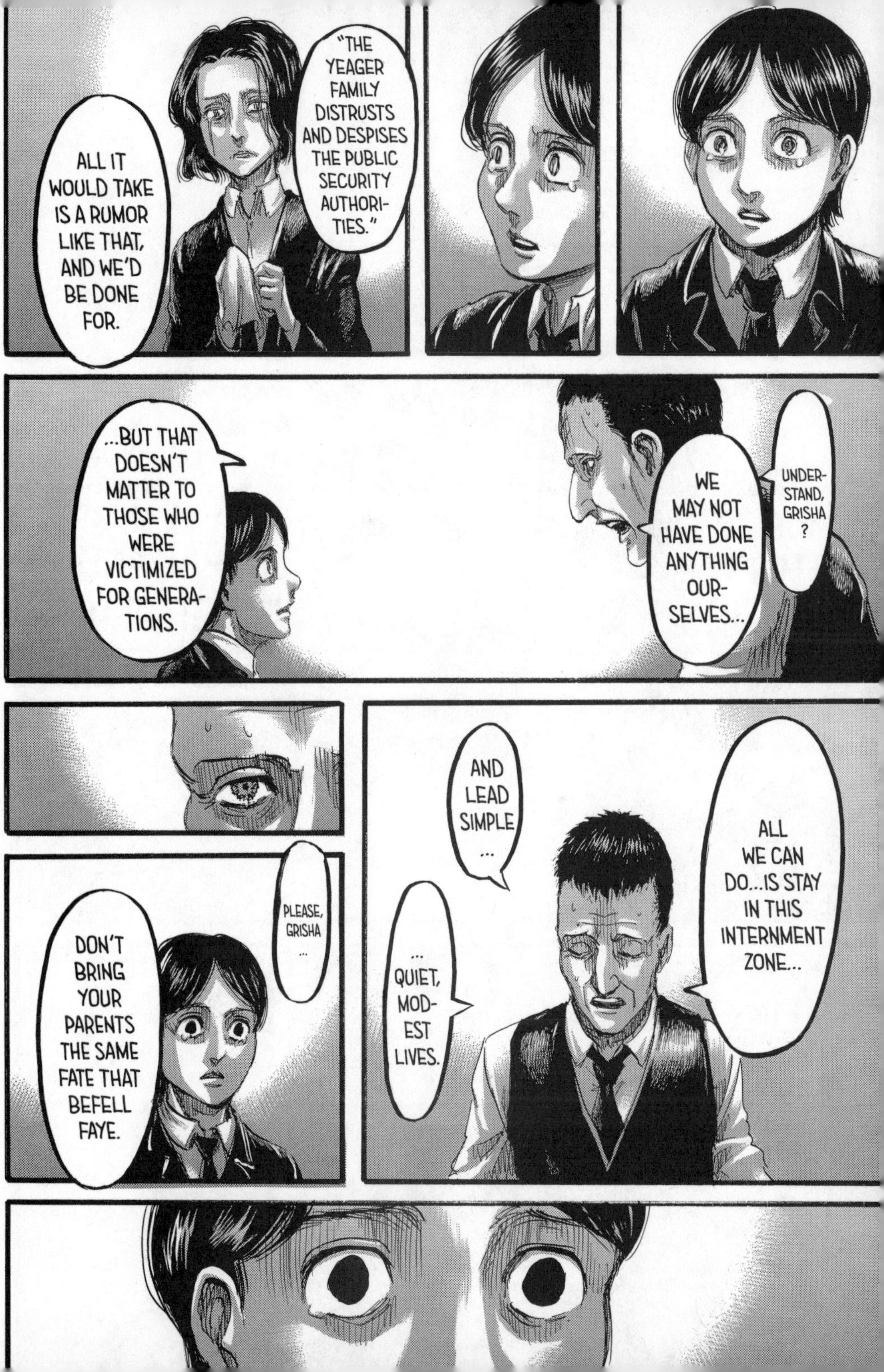
"THE YEAGER FAMILY DISTRUSTS AND DESPISES THE PUBLIC SECURITY AUTHORITIES."
ALL IT WOULD TAKE IS A RUMOR LIKE THAT, AND WE'D BE DONE FOR.
UNDERSTAND, GRISHA?
WE MAY NOT HAVE DONE ANYTHING OURSELVES...
...BUT THAT DOESN'T MATTER TO THOSE WHO WERE VICTIMIZED FOR GENERATIONS.
ALL WE CAN DO...IS STAY IN THIS INTERNMENT ZONE...
AND LEAD SIMPLE...
...QUIET, MODEST LIVES.
PLEASE, GRISHA...
DON'T BRING YOUR PARENTS THE SAME FATE THAT BEFELL FAYE.

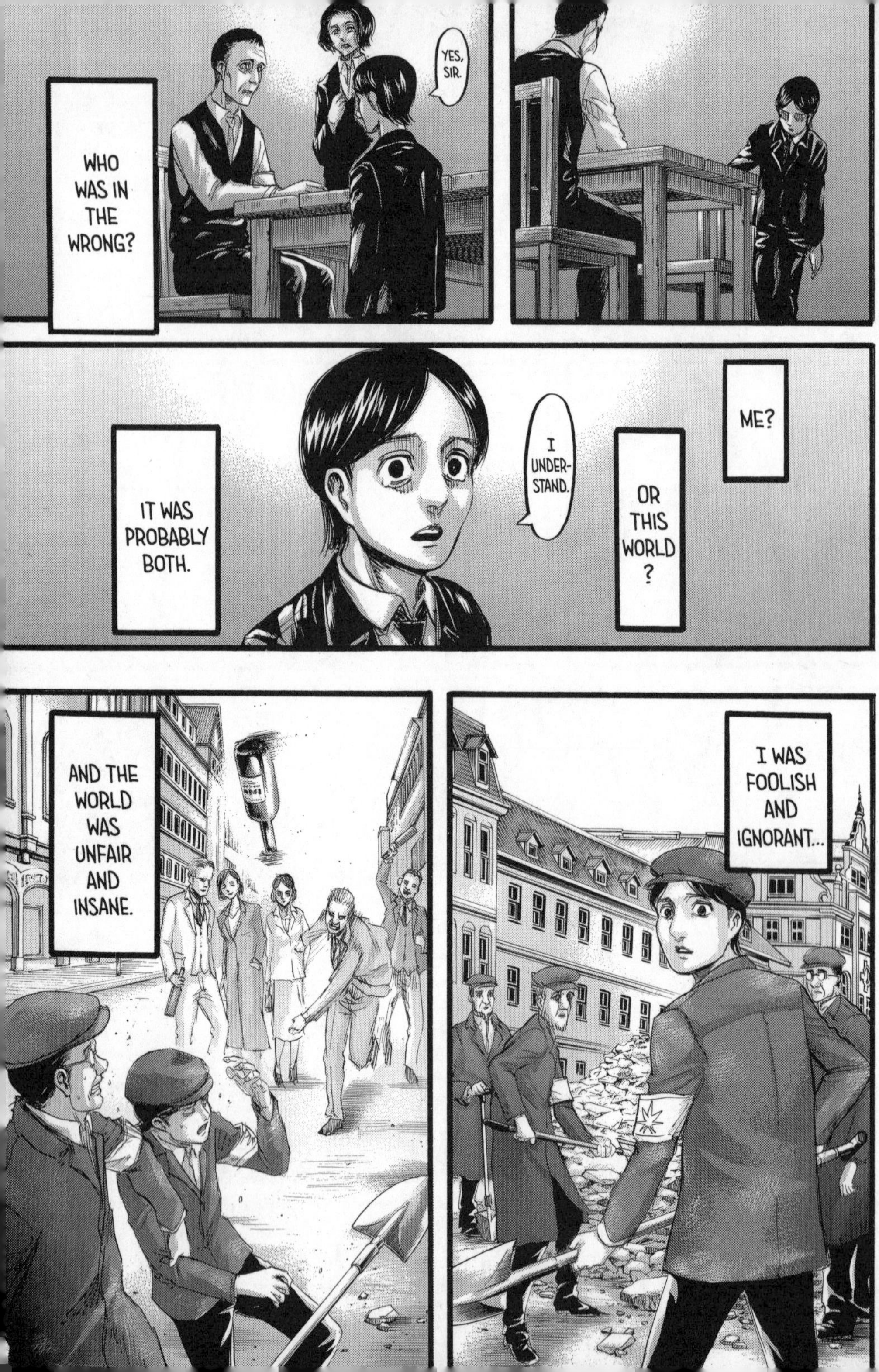
YES, SIR.
WHO WAS IN THE WRONG?
ME?
OR THIS WORLD?
I UNDER-STAND.
IT WAS PROBABLY BOTH.
I WAS FOOLISH AND IGNORANT...
AND THE WORLD WAS UNFAIR AND INSANE.

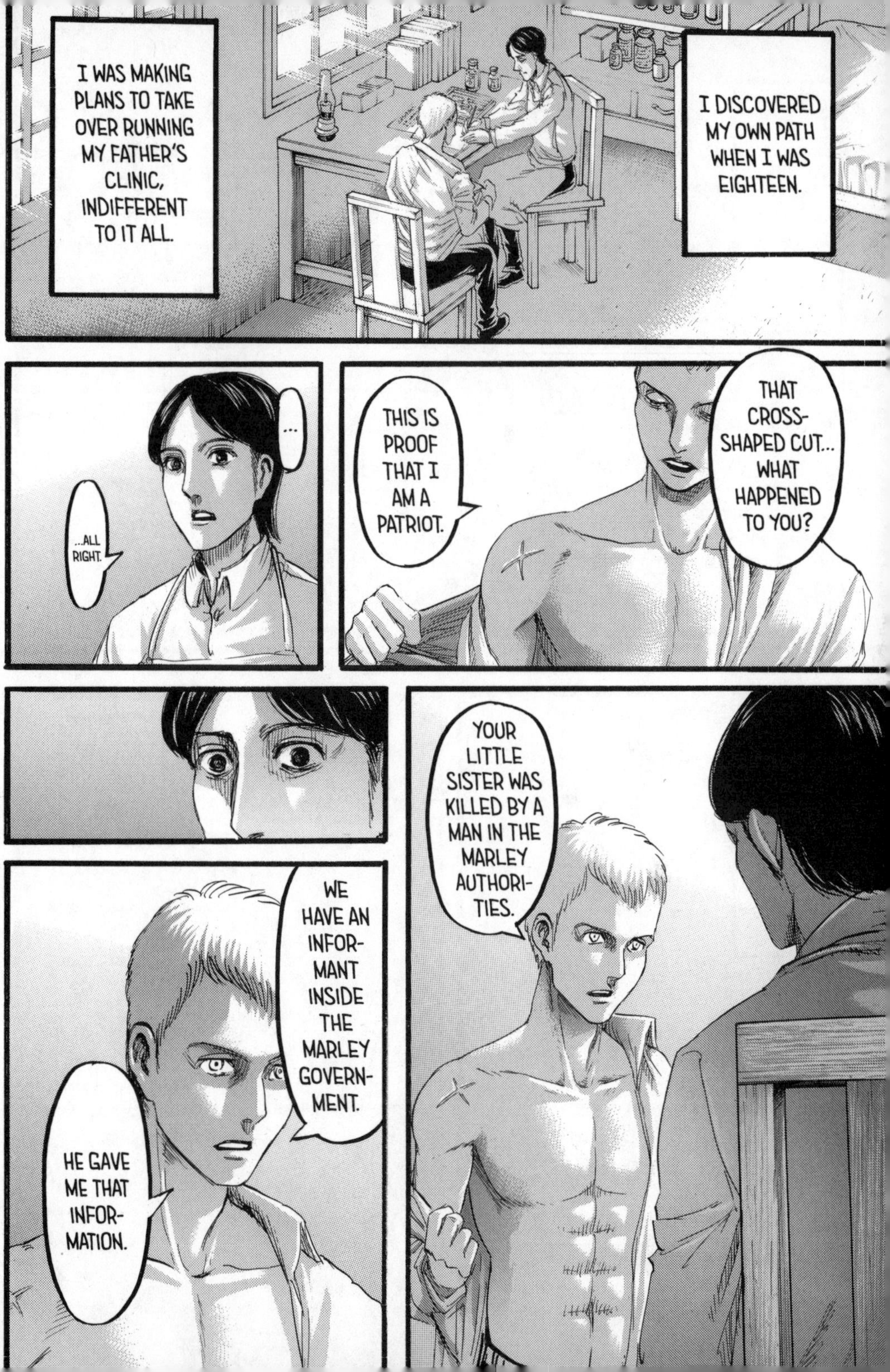

I DISCOVERED MY OWN PATH WHEN I WAS EIGHTEEN.
I WAS MAKING PLANS TO TAKE OVER RUNNING MY FATHER'S CLINIC, INDIFFERENT TO IT ALL.
THAT CROSS-SHAPED CUT... WHAT HAPPENED TO YOU?
THIS IS PROOF THAT I AM A PATRIOT.
...
...ALL RIGHT.
YOUR LITTLE SISTER WAS KILLED BY A MAN IN THE MARLEY AUTHORITIES.
WE HAVE AN INFORMANT INSIDE THE MARLEY GOVERNMENT.
HE GAVE ME THAT INFORMATION.

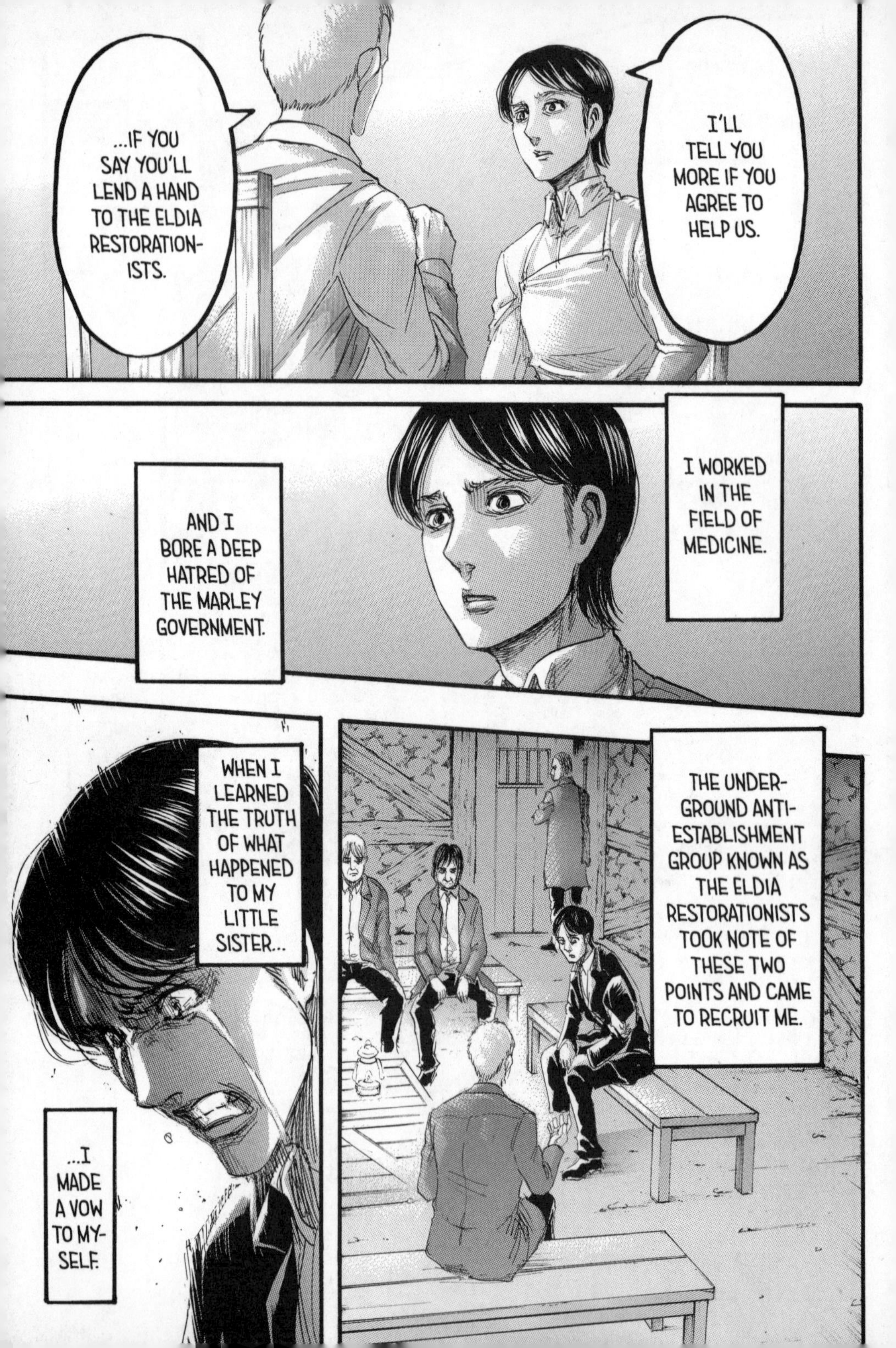
I'LL TELL YOU MORE IF YOU AGREE TO HELP US.
...IF YOU SAY YOU'LL LEND A HAND TO THE ELDIA RESTORATION-ISTS.
I WORKED IN THE FIELD OF MEDICINE.
AND I BORE A DEEP HATRED OF THE MARLEY GOVERNMENT.
THE UNDER-GROUND ANTI-ESTABLISHMENT GROUP KNOWN AS THE ELDIA RESTORATIONISTS TOOK NOTE OF THESE TWO POINTS AND CAME TO RECRUIT ME.
WHEN I LEARNED THE TRUTH OF WHAT HAPPENED TO MY LITTLE SISTER...
...I MADE A VOW TO MY-SELF.

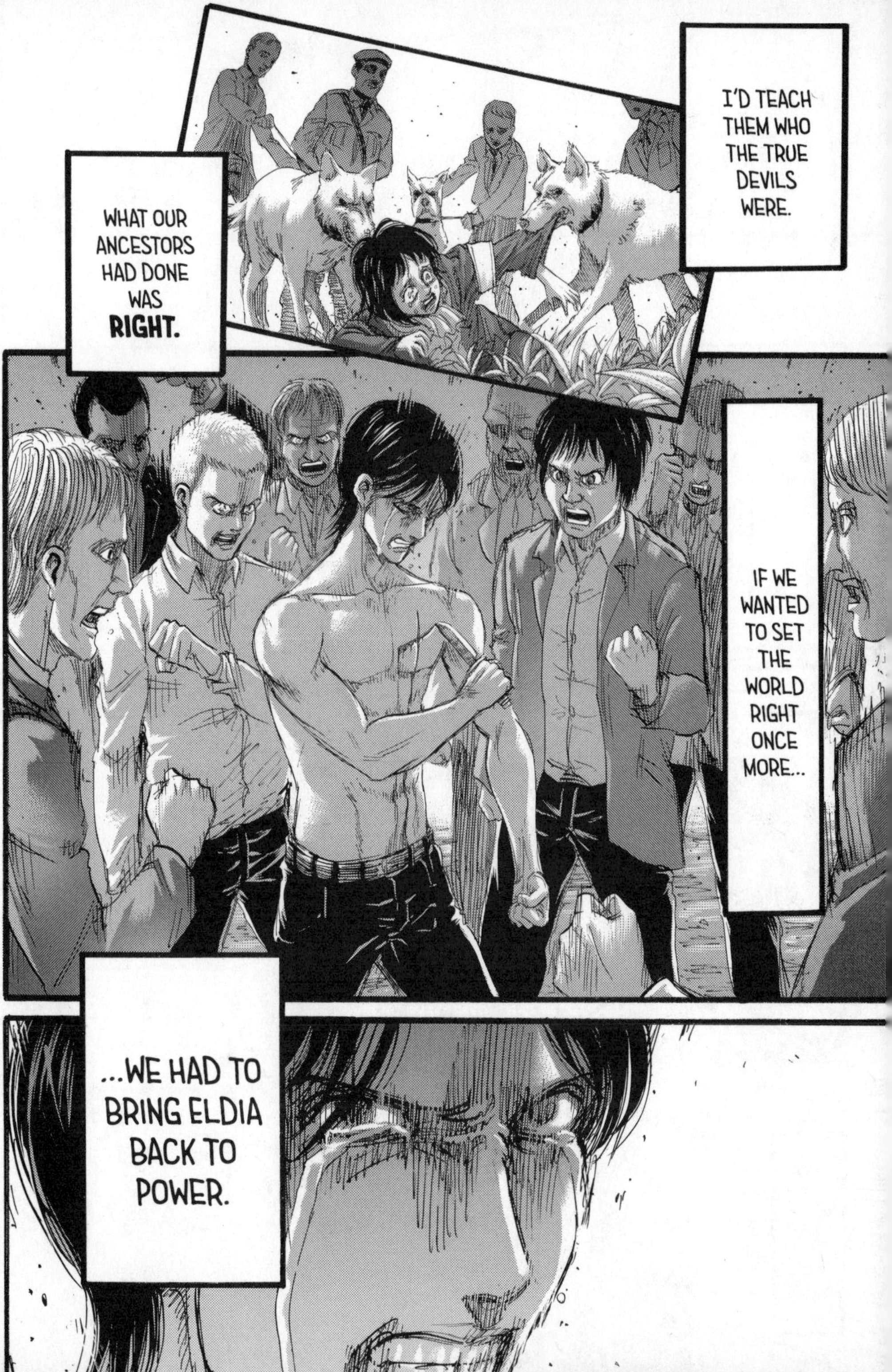
I'D TEACH THEM WHO THE TRUE DEVILS WERE.
WHAT OUR ANCESTORS HAD DONE WAS **RIGHT.**
IF WE WANTED TO SET THE WORLD RIGHT ONCE MORE...
...WE HAD TO BRING ELDIA BACK TO POWER.

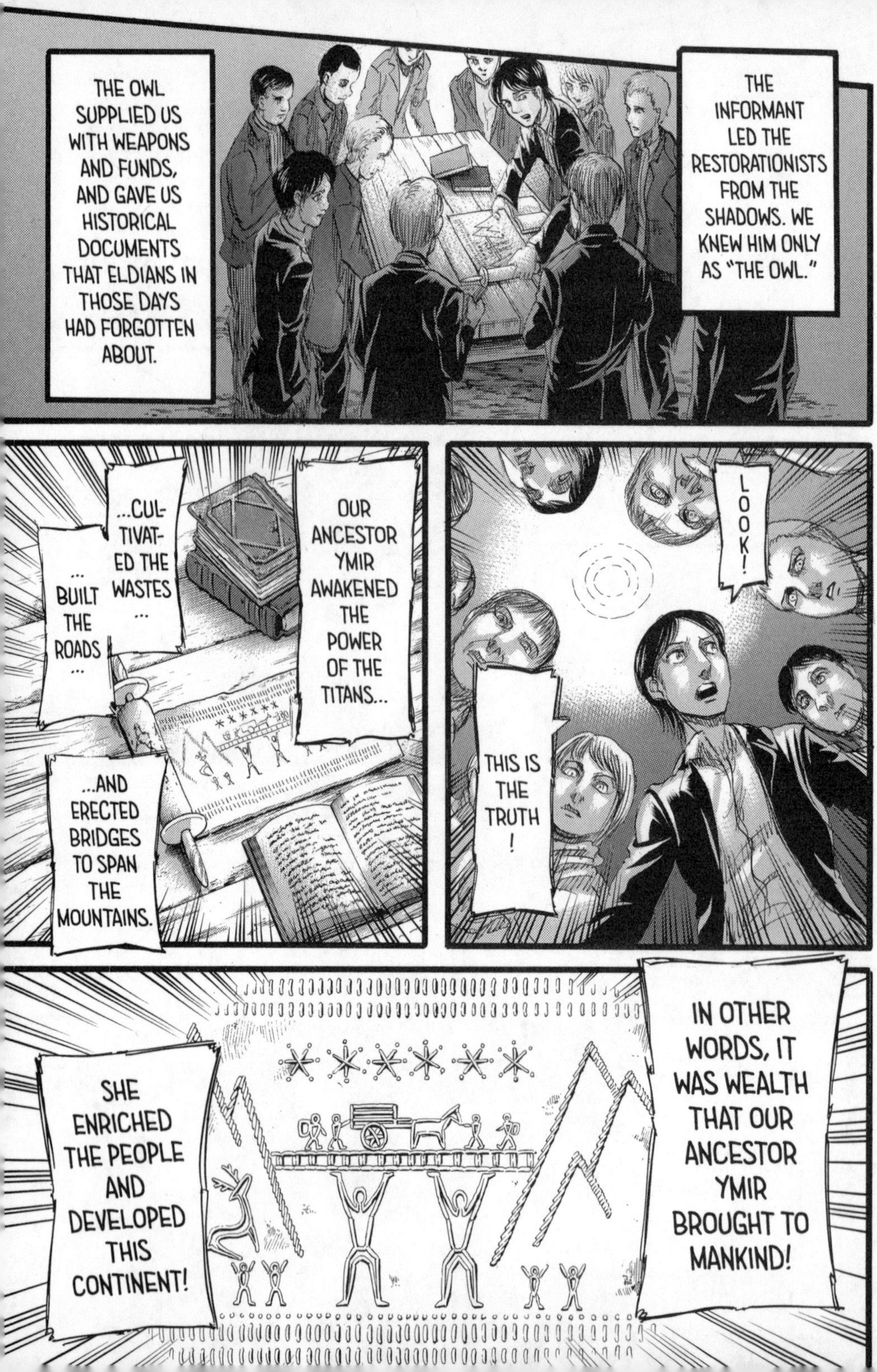
THE INFORMANT LED THE RESTORATIONISTS FROM THE SHADOWS. WE KNEW HIM ONLY AS "THE OWL."
THE OWL SUPPLIED US WITH WEAPONS AND FUNDS, AND GAVE US HISTORICAL DOCUMENTS THAT ELDIANS IN THOSE DAYS HAD FORGOTTEN ABOUT.
LOOK!
THIS IS THE TRUTH!
OUR ANCESTOR YMIR AWAKENED THE POWER OF THE TITANS...
...CULTIVATED THE WASTES...
...BUILT THE ROADS...
...AND ERECTED BRIDGES TO SPAN THE MOUNTAINS.
IN OTHER WORDS, IT WAS WEALTH THAT OUR ANCESTOR YMIR BROUGHT TO MANKIND!
SHE ENRICHED THE PEOPLE AND DEVELOPED THIS CONTINENT!

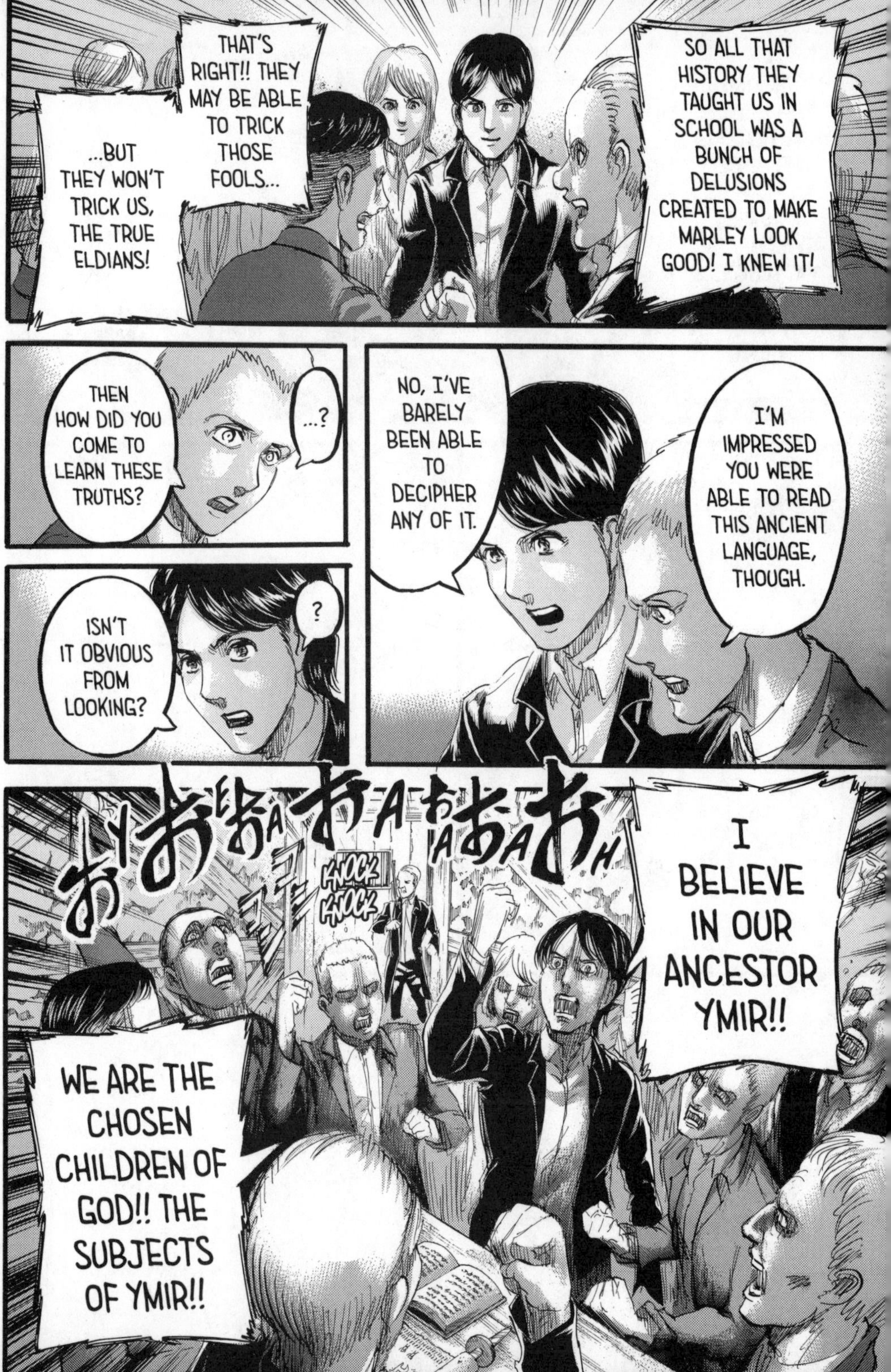
SO ALL THAT HISTORY THEY TAUGHT US IN SCHOOL WAS A BUNCH OF DELUSIONS CREATED TO MAKE MARLEY LOOK GOOD! I KNEW IT!
THAT'S RIGHT!! THEY MAY BE ABLE TO TRICK THOSE FOOLS...
...BUT THEY WON'T TRICK US, THE TRUE ELDIANS!
I'M IMPRESSED YOU WERE ABLE TO READ THIS ANCIENT LANGUAGE, THOUGH.
NO, I'VE BARELY BEEN ABLE TO DECIPHER ANY OF IT.
...?
THEN HOW DID YOU COME TO LEARN THESE TRUTHS?
?
ISN'T IT OBVIOUS FROM LOOKING?
I BELIEVE IN OUR ANCESTOR YMIR!!
KNOCK KNOCK
WE ARE THE CHOSEN CHILDREN OF GOD!! THE SUBJECTS OF YMIR!!

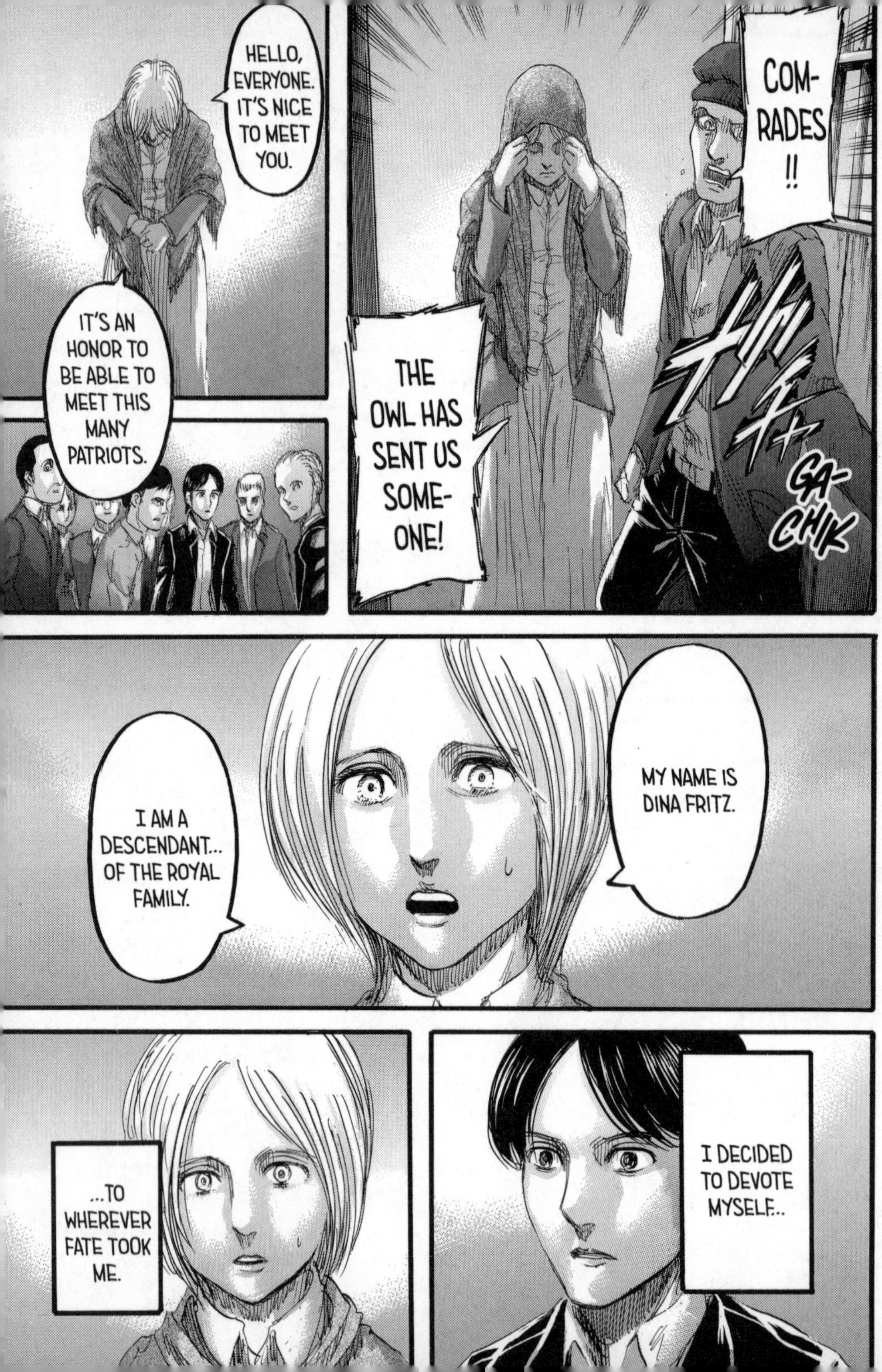
COM-RADES!!
THE OWL HAS SENT US SOME-ONE!
GA-CHIK
HELLO, EVERYONE. IT'S NICE TO MEET YOU.
IT'S AN HONOR TO BE ABLE TO MEET THIS MANY PATRIOTS.
MY NAME IS DINA FRITZ.
I AM A DESCENDANT... OF THE ROYAL FAMILY.
I DECIDED TO DEVOTE MYSELF...
...TO WHEREVER FATE TOOK ME.

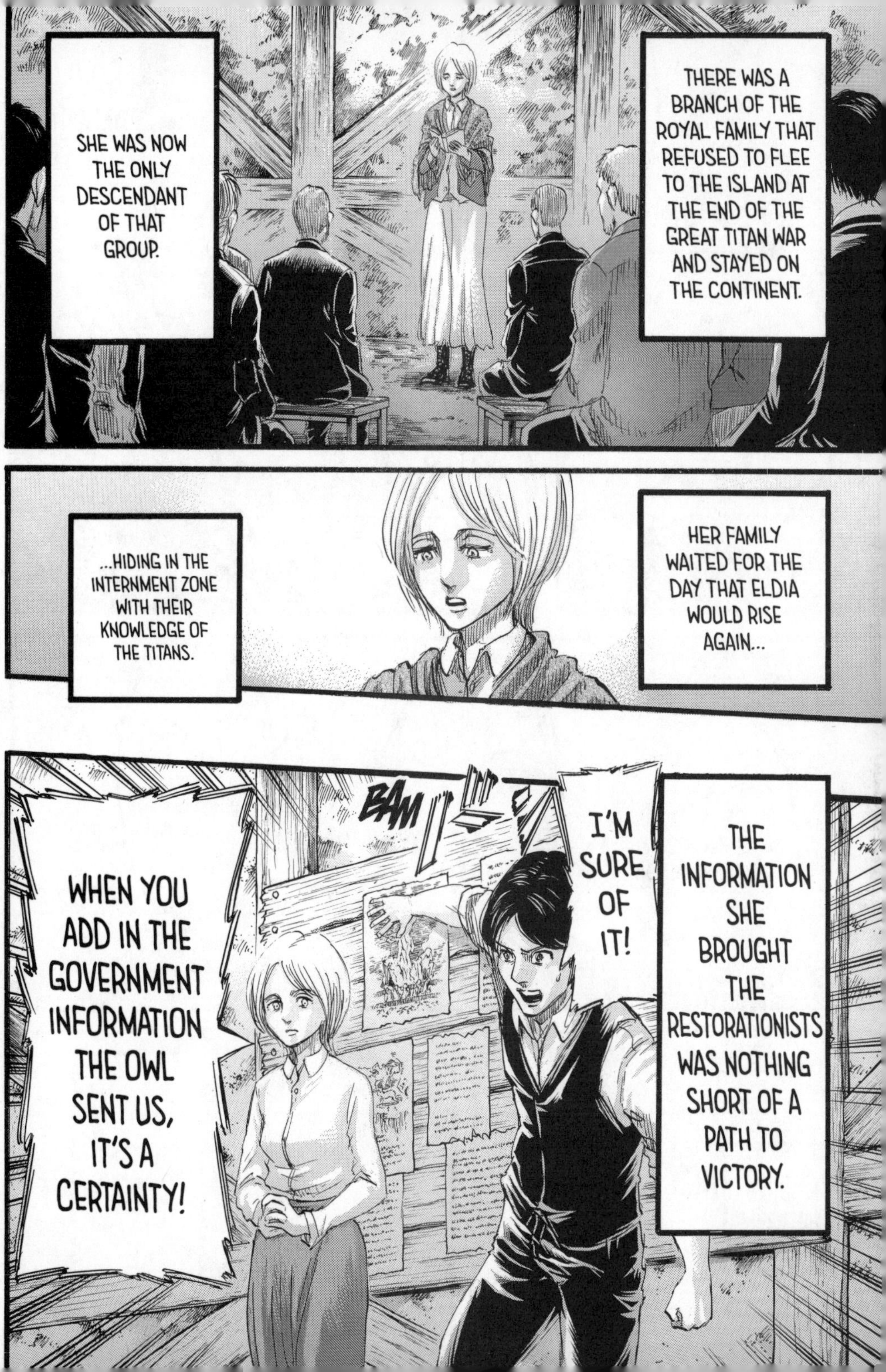
THERE WAS A BRANCH OF THE ROYAL FAMILY THAT REFUSED TO FLEE TO THE ISLAND AT THE END OF THE GREAT TITAN WAR AND STAYED ON THE CONTINENT.
SHE WAS NOW THE ONLY DESCENDANT OF THAT GROUP.
HER FAMILY WAITED FOR THE DAY THAT ELDIA WOULD RISE AGAIN...
...HIDING IN THE INTERNMENT ZONE WITH THEIR KNOWLEDGE OF THE TITANS.
THE INFORMATION SHE BROUGHT THE RESTORATIONISTS WAS NOTHING SHORT OF A PATH TO VICTORY.
I'M SURE OF IT!
BAM
WHEN YOU ADD IN THE GOVERNMENT INFORMATION THE OWL SENT US, IT'S A CERTAINTY!

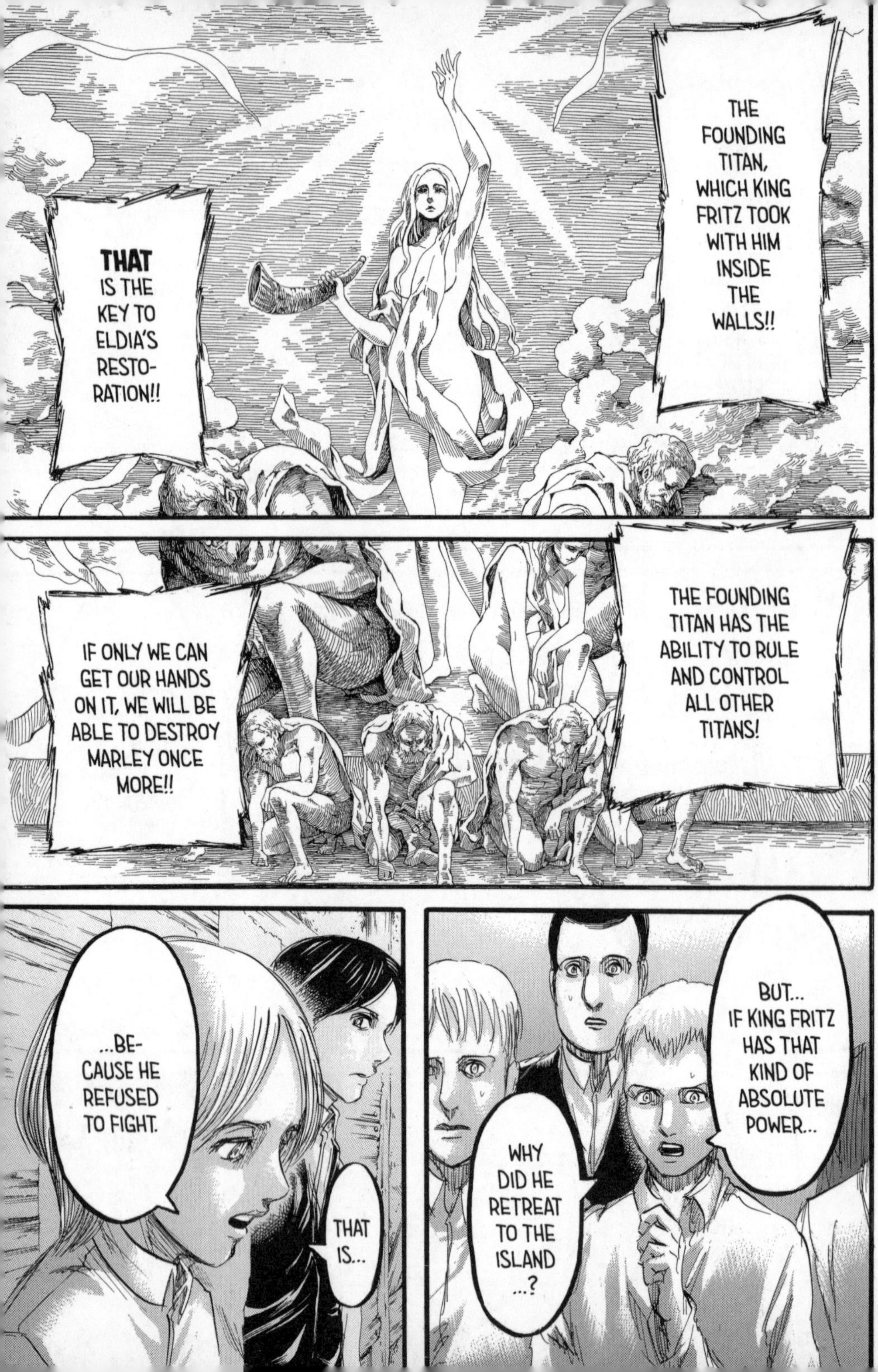
THE FOUNDING TITAN, WHICH KING FRITZ TOOK WITH HIM INSIDE THE WALLS!!
THAT IS THE KEY TO ELDIA'S RESTORATION!!
THE FOUNDING TITAN HAS THE ABILITY TO RULE AND CONTROL ALL OTHER TITANS!
IF ONLY WE CAN GET OUR HANDS ON IT, WE WILL BE ABLE TO DESTROY MARLEY ONCE MORE!!
BUT... IF KING FRITZ HAS THAT KIND OF ABSOLUTE POWER...
WHY DID HE RETREAT TO THE ISLAND ...?
THAT IS...
...BECAUSE HE REFUSED TO FIGHT.

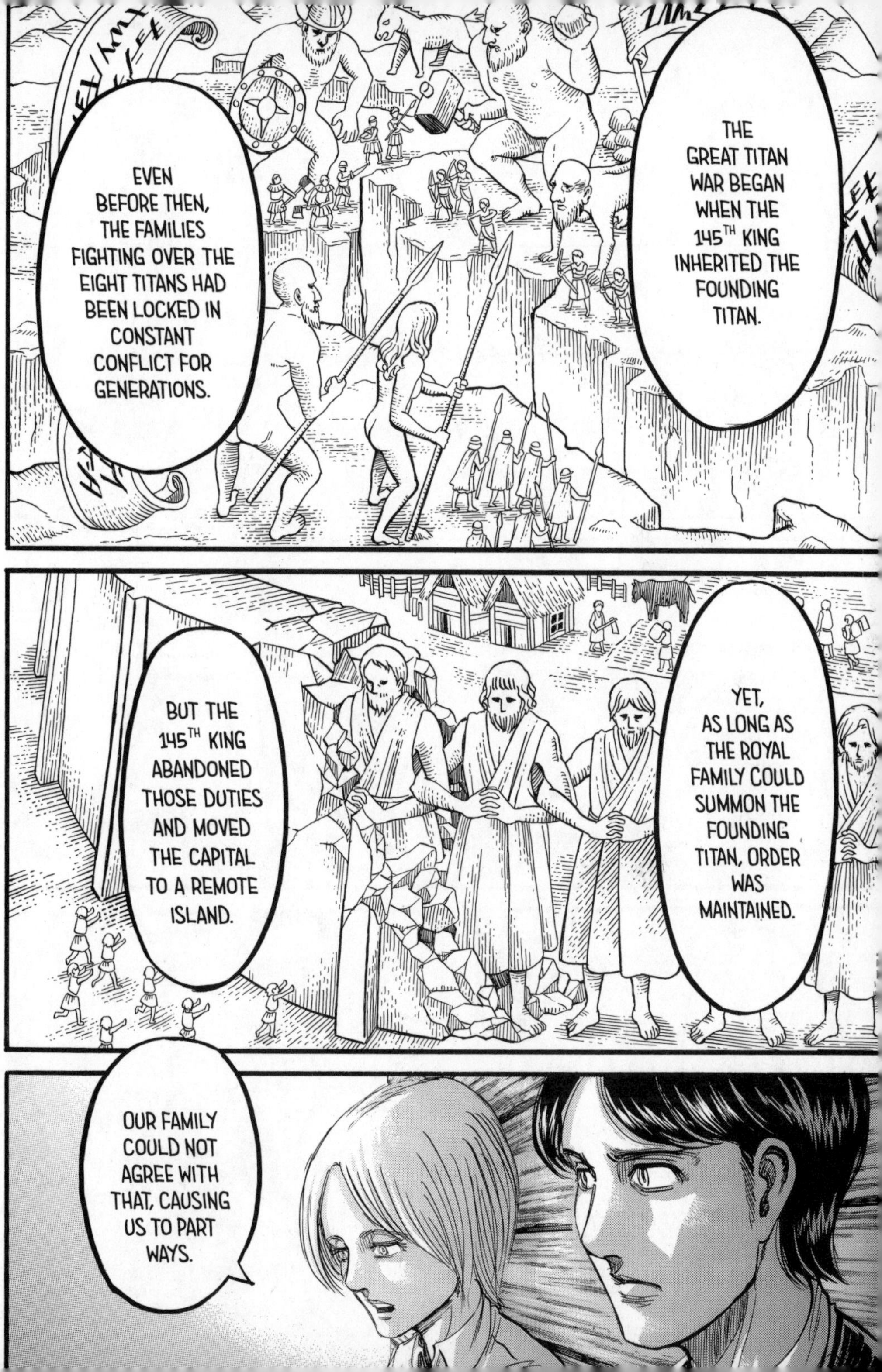
THE GREAT TITAN WAR BEGAN WHEN THE 145TH KING INHERITED THE FOUNDING TITAN.
EVEN BEFORE THEN, THE FAMILIES FIGHTING OVER THE EIGHT TITANS HAD BEEN LOCKED IN CONSTANT CONFLICT FOR GENERATIONS.
YET, AS LONG AS THE ROYAL FAMILY COULD SUMMON THE FOUNDING TITAN, ORDER WAS MAINTAINED.
BUT THE 145TH KING ABANDONED THOSE DUTIES AND MOVED THE CAPITAL TO A REMOTE ISLAND.
OUR FAMILY COULD NOT AGREE WITH THAT, CAUSING US TO PART WAYS.

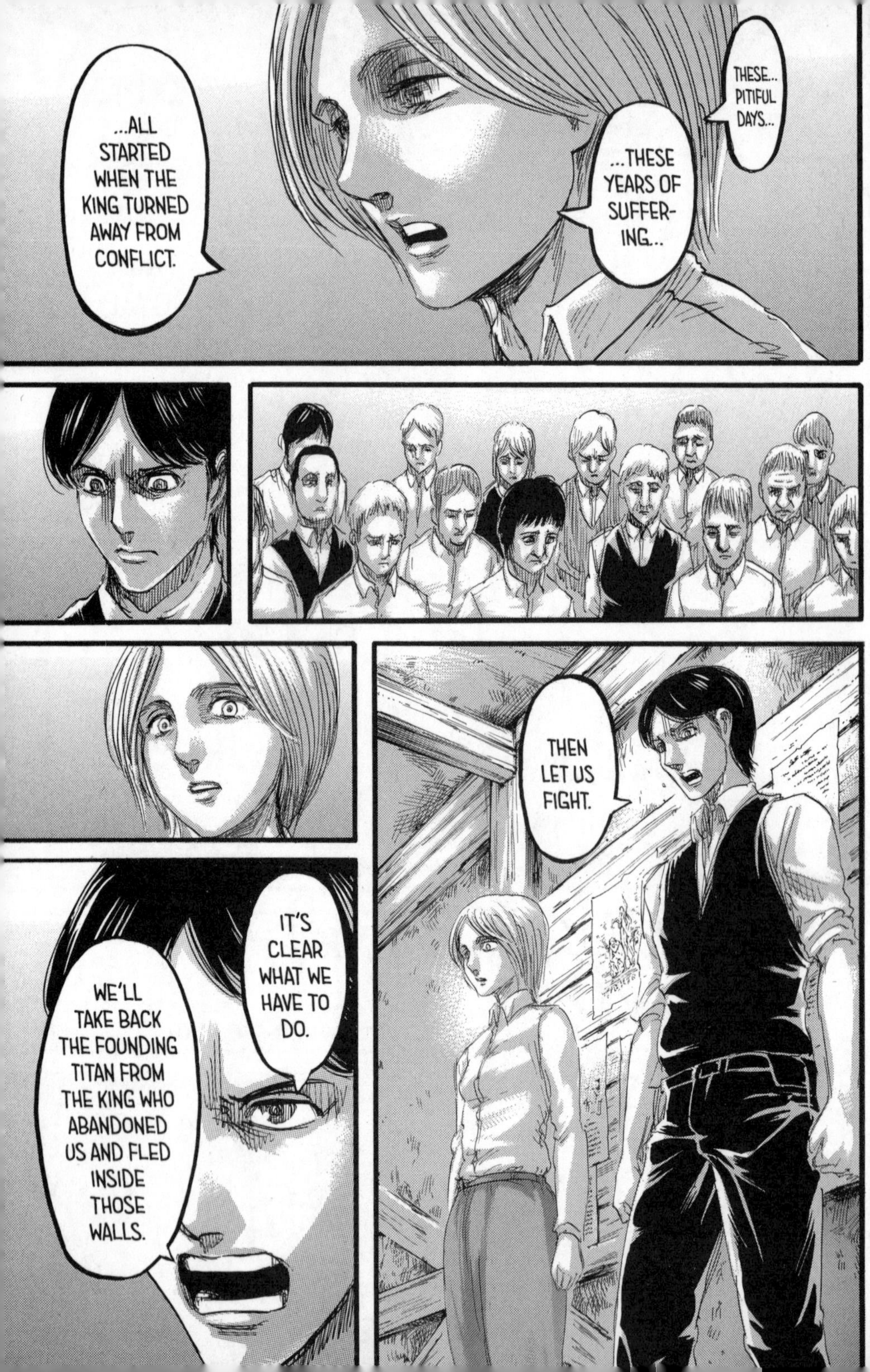

THESE... PITIFUL DAYS...
...THESE YEARS OF SUFFER-ING...
...ALL STARTED WHEN THE KING TURNED AWAY FROM CONFLICT.
THEN LET US FIGHT.
IT'S CLEAR WHAT WE HAVE TO DO.
WE'LL TAKE BACK THE FOUNDING TITAN FROM THE KING WHO ABANDONED US AND FLED INSIDE THOSE WALLS.

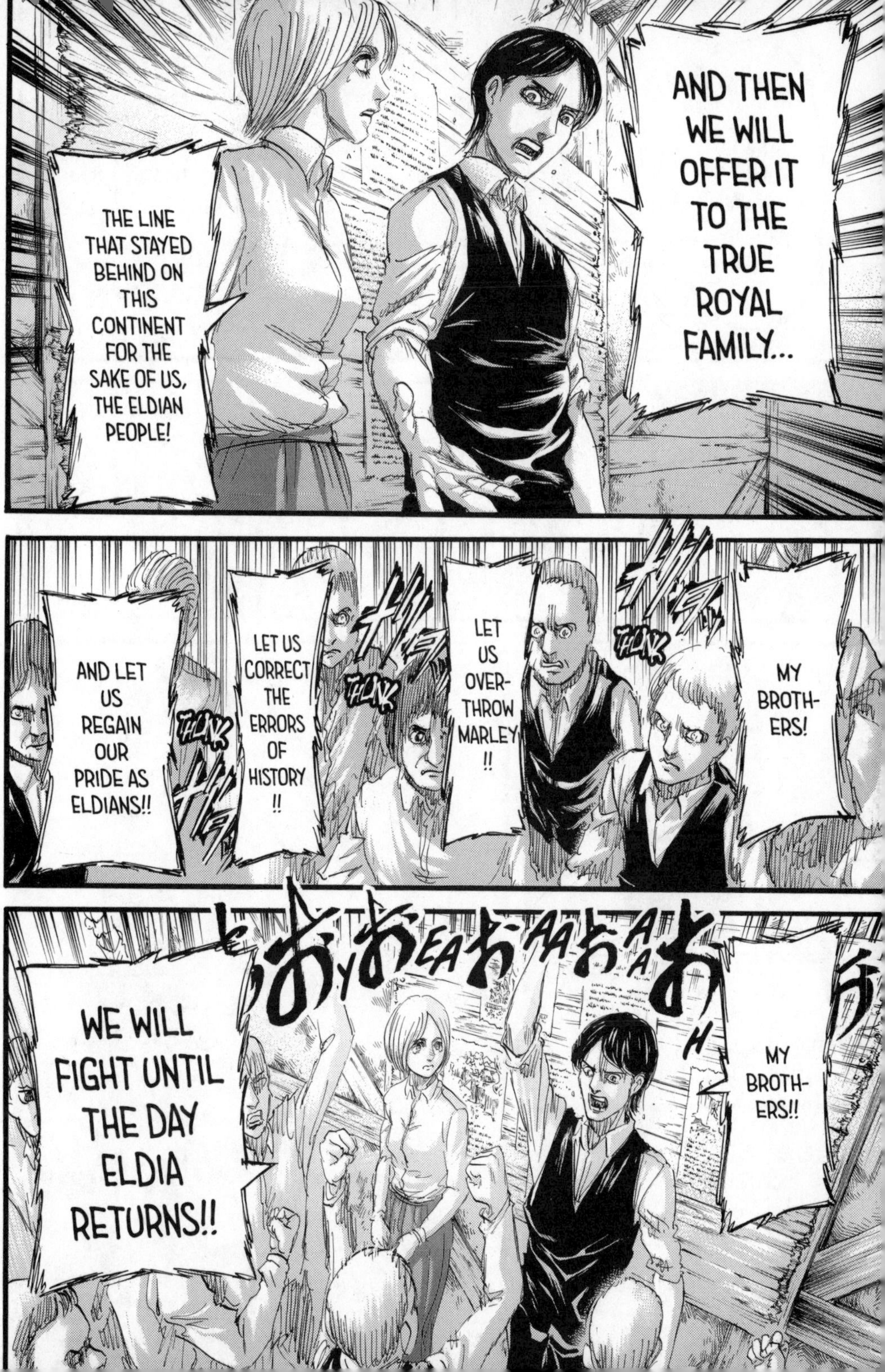
AND THEN WE WILL OFFER IT TO THE TRUE ROYAL FAMILY...
THE LINE THAT STAYED BEHIND ON THIS CONTINENT FOR THE SAKE OF US, THE ELDIAN PEOPLE!
MY BROTHERS!
THUNK
LET US OVERTHROW MARLEY!!
THUNK
LET US CORRECT THE ERRORS OF HISTORY!!
THUNK
AND LET US REGAIN OUR PRIDE AS ELDIANS!!
MY BROTHERS!!
WE WILL FIGHT UNTIL THE DAY ELDIA RETURNS!!

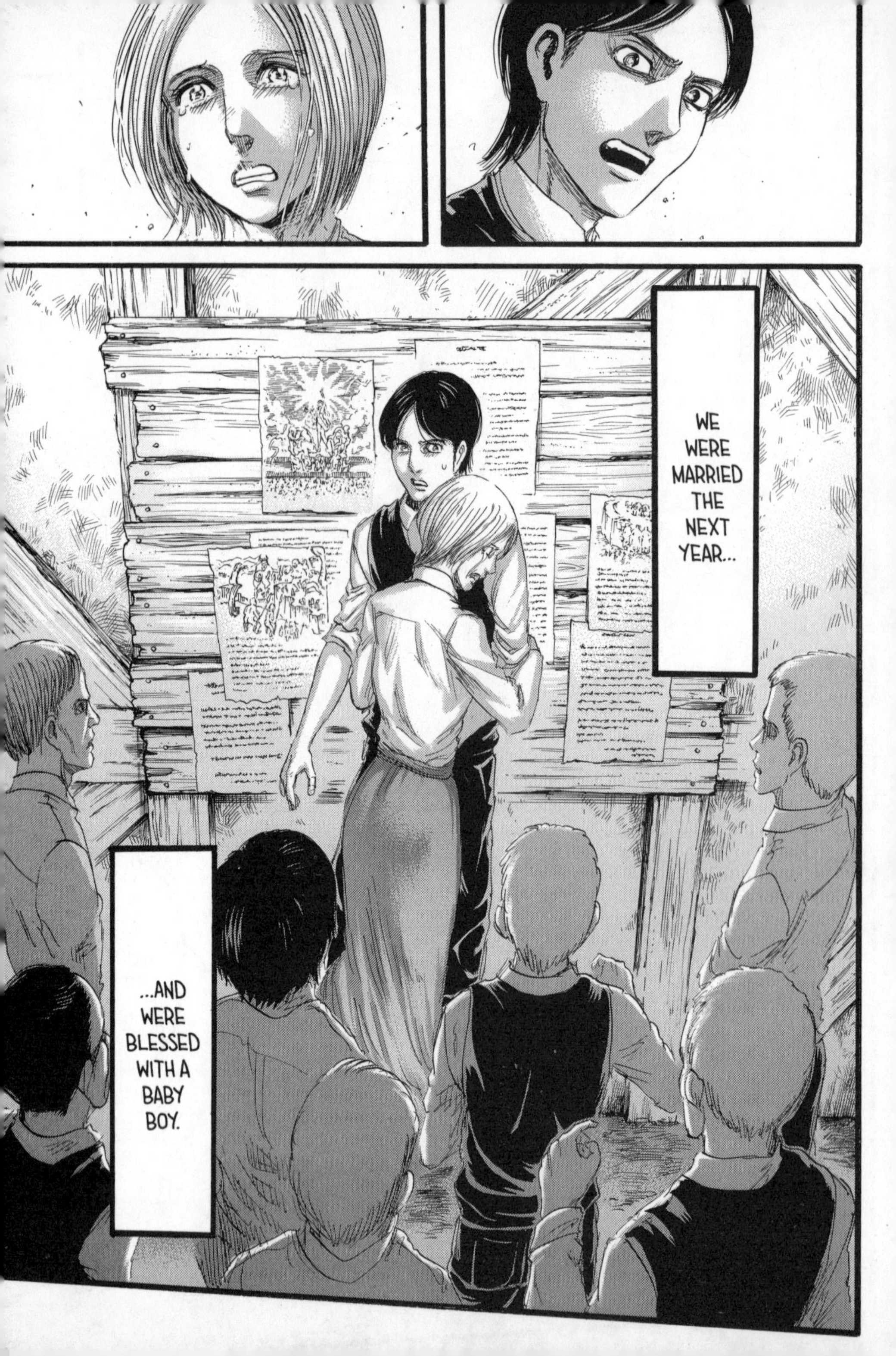
WE WERE MARRIED THE NEXT YEAR...
...AND WERE BLESSED WITH A BABY BOY.

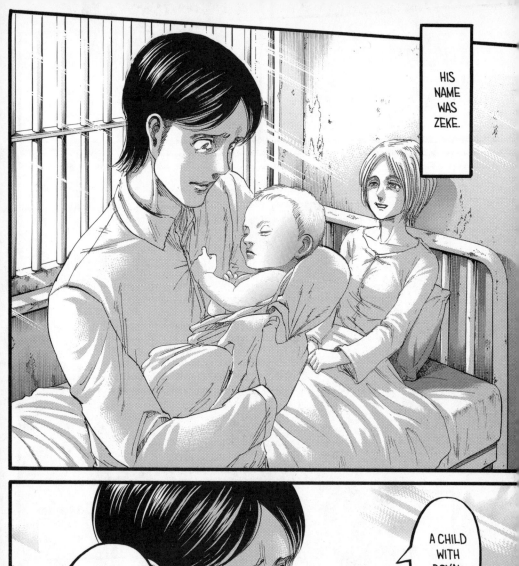

HIS NAME WAS ZEKE.

A CHILD WITH ROYAL BLOOD...

I'M SURE HE'LL ONE DAY HELP LEAD US TO VICTORY.

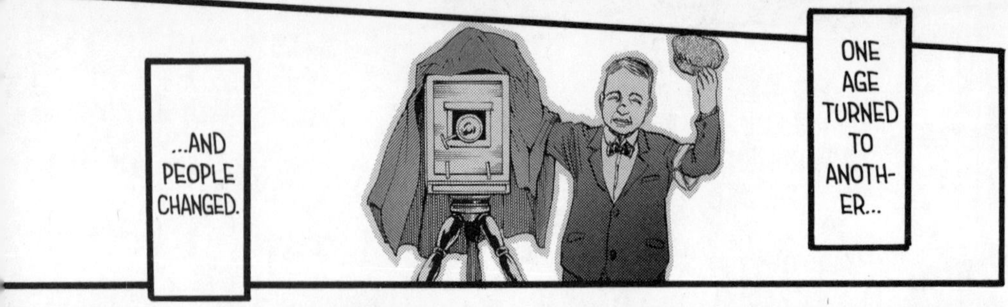
ONE AGE TURNED TO ANOTH-ER...
...AND PEOPLE CHANGED.

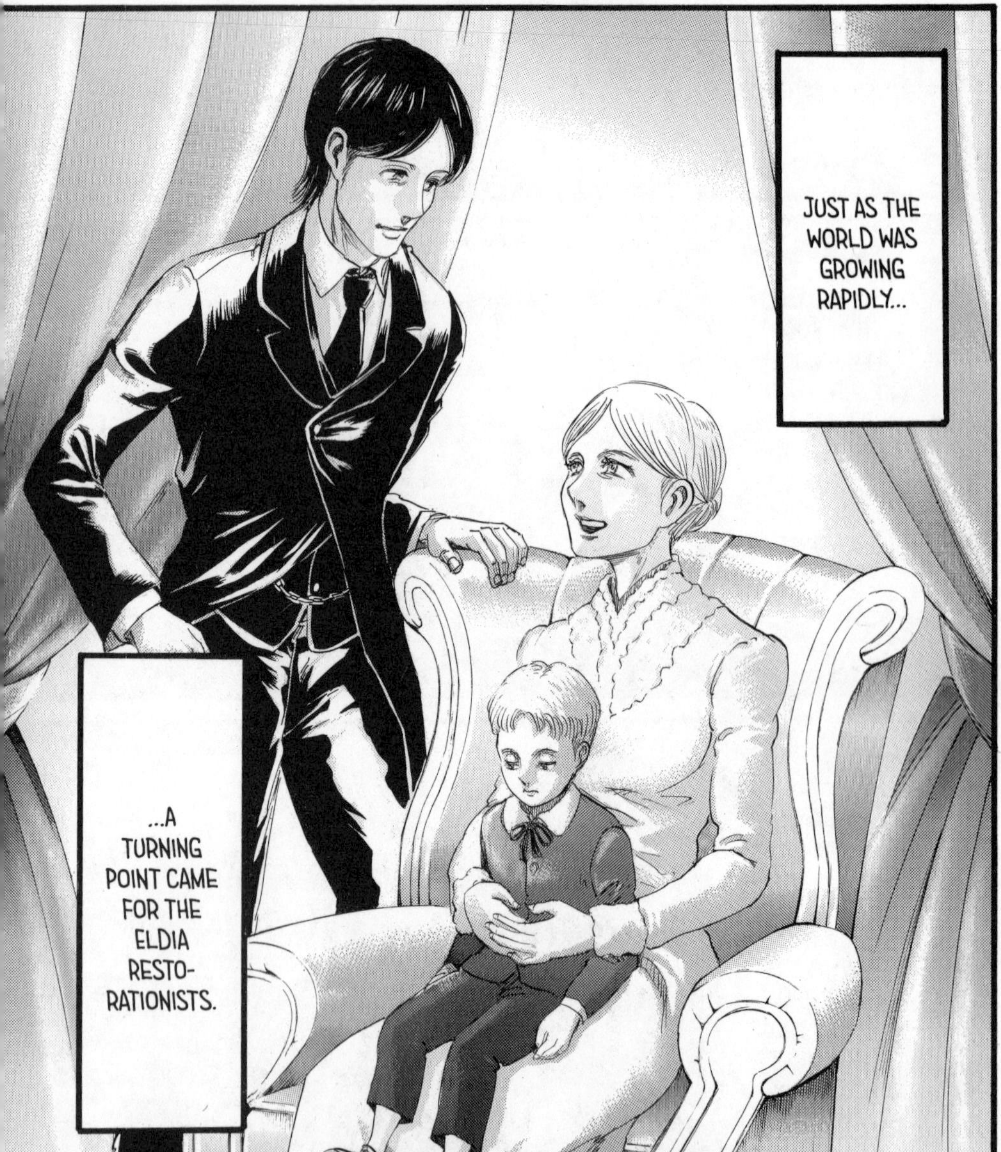
JUST AS THE WORLD WAS GROWING RAPIDLY...
...A TURNING POINT CAME FOR THE ELDIA RESTO-RATIONISTS.

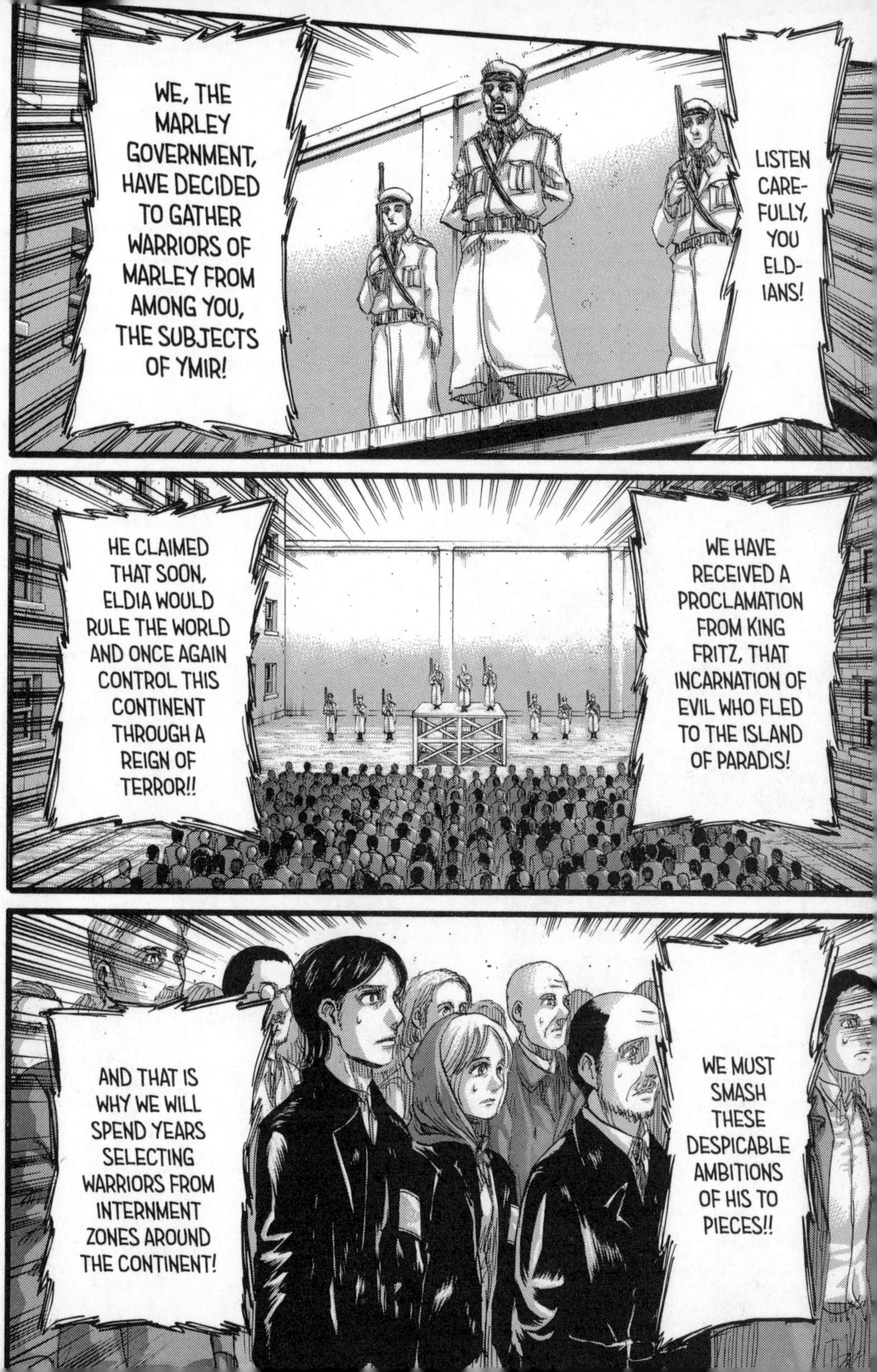
LISTEN CAREFULLY, YOU ELDIANS!
WE, THE MARLEY GOVERNMENT, HAVE DECIDED TO GATHER WARRIORS OF MARLEY FROM AMONG YOU, THE SUBJECTS OF YMIR!
WE HAVE RECEIVED A PROCLAMATION FROM KING FRITZ, THAT INCARNATION OF EVIL WHO FLED TO THE ISLAND OF PARADIS!
HE CLAIMED THAT SOON, ELDIA WOULD RULE THE WORLD AND ONCE AGAIN CONTROL THIS CONTINENT THROUGH A REIGN OF TERROR!!
WE MUST SMASH THESE DESPICABLE AMBITIONS OF HIS TO PIECES!!
AND THAT IS WHY WE WILL SPEND YEARS SELECTING WARRIORS FROM INTERNMENT ZONES AROUND THE CONTINENT!

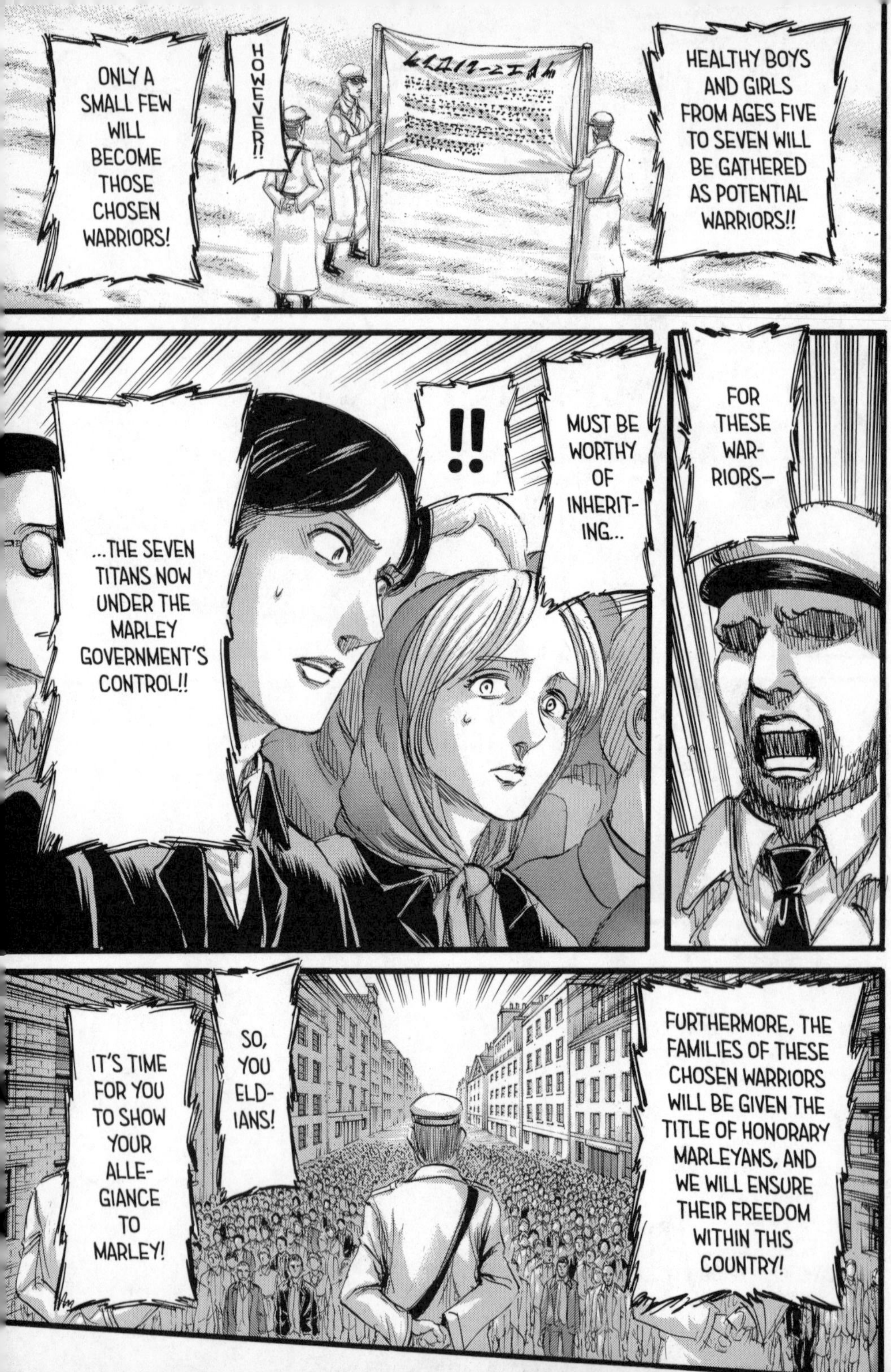
HEALTHY BOYS AND GIRLS FROM AGES FIVE TO SEVEN WILL BE GATHERED AS POTENTIAL WARRIORS!!
HOWEVER!!
ONLY A SMALL FEW WILL BECOME THOSE CHOSEN WARRIORS!
FOR THESE WARRIORS—
MUST BE WORTHY OF INHERITING...
!!
...THE SEVEN TITANS NOW UNDER THE MARLEY GOVERNMENT'S CONTROL!!
FURTHERMORE, THE FAMILIES OF THESE CHOSEN WARRIORS WILL BE GIVEN THE TITLE OF HONORARY MARLEYANS, AND WE WILL ENSURE THEIR FREEDOM WITHIN THIS COUNTRY!
SO, YOU ELDIANS!
IT'S TIME FOR YOU TO SHOW YOUR ALLEGIANCE TO MARLEY!

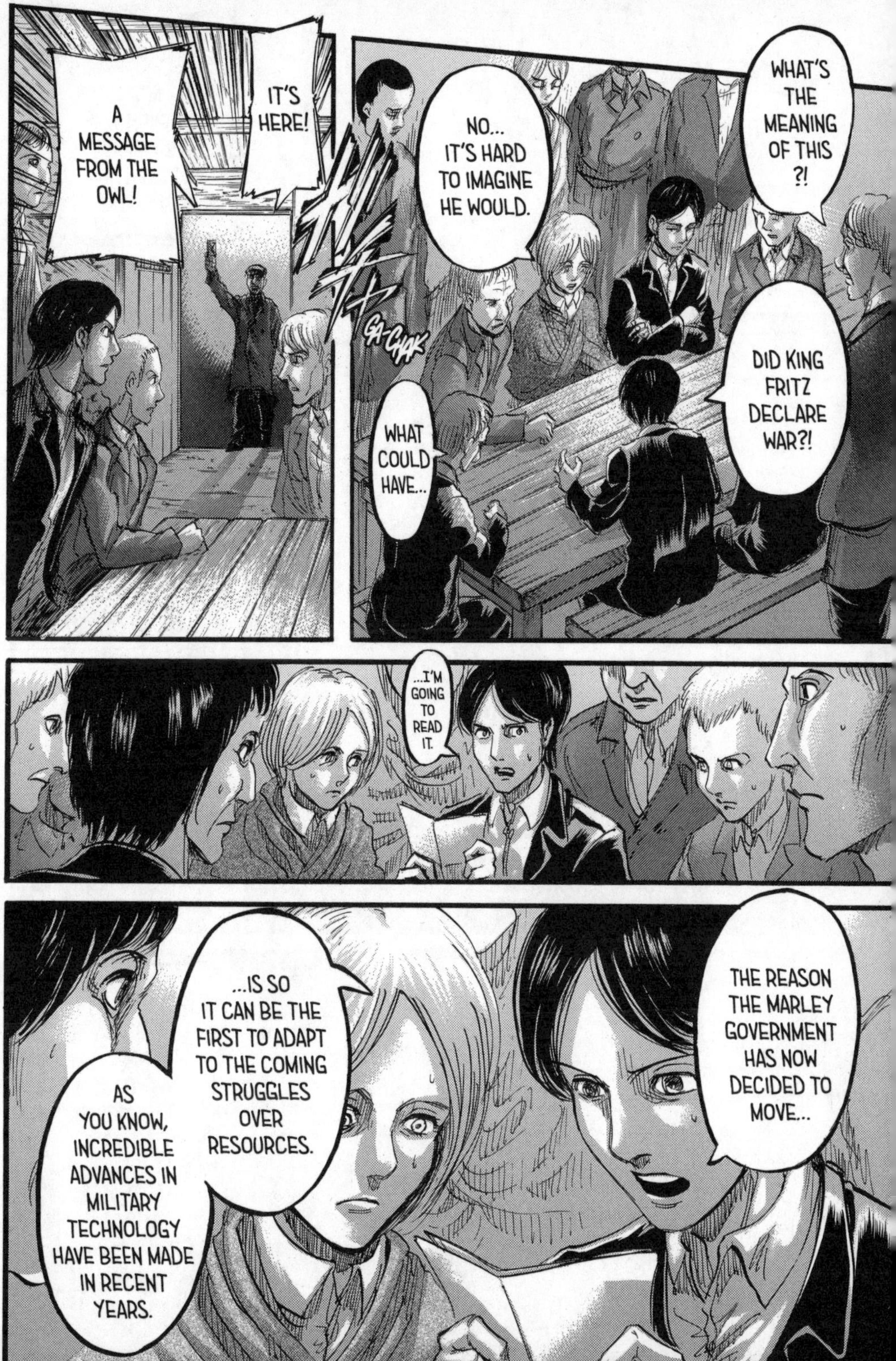
WHAT'S THE MEANING OF THIS?!
DID KING FRITZ DECLARE WAR?!
NO... IT'S HARD TO IMAGINE HE WOULD.
WHAT COULD HAVE...
GA-CHAK
IT'S HERE!
A MESSAGE FROM THE OWL!
...I'M GOING TO READ IT.
THE REASON THE MARLEY GOVERNMENT HAS NOW DECIDED TO MOVE...
...IS SO IT CAN BE THE FIRST TO ADAPT TO THE COMING STRUGGLES OVER RESOURCES.
AS YOU KNOW, INCREDIBLE ADVANCES IN MILITARY TECHNOLOGY HAVE BEEN MADE IN RECENT YEARS.

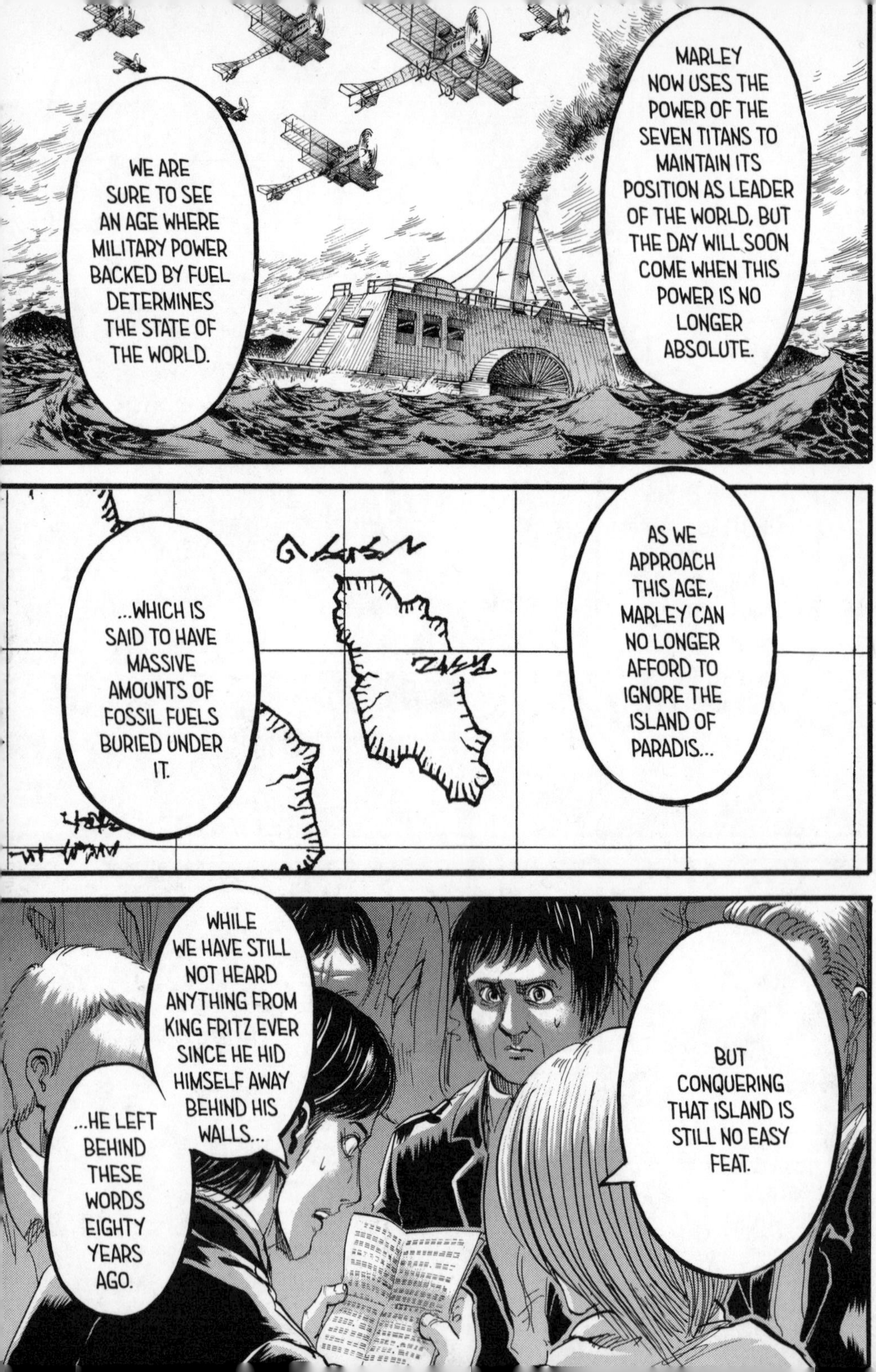
MARLEY NOW USES THE POWER OF THE SEVEN TITANS TO MAINTAIN ITS POSITION AS LEADER OF THE WORLD, BUT THE DAY WILL SOON COME WHEN THIS POWER IS NO LONGER ABSOLUTE.
WE ARE SURE TO SEE AN AGE WHERE MILITARY POWER BACKED BY FUEL DETERMINES THE STATE OF THE WORLD.
AS WE APPROACH THIS AGE, MARLEY CAN NO LONGER AFFORD TO IGNORE THE ISLAND OF PARADIS...
...WHICH IS SAID TO HAVE MASSIVE AMOUNTS OF FOSSIL FUELS BURIED UNDER IT.
BUT CONQUERING THAT ISLAND IS STILL NO EASY FEAT.
WHILE WE HAVE STILL NOT HEARD ANYTHING FROM KING FRITZ EVER SINCE HE HID HIMSELF AWAY BEHIND HIS WALLS...
...HE LEFT BEHIND THESE WORDS EIGHTY YEARS AGO.

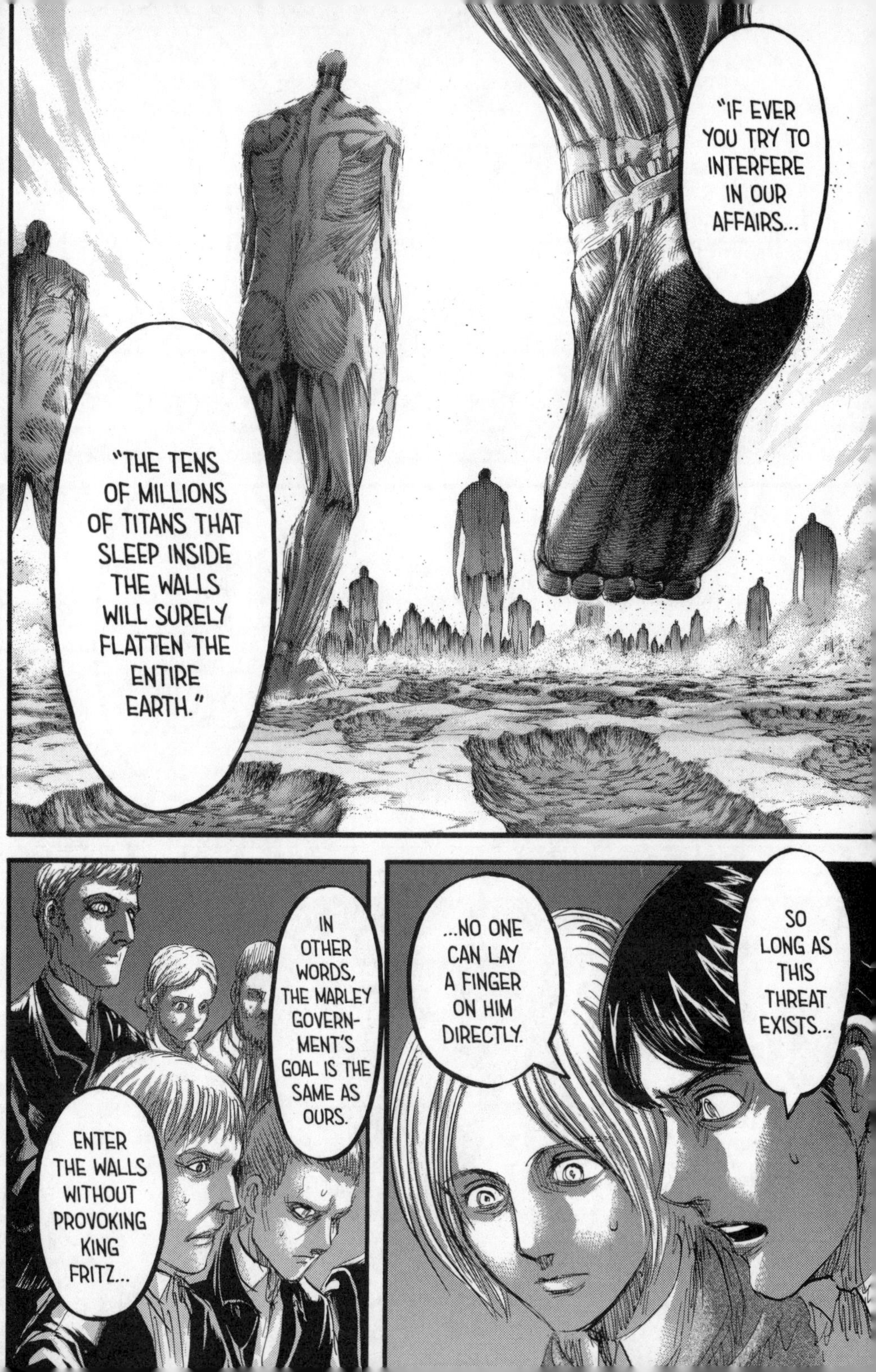
"IF EVER YOU TRY TO INTERFERE IN OUR AFFAIRS...
"THE TENS OF MILLIONS OF TITANS THAT SLEEP INSIDE THE WALLS WILL SURELY FLATTEN THE ENTIRE EARTH."
SO LONG AS THIS THREAT EXISTS...
...NO ONE CAN LAY A FINGER ON HIM DIRECTLY.
IN OTHER WORDS, THE MARLEY GOVERN-MENT'S GOAL IS THE SAME AS OURS.
ENTER THE WALLS WITHOUT PROVOKING KING FRITZ...

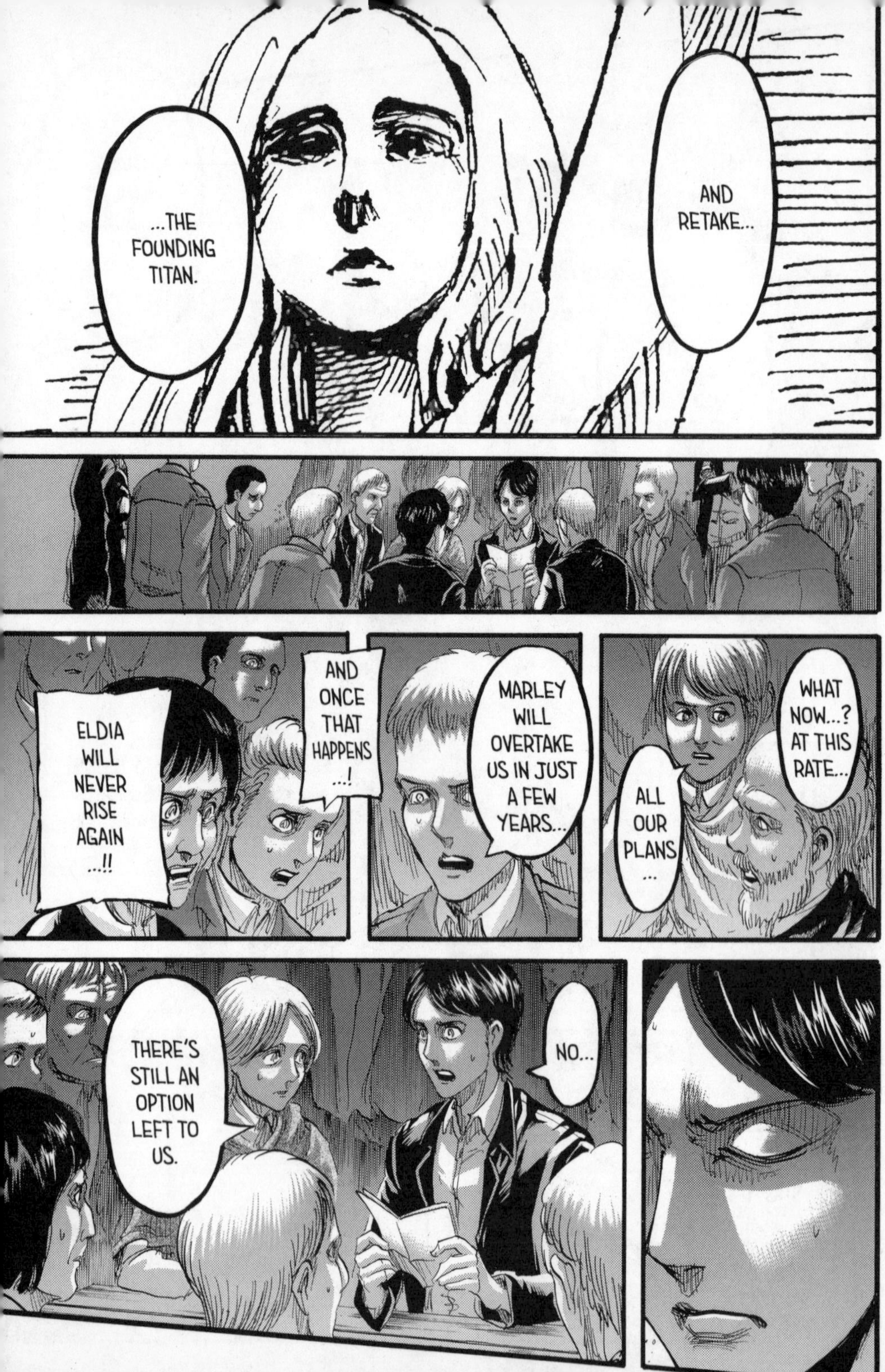
AND RETAKE...
...THE FOUNDING TITAN.
WHAT NOW...? AT THIS RATE...
ALL OUR PLANS ...
MARLEY WILL OVERTAKE US IN JUST A FEW YEARS...
AND ONCE THAT HAPPENS ...!
ELDIA WILL NEVER RISE AGAIN ...!!
NO...
THERE'S STILL AN OPTION LEFT TO US.

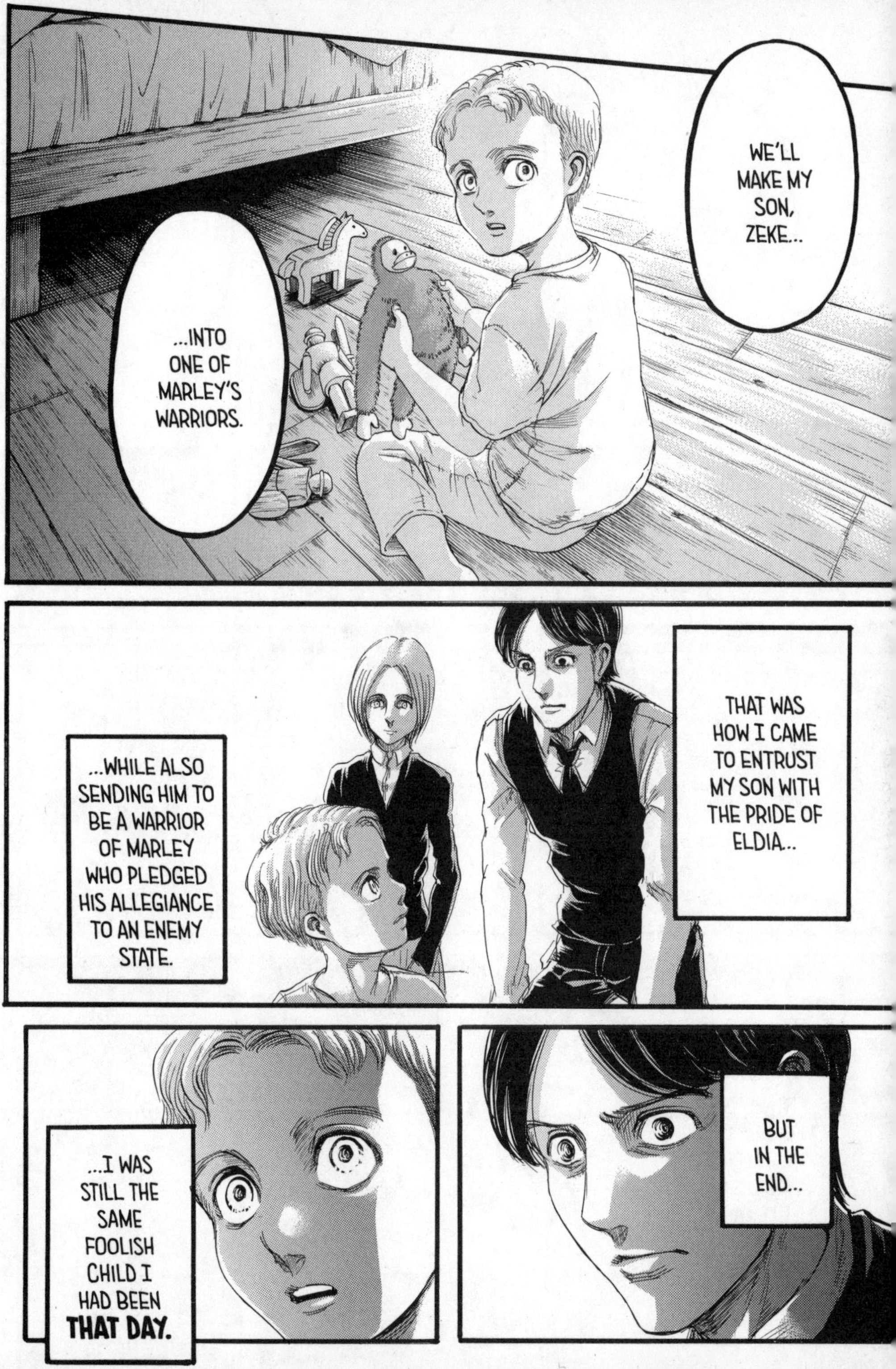
WE'LL MAKE MY SON, ZEKE...
...INTO ONE OF MARLEY'S WARRIORS.
THAT WAS HOW I CAME TO ENTRUST MY SON WITH THE PRIDE OF ELDIA...
...WHILE ALSO SENDING HIM TO BE A WARRIOR OF MARLEY WHO PLEDGED HIS ALLEGIANCE TO AN ENEMY STATE.
BUT IN THE END...
...I WAS STILL THE SAME FOOLISH CHILD I HAD BEEN **THAT DAY.**

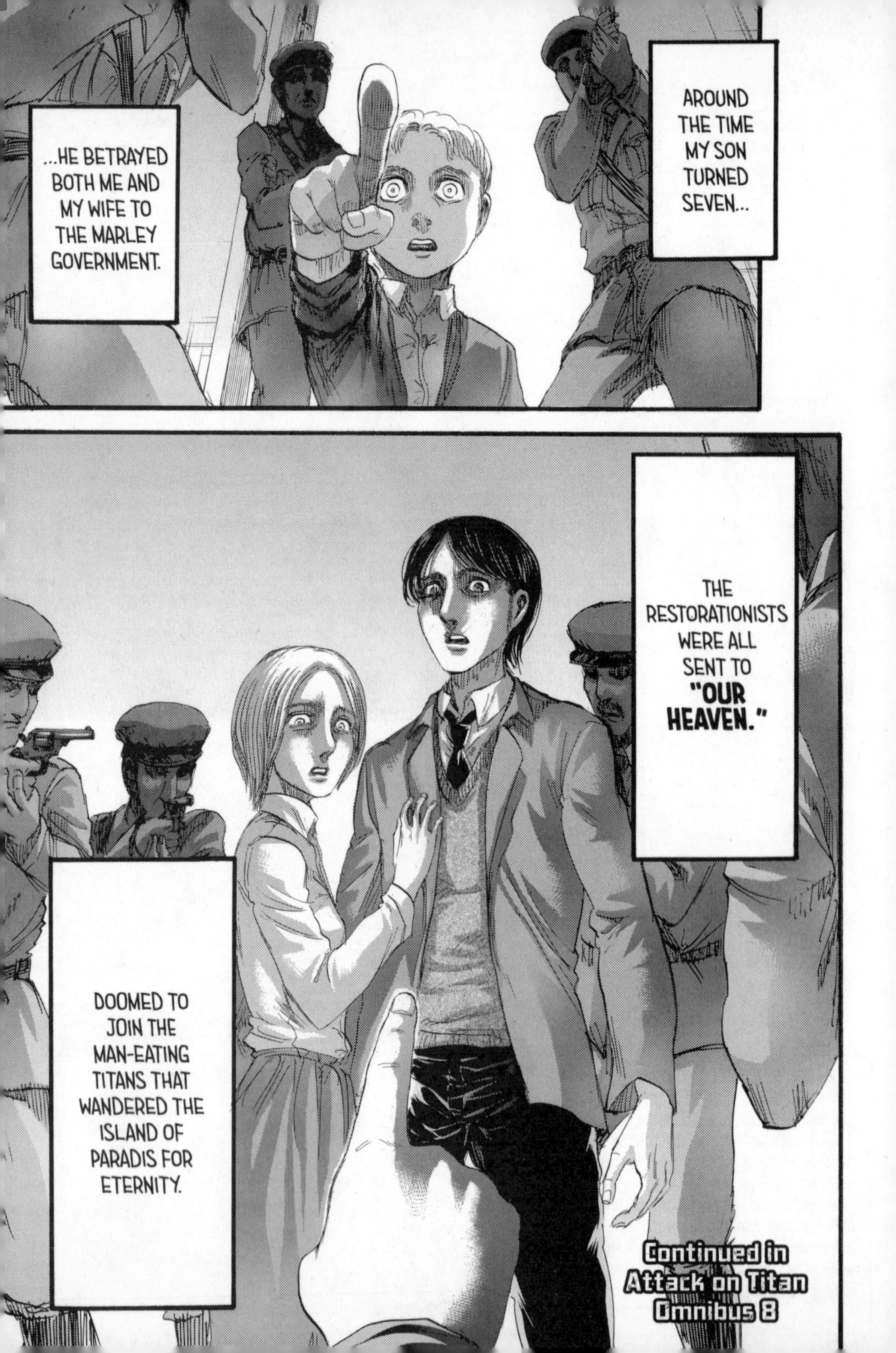
AROUND THE TIME MY SON TURNED SEVEN...
...HE BETRAYED BOTH ME AND MY WIFE TO THE MARLEY GOVERNMENT.
THE RESTORATIONISTS WERE ALL SENT TO **"OUR HEAVEN."**
DOOMED TO JOIN THE MAN-EATING TITANS THAT WANDERED THE ISLAND OF PARADIS FOR ETERNITY.
Continued in Attack on Titan Omnibus 8

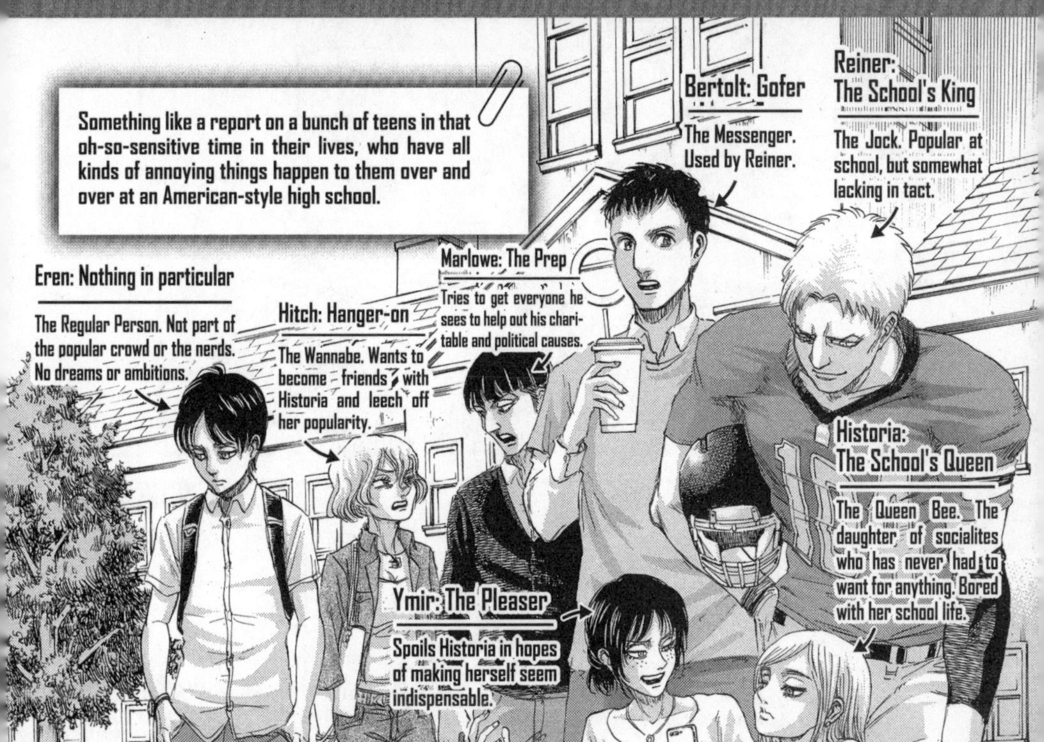
Something like a report on a bunch of teens in that oh-so-sensitive time in their lives, who have all kinds of annoying things happen to them over and over at an American-style high school.
Reiner: The School's King
The Jock. Popular at school, but somewhat lacking in tact.
Bertolt: Gofer
The Messenger. Used by Reiner.
Marlowe: The Prep
Tries to get everyone he sees to help out his charitable and political causes.
Hitch: Hanger-on
The Wannabe. Wants to become friends with Historia and leech off her popularity.
Eren: Nothing in particular
The Regular Person. Not part of the popular crowd or the nerds. No dreams or ambitions.
Historia: The School's Queen
The Queen Bee. The daughter of socialites who has never had to want for anything. Bored with her school life.
Ymir: The Pleaser
Spoils Historia in hopes of making herself seem indispensable.
INGEKI

WHAT ARE SCHOOL CASTES?

The hierarchical relationships observed between students within the society that is a school can be seen as a caste system. This system is most notable in middle schools and high schools, and is an important element in regulating friendships and romantic relationships. As the lower castes can easily become targets for bullying, one's place within the class can sometimes become a matter of life and death.

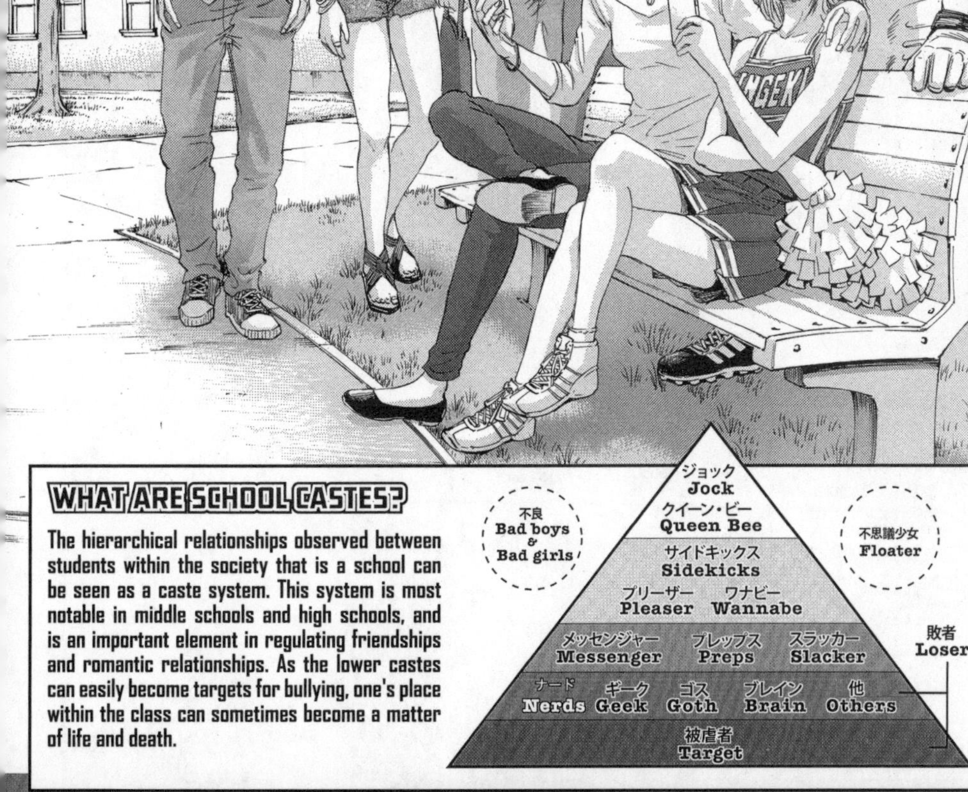
ジョック
Jock
クイーン・ビー
Queen Bee
サイドキックス
Sidekicks
プリーザー
Pleaser
ワナビー
Wannabe
メッセンジャー
Messenger
プレップス
Preps
スラッカー
Slacker
ナード
Nerds
ギーク
Geek
ゴス
Goth
ブレイン
Brain
他
Others
被虐者
Target
不良
Bad boys & Bad girls
不思議少女
Floater
敗者
Loser

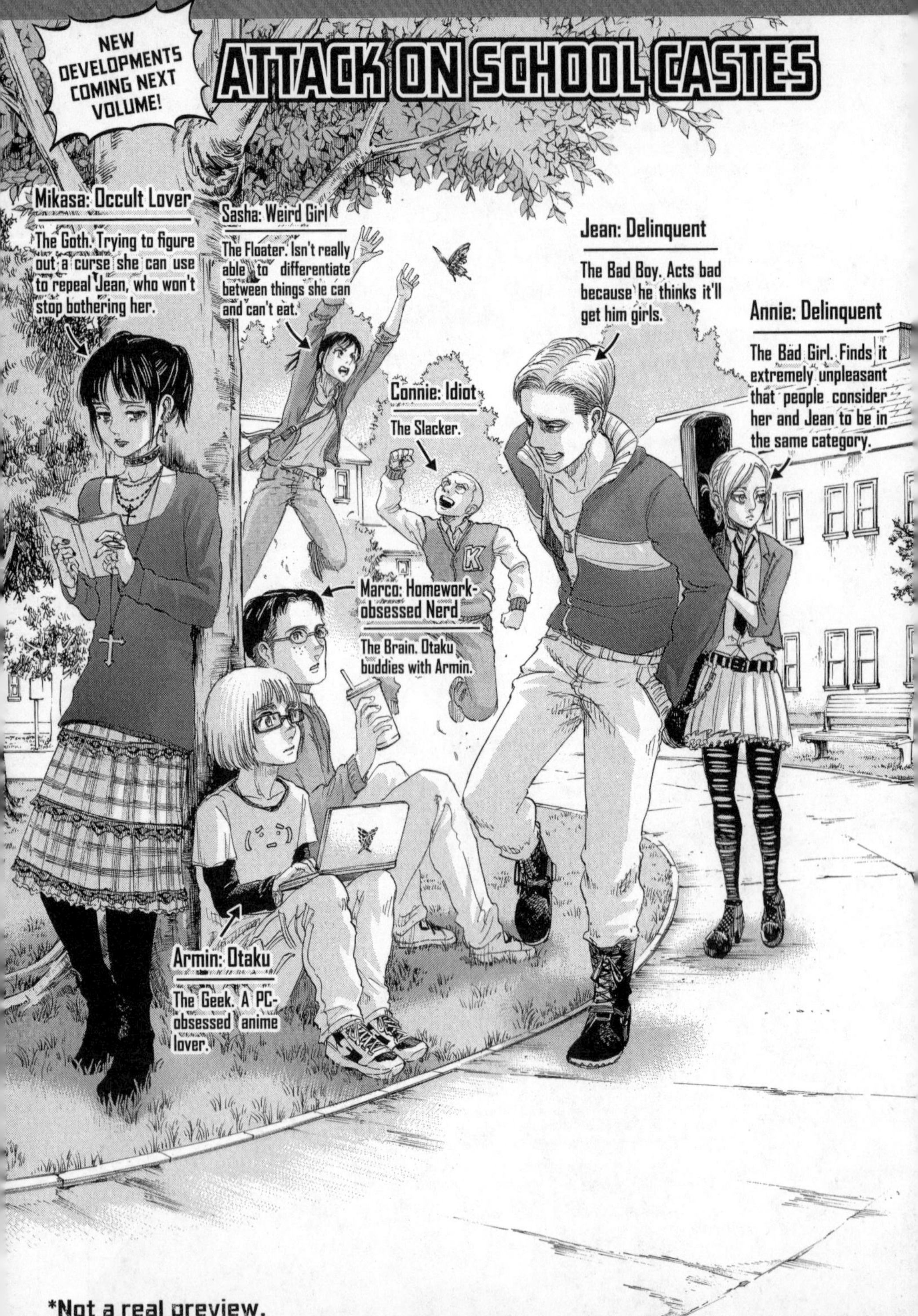
ATTACK ON SCHOOL CASTES
NEW DEVELOPMENTS COMING NEXT VOLUME!
Jean: Delinquent
The Bad Boy. Acts bad because he thinks it'll get him girls.
Annie: Delinquent
The Bad Girl. Finds it extremely unpleasant that people consider her and Jean to be in the same category.
Connie: Idiot
The Slacker.
Sasha: Weird Girl
The Floater. Isn't really able to differentiate between things she can and can't eat.
Mikasa: Occult Lover
The Goth. Trying to figure out a curse she can use to repeal Jean, who won't stop bothering her.
Marco: Homework-obsessed Nerd
The Brain. Otaku buddies with Armin.
Armin: Otaku
The Geek. A PC-obsessed anime lover.
*Not a real preview.

ATTACK on TITAN

ATTACK on TITAN

ATTACK on TITAN

ATTACK on TITAN

A Kodansha Trade Paperback Orig[...]

Published in the United States by
Kodansha USA Publishing, LLC, New York.

Publication rights for this English edition arranged through
Kodansha Ltd., Tokyo.

First published in Japan in 2016 by Kodansha Ltd., Tokyo
as *Shingeki no kyojin*, volumes 19, 20, and 21.

ISBN 978-1-64651-488-5

Original cover design by Takashi Shimoyama/Manami Fukunaga (Red Rooster)

Printed in the United States of America.

9 8 7 6 5 4 3 2 1

Translation: Ko Ransom
Lettering: Steve Wands
Additional Lettering: Evan Hayden
Editing: Tiff Joshua TJ Ferentini
Kodansha USA Publishing edition cover design by Adam Del Re
Kodansha USA Publishing edition logo design by Phil Balsman

Publisher: Kiichiro Sugawara

Director of Publishing Services: Ben Applegate
Director of Publishing Operations: Dave Barrett
Associate Director of Publishing Operations: Stephen Pakula
Publishing Services Managing Editors: Alanna Ruse, Madison Salters
Senior Production Manager: Angela Zurlo

KODANSHA.US

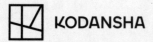